THE WORKS
OF
VICTOR HUGO

One Volume Edition

*Poems, Novels
Stories of Crime
Dramas aud Essays on Humanity*

P. F. COLLIER & SON CORPORATION
NEW YORK

COPYRIGHT, 1928,
BY
WALTER J. BLACK, INC.

PRINTED IN THE UNITED STATES OF AMERICA

VICTOR HUGO

TABLE OF CONTENTS

POEMS

	PAGE
The Fallen Veil	1
Zara, the Bather	2
Gastibelza	3
The Feast of Freedom	5
The Grandmother	6
The Giant in Glee	7
The Cymbaleer's Bride	8
Children of Cain	10
Eviradnus	11
The Adventurer	11
In Holy Rage	12
In the Forest	13
A Weird Meal	15
Unmarried	17
The Evil Pair	18
Love and Feast	20
Legion of Death	21
A Noise on the Floor	25
The Spectral Knight	26
Kiss for Fodder	26
Three Heads	27
A Minstrel without Shame	29
The Odour of Crime	30
Hell's Partition	32
Spirit of the Abyss	33
Colossal Hands	37
No Baptism	39
March of the Halberdiers	40
Hero of Gentle Mien	41
Night and a Cabin	42
Song of the Gilders	45

POEMS—*Continued*

	PAGE
SAGA OF THE BEAST	47
THE BABE	47
THE HERMIT	49
THE HOUNDS	50
OUT OF RED JAWS	53

NOVELS

THE HUNCH-BACK OF NOTRE-DAME

BOOK I—THE PLAY

I.	THE GREAT HALL	57
II.	PIERRE GRINGOIRE	66
III.	THE CARDINAL	72
IV.	MASTER JACQUES COPPENOLE	77
V.	QUASIMODO	83
VI.	ESMERALDA	87

BOOK II—LOVE

I.	FROM CHARYBDIS TO SCYLLA	89
II.	THE GRÈVE	91
III.	BESOS PARA GOLPES	92
IV.	INCONVENIENCES OF FOLLOWING A PRETTY WOMAN	99
V.	THE REST OF THE INCONVENIENCES . .	102
VI.	THE BROKEN JUG	103
VII.	A WEDDING NIGHT	116

BOOK III—THE CATHEDRAL

I.	NOTRE-DAME	122
II.	A BIRD'S-EYE VIEW OF PARIS	127

BOOK IV—GRATITUDE

I.	KIND SOULS	144
II.	CLAUDE FROLLO	147
III.	IMMANIS PECORIS CUSTOS, IMMANIOR IPSE	150

THE HUNCH-BACK OF NOTRE-DAME
(*Continued*)

BOOK IV—GRATITUDE—*Continued*

		PAGE
IV.	The Dog and His Master	155
V.	More about Claude Frollo	156
VI.	Unpopularity	160

BOOK V—THE NEW POWER

| I. | Abbas Beati Martini | 163 |
| II. | The One Will Kill the Other | 170 |

BOOK VI—THE PILLORY

I.	An Impartial Glance at the Ancient Magistracy	180
II.	The Rat-hole	187
III.	The Story of a Wheaten Cake	190
IV.	A Tear for a Drop of Water	204
V.	End of the Story of the Cake	210

BOOK VII—THE INSCRIPTION

I.	On the Danger of Confiding a Secret	211
II.	Showing a Priest and a Philosopher	220
III.	The Bells	226
IV.	'Ana'tkh	228
V.	The Two Men Dressed in Black	237
VI.	The Effect Produced by Seven Oaths	241
VII.	The Spectre Monk	243
VIII.	The Advantage of Windows	248

BOOK VIII—HEARTS

I.	The Crown Changed to a Dry Leaf	254
II.	Sequel to the Crown	261
III.	End of the Crown	264
IV.	Lasciate Ogni Speranza	266
V.	The Mother	276
VI.	Three Men's Hearts Differently Constituted	278

THE HUNCH-BACK OF NOTRE-DAME
(Continued)

BOOK IX—ACCUMULATED AFFLICTIONS

		PAGE
I.	Delirium	291
II.	Deformed, Blind, Lame	298
III.	Deaf	301
IV.	Earthenware and Crystal	303
V.	The Key to the Porte-Rouge	310
VI.	The Key to the Porte-Rouge (*Continued*)	311

BOOK X—THE KING

I.	Gringoire Has Several Capital Ideas	313
II.	Turn Vagabond!	320
III.	Joy Forever!	322
IV.	An Awkward Friend	327
V.	The Retreat	340
VI.	"The Chive in the Cly"	361
VII.	Chateaupers to the Rescue	362

BOOK XI—MARRIAGE

I.	The Little Shoe	363
II.	La Creatura Bella Bianco Vestita	386
III.	Marriage of Phœbus	392
IV.	Marriage of Quasimodo	392

STORIES OF CRIME

Last Days of a Condemned Man	395
Claude Gueux King of Thieves	430
Monster and Infanticide	441
A Woman of the Streets	454
Fieschi the Explorer	457
Lecomte the Assassin	459
Henri the Regicide	467
The Crypt of Pain	472
Count Mortier the Madman	491
An Over-night Criminal	493

STORIES OF CRIME—*Continued*

	PAGE
PRASLIN, DUCHESS-SLAYER	500
HUBERT, THE SPY	506
THE NINETY-FOUR THOUSAND FRANC FRAUD	524

NINETY-THREE

PART I—AT SEA

BOOK I—THE WOOD OF LA SAUDRAIE

BOOK II—THE CORVETTE "CLAYMORE"

I.	ENGLAND AND FRANCE IN CONCERT	545
II.	NIGHT ON THE VESSEL	547
III.	NOBLE AND PLEBEIAN IN CONCERT	548
IV.	TORMENTUM BELLI	552
V.	VIS ET VIR	554
VI.	THE TWO SCALES OF THE BALANCE	557
VII.	HE WHO SETS SAIL	559
VIII.	9=380	561
IX.	SOME ONE ESCAPES	564
X.	DOES HE ESCAPE?	565

BOOK III—HALMALO

I.	SPEECH IS THE "WORD"	567
II.	THE PEASANT'S MEMORY	570

BOOK IV—TELLMARCH

I.	THE TOP OF THE DUNE	577
II.	AURES HABET, ET NON AUDIET	578
III.	USEFULNESS OF BIG LETTERS	580
IV.	THE CAIMAND	581
V.	SIGNED GAUVAIN	585
VI.	THE WHIRLIGIGS OF CIVIL WAR	587
VII.	"NO MERCY!" "NO QUARTER!"	590

PART II—IN PARIS

BOOK I—CIMOURDAIN

I.	THE STREETS OF PARIS AT THAT TIME	594
II.	CIMOURDAIN	598
III.	A CORNER NOT DIPPED IN STYX	603

NINETY-THREE (*Continued*)

BOOK II—THE PUBLIC HOUSE OF THE RUE DU PAON

		PAGE
I.	Minos, Æacus, and Rhadamanthus	604
II.	Magna Testantur Voce Per Umbras	606
III.	A Stirring of the Inmost Nerves	616

BOOK III—THE CONVENTION

I.	Only One	622
II.	The Tricolour	623
III.	Architecture	624
IV.	Giants Meet	627
V.	Lowlands	631
VI.	Visionaries	631
VII.	Sentences	632
VIII.	The Scene	634
IX.	Results	635
X.	Gathering Foes	636
XI.	Destiny	638
XII.	Wind-swept	638
XIII.	Marat	639

PART III—LA VENDÉE

BOOK I—LA VENDÉE

I.	The Forests	643
II.	The Peasants	644
III.	Connivance of Men and Forests	645
IV.	Their Life Underground	647
V.	Their Life in Warfare	648
VI.	The Spirit of the Place	651
VII.	La Vendée Ended Brittany	653

BOOK II—THE THREE CHILDREN

I.	Plusquam Civilia Bella	655
II.	Dol	659
III.	Small Armies and Great Battles	663

NINETY-THREE (*Continued*)

BOOK II—THE THREE CHILDREN—*Continued*

		PAGE
IV.	"It is the Second Time"	668
V.	The Drop of Cold Water	669
VI.	A Healed Breast; a Bleeding Heart	671
VII.	The Two Poles of the Truth	675
VIII.	Dolorosa	678
IX.	A Provincial Bastile	680
X.	The Hostages	686
XI.	Terrible as the Antique	689
XII.	Possible Escape	691
XIII.	What the Marquis Was Doing	693
XIV.	What Imanus Was Doing	694

BOOK III—THE MASSACRE OF SAINT BARTHOLOMEW

I.	The Children	696
II.	The Journey	697
III.	The Good God	699
IV.	The Gallop	700
V.	The Book	702
VI.	Extermination	703
VII.	Sleep	704

BOOK IV—THE MOTHER

I.	Death Passes	705
II.	Death Speaks	707
III.	Mutterings among the Peasants	709
IV.	A Mistake	712
V.	Vox in Deserto	713
VI.	The Situation	714
VII.	Preliminaries	716
VIII.	The Word and the Roar	718
IX.	Titans against Giants	721
X.	Radoub	723
XI.	Desperate	727
XII.	Deliverance	729
XIII.	The Executioner	731
XIV.	Imânus also Escapes	732
XV.	A Watch and a Key	733

NINETY-THREE (*Continued*)
BOOK V—IN DÆMONE DEUS

		PAGE
I.	FOUND, BUT LOST	736
II.	FROM THE DOOR OF STONE TO THE IRON DOOR	740
III.	WHERE WE SEE THE CHILDREN WAKE	741

BOOK VI—AFTER THE VICTORY THE COMBAT BEGINS

I.	LANTENAC TAKEN	744
II.	GAUVAIN'S SELF-QUESTIONING	746
III.	THE COMMANDANT'S MANTLE	753

BOOK VII—FEUDALITY AND REVOLUTION

I.	THE ANCESTOR	755
II.	THE COURT-MARTIAL	759
III.	THE VOTES	761
IV.	CIMOURDAIN THE MASTER	764
V.	THE DUNGEON	765
VI.	WHEN THE SUN ROSE	770

DRAMAS

HERNANI	777
ACT FIRST: THE KING	777
ACT SECOND: THE BANDIT	789
ACT THIRD: THE OLD MAN	799
ACT FOURTH: THE TOMB	817
ACT FIFTH: THE NUPTIALS	832
RUY BLAS	844
ACT FIRST: DON SALLUSTE	844
ACT SECOND: THE QUEEN OF SPAIN	862
ACT THIRD: RUY BLAS	875
ACT FOURTH: DON CÆSAR	891
ACT FIFTH: THE TIGER AND THE LION	909

ESSAYS ON HUMANITY

CAPITAL PUNISHMENT	917
THE MINDS AND THE MASSES	926
THE PEOPLE	926
SOCIALISM	926
LIBERTY	928

ESSAYS ON HUMANITY (*Continued*)

	PAGE
Light	929
Literature	930
Macchiavelli	931
Progress	932
The Ideal	933
Fraternization	934
The Face of Cain	941
The Advent	941
Splendour in the Distance	943
History	946
Change	952
Guidance	955
The Souls	957
Production	957
Boundlessness	963
Mirabeau	964
Voltaire	991
Sir Walter Scott	998

The Fallen Veil

The Sister

What has happened, my brothers?
    Your spirit to-day
Some secret sorrow damps:
There's a cloud on your brow. What
    has happened? Oh, say,
For your eyeballs glare out with a sin-
    ister ray
Like the light of funeral lamps.
And the blades of your poinards are
    half unsheathed
In your belt—and ye frown on me!
There's a woe untold, there's a pang
    unbreathed
In your bosom, my brothers three!

Eldest Brother

Gulnara, make answer! Hast thou,
    since the dawn,
To the eye of a stranger thy veil with-
    drawn?

The Sister

As I came, oh, my brother! at noon—
    from the bath—
As I came—it was noon, my lords—
And your sister had then, as she con-
    stantly hath,
Drawn her veil close around her, aware
    that the path
Is beset by these foreign hordes.
But the weight of the noonday's sultry
    hour
Near the mosque was so oppressive
That—forgetting a moment the eye of
    the Giaour—
I yielded to th' heat excessive.

Second Brother

Gulnara, make answer! Whom, then,
    hast thou seen,
In a turban of white and a caftan of
    green?

The Sister

Nay, *he* might have been there; but I
    muffled me so,
He could scarcely have seen my
    figure.—
But why to your sister thus dark do
    you grow?
What words to yourselves do you mut-
    ter thus low,
Of "blood" and "an intriguer"?
Oh! ye cannot of murder bring down
    the red guilt
On your souls, my brothers, surely!
Though I fear—from the hands that
    are chafing the hilt,
And the hints you give obscurely.

Third Brother

Gulnara, this evening when sank the red
    sun,
Didst thou mark how like blood in de-
    scending it shone?

The Sister

Mercy! Allah! have pity! oh, spare!
    See! I cling to your knees repenting!
Kind brothers, forgive me! for mercy,
    forbear!
Be appeased at the cry of a sister's de-
    spair,

For our mother's sake relenting.
O God! must I die? They are deaf
   to my cries!
Their sister's life-blood shedding;
They have stabbed me each one — I
   faint—o'er my eyes
A *veil of Death* is spreading!

THE BROTHERS

Gulnara farewell! take *that* veil; 'tis
   the gift
Of thy brothers—a veil thou wilt never
   lift!

ZARA, THE BATHER

IN a swinging hammock lying,
    Lightly flying,
Zara, lovely indolent,
   O'er a fountain's crystal wave
    There to lave
Her young beauty—see her bent.

As she leans, so sweet and soft,
    Flitting oft,
O'er the mirror to and fro,
   Seems that airy floating bat
    Like a feather
From some sea-gull's wing of snow.

Every time the frail boat laden
    With the maiden
Skims the water in its flight,
   Starting from its trembling sheen,
    Swift are seen
A white foot and neck so white.

As that lithe foot's timid tips
    Quick she dips,
Passing, in the rippling pool,

(Blush, oh! snowiest ivory!)
    Frolic, she
Laughs to feel the pleasant cool.

Here displayed, but half concealed—
    Half revealed,
Each bright charm shall you behold,
   In her innocence emerging,
    As a-verging
On the wave her hands grow cold.

For no star howe'er divine
    Has the shine
Of a maid's pure loveliness,
   Frightened if a leaf but quivers
    As she shivers,
Veiled with nought but dripping trees.

By the happy breezes fanned
    See her stand,—
Blushing like a living rose,
   On her bosom swelling high
    If a fly
Dare to seek a sweet repose.

In those eyes which maiden pride
    Fain would hide,
Mark how passion's lightnings sleep!
   And their glance is brighter far
    Than the star
Brightest in heaven's bluest deep.

O'er her limbs the glittering current
    In soft torrent
Rains adown the gentle girl,
   As if, drop by drop, should fall,
    One and all
From her necklace every pearl.

Lengthening still the reckless pleasure
    At her leisure,
Care-free Zara ever slow
   As the hammock floats and swings

  Smiles and sings,
To herself, so sweet and low.

"Oh, were I a capitana,
  Or sultana,
Amber should be always mixt
 In my bath of jewelled stone,
  Near my throne,
Griffins twain of gold betwixt.

"Then my hammock should be silk,
  White as milk;
And, more soft than down of dove,
 Velvet cushions where I sit
  Should emit
Perfumes that inspire love.

"Then should I, no danger near,
  Free from fear,
Revel in my garden's stream;
 Nor amid the shadows deep
  Dread the peep
Of two dark eyes' kindling gleam.

"He who thus would play the spy,
  On the die
For such sight his head must throw;
 In his blood the sabre naked
  Would be slakéd,
Of my slaves of ebon brow.

"Then my rich robes trailing show
  As I go,
None to chide should be so bold;
 And upon my sandals fine
  How should shine
Rubies worked in cloth-of-gold!"

Fancying herself a queen,
  All unseen,
Thus vibrating in delight;
 In her indolent coquetting
  Quite forgetting
How the hours wing their flight.

As she lists the showery tinkling
  Of the sprinkling
By her wanton curvets made,
 Never pauses she to think
  Of the brink
Where her wrapper white is laid.

To the harvest-fields the while,
  In long file,
Speed her sisters' lively band,
 Like a flock of birds in flight
  Streaming light,
Dancing onward hand in hand.

And they're singing, every one,
  As they run;
This the burden of their lay:
 "Fie upon such idleness!
  Not to dress
Earlier on harvest-day!"

GASTIBELZA

GASTIBELZA, the man with the carabine,
 Sung in this wise:
"Hath one of you here known Doña
 Sabine
With the gentle eyes?
Ay, dance and sing! For the night
 draws nigh
O'er hill and lea.
—*The wind that wails o'er yon mountain high
Will madden me.*

"Hath one of you here known Doña
 Sabine,
 To me so dear?

Her mother, the old, old, Maugrabine,
　Erst made one fear,
For each night from the haunted cavern
　　she'd cry
　With an owlet's glee.
—*The wind that wails o'er yon moun-
　　tain high
　Will madden me!*

"Ay, dance ye and sing! The hour's
　　delight
　One needs must use.
How young she was, and those eyes
　　how bright,
　Which made one muse.—
To this old man whom a child leads by,
　A coin cast ye!
—*The wind that wails o'er yon moun-
　　tain high
　Will madden me!*

"In sooth the queen for envy had wept,
　Had she seen her, alack!
As o'er Toledo's bridge she light-tript
　In a corset black.
A chaplet of beads that charmed one's
　　eye,
　From her neck hung free.
—*The wind that wails o'er yon moun-
　　tain high
　Will madden me!*

"The King, bedazed with her loveliness,
　Bespake one there:
'For one only smile, for one only kiss,
　One tress of her hair,
I would give my Spain and gold realms
　　that lie
　O'er yonder sea!'
—*The wind that wails o'er yon moun-
　　tain high
　Will madden me!*

"I know not well if I loved this sweet,
　But well I know,
If but one glance of her soul might
　　greet
　My soul, I would go
On the galleys to toil, on the galleys
　　to die,
　Right cheerfully.
—*The wind that wails o'er yon moun-
　　tain high
　Will madden me!*

"One summer morn when all heaven
　　was bright,
　All earth was gay,
To the stream with her sister for dear
　　delight,
　This sweet must stray.
The foot of her comrade I there did
　　spy,
　And saw *her* knee.
—*The wind that wails o'er yon moun-
　　tain high
　Will madden me!*

"When thus of me, a poor shepherd, was
　　seen
　This glorious May,
Methought, 'tis Cleopatra the queen
　Who once, they say,
Won Cæsar, great Emperor of Ger-
　　many,
　Her slave to be.
—*The wind that wails o'er yon moun-
　　tain high
　Will madden me!*

"Dance ye and sing—lo, the night doth
　　fall!
　Sabine, one while
Her dovelike beauty, her soul, her all,
　Her angel-smile,

For a ring of gold to the Count hath sold—
Saldane is he.
—*The wind that wails o'er yon mountain high
Will madden me!*

"On this bench for a moment suffer me rest,—
Full-weary each limb.
With this Count then fled this loveliest—
Alas! with him!
By the road that leads . . . but I know not, I,
Where then fled she.
—*The wind that wails o'er yon mountain high
Will madden me!*

"I saw her pass at the death of day,
And all was night.
And now I wander and weary alway,
In pain's despite.
My soul's on quest; my dagger's put by,
Ne'er-used to be.
—*The wind that wails o'er yon mountain high
Has maddened me!*"

THE FEAST OF FREEDOM

TO YE KINGS

When the Christians were doomed to the lions of old
By the priest and prætor, combined to uphold
    An idolatrous cause,
Forth they came while the vast Colosseum throughout
Gathered thousands looked on, and they fell 'mid the shout
    Of "the People's" applause.

On the eve of that day of their evenings the last!
At the gates of their dungeon a gorgeous repast,
    Rich, unstinted, unpriced,
That the doomed might (forsooth) gather strength ere they bled,
With an ignorant pity the gaolers would spread
    For the martyrs of Christ.

Oh, 'twas strange for a pupil of Paul to recline
On voluptuous couch, while Falernian wine
    Fill'd his cup to the brim!
Dulcet music of Greece, Asiatic repose,
Spicy fragrance of Araby, Italian rose,
    All united for him!

Every luxury known through the earth's wide expanse,
In profusion procured was put forth to enhance
    The repast that they gave;
And no Sybarite, nursed in the lap of delight,
Such a banquet ere tasted as welcomed that night
    The elect of the grave.

And the lion, meantime, shook his ponderous chain,
Loud and fierce howled the tiger, impatient to stain
    The bloodthirsty arena;
Whilst the women of Rome, who applauded those deeds

And who hailed the forthcoming en-
    joyment, must needs
        Shame the restless hyæna.

They who figured as guests on that ul-
    timate eve,
In their turn on the morrow were des-
    tined to give
        To the lions their food;
For, behold, in the guise of a slave at
    that board,
Where his victims enjoyed all that life
    can afford,
        Death administering stood.

Such, O monarchs of earth! was your
    banquet of power,
But the tocsin has burst on your fes-
    tival hour—
        'Tis your knell that it rings!
To the popular tiger a prey is decreed,
And the maw of Republican hunger will
    feed
        On *a banquet of Kings!*

THE GRANDMOTHER

STILL asleep! We have been since the
    noon thus alone.
    Oh, the hours we have ceased to
        number!
Wake, grandmother! — speechless say
    why thou art grown.
Then, thy lips are so cold!—the Ma-
    donna of stone
    Is like thee in thy holy slumber.
We have watched thee in sleep, we have
    watched thee at prayer,
    But what can now betide thee?
Like thy hours of repose all thy orisons
    were,

And thy lips would still murmur a
    blessing whene'er
    Thy children stood beside thee.

Now thine eye is unclosed, and thy
    forehead is bent
    O'er the hearth, where ashes smoul-
        der;
And behold, the watch-lamp will be
    speedily spent.
Art thou vexed? have we done aught
    amiss? Oh, relent!
    But—parent, thy hands grow colder!
Say, with ours wilt thou let us rekindle
    in thine
    The glow that has departed?
Wilt thou sing us some songs of the
    days of lang syne?
Wilt thou tell us some tale, from those
    volumes divine,
    Of the brave and noble-hearted?

Of the dragon who, crouching in forest
    green glen,
    Lies in wait for the unwary—
Of the maid who was freed by her
    knight from the den
Of the ogre, whose club was uplifted,
    but then
    Turned aside by the wand of a fairy?
Wilt thou teach us spell-words that pro-
    tect from all harm,
    And thoughts of evil banish?
What goblins the sign of the cross may
    disarm?
What saint it is good to invoke? and
    what charm
    Can make the demon vanish?

Or unfold to our gaze thy most won-
    derful book,
    So feared by hell and Satan;

At its hermits and martyrs in gold
   let us look,
At the virgins, and bishops with pas-
   toral crook,
   And the hymns and the prayers in
      Latin.
Oft with legends of angels, who watch
   o'er the young,
Thy voice was wont to gladden;
Have thy lips yet no language—no wis-
   dom thy tongue?
Oh, see! the light wavers, and sinking,
   hath flung
   On the wall forms that sadden.

Wake! awake! evil spirits perhaps may
   presume
   To haunt thy holy dwelling;
Pale ghosts are, perhaps, stealing into
   the room—
Oh, would that the lamp were relit!
   with the gloom
   These fearful thoughts dispelling.
Thou hast told us our parents lie sleep-
   ing beneath
   The grass, in a churchyard lonely:
Now, thine eyes have no motion, thy
   mouth has no breath,
And thy limbs are all rigid! Oh, say,
   Is this death,
Or thy prayer or thy slumber only?

Envoy

Sad vigil they kept by that grand-
   mother's chair,
   Kind angels hovered o'er them—
And the dead-bell was tolled in the
   hamlet—and there,
On the following eve, knelt that inno-
   cent pair,
   With the missal-book before them.

THE GIANT IN GLEE

Ho, warriors! I was reared in the land
   of the Gauls;
O'er the Rhine my ancestors came
   bounding like balls
Of the snow at the Pole, where, a babe,
   I was bathed
Ere in bear and in walrus-skin I was
   enswathed.

Then my father was strong, whom the
   years lowly bow,—
A bison could wallow in the grooves of
   his brow.
He is weak, very old—he can scarcely
   uptear
A young pine-tree for staff since his legs
   cease to bear;

But here's to replace him!—I can toy
   with his axe;
As I sit on the hill my feet swing in
   the flax,
And my knee caps the boulders and
   troubles the trees.
How they shiver, yea, quake if I happen to sneeze!

I was still but a springald when, cleaving the Alps,
I brushed snowy periwigs off granitic
   scalps,
And my head, o'er the pinnacles,
   stopped the fleet clouds,
Where I captured the eagles and caged
   them by crowds.

There were tempests! I blew them back
   unto their source!
And put out their lightnings! More
   than once in a course,

Through the ocean I went wading after
    the whale,
And stirred up the bottom as did never
    a gale.

Fond of rambling, I hunted the shark
    'long the beach,
And no osprey in ether soared out of
    my reach;
And the bear that I pinched 'twixt my
    finger and thumb,
Like the lynx and the wolf, perished
    harmless and dumb.

But these pleasures of childhood have
    lost all their zest;
It is warfare and carnage that now I
    love best:
The sounds that I wish to awaken and
    hear
Are the cheers raised by courage, the
    shrieks due to fear;

When the riot of flames, ruin, smoke,
    steel and blood,
Announces an army rolls along as a
    flood,
Which I follow, to harry the clamorous
    ranks,
Sharp-goading the laggards and press-
    ing the flanks,
Till, a thresher 'mid ripest of corn, up
    I stand
With an oak for a flail in my unflagging
    hand.

Rise the groans! rise the screams! on
    my feet fall vain tears
As the roar of my laughter redoubles
    their fears.
I am naked. At armour of steel I
    should joke—

True, I'm helmed—a brass pot you
    could draw with ten yoke.

I look for no ladder to invade the king's
    hall—
I stride o'er the ramparts, and down
    the walls fall,
Till choked are the ditches with the
    stones, dead and quick,
Whilst the flagstaff I use 'midst my
    teeth as a pick.

Oh, when cometh my turn to succumb
    like my prey,
May brave men my body snatch away
    from th' array
Of the crows—may they heap on the
    rocks till they loom
Like a mountain, befitting a colossus'
    tomb!

THE CYMBALEER'S BRIDE

My lord the Duke of Brittany
    Has summoned his barons bold—
Their names make a fearful litany!
Among them you will not meet any
    But men of giant mould.

Proud earls, who dwell in donjon keep,
    And steel-clad knight and peer,
Whose forts are girt with a moat cut
    deep—
But none excel in soldiership
    My own loved cymbaleer.

Clashing his cymbals, forth he went,
    With a bold and gallant bearing;
Sure for a captain he was meant,
To judge his pride with courage blent,
    And the cloth of gold he's wearing.

But in my soul since then I feel
  A fear in secret creeping;
And to my patron saint I kneel,
  That she may recommend his weal
    To his guardian-angel's keeping.

I've begged our abbot Bernardine
  His prayers not to relax;
And to procure him aid divine
I've burnt upon Saint Gilda's shrine
  Three pounds of virgin wax.

Our Lady of Loretto knows
  The pilgrimage I've vowed:
"To wear the scallop I propose,
If health and safety from the foes
  My lover be allowed."

No letter (fond affection's gage!)
  From him could I require,
The pain of absence to assuage—
A vassal-maid can have no page,
  A liegeman has no squire.

This day will witness, with the duke's,
  My cymbaleer's return:
Gladness and pride beam in my looks,
Delay my heart impatient brooks,
  All meaner thoughts I spurn.

Back from the battlefield elate
  His banner brings each peer;
Come, let us see, at the ancient gate,
The martial triumph pass in state—
  With the princes my cymbaleer.

We'll have from the rampart walls a
    glance
  Of the air his steed assumes;
His proud neck swells, his glad hoofs
    prance,
And on his head unceasing dance,
  In a gorgeous tuft, red plumes!

Be quick, my sisters! dress in haste!
  Come, see him bear the bell,
With laurels decked, with true love
    graced,
While in his bold hands, fitly placed,
  The bounding cymbals swell!

Mark well the mantle that he'll wear,
  Embroidered by his bride!
Admire his burnished helmet's glare,
O'ershadowed by the dark horsehair
  That waves in jet folds wide!

The gypsy (spiteful wench!) foretold,
  With a voice like a viper hissing
(Though I had crossed her palm with
    gold),
That from the ranks a spirit bold
  Would be to-day found missing.

But I have prayed so much, I trust
  Her words may prove untrue;
Though in a tomb the hag accurst
Muttered: "Prepare thee for the
    worst!"
  Whilst the lamp burnt ghastly blue.

My joy her spells shall not prevent.
  Hark! I can hear the drums!
And ladies fair from silken tent
Peep forth, and every eye is bent
  On the cavalcade that comes!

Pikemen, dividing on both flanks,
  Open the pageantry;
Loud, as they tread, their armour
    clanks,
And silk-robed barons lead the ranks—
  The pink of gallantry!

In scarves of gold the priests admire:
  The heralds on white steeds;
Armorial pride decks their attire,

Worn in remembrance of some sire
    Famed for heroic deeds.

Feared by the Paynim's dark divan,
    The Templars next advance;
Then the tall halberds of Lausanne,
    Foremost to stand in battle van
    Against the foes of France.

Now hail the duke, with radiant brow,
    Girt with his cavaliers;
Round his triumphant banner bow
Those of his foe. Look, sisters, now!
    Here come the cymbaleers!

She spoke—with searching eye surveyed
    Their ranks—then, pale, aghast,
Sunk in the crowd! Death came in aid—
'Twas mercy to that loving maid—
    The cymbaleers had passed!

CHILDREN OF CAIN

Then, with his children, clothed in skins of brutes,
Dishevelled, livid, rushing through the storm,
Cain fled before Jehovah. As night fell
The dark man reached a mount in a great plain,
And his tired wife and his sons, out of breath,
Said: "Let us lie down on the earth and sleep."
Cain, sleeping not, dreamed at the mountain foot.
Raising his head, in that funereal heaven
He saw an eye, a great eye, in the night
Open, and staring at him in the gloom.

"I am too near," he said, and tremblingly woke up
His sleeping sons again, and his tired wife,
And fled through space and darkness. Thirty days
He went, and thirty nights, nor looked behind;
Pale, silent, watchful, shaking at each sound;
No rest, no sleep, till he attained the strand
Where the sea washes that which since was Asshur.
"Here pause," he said, "for this place is secure;
Here may we rest, for this is the world's end."
And he sat down; when, lo! in the sad sky,
The self-same Eye on the horizon's verge,
And the wretch shook as in an ague fit.
"Hide me!" he cried; and all his watchful sons,
Their finger on their lip, stared at their sire.
Cain said to Jabal (father of them that dwell
In tents): "Spread here the curtain of thy tent."
And they spread wide the floating canvas roof,
And made it fast and fixed it down with lead.
"You see nought now," said Zillah then, fair child,
The daughter of his eldest, sweet as day.
But Cain replied, "That Eye—I see it still."
And Jubal cried (the father of those

That handle harp and organ): "I will build
A sanctuary;" and he made a wall of bronze,
And set his sire behind it. But Cain moaned,
"That Eye is glaring at me ever." Henoch cried:
 Then must we make a circle vast of towers,
So terrible that nothing dare draw near;
Build we a city with a citadel;
Build we a city high and close it fast."
Then Tubal Cain (instructor of all them
That work in brass and iron) built a tower—
Enormous, superhuman. While he wrought,
His fiery brothers from the plain around
Hunted the sons of Enoch and of Seth;
They plucked the eyes out of whoever passed,
And hurled at even arrows to the stars.
They set strong granite for the canvas wall,
And every block was clamped with iron chains.
It seemed a city made for hell. Its towers,
With their huge masses, made night in the land.
The walls were thick as mountains. On the door
They graved: "Let not God enter here."
 This done,
And having finished to cement and build
In a stone tower, they set him in the midst.
To him, still dark and haggard, "Oh, my sire,
Is the Eye gone?" quoth Zillah tremblingly.
But Cain replied: "Nay, it is even there."
Then added: "I will live beneath the earth,
As a lone man within his sepulchre.
I will see nothing; will be seen of none."
They digged a trench, and Cain said:
 " 'Tis enow,"
As he went down alone into the vault;
But when he sat, so ghost-like, in his chair,
And they had closed the dungeon o'er his head,
The Eye was in the tomb and fixed on Cain.

EVIRADNUS

The Adventurer

What was it Sigismond and Ladislāus said?

I know not if the rock, or tree o'erhead,
Had heard their speech;—but when the two spake low,
Among the trees, a shudder seemed to go
Through all their branches, just as if that way
A beast had passed to trouble and dismay.
Darker the shadow of the rock was seen,
And then a morsel of the shade, between
The sombre trees, took shape as it would seem
Some spectre walking in the sunset's gleam.

'Tis not a monster rising from its lair,
Nor phantom of the foliage and the air,
'Tis not a morsel of the granite's shade
That walks in deepest hollows of the glade.
'Tis not a vampire nor a spectre pale,
But living man in rugged coat of mail.
It is Alsatia's noble Chevalier,
Eviradnus the brave, that now is here.

The men who spoke he recognized the while
He rested in the thicket; words of guile
Most horrible were theirs as they passed on,
And to the ears of Eviradnus one—
One word had come which roused him. Well he knew
The land which lately he had journeyed through.

He down the valley went unto the inn
Where he had left his horse and page, Gasclin.
The horse had wanted drink, and lost a shoe;
And now, "Be quick!" he said, "with what you do,
For business calls me, I must not delay."
He strides the saddle and he rides away.

IN HOLY RAGE

Eviradnus was growing old apace,
The weight of years had left its hoary trace,
But still of knights the most renowned was he,
Model of bravery and purity.
His blood he spared not; ready day or night
To punish crime, his dauntless sword shone bright
In his unblemished hand; holy and white
And loyal all his noble life had been,
A Christian Samson coming on the scene.
With fist alone the gate he battered down
Of Sickingen in flames, and saved the town.
'Twas he, indignant at the honour paid
To crime, who with his heel an onslaught made
Upon Duke Lupus' shameful monument,
Tore down the statue he to fragments rent;
Then column of the Strasburg monster bore
To bridge of Wasselonne, and threw it o'er
Into the waters deep. The people round
Blazon the noble deeds that so abound
From Altorf unto Chaux-de-fonds, and say,
When he rests musing in a dreamy way,
"Behold, 'tis Charlemagne!" Tawny to see
And hairy, and seven feet high was he,
Like John of Bourbon. Roaming hill or wood
He looked like a wolf endeavouring to do good.
Bound up in duty, he of nought complained,
The cry for help his aid at once obtained.
Only he mourned the baseness of mankind,
And—that the beds too short he e'er must find.
When people suffer under cruel kings,
With pity moved, he to them succour brings.
'Twas he defended Alix from her foes

As sword of Urraca—he ever shows
His strength is for the feeble and oppressed;
Father of orphans he, and all distressed!
Kings of the Rhine in strongholds were by him
Boldly attacked, and tyrant barons grim.
He freed the towns—defying in his lair
Hugo The Eagle; boldly did he dare
To break the collar of Saverne, the ring
Of Colmar, and the iron torture-thing
Of Schlestadt, and the chain that Haguenau bore.
Confront with evil he an aspect wore
Good but most terrible. In the dread scale
Which princes weighted with their horrid tale
Of craft and violence, and blood and ill,
And fire and shocking deeds, his sword was still
God's counterpoise displayed. Ever alert
More evil from the wretched to avert,
Those hapless ones who 'neath Heaven's vault at night
Raise suppliant hands. His lance loved not the plight
Of mouldering in the rack, of no avail,
His battle-axe slipped from supporting nail
Quite easily; 'twas ill for action base
To come so near that he the thing could trace.
The steel-clad champion death drops all around
As glaciers water. Hero ever found
Eviradnus is kinsman of the race
Of Amadys of Gaul, and knights of Thrace.
He smiles at age. For he who never asked
For quarter from mankind—shall he be tasked
To beg of Time for mercy? Rather he
Would girdle up his loins, like Baldwin be.
Aged he is, but of a lineage rare;
The least intrepid of the birds that dare
Is not the eagle barbed. What matters age,
The years but fire him with a holy rage.
Though late from Palestine, he is not spent,—
With age he wrestles, firm in his intent.

In the Forest

If in the wood a traveller there had been
That eve, had lost himself, strange sight he'd seen.
Quite in the forest's heart a lighted space
Arose to view; in that deserted place
A lone, abandoned hall with light aglow
The long neglect of centuries did show.
The castle-towers of Corbus in decay
Were girt by weeds and growths that had their way;
Couch-grass and ivy, and wild eglantine
In subtle scaling warfare all combine.
Subject to such attacks three hundred years,
The donjon yields, and ruin now appears.
E'en as by leprosy the wild boars die,
In moat the crumbled battlements now lie;
Around the snake-like bramble twists its rings;
Freebooter sparrows come on daring wings
To perch upon the swivel-gun, nor heed
Its murmuring growl when pecking in their greed
The mulberries ripe. With insolence the thorn

Thrives on the desolation so forlorn.
But winter brings revenges; then the Keep
Wakes all vindictive from its seeming sleep,
Hurls down the heavy rain, night after night,
Thanking the season's all-resistless might;
And, when the gutters choke, its gargoyles four
From granite mouths in anger spit and pour
Upon the hated ivy hour by hour.

As to the sword rust is, so lichens are
To towering citadel with which they war.
Alas! for Corbus—dreary, desolate,
And yet its woes the winters mitigate.
It rears itself among convulsive throes
That shake its ruins when the tempest blows.
Winter, the savage warrior, pleases well,
With its storm clouds, the mighty citadel,—
Restoring it to life. The lightning flash
Strikes like a thief and flies; the winds that crash
Sound like a clarion, for the Tempest bluff
Is Battle's sister. And when wild and rough,
The north wind blows, the tower exultant cries
"Behold me!" When hail-hurling gales arise
Of blustering Equinox, to fan the strife,
It stands erect, with martial ardour rife,
A joyous soldier! When like yelping hound
Pursued by wolves, November comes to bound
In joy from rock to rock, like answering cheer
To howling January now so near—
"Come on!" the Donjon cries to blasts o'erhead—
It has seen Attila, and knows not dread.
Oh, dismal nights of contest in the rain
And mist, that furious would the battle gain,
The tower braves all, though angry skies pour fast
The flowing torrents, river-like and vast.
From their eight pinnacles the gorgons bay
And scattered monsters, in their stony way,
Are growling heard; the rampart lions gnaw
The misty air and slush with granite maw,
The sleet upon the griffins spits, and all
The Saurian monsters, answering to the squall,
Flap wings; while through the broken ceiling fall
Torrents of rain upon the forms beneath,
Dragons and snak'd Medusas gnashing teeth
In the dismantled rooms. Like armoured knight
The granite Castle fights with all its might,
Resisting through the winter. All in vain,
The heaven's bluster, January's rain,
And those dread elemental powers we call
The Infinite — the whirlwinds that appal—
Thunder and waterspouts; and winds that shake
As 'twere a tree its ripened fruit to take.

The winds grow wearied, warring with
  the tower,
The noisy North is out of breath, nor
  power
Has any blast old Corbus to defeat,
It still has strength their onslaughts
  worst to meet.
Thus, spite of briars and thistles, the
  old tower
Remains triumphant through the darkest hour;
Superb as pontiff, in the forest shown,
Its rows of battlements make triple
  crown;
At eve, its silhouette is finely traced
Immense and black—showing the Keep
  is placed
On rocky throne, sublime and high;
  east, west,
And north and south, at corners four,
  there rest
Four mounts; Aptar, where flourishes
  the pine,
And Toxis, where the elms grow green
  and fine;
Crobius and Bleyda, giants in their
  might,
Against the stormy winds to stand and
  fight,
And these above its diadem uphold
Night's living canopy of clouds unrolled.

The herdsman fears, and thinks its
  shadow creeps
To follow him; and superstition keeps
Such hold that Corbus as a terror reigns;
Folks say the Fort a target still remains
For the Black Archer—and that it contains
The cave where the Great Sleeper still
  sleeps sound.
The country people all the castle round
Are frightened easily, for legends grow
And mix with phantoms of the mind;
  we know
The hearth is cradle of such fantasies,
And in the smoke the cotter sees arise
From low-thatched hut he traces cause
  of dread.
Thus rendering thanks that he is lowly
  bred,
Because from such none look for valorous deeds,
The peasant flies the Tower, although it
  leads
A noble knight to seek adventure there,
And, from his point of honour, dangers
  dare.

Thus very rarely passer-by is seen;
But—it might be with twenty years between,
Or haply less—at unfixed interval
There would a semblance be of festival.
A Seneschal and usher would appear,
And troops of servants many baskets
  bear.
Then were, in mystery, preparations
  made,
And they departed—for till night none
  stayed.
But 'twixt the branches gazers could
  descry
The blackened hall lit up most brilliantly.
None dared approach—and this the reason why.

A Weird Meal

When died a noble Marquis of Lusace
'Twas the custom for the heir who filled
  his place
Before assuming princely pomp and
  power

To sup one night in Corbus' olden tower.
From this weird meal he passed to the degree
Of Prince and Margrave; nor could ever he
Be thought brave knight, or she — if woman claim
The rank—be reckoned of unblemished fame
Till they had breathed the air of ages gone,
The funeral odours, in the nest alone
Of its dead masters. Ancient was the race;
To climb the upward stem of proud Lusace
Gives one a vertigo; descended they
From ancestor of Attila, men say;
Their race to him—through Pagans—they trace back;
Becoming Christians, they their line could track
Through Lechus, Plato, Otho to combine
With Ursus, Stephen, in a lordly line.
Of all those masters of the country round
That were on Northern Europe's boundary found—
At first were waves, and then the dykes were reared—
Corbus in double majesty appeared,
Castle on hill and town upon the plain;
And one who mounted on the tower could gain
A view beyond the pines and rocks, of spires
That pierce the shade the distant scene acquires;
A walled town is it, but 'tis not ally
Of the old citadel's proud majesty;
Unto itself belonging this remained.
Often a castle was thus self-sustained

And equalled towns; witness in Lombardy
Crama, and Prato in fair Tuscany,
And in Apulia Barletta too;—and each one
Was powerful as a town, and dreaded none.
Corbus ranked thus; its precincts seemed to hold
The reflex of its mighty kings of old;
Their great events had witness in these walls,
Their marriages were here and funerals,
And mostly here it was that they were born;
And here crowned Barons ruled with pride and scorn;
Cradle of Scythian majesty this place.
Now each new master of this ancient race
A duty owed to ancestors which he
Was bound to carry on. The law's decree
It was that he should pass alone the night
Which made him king, as in their solemn sight.
Just at the forest's edge a clerk was met
With wine in sacred cup and purpose set,
A wine mysterious, which the heir must drink
To cause deep slumber till the day's soft brink.
Then to the castle tower he wends his way,
And finds a supper laid with rich display.
He sups and sleeps: when to his slumbering eyes
The shades of kings from Bela all arise.

None dare the tower to enter on this night,
But when the morning dawns, crowds are in sight
The dreamer to deliver,—whom half dazed,
And with the visions of the night amazed,
They to the old church take, where rests the dust
Of Borivorus; then the bishop must,
With fervent blessings on his eyes and mouth,
Put in his hands the stony hatchets both,
With which — even like death impartially—
Struck Attila, with one arm dexterously
The south, and with the other arm the north.

This day the town the threatening flag set forth
Of Marquis Swantibore, the monster he
Who in the wood tied up his wife, to be
Devoured by wolves, together with the bull
Of which with jealousy his heart was full.

Even when woman took the place of heir
The tower of Corbus claimed the supper there;
'Twas law—the woman trembled, but must dare.

Unmarried

Niece of the Marquis—John the Striker named—
Mahaud to-day the marquisate has claimed.
A noble dame—the crown is hers by right:
As woman she has graces that delight.
A queen devoid of beauty is not queen,
She needs the royalty of beauty's mien;
God in His harmony has equal ends
For cedar that resists, and reed that bends,
And good it is a woman sometimes rules,
Holds in her hand the power, and manners schools,
And laws and mind;—succeeding master proud,
With gentle voice and smile she leads the crowd,
The sombre human troop. But sweet Mahaud
On evil days had fallen; gentle, good,
Alas! she held the sceptre like a flower;
Timid yet gay, imprudent for the hour,
And careless too. With Europe all in throes,
Though twenty years she now already knows,
She has refused to marry, although oft
Entreated. It is time an arm less soft
Than hers — a manly arm — supported her;
Like to the rainbow she, one might aver,
Shining on high between the cloud and rain,
Or like the ewe that gambols on the plain
Between the bear and tiger; innocent,
She has two neighbours of most foul intent:
For foes the Beauty has, in life's pure spring,
The German Emperor and the Polish King.

The Evil Pair

The difference this betwixt the evil pair,
Faithless to God—for laws without a care—
One was the claw, the other one the will
Controlling. Yet to mass they both went still,
And on the rosary told their beads each day.
But none the less the world believed that they
Unto the powers of hell their souls had sold.
Even in whispers men each other told
The details of the pact which they had signed
With that dark power, the foe of human kind;
In whispers, for the crowd had mortal dread
Of them so high, and woes that they had spread.
One might be vengeance and the other hate,
Yet lived they side by side, in powerful state
And close alliance. All the people near
From red horizon dwelt in abject fear,
Mastered by them; their figures darkly grand
Had ruddy reflex from the wasted land,
And fires, and towns they sacked. Besides the one,
Like David, poet was, the other shone
As fine musician—rumour spread their fame,
Declaring them divine, until each name
In Italy's fine sonnets met with praise.
The ancient hierarch in those old days
Had custom strange, a now forgotten thing,
It was a European plan that King
Of France was marquis, and th' imperial head
Of Germany was duke; there was no need
To class the other kings, but barons they,
Obedient vassals unto Rome, their stay.
The King of Poland was but simple knight,
Yet now, for once, had strange unwonted right,
And, as exception to the common state,
This one Sarmatian King was held as great
As German Emperor; and each knew how
His evil part to play, nor mercy show.
The German had one aim, it was to take
All the land he could, and it his own to make.
The Pole, already having Baltic shore,
Seized Celtic ports, still needing more and more.
On all the Northern Sea his crafts roused fear;
Iceland beheld his demon navy near.
Antwerp the German burnt; and Prussias twain
Bowed to his yoke. The Polish King was fain
To help the Russian Spotocus—his aid
Was like the help that in their common trade
A sturdy butcher gives a weaker one.
The King it is who seizes, and this done,
The Emperor pillages, usurping right
In war Teutonic, settled but by might.
The King in Jutland cynic footing gains,
The weak coerced, the while with cunning pains
The strong are duped. But 'tis a law they make

That their accord themselves should never break.
From Arctic seas to cities Transalpine,
Their hideous talons, curved for sure rapine,
Scrape o'er and o'er the mournful continent,
Their plans succeed, and each is well content.
Thus under Satan's all paternal care
They brothers are, this royal bandit pair.
Oh, noxious conquerors! with transient rule
Chimera heads—ambition can but fool.
Their misty minds but harbour rottenness
Loathsome and fetid, and all barrenness—
Their deeds to ashes turn, and, hydra-bred,
The mystic skeleton is theirs to dread.
The daring German and the cunning Pole
Noted to-day a woman had control
Of lands, and watched Mahaud like evil spies;
And from the Emp'ror's cruel mouth—with dyes
Of wrath empurpled—came these words of late:
"The empire wearies of the wallet weight
Hung at its back—this High and Low Lusace,
Whose hateful load grows heavier apace,
That now a woman holds its ruler's place."
Threatening, and blood suggesting, every word;
The watchful Pole was silent—but he heard.

Two monstrous dangers; but the heedless one
Babbles and smiles, and bids all care begone—
Likes lively speech—while all the poor she makes
To love her, and the taxes off she takes.
A life of dance and pleasure she has known—
A woman always; in her jewelled crown
It is the pearl she loves—not cutting gems,
For these can wound, and mark men's diadems.
She pays the hire of Homer's copyists,
And in the Courts of Love presiding, lists.

Quite recently unto her Court have come
Two men—unknown their names or native home,
Their rank or race; but one plays well the lute,
The other is a troubadour; both suit
The taste of Mahaud, when on summer eve,
'Neath opened windows, they obtain her leave
To sing upon the terrace, and relate
The charming tales that do with music mate.
In August the Moravians have their fête,
But it is radiant June in which Lusace
Must consecrate her noble Margrave race.
Thus in the weird and old ancestral tower
For Mahaud now has come the fateful hour,
The lonely supper which her state decrees.

What matters this to flowers, and birds, and trees,
And clouds and fountains? That the people may
Still bear their yoke—have kings to rule alway?
The water flows, the wind in passing by
In murmuring tones takes up the questioning cry.

LOVE AND FEAST

The old stupendous hall has but one door,
And in the dusk it seems that more and more
The walls recede in space unlimited.
At the far end there is a table spread
That in the dreary void with splendour shines;
For ceiling we behold but rafter lines.
The table is arranged for one sole guest,
A solitary chair doth near it rest,
Throne-like, 'neath canopy that droopeth down
From the black beams; upon the walls are shown
The painted histories of the olden might,
The Wendish King Thassilo's sturdy fight
On land with Nimrod, and on ocean wide
With Neptune. Rivers too personified
Appear—the Rhine as by the Meuse betrayed,
And fading groups of Odin in the shade,
And the wolf Fenrir and the Asgard snake.
One might the place for dragon's stable take.
The only lights that in the shed appear
Spring from the table's giant chandelier
With seven iron branches — brought from hell
By Attila Archangel, people tell,
When he had conquered Mammon—and they say
That seven souls were the first flames that day.
This banquet hall looks an abyss outlined
With shadowy vagueness, though indeed we find
In the far depth upon the table spread
A sudden, strong, and glaring light is shed,
Striking upon the goldsmith's burnished works,
And on the pheasants killed by traitor hawks.
Loaded the table is with viands cold,
Ewers and flagons, all enough of old
To make a love feast. All the napery
Was Friesland's famous make; and fair to see
The dishes, silver-gilt and bordered round
With flowers; for fruit, here strawberries were found
And citrons, apples too, and nectarines.
The wooden bowls were carved in cunning lines
By peasants of the Murg, whose skilful hands
With patient toil reclaim the barren lands
And make their gardens flourish on a rock,
Or mountain where we see the hunters flock.
A golden cup, with handles Florentine,
Shows horned Acteons, armed and booted fine,
Who fight with sword in hand against the hounds.

Roses and gladioles make up bright mounds
Of flowers, with juniper and aniseed;
While sage, all newly cut for this great need,
Covers the Persian carpet that is spread
Beneath the table, and so helps to shed
Around a perfume of the balmy spring.
Beyond is desolation withering.
One hears within the hollow dreary space
Across the grove, made fresh by summer's grace,
The wind that ever is with mystic might
A spirit ripple of the Infinite.
The glass restored to frames to creak is made
By blustering wind that comes from neighbouring glade.
Strange, in this dream-like place, so drear and lone,
The guest expected was a living one!
The seven lights from seven arms make glow
Almost with life the staring eyes that show
On the dim frescoes—and along the walls
Is here and there a stool, or the light falls
O'er some long chest, with likeness to a tomb;
Yet were displayed amid the mournful gloom
Some copper vessels, and some crockery ware.
The door—as if it must, yet scarcely dare—
Had opened widely to the night's fresh air.

No voice is heard, for man has fled the place;
But Terror crouches in the corners' space.
And waits the coming guest. This banquet hall
Of Titans is so high, that he who shall
With wandering eye look up from beam to beam
Of the confused wild roof will haply seem
To wonder that the stars he sees not there.
Giants the spiders are, that weave with care
Their hideous webs, which float the joists amid,
Joists whose dark ends in griffins' jaws are hid.
The light is lurid, and the air like death,
And dark and foul. Even Night holds its breath
Awhile. One might suppose the door had fear
To move its double leaves—their noise to hear.

Legion of Death

But the great hall of generations dead
Has something more sepulchral and more dread
Than lurid glare from seven-branched chandelier
Or table lone with stately daïs near—
Two rows of arches o'er a colonnade
With knights on horseback all in mail arrayed,
Each one disposed with pillar at his back
And to another vis-à-vis. Nor lack
The fittings all complete; in each right hand
A lance is seen; the armoured horses stand

With chamfrons laced, and harness buckled sure;
The cuissarts' studs are by their clamps secure;
The dirks stand out upon the saddle-bow;
Even unto the horses' feet do flow
Caparisons,—the leather all well clasped,
The gorget and the spurs with bronze tongues hasped,
The shining long sword from the saddle hung,
The battle-axe across the back was flung.
Under the arm a trusty dagger rests,
Each spiked knee-piece its murderous power attests.
Feet press the stirrups—hands on bridle shown
Proclaim all ready, with the visors down,
And yet they stir not, nor is audible
A sound to make the sight less terrible.

Each monstrous horse a frontal horn doth bear,
If e'er the Prince of Darkness herdsman were
These cattle black were his by surest right,
Like things but seen in horrid dreams of night.
The steeds are swathed in trappings manifold,
The arméd knights are grave, and stern, and cold,
Terrific too; the clench'd fists seem to hold
Some frightful missive, which the phantom hands
Would show, if opened out at Hell's commands.
The dusk exaggerates their giant size.

The shade is awed—the pillars coldly rise.
Oh, Night! why are these awful warriors here?

Horses and horsemen that make gazers fear
Are only empty armour. But erect
And haughty mien they all affect
And threatening air—though shades of iron still.
Are they strange larvæ—these their statues ill?
No. They are dreams of horror clothed in brass,
Which from profoundest depths of evil pass
With futile aim to dare the Infinite!
Souls tremble at the silent spectre sight,
As if in this mysterious cavalcade
They saw the weird and mystic halt was made
Of them who at the coming dawn of day
Would fade, and from their vision pass away.
A stranger looking in, these masks to see,
Might deem from Death some mandate there might be
At times to burst the tombs—the dead to wear
A human shape, and mustering ranks appear
Of phantoms, each confronting other shade.

Grave-clothes are not more grim and sombre made
Than are these helms, the deaf and sealed-up graves
Are not more icy than these arms; the staves

Of hideous biers have not their joints more strong
Than are the joinings of these legs; the long
Scaled gauntlet fingers look like worms that shine,
And battle robes to shroud-like folds incline.
The heads are skull-like, and the stony feet
Seem for the charnal house but only meet.
The pikes have death's-heads carved, and seem to be
Too heavy; but the shapes defiantly
Sit proudly in the saddle—and perforce
The rider looks united to the horse
Upon whose flanks the mail and harness cross.
The cap of Marquis beams near Ducal wreath,
And on the helm and gleaming shield beneath
Alternate triple pearls with leaves displayed
Of parsley, and the royal robes are made
So large that with the knightly hauberk they
Seem to o'erspread the palfrey every way.
To Rome the oldest armour might be traced,
And men and horses' armour interlaced
Blent horribly; the man and steed we feel
Made but one hydra with its scales of steel.

Yet is there history here. Each coat of mail
Is representant of some stirring tale.
Each delta-shaped escutcheon shines to show
A vision of the chief by it we know.
Here are the blood-stained Dukes' and Marquis' line,
Barbaric lords, who amid war's rapine
Bore gilded saints upon their banners still
Painted on fishes' skin with cunning skill.
Here Geth, who to the Slaves cried "Onward go,"
And Mundiaque and Ottocar—Plato
And Ladislaus Kunne; and Welf who bore
These words upon his shield his foes before:
"Nothing there is I fear." Otho blear-eyed,
Zultan and Nazamustus, and beside
The later Spignus, e'en to Spartibor
Of triple vision, and yet more and more
As if a pause at every age were made,
And Antæus' fearful dynasty portrayed.

What do they here so rigid and erect?
What wait they for—and what do they expect?
Blindness fills up the helm 'neath iron brows;
Like sapless tree no soul the hero knows.
Darkness is now where eyes with flame were fraught,
And pierced visor serves for mask of nought.
Of empty void is spectral giant made,
And each of these all-powerful knights displayed
Is only rind of pride and murderous sin;
Themselves are held the icy grave within.
Rust eats the casques enamoured once so much
Of death and daring—which knew kiss-like touch

Of banner—mistress so august and dear—
But not an arm can stir its hinges here;
Behold how mute are they whose threats were heard
Like savage roar—whose gnashing teeth and word
Deadened the clarion's tones; the helmets dread
Have not a sound, and all the armour spread,
The hauberks, that strong breathing seemed to sway,
Are stranded now in helplessness alway
To see the shadows, still prolonged, that seem
To take at night the image of a dream.

These two great files reach from the door afar
To where the table and the daïs are,
Leaving between their fronts a narrow lane.
On the left side the Marquises maintain
Their place, but the right side the Dukes retain,
And till the roof, embattled by Spignus,
But worn by time that even that subdues,
Should fall upon their heads, these forms will stand
The grades confronting—one on either hand.
While in advance beyond, with haughty head—
As if commander of this squadron dread—
All waiting signal of the Judgment Day,
In stone was seen in olden sculptors' way
Charlemagne the King, who on the earth had found
Only twelve knights to grace his Table Round.

The crests were an assembly of strange things,
Of horrors such as nightmare only brings.
Asps, and spread eagles without beak or feet,
Sirens and mermaids here and dragons meet,
And antlered stags and fabled unicorn,
And fearful things of monstrous fancy born.
Upon the rigid form of morion's sheen
Winged lions and the Cerberus are seen,
And serpents winged and finned; things made to fright
That timid foe, alone by sense of sight.
Some leaning forward and the others back,
They looked a growing forest that did lack
No form of terror; but these things of dread
That once on barons' helms the battle led
Beneath the giant banners, now are still,
As if they gaped and found the time but ill,
Wearied the ages passed so slowly by,
And that the gory dead no more did lie
Beneath their feet—pined for the battle-cry,
The trumpet's clash, the carnage and the strife,
Yawning to taste again their dreadful life.
Like tears upon the palfreys' muzzles were
The hard reflections of the metal there;
From out these spectres, ages past exhumed,

And as their shadows on the roof-beams loomed,
Cast by the trembling light, each figure wan
Seemed growing, and a monstrous shape to don,
So that the double range of horrors made
The darkened zenith clouds of blackest shade,
That shaped themselves to profiles terrible.

All motionless the coursers horrible,
That formed a legion lured by Death to war,
These men and horses masked, how dread they are!
Absorbed in shadows of the eternal shore,
Among the living all their tasks are o'er.
Silent, they seem all mystery to brave,
These sphynxes whom no beacon light can save
Upon the threshold of the gulf so near,
As if they faced the great enigma here;
Ready with hoofs, between the pillars blue,
To strike out sparks, and combats to renew,
Choosing for battle-field the shades below,
Which they provoked by deeds we cannot know,
In that dark realm thought dares not to expound
False masks from heaven lowered to depths profound.

A NOISE ON THE FLOOR

This is the scene on which now enters in Eviradnus; and follows page Gasclin.

The outer walls were almost all decayed,
The door, for ancient Marquises once made—
Raised many steps above the courtyard near—
Commanded view of the horizon clear.
The forest looked a great gulf all around,
And on the rock of Corbus there were found
Secret and blood-stained precipices tall.
Duke Plato built the tower and banquet hall
Over great pits,—so was it Rumour said.
The flooring sounds 'neath Eviradnus' tread
Above abysses many.
    "Page," said he,
"Come here, your eyes than mine can better see,
For sight is woman-like and shuns the old;
Ah! he can see enough, when years are told,
Who backward looks. But, boy, turn towards the glade
And tell me what you see."
    The boy obeyed,
And leaned across the threshold, while the bright,
Full moon shed o'er the glade its white, pure light.
"I see a horse and woman on it now,"
Said Gasclin, "and companions also show."
"Who are they?" asked the seeker of sublime
Adventures. "Sir, I now can hear like chime
The sound of voices, and men's voices too,
Laughter and talk; two men there are in view,

Across the road the shadows clear I
    mark
Of horses three."
            "Enough. Now, Gasclin, hark!"
Exclaimed the knight, "you must at
    once return
By other path than that which you dis-
    cern,
So that you be not seen. At break of
    day
Bring back our horses fresh, and every
    way
Caparisoned; now leave me, boy, I say."
The page looked at his master like a son,
And said to him, "Oh, if I might stay
    on,
For they are two."
        "Go—I suffice alone!"

The Spectral Knight

And lone the hero is within the hall
And nears the table where the glasses all
Show in profusion; all the vessels there,
Goblets and glasses gilt, or painted fair,
Are ranged for different wines with prac-
    tised care.
He thirsts; the flagons tempt; but there
    must stay
One drop in emptied glass, and 'twould
    betray
The fact that some one living had been
    here.
Straight to the horses goes he, pauses
    near
That which is next the table shining
    bright,
Seizes the rider — plucks the phantom
    knight
To pieces—all in vain its panoply
And pallid shining to his practised eye;
Then he conveys the severed iron re-
    main
To corner of the hall where darkness
    reigns;
Against the wall he lays the armour low
In dust and gloom like hero vanquished
    now—
But keeping pond'rous lance and shield
    so old,
Mounts to the empty saddle, and be-
    hold!
A statue Eviradnus has become,
Like to the others in their frigid home.
With visor down scarce breathing
    seemed maintained.

Throughout the hall a death-like silence
    reigned.

Kiss for Fodder

Listen! like hum from unseen nests we
    hear
A mirthful buzz of voices coming near,
Of footsteps—laughter—from the trem-
    bling trees.
And now the thick-set forest all receives
A flood of moonlight—and there gently
    floats
The sound of a guitar of Innsbruck;
    notes
Which blend with chimes—vibrating to
    the hand—
Of tiny bell—where sounds a grain of
    sand.
A man's voice mixes with the melody,
And vaguely melts to song in harmony.

"If you like we'll dream a dream.
    Let us mount on palfreys two;
    Birds are singing,—let it seem
    You lure me—and I take you.

"Let us start—'tis eve, you see,
    I'm thy master and thy prey.

My bright steel shall pleasure be;
  Yours, it shall be love, I say.

"Journeying leisurely we go,
  We will make our steeds touch heads,
Kiss for fodder,—and we so
  Satisfy our horses' needs.

"Come! the two delusive things
  Stamp impatiently it seems,
Yours has heavenward soaring wings,
  Mine is of the land of dreams.

"What's our baggage? only vows,
  Happiness, and all our care.
And the flower that sweetly shows
  Nestling lightly in your hair.

"Come, the oaks all dark appear,
  Twilight now will soon depart,
Railing sparrows laugh to hear
  Chains thou puttest round my heart.

"Not my fault 'twill surely be
  If the hills should vocal prove,
And the trees when us they see,
  All should murmur—let us love!

"Oh, be gentle!—I am dazed,
  See the dew is on the grass,
Wakened butterflies amazed
  Follow thee as on we pass.

"Envious night-birds open wide
  Their round eyes to gaze awhile,
Nymphs that lean their urns beside
  From their grottoes softly smile,

"And exclaim, by fancy stirred,
  'Hero and Leander they;

We in listening for a word
  Let our water fall away.'

"Let us journey Austrian way,
  With the daybreak on our brow;
I be great, and you I say
  Rich, because we love shall know.

"Let us over countries rove,
  On our charming steeds content,
In the azure light of love,
  And its sweet bewilderment.

"For the charges at our inn,
  You with maiden smiles shall pay;
I the landlord's heart will win
  In a scholar's pleasant way.

"You, great lady—and I, Count—
  Come, my heart has opened quite.
We this tale will still recount,
  To the stars that shine at night."

The melody went on some moments more
Among the trees the calm moon glistened o'er,
Then trembled and was hushed; the voice's thrill
Stopped like alighting birds, and all was still.

THREE HEADS

Quite suddenly there showed across the door,
Three heads which all a festive aspect wore.
Two men were there; and, dressed in cloth of gold,
A woman. Of the men one might have told

Some thirty years, the other younger seemed,
Was tall and fair, and from his shoulder gleamed
A gay guitar with ivy leaves enlaced.
The other man was dark, but pallid-faced
And small. At the first glance they seemed to be
But made of perfume and frivolity.
Handsome they were, but through their comely mien
A grinning demon might be clearly seen.
April has flowers where lurk the slugs between.

"Big Joss and little Zeno, pray come here;
Look now—how dreadful! can I help but fear!"
Madame Mahaud was speaker. Moonlight there
Caressingly enhanced her beauty rare,
Making it shine and tremble, as if she
So soft and gentle were of things that be
Of air created, and are brought and ta'en
By heavenly flashes. Now, she spoke again:
"Certes, 'tis heavy purchase of a throne,
To pass the night here utterly alone.
Had you not slyly come to guard me now,
I should have died of fright outright I know."
The moonbeams through the open door did fall,
And shine upon the figure next the wall.
Said Zeno, "If I played the Marquis part,
I'd send this rubbish to the auction mart;

Out of the heap should come the finest wine,
Pleasure and gala-fêtes, were it all mine."
And then with scornful hand he touched the thing,
And made the metal like a soul's cry ring.
He laughed—the gauntlet trembled at his stroke.
"Let rest my ancestors"—'twas Mahaud spoke;
Then murmuring added she, "For you are much
Too small their noble armour here to touch."
And Zeno paled, but Joss with laugh exclaimed,
"Why, all these good black men so grandly named
Are only nests for mice. By Jove, although
They lifelike look and terrible, we know
What is within; just listen, and you'll hear
The vermins' gnawing teeth, yet 'twould appear
These figures once were proudly named Otho,
And Ottocar, and Bela, and Plato.
Alas! the end's not pleasant—puts one out;
To have been kings and dukes—made mighty rout—
Colossal heroes filling tombs with slain,
And, Madame, this to only now remain;
A peaceful nibbling rat to calmly pierce
A prince's noble armour proud and fierce."

"Sing, if you will—but do not speak so loud;

Besides, such things as these," said fair Mahaud,
"In your condition are not understood."
"Well said," made answer Zeno, " 'tis a place
Of wonders—I see serpents, and can trace
Vampires, and monsters swarming, that arise
In mist, through chinks, to meet the gazer's eyes."
Then Mahaud shuddered, and she said:
"The wine
The Abbé made me drink as task of mine,
Will soon enwrap me in the soundest sleep—
Swear not to leave me—that you here will keep."
"I swear," cried Joss, and Zeno, "I also;
But now at once to supper let us go."

A Minstrel Without Shame

With laugh and song they to the table went.
Said Mahaud gaily: "It is my intent
To make Joss chamberlain. Zeno shall be
A constable supreme of high degree."
All three were joyous, and were fair to see.
Joss ate—and Zeno drank; on stools the pair,
With Mahaud musing in the regal chair.
The sound of separate leaf we do not note—
And so their babble seemed to idly float,
And leave no thought behind. Now and again
Joss his guitar made trill with plaintive strain
Or Tyrolean air; and lively tales they told
Mingled with mirth all free, and frank, and bold.
Said Mahaud: "Do you know how fortunate
You are?" "Yes, we are young at any rate—
Lovers half crazy—this is truth at least."
"And more, for you know Latin like a priest,
And Joss sings well."
          "Ah, yes, our master true,
Yields us these gifts beyond the measure due."
"Your master!—who is he?" Mahaud exclaimed.
"Satan, we say—but Sin you'd think him named,"
Said Zeno, veiling words in raillery.
"Do not laugh thus," she said with dignity;
"Peace, Zeno. Joss, you speak, my chamberlain."
"Madame, Viridis, Countess of Milan,
Was deemed superb; Diana on the mount
Dazzled the shepherd boy; ever we count
The Isabel of Saxony so fair,
And Cleopatra's beauty all so rare—
Aspasia's, too, that must with theirs compare—
That praise of them no fitting language hath.
Divine was Rhodope—and Venus' wrath
Was such at Erylesis' perfect throat,
She dragged her to the forge where Vulcan smote
Her beauty on his anvil. Well, as much
As star transcends a sequin, and just such

As temple is to rubbish-heap, I say
You do eclipse their beauty every way.
Those airy sprites that from the azure smile
Peris and elfs the while they men beguile,
Have brows less youthful pure than yours; besides
Dishevelled they whose shaded beauty hides
In clouds."
    "Flatt'rer," said Mahaud, "you but sing
Too well."
    Then Joss more homage sought to bring;
"If I were angel under heav'n," said he,
"Or girl or demon, I would seek to be
By you instructed in all art and grace,
And as in school but take a scholar's place.
Highness, you are a fairy bright, whose hand
For sceptre vile gave up your proper wand."
Fair Mahaud mused—then said, "Be silent now;
You seem to watch me; little 'tis I know,
Only that from Bohemia Joss doth come,
And that in Poland Zeno hath his home.
But you amuse me; I am rich, you poor—
What boon shall I confer and make secure?
What gift? ask of me, poets, what you will
And I will grant it—promise to fulfil."
"A kiss," said Joss.
    "A kiss!" quick anger wrought
In Mahaud at the minstrel's shameless thought,
And flush of indignation warmed her cheek.
"You do forget to whom it is you speak,"
She cried.
    "Had I not known your high degree,
Should I have asked this royal boon," said he,
"Obtained or given, a kiss must ever be.
No gift like king's—no kiss like that of queen!"
Queen! And on Mahaud's face a smile was seen.

The Odour of Crime

But now the potion proved its subtle power,
And Mahaud's heavy eyelids 'gan to lower.
Zeno, with finger on his lip, looked on—
Her head next drooped, and consciousness was gone.
Smiling she slept, serene and very fair,
He took her hand, which fell all unaware.
"She sleeps," said Zeno, "now let chance or fate
Decide for us which has the marquisate,
And which the girl."
    Upon their faces now
A hungry tiger's look began to show.
"My brother, let us speak like men of sense,"
Said Joss, "while Mahaud dreams in innocence,
We grasp all here—and hold the foolish thing—
Our Friend below to us success will bring.
He keeps his word; 'tis thanks to him I say,

No awkward chance has marred our plans to-day.
All has succeeded—now no human power
Can take from us this woman and her dower.
Let us conclude. To wrangle and to fight
For just a yes or no, or to prove right
The Arian doctrines, all the time the Pope
Laughs in his sleeve at you—or with the hope
Some blue-eyed damsel with a tender skin
And milkwhite dainty hands by force to win—
This might be well in days when men bore loss
And fought for Latin or Byzantine Cross;
When Jack and Rudolf did like fools contend,
And for a simple wench their valour spend—
When Pepin held a synod at Leptine,
And times than now were much less wise and fine.
We do no longer heap up quarrels thus,
But better know how projects to discuss.
Have you the needful dice?"
    "Yes, here they wait
For us."
      "Who wins shall have the Marquisate;
Loser, the girl."
    "Agreed."
      "A noise I hear?"
"Only the wind that sounds like some one near—
Are you afraid?" said Zeno.
    "Naught I fear
Save fasting — and that solid earth should gape.
Let's throw and fate decide—ere time escape."
Then rolled the dice.
    " 'Tis four."
      'Twas Joss to throw.
"Six!—and I neatly win, you see; and lo!
At bottom of this box I've found Lusace,
And henceforth my orchestra will have place;
To it they'll dance. Taxes I'll raise, and they
In dread of rope and forfeit well will pay;
Brass trumpet-calls shall be my flutes that lead,
Where gibbets rise the imposts grow and spread."
Said Zeno, "I've the girl and so is best."
"She's beautiful," said Joss.
    "Yes, 'tis confess'd."
"What shall you do with her?" asked Joss.
    "I know.
Make her a corpse," said Zeno; "marked you how
The jade insulted me just now! Too small
She called me—such the words her lips let fall.
I say, that moment ere the dice I threw
Had yawning Hell cried out, 'My son, for you
The chance is open still: take in a heap
The fair Lusace's seven towns, and reap
The corn, and wine, and oil of counties ten,
With all their people diligent, and then
Bohemia with its silver mines, and now

The lofty land whence mighty rivers flow
And not a brook returns; add to these counts
The Tyrol with its lovely azure mounts
And France with her historic fleurs-de-lis;
Come now, decide, what 'tis your choice must be?'
I should have answered, 'Vengeance! give to me
Rather than France, Bohemia, or the fair
Blue Tyrol! I my choice, O Hell! declare
For government of darkness and of death,
Of grave and worms.' Brother, this woman hath
As marchioness with absurdity set forth
To rule o'er frontier bulwarks of the north.
In any case to us a danger she,
And having stupidly insulted me
'Tis needful that she die. To blurt all out—
I know that you desire her; without doubt
The flame that rages in my heart warms yours;
To carry out these subtle plans of ours,
We have become as gipsies near this doll,
You as her page—I dotard to control—
Pretended gallants changed to lovers now.
So, brother, this being fact for us to know
Sooner or later, 'gainst our best intent
About her we should quarrel. Evident
Is it our compact would be broken through.
There is only one thing for us to do,
And that is, kill her."
    "Logic very clear,"
Said musing Joss, "but what of blood shed here?"
Then Zeno stooped and lifted from the ground
An edge of carpet—groped until he found
A ring, which, pulled, an opening did disclose,
With deep abyss beneath; from it there rose
The odour rank of crime. Joss walked to see
While Zeno pointed to it silently.
But eyes met eyes, and Joss, well pleased, was fain
By nod of head to make approval plain.

Hell's Partition

If sulphurous light had shone from this vile well
One might have said it was a mouth of hell,
So large the trap that by some sudden blow
A man might backward fall and sink below.
Who looked could see a harrow's threatening teeth,
But lost in night was everything beneath.
Partitions blood-stained have a reddened smear,
And Terror unrelieved is master here.
One feels the place has secret histories
Replete with dreadful murderous mysteries,
And that this sepulchre, forgot to-day,
Is home of trailing ghosts that grope their way

Along the walls where spectre reptiles crawl.
"Our fathers fashioned for us after all
Some useful things," said Joss; then Zeno spoke:
"I know what Corbus hides beneath its cloak,
I and the osprey know its ancient walls
And how was justice done within its halls."
"And are you sure that Mahaud will not wake?"
"Her eyes are closed as now my fist I make;
She is in mystic and unearthly sleep;
The potion still its power o'er her must keep."
"But she will surely wake at break of day?"
"In darkness."
  "What will all the courtiers say
When in the place of her they find two men?"
"To them we will declare ourselves—and then
They at our feet will fall."
  "Where leads this hole?"
"To where the crow makes feast and torrents roll,
To desolation. Let us end it now."

These young and handsome men had seemed to grow
Deformed and hideous—so doth foul black heart
Disfigure man, till beauty all depart.
So too the hell within the human face
Transparent is. They nearer move apace;
And Mahaud soundly sleeps as in a bed.
"To work."

Joss seizes her and holds her head
Supporting her beneath her arms, in his;
And then he dared to plant a monstrous kiss
Upon her rosy lips,—while Zeno bent
Before the massive chair, and with intent
Her robe disordered as he raised her feet;
Her dainty ankles thus their gaze to meet.
And while the mystic sleep was all profound,
The pit gaped wide like grave in burial ground.

SPIRIT OF THE ABYSS

Bearing the sleeping Mahaud they moved now
Silent and bent with heavy step and slow.
Zeno faced darkness—Joss turned towards the light—
So that the hall to Joss was quite in sight.
Sudden he stopped—and Zeno, "What now!" called,
But Joss replied not, though he seemed appalled,
And made a sign to Zeno, who with speed
Looked back. Then seemed they changed to stone indeed,
For both perceived that in the vaulted hall
One of the grand old knights ranged by the wall
Descended from his horse. Like phantom he
Moved with a horrible tranquillity.
Masked by his helm towards them he came; his tread

Made the floor tremble—and one might
    have said
A spirit of th' abyss was here; between
    Them and the pit he came—a barrier
    seen;
Then said, with sword in hand and visor
    down,
In measured tones that had sepulchral
    grown
As tolling bell. "Stop, Sigismond, and
    you,
King Ladislāus;" at those words, though
    few,
They dropped the Marchioness, and in
    such a way
That at their feet like rigid corpse she
    lay.

The deep voice speeking from the vi-
    sor's grate
Proceeded—while the two in abject state
Cowered low. Joss paled, by gloom and
    dread o'ercast.
And Zeno trembled like a yielding mast.
"You two who listen now must recollect
The compact all your fellow-men sus-
    pect.
'Tis this: 'I, Satan, god of darkened
    sphere,
The king of gloom and winds that bring
    things drear,
Alliance make with my two brothers
    dear,
The Emperor Sigismond and Polish
    King
Named Ladislāus. I to surely bring
Aid and protection to them both alway,
And never to absent myself or say
I'm weary. And yet more—I, being lord
Of sea and land, to Sigismond award
The earth; to Ladislāus all the sea.
With this condition that they yield to
    me
When I the forfeit claim—the King his
    head,
But shall the Emperor give his soul in-
    stead.' "

Said Joss, "Is't he?—Spectre with flash-
    ing eyes,
And art thou Satan come us to sur-
    prise?"
"Much less am I and yet much more.
Oh, kings of crimes and plots! your day
    is o'er,
But I your lives will only take to-day;
Beneath the talons black your souls
    let stay
To wrestle still."
        The pair looked stupefied
And crushed. Exchanging looks 'twas
    Zeno cried,
Speaking to Joss, "Now who—who can
    it be?"
Joss stammered, "Yes, no refuge can I
    see;
The doom is on us. But oh, spectre!
    say
Who are you?"
        "I'm the judge."
        "Then mercy, pray."
The voice replied: "God guides His
    chosen hand
To be th' Avenger in your path to stand.
Your hour has sounded, nothing now in-
    deed
Can change for you the destiny decreed,
Irrevocable quite. Yes, I looked on.
Ah! little did you think that any one
To this unwholesome gloom could
    knowledge bring
That Joss a kaiser was, and Zeno king.
You spoke just now—but why?—too
    late to plead.
The forfeit's due and hope should all be
    dead.

Incurables! For you I am the grave.
Oh, miserable men! whom naught can save.
Yes, Sigismond a kaiser is, and you
A king, O Ladislāus!—it is true.
You thought of God but as a wheel to roll
Your chariot on; you who have king's control
O'er Poland and its many towns so strong.
You, Milan's Duke, to whom at once belong
The gold and iron crowns. You, Emperor made
By Rome, a son of Hercules, 'tis said;
And you of Spartibor. And your two crowns
Are shining lights; and yet your shadow frowns
From every mountain land to trembling sea.
You are at giddy heights twin powers to be
A glory and a force for all that's great—
But 'neath the purple canopy of state,
Th' expanding and triumphant arch you prize,
'Neath royal power that sacred veils disguise,
Beneath your crowns of pearls and jewelled stars,
Beneath your exploits terrible and wars,
You, Sigismond, have but a monster been,
And, Ladislāus, you are scoundrel seen.
Oh, degradation of the sceptre's might
And sword's—when Justice has a hand like night,
Foul and polluted; and before this thing,
This hydra, do the Temple's hinges swing—
The throne becomes the haunt of all things base!
Oh, age of infamy and foul disgrace!
Oh, starry heavens looking on the shame,
No brow but reddens with resentful flame—
And yet the silent people do not stir!
Oh, million arms! what things do you deter—
Poor sheep, whom vermin-majesties devour,
Have you not nails with strong desiring power
To rend these royalties, that you so cower?
But two are taken,—such as will amaze
E'en hell itself, when it on them shall gaze.
Ah, Sigismond and Ladislāus, you
Were once triumphant, splendid to the view,
Stifling with your prosperity—but now
The hour of retribution lays you low.
Ah, do the vulture and the crocodile
Shed tears! At such a sight I fain must smile.
It seems to me 'tis very good sometimes
That princes, conquerors stained with bandits' crimes,
Sparkling with splendour, wearing crowns of gold,
Should know the deadly sweat endured of old,
That of Jehoshaphat; should sob and fear,
And after crime th' unclean be brought to bear.
'Tis well—God rules—and thus it is that I
These masters of the world can make to lie

In ashes at my feet. And this was he
Who reigned—and this a Cæsar known
    to be!
In truth, my old heart aches with very
    shame
To see such cravens with such noble
    name.
But let us finish—what has just passed
    here
Demands thick shrouding, and the time
    is near.
Th' accursed dice that rolled at Calvary
You rolled a woman's murder to decree:
It was a dark disastrous game to play;
But not for me a moral to essay.
This moment to the misty grave is due,
And far too vile and little human you
To see your evil ways. Your fingers
    lack
The human sense to test your actions
    black.
What use in darkness mirror to uphold?
What use that now your deeds should be
    retold?
Drink of the darkness—greedy of the
    ill
To which from habit you're attracted
    still,
Not recognizing in the draught you take
The stench that your atrocities must
    make.
I only tell you that this burthened age
Tires of your Highnesses, that soil its
    page,
And of your villainies—and this is why
You now must swell the stream that
    passes by
Of refuse filth. Oh, horrid scene to
    show
Of these young men and that young
    girl just now!
Oh! can you really be of human kind
Breathing pure air of heaven? Do we
    find
That you are men? Oh, no! for when
    you laid
Foul lips upon the mouth of sleeping
    maid,
You seemed but ghouls that had come
    furtively
From out the tombs; only a horrid lie
Your human shape; of some strange
    frightful beast
You have the soul. To darkness I at
    least
Remit you now. Oh, murderer Sigis-
    mond
And Ladislāus pirate, both beyond
Release—two demons that have broken
    ban!
Therefore 'tis time their empire over
    man,
And converse with the living, should be
    o'er;
Tyrants, behold your tomb your eyes
    before;
Vampires and dogs, your sepulchre is
    here.
Enter."
        He pointed to the gulf so near.

All terrified upon their knees they fell.
"Oh! take us not in your dread realm
    to dwell,"
Said Sigismond. "But, phantom! do us
    tell
What thou wouldst have from us—we
    will obey.
Oh, mercy!—'tis for mercy now we
    pray."
"Behold us at your feet, oh, spectre
    dread!"
And no old crone in feebler voice could
    plead
Than Ladislāus did.

But not a word
Said now the figure motionless, with sword
In hand. This sovereign soul seemed to commune
With self beneath his metal sheath; yet soon
And suddenly, with tranquil voice said he,
"Princes, your craven spirit wearies me.
No phantom—only man am I. Arise!
I like not to be dreaded otherwise
Than with the fear to which I'm used; know me,
For it is Eviradnus that you see!"

Colossal Hands

As from the mist a noble pine we tell
Grown old upon the heights of Appenzel,
When morning freshness breathes round all the wood,
So Eviradnus now before them stood,
Opening his vizor, which at once revealed
The snowy beard it had so well concealed.
Then Sigismond was still as dog at gaze,
But Ladisläus leaped, and howl did raise,
And laughed and gnashed his teeth, till, like a cloud
That sudden bursts, his rage was all avowed.
" 'Tis but an old man after all!" he cried.

Then the great knight, who looked at both, replied,
"Oh, kings! an old man of my time can cope
With two much younger ones of yours, I hope.
To mortal combat I defy you both
Singly; or, if you will, I'm nothing loth
With two together to contend; choose here
From out the heap what weapon shall appear
Most fit. As you no cuirass wear, I see,
I will take off my own, for all must be
In order perfect—e'en your punishment."

Then Eviradnus, true to his intent,
Stripped to his Utrecht jerkin; but the while
He calmly had disarmed—with dexterous guile
Had Ladisläus seized a knife that lay
Upon the damask cloth, and slipped away
His shoes; then barefoot, swiftly, silently
He crept behind the knight, with arm held high.
But Eviradnus was of all aware,
And turned upon the murderous weapon there,
And twisted it away; then in a trice
His strong colossal hand grasped like a vice
The neck of Ladisläus, who the blade
Now dropped; over his eyes a misty shade
Showed that the royal dwarf was near to death.

"Traitor!" said Eviradnus in his wrath,
"I rather should have hewn your limbs away,
And left you crawling on your stumps;

I say,—
But now die fast."

    Ghastly, with starting eyes,
The King without a cry or struggle dies.
One dead—but lo! the other stands bold-faced,
Defiant; for the knight, when he unlaced
His cuirass, had his trusty sword laid down,
And Sigismond now grasps it as his own.
The monster youth laughed at the silv'ry beard,
And, sword in hand, a murderer glad appeared.
Crossing his arms, he cried, " 'Tis my turn now!"
And the black mounted knights in solemn row
Were judges of the strife. Before them lay
The sleeping Mahaud—and not far away
The fatal pit, near which the champion knight
With evil Emperor must contend for right,
Though weaponless he was. And yawned the pit
Expectant which should be engulphed in it.
"Now we shall see for whom this ready grave,"
Said Sigismond, "you dog, whom nought can save!"
Aware was Eviradnus that if he
Turned for a blade unto the armoury,
He would be instant pierced—what can he do?
The moment is for him supreme. But, lo!
He glances now at Ladislaüs dead,
And with a smile triumphant and yet dread,
And air of lion caged to whom is shown
Some loophole of escape, he bends him down.
"Ha! ha! no other club than this I need!"
He cried, as seizing in his hands with speed
The dead King's heels, the body lifted high,
Then to the frightened Emperor he came nigh,
And made him shake with horror and with fear,
The weapon all so ghastly did appear.
The head became the stone to this strange sling,
Of which the body was the potent string;
And while 'twas brandished in a deadly way,
The dislocated arms made monstrous play
With hideous gestures, as now upside down
The bludgeon corpse a giant force had grown.
" 'Tis well!" said Eviradnus, and he cried,
"Arrange between yourselves, you two allied;
If hell-fire were extinguished, surely it
By such a contest might be all relit;
From kindling spark struck out from dead King's brow,
Batt'ring to death a living Emperor now."

And Sigismond, thus met and horrified,
Recoiled to near the unseen opening wide:

The human club was raised, and struck
    again . . .
And Eviradnus did alone remain
All empty-handed—but he heard the
    sound
Of spectres two falling to depths pro-
    found;
Then, stooping o'er the pit, he gazed be-
    low,
And, as half-dreaming now, he mur-
    mured low
"Tiger and jackal meet their portion
    here,
'Tis well together they should disap-
    pear!"

. . . .

Then lifts he Mahaud to the ducal chair,
And shuts the trap with noiseless, gentle
    care;
And puts in order everything around,
So that, on waking, nought should her
    astound.

NO BAPTISM

FINDING that earthquakes far too much
    prevailed,
The Spanish kings with sacred rites as-
    sailed
Volcanic mountains of the New World
    land,
Baptising them; and to the priestly hand
They all submitted, saving only one,
But Momotombo would not have it
    done.
Divers the surpliced priests who—choice
    of Rome—
Essayed to reach the frowning moun-
    tain's dome,
Bearing the Sacrament the Church de-
    crees,
With eyes on Heaven fixed, but of all
    these—
And many were they—none were heard
    of more.

"Oh Momotombo, thou colossus hoar,
Who ponderest by the sea, whilst thou
    hast made
Tiara of thy crater's flame and shade,
Why, when thy dreadful threshold we
    draw near,
And bring thee God, why wilt thou not
    us hear?"
Stayed was the belching of its lava tide,
While gravely Momotombo thus replied:

"I liked not much the god you chased
    away,
His jaws were black with gory rot al-
    way.
Eater of human flesh was he, this god,
And miser hiding gold beneath the sod.
His cave, the porch to frightful yard,
    was made
Sepulchral Temple where his Pontiff
    stayed,
The slaughterer deaf, deformed, of hide-
    ous mien,
Bleeding between his teeth was ever
    seen
A corpse, while round his wrists the ser-
    pents twined;
And horrid skeletons of human kind
Grinn'd at his feet. Oh cruel were the
    ways
Of shocking murder in those dreadful
    days,
Blackening of the firmament sublime.
    At this
I groaned from out the depths of my
    abyss.

Thus when came proudly o'er the trembling sea
White men, from that side whence unfailingly
The morning ever breaks, it seemed to me
That to receive them well were only wise.
'White men,' said I, 'resemble azure skies,
Surely the colour of their souls we trace,
It must be like the colour of their face,
The god that these men worship must be good;
Murders will cease,' and I in happy mood
Rejoiced—the ancient priest I hated so;
But when the new one's work began to show,
When I could see the Inquisition flame,
That ne'er was quenched, taking the Holy name,
A mournful torch that to my level reached,
Just Heaven! when thus you daily taught and preached,
And Torquemada tried with fiery might
To dissipate the darkness of the night
Of savage heathendom—when I saw then
How He would civilize—at Lima, when
I saw the osier giants, in the strife,
Filled to the brim with childish baby life
Crackling above the mighty furnace heat,
And curls of smoke round burning women meet,
Choked by the stench of every horrid deed,
Auto-da-fé according to your creed,
I—who but shadow brightly burn away—
Repented of my gladness, forced to say,
When looking at the strangers' god more near,
'To change is not worth while it doth appear!'"

MARCH OF THE HALBERDIERS

WHEN the regiment of Halberdiers
  Is proudly marching by,
The eagle of the mountain screams
  From out his stormy sky;
Who speaketh to the precipice,
  And to the chasm sheer;
Who hovers o'er the thrones of kings,
  And bids the caitiffs fear.
King of the peak and glacier,
  King of the cold, white scalps—
He lifts his head, at that close tread,
  The eagle of the Alps.

O shame! those men that march below—
  O ignominy dire!
Are the sons of my free mountains
  Sold for imperial hire.
Ah! the vilest in the dungeon!
  Ah! the slave upon the seas—
Is great, is pure, is glorious,
  Is grand compared with these,
Who, born amid my holy rocks
  In solemn places high,
Where the tall pines bend like rushes
  When the storm goes sweeping by;

Yet give the strength of foot they learned
  By perilous path and flood,
And from their blue-eyed mothers won,
  The old, mysterious blood;
The daring that the good south wind
  Into their nostrils blew,

And the proud swelling of the heart
  With each pure breath they drew;
The graces of the mountain glens,
  With flowers in summer gay;
And all the glories of the hills
  To earn a lackey's pay.

Their country free and joyous—
  She of the rugged sides—
She of the rough peaks arrogant
  Whereon the tempest rides:
Mother of the unconquered thought
  And of the savage form,
Who brings out of her sturdy heart
  The hero and the storm;
Who giveth freedom unto man,
  And life unto the beast;
Who hears her silver torrents ring
  Like joy-bells at a feast;

Who hath her caves for palaces,
  And where her châlets stand—
The proud, old archer of Altorf,
  With his good bow in his hand.
Is she to suckle gaolers?
  Shall shame and glory rest,
Amid her lakes and glaciers,
  Like twins upon her breast?
Shall the two-headed eagle,
  Marked with her double blow,
Drink of her milk through all those hearts
  Whose blood he bids to flow?

Say, was it pomp ye needed,
  And all the proud array
Of courtly joust and high parade
  Upon a gala day?
Look up; have not my valleys
  Their torrents white with foam—
Their lines of silver bullion
  On the blue hillocks of home?
Doth not sweet May embroider

My rocks with pearls and flowers?
  Her fingers trace a richer lace
Than yours in all my bowers.

Are not my old peaks gilded
  When the sun arises proud,
And each one shakes a white mist plume
  Out of the thunder-cloud?
O neighbour of the golden sky—
  Sons of the mountain sod—
Why wear a base king's colours
  For the livery of God?
O shame! despair! to see my Alps
  Their giant shadows fling
Into the very waiting-room
  Of tyrant and of king!

O thou deep heaven, unsullied yet,
  Into thy gulfs sublime—
Up azure tracks of flaming light—
  Let my free pinion climb;
Till from my sight, in that clear light,
  Earth and her crimes be gone—
The men who act the evil deeds—
  The caitiffs who look on.
Far, far into that space immense,
  Beyond the vast white veil,
Where distant stars come out and shine,
  And the great sun grows pale.

HERO OF GENTLE MIEN

My father, hero of benignant mien,
On horseback visited the gory scene,
After the battle as the evening fell,
And took with him a trooper loved right well,
Because of bravery and presence bold.
The field was covered with the dead, all cold,

And shades of night were deepening: came a sound,
  Feeble and hoarse, from something on the ground;
It was a Spaniard of the vanquished force,
Who dragged himself with pain beside their course;
Wounded and bleeding, livid and half dead,
"Give me to drink—in pity, drink!" he said.
My father, touched, stretched to his follower now,
A flask of rum that from his saddle-bow
Hung down: "The poor soul—give him drink," said he.
But while the trooper prompt, obediently
Stooped towards the other, he of Moorish race
Pointed a pistol at my father's face,
And with a savage oath the trigger drew;
The hat flew off, a bullet passing through.
As swerved his charger in a backward stride,
"Give him to drink the same," my father cried.

NIGHT AND A CABIN

'Tis night—within the close stout cabin door,
  The room is wrapped in shade save where there fall
Some twilight rays that creep along the floor,
  And show the fisher's nets upon the wall.

In the dim corner, from the oaken chest,
  A few white dishes glimmer; through the shade
Stands a tall bed with dusky curtains dressed,
  And a rough mattress at its side is laid.

Five children on the long low mattress lie—
  A nest of little souls, it heaves with dreams;
In the high chimney the last embers die,
  And redden the dark room with crimson gleams.

The mother kneels and thinks, and pale with fear,
  She prays alone, hearing the billows shout:
While to wild winds, to rocks, to midnight drear,
  The ominous old ocean sobs without.

. . . . . .

Poor wives of fishers! Ah! 'tis sad to say,
  Our sons, our husbands, all that we love best,
Our hearts, our souls, are on those waves away,
  Those ravening wolves that know not ruth, nor rest.

Think how they sport with these beloved forms;
  And how the clarion-blowing of the wind unties
Above their heads the tresses of the storms:
  Perchance even now the child, the husband dies.

For we can never tell where they may be
　Who, to make head against the tide and gale,
Between them and the starless, soulless sea
　Have but one bit of plank, with one poor sail.

Terrible fear! We seek the pebbly shore,
　Cry to the rising billows, "Bring them home."
Alas! what answer gives their troubled roar,
　To the dark thought that haunts us as we roam.

Janet is sad: her husband is alone,
　Wrapped in the black shroud of this bitter night:
His children are so little, there is none
　To give him aid. "Were they but old, they might."
Ah, mother! when they too are on the main,
　How wilt thou weep: "Would they were young again!"

She takes his lantern—'tis his hour at last:
　She will go forth, and see if the day breaks,
And if his signal-fire be at the mast;
　Ah, no—not yet—no breath of morning wakes.

No line of light o'er the dark water lies;
　It rains, it rains, how black is rain at morn;
The day comes trembling, and the young dawn cries—
　Cries like a baby fearing to be born.

Sudden her humane eyes that peer and watch
　Through the deep shade, a mouldering dwelling find,
No light within—the thin door shakes—the thatch
　O'er the green walls is twisted of the wind.

Yellow, and dirty, as a swollen rill,
　"Ah, me," she saith, "here does that widow dwell;
Few days ago my good man left her ill:
　I will go in and see if all be well."

She strikes at the door, she listens, none replies,
　And Janet shudders. "Husbandless, alone,
And with two children—they have scant supplies.
　Good neighbour! She sleeps heavy as a stone."

She calls again, she knocks, 'tis silence still;
　No sound—no answer—suddenly the door,
As if the senseless creature felt some thrill
　Of pity, turned—and open lay before.

She entered, and her lantern lighted all
　The house so still, but for the rude waves' din.
Through the thin roof the plashing rain-drops fall,
　But something terrible is couched within.

．　．　．　．　．　．

"So, for the kisses that delight the flesh,

For mother's worship, and for children's bloom,
For song, for smile, for love so fair and
   fresh,
For laugh, for dance, there is one
   goal—the tomb."

And why does Janet pass so fast away?
   What hath she done within that house
      of dread?
   What foldeth she beneath her mantle
      grey?
   And hurries home, and hides it in her
      bed:
   With half-averted face, and nervous
      tread,
   What hath she stolen from the awful
      dead?

The dawn was whitening over the sea's
      verge
   As she sat pensive, touching broken
      chords
Of half-remorseful thought, while the
      hoarse surge
   Howled a sad concert to her broken
      words.

"Ah, my poor husband! we had five be-
      fore,
   Already so much care, so much to
      find,
For he must work for all. I give him
      more.
   What was that noise? His step! Ah,
      no! the wind.

"That I should be afraid of him I love!
   I have done ill. If he should beat
      me now,
I would not blame him. Did not the
      door move?

Not yet, poor man." She sits with
      careful brow
Wrapped in her inward grief; nor hears
      the roar
   Of winds and waves that dash against
      his prow,
Nor the black cormorant shrieking on
      the shore.

Sudden the door flies open wide, and
      lets
   Noisily in the dawn-light scarcely
      clear,
And the good fisher, dragging his damp
      nets,
   Stands on the threshold, with a joy-
      ous cheer.

" 'Tis thou!" she cries, and, eager as a
      lover,
   Leaps up and holds her husband to
      her breast;
Her greeting kisses all his vesture cover;
" 'Tis I, good wife!" and his broad face
      expressed

How gay his heart that Janet's love
      made light.
   "What weather was it?" "Hard."
      "Your fishing?" "Bad.
The sea was like a nest of thieves to-
      night;
   But I embrace thee, and my heart is
      glad.

"There was a devil in the wind that
      blew;
   I tore my net, caught nothing, broke
      my line,
And once I thought the bark was broken
      too;
   What did you all the night long, Janet
      mine?"

She, trembling in the darkness, an-
    swered, "I!
  Oh, nought—I sew'd, I watch'd, I was
    afraid,
  The waves were loud as thunders from
    the sky;
  But it is over." Shyly then she said—

"Our neighbour died last night; it must
    have been
  When you were gone. She left two
    little ones,
  So small, so frail—William and Made-
    line;
  The one just lisps, the other scarcely
    runs."

The man looked grave, and in the cor-
    ner cast
  His old fur bonnet, wet with rain and
    sea,
  Muttered awhile, and scratched his
    head,—at last:
  "We have five children, this makes
    seven," said he.

"Already in bad weather we must sleep
  Sometimes without our supper. Now!
    Ah, well—
  'Tis not my fault. These accidents are
    deep;
  It was the good God's will. I cannot
    tell.

"Why did he take the mother from
    those scraps,
  No bigger than my fist. 'Tis hard to
    read;
  A learned man might understand, per-
    haps—
  So little, they can neither work nor
    need.

"Go fetch them, wife; they will be
    frightened sore,
  If with the dead alone they waken
    thus.
  That was the mother knocking at our
    door,
  And we must take the children home
    to us.

"Brother and sister shall they be to
    ours,
  And they will learn to climb my knee
    at even;
  When He shall see these strangers in
    our bowers,
  More fish, more food, will give the
    God of Heaven.

"I will work harder; I will drink no
    wine—
  Go fetch them. Wherefore dost thou
    linger, dear?
  Not thus were wont to move those feet
    of thine."
  She drew the curtain, saying, "They
    are here!"

SONG OF THE GILDERS

We are the gilders of the prows.
Wheel-like awhirl, strong winds arouse
The verdant sea's rotundity,
Mingling the shadows and the gleams,
And 'mid the folds of sombre streams
Drawing slant vessels steadfastly.

The shrilling squall close-circling flies,
The tortuous winds deep guiles devise,
The Archer black in his horn doth blow;
These sounds bode death's dark mys-
    tery,

And through these prodigies 'tis we
That make the golden spectres go.

For the ship's prow is like a ghost.
Still wave-engirdled, tempest-tossed;
Proudly from our bazaars she sails
To serve the lightnings with a mark,
And midst the hazards of the dark
To be an eye that never fails.

King, 'neath the plane-trees pleasure thee;
Sultan to the Sultanas see,
And hide beneath long veils the grace
Of myriad girls with names untold
Who yestermorn stark-bare were sold
By auction on the market-place.

What cares the wave? What cares the air!
This girl is dark and that is fair,
Of Halep she, or Ispahan;
Before thy face they all make quake;
What heed thereof forsooth should take
The vast mysterious ocean!

Ye have each one your revelry.
Be thou the prince, the tempest he.
He lightning hath, the yataghan
Thou, to chastise your multitudes;
Beneath its lord the people broods,
The wave beneath the hurricane.

For one and the other do we strive.
This double task is ours alive;—
And thus we sing: O stern Emir,
Thine eyes of steel, thy heart of ice
Keep not the little swallow's eyes
From trustful sleep when night is near.

For holy Nature is eterne
And tranquil; living souls that yearn
God sheltereth beneath His wing;

Amid the all-serene sweet shade,
With hearts for ever undismayed
By spectral terrors, do we sing.

Unto our lords we leave the palm
And statelier laurel! We are calm
And steadfast while within their hand
They have not ta'en the minished stars,
And the swift flight of the cloud-cars
Depends not on a king's command.

The summer glows, the flowers bloom bright,
Small rose-buds tip the bosoms white;
One hunts, one laughs; 'the craftsmen still
Sing, and the priests still sigh and sleep;
Slight shadowy fawns through copses deep
Fleeing, make greyhounds strain and thrill.

If soothly, Sultan, thou hadst quaffed
All proffered pleasures, the sweet draugh'.
Would surely quickly poison thee!
Live thou and reign,—thy life is sweet.
Couched on the moss the roebuck fleet
In forest slumbers dreamfully.

Who mounts aloft must needs descend;
The hours are flame, dust is their end;
The tomb saith unto man: "Behold!"—
Times change, blithe birds not alway sing,
Waves lisp, and straight are thundering,
While aye around are omens rolled:

The hour is sultry; women bare
Lave lovely limbs nigh blooms less fair;
All lightest sorrows now repose;

O'er blue tranced lakes white clouds are driven;
With the most golden star of heaven;
Crowneth itself earth's reddest rose.

Thy galley we have gold-arrayed
By sixty pairs of oars is swayed
Which from Lepanto, 'mid the surge,
Subdue the tempest and the tide,
And each of which is hotly plied
By four slaves shackled, 'neath the scourge.

SAGA OF THE BEAST

The Babe

A LION in his jaws caught up a child—
Not harming it—and to the woodland, wild
With secret streams and lairs, bore off his prey;
The beast, as one might cull a flower in May,
Had plucked this bud, not thinking wrong or right,
Mumbling its stalk, too proud or kind to bite,—
A lion's way, roughly compassionate.
Yet truly dismal was the victim's fate;
Thrust in a cave that rumbled with each roar,
His food wild herbs, his bed the earthly floor,
He lived, half-dead with daily frightening.
It was a rosy boy, son of a king;
A ten-year lad with bright eyes shining wide,
And save this son his majesty beside
Had but one girl—two years of age—and so

The monarch suffered, being old, much woe,
His heir the monster's prey, while the whole land
In dread both of the beast and king did stand;
Sore terrified were all:—
    By came a Knight
That road, who halted, asking "What's the fright?"
They told him, and he spurred straight for the den:
Oh, such a place, the sunlight entering in
Grew pale and crept, so grim a sight was shown
Where the gaunt Lion on the rock lay prone:
The wood, at this part thick of growth and wet,
Barred out the sky with black trunks closely set;
Forest and forester matched wondrous well!
Great stones stood near, with ancient tales to tell—
Such as make moorlands weird in Brittany—
And at its edge a mountain you might see,
One of those iron walls which shut off heaven;
The Lion's den was a deep cavern driven
Into the granite ridge, fenced round with oaks:
Cities and caverns are discordant folks,
They bear each other grudges! this did wave
A leafy threat to trespasser,—"Hence, knave!
Or meet my Lion!"
    In the champion went.
The den had all the sombre sentiment

Which palaces display—deaths—murderings—
Terrors—you felt "here lives one of the kings:"
Bones strewn around showed that this mighty lord
Denied himself nought which his woods afford.
A rock-rift pierced by stroke of lightning gave
Such misty glimmer as a den need have:
What eagles might think dawn and owls the dusk
Makes day enough for kings of claw and tusk.
All else was regal, though! you understood
Why the majestic brute slept, as he should,
On leaves, with no lace curtains to his bed;
And how his wine was blood—nay, or instead,
Spring-water lapped *sans* napkin, spoon, or cup,
Or lackeys:—
    Being from spur to crest mailed up,
The champion enters.
    In the den he spies
Truly a Mighty One! Crowned to the eyes
With shaggy golden fell—the Beast!—it muses
With look infallible; for, if he chooses,
The master of a wood may play at Pope,
And this one had such claws, there was small hope
To argue with him on the point of creed!
The Knight approached—yet not too fast, indeed;
His footfall clanged, flaunted his rose-red feather,
None the more notice took the Beast of either,
Still in his own reflections plunged profound;
Theseus a-marching upon that black ground
Of Sisyphus, Ixion, and dire hell,
Saw such a scene, murk and implacable:
But duty whispered "Forward!" so the Knight
Drew out his sword: the Lion at that sight
Lifted his head in slow wise, grim to see;

The Knight said: "Greeting! monstrous brute! to thee;
In this foul hole thou hast a child in keeping,—
I search its noisome nooks with glances sweeping
But spy him not. That child I must reclaim,
Friends are we if thou renderest up the same;
If not—I too am lion, thou wilt find;
The king his lost son in his arms shall bind;
While here thy wicked blood runs, smoking-hot,
Before another dawn."
    "I fancy not,"
Pensive the Lion said.
    The Knight strode near,
Brandished his blade and cried: "Sire! have a care!"
The Beast was seen to smile—ominous sight!—
Never make lions smile! Then joined they fight,

The man and monster, in most desperate duel,
Like warring giants, angry, huge, and cruel;
Like tigers crimsoning an Indian wood,
The man with steel, the beast with claws as good;
Fang against falchion, hide to mail, that lord
Hurled himself foaming on the flashing sword:
Stout though the Knight, the Lion stronger was,
And tore that brave breast under its cuirass,
And striking blow on blow with ponderous paw,
Forced plate and rivet off, until you saw
Through all the armour's cracks the bright blood spirt,
As when clenched fingers make a mulberry squirt;
And piece by piece he stripped the iron sheath,
Helm, armlets, greaves—gnawed bare the bones beneath
Scrunching that hero, till he sprawled—alas!
Beneath his shield, all blood, and mud, and mess:
Whereat the Lion feasted:—then it went
Back to its rocky couch and slept content.

The Hermit

Next came a hermit:
    He found out the cave;
With girdle, gown, and cross—trembling and grave—
He entered. There that Knight lay, out of shape,
Mere pulp: the Lion waking up did gape,
Opened his yellow orbs, heard some one grope,
And—seeing the woollen coat bound with a rope,
A black peaked cowl, and inside that a man—
He finished yawning and to growl began:
Then, with a voice like prison-gates which creak,
Roared, "What would'st thou?"
    "My King"
      "King?"
        "May I speak?"
"Of whom?"
    "The Prince."
      "Is that what makes a King?"
The monk bowed reverence, "Majesty! I bring
A message—wherefore keep this child?"
"For that
Whene'er it rains I've some one here to chat."
"Return him."
    "Not so."
      "What then wilt thou do?
Would'st eat him?"
      "Ay—if I have naught to chew!"
"Sire! think upon His Majesty in woe!"
"They killed my dam," the Beast said, "long ago."
"Bethink thee, sire, a king implores a king."
"Nonsense—he talks—he's man! when my notes ring
A Lion's heard!"
    "His only boy!"
      "Well, well!
He hath a daughter."

"She's no heir."
"I dwell
Alone in this my home, 'mid wood and rock,
Thunder my music, and the lightning-shock
My lamp;—let his content him."
"Ah! show pity."
"What means that word? is't current in your city?"
"Lion thou'dst wish to go to heaven—see here!
I offer thee indulgence, and, writ clear,
God's passport to His paradise!"
"Get forth,
Thou holy rogue," thundered the Beast in wrath:
The hermit disappeared.

THE HOUNDS

Thereat left free,
Full of a lion's vast serenity
He slept again, leaving still night to pass:
The moon rose, starting spectres on the grass,
Shrouding the marsh with mist, blotting the ways,
And melting the black woodland to grey maze;
No stir was seen below, above no motion
Save of the white stars trooping to the ocean:
And while the mole and cricket in the brake
Kept watch, the Lion's measured breath did make
Slow symphony that kept all creatures calm.
Sudden—loud cries and clamours! striking qualm
Into the heart of the quiet, horn and shout
Causing the solemn wood to reel with rout,
And all the nymphs to tremble in their trees.
The uproars of a midnight chase are these
Which shakes the shades, the marsh, mountain and stream,
And breaks the silence of their sombre dream.
The thicket flashed with many a lurid spark
Of torches borne 'mid wild cries through the dark;
Hounds, nose to earth, ran yelping through the wood,
And armed groups, gathering in the alleys, stood.
Terrific was the noise that rolled before;
It seemed a squadron; nay, 'twas something more —
A whole battalion, sent by that sad king
With force of arms his little Prince to bring,
Together with the Lion's bleeding hide.

Which here was right or wrong? who can decide?
Have beasts or men most claim to live? God wots!
He is the unit, we the cypher-dots.

Well warmed with meat and drink those soldiers were,
Good hearts they bore—and many a bow and spear;
Their number large, and by a captain led
Valiant, whilst some in foreign wars had bled,

And all were men approved and firm in fight;
The Lion heard their cries, affronting night,
For by this time his awful lids were lifted;
But from the rock his chin he never shifted,
And only his great tail wagged to and fro.

Meantime, outside the cavern, startled so,
Came close the uproar of this shouting crowd.
As round a web flies buzzing in a cloud,
Or hive-bees swarming o'er a bear ensnared,
This hunter's legion buzzed, and swarmed, and flared.
In battle order all their ranks were set:
'Twas understood the Beast they came to get,
Fierce as a tiger's cunning—strong to seize—
Could munch up heroes as an ape cracks fleas,
Could with one glance make Jove's own bird look down;
Wherefore they laid him siege as to a town.
The spearmen followed in close array,
The archers held their arrows on the string;
Silence was bid, lest any chattering
Should mask the Lion's footstep in the wood;
The dogs—who know the moment when 'tis good
To hold their peace—went first, nose to the ground,
Giving no tongue; the torches all around
Hither and thither flickered, their long beams
Through sighing foliage sending ruddy gleams;—
Such is the order a great hunt should have:
And soon between the trunks they spy the cave,
A black, dim-outlined hole, deep in the gloom,
Gaping, but blank and silent as the tomb,
Wide open to the night, as though it feared
As little all that clamour as it heard.
There's smoke where fire smoulders, and a town,
When men lay seige, rings tocsin up and down;
Nothing so here! therefore with vague dismay
Each stood, and grasp on bow or blade did lay,
Watching the sombre stillness of that chasm:
The dogs among themselves whimpered: a spasm
From the horror lurking in all voiceless places—
Worse than the rage of tempests—blanched all faces:
Yet they were there to find and fight this Thing,
So they advance, each bush examining,
Dreading full sore the very prey they sought;
The pioneers held high the lamps they brought:
"There! that is it! the very mouth of the den!"
The trees all round it muttered, warning men:

Still they kept step and neared it—look you now,
Company's pleasant, and there were a thou—
Good Lord! all in a moment, there's its face!
Frightful!—they saw the Lion! Not one pace
Further stirred any man; the very trees
Grew blacker with his presence, and the breeze
Blew shudders into all hearts present there:
Yet, whether 'twas from valour or wild fear,
The archers drew—and arrow, bolt, and dart
Made target of the Beast. He, on his part—
As calm as Pelion in the rain or hail—
Bristled majestic from the nose to tail,
And shook full fifty missiles from his hide;
Yet any meaner brute had found beside
Enough still sticking fast to make him yell
Or fly; the blood was trickling down his fell,
But no heed took he, glaring steadfastly;
And all those men of war, amazed to be
Thus met by so stupendous might and pride,
Thought him no beast, but some god brutified.
The hounds, tail down, slunk back behind the spears;
And then the Lion, 'mid the silence, rears
His awful face, and over wood and marsh
Roared a vast roar, hoarse, vibrant, vengeful, harsh,—
A rolling, raging peal of wrath, which spread
From the quaking earth to the echoing vault o'erhead,
Making the half-awakened thunder cry
"Who thunders there?" from its black bed of sky.

This ended all!—sheer horror cleared the coast:
As fogs are driven by wind, that valorous host
Melted, dispersed to all the quarters four,
Clean panic-stricken by that monstrous roar;
Each with one impulse—leaders, rank and file,
Deeming it haunted ground, where Earth somewhile
Is wont to breed marvels of lawless might—
They scampered, mad, blind, reckless, wild with fright.
Then quoth the Lion, "Woods and mountains! see,
A thousand men enslaved fear one Beast free!'
As lava to volcanoes, so a roar
Is to these creatures; and, the eruption o'er
In heaven-shaking wrath, they mostly calm.
The gods themselves to lions yield the palm
For magnanimity. When Jove was king,
Hercules said, "Let's finish off the thing,
Not the Nemæan merely; every one
We'll strangle—all the lions." Whereupon

The lions yawned a "much obliged!"
  his way.

But this Beast, being whelped by night,
  not day—
Offspring of glooms—was sterner; one
  of those
Who go down slowly when their storm's
  at close;
His anger had a savage ground-swell
  in it:
He loved to take his naps, too, to the
  minute,
And to be roused up thus with horn
  and hound,—
To find an ambush sprung—to be
  hemmed round—
Targetted—'twas an insult to his grove!
He paced towards the hill, climbed high
  above,
Lifted his voice, and, as the sowers sow
The seeds down wind, thus did that
  Lion throw
His message far enough the town to
  reach.

"King! your behaviour really passes
  speech!
Thus far no harm I've wrought to him
  your son;
But now I give you notice—when night's
  done
I will make entry at your city-gate,
Bringing the Prince alive; and those
  who wait
To see him in my jaws—your lackey-
  crew—
Shall see me eat him in your palace
  too!"

Quiet the night passed, while the stream-
  lets bubbled,
And the clouds sailed across the vault
  untroubled.

Next morning this is what was viewed
  in town:

Dawn coming — people going — some
  adown
Praying, some crying; pallid cheeks,
  swift feet,
And a huge Lion stalking through the
  street.

Out of Red Jaws

The quaking townsmen in the cellars
  hid;
How make resistance? briefly, no one
  did;
The soldiers left their posts, the gates
  stood wide;
'Twas felt the Lion had upon his side
A majesty so godlike, such an air—
That den, too, was so dark and grim a
  lair—
It seemed scarce short of rash impiety
To cross its path as the fierce Beast
  went by.
So to the palace and its gilded dome
With stately steps unchallenged did he
  roam,
In many a spot with those vile darts
  scarred still,
As you may note an oak scored with
  the bill,
Yet nothing recks that giant-trunk; so
  here
Paced this proud wounded Lion, free of
  fear,
While all the people held aloof in dread,
Seeing the scarlet jaws of that great
  head

Hold up the princely boy—aswoon.
　　　Is't true
Princes are flesh and blood?　Ah, yes! and you
Had wept with sacred pity, seeing him
Swing in the Lion's mouth, body and limb:
The tender captive gripped by those grim fangs,
On either side the jowl helplessly hangs,
Deathlike, albeit he bore no wound of tooth.
And for the brute thus gagged it was, in sooth,
A grievous thing to wish to roar, yet be
Muzzled and dumb, so he walked savagely,
His pent heart blazing through his burning eyes,
While not one bow is stretched, no arrow flies;
They dreaded, peradventure, lest some shaft
Shot with a trembling hand and faltering craft
Might miss the Beast and pierce the Prince:
　　　So, still
As he had promised, roaring from his hill,
This Lion, scorning town and townsfolk sick
To view such terror, goes on straight and quick
To the King's house, hoping to meet there one
Who dares to speak with him:—outside is none!
The door's ajar, and flaps with every blast;
He enters it — within those walls at last!—
No man!

For, certes, though he raged and wept,
His Majesty, like all, close shelter kept,
Solicitous to live, holding his breath
Specially precious to the realm: now death
Is not thus viewed by honest beasts of prey,
And when the Lion found *him* fled away,
Ashamed to be so grand, man being so base,
He muttered to himself in that dark place
Where lions keep their thoughts: "This wretched King!
'Tis well, I'll eat his boy!"　Then, wandering,
Lordly he traversed courts and corridors,
Paced beneath vaults of gold on shining floors,
Glanced at the throne deserted, stalked from hall
To hall—green, yellow, crimson—empty all!
Rich couches void, soft seats unoccupied!
And as he walked he looked from side to side
To find some pleasant nook for his repast,
Since appetite was come to munch at last
The princely morsel:—Ah! what sight astounds
That grisly lounger?
　　　In the palace grounds
An alcove on a garden gives, and there
A tiny thing—forgot in the general fear,
Lulled in the flower-sweet dreams of infancy,
Bathed with soft sunlight falling brokenly

Through leaf and lattice—was that moment waking;
A little lovely maid, most dear and taking,
The Prince's sister; all alone—undressed—
She sate up singing: children sing so best.

A voice of joy, than silver lute-string softer!
A mouth all rose-bud, blossoming in laughter!
A baby-angel hard at play! a dream
Of Bethlehem's cradle, or what nests would seem
If girls were hatched!—all these! Eyes, too, so blue
That sea and sky might own their sapphire new!
Neck bare, arms bare, pink legs and stomach bare!
Nought hid the roseate satin skin, save where
A little white-laced shift was fastened free;
She looked as fresh, singing thus peacefully,
As stars at twilight or as April's heaven;
A floweret — you had said — divinely given,
To show on earth how God's own lilies grow;
Such was this beauteous baby-maid; and so
The Beast caught sight of her and stopped—

And then
Entered:—the floor creaked as he stalked straight in.

Above the playthings by the little bed
The Lion put his shaggy massive head,
Dreadful with savage might and lordly scorn,
More dreadful with that princely prey so borne;
Which she, quick spying, "Brother! brother!" cried,
"Oh, my own brother!" and, unterrified—
Looking a living rose that made the place
Brighter and warmer with its fearless grace—
She gazed upon that monster of the wood,
Whose yellow balls not Typhon had withstood.
And—well! who knows what thoughts these small heads hold?
She rose up in her cot—full height, and bold,
And shook her pink fist angrily at him.
Whereon—close to the little bed's white rim,
All dainty silk and laces—this huge Brute
Set down her brother gently at her foot,
Just as a mother might, and said to her—
"Don't be put out, now! there he is, Dear!—there!"

The Hunchback of Notre-Dame

BOOK I

THE PLAY

CHAPTER I

THE GREAT HALL

THREE hundred and forty-eight years, six months, and nineteen days ago to-day the Parisians were wakened by the sound of loud peals from all the bells within the triple precincts of the City, the University, and the Town.

And yet the 6th of January, 1482, is not a day of which history takes much note. There was nothing extraordinary about the event which thus set all the bells and the citizens of Paris agog from early dawn. It was neither an attack from the Picards or the Burgundians, nor some shrine carried in procession, nor was it a student revolt in the Ville de Laas, nor an entry of "our greatly to be dreaded lord the king," nor even the wholesale slaughter of a band of thieves before the Palace of Justice. Neither was it the arrival, so frequent during the fifteenth century, of some plumed and laced embassy. It was scarcely two days since the last cavalcade of this sort, that of the Flemish ambassadors empowered to arrange a marriage between the Dauphin and Margaret of Flanders, had entered Paris, to the great annoyance of Cardinal Bourbon, who, to please the king, was forced to smile upon all this rustic rout of Flemish burgomasters, and to entertain them at his own mansion with "a very fine morality and farce," while a driving rain-storm drenched the splendid tapestries at his door.

That which "stirred the emotions of the whole populace of Paris," as Jehan de Troyes expresses it, on January 6, was the double festival, celebrated from time immemorial, of Epiphany and the Feast of Fools.

Upon that day there was to be a bonfire at the Grève, a Maypole at the Braque chapel, and a mystery or miracle play at the Palace of Justice. All these things had been proclaimed at the cross-roads, to the sound of trumpets, by the provost's men, in fine coats of purple camlet, with big white crosses on the breast.

A crowd of citizens with their wives and daughters had therefore been making their way from every quarter, towards the places named, ever since early dawn. Each had decided for himself, in favour of the bonfire, the Maypole, or the mystery. It must be confessed, to the glory of the proverbial good sense of Parisian idlers, that the majority of the crowd turned towards the bonfire, which was most seasonable, or towards the miracle play which was to be performed in the great hall of the law courts, well roofed in and between four walls; and that most of the pleasure-seekers agreed to leave the poor Maypole with its scanty blossoms to shiver alone beneath the January sky, in the cemetery of the Braque chapel.

The people swarmed most thickly in the avenues leading to the law courts, because it was known that the Flemish ambassadors who arrived two nights before proposed to be present at the performance of the miracle play and election of the Lord of Misrule, which was also to take place in the great hall.

It was no easy matter to make a way into the great hall upon that day, although it was then held to be the largest enclosure under cover in the world (to be sure, Sauval had not yet measured the great hall of the castle at Montargis). The courtyard, filled with people, looked to the spectators at the windows like a vast sea into which five or six streets, like the mouths of so many rivers, constantly disgorged new waves of heads. The billowing crowd, growing ever greater, dashed against houses projecting here and there like so many promontories in the irregular basin of the court. In the middle of the lofty Gothic façade of the Palace was the great staircase, up and down which flowed an unending double stream, which, after breaking upon the intermediate landing, spread in broad waves over its two side slopes; the great staircase, I say, poured a steady stream into the courtyard, like a waterfall into a lake. Shouts, laughter, and the tramp of countless feet made a great noise and a great hubbub. From time to time the hubbub and the noise was redoubled; the current which bore this throng towards the great staircase was turned back, eddied, and whirled. Some archer had dealt a blow, or the horse of some provost's officer had administered a few kicks to restore order,—an admirable tradition, which provost has bequeathed to constable, constable to marshalsea, and marshalsea to our present Parisian police.

At doors, windows, in garrets, and on roofs swarmed thousands of good plain citizens, quiet, honest people, gazing at the Palace, watching the throng, and asking nothing more; for many people in Paris are quite content to look on at others, and there are plenty who regard a wall behind which something is happening as a very curious thing.

If it could be permitted to us men of 1830 to mingle in fancy with those fifteenth-century Parisians, and to enter with them, pushed, jostled, and elbowed, the vast hall of the Palace of Justice, all too small on the 6th of January, 1482, the sight would not be without interest or charm, and we should have about us only things so old as to seem brand-new.

With the reader's consent we will endeavour to imagine the impression he would have received with us in crossing the threshold of that great hall amidst that mob in surcoats, cassocks, and coats of mail.

And first of all there is a ringing in our ears, a dimness in our eyes. Above our heads, a double roof of pointed arches, wainscotted with carved wood, painted in azure, sprinkled with golden *fleurs-de-lis;* beneath our feet, a pavement of black and white marble laid in alternate blocks. A few paces from us, a huge pillar, then another,—in all seven pillars down the length of the hall, supporting the spring of the double arch down the centre. Around the first four columns are tradesmen's booths, glittering with glass and tinsel; around the last three, oaken benches worn and polished by the breeches of litigants and the gowns of attorneys. Around the hall, along the lofty wall, between the doors, between the casements, between the pillars, is an unending series of statues of all the kings of France, from Pharamond down,—the sluggard kings, with loosely hanging arms and downcast eyes; the brave and warlike kings, with head and hands boldly raised to heaven. Then in the long pointed windows, glass of a thousand hues; at the wide portals of the hall, rich doors finely carved; and the whole—arches, pillars, walls, cornices, wainscot, doors, and statues—covered from top to bottom with a gorgeous colouring of blue and gold, which, somewhat tarnished even at the date when we see it, had almost disappeared under dust and cobwebs in the year of grace 1549, when Du Breuil admired it from tradition.

Now, let us imagine this vast oblong hall, lit up by the wan light of a January day, taken possession of by a noisy motley mob who drift along the walls and ebb and flow about the seven columns, and we may have some faint idea of the general effect of the picture, whose strange details we will try to describe somewhat more minutely.

It is certain that if Ravaillac had not assassinated Henry IV., there would have been no documents relating to his case laid away in the Rolls Office in the Palace of Justice; no accomplices interested to make away with the said documents, accordingly no incendiaries, forced for want of better means to burn the Rolls Office in order to burn up the documents, and to burn the Palace of Justice in order to burn the Rolls Office; consequently, therefore, no fire in 1618. The old Palace would still be standing, with its great hall; I might say to my reader, "Go and look at it," and we should thus both of us be spared the need,—I of writing, and he of reading, an indifferent description; which proves this novel truth,—that great events have incalculable results.

True, Ravaillac may very possibly have had no accomplices; or his accomplices, if he chanced to have any, need have had no hand in the fire of 1618. There are two other very plausible explanations: first, the huge "star of fire, a foot broad and a foot and a half high," which fell, as every one knows, from heaven upon the Palace after midnight on the 7th of March; second, Théophile's verses:—

"In Paris sure it was a sorry game
When, fed too fat with fees, the
  frisky Dame
Justice set all her palace in a
  flame."

Whatever we may think of this triple explanation,—political, physical, and poetical,—of the burning of the Palace of Justice in 1618, one unfortunate fact remains: namely, the fire. Very little is now left, thanks to this catastrophe, and thanks particularly to the various and successive restorations which have finished what it spared,—very little is now left of this first home of the King of France, of this palace, older than the Louvre, so old even in the time of Philip the Fair that search had to be made for traces of the magnificent buildings erected by King Robert and described by Helgaldus. Almost everything is gone. What has become of the chancery office, Saint Louis' bridal chamber; the garden where he administered justice, "clad in a camlet coat, a sleeveless surcoat of linsey-woolsey, and over it a mantle of black serge, reclining upon carpets, with Joinville?" Where is the chamber of the Emperor Sigismond, that of Charles IV., and that of John Lackland? Where is the staircase from which Charles VI. issued his edict of amnesty; the flag-stone upon which Marcel slew, in the dauphin's presence, Robert of Clermont and the Marshal of Champagne; the wicket-gate where the bulls of Benedict the antipope were destroyed, and through which departed those who brought them, coped and mitred in mockery, thus doing public penance throughout Paris; and the great hall, with its gilding, its azure, its pointed arches, its statues, its columns, its great vaulted roof thickly covered with carvings; and the golden room; and the stone lion, which stood at the door, his head down, his tail between his legs, like the lions around Solomon's throne, in the humble attitude that befits strength in the presence of justice; and the beautiful doors; and the gorgeous windows; and the wrought-iron work which discouraged Biscornette; and Du Hancy's dainty bits of carving? What has time done, what have men done with these marvels? What has been given us in exchange for all this,—for all this ancient French history, all this Gothic art? The heavy elliptic arches of M. de Brosse, the clumsy architect of the St. Gervais portal,—so much for art; and for history we have the gossipy memories of the big pillar still echoing and re-echoing with the tittle-tattle of the Patrus.

This is not much. Let us go back to the genuine great hall of the genuine old Palace.

The two ends of this huge parallelogram were occupied, the one by the famous marble table, so long, so broad, and so thick, that there never was seen, as the old Court Rolls express it in a style which would give Gargantua an appetite, "such another slice of marble in the world;" the other by the chapel in which Louis XI. had his statue carved kneeling before the Virgin, and into which, wholly indifferent to the fact that he left two vacant spaces in the procession of royal images, he ordered the removal of the figures of Charlemagne and Saint Louis, believing these two saints to be in high favour with Heaven as being kings of France. This chapel, still quite new, having been built scarcely six years, was entirely in that charming school of refined and delicate architecture, of marvellous sculpture, of fine, deep chiselling, which marks the end of the Gothic era in France, and lasts until towards the middle of the sixteenth century in the fairy-like fancies of the Renaissance. The small rose-window over the door was an especial masterpiece of delicacy and grace; it seemed a mere star of lace.

In the centre of the hall, opposite the great door, a daïs covered with gold brocade, placed against the wall, to which a private entrance was arranged by means of a window from the passage to the gold room, had been built for the Flemish envoys and other great personages invited to the performance of the mystery.

This mystery, according to custom, was to be performed upon the marble table. It had been prepared for this at dawn; the superb slab of marble, scratched and marked by lawyers' heels, now bore a high wooden cage-like scaffolding, whose upper surface, in sight of the entire hall, was to serve as stage, while the interior, hidden by tapestry hangings, was to take the place of dressing-room for the actors in the play. A ladder placed outside with frank simplicity formed the means of communication between the dressing-room and stage, its rough rounds doing service for entrance as well as exit. There was no character however unexpected, no sudden change, and no dramatic effect, but was compelled to climb this ladder. Innocent and venerable infancy of art and of machinery!

Four officers attached to the Palace, forced guardians of the people's pleasures on holidays as on hanging days, stood bolt upright at the four corners of the marble table.

The play was not to begin until the twelfth stroke of noon rang from the great Palace clock. This was doubtless very late for a theatrical performance; but the ambassadors had to be consulted in regard to the time.

Now, this throng had been waiting since dawn. Many of these honest sightseers were shivering at earliest daylight at the foot of the great Palace staircase. Some indeed declared that they had spent the night lying across the great door, to be sure of getting in first. The crowd increased every moment, and, like water rising above its level, began to creep up the walls, to collect around the columns, to overflow the entablatures, the cornices, the window-sills, every projection of the architecture, and every bit of bold relief in the carvings. Then, too, discomfort, impatience, fatigue, the day's license of satire and folly, the quarrels caused ever and anon by a sharp elbow or a hob-nailed shoe, the weariness of waiting lent, long before the hour when the ambassadors were due, an acid, bitter tone to the voices of these people, shut up, pent in, crowded, squeezed, and stifled as they were. On every hand were heard curses and complaints against the Flemish, the mayor of Paris, Cardinal Bourbon, the Palace bailiff, Madame Margaret of Austria, the ushers, the cold, the heat, the bad weather, the Lord of Misrule, the columns, the statues, this closed door, that open window,—all to the vast amusement of the groups of students and lackeys scattered through the crowd, who mingled their mischief and their malice with all this discontent, and administered, as it were, pin-pricks to the general bad humour.

Among the rest there was one group of these merry demons who, having broken the glass from a window, had boldly seated themselves astride the sill, distributing their glances and their jokes by turns, within and without, between the crowd in the hall and the crowd in the courtyard. From their mocking gestures, their noisy laughter, and the scoffs and banter which they exchanged with their comrades, from one end of the hall to the other, it was easy to guess that these young students felt none of the weariness and fatigue of the rest of the spectators, and that they were amply able, for their own private amusement, to extract from what they had before their eyes a spectacle quite diverting enough to make them wait patiently for that which was to come.

"By my soul, it's you, Joannes Frollo de Molendino!" cried one of them to a light-haired little devil with a handsome but evil countenance, who was clinging to the acanthus leaves of a capital; "you are well named, Jehan du Moulin, for your two arms and your two legs look like the four sails fluttering in the wind. How long have you been here?"

"By the foul fiend!" replied Joannes Frollo, "more than four hours, and I certainly hope that they may be deducted from my time in purgatory. I heard the King of Sicily's eight choristers intone the first verse of high mass at seven o'clock in the Holy Chapel."

"Fine choristers they are!" returned the other; "their voices are sharper than the points of their caps. Before he endowed a Mass in honour of Saint John, the king might well have inquired whether Saint John liked his Latin sung with a southern twang."

"He only did it to give work to these confounded choristers of the King of Sicily!" bitterly exclaimed an old woman in the crowd beneath the window. "Just fancy! a thousand pounds Paris for a Mass! and charged to the taxes on all salt-water fish sold in the Paris markets too!"

"Silence, old woman!" said a grave and reverend personage who was holding his nose beside the fishwoman; "he had to endow a Mass. You don't want the king to fall ill again, do you?"

"Bravely spoken, Master Gilles Lecornu, sir furrier of the king's robes!" cried the little scholar clinging to the capital.

"Lecornu! Gilles Lecornu!" said some.

"*Cornutus et hirsutus*," replied another.

"Oh, no doubt!" continued the little demon of the capital. "What is there to laugh at? An honourable man is Gilles Lecornu, brother of Master Jehan Lecornu, provost of the king's palace, son of Master Mahiet Lecornu, head porter of the Forest of Vincennes,—all good citizens of Paris, every one of them married, from father to son!"

The mirth increased. The fat furrier, not answering a word, strove to escape the eyes fixed on him from every side, but he puffed and perspired in vain; like a wedge driven into wood, all his efforts only buried his broad apoplectic face, purple with rage and spite, the more firmly in the shoulders of his neighbours.

At last one of the latter, fat, short, and venerable as himself, came to his rescue.

"Abominable! Shall students talk thus to a citizen! In my day they would have been well whipped with the sticks which served to burn them afterwards."

The entire band burst out:—

"Hollo! who sings that song? Who is this bird of ill omen?"

"Stay, I know him," said one; "it's Master Andry Musnier."

"He is one of the four copyists licensed by the University!" said another.

"Everything goes by fours in that shop," cried a third,— "four nations, four faculties, four great holidays, four proctors, four electors, four copyists."

"Very well, then," answered Jehan Frollo; "we must play the devil with them by fours."

"Musnier, we'll burn your books."

"Musnier, we'll beat your servant."

"Musnier, we'll hustle your wife."

"That good fat Mademoiselle Oudarde."

"Who is as fresh and as fair as if she were a widow."

"Devil take you!" growled Master Andry Musnier.

"Master Andry," added Jehan, still hanging on his capital, "shut up, or I'll fall on your head!"

Master Andry raised his eyes, seemed for a moment to be measuring the height of the column, the weight of the rascal, mentally multiplied that weight by the square of the velocity, and was silent.

Jehan, master of the field of battle, went on triumphantly:—

"I'd do it, though I am the brother of an archdeacon!"

"Fine fellows, our University men are, not even to have insisted upon our rights on such a day as this! For, only think of it, there is a Maypole and a bonfire in the Town; a miracle play, Lord of Misrule, and Flemish embassy in the City; and at the University—nothing!"

"And yet Maubert Square is big enough!" answered one of the scholars established on the window-seat.

"Down with the rector, the electors, and the proctors!" shouted Joannes.

"We must build a bonfire to-night in the Gaillard Field," went on the other, "with Master Andry's books."

"And the desks of the scribes," said his neighbour.

"And the beadles' maces!"

"And the deans' spittoons!"

"And the proctors' cupboards!"

"And the electors' bread-bins!"

"And the rector's footstools!"

"Down with them!" went on little Jehan, mimicking a droning psalm-tune; "down with Master Andry, the beadles, and the scribes; down with theologians, doctors, and decretists; proctors, electors, and rector!"

"Is the world coming to an end?" muttered Master Andry stopping his ears as he spoke.

"Speaking of the rector, there he goes through the square!" shouted one of those in the window.

Every one turned towards the square.

"Is it really our respectable rector, Master Thibaut?" asked Jehan Frollo du Moulin, who, clinging to one of the inner columns, could see nothing of what was going on outside.

"Yes, yes," replied the rest with one accord, "it is really he, Master Thibaut, the rector."

It was indeed the rector and all the dignitaries of the University going in procession to meet the embassy, and just at this moment crossing the Palace yard. The scholars, crowding in the window, greeted them, as they passed, with sarcasms and mock applause. The rector, who walked at the head of his company, received the first volley, which was severe:—

"Good-morning, Sir Rector! Hollo there! Good-morning, I say!"

"How does he happen to be here, the old gambler? Has he forsaken his dice?"

"How he ambles along on his mule! The animal's ears are not so long as his."

"Hollo there! Good-day to you, Master Rector Thibaut! *Tybalde aleator!* old fool! old gambler!"

"God keep you! did you throw many double sixes last night?"

"Oh, look at his lead-coloured old face, wrinkled and worn with love of cards and dice!"

"Whither away so fast, Thibaut, *Tybalde ad dados*, turning your back on the University and trotting straight towards town?"

"He's probably going to look for a lodging in Tybaldy Street," shouted Jehan du Moulin.

The entire band repeated the silly joke in a shout like thunder, and with frantic clapping of hands.

"You're going to look for a lodging in Tybaldy Street, are you not, Sir Rector, you devil's advocate?"

Then came the turn of the other officials.

"Down with the beadles! down with the mace-bearers!"

"Say, you Robin Poussepain, who's that fellow yonder?"

"That's Gilbert de Suilly, *Gilbertus de Soliaco*, Chancellor of the College of Autun."

"Stay, here's my shoe; you've got a better place than I; fling it in his face."

"*Saturnalitias mittimus ecce nuces.*"

"Down with the six theologians in the white surplices!"

"Are those theologians? I thought they were six white geese given to the city by Saint Geneviève for the fief of Roogny."

"Down with the doctors!"

"Down with all cardinal and jocose disputations."

"Take my cap, Chancellor of St. Geneviève! You did me an injustice,—and that's the truth; he gave my place in the nation of Normandy to little Ascanio Falzaspada, who belongs to the province of Bourges, being an Italian."

"Rank injustice," exclaimed all the students. "Down with the Chancellor of St. Geneviève."

"Ho there, Master Joachim de Ladehors! Ho there, Louis Dahuille! Hollo, Lambert Hoctement!"

"May the devil smother the proctor of the German nation!"

"And the chaplains of the Holy Chapel, with their grey amices, *cum tunicis grisis!*"

"*Seu de pellibus grisis fourratis!*"

"Ho there! you Masters of Arts! See all the fine black copes! See all the fine red copes!"

"That makes a fine tail for the rector!"

"You would think it was a Venetian doge on his way to wed the sea."

"I say, Jehan! look at the Canons of St. Geneviève!"

"Deuce take all Canons!"

"Abbot Claude Choart! Doctor Claude Choart! Are you looking for Marie la Giffarde?"

"She lives in Glatigny Street."

"She's bedmaker to the king of scamps."

"She's paying her four farthings, *quatuor denarios.*"

"*Aut unum bombum.*"

"Would you like her to pay you in the nose?"

"Comrades! there goes Master Simon

Sanguin the Elector from Picardy, with his wife behind him!"

"Post equitem sedet atra cura."

"Cheer up, Master Simon!"

"Good-day to you, Sir Elector!"

"Good-night to you, Madame Electress!"

"How lucky they are to see so much!" sighed Joannes de Molendino, still perched among the foliage of his column.

Meanwhile, the licensed copyist to the University, Master Andry Musnier, leaned towards the ear of the furrier of the king's robes, Master Gilles Lecornu.

"I tell you, sir, this is the end of the world. The students never were so riotous before; it's the cursed inventions of the age that are ruining us all,—artillery, bombards, serpentines, and particularly printing, that other German pest. No more manuscripts, no more books! Printing is death to bookselling. The end of the world is at hand."

"So I see by the rage for velvet stuffs," said the furrier.

At this instant the clock struck twelve.

"Ha!" cried the entire throng with but a single voice.

The students were silent. Then began a great stir; a great moving of feet and heads; a general outbreak of coughing and handkerchiefs; everybody shook himself, arranged himself, raised himself on tiptoe, placed himself to the best advantage. Then came deep silence; every neck was stretched, every mouth was opened wide, every eye was turned towards the marble table. Nothing was to be seen there. The four officers still stood stiff and motionless as four coloured statues. Every eye turned towards the daïs reserved for the Flemish ambassadors. The door was still shut and the daïs empty. The throng has been waiting since dawn for three things: noon, the Flemish embassy, and the mystery. Noon arrived punctually. Really it was too bad.

They waited one, two, three, five minutes, a quarter of an hour; nothing happened. The daïs was still deserted, the theatre mute. Rage followed in the footsteps of impatience. Angry words passed from mouth to mouth, though still in undertones, to be sure. "The mystery! the mystery!" was the low cry.

Every head was in a ferment. A tempest, as yet but threatening, hung over the multitude. Jehan du Moulin drew forth the first flash.

"The mystery! and to the devil with the Flemish!" he shouted at the top of his voice, writhing and twisting around his capital like a serpent.

The crowd applauded.

"The mystery!" repeated the mob; "and deuce take Flanders!"

"We insist on the mystery at once," continued the student; "or else it's my advice to hang the Palace bailiff by way of a comedy and morality."

"Well said," cried the people; "and let us begin the hanging with his men."

Loud cheers followed. The four poor devils began to turn pale and to exchange glances. The mob surged towards them, and the frail wooden railing parting them from the multitude bent and swayed beneath the pressure.

It was a critical moment.

"To the sack with them! to the sack!" was the cry from every side.

At that instant the hangings of the

dressing-room, which we have already described, were raised, giving passage to a personage the mere sight of whom suddenly arrested the mob, changing rage to curiosity as if by magic.

"Silence! Silence!"

This person, but little reassured, and trembling in every limb, advanced to the edge of the table, with many bows, which, in proportion as he approached, grew more and more like genuflections. However, peace was gradually restored. There remained only that slight murmur always arising from the silence of a vast multitude.

"Sir citizens," said he, "and fair citizenesses, we shall have the honour to declaim and perform before his Eminence the Cardinal a very fine morality entitled, 'The Wise Decision of Mistress Virgin Mary.' I am to enact Jupiter. His Eminence is at this moment escorting the very honourable embassy of his Highness the Duke of Austria, which is just now detained to listen to the speech of the Rector of the University at the Donkeys' Gate. As soon as the most eminent Cardinal arrives, we will begin."

It is plain that it required nothing less than the intervention of Jupiter himself to save the poor unfortunate officers of the bailiff. If we had had the good luck to invent this very truthful history, and consequently to be responsible for it to our lady Criticism, the classic rule, *Nec deus intersit*, could not be brought up against us at this point. Moreover, Lord Jupiter's costume was very handsome, and contributed not a little to calm the mob by attracting its entire attention. Jupiter was clad in a brigandine covered with black velvet, with gilt studs; on his head was a flat cap trimmed with silver-gilt buttons; and had it not been for the paint and the big beard which covered each half of his face, had it not been for the roll of gilded cardboard, sprinkled with spangles and all bristling with shreds of tinsel, which he carried in his hand, and in which practised eyes readily recognized the thunder, had it not been for his flesh-coloured feet bound with ribbons in Greek fashion, he might have stood favourable comparison, for severity of bearing, with any Breton archer in the Duke of Berry's regiment.

CHAPTER II

Pierre Gringoire

But as he spoke, the satisfaction, the admiration excited by his dress, were destroyed by his words; and when he reached the fatal conclusion "as soon as the most eminent Cardinal arrives, we will begin," his voice was drowned in a storm of hoots.

"Begin at once! The mystery! the mystery at once!" screamed the people. And over all the other voices was heard that of Johannes de Molendino piercing the uproar, like the fife in a *charivari* at Nismes. "Begin at once!" shrieked the student.

"Down with Jupiter and Cardinal Bourbon!" shouted Robin Poussepain and the other learned youths perched in the window.

"The morality this instant!" repeated the mob; "instantly! immediately! To the sack and the rope with the actors and the Cardinal!"

Poor Jupiter, haggard, terrified, pale

beneath his paint, let his thunderbolt fall, and seized his cap in his hand. Then he bowed, trembled, and stammered out: "His Eminence—the ambassadors—Madame Margaret of Flanders—" He knew not what to say. In his secret heart he was mightily afraid of being hanged.

Hanged by the populace for waiting, hanged by the Cardinal for not waiting,—on either hand he saw a gulf; that is to say, a gallows.

Luckily, some one appeared to extricate him from his embarrassing position and assume the responsibility.

An individual, standing just within the railing, in the vacant space about the marble table, and whom nobody had as yet observed,—so completely was his long slim person hidden from sight by the thickness of the pillar against which he leaned,—this individual, we say, tall, thin, pale, fair-haired, still young, although already wrinkled in brow and cheeks, with bright eyes and a smiling mouth, clad in black serge, worn and shining with age, approached the table and made a sign to the poor victim. But the latter, in his terror and confusion, failed to see him.

The new-comer took another step forward.

"Jupiter!" said he, "my dear Jupiter!"

The other did not hear him.

At last the tall fair-haired fellow, growing impatient, shouted almost in his ear,—

"Michel Giborne!"

"Who calls me?" said Jupiter, as if suddenly wakened.

"I," replied the person dressed in black.

"Ah!" said Jupiter.

"Begin directly," continued the other. "Satisfy the public; I take it upon myself to pacify the bailiff, who will pacify the Cardinal."

Jupiter breathed again.

"Gentlemen and citizens," he shouted at the top of his lungs to the crowd who continued to hoot him, "we will begin at once."

"*Evoe, Jupiter! Plaudite, cives!*" cried the students.

"Noël! Noël!" cried the people.

Deafening applause followed, and the hall still trembled with the plaudits when Jupiter had retired behind the hangings.

But the unknown person who had so miraculously changed "the tempest to a calm," as our dear old Corneille says, had modestly withdrawn into the shadow of his pillar, and would doubtless have remained there invisible, motionless, and mute as before, had he not been drawn forward by two young women, who, placed in the foremost rank of the spectators, had observed his colloquy with Michel Giborne-Jupiter.

"Master," said one of them, beckoning him to come nearer.

"Be quiet, my dear Liénarde," said her neighbour, pretty, fresh, and emboldened by all her Sunday finery. "That is no scholar, he is a layman; you must not call him *Master*, but *Sir*."

"Sir," said Liénarde.

The stranger approached the railing. "What do you wish of me, young ladies?" he asked eagerly.

"Oh, nothing!" said Liénarde, much confused; "it is my neighbour Gisquette la Gencienne who wants to speak to you."

"Not at all," replied Gisquette, blushing; "it was Liénarde who called you Master; I told her that she should say Sir."

The two young girls cast down their eyes. The stranger, who desired nothing better than to enter into conversation with them, looked at them with a smile.

"Then you have nothing to say to me, young ladies?"

"Oh, nothing at all!" answered Gisquette.

The tall fair-haired youth drew back a pace; but the two curious creatures had no idea of losing their prize.

"Sir," said Gisquette hastily, and with the impetuosity of water rushing through a floodgate or a woman coming to a sudden resolve, "so you know that soldier who is to play the part of Madame Virgin in the mystery?"

"You mean the part of Jupiter?" replied the unknown.

"Oh, yes," said Liénarde, "isn't she silly? So you know Jupiter?"

"Michel Giborne?" replied the unknown. "Yes, madame."

"He has a fine beard!" said Liénarde.

"Will it be very interesting—what they are going to recite up there?" asked Gisquette, shyly.

"Very interesting indeed," replied the stranger, without the least hesitation.

"What is it to be?" said Liénarde.

" 'The Wise Decision of Madame Virgin Mary,' a morality, if you please, madame."

"Ah, that's another thing," replied Liénarde.

A short pause followed. The stranger first broke the silence:—

"It is quite a new morality, which has never yet been played."

"Then it is not the same," said Gisquette, "that was given two years ago, on the day of the legate's arrival, and in which three beautiful girls took the part of—"

"Sirens," said Liénarde.

"And all naked," added the young man. Liénarde modestly cast down her eyes; Gisquette looked at her, and did the same. He continued with a smile,—

"That was a very pretty sight. This, now, is a morality, written expressly for the young Flemish madame."

"Will they sing pastorals?" asked Gisquette.

"Fie!" said the stranger, "in a morality! You must not mix up different styles. If it were a farce, that would be another thing."

"What a pity!" replied Gisquette. "That day there were wild men and women at the Ponceau Fountain, who fought together and made all sorts of faces, singing little motets and pastorals all the while."

"What suits a legate," said the stranger, somewhat drily, "will hardly suit a princess."

"And close by them," added Liénarde, "were several bass instruments which played grand melodies."

"And to refresh the passers-by," continued Gisquette, "the fountain streamed wine, milk and hippocras, from three mouths, for all to drink who would."

"And a little way beyond that fountain," went on Liénarde, "at the Trinity, there was a passion-play, performed by mute characters."

"How well I remember it!" exclaimed

Gisquette,—"God on the cross, and the two thieves to right and left."

Here the young gossips, growing excited at the recollection of the arrival of the legate, both began to talk at once.

"And farther on, at the Painters' Gate, there were other persons richly dressed."

"And at the Fountain of the Holy Innocents, that hunter chasing a doe, with a great noise of dogs and hunting-horns!"

"And at the Paris shambles, those scaffolds representing the fortress at Dieppe!"

"And when the legate passed by, you know, Gisquette, there was an attack, and all the English had their throats cut."

"And over against the Châtelet Gate there were very fine persons!"

"And on the Money-brokers' Bridge, which was hung all over with tapestries!"

"And when the legate passed by, they let loose more than two hundred dozen of all sorts of birds; it was very fine, Liénarde."

"It will be finer to-day," replied their listener at last, seeming to hear them with some impatience.

"Then you promise us that this play will be a fine one?" said Gisquette.

"To be sure," he answered. Then he added with a certain emphasis: "Young ladies, I am the author of it."

"Really?" said the young girls, much amazed.

"Really!" replied the poet, drawing himself up; "that is, there are two of us: Jehan Marchand, who sawed the planks and built the frame and did all the carpenter's work, and I, who wrote the piece. My name is Pierre Gringoire."

The author of the "Cid" could not have said "Pierre Corneille" with any greater degree of pride.

Our readers may have noticed that some time had already passed since Jupiter had gone behind the hangings, and before the author of the new morality revealed himself so abruptly to the simple admiration of Gisquette and Liénarde. Strange to say, all that multitude, which a few instants previous was so furiously uproarious, now waited calmly for the fulfillment of the actor's promise, which proves that enduring truth, still verified in our own theatres, that the best way to make your audience wait patiently is to assure them that you will begin directly.

However, student Joannes was not asleep.

"Hollo, ho!" he cried out suddenly, in the midst of the calm expectation which followed on confusion. "Jupiter, Madame Virgin, devilish mountebanks! are you mocking us? The play! the play! Begin, or we will stir you up again!"

This was quite enough.

The sound of musical instruments pitched in various keys was heard from the interior of the scaffolding. The tapestry was raised; four characters painted and clad in motley garb came out, climbed the rude stage ladder, and gaining the upper platform, ranged themselves in line before the public, bowing low; then the symphony ceased. The mystery was about to begin.

These four personages, having been abundantly repaid for their bows by applause, began, amid devout silence, a prologue which we gladly spare the reader. Moreover, as happens even nowadays, the audience was far more interested in the costumes of the actors than in the speeches which they recited; and, to tell the truth, they were quite right. They were all four dressed in gowns partly yellow and partly white, which only differed from each other in material; the first was of gold and silver brocade, the second of silk, the third of wool, the fourth of linen. The first of these characters had a sword in his right hand, the second two golden keys, the third a pair of scales, the fourth a spade; and to aid those indolent understandings which might not have penetrated the evident meaning of these attributes, might be read embroidered in big black letters—on the hem of the brocade gown, "I AM NOBILITY;" on the hem of the silk gown, "I AM RELIGION," on the hem of the woolen gown, "I AM TRADE;" and on the hem of the linen gown, "I AM LABOUR." The sex of the two male allegories was clearly shown to every sensible beholder by their shorter gowns and by their peculiar headdress,—a flat cap called a *cramignole*; while the two feminine allegories, clad in longer garments, wore hoods.

One must also have been wilfully dull not to gather from the poetical prologue that Labour was wedded to Trade, and Religion to Nobility, and that the two happy pairs owned in common a superb golden dolphin, which they desired to bestow only on the fairest of the fair. They were therefore journeying through the world in search of this beauty; and having in turn rejected the Queen of Golconda, the Princess of Trebizond, the daughter of the Cham of Tartary, etc., Labour and Religion, Nobility and Trade, were now resting on the marble table in the Palace of Justice, spouting to their simple audience as many long sentences and maxims as would suffice the Faculty of Arts for all the examinations, sophisms, determinances, figures, and acts required of all the bachelors in taking their degrees.

All this was indeed very fine.

But in the crowd upon whom the four allegorical personages poured such floods of metaphor, each trying to outdo the other, there was no more attentive ear, no more anxious heart, no more eager eye, no neck more outstretched, than the eye, the ear, the neck, and the heart of the author, the poet, the worthy Pierre Gringoire, who could not resist, a moment previous, the delight of telling his name to two pretty girls. He had withdrawn some paces from them, behind his pillar; and there he listened, looked, and enjoyed. The kindly plaudits which greeted the opening lines of his prologue still rang in his innermost soul, and he was completely absorbed in that kind of ecstatic contemplation with which an author watches his ideas falling one by one from the actor's lips amid the silence of a vast assembly. Good Pierre Gringoire!

We regret to say that this first ecstasy was very soon disturbed. Gringoire had scarcely placed his lips to this intoxicating draught of joy and triumph, when a drop of bitterness was blended with it.

A ragged beggar, who could reap no harvest, lost as he was in the midst of the crowd, and who doubtless failed to find sufficient to atone for his loss in the pockets of his neighbours, hit upon the plan of perching himself upon some conspicuous point, in order to attract eyes and alms. He therefore hoisted himself, during the first lines of the programme, by the aid of the columns of the daïs, up to the top of the high railing running around it; and there he sat, soliciting the attention and the pity of the multitude, by the sight of his rags, and a hideous sore which covered his right arm. Moreover, he uttered not a word.

His silence permitted the prologue to go on without interruption, and no apparent disorder would have occurred if ill luck had not led the student Joannes to note the beggar and his grimaces, from his own lofty post. A fit of mad laughter seized upon the young rogue, who, regardless of the fact that he was interrupting the performance and disturbing the general concentration of thought, cried merrily,—

"Just look at that impostor asking for alms!"

Any one who has thrown a stone into a frog-pond or fired a gun into a flock of birds, can form some idea of the effect which these incongruous words produced in the midst of the universal attention. Gringoire shuddered as at an electric shock. The prologue was cut short, and every head was turned, in confusion, towards the beggar, who, far from being put out of countenance, regarded this incident as a good occasion for a harvest, and began to whine, with an air of great distress, his eyes half closed, "Charity, kind people!"

"Why, upon my soul," continued Joannes, "it is Clopin Trouillefou! Hollo there, my friend! Did you find the wound on your leg inconvenient, that you have transferred it to your arm?"

So saying, with monkey-like skill he flung a small silver coin into the greasy felt hat which the beggar held with his invalid arm. The beggar accepted the alms and the sarcasm without wincing, and went on in piteous tones, "Charity, kind people!"

This episode greatly distracted the attention of the audience; and many of the spectators, Robin Poussepain and all the students at their head, joyfully applauded the odd duet, improvised, in the middle of the prologue, by the student with his shrill voice and the beggar with his imperturbable whine.

Gringoire was much displeased. Recovering from his first surprise, he began shouting to the characters on the stage: "Go on! What the deuce! Go on!" not even condescending to cast a look of scorn at the two interrupters.

At this moment he felt himself pulled by the hem of his surtout; he turned, in rather an ill-humour, and had hard work to force a smile, as he needs must do. It was the fair arm of Gisquette la Gencienne, which, passed through the rails, thus entreated his attention.

"Sir," said the young girl, "will they go on?"

"Of course," replied Gringoire, quite shocked at the question.

"In that case, sir," she went on, "would you have the kindness to explain to me—"

"What they are going to say?" interrupted Gringoire. "Well! listen."

"No," said Gisquette, "but what they have already said."

Gringoire started violently, like a man touched on a sensitive spot.

"Plague take the foolish, stupid little wench!" he muttered between his teeth.

From that moment Gisquette was lost in his estimation.

However, the actors had obeyed his command, and the public, seeing that they had begun to speak again, again began to listen, not without necessarily losing many beauties from this kind of rough joining of the two parts of the piece, so abruptly dissevered. Gringoire brooded bitterly over this fact in silence. Still, quiet was gradually restored, the student was silent, the beggar counted a few coins in his hat, and the play went on.

It was really a very fine work, and one which it seems to us might well be made use of to-day, with a few changes. The plot, somewhat long and somewhat flat,—that is, written according to rule, —was simple; and Gringoire, in the innocent sanctuary of his innermost soul, admired its clearness. As may be imagined, the four allegorical characters were rather fatigued after traversing three quarters of the globe without managing to dispose of their golden dolphin creditably. Thereupon ensued fresh eulogies of the marvellous fish, with a thousand delicate allusions to the young lover of Margaret of Flanders, then very sadly secluded at Amboise, and little suspecting that Labour and Religion, Nobility and Trade, had just travelled around the world for his sake. The aforesaid dauphin was young, was handsome, was strong, and especially (magnificent source of all royal virtues!) he was the son of the Lion of France. I declare that this bold metaphor is admirable; and that the natural history of the theatre, on a day of allegories and royal epithalamia, is not to be alarmed at the thought of a dolphin being the son of a lion. It is just these rare and Pindaric mixtures which prove the degree of enthusiasm. Nevertheless, to play the critic, we must confess that the poet might have managed to develop this beautiful idea in less than two hundred lines. True, the mystery was to last from noon until four o'clock, by the order of the provost; something must be done to fill up the time. Besides, the people listened patiently.

All at once, in the very middle of a quarrel between Mademoiselle Trade and Madame Nobility, just as Master Labour pronounced this wonderful line,—

"Ne'er saw the woods a beast more beautiful."

the door leading to the platform, which had hitherto remained so inopportunely closed, was still more inopportunely opened, and the ringing voice of the usher abruptly announced "His Eminence, Cardinal Bourbon!"

Chapter III

THE CARDINAL

Poor Gringoire! The noise of all the big cannon crackers fired on St. John's day, the discharge of twenty crooked arquebuses, the report of that famous serpentine of the Tower of Billy, which, during the siege of Paris, on Sunday, Sept. 29, 1465, killed seven Burgundians at one shot, the explosion of all the gunpowder stored at the Temple Gate, would have rent his ears less rudely, at that solemn and dramatic moment, than did those few words dropping from the mouth of an usher: "His Eminence, Cardinal Bourbon!"

Not that Pierre Gringoire feared the Cardinal or scorned him; he was neither so weak nor so conceited. A genuine eclectic, as he would be called nowadays, Gringoire was one of those firm and lofty, calm and temperate souls, who always contrive to choose a happy medium (*stare in dimidio rerum*), and who are full of sense and liberal philosophy, although they have a high regard for cardinals. Precious and perpetual race of philosophers, to whom, as to another Ariadne, wisdom seems to have given a guiding clew which they have gone on unwinding from the beginning of the world, as they journeyed through the labyrinth of human things! They are to be found in every age, ever the same; that is, always in harmony with the age. And, to say nothing of our Pierre Gringoire, who would represent them in the fifteenth century if we could succeed in portraying him as he deserves, it is assuredly their spirit which animated Father du Breul in the sixteenth, when he wrote these simple and sublime words, worthy of all the ages: "I am a Parisian in nationality and a Parrhisian in speech; *Parrhisia* being a Greek word signifying 'freedom of speech;' the which I have used even towards the cardinals, uncle and brother to the Prince of Conty; always with due respect to their greatness, and without offending any man among their followers, which is much."

The disagreeable effect which the Cardinal produced on Pierre Gringoire, therefore, partook neither of hatred nor of scorn. Quite the contrary; our poet had too much good sense and too threadbare a coat not to attach especial value to the fact that many an allusion in his prologue, and particularly those in glorification of the dauphin, son of the Lion of France, might be heard by a most eminent ear. But interest is not all-powerful in the noble nature of poets. Let us suppose the entity of the poet to be represented by the number ten: it is certain that a chemist, who should analyze and pharmacopœize it, as Rabelais says, would find it to be composed of one part self-interest to nine parts of self-esteem. Now, at the moment that the door was thrown open to admit the Cardinal, Gringoire's nine parts of self-esteem, swollen and inflated by the breath of public admiration, were in a state of abnormal development, before which the imperceptible molecule of self-interest, which we just now discovered in the constitution of poets, vanished and faded into insignificance, precious ingredient though it was,—the ballast of reality and humanity, without which they would never descend to earth. Gringoire enjoyed feeling, seeing, handling, as it were, an entire assembly, —of rascals, it is true, but what did that matter? They were stupefied, petrified, and almost stifled by the incommensurable tirades with which every portion of his epithalamium bristled. I affirm that he himself partook of the general beatitude, and that, unlike La Fontaine, who, on witnessing a performance of his own comedy, "The Florentine," inquired, "What clown wrote that rhapsody?" Gringoire would fain have asked his neighbour, "Whose is this masterpiece?" You may judge of the effect produced on him by the abrupt and untimely arrival of the Cardinal.

His fears were but too soon realized. The entrance of his Eminence distracted the audience. Every head was turned towards the platform. No one listened. "The Cardinal! the Cardinal!" repeated every tongue. The unfortunate prologue was a second time cut short.

The Cardinal paused for a moment on the threshold. While he cast an indifferent glance over the assembly, the uproar increased. Every one wished to get a better view of him. Every one tried to see who could best stretch his neck over his neighbour's shoulders.

He was indeed a great personage, and one the sight of whom was well worth any other spectacle. Charles, Cardinal Bourbon, Archbishop and Count of Lyons, Primate of the Gauls, was at the same time allied to Louis XI. through his brother, Pierre, Lord of Beaujeu, who had married the eldest daughter of the king, and allied to Charles the Bold through his mother, Agnes of Burgundy. Now, the dominant feature, the characteristic and distinctive trait in the character of the Primate of the Gauls, was his courtier-like spirit and his devotion to those in power. It is easy to imagine the countless difficulties in which his double kinship had involved him, and all the temporal reefs between which his spiritual bark had been forced to manœuvre lest it should founder upon either Louis or Charles,—that Charybdis and that Scylla which had swallowed up the Duke of Nemours and the Constable of Saint-Pol. Heaven be thanked, he had escaped tolerably well from the voyage, and had reached Rome without accident. But although he was safe in port, and indeed because he was safe in port, he never recalled without a tremor the various haps and mishaps of his political life, so long full of alarms and labours. He was therefore wont to say that the year 1476 had been to him both black and white; meaning that in one and the same year he had lost his mother, the Duchess of Bourbonnais, and his cousin, the Duke of Burgundy, and that one loss had consoled him for the other.

However, he was a very good fellow; he led a joyous life as cardinal, cheered himself willingly with the royal wine of Chaillot, was not averse to Richarde lo Garmoise and Thomasse la Saillarde, preferred to bestow alms upon pretty maids rather than aged matrons, and for all these reasons was very agreeable to the populace of Paris. He always went surrounded by a small court of bishops and priests of lofty lineage, gallant, jovial, and fond of feasting on occasion; and more than once the good devotees of St. Germain d'Auxerre, as they passed by night beneath the brightly lighted windows of Bourbon's house, had been scandalized on hearing the same voices which had sung vespers for them that day, now chanting to the clink of glasses the Bacchic adage of Benedict III.,—that pope who added a third crown to the tiara,—*"Bibamus papaliter."*

It was undoubtedly this popularity, so justly acquired, which saved him, on his entrance, from any unpleasant reception on the part of the mob, so malcontent but a moment before, and but little inclined to respect a cardinal on the very day when they were to elect a pope. But Parisians are not given to hoarding up grudges; and then, by insisting that the play should begin, the good citizens had shown their authority, thus getting the better of the Cardinal: and this triumph sufficed them. Besides, Cardinal Bourbon was a remarkably handsome man; he had a very gorgeous red robe which was most becoming; which is as much as to say that all the women, and consequently the better half of the audience, were on his side. Certainly, it would have been unjust, and in very bad taste, to hoot a cardinal for being late at the play, when he is handsome and wears his red robe gracefully.

He entered, therefore, bowed to the assembly with the hereditary smile of the grandee to the people, and walked slowly towards his scarlet velvet armchair with an air of being absorbed in thoughts of far other things. His escort, or what we should now call his staff of bishops and priests, flocked after him upon the daïs, not without renewed curiosity and confusion on the part of the groundlings. Every man tried to point them out and name them; every man knew at least one among them: this one, the Bishop of Marseilles, Alaudet, if I remember rightly; that one, the Dean of St. Denis; another, Robert de Lespinasse, Abbot of St. Germain des Prés, the libertine brother of one of the mistresses of Louis XI.,—all with endless mistakes and mispronunciations. As for the students, they swore roundly. It was their day, their Feast of Fools, their saturnalia, the annual orgies of the basoche and the schools. No iniquity but was allowable and sacred upon that day. And then there were plenty of giddy girls in the crowd,—Simone Quatrelivres, Agnès la Gadine, Robine Piédebou. Was it not the least that they could do to swear at their ease and blaspheme a little on so fine a day, in so goodly a company of churchmen and courtesans? Neither were they slow to seize the opportunity; and in the midst of the uproar came a terrific outburst of oaths and obscenities from their lawless lips,—the lips of a set of students and scholars restrained all the rest of the year by their dread of the hot iron of Saint Louis. Poor Saint Louis! how they set him at defiance in his own Palace of Justice! Each of them selected from the new-comers on the daïs a black or grey, a white or purple gown for his own especial victim. As for Joannes Frollo de Molendino, in his quality of brother to an archdeacon he boldly attacked the red cassock, and bawled at the top of his voice, fixing his impudent eyes full on the Cardinal, *"Cappa repleta mero!"*

All these details, boldly set down here for the edification of the reader, were so covered by the general noise and confusion, that they were lost before they reached the daïs; besides which, the Cardinal would have paid but little heed to them, had he heard them, the license of that particular day was so well established a fact in the history of public morals. He had, moreover,—and his countenance showed how fully it absorbed him,—quite another care following him closely, and stepping upon the platform almost at the same moment as himself; namely, the Flemish embassy.

Not that he was much of a politician, or that he troubled himself much about the possible results of the marriage of his cousin, Lady Margaret of Burgundy, with his cousin Charles, Dauphin of Vienna; he cared very little about the duration of the friendship patched up between the Duke of Austria and the King of France, or about the King of England's opinion of the slight put upon his daughter! and he tested the royal vintage of Chaillot every evening, without suspecting that a few flasks of that same wine (slightly doctored and improved by Doctor Coictier, to be sure), cordially presented to Edward IV. by Louis XI. would one fine day rid Louis XI. of Edward IV. The very honourable embassy of the Duke of Austria brought none of these cares to the Cardinal's mind, but it troubled him in another way. It was indeed rather hard, and we have already spoken a word in regard to it in an earlier page of this book, to be forced to welcome and entertain—he, Charles of Bourbon—these nondescript citizens; he, a cardinal, to condescend to aldermen; he, a Frenchman and a boon companion, to befriend Flemish beer-drinkers, and that in public too! This was assuredly one of the most painful farces he had ever been compelled to play for the king's pleasure.

Still, he turned to the door with the best grace in the world (so well had he trained himself) when the usher announced in ringing tones, "The envoys from the Duke of Austria!" Needless to say that the entire audience did the same.

Then entered, two by two, with a gravity in vivid contrast to the lively ecclesiastical escort of Charles of Bourbon, the forty-eight ambassadors of Maximilian of Austria, headed by the reverend father in God, Jehan, Abbot of Saint-Bertin, Chancellor of the Golden Fleece, and Jacques de Goy, Lord of Dauby, high bailiff of Ghent. A profound silence fell upon the assembly, followed by stifled laughter at all the absurd names and all the commonplace titles which each of these personages calmly transmitted to the usher, who instantly hurled names and titles pell-mell, and horribly mangled, at the heads of the crowd. There were Master Loys Roelof, alderman of the city of Louvain; Master Clays d'Etuelde, alderman of Brussels; Master Paul de Baeurst, Lord of Voirmizelle, president of Flanders; Master Jehan Coleghens, burgomaster of the city of Antwerp; Master George de la Moere, head sheriff of the *kuere* of the town of Ghent; Master Gheldolf van der Hage, head sheriff of the court of equity of the same town; and the Lord of Bierbecque, and Jehan Pinnock, and Jehan Dymaerzelle, etc., etc., etc.: bailiffs, aldermen, burgomasters; burgomasters, aldermen, bailiffs; all stiff, starched, and strait-laced, dressed in their Sunday best of velvet and damask, wearing flat black velvet caps on their heads, with large tassels of gold thread from Cyprus; honest Flemish figures after all, severe and dignified faces, of the race of those whom Rembrandt portrayed so gravely and forcibly against the dark background of his "Night Watch,"—personages every one of whom bore it written upon his brow that Maximilian of Austria was right in "confiding fully," as his proclamation had it, "in their good sense, valour, experience, loyalty, and good qualities."

But there was one exception. This

was a man with a cunning, intelligent, crafty face, the face of a monkey combined with that of a diplomatist, to meet whom the Cardinal stepped forward three paces, bowing low, and yet who bore a name no more high sounding than "Guillaume Rym, councillor and pensionary of the town of Ghent."

Few persons there knew what Guillaume Rym was,—a rare genius, who in time of revolution would have appeared with renown in the foremost rank, but who in the fifteenth century was reduced to the lowest intrigues, and to "living by sapping and mining" as the Duke of St. Simon expresses it. However, he was appreciated by the greatest "sapper" in Europe; he planned and plotted with Louis XI. on familiar terms, and often laid his hand on the king's secret necessities.

All these things were utterly unknown to this throng, who marvelled at the politeness shown by the Cardinal to this scurvy Flemish bailiff.

Chapter IV

MASTER JACQUES COPPENOLE

As the pensionary of Ghent and his Eminence were exchanging very low bows, and a few words in still lower voices, a tall, broad-faced, square-shouldered man entered boldly after Guillaume Rym; he reminded one of a dog in pursuit of a fox. His felt hat and leather jerkin looked very shabby in the midst of the velvet and silk which surrounded him. Supposing him to be some groom who had lost his way, the usher stopped him.

"Hollo, my friend! there's no passing here."

The man in the leather coat shouldered him aside.

"What does the fellow mean?" he said in a tone which made the entire hall aware of this strange colloquy. "Don't you see that I belong to the party?"

"Your name?" asked the usher.

"Jacques Coppenole."

"Your titles?"

"Hosier at the sign of the Three Little Chains, at Ghent."

The usher started back. It was bad enough to have to announce aldermen and burgomasters; but a hosier, that was hard indeed! The Cardinal was on thorns. Every one was looking and listening. For two days past his Eminence had been labouring to lick these Flemish bears into some presentable shape, and this outburst was hard upon him. However, Guillaume Rym, with his crafty smile, leaned towards the usher.

"Announce Master Jacques Coppenole, clerk to the aldermen of the town of Ghent," he whispered softly.

"Usher," added the Cardinal in a loud voice, "announce Master Jacques Coppenole, clerk to the aldermen of the illustrious town of Ghent."

This was a mistake. Guillaume Rym, if left to himself, would have evaded the difficulty; but Coppenole had overheard the Cardinal.

"No, by God's cross!" he cried in his voice of thunder. "Jacques Coppenole, hosier. Do you hear me, usher? Nothing more, nothing less. By God's cross! a hosier is good enough for me. The archduke himself has more than once sought his gauntlet in my hose."

There was a burst of laughter and applause. A pun is always instantly appreciated in Paris, and consequently always applauded.

Let us add that Coppenole was a man of the people, and that the audience about him consisted of the people only; thus the sympathy between them was prompt, electric, and they were at once on an equal footing. The proud exclamation of the Flemish hosier, while it mortified the courtiers, stirred in every humble soul a certain sense of dignity still vague and indistinct in the fifteenth century. This hosier, who had just bearded the Cardinal himself, was their equal! A very pleasant thought for poor devils who were want to respect and obey the servants of the officers of the bailiff of the Abbot of St. Geneviève, train-bearer to the Cardinal.

Coppenole bowed haughtily to his Eminence, who returned the salutation of the all-powerful citizen dreaded by Louis XI. Then, while Guillaume Rym, "a wise and wily man," as Philippe de Comines has it, watched them both with a smile full of raillery and superiority, they took each his place,—the Cardinal troubled and disconcerted, Coppenole calm and erect, doubtless thinking that after all his title of hosier was quite as good as any other, and that Mary of Burgundy, mother of that Margaret whose marriage he was now negotiating, would have feared him less as cardinal than as hosier; for no cardinal would have led on the men of Ghent against the favourites of the daughter of Charles the Bold; no cardinal could have hardened the hearts of the masses against her tears and her prayers, by a single word, when the heiress of Flanders besought her people to grant their pardon, at the very foot of their scaffold; while the hosier had but to lift his leathern elbow to cause both your heads to fall, O ye illustrious lords, Guy d'Hymbercourt and Chancellor Guillaume Hugonet!

But all was not over yet for the poor Cardinal, who must needs drink to the dregs the bitter cup of compassion with such low company.

The reader may perhaps recall the impudent beggar who clung to the fringes of the Cardinal's daïs at the opening of the prologue. The arrival of the distinguished guests did not cause him to relax his hold; and while prelates and ambassadors were packed as close as Dutch herrings in the seats upon the platform, he made himself quite comfortable, and coolly crossed his legs upon the architrave. Such insolence was unusual, and no one noted it at the moment, attention being -fixed elsewhere. He for his part saw nothing in the hall; he swayed his head to and fro with the careless ease of a Neapolitan, repeating ever and anon amid the din, as if mechanically, "Charity, kind people!" and certainly he was the only one in the entire audience who did not deign to turn his head to listen to the altercation between Coppenole and the usher. Now, as chance would have it, the master hosier of Ghent, with whom the people already sympathized strongly, and upon whom all eyes were fixed, seated himself in the front row upon the platform, just above the beggar; and they were not a little amazed to see the Flemish ambassador, after glancing at the rascal beneath him, give him a friendly slap upon his tattered shoulder.

The beggar turned; surprise, recognition, delight, were visible in both faces, then, without paying the slightest heed to the throng of spectators, the hosier and the scurvy knave fell to talking in low tones, clasping each other's hands; while the rags of Clopin Trouillefou, displayed against the cloth of gold of the daïs, produced the effect of a caterpillar upon an orange.

The novelty of this strange scene excited such an outburst of mirth in the hall that the Cardinal quickly perceived it; he bent forward, and, unable from his position to catch more than a glimpse of Trouillefou's disgraceful garments, he quite naturally supposed that the beggar was asking alms, and indignant at his audacity, he exclaimed, "Sir Bailiff of the Palace, throw me that rascal into the river!"

"By God's cross! Sir Cardinal," said Coppenole, without releasing Clopin's hand, "he is my friend."

"Noël! Noël" cried the mob. From that instant Master Coppenole was "in high favour with the people," in Paris as in Ghent; "for men of his cut always are," says Philippe de Comines, "when they are thus disorderly."

The Cardinal bit his lip. He bent towards his neighbour, the Abbot of St. Geneviève, and said in an undertone:—

"Pleasant ambassadors are these sent us by the archduke to announce the coming of Lady Margaret!"

"Your Eminence," replied the abbot, "wastes his courtesies upon these Flemish grunters,—*Margaritas ante porcos.*"

"Say rather," replied the Cardinal with a smile, "*Porcos ante Margaritam.*"

All the little court in priestly robes went into ecstasies over the joke. The Cardinal felt slightly comforted: he was quits with Coppenole; his pun also had been applauded.

Now, let those of our readers who have the power of generalizing an image and an idea, as it is the pleasant fashion to express it, allow us to ask them if they have a distinct conception of the spectacle afforded, at the moment that we claim their attention, by the vast parallelogram of the great hall of the Palace: In the centre of the hall, against the western wall, a broad and magnificent platform covered with gold brocade, upon which stepped in procession, through a small arched doorway, a number of grave and reverend personages successively announced by the nasal voice of an usher; on the foremost benches, already seated, various venerable figures wrapped in ermine, velvet, and scarlet; around the daïs, where all was dignity and silence, below, in front, everywhere, a great crowd and a great uproar; a thousand eyes from the crowd fixed upon every face on the platform, a thousand murmurs upon the announcement of every name. Certainly the sight is a strange one, and well worthy the attention of the spectators. But below there, at the extreme end, what is that kind of trestle-work with four motley puppets above and four more below? Who is that pale-faced man in a black coat beside the boards? Alas! dear reader, that is Pierre Gringoire and his prologue.

We had all entirely forgotten him.

This was precisely what he feared.

From the instant that the Cardinal entered, Gringoire had never ceased working for the salvation of his prologue. He at first enjoined the actors, who remained in suspense, to go on, and to raise their voices; then, seeing that no one was listening, he stopped them; and then, after the interruption had lasted nearly fifteen minutes, he began to stamp, to struggle, to question Gisquette and Liénarde, and to encourage his neighbours to call for the prologue. All in vain; not an eye would move from the Cardinal, the embassy, and the daïs,—the sole centre of that vast circle of visual rays. We must therefore believe, and we say it with regret, that the prologue was beginning to be somewhat tedious to the audience at the moment that his Eminence caused so terrible a diversion. After all, the spectacle was the same upon the daïs as upon the marble table,—the conflict between Labour and Religion, Nobility and Trade; and many people preferred to see them simply, in living, breathing reality, elbowing and pushing, in flesh and blood, in this Flemish embassy, in this Episcopal court, beneath the Cardinal's robe, beneath the jacket of Coppenole, rather than painted and decked out, speaking in artificial verse, and as it were stuffed with straw beneath the white and yellow tunics in which Gringoire had arrayed them.

However, when our poet saw that peace was beginning to reign once more, he hit upon a stratagem which might have saved all.

"Sir," said he, turning towards one of his neighbours, a good fat fellow with a patient face, "suppose they begin again?"

"Begin what?" said the neighbour.

"Why, the mystery!" said Gringoire.

"If you like," responded his neighbour.

This lukewarm approval was enough for Gringoire, and acting for himself he began to shout, mixing with the crowd as much as he could, "Go on with the miracle-play! Go on!"

"The devil!" said Joannes de Molendino, "what are they bawling about over there?" (For Gringoire made noise enough for four.) "Say, boys, isn't the play done? They want to have it all over again; it's not fair."

"No, no!" cried the students. "Down with the mystery! down with it!"

But Gringoire seemed ubiquitous, and shouted louder than before, "Go on, go on!"

These outcries attracted the attention of the Cardinal.

"Bailiff," he said to a tall dark man seated near him, "are those devils caught in a font of holy water, that they make such an infernal noise?"

The Bailiff of the Palace was a species of amphibious magistrate, a sort of bat of the judicial order, partaking at once of the nature of the rat and the bird, the judge and the soldier.

He approached his Eminence, and, not without serious fears of his displeasure, stammered out an explanation of the popular misconduct,—that noon had come before his Eminence, and that the actors were obliged to begin without awaiting his Eminence.

The Cardinal burst out laughing.

"Upon my word, the Rector of the University had better have done as much. What say you, Master Guillaume Rym?"

"My lord," replied Guillaume Rym, "let us be content that we have escaped half the play. It is just so much gained."

"May those rascals go on with their performance?" asked the bailiff.

"Go on, go on," said the Cardinal; "it's all the same to me. I will read my breviary meantime."

The bailiff advanced to the edge of the platform and cried aloud, after imposing silence by a wave of his hand: "Citizens, commoners, and residents: to satisfy those who wish the play to begin again and those who wish it to end, his Eminence orders that it be continued."

Both parties were forced to submit. However, the author and the audience long cherished a grudge against the Cardinal.

The characters on the stage accordingly resumed their recital, and Gringoire hoped that the rest of his work at least would be heard. This hope soon proved as illusory as all the rest. Silence was indeed restored to a certain extent among the audience; but Gringoire had not remarked that, at the moment when the Cardinal gave the order to go on, the daïs was far from being filled, and that in the train of the Flemish embassy came other personages forming part of the procession, whose names and titles, shouted out in the midst of his prologue by the intermittent cry of the usher, made many ravages in it. Imagine the effect, in the midst of a play, of the shrill voice of an usher uttering between two rhymes, and often between two hemistichs, such parentheses as these:—

"Master Jacques Charmolue, king's attorney in the Ecclesiastical Court!"

"Jehan de Harlay, esquire, keeper of the office of captain of the watch of the city of Paris!"

"Master Galiot de Genoilhac, knight, Lord of Brussac, chief of the king's ordinance!"

"Master Dreux-Raguier, inspector of the woods and waters of our lord the king, in the lands of France, Champagne, and Brie!"

"Master Louis de Graville, knight, councillor, and chamberlain to the king, admiral of France, keeper of the forest of Vincennes!"

Master Denis le Mercier, guardian of the Home for the Blind of Paris!" etc.

This at last became unendurable.

This strange accompaniment, which made it very hard to follow the play, enraged Gringoire all the more because he could not blind himself to the fact that the interest was constantly increasing, and that all his work needed was to be heard. It was indeed difficult to conceive of a more ingenious and more dramatic context. The four characters of the prologue were lamenting their terrible embarrassment, when Venus in person (*vera incessu patuit dea*) appeared before them, clad in a fine coat of mail, emblazoned with the ship from the seal of the city of Paris. She came herself to claim the dolphin promised to the fairest of the fair. Jupiter, whose thunder was heard muttering in the dressing-room below, supported her claim, and the goddess was about to triumph,—that is, speaking without metaphor, to marry the Dauphin,—when a young child, habited in white damask and holding a daisy (an obvious allusion to the Lady of Flanders), came to contest the prize with Venus. Theatrical effect and sudden change of affairs! After some controversy, Venus, Margaret, and those behind the scenes agreed to refer the matter to the wise decision of the Holy Virgin. There was also another fine part, that of Don Pedro, King of Mesopotamia; but amid so many interruptions it was difficult to discover the object of his introduction. All these characters came up the ladder.

But it all was in vain; none of these beauties were appreciated or understood. With the Cardinal's entrance, an invisible and magical cord seemed suddenly to draw all eyes from the marble table to the daïs, from the southern to the western portion of the hall. Nothing could free the audience from the spell; every eye was fixed, and the new-comers and their accursed names, and their faces and their dresses, were a perpetual source of distraction. It was heartrending. Save for Gisquette and Liénarde, who occasionally turned away when Gringoire pulled them by the sleeve; save for the patient fat neighbour, no one listened to, no one looked at, the poor forsaken morality. Gringoire saw nothing but profiles.

With what bitterness he saw his whole framework of fame and poetry crumble away bit by bit! And to think that this very mob had been on the point of revolting against the bailiff, from sheer impatience to hear his work! Now that they had it, they cared nothing for it,—this same performance which began amid such universal applause! Eternal ebb and flow of popular favour! To think that they had come so near hanging the bailiff's men! What would he not have given to recover that golden hour!

The usher's brutal monologue ceased at last; every one had arrived, and Gringoire breathed again; the actors went bravely on.

But then what should Master Coppenole, the hosier, do but rise suddenly; and Gringoire heard him utter, amid universal attention, this abominable speech:—

"Citizens and squires of Paris, I know not, by God's cross! what we are doing here. I do indeed see in yonder corner, upon those boards, people who look as if they were spoiling for a fight. I don't know whether that is what you call a 'mystery,' but it is not at all amusing: they abuse one another, and get no farther. For full fifteen minutes I have been waiting for the first blow; nothing comes; they are cowards, who deal in no other weapons than insults. You ought to fetch a few wrestlers from London or Rotterdam, and then you'd have a treat! You would see blows that could be heard all over the place; but those fellows yonder are a disgrace. They might at least give us a Morris-dance or some other mummery! This is not what I was told I should see; I was promised a Feast of Fools and the election of a Lord of Misrule. We have our Lord of Misrule in Ghent, too; and we're not behind you in that, by God's cross! But this is how we do it: we collect a crowd, as you do here; then every man in his turn puts his head through a hole and pulls a face at the rest; he who makes the ugliest is chosen pope by popular acclaim; there! It's very amusing. Would you like to choose your pope after the fashion of my country? At least it would be better than listening to those chatterboxes. If they will come and make their grimaces through the window, they can join the game. What say you, Sir Citizens? There are quite enough absurd specimens of both sexes here to give us a good Flemish laugh, and we have ugly mugs enough to hope for some fine grimaces."

Gringoire longed to answer; but amazement, anger, indignation, robbed him of speech. Moreover, the proposal of the popular hosier was greeted with such enthusiasm by those plain citizens who were flattered at being dubbed "Squires," that all opposition was useless. Nothing remained but to follow the current. Gringoire hid his face in his hands, not being lucky enough to have a cloak to cover his head, like Agamemnon of Timanthes.

Chapter V

QUASIMODO

In the twinkling of an eye, all was ready for the execution of Coppenole's idea. Citizens, students, and lawyers' clerks set briskly to work. The little chapel opposite the marble table was chosen as the stage for the grimaces. A broken pane in the pretty rose-window over the door left free a circle of stone, through which it was agreed that the contestants should thrust their heads. To reach it, all were obliged to climb upon a couple of casks, which had been discovered somewhere and set one upon the other. It was settled that all candidates, men or women (for a papess might be chosen), lest the effect of their grimaces should be weakened, should cover their faces and remain hidden in the chapel until the proper moment to appear. In less than an instant the chapel was filled with aspirants, upon whom the door was closed.

Coppenole, from his seat, directed everything, arranged everything. During the confusion the Cardinal, no less disconcerted than Gringoire, withdrew with all his train, feigning business and vespers; the same crowd which had been so stirred by his coming, showing not the least emotion at his departure. Guillaume Rym was the only one who observed his Eminence's flight. Popular attention, like the sun, pursued its course; starting from one end of the hall, after pausing for some time in the centre, it was now at the other end. The marble table, the brocaded daïs, had had their day; it was the turn of Louis XI.'s chapel. The field was now clear for every kind of folly. No one remained but the Flemings and the vulgar herd.

The wry faces began. The first to appear at the window, with eyelids inverted until they showed the red, a cavernous mouth, and a forehead wrinkled like the boots of a hussar under the Empire, produced such inextinguishable laughter, that Homer would have taken all these clowns for gods. And yet, the great hall was anything but an Olympus, and Gringoire's poor Jupiter knew this better than any one. A second, a third wry face followed, then another, and another; and still the shouts of laughter and stamps of delight increased. There was a certain peculiar intoxication in the spectacle, a certain potent ecstasy and fascination which it would be hard to explain to the reader of our own day and society. Let him imagine a series of faces presenting in turn every geometric form, from the triangle to the trapezium, from the cone to the polyhedron; every human expression, from rage to lust; every age, from the wrinkles of the new-born babe to the furrows of the old and dying; every religious phantasmagoria, from Faunus to Beelzebub; every animal profile, from the jaws of the dog to the beak of the bird, from the boar's head to the pig's snout. Let him picture to himself all the grotesque heads carved on the Pont Neuf, those petrified nightmares from the hand of Germain Pilon, taking breath and life, and coming in turn to gaze at you with fiery eyes; all the masks from a Venetian carnival passing before your glass,— in one word, a human kaleidoscope.

The revelry became more and more Flemish. Téniers could have given but an imperfect idea of it! Imagine Salvator Rosa's battle-piece turned into a bacchanal feast. There were no longer students, ambassadors, townspeople, men, or women; no longer a Clopin Trouillefou, a Gilles Lecornu, a Simone Quatrelivres, or a Robin Poussepain. All distinctions died in the common license. The great hall ceased to be anything but a vast furnace of effrontery and mirth, wherein every mouth was a cry, every face a grimace, every individual a posture; the sum total howled and yelled. The strange faces which took their turn in gnashing their teeth through the rose-window were like so many brands cast into the flames; and from this effervescent mob arose, like steam from a furnace, a sharp, shrill, piercing sound, like the buzz of a gnat's wings.

"Oh, confound it!"
"Just look at that face!"
"That's nothing!"
"Let's have another!"
"Guillemette Maugerepuis, do look at that bull's head! it only lacks horns. It is not your husband."
"Another!"
"By the Pope's head! what's the meaning of that contortion?"
"Hollo there! that's not fair. You should show only your face."
"That damned Perrette Callebotte! She is just capable of such a thing."
"Noël! Noël!"
"I'm smothering!"
"There's a fellow whose ears are too big to go through!"

But we must do justice to our friend Jehan. Amidst this uproar he was still to be seen perched upon his pillar, like a cabin-boy on a topsail. He exerted himself with incredible fury. His mouth was opened wide, and there issued from it a yell which no one heard,—not that it was drowned by the general clamour, tremendous though it was; but because it undoubtedly reached the limit of audible shrillness,—the twelve thousand vibrations of Sauveur or the eight thousand of Biot.

As for Gringoire, the first moment of depression over, he recovered his composure. He braced himself to meet adversity. "Go on!" he cried for the third time to his actors, whom he regarded as mere talking-machines; then, as he strode up and down in front of the marble table, he was seized with a desire to appear in his turn at the chapel window, were it only for the pleasure of making faces at that ungrateful mob. "But no, that would be unworthy of us; no vengeance. Let us struggle on to the end," he murmured; "the power of poetry over the people is great; I will bring them back. Let us see whether wry faces or polite learning will triumph."

Alas! he was left the only spectator of his play.

It was even worse than before. Now he saw nothing but people's backs. I am wrong. The patient fat man, whom he had already consulted at a critical moment, was still turned towards the theatre. As for Gisquette and Liénarde, they had long since deserted.

Gringoire was touched to the heart by the fidelity of his only listener. He went up to him and addressed him, shaking him slightly by the arm; for the worthy man was leaning against the railing in a light doze.

"Sir," said Gringoire, "I thank you."

"Sir," replied the fat fellow with a yawn, "for what?"

"I see what annoys you," resumed the poet; "it is all this noise which prevents you from hearing readily. But be calm! your name shall be handed down to posterity. Your name, if you please?"

"Renauld Château, Keeper of the Seals of the Châtelet, at Paris, at your service."

"Sir, you are the sole representative of the muses here," said Gringoire.

"You are too kind, sir," replied the Keeper of the Seals of the Châtelet.

"You are the only man," added Gringoire, "who has paid proper attention to the play. How do you like it?"

"Ha, ha!" replied the fat magistrate, who was but half awake, "jolly enough, in truth!"

Gringoire was forced to content himself with this eulogy; for a storm of applause, mingled with prodigious shouts, cut short their conversation. The Lord of Misrule was elected.

"Noël! Noël! Noël!" shouted the people on all sides.

That was indeed a marvellous grin which now beamed through the hole in the rose-window. After all the pentagonal, hexagonal, and heteroclitic faces which had followed one another in quick succession at the window without realizing that ideal of the grotesque constructed by imagination exalted by revelry, it required nothing less to gain the popular vote than the sublime grimace which had just dazzled the assembly. Master Coppenole himself applauded; and Clopin Trouillefou, who had competed for the prize (and Heaven knows to what intensity of ugliness his features could attain), confessed himself conquered. We will do the same. We will not try to give the reader any idea of that tetrahedron-like nose, of that horseshoe-shaped mouth; of that small left eye overhung by a bushy red eyebrow, while the right eye was completely hidden by a monstrous wart; of those uneven, broken teeth, with sad gaps here and there like the battlements of a fortress; of that callous lip, over which one of these teeth projected like an elephant's tusk; of that forked chin; and especially of the expression pervading all this,—that mixture of malice, amazement, and melancholy. Imagine, if you can, that comprehensive sight.

The vote was unanimous; the crowd rushed into the chapel. They returned leading the fortunate Lord of Misrule in triumph. But it was then only that surprise and admiration reached their highest pitch; the grimace was his natural face.

Or rather the entire man was a grimace. A large head bristling with red hair; between his shoulders an enormous hump, with a corresponding prominence in front; legs and thighs so singularly crooked that they touched only at the knees, and, seen from the front, resembled two reaping-hooks united at the handle; broad feet, huge hands; and, with all this deformity, a certain awe-inspiring air of vigour, agility, and courage; strange exception to the rule which declares power, as well as beauty, to be the result of harmony,—such was the pope whom the fools had chosen to reign over them.

He looked like a giant broken to pieces and badly cemented together.

When this species of Cyclop appeared upon the threshold of the chapel, motionless, thickset, almost as broad as he was long, "the square of his base," as a great man once expressed it, the people recognized him instantly, by his partly-coloured red and purple coat spangled with silver, and particularly by the perfection of his ugliness, and cried aloud with one voice:—

"It is Quasimodo, the bell-ringer! It is Quasimodo, the humpback of Notre-Dame! Quasimodo, the one-eyed! Quasimodo, the bandy-legged! Noël! Noël!"

The poor devil evidently had an abundance of nicknames to choose from.

"Let all pregnant women beware!" cried the students.

"Or all those who hope to be so," added Joannes.

In fact, the women hid their faces.

"Oh, the ugly monkey!" said one of them.

"As wicked as he is ugly," added another.

"He's the very devil," added a third.

"I am unlucky enough to live near Notre-Dame. I hear him prowling among the gutters by night."

"With the cats."

"He's always on our roofs."

"He casts spells upon us through the chimneys."

"The other evening he came and pulled a face at me through the window. I thought it was a man. He gave me such a fright!"

"I'm sure he attends the Witches' Sabbath. Once he left a broomstick on my leads."

"Oh, what a disagreeable humpback's face he has!"

"Oh, the villainous creature!"

"Faugh!"

The men, on the contrary, were charmed, and applauded.

Quasimodo, the object of this uproar, still stood at the chapel door, sad and serious, letting himself be admired.

A student (Robin Poussepain, I think) laughed in his very face, and somewhat too close. Quasimodo merely took him by the belt and cast him ten paces away through the crowd; all without uttering a word.

Master Coppenole, lost in wonder, approached him.

"By God's cross and the Holy Father! you are the most lovely monster that I ever saw in my life. You deserve to be pope of Rome as well as of Paris."

So saying, he laid his hand sportively upon his shoulder. Quasimodo never budged. Coppenole continued:—

"You're a rascal with whom I have a longing to feast, were it to cost me a new douzain of twelve pounds Tours. What say you?"

Quasimodo made no answer.

"By God's cross!" said the hosier, "you're not deaf, are you?"

He was indeed deaf.

Still, he began to lose his temper at Coppenole's proceedings, and turned suddenly towards him, gnashing his teeth so savagely that the Flemish giant recoiled, like a bull-dog before a cat.

Then a circle of terror and respect, whose radius was not less than fifteen geometric paces, was formed about the strange character. An old woman explained to Master Coppenole that Quasimodo was deaf.

"Deaf!" said the hosier, with his hearty Flemish laugh. "By God's cross! but he is a perfect pope!"

"Ha! I know him now," cried Jehan, who had at last descended from his capital to view Quasimodo more closely; "it's my brother the archdeacon's bell-ringer. Good-day, Quasimodo!"

"What a devil of a fellow!" said Robin Poussepain, till aching from his fall. "He appears: he's a humpback; he walks: he's bandy-legged; he looks at you: he is blind of one eye; you talk to him: he is deaf. By the way, what use does this Polyphemus make of his tongue?"

"He talks when he likes," said the old woman; "he grew deaf from ringing the bells. He is not dumb."

"That's all he lacks," remarked Jehan.

"And he has one eye too many," said Robin Poussepain.

"Not at all," judiciously observed Jehan. "A one-eyed man is far more incomplete than a blind one. He knows what he lacks."

But all the beggars, all the lackeys, all the cutpurses, together with the students, had gone in procession to fetch, from the storeroom of the basoche, the pasteboard tiara and mock robes of the Pope of Fools, or Lord of Misrule. Quasimodo submitted to be arrayed in them without a frown, and with a sort of proud docility. Then he was seated upon a barrow painted in motley colours. Twelve officers of the fraternity of fools raised it to their shoulders; and a sort of bitter, scornful joy dawned upon the morose face of the Cyclop when he saw beneath his shapeless feet the heads of so many handsome, straight, and well-made men. Then the howling, tatterdemalion train set out, as was the custom, to make the tour of the galleries within the Palace before parading the streets and public squares.

Chapter VI

ESMERALDA

We are delighted to be able to inform our readers that during the whole of this scene Gringoire and his play had stood their ground. His actors, spurred on by him, had not stopped spouting his verses, and he had not given over listening. He had resigned himself to the uproar, and was determined to go on to the bitter end, not despairing of recovering some portion of public attention. This ray of hope revived when he saw Quasimodo, Coppenole, and the deafening escort of the Lord of Misrule leave the hall with a tremendous noise. The crowd followed eagerly on their heels. "Good!" said he to himself; "now we have got rid of all the marplots." Unfortunately, all the marplots meant the whole audience. In the twinkling of an eye, the great hall was empty.

To be exact, there still remained a handful of spectators, some scattered, others grouped around the pillars, women, old men, or children, who had had enough of the tumult and the hurly-burly. Some few students still lingered, astride of the window-frames, gazing into the square.

"Well," thought Gringoire, "here are still enough to hear the end of my mystery. There are but few, but it is a picked public, an intellectual audience."

A moment later, a melody meant to produce the greatest effect at the appearance of the Holy Virgin was missing. Gringore saw that his musicians had been borne off by the procession of the Lord of Misrule. "Proceed," he said stoically.

He went up to a group of townspeople who seemed to him to be talking about his play. This is the fragment of conversation which he caught:—

"You know, Master Cheneteau, the Hôtel de Navarre, which belonged to M. de Nemours?"

"Yes, opposite the Braque Chapel."

"Well, the Treasury Department has just let it to Guillaume Alexandre, the painter of armorial bearings, for six pounds and eight pence Paris a year."

"How high rents are getting to be!"

"Well, well!" said Gringoire with a sigh; "the rest are listening."

"Comrades!" shouted one of the young scamps in the window; "Esmeralda! Esmeralda is in the square!"

This cry had a magical effect. Every one in the hall rushed to the windows, climbing up the walls to get a glimpse, and repeating, "Esmeralda! Esmeralda!"

At the same time a great noise of applause was heard outside.

"What do they mean by their 'Esmeralda'?" said Gringoire, clasping his hands in despair. "Oh, heavens! I suppose it's the turn of the windows now!"

He turned back again to the marble table, and saw that the play had stopped. It was just the moment when Jupiter should have appeared with his thunder. Now Jupiter stood motionless at the foot of the stage.

"Michel Giborne!" cried the angry poet, "what are you doing there? Is that put down in your part? Go up, I tell you!"

"Alas!" said Jupiter, "one of the students has taken away the ladder."

Gringoire looked. It was but too true. All communication was cut off between his plot and its solution.

"The rascal!" he muttered; "and why did he carry off that ladder?"

"That he might see Esmeralda," piteously responded Jupiter. "He said, 'Stay, there's a ladder which is doing no one any good!' and he took it."

This was the finishing stroke. Gringoire received it with submission.

"May the devil seize you!" said he to the actors; "and if I am paid, you shall be too."

Then he beat a retreat, with drooping head, but last to leave, like a general who has fought a brave fight.

And as he descended the winding Palace staircase, he muttered between his teeth: "A pretty pack of donkeys and clowns these Parisians are! They come to hear a miracle play, and then pay no heed to it! Their whole minds are absorbed in anybody and everybody,—in Clopin Trouillefou, the Cardinal, Coppenole, Quasimodo, the devil! but in Madame Virgin Mary not a whit. If I had known, I'd have given you your fill of Virgin Marys, you boobies! And I,—to come to see faces, and to see nothing but backs! to be a poet, and to have the success of an apothecary! True, Homer begged his way through Greek villages, and Naso died in exile among the Muscovites. But may the devil flay me if I know what they mean by their 'Esmeralda'! What kind of a word is that, anyhow? It must be Egyptian!"

BOOK II

Love

Chapter I

FROM CHARYBDIS TO SCYLLA

Night comes on early in January. The streets were already dark when Gringoire left the Palace. This nightfall pleased him. He longed to find some dark and solitary alley where he might meditate at his ease, and let the philosopher apply the first healing balm to the poet's wounds. Besides, philosophy was his only refuge; for he knew not where to find shelter. After the total failure of his first theatrical effort he durst not return to the lodging which he had occupied, opposite the Hay-market, in the Rue Grenier-sur-l'Eau, having reckoned upon what the provost was to give him for his epithalamium to pay Master Guillaume Doulx-Sire, farmer of the taxes on cloven-footed animals in Paris, the six months' rent which he owed him, namely, twelve Paris pence,—twelve times the worth of everything that he owned in the world, including his breeches, his shirt, and his hat.

After a moment's pause for reflection, temporarily sheltered under the little gateway of the prison of the treasurer of the Sainte-Chapelle, as to what refuge he should seek for the night, having all the pavements of Paris at his disposition, he remembered having noticed, the week before in the Rue de la Savaterie, at the door of a Parliamentary Councillor, a stone block for mounting a mule, and having said to himself that this stone would, on occasion, make a very excellent pillow for a beggar or a poet. He thanked Providence for sending him so good an idea; but as he prepared to cross the Palace courtyard on his way to the crooked labyrinth of the city, formed by the windings of all those antique sisters, the Rues de la Barillerie, de la Vieille-Draperie, de la Savaterie, de la Juiverie, etc., still standing at the present day with their nine-story houses, he saw the procession of the Lord of Misrule, which was also just issuing from the Palace and rushing across the courtyard, with loud shouts, an abundance of glaring torches, and his (Gringoire's) own music. This sight opened the wound to his self-esteem; he fled. In the bitterness of dramatic misfortune, all that recalled the day's festival incensed him, and made his wound bleed afresh.

He meant to cross St. Michael's Bridge; some children were careering up and down there with rockets and crackers.

"A plague on all fireworks!" said Gringoire; and he turned towards Exchange Bridge. The houses at the head of the bridge were adorned with three large banners representing the king, the dauphin, and Margaret of Flanders, and six little bannerets with portraits of the Duke of Austria, Cardinal Bourbon, M. de Beaujeu, and Madame Jeanne de France, the Bastard of Bourbon, and I know not who besides,—all lighted up by torches. The mob gazed in admiration.

"Lucky painter, Jehan Fourbault!" said Gringoire, with a heavy sigh; and he turned his back on banners and bannerets. A street opened directly before him: it looked so dark and deserted that he hoped it would afford a way of escape from every echo as well as every reflection of the festival: he plunged down it. In a few moments he struck his foot against something, stumbled, and fell. It was the big bunch of hawthorn which the members of the basoche had that morning placed at the door of a president of the Parliament, in honour of the day. Gringoire bore this new misfortune bravely; he rose and walked to the bank of the river. Leaving behind him the civil and criminal towers, and passing by the great walls of the royal gardens, along the unpaved shore where the mud was ankle-deep, he reached the western end of the city, and for some time contemplated the islet of the Passeur aux Vaches, which has since vanished beneath the bronze horse on the Pont Neuf. The islet lay before him in the darkness,— a black mass across the narrow strip of whitish water which lay between him and it. The rays of a tiny light dimly revealed a sort of beehive-shaped hut in which the cows' ferryman sought shelter for the night.

"Lucky ferryman!" thought Gringoire; "you never dream of glory, and you write no wedding songs! What are the marriages of kings and Burgundian duchesses to you? You know no Marguerites save those which grow upon your turf in April for the pasturage of your cows! and I, poet that I am, am hooted, and I shiver, and I owe twelve pence, and the soles of my shoes are so thin that you might use them for glasses in your lantern. Thanks, ferryman! Your hut rests my eyes and makes me forget Paris."

He was roused from his almost lyric ecstasy by a huge double-headed St. John's cracker, which was suddenly sent up from the blessed cabin. The ferryman was taking his part in the festivities of the day, and setting off a few fireworks.

The explosion set Gringoire's teeth on edge.

"Accursed festival!" he exclaimed, "will you pursue me forever,—oh, my God! even to the ferryman's house?"

He gazed at the Seine at his feet and a horrible temptation overcame him.

"Ah!" said he, "how cheerfully I

would drown myself if the water were not so cold!"

Then he took a desperate resolve. It was, since he could not escape from the Lord of Misrule, Jehan Fourbault's flags, the bunches of hawthorn, the rockets, and squibs, to plunge boldly into the very heart of the gaiety and go directly to the Grève.

"At least," thought he, "I may find some brands from the bonfire to warm myself and I may sup on some crumbs from the three great sugar escutcheons which were to be served on the public sideboard."

Chapter II

THE GRÈVE

But very slight traces now remain of the Grève as it existed at the time of which we write; all that is left is the picturesque little tower at the northern corner of the square; and that, already buried beneath the vulgar whitewash which incrusts the sharp edges of its carvings, will soon disappear perhaps, drowned in that flood of new houses which is so rapidly swallowing up all the old fronts in Paris.

People who, like ourselves, never pass through the Grève without giving a glance of sympathy and pity to the poor little tower, choked between two hovels of the time of Louis XV., may readily reconstruct in fancy the entire mass of buildings to which it belonged, and as it were restore the old Gothic square of the fifteenth century.

It was, as it still is, an irregular square, bounded on one side by the quay, and on the other three by a number of tall, narrow, gloomy houses. By day one might admire the variety of its edifices, all carved in stone or wood, and presenting perfect specimens of the various kinds of mediæval domestic architecture, going back from the fifteenth to the eleventh century, from the casement window which was beginning to supersede the pointed arch, to the semicircular arch of the Romance period, which gave way to the pointed arch, and which still occupied below it the first story of that old house called Roland's Tower, on the corner of the square nearest the Seine, close to the Rue de la Tannerie. At night, nothing could be seen of this mass of buildings but the dark indented line of the roofs stretching their chain of acute angles round the square. For it is one of the radical differences between the modern and ancient towns, that nowadays the fronts of the houses face upon the squares and streets, and in old times it was the gable ends. In two centuries the houses have turned round.

In the middle of the eastern side of the square stood a heavy and hybrid construction composed of three houses together. It was known by three names, which explain its history, its purpose, and its architecture. The Dauphin's House, because Charles V. occupied it while dauphin; the Trades House, because it was used as Town Hall; the Pillar House (*domus ad piloria*), on account of a series of thick columns which supported its three stories. There the city found everything required for a well-to-do town like Paris—a chapel in which to pray to God; a court of special pleas, where audience was given, and if necessary "the king's men put down;" and in the garrets an "arsenal" full of artillery. For the citizens of Paris, knowing that it is not always enough to pray and plead for the liberties of the town, always had a good rusty arquebus or two in reserve in an attic of the Town Hall.

Even then the Grève had the same forbidding aspect which the detestable ideas clinging about it awaken, and the gloomy Town Hall built by Dominique Bocador, which has taken the place of the Pillar House, still gives it. It must be confessed that a permament gibbet and pillory,—"a justice and a ladder," as they were then called,—standing side by side in the middle of the flagstones, largely contributed to make men turn away from that fatal square where so many beings full of life and health have died in agony; where the Saint Vallier's fever was destined to spring to life some fifty years later,—that disease which was nothing but dread of the scaffold, the most monstrous of all maladies, because it came not from God, but from man.

It is a consoling thought (let us say in passing) that the death penalty, which three hundred years ago still cumbered the Grève, the Markets, the Place Dauphine, the Cross du Trahoir, the Pigmarket, the hideous Montfaucon, the Sergeants' Barrier, Cats' Square, St. Denis Gate, Champeaux, Baudet Gate, and St. Jacques Gate, with its iron wheels, its stone gibbets and all its machinery of torture, permanently built into the pavement; not to mention the countless pillories belonging to provosts, bishops, chapters, abbots, and priors administering justice; to say nothing of the legal drownings in the river Seine,— it is a consolation that in the present day, having successively lost all the pieces of her armour, her refinements of torture, her purely capricious and wilful penal laws, her torture for the administration of which she made afresh every five years a leather bed at the Grand-Châtelet, that ancient sovereign of feudal society, almost outlawed and exiled from our cities, hunted from code to code, driven from place to place, now possesses in one vast Paris but one dishonoured corner of the Grève, but one wretched guillotine, furtive, timid, and ashamed, seeming ever in dread of being taken in the very act, so swiftly does it vanish after it has dealt its deadly stroke!

Chapter III

besos para golpes

When Pierre Gringoire reached the Grève, he was benumbed. He had come by way of the Millers' Bridge to avoid the mob on Exchange Bridge and Jehan Fourbault's flags; but the wheels of all the bishop's mills had bespattered him as he crossed, and his coat was soaked; moreover, it seemed to him that the failure of his play had made him more sensitive to cold than ever. He therefore made haste to draw near the bonfire which still blazed gloriously in the middle of the square; but a considerable crowd formed a circle round about it.

"Damned Parisians!" said he to himself (for Gringoire, like all true dramatic poets, was given to monologues), "there they stand blocking my way to the fire! and yet I greatly need a good warm chimney-corner; my shoes leak, and all those cursed mills have dripped upon me! Deuce take the Bishop of Paris and his mills! I would really like to know what a bishop wants with a mill! does he expect to turn miller? If he is merely waiting for my curse, I give it to him cheerfully, and to his cathedral and his mills into the bargain! Now just let's see if any of those boors will disturb themselves for me! What on earth are they doing there? Warming themselves indeed; a fine amusement! Watching to see a hundred fagots burn; a fine sight, truly!"

Looking more closely, he saw that the circle was far larger than was necessary for the crowd to warm themselves at the royal bonfire, and that the large number of spectators was not attracted solely by the beauty of the hundred blazing fagots.

In the vast space left free between the crowd and the fire a young girl was dancing.

Whether this young girl was a human being, or a fairy, or an angel, was more than Gringoire, cynic philosopher and sarcastic poet though he was, could for a moment decide, so greatly was he fascinated by the dazzling vision.

She was not tall, but seemed to be, so proudly erect did she hold her slender figure. She was brown, but it was evident by daylight her skin must have that lovely golden gleam peculiar to Spanish and Roman beauties. Her tiny foot was Andalusian too, for it fitted both snugly and easily into its dainty shoe. She danced, she turned, she twirled, upon an antique Persian carpet thrown carelessly beneath her feet; and every time her radiant figure passed, as she turned, her great black eyes sent forth lightning flashes.

Upon her every eye was riveted, every mouth gaped wide; and in very truth, as she danced to the hum of the tambourine which her round and graceful arms held high above her head, slender, quick and active as any wasp, with smoothly fitting golden bodice, her many-coloured full skirts, her bare shoulders, her shapely legs, from which her skirts now and then swung away, her black hair, her eyes of flame, she seemed more than mortal creature.

"Indeed," thought Gringoire, "she is a salamander, a nymph, a goddess, a bacchante from Mount Mænalus!"

At this moment one of the salamander's tresses was loosened, and a bit of brass which had been fastened to it fell to the ground.

"Alas, no!" said he, "she's a gipsy."

All illusion had vanished.

She began to dance once more. She picked up two swords, and balancing them by their points on her forehead, she twirled them in one direction while she herself revolved in another; she was indeed but a gipsy girl. But great as was Gringoire's disenchantment, the picture was far from being destitute of all charm and beauty; the bonfire lit it up with a crude red light, which flickered brightly upon the circle of surrounding figures and the young girl's brown face, casting wan reflections, blended with alternating shadows, into the farthest corners of the square,—on one side upon the black and weather-beaten front of the Pillar House, and on the other upon the cross-beam of the stone gibbet.

Among the myriad faces dyed scarlet by the flames, there was one which seemed absorbed even beyond all the rest in gazing at the dancer. It was the face of a man, austere, calm, and sombre. This man, whose dress was hidden by the crowd about him, seemed not more than thirty-five years old, and yet he was bald; he had but a few grey and scanty locks of hair about his temples; his broad, high forehead was already beginning to be furrowed with wrinkles, but in his deep-set eyes sparkled an extraordinary spirit of youth, an ardent love of life and depth of passion. He kept them fixed on the gipsy; and while the giddy young damsel danced and fluttered to the delight of all, his thoughts seemed to become more and more melancholy. From time to time a smile and a sigh met upon his lips, but the smile was far sadder than the sigh.

The young girl stopped at last, breathless, and the people applauded eagerly.

"Djali!" said the gipsy.

Then Gringoire saw a pretty little white goat, active, alert, and glossy, with gilded horns, gilded hoofs, and a gilded collar, which he had not before observed, and which had hitherto remained quietly crouching on a corner of the carpet, watching its mistress as she danced.

"Djali," said the dancer. "it's your turn now."

And sitting down, she gracefully offered the goat her tambourine.

"Djali," she added, "what month in the year is this?"

The goat raised its fore-foot and struck once upon the tambourine. It was indeed the first month of the year. The crowd applauded.

"Djali," resumed the young girl, turning her tambourine another way, "what day of the month is it?"

Djali lifted his little golden hoof and struck it six times upon the tambourine.

"Djali," continued the daughter of Egypt, with still another twist of the tambourine, "what time of day is it?"

Djali gave seven blows, and at the same instant the clock on the Pillar House struck seven.

The people were lost in wonder.

"There is sorcery in this," said a forbidding voice from the throng. It was the voice of the bald man, who had never taken his eyes from the gipsy.

She trembled, and turned towards him; but fresh plaudits broke out, and drowned the surly exclamation.

They even effaced it so completely from her mind that she went on questioning her goat.

"Djali, how does Master Guichard Grand-Remy, the captain of the city pistoleers, walk in the procession at Candlemas?"

Djali rose on his hind-legs and began to bleat, walking as he did so with an air of polite gravity that the whole ring of spectators burst into a laugh at this parody of the selfish devotion of the captain of pistoleers.

"Djali," continued the young girl, encouraged by her increasing success, "show us how Master Jacques Charmolue, king's attorney in the Ecclesiastical Court, preaches."

The goat sat up and began to bleat, waving his fore-feet in so strange a fashion that, except for the bad French and the bad Latin, Jacques Charmolue himself stood before you,—gesture, accent, and attitude.

And the crowd applauded louder than before.

"Sacrilege! Profanation!" exclaimed the voice of the bald-headed man.

The gipsy turned again.

"Ah!" said she, "it is that ugly man!" Then projecting her lower lip beyond the upper one, she made a little face which seemed habitual with her, pirouetted on her heel, and began to collect the gifts of the multitude in her tambourine.

Big pieces of silver, little pieces of silver, pennies, and farthings, rained into it. Suddenly she passed Gringoire. He put his hand in his pocket so heedlessly that she stopped. "The devil!" said the poet, as he found reality at the bottom of his pocket,—that is to say, an empty void. But there stood the pretty girl, looking at him with her big eyes, holding out her tambourine, and waiting. Gringoire was in agony.

If he had had the wealth of Peru in his pocket, he would certainly have given it to the dancing-girl; but Gringoire did not possess the wealth of Peru, and moreover America had not then been discovered.

Luckily an unexpected event came to his rescue.

"Will you be gone, you gipsy grasshopper?" cried a sharp voice from the darkest corner of the square.

The young girl turned in terror. This was not the voice of the bald-headed man; it was a woman's voice,—the voice of a malicious and bigoted person.

However, the cry which alarmed the gipsy delighted a band of roving children.

"It's the recluse of the Tour-Roland," they shouted with riotous laughter.

"It's the nun scolding! Hasn't she had her supper? Let's carry her some bits from the city sideboard!"

All rushed towards the Pillar House.

Gringoire seized the occasion of the dancer's distress to disappear. The children's shouts reminded him that he too had not supped. He therefore hastened to the sideboard. But the little scamps had better legs than he; when he arrived, they had swept the table clear. There was not even a paltry cake at five cents the pound remaining. Nothing was left on the wall but the delicate *fleurs-de-lis*, twined with rose branches, painted in 1434 by Mathieu Biterne. That was a meagre repast.

It's a tiresome matter to go to bed without supper; it is still less agreeable to have no supper and not to know where to find a bed. This was Gringoire's condition. No bread, no shelter; he was goaded on every hand by necessity, and he found necessity very crabbed and cross. He had long since discovered the truth that Jupiter created mankind in a fit of misanthropy, and that throughout a wise man's life fate keeps his philosophy in a state of siege. As for himself, the blockade had never been so complete. He heard his stomach sounding a parley, and he thought it very improper for an evil destiny to overcome his philosophy by famine.

He was becoming more and more absorbed in these melancholy reflections, when a peculiar although melodious song suddenly roused him from them. The young gipsy girl was singing.

Her voice was like her dancing, like her beauty. It was charming, and not to be defined,—possessing a pure and sonorous quality, something ethereal and airy. There was a constant succession of bursts of melody, of unexpected cadences, then of simple phrases mingled with shrill sibilant notes: now runs and trills which would have baffled a nightingale, but which never ceased to be harmonious; then softly undulating octaves rising and falling like the bosom of the youthful singer.

Her fine features expressed every caprice of her song with singular flexibility, from the most lawless inspiration to the chastest dignity. At one instant she seemed a mad woman, at the next a queen.

The words which she sang were in a language unknown to Gringoire, and apparently one with which she was not herself familiar, so little connection had the expression which she lent her song with the meaning of the words. Thus these four lines in her mouth became wildly gay:—

"Un cofre de gran riqueza
Hallaron dentro un pilar,
Dentro del, nuevas banderas
Con figuras de espantar."

And a moment later, the tone in which she uttered the words,—

"Alarabes de cavallo
Sin poderse menear,
Con espadas, y los cuellos,
Ballestas de buen echar."

brought the tears into Gringoire's eyes. And yet her song was full of joy, and she seemed to sing like a bird, from sheer happiness and freedom from care.

The gipsy's song had troubled Gringoire's reverie, but as the swan troubles the water. He listened in a sort of ecstasy which rendered him oblivious of all else. It was the first instant, for some hours, in which he had felt no pain.

The moment was brief.

The same woman's voice which had cut short the girl's dance now interrupted her song.

"Will you hold your tongue, you infernal cricket?" she cried, still from the dark corner of the square.

The poor "cricket" stopped short. Gringoire clapped his hands to his ears.

"Oh," he exclaimed, "cursed be that rusty saw, which breaks the lyre!"

And the other listeners grumbled with him.

"Deuce take the nun!" said more than one. And the invisible old marplot might have had reason to repent of her aggressions had not their thoughts been diverted at that very moment by the procession of the Lord of Misrule, which, having traversed many a street and square, now appeared in the Grève with all its torches and all its noise.

This procession, which our readers saw as it started from the Palace, had taken shape as it marched, enlisting all the available vagabonds and scamps and idle thieves in Paris; so that it presented quite a respectable appearance when it reached the Grève.

First came the barn-stormers, the chief cackling cove at the head, on horseback, with his aids on foot, holding his stirrup and bridle. Behind walked the rest of the barn-stormers, male and female, with their little ones clamouring on their backs; all, men, women, and children, in rags and tatters. Then came the thieves' brotherhood: that is, all the robbers in France, ranged according to their degree, the least expert coming first. Thus they filed along four by four, armed with the various insignia of their degrees. In this singular faculty, most of them maimed, some halt, some with but one arm, were shoplifters, mock pilgrims, tramps who pretended to have been bitten by wolves, dummy chuckers, thimble-riggers, sham Abrams, Jeremy Diddlers, sham cripples, mumpers, pall-yards, show-fall pitchers, rogues pretending to have been burned out, cadgers, old soldiers, high-flyers, swell mobsmen, gonnofs, flash coves,—a list long enough to weary Homer himself. In the centre of the conclave of gonnofs and flash coves might dimly be distinguished the head of the thieves' brotherhood, the "Grand Coëre," or king of rogues, squatting in a small cart, drawn by two big dogs. After the fraternity of thieves came the Empire of Galilee. Guillaume Rousseau, Emperor of the Galilees, marched majestic in his purple robes stained with wine, preceded by mountebanks fighting and dancing Pyrrhic dances, surrounded by his mace-bearers, tools, and the clerks of the Court of Exchequer. Last came the basoche (the corporation of lawyers' clerks), with their sheaves of maize crowned with flowers, their black gowns, their music worthy of a Witches' Sabbath, and their huge yellow wax candles. In the midst of this throng the high officials of the fraternity of fools bore upon their shoulders a barrow more heavily laden with tapers than the shrine of St. Geneviève in time of plague; and upon this barrow rode resplendent, with crosier, cope, and mitre, the new Lord of Misrule, the bell-ringer of Notre-Dame, Quasimodo the Humpback.

Each division of this grotesque procession had its own peculiar music. The barn-stormers drew discordant notes from their balafos and their African tabours. The thieves, a far from musical race, were still using the viol, the cowherd's horn, and the quaint rubeb of the twelfth century. Nor was the Empire of Galilee much more advanced; their music was almost wholly confined to some wretched rebec dating back to the infancy of the art, still imprisoned within the *re-la-mi*. But it was upon the Lord of Misrule that all the musical riches of the period were lavished in one magnificent cacophony. There were treble rebecs, counter-tenor rebecs, tenor rebecs, to say nothing of flutes and brass instruments. Alas! our readers may remember that this was Gringoire's orchestra.

It is difficult to convey any idea of the degree of proud and sanctimonious rapture which Quasimodo's hideous and painful face had assumed during the journey from the Palace to the Grève. This was the first thrill of vanity which he had ever felt. Hitherto he had known nothing but humiliation, disdain of his estate, and disgust for his person. Therefore, deaf as he was, he enjoyed, like any genuine pope, the plaudits of that mob which he had hated because he felt that it hated him. What mattered it to him that his subjects were a collection of fools, cripples, thieves, and beggars! They were still subjects and he a sovereign! And he took seriously all the mock applause, all the satirical respect with which, it must be confessed, there was a slight mixture of very real fear in the hearts of the throng. For the humped back was strong; for the bandy legs were nimble;

for the deaf ears were malicious,—three qualities which tempered the ridicule.

Moreover, we are far from fancying that the new Lord of Misrule realized clearly either his own feelings or those which he inspired. The spirit lodged in that imperfect body was necessarily something dull and incomplete. Therefore what he felt at this instant was absolutely vague, indistinct, and confused to him. Joy only pierced the cloud; pride prevailed. The sombre and unhappy face was radiant.

It was not therefore without surprise and fright that, at the moment when Quasimodo in his semi-intoxication passed triumphantly before the Pillar House, the spectators saw a man dart from the crowd and snatch from his hands, with a gesture of rage, his gilded crosier, the badge of his mock papacy.

This man, this rash fellow, was no other than the bald-headed character who, the instant before, mingling with the group about the gipsy girl, had chilled her blood with his words of menace and hatred. He was clad now in ecclesiastical garb. Just as he stepped forward from the crowd, Gringoire, who had not noticed him until then, recognized him. "Why!" said he with an exclamation of amazement, "it is my master in Hermes, Don Claude Frollo, the archdeacon! What the devil does he want with that ugly one-eyed man? He'll be swallowed up alive!"

Indeed, a cry of terror rose. The terrible Quasimodo flung himself headlong from his barrow, and the women turned away their eyes that they might not see the archdeacon rent limb from limb.

He made but one bound towards the priest, gazed at him, and fell on his knees.

The priest tore from him his tiara, broke his crosier and rent his tinsel cope.

Quasimodo still knelt, with bowed head and clasped hands.

Then followed between them a strange dialogue in signs and gestures, for neither spoke,—the priest, erect, angry, threatening, imperious; Quasimodo, prostrate, humble, suppliant. And yet it is very certain that Quasimodo could have crushed the priest with his thumb.

At last the archdeacon, rudely shaking Quasimodo's powerful shoulder, signed to him to rise and follow.

Quasimodo rose.

Then the fraternity of fools, their first stupor over, strove to defend their pope, so abruptly dethroned. The thieves, the Galilees, and all the lawyers' clerks yelped about the priest.

Quasimodo placed himself before the priest, put the muscles of his fists into play, and glared at his assailants, gnashing his teeth like an enraged bear.

The priest resumed his wonted sombre gravity, beckoned to Quasimodo, and withdrew silently.

Quasimodo walked before him, scattering the crowd as he passed.

When they had made their way through the people and the square, a swarm of curious idlers attempted to follow them. Quasimodo then took up the position of rearguard, and followed the archdeacon backwards, short, thickset, crabbed, monstrous, bristling, gathering himself together, licking his tusks, growling like a wild beast, and driving the crowd before him in waves, with a gesture or a look.

They vanished down a dark, narrow street, where none dare venture after them; so effectually did the mere image of Quasimodo grinding his teeth bar the way.

"Strange enough!" said Gringoire; "but where the deuce am I to find supper?"

Chapter IV

THE INCONVENIENCES OF FOLLOWING A PRETTY WOMAN IN THE STREET AT NIGHT

Gringoire determined to follow the gipsy girl at any risk. He had seen her go down the Rue de la Coutellerie with her goat; he therefore went down the Rue de la Coutellerie.

"Why not?" said he to himself.

Gringoire, being a practical philosopher of the streets of Paris, had observed that nothing is more favourable to reverie than the pursuit of a pretty woman when you don't know where she is going. In this voluntary surrender of your own free will, this caprice yielding to another caprice, all unconscious of submission, there is a mixture of odd independence and blind obedience, a certain happy medium between slavery and liberty, which pleased Gringoire, a mind essentially mixed, undetermined, and complex, carrying everything to extremes, forever wavering betwixt all human propensities, and neutralizing them the one by the other. He frequently compared himself to Mahomet's tomb, attracted in opposite directions by two loadstones, and perpetually trembling between top and bottom, between the ceiling and the pavement, between descent and ascent, between the zenith and the nadir.

If Gringoire were living now, what a golden mean he would observe between the classic and romantic schools! But he was not sufficiently primitive to live three hundred years, and 't is a pity. His absence leaves a void but too deeply felt to-day.

However, nothing puts a man in a better mood for following people in the street (especially when they happen to be women), a thing Gringoire was always ready to do, than not knowing where he is to sleep.

He accordingly walked thoughtfully along behind the young girl, who quickened her pace and urged on her pretty goat, as she saw the townspeople were all going home, and the taverns—the only shops open upon this general holiday—were closing.

"After all," thought he, "she must have a lodging somewhere; gipsies are generous. Who knows—"

And there were some very pleasant ideas interwoven with the points of suspension that followed this mental reticence.

Still, from time to time, as he passed the last belated groups of citizens shutting their doors, he caught fragments of their talk, which broke the chain of his bright hypotheses.

Now, it was two old men chatting together.

"Master Thibaut Fernicle, do you know it is cold?"

(Gringoire had known this since the winter first set in.)

"Yes, indeed, Master Boniface Disome! Are we going to have another winter like the one we had three years ago, in '80, when wood cost eight pence the measure?"

"Bah! that's nothing, Master Thibaut, to the winter of 1407, when it froze from St. Martin's Day to Candlemas, and with such fury that the parliamentary registrar's pen froze, in the Great Chamber, between every three words, which was a vast impediment to the registration of justice!"

Farther on, two neighbour women gossiped at their windows; the candles in their hands flickered faintly through the fog.

"Did your husband tell you of the accident, Mademoiselle la Boudraque?"

"No. What was it, Mademoiselle Turquant?"

"The horse of M. Gilles Godin, the notary from the Châtelet, took fright at the Flemish and their procession, and knocked down Master Philippot Avrillot, lay brother of the Celestines."

"Is that really so?"

"Indeed it is."

"And such a plebeian animal! It's a little too much. If it had only been a cavalry horse, it would not be so bad!"

And the windows were closed. But Gringoire had already lost the thread of his ideas.

Luckily, he soon recovered and readily resumed it, thanks to the gipsy girl, thanks to Djali, who still went before him,—two slender, delicate, charming creatures, whose tiny feet, pretty forms, and graceful manners he admired, almost confounding them in his contemplation; thinking them both young girls from their intelligence and close friendship; considering them both goats from the lightness, agility, and grace of their step.

But the streets grew darker and more deserted every instant. The curfew had long since sounded and it was only at rare intervals that a passenger was seen upon the pavement or a light in any window. Gringoire had involved himself, by following in the footsteps of the gipsy, in that inextricable labyrinth of lanes, cross-streets, and blind alleys, which encircles the ancient sepulchre of the Holy Innocents, and which is much like a skein of thread tangled by a playful kitten.

"Here are streets with but little logic!" said Gringoire, lost in the myriad windings which led back incessantly to their original starting-point, but amid which the damsel pursued a path with which she seemed very familiar, never hesitating, and walking more and more swiftly. As for him, he would not have had the least idea where he was, if he had not caught a glimpse, at the corner of a street, of the octagonal mass of the pillory of the Markets, whose pierced top stood out in sharp, dark outlines against a window still lighted in the Rue Verdelet.

A few moments before, he had attracted the young girl's attention; she had several times turned her head anxiously towards him; once she had even stopped short, and taken advantage of a ray of light which escaped from a half-open bake-shop, to study him earnestly from head to foot; then, having cast that glance, Gringoire saw her make the little grimace which he had already noted, and then she passed on.

It gave Gringoire food for thought. There was certainly a leaven of scorn and mockery in that dainty grimace. He therefore began to hang his head, to count the paving-stones, and to follow the young girl at a somewhat greater distance, when at the turn of a street which hid her from his sight, he heard her utter a piercing scream.

He hastened on.

The street was full of dark shadows. Still, a bit of tow soaked in oil, which burned in an iron cage at the foot of the image of the Holy Virgin at the street corner enabled Gringoire to see the gipsy girl struggling in the arms of two men who were trying to stifle her cries. The poor little goat, in great alarm, lowered its horns and bleated piteously.

"This way, gentlemen of the watch!" shouted Gringoire; and he rushed boldly forward. One of the men who held the girl turned towards him. It was the formidable figure of Quasimodo.

Gringoire did not take flight, but neither did he advance another step.

Quasimodo approached him, flung him four paces away upon the pavement with a single back stroke, and plunged rapidly into the darkness, bearing the girl, thrown over one arm like a silken scarf. His companion followed him, and the poor goat ran behind, with its plaintiff bleat.

"Murder! murder!' shrieked the unfortunate gipsy.

"Halt, wretches, and let that wench go!" abruptly exclaimed, in a voice of thunder, a horseman who appeared suddenly from the next cross-street.

It was a captain of the king's archers, armed from head to foot, and broadsword in hand.

He tore the gipsy girl from the arms of the astonished Quasimodo, laid her across his saddle, and just as the redoubtable humpback, recovering from his surprise, rushed upon him to get back his prey, some fifteen or sixteen archers, who were close behind their captain, appeared, two-edged swords in hand. They were a squadron of the royal troops going on duty as extra watchmen, by order of Master Robert d'Estouteville, provost's v arden of Paris.

Quasimodo was surrounded, seized, garotted. He roared, he foamed at the mouth, he bit; and had it been daylight, no doubt his face alone, made yet more hideous by rage, would have routed the whole squadron. But by night he was stripped of his most tremendous weapon,—his ugliness.

His companion had disappeared during the struggle.

The gipsy girl sat gracefully erect upon the officer's saddle, placing both hands upon the young man's shoulders, and gazing fixedly at him for some seconds, as if charmed by his beauty and the timely help which he had just rendered her.

Then breaking the silence, she said, her sweet voice sounding even sweeter than usual:

"What is your name, Mr. Officer?"

"Captain Phœbus de Châteaupers, at your service, my pretty maid!" replied the officer, drawing himself up.

"Thank you," said she.

And while Captain Phœbus twirled his moustache, cut in Burgundian fashion, she slipped from the horse like an arrow falling to the earth, and fled.

A flash of lightning could not have vanished more swiftly.

"By the Pope's head!" said the captain, ordering Quasimodo's bonds to be tightened, "I had rather have kept the wench."

"What would you have, Captain?" said one of his men; "the bird has flown, the bat remains."

Chapter V

THE REST OF THE INCONVENIENCES

Gringoire, still dizzy from his fall, lay stretched on the pavement before the figure of the Blessed Virgin at the corner of the street. Little by little he regained his senses; at first he was for some moments floating in a sort of half-drowsy reverie which was far from unpleasant, in which the airy figures of the gipsy and her goat were blended with the weight of Quasimodo's fist. This state of things did not last long. A somewhat sharp sensation of cold on that part of his body in contact with the pavement roused him completely, and brought his mind back to realities once more.

"Why do I feel so cold?" said he, abruptly. He then discovered that he was lying in the middle of the gutter.

"Deuce take the humpbacked Cyclop!" he muttered; and he tried to rise. But he was too dizzy and too much bruised; he was forced to remain where he was. However, his hand was free; he stopped his nose and resigned himself to his fate.

"The mud of Paris," thought he (for he felt very sure that the gutter must be his lodging for the night).

"And what should we do in a lodging if we do not think?"

"the mud of Paris is particularly foul; it must contain a vast amount of volatile and nitrous salts. Moreover, such is the opinion of Master Nicolas Flamel and of the Hermetics—"

The word "Hermetics" suddenly reminded him of the archdeacon, Claude Frollo. He recalled the violent scene which he had just witnessed,—how the gipsy struggled with two men, how Quasimodo had a companion; and the morose and haughty face of the archdeacon passed confusedly through his mind. "That would be strange!" he thought. And he began to erect, upon these data and this basis, the fantastic edifice of hypothesis, that card-house of philosophers; then suddenly returning once more to reality, "But there! I am freezing!" he exclaimed.

The situation was in fact becoming more and more unbearable. Every drop of water in the gutter took a particle of heat from Gringoire's loins, and the temperature of his body and the temperature of the gutter began to balance each other in a very disagreeable fashion.

An annoyance of quite another kind all at once beset him.

A band of children, those little barefoot savages who have haunted the streets of Paris in all ages under the generic name of "gamins," and who, when we too were children, threw stones at us every day as we hastened home from school because our trousers were destitute of holes,—a swarm of these young scamps ran towards the crossroads where Gringoire lay, with shouts and laughter which seemed to show but little regard for their neighbour's sleep. They dragged after them a shapeless sack, and the mere clatter of their wooden shoes would have been enough to rouse the dead. Gringoire, who was not quite lifeless yet, rose to a sitting position.

"Hollo, Hennequin Dandèche! Hollo there, Jehan-Pincebourde!" they bawled at the top of their voices; "old Eustache Moubon, the junk-man at the corner, has just died; we've got his mattress; we're going to build a bonfire. This is the Flemings' day!"

And lo, they flung the mattress directly upon Gringoire, near whom they stood without seeing him. At the same time one of them snatched up a wisp of straw which he lighted at the good Virgins lamp.

"Christ's body!" groaned Gringoire, "am I going to be too hot next?"

It was a critical moment. He would soon be caught betwixt fire and water. He made a supernatural effort,—such an effort as a coiner of false money might make when about to be boiled alive and struggling to escape. He rose to his feet, hurled the mattress back upon the little rascals, and fled.

"Holy Virgin!" screamed the boys; "the junk-dealer has returned!"

And they too took to their heels.

The mattress was left mistress of the battlefield. Belleforêt, Father le Juge, and Corrozet affirm that it was picked up next day with great pomp by the clergy of the quarter, and placed in the treasury of the Church of the Holy Opportunity, where the sacristan earned a handsome income until 1789 by his tales of the wonderful miracle performed by the statue of the Virgin at the corner of the Rue Mauconseil, which had by its mere presence, on the memorable night of Jan. 6, 1482, exorcised the spirit of the defunct Eustache Moubon, who, to outwit the devil, had, in dying, maliciously hidden his soul in his mattress.

Chapter VI

THE BROKEN JUG

AFTER running for some time as fast as his legs would carry him, without knowing whither, plunging headlong around many a street corner, striding over many a gutter, traversing many a lane and blind alley, seeking to find escape and passage through all the windings of the old streets about the markets, exploring in his panic fear what the elegant Latin of the charters calls *tota via, cheminum et viaria,* our poet came to a sudden stop, partly from lack of breath, and partly because he was collared as it were by a dilemma which had just dawned upon his mind. "It strikes me, Pierre Gringoire," said he to himself, laying his finger to his forehead, "that you are running as if you had lost your wits. Those little scamps were quite as much afraid of you as you were of them. It strikes me, I tell you, that you heard the clatter of their wooden shoes as they fled to the south, while you took refuge to the north. Now, one of two things: either they ran away, and then the mattress, which they must have forgotten in their fright, is just the hospitable bed which you have been running after since morning, and which Our Lady miraculously sends you to reward you for writing a morality in her honour, accompanied by triumphal processions and mummeries; or else the boys did not run away, and in that case they have set fire to the mattress; and there you have just exactly the good fire that you need to cheer, warm, and dry you. In either case, whether as a good fire or a good bed, the mattress is a gift from Heaven. The Blessed Virgin Mary, at the corner of the Rue Mauconseil, may have killed Eustache Moubon for this very purpose; and it is sheer madness in you to betake yourself to such frantic flight, like a Picard running before a Frenchman, leaving behind what you are seeking before you; and you are a fool!"

Then he retraced his steps, and fumbling and ferreting his way, snuffing the breeze, and his ear on the alert, he strove to find the blessed mattress once more, but in vain. He saw nothing but intersecting houses, blind alleys, and crossings, in the midst of which he doubted and hesitated continually, more hindered and more closely entangled in this confusion of dark lanes than he would have been in the very labyrinth of the Hôtel des Tournelles. At last he lost patience, and exclaimed solemnly: "Curse all these crossings! The devil himself must have made them in the likeness of his pitchfork."

This outburst comforted him somewhat, and a sort of reddish reflection which he observed at this instant at the end of a long, narrow lane, quite restored his wonted spirits. "Heaven be praised!" said he; "yonder it is! There's my mattress burning briskly." And comparing himself to the boatman foundering by night, he added piously: "*Salve, salve, maris stella!*"

Did he address this fragment of a litany to the Holy Virgin, or to the mattress? That we are wholly unable to say.

He had taken but a few steps down the long lane, which was steep, unpaved, and more and more muddy and sloping, when he remarked a very strange fact. It was not empty: here and there, along its length, crawled certain vague and shapeless masses, all proceeding towards the light which flickered at the end of the street, like those clumsy insects which creep at night from one blade of grass to another towards a shepherd's fire.

Nothing makes a man bolder than the sense of an empty pocket. Gringoire continued to advance, and had soon overtook that larva which dragged itself most lazily along behind the others. As he approached, he saw that it was nothing but a miserable cripple without any legs, strapped into a bowl, and hopping along as best he might on his hands, like a wounded spider which has but two legs left. Just as he passed this kind of human insect, it uttered a piteous appeal to him; "*La buona mancia, signor! la buona mancia!*"

"Devil fly away with you," said Gringoire, "and with me too, if I know what you're talking about!"

And he passed on.

He came up with another of these perambulating masses, and examined it. It was another cripple, both lame and one-armed, and so lame and so armless that the complicated system of crutches and wooden limbs which supported him made him look like a mason's scaffolding walking off by itself. Gringoire, who loved stately and classic similes, compared the fellow, in fancy, to Vulcan's living tripod.

The living tripod greeted him as he

passed, by holding his hat at the level of Gringoire's chin, as if it had been a barber's basin, and shouting in his ears: *"Señor caballero, para comprar un pedaso de pan!"*

"It seems," said Gringoire, "that he talks too; but it's an ugly language, and he is better off than I am if he understands it."

Then, clapping his hand to his head with a sudden change of idea: "By the way, what the devil did they mean this morning by their 'Esmeralda'?"

He tried to quicken his pace; but for the third time something blocked the way. This something, or rather this some one, was a blind man, a little blind man, with a bearded Jewish face, who, feeling about him with a stick, and towed by a big dog, snuffled out to him with a Hungarian accent: *"Facitote caritatem!"*

"That's right!" said Pierre Gringoire; "here's one at last who speaks a Christian tongue. I must have a very charitable air to make all these creatures come to me for alms when my purse is so lean. My friend (and he turned to the blind man), I sold my last shirt last week; that is to say, since you understand the language of Cicero, *'Vendidi hebdomade nuper transita meam ultimam chemisam!'* "

So saying, he turned his back on the blind man and went his way. But the blind man began to mend his steps at the same time; and lo and behold! the cripple and the man bound into the bowl hurried along after them with a great clatter of bowl and crutches over the pavement.

Then all three, tumbling over each other in their haste at the heels of poor Gringoire, began to sing their several songs:

"Caritatem!" sang the blind man.

"La buona mancia!" sang the man in the bowl.

And the lame man took up the phrase with, *"Un pedaso de pan!"*

Gringoire stopped his ears, exclaiming, "Oh, tower of Babel!"

He began to run. The blind man ran. The lame man ran. The man in the bowl ran.

And then, the farther he went down the street, the more thickly did cripples, blind men, and legless men swarm around him, with armless men, one-eyed men, and lepers with their sores, some coming out of houses, some from adjacent streets, some from cellar-holes, howling, yelling, bellowing, all hobbling and limping, rushing towards the light, and wallowing in the mire like slugs after a shower.

Gringoire, still followed by his three persecutors and not knowing what would happen next, walked timidly through the rest, going around the lame, striding over the cripples, his feet entangled in this ant-hill of deformity and disease, like that English captain caught fast by an army of land-crabs.

He thought of retracing his steps; but it was too late. The entire legion had closed up behind him, and his three beggars pressed him close. He therefore went on, driven alike by this irresistible stream, by fear, and by a dizzy feeling which made all this seem a horrible dream.

At last he reached the end of the street. It opened into a vast square, where a myriad scattered lights twinkled through the dim fog of night. Gringoire hurried forward, hoping by the swiftness of his legs to escape the three infirm spectres who had fastened themselves upon him.

"*Onde vas, hombre?*" cried the lame man, throwing away his crutches, and running after him with the best pair of legs that ever measured a geometric pace upon the pavements of Paris.

Then the man in the bowl, erect upon his feet, clapped his heavy iron-bound bowl upon Gringoire's head, and the blind man glared at him with flaming eyes.

"Where am I?" asked the terrified poet.

"In the Court of Miracles," replied a fourth spectre, who had just accosted them.

"By my soul!" replied Gringoire; "I do indeed behold blind men seeing and lame men running; but where is the Saviour?"

They answered with an evil burst of laughter.

The poor poet glanced around him. He was indeed in that fearful Court of Miracles, which no honest man had ever entered at such an hour; the magic circle within whose lines the officers of the Châtelet, and the provost's men who ventured to penetrate it, disappeared in morsels; a city of thieves, a hideous wart upon the face of Paris; the sewer whence escaped each morning, returning to stagnate at night, that rivulet of vice, mendicity, and vagrancy, perpetually overflowing the streets of every great capital; a monstrous hive, receiving nightly all the drones of the social order with their booty; the lying hospital, where the gipsy, the unfrocked monk, the ruined scholar, the scape-grace of every nation, Spanish, Italian, and German, and of every creed, Jew, Christian, Mahometan, and idolater, covered with painted sores, beggers by day, were transformed into robbers by night,—in short, a huge cloak-room, used at this period for the dressing and undressing of all the actors in the everlasting comedy enacted in the streets of Paris by theft, prostitution, and murder.

It was a vast square, irregular and ill-paved, like every other square in Paris at that time. Fires, around which swarmed strange groups, gleamed here and there. People came and went, and shouted and screamed. There was a sound of shrill laughter, of the wailing of children and the voices of women. The hands, the heads of this multitude, black against the luminous background, made a thousand uncouth gestures. At times, a dog which looked like a man, or a man who looked like a dog, passed over the space of ground lit up by the flames, blended with huge and shapeless shadows. The limits of race and species seemed to fade away in this city as in some pandemonium. Men, women, beasts, age, sex, health, disease, all seemed to be in common among these people; all was blended, mingled, confounded, superimposed; each partook of all.

The feeble flickering light of the fires enabled Gringoire to distinguish, in spite of his alarm, all around the vast square a hideous framing of ancient houses whose worm-eaten, worn, misshapen fronts, each pierced by one or two lighted garret windows, looked to him in the darkness like the huge heads of old women ranged in a circle, monstrous and malign, watching and winking at the infernal revels.

It was like a new world, unknown, unheard of, deformed, creeping, swarming, fantastic.

Gringoire, more and more affrighted, caught by the three beggars, as if by three pairs of pincers, confused by the mass of other faces which snarled and grimaced about him,—the wretched Gringoire tried to recover sufficient presence of mind to recall whether it was Saturday or not. But his efforts were in vain; the thread of his memory and his thoughts was broken; and doubting everything, hesitating between what he saw and what he felt, he asked himself the unanswerable questions: "If I be I, are these things really so? If these things be so, am I really I?"

At this instant a distinct cry arose from the buzzing mob which surrounded him: "Take him to the king! take him to the king!"

"Holy Virgin!" muttered Gringoire, "the king of this region should be a goat."

"To the king! to the king!" repeated every voice.

He was dragged away. Each one vied with the other in fastening his claws upon him. But the three beggars never loosed their hold, and tore him from the others, howling, "He is ours!"

The poet's feeble doublet breathed its last in the struggle.

As they crossed the horrid square his vertigo vanished. After walking a few steps, a sense of reality returned. He began to grow accustomed to the atmosphere of the place. At first, from his poetic head, or perhaps, quite simply and quite prosaically, from his empty stomach, there had arisen certain fumes, a vapour as it were, which, spreading itself between him and other objects, prevented him from seeing anything save through a confused nightmare mist, through those dreamlike shadows which render every outline vague, distort every shape, combine all objects into exaggerated groups, and enlarge things into chimeras and men into ghosts. By degrees this delusion gave way to a less wild and less deceitful vision. Reality dawned upon him, blinded him, ran against him, and bit by bit destroyed the frightful poetry with which he had at first fancied himself surrounded. He could not fail to see that he was walking, not in the Styx, but in the mire; that he was pushed and elbowed, not by demons but by thieves; that it was not his soul, but merely his life which was in danger (since he lacked that precious conciliator which pleads so powerfully with the bandit for the honest man,—a purse). Finally, examining the revels more closely and with greater calmness, he descended from the Witches' Sabbath to the pot-house.

The Court of Miracles was indeed only a pot-house, but a pot-house of thieves, as red with blood as with wine.

The spectacle presented to his eyes when his tattered escort at last landed him at his journey's end was scarcely fitted to bring him back to poetry, even were it the poetry of hell. It was more than ever the prosaic and brutal reality of the tavern. If we were not living in the fifteenth century, we should say that Gringoire had fallen from Michael Angelo to Callot.

Around a large fire burning upon a great round flagstone, and lapping with its flames the rusty legs of a trivet empty for the moment, stood a number of worm-eaten tables here and there, in dire confusion, no lackey of any geometrical pretensions having deigned to adjust their parallelism, or at least to see that they did not cross each other at angles too unusual. Upon these tables glittered various pots and jugs dripping with wine and beer, and around these jugs were seated numerous Bacchanalian faces, purple with fire and wine. One big-bellied man with a jolly face was administering noisy kisses to a brawny, thickset woman. A rubbie, or old vagrant, whistled as he loosed the bandages from his mock wound, and rubbed his sound, healthy knee, which had been swathed all day in ample ligatures. Beyond him was a mumper, preparing his "visitation from God"—his sore leg—with suet and ox-blood. Two tables farther on, a sham pilgrim, in complete pilgrim dress, was spelling out the lament of Sainte-Reine, not forgetting the snuffle and the twang. In another place a young scamp who imposed on the charitable by pretending to have been bitten by a mad dog, was taking a lesson of an old dummy chucker in the art of frothing at the mouth by chewing a bit of soap. By their side a dropsical man was reducing his size, making four or five doxies hold their noses as they sat at the same table, quarrelling over a child which they had stolen during the evening,—all circumstances which, two centuries later, "seemed so ridiculous to the court," as Sauval says, "that they served as diversion to the king, and as the opening to a royal ballet entitled 'Night,' divided into four parts, and danced at the Petit Bourbon Theatre." "Never," adds an eye-witness in 1653, "have the sudden changes of the Court of Miracles been more happily hit off. Benserade prepared us for them by some very fine verses."

Coarse laughter was heard on every hand, with vulgar songs. Every man expressed himself in his own way, carping and swearing, without heeding his neighbour. Some hobnobbed, and quarrels arose from the clash of their mugs, and the breaking of their mugs was the cause of many torn rags.

A big dog squatted on his tail, gazing into the fire. Some children took their part in the orgies. The stolen child cried and screamed; while another, a stout boy of four, sat on a high bench, with his legs dangling, his chin just coming above the table, and not speaking a word. A third was gravely smearing the table with melted tallow as it ran from the candle. Another, a little fellow crouched in the mud, almost lost in a kettle which he was scraping with a potsherd, making a noise which would have distracted Stradivarius.

A cask stood near the fire, and a beggar sat on the cask. This was the king upon his throne.

The three who held Gringoire led him up to his cask, and all the revellers were hushed for a moment, except the caldron inhabited by the child.

Gringoire dared not breathe or raise his eyes.

"*Hombre, quita tu sombrero!*" said one of the three scoundrels who held him; and before he had made up his mind what this meant, another snatched his hat,—a shabby headpiece, to be sure, but still useful on sunny or on rainy days. Gringoire sighed.

But the king, from the height of his barrel, addressed him,—

"Who is this varlet?"

Gringoire started. The voice, although threatening in tone, reminded him of another voice which had that same morning dealt the first blow to his mystery by whining out from the audience, "Charity, kind souls!" He lifted his head. It was indeed Clopin Trouillefou.

Clopin Trouillefou, decked with his royal insignia, had not a tatter more or less than usual. The wound on his arm had vanished.

In his hand he held one of those whips with whit-leather thongs then used by serjeants of the wand to keep back the crowd, and called "boullayes." Upon his head he wore a circular coif closed at the top; but it was hard to say whether it was a child's pad or a king's crown, so similar are the two things.

Still, Gringoire, without knowing why, felt his hopes revive when he recognized this accursed beggar of the Great Hall in the king of the Court of Miracles.

"Master," stuttered he, "My lord— Sire— How shall I address you?" he said at last, reaching the culminating point of his crescendo, and not knowing how to rise higher or to redescend. "My lord, your Majesty, or comrade. Call me what you will; but make haste. What have you to say in your defence?"

"'In your defence,'" thought Gringoire; "I don't like the sound of that." He resumed stammeringly, "I am he who this morning—"

"By the devil's claws!" interrupted Clopin, "your name, varlet, and nothing more. Hark ye. You stand before three mighty sovereigns: me, Clopin Trouillefou, King of Tunis, successor to the Grand Coëre, the king of rogues, lord paramount of the kingdom of Cant; Mathias Hungadi Spicali, Duke of Egypt and Bohemia, that yellow old boy you see yonder with a clout about his head, Guillaume Rousseau, Emperor of Galilee, that fat fellow who pays no heed to us, but caresses that wanton. We are your judges. You have entered the kingdom of Cant, the land of thieves, without being a member of the confraternity; you have violated the privileges of our city. You must be punished, unless you be either prig, mumper, or cadger; that is, in the vulgar tongue of honest folks, either thief, beggar, or tramp. Are you anything of the sort? Justify yourself; state your character."

"Alas!" said Gringoire, "I have not that honour. I am the author—"

"Enough!" cried Trouillefou, not allowing him to finish his sentence. "You must be hanged. Quite a simple matter, my honest citizens! As you treat our people when they enter your domain, so we treat yours when they intrude among us. The law which you mete out to vagabonds, the vagabonds mete out to you. It is your own fault if it be evil. It is quite necessary that we should occasionally see an honest man grin through a hempen collar; it makes the thing honourable. Come, friend, divide your rags cheerfully among these young ladies. I will have you hanged to amuse the vagabonds, and you shall give them your purse to pay for a drink. If you have any mummeries to perform, over yonder in that mortar there's a capital God the Father, in stone, which we stole from the Church of Saint-Pierre-aux-Bœufs. You have four minutes to fling your soul at his head."

This was terrible speech.

"Well said, upon my soul! Clopin Trouillefou preaches as well as any pope!" exclaimed the Emperor of Galilee, smashing his jug to prop up his table.

"Noble emperors and kings," said Gringoire with great coolness (for his courage had mysteriously returned, and he spoke firmly), "you do not consider what you're doing. My name is Pierre Gringoire; I am the poet whose play was performed this morning in the Great Hall of the Palace."

"Oh, is it you, sirrah?" said Clopin. "I was there, God's wounds! Well, comrade, because you bored us this morning, is that any reason why we should not hang you to-night?"

"I shall have hard work to get off," thought Gringoire. But yet he made one more effort. "I don't see," said he, "why poets should not be classed with vagabonds. Æsop was a vagrant; Homer was a beggar; Mercury was a thief—"

Clopin interrupted him: "I believe you mean to cozen us with your lingo. Good God! be hanged, and don't make such a row about it!"

"Excuse me, my lord King of Tunis," replied Gringoire, disputing every inch of the ground. "Is it worth while— An instant— Hear me— You will not condemn me unheard—"

His melancholy voice was indeed lost in the uproar around him. The little boy scraped his kettle more vigorously than ever; and, to cap the climax, an old woman had just placed a frying-pan full of fat upon the trivet, and it crackled over the flames with a noise like the shouts of an army of children in chase of some masquerader.

However, Clopin Trouillefou seemed to be conferring for a moment with the Duke of Egypt and the Emperor of Galilee, the latter being entirely drunk. Then he cried out sharply, "Silence, I say!" and as the kettle and the frying-pan paid no heed, but kept up their duet, he leaped from his cask, dealt a kick to the kettle, which rolled ten paces or more with the child, another kick to the frying-pan, which upset all the fat into the fire, and then gravely reascended his throne, utterly regardless of the little one's stifled sobs and the grumbling of the old woman whose supper had vanished in brilliant flames.

Trouillefou made a sign, and the duke, the emperor, the arch thieves, and the gonnofs ranged themselves around him in the form of a horseshoe, Gringoire, still roughly grasped by the shoulders, occupying the centre. It was a semi-circle of rags, of tatters, of tinsel, of pitchforks, of axes, of staggering legs, of bare brawny arms, of sordid, dull, stupid faces. In the middle of this Round Table of beggary Clopin Trouillefou reigned pre-eminent, as the doge of this senate, the king of this assembly of peers, the pope of this conclave,—pre-eminent in the first place by the height of his cask, then by a peculiarly haughty, savage, and tremendous air, which made his eyes flash, and amended in his fierce profile the bestial type of the vagrant. He seemed a wild boar among swine.

"Hark ye," he said to Gringoire, caressing his shapeless chin with his horny hand; "I see no reason why you should not be hanged. To be sure, you seem to dislike the idea, and it's very plain that you worthy cits are not used to it; you've got an exaggerated idea of the thing. After all, we wish you no harm. There is one way of getting you out of the difficulty for the time being. Will you join us?"

My reader may fancy the effect of this proposal upon Gringoire, who saw his life escaping him, and had already begun to lose his hold upon it. He clung to it once more with vigour.

"I will indeed, with all my heart," said he.

"Do you agree," resumed Clopin, "to enroll yourself among the gentry of the chive."

"Of the chive, exactly," answered Gringoire.

"Do you acknowledge yourself a member of the rogues' brigade?" continued the King of Tunis.

"Of the rogues' brigade."

"A subject of the kingdom of Cant?"

"Of the kingdom of cant."

"A vagrant?"

"A vagrant."

"At heart?"

"At heart."

"I would call your attention to the fact," added the king, "that you will be hanged none the less."

"The devil!" said the poet.

"Only," continued Clopin, quite unmoved, "you will be hanged later, with more ceremony, at the cost of the good city of Paris, on a fine stone gallows, and by honest men. That is some consolation."

"As you say," responded Gringoire.

"There are other advantages. As a member of the rogues' brigade you will have to pay no taxes for pavements, for the poor, or for lighting the streets, to all of which the citizens of Paris are subject."

"So be it," said the poet, "I consent. I am a vagrant, a Canter, a member of the rogues' brigade, a man of the chive,—what you will; and I was all this long ago, Sir King of Tunis, for I am a philosopher; *et omnia in philosophia, omnes in philosopho continentur,* as you know."

The King of Tunis frowned.

"What do you take me for, mate? What Hungarian Jew's gibberish are you giving us? I don't know Hebrew. I'm no Jew, if I am a thief. I don't even steal now; I am above that; I kill. Cut-throat, yes; cutpurse, no."

Gringoire tried to slip in some excuse between these brief phrases which anger made yet more abrupt.

"I beg your pardon, my lord. It is not Hebrew, it is Latin."

"I tell you," replied Clopin, furiously, "that I am no Jew, and that I will have you hanged,—by the synagogue, I will! —together with that paltry Judean cadger beside you, whom I mightily hope I may some day see nailed to a counter, like the counterfeit coin that he is!"

So saying, he pointed to the little Hungarian Jew with beard, who had accosted Gringoire with his *"Facitote caritatem,"* and who, understanding no other language, was amazed at the wrath which the King of Tunis vented upon him.

At last my lord Clopin became calm.

"So, varlet," said he to our poet, "you wish to become a vagrant?"

"Undoubtedly," replied the poet.

"It is not enough merely to wish," said the surly Clopin; "good-will never added an onion to the soup, and is good for nothing but a passport to paradise; now, paradise and Cant are two distinct things. To be received into the kingdom of Cant, you must prove that you are good for something; and to prove this you must fumble the snot."

"I will fumble," said Gringoire, "as much as ever you like."

Clopin made a sign. A number of Canters stepped from the circle and returned immediately, bringing a couple of posts finished at the lower end with broad wooden feet, which made them stand firmly upon the ground; at the upper end of the two posts they arranged a crossbeam, the whole forming a very pretty portable gallows, which Gringoire had the pleasure of seeing erected before him in the twinkling of an eye. Nothing was wanting, not even the rope, which swung gracefully from the crossbeam.

"What are they going to do?" wondered Gringoire with some alarm. A sound of bells which he heard at the same moment put an end to his anxiety; it was a manikin, or puppet, that the vagrants hung by the neck to the cord,—a sort of scarecrow, dressed in red, and so loaded with little bells and hollow brasses that thirty Castilian mules might have been tricked out with them. These countless tinklers jingled for some time with the swaying of the rope, then the sound died away by degrees, and finally ceased when the manikin had been restored to a state of complete immobility by that law of the pendulum which has superseded the clepsydra and the hour-glass.

Then Clopin, showing Gringoire a rickety old footstool, placed under the manikin, said,—

"Climb up there!"

"The devil!" objected Gringoire; "I shall break my neck. Your stool halts like one of Martial's couplets; one foot has six syllables and one foot has but five."

"Climb up!" repeated Clopin.

Gringoire mounted the stool, and succeeded, though not without considerable waving of head and arms, in recovering his centre of gravity.

"Now," resumed the King of Tunis, "twist your right foot round your left leg, and stand on tiptoe with your left foot."

"My lord," said Gringoire, "are you absolutely determined to make me break a limb?"

Clopin tossed his head.

"Hark ye, mate; you talk too much. I will tell you in a couple of words what I expect you to do: you are to stand on tiptoe, as I say; in that fashion you can reach the manikin's pockets; you are to search them; you are to take out a purse which you will find there; and if you do all this without ringing a single bell, it is well: you shall become a vagrant. We shall have nothing more to do but to baste you with blows for a week."

"Zounds! I shall take good care," said Gringoire. "And if I ring the bells?"

"Then you shall be hanged. Do you understand?"

"I don't understand at all," answered Gringoire.

"Listen to me once more. You are to search the manikin and steal his purse; if but a single bell stir in the act, you shall be hanged. Do you understand that?"

"Good," said Gringoire, "I understand that. What next?"

"If you manage to get the purse without moving the bells, you are a vagrant, and you shall be basted with blows for seven days in succession. You understand now, I suppose?"

"No, my lord; I no longer understand. Where is the advantage? I shall be hanged in the one case, beaten in the other?"

"And as a vagrant," added Clopin, "and as a vagrant; does that count for nothing? It is for your own good that we shall beat you, to harden you against blows."

"Many thanks," replied the poet.

"Come, make haste," said the king, stamping on his cask, which re-echoed like a vast drum.

"Fumble the snot, and be done with it! I warn you, once for all, that if I hear but one tinkle you shall take the manikin's place."

The company of Canters applauded Clopin's words, and ranged themselves in a ring around the gallows, with such pitiless laughter that Gringoire saw that he amused them too much not to have everything to fear from them. His only hope lay in the slight chance of succeeding in the terrible task imposed upon him; he decided to risk it, but not without first addressing a fervent prayer to the manikin whom he was to plunder, and who seemed more easily moved than the vagrants. The myriad little bells with their tiny brazen tongues seemed to him like so many vipers with gaping jaws, ready to hiss and sting.

"Oh," he murmured, "is it possible that my life depends upon the slightest quiver of the least of these bells! Tinkle not, ye tinklers! Jingle not, ye jinglers!"

He made one more attempt to melt Trouillefou.

"And if a breeze spring up?" he asked.

"You will be hanged," answered the other, without hesitating.

Seeing that neither respite, delay, nor subterfuge was possible, he made a desperate effort; he twisted his right foot round his left leg, stood tiptoe on his left foot, and stretched out his arm, but just as he touched the manikin, his body, now resting on one foot, tottered upon the stool, which had but three; he strove mechanically to cling to the figure, lost his balance, and fell heavily to the ground, deafened and stunned by the fatal sound of the myriad bells of the manikin, which, yielding to the pressure of his hand, first revolved upon its own axis, then swung majestically to and fro between the posts.

"A curse upon it!" he cried as he fell; and he lay as if dead, face downwards.

Still he heard the fearful peal above his head, and the devilish laughs of the vagrants, and the voice of Trouillefou, as it said, "Lift up the knave, and hang him with a will."

He rose. The manikin had already been taken down to make room for him.

The Canters made him mount the

stool. Clopin stepped up to him, passed the rope round his neck, and clapping him on the shoulder, exclaimed,—

"Farewell, mate. You can't escape now, though you have the digestion of the Pope himself."

The word "mercy" died on Gringoire's lips. He gazed around him, but without hope; every man was laughing.

"Bellevigne de l'Etoile," said the King of Tunis to a huge vagrant who started from the ranks, "climb upon the crossbeam."

Bellevigne de l'Etoile nimbly climbed the crossbeam, and in an instant Gringoire, raising his eyes, with terror beheld him squatting upon it, above his head.

"Now," continued Clopin Trouillefou, "when I clap my hands, do you, Andry le Rouge, knock away the footstool from under him; you, François Chant-Prune, hang on to the knave's feet; and you, Bellevigne, jump down upon his shoulders; and all three at once, do you hear?"

Gringoire shuddered.

"Are you ready?" said Clopin Trouillefou to the three Canters prepared to fall upon Gringoire. The poor sufferer endured a moment of horrible suspense, while Clopin calmly pushed into the fire with his foot a few vine-branches which the flame had not yet kindled. "Are you ready?" he repeated; and he opened his hands to clap. A second more, and all would have been over.

But he paused, as if struck by a sudden thought.

"One moment," said he; "I forgot! It is our custom never to hang a man without asking if there be any woman who'll have him. Comrade, it's your last chance. You must marry a tramp or the rope."

This gipsy law, strange as it may seem to the reader, is still written out in full in the ancient English code. (See "Burington's Observations.")

Gringoire breathed again. This was the second time that he had been restored to life within the half-hour; so he dared not feel too confident.

"Hollo!" cried Clopin, remounting his cask; "hollo there, women, females! is there among you, from the old witch to her cat, a wench who'll take this scurvy knave? Hollo, Colette la Charonne! Elisabeth Trouvain! Simone Jodouyne! Marie Piédebou! Thonne la Longue! Bérarde Fanouel! Michelle Genaille! Claude Ronge-Oreille! Mathurine Girorou! Hollo! Isabeau la Thierrye! Come and look! a man for nothing! who'll take him?"

Gringoire, in his wretched plight, was doubtless far from tempting. The vagabond women seemed but little moved by the offer. The luckless fellow heard them answer: "No! no! hang him; that will make sport for us all."

Three, however, stepped from the crowd to look him over. The first was a stout, square-faced girl. She examined the philosopher's pitiable doublet most attentively. The stuff was worn, and more full of holes than a furnace for roasting chestnuts. The girl made a wry face. "An old clout!" she grumbled, and, addressing Gringoire, "Let's look at your cloak?"

"I have lost it," said Gringoire.

"Your hat?"

"Some one took it from me."

"Your shoes?"

"The soles are almost worn through."

"Your purse?"

"Alas!" faltered Gringoire, "I have not a penny."

"Be hanged to you then, and be thankful!" replied the tramp, turning her back on him.

The second, old, weather-beaten, wrinkled, and ugly, hideous enough to be conspicuous even in the Court of Miracles, walked round and round Gringoire. He almost trembled lest she should accept him. But she muttered, "He's too thin," and took her leave.

The third was a young girl, quite rosy and not very ugly. "Save me!" whispered the poor devil.

She looked at him a moment with a compassionte air, then looked down, began to plait up her skirt, and seemed uncertain. He watched her every motion; this was his last ray of hope. "No," said the young woman at last; "no! Guillaume Longuejoue would lick me," and she went back to the crowd.

"Comrade," said Clopin Trouillefou, "you're down on your luck."

Then, standing erect upon his cask, he cried, "Will no one take this lot?" mimicking the tone of an auctioneer, to the great entertainment of all; "will no one take it? Going, going, going!" and turning to the gallows with a nod, "Gone!"

Bellevigne de l'Etoile, Andry le Rouge, and François Chant-Prune approached Gringoire.

At this instant a shout rose from the thieves: "Esmeralda! Esmeralda!"

Gringoire trembled, and turned in the direction of the cry. The crowd opened and made way for a pure and radiant figure.

It was the gipsy girl.

"Esmeralda!" said Gringoire, astounded, amidst his contending emotions, at the suddenness with which that magic word connected all the various recollections of his day.

This rare creature seemed to exercise sovereign sway through her beauty and her charm even in the Court of Miracles. Thieves, beggars, and harlots stood meekly aside to let her pass, and their brutal faces brightened at her glance.

She approached the victim with her light step. Her pretty Djali followed her. Gringoire was more dead than alive. She gazed at him an instant in silence.

"Are you going to hang this man?" she gravely asked Clopin.

"Yes, sister," replied the King of Tunis, "unless you'll take him for your husband."

She pouted her pretty lower lip.

"I'll take him," said she.

Gringoire here firmly believed that he had been dreaming ever since morning, and that this was the end of the dream.

In fact, the sudden change of fortune, though charming, was violent.

The slip-noose was unfastened, the poet was helped from his stool. He was obliged to seat himself, so great was his agitation.

The Duke of Egypt, without uttering a word, brought forward an earthen jug. The gipsy girl offered it to Gringoire. "Throw it down," she said to him.

The jug was broken into four pieces.

"Brother," then said the Duke of Egypt, laying his hands on their heads, "she is your wife; sister, he is your husband. For four years. Go!"

Chapter VII

A WEDDING NIGHT

A FEW moments later our poet found himself in a small room with a vaulted roof, very snug, very warm, seated before a table which seemed to ask nothing better than to borrow a few stores from a hanging cupboard close by; with a good bed in prospect, and alone with a pretty girl. The adventure partook of the nature of magic. He began seriously to think himself the hero of some fairy-tale; now and then he gazed about him as if in search of the fairy chariot, drawn by two winged steeds, which could alone have transported him so swiftly from Tartarus to Paradise. Occasionally his eyes were riveted on the holes in his doublet, to bring himself back to actual things, and lest he should quite lose sight of land. His reason, floating in imaginary realms, had only this thread to cling to.

The young girl apparently took no notice of him: she came and went, moved a stool, chatted with her goat, smiled, and pouted. Finally she seated herself at the table, and Gringoire could study her at his leisure.

You were once a child, reader, and you may be lucky enough to be one still. You must more than once (and for my part I spent whole days at it,— the best days of my life) have pursued from bush to bush, on the brink of some brisk stream, in bright sunshine, some lovely green or azure dragon-fly, which checked its flight at sharp angles, and kissed the tip of every twig. You will remember the loving curiosity with which your mind and your eye followed that buzzing, whizzing little whirlwind, with blue and purple wings, between which floated an intangible form, veiled by the very swiftness of its motion. The airy creature, vaguely seen amid the quivering wings, seemed to you chimerical, imaginary, impossible to touch, impossible to see. But when the dragon-fly at last rested on the tip of a reed, and you could examine, holding your breath meanwhile, its slender gauzy wings, its long enamelled robes, its crystal globe-like eyes, what amazement you felt, and what fear lest it should again fade to a shadow and the creature turn to a chimera! Recall these sensations, and you will readily appreciate what Gringoire felt as he beheld in visible, palpable form that Esmeralda of whom he had hitherto had but a glimpse amidst the eddying dance and song, and a confused mass of people.

Becoming more and more absorbed in his reverie, he thought: "This, then, is 'Esmeralda'! a celestial creature! a street dancer! So much and so little! It was she who put the finishing stroke to my play this morning; it was she who saved my life this evening. My evil genius! my good angel! A pretty woman, upon my word! And she must love me to distraction to take me in this fashion. By-the-by," said he, rising suddenly with that sense of truth which formed the basis of his character and his philosophy, "I don't quite know how it came about, but I am her husband!"

With this idea in mind and in his eyes, he approached the young girl in so military and lover-like fashion that she shrank away from him.

"What do you want?" she said.

"Can you ask me, adorable Esmeralda?" replied Gringoire in such impassioned tones that he himself was astounded at his own accents.

The gipsy girl stared at him. "I don't know what you mean."

"Oh, come now!" added Gringoire, becoming more and more excited, and thinking that after all he was only dealing with the ready-made virtue of the Court of Miracles; "am I not yours, sweet friend? Are you not mine?"

And, quite innocently, he clasped her by the waist.

The girl's bodice slipped through his hands like a snake's skin. She leaped from one end of the little cell to the other, stooped, and rose with a tiny dagger in her hand, before Gringoire had time to see whence this dagger came,— proud, angry, with swelling lips, dilated nostrils, cheeks red as crabapples, and eyes flashing lightning. At the same time the white goat placed itself before her, and presented a battlefront to Gringoire, bristling with two pretty, gilded, and very sharp horns. All this took place in the twinkling of an eye.

The damsel had turned wasp, and asked nothing better than to sting.

Our philosopher stood abashed, glancing alternately at the girl and the goat in utter confusion. "Holy Virgin!" he exclaimed at last, when surprise allowed him to speak, "here's a determined pair!"

The gipsy girl broke the silence in her turn. "You must be a very bold rascal!"

"Forgive me, mademoiselle," said Gringoire with a smile. "But why did you marry me, then?"

"Was I to let them hang you?"

"So," replied the poet, somewhat disappointed in his amorous hopes, "you had no other idea in wedding me than to save me from the gibbet?"

"And what other idea should I have had?"

Gringoire bit his lips. "Well," said he, "I am not quite such a conquering hero as I supposed. But then, what was the use of breaking that poor jug?"

But Esmeralda's dagger and the goat's horns still remained on the defensive.

"Mademoiselle Esmeralda," said the poet, "let us come to terms. I am not clerk of the Châtelet, and I shall not pick a quarrel with you for carrying concealed weapons in Paris, in the face of the provost's orders and prohibition. Yet you must know that Noël Lescrivain was sentenced to pay ten Paris pence only a week ago for wearing a broadsword. Now, that is none of my business, and I will come to the point. I swear to you, by all my hopes of paradise, that I will not come near you without your sovereign leave and permission; but give me some supper."

To tell the truth, Gringoire, like Despréaux, was "very little of a Don Juan." He was not one of the chivalric, musketeering kind who take girls by storm. In the matter of love, as in all other matters, he was always for temporizing and compromising; and a good supper, in friendly society, struck him, especially when he was hungry, as an excellent interlude between the prologue and the issue of an intrigue.

The gipsy made no answer. She gave her usual scornful little pout, cocked her head like a bird, then burst out laughing, and the dainty dagger disappeared as it came, Gringoire being still unable to discover where the bee hid her sting.

A moment late, a rye loaf, a slice of bacon, a few withered apples, and a jug of beer were on the table. Gringoire began to eat greedily. Judging by the fierce clatter of his iron fork against his earthen-plate, all his love had turned to hunger.

The young girl seated near him looked on in silence, evidently absorbed in other thoughts, at which she occasionally smiled, while her gentle hand caressed the intelligent head of the goat as it rested idly against her knee.

A yellow wax candle lit up this scene of voracity and reverie.

However, the first cravings of hunger appeased, Gringoire felt somewhat ashamed to find that there was but one apple left. "You don't eat, Mademoiselle Esmeralda?"

She answered by a shake of the head, and her pensive gaze was fixed on the arched roof of the cell.

"What the deuce is she thinking about?" thought Gringoire; and, looking to see what she was looking at: "It can't be the wry face of that stone dwarf carved upon yonder keystone which so absorbs her attention. What the devil! I'm sure I can stand the comparison!"

He raised his voice: "Mademoiselle!" She did not seem to hear him.

He spoke still louder: "Mademoiselle Esmeralda!"

Labour lost. The girl's mind was elsewhere, and Gringoire's voice had no power to call it back. Luckily the goat interfered, by softly pulling her mistress by the sleeve.

"What do you want, Djali?" said the gipsy, hastily, as if roused suddenly.

"The creature is hungry," said Gringoire, delighted to open the conversation.

Esmeralda began to crumble some bread, which Djali nibbled daintily from the hollow of her hand.

However, Gringoire gave her no time to resume her reverie. He risked a delicate question:—

"Then you don't want me for your husband?"

The young girl looked steadily at him, and replied, "No."

"For your lover?" continued Gringoire.

She pouted, and answered, "No."

"For your friend?" went on Gringoire.

She looked at him fixedly once more, and after an instant's reflection said, "Perhaps."

This "perhaps," so dear to philosophers, emboldened Gringoire.

"Do you know what friendship is?" he asked.

"Yes," answered the gipsy; "it is to be brother and sister; two souls which meet without mingling, two fingers of one hand."

"And love?" continued Gringoire.

"Oh, love!" said she, and her voice trembled and her eye brightened. "That is to be two and yet but one. A man and a woman blended into an angel. It is heaven itself."

The street dancer assumed a beauty, as she spoke, which struck Gringoire strangely, and seemed to him in perfect harmony with the almost Oriental exaltation of her words. Her pure rosy lips half smiled; her serene and innocent brow was clouded for the moment by her thought, as when a mirror is dimmed by a breath; and from her long, dark, drooping lashes flashed an ineffable light, which lent her profile that ideal sweetness which Raphael has since found at the mystic meeting-point of the virgin, the mother, and the saint.

Nevertheless, Gringoire kept on,—

"What must one be to please you, then?"

"He must be a man."

"And I," said he,—"what am I?"

"A man with a helmet on his head, a sword in his hand, and golden spurs on his heels."

"Good!" said Gringoire; "dress makes the man. Do you love any one?"

"As a lover?"

"As a lover."

She looked pensive for a moment; then she said with a peculiar expression, "I shall know soon."

"Why not to-night?" said the poet, tenderly; "why not me?"

She cast a serious glance at him.

"I can only love a man who can protect me."

Gringoire flushed, and was silent. It was evident that the young girl alluded to the slight assistance which he had afforded her in the critical situation in which she had found herself a couple of hours previous. This memory, blotted out by the other adventures of the evening, returned to him. He struck his brow.

"By-the-by, mademoiselle, I ought to have begun there. Forgive me my foolish distractions. How did you manage to escape from Quasimodo's claws?"

This question made the gipsy shudder.

"Oh, the horrid hunchback!" she cried, hiding her face in her hands.

And she shivered as if icy cold.

"Horrid, indeed," said Gringoire, not dropping the subject; "but how did you contrive to escape him?"

Esmeralda smiled, sighed, and was silent.

"Do you know why he pursued you?" continued Gringoire, trying to get an answer by a roundabout way.

"I don't know," said the girl. And she added quickly, "But you followed me too; why did you follow me?"

"In good faith," replied Gringoire, "I have forgotten."

There was a pause. Gringoire slashed the table with his knife. The girl smiled, and seemed to be gazing at something through the wall. All at once she began to sing in a voice which was scarcely articulate,—

"Quando las pintadas aves
Mudas estan, y la tierra—"

She broke off abruptly, and began to fondle Djali.

"That's a pretty creature of yours," said Gringoire.

"It is my sister," she replied.

"Why do they call you 'Esmeralda'?" the poet ventured to ask.

"I've no idea."

"But why do they?"

She drew from her bosom a small oblong bag fastened to her neck by a string of beads made of some sweet-scented gum. This bag gave forth a strong smell of camphor; it was made of green silk, and had in the centre a large bit of green glass, in imitation of an emerald.

"Perhaps it is on account of that," said she.

Gringoire tried to take the bag. She drew back.

"Don't touch it! It's an amulet. You

will injure the charm, or the charm you."

The poet's curiosity was more and more eagerly aroused.

"Who gave it to you?"

She put her finger to her lip and hid the amulet in her bosom. He tried her with other questions, but she scarcely answered him.

"What does the word 'Esmeralda' mean?"

"I don't know," said she.

"To what language does it belong?"

"I think it is a gipsy word."

"So I suspected," said Gringoire; "you are not a native of France?"

"I know nothing about it."

"Are your parents living?"

She began to sing, to an ancient air:—
"A bird is my mother,
My father another.
Nor boat nor bark need I
As over the sea I fly;
A bird is my mother,
My father another."

"Very good," said Gringoire. "At what age did you come to France?"

"When I was very small."

"To Paris?"

"Last year. Just as we entered the Papal Gate, I saw the reed warbler skim through the air; it was the last of August. I said: It will be a hard winter."

"So it has been," said Gringoire, charmed at this beginning of conversation; "I have spent it in blowing on my fingers to keep them warm. So you have the gift of prophecy?"

She fell back into her laconicism.

"No."

"Is that man whom you call the Duke of Egypt, the head of your tribe?"

"Yes."

"But it was he who married us," timidly remarked the poet.

She made her usual pretty grimace.

"I don't even know your name."

"My name? You shall have it, if you wish: Pierre Gringoire."

"I know a nicer one," said she.

"Cruel girl!" replied the poet. "Never mind, you shall not vex me. Stay; perhaps you will love me when you know me better; and then you told me your history so confidingly that I owe you somewhat of mine. You must know, then, that my name is Pierre Gringoire, and that I am the son of the notary of Gonesse. My father was hanged by the Burgundians and my mother ripped up by the Picards, at the time of the siege of Paris, now twenty years ago. At the age of six years, therefore, I was left an orphan, with no sole to my foot but the pavement of Paris. I don't know how I managed to exist from six to sixteen. A fruit-seller would give me a plum, a baker would throw me a crust; at nightfall I would contrive to be caught by the watch, who put me in prison, and there I found a bundle of straw. All this did not hinder me from growing tall and thin, as you see. In winter time I warmed myself in the sun, under the portico of the Hôtel de Sens, and I thought it very absurd that the bale-fires of St. John should be deferred until the dog-days. At the age of sixteen I wished to learn a trade. I tried everything in turn. I became a soldier, but I was not brave enough. I turned monk, but I was not pious enough; and then, I'm no drinker. In despair, I became a carpenter's apprentice, but I was not strong enough. I had more liking for the schoolmaster's trade; true, I did not know how to read but that was no hindrance. After a time, I discovered that I lacked some necessary quality for everything; and seeing that I was good for nothing, I became a poet and composer of rhymes, of my own free will. That is a trade that one can always take up when one is a vagabond; and it is better than stealing, as certain thievish young friends of mine advised. By good luck, I one fine day encountered Don Claude Frollo, the reverend archdeacon of Notre-Dame. He took an interest in me, and it is to him I owe it that I am now a genuine man of letters, knowing Latin, from Cicero's Offices to the necrology of the Celestine Fathers, and being ignorant of neither scholastics, poetry, nor rhythm, that sophism of sophisms. I am the author of the miracle-play performed to-day with great triumph, and before a great concourse of people, in the hall of the Palace. I have also written a book which will make six hundred pages, on the wonderful comet of 1465, which drove one man mad. I have also had other successes. Being somewhat of an engineer, I worked on Jean Maugue's great bomb, which you know burst on Charenton Bridge the day that it was to be tested, and killed twenty-four of the curious spectators. You see that I am by no means a bad match. I know a great many sorts of delightful tricks which I will teach your goat; for instance, how to take off the Bishop of Paris, that accursed Parisian whose mills bespatter all those who pass over the Millers' Bridge. And then, my miracle-play will bring me in plenty of ready money if they pay me. Finally, I am at your service, I and my wit and my science and my learning,—ready to live with you, lady, as it may please you: soberly or merrily; as husband and wife if you see fit; as brother and sister if you prefer."

Gringoire ceased, awaiting the effect of this speech upon the young girl. Her eyes were bent on the floor.

"'Phœbus,'" she said in an undertone. Then, turning to the poet, "'Phœbus;' what does that mean?"

Gringoire, scarcely comprehending the connection between his words and this question, was nothing loath to display his erudition. He answered, drawing himself up,—

"It is a Latin word signifying 'sun.'"

"'Sun'?" she repeated.

"It is the name of a certain handsome archer who was a god," added Gringoire.

"A god!" repeated the gipsy; and there was something pensive and passionate in her tone.

At this moment, one of her bracelets became unfastened and fell. Gringoire stooped quickly to pick it up; when he rose, the girl and the goat had disappeared. He heard a bolt slide across a small door, doubtless communicating with a neighbouring cell, which was fastened on the other side.

"At least, I hope she has left me a bed!" said our philosopher.

He walked around the room. There was nothing fit to sleep upon except a long wooden chest; and even that had a carved lid, which gave Gringoire a feeling, when he stretched himself out upon it, very like that experienced by Micromegas when he slept at full length upon the Alps.

"Come," said he, making himself as comfortable as he could, "I must submit to fate. But this is an odd wedding night. It is a pity; there was something simple and antediluvian about this marriage with a broken jug, which I liked."

BOOK III

THE CATHEDRAL

CHAPTER I

NOTRE-DAME

THE Church of Notre-Dame at Paris is doubtless still a sublime and majestic building. But, much beauty as it may retain in its old age, it is not easy to repress a sigh, to restrain our anger, when we mark the countless defacements and mutilations to which men and Time have subjected that venerable monument, without respect for Charlemagne, who laid its first stone, or Philip Augustus, who laid its last.

Upon the face of this aged queen of French cathedrals, beside every wrinkle we find a scar. *"Tempus edax, homo edacior;"* which I would fain translate thus: "Time is blind, but man is stupid."

Had we leisure to study with the reader, one by one, the various marks of destruction graven upon the ancient church, the work of Time would be the lesser, the worse that of Men, especially of "men of art," since there are persons who have styled themselves architects during the last two centuries.

And first of all, to cite but a few glaring instances, there are assuredly few finer pages in the history of architecture than that façade where the three receding portals with their pointed arches, the carved and denticulated plinth with its twenty-eight royal niches, the huge central rose-window flanked by its two lateral windows as is the priest by his deacon and subdeacon, the lofty airy gallery of trifoliated arcades supporting a heavy platform upon its slender columns, and lastly the two dark and massive towers with their penthouse roofs of slate, harmonious parts of a magnificent whole, one above the other, five gigantic stages, unfold themselves to the eye, clearly and as a whole, with their countless details of sculpture, statuary, and carving, powerfully contributing to the calm grandeur of the whole; as it were, a vast symphony in stone; the colossal work of one man and one nation, one and yet complex, like the Iliad and the old Romance epics, to which it is akin; the tremendous sum of the joint contributions of all the forces of an entire epoch, in which every stone reveals, in a hundred forms, the fancy of the workman disciplined by the genius of the artist,—a sort of human creation, in brief, powerful and prolific as the Divine creation, whose double characteristics, variety and eternity, it seems to have acquired.

And what we say of the façade, we

must also say of the whole church; and what we say of the cathedral church of Paris must also be said of all the Christian churches of the Middle Ages. Everything is harmonious which springs from that spontaneous, logical, and well-proportioned art. To measure a toe, is to measure the giant.

Let us return to the façade of Notre-Dame as we see it at the present day, when we make a pious pilgrimage to admire the solemn and mighty cathedral, which, as its chroniclers declare, inspires terror: *"Quæ mole sua terrorem incutit spectantibus."*

This façade now lacks three important things: first, the eleven steps which formerly raised it above the level of the ground; next, the lower series of statues which filled the niches over the doors; and lastly, the upper row of the twenty-eight most ancient kings of France, which adorned the gallery of the first story, from Childebert down to Philip Augustus, each holding in his hand "the imperial globe."

The stairs were destroyed by Time, which, with slow and irresistible progress, raised the level of the city's soil; but while this flood-tide of the pavements of Paris swallowed one by one the eleven steps which added to the majestic height of the edifice, Time has perhaps given to the church more than it took away, for it is Time which has painted the front with that sober hue of centuries which makes the antiquity of churches their greatest beauty.

But who pulled down the two rows of statues? Who left those empty niches? Who carved that new and bastard pointed arch in the very centre of the middle door? Who dared to insert that clumsy, tasteless wooden door, carved in the style of Louis XV., side by side with the arabesques of Biscornette? Who but men, architects, the artists of our day?

And if we step into the interior of the edifice, who overthrew that colossal figure of Saint Christopher, proverbial among statues by the same right as the Great Hall of the Palace among halls, as the spire of Strasburg among steeples? And those myriad statues which peopled every space between the columns of the choir and the nave, kneeling, standing, on horseback, men, women, children, kings, bishops, men-at-arms,—of stone, of marble, of gold, of silver, of copper, nay, even of wax,—who brutally swept them away? It was not the hand of Time.

And who replaced the old Gothic altar, with its splendid burden of shrines and reliquaries, by that heavy marble sarcophagus adorned with clouds and cherubs, looking like a poor copy of the Val-de-Grâce or the Hôtel des Invalides? Who was stupid enough to fasten that clumsy stone anachronism into the Carlovingian pavement of Hercandus? Was it not Louis XIV., fulfilling the vow of Louis XIII.?

And who set cold white panes in place of that stained glass of gorgeous hue, which led the wondering gaze of our fathers to roam uncertain 'twixt the rose-window of the great door and the ogives of the chancel? And what would a precentor of the sixteenth century say if he could see the fine coat of yellow wash with which our Vandal archbishops have smeared their cathedral? He would remember that this was the colour with which the executioner formerly painted those buildings judged "infamous;" he would recall the hotel of the Petit-Bourbon, dedaubed with yellow in memory of the Constable's treason; " a yellow of so fine a temper," says Sauval, "and so well laid on, that more than a hundred years have failed to wash out its colour." He would fancy that the sacred spot had become accursed, and would turn and flee.

And if we climb higher in the cathedral, without pausing to note a thousand barbarous acts of every kind, what has become of that delightful little steeple which rested upon the point of intersection of the transept, and which, no less fragile and no less daring than its neighbour, the spire of the Sainte-Chapelle (also destroyed), rose yet nearer heaven than the towers, slender, sharp, sonorous, and daintily wrought? An architect of good taste (1787) amputated it, and thought it quite enough to cover the wound with that large leaden plaster which looks like the lid of a stewpan. Thus was the marvellous art of the Middle Ages treated in almost every land, but particularly in France. We find three sorts of injury upon its ruins, these three marring it to different depths: first, Time, which has made insensible breaches here and there, mildewed and rusted the surface everywhere; then, political and religious revolutions, which, blind and fierce by nature, fell furiously upon it, rent its array of sculpture and carving, shivered its rose-windows, shattered its necklaces of arabesques and quaint figures, tore down its statues,—sometimes because of their mitre, sometimes because of their crown; lastly, changing fashion, ever more grotesque and absurd, from the anarchic and splendid deviations of the Renaissance down to the necessary decline of architecture. Fashion did more harm than revolutions. Fashion cut into the living flesh, attacked the very skeleton and framework of art; it chopped and hewed, dismembered, slew the edifice, in its form as well as in its symbolism, in its logic no less than in its beauty. But fashion restored,—a thing which neither time nor revolution ever pretended to do. Fashion, on the plea of "good taste," impudently adapted to the wounds of Gothic architecture the paltry gewgaws of a day,—marble ribbons, metallic plumes, a veritable leprosy of egg-shaped mouldings, of volutes, wreaths, draperies, spirals, fringes, stone flames, bronze clouds, lusty cupids, and bloated cherubs, which began to ravage the face of art in the oratory of Catherine de Médicis, and destroyed it, two centuries later, tortured and distorted, in the Dubarry's boudoir.

There are thus, to sum up the points to which we have alluded, three sorts of scars now disfiguring Gothic architecture,—wrinkles and warts upon the epidermis (these are the work of time); wounds, brutal injuries, bruises, and fractures (these are the work of revolution from Luther to Mirabeau); mutilations, amputations, dislocations of the frame, "restorations" (these are the Greek, Roman, Barbaric work of professors according to Vitruvius and Vignole). Academies have murdered the magnificent art which the Vandals produced. To centuries, to revolutions which at least laid waste with impartiality and grandeur, are conjoined the host of scholastic architects licensed and sworn, degrading all they touch with the discernment and selection of bad taste, substituting the tinsel of Louis XV. for Gothic lace-work, for the greater glory of the Parthenon. This is the donkey's kick at the dying lion. It is the old oak, decaying at the crown, pierced, bitten, and devoured by caterpillars.

How different from the time when Robert Cenalis, comparing Notre-Dame at Paris to the famous temple of Diana at Ephesus, "so loudly boasted by the ancient pagans," which immortalized Erostrates, held the cathedral of the Gauls to be "more excellent in length, breadth, height, and structure!"

Notre-Dame at Paris is not, however, what can be called a complete, definite monument, belonging to a class. It is neither a Roman nor a Gothic church. The edifice is not a typical one. It has not, like the abbey at Tournus, the sober massive breadth, the round expansive arch, the icy bareness, the majestic simplicity of those buildings based on the semicircular arch. It is not, like the cathedral at Bourges, the magnificent, airy, multiform, bushy, sturdy, efflorescent product of the pointed arch. It is impossible to class it with that antique order of dark, mysterious, low-studded churches, apparently crushed by the semicircular arch,—almost Egyptian, save for the ceiling; all hieroglyphic, all sacerdotal, all symbolic, more loaded in their ornamentation with lozenges and zig-zags than with flowers, with flowers than with animals, with animals than with men: less the work of the architect than of the bishop; the first transformation of the art, bearing the deep impress of theocratic and military discipline, taking root in the Lower Empire, and ceasing with William the Conqueror. It is impossible to place our cathedral in that other family of lofty, aerial churches, rich in stained glass and sculpture; of pointed forms and daring attitudes; belonging to the commoners and plain citizens, as political symbols; free, capricious, lawless, as works of art; the second transformation of architecture, no longer hieroglyphic, unchangeable, sacerdotal, but artistic, progressive, and popular, beginning with the close of the Crusades and ending with Louis XI. Notre-Dame at Paris is not of purely Roman race like the former, nor of purely Arab breed like the latter.

It is a building of the transition period. The Saxon architect had just reared the pillars of the nave, when the pointed arch, brought back from the Crusades, planted itself as conqueror upon those broad Roman capitals which were never meant to support anything but semi-circular arches. The pointed arch, thenceforth supreme, built the rest of the church. And still, inexperienced and shy at first, it swelled, it widened, it restrained itself, and dared not yet shoot up into spires and lancets, as it did later on in so many marvellous cathedrals. It seemed sensible of the close vicinity of the heavy Roman columns.

Moreover, these buildings of the transition from Roman to Gothic are no less valuable studies than the pure types. They express a gradation of the art which would otherwise be lost. They represent the ingrafting of the pointed arch upon the semicircular.

Notre-Dame at Paris, in particular, is a curious example of this variety. Every face, every stone of the venerable monument is a page not only of the history of the country, but also of the history of science and art. Thus, to allude only to leading details, while the little Porte Rouge attains almost the extreme limit of the Gothic refinements of the fifteenth century, the pillars of the nave, in their size and gravity of style, go back to the Carlovingian Abbey of Saint-Germain des Prés. One would say that there was an interval of six centuries between that door and those pillars. Even the Hermetics find among the symbols of the great door a satisfactory epitome of their science, of which the Church of Saint-Jacques de la Boucherie formed so complete a hieroglyph. Thus, the Roman abbey, the philosophers' church, Gothic art, Saxon art, the clumsy round pillar, which recalls Gregory VII., the hermetic symbolism by which Nicolas Flamel paved the way for Luther, papal unity, schism, Saint-Germain des Prés, Saint-Jacques de la Boucherie, are all confounded, combined, and blended in Notre-Dame. This central and generative church is a kind of chimera among the old churches of Paris; it has the head of one, the limbs of another, the trunk of a third, something of all.

We repeat it; these hybrid constructions are by no means the least interesting to the artist, the antiquary, and the historian. They show us to how great an extent architecture is a primitive thing, in that they demonstrate (as the Cyclopean remains, the pyramids of Egypt, the vast pagodas of India demonstrate) that the greatest products of architecture are not so much individual as they are social works; rather the children of nations in labour than the inspired efforts of men of genius; the legacy of a race; the accumulated wealth of centuries; the residuum of the successive evaporations of human society, —in a word, a species of formation. Every wave of time adds its alluvium, every race leaves a fresh layer on the monument, every individual brings his stone. Thus the beavers work, thus work the bees, thus works man. The great symbol of architecture, Babel, is a beehive.

Great buildings, like great mountains, are the work of centuries. Art is often transformed while they are still pending, —*pendent opera interrupta;* they go on quietly, in harmony with the changes in the art. The new form of art takes up the monument where it finds it, becomes a part of it, assimilates it to itself, develops it according to its fancy, and finishes it if it can. The thing is done without effort, without reaction, in accordance with a natural and tranquil law. It is like a budding graft, like circulating sap, like renewed vegetation. Certainly, there is matter for many big books, and often for the universal history of humanity, in these successive weldings of various forms of art at various levels upon one and the same structure. The man, the artist, and the individual are obliterated in these huge anonymous piles; they represent the sum total of human intelligence. Time is the architect, the nation is the mason.

Considering here Christian European architecture only, that younger sister of the grand piles of the Orient, we may say that it strikes the eye as a vast formation divided into three very distinct zones or layers, one resting upon the other; the Roman zone, the Gothic zone, the zone of the Renaissance, which may be called the Greco-Roman. The

Roman stratum, which is the oldest and the lowest, is occupied by the semicircular arch, which reappears, together with the Greek column, in the modern and uppermost stratum of the Renaissance. The pointed arch is between the two. The buildings belonging to any one of these three strata are perfectly distinct, uniform, and complete. Such are the Abbey of Jumiéges, the Cathedral of Rheims, the Church of the Holy Cross at Orleans. But the three zones are blended and mingled at the edges, like the colours in the solar spectrum. Hence, we have certain complex structures, buildings of gradation and transition, which may be Roman at the base, Gothic in the middle, and Greco-Roman at the top. This is caused by the fact that it took six hundred years to build such a fabric. This variety is rare. The donjon-keep at Etampes is a specimen. But monuments of two formations are more frequent. Such is Notre-Dame at Paris, a structure of the pointed arch, its earliest columns leading directly to that Roman zone, of which the portal of Saint-Denis and the nave of Saint-Germain des Prés are perfect specimens. Such is the charming semi-Gothic chapter-house of Bocherville, where the Roman layer reaches midway. Such is the cathedral of Rouen, which would be wholly Gothic if the tip of its central spire did not dip into the zone of the Renaissance.

However, all these gradations and differences affect the surface only of an edifice. Art has but changed its skin. The construction itself of the Christian church is not affected by them. The interior arrangement, the logical order of the parts, is still the same. Whatever may be the carved and nicely wrought exterior of a cathedral, we always find beneath it, if only in a rudimentary and dormant state, the Roman basilica. It rises forever from the ground in harmony with the same law. There are invariably two naves intersecting each other in the form of a cross, the upper end being rounded into a chancel or choir; there are always side aisles, for processions and for chapels, a sort of lateral galleries or walks, into which the principal nave opens by means of the spaces between the columns. This settled, the number of chapels, doors, steeples, and spires may be modified indefinitely according to the fancy of the century, the people, and the art. The performance of divine service once provided for and assured, architecture acts its own pleasure. Statues, stained glass, rose-windows, arabesques, denticulations, capitals, and bas-reliefs,—it combines all these flowers of the fancy according to the logarithm that suits it best. Hence the immense variety in the exteriors of those structures within which dwell such unity and order. The trunk of the tree is fixed; the foliage is variable.

Chapter II

A Bird's-Eye View of Paris

In the last chapter we strove to restore the wonderful Church of Notre-Dame at Paris for the reader's pleasure. We briefly pointed out the greater part of the charms which it possessed in the fifteenth century and which it now lacks; but we omitted the chief beauty, —the view of Paris then to be had from the top of its towers.

It was, indeed, when after long fumbling in the gloomy spiral staircase which pierces perpendicularly the thick wall of the steeples you finally emerged suddenly upon one of the two lofty platforms bathed in sunshine and daylight, —it was, indeed, a fine picture which lay unrolled before you on every hand; a spectacle *sui generis*, as those of our readers can readily imagine who have been so fortunate as to see one of the few Gothic cities still left entire, complete, and homogeneous, such as Nuremberg in Bavaria, and Vittoria in Spain; or even smaller examples, if they be but well preserved, like Vitré in Brittany, and Nordhausen in Prussia.

The Paris of three hundred and fifty years ago, the Paris of the fifteenth century, had already attained to vast dimensions. We modern Parisians are apt to deceive ourselves in regard to the ground which we imagine we have gained since then. Paris has not grown much more than a third larger since the days of Louis XI. It has certainly lost far more in beauty than it has gained in size.

Paris was born, as every one knows, on that island of the City which is shaped like a cradle. The shores of that island were her first enclosure, the Seine her first moat. Paris remained for several centuries in the state of an island, with two bridges, one on the north, the other on the south, and two bridge-heads, at once her gates and her fortresses: the Grand-Châtelet on the right bank, the Petit Châtelet on the left. With the first line of kings, being pressed for room in her island, back of which she no longer could return, Paris crossed the water. Then, beyond the two Châtelets, the first enclosing line of walls and towers began to encroach upon the country region on either side the Seine. Some traces of this ancient boundary wall still existed in the last century; now, nothing but the memory of it survives, and here and there a local tradition, like the Porte des Baudets or Baudoyer, *Porta Bagauda*. Little by little the flood of houses, perpetually driven from the centre of the city, overflowed, made breaches in, and wore away this enclosure. Philip Augustus made a new embankment, and confined Paris within a circular chain of great towers, tall and solid. For more than a hundred years the houses pressed one upon the other, accumulated and raised their level within this basin, like water in a reservoir. They began to grow higher; they added story to story; they climbed one upon the other; they leaped up in height like any repressed fluid, vying each with the other in raising its head above its neighbour's to get a little air. The streets became deeper and narrower; every vacant space was filled up and disappeared. The houses at last leaped the wall of Philip Augustus, scattered merrily over the plain irregularly and all awry, like so many school-boys let loose. There they strutted proudly about, cut themselves gardens from the fields, and took their ease. By 1367 the city had extended so far into the suburbs that a new boundary wall was needed, particularly on the right bank of the river; Charles V. built it. But a city like Paris is in a perpetual state of growth. It is only such cities which ever become capitals. They are funnels into which flow all the geographical, political, and intellectual watersheds of a country, all the natural tendencies of a nation; wells of civilization, as it were, and also sewers, into which trade, commerce, intellect, population, all the vigour, all the life, all the soul of a nation unceasingly filter and collect, drop by drop, century after century. Charles V.'s boundary wall followed in the footsteps of that of Philip Augustus. By the end of the fifteenth century, it was overtaken, left behind, and the suburbs advanced yet farther. In the sixteenth, the wall seemed to recede visibly, and to be more and more deeply buried in the old city, so thickly did the new town spring up outside it. Thus, in the fifteenth century, to stop there, Paris had already worn out the three concentric circles of walls, which in the time of Julian the Apostate were, as we may say, in the germ, in the Grand-Châtelet and the Petit-Châtelet. The mighty city rent asunder its four girdles of ramparts in succession, like a child outgrowing his last year's clothes. Under Louis XI., groups of the ruined towers belonging to the old enclosure rose here and there from the sea of houses like hill-tops after a flood,— archipelagoes, as it were, of the old Paris submerged beneath the new.

Since then Paris has, unfortunately for us, undergone another transformation, but has crossed only one more wall, that of Louis XV.,—that miserable rampart of lath and plaster, worthy of the king who built it, worthy of the poet who celebrated it in a verse defying translation:—

"Le mur murant Paris rend
Paris murmurant."

In the fifteenth century, Paris was still divided into three quite distinct and separate cities, each possessing its own physiognomy, peculiar features, manners, customs, privileges, and history,— the City, the University, and the Town. The City, which occupied the island, was the oldest, the smallest, and the mother of the other two, crowded in between them (if we may be allowed the comparison) like a little old woman between two tall, handsome daughters. The University covered the left bank of the Seine, from the Tournelle to the Tour de Nesle,—points corresponding in the Paris of to-day to the Wine-market and the Mint. Its precincts infringed boldly upon the region where Julian built his baths. St. Geneviève's Mount was included in this division. The culminating point of this curve of walls was the Porte Papale; that is, just about where the Pantheon now stands. The Town, which was the largest of the three parts of Paris, held possession of the right bank of the river. Its quay, broken and interrupted at various points, ran along the Seine, from the Tour de Billy to the Tour du Bois; that is, from the present site of the Public Granaries to the present site of the Tuileries. These four points, at which the river intersected the precincts of the capital; the Tournelle and the Tour de Nesle on the left, the Tour de Billy and the Tour du Bois on the right, were called the "Four Towers of Paris," by way of distinction. The Town extended even farther into the country than the University. The extreme limits of the Town (in the time of Charles V.) were the Portes Saint-Denis and Saint-Martin, the situation of which has not been changed.

As we have just observed, each of

these three great divisions of Paris was a city in itself, but a city too individual to be complete,—a city which could not dispense with the aid of the other two. Thus, they were utterly unlike in aspect. Churches abounded in the City, palaces in the Town, and colleges in the University. To pass over the minor eccentricities of old Paris and the caprices of those persons holding right of road, we may make the general statement—speaking only of the great masses in the chaos of communal jurisdictions —that the island was subject to the bishop, the right bank of the river to the provost, and the left bank to the rector; the Provost or Mayor of Paris, a royal and not a municipal officer, having authority over them all. The City contained Notre-Dame, the Town the Louvre and the Hôtel de Ville, and the University the College of the Sorbonne. The Town contained the Markets, the City the Hospital, the University the Pré-aux-Clercs. For any offence committed by a student on the left bank of the river, he was tried upon the island at the Palace of Justice, or law courts, and punished on the right bank, at Montfaucon, unless the rector, finding the University strong and the king weak, interfered; for it was one of the privileges of the students to be hanged in their own domain.

(The majority of these privileges, it may be noted in passing,—and there were many more desirable than this,— had been extorted from various kings by riots and revolts. This is the traditional course of things: a French proverb declares that the king only grants what the people wrest from him. There is an ancient charter which states the fact with much simplicity; speaking of loyalty, it says: *"Civibus fidelitas in reges, quæ tamen aliquoties seditionibus interrupta, multa peperit privilegia."*)

In the fifteenth century, the Seine washed the shores of five islets within the precincts of Paris: the Ile Louviers, where there were then trees, and where there is now nothing but wood; the Ile aux Vaches and the Ile Notre-Dame, both deserted, save for a single structure, both held in fee by the bishop (in the seventeenth century, these two islands were made into one, now known as the Ile Saint-Louis); and lastly, the City, and at its extreme end the islet of the Passeur aux Vaches, since submerged beneath the platform of the Pont-Neuf. The City had then five bridges: three on the right,—the Pont Notre-Dame and Pont au Change, of stone, the Pont aux Meuniers, of wood; two on the left side,—the Petit-Pont, of stone, the Pont Saint-Michel, of wood: all built over with houses. The University had six gates, built by Philip Augustus; starting from the Tournelle, there were the Porte Saint-Victor, the Porte Bordelle, the Porte Papale, the Porte Saint-Jacques, the Porte Saint-Michel, the Porte Saint-Germain. The Town had six gates, built by Charles V.; starting from the Tour de Billy, there were the Porte Saint-Antoine, the Porte du Temple, the Porte Saint-Martin, the Porte Saint-Denis, the Porte Montmartre, and the Porte Saint-Honoré. All these gates were strong, and handsome also, which does not detract from strength. A broad, deep moat, whose waters ran rapidly during winter floods, washed the foot of the walls all around Paris, the Seine providing the water. At night the gates were closed, the river barred at each end of the town by great iron chains, and Paris slept in peace.

A bird's-eye view of these three boroughs—the City, the University, and the Town—presented an inextricable network of streets strangely entangled. But still, even at first sight, it was apparent that these three fragments of a city formed but one body. One saw at once two long parallel streets, without break or deviation, running almost in a straight line, and traversing the three towns from end to end, from north to south, perpendicular to the Seine, connecting them, uniting them, infusing, pouring, and incessantly decanting the people of the one into the precincts of the other, and making of the three but one. One of these two streets led from the Porte Saint-Jacques to the Porte Saint-Martin; it was known as Rue Saint-Jacques in the University, Rue de la Juiverie in the City, Rue Saint-Martin in the Town; it crossed the water twice under the name of the Petit-Pont and the Pont Notre-Dame.

The other, known as Rue de la Harpe on the left bank of the river, Rue de la Barillerie on the island, Rue Saint-Denis on the right bank, Pont Saint-Michel over one arm of the Seine, Pont au Change over the other, ran from the Porte Saint-Michel in the University to the Porte Saint-Denis in the Town. And yet, under all these various names, they were still the same two streets, the two parent streets, the two original streets, the two arteries of Paris. All the other veins of the triple town proceeded from or emptied into them.

Independently of these two diametrical main streets, traversing the entire breadth of Paris, and common to the whole capital, the University and Town had each its individual street, traversing its length, parallel to the Seine, and crossing the two arterial streets at right angles. Thus, in the Town, one could go in a straight line from the Porte Saint-Antoine to the Porte Saint-Honoré; in the University, from the Porte Saint-Victor the the Porte Saint-Germain. These two great roads, crossing the two first mentioned, made the canvas upon which was wrought the knotted and tangled Dædalian web of the streets of Paris. By careful study of the unintelligible design of this network, one might also distinguish—like two sheaves of wheat stretching, one into the University, the other into the Town —two bunches of great streets leading from the bridges to the gates. Something of this geometric plan still exists.

We shall now attempt to give some idea of the general view seen from the top of the towers of Notre-Dame.

To the spectator who reached this pinnacle in a breathless condition, all was at first a dazzling sea of roofs, chimneys, streets, bridges, squares, spires, and steeples. Everything burst upon his vision, at once,—the carved gable, the steep roof, the turret hanging from the angles of the walls, the eleventh-century stone pyramid, the fifteenth-century slate obelisk, the round bare tower of the donjon-keep, the square elaborately wrought tower of the church, the great, the small, the massive, and the light. The eye wandered for a time, plunging deep down into this labyrinth, where there was no one thing destitute of originality, purpose, genius, and beauty, nothing uninspired by art, from the tiniest house with carved and painted front, outside timbers, surbased door, and overhanging stories, to the royal Louvre, which then had a colonnade of towers. But the principal masses to be seen when the eye became wonted to this medley of buildings were as follows:—

First, the City. "The island of the City," as says Sauval, who, in spite of his nonsense, sometimes hits upon a happy phrase,—"the island of the City is shaped like a huge ship buried in the mud and stranded in the current towards the middle of the Seine." We have just explained that in the fifteenth century this ship was moored to the shores of the stream by five bridges. This likeness to a vessel also struck the heraldic scribes; for it is thence, and not from the Norman siege, say Favyn and Pasquier, that the ship blazoned on the ancient shield of Paris is taken. To him who can decipher it, the science of heraldry is another algebra, the science of heraldry is a language. The whole history of the second half of the Middle Ages is written out in heraldry, as is the history of the first half in the symbolism of the Roman Church. The hieroglyphs of feudalism follow those of theocracy.

The City, then, first fell upon the eye with its stern to the east and its prow to the west. Facing the prow, the spectator saw a countless collection of ancient roofs, above which rose, broad and round, the leaden bolster of the Sainte-Chapelle, like an elephant's back laden with its tower. Only in this case the tower was the most daring, the most daintily wrought, the most delicately carved spire that ever gave glimpses of the sky through its lace-like cone. In front of Notre-Dame, close at hand, three streets emptied into the space in front of the cathedral,—a beautiful square lined with old houses. Over the southern side of this square hung the wrinkled and frowning front of the Hospital, or Hôtel-Dieu, and its roof, which seemed covered with warts and pimples. Then to the left, to the right, to the east, to the west, throughout the City limits, narrow as they were, rose the steeples of its one-and-twenty churches of every age, of every form and every size, from the low, worm-eaten Roman campanile of Saint-Denis du Pas (*carcer Glaucini*) to the slender spires of Saint-Pierre aux Bœufs and Saint-Landry. Behind Notre-Dame were revealed, on the north, the cloisters with their Gothic galleries; on the south, the semi-Roman palace of the bishop; on the east, the borders of the Terrain, a plot of waste land. Amid this accumulation of houses, by the tall mitres made of openwork stone, which crowned the highest windows of the palace, then placed even in the very roof, the eye could also distinguish the hotel given by the town in the reign of Charles VI. to Juvénal des Ursins; a little farther away, the tarred booths of the Palus Market; elsewhere, again, the new chancel of Saint-Germain le Vieux, pieced out in 1458 with a bit of the Rue aux Febves; and then, at intervals, a square crowded with people; a pillory set up at some street corner; a fine fragment of the pavement of Philip Augustus,—superb flagging laid in the middle of the road, and furrowed to prevent horses from slipping, which was so ill replaced in the sixteenth century by the wretched flints and pebbles known as the "pavement of the League;" a deserted back yard with one of those open turret staircases which were common in the fifteenth century, and an example of which may still be seen in the Rue des Bourdonnais. Finally, to the right of the Sainte-Chapelle, towards the west, the Palace of Justice reared its group of towers on the water's edge. The tall trees of the king's gardens, which covered the western end of the City, hid the Ile du Passeur. As for the water, from the top of the towers of Notre-Dame it was barely visible on either side of the City: the Seine was concealed by bridges, the bridges by houses.

And if the spectator looked beyond those bridges, the roofs of which were of a greenish tint, mouldy before their time by the damp vapours rising from the water, if he turned to the left in the direction of the University, the first building which attracted him was a broad, low group of towers, the Petit-Châtelet, whose wide-mouthed porch swallowed up the end of the Petit-Pont; then, if his eye followed the shore from east to west, from the Tournelle to the Tour de Nesle, he saw a long line of houses with carved beams and stained-glass windows, overhanging the pavement story upon story, an endless zigzag of homely gables, often interrupted by the mouth of some street, and sometimes also by the front or the projecting corner of a huge stone mansion, spreading out its courtyards and gardens, its wings and its main buildings, quite at its ease amid this mob of narrow crowded houses, like a great lord in a rabble of rustic clowns. There were five or six of these mansions on the quay, from the house of Lorraine, which shared the great monastery enclosure next the Tournelle with the Bernardines, to the family mansion of the de Nesles, the main tower of which bounded Paris on that side, and whose painted roofs for three months in the year slivered the scarlet disk of the setting sun with their dark triangles.

This side of the Seine, moreover, was the less commercial of the two; students were noisier and more numerous than labourers, and, properly speaking, the quay extended only from the Pont Saint-Michel to the Tour de Nesle. The rest of the river-bank was now a bare beach, as beyond the Bernardine monastery, and then again a mass of houses washed by the water, as between the two bridges.

There was a vast clamour of washerwomen; they shouted, chattered, and sang from morning till night along the shore, and beat the linen hard, as they do in our day. This is not the least part of the gaiety of Paris.

The University presented a huge mass to the eye. From one end to the other it was a compact and homogeneous whole. The myriad roofs, close-set, angular, adherent, almost all composed of the same geometrical elements, looked from above like a crystallization of one substance. The fantastic hollows of the streets divided this pasty of houses into tolerably equal slices. The forty-two colleges were distributed about quite evenly, there being some in every quarter. The delightfully varied pinnacles of these fine structures were the product of the same art as the simple roofs which they crowned, being really but a multiplication of the square or cube of the same geometrical figure. In this way they made the sum total more intricate without rendering it confused, and completed without overloading the general effect. Geometry is harmony. Certain handsome mansions here and there stood out superbly among the picturesque garrets on the left bank of the river, —the Nevers house, the house of Rome, the Rheims house, which have all disappeared; the Hôtel de Cluny, still standing for the consolation of artists, and the tower of which was so stupidly lowered some years since. That Roman palace near Cluny, with its beautiful arches, was formerly the Baths of Julian. There were also a number of abbeys of a beauty more religious, a grandeur more severe, than the mansions, but no less splendid, no less spacious. Those first attracting the eye were the monastery of the Bernardines, with its three spires; Sainte-Geneviève, whose square tower, still standing, makes us regret the rest so much; the Sorbonne, half college, half monastery, of which the fine nave still remains; the elegant quadrangular cloister of the Mathurin friars; its neighbour, the cloister of St. Benedict, within the walls of which a theatre has been knocked up in the interval between the seventh and eighth editions of this book; the Franciscan abbey, with its three enormous gables side by side; the house of the Austin friars, whose graceful spire was, after the Tour de Nesle, the second lofty landmark on this side of Paris, looking westward. The colleges, which are in fact the connecting link between the convent and the world, formed the central point in the series of buildings between secular and religious houses, with a severity full of elegance, their sculptures being less meaningless than those of the palaces, their architecture not so sober as that of the monasteries. Unfortunately, scarcely anything is left of these monuments in which Gothic art hit so happy a medium between richness and economy; the churches (and they were many and splendid in the University quarter, representing every period of architecture, from the semicircular arches of St. Julian to the painted arches of St. Severius) predominated over everything else; and, like one harmony the more in that mass of harmonies, they broke through the varied sky-line of gables ever and anon with their sharp spires, their open steeples, and their slender pinnacles, whose line was but a magnificent exaggeration of the steep pitch of the roofs.

The ground on which the University stood was hilly. St. Geneviève's Mount formed a huge wen to the southeast; and it was a sight well worth seeing, to look down from the top of Notre-Dame upon that crowd of narrow, winding streets (now the Latin Quarter), and those close clusters of houses which, scattered in every direction from the summit of the height, seemed hurrying haphazard and almost perpendicularly down its sides to the water's edge, some apparently falling, others climbing up again, all clinging together for mutual support. The constant ebb and flow of a myriad black dots crossing and recrossing each other on the pavement lent a shimmering and indistinct look to everything; these were the people seen from a height and a distance.

Lastly, in the spaces between these

roofs, these spires, these unnumbered and irregular structures which curved and twisted and indented the outline of the University in so odd a fashion, might be seen at intervals a big bit of mossy wall, a thick round tower, or an embattled city gate, representing the fortress: this was the wall of Philip Augustus. Beyond were the green fields, and beyond these ran the roads, along which stretched a few suburban houses, becoming fewer in number as the distance increased. Some of these suburbs were of considerable importance: there was first, starting from the Tournelle, the borough of Saint-Victor, with its single arched bridge across the Bièvre; its abbey, where one might read the epitaph of Louis the Fat,—*epitaphium Ludovici Grossi;* and its church with an octagonal steeple flanked by four eleventh-century belfries (there is a similar one at Etampes, which has not yet been destroyed); then the borough of Saint-Marceau, which possessed three churches and a convent; then, leaving the Gobelins factory and its four white walls on the left, came the suburb of Saint-Jacques, with the beautiful carved cross in the market-place; the Church of Saint-Jacques du Haut-Pas, which was then Gothic, pointed and delightful; Saint-Magloire, with a fine fourteenth-century nave, which Napoleon turned into a hayloft; Notre-Dame des Champs, where there were Byzantine mosaics; lastly, leaving in the open country the Carthusian monastery, a rich edifice of the same date as the Palace of Justice, with its little private gardens, and the ill-famed ruins of Vauvert, the eye fell, to the westward, upon the three Roman spires of Saint-Germain des Prés. The borough of Saint-Germain, even then a large parish, included fifteen or twenty streets in the rear; the sharp spire of Saint-Sulpice formed one of the boundaries of the borough. Close beside it might be seen the square enclosure of the Saint-Germain fair-ground, where the market now stands; then the abbot's pillory, a pretty little round tower neatly capped with a leaden cone; the tile-kiln was farther on, as were the Rue du Four, leading to the town ovens, the mill on its knoll, and the hospital for lepers, —a small isolated building shunned by all. But the thing which particularly attracted and held attention was the abbey itself. It is certain that this monastery which held high rank both as a church and as a manor, this abbatial palace where the bishops of Paris held themselves happy to be allowed to pass a night, that refectory to which the architect had given the air, the beauty, and the splendid rose-window of a cathedral, that elegant Lady Chapel, that vast dormitory, those great gardens, that portcullis, that drawbridge, the battlements which intrenched upon the verdure of the surrounding fields, the courtyards glittering with men-at-arms mingled with golden copes, all grouped and combined around the three tall spires with their semicircular arches, firmly planted upon a Gothic chancel, made a magnificent figure on the horizon.

When at length, after close study of the University, the spectator turned towards the Town, the character of the view changed abruptly. The Town, in fact, though much larger than the University, was less of a unity. At the first glance it seemed to be divided into several strangely distinct masses. First, to the east, in that part of the town which still retains the name of the Marais, derived from the marsh in which Camulogenes mired Cæsar, there were a number of palaces. The buildings extended to the water's edge. Four mansions, so close together as to be almost connected,—the homes of the Jouy, Sens, Barbeau families, and the queen's residence,—mirrored their slated roofs, broken by slender turrets, in the Seine. These four buildings occupied the region between the Rue des Nonaindières and the Celestine Abbey, whose spire formed a graceful contrast to their line of battlements and gables. Certain moss-grown structures, overhanging the water in front of these sumptuous mansions, did not hide the fine outlines of their façades, their broad square windows with stone casements, their porches with pointed arches overloaded with statues, the sharp clear-cut edges of their walls, and all those dainty architectural accidents which make Gothic art seem as if it began a fresh series of combinations with every new building. Behind these palaces, stretched on every hand, here broken, palisaded, and crenelated like a citadel, here concealed amid tall trees like a monastery, the vast and varied wall around that marvellous Hôtel Saint-Pol, where the king had sufficient space to lodge luxuriously twenty-two princes of the rank of the Dauphin and the Duke of Burgundy, with their servants and suites, to say nothing of great lords, and the Emperor himself when he visited Paris, and the lions, which had a separate residence in the royal establishment. Let us say here that the apartment of a prince at this period comprised no less than eleven rooms, from the audience chamber to the oratory, not to mention the galleries, baths, stove-rooms, and other "superfluous places" with which each apartment was provided; not to mention the private gardens for each guest of the king; not to mention the kitchens, cellars, offices, and general refectories of the house; the servants' quarters, where there were twenty-two offices, from the bakehouse to the wine-cellars; the games of various sorts, mall, tennis, riding at the ring, etc.; aviaries, fish-ponds, poultry-yards, stables, cow-houses, libraries, arsenals, and foundries. Such was a royal palace of that period, a Louvre, a Hôtel Saint-Pol,—a city within a city.

From the tower where in fancy we stand, the Hôtel Saint-Pol, almost half concealed by the four great mansions just mentioned, was yet very vast and very wonderful to behold. Although skilfully joined to the main building by long glazed and columned galleries, the three residences which Charles V. had added to his palace were readily to be distinguished: the Hôtel du Petit-Muce, with the open-work balustrade so gracefully bordering its roof; the house of the Abbot of St. Maur, having the aspect of a stronghold, a great tower, bastions, loop-holes, iron cowls, and over the wide Saxon gateway, the abbot's escutcheon between the two grooves for the drawbridge; the residence of the Count d'Etampes, whose donjon-keep, in ruins at the top, was round and notched like a cock's comb; here and there three or four low bushy old oak-trees grew close together, looking like huge cauliflowers; swans sported in the clear waters of the fish-ponds, rippled with light and shade; numerous courtyards afforded picturesque glimpses; the Hôtel des Lions, with its low pointed arches resting upon short Saxon pillars, its iron portcullises and its never-ending roar; rising above all this, the scaly spire of the Ave-Maria; to the left, the house of the provost of Paris, flanked by four delicately designed turrets; in the centre, in the background, the Hôtel Saint-Pol itself, properly so called, with its myriad façades, its successive embellishments from Charles V.'s day down, the hybrid excrescences with which the caprice of architects had loaded it during the lapse of two centuries, with all the chancels of its chapels, all the gables of its galleries, its endless weathercocks, and its two tall adjacent towers, whose conical roofs, bordered with battlements at their base, looked like cocked hats.

Still climbing the various stages of this amphitheatre of palaces rising in the distance, after crossing a deep ravine cut through the house-roofs of the Town, which marked the passage of the Rue Saint-Antoine, the eye fell upon the D'Angoulême mansion, a vast structure built at different periods, and containing very new and shining portions, which harmonized with the general effect no better than a red patch with a blue doublet. Still, the oddly steep, high roof of the modern palace, bristling with carved gutters, covered with sheets of lead over which rolled sparkling incrustations of gilded copper in a thousand fanciful arabesques,—the curiously damascened roof soared airily and gracefully aloft in the midst of the dark ruins of the ancient edifice, whose antique towers, bulging like casks, from old age, were bowed down by the weight of years and rent asunder from top to bottom. Behind them rose the forest of spires of the Palace of the Tournelles. No view in the world, not even from Chambord or the Alhambra, could be more magical, more airy, more enchanting than this wilderness of spires, steeples, chimneys, vanes, winding staircases, wrought lanterns which looked as if struck out with a die, pavilions and spindle-shaped turrets, or tournelles, all varying in form, height, and position. It might well be compared to a gigantic stone chess-board.

That group of enormous inky-black towers, one melting into the other, and as it were bound together by a circular moat; that donjon-keep more thickly pierced with loopholes than with windows; that drawbridge forever raised and that portcullis forever down, to the right of the Tournelles, is the Bastille. Those black muzzles peering from the battlements, and which from this distance might pass for gutter-spouts, are cannon.

Within gunshot, below the terrible edifice, is the Porte Saint-Antoine, quite hidden between its two towers.

Beyond the Tournelles, as far as the wall of Charles V., stretched an expanse of beds of shrubs and flowers, and velvety lawns, the royal parks, amidst which the Dædalus garden, given by Louis XI. to Coictier, was easily to be distinguished by its labyrinth of trees and winding walks. The doctor's laboratory rose from the maze like a great solitary column with a tiny house for capital. In this small dwelling dread predictions of astrology were concocted.

The Place Royale now stands upon this spot.

As we have just observed, the region

of the Palace—some idea of which we have striven to give the reader, although alluding to its principal features only—filled up the angle formed on the east by the Seine and the boundary wall of Charles V. The heart of the Town was occupied by a group of common houses. There the three bridges leading from the City discharged themselves upon the right bank; and bridges lead to the building of houses rather than of palaces. This collection of ordinary houses, crowded together like cells in a hive, was not without a beauty of its own. The roofs of a great city have a certain grandeur, like the waves of the sea. In the first place, the streets, crossed and intertangled, formed a hundred droll figures; around the markets, they looked like a myriad-rayed star. The Rues Saint-Denis and Saint-Martin, with their endless ramifications, climbed the hill side by side, like two great trees with intermingling branches; and then crooked lines, like the Rues de la Plâtrerie, de la Verrerie, de la Tixeranderie, etc., twisted and wound in and out among the whole. There were also fine structures piercing through the fixed swell of this sea of gables. At the end of the Pont aux Changeurs, behind which the Seine foamed beneath the wheels of the Pont aux Meuniers, there was the Châtelet, no longer a Roman tower, as in the days of Julian the Apostate, but a feudal tower of the thirteenth century, and constructed of a stone so hard that three hours' work with the pick could not remove a piece the size of a man's fist; there was the superb square bell-tower of Saint-Jacques de la Boucherie, all its angles softened by sculptures, even then worthy of admiration, although it was not finished in the fifteenth century. (It lacked particularly those four monsters which even yet, perched on the corners of its roof, look like four sphinxes giving modern Paris the riddle of the ancient Paris to solve. Rault the sculptor put them up in 1526, and he was paid only twenty francs for his pains!) There was the Pillar House, opening on the Grève, of which we have already given the reader some idea; there was Saint-Gervais, which a porch "in good taste" has since spoiled; Saint-Méry, whose old pointed arches were a close approach to the semicircular; Saint-Jean, whose magnificent spire had passed into a proverb; there were at least twenty other edifices, which did not disdain to bury their marvels in this wilderness of deep, dark, and narrow streets. Add to this the carved stone crosses, even more abundant at cross-roads than gibbets; the Cemetery of the Innocents, whose wall, a fine specimen of architecture, was visible from a distance, over the house-tops; the market pillory, the top of which peeped between two chimneys in the Rue de la Cossonnerie; the "ladder" of the Croix-du-Trahoir at the cross-roads, always black with people; the circular booths of the Corn-market; the remains of the ancient wall of Philip Augustus, visible here and there, lost among the houses, towers overgrown with ivy, ruined gates, crumbling, shapeless fragments of masonry; the quay with its countless shops and its bloody knackers' yards; the Seine, covered with boats, from the Port au Foin to For-l'Evêque, —and you will have a dim idea of what the central portion of the town was in 1482.

Together with these two quarters,—the one of princely mansions, the other of ordinary houses,—the third element in the view of the Town was a long belt of abbeys bordering almost its entire circumference from east to west, and forming a second inner circle of convents and chapels in addition to the circle of fortifications enclosing Paris. Thus, close beside the Tournelles Park, between the Rue Saint-Antoine and the old Rue du Temple, there was a Sainte-Catherine with its immense grounds, bounded only by the city walls. Between the old and the new Rue du Temple there was the Temple,—a gloomy group of towers, tall, straight, lonely in the midst of a vast battlement enclosure. Between the Rue Neuve du Temple and the Rue Saint-Martin there was the Abbey of Saint-Martin, in its gardens, a superb fortified church, whose engirdling towers, whose coronet of spires, only yielded in strength and splendour to those of Saint-Germain des Prés. Between the Rues Saint-Martin and Saint-Denis were the precincts of the Convent of the Trinity. Lastly, between the Rue Saint-Denis and the Rue Montorgueil was the Convent of the Daughters of God. Close by might be seen the rotting roofs and unpaved district of the Court of Miracles. This was the only profane link in this pious chain of convents.

Lastly, the fourth division clearly outlined in the conglomeration of housetops on the right bank of the river, and occupying the western angle formed by the boundary wall and the shore down stream, was still another cluster of palaces and elegant residences, nestling in the shadow of the Louvre. The old Louvre of Philip Augustus, that overgrown structure around whose great tower were grouped twenty-three towers almost as large, to say nothing of smaller turrets, seemed from a distance to be framed in the Gothic summits of the Hôtel d'Alençon and of the Petit-Bourbon. This hydra of towers, the giant guardian of Paris, with its twenty-four heads always reared aloft, with its monstrous cruppers covered with lead or scaly with slates, all dimpling and rippling with metallic reflections, made a surprising finish to the outline of the Town on the west.

An immense mass, therefore,—what the Romans called an *insula*,—of plain, homely houses, flanked on either hand by blocks of palaces, crowned, the one by the Louvre, the other by the Tournelles, bounded on the north by a long line of abbeys and cultivated fields, blending and mingling together as one gazed at them; above these countless buildings, whose tiled and slated roofs stood out in such strange outlines one against the other, the crimped, twisted, ornamented steeples of the forty-four churches of the right bank of the river; myriads of crooked streets, bounded on one side by a line of high walls with square towers (that of the University had round towers), on the other by the Seine intersected by bridges, and bearing along a wilderness of boats,—such was the Town in the fifteenth century.

Outside the walls, some few suburbs crowded to the gates; but there were not so many houses, nor were they so close together, as in the University quarter. There were, behind the Bastille, some twenty huts, built close around the Cross of Faubin with its curious carvings, and the Abbey of Saint-Antoine des Champs with its buttresses; then came Popincourt, hidden in wheat-fields; then Courtille, a jolly village of taverns; the borough of Saint-Laurent, with its church, whose steeple at a distance seemed to be a part of the pointed towers of the Porte Saint-Martin; the Faubourg Saint-Denis, with the vast enclosure of Saint-Ladre; outside the Porte Montmartre, Grange-Batelière, surrounded by white walls; behind it, with its chalky slopes, Montmartre, which then held almost as many churches as windmills, and which has kept only the mills,—for society now prefers material to spiritual bread. Lastly, beyond the Louvre the Faubourg Saint-Honoré, even then of considerable extent, stretched away into the fields, and Little Britain looked green in the distance, and the Pig-market was plainly visible, in the midst of it the horrible caldron for boiling alive coiners of counterfeit money. Between Courtille and Saint-Laurent the eye noted, on the summit of a height situated in the midst of bare plains, a sort of structure looking from a distance like a ruined colonnade standing upon bare foundations. It was neither a Parthenon nor a temple to Olympian Jove; it was Montfaucon.

Now, if the list of so many buildings, brief as we have tried to make it, has not destroyed, as fast as we constructed it, in the reader's mind the general outlines of old Paris, we will sum up our description in a few words. In the centre, the island of the City, shaped like a huge turtle, and protruding its bridges, scaly with tiles, like feet, from under its grey shell of roofs. To the left, the close, compact, crowded, monolithic trapezium of the University; to the right, the vast semicircle of the Town, where houses and gardens were much more mingled,—the three districts, City, University and Town, veined with countless streets. In and out, through the whole, ran the Seine,—"the nourishing Seine," as Father du Breuil calls it,—obstructed with islands, bridges, and boats; all around an immense plain, green with a thousand different crops, and sprinkled with lovely villages: to the left, Issy, Vanvres, Vaugirard, Montrouge, Gentilly with its round tower and its square tower, etc.; to the right, a score of others, from Conflans to Ville-l'Evêque; on the horizon, a line of hills arranged in a circle like the rim of the basin. Finally, in the distance, to the eastward, Vincennes and its seven quadrangular towers; to the south, Bicêtre, and its pointed turrets; to the north, Saint-Denis and its spire; to the west, Saint-Cloud and its donjon. Such was Paris as seen from the top of the towers of Notre-Dame by the ravens who lived in 1482.

And yet it was of this city that Voltaire said that "before the time of Louis XIV. it possessed but four handsome public buildings": the dome of the Sorbonne, the Val-de-Grâce, the modern Louvre, and the fourth I have forgotten, —possibly the Luxembourg. Fortunately, Voltaire wrote "Candide" all the same, and is still, in spite of this criticism, of all men who have succeeded one another in the long series of humanity, the one who was most perfect master of sardonic laughter. This proves, moreover, that one may be a great genius and yet understand nothing of other people's art. Did not

Molière think he honoured Raphael and Michael Angelo when he called them "those Mignards of their age"?

Let us return to Paris and the fifteenth century.

It was not only a beautiful city; it was a uniform, consistent city, an architectural and historic product of the Middle Ages, a chronicle in stone. It was a city formed of two strata only,— the bastard Roman and the Gothic; for the pure Roman stratum had long since disappeared, except in the Baths of Julian, where it still broke through the thick crust of the Middle Ages. As for the Celtic stratum, no specimen was now to be found even in the digging of wells.

Fifty years later, when the Renaissance added to this severe and yet varied unity the dazzling luxury of its fantasy and its systems, its riotous wealth of Roman semicircular arches, Greek columns, and Gothic foundations, its tender and ideal sculpture, its peculiar taste for arabesques and acanthus-leaves, its architectural paganism, contemporary with Luther, Paris was perhaps still more beautiful, although less harmonious to the eye and intellect. But this splendid moment was of brief duration, the Renaissance was not impartial; not content with building up, it desired to pull down: true, it needed space. Thus Gothic Paris was complete for an instant only. Saint-Jacques de la Boucherie was scarcely finished when the destruction of the old Louvre began.

Since then the great city has grown daily more and more deformed. Gothic Paris, which swallowed up the Paris of the bastard Roman period, vanished in its turn; but who can say what manner of Paris has replaced it?

There is the Paris of Catherine de Médicis, at the Tuileries; the Paris of Henry II., at the Hôtel de Ville, or Town Hall,—two buildings still in the best taste; the Paris of Henry IV., at the Place Royale,—brick fronts, with stone corners and slated roofs, tricoloured houses; the Paris of Louis XIII., at the Val-de-Grâce,—a squat, dumpy style of architecture, basket-handle vaults, something corpulent about the columns, something crook-backed about the dome; the Paris of Louis XIV., at the Invalides,—grand, rich, gilded, and cold; the Paris of Louis XV., at Saint-Sulpice,—volutes, knots of ribbon, clouds, vermicelli, and chiccory, all in stone; the Paris of Louis XVI., at the Pantheon, —a poor copy of St. Peter's at Rome (the building has settled awkwardly, which has not corrected its lines); the Paris of the Republic at the Medical School,—a poor bit of Greek and Roman taste, no more like the Coliseum or the Parthenon than the Constitution of the year III. is like the laws of Minos; it is known in architecture as "the Messidor style;" the Paris of Napoleon, at the Place Vendôme: this is sublime,— a bronze column made from captured cannon; the Paris of the Restoration, at the Exchange,—a very white colonnade supporting a very smooth frieze; the whole thing is square, and cost twenty million francs.

For each of these characteristic structures we find a certain number of houses similar in taste, style, and attitude, scattered through different quarters of the city, and easily to be recognized and dated by a trained observer. Any one who has the art of seeing can trace the spirit of a century and the physiognomy of a king even in a door-knocker.

Paris of the present day, therefore, has no general character of its own. It is a collection of specimens of various ages, and the best ones have disappeared. The capital increases in houses only, and what houses! At the rate at which Paris moves, it will be renewed every fifty years. Thus the historic significance of its architecture dies daily. Monuments of art are becoming more and more rare, and it seems as if we saw them swallowed up by degrees, lost among the houses. Our fathers had a Paris of stone; our children will have a Paris of plaster.

As for the modern monuments of new Paris, we would gladly forbear to speak of them. This is not because we do not admire them as they deserve. M. Soufflot's Sainte-Geneviève is assuredly the best fancy cake that was ever made of stone. The Palace of the Legion of Honour is also a very elegant piece of confectionery. The dome of the Cornmarket is an English jockey-cap on a large scale. The towers of Saint-Sulpice are two big clarionets, and that is a very good shape in its way; the telegraph wire, twisting and wriggling, makes a pretty diversity upon their roof. Saint-Roch has a doorway only comparable in magnificence to that of the church of Saint-Thomas d'Aquin. It has also a Calvary in high relief in a cellar, and a sun made of gilded wood. These are very marvellous matters. The lantern in the labyrinth of the Botanical Garden, too, is very ingenious. As for the Exchange, which has a Greek colonnade, Roman semicircular arches over its doors and windows, and a great elliptic vault of the period of the Renaissance, it is undoubtedly a very correct and very pure piece of architecture: the proof being, that it is crowned with an attic such as Athens never saw,—a beautiful straight line gracefully broken here and there by chimney-pots. Let us add, that if it be the rule that the architectural design of a building should be adapted to its purpose, so that this purpose shall be self-evident from one look at the edifice, we cannot too much wonder at a public building which might be indifferently a royal palace, a House of Commons, a town-hall, a college, a riding-school, a warehouse, a courthouse, a museum, a barrack, a tomb, a temple, or a theatre. And, after all, it is an Exchange! Moreover, a building should be appropriate to the climate. This is evidently built for our cold and rainy sky. It has a roof almost as flat as if it were in the Orient, so that in winter, when it snows, the roof can be swept; and it is evident that roofs were made to be swept. As for that purpose to which we alluded just now, it fulfils it marvellously well; it is an Exchange in France, as it would have been a temple in Greece. True, the architect took great pains to hide the face of the clock, which would have destroyed the purity of the fine lines of the front; but, to make amends for this, there is that colonnade which runs round the building, and under which, on high holidays or religious festivals, the theories of stock-brokers and jobbers may be solemnly unfolded.

These are doubtless very superb structures. Add any number of fine streets, entertaining and diversified like the Rue de Rivoli, and I am not without hope that Paris, seen from a balloon, may yet present that richness of outline, that wealth of detail, that diversity of aspect, that union of the grandiose and simple, of the unexpected and the beautiful, which characterize a checker-board.

Nevertheless, admirable as Paris of the present day may seem to you, recall Paris of the fifteenth century; reconstruct it in imagination; gaze at the sky through that amazing thicket of spires, steeples, and towers; let the Seine flow through the centre of the vast city, interrupt its course with islands, let it curve around the arches of its bridges in broad pools of green and yellow more variable than a serpent's skin; draw distinctly on the blue horizon the Gothic profile of old Paris; let its outlines shimmer in the fog which clings about its many chimneys; drown it in profound darkness, and watch the strange play of lights and shadows in this gloomy labyrinth of buildings; throw a moonbeam upon it which shall reveal it dimly and lift the great heads of the towers above the fog; or recall that dark picture, light up the myriad sharp angles of spire and gable as they lurk in the shadow, and make them all stand out, more indented than a shark's jaw, against the coppery sunset sky,—and then compare the two.

And if you would receive an impression from the old city which the modern one can never give you, climb, some holiday morning, say at sunrise on Easter or Whitsunday,—climb to some high point whence you overlook the whole town, and listen to the call of the chimes. See, at a signal from the sky,—for it is the sun that gives it,—those countless churches quiver simultaneously. At first a scattered tolling passes from church to church, as when musicians give notice that they are about to begin. Then, all at once, see,—for at certain moments it seems as if the ear had also its vision,—see as it were a column of sound, a vapour of harmony rise at one and the same moment from every tower. At first the vibrations of each bell ascend straight, pure, and as it were apart from the rest, into the clear morning sky; then, little by little, as they increase, they melt into one another, are blended, united, and combined into one magnificent harmony. It ceases to be anything but a mass of sonorous vibrations incessantly set loose from countless spires, floating, undulating, bounding, whirling over the city, and prolonging the deafening circle of its oscillations far beyond the horizon. Yet that sea of harmonies is not a chaos. Deep and wide as it may be, it has not lost its transparency; you may see each group of notes, as it escapes from the several chimes of bells, take its own meandering course. You may follow the dialogue, by turns solemn and shrill, between the small bell and the big bell; you may see the octaves bound from spire to spire; you watch them spring winged, light, and sibilant from the silver bell, fall maimed and halting from the wooden bell; you admire in their midst the rich gamut perpetually running up and down the seven bells of Saint-Eustache; you behold quick, clear notes dart through the whole in three or four luminous zigzags, and then vanish like lightning flashes. Yonder is the Abbey of Saint-Martin, shrill and cracked of voice; here is the surly, ominous voice of the Bastille; at the other end the great tower of the Louvre, with its counter-tenor. The royal peal of the Palace flings resplendent trills on every hand, without a pause; and upon them fall at regular intervals dull strokes from the belfry of Notre-Dame, which strike sparks from them as the hammer from the anvil. At intervals you see passing tones of every form, coming from the triple peal of Saint-Germain des Prés. Then again, from time to time this mass of sublime sounds half opens and makes way for the *stretto* of the Ave-Maria, which tinkles and flashes like a starry plume. Below, in the very heart of the harmony, you vaguely catch the inner music of the churches as it escapes through the vibrating pores of their vaulted roofs. Certainly, this is an opera worth hearing. Usually, the noise which rises up from Paris by day is the talking of the city; by night, it is the breathing of the city; but this,—this is the singing of the city. Hearken then to this *tutti* of the steeples; over all diffuse the murmur of half a million men, the never-ending murmur of the river, the endless sighing of the wind, the grave and distant quartet of the four forests ranged upon the hills in the horizon like huge organ-cases; drown, as in a demi-tint, all that would otherwise be too harsh and shrill in the central chime,—and then say if you know of anything on earth richer, more joyous, more mellow, more enchanting than this tumult of bells and chimes; than this furnace of music; than these ten thousand brazen voices singing together through stone flutes three hundred feet in length; than this city which is but an orchestra; than this symphony which roars like a tempest.

BOOK IV

Gratitude

Chapter I

KIND SOULS

It was some sixteen years previous to the date of this story, on a fine morning of the first Sunday after Easter, known in France as Quasimodo Sunday, that a living creature was laid, after Mass, in the Church of Notre-Dame, upon the bedstead fixed in the square outside, to the left of the entrance, opposite that "great image" of Saint Christopher, which the carven stone figure of Master Antoine des Essarts, knight, had contemplated on his knees until the year 1413, when it was thought proper to pull down both saint and believer. Upon this bed it was customary to expose foundlings to public charity. Whoever chose to take them, did so. In front of the bedstead was a copper basin for alms.

The sort of living creature lying on the board upon this Sunday morning, in the year of our Lord 1467, seemed to excite in a high degree the curiosity of the somewhat numerous group of people who had gathered around the bed. This group was largely composed of members of the fair sex. They were almost all old women.

In the foremost rank, and bending over the bed, were four who by their grey hoods and gowns seemed to belong to some religious community. I know no reason why history should not hand down to posterity the names of these four discreet and venerable dames. They were Agnès la Herme, Jehanne de la Tarme, Henriette la Gaultière, and Gauchère la Violette, all four widows, all four good women from the Etienne Haudry Chapel, who had come out for the day by their superior's permission, and conformably to the statutes of Pierre d'Ailly, to hear the sermon.

However, if these worthy Haudriettes were, for the time being, obeying the statutes of Pierre d'Ailly, they were certainly wilfully violating those of Michel de Brache and the Cardinal of Pisa, which so barbarously condemned them to silence.

"What on earth is it, sister?" said Agnès to Gauchère, gazing at the little foundling as it shrieked and writhed upon its bed, terrified by so many observers.

"What is the world coming to," said Jehanne, "if that is the way the children look nowadays?"

"I don't know much about children," added Agnès; "but it must surely be a sin to look at this thing."

"It's no child, Agnès."

"It's a deformed monkey," remarked Gauchère.

"It's a miracle," continued Henriette la Gaultière.

"Then," observed Agnès, "it's the third since Lætare Sunday; for it's not a week since we had the miracle of the mocker of pilgrims divinely punished by Our Lady of Aubervilliers, and that was the second miracle of the month."

"This foundling, as they call it, is a regular monster of abomination," added Jehanne.

"He howls fit to deafen a chorister," said Gauchère. "Will you hold your tongue, you little screamer!"

"To think that the Bishop of Rheims should send this monstrosity to the Bishop of Paris," went on La Gaultière, clasping her hands.

"I believe," said Agnès la Herme, "that it's a beast, an animal, a cross between a Jew and a pig; something, in fact, which is not Christian, and should be burned or drowned."

"I'm sure I hope," exclaimed La Gaultière, "that no one will offer to take it."

"Oh, good gracious!" cried Agnès, "I pity those poor nurses in the Foundling Hospital at the end of the lane, as you go down to the river, just next door to his lordship the bishop, if this little monster is given to them to suckle. I'd rather nurse a vampire."

"What a simpleton you are, poor La Herme!" cried Jehanne; "don't you see, sister, that this little wretch is at least four years old, and that he would have less appetite for your breast than for a piece of roast meat."

In fact, "the little monster" (for we ourselves should find it hard to describe him otherwise) was no new-born baby. He was a very bony and very uneasy little bundle, tied up in a linen bag marked with the monogram of M. Guillaume Chartier, then Bishop of Paris, with a head protruding from one end. This head was a most misshapen thing; there was nothing to be seen of it but a shock of red hair, an eye, a mouth, and teeth. The eye wept, the mouth shrieked, and the teeth seemed only waiting a chance to bite. The whole body kicked and struggled in the bag, to the amazement of the crowd, which grew larger and changed continually around it.

Dame Aloïse de Gondelaurier, a rich and noble lady, leading a pretty girl of some six years by the hand, and trailing a long veil from the golden horn of her headdress, stopped as she passed the bed, and glanced for an instant at the miserable creature, while her lovely little daughter Fleur-de-Lys de Gondelaurier, arrayed in silk and velvet, spelled out with her pretty little finger the permanent inscription fastened to the bedstead: "For Foundlings."

"Really," said the lady, turning away in disgust, "I thought they only put children here!"

She turned her back, throwing into the basin a silver coin which jingled loudly among the copper pence, and made the four good women from the Etienne Haudry Home stare.

A moment later, the grave and learned Robert Mistricolle, prothonotary to the king, passed with a huge missal under one arm and his wife under the other (Damoiselle Guillemette la Mairesse), being thus armed on either hand with his spiritual and his temporal advisers.

"A foundling," said he, after examination, "found apparently on the shores of the river Phlegethon!"

"It sees with but one eye," remarked Damoiselle Guillemette; "there is a wart over the other."

"That is no wart," replied Master Robert Mistricolle; "that is an egg which holds just such another demon, who also bears another little egg containing another demon, and so on *ad infinitum.*"

"How do you know?" asked Guillemette la Mairesse.

"I know it for very good reasons," answered the prothonotary.

"Mr. Prothonotary," inquired Gauchère la Violette, "what do you predict from this pretended foundling?"

"The greatest misfortunes," replied Mistricolle.

"Ah, good heavens!" said an old woman in the audience; "no wonder we had such a great plague last year, and that they say the English are going to land at Harfleur!"

"Perhaps it will prevent the queen from coming to Paris in September," added another; "and trade's so bad already!"

"It is my opinion," cried Jehanne de la Tarme, "that it would be better for the people of Paris if this little sorcerer here were laid on a fagot rather than a board,"

"A fine flaming fagot!" added the old woman.

"That would be more prudent," said Mistricolle.

For some moments a young priest had been listening to the arguments of the Haudriettes and the sententious decrees of the prothonotary. His was a stern face, with a broad brow and penetrating eye. He silently put aside the crowd, examined the "little sorcerer," and stretched his hand over him. It was high time; for all the godly old women were already licking their lips at the thought of the "fine flaming fagot."

"I adopt this child," said the priest.

He wrapped it in his cassock and bore it away. The spectators looked after him with frightened eyes. A moment later he had vanished through the Porte Rouge, which then led from the church to the cloisters.

When their first surprise was over, Jehanne de la Tarme whispered in La Gaultière's ear,—

"I always told you, sister, that that young scholar Monsieur Claude Frollo was a wizard."

Chapter II

CLAUDE FROLLO

INDEED, Claude Frollo was no ordinary character. He belonged to one of those middle-class families called indifferently, in the impertinent language of the last century, the better class of citizens, or petty nobility. This family had inherited from the brothers Paclet the estate of Tirechappe, which was held of the Bishop of Paris, and the twenty-one houses belonging to which had been the subject of so many suits before the judge of the bishop's court during the thirteenth century. As holder of this fief, Claude Frollo was one of the one hundred and forty-one lords and nobles claiming quit-rents in Paris and its suburbs; and his name was long to be seen inscribed, in that capacity, between those of the Hôtel de Tancarville, belonging to Master François le Rez, and the College of Tours, in the cartulary deposited for safe keeping at Saint-Martin des Champs.

Claude Frollo had from early childhood been destined by his parents to enter the ranks of the clergy. He was taught to read in Latin; he was trained to look down and speak low. While still very young his father put him at the convent School of Torchi in the University. There he grew up on the missal and the lexicon.

He was moreover a sad, serious, sober, child, who loved study and learned quickly. He never shouted at play, took little part in the riotous frolics of the Rue du Fouarre, knew not what it was to *"dare alapas et capillos laniare,"* and had no share in the mutiny of 1463, which historians gravely set down as the "sixth disturbance at the University." It seldom occurred to him to tease the poor scholars of Montaigu about their capotes,—the little hoods from which they took their name,—or the bursars of the College of Dormans about their shaven pates, and their motley garb of grey, blue, and violet cloth, *"azurini coloris et bruni,"* as the charter of Cardinal des Quatre-Couronnes words it.

But, on the other hand, he was faithful to the great and little schools in the Rue Saint-Jean de Beauvais. The first scholar to be seen by the Abbot of Saint-Pierre de Val, as he began his lecture on canon law, was always Claude Frollo, glued to a column in the Saint-Vendregesile School, directly opposite the speaker's chair, armed with his inkhorn, chewing his pen, scribbling on his threadbare knee, and in winter blowing on his fingers to keep them warm. The first auditor whom Master Miles d'Isliers, doctor of decretals, saw hurrying up all out of breath every Monday morning at the opening of the doors of the Chef-Saint-Denis School, was Claude Frollo. Accordingly, at the age of sixteen the young scholar was quite able to argue matters of mystical theology with a father of the Church, of canonical theology with a father of the Councils, and of scholastic theology with a doctor of the Sorbonne.

Theology mastered, he plunged into decretals. After the "Master of Sentences," he fell upon the "Capitularies of Charlemagne;" and devoured in turn, in his appetite for knowledge, decretal after decretal,—those of Theodore, Bishop of Hispala; those of Bouchard, Bishop of Worms; those of Yves, Bishop of Chartres; then the decree of Gratian, which followed the "Capitularies of Charlemagne;" then the collection of Gregory IX.; then the epistle *"Super Specula,"* of Honorius III. He gained a clear idea of, he became familiar with, that vast and bewildering period when civil law and canon law were struggling and labouring amid the chaos of the Middle Ages,—a period beginning with Bishop Theodore in 618, and ending with Pope Gregory in 1227.

Decretals digested, he turned to medicine and the liberal arts. He studied the science of herbs, the science of salves; he became skilled in fevers and bruises, in wounds and sores. Jacques d'Espars would have given him the degree of doctor of medicine; Richard Hellain, that of surgeon. He also took all the degrees in all the other arts. He studied languages, Latin, Greek, and Hebrew,—a triple shrine then but little worshipped. His was a genuine thirst for acquiring and treasuring the facts of science. At eighteen, he had done with the four faculties; life seemed to the youth to have but one purpose,—to gain knowledge.

It was about this time that the excessive heat of the summer of 1466 caused an epidemic of the plague, which carried off more than forty thousand souls in the viscounty of Paris, and among others, says Jehan de Troyes, "Master Arnoul, astrologian to the king, who was a very virtuous, wise, and pleasant man." A rumour spread through the University that the Rue Tirechappe was especially subject to the disease. There Claude's parents lived, in the heart of their estate. The young scholar hastened in alarm to the paternal mansion. On entering, he found that his father and mother had died the night before. A baby brother was still living, and lay crying in his cradle. He was all that was left to Claude of his family. The youth took the child in his arms and walked thoughtfully away. Hitherto, he had lived for science only; he now began to live in the present.

This catastrophe marked an epoch in his existence. An orphan, the eldest, the head of a family at the age of nineteen, he was recalled from scholastic dreams to actual realities. Then, moved by pity, he was filled with love and devotion for this child, his brother; and a human affection was a strange sweet thing to him who had loved nothing but books before.

This affection grew to a singular degree; in so virgin a soul it was like a first love. Parted in infancy from his parents, whom he scarcely knew, cloistered and as it were immured among his books, eager to study and to learn everything, hitherto paying exclusive attention to his intellect, which delighted in literature, the poor student had had no time to learn that he had a heart. This little fatherless, motherless brother, this baby dropped unawares from heaven into his arms, made a new man of him. He saw that there were other things in the world than the speculations of the Sorbonne and the verses of Homer; that man required affection; that life without tenderness and without love was only a noisy, miserable, unfeeling machine. Only he fancied—for he was at the age when illusions are still replaced by illusions only—that the ties of family and kindred were all that was necessary, and that a little brother to love was enough to fill up a whole life.

He therefore yielded to his love for little Jehan with the passion of a character which was already energetic, ardent, and concentrated. The poor frail creature, a pretty, fair-haired, rosy, curly-locked child, an orphan, stirred him to the very soul; and like the serious thinker that he was, he began to meditate about Jehan with infinite compassion. He thought and cared for him as for something very fragile and very precious. He was more than a brother to the boy; he became a mother to him.

Little Jehan was not yet weaned when he lost his mother; Claude put him out to nurse. Besides the estate of Tirechappe, he had inherited from his father the fief of Moulin, which was held of the square tower of Gentilly; it consisted of a mill upon a hill, near the Château de Winchestre (now Bicêtre). The miller's wife was just then nursing a fine child; it was not far from the University. Claude himself carried little Jehan thither.

Henceforth, feeling that he had a burden to bear, he took life very soberly. The thought of his little brother became not only the refreshment, but the object of his studies. He resolved to devote himself wholly to the future of one for whom he must be answerable to God, and to have no other wife, no other child, than the happiness and prosperity of his brother. He accordingly became more than ever attached to his clerical calling. His merits, his learning, his position as the direct vassal of the Bishop of Paris, opened wide all the doors of the Church to him. At the age of twenty, by a special dispensation from the Holy See, he was a priest, and served as the youngest of the chaplains of Notre-Dame at the altar called, from the lateness of the Mass said at it, *altare pigrorum.*

There, more than ever buried in his dear books, which he only left to make a hasty visit to the mill, this mixture of wisdom and austerity, so rare at his age, soon made him respected and admired by the cloisters. From the convent, his reputation as a learned man spread to the people, among whom it had been somewhat changed—a frequent occurrence in those days—to the renown of a sorcerer.

It was as he was returning, on Quasimodo, or Low Sunday, from saying the sluggards' mass at their altar, which was close by the gate of the choir leading into the nave, to the right, near the image of the Virgin, that his attention was aroused by the group of old women chattering round the bed for foundlings.

He approached the unfortunate little being who seemed to be so much hated and so much threatened. Its distress, its deformity, its desertion, the thought of his own little brother, the wild dread, which at once struck him, that if he should die his dear little Jehan might also be flung upon that board to suffer, —all this rushed into his heart at once; a great wave of pity swept over him and he carried off the child.

When he took the child from the sack, he found it terribly deformed indeed. The poor little imp had a wart over his left eye, his head was buried between his shoulders, his spine was curved, his breastbone prominent, his legs crooked; but he seemed lively; and although it was impossible to say in what language he babbled, his cries proclaimed a certain amount of health and vigour. Claude's pity increased at the sight of so much ugliness; and he vowed in his inmost soul that he would educate this child for love of his own brother, so that whatever faults little Jehan might in the future commit, he might always have to his credit this charitable deed done for his benefit. It was a sort of investment of good works in his little brother's name; it was part of the stock of good deeds which he decided to lay up for him in advance, in case the young rascal should one day run short of this sort of money,—the only coin which will be accepted at the tollgate of paradise.

He baptized his adopted child, and named him Quasimodo, either because he wished to mark in this way the day upon which the child was found, or because he wished to show by this name how imperfect and incomplete the poor little creature was. Indeed, Quasimodo, one-eyed, humpbacked, and knock-kneed, was hardly more than an "apology."

Chapter III

IMMANIS PECORIS CUSTOS, IMMANIOR IPSE

Now, in 1482, Quasimodo had grown up. He had been made, some years previous, bell-ringer of Notre-Dame, thanks to his adopted father Claude Frollo, who had become archdeacon of Josas, thanks to his liege lord Sir Louis de Beaumont, who had become Bishop of Paris in 1472, on the death of Guillaume Chartier, thanks to his patron Olivier le Daim, barber to Louis XI., king by the grace of God.

Quasimodo, therefore, was ringer of Notre-Dame.

In time, a peculiar bond of intimacy grew up between the ringer and the church. Cut off forever from the world by the double faculty of his unknown birth and his deformity, confined from infancy in this doubly insuperable circle, the poor wretch became used to seeing nothing of the world outside the religious walls which had received him into their shadow. Notre-Dame had been to him by turns, as he grew and developed, egg, nest, home, country, universe.

And it is certain that there was a sort of mysterious and pre-existing harmony between this creature and the structure. When, still a child, he dragged himself tortuously and jerkingly along beneath its gloomy arches, he seemed, with his human face and animal-like limbs, to be some reptile native to that damp dark pavement upon which the Roman capitals cast so many grotesque shadows.

Later on, the first time that he mechanically grasped the bell-rope in the tower, and clung to it, and set the bell ringing, he seemed to Claude, his adopted father, like a child whose tongue is loosed, and who begins to talk.

It was thus, little by little, growing ever after the pattern of the cathedral, living there, sleeping there, seldom leaving its precincts, forever subject to its mysterious influence, he came to look like it, to be imbedded in it, to form, as it were, an integral part of it. His sharp angles (if we may be pardoned the simile) fitted into the re-entering angles of the building, and he seemed not only to inhabit it, but to be its natural tenant. He might almost be said to have assumed its form, as the snail assumes the form of its shell. It was his dwelling, his hole, his wrapper. There was so deep an instinct of sympathy between him and the old church, there were so many magnetic affinities between them, that he in some sort clung to it, as the tortoise to its shell. The rugged cathedral was his shell.

It is useless to warn the reader not to take literally the figures of speech which we are forced to use here to express this singular, symmetrical, direct, almost consubstantial union of a man and an edifice. It is also useless to speak of the degree of familiarity with the whole cathedral which he had acquired during so long and intimate a cohabitation. This dwelling was his own. It contained no deeps which Quasimodo had not penetrated, no heights which he had not scaled. He often climbed the façade several stories high by the mere aid of projecting bits of sculpture. The towers upon the outer face of which he was frequently seen crawling like a lizard gliding over a perpendicular wall (those twin giants, so lofty, so threatening, so terrible) had no vertigoes, no terrors, no giddiness for him; they were so docile to his hand, so easily climbed, that he might be said to have tamed them. By dint of jumping, clambering, sporting amid the abysses of the huge cathedral, he had become, as it were, a monkey and a goat, like the calabrian child who swims before he walks, and plays with the sea while but an infant.

Moreover not only his body but also his spirit seemed to be moulded by the cathedral. What was the state of that soul? What bent had it assumed, what form had it taken under its knotty covering in this wild life? It would be hard to tell. Quasimodo was born blind of one eye, humpbacked, lame. It was only by great patience and great painstaking that Claude Frollo had succeeded in teaching him to speak. But a fatality followed the poor foundling. Bell-ringer of Notre-Dame at the age of fourteen, a new infirmity soon put the finishing touch to his misfortunes; the bells had broken the drums of his ears; he became deaf. The only avenue which Nature had left him open to the world was suddenly closed forever.

In closing, it shut off the only ray of joy and light which still reached Quasimodo's soul. That soul relapsed into utter darkness. The miserable lad's melancholy became as complete and as hopeless as his deformity. Add to this that his deafness made him in some sort dumb; for that he might not be an object of laughter to others, from the moment that he realized his deafness he firmly resolved to observe a silence which he scarcely ever broke save when alone. Of his own free will he bound that tongue which Claude Frollo had worked so hard to set free. Hence it resulted that, when necessity constrained him to speak, his tongue was stiff and awkward, like a door whose hinges have rusted.

If now we strive to penetrate Quasimodo's soul through this hard thick bark; could we sound the depths of that misshapen organism; could we hold a torch behind those non-transparent organs, explore the dark interior of that opaque being, illuminate its obscure corners, its absurd blind alleys, and cast a strong light suddenly upon the Psyche imprisoned at the bottom of this well, we should doubtless find the poor thing in some constrained attitude, stunted and rickety, like those prisoners under the leads of Venice, who grew old bent double in a stone coffer too short and too low for them either to lie down or to stand up.

The spirit certainly wastes away in a misshapen body. Quasimodo barely felt within him the blind stirring of a soul made in his own image. His impressions of objects underwent a considerable refraction before they reached his mind. His brain was a peculiar medium; the ideas which traversed it came forth greatly distorted. The reflection resulting from that refraction was necessarily divergent, and deviated from the right path.

Hence endless optical illusions, endless aberrations of opinion, endless digressions into which his thoughts, sometimes foolish, and sometimes idiotic, would wander.

The first effect of this unfortunate condition of things was to disturb his views of all outward objects. He had scarcely any direct perception of them. The external world seemed much farther away from him than it does from us.

The second effect of his misfortune was to make him mischievous.

He was mischievous because he was an untrained savage; he was a savage because he was ugly. There was a logic in his nature as in ours.

His strength, wonderfully developed as it was, was the cause of still greater mischief. *"Malus puer robustus,"* says Hobbes.

But we must do him the justice to say that this mischievous spirit was not innate. From his first intercourse with men he had felt, had seen himself despised, scorned, repulsed. To him, human speech meant nothing but mockery or curses. As he grew up, he encountered nothing but hate. He caught the infection. He acquired the universal malevolence. He adopted the weapon with which he had been wounded.

After all, he never turned his face to the world of men save with regret; his cathedral was enough for him. It was peopled with marble figures, kings, saints, and bishops who at least did not laugh at him, and never looked upon him otherwise than with peace and goodwill. The other statues, those of monsters and demons, did not hate Quasimodo; he looked too much like them for that. They rather mocked at other men. The saints were his friends, and blessed him. The monsters were his friends, and protected him. Thus he had long conversations with them. He would sometimes pass whole hours squatting before one of these statues, in solitary chat with it. If any one came by, he would fly like a lover surprised in his serenade.

And the cathedral was not only company for him, it was the universe; nay, more, it was Nature itself. He never dreamed that there were other hedgerows than the stained-glass windows in perpetual bloom; other shade than that of the stone foliage always budding, loaded with birds in the thickets of Saxon capitals; other mountains than the colossal towers of the church; or other ocean than Paris roaring at their feet.

But that which he loved more than all else in the motherly building, that which awakened his soul and bade it spread its poor stunted wings folded in such misery where it dwelt in darkness, that which sometimes actually made him happy, was the bells. He loved them, he caressed them, he talked to them, he understood them. From the chime in the steeple over the transept to the big bell above the door, he had a tender feeling for them all. The belfry of the transept and the two towers were to him like three great cages, in which the birds, trained by him, sang for him alone; and yet it was these very bells which made him deaf. But mothers often love that child best which has cost them most pain.

To be sure, their voice was the only one which he could now hear. For this reason the big bell was his best beloved. She was his favourite of that family of noisy damsels who fluttered about his head on holidays. This big bell had been christened Marie. She hung alone in the south tower with her sister Jacqueline, a bell of less size enclosed in a smaller cage close beside her own. This Jacqueline was named for the wife of Jehan Montague, who gave the bell to the church; which did not prevent him from figuring at Montfaucon without a head. In the second tower there were six other bells; and lastly, the six smallest dwelt in the belfry over the transept with the wooden bell, which was only rung from the afternoon of Maundy Thursday till the morning of Holy Saturday or Easter Eve. Thus Quasimodo had fifteen bells in his harem; but big Marie was his favourite.

It is impossible to give any idea of his joy on those days when full peals were rung. When the archdeacon dismissed him with the word "Go," he ran up the winding staircase more rapidly than any one else could have gone down. He reached the aerial chamber of the big bell, breathless; he gazed at it an instant with love and devotion, then spoke to it gently, and patted it, as you would a good horse about to take a long journey. He condoled with it on the hard work before it. After these initiatory caresses he called to his assistants, stationed on a lower story of the tower, to begin. They then hung upon the ropes, the windlass creaked, and the enormous mass of metal moved slowly. Quasimodo, panting with excitement, followed it with his eye. The first stroke of the clapper upon its brazen wall made the beam on which he stood quiver. Quasimodo vibrated with the bell. "Here we go! There we go!" he shouted with a mad burst of laughter. But the motion of the great bell grew faster and faster, and as it traversed an ever-increasing space, his eye grew bigger and bigger, more and more glittering and phosphorescent. At last the full peal began; the whole tower shook: beams, leads, broad stones, all rumbled together, from the piles of the foundation to the trefoils at the top. Then Quasimodo's rapture knew no bounds: he came and went; he trembled and shook from head to foot with the tower. The bell, let loose, and frantic with liberty, turned its jaws of bronze to either wall of the tower in turn,—jaws from which issued that whirlwind whose roar men heard for four leagues around. Quasimodo placed himself before those gaping jaws! he rose and fell with the swaying of the bell, inhaled its tremendous breath, gazed now at the abyss swarming with people like ants, two hundred feet below him, and now at the huge copper clapper which from second to second bellowed in his ear. That was the only speech which he could hear, the only sound that broke the universal silence reigning around him. He basked in it as a bird in the sunshine. All at once the frenzy of the bell seized him; his look became strange; he waited for the passing of the bell as a spider lies in wait for a fly, and flung himself headlong upon it. Then, suspended above the gulf, launched upon the tremendous vibration of the bell, he grasped the brazen monster by its ears, clasped it with his knees, spurred it with his heels, doubling the fury of the peal with the whole force and weight of his body. As the tower shook, he shouted and gnashed his teeth, his red hair stood erect, his chest laboured like a blacksmith's bellows, his eye flashed fire, the monstrous steed neighed and panted under him; and then the big bell of Notre-Dame and Quasimodo ceased to exist: they became a dream, a whirlwind, a tempest; vertigo astride of uproar; a spirit clinging to a winged crupper; a strange centaur, half man, half bell; a sort of horrid Astolpho, borne aloft by a prodigious hippogriff of living bronze.

The presence of this extraordinary being pervaded the whole cathedral with a peculiar breath of life. It seemed, at least in the opinion of the grossly superstitious mob, as if mysterious emanations issued from him, animating every stone in Notre-Dame and making the very entrails of the old church throb and palpitate. His mere presence there was enough to lead the vulgar to fancy that the countless statues in the galleries and over the doors moved and breathed. And in very truth the cathedral seemed a creature docile and obedient to his hand: it awaited his pleasure to lift up its mighty voice; it was possessed and filled with Quasimodo as with a familiar spirit. He might be said to make the vast edifice breathe. He was indeed omnipresent in it, he multiplied himself at every point of the structure. Sometimes the terrified spectator saw an odd dwarf on the extreme pinnacle of one of the towers, climbing, creeping, writhing, crawling on all fours, descending head-first into the abyss, leaping from one projection to another, and diving deep into the maw of some sculptured gorgon: it was Quasimodo hunting for daws' nests. Sometimes a visitor stumbled over a sort of living nightmare, crouching and scowling in a dark corner of the church; it was Quasimodo absorbed in thought. Sometimes an enormous head and a bundle of ill-adjusted limbs might be seen swaying frantically to and fro from a rope's end under a belfry: it was Quasimodo ringing the Vespers or the Angelus. Often by night a hideous form was seen wandering along the frail delicately wrought railing which crowns the towers and runs round the top of the chancel: it was still the hunchback of Notre-Dame. Then, so the neighbours said, the whole church took on a fantastic, supernatural, horrible air,—eyes and mouths opened wide here and there; the dogs and dragons and griffins of stone which watch day and night, with outstretched necks and gaping jaws, around the monstrous cathedral, barked loudly. And if it were a Christmas night, while the big bell, which seemed uttering its death-rattle, called the faithful to attend the solemn midnight mass, the gloomy façade assumed such an aspect that it seemed as if the great door were devouring the crowd while the rose-window looked on. And all this was due to Quasimodo. Egypt would have taken him for the god of the temple; the Middle Ages held him to be its demon: he was its soul.

So much so that to those who knew that Quasimodo once existed, Notre-Dame is now deserted, inanimate, dead. They feel that something has gone from it. That immense body is empty; it is a skeleton; the spirit has left it, the abode remains, and that is all. It is like a skull; the sockets of the eyes are still there, but sight is gone.

Chapter IV

THE DOG AND HIS MASTER

There was, however, one human being whom Quasimodo excepted from his malice and hatred of mankind in general, and whom he loved as much as, perhaps more than, his cathedral: this was Claude Frollo.

This was very natural. Claude Frollo had taken him, adopted him, fed him, brought him up. While still a child, it was between Claude Frollo's legs that he found shelter when dogs and boys barked at him and tormented him. Claude Frollo taught him to speak, to read, and to write. Claude Frollo even made him bell-ringer. Now, to give the big bell in marriage to Quasimodo was like giving Juliet to Romeo.

Therefore Quasimodo's gratitude was profound, passionate, boundless; and although the face of his adopted father was often clouded and severe, although his speech was usually brief, harsh, and imperative, this gratitude never for an instant failed him. In Quasimodo the archdeacon had the most submissive of slaves, the most docile of servants, the most watchful of guardians. When the poor bell-ringer became deaf, the two contrived a language of signs, mysterious and incomprehensible to every one else. Thus the archdeacon was the only human being with whom Quasimodo kept up any communication. He had relations with but two things in the world,—Notre-Dame and Claude Frollo.

There is nothing to which we can compare the archdeacon's empire over the ringer or the ringer's devotion to the archdeacon. One sign from Claude, and the idea that it would please him, would have been enough for Quasimodo to hurl himself from the top of the cathedral towers. It was wonderful to see so much physical strength brought to such rare development in Quasimodo, and blindly placed by him at the disposal of another. This was doubtless partly due to filial love, domestic affection; it was also due to the fascination exercised by one mind upon another. It was a poor, clumsy, awkward nature, with bowed head and suppliant eyes, before a profound and lofty, superior, and all-powerful intellect. Lastly, and above all, it was gratitude,—gratitude so pushed to its extremest limits that we know of nothing to which it may be compared. This virtue is not one of those which are to be found in the finest examples among men. Let us say therefore that Quasimodo loved the archdeacon as no dog, no horse, no elephant, ever loved its master.

Chapter V

MORE ABOUT CLAUDE FROLLO

In 1482 Quasimodo was about twenty years old, Claude Frollo about thirty-six. The one had grown up, the other had grown old.

Claude Frollo was no longer the simple scholar of the College of Torchi, the tender protector of a little child, the dreamy young philosopher who knew many things and was ignorant of many more. He was now an austere, grave, morose priest; a keeper of other men's consciences; the archdeacon of Josas, second acolyte to the bishop, having charge of the two deaneries of Montlhéry and Châteaufort, and one hundred and seventy-four of the rural clergy. He was a gloomy and awe-inspiring personage, before whom choir-boys in alb and petticoat, the precentors, the monks of St. Augustine, and those clerks who officiated at the early service at Notre-Dame, trembled when he passed slowly by beneath the lofty arches of the choir, majestic, pensive, with folded arms, and head so bent upon his bosom that nothing of his face could be seen but the high bald forehead.

Now, Don Claude Frollo had not given up either science or the education of his younger brother,—those two occupations of his life. But time had imparted a slight bitterness to these things once so sweet. "The best bacon in the world," says Paul Diacre, "grows rancid at last." Little Jehan Frollo, surnamed "du Moulin," from the place where he was put to nurse, had not grown up in the path in which Claude would fain have led him. The big brother expected him to be a pious, docile, studious, honourable pupil. Now, the little brother, like those young trees which foil the gardener's every effort and turn obstinately towards the sun and air,— the little brother only grew and flourished, only put forth fine leafy and luxuriant branches, in the direction of idleness, ignorance, and debauchery. He was a perfect imp, utterly lawless, which made Don Claude frown; but very shrewd and witty, which made the big brother smile. Claude had confided him to that same College of Torchi where he had passed his own early years in study and meditation; and it cost him many a pang that this sanctuary once so edified by the name of Frollo should now be scandalized by it. He sometimes read Jehan very long and very severe lectures on this text, but the latter bore them without wincing. After all, the young scamp had a good heart, as every comedy shows us is always the case.

But the lecture over, he resumed his riotous ways with perfect tranquillity. Now it was a yellow beak (as newcomers at the University were called) whom he mauled for his entrance fee,— a precious tradition which has been carefully handed down to the present day. Now he headed a band of students who had fallen upon some tavern in classic style, *quasi classico excitati,* then beaten the landlord "with offensive cudgels," and merrily sacked the house, even to staving in the casks of wine in the cellar; and then it was a fine report in Latin which the submonitor of Torchi brought ruefully to Don Claude, with this melancholy marginal note: *"Rixa; prima causa vinum optimum potatum."* Lastly, it was reported—horrible to relate of a sixteen-year-old lad—that his excesses often took him even to the Rue de Glatigny.

Owing to all this, Claude, saddened and discouraged in his human affections, threw himself with all the greater ardour into the arms of Science,—that lady who at least does not laugh in your face, and always repays you, albeit in coin that is sometimes rather hollow, for the attentions that you have bestowed on her. He therefore became more and more learned, and at the same time, as a natural consequence, more and more rigid as a priest, more and more melancholy as a man. With each of us there are certain parallelisms between our intellect, our morals, and our character, which are developed continuously, and only interrupted by great upheavals in our life.

Claude Frollo having traversed in his youth almost the entire circle of human knowledge, positive, external, and legitimate, was forced, unless he stopped *ubi defuit orbis,* to go farther afield and seek other food for the insatiate activity of his mind. The antique symbol of the serpent biting its own tail is especially appropriate to science. It seemed that Claude Frollo had experienced this. Many worthy persons affirmed that having exhausted the *fas* of human knowledge, he had ventured to penetrate into the *nefas.* He had, so they said, successively tasted every apple on the tree of knowledge, and whether from hunger or disgust, had ended by biting into the forbidden fruit. He had taken his place by turns, as our readers have seen, at the conferences of the theologians of the Sorbonne, the assemblies of the philosophers at the image of Saint-Hilaire, at the disputes of the decretists at the image of Saint-Martin, at the meetings of the doctors at the holy-water font in Notre-Dame, *ad cupam Nostræ-Dominæ.* All the permissible and approved meats which those four great kitchens called the four faculties could prepare and serve up to the understanding he had devoured, and satiety had ensued before his hunger was appeased. Then he had dug farther and deeper, beneath all this finite, material, limited science; he had possibly risked his soul, and had seated himself in the cavern at that mysterious table of the alchemists, astrologers, and hermetics, headed by Averroës, Guillaume de Paris, and Nicolas Flamel, in the Middle Ages, and prolonged in the East, by the light of the seven-branched candlestick, to Solomon, Pythagoras, and Zoroaster.

At least this is what people imagined, whether rightly or wrongly.

Certain it is that the archdeacon often

visited the Cemetery of the Holy Innocents, where, to be sure, his father and mother were buried, with the other victims of the pest in 1466; but he seemed far less interested in the cross over their grave than in the strange characters carved upon the tomb of Nicolas Flamel and Claude Pernelle which stood close by.

Certain it was that he was often seen walking slowly along the Rue des Lombards and furtively entering a small house at the corner of the Rue des Ecrivains and the Rue Marivault. This was the house which Nicolas Flamel built, where he died about 1417, and which having remained empty ever since, was now beginning to fall into decay; so badly had the hermetics and alchemists of every nation injured the walls merely by writing their names upon them. Certain of the neighbours even declared that they had once seen, through a venthole, archdeacon Claude, digging, turning over, and spading the earth in those two cellars whose buttresses were scribbled all over with endless rhymes and hieroglyphics by Nicolas Flamel himself. It was supposed that Flamel had buried the philosopher's stone in these cellars; and alchemists, for two centuries back, from Magistri down to Father Pacificus, never ceased delving at the soil, until the house, so severely rummaged and ransacked, ended by crumbling into dust beneath their feet.

Certain it is also that the archdeacon was seized with a singular passion for the symbolical doorway of Notre-Dame, that page of conjury written in stone by Bishop Guillaume de Paris, who was undoubtedly damned for having added so infernal a frontispiece to the holy poem perpetually sung by the rest of the structure. Archdeacon Claude also passed for having fathomed the mystery of the colossal figure of Saint Christopher, and that tall enigmatical statue then standing at the entrance to the square in front of the cathedral, which people called in derision, "Monsieur Legris." But what every one might have observed, was the interminable hours which he often passed, sitting on the parapet of this same square, gazing at the carvings of the porch, sometimes studying the foolish virgins with their lamps turned upside down, sometimes the wise virgins with the lamps upright; at other times calculating the angle of vision of the daw to the left of the porch and gazing at a mysterious point inside the church where the philosopher's stone must assuredly be hidden, if it be not in the cellar of Nicolas Flamel. It was, let us say in passing, a singular fate for the Church of Notre-Dame at this period to be so loved, in different degrees and with such devotion, by two beings so dissimilar as Claude and Quasimodo. Loved by the one, a sort of instinctive and savage half-man, for its beauty, for its stature, for the harmonies that proceeded from its magnificent mass; loved by the other, a man of scholarly and impassioned fancy, for its significance, for its myth, for its hidden meaning, for the symbolism scattered throughout the sculptures of its front, like the first text under the second in a palimpsest—in short, for the riddle which it forever puts to the intellect.

Certain it is, lastly, that the archdeacon had arranged for himself, in that one of the two towers which looks upon the Grève, close beside the belfry a very secret little cell, where none might enter without his leave, not even the bishop, it was said. This cell, contrived in old times, had been almost at the very summit of the tower, among the daws' and ravens' nests, by Bishop Hugh of Besançon, who practised sorcery there in his time. What this cell contained, no one knew; but from the shore of the Terrain there was often seen at night, through a small dormer-window at the back of the tower, a strange, red, intermittent light, appearing, disappearing, and reappearing at brief and regular intervals, and seeming to follow the blasts of a bellows, and to proceed rather from the flame of a fire than from the light of a candle. In the darkness, at that height, it produced a singular effect; and the gossips would say, "There's the archdeacon blowing again! Hell is sparkling up there!"

After all, there was no great proof of sorcery in all this; but still there was so much smoke that it might well be supposed there was fire, and the archdeacon had quite a formidable fame. And yet we must say that Egyptian arts, necromancy, and magic, even of the whitest and most innocent kind, had no more relentless enemy, no more pitiless accuser than himself, before the officials of Notre-Dame. Whether this were genuine horror, or the game played by the robber who shouts, "Stop, thief!" it did not prevent the archdeacon from being considered by the wise heads of the chapter as a soul which had ventured into the outskirts of hell, as one lost in the dark caves of the Cabala,—groping in the obscurity of the occult sciences. Nor were the people deceived: with every one who had a grain of sense, Quasimodo passed for the devil, Claude Frollo for the sorcerer. It was plain that the bell-ringer was bound to serve the archdeacon for a given time, at the end of which he would carry off his soul by way of payment. The archdeacon was therefore, in spite of the extreme austerity of his life, in very bad odour with pious people; and there was no devout nose so inexperienced as not to smell in him the magician.

And if, as he grew old, there were voids in his science, there were others in his heart. At least, so one was led to believe on looking at that face in which his soul never shone forth save through a dark cloud. Whence came that broad bald brow, that head forever bowed, that breast forever heaved by sighs? What secret thought made his lips smile so bitterly at the very moment that his frowning brows met like two bulls about to tussle? Why were his few remaining hairs already grey? What was that inward fire which sometimes broke forth in his eye to such a degree that it looked like a hole pierced in the wall of a furnace?

These signs of intense moral preoccupation had acquired a high pitch of intensity at the very time of this story. More than once a choir-boy had taken to his heels in alarm on finding him alone in the church, so strange and wild was his look. More than once, in the choir, during divine service, his neighbour in the stalls had heard him mingle unintelligible parentheses with the church music. More than once the laundress of the Terrain, employed "to wash the chapter," had remarked, not without terror, marks of nails and clinched fingers in the surplice of the archdeacon of Josas.

In other respects he redoubled his severity, and had never been more exemplary. From disposition as well as by profession he had always held himself aloof from women; he seemed now to hate them more than ever. The mere rustle of a silk petticoat made him pull his hood over his eyes. He was so jealous of his austerity and reserve upon this point that when Madame de Beaujeu, daughter of the king, came, in the month of December, 1481, to visit the convent of Notre-Dame, he gravely opposed her entrance, reminding the bishop of that statute in the Black Book, dated on the eve of St. Bartholomew, 1334, which forbids all access to the cloister to every woman "whatsoever, old or young, mistress or maid;" upon which the bishop was constrained to quote to him the ordinance of the legate Odo, which excepts certain great ladies, *"aliquæ magnates mulieres, quæ sine scandalo vitari non possunt."* And the archdeacon still protested, objecting that the legate's decree, which went back to 1207, antedated the Black Book by one hundred and twenty-seven years, and was consequently annulled by it; and he refused to appear before the princess.

It was moreover remarked that his horror of the gipsies seemed to have increased for some time past. He had solicited from the bishop an edict expressly forbidding the tribe from coming to dance and play the tambourine in the square before the cathedral; and he had also searched in the musty official papers, to collect all cases of witches and wizards condemned to be burned or hanged for complicity in conjury with goats, swine, or rams.

Chapter VI

UNPOPULARITY

The archdeacon and the bell-ringer, as we have already observed, were not held in much favour by the great and little folk about the cathedral. When Claude and Quasimodo went forth together, as they frequently did, and were seen in company, the man behind the master, traversing the cool, narrow, shady streets about Notre-Dame, more than one malicious speech, more than one satirical exclamation and insulting jest stung them as they passed, unless Claude Frollo, as seldom happened, walked with head erect, displaying his stern and almost majestic brow to the abashed scoffers.

Both were in their district like the "poets" of whom Régnier speaks:—

"All sorts of folks will after poets hie,
As after owls our song-birds shriek and fly."

Now a sly brat would risk his bones for the ineffable delight of burying a pin in Quasimodo's hump: and now a lovely young girl, full of fun, and bolder than need be, would brush against the priest's black gown, singing in his ear the sarcastic song,—

"Hide, hide, for the devil is caught."

Sometimes a squalid group of old women, squatting in a row in the shade upon the steps of some porch, scolded roundly as the archdeacon and the bell-ringer went by, and flung after them with curses this encouraging greeting:

"Well, one of them has a soul as misshapen as the other one's body!" Or else it would be a band of students and beetle-crushers playing at hop-scotch, who jumped up in a body and hailed them in classic fashion with some Latin whoop and hoot: *"Eia! eia! Claudius cum Claudo!"*

But usually all insults were unheeded by both priest and ringer. Quasimodo was too deaf and Claude too great a dreamer to hear all these gracious speeches.

The Hunchback of Notre-Dame

BOOK V

THE NEW POWER

CHAPTER I

ABBAS BEATI MARTINI

DON CLAUDE's renown had spread far and wide. It procured him, at about the period when he refused to see Madame de Beaujeu, the honour of a visit which he long remembered.

It was on a certain evening. He had just retired after divine service to his canonic cell in the convent of Notre-Dame. This apartment, aside from a few glass phials banished to a corner, and full of somewhat suspicious powder, which looked vastly like gunpowder, contained nothing strange or mysterious. There were inscriptions here and there upon the walls, but they were merely scientific statements, or pious extracts from well-known authors. The archdeacon had just seated himself, by the light of a three-beaked copper lamp, before a huge chest covered with manuscripts. His elbow rested on a wide-open book by Honorius d'Autun, *"De Prædestinatione et libero arbitrio,"* and he was very meditatively turning the leaves of a printed folio which he had brought upstairs with him,—the only product of the press which his cell contained. In the midst of his reverie there was a knock at the door. "Who is there?" cried the sage in the gracious tone of a hungry dog disturbed while eating his bone.

A voice answered from without; "Your friend, Jacques Coictier." He at once opened the door.

It was indeed the king's physician,— a person of some fifty years of age, whose harsh expression was only corrected by a crafty look. Another man was with him. Both wore long slate-coloured robes furred with minever, belted and clasped, with caps of the same stuff and colour. Their hands were hidden in their sleeves, their feet under their gowns, their eyes beneath their bonnets.

"God help me, gentlemen!' said the archdeacon, showing them in; "I did not expect so honourable a visit at such an hour." And while speaking in this courteous fashion, he cast an anxious and searching glance from the physician to his companion.

"It is never too late to visit so distinguished a scholar as Don Claude Frollo de Tirechappe," replied Doctor Coictier, who, being a native of Franche-Comté, drawled all his sentences until they dragged as majestically as the long train of a lady's dress.

Then began between the doctor and the archdeacon one of those congratulatory prefaces with which it was at this period customary to precede every conversation between learned men, and which did not hinder them from hating each other most cordially. However, it is just so to-day: the lips of every learned man who compliments another scholar are like a cup of honeyed poison.

Claude Frollo's congratulations to Jacques Coictier dwelt particularly on the numerous worldly advantages which that worthy physician in the course of his much-envied career had contrived to extract from every royal malady,—the result of a better and surer alchemy than the search for the philosopher's stone.

"Truly, Doctor Coictier, I was delighted to hear of the bishopric of your nephew, my reverend lord Pierre Versé. Has he not been made Bishop of Amiens?"

"Yes, archdeacon; by the favour and mercy of God."

"Do you know that you cut a very fine figure on Christmas Day, at the head of your associates of the Court of Exchequer, Mr. President?"

"Vice-president, Don Claude. Nothing more, alas!"

"How is your superb house in the Rue Saint-André des Arcs getting on? It's another Louvre. I particularly admire the apricot-tree carved over the door, and the pleasing pun in the motto, 'A L'Abri Cotier.'"

"Alas! Master Claude, all that stonework costs me dear. I am being ruined as fast as the house grows."

"Pooh! Haven't you your revenues from the jail and the Palace bailiwick, and the rent of all the houses, butchers' stalls, booths, and shops within the boundary wall? That's a fine milchcow for you."

"My Poissy castellany brought me in nothing this year."

"But your toll-gates at Triel, Saint-James, and Saint-Germain-en-Laye are still good."

"A hundred and twenty pounds, and not even Paris pounds at that."

"But you have your place as Councillor to the King. That's a permanent thing."

"Yes, Brother Claude; but that confounded manor of Poligny, which people make such a talk about, doesn't bring me in sixty crowns, take it one year with another."

In the compliments paid to Jacques Coictier by Don Claude there was the sarcastic, sour, slightly mocking tone, the cruel, acid smile of an unfortunate and superior person sporting for a moment, by way of amusement, with the fat prosperity of a vulgar fellow. The other did not observe this.

"By my soul," said Claude at last, pressing his hand, "I am glad to see you in such robust health!"

"Thank you, Master Claude."

"By the way," cried Don Claude, "how goes it with your royal patient?"

"He does not pay his doctor enough," answered the physician, casting a side glance at his comrade.

"Do you think so, friend Coictier?" said his comrade.

These words, uttered in tones of surprise and reproach, drew the archdeacon's attention to the stranger, although, to tell the truth, he had not been wholly unobservant of him for a single instant since he had crossed his threshold. Had there not been a thousand reasons for his conciliating Doctor Jacques Coictier, the all-powerful physician of King Louis XI., he would never have admitted him in such company. Therefore his mien was anything but cordial when Jacques Coictier said,—

"By the way, Don Claude, I bring you a brother worker, who was anxious to see you, being familiar with your fame."

"A gentleman of science?" inquired the archdeacon, fixing his piercing eye upon Coictier's companion. The stranger returned his gaze with an equally searching and defiant look.

As well as the feeble light of the lamp allowed one to judge, he was an elderly man of some sixty years, and of medium height, apparently quite ill and broken. His profile, although not at all aristocratic, was still strong and severe; his eye flashed from beneath a very prominent brow, like a light from the depths of a cave; and under the flat cap which drooped over his face, the broad forehead of a man of genius was visible.

He took upon himself to answer the archdeacon's question.

"Reverend sir," he said in grave tones, "your renown has reached me, and I desired to consult you. I am only a poor country gentleman, who takes off his shoes before venturing into the presence of learned men. You must know my name. I am Father Tourangeau."

"An odd name for a gentleman!" thought the archdeacon. Still, he felt that he had before him a strong and serious character. The instinct of his lofty intellect led him to guess that a spirit no less lofty lurked beneath the furred cap of Father Tourangeau; and as he studied his grave face, the ironical smile which the presence of Jacques Coictier had forced to his sullen lips faded slowly, as twilight fades from the sky at night. He reseated himself silently and moodily in his great armchair, his elbow resumed its wonted place upon the table, and his head on his hand. After a few moments of meditation he signed to the two visitors to be seated, and addressed Father Tourangeau:—

"You came to consult me, sir; and upon what branch of science?"

"Your reverence," replied Father Tourangeau, "I am ill; very ill. You are said to be a great doctor, and I come to you for medical advice."

"Medical advice!" said the archdeacon, shaking his head. He seemed communing with himself an instant, then added: "Father Tourangeau, if that be your name, turn your head. You will find my answer ready written on the wall."

Father Tourangeau obeyed, and read this inscription on the wall above his head: "Medicine is the daughter of dreams.—JAMBLIQUE."

But Doctor Coictier listened to his comrade's question with a displeasure only increased by Don Claude's answer. He bent to Father Tourangeau's ear and said, low enough not to be overheard by the archdeacon, "I told you he was a madman; but you insisted on seeing him!"

"Because this madman may well be right, Doctor Jacques!" replied the stranger, in the same tone, and with a bitter smile.

"As you please," answered Coictier, drily. Then turning to the archdeacon: "You are an apt workman, Don Claude, and you handle Hippocrates as deftly as a monkey does a nut. Medicine a dream, indeed! I doubt me the druggists and the old masters would stone you well, were they here. Then you deny the influence of philters on the blood, of ointments on the flesh! You deny that everlasting pharmacy of flowers and metals which we call the world, made expressly for that eternal sufferer whom we call man!"

"I deny," said Don Claude, coldly, "neither drugs nor disease. I deny the physician."

"Then it is false," continued Coictier, with warmth, "that gout is an inward eruption, that a cannon-wound may be cured by the application of a roasted mouse, that young blood properly infused restores youth to old veins; it is false to say that two and two make four, and that emprostathonos follows opistathonos."

The archdeacon quietly replied, "There are certain things which I regard in a certain way."

Coictier turned red with rage.

"There, there, my good Coictier, don't be angry!" said Father Tourangeau. "The archdeacon is our friend."

Coictier calmed himself, muttering,—

"After all, he's a madman!"

"Odzooks, Master Claude!" continued Father Tourangeau, after a pause, "you embarrass me mightily. I had two pieces of advice to ask of you,—one concerning my health, the other concerning my star."

"Sir," responded the archdeacon, "if that be your object, you would have done as well not to waste your breath in climbing my stairs. I am no believer in medicine: I am no believer in astrology!"

"Indeed!" said the stranger with surprise.

Coictier laughed a forced laugh. "You see now that he's mad," he whispered to Father Tourangeau. "He doesn't believe in astrology!"

"How can any-one imagine," continued Don Claude, "that every star-ray is a thread which leads to some man's head!"

"Pray, in what do you believe, then?" exclaimed Father Tourangeau.

The archdeacon for an instant seemed uncertain, then with a gloomy smile, which seemed to belie his answer, said: "credo in Deum."

"Dominum nostrum," added Father Tourangeau, making the sign of the cross.

"Amen," said Coictier.

"Reverend sir," resumed the stranger, "I am delighted to find you so good a Christian. But, great scholar that you are, have you reached such a point that you no longer believe in science?"

"No," said the archdeacon, seizing Father Tourangeau by the arm, while a lightning flash of enthusiasm kindled his dull eye,—"no, I do not deny science. I have not crawled flat on my face all these years, digging the earth with my nails, amid the countless mazes of the cavern, without seeing far before me, at the end of the dark tunnel, a light, a flame, something, doubtless the reflection of the dazzling central laboratory where sages and patient souls have taken God by surprise."

"Come, then," interrupted Tourangeau, "what do you consider true and certain?"

"Alchemy."

Coictier cried out: "Good God, Don

Claude! alchemy has its good points, no doubt; but why should you blaspheme against medicine and astrology?"

"Your science of mankind is naught; your science of heaven naught!" said the archdeacon, authoritatively.

"You treat Epidaurus and Chaldea very cavalierly," replied the doctor with a sneer.

"Hear me, Master Jacques. I speak in good faith. I am not the king's physician, and his Majesty did not give me the Dædalus garden as a convenient spot whence I might study the constellations. Don't be angry, and listen to me. What new truth did you ever derive,—I don't say from medicine, which is far too foolish a matter, but from astrology? Tell me the virtues of the vertical boustrophedon, the discoveries of the number Ziruph and the number Zephirod."

"Would you deny," said Coictier, "the sympathetic power of the clavicle, and that the Cabala is derived from it?"

"An error, Master Jacques! None of your formulæ lead to reality; while alchemy has its indubitable discoveries. Can you contest such results as these, —ice buried beneath the ground for a thousand years is transformed to rock crystal; lead is the progenitor of all the metals,—for gold is not metal, gold is light; lead requires but four periods of two hundred years each to pass successively from the state of lead to the state of red arsenic, from red arsenic to tin, from tin to silver? Are these facts or are they not? But to believe in clavicles, planets, and stars is as absurd as to believe with the natives of far Cathay that the golden oriole turns into a mole, and grains of wheat into mollusks of the genus Cypræa!"

"I have studied hermetics," cried Coictier, "and I affirm—"

The fiery archdeacon did not permit him to finish his speech. "And I have studied medicine, astrology, and hermetics. Here alone is truth [as he spoke he took from the press a phial filled with the powder of which we spoke some pages back], here alone is light! Hippocrates is a dream; Urania is a dream; Hermes is a mere idea. Gold is the sun; to make gold, is to become God. This is the only wisdom. I have sounded the depths of medicine and astrology, I tell you. They are naught, naught! The human body is a mere shadow; the stars are shadows!"

And he fell back upon his seat in a striking and imposing attitude. Father Tourangeau watched him in silence. Coictier forced himself to sneer, shrugged his shoulders slightly, and repeated in a low voice,—

"A madman!"

"And," said Tourangeau suddenly, "the splendid goal,—have you attained that? Have you made gold?"

"Had I made it," replied the archdeacon, pronouncing his words slowly, like a man who is reflecting, "the King of France would be called Claude, and not Louis."

The stranger frowned.

"What do I say?" added Don Claude with a scornful smile. "What would the throne of France avail me when I could reconstruct the Empire of the East?"

"Well, well," said the stranger.

"Oh, poor fool!" muttered Coictier.

The archdeacon went on, apparently replying to his own thoughts only:—

"But no, I still crawl; I bruise my face and knees on the sharp stones of the subterranean way. I see dimly; I do not behold the full splendour! I do not read; I spell!"

"And when you can read," asked the stranger, "shall you make gold?"

"Who can doubt it?" said the archdeacon.

"In that case, Notre-Dame knows that I am in great need of money, and I would fain learn to read your books. Tell me, reverend master, is your science hostile or displeasing to Notre-Dame?"

To this question from the stranger Don Claude merely answered with a quiet dignity,—

"Whose archdeacon am I?"

"True, my master. Well; will it please you to initiate me? Let me spell with you?"

Claude assumed the majestic and pontifical attitude of a Samuel.

"Old man, it needs more years than still remain to you to undertake the journey through mysterious things. Your head is very grey! None ever leave the cavern without white hairs, but none enter save with dark hair. Science is skilled in furrowing, withering, and wrinkling human faces; it needs not that old age should bring to her faces ready wrinkled. Yet if you long to submit yourself to discipline at your age, and to decipher the dread alphabet of sages, come to me; it is well: I will try what I can do. I will not bid you, you poor old man, go visit the sepulchres in the Pyramids, of which ancient Herodotus speaks, nor the brick tower of Babylon, nor the huge white marble sanctuary of the Indian temple of Eklinga. Neither I nor you have seen the Chaldean edifices constructed after the sacred form of Sikra, or the Temple of Solomon, which is destroyed, or the stone doors of the tomb of the kings of Israel, which are shattered. We will be content with the fragments of the book of Hermes which we have at hand. I will explain to you the statue of Saint Christopher, the symbolism of the sower, and that of the two angels at the door of the Sainte-Chapelle, one of whom has his hand in a vase and the other in a cloud—"

Here Jacques Coictier, who had been disconcerted by the archdeacon's spirited replies, recovered himself, and interrupted in the triumphant tone of one wise man setting another right: *"Erras, amice Claudi.* The symbol is not the number. You take Orpheus for Hermes."

"It is you who err," gravely answered the archdeacon. "Dædalus is the basement; Orpheus is the wall; Hermes is the building itself,—is the whole. Come when you will," he added, turning to Tourangeau; "I will show you the particles of gold remaining in the bottom of Nicolas Flamel's crucible, and you may compare them with the gold of Guillaume de Paris. I will teach you the secret virtues of the Greek word *peristera.* But first of all, you must read in turn the marble letters of the alphabet, the granite pages of the book. We will go from the porch of Bishop Guillaume and of Saint-Jean le Rond to the Sainte-Chapelle, then to the house of Nicolas Flamel in the Rue Marivault, to his tomb, which is in the Cemetery of the Holy Innocents, to his two almshouses in the Rue Montmorency. You shall read the hieroglyphics which cover the four great iron andirons in the porch of the Saint-Gervais Hospital, and those in the Rue de la Ferronnerie. We will spell over together once more the façades of Saint-Côme, Sainte-Geneviève des Ardents, Saint-Martin, Saint-Jacques de la Boucherie—"

For some time Tourangeau, intelligent though his appearance was, had seemed as if he failed to follow Don Claude. He now interrupted him with the words,—

"Odzooks! What sort of books can yours be?"

"Here is one of them," said the archdeacon.

And opening the window of his cell, he pointed to the vast Church of Notre-Dame, which, with its two towers outlined in black against a starry sky, its stone sides and monstrous hiproof, seemed like some huge double-headed sphinx crouching in the heart of the town.

The archdeacon silently gazed at the gigantic edifice; then with a sigh, stretching his right hand towards the printed book which lay open on the table, and his left hand towards Notre-Dame, with a melancholy glance from book to church, he said, "Alas! the one will kill the other."

Coictier, who had eagerly approached the book, could not repress the words, "Why! But what is there so terrible about this: *'Glossa in epistolas D. Pauli. Norimbergæ, Antonius Koburger. 1474.'* This is nothing new. It is a book by Pierre Lombard, the Master of Maxims. Is it because it is printed?"

"That's it," replied Claude, who seemed absorbed in deep meditation, and stood with his forefinger on the folio from the famous presses of Nuremberg. Then he added these mysterious words: "Alas! alas! Small things overcome great ones: the Nile rat kills the crocodile, the swordfish kills the whale, the book will kill the building."

The convent curfew rang just as Doctor Jacques once more whispered in his comrade's ear his perpetual refrain: "He is mad." To which his comrade now made answer, "I believe he is."

No stranger was allowed to linger in the convent at this hour. The two visitors withdrew. "Master," said Father Tourangeau as he took leave of the archdeacon, "I like scholars and great minds, and I hold you in singular esteem. Come to-morrow to the Palace of the Tournelles, and ask for the Abbot of Saint-Martin de Tours."

The archdeacon returned to his cell in amazement, realizing at last who this Father Tourangeau really was, and calling to mind this passage from the cartulary of Saint-Martin de Tours: *"Abbas beati Martini,* SCILICET REX FRANCIÆ, *est canonicus de consuetudine et habet parvam præbendam quam habet sanctus Venantius et debet sedere in sede thesaurarii."*

It is said that from this time forth the archdeacon held frequent meetings with Louis XI., when his Majesty came to Paris, and that Don Claude's credit much eclipsed that of Olivier le Daim and Jacques Coictier, the latter of whom, as was his wont, roundly reproached the king on this score.

Chapter II

THE ONE WILL KILL THE OTHER

Our fair readers will pardon us for pausing a moment to search for the hidden meaning of those enigmatical words of the archdeacon: "The one will kill the other. The book will kill the building."

In our opinion this thought had two phases. In the first place it was the thought of a priest. It was the terror of a true ecclesiastic at sight of a new agent,—printing. It was the fear and confusion of the man of the sanctuary at sight of Gutenberg's light-giving press. It was the pulpit and the manuscript, the spoken word and the written word, taking fright at the printed word; something similar to the stupor of a sparrow who should see the angel Legion spread his six million wings. It was the cry of the prophet who already hears the busy noise and stir of humanity set free, who sees in the future intellect undermining faith, opinion superseding belief, the world shaking off the yoke of Rome; the presage of the philosopher who sees human ideas, volatilized by the press, evaporated from the theocratic receiver; the dread of the soldier who examines the iron battering-ram and says: The tower must fall. It meant that one power was about to succeed another power. It meant: The press will kill the church.

But underlying this idea, doubtless the first and simplest, there was, to our thinking, another and more recent one, a corollary of the first, less easily seen and more easily contested; a point of view quite as philosophic, but not that of the priest alone,—that of the scholar and the artist as well. It was the presentiment that human thought, in changing its form, would also change its mode of expression; that the leading idea of each generation would no longer be written with the same material and in the same fashion; that the book of stone, so solid and so enduring, must make way for the book of paper, still more solid and enduring. Looked at in this light, the archdeacon's vague statement had another meaning; it meant that one art would dethrone another art. It meant: Printing will destroy architecture.

Indeed, from the beginning of things down to the fifteenth century of the Christian era inclusive, architecture was the great book of humanity, the chief expression of man in his various stages of development, whether as force or as intellect.

When the memory of the earliest races became surcharged, when mankind's burden of recollections became so great and so bewildering that mere speech, naked and winged, was in danger of losing a part on the road, men wrote them upon the ground in the way which was at once plainest, most enduring, and most natural. Every tradition was sealed beneath a monument.

The first monuments were mere fragments of rock "which the iron had not touched," says Moses. Architecture began like all writing. A stone was placed on end, and it was a letter, and each letter was a hieroglyph; and upon each hieroglyph rested a group of ideas, like the capital on a column. Thus did the first races, everywhere, at the same moment, over the entire surface of the world. We find the "cromlech" of the Celts in Asiatic Siberia and in American pampas.

Later on, words were formed; stone was added to stone, these granite syllables were coupled together, the verb essayed a few combinations. The Celtic dolmen and cromlech, the Etruscan tumulus, the Hebrew galgal, are words. Some of them, particularly the tumulus, are proper names. Sometimes, when there was plenty of stone and a vast stretch of coast, a phrase was written. The immense pile of Karnac is an entire formulary.

Finally, men made books. Traditions gave birth to symbols, which hid them as the leaves hide the trunk of a tree; all these symbols, in which humanity believed, grew, multiplied, crossed one another, became more and more complicated; the first monuments were no longer sufficient to contain them; they overflowed them on every side; these monuments barely sufficed to express the primitive tradition, as bare, as simple, and as plain as themselves. Symbolism must needs expand into an edifice. Architecture, therefore, was developed parallel with human thought; it became a thousand-headed, thusand-armed giantess, and fixed all that floating symbolism in an eternal, visible, palpable form. While Dædalus, that is, force, measured; while Orpheus, which is to say, intellect, sang, the column, which is a letter, the arcade, which is a syllable, the pyramid, which is a word, set in motion alike by a geometric and a poetic law, grouped, combined, blended, rose, fell, were juxtaposed upon the ground, placed in rows one above another in air, until they had written, at the dictation of the universal idea of an epoch, those marvellous books which were also marvellous buildings,—the pagoda at Eklinga, the Egyptian Rhamseïon, the Temple of Solomon.

The original idea, the word, was not only at the base of all these buildings, but also in their form. Solomon's Temple, for instance, was not merely the binding of the Holy Book, it was the Holy Book itself. In each of its concentric halls the priests could read the Word translated and made manifest; and thus they followed its transformations from sanctuary to sanctuary, until they grasped it in its innermost tabernacle in its most concrete form, which was again architectural,—the arch. Thus the Word was contained within the edifice; but its image was upon its exterior as the human figure is upon the case of a mummy.

And not only the form of the structure, but the site which was chosen for it, revealed the thought which it represented. According as the symbol to be expressed was graceful and pleasing or gloomy and severe, Greece crowned her mountains with a temple harmonious to the eye; India excavated hers, to carve within them those misshapen subterranean pagodas upborne by gigantic rows of granite elephants.

Thus, for the first six thousand years of the world's history, from the most immemorial pagoda of Hindustan to the Cologne Cathedral, architecture was the great writing of mankind. And this is so true that not only every religious symbol, but even each human thought, had its page and its monument in this vast book.

All civilization begins with theocracy

and ends with democracy. This law of liberty succeeding to unity is written in architecture. For,—let us dwell upon this point,—we must not suppose that the mason's work is only potent to build the temple, to express myth and priestly symbols, to transcribe the mysterious tables of the law in hieroglyphic characters upon its pages of stone. Were it so, as in every human society there comes a moment when the sacred symbol is worn away and obliterated by free thought, when the man slips away from the priest, when the excrescences of philosophies and systems eat away the face of religion, architecture could not reproduce this new state of the human mind; its leaves, closely written on the right side, would be blank upon the other, its work would be mutilated, its book would be imperfect. But it is not so.

Let us take for example the Middle Ages, which we see more clearly from their being nearer to us. During its first period, while theocracy was organizing Europe, while the Vatican rallied and reclassified around it the elements of a Rome made up from the Rome which lay crumbling about the Capitol, while Christianity was seeking the various stages of society amid the rubbish-heaps of previous civilizations, and was rebuilding from its ruins a new hierarchic universe whose high priest was the keystone of a vault, there was first heard springing into place amid this chaos, then little by little seen arising beneath the inspiration of Christianity, under the hand of the barbarians, fragments of dead schools of architecture, Greek and Roman,—that mysterious Roman architecture, the sister of the theocratic edifices of Egypt and India, the unalterable emblem of pure Catholicism, the unchanging hieroglyph of papal unity. All the thought of that time, in fact, is written in this sombre Roman style. Authority, unity, the impenetrable, the absolute, Gregory VII., are everywhere evident; everywhere we find the priest, never the man; everywhere the caste, never the people. Next came the Crusades. This was a great popular movement; and every great popular movement, whatever its cause and purpose, always releases the spirit of liberty from its final precipitate. Novelties are at hand. Here begins the stormy period of the Jacqueries, the Pragueries, and the Leagues. Authority is shaken, unity is divided. Feudality insists upon sharing with theocracy, until the people shall inevitably rise, and, as usual, seize the lion's portion; *Quia nominor leo*. The nobility then penetrate the ranks of the priesthood, the commonalty those of the nobility. The face of Europe is changed. Well! the face of architecture is also changed. Like civilization, it has turned the page, and the new spirit of the times finds architecture ready to write at its dictation. It returned from the Crusades with the pointed arch, as the nations did with liberty. Then, while Rome was being slowly dismembered, Roman architecture died. The hieroglyph forsook the cathedral, and went forth to emblazon the donjon and lend a glory to feudalism. The cathedral itself, that edifice once so dogmatic, henceforth invaded by the burghers, by the Commons, by liberty, escapes from the priest and falls into the power of the artist. The artist builds it in his own way.

Farewell to mystery, myth, and law! Fancy and caprice have full sway. If the priest have but his basilica and his altar, he has nothing to say; the four walls belong to the artist. The architectural book no longer belongs to the priesthood, to religion, to Rome; it is the property of the imagination, of poetry, of the people. Hence the rapid and innumerable changes in this style of architecture which has existed but for three centuries, and which are so striking after the stagnant immobility of the Roman school, which has lived through six or seven. But art advances with giant pace. The genius and originality of the people do the work formerly assigned to the bishops. Each race, as it passes, writes its line in the book; it erases the old Roman hieroglyphs from the frontispiece of the cathedrals, and barely permits the dogma to peep here and there from beneath the new symbolism overlying it. The popular drapery scarcely permits us to guess at the religious framework. No idea can be given of the liberties then taken by architects even in regard to the Church. We find capitals interwoven with monks and nuns in shameful attitudes, as in the Salle des Cheminées of the Palace of Justice at Paris; we find Noah's adventures carved at full length, as under the great porch at Bourges; or we find a tipsy monk, with the ears of an ass, and a glass in his hand, laughing in the face of an entire community, as in the lavatory of the Abbey of Bocherville. There was at this time a license for thoughts written in stone, comparable only to the present freedom of the press. It was the freedom of architecture.

This liberty was carried to great lengths. Sometimes a doorway, a façade, an entire church, offers a symbolic meaning absolutely foreign to religion, nay, even hostile to the Church. Guillaume de Paris in the thirteenth century, Nicolas Flamel in the fifteenth, wrote such seditious pages. Saint-Jacques de la Boucherie was a church of opposition throughout.

In those days thought was free in this direction only; it was therefore never written out in full except upon those books called buildings. Accepted in the form of a building, it would have been burned in the market-place by the executioner had any one been rash enough to risk it in the manuscript form; the thought expressed in the porch of a church would have witnessed the torture of the same thought expressed in the shape of a book. Thus, having only this one way, mason-work, to see the light, it bloomed forth in this way on every hand. Hence the vast quantity of cathedrals which once covered Europe,—a number so prodigious that we can hardly credit it even after verifying it. All the material and all the intellectual forces of society tended to one and the same end,—architecture. In this way, under pretext of building churches to God, the art grew to magnificent proportions.

Then, whoever was born a poet, turned architect. The genius scattered through the masses, repressed on every hand by feudalism as beneath a carapace of iron bucklers, finding no issue save in the direction of architecture, emerged through that art, and its Iliad took the form of cathedrals. All the other arts obeyed and submitted to the sway of architecture. They were the workmen who executed the great work. The architect, the poet, the master singer, summed up in his own person the sculpture which carved his façades, the painting which lit up his window-panes, the music which set his bells in motion and blew his organs. Even the poor poetry, properly so called, which persisted in vegetating in manuscript, was obliged to take some part, to enter into the structure in the form of canticle or prose hymn,—the same part, after all, played by the tragedies of Æschylus at the sacerdotal feasts of Greece, by the book of Genesis in Solomon's Temple.

So, down to the days of Gutenberg, architecture was the principal, the universal writing. In this granite volume, begun by the East, continued by Greek and Roman antiquity, the Middle Ages wrote the final page. Moreover, this phenomenon of an architecture of the people taking the place of an architecture of caste and rank, which we have observed in the Middle Ages, is reproduced with every analogous movement of the human intellect in the other great epochs of history. Thus, to state but briefly here a law which requires volumes for its development, in the Orient, the cradle of the primitive races, after Hindu architecture came Phœnician architecture, that opulent mother of Arab architecture; in antiquity, after Egyptian architecture, of which the Etruscan style and cyclopean monuments are but one variety, came Greek architecture, whose Roman style is but an overloaded prolongation of the Carthaginian dome; in modern times, after Roman architecture, came Gothic architecture. And by dividing these three series, we shall find in the three elder sisters (Hindu architecture, Egyptian architecture, Roman architecture) the same symbolism,—that is to say, theocracy, caste, unity, dogma, myth, God; and in the three younger sisters (Phœnician architecture, Greek architecture, Gothic architecture), whatever may be the diversity of form inherent in their nature, the meaning is always the same,—that is to say, liberty, humanity, mankind.

Whether he be known as Brahmin, Magian, or Pope, we are always conscious of the priest, nothing but the priest, in Hindu, Egyptian, or Roman structures. It is not so with the architecture of the people; their work is richer and less saintly. In the Phœnician school we are conscious of the tradesman; in the Grecian, of the republican; in the Gothic, of the burgher.

The general characteristics of all theocratic architecture are immutability, a horror of progress, a retention of traditional lines, a consecration of primitive types, a constant tendency of all human and natural forms towards the incomprehensible caprices of symbolism. These are obscure books, which only the initiated can decipher. Moreover, in them every form, every deformity even, has a meaning which makes it inviolable. Do not ask the Hindu, Egyptian, or Roman edifices to change their design or correct their statues. All perfection is to them impious. In these pieces of architecture the rigour of the dogma seems to overlie the stone like a second petrifaction. The general characteristics of popular edifices, on the contrary, should be variety, progress, originality, opulence, perpetual motion. They are sufficiently removed from religion to think of their beauty, to care for it, continually to alter and improve their adornment of statues or arabesques. They belong to this age. They have a human quality which they perpetually mingle with the divine symbolism under whose inspiration they are still produced. Hence edifices pervious to every soul, every intellect, and every imagination, still symbolical, but as easy to understand as Nature herself. Between theocratic architecture and this there is the difference that there is between a sacred language and a profane one, between hieroglyphics and art, between Solomon and Phidias.

If we sum up what we have thus far very hastily shown, omitting countless minor evidences and objections, we are led to these conclusions,—that architecture was, up to the fifteenth century, the chief register of humanity; that during this space of time no idea of any elaboration appeared in the world without being built into masonry; that every popular idea as well as every religious law has had its monument; in fact, that the human race has never had an important thought which it has not written in stone. And why? It is because every thought, whether religious or philosophic, is interested in its own perpetuation; because an idea which has stirred one generation desires to stir others, and to leave its trace. Now, what a precarious immortality is that of the manuscript! How far more solid, lasting, and enduring a book is a building! A torch and a Turk are enough to destroy the written words; it takes a social or a terrestrial revolution to destroy the constructed word. The barbarians passed over the Coliseum, the Deluge perhaps over the Pyramids.

In the fifteenth century everything changed.

Human thought discovered a means of perpetuation, not only more durable and more resisting than architecture, but also simpler and easier. Architecture was dethroned. To the stone letters of Orpheus succeeded the leaden letters of Gutenberg.

"The book will destroy the building."

The invention of printing was the greatest event in history. It was the primal revolution. It was the renewed and renovated form of expression of humanity; it is human thought laying off one form and assuming another; it is the entire and final changing of the skin of that symbolic serpent which ever since Adam has represented intellect.

Under the form of printing, thought is more imperishable than ever; it is volatile, intangible, indestructible. It is mingled with the air. In the day of architecture it became a mountain, and took armed possession of a century and a place. Now it becomes a flock of birds, is scattered to the four winds, and occupies at once all points of the horizon and all space.

We repeat it; who does not see that in this way it is far more indelible than before? From being solid, it has become perennial. It has passed from duration to immortality. A great body may be demolished, but how can ubiquity be rooted out? Had a flood come, the mountain would have disappeared beneath the waves long before the birds ceased to fly above it; and if but a single ark should float on the surface of the cataclysm, they would rest upon it, survive with it, watch with it the going down of the waters; and the new world which rose from that chaos would, on awakening, behold, hovering aloft, winged and living, the thought of the world which had been swallowed up.

And when we see that this mode of expression is not only the most preservative, but also the simplest, most convenient, and most practicable of all; when we consider that it entails no great amount of luggage, and requires no cumbrous apparatus; when we compare a thought obliged, in order to translate itself into an edifice, to set in motion four or five other arts, tons of gold, a whole mountain of stone, a whole forest of timber, a whole nation of workmen, —when we compare this with the thought which is made into a book, and which needs nothing but a little paper, a little ink, and a pen, why should we wonder that the human intellect gave up architecture for printing? Cross the original bed of a stream by a canal dug below its level, the stream will forsake its bed.

So, too, see how from the time of the discovery of printing, architecture gradually decayed, withered, and dried away. How plainly we can see the water sinking, the sap drying up, the thought of the time and of the people withdrawing from it! The sense of chill is almost imperceptible in the fifteenth century; the press was still too weak, and could only draw off somewhat of the superabundant life of mighty architecture. But with the dawn of the sixteenth century the disease of architecture becomes apparent; it has ceased to be the essential expression of society; in distress, it becomes classic art; from being Gallican, European, indigenous, it becomes Greek and Roman; from being real and modern, it becomes pseudo-antique. It it this decline which is known as the Renaissance, or revival. And yet it is a magnificent decline; for the old Gothic genius, that sun which is setting behind the gigantic press of Mayence, for some time longer pierces with its last rays all this hybrid heap of Latin arcades and Corinthian columns.

It is this setting sun which we take for the light of dawn.

And yet, from the moment that architecture becomes an art, like any other art, that it ceases to be the sum total of art, the supreme, the tyrant art, it loses the power to hold the other arts. They therefore gain their liberty, break the yoke of the architect, and go each its own way. Each of them gains by this divorce. Isolation enlarges everything. Carving becomes sculpture, picture-making becomes painting, the canon becomes music. It might be compared to an empire torn limb from limb at the death of its Alexander, whose provinces become kingdoms.

Hence Raphael, Michael Angelo, Jean Goujon, Palestrina,—those splendours of the dazzling sixteenth century.

At the same time with the arts, thought gained freedom in all directions. The heresiarchs of the Middle Ages had already made large inroads upon Catholicism. The sixteenth century destroyed religious unity. Before the invention of printing, the Reformation would have been but a schism; the invention of printing made it a revolution. Take away the press, and heresy is unnerved. Whether it be due to Providence or to fate, Gutenberg was the precursor of Luther.

But when the sun of the Middle Ages had wholly set, when Gothic genius had forever faded from the horizon of art, architecture grew daily dimmer, duller, and fainter. The printed book, that undying worm of the great edifice, sucked its life-blood and devoured it. It grew visibly thinner, barer, and poorer. It was commonplace, it was paltry, it was null. It ceased to express anything, even the memory of the art of former ages. Reduced to itself, abandoned by the other arts because human thought has abandoned it, it calls in journeymen for lack of artists; plain glass takes the place of painted windows; the stonecutter succeeds the sculptor. Farewell to all vigour, originality, life, and intellect. Architecture now crawled, like a pitiful beggar of the studios, from copy to copy. Michael Angelo, who had doubtless foreseen its death from the dawn of the sixteenth century, had a last inspiration,—the in-inspiration of despair. That Titan of art piled the Pantheon upon the Parthenon, and created St. Peter's Church at Rome. It is a great work, which deserved to remain unique,—the last original creation of architecture, the signature of a colossal artist at the foot of the vast registry of stone which it closed. Michael Angelo dead, what did this wretched architecture do, which survived itself in a spectral, ghost-like state? It took St. Peter's at Rome, copied it, and parodied it. It was mere mania. It was pitiable. Every century had its St. Peter's; in the seventeenth century it was the Val-de-Grâce, in the eighteenth, Sainte-Geneviève. Every country had its St. Peter's. London had its own; St. Petersburg had its own; Paris had two or three,— a worthless legacy, the last unmeaning drivel of a great art grown old and reduced to dotage before it died!

If in place of characteristic monuments, such as those to which we have just referred, we examine the general aspect of art from the sixteenth to the eighteenth centuries, we observe the same phenomena of decline and decay. From Francis II. down, the architectural form of the edifice becomes less and less apparent, the geometric form growing more and more prominent, like the skeleton of an emaciated invalid. The beautiful lines of art give way to the cold and inexorable lines of geometry. A building ceases to be a building; it is a polyhedron. Architecture, however, struggles to disguise this nakedness. We have the Greek pediment put down upon the Roman pediment, and *vice versa*. We still have the Pantheon within the Parthenon; we still have St. Peter's. We have the brick houses of the reign of Henry IV. with brick corners, as in the Place Royale and Place Dauphine. We have the churches of the reign of Louis XIII., heavy, clumsy, surbased, short, and broad, loaded with a dome as with a hump. We have the Mazarin architecture,—the wretched Italian Pasticcio of the "Four Nations." We have the palaces of the reign of Louis XIV., —long barracks built for courtiers, stiff, cold, and stupid. Lastly, we have the style of Louis XV., with its chiccory and vermicelli, and all the warts and fungi which disfigure that decrepit, toothless, coquettish old architecture. From the days of Francis II. to those of Louis XIV. the evil increased in geometrical ratio. Art was nothing but skin and bones. It was dying a wretched lingering death.

But what was printing doing? All the life which architecture lost, flushed its veins. In proportion as architecture degenerated, printing throve and flourished. The capital of forces which human thought had expended in building, it henceforth expended in books. So from the dawn of the sixteenth century onward, the press, grown to the level of the declining architecture, wrestled with it and slew it. In the seventeenth century it was already sufficiently supreme, sufficiently triumphant, sufficiently sure of victory, to give the world the spectacle of a great literary age. In the eighteenth century, after a long interval of rest at the court of Louis XIV., it once more grasped the old sword of Luther, armed Voltaire with it, and hastened tumultuously forth to attack that ancient Europe whose architectural expression it had already destroyed. When the eighteenth century closed, it had uprooted everything. In the nineteenth, it will reconstruct.

Now, we ask which of the two arts has really represented human thought for three centuries past? Which translates it? Which expresses, not only its literary and scholastic fancies, but its vast, profound, universal movement? Which constantly superposes itself, without rupture or void, upon mankind, which moves apace, a thousand-footed monster,—Architecture, or Printing?

Printing. Let no one be deceived: architecture is dead, irrevocably dead; killed by the printed book; killed because it was less enduring; killed because it was more costly. Every cathedral represents a thousand million francs. Think, then, what a capital would be required to rewrite the architectural book; to make thousands of structures once more cover the earth as thick as ant-hills; to bring back the days when the number of monumental works was such that, in the words of an eye-witness, "You would have thought that the world had shaken off her old garments, to clothe herself in a white array of churches," *Erat enim ut si mundus, ipse excutiendo semet, rejecta vetustate, candidam ecclesiarum vestem indueret.*"
—Glaber Radulphus.

A book is so soon made, costs so little, and may go so far! Why should we be surprised that all human thought flows that way? We do not mean to say that architecture may not yet produce a fine specimen here and there, a single masterpiece. We may still, I suppose, have from time to time, under the reign of printing, a column made by an entire army, of molten cannon, as during the reign of architecture we had Iliads and Romanceros, Mahâbhâratas, and Nibelungen-Lieds made by a whole nation, out of collected and blended rhapsodies.

The great accident of an architect of genius may occur in the twentieth century, as that of Dante did in the thirteenth; but architecture will never again be the social art, the collective art, the dominant art. The great poem, the great edifice, the great work of humanity, will no longer be built; it will be printed.

And in the future, should architecture accidentally revive, it will never again be supreme. It must bow to the sway of literature, formerly subject to it. The respective positions of the two arts will be reversed. It is certain that the rare poems to be found during the architectural period are like monuments. In India, Vyâsa was as manifold, strange, and impenetrable as a pagoda. In Egypt, poetry had, like the buildings, a grandeur and quietness of outline; in ancient Greece, beauty, serenity, and calm; in Christian Europe, the Catholic majesty, popular simplicity, the rich and luxuriant vegetation of a period of renewal. The Bible is like the Pyramids, the Iliad like the Parthenon, Homer like Phidias. Dante in the thirteenth century is the last Roman church; Shakspeare in the sixteenth the last Gothic cathedral.

Thus, to sum up what we have so far said in a manner necessarily brief and imperfect, mankind has two books, two registers, two testaments: architecture and printing,—the Bible of stone and the Bible of paper. Undoubtedly, when we examine these two Bibles, so widely opened during the lapse of centuries, we may be permitted to regret the visible majesty of the granite writing, of those gigantic alphabets formed into colonnades, pylons, and obelisks, of those human mountains which covered the world of the past, from the pyramid to the belfry, from Cheops to Strasburg. We should re-read the past upon those marble pages. We should admire and unceasingly re-turn the leaves of the book written by architecture; but we should not deny the grandeur of the structure reared by printing in its turn.

That structure is colossal. I know not what maker of statistics has calculated that by placing one upon another all the volumes issued from the press since the days of Gutenberg, we might fill up the space between the earth and the moon; but this is not the sort of grandeur which we mean. Still, when we try to form a mental image of all the products of printing down to our own day, does not the sum total seem a vast construction, resting upon the entire universe, at which humanity labours without respite, and whose monstrous summit is lost in the thick mists of the future? It is the ant-hill of intellects. It is the hive where all wit and imagination, those golden bees, store up their honey. The structure has a thousand stories. Here and there, opening on its staircases, we see the dark caves of learning intersecting one another within it. All over its surface art has woven its arabesques, its rose-windows, and its lace-work, to captivate the eye. There each individual work, fanciful and unique as it may seem, has its place and its purpose. Harmony results from the union of all. From the cathedral of Shakspeare to the mosque of Byron, a myriad spires are heaped pell-mell upon this metropolis of universal thought. At its base are inscribed some antique titles of humanity which architecture failed to register. At the left of the entrance is fastened the old white bas-relief of Homer; at the right the polyglot Bible rears its seven heads. The hydra of the Romancero bristles up beyond, with certain other hybrid forms, like the Vedas and the Nibelungen. Moreover, the vast edifice remains forever unfinished. The press, that gigantic machine which untiringly sucks up all the intellectual sap of society, unceasingly vomits forth fresh material for its work. All mankind are on the scaffolding. Every mind is a mason. The humblest stops up his hole or lays his stone. Every day a fresh course is laid. Independently of the original and individual contributions of each writer, there are collective supplies. The eighteenth century gave the "Encyclopædia," The French Revolution gave the "Moniteur." Assuredly, it is a structure which will gather and grow in unending spirals. Here, too, there is a confusion of tongues, an incessant activity, an indefatigable industry, a frantic co-operation of all humanity; it is the refuge promised to intellect against another deluge, against a flood of barbarians. It is the second Tower of Babel of the human race.

BOOK VI

The Pillory

Chapter I

AN IMPARTIAL GLANCE AT THE ANCIENT MAGISTRACY

A very lucky fellow, in the year of grace 1482, was that noble gentleman Robert d'Estouteville, knight, Lord of Beyne, Baron of Ivry and St. Andry in La Marche, councillor and chamberlain to the king, and keeper of the provosty of Paris. It was some seventeen years since he received from the king, Nov. 7, 1465, the year of the comet, the handsome appointment of provost of Paris, which was regarded rather as a dignity than an office. *"Dignitas,"* says Joannes Loemnœus, *"quæ cum non exigua potestate politiam concernente, atque prærogativis multis et juribus conjuncta est."* It was an extraordinary thing in 1482 for a gentleman to hold a commission from the king; and a gentleman, too, whose appointment dated back to the time of the marriage of Louis XI.'s natural daughter to the Bastard of Bourbon. On the same day that Robert d'Estouteville succeeded Jacques de Villiers as provost of Paris, Master Jehan Dauvet took the place of Master Hélye de Thorrettes as first president of the court of Parliament, Jehan Jouvenel des Ursins supplanted Pierre de Morvilliers in the office of Lord Chancellor of France, Regnault des Dormans deprived Pierre Puy of his place as referendary in ordinary to the king's household. Now, through how many hands had the presidency, chancellorship, and referendaryship not passed since Robert d'Estouteville was made provost of Paris! The office was "granted into his keeping," said the letters-patent; and certainly he kept it well. He clung to it, he identified himself with it, he made himself so much a part of it that he escaped that passion for change which possessed Louis XI., the suspicious, stingy, industrious king, who insisted on keeping up the elasticity of his power by constant removals and appointments. Nay, more: the worthy knight had obtained the reversion of his office for his son, and for the last two years the name of the noble Jacques d'Estouteville, Esquire, had figured beside his own at the head of the ordinary of the provosty of Paris. Assuredly a rare and signal mark of favour! True, Robert d'Estouteville was a good soldier; he had loyally raised his standard against "the league of the public weal," and had offered the queen a very marvellous stag made of sweetmeats on the day she entered Paris, in 14——. Besides, he had a good friend in Master Tristan l'Hermite, provost of the marshals of the king's household. Master Robert, therefore, led a very smooth and pleasant life. In the first place, he had a capital salary, to which were attached and hung, like so many additional bunches of grapes to his vine, the revenues of the civil and criminal registries of the provostship, besides the civil and criminal revenues of the Inferior Courts of the Châtelet, not to mention some slight toll on the Pont de Mantes and Pont de Corbeil, the tax on all the onions, leeks, and garlic brought into Paris, and the tax on wood meters and salt measures. Add to this the pleasure of displaying his fine suit of armour within the city limits, and showing off among the party-coloured red and tan robes of the sheriffs and district police which you may still admire carved upon his tomb at the Abbey of Valmont in Normandy, as you may also see his embossed morion at Montlhéry. And then,—was it nothing to have supreme power over the twelve serjeants, the porter and warder of the Châtelet, the two auditors of the Châtelet, *auditores castelleti,* the sixteen commissaries of the sixteen quarters of the city, the jailer of the Châtelet, the four enfeoffed serjeants, the hundred and twenty mounted police, the hundred and twenty vergers, the captain of the watch, his under-watch, counter-watch, and rear-watch? Was it nothing to administer high and low justice, to exercise the right to turn, hang, and draw, to say nothing of the minor jurisdiction "in the first instance" (*in prima instantia,* as the charters say) of that viscounty of Paris, so gloriously provided with seven noble bailiwicks? Can anything be imagined more agreeable than to give judgments and degrees, as Master Robert d'Estouteville did daily at the Grand-Châtelet, under the broad flat arches of Philip Augustus; and to return, as he was wont to do every evening, to that charming house in the Rue Galilée, within the precincts of the royal palace, which he held in right of his wife, Madame Ambroise de Loré, there to rest from the labour of sending some poor devil to pass his night in "that little lodge in the Rue de l'Escorcherie, wherein the provosts and sheriffs of Paris were used to make their prison, —the same measuring eleven feet in length, seven feet and four inches in width, and eleven feet in height?"

And not only had Master Robert d'Estouteville his private court as provost and viscount of Paris, but he also had his share, both active and passive, in the king's own high justice. There was no head of any note but had passed through his hands before falling into those of the executioner. It was he who went to the Bastille Saint-Antoine, in search of M. de Nemours, to take him to the Markets; and he who conducted M. de Saint-Pol to the Grève, the latter gentleman sulking and fretting, to the great delight of the provost, who had no love for the constable.

Here, certainly, was more than enough to make life happy and illustrious, and to justify in the future a memorable page in the interesting history of the provosts of Paris, wherein we learn that Oudard de Villeneuve had a house in the Rue des Boucheries, that Guillaume de Hangest bought big and little Savoy, that Guillaume Thiboust gave the nuns of Sainte-Geneviève his houses in the Rue Clopin, that Hugues Aubriot lived at Hôtel du Porc-Epic, and other domestic facts.

And yet, with all these motives for taking life patiently and pleasantly, Master Robert d'Estouteville waked on the morning of Jan. 7, 1482, in a very sulky and disagreeable mood. Whence came this ill-humour? He could not have told you himself. Was it because the sky was overcast; because the buckle of his old Montlhéry belt was fastened amiss, and girt his provostship's goodly portliness in too military a fashion; because he had seen a band of ragamuffins march through the street below his window, mocking him as they passed in double file, wearing doublets without shirts, crownless hats, and wallet and flask at their side? Was it a vague presentiment of the three hundred and seventy pounds, sixteen pence, and eight farthings which the future king, Charles VIII., was to cut off from the revenues of the provosty? The eader can take his choice; as for us, we incline to the belief that he was out of temper simply because he was out of temper.

Besides, it was the day after a holiday,—a stupid day for everybody, and especially for the magistrate, whose duty it was to sweep away all the dirt, actual and metaphorical, caused by a popular holiday in Paris. And then, he was to hold court at the Grand-Châtelet. Now, we have noticed that judges usually so arrange matters that the day upon which they hold court is also the day on which they are out of temper, in order that they may always have some one upon whom to vent their rage, in the name of the king, law, and justice.

However, the court had opened without him. His deputies, in the civil, criminal, and private courts, were doing his work for him, as was the custom; and ever since eight o'clock in the morning some scores of citizens, men and women, crowded and crammed into a dark corner of the lower court-room of the Châtelet, between a stout oaken railing and the wall, had blissfully looked on at the varied and attractive spectacle of the administration of civil and criminal law by Master Florian Barbedienne, auditor of the Châtelet, and provost's deputy, whose sentences were delivered pell-mell and somewhat at random.

The hall was small and low, with a vaulted roof. A table branded with *fleur-de-lis* stood at the back of it, with a large carved oaken arm-chair, which belonged to the provost and was empty, and a stool on the left for the auditor, Master Florian. Below sat the clerk, scribbling; opposite him were the people; and before the door and table were a number of the provost's officers, in frocks of purple camlet, with white crosses. Two officers from the Commonalty Hall, arrayed in party-coloured

red and blue kersey jackets, stood sentry before a half-open door, behind the table. A single arched window, deep set in the thick wall, cast a ray of pale January sunshine upon two grotesque figures,—the comical stone demon carved as a tailpiece to the keystone of the vaulted roof, and the judge seated at the end of the hall upon the *fleurs-de-lis*.

Now, picture to yourself at the provost's table, between two bundles of papers, leaning on his elbows, his feet on the train of his plain brown cloth gown, his face framed in its white lamb's-wool wig, of which his eyebrows seemed to be a fragment, red-faced, stern, winking and blinking, majestically bearing the burden of his fat cheeks, which met under his chin, Master Florian Barbedienne, auditor of the Châtelet.

Now, the auditor was deaf,—a slight defect for an auditor. Master Florian gave judgment, nevertheless, without appeal, and very properly too. It is certainly quite enough if a judge look as if he were listening; and the venerable auditor fulfilled this condition—the only one requisite to the due administration of justice—all the better for the fact that his attention was not to be distracted by any noise.

Moreover, he had a merciless comptroller of his sayings and doings, among the audience, in the person of our friend Jehan Frollo du Moulin, the little student of the previous day, that pedestrian who was sure to be found anywhere in Paris except in front of his professors' desk.

"Stay," he whispered to his comrade, Robin Poussepain, who was chuckling beside him while he commented on the scenes unrolled before them, "there's Jehanneton du Buisson,—the pretty daughter of that loafer from the New Market! Upon my soul, he has condemned her, the old wretch! Then his eyes can't be any better than his ears. Fifteen pence and four Paris farthings, for wearing two strings of beads! That's rather dear. '*Lex duri carminis.*' Who's that fellow? Robin Chief-de-Ville, hauberk-maker,—for having been passed and received as a master of the said trade? It's his entrance-fee. Hollo! two gentlemen among these varlets,—Aiglet de Soins, Hutin de Mailly. Two esquires, *Corpus Christi!* Ah, ha! they've been playing at dice. When shall I see our rector here? A hundred Paris pounds fine to the king! Barbedienne hits hard, like a deaf man as he is! I wish I may be my brother the archdeacon if this prevent me from gambling,—gambling by day, gambling by night, living a gambler, dying a gambler, and gambling away my soul when my last rag's gone! Holy Virgin! what a lot of girls! One after the other, my lambs! Ambroise Lécuyère! Isabeau la Paynette! Bérarde Gironin! I know them all, by heaven! Fine 'em! fine 'em! That'll teach you to wear gilt belts! Ten Paris pence, coquettes! Oh, what an old dog of a judge! deaf and imbecile! Oh, Florian, you blockhead! Oh, Barbedienne, you booby! See him sit at table! He gobbles the suitor, he gobbles the suit, he minces, he munches, he stuffs himself, he fills himself full. Fines, estrays, taxes, expenses, legal costs, wages, damages, torture, prison and jail and stocks, are Christmas cakes and Saint John's marchpane to him! Just look at him, the pig! Now, then, good! Still another amorous dame! Thibaud-la-Thibaude, and no one else,—for leaving the Rue Glatigny! Who is that fellow? Gieffroy Mabonne, bowman of the guard. He swore by the Holy Name, did he?—A fine, Thibaude! a fine, Gieffroy! Fine 'em both! Deaf old fool! he must have mixed the two charges up! Ten to one, he'll fine the woman for swearing, and the bowman for making love! Attention, Robin Poussepain! Whom are they bringing in now? What a lot of serjeants! By Jupiter! all the hounds in the pack are here. This must be the best head of game they've got,—a wild boar. It *is* one, Robin, it is indeed,—and a fine one too! By Hercules! it's our yesterday's prince, our Lord of Misrule, our bell-ringer, our one-eyed, humpbacked pet, our wryface! It's Quasimodo!"

It was no less a personage, indeed.

It was Quasimodo, bound, corded, tied, garotted, and well guarded. The squad of men who had him in charge were assisted by the captain of the watch in person, wearing the arms of France embroidered on his breast, and the city arms on his back. There was nothing, however, about Quasimodo, except his deformity, which could justify this display of halberds and arquebuses; he was sombre, silent, and quiet. His solitary eye merely cast an occasional crafty, angry glance at the bonds which held him.

He gazed around him with the same expression, but so dull and sleepy was it that the women only pointed him out to each other to mock at him.

But Master Florian, the auditor, was attentively turning over the brief containing the charge against Quasimodo, which the clerk had just handed him, and having examined the papers, seemed to be meditating for a moment. Thanks to this precaution, which he was always careful to take just before proceeding to an examination, he knew in advance the name, condition, and crimes of the prisoner, had his answer ready for replies which he expected, and succeeded in extricating himself from all intricacies of the examination without making his deafness too apparent. The brief therefore was to him like the blind man's dog. If he chanced to betray his infirmity by an occasional incoherent remark or an unintelligible question, it passed with some for profundity, and with others for imbecility. In either case, the honour of the magistracy was unimpeached; for it is much better that a judge should be considered stupid or profound than deaf. He accordingly took great pains to hide his deafness from all, and usually succeeded so well that he had actually come to deceive himself,—a thing, moreover, which is easier than you would think. All hunchbacks carry their heads high, all stammerers are fond of speechifying, all deaf people speak in low tones. As for him, at most he thought himself a little hard of hearing. This was the sole concession which he was willing to make to the public opinion upon this point, in his moments of perfect frankness and self-examination.

Having therefore considered Quasimodo's case, he threw back his head and half closed his eyes, in order to look more majestic and impartial, so that for the time being he was both deaf and blind,—a twofold condition, without which there can be no perfect judge. In this magisterial attitude he began his cross-examination.

"Your name?"

Now, here was a case which had not been "provided for by the law,"—that of one deaf man questioning another.

Quasimodo, quite unconscious of the question, continued to gaze fixedly at the judge, and made no answer. The judge, deaf, and wholly unaware of the prisoner's deafness, supposed that he had answered, as all prisoners were wont to do, and went on, with his mechanical and stupid assurance,—

"Good! Your age?"

Quasimodo made no answer. The judge was satisfied, and continued,—

"Now, your business?"

Still the same silence. The audience began to whisper and look at each other.

"That will do," resumed the imperturbable auditor, when he supposed that the prisoner had ended his third answer. "You are accused, before us: *primo,* of making a nocturnal disturbance; *secundo,* of an indecent assault upon the person of a light woman, *in præjudicium meretricis; tertio,* of rebellion and disloyalty towards the archers of the guard of our lord the king. What have you to say for yourself on all these points? Clerks, have you written down all that the prisoner has said thus far?"

At this unfortunate question a shout of laughter burst from both clerk and audience, so violent, so hearty, so contagious, so universal, that even the two deaf men could not fail to notice it. Quasimodo turned away, shrugging his hump in disdain; while Master Florian, equally surprised, and supposing the laughter of the spectators to be provoked by some irreverent reply from the prisoner, made apparent to him by that shrug, addressed him most indignantly,—

"Such an answer as that, you rascal, deserves a halter! Do you know to whom you speak?"

This sally was scarcely adapted to silence the outburst of merriment. It seemed to all so absurd and ridiculous that the contagious laughter spread to the very serjeants from the Commonalty Hall, the kind of men-at-arms whose stupidity is their uniform. Quasimodo alone preserved his gravity, for the very good reason that he understood nothing of what was going on around him. The judge, more and more indignant, felt obliged to proceed in the same strain, hoping in this way to strike the prisoner with a terror which would react upon the audience and restore them to a due sense of respect for him.

"So then, perverse and thievish knave, you venture to insult the auditor of the Châtelet, the chief magistrate of the police courts of Paris, appointed to inquire into all crimes, offences, and misdemeanours; to control all trades and prevent monopoly; to keep the pavements in repair; to put down hucksters of poultry, fowl, and wild game; to superintend the measuring of logs and firewood; to cleanse the city of mud and the air of contagious diseases,—in a word, to watch continually over the public welfare, without wages or hope of salary! Do you know that my name is Florian Barbedienne, and that I am the lord provost's own deputy, and, moreover, commissary, comptroller, and examiner with equal power in provosty, bailiwick, court of registration, and presidial court?"

There is no reason why a deaf man talking to a deaf man should ever cease. Heaven knows when Master Florian, thus launched on the full flood of his own eloquence, would have paused, if the low door at the back of the room had not suddenly opened and admitted the provost himself.

At his entrance Master Florian did not stop short, but turning half round on his heel and abruptly addressing to the provost the harangue with which but a moment before he was overwhelming Quasimodo, he said: "My lord, I demand such sentence as it may please you to inflict upon the prisoner here present, for his grave and heinous contempt of court."

And he sat down again quite out of breath, wiping away the big beads of moisture which ran down his face like tears, wetting the papers spread out before him. Master Robert d'Estouteville frowned, and commanded Quasimodo's attention by a sign so imperious and significant that even the deaf man understood something of his meaning.

The provost addressed him severely: "What brings you here, scoundrel?"

The poor wretch, supposing that the provost asked his name, broke his wonted silence, and answered in a hoarse and guttural voice, "Quasimodo."

The answer had so little to do with the question than an irresistible laugh again ran round the room, and Master Robert cried out, red with rage,—

"Would you mock me too, you arrant knave?"

"Bell-ringer of Notre-Dame," replied Quasimodo, fancying himself called upon to explain to the judge who he was.

"Bell-ringer, indeed!" responded the provost, who, as we have already said, had waked in an ill enough humour that morning not to require any fanning of the flames of his fury by such strange answers. "Bell-ringer! I'll have a peal of switches rung upon your back through all the streets of Paris! Do you hear me, rascal?"

"If you want to know my age," said Quasimodo, "I believe I shall be twenty on Saint Martin's Day."

This was too much; the provost could bear it no longer.

"Oh, you defy the provost's office, do you, wretch! Vergers, take this scamp to the pillory in the Grève; beat him well, and then turn him for an hour. He shall pay me for this, odzooks! And I order this sentence to be proclaimed, by the aid of four sworn trumpeters, throughout the seven castellanies of the viscounty of Paris."

The clerk at once wrote down the sentence.

"A wise sentence, by God!" exclaimed the little student, Jehan Frollo du Moulin, from his corner.

The provost turned, and again fixed his flashing eyes upon Quasimodo: "I believe the scamp said 'By God!' Clerk, add a fine of twelve Paris pence for swearing, and let half of it go to the Church of Saint Eustache; I am particularly fond of Saint Eustache."

In a few moments the sentence was drawn up. It was simple and brief in tenor. The common law of the provosty and viscounty of Paris had not yet been elaborated by the president, Thibaut Baillet, and by Roger Barmue, the king's advocate; it was not then obscured by that mass of quirks and quibbles which these two lawyers introduced at the beginning of the sixteenth century. Everything about it was clear, expeditious, and explicit. It went straight to the mark, and at the end of every path, unconcealed by brambles or briers, the wheel, the gallows, or the pillory were plainly to be seen from the very outset. At least, you knew what was coming.

The clerk handed the sentence to the provost, who affixed his seal to it, and left the room to continue his round of the courts, in a state of mind which must have added largely that day to the population of the jails of Paris. Jehan Frollo and Robin Poussepain laughed in their sleeves. Quasimodo looked on with indifference and surprise.

But the clerk, just as Master Florian Barbedienne was reading the sentence in his turn before signing it, felt a twinge of pity for the poor devil of a prisoner, and in the hope of gaining some diminution of his punishment, leaned as close as he could to the auditor's ear, and said, pointing to Quasimodo, "That fellow is deaf."

He hoped that their common infirmity might rouse Master Florian's interest in the prisoner's favour. But, in the first place, we have already observed that Master Florian did not care to have his deafness noticed. In the next place, he was so hard of hearing that he caught not one word of what the clerk said to him; and yet, he wanted to have it appear that he heard, and therefore answered. "Oho! that's a different matter; I did not know that. Give him another hour in the pillory, in that case."

And he signed the sentence with this modification.

"Well done!" said Robin Poussepain, who bore Quasimodo a grudge; "that will teach him to maltreat folks."

Chapter II

THE RAT-HOLE

WITH the reader's permission, we will return to the Grève which we left yesterday with Gringoire, to follow Esmeralda.

It is ten o'clock in the morning; everything smacks of the day after a holiday. The pavement is covered with fragments,—ribbons, scraps, feathers from the plumes, drops of wax from torches, crumbs from the public feast. A number of citizens are lounging here and there, occasionally stirring the dying embers of the bonfire with their feet, going into ecstasies over the Pillar House, as they recall the fine hangings of the previous day, and staring at the nails which held them, the last remnant of their pleasure. The venders of cider and beer roll their barrels through the various groups. A few busy passers come and go. The shop-keepers chat and gossip with one another at the door of their shops. The festival, the ambassadors, Coppenole, the Lord of Misrule, are on every tongue, each vying with the other in the severity of his criticisms and the loudness of his laughter. And yet four mounted police, who have just stationed themselves at the four corners of the pillory, have already collected about them a goodly portion of the populace scattered about the square, and willing to stand stupidly still for any length of time, in the hope of witnessing some petty punishment.

If now the reader, having looked upon this lively and noisy scene enacting in every part of the square, will turn his gaze towards that ancient half-Gothic, half-Roman structure known as Tour-Roland, which forms the western angle of the quay, he may perceive at the corner of its façade a large public breviary, richly illuminated, protected from the rain by a small pent-house, and from thieves by a grating, which, however, allows the passer-by to turn over its leaves. Beside this breviary is a narrow arched window, guarded by two iron bars placed crosswise, and looking out upon the square,—the only opening through which a little air and light reach a tiny cell without a door, built on the ground-floor, in the thickness of the wall of the old house, and filled with a peace made more profound, a silence made more melancholy, by the fact that a public square, the noisiest and most thickly peopled place in all Paris, swarms and shrieks just outside.

This cell has been celebrated throughout Paris for almost three centuries; since Madame Rolande, of the Tour-Roland, being in mourning for her father, who died while on a Crusade, had it hewed out of the wall of her own house and shut herself up in it forever, keeping no part of her palace but this one lodging, the door of which was walled up and the window open, in winter as in summer, giving all the rest of her property to God and the poor. The desolate dame did indeed await death for twenty years within this premature tomb, praying night and day for her father's soul, sleeping upon a bed of ashes, without even a stone for a pillow, clad in black sack-cloth, and living on such portions of bread and water as the pity of the passers-by placed on her window-sill; thus accepting charity after having bestowed it. At her death, as she was about to pass to another tomb, she bequeathed this one in perpetuity to all afflicted women, mothers, widows, or daughters, who had great need to pray for others or themselves, and who wished to bury themselves alive in token of their great grief or great penitence. The poor of her time paid her the best of funeral rites in their tears and blessings; but, to their great regret, the pious dame could not be canonized a saint, for lack of patronage. Those of them who were inclined to be impious hoped that the matter might be more readily arranged in paradise than at Rome, and quite simply prayed to God instead of to the Pope, for the deceased. Most of them were satisfied with holding her memory sacred and making relics of her rags. The city, for its part, founded for the lady's sake a public breviary, which was fastened to the wall near the window of the cell, so that those who passed might occasionally stop, if only to pray, that so the prayer might lead them to think of alms, and that the poor recluses, the heirs of Madame Rolande's cell, might not die of hunger and neglect.

Nor was this sort of tomb a great rarity in the cities of the Middle Ages. There might frequently be found, in the most crowded street, in the most motley and clamorous market-place, in the very midst of the confusion, under the horses' feet, under the cart-wheels, as it were, a cellar, a well, a walled and grated cell, within which some human being prayed night and day, voluntarily vowed to everlasting lamentation, to some extraordinary expiation. And all the reflections which would be roused to-day by so singular a sight,—that horrid cell, a sort of connecting link between the house and the tomb, the cemetery and the city; that living creature cut off from human companionship and thenceforth reckoned with the dead; that lamp consuming its last drop of oil in darkness; that remnant of life flickering in a grave; that breath, that voice, that perpetual prayer, in a coffin of stone; that face forever turned towards the other world; that eye already illumined by another sun; that ear glued to the wall of the tomb; that soul imprisoned in that body; that body imprisoned in that dungeon; and beneath that double casing of flesh and stone the murmur of that suffering soul,—nothing of all this was noted by the crowd.

The unreasoning and far from subtile piety of that day could not conceive of so many sides to an act of religion. It viewed the thing as a whole, and honoured, venerated, sanctified the sacrifice if need be, but did not analyze the suffering, and pitied it but slightly. It occasionally bestowed some pittance on the wretched penitent, looked through the hole to see if he were still alive, knew not his name, hardly knew how many years it was since he began to die, and to the stranger who asked about the living skeleton rotting in that cellar, the neighbours simply answered, "That is the recluse."

People saw things in this way then,—without metaphysics, without exaggeration, without magnifying-glass, with the naked eye. The microscope had not yet been invented, either for material or for spiritual things.

Besides, although people marvelled so little at them, instances of this kind of claustration in the heart of a town were really very frequent, as we just now observed. Paris contained a goodly number of these cells for praying to God and doing penance; they were almost all occupied. It is true that the clergy did not care to leave them empty, as that would imply luke-warmness among the faithful; and they therefore put lepers into them when they had no penitents. Besides the cell in the Grève, there was one at Montfaucon, one at the charnel-house of the Cemetery of the Innocents, another,—I've forgotten just where,—at Clichon House, I believe; others again in many other places, traces of which may yet be found in popular tradition, for lack of monuments. The University also had cells of its own. On St. Geneviève's Mount a kind of mediæval Job for thirty years sang the seven penitential psalms upon a dunghill, at the bottom of a cistern, beginning again whenever he reached the end, chanting louder by night,—*magna voce per umbras*; and even now the antiquary fancies that he hears his voice when he enters the street known as Rue Puits-qui-parle ("Talking Well").

But to keep to the cell of the Tour-Roland, we should mention that it had never wanted for recluses. Since Madame Rolande's death, it had seldom been vacant for more than a year. Many women had gone thither to weep, until death, for parents, lovers, or sins. Parisian malice, which interferes with everything, even those things which concern it least, asserted that very few widows had ever been seen within its walls.

As was the fashion of that period, a Latin inscription on the wall informed the learned passers-by of the pious purpose of this cell. The custom was retained until the middle of the sixteenth century, of explaining the purpose of a building in a brief device inscribed above the door. Thus we still read in France, over the gate of the prison belonging to the manor of the Lord of Tourville: *"Sileto et spera;"* in Ireland, under the escutcheon over the great door of Fortescue Castle: *"Forte scutum, salus ducum;"* and in England, over the main entrance to the hospitable manor of Earl Cowper: *"Tuum est."* In those days every edifice embodied a thought.

As there was no door to the walled cell in the Tour-Roland, some one had carved in Roman capitals over the window these two words:—

"TU, ORA."

Hence the people, whose mind never grasps such nice distinctions, and who are quite ready to translate *Ludovico Magno* into the Porte Saint-Denis, gave this dark, damp, gloomy cavern the name of the *"Trou-aux-Rats,"* or the Rat-Hole,—an explanation possibly less sublime, but certainly more picturesque than the other.

Chapter III

THE STORY OF A WHEATEN CAKE

AT the time of which this story treats, the cell in the Tour-Roland was occupied. If the reader wish to know by whom, he has but to listen to the conversation of three worthy gossips, who, at the moment when we drew his attention to the Rat-Hole, were walking directly that way, going from the Châtelet towards the Grève, along the water's edge.

Two of these women were dressed like good citizens of Paris. Their fine white gorgets; their petticoats of striped linsey-woolsey, red and blue; their white knitted stockings, with coloured clocks, pulled well up over the leg; their squaretoed shoes of tan-coloured leather with black soles; and above all their headdress,—a sort of tinsel horn overloaded with ribbons and lace, still worn by the women of Champagne and by the grenadiers of the Russian Imperial Guard,—proclaiming that they belonged to that class of rich tradesfolk occupying the middle ground between what servants call "a woman" and what they call "a lady." They wore neither rings nor gold crosses; and it was easy to see that this was not from poverty, but quite simply from fear of a fine. Their companion was attired in much the same style; but there was something in her appearance and manner which bespoke the country notary's wife. It was evident by the way in which her girdle was arranged high above her hips, that she had not been in Paris long; add to this a pleated gorget, knots of ribbon on her shoes, the fact that the stripes of her petticoat ran breadthwise, and a thousand other enormities revolting to good taste.

The first two walked with the gait peculiar to Parisian women showing Paris to their country friends. The country-woman held by the hand a big boy, who grasped in his hand a large cake. We regret that we must add that, owing to the severity of the season, his tongue did duty as a pocket-handkerchief. The child loitered ("*non passibus æquis*," as Virgil has it), and stumbled constantly, for which his mother scolded him well. True, he paid far more attention to the cake than to the pavement. Undoubtedly he had some grave reason for not biting it (the cake), for he contented himself with gazing affectionately at it. But his mother should have taken charge of the cake. It was cruel to make a Tantalus of the chubby child.

But the three damsels (for the term "dame" was then reserved for noble ladies) were all talking at once.

"Make haste, Damoiselle Mahiette," said the youngest of the three, who was also the biggest, to the country-woman. "I am mightily afraid we shall be too late; they told us at the Châtelet that he was to be taken directly to the pillory."

"Nonsense! What do you mean, Damoiselle Oudarde Musnier?" replied the other Parisian. "He is to spend two hours in the pillory. We have plenty of time. Did you ever see any one pilloried, my dear Mahiette?"

"Yes," said the country-woman, "at Rheims."

"Pooh! What's your pillory at Rheims? A miserable cage, where they turn nothing but peasants! A fine sight, truly!"

"Nothing but peasants!" said Mahiette, "in the Cloth-market! at Rheims! We've seen some very fine criminals there,—people who had killed both father and mother! Peasants, indeed! What do you take us for, Gervaise?"

The country-lady was certainly on the eve of losing her temper in defence of her pillory. Fortunately the discreet Damoiselle Oudarde Musnier changed the subject in time:—

"By-the-bye, Damoiselle Mahiette, what do you say to our Flemish ambassadors? Have you any as fine at Rheims?"

"I confess," answered Mahiette, "that there is no place like Paris for seeing such Flemings as those."

"Did you see among the embassy that great ambassador who is a hosier?" asked Oudarde.

"Yes," responded Mahiette. "He looks like a regular Saturn."

"And that fat one with the smooth face?" added Gervaise. "And that little fellow with small eyes and red lids, as ragged and hairy as a head of thistle?"

"Their horses were the finest sight," said Oudarde, "dressed out in the fashion of their country."

"Oh, my dear," interrupted the rustic Mahiette, assuming an air of superiority in her turn, "what would you say if you had seen, in 1461, at the coronation at Rheims, now eighteen years ago, the horses of the princes and of the king's escort? Housings and trappings of every description: some of damask cloth, of fine gold, trimmed with sable; others, of velvet, trimmed with ermines' tails; others, loaded down with goldsmiths' work and great gold and silver bells! And the money that it must have cost! And the lovely page-boys that rode on them!"

"That does not alter the fact," drily responded Damoiselle Oudarde, "that the

Flemings have very fine horses, and that they had a splendid supper last night given them by the mayor at the City Hall, where they were treated to sugar-plums, hippocras, spices, and other rarities."

"What are you talking about, neighbour!" cried Gervaise. "It was at the Petit-Bourbon, with the Cardinal, that the Flemings supped."

"Not at all. At the City Hall."

"Yes, indeed. At the Petit-Bourbon!"

"So surely was it at the City Hall," returned Oudarde, sharply, "that Doctor Scourable made them a speech in Latin with which they seemed mightily pleased. It was my husband, who is one of the licensed copyists, who told me so."

"So surely was it at the Petit-Bourbon," replied Gervaise, with no whit less of animation, "that I can give you a list of what the Cardinal's attorney treated them to: Twelve double quarts of hippocras, white, yellow, and red; twenty-four boxes of double gilt Lyons marchpane; as many wax torches of two pounds each, and six half-casks of Beaune wine, red and white, the best to be found. I hope that's decisive." I have it from my husband, who is captain of fifty men in the Commonalty Hall, and who was only this morning comparing the Flemish ambassadors with those sent by Prester John and the Emperor of Trebizond, who came from Mesopotamia to Paris during the reign of the last king, and who had rings in their ears."

"It is true that they supped at the City Hall," replied Oudarde, but little moved by this display of eloquence, "that no one ever saw such an exhibition of meats and sugar-plums before."

"But I tell you that they were served by Le Sec, one of the city guard, at the Petit-Bourbon, and that's what misled you."

"At the City Hall, I say!"

"At the Petit-Bourbon, my dear! For didn't they illuminate the word 'Hope,' which is written over the great entrance, with magical glasses?"

"At the City Hall! at the City Hall! Don't I tell you that Husson-le-Voir played the flute?"

"I tell you, no!"

"I tell you, yes!"

"And I tell you, no!"

The good fat Oudarde was making ready to reply, and the quarrel might have come to blows, if Mahiette had not suddenly exclaimed, "Only see those people crowding together at the end of the bridge! There's something in the midst of them, at which they're all looking."

"Truly," said Gervaise, "I do hear the sound of a tambourine. I verily believe it's that little Smeralda playing her tricks with her goat. Come quick, Mahiette! Make haste and pull your boy along faster. You came here to see all the sights of Paris. Yesterday you saw the Flemings; to-day you must see the gipsy girl."

"The gipsy," said Mahiette, turning back abruptly, and grasping her son's arm more firmly. "Heaven preserve us! She might steal my child!—Come, Eustache!"

And she set out running along the quay towards the Grève, until she had left the bridge far behind her. But the child, whom she dragged after her, stumbled, and fell upon his knees; she stopped, out of breath. Oudarde and Gervaise rejoined her.

"That gipsy girl steal your child!" said Gervaise. "What a strange idea!"

Mahiette shook her head with a pensive air.

"The queer part of it is," observed Oudarde, "that the nun has the same opinion of the gipsies."

"What do you mean by the nun?" said Mahiette.

"Why!" said Oudarde, "Sister Gudule."

"And who," returned Mahiette, "is Sister Gudule?"

"You must indeed be from Rheims, not to know that!" replied Oudarde. "She is the recluse of the Rat-Hole."

"What!" asked Mahiette, "the poor woman to whom we are carrying this cake?"

Oudarde nodded.

"Exactly so. You will see her presently at her window on the Grève. She feels just as you do about those gipsy vagabonds who go about drumming on the tambourine and telling people's fortunes. No one knows what gave her such a horror of gipsies. But you, Mahiette,—why should you take to your heels in such haste at the mere sight of them?"

"Oh," said Mahiette, clasping her child to her bosom, "I could not bear to have the same thing happen to me that happened to Paquette la Chantefleurie."

"Oh, do tell us the story, my dear Mahiette," said Gervaise, taking her arm.

"Gladly," answered Mahiette; "but you must indeed be from Paris, not to know that! You must know, then,— but we need not stand here to tell the tale,—that Paquette la Chantefleurie was a pretty girl of eighteen when I was one too; that is to say, some eighteen years ago, and it is her own fault if she is not now, like me, a happy, hale, and hearty mother of six-and-thirty, with a husband and a son. However, from the time she was fourteen, it was too late! She was the daughter of Guybertaut, minstrel to the boats at Rheims, the same who played before King Charles VII., at his coronation, when he sailed down the river Vesle from Sillery to Muison, and, more by token, the Maid of Orleans was in the boat with him. Her old father died when Paquette was still a mere child; then she had no one but her mother, a sister to Pradon, the master brazier and coppersmith at Paris, in the Rue Parin-Garlin, who died last year. You see that she came of an honest family. The mother was a good, simple woman, unfortunately, and taught Paquette nothing but a little fringe-making and toy-making, which did not keep the child from growing very tall and remaining very poor. The two lived at Rheims, on the water's edge, in the Rue Folle-Peine. Note this. I think this was what brought ill-luck to Paquette. In '61, the year of the coronation of our King Louis XI.,—may Heaven preserve him!—Paquette was so merry and so pretty that every one knew her as Chantefleurie. Poor girl! She had lovely teeth, and she liked to laugh, so that she might show them. Now, a girl who likes to laugh is on the high-road to weep; fine teeth spoil fine eyes. Such was Chantefleurie. She and her mother had hard work to earn a living;

they were greatly reduced after the minstrel's death; their fringe-making did not bring them in more than six farthings a week, which doesn't make quite two pence. Where was the time when Father Guybertaut earned twelve Paris pence at a single coronation for a single song? One winter (it was that same year of '61), when the two women had not a stick of firewood and it was bitterly cold, the cold gave Chantefleurie such a fine colour that the men called her Paquette,—some called her Pâquerette,—and she went to the bad. —Eustache! don't you let me see you nibble that cake!—We soon saw that she was ruined, when she came to church one fine Sunday with a gold cross on her neck. At fourteen years of age! Think of that! First it was the young Vicomte de Cormontreuil, whose castle is about three quarters of a league away from Rheims; then M. Henri de Triancourt, the king's equerry; then something lower, Chiart de Beaulin, serjeant-at-arms; then, still lower, Guery Aubergeon, the king's carver; then, Macé de Frépus, the dauphin's barber; then, Thévenin-le-Moine, the king's cook; then, still descending to older and meaner men, she fell into the hands of Guillaume Racine, viol-player, and of Thierry-de-Mer, the lanternmaker. Then—poor Chantefleurie!— she became common property; she had come to the last copper of her gold piece. How shall I tell you, ladies? At the time of the coronation, in that same year '61, it was she who made the king of ribalds' bed,—that selfsame year!"

Mahiette sighed, and wiped a tear from her cheek.

"No very uncommon story," said Gervaise; "and I don't see that it has anything to do with gipsies, or with children."

"Patience!" replied Mahiette: "we shall soon come to the child. In '66, sixteen years ago this very month, on Saint Paula's Day, Paquette gave birth to a little girl. Poor thing! Great was her joy; she had long wished for a child. Her mother, good woman, who never knew how to do anything but shut her eyes to her daughter's faults,—her mother was dead. Paquette had no one left to love, no one to love her. Five years had passed since her fall, and Chantefleurie was but a miserable creature. She was alone, alone in the world, pointed at, hooted after in the street, beaten by the police, mocked by little ragged boys. And then, she was now twenty years old; and twenty is old age to such women. Vice had ceased to bring her in much more than her fringemaking used to do; every fresh wrinkle took away another coin. Winter was once more a hard season for her; wood was again scarce upon her hearth, and bread in her cupboard. She could no longer work; for when she took to a life of pleasure she learned to be lazy, and she suffered far more than before, because in learning to be lazy she became accustomed to pleasure,—at least, that's the way the priest of Saint-Remy explains it to us that such women feel cold and hunger more than other poor folks do when they are old."

"Yes," remarked Gervaise; "but the gipsies?"

"One moment, Gervaise!" said Oudarde, whose attention was less impatient. "What would there be left for the end, if everything came at the beginning? Go on, Mahiette, please. Poor Chantefleurie!"

Mahiette continued:—

"So she was very wretched, very unhappy, and her tears wore deep furrows in her cheeks. But in her shame, her disgrace, and her misery, it seemed to her that she should feel less ashamed, less disgraced, and less miserable, if she had something to love or some one to love her. It must be a child; for only a child could be innocent enough for that. She recognized this after trying to love a thief,—the only man who would have anything to say to her; but after a little she saw that even the thief despised her. Women of that sort must have a lover or a child to fill up their hearts, otherwise they are very unhappy. As she could not have a lover, she gave herself up to longing for a child; and as she had never given over being pious, she prayed night and day that the good God would give her one. The good God had pity on her, and gave her a little girl. I cannot describe to you her delight; she covered it with a perfect rain of tears, kisses, and caresses. She nursed her child herself, made swaddling-clothes for it of her own coverlet,—the only one she had on her bed,—and no longer felt cold or hungry. She grew handsome again. An old maid makes a young mother. She took to her former courses; her old friends came back to see her, and she readily found customers for her wares, and with the price of all these iniquities she bought baby linen, caps, and bibs, lace gowns and little satin bonnets, without ever thinking of buying herself another coverlet.—Master Eustache didn't I tell you not to eat that cake?—It is certain that little Agnès,—that was the child's name, her given name; for as to a surname, Chantefleurie had long since ceased to have one,—it is certain that the little thing was more tricked out with ribbons and embroidery than a dauphiness from Dauphiny! Among other things, she had a pair of tiny shoes, the like of which even King Louis XI. himself surely never had! Her mother sewed and embroidered them herself; she put all the dainty arts of her fringe-making into them, and as many intricate stitches as would make a gown for the Holy Virgin. They were the two sweetest little pink shoes imaginable. They were no longer than my thumb, and you must have seen the child's tiny feet slip out of them, or you would never have believed they could have gone in. To be sure, those little feet were so small, so pink, and so pretty!—pinker than the satin of the shoes! When you have children of your own, Oudarde, you will know that there is nothing prettier than those little feet and hands!"

"I ask nothing better," said Oudarde, sighing; "but I must wait the good pleasure of Master Andry Musnier."

"Besides," resumed Mahiette, "Paquette's child had not merely pretty feet. I saw her when she was only four months old; she was a perfect love! Her eyes were bigger than her mouth, and she had the finest black hair, which curled already! She would have made a splendid brunette if she had lived to be sixteen. Her mother became more and more crazy about her every day. She fondled her, kissed her, tickled her, washed her, decked her out, almost ate her up! She lost her head over her; she thanked God for her. Her pretty little pink feet particularly were an endless wonder, the cause of a perfect delirium of joy! Her lips were forever pressed to them; she could never cease admiring their smallness. She would put them into the tiny shoes, take them out again, admire them, wonder at them, hold them up to the light, pity them when they tried to walk upon the bed, and would gladly have spent her life on her knees, putting the shoes on and off those feet, as if they had been those of an infant Jesus."

"A very pretty story," said Gervaise in a low voice; "but what has all this to do with the gipsies?"

"This," replied Mahiette. "There came one day to Rheims some very queer-looking men on horseback. They were beggars and vagrants roaming about the country, under the lead of their duke and their counts. They were swarthy, all had curly hair, and silver rings in their ears. The women were even uglier than the men. Their faces were blacker, and always uncovered; they wore shabby blouses, with an old bit of cloth woven of cords tied over their shoulders, and their hair hung down like a horse's tail. The children wallowing under their feet would have frightened a monkey. A band of outlaws! They all came in a direct line from Lower Egypt to Rheims by way of Poland. People said that the Pope had confessed them, and ordered them, by way of penance, to travel through the world for seven years in succession, without ever sleeping in beds. So they called themselves penitents, and smelt horribly. It seems that they were once Saracens, so they must have believed in Jupiter; and they demanded ten Tours pounds from every crosiered and mitred archbishop, bishop, and abbot. It was a papal bull that gave them this right. They came to Rheims to tell fortunes in the name of the King of Algiers and the Emperor of Germany. You may imagine that this was quite enough reason for forbidding them to enter the town. So the whole band encamped near the Porte de Braine with a good grace, on that hill where there is a mill, close by the old chalk-pits; and every one in Rheims made haste to visit them. They looked into your hand and told you marvellous things; they were quite capable of predicting to Judas that he should be pope! And yet there were evil reports of their having stolen children, cut purses, and eaten human flesh. Wise folks said to the simple, 'Keep away from them!' and then went themselves in secret. It was a perfect rage. The fact is, they said things that would have amazed a cardinal. Mothers boasted loudly of their children, after the gipsies had read all sorts of miracles written in their hands in Turkish and in heathen tongues. One had an emperor for her son, another a pope, and another a captain. Poor Chantefleurie was seized with curiosity; she longed to know what her child would be, and whether her pretty little Agnès would not one day be Empress of Armenia, or something of that sort. So she carried her to the gipsies; and the gipsies admired the child, caressed her, and kissed her with their black mouths, and wondered at her little hand, alas! to the great delight of her mother. They were particularly charmed with her pretty feet and her pretty shoes. The child was not a year old then. She already lisped a few words, laughed at her mother like a little madcap, was round and fat, and had a thousand enchanting little tricks like those of the angels in paradise. She was sorely afraid of the gipsy women, and cried. But her mother kissed her the harder, and went away charmed with the good luck which the fortune-tellers had promised her Agnès. She was to be beautiful, virtuous, and a queen. She therefore returned to her garret in the Rue Folle-Peine, quite proud of carrying a queen in her arms. Next day she took advantage of a moment while the child was asleep on her bed (for she always had it sleep in her own bed), softly left the door ajar, and ran out to tell a neighbour in the Rue de la Séchesserie that her daughter Agnès would one day have the King of England and the Duke of Ethiopia to wait upon her at table, and a hundred other surprising things. On her return, hearing no sound as she climbed the stairs, she said to herself, 'Good! baby is still asleep.' She found the door much wider open than she had left it; but she went in, poor mother! and ran to the bed. The child was gone; the place was empty. There was nothing left of the child but one of her pretty little shoes. She rushed from the room, flew down the stairs, and began to beat the walls with her head, crying, 'My child! my child! Where is my child? Who has taken away my child?' The street was deserted, the house stood alone; no one could give her any information. She went through the town, searched every street, ran up and down all day long, mad, distracted, terrible, staring in at doors and windows, like a wild beast that has lost its young. She was breathless, dishevelled, fearful to look upon, and there was a fire in her eyes which dried her tears. She stopped the passers-by, and cried, 'My daughter! my daughter! my pretty little daughter! If any one will give me back my daughter, I will be his servant, the servant of his dog, and he shall devour my heart if he will.' She met the priest of Saint-Remy, and said to him: 'I will dig the ground with my nails, only give me back my child!' It was heartrending, Oudarde; and I saw a very hard-hearted man, Master Ponce Lacabre, the attorney, weep. Ah, poor mother! When night came, she went home. During her absence a neighbour had seen two gipsy women go slyly upstairs with a bundle in their arms, then shut the door again and hurry away. After they had gone, a child's cries were heard, coming from Paquette's room. The mother laughed wildly, flew over the stairs as if she had wings, burst open her door, and went in. A frightful thing had happened, Oudarde! Instead of her lovely little Agnès, so rosy and so fresh, who was a gift from the good God, there lay a hideous little monster, blind, lame, deformed, squalling, and crawling about the brick floor. She hid her eyes in horror. 'Oh!' she exclaimed, 'can the witches have changed my daughter into this horrible beast?' The little club-foot was hastily removed; he would have driven her mad. He was the monstrous offspring of some gipsy woman given over to the devil. He seemed to be about four years old, and spoke a language which was no human tongue; such words were quite impossible. Chantefleurie flung herself upon the little shoe,—all that was left her of all that she had loved. She lay there so long, motionless, silent, apparently not breathing, that the neighbours thought she must be dead. Suddenly she trembled from head to foot, covered her precious relic with frantic kisses, and burst into sobs as if her heart were broken. I assure you that we all wept with her. She said: 'Oh, my little girl! my pretty little girl! where are you?' And that would have wrung your hearts. I cry now when I think of it. Our children, you see, are the very marrow of our bones.—My poor Eustache! you are so handsome! If you only knew what a darling he is! Yesterday he said to me, 'I mean to be one of the city guard, I do.' Oh, my Eustache! if I were to lose you!—Chantefleurie got up all at once and began to run about Rheims, shouting, 'To the gipsy camp! to the gipsy camp! Guard, burn the witches!' The gipsies were gone. It was night. No one could follow them. Next day, two leagues away from Rheims, on a heath between Gueux and Tilloy, were found the remains of a great fire, some ribbons which had belonged to Paquette's child, drops of blood, and some goats' dung. The night just passed happened to be a Saturday night. No one doubted any longer that the gipsies had kept their Sabbath on that heath, and that they had devoured the child in company with Beelzebub, as the Mahometans do. When Chantefleurie heard these horrible things, she did not shed a tear; she moved her lips as if to speak, but could not. Next day her hair was grey. On the following day she had disappeared."

"A terrible story indeed," said Oudarde, "and one that would make a Burgundian weep!"

"I am no longer surprised," added Gervaise, "that the fear of the gipsies haunts you so."

"And you had all the more reason," continued Oudarde, "to run away with your Eustache just now, because these are also Polish gipsies."

"Not at all," said Gervaise; "they say they came from Spain and Catalonia."

"Catalonia? That may be," replied Oudarde; "Polonia, Catalonia, Valonia, —those places are all one to me; I always mix them up. There's one thing sure; they are gipsies."

"And their teeth are certainly long enough to eat little children. And I should not be a bit surprised if Smeralda ate a little too, for all her dainty airs. Her white goat plays too many clever tricks to be all right."

Mahiette walked on in silence. She was absorbed in that sort of reverie which seems to be the continuation of a painful story, and which does not cease until it has imparted its own emotion, throb by throb, to the innermost fibres of the heart. Gervaise, however, addressed her: "And did no one ever know what became of Chantefleurie?" Mahiette made no answer. Gervaise repeated the question, shaking her arm and calling her by name as she did so. Mahiette seemed to wake from her dream.

"What became of Chantefleurie?" she said, mechanically repeating the words whose sound was still fresh in her ear; then, making an effort to fix her attention upon the meaning of the words, she said quickly, "Oh, no one ever knew."

She added, after a pause:—

"Some said they saw her leave Rheims at dusk by the Porte Fléchembault; others, at daybreak, by the old Porte Basée. A poor man found her gold cross hanging to the stone cross in the fair-grounds. It was that trinket which caused her ruin in '61. It was a gift from the handsome Vicomte de Cormontreuil, her first lover. Paquette never would part with it, however poor she might be. She clung to it like her own life. So when this cross was found, we all thought that she was dead. Still, there were people at Cabaret-les-Vautes who said they saw her pass by on the road to Paris, walking barefoot over the stones. But in that case she must have left town by the Porte de Vesle, and all these stories don't agree; or, rather, I believe she did actually leave by the Porte de Vesle, but that she left this world."

"I don't understand you," said Gervaise.

"The Vesle," replied Mahiette, with a melancholy smile, "is the river."

"Poor Chantefleurie!" said Oudarde, with a shudder; "drowned!"

"Drowned!" returned Mahiette; "and who could have told good father Guybertaut, when he floated down the river beneath the Pont de Tinquex, singing in his boat, that his dear little Paquette would one day pass under that same bridge, but without boat or song?"

"And the little shoe?" asked Gervaise.

"It disappeared with the mother," replied Mahiette.

"Poor little shoe!" said Oudarde.

Oudarde, a fat and tender-hearted woman, would have been quite content to sigh in company with Mahiette; but Gervaise, who was more curious, had not come to the end of her questions.

"And the monster?" she suddenly said to Mahiette.

"What monster?" asked the latter.

"The little gipsy monster left by the witches in Chantefleurie's room in exchange for her daughter. What did you do with it? I really hope you drowned it too."

"Not a bit of it," replied Mahiette.

"What! You burned it then? After all, that was better. A sorcerer's child!"

"Nor that either, Gervaise. My lord the archbishop took an interest in the gipsy child; he exorcised it, blessed it, carefully took the devil out of the boy's body, and sent him to Paris to be exposed upon the wooden bed at Notre-Dame, as a foundling."

"These bishops," grumbled Gervaise, "never do anything like other people, just because they are so learned. Just think, Oudarde, of putting the devil among the foundlings! For that little monster is sure to have been the devil. Well, Mahiette, what did they do with him in Paris! I'm sure no charitable person would take him."

"I don't know," replied the native of Rheims; "it was just at that very time that my husband bought the tabellion's office at Beru, two leagues away from town, and we thought no more about the matter; particularly as near Beru there are the two hills of Cernay, which quite hide the spires of the Rheims cathedral."

While talking thus, the three worthy women had reached the Grève. In their preoccupation, they had passed the public breviary of the Tour-Roland without stopping, and were proceeding mechanically towards the pillory, around which the crowd increased momentarily. Probably the sight which at this instant attracted every eye would have made them completely forget the Rat-Hole, and the visit which they meant to pay, if the sturdy six-year-old Eustache, whom Mahiette led by the hand, had not suddenly reminded them of it by saying, as if some instinct warned him that the Rat-Hole lay behind him, "Mother, may I eat the cake now?"

Had Eustache been more crafty, that is to say less greedy, he would have waited still longer, and would not have risked the timid question, "Mother, may I eat the cake now?" until they were safe at home again, at Master Andry Musnier's house, in the University, in the Rue Madame-la-Valence, when both branches of the Seine and the five bridges of the City would have been betwixt the Rat-Hole and the cake.

This same question, a very rash one at the time that Eustache asked it, roused Mahiette's attention.

"By the way," she exclaimed, "we are forgetting the recluse! Show me your Rat-Hole, that I may carry her my cake."

"Directly," said Oudarde. "It's a true charity."

This was not at all to Eustache's liking.

"Oh, my cake! my cake!" he whined, hunching up first one shoulder and then the other,—always a sign of extreme displeasure in such cases.

The three women retraced their steps, and as they approached the Tour-Roland, Oudarde said to the other two:—

"It will never do for all three of us to peep in at the hole at once, lest we should frighten the nun. You two must pretend to be reading the Lord's Prayer in the breviary while I put my nose in at the window; the nun knows me slightly. I'll tell you when to come."

She went to the window alone. As soon as she looked in, profound pity was expressed in every feature, and her bright frank face changed colour as quickly as if it had passed from sunlight into moonlight; her eyes grew moist, her mouth quivered as if she were about to weep. A moment later, she put her finger to her lips and backoned to Mahiette.

Mahiette silently joined her, on tiptoe as if by the bedside of a dying person.

It was indeed a sad sight which lay before the two women, as they gazed without moving or breathing through the grated window of the Rat-Hole.

The cell was small, wider than it was long, with a vaulted roof, and seen from within looked like the inside of an exaggerated bishop's mitre. Upon the bare stone floor, in a corner, sat, or rather crouched a woman. Her chin rested on her knees, which her crossed arms pressed closely against her breast. Bent double in this manner, clad in brown sackcloth, which covered her loosely from head to foot, her long grey locks drawn forward and falling over her face, down her legs to her feet, she seemed at first sight some strange shape outlined against the dark background of the cell, a sort of blackish triangle, which the ray of light entering at the window divided into two distinct bands of light and shadow. She looked like one of those spectres, half darkness and half light, which we see in dreams, and in the extraordinary work of Goya,— pale, motionless, forbidding, cowering upon a tomb or clinging to the grating of a dungeon. It was neither man, nor woman, nor living being, nor any definite form; it was a figure; a sort of vision in which the real and the imaginary were blended like twilight and daylight. Beneath her dishevelled hair, which fell to the ground, the outlines of a stern and emaciated profile were barely visible; the tip of one bare foot just peeped from the hem of her garment, seeming to be curled up on the hard, cold floor. The little of human form which could be dimly seen beneath that mourning garb made the beholder shudder.

This figure, which seemed rooted to the ground, appeared to have neither motion, thought, nor breath. In that thin sackcloth, in January, lying half naked on a granite floor, without fire, in the darkness of a dungeon, whose slanting window never admitted the sun, only the icy blast, she did not seem to suffer, or even to feel.

She seemed to have been turned to stone like her cell, to ice like the season. Her hands were clasped, her eyes were fixed. At the first glance, she seemed a spectre, at the second, a statue.

And yet at intervals her blue lips were parted by a breath, and trembled; but they seemed as dead and as destitute of will as leaves blowing in the wind.

Yet her dull eyes gazed with an ineffable expression, a deep, mournful, serious, perpetually fixed expression, on a corner of the cell hidden from those outside; her look seemed to connect all the sombre thoughts of her distressed soul with some mysterious object.

Such was the creature who was called "the recluse" from her habitation, and "the nun" from her dress.

The three women—for Gervaise had joined Mahiette and Oudarde—peered through the window. Their heads cut off the faint light which entered the dungeon; but the wretched inmate seemed unconscious of her loss, and paid no attention to them. "Don't disturb her," said Oudarde in low tones; "she is in one of her ecstatic fits; she is praying."

But Mahiette still gazed with ever-increasing anxiety at the wan, wrinkled face, and those dishevelled locks, and Her eyes filled with tears. "How strange that would be!" she muttered.

She put her head through the iron bars, and at last contrived to get a glimpse of the corner upon which the unhappy woman's eyes were forever riveted.

When she withdrew her head from the window, her face was bathed in tears.

"What is that woman's name?" she asked Oudarde.

Oudarde answered,—

"We call her Sister Gudule."

"And I," returned Mahiette,—"I call her Paquette Chantefleurie."

Then, putting her finger to her lip, she signed to the amazed Oudarde to put her head through the aperture and look.

Oudarde looked, and saw, in the corner upon which the recluse's eye was fixed in such sad ecstasy, a tiny pink satin shoe, embroidered with gold and silver spangles.

Gervaise looked in after Oudarde, and then the three women began to weep at the sight of that miserable mother.

However, neither their looks nor their tears disturbed the recluse. Her hands were still clasped, her lips dumb, her eyes set; and to those who knew her story it was heartrending to see her sit and gaze at that little shoe.

The three had not yet breathed a word; they dared not speak, even in a whisper. This profound silence, this great grief, this entire oblivion of all but one thing, affected them like the high altar at Easter or at Christmastide. They were silent, absorbed, ready to fall upon their knees. They felt as if they had just gone into church on Holy Saturday and heard the *Tenebræ*.

At last Gervaise, the most curious, and consequently the least sensitive of the three, made an attempt to draw the recluse into conversation: "Sister! Sister Gudule!"

She repeated the call three times, raising her voice each time. The recluse did not stir; there was not a word, not a look, not a sign of life.

Oudarde, in her turn, in a gentler and more affectionate tone, said, "Sister! holy Sister Gudule!"

The same silence, the same absolute repose as before.

"What a strange woman!" cried Gervaise; "I don't believe she would mind a cannonade!"

"Perhaps she's deaf," said Oudarde.

"Maybe blind," added Gervaise.

"Perhaps dead," said Mahiette.

Certainly, if the soul had not already quitted that inert, torpid, lethargic body, it had at least withdrawn into it and concealed itself in depths to which the perceptions of the external organs did not penetrate.

"We shall have to leave the cake on the window-sill," said Oudarde; "but then some boy will steal it. How can we rouse her?"

Eustache, who had thus far been absorbed in a little wagon drawn by a big dog, which was just passing, suddenly noticed that his three companions were looking at something through the window, and, seized by curiosity in his turn, he scrambled upon a post, stood on tiptoe, and put his fat, rosy face to the opening, shouting,

"Mother, let me see, too!"

At the sound of this childish voice, clear, fresh, and ringing, the recluse trembled. She turned her head with the abrupt, quick, motion of a steel spring, her long, thin hands brushed the hair from her face, and she fixed her astonished, unhappy, despairing eyes upon the child. The look was like a flash of lightning.

"Oh, my God!" she instantly exclaimed, hiding her head upon her knees, and it seemed as if her hoarse voice tore her chest, "at least do not show me those of others!"

"Good-morning, madame," said the child, gravely.

But the shock had, as it were, aroused the recluse. A long shudder ran through her entire frame from head to foot; her teeth chattered; she half raised her head, and said, as she pressed her elbows to her sides and took her feet in her hands as if to warm them,—

"Oh, how bitterly cold!"

"Poor woman!" said Oudarde, pitifully; "would you like a little fire?"

She shook her head in token of refusal.

"Well," added Oudarde, offering her a bottle, "here is some hippocras, which will warm you; drink."

She again shook her head, looked steadily at Oudarde, and answered, "Water."

Oudarde insisted. "No, sister, water is no fit drink for January. You must drink a little hippocras, and eat this wheaten cake, which we have made for you."

She put aside the cake which Mahiette offered her, and said, "Some black bread."

"Come," said Gervaise feeling a charitable impulse in her turn, and unfastening her wollen mantle, "here is a covering somewhat warmer than yours. Throw this over your shoulders."

She refused the mantle as she had the bottle and the cake, and answered, "A cloth."

"But," resumed the kind-hearted Oudarde, "you must have seen that yesterday was a holiday."

"I knew it," said the recluse; "for two days I have had no water in my jug."

She added after a pause: "On a holiday, every one forgets me. They do well. Why should people remember me, who never think of them? When the fire goes out, the ashes are soon cold."

And as if wearied by so many words, she let her head fall upon her knees once more. The simple and charitable Oudarde, who interpreted her last words as another complaint of the cold, answered innocently, "Then wouldn't you like a little fire?"

"Fire!" said the recluse in a singular tone; "and will you give me a little for the poor baby too,—the baby who has been under ground these fifteen years?"

She trembled in every limb, her voice quivered, her eyes flashed; she had risen to her knees; she suddenly stretched her thin white hand towards the child, who was looking at her in surprise.

"Take away that child!" she cried. "The gipsy woman will soon pass by."

Then she fell face downwards, and her forehead struck the floor, with the sound of one stone upon another. The three women thought her dead. But a moment later she stirred, and they saw her drag herself upon her hands and knees to the corner where the little shoe lay. They dared not look longer; they turned away their eyes; but they heard a thousand kisses and a thousand sighs, mingled with agonizing cries and dull blows like those of a head dashed against a wall; then after one of these blows, so violent that they all three started, they heard nothing more.

"Has she killed herself?" said Gervaise, venturing to put her head through the bars. "Sister! Sister Gudule!"

"Sister Gudule!" repeated Oudarde.

"Oh, heavens! She does not move!" exclaimed Gervaise. "Can she indeed be dead? Gudule! Gudule!"

Mahiette, until now so choked by emotion that she could not speak, made an effort. "Wait a minute," she said; then going to the window, she cried, "Paquette! Paquette Chantefleurie!"

A child who innocently blows on an ill-lighted firecracker and makes it explode in his face, is no more alarmed than was Mahiette at the effect of the name so suddenly flung into Sister Gudule's cell.

The recluse trembled from head to foot, sprang to her bare feet, and rushed to the window with such flaming eyes that Mahiette, Oudarde, the other woman and the child retreated to the farthest edge of the quay.

But still the forbidding face of the recluse remained pressed against the window-bars. "Oh! oh!" she screamed with a terrible laugh, "the gipsy woman calls me!"

At this instant the scene which was passing at the pillory caught her wild eye. Her brow wrinkled with horror; she stretched her skeleton arms from her cell and cried in a voice which sounded like a death rattle. "Have you come again, you daughter of Egypt? Is it you who call me, you child-stealer? Well! may you be accursed! accursed! accursed! accursed!"

Chapter IV

A tear for a drop of water

These words were, so to speak, the connecting link between two scenes which up to this instant had gone on simultaneously, each upon its own particular stage: one, of which we have just read, at the Rat-Hole; the other, of which we shall now read, at the pillory. The former was witnessed only by the three women whose acquaintance the reader has just made; the spectators of the latter consisted of the crowd of people whom we saw some time since gathering in the Grève, about the gibbet and the pillory.

This crowd, whom the sight of the four officers posted at the four corners of the pillory ever since nine in the morning led to expect an execution of some sort, perhaps not a hanging, but a whipping, cropping of ears, or something of the sort,—this crowd had grown so rapidly that the four officers, too closely hemmed in, were more than once obliged to drive the people back by a free use of their whips and their horses' heels.

The populace, well accustomed to wait for public executions, betrayed no great impatience. They amused themselves by looking at the pillory,—a very simple structure, consisting of a cube of masonry some ten feet high, and hollow within. A very steep flight of stairs of unhewn stone, called the ladder, led to the upper platform, upon which was a horizontal wheel made of oak. The victim was bound to this wheel in a kneeling posture, with his hands behind him. A wooden shaft, set in motion by a capstan concealed inside the machine, made the wheel revolve horizontally, thus presenting the prisoner's face to each side of the square in turn. This was called "turning" a criminal.

It is evident that the pillory of the Grève was far from possessing all the attractions of the pillory of the Markets. There was nothing architectural or monumental about it. It had no roof with an iron cross, no octagonal lantern, no slender columns expanding at the edge of the roof into capitals composed of acanthus-leaves and flowers, no huge fantastic gutter-spouts, no carved woodwork, no delicate sculpture cut deep into the stone.

Here the spectator must needs be content with the four rough walls, two stone facings, and a shabby stone gibbet, plain and bare.

The treat would have been a sorry one for lovers of Gothic architecture. It is true that no one was ever less interested in monuments than your good cockney of the Middle Ages, who paid very little heed to the beauty of a pillory.

The victim appeared at last, tied to the tail of a cart; and when he had been hoisted to the top of the platform, where he could be seen from all parts of the square bound to the wheel of the pillory with straps and ropes, a prodigious hooting, mingled with shouts and laughter, burst from the spectators. They had recognized Quasimodo.

It was indeed he. It was a strange reverse. He was now pilloried on the same place where he was the day before hailed, acclaimed, and proclaimed Pope and Prince of Fools, Lord of Misrule, and attended by the Duke of Egypt, the King of Tunis, the Emperor of Galilee! One thing is certain; there was not a soul in the crowd, not even himself, in turn triumphant and a victim, who could distinctly draw a mental comparison between these two situations. Gringoire and his philosophy were wanting to the spectacle.

Soon Michel Noiret, sworn trumpeter to our lord the king, imposed silence on all beholders, and proclaimed the sentence, according to the provost's order and command. He then retired behind the cart, with his men in livery coats.

Quasimodo, utterly impassive, never winked. All resistance on his part was rendered impossible by what was then called, in the language of criminal law, "the vehemence and firmness of the bonds;" which means that the chains and thongs probably cut into his flesh. This, by-the-bye, is a tradition of the jail and the convict prison which is not yet lost, and which the handcuffs still preserve as a precious relic among us, civilized, mild, and humane as we are (not to mention the guillotine and the galleys).

He allowed himself to be led, pushed, carried, lifted, tied, and re-tied. His face revealed nothing more than the surprise of a savage or an idiot. He was known to be deaf; he seemed to be blind.

He was placed upon his knees on the circular plank; he made no resistance. He was stripped of shirt and doublet to the waist; he submitted. He was bound with a fresh system of straps and buckles; he suffered himself to be buckled and bound. Only from time to time he breathed heavily, like a calf whose head hangs dangling from the back of the butcher's cart.

"The booby!" said Jehan Frollo du Moulin to his friend Robin Poussepain (for the two students had followed the victim, as a matter of course); "he understands no more about it than a cockchafer shut up in a box!"

A shout of laughter ran through the crowd when Quasimodo's hump, his camel breast, his horny, hairy shoulders, were bared to view. During this burst of merriment, a man in the city livery, short of stature, and strong, mounted the platform and took his place by the prisoner's side. His name was soon circulated among the spectators. It was Master Pierrat Torterue, sworn torturer of the Châtelet.

He began by placing on one corner

of the pillory a black hour-glass, the upper part of which was full of red sand, which dropped slowly into the lower half; then he took off his party-coloured coat, and there was seen hanging from his right hand a slim, slender whip with long white thongs, shining, knotted, braided, armed with metal tips. With his left hand he carelessly rolled his right shirt-sleeve up to his armpit.

Meanwhile Jehan Frollo shouted, lifting his fair curly head high above the crowd (he had climbed Robin Poussepain's shoulders for the express purpose), "Come and see, gentlemen and ladies! They are going straightway to flog Master Quasimodo, the bell-ringer of my brother the archdeacon of Josas, a strange specimen of Oriental architecture, with a dome for his back and twisted columns for legs."

All the people laughed, especially the children and the young girls.

At last the executioner stamped his foot. The wheel began to turn. Quasimodo reeled in spite of his bonds. The astonishment suddenly depicted upon his misshapen face redoubled the bursts of laughter around him.

Suddenly, just as the wheel in its revolution presented to Master Pierrat Quasimodo's mountainous back, Master Pierrat raised his arm; the thin lashes hissed through the air like a brood of vipers, and fell furiously upon the wretched man's shoulders.

Quasimodo started as if roused abruptly from a dream. He began to understand. He writhed in his bonds; surprise and pain distorted the muscles of his face, but he did not heave a sigh. He merely bent his head back, to the right, then to the left, shaking it like a bull stung in the flank by a gad-fly.

A second blow followed the first, then a third, and another, and another, and so on and on. The wheel did not cease from turning, or the blows from raining down.

Soon the blood spurted; it streamed in countless rivulets over the hunchback's shoulders; and the slender thongs, as they rent the air, sprinkled it in drops among the crowd.

Quasimodo had resumed, apparently at least, his former impassivity. He had tried at first, secretly and without great visible effort, to burst his bonds. His eye kindled, his muscles stiffened, his limbs gathered all their force, and the straps and chains stretched. The struggle was mighty, prodigious, desperate; but the tried and tested fetters of the provosty held firm. They cracked; and that was all. Quasimodo fell back exhausted. Surprise gave way, upon his features, to a look of bitter and profound dejection. He closed his single eye, dropped his head upon his breast, and feigned death.

Thenceforth he did not budge. Nothing could wring a movement from him, —neither his blood, which still flowed, nor the blows, which increased in fury, nor the rage of the executioner, who became excited and intoxicated by his work, nor the noise of the horrid lashes, keener and sharper than the sting of wasps.

At last an usher from the Châtelet, dressed in black, mounted on a black horse, who had been posted beside the ladder from the beginning of the execution of the sentence, extended his ebony wand towards the hour-glass. The executioner paused. The wheel stopped. Quasimodo's eye reopened slowly.

The flagellation was ended. Two attendants of the execution washed the victim's bleeding shoulders, rubbed them with some salve which at once closed all the wounds, and threw over his back a piece of yellow cloth cut after the pattern of a priest's cope. Meanwhile Pierrat Torterue let his red lashes soaked with blood drip upon the pavement.

But all was not over for Quasimodo. He had still to spend in the pillory that hour so judiciously added by Master Florian Barbedienne to the sentence of Master Robert d'Estouteville, —all to the greater glory of Jean de Cumène's old physiological and psychological pun: *"Surdus absurdus."*

The hour-glass was therefore turned, and the hunchback was left bound to the plank as before, in order that justice might be executed to the utmost.

The people, particularly in the Middle Ages, were to society what the child is to a family. So long as they remain in their primitive condition of ignorance, of moral and intellectual nonage, it may be said of that as of a child,—

"That age is without pity."

We have already shown that Quasimodo was the object of universal hatred, —for more than one good reason, it is true. There was hardly a single spectator in the crowd who had not—or did not think he had—grounds for complaint against the malicious hunchback of Notre-Dame. Every one was delighted to see him in the pillory; and the severe punishment which he had just received, and the piteous state in which it had left him, far from softening the hearts of the populace, had made their hatred keener by adding to it a spice of merriment.

Thus, "public vengeance," as the legal jargon still styles it, once satisfied, a thousand private spites took their turn at revenge. Here, as in the Great Hall, the women made themselves especially conspicuous. All bore him a grudge,— some for his mischief, others for his ugliness. The latter were the more furious.

"Oh, you image of Antichrist!" said one.

"Broomstick-rider!" cried another.

"What a fine tragic face!" yelled a third. "It would surely make you Lord of Misrule, if to-day were only yesterday."

"That's right," added an old woman. "This is the pillory face. When shall we have the gallows face?"

"When shall we see you buried a hundred feet below ground, with your big bell upon your head, you cursed bell-ringer?"

"And to think that it's this demon that rings the Angelus!"

"Oh, you deaf man! you blind man! you hunchback! you monster!"

And the two students, Jehan du Moulin and Robin Poussepain, sang at the top of their voices the old popular refrain:—

"A halter for the gallows-bird!
A fagot for the ugly ape!"

Countless other insults rained upon him, mingled with hoots, curses, laughter, and occasional stones.

Quasimodo was deaf, but his sight was capital, and the fury of the mob was no less forcibly painted on their faces than in their words. Besides, the stones which struck him explained the peals of laughter.

He bore it for a time; but little by little his patience, which had resisted the torturer's whip, gave way, and rebelled against all these insect stings. The Asturian bull, which pays but little heed to the attacks of the picador, is maddened by the dogs and the banderillos.

At first he glanced slowly and threateningly around the crowd; but, bound fast as he was, his glance was impotent to drive away those flies which galled his wounds. Then he struggled in his fetters, and his frantic efforts made the old pillory wheel creak upon its timbers. All this only increased the shouts and derision of the crowd.

Then the wretched man, unable to break the collar which held him chained like a wild beast, became quiet again; only at intervals a sigh of rage heaved his breast. His face showed no trace of mortification or shame. He was too far removed from the existing state of society, and too nearly allied to a state of nature, to know what shame was. Besides, it is doubtful if infamy be a thing which can be felt by one afflicted with that degree of deformity. But rage, hate, despair, slowly veiled the hideous face with a cloud which grew darker and darker, more and more heavily charged with an electricity revealed by countless flashes from the eye of the Cyclop.

However, this cloud was lightened for a moment as a mule passed through the crowd, bearing a priest on his back. As soon as he saw that mule and that priest, the poor sufferer's face softened. The fury which convulsed it gave way to a strange smile, full of ineffable sweetness, affection, and tenderness. As the priest approached, this smile became more pronounced, more distinct, more radiant. It was as if the unhappy man hailed the coming of a Saviour. Yet, when the mule was near enough to the pillory for his rider to recognize the prisoner, the priest cast down his eyes, turned back abruptly, spurred his animal on either side as if in haste to avoid humiliating appeals, and very far from anxious to be greeted and recognized by a poor devil in such a plight.

The priest was the archdeacon Don Claude Frollo.

The cloud grew darker than ever upon the face of Quasimodo. The smile lingered for some time, although it became bitter, dejected, profoundly sad.

Time passed. He had been there at least an hour and a half, wounded, ill-treated, incessantly mocked, and almost stoned to death.

Suddenly he again struggled in his chains with renewed despair, which made all the timbers that held him quiver; and breaking the silence which he had hitherto obstinately kept, he cried in a hoarse and furious voice more like the bark of a dog than a human cry, and which drowned the sound of the hooting, "Water!"

This exclamation of distress, far from exciting compassion, only increased the amusement of the good Parisian populace who surrounded the ladder, and who, it must be confessed, taken in the mass and as a multitude, were at this time scarcely less cruel and brutish than that horrible tribe of Vagrant Vagabonds to whom we have already introduced the reader, and who were simply the lowest stratum of the people. Not a voice was raised around the wretched sufferer, except to mock at his thirst.

Certainly he was at this moment more grotesque and repulsive than he was pitiable, with his livid and streaming face, his wild eye, his mouth foaming with rage and suffering, and his tongue protruding. It must also be acknowledged, that, even had there been in the throng any charitable soul tempted to give a cup of cold water to the miserable creature in his agony, so strong an idea of shame and ignominy was attached to the infamous steps of the pillory, that this alone would have sufficed to repel the Good Samaritan.

In a few minutes Quasimodo cast a despairing look upon the crowd, and repeated in a still more heart-rending voice, "Water!"

Every one laughed.

"Drink that!" shouted Robin Poussepain, flinging in his face a sponge which had been dragged through the gutter. "There, you deaf monster! I owe you something."

A woman aimed a stone at his head:—

"That will teach you to wake us at night with your cursed chimes!"

"Well, my boy!" howled a cripple, striving to reach him with his crutch, "will you cast spells on us again from the top of the towers of Notre-Dame?"

"Here's a porringer to drink out of!" added a man, letting fly a broken jug at his breast. " 'Twas you who made my wife give birth to a double-headed child, just by walking past her."

"And my cat have a kitten with six feet!" shrieked an old woman, hurling a tile at him.

"Water!" repeated the gasping Quasimodo for the third time.

At this moment he saw the crowd separate. A young girl, oddly dressed, stepped from their midst. She was accompanied by a little white goat with gilded horns, and held a tambourine in her hand.

Quasimodo's eye gleamed. It was the gipsy girl whom he had tried to carry off the night before,—a freak for which he dimly felt that he was even now being punished; which was not in the least true, since he was only punished for the misfortune of being deaf, and having been tried by a deaf judge. He did not doubt that she too came to be avenged, and to take her turn at him with the rest.

He watched her nimbly climb the ladder. Rage and spite choked him. He longed to destroy the pillory; and had the lightning of his eye had power to blast, the gipsy girl would have been reduced to ashes long before she reached the platform.

Without a word she approached the sufferer, who vainly writhed and twisted to avoid her, and loosening a gourd from her girdle, she raised it gently to the parched lips of the miserable wretch.

Then from that eye, hitherto so dry and burning, a great tear trickled, and rolled slowly down the misshapen face, so long convulsed with despair. It was perhaps the first that the unfortunate man had ever shed.

But he forgot to drink. The gipsy girl made her customary little grimace of impatience, and smilingly pressed the neck of the gourd to Quasimodo's jagged mouth.

He drank long draughts; his thirst was ardent.

When he had done, the poor wretch put out his black lips, doubtless to kiss the fair hand which had helped him. But the girl, perhaps not quite free from distrust, and mindful of the violent attempt of the previous night, withdrew her hand with the terrified gesture of a child who fears being bitten by a wild animal.

Then the poor deaf man fixed upon her a look of reproach and unutterable sorrow.

It would anywhere have been a touching sight, to see this lovely girl, fresh, pure, charming, and yet so weak, thus devoutly hastening to the help of so much misery, deformity, and malice. Upon a pillory, the sight was sublime.

The people themselves were affected by it, and began to clap their hands and shout,—

"Noël! Noël!"

It was at this instant that the recluse saw, from the window of her cell, the gipsy girl upon the pillory, and hurled her ominous curse at her head:—

"May you be accursed, daughter of Egypt! accursed! accursed!"

Chapter V

END OF THE STORY OF THE CAKE

Esmeralda turned pale, and descended from the pillory with faltering steps. The voice of the recluse still pursued her:—

"Come down! come down, you gipsy thief! You will go up again!"

"The nun has one of her ill turns to-day," muttered the people, and they said no more; for women of this sort were held in much awe, which made them sacred. No one liked to attack those who prayed night and day.

The hour had come to release Quasimodo. He was unbound, and the mob dispersed.

Near the great bridge, Mahiette, who was returning home with her two companions, stopped suddenly:—

"By the way, Eustache, what have you done with the cake?"

"Mother," said the child, "while you were talking to the woman in that hole, there came a big dog and bit a piece out of my cake; so then I took a bite too."

"What, sir!" she continued, "did you eat it all?"

"Mother, it was the dog. I told him not to eat it, but he wouldn't mind me. So then I took a bite too; that's all!"

"What a bad boy you are!" said his mother, smiling and scolding at once. "Only think, Oudarde! he ate every cherry on the tree in our orchard at Charlerange; so his grandfather says that he is sure to be a soldier. Let me catch you at it again, Master Eustache! Get along, you greedy boy!"

BOOK VII

THE INSCRIPTION

CHAPTER I

ON THE DANGER OF CONFIDING A SECRET TO A GOAT

SEVERAL weeks had passed. It was early in March. The sun, which Dubartas, that classic father of periphrase, had not yet dubbed "the grand duke of candles," was none the less bright and gay. It was one of those spring days which are so full of sweetness and beauty that all Paris, flocking into the squares and parks, keeps holiday as if it were a Sunday. On such clear, warm, peaceful days, there is one particular hour when the porch of Notre-Dame is especially worthy of admiration. It is the moment when the sun, already sinking towards the west, almost exactly faces the cathedral. Its rays, becoming more and more level, withdraw slowly from the pavement of the square, and climb the perpendicular face of the church, the shadows setting off the countless figures in high relief, while the great central rose-window flames like the eye of a Cyclop lighted up by reflections from his forge.

It was just that hour.

Opposite the lofty cathedral, reddened by the setting sun, upon the stone balcony built over the porch of a handsome Gothic house at the corner of the square and the Rue du Parvis, a group of lovely young girls were laughing and chatting gracefully and playfully. By the length of the veil which hung from the peak of their pointed coif, twined with pearls, down to their heels, by the fineness of the embroidered tucker which covered their shoulders, but still revealed, in the pleasing fashion of the day, the swell of their fair virgin bosoms, by the richness of their under petticoats, even costlier than their upper garments (wonderful refinement!), by the gauze, the silk, the velvet in which they were arrayed, and especially by the whiteness of their hands, which proved that they led a life of idle ease, it was easy to guess that these were rich heiresses. They were in fact Damoiselle Fleur-de-Lys de Gondelaurier and her companions, Diane de Christeuil, Amelotte de Montmichel, Colombe de Gaillefontaine, and the little De Champchevrier, all daughters of noble houses, just now visiting the widowed Madame de Gondelaurier, on account of Monseigneur de Beaujeu and his wife, who were coming to Paris in April to choose maids of honour to meet the Dauphiness Marguerite in Picardy and receive her from the hands of the Flemings. Now, all the country squires for thirty miles around aspired to win this favour for their daughters, and many of them had already been brought or sent to Paris. The damsels in question were intrusted by their parents to the discreet and reverend care of Madame Aloïse de Gondelaurier, the widow of a former officer of the king's crossbowmen, living in retirement, with her only daughter, in her house on the square in front of Notre-Dame.

The balcony upon which the young

girls sat opened from a room richly hung with fawn-coloured Flemish leather stamped with golden foliage. The transverse beams on the ceiling, diverted the eye by countless grotesque carvings, painted and gilded. Splendid enamels glittered here and there upon sculptured presses. A boar's head made of earthenware crowned a superb sideboard, the two steps of which showed that the mistress of the house was the wife or widow of a knight banneret. At the end of the room, beside a tall chimney-piece covered with armorial bearings and escutcheons, sat, in a rich red velvet arm-chair, Madame de Gondelaurier, whose fifty-five years were as plainly written in her garments as on her face. Near her stood a young man of aristocratic though somewhat arrogant and swaggering mien,—one of those fine fellows about whom all women agree, although serious men and physiognomists shrug their shoulders at them. This youthful cavalier wore the brilliant uniform of a captain of the archers of the household troops, which is too much like the dress of Jupiter, described in the first part of this story, for us to inflict a second description of it upon the reader.

The damsels were seated, some in the room, some upon the balcony, the former upon squares of Utrecht velvet with golden corner-pieces, the latter on oaken stools carved with flowers and figures. Each held upon her knees a portion of a large piece of tapestry, at which they were all working together, and a long end of which trailed over the matting that covered the floor.

They talked together in the undertone and with the suppressed laughter common to a group of young girls when there is a young man among them. The young man whose presence sufficed to call forth all these feminine wiles seemed, for his part, to pay but little heed to them; and while these lovely girls vied with one another in trying to attract his attention, he seemed chiefly occupied in rubbing up his belt-buckle with his buckskin glove.

From time to time the elderly lady addressed some remark to him in a very low voice, and he replied as best he could, with awkward and forced courtesy. By Madame Aloïse's smiles and little significant signs, as well as by the glances which she cast at her daughter Fleur-de-Lys while she whispered to the captain, it was easy to see that she was talking of the recent betrothal, and of the marriage, doubtless to come off soon, between the young man and Fleur-de-Lys; and by the officer's coldness and embarrassment, it was plain that on his side at least there was no question of love. His whole manner expressed a weariness and constraint such as the young officers of our day would aptly translate by saying that he was "deucedly bored!"

The good lady, utterly infatuated with her daughter, like the silly mother that she was, did not perceive the officer's lack of enthusiasm, and did her best to point out to him in a whisper the infinite perfection with which Fleur-de-Lys plied her needle or wound her skeins of silk.

"There, cousin," she said, plucking him by the sleeve that she might speak in his ear, "just look at her now! See how gracefully she stoops!"

"To be sure," replied the young man;

and he relapsed into his cold and careless silence.

A moment after, he was forced to bend anew, and Dame Aloïse said,—

"Did you ever see a merrier or more attractive face than that of your betrothed? Could any one have a fairer, whiter skin? Aren't those clever hands; and isn't her neck a perfect match in grace for a swan's? How I envy you at times! and how lucky it is for you that you are a man, wicked scamp that you are! Isn't my Fleur-de-Lys adorably lovely, and aren't you dead in love with her?"

"Of course," he replied, with his mind upon other things.

"But why don't you talk to her?" suddenly observed Madame Aloïse, giving him a push. "Say something to her; you are wonderfully shy all of a sudden."

We can assure our readers that shyness was neither one of the captain's failings nor good points; but he tried to do what was required of him.

"Fair cousin," said he, approaching Fleur-de-Lys, "what is the subject of your tapestry-work?"

"Fair cousin," answered Fleur-de-Lys in an injured tone, "I have told you three times already: it is Neptune's grotto."

It was plain that Fleur-de-Lys was far more clear-sighted than her mother in regard to the captain's cold and careless manners. He felt that he must needs make a little conversation.

"And what is all this Neptune-work for?" he asked.

"For the Abbey of Saint-Antoine des Champs," said Fleur-de-Lys, without raising her eyes.

The captain picked up a corner of the tapestry.

"And who, my fair cousin, is that fat fellow with puffy cheeks, blowing his trumpet so vigorously?"

"That is Triton," she answered.

There was still a somewhat offended tone about Fleur-de-Lys' brief words. The captain saw that he must absolutely whisper something in her ear,—a compliment, a bit of nonsense, never mind what. He bent towards her accordingly, but his imagination suggested nothing tenderer or more familiar than this: "Why does your mother always wear a petticoat wrought with coats-of-arms, such as our grandmothers wore in the time of Charles VII.? Do tell her, fair cousin, that it is no longer the fashion, and that her laurel-tree and her hinges emblazoned all over her gown make her look like a walking mantelpiece. Really, nobody sits upon their banner in that way now, I swear they don't."

Fleur-de-Lys raised her lovely eyes full of reproach.

"Is that all you have to swear to me?" she said in a low voice.

Meantime good Dame Aloïse, enchanted to see them chatting thus confidently, said, as she played with the clasps of her prayer-book,—

"What a touching picture of love!"

The captain, more and more embarrassed, fell back on the tapestry. "That really is a beautiful piece of work!" he exclaimed.

Upon this remark, Colombe de Gaillefontaine, another charming, fair-haired, white-skinned girl, in a high-necked blue damask gown, timidly ventured to address Fleur-de-Lys, in the hope that the handsome captain would reply: "My dear Gondelaurier, have you seen the tapestries at the Roche-Guyon house?"

"Isn't that the house with the garden, which belongs to the linen-dealer of the Louvre?" asked Diane de Christeuil with a laugh; for she had fine teeth, and consequently laughed on every occasion.

"And where there is that big old tower belonging to the ancient wall of Paris," added Amelotte de Montmichel, a pretty, curly-haired, rosy-cheeked brunette, who was as much given to sighing as the other was to laughing, without knowing why.

"My dear Colombe," put in Dame Aloïse, "are you talking of the house which belonged to M. de Bacqueville in the reign of King Charles VI.? It does indeed contain some superb high-warp tapestries."

"Charles VI.! Charles VI.!" muttered the young captain, twirling his moustache. "Heavens! What a memory the good lady has for by-gone things!"

Madame de Gondelaurier went on: "Beautiful tapestries, indeed. Such magnificent work that it is thought to be unique!"

At this instant Bérangère de Champchevrier, a slender little girl of seven, who was gazing into the square through the trefoils of the balcony railing, cried out,—

"Oh, look, pretty godmamma Fleur-de-Lys, see that dear dancing-girl dancing down there on the pavement, and playing on the tambourine among those common clowns!"

The shrill jingle of a tambourine was in fact heard by all.

"Some gipsy girl," said Fleur-de-Lys, turning nonchalantly towards the square.

"Let us see! let us see!" exclaimed her lively companions; and they all ran to the edge of the balcony, while Fleur-de-Lys, musing over her lover's coldness, followed them slowly, and her lover, relieved by this incident, which cut short an embarrassing conversation, returned to the farther end of the room with the satisfied air of a soldier released from duty. Yet it was a delightful and an easy duty to wait upon the fair Fleur-de-Lys, and so it had once seemed to him; but the captain had gradually wearied of it; the prospect of a speedy marriage grew less and less attractive day by day. Besides, he was of an inconstant humour, and—must we own it? —his taste was somewhat vulgar. Although of very noble birth, he had contracted while in harness more than one of the habits of the common soldier. He loved the tavern and all its accompaniments. He was never at his ease except among coarse witticisms, military gallantries, easy-going beauties, and facile conquests. He had received some education and some polish from his family; but he had roamed the country too young, joined the garrison too young, and every day the veneer of the gentleman was worn away a little more by the hard friction of his military baldric. Although he still visited her occasionally, from a lingering spark of common respect, he felt doubly embarrassed in Fleur-de-Lys' presence: first, because by dint of distributing his love in all sorts of places he had very little left for her; and next, because amid so many stately, starched, and modest dames he trembled continually lest his lips, accustomed to oaths, should suddenly lose all restraint and break out into the language of the tavern. Fancy what the effect would be!

However, with all this were mingled great pretensions to elegance in dress and to a fine appearance. Let those who can reconcile these things. I am only the historian.

He had been standing for some moments, thinking or not thinking, leaning silently against the carved chimney-piece, when Fleur-de-Lys, turning suddenly, spoke to him. After, all, the poor girl only looked black at him in self-defence.

"Fair cousin, didn't you tell us of a little gipsy girl whom you rescued from a dozen robbers some two months since, while you were on the night patrol?"

"I think I did, fair cousin," said the captain.

"Well," she continued, "it may be that same gipsy girl who is dancing in the square below. Come and see if you recognize her, fair Cousin Phœbus!"

He perceived a secret desire for reconciliation in this gentle invitation to return to her side, and in the pains she took to call him by his Christian name. Captain Phœbus de Châteaupers (for it is he whom the reader has had before him from the beginning of this chapter) slowly approached the balcony. "There," said Fleur-de-Lys, tenderly, laying her hand upon Phœbus's arm, "look at that little thing dancing in the ring. Is that your gipsy girl?"

Phœbus looked, and said,—

"Yes; I know her by her goat."

"Oh, yes! what a pretty little goat!" said Amelotte, clasping her hands in admiration.

"Are its horns really, truly gold?" asked Bérangère.

Without moving from her easy-chair, Dame Aloïse took up the word: "Isn't it one of those gipsies who came here last year through the Porte Gibard?"

"Mother," said Fleur-de-Lys, gently, "that gate is now called Porte d'Enfer."

Mademoiselle de Gondelaurier knew how much her mother's superannuated modes of speech shocked the captain. In fact, he began to sneer, and muttered between his teeth: "Porte Gibard! Porte Gibard! That's to admit King Charles VI."

"Godmamma," cried Bérangère, whose restless eyes were suddenly raised to the top of the towers of Notre-Dame, "what is that black man doing up there?"

All the girls looked up. A man was indeed leaning on his elbows on the topmost balustrade of the northern tower, overlooking the Grève. He was a priest. His dress was distinctly visible, and his face rested on his hands. He was as motionless as a statue. His eye was fixed intently on the square.

There was something in his immobility like a kite which has just discovered a nest of sparrows, and gazes at it.

"It is the archdeacon of Josas," said Fleur-de-Lys.

"You have good eyes if you can recognize him from this distance!" remarked Mademoiselle Gaillefontaine.

"How he watches the little dancer," added Diane de Christeuil.

"The gipsy girl had better beware," said Fleur-de-Lys, "for he is not fond of gipsies."

"'Tis a great pity the man should stare at her so," added Amelotte de Montmichel, "for she dances ravishingly."

"Fair Cousin Phœbus," suddenly said Fleur-de-Lys, "as you know this little gipsy girl, pray beckon to her to come up. It will amuse us."

"Oh, yes!" cried all the girls, clapping their hands.

"What nonsense!" replied Phœbus. "She has doubtless forgotten me, and I don't even know her name. Still, if you wish it, ladies, I will make an attempt;" and leaning over the balcony-rail, he called, "Little one!"

The dancer was not playing her tambourine at the moment. She turned her head towards the point whence this call came, her sparkling eye fell on Phœbus, and she stopped short.

"Little one!" repeated the captain; and he signed to her to come.

The young girl looked at him again; then she blushed as if her cheeks were on fire, and putting her tambourine under her arm, she moved through the astonished spectators towards the door of the house to which Phœbus called her, with slow, hesitating steps, and the troubled gaze of a bird yielding to the fascination of a snake.

A moment later, the tapestry hanging before the door was lifted, and the gipsy appeared on the threshold of the room, red, abashed, breathless, her large eyes cast down, and not daring to advance another step.

Bérangère clapped her hands.

But the dancer stood motionless at the door. Her appearance produced a strange effect upon the group of young girls. It is certain that a vague and indistinct desire to please the handsome officer animated them all alike; that his splendid uniform was the aim of all their coquetries; and that so long as he was present there was a certain secret lurking rivalry among them, which they hardly confessed to themselves, but which none the less appeared every instant in their gestures and words. Still, as they were possessed of an almost equal share of beauty, the contest was a fair one, and each might well hope for victory. The gipsy's arrival abruptly destroyed this equilibrium. Her beauty was so remarkable that when she appeared on the threshold of the room she seemed to diffuse a sort of light peculiar to herself. Shut into this room, in this dark frame of hangings and wainscotting, she was incomparably more beautiful and more radiant than in the public square. She was like a torch brought from broad daylight into darkness. The noble maidens were dazzled in spite of themselves. Each of them felt her beauty in some sort impaired. Therefore their battle-front (if we may be pardoned the expression) changed at once, without exchanging a word. Still, they understood one another to perfection. The instincts of women read and reply to one another more rapidly than the understandings of men. An enemy had arrived; all felt it, all rallied for mutual support. A drop of wine is enough to redden a whole glass of water; the entrance of a prettier woman than themselves is enough to tinge a whole party of pretty women with a certain amount of ill-humour,—especially when there is but one man present.

Thus their reception of the gipsy girl was marvellously cold. They examined her from head to foot, then looked at one another, and that was enough: they understood one another. But the young girl waited for them to speak, so much agitated that she dared not raise her eyes.

The captain was the first to break the silence.

"On my word," he said in his tone of bold assurance, "a charming creature! What do you think of her, fair cousin?"

The observation, which a more delicate admirer would at least have uttered in an undertone, was not adapted to soothe the feminine jealousies arrayed against the gipsy girl.

Fleur-de-Lys answered the captain with a sweet affectation of disdain: "She's not bad-looking."

The others whispered together.

At last Madame Aloïse, who was not the least jealous of the party since she was jealous for her daughter, addressed the dancer. "Come in, little one."

"Come in, little one!" repeated, with comic dignity, Bérangère, who would have reached about to the gipsy's waist.

Esmeralda approached the noble lady.

"My pretty child," said Phœbus with emphasis, taking a few steps towards her, "I don't know whether I have the supreme happiness of being recognized by you—"

She interrupted him with a smile and a glance of infinite sweetness,—

"Oh, yes!"

"She has a good memory," observed Fleur-de-Lys.

"Now, then," continued Phœbus, "you escaped very nimbly the other night. Did I frighten you?"

"Oh, no!" said the gipsy.

There was an indefinite something in the tone in which this "Oh, no!" was uttered directly after the "Oh, yes!" which wounded Fleur-de-Lys.

"You left me in your place, my beauty," resumed the captain, whose tongue was loosened when he talked to a girl from the streets, "a very surly knave, blind of one eye, and a hunchback, the bishop's bell-ringer, I believe. They tell me he's the archdeacon's son, and a devil. He has a droll name; they call him Ember Days, Palm Sunday, Shrove Tuesday, or something of the sort! He's named for some high holiday or other! He took the liberty of carrying you off; as if you were a mate for such as he! That was coming it rather strong. What the devil did that screech-owl want with you, eh? Tell me!"

"I don't know," answered she.

"Did any one ever hear of such insolence,—a bell-ringer to carry off a girl as if he were a viscount! a common fellow to poach the game of gentlemen! A pretty state of things, indeed! However, he paid dearly for it. Master Pierrat Torterue is the roughest groom that ever combed and curried a knave; and I can tell you, if it will please you, that he gave your bell-ringer's hide a most thorough dressing."

"Poor man!" said the gipsy, reminded by these words of the scene at the pillory.

The captain burst out laughing. "By the great horn-spoon! your pity is as much out of place as a feather on a pig's tail. May I be as fat as a pope, if—"

He stopped short. "Excuse me, ladies! I was just about to utter a folly."

"Fie, sir!" said Gaillefontaine.

"He speaks to that creature in her own tongue!" added Fleur-de-Lys in a low voice, her anger growing every instant. Nor was this wrath diminished when she saw the captain, charmed with the gipsy and above all with himself, turn on his heel, repeating with the coarse and frank gallantry of a soldier,—

"A lovely girl, upon my soul!"

"Very badly dressed," said Diane de Christeuil, smiling to show her fine teeth.

This remark was a ray of light to the others. It showed them the gipsy's vulnerable point: unable to carp at her beauty, they attacked her dress.

"Why, that's true, little one," said Montmichel; "where did you learn to run about the streets in this way, without a wimple or a neckerchief?"

"Your skirt is so short it fairly makes me shiver," added Gaillefontaine.

"My dear," continued Fleur-de-Lys, somewhat sharply, "you will be taken up one of these days, by the serjeants of the dozen, for your gilded belt."

"Little one, little one," resumed Christeuil with a pitiless smile, "if you wore a decent pair of sleeves upon your arms, they would be less sunburnt."

It was indeed a scene worthy of a more intelligent spectator than Phœbus, to see how these beautiful girls, with their angry, venomous tongues, glided and twisted and twined about the street dancer; they were cruel and yet gracious; they maliciously searched and scanned her shabby, fantastic garb of rags and tinsel. Their laughter, their mockery, and their sneers were endless. Sarcasms rained upon the gipsy, with wicked glances and a haughty pretence of benevolence. They were like those young Roman damsels who amused themselves by plunging golden pins into the bosom of a beautiful slave girl. They were like elegant greyhounds, hanging, with distended nostrils and fiery eyes, about a poor wood-deer which their master's eye forbids them to devour.

After all, what was a miserable street dancer to these daughters of noble houses? They seemed to pay no heed to her presence, and spoke of her, before her, to her, in loud tones as of something rather dirty, rather low, but still rather pretty.

The gipsy was not insensible to these pin-pricks. Now and then a flush of shame, a flash of anger, kindled in her eyes or on her cheeks; a scornful word seemed trembling on her lips; she made that little grimace with which the reader is familiar, in token of her contempt, but she stood motionless; she fixed a sad, sweet look of resignation upon Phœbus. This look was also full of happiness and affection. She seemed to be restraining herself, for fear she should be turned out.

Phœbus also laughed, and took the gipsy's part with a mixture of impertinence and pity.

"Let them talk, little one," he repeated, jingling his golden spurs; "no doubt your dress is somewhat extravagant and peculiar; but what does that matter to such a charming girl as you are?"

"Good gracious!" exclaimed the fair-haired Gaillefontaine, straightening her swan-like neck with a bitter smile, "I see that the officers of the king's guard easily take fire at the bright eyes of a gipsy."

"Why not?" said Phœbus.

At this answer, carelessly uttered by the captain, like a stone cast at random, which falls unnoted, Colombe began to laugh, as did Diane and Amelotte and

Fleur-de-Lys, into whose eyes tears started at the same time.

The gipsy, whose eyes had drooped at the words of Colombe de Gaillefontaine, now raised them beaming with pride and pleasure, and fixed them again upon Phœbus. She was beautiful indeed at this moment.

The old lady, who was watching this scene, felt offended, though she did not know why.

"Holy Virgin!" she suddenly exclaimed, "what is this thing poking about under my feet? Oh, the ugly beast!"

It was the goat, which had entered in search of its mistress, and which, in its haste to reach her, had caught its horns in the mass of folds which the noble dame's draperies formed about her feet when she was seated.

This caused a diversion. The gipsy girl, without speaking, released her pet.

"Oh, there's the little goat with the golden feet!" cried Bérangère, jumping with joy.

The gipsy girl crouched upon her knees and pressed her cheek against the goat's fond head. She seemed to be begging its pardon for having thus deserted it.

But Diane whispered in Colombe's ear,—

"Gracious! why didn't I think of it before? It's the gipsy girl with the goat, of whom I have so often heard. They say she is a witch, and that her goat performs very marvellous tricks."

"Very well," said Colombe, "the goat must now amuse us, in its turn, by performing some miracle."

Diane and Colombe addressed the gipsy eagerly,—

"Little one, make your goat perform some miracle."

"I don't know what you mean," replied the dancer.

"A miracle, a piece of magic, some witchcraft."

"I don't understand;" and she began to fondle the pretty creature, repeating, "Djali! Djali!"

At this instant Fleur-de-Lys noticed an embroidered leather bag hanging from the goat's neck.

"What is that?" she asked.

The gipsy raised her large eyes to the girl's face and replied gravely, "That is my secret."

"I should very much like to know what your secret is," thought Fleur-de-Lys.

Meanwhile the good lady rose angrily, saying,—

"Come, gipsy, if neither you nor your goat can dance for us, why do you loiter here?"

The gipsy, without answering, moved slowly towards the door; but the nearer she came to it, the slower grew her steps. An irresistible magnet seemed to hold her back. All at once she turned her eyes wet with tears upon Phœbus, and paused.

"Zounds!" cried the captain; "you mustn't go in that way. Come back, and dance something for us. By the way, my beauty, what is your name?"

"Esmeralda," said the dancer, without taking her eyes from his face.

At this strange name the young girls burst into a fit of laughter.

"A terrible name for a girl," said Diane.

"You see now," added Amelotte, "that she is an enchantress."

"My dear," solemnly exclaimed Dame Aloïse, "your parents never fished out that name for you from the baptismal font."

Some moments previous, however, Bérangère, unheeded by the rest, had lured the goat into one corner of the room by a bit of marchpane. In an instant they were good friends. The curious child had removed the bag from the goat's neck, had opened it, and emptied its contents upon the matting; they consisted of an alphabet, each letter being written upon a separate square of boxwood. No sooner were these playthings scattered over the floor, than the child was amazed to see the goat, one of whose "miracles" this undoubtedly was, select certain letters with her golden hoof and arrange them, by a series of gentle pushes, in a particular order. In a moment a word was spelled out which the goat seemed to have been trained to write, so little did she hesitate in the task; and Bérangère exclaimed suddenly, clasping her hands in admiration,—

"Godmamma Fleur-de-Lys, do see what the goat has just done!"

Fleur-de-Lys looked, and shuddered. The letters arranged upon the floor spelled this word:—

"PHŒBUS."

"Did the goat do that?" she asked in an altered tone.

"Yes, godmamma," answered Bérangère.

It was impossible to doubt her, for the child could not spell.

"This is her secret!" thought Fleur-de-Lys.

Meantime, at the child's shout, the whole party hastened to her side,—the mother, the girls, the gipsy, and the officer.

The gipsy saw the folly which her goat had committed. She turned first red, then pale, and trembled like a criminal before the captain, who regarded her with a smile of mingled satisfaction and surprise.

"Phœbus," whispered the astonished girls. "Why, that's the captain's name!"

"You have a marvellous memory!" said Fleur-de-Lys to the stupefied gipsy. Then bursting into sobs, she stammered out in an agony, hiding her face in her lovely hands, "Oh, she is a witch!" and she heard a voice more bitter yet, which said to her inmost heart, "She is your rival!"

She fell fainting to the floor.

"My daughter! my daughter!" screamed the terrified mother. "Begone, you devilish gipsy!"

Esmeralda picked up the unlucky letters in the twinkling of an eye, made a sign to Djali, and went out at one door as Fleur-de-Lys was borne away by another.

Captain Phœbus, left alone, hesitated a moment between the two doors; then he followed the gipsy.

Chapter II

SHOWING THAT A PRIEST AND A PHILOSOPHER ARE TWO VERY DIFFERENT PERSONS

The priest whom the girls had noticed on the top of the north tower, leaning over to look into the square and watching the gipsy's dance so closely, was no other than Claude Frollo.

Our readers have not forgotten the

mysterious cell which the archdeacon reserved to himself in that tower. (I do not know, let me observe by the way, whether or not this be the same cell, the interior of which may still be seen through a tiny grated loop-hole, opening to the eastward, at about the height of a man from the floor, upon the platform from which the towers spring; a mere hole, now bare, empty, and dilapidated, the ill-plastered walls "adorned" here and there, at the present time, with a few wretched yellow engravings, representing various cathedral fronts. I presume that this hole is conjointly inhabited by bats and spiders, and that consequently a double war of extermination is waged against flies.)

Every day, an hour before sunset, the archdeacon climbed the tower stairs and shut himself up in this cell, where he often passed whole nights. On this especial day, just as, having reached the low door of his retreat, he was fitting into the lock the complicated little key, which he always carried about with him in the purse hanging at his side, the sound of tambourine and castanets struck upon his ear. The sound came from the square in front of the cathedral. The cell, as we have already said, had but one window looking upon the roof of the church. Claude Frollo hastily withdrew the key, and an instant later he was upon the top of the tower, in the gloomy and meditative attitude in which the ladies had seen him.

There he was, serious and motionless, absorbed in one sight, one thought. All Paris lay beneath his feet, with its countless spires and its circular horizon of gently sloping hills, with its river winding beneath its bridges, and its people flowing through its streets, with its cloud of smoke and its mountainous chain of roofs crowding Notre-Dame close with their double rings of tiles; but of this whole city the archdeacon saw only one corner,—the square in front of the cathedral; only one figure in all that crowd,—the gipsy.

It would have been hard to explain the nature of his gaze, and the source of the fire which flashed from his eyes. It was a fixed gaze, and yet it was full of agitation and trouble. And from the perfect repose of his whole body, scarcely shaken by an occasional involuntary shiver, like a tree stirred by the wind; from the stiffness of his elbows, more stony than the railing upon which they rested; from the rigid smile which contracted his face, you would have said that there was nothing living about Claude Frollo but his eyes.

The gipsy danced; she twirled her tambourine upon the tip of her finger, and tossed it into the air as she danced her Provençal sarabands: light, alert, and gay, quite unconscious of the weight of that terrible gaze which fell perpendicularly upon her head.

The crowd swarmed about her. Now and then a man accoutred in a loose red and yellow coat waved the people back into a circle, then sat down again in a chair a few paces away from the dancer, and let the goat lay its head upon his knees. This man seemed to be the gipsy's comrade. From the lofty point where he stood, Claude Frollo could not distinguish his features.

From the moment that the archdeacon observed this stranger, his attention seemed to be divided between him and the dancer, and his face grew blacker and blacker. Suddenly he straightened himself up, and trembled from head to foot. "Who is that man?" he muttered between his teeth. "I have always seen her alone till now!"

Then he plunged down the winding stairs once more. As he passed the half-open belfry door, he saw something which struck him: he saw Quasimodo, who, leaning from an opening in one of those slate pent-houses which look like huge Venetian blinds, was also gazing steadily out into the square. He was so absorbed in looking that he paid no heed to his foster father's presence. His savage eye had a strange expression; it looked both charmed and gentle. "How strange!" murmured Claude. "Can he be looking at the gipsy?" He continued his descent. In a few moments the anxious archdeacon came out into the square through the door at the foot of the tower.

"What has become of the gipsy girl?" he said, joining the group of spectators called together by the sound of the tambourine.

"I don't know," answered one of his neighbours. "She has just vanished. I think she has gone to dance some sort of a fandango in the house over opposite, where they called her in."

In the gipsy's place, upon the same carpet whose pattern had but just now seemed to vanish beneath the capricious figures of her dance, the archdeacon saw no one but the red-and-yellow man, who, hoping to gain a few coppers in his turn, was walking round the ring, his elbows on his hips, his head thrown back, his face scarlet, his neck stretched to its utmost extent, and a chair between his teeth. Upon this chair was fastened a cat, lent by a neighbouring woman, which spit and squalled in desperate alarm.

"By'r Lady!" cried the archdeacon, as the mountebank, dripping with perspiration, passed him with his pyramid of chair and cat, "what is Master Pierre Gringoire doing here?"

The archdeacon's stern voice so agitated the poor wretch that he lost his balance, and his entire structure, chair, cat, and all, fell pell-mell upon the heads of the spectators, amid a storm of inextinguishable shouts and laughter.

Master Pierre Gringoire (for it was indeed he) would probably have had a serious account to settle with the mistress of the cat, and the owners of all the bruised and scratched faces around him, if he had not hastily availed himself of the confusion to take refuge in the church, where Claude Frollo had beckoned him to follow.

The cathedral was dark and deserted; the side aisles were full of shadows, and the lamps in the chapels began to twinkle like stars, so black had the arched roofs grown. Only the great rose-window in the front, whose myriad hues were still bathed in a ray from the setting sun, gleamed through the darkness like a mass of diamonds, and threw a dazzling reflection to the farther end of the nave.

When they had gone a few paces, Don Claude leaned his back against a pillar and looked steadily at Gringoire. It was not such a look as Gringoire had dreaded, in his shame at being caught by a grave and learned person in this merryandrew attire. The priest's glance had nothing mocking or ironical about it; it was serious, calm, and piercing.

The archdeacon was first to break the silence.

"Come hither, Master Pierre. You have may matters to explain to me. And, first of all, how comes it that I have not seen you for these two months past, and that I now find you in the streets, in a pretty plight indeed,—half red and half yellow, like a Caudebec apple?"

"Sir," said Gringoire, in piteous tones, "it is in sooth a monstrous garb, and I feel as much abashed as a cat with a calabash on her head. 'Tis very ill done, I feel, to expose the gentlemen of the watch to the risk of cudgelling the shoulders of a Pythagorean philosopher under this loose coat. But what else could I do, my reverend master? The blame belongs entirely to my old doublet, which basely deserted me at the very beginning of winter, on the plea that it was falling to pieces, and must needs take a little rest in some ragpicker's basket. What could I do? Civilization has not yet reached the point where a man may go naked, as Diogenes of old desired. Besides, the wind blew very cold, and the month of January is not a good time to introduce such a new measure to mankind with any hope of success. This coat offered itself; I accepted it, and left behind my old black frock, which, for a Hermetic like myself, was far from being hermetically closed. So here I am in the dress of a mountebank, like Saint Genest. How can I help it? It is an eclipse; but even Apollo kept the swine of Admetus."

"A fine trade you have there," replied the archdeacon.

"I confess, master, that it is far better to philosophize and poetize, to blow the flame in the furnace, or to receive it from heaven, than to carry cats upon your shield; so, when you addressed me, I felt as silly as any donkey before a turnspit. But what was I to do, sir? A man must live; and the finest Alexandrine verses are not such good eating as a bit of Brie cheese. Now, I wrote that famous epithalamium for Margaret of Flanders, which you know all about, and the city has never paid me, under the pretext that it was not very good; as if one could furnish such tragedies as those of Sophocles for four crowns! I almost starved to death. Luckily, I discovered that I had rather a strong jaw. I said to this jaw of mine, 'Perform some feats of strength and balancing; feed yourself,' —*Ale te ipsam*. A lot of tatterdemalions, with whom I have made friends, taught me some score of Herculean tricks, and now I give my teeth every night the bread which I have earned through the day by the sweat of my brow. After all (*concedo*), I confess that it is a sad waste of my intellectual faculties, and that man was never made to spend his life in drumming on the tambourine and biting into chairs. But, reverend master, it is not enough to spend one's life; one must earn his living."

Don Claude listended in silence. All at once his sunken eyes assumed so sagacious and penetrating an expression that Gringoire felt that the look searched his inmost soul.

"Very good, Master Pierre; but how comes it that you are now keeping company with that gipsy dancing-girl?"

"I' faith" said Gringoire, "because she is my wife and I am her husband."

The priest's gloomy eyes blazed with wrath.

"Have you done this, miserable fellow?" cried he, furiously seizing Gringoire by the arm! "can you have been so forsaken of God as to have laid your hands upon that girl?'

"By my hopes of paradise, my lord," replied Gringoire, trembling in every limb, "I swear to you that I have never laid a finger upon her, if that is what disturbs you."

"Then, what do you mean by talking about husband and wife?" said the priest.

Gringoire hastily gave him as brief an account as possible of his adventure in the Court of Miracles, and his marriage with the broken jug, all of which the reader already knows. It seemed, moreover, that this marriage had as yet had no result, the gipsy always contriving to slip away and leave him as she had done on their wedding night. "It is very mortifying," said he in conclusion, "but that's the consequence of my being so unlucky as to marry a maid."

"What do you mean?" asked the archdeacon, who had gradually grown calmer as he listened to this tale.

"That's not easy to explain," replied the poet. "It's a superstition. My wife, according to an old prig whom we call the Duke of Egypt, is a foundling or a lost child, which comes to the same thing in the end. She wears about her neck an amulet which they say will some day restore her to her parents, but which will lose its virtue should the young girl lose hers. Hence it follows that we are both leading the most virtuous of lives."

"Then," continued Claude, whose brow had cleared more and more, "you think, Master Pierre, that this creature has never been approached by any man?"

"What chance, Don Claude, could any man have against a superstition? She has a mania upon this point. I certainly consider it a great rarity to find such nun-like prudery fiercely maintained in the midst of those gipsy girls, who are so easily tamed. But she has three safeguards,—the Duke of Egypt, who has taken her under his protection, perhaps intending to sell her to some gentleman priest; her whole tribe, who hold her in singular veneration, as if she were another Virgin Mary; and a certain dainty little dagger, which the hussy always carries somewhere about her, in spite of the provost's orders against wearing concealed weapons, and which always springs into her hand if you do but clasp her waist. She's a regular wasp, I can tell you!"

The archdeacon pressed Gringoire with questions.

In Gringoire's opinion Esmeralda was a charming, harmless creature, pretty, if it were not for a grimace which she was always making; a simple, affectionate girl, ignorant of all evil, and enthusiastic about everything; particularly fond of dancing, of noise, of the open air; a sort of woman bee, with invisible wings to her feet, and living in a whirl. She owed this nature to the wandering life which she had always led. Gringoire had managed to find out that while still a child she had travelled through Spain and Catalonia, to Sicily; he even fancied that she was taken, by the caravan of gipsies to which she belonged, to the kingdom of Algiers, a country situated in Achaia, which Achaia, on one side borders Albania and Greece, on the other the Sicilian sea, which is the road to Constantinople. The gipsies, said Gringoire, are vassals of the King of Algiers, in his capacity of chief of the nation of white Moors. One thing is certain, that Esmeralda came to France when very young, by way of Hungary. From all these countries the girl had gathered scraps of strange tongues, queer songs and notions, which made her conversation as motley a piece of patchwork as her dress, half Parisian and half African. Moreover, the people of those quarters of the town which she frequented, loved her for her gaiety, her gracefulness, her lively ways, her dances, and her songs. She knew but two persons in the whole city who disliked her, of whom she often spoke with terror,—the nun of the Tour-Roland, a dreadful recluse who had some special spite against all gipsies, and cursed the poor dancer every time she passed her window; and a priest, who never met her without looking at her and speaking to her in a way that frightened her. This latter circumstance greatly troubled the archdeacon, although Gringoire paid but little heed to his agitation; so completely had two months sufficed to blot from the careless poet's mind the singular details of that evening upon which he first met the gipsy, and the archdeacon's presence on that occasion. Except for this, the little dancer feared nothing; she never told fortunes, which prevented all danger of a trial for witchcraft, such as was frequently brought against the other gipsy women. And then, Gringoire took the place of a brother, if not of a husband to her. After all, the philosopher bore this kind of Platonic marriage very patiently. At any rate, it ensured him food and lodging. Every morning he set forth from the vagrant's headquarters, generally in Esmeralda's company; he helped her to reap her harvest of coin along the streets; every night he shared the same roof with her, allowing her to bolt herself into her tiny cell, and slept the sleep of the just. A very pleasant life, take it all in all, he thought, and very conducive to reverie. And then, in his innermost soul the philosopher was not so absolutely sure that he was desperately in love with the girl. He loved her goat almost as well. It was a charming animal, gentle, intelligent, quick,—a learned goat. Nothing was more common in the Middle Ages than these learned animals, at which men marvelled vastly, and which often conducted their instructors to the stake. And yet, the sorceries of the goat with the golden hoofs were very innocent tricks. Gringoire explained them to the archdeacon, whom these particulars seemed to interest greatly. All that was necessary, in most cases, was to hold the tambourine out to the goat in such or such a fashion, to make the creature perform the desired trick. It had been trained to do all this by the gipsy girl, who had such rare skill as an instructor that it took her only two months to teach the goat to write the word "Phœbus" with movable letters.

"Phœbus," said the priest; "and why 'Phœbus?'"

"I don't know," answered Gringoire. "It may be a word which she thinks has some secret magic virtue. She often repeats it in an undertone when she thinks she is alone."

"Are you sure," returned Claude, with his penetrating glance, "that it is a word, and not a name?"

"Whose name?" said the poet.

"How do I know?" said the priest.

"This is what I believe, sir. These gipsies are a kind of fire-worshippers, and worship the sun. Hence, 'Phœbus.'"

"That is not so clear to me as to you, Master Pierre."

"Never mind; it doesn't concern me. Let her mumble her 'Phœbus' as much as she likes. I'm sure of one thing; and that is, that Djali is almost as fond of me as of her."

"Who is Djali?"

"That's the goat."

The archdeacon rested his chin on his hand, and seemed for a moment lost in thought. Suddenly he turned abruptly to Gringoire.

"And you swear that you have never touched her?"

"Who?" said Gringoire,—"the goat?"

"No, that woman."

"My wife? I swear I never have."

"And you are often alone with her?"

"A good hour every evening."

Don Claude frowned.

"Oh! oh! *Solus c....t sola non cogitabuntur orare Pater r·ster.*"

"By my soul! I might repeat the *Pater,* and the *Ave Maria,* and the *Credo in Deum patrem omnipotentem,* without her taking any more notice of me than a hen would of a church."

"Swear to me by your mother's soul," repeated the archdeacon, vehemently, "that you have never laid the tip of your finger upon the girl."

"I will swear it by my father's head as well, if you like. But, my reverend master, let me ask one question in my turn."

"Speak, sir."

"What difference does it make to you?"

The archdeacon's pale face turned red as a girl's cheek. For a moment he made no answer; then, with evident embarrassment, he said,—

"Hark ye, Master Pierre Gringoire. You are not yet damned, so far as I know. I am interested in you, and wish you well. Now, the slighest contact with that devilish gipsy girl would make you the slave of Satan. You know that it is always the body which destroys the soul. Woe betide you if you approach that woman. That is all."

"I tried it once," said Gringoire, scratching his ear. "That was the first day; but I got stung."

"Had you the effrontery, Master Pierre?"

And the priest's face clouded.

"Another time," said the poet, smiling, "I peeped through her keyhole before I went to bed, and I saw, in her shift, as delicious a damsel as ever made a bed creak beneath her naked foot."

"Go to the devil!" cried the priest, with a terrible look; and pushing away the amazed Gringoire by the shoulders, he was soon lost to sight beneath the gloomiest arches of the cathedral.

Chapter III

THE BELLS

EVER since the morning when he was pilloried, the people living in the neighbourhood of Notre-Dame fancied that

Quasimodo's zeal for bell-ringing had grown very cold. Up to that time he had pulled the bells upon every occasion and no occasion at all; their music sounded from prime to complines; the belfry rang a peal for high mass, or the bells sounded a merry chime for a wedding or a christening, mingling and blending in the air like a rich embroidery of all sorts of melodious sounds. The old church, resonant and re-echoing, was forever sounding its joy-bells. There seemed to be an ever-present spirit of noise and caprice, which shouted and sang through those brazen tongues. Now that spirit seemed to have vanished; the cathedral seemed sombre, and given over to silence; for festivals and funerals there was still the simple tolling dry and bare, such as the ritual required, and nothing more; of the double noise which a church sends forth, from its organ within and its bells without, only the organ remained. It seemed as if there were no musician left in the belfry towers. And yet, Quasimodo was still there. What had happened to him? Did the shame and despair felt upon the pillory still rankle within him; did the executioner's lashes still tingle in his soul; and had the agony caused by such treatment killed all emotion within him, even his passion for the bells? Or had big Marie a rival in the heart of the ringer of Notre-Dame, and were the big bell and her fourteen sisters neglected for a fairer and more attractive object?

It happened that in this year of grace 1482 the Feast of the Annunciation fell upon Tuesday, the 25th of March. On that day the air was so pure and so clear that Quasimodo felt some slight return of his love for the bells. He therefore climbed up into the north tower, while below, the beadle threw wide open the church doors, which were then made of huge panels of hard wood covered with leather, edged with gilded iron nails, and framed in carvings "very cunningly wrought."

The high belfry cage reached, Quasimodo gazed at the six bells for some time with a sad shake of the head, as if mourning over the strange thing which had come between his heart and them. But when he had set them swinging; when he felt that cluster of bells vibrating beneath his touch; when he saw —for he could not hear—the quivering octave run up and down that sonorous scale as a bird hops from twig to twig; when the demon of music, that demon which shakes a dazzling sheaf of runs, trills, and arpeggios, had taken possession of the poor deaf fellow,—then he was happy again; he forgot everything; and as his heart swelled with bliss his face grew radiant.

He came and went, he clapped his hands, he ran from one rope to another, he encouraged the six singers with voice and gesture, as the leader of an orchestra spurs on intelligent performers.

"Go on," he cried; "go on, Gabrielle! Pour all your music into the public square; this is a high holiday. Thibauld, no laziness! your pace is slackening; go on, go on, I say! Are you growing rusty, sluggard? That's good! quick! quick! don't let me see the clapper. Make them all as deaf as I am. That's it, Thibauld! bravely done! Guillaume! Guillaume! you are the biggest of them all, and Pasquier is the smallest, and yet Pasquier rings the best. I'll wager that they who can hear, hear him better than they do you. Good! good! my Gabrielle! louder! louder! Hollo! what are you two doing up there, you Sparrows? I don't see you make the very least noise. What are those brazen beaks about yonder, that they seem to yawn when they should be singing? There, work away! 'Tis the Feast of the Annunciation. The sun shines bright; we want a fine peal of bells. Poor Guillaume! you're quite out of breath, my fat lad."

He was wholly absorbed in urging on his bells, all six of which bounded to and fro as best they could, and shook their shining sides, like a noisy team of Spanish mules goaded by the sharp voice of their driver.

All at once, as his gaze fell between the broad slate scales which covered the steep belfry wall up to a certain height, he saw in the square below a young girl quaintly attired, who paused, spread a carpet on the ground, upon which a little goat took its place, and a group of spectators formed about them. This sight suddenly changed the course of his ideas, and chilled his musical enthusiasm as a blast of wind chills melted resin. He stopped, turned his back on the chime of bells, and crouched behind the slated eaves, fixing on the dancing-girl that dreamy, tender, gentle look which had once before astonished the archdeacon. The neglected bells ceased suddenly and all at once, to the great disappointment of the lovers of chimes, who were eagerly listening to the peal from the Pont au Change, and who now went away as much amazed as a dog that has been shown a bone and then receives a stone.

Chapter IV

'ANA'TKH

It happened that on a fine morning in that same month of March,—I believe it was Saturday, the 29th,—Saint Eustache's Day, our young friend the student, Jehan Frollo du Moulin, noticed while dressing that his breeches, which contained his purse, gave forth no clink of metal. "Poor purse!" said he, pulling it from his pocket; "what! not the smallest coin! How cruelly have the dice, Venus, and mugs of beer gutted thee! How empty, wrinkled, and flat you are! You look like the breast of a Fury! I just ask you, Master Cicero and Master Seneca, whose dog's-eared works I see scattered over the floor, what does it avail me to know, better than any governor of the Mint or any Jew from the Pont au Change, that one golden crown-piece is worth thirty-five unzains at twenty-five pence and eight Paris farthings each, and that another is worth thirty-six unzains at twenty-six pence and six Tours farthings each, if I have not a paltry copper to stake upon the double-six? Oh, Consul Cicero! that is not a calamity to be overcome by periphrases,—by *quemadmodum* and *verum enim vero*."

He dressed himself sadly. A thought struck him as he laced his shoes, but he at first rejected it; however, it recurred to him, and he put on his waistcoat wrong side out,—an evident sign of some violent mental conflict. At last he dashed down his cap, exclaimed, "So much the worse! Come what will, I will go to my brother. I shall catch a lecture, but I shall also catch a crown."

Then he hastily put on his cassock with furred shoulder-pads, picked up his cap, and dashed out of the room.

He went down the Rue de la Harpe towards the City. As he passed the Rue de la Huchette, the smell of those wonderful spits perpetually revolving there tickled his olfactories, and he cast an affectionate glance at the gigantic cookshop which once drew from the Franciscan friar Calatagirone the pathetic exclamation, — *"Veramente, queste rotisserie sono cosa stupenda!"* But Jehan had no money to pay for breakfast; and with a deep sigh he entered the door of the Petit-Châtelet,— that huge double trefoil of massive towers which guarded the entrance to the City.

He did not even take time to throw a stone as he passed, as was customary, at the wretched statue of that Périnet Leclerc who deliverd over the Paris of Charles VI. to the English,—a crime which his effigy, its surface defaced by stones and covered with mud, has expiated for three centuries, at the corner of the Rues de la Harpe and de Buci, as in a perpetual pillory.

Crossing the Petit-Pont, and striding down the Rue Neuve-Sainte-Geneviève, Jehan de Molendino found himself face to face with Notre-Dame. Then his former indecision overcame him, and he walked around the statue of Monsieur Legris for several moments, repeating in agony, "The lecture is a certainty; the crown-piece is doubtful!"

He stopped a beadle as he came from the cloister.

"Where is the archdeacon of Josas?"

"I think that he is in his cell in the tower," said the beadle; "and I don't advise you to disturb him, unless you come from some such person as the pope or the king."

Jehan clapped his hands.

"The devil! what a splendid opportunity to see the famous abode of sorceries!"

Strengthened by this thought, he boldly entered the little black door, and began to climb the winding staircase of Saint-Gilles, which leads to the upper stories of the tower. "We'll see!" said he as he climbed. "By the Holy Virgin's shoestrings! it must be something very queer which my reverend brother keeps so closely hidden. They say that he lights the fires of hell up there, and cooks the philosopher's stone over the blaze. My word! I care no more for the philosopher's stone than for any common pebble; and I should rather find a good omelet of Easter eggs over his fire than the biggest philosopher's stone in the world!"

Reaching the gallery of little columns, he stopped a moment to take breath, and to swear at the interminable staircase by I know not how many millions of cartloads of devils; then he resumed his ascent by the little door of the north tower, now closed to the public. A few moments later, after passing the belfry cage, he reached a small landing-place built in a lateral recess, and under the arch, a low pointed door,—an opening cut through the circular wall of the staircase enabling him to see its enormous lock and strong iron framework. Persons desirous of visiting this door at the present time may recognize it by the inscription in white letters on the black wall, "I adore Coralie. 1823.

Signed, Eugène." The word "signed" is in the original.

"Oho!" said the student; "this must be the place."

The key was in the lock. The door was ajar; he pushed it gently, and put his head through the opening.

The reader has doubtless seen the admirable works of Rembrandt, that Shakspeare of painting. Among many marvellous engravings, there is one especial etching which is supposed to represent Doctor Faustus, and at which it is impossible to look without being dazzled. It represents a dark cell; in the foreground is a table covered with hideous objects,—skulls, globes, alembics, compasses, hieroglyphic parchments. The Doctor is at this table, dressed in his coarse great-coat, a furred bonnet pulled down to his eyebrows. He is painted at half-length. He has half risen from his vast arm-chair, his clinched fists rest on the table, and he stares with curiosity and terror at a large luminous circle, composed of magical letters, which gleams on the opposite wall like the solar spectrum in the camera obscura. The cabalistic sun seems to shimmer as we look, and fills the gloomy cell with its mysterious radiance. It is horrible, and the same time beautiful.

Something very similar to Faust's cell appeared to Jehan when he ventured to put his head in at the half-open door. This, too, was a dark and dimly lighted dwelling. There, too, were the large chair and large table, the compasses and alembics, skeletons of animals hanging from the roof, a globe rolling over the floor, hippocamps pell-mell with glass jars in which quivered leaf gold, death's-heads lying on vellum scrawled over with figures and letters, thick manuscripts, open, and piled one upon another, without regard to the fragile corners of the parchment,—in short, all the rubbish of science, and over all this litter, dust and cobwebs; but there was no circle of luminous letters, no rapt doctor gazing at the flaming vision as the eagle looks upon the sun.

And yet the cell was not deserted. A man sat in the arm-chair, leaning over the table. Jehan, to whom his back was turned, could see only his shoulders and the back of his skull; but he found no difficulty in recognizing the bald head, which Nature had endowed with an enduring tonsure, as if wishing to mark by this outward symbol the archdeacon's irresistible clerical vocation.

Jehan recognized his brother; but the door had opened so softly that nothing warned Don Claude of his presence. The curious student took advantage of this fact to examine the cell at his leisure. A large stove, which he had not at first observed, stood to the left of the arm-chair, under the dormer-window. The rays of light which penetrated that aperture passed through a round cobweb covering the pointed arch of the window with its delicate tracery, in the centre of which the insect architect lay motionless, like the nave of this wheel of lacework. Upon the stove were heaped in confusion all sorts of vessels,—earthen flasks, glass retorts, and charcoal matrasses. Jehan noticed, with a sigh, that there was not a single saucepan.

"The kitchen utensils are cold!" thought he.

Moreover, there was no fire in the stove, and it even seemed as if none had been lighted for a long time. A glass mask, which Jehan noted among the alchemist's tools, and doubtless used to protect the archdeacon's face when handling any dangerous substance, lay in one corner, covered with dust, and apparently forgotten. Beside it lay an equally dusty pair of bellows, upon the upper surface of which was the motto, inlaid in copper, "*Spira, spera.*"

Other mottoes were written on the walls, after the manner of the Hermetics, in great number,—some in ink, others engraved with a metal point. Moreover, Gothic letters, Hebrew letters, Greek letters, and Roman letters were used indiscriminately,—the inscriptions overlapping each other at haphazard, the newest effacing the oldest, and all entangled together, like the branches in a thicket, like the pikes in an affray. There was a confused medley of all human philosophy, thought, and knowledge. Here and there one shone out among the rest like a flag among the spear-heads. They were for the most part brief Greek or Latin devices, such as the Middle Ages expressed so well: "*Unde? inde?*" "*Homo homini monstrum.*" "*Astra, castra, nomen, numen.*" "Μέγα βιβλίον, μέγα κακόν." "*Sapere aude.*" "*Flat ubi vult.*" etc. Sometimes a single word without any apparent meaning, "'Ἀναγκοφαγία," which possibly hid a bitter allusion to the monastic system; sometimes a simple maxim of clerical discipline in the form of a regular hexameter, "*Cælestem dominum, terrestrem dicito domnum.*" There were also Hebrew hieroglyphics, of which Jehan, who did not even know much Greek, could make nothing; and the whole was crisscrossed in every direction with stars, figures of men and animals, and intersecting triangles, which contributed not a little to make the blotted wall of the cell look like a sheet of paper which a monkey had bedaubed with an inky pen.

The entire abode, moreover, had a look of general desertion and decay, and the bad condition of the implements led to the conjecture that their owner had for some time been distracted from his labours by other cares.

This owner, however, bending over a huge manuscript adorned with quaint paintings, seemed tormented by a thought which mingled constantly with his meditations,—at least, so Jehan judged from hearing him exclaim, with the pensive pauses of a man in a brown study thinking aloud:—

"Yes, Manu said it, and Zoroaster taught it,—the sun is the offspring of fire, the moon of the sun; fire is the central soul of the great whole; its elementary atoms perpetually overflow, and flood the world in boundless currents! At the points where these currents cross in the heavens, they produce light; at their points of intersection on the earth, they produce gold. Light, gold; the same thing! From fire to the concrete state. The difference between the visible and palpable, between the fluid and solid of the same substance, between steam and ice,—nothing more. These are not mere dreams,—it is the general law of Nature. But how are we to wrest from science the secret of this general law? Why, this light which irradiates my hand is gold! these selfsame atoms, expanded in harmony with a certain law, only require to be condensed in accordance with another law.

And how? Some have fancied it was by burying a sunbeam. Averroës,—yes, it was Averroës,—Averroës interred one under the first column to the left in the sanctuary of the Koran, in the great mosque of Cordova; but the vault may not be opened to see if the operation be successful, until eight thousand years have passed."

"The deuce!" said Jehan aside, "that's a long time to wait for a crown."

"Others have thought," continued the musing archdeacon, "that it was better to work with a ray from Sirius. But it is not easy to get such a ray pure, on account of the simultaneous presence of other stars which blend with it. Flamel! What a name for one of the elect, *Flamma!*—Yes, fire. That is all: the diamond lurks in the coal; gold is to be found in fire. But how to extract it? Magistri declares that there are certain feminine names possessing so sweet and mysterious a spell that it is enough to pronounce them during the operation. Let us read what Manu says under this head: 'Where women are reverenced, the divinities rejoice; where they are scorned, it is vain to pray to God. A woman's mouth is ever pure; it is like running water, it is like a sunbeam. A woman's name should be agreeable, soft, fantastic; it should end with long vowels, and sound like words of blessing.' Yes, the sage is right,—indeed, Maria, Sophia, Esmeral— Damnation! again that thought!"

And he closed the book violently.

He passed his hand across his brow, as if to drive away the idea which possessed him; then he took from the table a nail and a small hammer, the handle of which was curiously painted with cabalistic letters.

"For some time," said he with a bitter smile, "I have failed in all my experiments; a fixed idea possesses me, and is burned into my brain as with a red-hot iron. I have not even succeeded in discovering the lost secret of Cassiodorus, whose lamp burned without wick or oil. And yet it is a simple matter!"

"A plague upon him!" muttered Jehan.

"A single wretched thought, then," continued the priest, "is enough to make a man weak and mad! Oh, how Claude Pernelle would laugh me to scorn,—she who could not for an instant turn Nicholas Flamel from his pursuit of the great work! Why, I hold in my hand the magic hammer of Ezekiel! At every blow which the terrible rabbi, in the seclusion of his cell, struck on this nail with his hammer, that one of his foes whom he had condemned, were he two thousand leagues away, sank an arm's-length into the earth, which swallowed him up. The King of France himself, having one night knocked heedlessly at the magician's door, sank knee-deep into the pavement of his own city of Paris. Well, I have the hammer and the nail, and they are no more powerful tools in my hand than a cooper's tiny mallet would be to a smith; and yet I only need to recover the magic word uttered by Ezekiel as he struck his nail."

"Nonsense!" thought Jehan.

"Let me see, let me try," resumed the archdeacon, eagerly. "If I succeed, I shall see a blue spark flash from the head of the nail. *'Emen-Hétan! Emen-Hétan!'* That's not it. *'Sigéani. Sigéani!'* May this nail open the gate of the tomb for every one who bears the name of Phœbus! A curse upon it! Always, always and forever the same idea!"

And he threw the hammer from him angrily. Then he sank so far forward over the table that Jehan lost sight of him behind the huge back of the chair. For some moments he saw nothing but his fist convulsively clinched upon a book. All at once Don Claude rose, took up a pair of compasses, and silently engraved upon the wall, in capital letters, this Greek word:—

'ANA'TKH

"My brother is mad," said Jehan to himself; "it would have been much simpler to write *Fatum*; every one is not obliged to understand Greek."

The archdeacon resumed his seat in his arm-chair, and bowed his head on his hands, like a sick man whose brow is heavy and burning.

The student watched his brother in surprise. He, who wore his heart on his sleeve, who followed no law in the world but the good law of Nature, who gave free rein to his passions, and in whom the fountain of strong feeling was always dry, so clever was he at draining it daily,—he could not guess the fury with which the sea of human passions bubbles and boils when it is denied all outlet; how it gathers and grows, how it swells, how it overflows, how it wears away the heart, how it breaks forth in repressed sobs and stifled convulsions, until it has rent its dikes and burst its bed. Claude Frollo's stern and icy exterior, that cold surface of rugged and inaccessible virtue, had always misled Jehan. The jovial student had never dreamed of the boiling lava which lies deep and fiery beneath the snowy front of Ætna.

We know not if he was suddenly made aware of these things; but, featherbrain though he was, he understood that he had seen what he was never meant to see, that he had surprised his elder brother's soul in one of its most secret moments, and that he must not let Claude discover it. Noting that the archdeacon had relapsed into his former immobility, he drew his head back very softly, and made a slight noise behind the door, as if he had just arrived, and wished to warn his brother of his approach.

"Come in!" cried the archdeacon from within the cell; "I expected you. I left the door on the latch purposely; come in, Master Jacques."

The student entered boldly. The archdeacon, much annoyed by such a visit in such a place, started in his chair. "What! is it you, Jehan?"

"It is a J, at any rate," said the student, with his merry, rosy, impudent face.

Don Claude's features resumed their usual severe expression.

"Why are you here?"

"Brother," replied the student, trying to put on a modest, unassuming, melancholy look, and twisting his cap with an innocent air, "I came to ask you—"

"What?"

"For a little moral lecture, which I sorely need." Jehan dared not add aloud, "And a little money, which I need still more sorely." The last part of his sentence was left unspoken.

"Sir," said the archdeacon in icy

tones, "I am greatly displeased with you."

"Alas!" sighed the student.

Don Claude turned his chair slightly, and looked steadily at Jehan.

"I am very glad to see you."

This was a terrible beginning. Jehan prepared for a severe attack.

"Jehan, I hear complaints of you every day. How about that beating with which you bruised a certain little Viscount Albert de Ramonchamp?"

"Oh!" said Jehan, "that was nothing,—a mischievous page, who amused himself with spattering the students by riding his horse through the mud at full speed!"

"How about that Mahiet Fargel," continued the archdeacon, "whose gown you tore? '*Tunicam dechiraverunt*,' the complaint says."

"Oh, pooh! a miserable Montaigu cape,—that's all!"

"The complaint says '*tunicam*,' and not '*cappettam*.' Do you know Latin?"

Jehan made no answer.

"Yes," resumed the priest, shaking his head, "this is what study and learning have come to now. The Latin language is hardly understood, Syriac is an unknown tongue, Greek is held in such odium that it is not considered ignorance for the wisest to skip a Greek word without reading it, and to say, '*Græcum est, non legitur.*'"

The student boldly raised his eyes: "Brother, would you like me to explain in good every-day French that Greek word written yonder on the wall?"

"Which word?"

'ΑΝΑ'ΤΚΗ

A slight flush overspread the archdeacon's dappled cheeks, like the puff of smoke which proclaims to the world the secret commotion of a volcano. The student scarcely noticed it.

"Well, Jehan!" stammered the elder brother with an effort, "what does the word mean?"

"FATE."

Don Claude turned pale again, and the student went on carelessly,—

"And that word below it, written by the same hand 'Αναγνεία, means 'impurity.' You see I know my Greek."

The archdeacon was still silent. This Greek lesson had given him food for thought.

Little Jehan, who had all the cunning of a spoiled child, thought this a favourable opportunity to prefer his request. He therefore assumed a very sweet tone, and began:—

"My good brother, have you taken such an aversion to me that you pull a long face for a few paltry cuffs and thumps distributed in fair fight to no one knows what boys and monkeys (*quibusdam marmosetis*)? You see, dear brother Claude, that I know my Latin."

But all this affectionate hypocrisy failed of its usual effect on the stern elder brother. Cerberus did not snap at the sop. The archdeacon's brow did not lose a single wrinkle.

"What are you driving at?" said he, drily.

"Well, then, to the point! This is it," bravely responded Jehan; "I want money."

At this bold declaration the archdeacon's face assumed quite a paternal and pedagogic expression.

"You know, Master Jehan, that our Tirechappe estate only brings us in reckoning the taxes and rents of th twenty-one houses, thirty-nine pounds eleven pence and six Paris farthings. It is half as much again as in the time of the Paclet brothers, but it is not much."

"I want money," stoically repeated Jehan.

"You know that it has been officially decided that our twenty-one houses were held in full fee of the bishopric, and that we can only buy ourselves off from this homage by paying two silver gilt marks of the value of six Paris pounds to the right reverend bishop. Now, I have not yet been able to save up those two marks. You know this."

"I know that I want money," repeated Jehan for the third time.

"And what would you do with it?"

This question made the light of hope shine in Jehan's eyes. He resumed his demure, caressing manner.

"See here, dear brother Claude; I do not come to you with any evil intention. I don't want to cut a dash at the tavern with your money, or to walk the streets of Paris in garments of gold brocade with my lackey, *cum meo laquasio*. No, brother; I want the money for a charity."

"What charity?" asked Claude with some surprise.

"There are two of my friends who want to buy an outfit for the child of a poor widow in the Haudry almshouse. It is a real charity. It will cost three florins; I want to give my share."

"Who are your two friends?"

"Pierre l'Assommeur and Baptiste Croque-Oison."

"Hum!" said the archdeacon; "those names are as fit for charity as a bombard for the high altar."

Certainly Jehan had chosen very suspicious names for his two friends, as he felt when it was too late.

"And then," added the sagacious Claude, "what kind of an outfit could you buy for three florins, and for the child of one of the women in the Haudry almshouse, too? How long have those widows had babies in swaddling-clothes?"

Jehan broke the ice once more:—

"Well, then, if I must tell you, I want the money to go to see Isabeau la Thierrye tonight, at the Val-d'Amour."

"Impure scamp!" cried the priest.

"'Ἀναγνεία,'" said Jehan.

This quotation, borrowed, perhaps maliciously, by the student from the wall of the cell, produced a strange effect upon the priest. He bit his lip, and his rage was extinguished in a blush.

"Begone!" said he to Jehan. "I am expecting someone."

The student made another effort,—

"Brother Claude, at least give me a few farthings for food."

"How far have you got in Gratian's decretals?" asked Don Claude.

"I've lost my copy-books."

"Where are you in the Latin humanities?"

"Somebody has stolen my copy of Horace."

"Where are you in Aristotle?"

"My faith, brother! what Father of the Church says that the errors of heretics have in all ages taken refuge in the brambles of Aristotle's metaphysics? Plague take Aristotle! I will not destroy my religion with his metaphysics."

"Young man," resumed the archdeacon, "at the king's last entry there was a gentleman called Philippe de

Comines, who had embroidered on his horse's housings this motto, which I advise you to consider: *'Qui non laborat non manducet.'* "

The student was silent for a moment, his finger to his ear, his eye fixed upon the ground, and an angry air.

Suddenly he turned to Claude with the lively quickness of a water wagtail,—

"So, good brother, you refuse to give me a penny to buy a crust from a baker?"

" *'Qui non laborat non manducet.'* "

At this reply from the inflexible archdeacon, Jehan hid his face in his hands like a woman sobbing, and exclaimed in accents of despair, "'Οτοτοτοτοτοί!"

"What do you mean by that, sir?" asked Claude, amazed at this outburst.

"Why," said the student,—and he looked up at Claude with impudent eyes into which he had just rubbed his fists to make them look red with crying,— "it is Greek! It is an anapæst of Æschylus which expresses grief perfectly."

And here he burst into laughter so absurd and so violent that it made the archdeacon smile. It was really Claude's fault; why had he so spoiled the child?

"Oh, good brother Claude," added Jehan, emboldened by this smile, "just see my broken buskins! Was there ever more tragic cothurnus on earth than boots with flapping soles?"

The archdeacon had promptly resumed his former severity.

"I will send you new boots, but no money."

"Only a paltry penny, brother," continued the suppliant Jehan. "I will learn Gratian by heart. I will believe heartily in God. I will be a regular Pythagoras of learning and virtue. But give me a penny, for pity's sake! Would you have me devoured by famine, which gapes before me with its jaws blacker, more noisome, deeper than Tartarus or a monk's nose?"

Don Claude shook his wrinkled brow: " *'Qui non laborat,—'* "

Jehan did not let him finish.

"Well, then," he cried, "to the devil! Hurrah for fun! I'll go to the tavern, I'll fight, I'll drink, and I'll go to see the girls!"

And upon this, he flung up his cap and cracked his fingers like castanets.

The archdeacon looked at him with a gloomy air.

"Jehan, you have no soul!"

"In that case, according to Epicurus, I lack an unknown quantity composed of unknown qualities."

"Jehan, you must think seriously of reform."

"Oh, come!" cried the student, gazing alternately at his brother and at the alembics on the stove; "is everything crooked here,—ideas as well as bottles?"

"Jehan, you are on a very slippery road. Do you know where you are going?"

"To the tavern," said Jehan.

"The tavern leads to the pillory."

"It's as good a lantern as any other, and perhaps it was the one with which Diogenes found his man."

"The pillory leads to the gallows."

"The gallows is a balance, with a man in one scale and the whole world in the other. It is a fine thing to be the man."

"The gallows leads to hell."

"That's a glorious fire."

"Jehan, Jehan, you will come to a bad end!"

"I shall have had a good beginning."

At this moment the sound of footsteps was heard on the stairs.

"Silence!" said the archdeacon, putting his finger to his lip: "here comes Master Jacques. Listen, Jehan," he added in a low voice; "take care you never mention what you may see and hear here. Hide yourself quickly under that stove, and don't dare to breathe."

The student crawled under the stove; there, a capital idea occurred to him.

"By the way, brother Claude, I want a florin for holding my breath."

"Silence! you shall have it."

"Then give it to me."

"Take it!" said the archdeacon, angrily, flinging him his purse.

Jehan crept farther under the stove, and the door opened.

Chapter V

THE TWO MEN DRESSED IN BLACK

The person who entered wore a black gown and a gloomy air. Our friend Jehan (who, as may readily be supposed, had so disposed himself in his corner that he could see and hear everything at his good pleasure) was struck, at the first glance, by the extreme melancholy of the new-comer's face and attire. Yet a certain amiability pervaded the countenance, albeit it was the amiability of a at or a judge,—a sickly amiability. The man was very grey, wrinkled, bordering on sixty years; had white eyebrows, hanging lip, and big hands. Then Jehan saw that he was a mere nobody,—that is, probably a doctor or a magistrate, and that his nose was very far away from his mouth, a sure sign of stupidity,—he curled himself up in his hiding-place, in despair at having to pass an indefinite length of time in so uncomfortable a position and in such poor company.

Meantime, the archdeacon did not even rise from his chair to greet this person. He signed to him to be seated on a stool near the door, and after a few moments' silence, which seemed the continuation of a previous meditation, he said in a somewhat patronizing tone, "Good-morning, Master Jacques."

"Your servant, master," replied the man in black.

In the two ways of pronouncing,—on the one hand that "Master Jacques," and on the other that distinctive "master,"—there was the difference that there is between *domine* and *domne*. It bespoke the greeting of teacher and pupil.

"Well," resumed the archdeacon after a fresh pause, which Master Jacques took care not to break, "have you succeeded?"

"Alas! master," said the other, with a sad smile, "I am still blowing away. As many ashes as I choose; but not a particle of gold."

Don Claude made an impatient gesture. "I'm not talking about that, Master Jacques Charmolue, but about the trial of your sorcerer, Marc Cenaine,—wasn't that what you called him?—the butler to the Court of Accounts. Does he confess his magic? Was the rack successful?"

"Alas! no," replied Master Jacques, still with the same sad smile, "we have not that consolation. The man is as hard as flint; we might boil him at the Pig-market before he would say a word. And yet, we have spared nothing to get at the truth; all his bones are out of joint already; we have left no stone unturned. As the old comic author, Plautus, says:—

'*Advorsum stimulos, laminas, crucesque, compedesque,
Nervos, catenas, carceres, numellas, pedicas, boias.*'

All in vain; the man is terrible indeed. I can't make him out!"

"You've not found anything new at his house?"

"Yes, indeed," said Master Jacques, fumbling in his purse; "this parchment. There are words written on it which we cannot comprehend. And yet the criminal lawyer, Philippe Lheulier, knows a little Hebrew, which he picked up in that affair of the Jews in the Rue Kantersten at Brussels."

So saying, Master Jacques unrolled a parchment.

"Give it to me," said the archdeacon. And casting his eyes over the writing, he exclaimed, "Clear magic, Master Jacques! *'Emen-Hétan!'* that is the cry of the vampires as they appear at their Sabbath. *'Per ipsum, et cum ipso, et in ipso!'*—that is the word of command which rechains the devil in hell. *'Hax, pax, max!'* this belongs to medicine: a prescription against the bite of mad dogs. Master Jacques, you are the king's proxy to the Ecclesiastical Court. This parchment is an abomination."

"We will return the man to the rack. Here again," added Master Jacques, rummaging in his wallet once more, "is something else which we found in Marc Cenaine's house."

It was a vessel similar to those which covered Don Claude's stove.

"Ah!" said the archdeacon, "an alchemist's crucible."

"I must confess," replied Master Jacques, with his shy, awkward smile, "that I tried it on my furnace, but I succeeded no better than with my own."

The archdeacon began to examine the vessel.

"What has he inscribed upon his crucible? *'Och! Och!'*—the word which drives away fleas! This Marc Cenaine is a dolt! I can easily believe that you will never make gold with this. Put it in your alcove in summer, for that's all it's fit for."

"Talking of mistakes," said the king's proxy, "I have just been studying the porch below before I came upstairs; is your reverence very sure that it is the opening of the book of physics which is represented there on the side towards the Hospital; and that, of the seven nude figures at the feet of the Virgin, the one with wings at his heels is meant for Mercury?"

"Yes," replied the priest; "it is so written by Augustin Nypho, that Italian doctor who had a bearded familiar spirit, which taught him everything. However, we will go down, and I will explain all this to you on the spot."

"Thanks, master," said Charmolue, bowing to the ground. "By the way, I forgot! When will it please you to have the little witch arrested?"

"What witch?"

"That gipsy girl whom you know well, who comes every day and dances in the square before the cathedral, despite the official prohibition. She has a goat which is possessed, and which has the devil's own horns; which reads and writes, and is as good a mathematician as Picatrix, and would be quite enough to hang an entire tribe of gipsies. The papers are ready; the case will be a short one, I warrant! A pretty creature, by my soul,—that dancing-girl! The finest black eyes! Two carbuncles! When shall we begin?"

The archdeacon was extremely pale.

"I will let you know," he stammered in a voice which was scarcely articulate; then he added, with an effort, "Devote yourself to Marc Cenaine."

"Never fear," said Charmolue, smiling; "I'll have him re-strapped to the leather bed when I go back. But he's a devil of a fellow; he would tire out Pierrat Torterue himself, and his hands are bigger than mine. As the worthy Plautus says:—

'Nudus vinctus, centum pondo, es
quando pendes per pedes.'

The torture of the wheel! That's the best thing we have. He shall take a turn at that."

Don Claude seemed absorbed in gloomy reverie. He turned to Charmolue with the words,—

"Master Pierrat,—Master Jacques, I mean,—devote yourself to Marc Cenaine."

"Yes, yes, Don Claude. Poor man! he must have suffered like Mummol. But then, what an idea, to go to the Witches' Sabbath,—a butler of the Court of Accounts, who must know Charlemagne's text, *'Stryga vel masca!'* As for that little girl,—Smelarda, as they call her,—I will await your orders. Ah! and as we pass through the porch you will also explain to me the meaning of the gardener painted in relief at the entrance to the church. The Sower, isn't it? Eh! master, what are you thinking about?"

Don Claude, lost in his own thoughts, did not hear him. Charmolue, following the direction of his gaze saw that it was fixed mechanically upon the large cobweb which covered the window. At this instant a rash fly, in search of the March sun, plunged headlong into the trap and was caught in it. At the vibration of its web the huge spider made a sudden sally from its central cell, and with one bound fell upon the fly, which it doubled up with its front antennæ, while its hideous proboscis dug out the head. "Poor fly!" said the king's proxy to the Ecclesiastical Court; and he raised his hand to save it. The archdeacon, with a start, held back his arm with convulsive force.

"Master Jacques," he cried, "do not interfere with the work of Fate!"

The attorney turned in alarm; he felt as if iron pincers had seized his arm. The priest's eye was fixed, wild, and flaming, and was still fastened upon the horrible little group of the spider and the fly.

"Oh, yes," added the priest in a voice which seemed to come from his very entrails, "this is a universal symbol. The insect flies about, is happy, is young; it seeks the spring sun, the fresh air, freedom; oh, yes, but it runs against the fatal web; the spider appears,—the hideous spider! Poor dancing-girl! poor predestined fly! Master Jacques, do not interfere! it is the hand of Fate! Alas! Claude, you are the spider. Claude, you are the fly as well! You flew abroad in search of learning, light, and sun; your only desire was to gain the pure air, the broad light of eternal truth; but in your haste to reach the dazzling window which opens into the other world,—the world of intellect, light, and learning,—blind fly! senseless doctor! you failed to see that subtle spider's web woven by Fate between the light and you; you plunged headlong into it, wretched fool! and now you struggle in its meshes, with bruised head and broken wings, in the iron grasp of destiny. Master Jacques, Master Jacques, let the spider do its work!"

"I assure you," said Charmolue, looking at him uncomprehendingly, "I will not touch it. But for mercy's sake, master, let go my arm! Your hand is like a pair of pincers."

The archdeacon did not hear him. "Oh, madman!" he resumed, without taking his eyes from the window. "And if you could have broken this dreadful web with your frail wings, do you think you could have reached the light? Alas! how could you have passed that pane of glass beyond it,—that transparent obstacle, that crystal wall harder than iron, which separates all philosophy from truth? Oh, vanity of science! How many sages have flown from afar to bruise their heads against it! How many contending systems have rushed pell-mell against that everlasting pane of glass!"

He ceased speaking. These last ideas, which had insensibly diverted his thoughts from himself to science, seemed to have calmed him. Jacques Charmolue completely restored him to a sense of reality by asking him this question: "Come, master, when are you going to help me to make gold? I long for success."

The archdeacon shook his head with a bitter smile:

"Master Jacques, read Michel Psellus, *'Dialogues de Energia et Operatione Dæmonum.'* Our work is not altogether innocent."

"Not so loud, master! I fear you are right," said Charmolue. "But I must needs dabble a little in hermetics, being only the king's proxy to the Ecclesiastical Court, at a salary of thirty Tours crowns a year. But speak lower."

At this moment the sound of champing and chewing proceeding from under the stove, attracted Charmolue's anxious ear.

"What was that?" he asked.

It was the student, who, greatly cramped and much bored in his hiding-place, had contrived to find an old crust of bread and a bit of mouldy cheese, and had set to work to devour them without more ado, by the way of consolation and of breakfast. As he was ravenously hungry, he made a great deal of noise, and smacked his lips loudly over every mouthful as to give the alarm to the lawyer.

"It is my cat," said the archdeacon, hastily, "feasting under there upon some mouse."

This explanation satisfied Charmolue.

"Indeed, master," he replied with a respectful smile, "every philosopher has had his familiar animal. You know what Servius says: *'Nullus enim locus sine genio est.'*"

But Don Claude, who feared some fresh outbreak from Jehan, reminded his worthy disciple that they had certain figures on the porch to study together and the two left the cell, to the great relief of the student, who began seriously to fear that his knees would leave their permanent mark upon his chin.

Chapter VI

THE EFFECT PRODUCED BY SEVEN OATHS IN THE OPEN AIR

"Te Deum Laudamus!" cried Master Jehan, as he stepped from his hiding-place; "the two screech-owls have gone. *Och! och! Hax! pax! max!* the fleas! the mad dogs! the devil! I've had enough of their talk! My head rings like a belfry. Mouldy cheese into the bargain! Now, then! let us be off; let us take our big brother's purse, and convert all these coins into bottles!"

He cast a look of tenderness and admiration into the interior of the precious purse, adjusted his dress, wiped his boots, dusted his poor shoulder-pads all grey with ashes, whistled a tune, frisked about, looked to see if there was nothing left in the cell which he might carry off, scraped up a few glass charms and trinkets from the top of the stove, thinking he might pass them off upon Isabeau la Thierrye for jewels, then gave a push to the door, which his brother had left ajar as a final favour, and which he left open in his turn as a final piece of mischief, and hopped down the winding stairs as nimbly as a bird.

In the midst of the shadows of the spiral staircase he elbowed something which moved aside with a growl; he took it for granted that it was Quasimodo, and this struck him as so droll that he held his sides with laughter all the rest of the way down. As he came out into the public square, he was still laughing.

He stamped his foot when he found himself on solid ground once more. "Oh," said he, "good and honourable pavement of Paris! Cursed stairs, which would put all the angels of Jacob's ladder out of breath! What was I thinking of when I poked myself into that stone gimlet which pierces the sky; and all to eat musty cheese, and to see the steeples of Paris through a garret window!"

He walked on a few paces, and saw the two screech-owls—that is to say, Don Claude and Master Jacques Charmolue—lost in contemplation of a bit of carving on the porch. He approached them on tiptoe, and heard the archdeacon say in a very low voice to Charmolue, "It was Guillaume de Paris who had a Job graven on that lapis-lazuli coloured stone, gilded at the edges. Job represents the philosopher's stone, which must also be tried and tortured before it can become perfect, as Raymond Lulle says: *'Sub conservatione formæ specificæ salva anima.'*"

"That's all one to me," said Jehan. "'Tis I who hold the purse."

At this instant he heard a loud ringing voice pronounce a terrible string of oaths just behind him.

"Zounds! Odds bodikins! By the Rood! By Cock and pye! Damme! 'Sdeath! Thunder and Mars!"

"By my soul," exclaimed Jehan, "that can be no other than my friend Captain Phœbus!"

The name of Phœbus reached the archdeacon's ears, just as he was explaining to the king's proxy the dragon hiding his tail in a bath from which rise smoke and a king's head. Don Claude shuddered, stopped short, to the great surprise of Charmolue, turned, and saw his brother Jehan talking to a tall officer at the door of the Gondelaurier house.

It was indeed Captain Phœbus de Châteaupers. He was leaning against the corner of his lady-love's house, and swearing like a pirate.

"My word! Captain Phœbus," said Jehan, taking him by the hand, "you swear with admirable spirit!"

"Thunder and Mars!" replied the captain.

"Thunder and Mars, yourself!" responded the student. "Now, then, my fine captain, what has caused such an outburst of elegant epithets?"

"Your pardon, good comrade Jehan," cried Phœbus, shaking him by the hand; "but a horse running at full speed cannot stop short. Now, I was swearing at full gallop. I have just come from those prudes; and when I leave them, I always have my mouth full of oaths; I must needs spit them out, or I should choke. Thunder and guns!"

"Will you take a drink?" asked the student. This proposition calmed the captain.

"With pleasure; but I've no money."

"But I have!"

"Pshaw! let me see!"

Jehan displayed the purse to the captain's eyes, with dignity and simplicity. Meanwhile the archdeacon, having left the amazed Charmolue, had approached them, and stood some paces distant, watching them both unobserved by them, so absorbed were they in looking at the purse.

Phœbus exclaimed, "A purse in your pocket, Jehan! That's like the moon in a pail of water. I see it, but it is not really there. It's only a shadow. By Heaven! I wager there's nothing but pebbles in it!"

Jehan answered coldly, "I'll show you the kind of pebbles that I pave my pocket with."

And without another word he emptied the purse upon a neighbouring post, with the air of a Roman saving his country.

"Good God!" muttered Phœbus; "gold pieces, big silver pieces, little silver pieces, crowns, shillings, and pence! It is dazzling!"

Jehan remained dignified and unmoved. A few pennies had rolled into the mud; the captain, in his enthusiasm, stooped to pick them up. Jehan restrained him, saying,—

"Fie, Captain Phœbus de Châteaupers!"

Phœbus counted the money, and turning solemnly to Jehan, asked, "Do you know, Jehan, that you have here twenty-three crowns? Whom did you rob last night in the Rue Coupe-Gueule?"

Jehan threw back his fair curly head, and said, half closing his eyes in scorn,—

"I have a brother who is an archdeacon and a fool."

"Confound it!" cried Phœbus; "so you have, the worthy fellow!"

"Let us take a drink," said Jehan.

"Where shall we go?" said Phœbus; "to the Pomme d'Eve!"

"No, Captain; let us go to the Vieille Science. An old woman who handles a saw to saw a handle,—that's a rebus; and I love that sort of thing."

"A plague on rebuses, Jehan! The wine is better at the Pomme d'Eve; and besides, at the door is a vine in the sun which cheers me as I drink."

"So be it," said the student; and taking Phœbus by the arm, the two friends set out for that tavern. It is needless to say that they first picked up the money, and that the archdeacon followed them.

The archdeacon followed them, sad and worn. Was this the Phœbus whose accursed name, since his interview with Gringoire, had mingled with all his thoughts? He knew not; but at any rate it was a Phœbus, and that magic name was enough to make the archdeacon follow the two heedless comrades with stealthy tread, listening to their every word and noting their least gesture with eager attention. Moreover, nothing was easier than to hear everything they said; for they spoke very loud, utterly regardless of the fact that they were taking the passers-by into their confidence. They talked of duels, women, drinking, and riots.

At the corner of a street the sound of a tambourine was heard from a neighbouring cross-way. Don Claude overheard the officer say to the student,—

"Thunder! We must hasten."

"Why, Phœbus?"

"I'm afraid the gipsy girl will see me."

"What gipsy girl?"

"That little thing with the goat."

"Smeralda?"

"Just so, Jehan. I alway forget her devil of a name. Make haste; she would be sure to recognize me. I don't wish to have that girl accost me in the street."

"Do you know her, Phœbus?"

Here the archdeacon saw Phœbus chuckle, put his mouth to Jehan's ear, and whisper a few words to him; then he burst out laughing, and shook his head with a triumphant air.

"Really?" said Jehan.

"Upon my soul!" said Phœbus.

"To-night?"

"To-night."

"Are you sure she will come?"

"Are you mad, Jehan? How can there be any doubt in such matters?"

"Captain Phœbus, you are a lucky soldier!"

The archdeacon heard every word of this conversation. His teeth chattered; he shook from head to foot. He stood still a moment, leaned against a post like a drunken man, then followed in the track of the two jolly scamps.

When he rejoined them they had changed the subject. He heard them singing at the top of their voices the old refrain:—

"The lads of Petty-Tiles, they say,
Like calves are butchered every day."

Chapter VII

THE SPECTRE MONK

The famous tavern known as the Pomme d'Eve was situated in the University, at the corner of the Rue de la Rondelle and the Rue du Bâtonnier. It was a large, low room on the ground-floor, with an arched roof, the central spring of which rested on a huge wooden pillar painted yellow; there were tables in every direction, shining pewter jugs hung on the wall; there were always plenty of topers, lots of girls, a window looking on the street, a vine at the door, and over the door a creaking piece of sheet iron, on which were painted a woman and an apple, rusted by the rain and swinging in the wind on an iron rod. This kind of weathercock, which overlooked the pavement, was the sign.

Night was falling; the streets were dark. The tavern, full of candles, flared from a distance like a forge in the gloom; a noise of glasses, of feasting, of oaths, and of quarrels escaped from the broken window-panes. Through the mist with which the heat of the room covered the glazed casement in front of the inn swarmed a myriad of confused figures, and from time to time a ringing burst of laughter was heard. People passing, intent on their own affairs, hastened by that noisy window without a glance; but now and then some little ragged boy would raise himself on tiptoe to the window-sill, and scream into the tavern the old mocking cry with which drunkards were often greeted at this period:—

"Back to your glasses,
Ye drunken, drunken asses."

One man, however, marched imperturbably up and down in front of the noisy tavern, looking continually, and never stirring farther away from it than a pikeman from his sentry-box. His cloak was pulled up to his very nose. This cloak he had just bought from the old-clothes man who lived hard by the Pomme d'Eve, doubtless to shield himself from the chill of the March evening, perhaps to hide his dress. From time to time he paused before the dim panes set in lead, listened, looked, and stamped his feet impatiently.

At last the tavern door opened. This seemed to be what he was waiting for. Two tipplers came out. The ray of light which escaped through the door, for a moment reddened their jovial faces. The man with the cloak took up his position under a porch on the other side of the street.

"Thunder and guns!" said one of the two drinkers. "It will strike seven directly. It is the hour for my appointment."

"I tell you," resumed his companion, with a thick utterance, "that I do not live in the Rue des Mauvaises-Paroles, *indignus qui inter mala verba habitat.* My lodgings are in the Rue Jean-Pain-Mollet, *in vico Johannis-Pain-Mollet.* You are more unreasonable than a unicorn, if you say to the contrary. Everybody knows that he who has once climbed upon a bear's back is never afraid; but you've a fine nose for scenting out dainty bits like Saint-Jacques de l'Hôpital."

"Jehan, my friend, you are drunk," said the other.

He replied, staggering, "So it pleases you to say, Phœbus; but it is well proven that Plato had the profile of a hunting-dog."

The reader has undoubtedly recognized our two worthy friends, the captain and the student. It seems that the man lurking in the shadow had also recognized them; for he followed with slow steps all the zig-zags which the student forced the captain to describe, the latter, a more hardened drinker, having preserved entire self-possession. By listening carefully, the man with the cloak was able to catch the whole of the following interesting conversation:—

"Body of Bacchus! do try to walk straight, Master Bachelor. You know that I shall have to leave you. Here it is seven o'clock. I have an appointment with a woman."

"Leave me then, do. I see fiery stars and spears. You are like the Château-de-Dampmartin, which burst with laughter."

"By my grandmother's warts, Jehan! your nonsense is rather too desperate. By-the-bye, Jehan, haven't you any money left?"

"Mr. Rector, there's no mistake: the little butcher's shop, *parva boucheria*."

"Jehan, friend Jehan! you know that I made an appointment to meet that little girl at the end of the Pont Saint-Michel; that I can't take her anywhere but to Mother Falourdel,—the old hag on the bridge; and that I must pay for the room; the white-whiskered old jade gives no credit. Jehan, for pity's sake, have we drunk up the priest's whole purse? Haven't you a penny left?"

"The consciousness that you have spent the rest of your time well is a good and savoury table-sauce."

"Thunder and blazes! A truce to your nonsense! Tell me, Jehan, you devil! have you any money left? Give it to me, by Heaven! or I will rob you, were you as leprous as Job and as mangy as Cæsar!"

"Sir, the Rue Galiache is a street which runs from the Rue de la Verrerie to the Rue de la Tixeranderie."

"Yes, yes, good friend Jehan, my poor comrade, the Rue Galiache,—that's all right, quite right, but in Heaven's name, come to your senses! I want only a few pence, and my appointment is for seven o'clock."

"Silence all around, and pay attention to my song:

'When the rats have eaten every case,
The king shall be lord of Arras race.
When the sea, so deep and wide,
Is frozen o'er at Saint John's tide,
Across the ice we then shall see
The Arras men their city flee.'"

"There, then, scholar of Antichrist, the foul fiend fly away with you!" cried Phœbus; and he gave the tipsy student a violent push, which sent him reeling against the wall, whence he fell gently to the pavement of Philip Augustus. With a remnant of that brotherly compassion which never quite forsakes the heart of a toper, Phœbus rolled Jehan with his foot over upon one of those pillows of the poor which Providence keeps in readiness at every street corner in Paris, and which the rich scornfully stigmatize as dunghills. The captain arranged Jehan's head on an inclined plane of cabbage-stalks, and the student instantly began to snore in a magnificent bass. However, all rancour was not yet dead in the captain's heart. "So much the worse for you if the devil's cart picks you up as it passes!" said he to the poor sleeping scholar; and he went his way.

The man in the cloak, who had not ceased following him, paused for a moment beside the prostrate student, as if uncertain; then, heaving a deep sigh, he also departed in the captain's wake.

Like them, we will leave Jehan to sleep under the friendly watch of the bright stars, and we too will follow them, if it so please the reader.

As he emerged into the Rue Saint-André-des-Arcs, Captain Phœbus discovered that some one was following him. As he accidentally glanced behind him, he saw a kind of shadow creeping behind him along the walls. He stopped, it stopped; he walked on again, the shadow also walked on. This troubled him but very little. "Pooh!" said he to himself, "I have not a penny about me."

In front of the Collège d'Autun, he came to a halt. It was at this college that he had passed through what he was pleased to call his studies, and from a habit learned in his student days he never passed the statue of Cardinal Pierre Bertrand without stopping to mock at it. He therefore paused before the statue as usual. The street was deserted, save for the shadow approaching slowly,—so slowly that he had ample time to observe that it wore a cloak and a hat. Coming close up to him, it stopped, and stood more motionless than the statue of Cardinal Bertrand itself; but it fastened upon Phœbus a pair of eyes full of that vague light seen at night in the pupil of a cat's eye.

The captain was brave, and would not have cared a farthing for a thief with a bludgeon in his hand; but this walking statue, this petrified man, froze his very blood. At that time there were current in society strange stories of the spectral monk, who prowled the streets of Paris by night. These tales now came confusedly to his mind, and for some moments he stood stupefied; at last he broke the silence with a forced laugh, saying,—

"Sir, if you are a robber, as I hope, you remind me of a heron attacking a nutshell; I am the son of a ruined family, my dear fellow. You've come to the wrong shop; you'd better go next door. In the chapel of that college there is a piece of the true cross set in silver."

The hand of the shadow was stretched from under the cloak, and swooped down upon Phœbus's arm with the grip of an eagle's talons. At the same time the shadow spoke:—

"Captain Phœbus de Châteaupers!"

"What! the devil!" said Phœbus; "do you know my name?"

"I not only know your name," replied the man in the cloak, with his sepulchral voice, "but I know that you have an appointment this evening?"

"Yes," answered the astonished Phœbus.

"At seven o'clock."

"In fifteen minutes."

"At Mother Falourdel's."

"Exactly so."

"The old hag of the Pont Saint-Michel."

"Saint Michel the archangel, as the Pater Noster says."

"Impious wretch!" muttered the spectre. "With a woman?"

"*Confiteor.*"

"Whose name is—"

"Esmeralda," said Phœbus, cheerfully. He had gradually recovered all his unconcern.

At this name the shadow's claws shook the captain's arm furiously.

"Captain Phœbus de Châteaupers, you lie!"

Any one who could at this moment have seen the captain's flaming face, his backward bound, so violent that it released him from the vice-like grasp that held him, the haughty air with which he clapped his hand to his sword-hilt, and the gloomy immobility of the man in the cloak in the presence of this rage,

—any one who saw all this would have trembled with fear. It was something like the fight between Don Juan and the statue.

"Christ and Satan!" cried the captain; "that is a word which seldom greets the ears of a Châteaupers! You dare not repeat it!"

"You lie!" said the shadow, coldly.

The captain gnashed his teeth. Spectre monk, phantom, superstitions, all were forgotten at this instant. He saw nothing but a man and an insult.

"Ha! it is well!" he stammered in a voice stifled by rage. He drew his sword; then, stuttering,—for anger makes a man tremble as well as fear, "Here! on the spot! Now then! swords! swords! Blood upon these stones!"

But the other never stirred. When he saw his adversary on his guard, and ready to burst with wrath, he said,—

"Captain Phœbus,"—and his voice quivered with bitterness,—"you forget your appointment."

The fits of passion of such men as Phœbus are like boiling milk,—a drop of cold water is enough to check their fury. At these simple words the sword which glittered in the captain's hand was lowered.

"Captain," continued the man, "to-morrow, the day after to-morrow, in a month, in ten years, you will find me ready to cut your throat; but keep your appointment first."

"Indeed," said Phœbus, as if trying to compound with his conscience, "a sword and a girl are both charming things to encounter by appointment; but I do not see why I should miss one for the sake of the other, when I might have both."

He replaced his sword in his scabbard.

"Go to your appointment," replied the stranger.

"Sir," answered Phœbus with some embarrassment, "many thanks for your courtesy. You are right in saying that to-morrow will be time enough for us to cut slashes and buttonholes in Father Adam's doublet. I am obliged to you for allowing me to pass another agreeable quarter of an hour. I did indeed hope to put you to bed in the gutter, and yet be in time for my fair one,—the more so that it is genteel to keep the women waiting a little in such cases. But you look to me like a determined dog, and it is safer to put the party off until to-morrow. I will therefore go to my appointment; it is for seven o'clock, as you know." Here Phœbus scratched his ear. "Ah, by my halidom! I forgot; I have not a penny to pay the toll for the use of the garret, and the old hag must be paid in advance. She won't trust me."

"Here is money to pay her."

Phœbus felt the stranger's cold hand slip a large piece of money into his. He could not help taking the money and squeezing the hand.

"By God!" he exclaimed, "you're a good fellow!"

"One condition," said the man. "Prove to me that I was wrong, and that you spoke the truth. Hide me in some corner where I can see whether this woman be really she whose name you mentioned."

"Oh," answered Phœbus, "with all my heart! We will take Saint Martha's room; you can look in very easily from the kennel beside it."

"Come on, then!" said the shadow.

"At your service," replied the captain. "I don't know whether or no you are Master Diabolus in *propria persona*: but let us be good friends for to-night; to-morrow I will pay you all my debts, of purse and sword."

They set forth at a rapid pace. In a few moments the sound of the river warned them that they stood on Pont Saint-Michel, then covered with houses.

"I will first introduce you," said Phœbus to his companion; "then I will go and fetch my charmer, who was to wait for me near the Petit-Châtelet."

His comrade made no answer; since they had walked side by side he had not said a word. Phœbus stopped before a low door and knocked loudly; a light appeared through the chinks of the door.

"Who is there?" cried a mumbling voice.

"By Saint Luke's face! By God's passion! By the Rood!" answered the captain.

The door opened instantly, and revealed to the new-comers an old woman and an old lamp, both in a very shaky state. The old woman was bent double, dressed in rags; her head shook; she had very small eyes, wore a dishclout on her head, and her hands, face, and neck were covered with wrinkles; her lips retreated under her gums, and she had tufts of white hair all around her mouth, which gave her the demure look of a cat.

The interior of the hovel was as dilapidated as its mistrees; there were whitewashed walls, black beams running across the ceiling, a dismantled fireplace, cobwebs in every corner; in the middle of the room stood a rickety collection of tables and chairs; a dirty child played in the ashes; and in the background a staircase, or rather a wooden ladder, led to a trap-door in the ceiling.

On entering this den Phœbus's mysterious companion pulled his cloak up to his eyes. But the captain, swearing all the time like a Turk, hastened "to make the sun flash from a crown-piece," as our all-accomplished Régnier says.

"Saint Martha's room," said he.

The old woman treated him like a lord, and put the coin away in a drawer. It was the money which the man in the black cloak had given Phœbus. While her back was turned, the ragged, dishevelled little boy, who was playing in the ashes, went adroitly to the drawer, took out the crown-piece, and put in its place a dried leaf which he had pulled from a fagot.

The old woman beckoned to the two gentlemen, as she called them, to follow her, and climbed the ladder before them. On reaching the upper floor, she placed her lamp upon a chest; and Phœbus, as one familiar with the house, opened a door leading to a dark hole. "Go in there, my dear boy," said he to his comrade. The man in the cloak obeyed without a word; the door closed behind him; he heard Phœbus bolt it, and a moment after go downstairs again with the old woman. The light had disappeared.

Chapter VIII

THE ADVANTAGE OF WINDOWS OVERLOOKING THE RIVER

Claude Frollo (for we presume that the reader, more clever than Phœbus, has discovered that this spectral monk was no other than the archdeacon), Claude Frollo groped about for some time in the gloomy hole into which the captain had bolted him. It was one of those nooks such as architects sometimes leave at the junction of the roof and outer wall. The vertical section of this kennel—as Phœbus had so aptly called it—would have formed a triangle. Moreover, there was neither window nor loop-hole, and the pitch of the roof was so steep that it was impossible to stand upright. Claude therefore squatted in the dust and mortar which crumbled beneath him. His head was burning; as he felt about him with his hands, he found upon the ground a bit of broken glass, which he pressed to his forehead, its coolness somewhat refreshing him.

What went on at this moment in the archdeacon's dark soul? God and himself alone knew.

According to what fatal order did he dispose in his thoughts Esmeralda, Phœbus, Jacques Charmolue, his young brother, so greatly loved, deserted by him in the mud, his archdeacon's gown, perhaps his reputation, dragged through the mire of Mother Falourdel's abode,—all these images, all these adventures? I cannot say; but it is certain that the ideas formed a horrible group in his mind.

He waited a quarter of an hour; he felt as if a century had been added to his age. All at once he heard the boards of the wooden staircase creak; some one was coming up. The trap-door opened; a light appeared. There was a considerable crack in the worm-eaten door of his prison; to this he glued his face. Thus he could see everything that happened in the next room. The cat-faced old woman first rose from the trap-door, lamp in hand; then came Phœbus, twirling his moustache; then a third person,—that lovely, graceful creature, Esmeralda. The priest saw her rise from below like a dazzling apparition. He trembled; a cloud came before his eyes; his veins swelled to bursting; everything swam before him; he saw and heard nothing more.

When he recovered his senses, Phœbus and Esmeralda were alone, seated on the wooden chest beside the lamp, whose light revealed to the archdeacon's eyes their two youthful figures, and a miserable pallet at the back of the garret.

Beside the pallet there was a window, through whose panes, shattered like a cobweb upon which rain has fallen, were seen a patch of sky, and the moon in the distance resting on a bed of soft clouds.

The young girl was blushing and trembling, and confused. Her long, drooping lashes shaded her flushed cheeks. The officer, to whose face she dared not raise her eyes, was radiant. Mechanically, and with a charming awkwardness, she drew meaningless lines on the bench with her finger-tips, and then looked at her finger. Her feet were hidden, for the little goat was lying upon them.

The captain was very gallantly arrayed; at his wrists and neck he wore embroidery, then considered very elegant.

Don Claude could scarcely hear what they said, for the throbbing of his temples.

Lovers' talk is very commonplace. It

is a perpetual "I love you." A very bare and very insipid phrase to an indifferent ear, unless adorned with a few grace-notes; but Claude was not an indifferent listener.

"Oh," said the girl, without raising her eyes, "do not despise me, my lord Phœbus! I feel that I am doing very wrong."

"Despise you, pretty child!" replied the officer with an air of extreme gallantry,—"despise you! By God's passion! and why?"

"For coming here with you."

"On that point, my beauty, we are not agreed. I should not despise you, but hate you."

The young girl gazed at him in affright. "Hate me! What have I done?"

"For requiring so much urging."

"Alas!" said she, "that is because I am breaking a sacred vow. I shall never find my parents! The amulet will lose its virtue; but what does that matter? Why should I need father or mother now?"

So saying, she fixed upon the captain her large dark eyes, moist with love and joy.

"Deuce take me if I understand you!" exclaimed Phœbus.

Esmeralda was silent for a moment, then a tear fell from her eyes, a sigh from her lips, and she said, "Oh, my lord, I love you!"

There was such an odour of chastity, such a charm of virtue about the young girl, that Phœbus did not feel wholly at his ease with her. But this speech emboldened him. "You love me!" said he, with transport; and he threw his arm around the gipsy's waist. He had only waited for such an opportunity.

The priest saw him, and tested with the tip of his finger the point of a dagger hidden in his bosom.

"Phœbus," continued the gipsy girl, gently removing the captain's stubborn hands from her girdle, "you are good, you are generous, you are kind; you saved me,—me, who am but a poor gipsy foundling. I have long dreamed of an officer who should save my life. It was of you I dreamed before I ever knew you, my Phœbus; the image of my dreams had a gorgeous uniform like yours, a grand air, a sword. Your name is Phœbus; it is a beautiful name. I love your name; I love your sword. Draw your sword, Phœbus, and let me see it."

"Child!" said the captain; and he unsheathed his rapier with a smile.

The gipsy girl studied the handle, the blade, examined the letters on the hilt with adorable curiosity, and kissed the sword, as she said,—

"You are a brave man's sword. I love my captain."

Phœbus again took advantage of the situation to imprint on her lovely bent neck a kiss which made the girl start up as red as a cherry. The priest ground his teeth in the darkness at the sight.

"Phœbus," resumed the gipsy, "let me talk to you. Walk about a little, so that I may have a good look at you, and hear your spurs jingle. How handsome you are!"

The captain rose to gratify her, while he scolded her with a smile of satisfaction:—

"What a child you are! By the way,

my charmer, did you ever see me in my full dress uniform?"

"Alas, no!" she replied.

"Well, that is really fine!"

Phœbus came back and sat down beside her, but much nearer than before.

"Look here, my dear—"

The gipsy gave him a few little taps on the lips with her pretty hand, with a childish playfulness full of gaiety and grace.

"No, no, I will not listen. Do you love me? I want you to tell me if you love me."

"Do I love you, angel of my life!" cried the captain, half kneeling before her. "My body, my soul, my blood, are yours. I am all yours,—all yours. I love you, and never loved any one but you."

The captain had so often repeated this phrase on many a similar occasion, that he uttered it in a breath, without making a single mistake. At this passionate declaration the gipsy turned towards the dirty ceiling, which took the place of heaven, a look of angelic happiness. "Oh," she murmured, "at such a moment one might well wish to die!"

Phœbus thought "the moment" a good one to steal another kiss, which inflicted fresh torment on the wretched archdeacon in his lair.

"To die!" exclaimed the amorous captain. "What are you talking about, my lovely angel? It is just the time to live, or Jupiter is but a paltry knave! Die at the beginning of such a pleasant thing! By Saint Luke's face, what a joke! that would never do! Listen, my dear Similar—Esmenarda— Forgive me! but you have such a vastly outlandish name that I can never get it straight. I'm forever getting entangled in it."

"Good Heavens!" said the poor girl, "and I thought the name pretty just for its oddness! But if you don't like it, I am quite ready to change it for anything you please."

"Ah, do not cry for such a trifle, my dearest! It's a name to which one has to get used, that's all. Once I have learned it by heart, it will be all right. Now listen, my dear Similar; I adore you passionately. I love you to such a degree that it is really marvellous. I know a little girl who is bursting with rage about it—"

The jealous damsel cut him short: "Who is she?"

"What difference does that make to us?" said Phœbus; "do you love me?"

"Oh!" said she.

"Well, then, that is all that is necessary. You shall see how I love you, too. May the great devil Neptune bestride me if I do not make you the happiest creature in the world. We will have a pretty little room somewhere! I will review my archers under your windows. They are all mounted, and make nothing of Captain Mignon's men. There are spearmen, cross-bowmen, and culverin men. I will take you to see the great Paris musters at the Grange de Rully. It's a very fine sight, —eighty thousand helmeted heads; thirty thousand bright harnesses, coats of mail, or brigandines; sixty-seven banners of the various guilds; the standards of the Parliament, the Chamber of Accounts, the Treasury, the Assistants in the Mint; in fact, the devil's own train! I will take you to see the lions at the king's palace, which are wild beasts; all the women like that."

For some moments the young girl, wrapped in her own delightful thoughts, had been dreaming to the sound of his voice, without heeding the meaning of his words.

"Oh, how happy you will be!" continued the captain; and at the same time he gently unclasped the gipsy's belt.

"What are you doing?" said she, quickly. This act of violence startled her from her reverie.

"Nothing," answered Phœbus; "I was merely saying that you must give up this ridiculous mountebank dress when you come to live with me."

"When I live with you, my Phœbus!" said the young girl, tenderly.

She again became pensive and silent.

The captain, made bold by her gentleness, took her by the waist without any resistance on her part, then began noiselessly to unlace the poor child's bodice, and so disarranged her neckerchief that the panting priest saw the gipsy's lovely shoulder issue from the gauze, plump and brown, like the moon rising through the mists on the horizon.

The young girl let Phœbus have his way. She did not seem conscious of what he was doing. The bold captain's eyes sparkled.

All at once she turned towards him.

"Phœbus," she said, with a look of infinite love, "instruct me in your religion."

"My religion!" cried the captain, bursting into laughter. "I instruct you in my religion! Thunder and guns! What do you want with my religion?"

"To be married to you," she answered.

The captain's face assumed an expression of mingled surprise, scorn, recklessness, and evil passion.

"Nonsense!" said he. "Why should we marry?"

The gipsy turned pale, and let her head sink sadly on her breast.

"My pretty love," tenderly added Phœbus, "what are all these foolish ideas? Marriage is nothing! Is any one less loving for not having spouted a little Latin in some priest's shop?"

So saying in his sweetest voice, he approached extremely near the gipsy girl; his caressing hands had resumed their place around the lithe, slender waist, and his eyes kindled more and more, and everything showed that Master Phœbus was about to enjoy one of those moments in which Jupiter himself commits so many follies that the good Homer is obliged to call in a cloud to help him.

But Don Claude saw all. The door was made of decayed puncheon staves, which left ample room between them for the passage of his hawk-like glance. The brown-skinned broad-shouldered priest, hitherto comdemned to the austere rule of the convent, shuddered and burned at this scene of love, darkness, and passion.

The young and lovely girl, her garments in disorder, abandoning herself to this ardent young man, made his veins run molten lead. An extraordinary agitation shook him; his eye sought, with lustful desire, to penetrate beneath all these unfastened pins. Any one who had at this moment seen the the face of the unhappy man glued to the worm-eaten bars, might have thought he saw a tiger glaring from his cage at some jackal devouring a gazelle. His pupils glowed like a candle through the cracks of the door.

Suddenly, with a rapid motion, Phœbus removed the gipsy's neckerchief. The poor child, who still sat pale and dreamy, sprang up with a start; she retreated hastily from the enterprising officer, and, glancing at her bare throat and shoulders, red, confused, and dumb with shame, she crossed her lovely arms over her bosom to cover it. But for the flame which mantled her cheeks, any one seeing her thus silent and motionless, might have thought her a statue of Modesty. Her eyes were downcast.

Meantime the captain's action had exposed the mysterious amulet which she wore about her neck.

"What's this?" said he, seizing this pretext to draw nearer to the beautiful creature whom he had alarmed.

"Do not touch it!" replied she, quickly "it is my protector. It will help me to find my family, if I am still worthy of it. Oh, leave me, Mr. Captain! My mother! my poor mother! Mother, where are you? Help me now! For Heaven's sake, Mr. Phœbus, give me back my neckerchief!"

Phœbus drew back, and said in a cold tone,—

"Oh, young lady! I see very plainly that you do not love me!"

"I do not love him!" exclaimed the unhappy creature, and at the same time she hung upon the captain, whom she drew to a seat by her side. "I not love you, my Phœbus? How can you say so, you wicked man, to break my heart? Oh, come! take me, take everything! Do with me what you will; I am yours. What do I care for the amulet! What is my mother to me now! You are my mother, for I love you! Phœbus, my adored Phœbus, do you see me? It is I, look at me; it is that little girl whom you cannot repulse, who comes,—who comes herself in search of you. My soul, my life, my person, are yours; I am all yours, my captain. No, then, we will not marry; it would trouble you; and what am I? A miserable child of the gutter; while you, my Phœbus, are a gentleman. A fine thing, truly,—a dancing-girl to marry an officer! I was mad. No, Phœbus, no; I will be your mistress, your amusement, your pleasure, when you will; always yours. I am only made for that,—to be soiled, despised, dishonoured; but what matter? I shall be loved. I shall be the proudest and happiest of women. And when I grow old or ugly, Phœbus, when I am no longer fit to love you, my lord, you will still suffer me to serve you. Others may embroider your scarves; but I, your servant, will take care of them. You will let me polish your spurs, brush your coat, dust your riding-boots. You will have this much pity for me, my Phœbus, will you not? Meantime, take me! There, Phœbus, all this belongs to you, only love me. We gipsy girls need nothing else,— nothing but air and love."

As she said this, she flung her arms around the officer's neck; she gazed up into his face imploringly, and with a lovely smile through her tears. Her delicate throat rubbed against his cloth doublet with its rough embroideries. She threw herself across his lap, her beautiful body half revealed. The enraptured captain pressed his burning lips to those beautiful brown shoulders. The young girl, her eyes fixed on the ceiling, her head thrown back, shuddered and trembled at his kiss.

All at once above the head of Phœbus she saw another head,—a livid, green, convulsed face, with the look of a soul in torment; beside this face there was a hand which held a dagger. It was the face and the hand of the priest; he had broken open the door, and he was there. Phœbus could not see him. The girl was motionless, frozen, mute, at the frightful apparition, like a dove which chances to raise its head at the instant when the sea-eagle glares into its nest with fiery eyes.

She could not even utter a cry. She saw the dagger descend upon Phœbus and rise again reeking.

"Malediction!" said the captain; and he fell.

She fainted.

As her eyes closed, as all consciousness left her, she fancied she felt a fiery touch upon her lips, a kiss more burning than the torturer's red-hot iron.

When she recovered her senses she was surrounded by the soldiers of the watch, some of whom were just carrying off the captain bathed in his own blood; the priest had vanished; the window at the back of the room, which opened upon the river, was wide open; some one picked up a cloak which he supposed belonged to the officer, and she heard the soldiers say,—

"She is a sorceress who has stabbed a captain."

BOOK VIII

Hearts

Chapter I

THE CROWN CHANGED TO A DRY LEAF

GRINGOIRE and the entire Court of Miracles were in a terrible state of anxiety. Esmeralda had not been heard from for a whole long month, which greatly grieved the Duke of Egypt and his friends the Vagrants; nor did any one know what had become of her goat, which redoubled Gringoire's grief. One night the gipsy girl had disappeared, and since then had given no sign of life. All search for her was vain. Some malicious dummy chuckers told Gringoire that they had met her that same evening near the Pont Saint-Michel, walking with an officer; but this husband, after the fashion of Bohemia, was an incredulous philosopher, and besides, he knew better than any one else how chaste his wife was. He had been able to judge what invincible modesty resulted from the two combined virtues of the amulet and the gipsy, and he had made a mathematical calculation of the resistance of that chastity multiplied into itself. He was therefore quite easy on this point.

But he could not explain her disappearance. It was a great grief to him, and he would have grown thin from fretting had such a thing been possible. He had forgotten everything else,— even his literary tastes, even his great work, *"De figuris regularibus et irregularibus,"* which he intended to have printed with the first money which he might have (for he raved about printing ever since he had seen the *"Didascalon"* of Hugues de Saint-Victor printed with the celebrated types of Vindelin de Spire).

One day, as he was walking sadly by the Tournelle, he noticed a crowd before one of the doors of the Palace of Justice.

"What's the matter?" he asked a young man who was just coming out.

"I don't know. sir," replied the young man. "I hear that they are trying a woman who murdered a man-at-arms. As it seems that there was witchcraft about it, the bishop and the judge of the Bishop's Court have interfered in the matter; and my brother, who is archdeacon of Josas, spends his entire time here. Now, I wanted to speak to him; but I could not get at him on account of the crowd, which annoys me mightily, for I am in need of money."

"Alas! sir," said Gringoire, "I wish I could lend you some; but if my breeches are full of holes, it is not from the weight of coins."

He dared not tell the young man that he knew his brother the archdeacon, whom he had not revisited since the scene in the church,—a neglect which embarrassed him.

The student went his way, and Gringoire followed the crowd, going up the stairs to the Great Hall. He considered that there was nothing like the sight of a criminal trial to dispel melancholy, the judges being generally most delightfully stupid. The people with whom he had mingled walked on and elbowed one another in silence. After a slow and tiresome progress through a long dark passage which wound through the Palace like the intestinal canal of the ancient edifice, he reached a low door opening into a hall, which his tall figure enabled him to examine over the moving heads of the mob.

The hall was huge and ill-lighted, which made it seem still larger. Evening was coming on; the long-pointed windows admitted but a faint ray of daylight, which faded before it reached the vaulted ceiling,—an enormous lattice-work of carved beams, whose countless figures seemed to move confusedly in the shadow. There were already several lighted candles here and there on the tables, and shining upon the heads of clerks bending over musty papers. The front of the hall was occupied by the crowd; to the right and left there were lawyers in their robes, and tables; in the background, upon a daïs, a number of judges, the last rows of whom were lost in the darkness; their faces were forbidding and unmoved. The walls were plentifully sprinkled with *fleurs-de-lis*. A huge crucifix was dimly visible over the heads of the judges, and everywhere there were pikes and halberds tipped with fire by the light of the candles.

"Sir," asked Gringoire of one of his neighbours, "who are all those people drawn up in line yonder, like prelates in council?"

"Sir," said the neighbour, "those are the councillors of the High Chamber on the right, and the councillors of inquiry on the left,—the referendaries in black gowns, and the masters in scarlet ones."

"Yonder, above them," added Gringoire, "who is that big red-faced fellow in such a perspiration?"

"That is the president."

"And those sheep behind him?" continued Gringoire, who, as we have already said, did not love the magistracy. This was perhaps partly due to the grudge which he had borne the Palace of Justice ever since his dramatic misadventure.

"Those are the masters of requests of the king's household."

"And that boar in front of them?"

"That is the clerk to the Court of Parliament."

"And that crocodile on the right?"

"Master Philippe Lheulier, advocate extraordinary to the king."

"And that big black cat on the left?"

"Master Jacques Charmolue, king's proxy to the Ecclesiastical Court, with the officials."

"Now, then, sir," said Gringoire, "what are all these worthy men doing here?"

"They are trying a case."

"Whom are they trying? I do not see the prisoner."

"It's a woman, sir. You cannot see her. She has her back to us, and is hidden from us by the crowd. Stay; there she is, where you see that group of halberds."

"Who is the woman?" asked Gringoire. "Do you know her name?"

"No, sir; I have only just got here. I merely suppose that there is sorcery in the case, because the judge of the Bishop's Court is present at the trial."

"Well," said our philosopher, "we will see all these men of the gown devour human flesh. It is as good a sight as any other."

"Sir," remarked his neighbour, "doesn't it strike you that Master Jacques Charmolue has a very amiable air?"

"Hum!" replied Gringoire. "I always suspect an amiability with pinched nostrils and thin lips."

Here their neighbours demanded silence from the two chatterers; an important piece of evidence was being heard.

"Gentlemen," said an old woman in the middle of the hall, whose face was so lost in the abundance of her garments that she looked like a walking rag-bag,—"gentlemen, the thing is as true as it is true that my name is Falourdel, and that I have lived for forty years on the Pont Saint-Michel, paying my rent, lord's dues, and quit-rents punctually; and the door is just opposite the house of Tassin-Caillart the dyer, which is on the side looking up stream; a poor old woman now, a pretty girl once, gentlemen. Some one said to me only a few days ago, 'Mother Falourdel, don't sit at your wheel and spin too much of an evening; the devil loves to comb old women's distaffs with his horn. It is very certain that the spectre monk who roamed about the Temple last year now haunts the City. Mother Falourdel, beware lest he knock at your door.' One evening I was spinning at my wheel; there was a knock at the door. I asked who was there. Some one swore roundly. I opened. Two men came in,—one in black, with a handsome officer. I could only see the eyes of the one in black,— two burning coals; all the rest was hat and cloak. This is what they said to me: 'The Saint Martha room.' That is my upstairs room, gentlemen,—my nicest one. They gave me a crown. I put the crown in my drawer, and I said, 'That shall be to buy tripe to-morrow at the Gloriette shambles.' We went up. When we got to the upper room, while my back was turned the black man disappeared. This startled me a little. The officer, who was as handsome as any great lord, went downstairs again with me. He left the house. By the time I had spun a quarter of a skein he was back with a lovely young girl,—a puppet who would have shone like the sun if her hair had been well dressed. She had with her a goat,—a big goat. I have forgotten now whether it was black or white. That bothered me. As for the girl, she was none of my business; but the goat! I don't like those animals; they have a beard and horns. They look like men. And then, they savour of sorcery. However, I said nothing. I had the crown-piece. That was right, my lord judge, wasn't it? I took the captain and the girl to the upper room, and I left them alone,— that is, with the goat. I went down and began to spin again. You must know that my house has a ground-floor and a floor above; it overlooks the river at the back, like all the rest of the houses on the bridge, and the window on the ground-floor and the one above both open upon the water. As I say, I was spinning. I don't know how I fell to thinking of the goblin monk, of whom the goat had reminded me; and then, that pretty girl was so queerly rigged out. All at once I heard a scream upstairs, and something fell on the floor, and the window opened. I ran to my window, which is just under it, and I saw a dark mass fall past me into the water. It was a phantom dressed like a priest. It was bright moonlight. I saw as plainly as possible. He swam away towards the City. Then, all in a tremble, I called the watch. Those gentlemen entered, and being somewhat merry, and not knowing what the matter was, they fell to beating me. But I soon explained things to them. We went upstairs, and what did we find? My poor room all stained with blood, the captain stretched out at full length with a dagger in his throat, the girl pretending to be dead, and the goat in a terrible fright. 'Well done!' said I; 'it will take me more than a fortnight to scrub up these boards. I shall have to scrape them; it will be a dreadful piece of work!' They carried off the officer,—poor young man!—and the girl, all dishevelled and in disorder. But stay; the worst of all is that next day, when I went to get the crown to buy my tripe, I found a withered leaf in its place."

The old woman paused. A murmur of horror ran round the room.

"The phantom, the goat, and all that, savour of sorcery," said one of Gringoire's neighbours.

"So does that withered leaf!" added another.

"No doubt," continued a third, "the girl was a witch, who was in league with the goblin monk to plunder officers."

Gringoire himself was inclined to consider the whole story both terrible and probable.

"Woman Falourdel," said the president, majestically, "have you nothing more to tell the court?"

"No, my lord," replied the old woman, "except that in the report my house was called a dirty, rickety hut, which is an outrageous way to talk. The houses on the bridge are not much to look at, because there are so many people there; but all the same even butchers don't scorn to live there, and some of them are rich folks, and married to very neat, handsome women."

The magistrate who had reminded Gringoire of a crocodile now rose.

"Silence!" said he. "I beg you, gentlemen, not to lose sight of the fact that a dagger was found upon the prisoner. Woman Falourdel, did you bring that leaf into which the crown-piece which the evil spirit gave you was changed?"

"Yes, my lord," replied she; "I found it. Here it is."

An usher handed the dead leaf to the crocodile, who shook his head mournfully, and passed it to the president, who sent it on to the king's proxy to the Ecclesiastical Court; and in this way it went the round of the room.

"It is a birch-leaf," said Master Jacques Charmolue. This was a fresh proof of magic.

A councillor next took up the word.

"Witness, two men went upstairs together in your house. The black man,—whom you first saw disappear, and afterwards swim the Seine in a priest's gown,—and the officer. Which of the two gave you the money?"

The old woman thought for a moment, and said, "It was the officer."

A confused clamour ran through the crowd.

"Ah!" thought Gringoire, "that shakes my conviction."

However, Master Philippe Lheulier, advocate extraordinary to the king, interfered afresh.

"I must remind you, gentlemen, that in his deposition, written at his bedside, the murdered officer, while he declares that he had a vague idea at the instant the man in black accosted him that it might easily be the goblin monk, added that the phantom had urged him to keep his appointment with the prisoner; and upon his remarking that he had no money, gave him the crown, which the said officer paid away to Mother Falourdel. Therefore, the crown was a coin from hell."

This conclusive observation seemed to dispel all the doubts of Gringoire and the other sceptics in the audience.

"Gentlemen, you have the brief," added the king's advocate, sitting down; "you can consult the statement of Phœbus de Châteaupers."

At the sound of this name the prisoner rose; her head appeared above the crowd. The terrified Gringoire recognized Esmeralda.

She was pale; her hair, once so gracefully braided and spangled with sequins, fell about her in disorder; her lips were livid; her hollow eyes were horrible. Alas!

"Phœbus!" said she, wildly, "where is he? Oh, gentlemen, before you kill me, in pity tell me if he still lives!"

"Be silent, woman!" replied the president; "that does not concern us."

"Oh, have mercy! Tell me if he is alive!" she repeated, clasping her beautiful but emaciated hands; and her chains rattled as she moved.

"Well," said the king's advocate, drily, "he is dying! Are you satisfied?"

The wretched girl fell back upon her seat, voiceless, tearless, white as a waxen image.

The president leaned towards a man standing at his feet, with a golden cap and a black gown, a chain about his neck, and a wand in his hand.

"Usher, bring in the other prisoner."

All eyes were turned upon a small door which opened, and to Gringoire's great dismay a pretty goat, with gilded horns and hoofs, appeared. The dainty creature paused a moment on the threshold, stretching her neck as if, perched on the point of a rock, she had a vast horizon before her. All at once she saw the gipsy girl, and leaping over the table and the head of a clerk with two bounds, she was at her knees; then she curled herself gracefully at the feet of her mistress, imploring a word or a caress; but the prisoner remained motionless, and even poor Djali could not win a look from her.

"Why, but— That is the ugly beast I told you about," said old Falourdel; " and I recognize the pair of them well enough!"

Jacques Charmolue interrupted her.

"If it please you, gentlemen, we will proceed to examine the goat."

Such was indeed the other prisoner. Nothing was simpler at that time than to bring a suit for witchcraft against an animal. Among other details, we find in the provost's accounts for 1466 a curious item of the costs of the trial of Gillet-Soulart and his sow, "executed for their demerits," at Corbeil. Everything is set down,—the cost of the pen in which the sow was imprisoned, the five hundred bundles of short fagots brought from the port of Morsant, the three pints of wine and the bread for the victim's last repast, fraternally shared by the executioner; even the eleven days' feeding and keep of the sow, at eight Paris pence each. Sometimes they went even beyond animals. The capitularies of Charlemagne and Louis the Debonair inflict severe penalties upon those fiery phantoms who take the liberty of appearing in mid-air.

Meantime the king's proxy to the Ecclesiastical Court cried aloud, "If the devil possessing this goat, and which has resisted every exorcism, persist in his evil deeds, if he terrify the court with them, we warn him that we shall be compelled to send him to the gibbet or the stake."

Gringoire was in a cold perspiration. Charmolue took from a table the gipsy girl's tambourine, and presenting it to the goat in a particular way, he asked the creature:

"What time is it?"

The goat looked at him with an intelligent eye, lifted her gilded hoof, and struck seven blows. It was indeed seven o'clock. A movement of terror ran through the crowd.

Gringoire could not restrain himself.

"She is lost!" he cried aloud; "you see that she doesn't know what she is doing."

"Silence among the people at the end of the hall!" said the usher, sharply.

Jacques Charmolue, by the aid of the same manœuvres with the tambourine, made the goat perform various other tricks as to the day of the month, the month of the year, etc., which the reader has already witnessed. And, by an optical illusion common to judicial debates, those same spectators who had perhaps more than once applauded the innocent pranks of Djali in the public streets, were terrified by them within the walls of the Palace of Justice. The goat was clearly the devil.

It was still worse when, the king's proxy having emptied out upon the floor a certain leather bag full of movable letters, which Djali wore about her neck, the goat selected with her foot the separate letters spelling out the fatal name "Phœbus." The spells to which the captain had fallen a victim seemed to be irresistibly demonstrated; and, in all eyes, the gipsy girl—that enchanting dancer who had so often dazzled the passers-by with her grace—was nothing but a horrible witch.

Moreover, she gave no sign of life; neither the pretty pranks of Djali, nor the threats of the magistrates, nor the muttered curses of the audience seemed to reach her ear.

In order to rouse her, an officer was forced to shake her most unmercifully, the president raising his voice solemnly as he said:—

"Girl, you are of the gipsy race, addicted to sorceries. You, with your accomplice, the bewitched goat involved in the charge, did, upon the night of the 29th of March last, murder and stab, in league with the powers of darkness, by the aid of charms and spells, a captain of the king's troops, one Phœbus de Châteaupers. Do you persist in denying this?"

"Horrible!" cried the young girl, hiding her face in her hands. "My Phœbus! oh, this is indeed hell!"

"Do you persist in your denial?" coldly asked the president.

"Certainly I deny it!" said she, in terrible accents; and she rose to her full height, her eyes flashing.

The president continued bluntly:—

"Then how do you explain the facts alleged against you?"

She answered in a broken voice,—

"I have told you already. I do not know. It was a priest,—a priest whom I do not know; an infernal priest who has long pursued me!"

"There it is," said the judge; "the goblin monk."

"Oh, my lords, have pity! I am only a poor girl."

"A gipsy," said the judge.

Master Jacques Charmolue said gently,—

"In view of the prisoner's painful obstinacy, I demand that she be put to the rack."

"Agreed," said the president.

The wretched girl shuddered. Still, she rose at the order of the halberdiers, and walked with quite firm step, preceded by Charmolue and the priests of the Bishop's Court, between two rows of halberds, towards a low door, which suddenly opened and closed behind her, making the unhappy Gringoire feel as if she had been devoured by some awful monster.

As she disappeared, a plaintive bleat was heard. It was the little goat mourning for her.

The hearing was over. A councillor

remarked that the gentlemen were tired, and that it would be a long time for them to wait until the torture was over; and the president replied that a magistrate should be ever ready to sacrifice himself to his duty.

"What a disagreeable, tiresome jade," said an old judge, "to force us to send her to the rack when we have not supped!"

Chapter II

SEQUEL TO THE CROWN CHANGED TO A DRY LEAF

After going up a few steps and down a few steps in corridors so dark that they were lighted with lamps at midday, Esmeralda, still surrounded by her dismal escort, was pushed by the serjeants of the Palace into a room of forbidding appearance. This room, round in form, occupied the ground-floor of one of these great towers which still rise above the layer of modern structures with which the new Paris has covered the old city. There were no windows in this vault, nor was there any opening save the low entrance closed by a huge iron door. Still, there was no lack of light; a furnace was built in the thickness of the wall; a vast fire had been kindled in it, which filled the vault with its red glow, and robbed a paltry candle, placed in a corner, of all its radiance. The iron grating which served to close the furnace was just now raised, only showing, at the mouth of the flaming chasm against the dark wall, the lower edge of its bars, like a row of sharp black teeth set at regular intervals, which made the furnace look like the mouth of one of those legendary dragons that spit forth fire. By the light which it cast, the prisoner saw, all around the room, terrible instruments whose use she did not understand. In the middle of the room was a leather mattress laid almost flat upon the ground, over which hung a strap with a buckle, attached to a copper ring held by a flat-nosed monster carved on the keystone of the vaulted ceiling. Pincers, nippers, and broad ploughshares filled the interior of the furnace, and glowed in a confused white-hot heap upon the living coals. The blood-red light of the furnace illuminated in the entire room nothing but a mass of horrible objects.

This Tartarus was known as "the torture-chamber."

Upon the bed sat carelessly Pierrat Torterue, the sworn torturer. His assistants, two square-faced gnomes with leather aprons and linen breeches, were stirring the iron instruments upon the coals.

In vain the poor girl strove to summon all her courage; as she entered the room a feeling of terror overcame her.

The serjeants of the Bailiff of the Palace ranged themselves on one side, the priests of the Bishop's Court on the other. A clerk, pen, ink, and paper, and a table were in one corner.

Master Jacques Charmolue approached the girl with a very sweet smile, saying,—

"Do you still persist in your denial, my dear child?"

"Yes," replied she in a faint voice.

"In that case," resumed Charmolue, "it will be our very painful duty to question you more urgently than we could wish. Be kind enough to take your seat on that bed. Master Pierrat, make room for the young lady, and close the door."

Pierrat rose with a grunt.

"If I close the door," he muttered, "my fire will go out."

"Very well, my dear fellow," replied Charmolue; "then leave it open."

But Esmeralda still stood. That leather bed, upon which so many wretches had writhed in torment, alarmed her. Terror froze the marrow in her bones; she stood there, stupefied and bewildered. At a sign from Charmolue, the two assistants took hold of her and seated her upon the bed. They did not hurt her; but when they touched her, when the leather touched her, she felt all the blood in her body flow back to her heart. She cast a desperate look around the room. She seemed to see all those monstrous tools of torture, which were to the instruments of every sort which she had hitherto seen, what bats, spiders, and wood-lice are to birds and insects, moving and advancing towards her from every direction, to crawl over her and bite her and pinch her.

"Where is the doctor?" asked Charmolue.

"Here," replied a black gown which she had not noticed before.

She shivered.

"Young lady," resumed the caressing voice of the king's proxy to the Ecclesiastical Court, "for the third time, do you persist in denying those things of which you are accused?"

This time she could only nod her head. Her voice failed her.

"You persist?" said Jacques Charmolue. "Then I am extremely sorry, but I must perform the duty of my office."

"Mr. Proxy," said Pierrat, abruptly, "with what shall we begin?"

Charmolue hesitated a moment, with the doubtful face of a poet in search of a rhyme.

"With the buskin," said he at last.

The unfortunate girl felt herself so wholly forsaken by God and man, that her head fell upon her breast like a lifeless thing destitute of all strength.

The torturer and the doctor approached her together. At the same time the two assistants began to rummage in their hideous arsenal.

At the clink of that frightful heap of iron, the unhappy creature trembled like a dead frog when galvanism is applied to it. "Oh," she murmured in so low a tone that no one heard it, "oh, my Phœbus!" Then she relapsed into her former immobility and marble-like silence. The sight would have rent any heart save the hearts of judges. She seemed some poor sinning soul questioned by Satan at the scarlet gates of hell. Could it be that this gentle, fair, and fragile creature, a poor grain of millet given over by human justice to be ground in the fearful mills of torture, was the miserable body upon which that frightful array of saws, wheels, and racks was to fasten,—the being whom the rough hands of executioners and pincers were to handle?

But the horny fingers of Pierrat Torterue's assistants had already brutally bared that charming leg and that tiny foot, which had so often amazed the by-standers with their grace and beauty in the streets of Paris.

"'Tis a pity!" growled the torturer, as he looked at the dainty and delicate limb.

Had the archdeacon been present, he would certainly have recalled at this moment his symbol of the spider and the fly. Soon the wretched victim saw, through a cloud which spread before her eyes, the buskin approach; soon she saw her foot, locked between the iron-bound boards, hidden by the hideous machine. Then terror restored her strength.

"Take it off!" she cried frantically; and starting up all dishevelled, "Mercy!"

She sprang from the bed to fling herself at the feet of the king's proxy; but her leg was held by the heavy mass of wood and iron, and she sank down upon the buskin, more helpless than a bee with a leaden weight upon its wing.

At a sign from Charmolue she was replaced upon the bed, and two coarse hands bound about her slender waist the strap which hung from the ceiling.

"For the last time, do you confess the facts in the case?" asked Charmolue with his unshaken benevolence.

"I am innocent."

"Then, young lady, how do you explain the circumstances brought against you?"

"Alas! sir, I do not know!"

"Then you deny everything?"

"Everything!"

"Proceed," said Charmolue to Pierrat.

Pierrat turned the handle of the screw-jack, the buskin contracted, and the wretched girl uttered one of those terrible shrieks which defy all orthography in any human language.

"Stop!" said Charmolue to Pierrat. "Do you confess?" said he to the gipsy.

"Everything!" cried the miserable girl. "I confess, I confess! Mercy!"

She had not calculated her strength when she braved the torture. Poor child! her life thus far had been so joyous, so sweet, so smooth, the first pang vanquished her.

"Humanity compels me to tell you," remarked the king's proxy, "that if you confess, you can look for nothing but death."

"I hope so, indeed!" said she. And she fell back upon the leather bed, almost fainting, bent double, suspended by the strap buckled around her waist.

"There, my beauty, hold up a little," said Master Pierrat, lifting her. "You look like the golden sheep which hangs on my Lord of Burgundy's neck."

Jacques Charmolue raised his voice,—

"Clerk, write. Young gipsy girl, you confess your complicity in the love-feasts, revels, and evil practices of hell, with wizards, demons, and witches? Answer!"

"Yes," said she, in so low a voice that it was scarcely more than a whisper.

"You confess that you have seen the ram which Beelzebub reveals in the clouds to summon his followers to the Witches' Sabbath, and which is only seen by sorcerers?"

"Yes."

"You confess that you have worshipped the heads of Bophomet, those abominable idols of the Templars?"

"Yes."

"That you have held constant intercourse with the devil in the shape of a tame goat, included in the trial?"

"Yes."

"And, finally, you acknowledge and confess that, with the help of the foul fiend and the phantom commonly called the goblin monk, on the night of the 29th of March last you did murder and assassinate a certain captain named Phœbus de Châteaupers?"

She raised her large steady eyes to the magistrate's face, and answered as if mechanically, without any effort or convulsion,—

"Yes."

It was plain that she was utterly broken.

"Write, clerk," said Charmolue; and addressing the torturers: "Release the prisoner, and lead her back to the court-room."

When the prisoner was "unshod," the king's proxy examined her foot, still numb with pain.

"Come!" said he; "there is no great harm done. You screamed in time. You can dance yet, my beauty."

Then he turned to his companions from the Bishop's Court—

"So justice is enlightened at last! That's a comfort, gentlemen! The young lady will bear witness that we have acted with the utmost gentleness."

Chapter III

END OF THE CROWN CHANGED TO A DRY LEAF

When she returned to the audience-chamber, pale and limping, she was greeted with a general buzz of pleasure. On the part of the audience, it was caused by that feeling of satisfied impatience which is felt at the theatre, at the end of the final intermission, when the curtain rises and the last act begins. On the part of the judges, it came from a prospect of supping ere long. The little goat also bleated with joy. She tried to run to meet her mistress, but she was tied to the bench.

Night had now fallen. The candles, whose number had not been increased, cast so little light that the walls of the court-room could not be seen. Shadows wrapped everything in a sort of mist. The apathetic faces of some of the judges could just be distinguished in the gloom. Opposite them, at the extreme end of the long hall, they could make out a vague white patch against the dark background. It was the prisoner.

She had dragged herself painfully to her place. When Charmolue had magisterially installed himself in his, he sat down, then rose, and said, without too great a show of vanity at his success, "The prisoner has confessed everything."

"Gipsy girl," began the president, "have you confessed all your crimes of sorcery, prostitution, and murder committed upon Phœbus Châteaupers?"

Her heart sank within her, and she sobbed aloud in the darkness.

"Whatever you please," she replied feebly; "but kill me quickly!"

"Sir Proxy to the Ecclesiastical Court," said the president, "the court is ready to hear your requisitions."

Master Charmolue drew forth a tremendous bundle of papers, and began to read, with many gestures, and the exaggerated emphasis common to lawyers, a Latin speech, in which all the evidence produced during the trial was set forth in Ciceronian periphrases, flanked by quotations from Plautus, his favourite comic author. We regret that we cannot present our readers with this remarkable piece of oratory. The speaker delivered it with wonderful effect. Long before he had ended the exordium, the perspiration poured down his face, and his eyes seemed starting from his head.

All at once, in the very middle of a period, he paused, and his glance, usually mild enough and even stupid, became withering·

"Gentlemen," he exclaimed (but in French, for this was not set down in his mauscript), "Satan plays so large a part in this affair, that yonder he stands, listening to our discussions and making a mock of their majesty. Behold!"

As he spoke, he pointed to the little goat, which, seeing Charmolue gesticulate, sincerely thought that it was but right for her to do the same, and sitting up on her haunches, was imitating to the best of her ability, with her forefeet and her bearded head, the pathetic pantomime of the king's proxy. This was, it may be remembered, one of her best tricks. This incident—this final proof—produced a great effect. The goat's feet were tied together, and the king's proxy resumed the thread of his eloquence.

His speech was very long, but the peroration was admirable. We give the concluding phrase; the reader may imagine Master Charmolue's hoarse voice and frantic gestures:—

"*Ideo, Domni, coram stryga demonstrata, crimine patente, intentione criminis existente, in nomine sanctæ ecclesiæ Nostræ-Dominæ Parisiensis, quæ est in saisina habendi omnimodam altam et bassam justitiam in illa hac intemerata Civitatis insula, tenore præsentium declaramus nos requirere, primo, aliquandam pecuniariam indemnitatem; secundo, amendationem honorabilem ante portalium maximum Nostræ-Dominæ, ecclesiæ cathedralis; tertio, sententiam in virtute cujus ista stryga cum sua capella, seu in trivio vulgariter dicto the Grève, seu in insula exeunte in fluvio se canæ, juxta pointam jardini regalis, executatæ sint!*"

He put on his cap and sat down.

"*Eheu!*" said the agonized Gringoire; "*bassa latinitas!*"

Another man in a black gown, near the prisoner, rose. This was her lawyer. The judges, being hungry, began to murmur.

"Be brief, Sir Lawyer," said the president.

"Mr. President," replied the lawyer, "the defendant having confessed her crime, I have but a few words to say to the bench. It is laid down in the Salic law that 'If a witch have devoured a man, and she be convicted of the crime, she shall pay a fine of eight thousand farthings, which make two hundred pence in gold.' May it please the court to sentence my client to pay this fine."

"That law is obsolete," said the king's proxy·

"*Nego,*" replied the lawyer.

"Put it to the vote!" said a councillor; "the crime is clear and it is late."

The question was put to the vote without leaving the hall. The judges nodded assent; they were in haste.

Their hooded heads were uncovered one after the other in the darkness, in response to the fatal question put to them in a low tone by the president. The poor prisoner seemed to be looking at them, but her dim eyes saw nothing.

The clerk began to write; then he handed the president a lengthy parchment.

The unhappy girl heard a stir among the people, the pikes clashed, and an icy voice said:—

"Gipsy girl, upon such day as it shall please the lord our king, at the hour of noon, you shall be taken in a trumbel, in your shift, barefoot, a rope around your neck, to the square before the great door of Notre-Dame, and shall there do proper penace, with a wax candle of the weight of two pounds in your hand; and thence you shall be taken to the Grève, where you shall be hanged and strangled on the city gibbet; and likewise this your goat; and you shall pay to the judges of the Bishop's Court three golden lions, in atonement for the crimes by you committed and by you confessed, of sorcery, magic, incontinence, and murder, upon the person of Lord Phœbus de Châteaupers! And may God have mercy on your soul!"

"Oh, it is a dream!" she murmured; and she felt rude hands bear her away.

Chapter IV

LASCIATE OGNI SPERANZA

In the Middle Ages, when a building was finished, there was almost as much of it below as above ground. Unless built upon piles, like Notre-Dame, a palace, a fortress, a church, had always a double foundation. In the case of cathedrals, it was almost like another and subterranean cathedral, low, dark, mysterious, blind and mute, beneath the upper nave, which blazed with light and echoed with the sound of organ and bells day and night; sometimes it was a sepulchre. In palaces and fortresses it was a prison; sometimes, too, a tomb, sometimes a combination of both. These mighty structures, whose mode of formation and slow growth we have explained elsewhere, had not merely foundations, but as it were roots which extended under the earth, branching out into rooms, galleries, staircases, in imitation of the building above. Thus churches, palaces, and fortresses were buried midway in the earth. The cellars of an edifice formed another edifice, into which one descended instead of ascending, and whose subterranean stories were evolved below the pile of upper stories of the monument, like those forests and mountains seen reversed in the mirroring water of a lake beneath the forests and mountains on its shore.

In the Bastille Saint-Antoine, the Palace of Justice at Paris, and the Louvre, these underground structures were prisons. The various stories of these prisons as they sank deeper into the ground became darker and more contracted. They formed so many zones presenting various degrees of horror. Dante could have found no better image of his hell. These tunnel-like dungeons usually ended in a deep hole like a tub, such as Dante chose for the abode of Satan, and where society placed those condemned to death. When once any poor wretch was buried there, he bade farewell to light, air, life, all hope; he never left it save for the gallows or the stake. Sometimes he lay there and rotted. Human justice styled this "forgetting." Between mankind and himself the prisoner felt that a mountain of stones and jailers weighed him down; and the entire prison, the massive fortress, became but a huge complicated lock which shut him off from the living world.

It was in a dungeon-hole of this kind, in one of the oubliettes dug by Saint Louis, the *in pace* of the Tournelle, that Esmeralda was placed when condemned to the gallows, doubtless lest she would try to escape, with the colossal Palace of Justice above her head. Poor fly, which could not have stirred the smallest one of the unhewn stones!

Certainly Providence and mankind were equally unjust. Such a lavish display of misery and torment was needless to crush so frail a creature.

There she lay, lost in the darkness, buried, entombed, immured. Whoever had seen her in that state, after having seen her laugh and dance in the sunshine, must have shivered. Cold as night, cold as death, not a breath of air to flutter her hair, not a human sound in her ear, not a ray of daylight in her eyes, bent double, crushed beneath her chains, crouching beside a jug and a loaf of bread, upon a little straw, in the pool of water formed beneath her by the damp oozing of her cell, motionless, nearly breathless, she was almost beyond all sense of suffering. Phœbus, the sun, high noon, the fresh air, the streets of Paris, her dancing always hailed with applause, the sweet prattle of love with the officer; then the priest, the old hag, the dagger, the blood, the torture, and the gallows,—all these things had hovered before her, now like a gay and golden vision, now like a monstrous nightmare; but they were now naught but a vague and horrible struggle lost in the darkness, or like distant music played above, on the earth, and no longer heard in the depths to which the wretched girl had fallen.

Since she had been there she had neither waked nor slept. In her misery, in her dungeon, she could no more distinguish waking from sleeping, a dream from reality, than she could day from night. All was mingled, broken, vague, floating confusedly before her mind. She felt nothing, knew nothing, thought nothing; at best, she only dreamed. Never did living creature pierce so far into the realm of nothingness.

Thus benumbed, frozen, petrified, she had scarcely noted the sound of a trap-door which was twice or thrice opened somewhere above her without even admitting a ray of light, and through which a hand had thrown a crust of black bread. And yet this was her only remaining means of communication with men,—the periodical visit of the jailer.

One thing only still mechanically caught her ear: over her head the dampness filtered through the mouldy stones of the roof, and at regular intervals a drop of water fell. She listened stupidly to the noise made by this drop of water as it dripped into the pool beside her.

This drop of water falling into the pool was the only movement still stirring around her, the only clock which marked the time, the only sound of all the noises made upon the surface of the earth which reached her.

To be exact, she did also feel from time to time, in this sink of mire and gloom, something cold crawling hither and thither over her foot or her arm, and she suddered.

How long had she been there? She did not know. She remembered a death sentence pronounced somewhere, against some one; then she was borne away, and she waked icy cold, in the midst of night and silence. She had dragged herself about on her hands and knees; then iron rings had cut her ankle, and chains had clanked. She discovered that there was a wall all about her, that there was a tiled floor under her, covered with water, and a bundle of straw; but neither lamp nor ventilator. There she seated herself upon the straw, and occasionally, for a change of position, on the last step of some stone stairs in her cell.

At one time she tried to count the dark moments measured for her by the drop of water; but soon this sad task of a diseased brain ceased of its own accord, and left her in a stupor.

At last, one day, or one night,—for midnight and noon wore the same hue in this tomb,—she heard above her a noise louder than that usually made by the turnkey when he brought her bread and water. She raised her head, and saw a reddish ray coming through the cracks in the sort of trap-door made in the room of the *"in pace."*

At the same time the heavy iron creaked, the trap-door grated on its rusty hinges, turned, and she saw a lantern, a hand, and the lower part of the bodies of two men, the door being too low for her to see their heads. The light hurt her so cruelly that she shut her eyes.

When she reopened them, the door was again closed, the lantern was placed on a step of the staircase, a man alone stood before her. A black gown fell to his feet; a cowl of the same colour hid his face. Nothing of his person was visible, neither his face nor his hands. He looked like a long black winding-sheet standing bolt upright, under which something seemed to move. She gazed fixedly for some moments at this spectre. Still, neither she nor he spoke. They seemed two statues confronting each other. Two things only seemed to live in the cave,—the wick of the lantern, which crackled from the dampness of the atmosphere, and the drop of water from the ceiling, which interrupted this irregular crackle with its monotonous plash, and made the light of the lantern quiver in concentric rings upon the oily water of the pool.

At last the prisoner broke the silence,—

"Who are you?"

"A priest."

The word, the accent, the sound of his voice, made her tremble.

The priest added in a hollow tone,—

"Are you prepared?"

"For what?"

"To die."

"Oh," said she, "will it be soon?"

"To-morrow."

Her head, which she had lifted with joy, again sank upon her breast.

"That is a very long time yet!" she

murmured; "why did they not make it to-day?"

"Then you are very unhappy?" asked the priest, after a pause.

"I am very cold," replied she.

She took her feet in her hands,—a common gesture with those wretched people who suffer from cold, and which we have already observed in the recluse of the Tour-Roland,—and her teeth chattered.

The priest seemed to cast his eyes about the cell, from beneath his hood.

"No light! no fire! in the water! It is horrible!"

"Yes," she answered, with the look of surprise which misfortune had imprinted on her face. "Daylight is for every one. Why is it that they give me nothing but night?"

"Do you know," resumed the priest, after a fresh pause, "why you are here?"

"I think I did know once," said she, passing her thin fingers over her brow as if to help her memory, "but I don't know now."

All at once she began to cry like a little child.

"I want to get out, sir. I am cold, I am frightened, and there are creatures which crawl all over me."

"Well, follow me."

So saying, the priest took her by the arm. The unfortunate creature was frozen to the marrow; but still that hand gave her a sensation of cold.

"Oh," she murmured, "it is the icy hand of death. Who are you?"

The priest threw back his hood; she looked. It was that evil face which had so long haunted her; that demon head which had appeared to her at he house of old Falourdel above the adored head of her Phœbus; that eye which she had last seen sparkle beside a dagger.

This apparition, always so fatal to her, and which had thus urged her on from misfortune to misfortune and even to torture, roused her from her torpor. The veil which had clouded her memory seemed rent in twain. Every detail of her mournful adventure, from the night scene at the house of Falourdel down to her condemnation at the Tournelle, rushed upon her mind at once, not vague and confused as heretofore, but clear, distinct, vivid, living, terrible. The sombre figure before her recalled those half-effaced memories almost blotted out by excess of suffering, as the heat of the fire brings back in all their freshness invisible letters traced on white paper with sympathetic ink. She felt as if every wound in her heart were torn open and bled together.

"Ha!" she cried, pressing her hands to her eyes with a convulsive shudder, "it is the priest!"

Then her arms fell listlessly at her side, and she sat with downcast head and eyes, mute and trembling.

The priest gazed at her with the eye of a kite which has long hovered high in the heavens above a poor meadowlark crouching in the wheat, gradually and silently descending in ever lessening circles, and, suddenly swooping upon his prey like a flash of lightning, grasps it panting in his clutch.

She murmured feebly,—

"Do your work! do your work! strike the last blow!" and her head sank between her shoulders in terror, like that of a lamb awaiting the butcher's axe.

"You look upon me with horror, then?" he asked at length.

She made no answer.

"Do you look on me with horror?" he repeated.

Her lips moved as if she smiled.

"Yes," said she, "the executioner jests with the prisoner. For months he has pursued me, threatened me, terrified me! But for him, my God, how happy I should have been! It is he who hurled me into this gulf of woe! Oh, heavens! it is he who killed,— it is he who killed *him*, my Phœbus!"

Here, bursting into sobs and raising her eyes to the priest, she cried,—

"Oh, wretch! who are you? What have I done to you? Do you hate me so much? Alas! what have you against me?"

"I love you!" exclaimed the priest.

Her tears ceased suddenly; she stared vacantly at him. He had fallen upon his knees, and devoured her face with eyes of flame.

"Do you hear? I love you!" he again exclaimed.

"What love!" said the miserable girl shuddering.

He replied,—

"The love of a damned man."

Both were silent for some moments, oppressed by the intensity of their emotions,—he mad, she stunned.

"Listen," said the priest at last, and a strange calm seemed to have taken possession of him. "You shall know all. I will tell you that which as yet I have hardly ventured to confess myself, when I secretly questioned my own soul in those dead hours of the night when the darkness is so profound that it seems as if even God could no longer see us. Listen. Before I met you, girl, I was happy."

"And I!" she faintly sighed.

"Do not interrupt me! Yes, I was happy,—at least I thought so. I was pure; my soul was filled with limpid light. No head was held higher or happier than mine. Priests consulted me on chastity, doctors on doctrines. Yes, science was all in all to me; it was a sister,—and a sister was all I asked. Not but that, as I grew older, other ideas came to me. More than once my flesh thrilled as a woman's form passed by. That force of sex and passion which, although in the pride of youth, I had imagined I had stifled forever, more than once has rebelled against the chain of the iron vows which bind me, —wretch that I am!—to the cold stones of the altar. But fasting, prayer, study, and monastic mortifications again made my spirit ruler of my body. And then I shunned women. I had only to open a book, and all the impure vapours of my brain were banished by the glorious sunbeams of science. In a few moments I felt the gross things of earth fly far away, and I was once more calm and serene, bathed in the tranquil light of eternal truth. So long as the demon sent only vague shadows to attack me, passing singly before me, in church, in the streets, or in the fields, and scarcely recurring in my dreams, I conquered him easily. Alas! if the victory be not still mine, God is to blame, who failed to make man and the devil of equal strength. Listen! One day—"

Here the priest paused, and the prisoner heard him utter agonizing sighs.

He continued:—

"One day I was leaning from the window of my cell. What book was I reading? Oh, all that is confused and vague to me now. I had been reading. The window looked upon a public square. I heard the sound of tambourine and music. Vexed at being thus disturbed in my reverie, I looked out. What I saw was seen by many others as well, and yet it was not a spectacle for mere mortal eyes. There, in the middle of the pavement,—it was noon, the sun shone brightly,—a creature was dancing,—a creature so beautiful that God would have preferred her to the Virgin, and chosen her to be his mother, and would have wished to be born of her, had she existed when he was made man! Her eyes were black and lustrous; amidst her black hair certain locks shone in the sun like threads of gold. Her feet moved so swiftly that they faded from sight like the spokes of a wheel revolving rapidly. About her head, in her black braids, there were metallic plates which glittered in the sun and made a crown of stars above her brow. Her gown, sprinkled with spangles, scintillated, blue, and sown with a thousand sparks like a summer night. Her pliant brown arms waved and twined about her waist like two scarves. Her figure was of surpassing beauty. Oh, how resplendent was that form which stood out like something luminous even in the very light of the sun itself! Alas! girl, it was you. Surprised, intoxicated, charmed, I suffered myself to gaze. I gazed so long that, all at once, I shuddered with terror. I felt that Fate had overtaken me."

The priest, oppressed, again paused a moment. Then he resumed:—

"Already half fascinated I tried to lay hold of something and to stay myself from falling. I recalled the traps which Satan had already laid for me. The creature before me possessed that superhuman beauty which could only proceed from heaven or from hell. That was no mere girl made of common clay, and dimly illumined within by the flickering rays of a woman's soul. It was an angel,—but of darkness, of flame, and not of light!

"Just as I was thinking thus, I saw close beside you a goat, a devilish beast, which looked at me and laughed. The midday sun made its horns seemed tipped with fire. Then I recognized the snare of the demon, and no longer doubted that you came from hell, and that you came for my perdition. I believed it."

Here the priest looked in the prisoner's face, and added coldly:—

"I believe so still. However, the charm worked little by little. Your dance went round and round in my brain; I felt the mysterious spell acting within me. All which should have waked slumbered in my soul, and, like men perishing in the snow, I found pleasure in the approach of this slumber. All at once you began to sing. What could I do, miserable man? Your singing was even more enchanting than your dancing. I strove to escape. Impossible. I was nailed, I was rooted to the spot. It seemed as if the marble of the floor had risen to my knees. I was forced to stay to the end. My feet were ice, my head burned. At last,— perhaps you pitied me,—you ceased to sing; you disappeared. The reflection of the dazzling vision, the echo of the enchanting music gradually faded from my eyes and ears. Then I sank into the corner of the window, stiffer and more helpless than a fallen statue. The vesper bell aroused me. I rose to my feet; I fled; but, alas! something within me had fallen which could never be raised up; something had overtaken me which I could not escape."

He paused once more, and then went on:—

"Yes, from that day forth there was another man within me, whom I did not know. I strove to apply all my remedies,—the cloister, the altar, work, books. Follies, all! Oh, how empty science seems when we beat against it in despair a head filled with frantic passion! Girl, do you know what I always saw between my book and me? You, your shadow, the image of the bright vision which had once passed before me. But that image was no longer of the same colour; it was gloomy, funereal, sombre as the black circle which long haunts the sight of the imprudent man who looks steadily at the sun.

"Unable to rid myself of it, forever hearing your song ring in my ears, forever seeing your feet dance over my breviary, forever feeling at night, in dreams, your form against mine, I longed to see you once more, to touch you, to know who you were, to see if you were indeed like the ideal image which I had formed of you,—to destroy perhaps my dream by confronting it with the reality. In any case, I hoped that a fresh impression might dispel the first, and the first had become unendurable. I sought you out; I saw you again. Misery! Having seen you twice, I longed to see you a thousand times,—I longed to see you forever. Then,—how may a man stop short upon that steep descent to hell? —then I ceased to be my own master. The other end of the cord which the demon had fastened to my wings was tied to his own foot. I became a wanderer and a vagrant like you. I waited for you beneath porches, I lurked at street corners, I watched you from the top of my tower. Every night I found myself more charmed, more desperate, more bewitched, nearer perdition!

"I had learned who you were,—a gipsy. How could I doubt your magic powers? I hoped that a criminal suit would set me free from your spell. A sorceress once enchanted Bruno d'Ast; he had her burned alive, and was cured. I knew it. I decided to try this remedy. I at first attempted to have you forbidden all access to the square in front of Notre-Dame, hoping that I might forget you if you no longer came thither. You paid no heed to the prohibition; you returned. Then I thought of carrying you off. One night, I tried to do so. There were two of us. We already had you in our grasp, when that miserable officer appeared. He rescued you. He thus began your misfortune, mine, and his own. Finally, not knowing what to do or what would become of me, I denounced you to the judges.

"I thought that I should be cured, like Bruno d'Ast. I also vaguely thought that a criminal trial would make you mine; that in a prison I should have you, should be able to hold you mine; that there you could not escape me; that you had possessed me so long that I might well possess you in my turn. When a man does wrong, he should do all the wrong he can; it is madness to stop half-way in crime! The extremity of guilt has its raptures of joy. A priest and a witch can mingle in delight upon the scanty straw of a cell!

"Accordingly I denounced you. It was then that I terrified you when we met. The plot which I was contriving against you, the storm which I was about to bring upon your head, burst from me in threats and in lightning flashes. And yet I still hesitated. My scheme had terrible sides which made me shrink.

"Perhaps I might have given it up; perhaps my odious thought might have withered in my brain, without bearing fruit. I thought that it would always be in my power to continue or to stay the prosecution; but every evil thought is inexorable, and insists upon becoming a deed. Where I supposed myself all-powerful, Fate was mightier than I. Alas, alas! it is she which captured you and delivered you over to the terrible wheels of the machine which I secretly constructed! Listen. I am near the end.

"One day—again the sun shone bright and warm—I saw a man pass who pronounced your name and laughed, and whose eyes were full of passion. Damnation! I followed him. You know the rest."

He ceased.

The young girl could only utter the words,—

"Oh, my Phœbus!"

"Not that name!" said the priest, seizing her angrily by the arm. "Do not utter that name! Oh, unhappy wretches that we are! it was that name which ruined us! or rather we have ruined each other by the inexplicable caprice of Fate! You suffer, do you not? You are cold, the darkness blinds you, the dungeon wraps you round; but perhaps you have still some ray of light in your innermost soul, were it but your childish love for that empty man who played with your heart, while I have a dungeon within me; within me all is winter, ice, despair; my soul is full of darkness.

"Do you know all that I have suffered? I was present at your trial. I sat upon the bench with the judges. Yes, beneath one of those priests' cowls were the contortions of the damned. When you were brought in, I was there; when you were cross-questioned, I was there. The den of wolves! It was my crime, it was my gibbet which I saw slowly rise above your head. At each witness, each proof, each plea, I was there; I counted your every step on the road of agony; I was there again when that savage beast— Oh, I did not foresee the torture! Listen. I followed you to the torture-chamber. I saw you stripped, and handled half naked by the infamous hands of the executioner. I saw your foot,—that foot upon which I would have given an empire to press a single kiss and die; that foot by which I would with rapture have been crushed,—I saw it enclosed in the horrid buskin which converts the limbs of a living creature into bleeding pulp. Oh, wretched me! As I saw these things, I grasped beneath my sackcloth a dagger, with which I slashed my breast. At the shriek which you uttered, I plunged it deep into my flesh; had you shrieked again, it would have pierced my heart. Look. I think it still bleeds."

He opened his cassock. His breast was indeed torn as if by a tiger's claw, and upon his side was a large, open wound.

The prisoner shrank from him in horror.

"Oh," said the priest, "have pity on me, girl! You think yourself unhappy. Alas! alas! You do not know the meaning of misery. Oh, to love a woman! to be a priest! to be abhorred! to love her with all the strength of your soul; to feel that you would give your blood, your life, your reputation, your salvation, immortality and eternity, this life and the next, for the least of her smiles; to regret that you are not a king, a genius, an emperor, an archangel, a god, to place at her feet a grander slave; to clasp her in your arms night and day, in your dreams and in your thoughts; and then to see her enamoured of a soldier's uniform, and to have nothing to offer her but a priest's dirty gown, which would terrify and disgust her; to be present with your jealousy and your rage while she lavishes upon a miserable idiotic braggart the treasures of her love and beauty! To see that body whose form inflames you, that bosom which has so much sweetness, that flesh tremble and blush under the kisses of another! Oh, Heaven! to love her foot, her arm, her shoulder; to think of her blue veins, of her brown skin, until one has writhed whole nights on the floor of one's cell, and to see all the caresses which you have dreamed of bestowing upon her end on the rack; to have succeeded only in stretching her upon the leather bed,—oh, these are indeed tongs heated red-hot in the fires of hell! Oh, happy is he who is sawn asunder between two planks, or torn in quarters by four horses! Do you know what agony he feels through long nights, whose arteries boil, whose heart seems bursting, whose head seems splitting, whose teeth tear his hands,—remorseless tormentors which turn him incessantly, as on a fiery gridiron, over a thought of love, jealousy, and despair! Mercy, girl! One moment's truce! Cast a handful of ashes upon the coals! Wipe away, I conjure you, the big drops of sweat that trickle from my brow! Child, torture me with one hand, but caress me with the other! Have pity, maiden,—have pity upon me!"

The priest wallowed in the water which lay on the floor, and beat his head against the edge of the stone stairs. The girl listened to him, looked at him.

When he ceased speaking, panting and exhausted, she repeated in a low tone,—

"Oh, my Phœbus!"

The priest dragged himself towards her on his knees.

"I entreat you," he cried; "if you have any feeling, do not repulse me! Oh, I love you! I am a miserable wretch! When you utter that name, unhappy girl, it is as if you ground the very fibres of my heart between your teeth! Have mercy! If you come from hell, I will go there with you.

"I have done everything to that end. The hell where you are will be paradise to me; the sight of you is more blissful than that of God! Oh, speak! Will you not accept me? I should have thought that on the day when a woman could repel such love the very mountains themselves would move! Oh, if you would but consent! Oh, how happy we might be! We would fly,—I would help you to escape.

"We would go somewhere; we would seek out that spot of earth where there was most sunshine, most trees, most blue sky. We would love each other; we would pour our two souls one into the other, and we would thirst inextinguishably each for the other, quenching our thirst forever and together at the inexhaustible cup of love."

She interrupted him with a loud burst of terrible laughter.

"Only look, father! There is blood upon your nails!"

The priest for some moments stood petrified, his eyes fixed on his hands.

"Ah, yes!" he replied at length, with strange gentleness; "insult me, mock me, overwhelm me! But come, come. We must hasten. To-morrow is the day, I tell you. The gallows in the Grève, you know! It is ever ready. It is horrible,—to see you borne in that tumbrel! Oh, have mercy! I never felt before how much I loved you. Oh, follow me! You shall take your time to love me after I have saved you. You shall hate me, too, as long as you will. But come. To-morrow! to-morrow! the gallows! your execution! Oh, save yourself! spare me!"

He seized her by the arm; he was frantic; he strove to drag her away.

She fixed her eyes steadily upon him.

"What has become of my Phœbus?"

"Ah!" said the priest, releasing her arm, "you are pitiless!"

"What has become of Phœbus?" she repeated coldly.

"He is dead!" cried the priest.

"Dead!" said she, still motionless and icy; "then why do you talk to me of living?"

He did not listen to her.

"Oh, yes," said he, as if speaking to himself, "he must indeed be dead. The blade entered very deeply. I think I touched his heart with the point. Oh, my very life hung upon that dagger!"

The young girl threw herself upon him like an angry tigress, and pushed him towards the stairs with supernatural strength.

"Begone, monster! begone, assassin! Leave me to die! May the blood of both of us forever stain your brow; Be yours, priest? Never! never! Nothing shall ever unite us,—not even hell! Go, accursed man! never!"

The priest had stumbled to the stairs. He silently freed his feet from the folds of his cassock, took up his lantern, and slowly ascended the steps leading to the door. He reopened the door and went out.

All at once the young girl saw his head reappear; his face wore a frightful expression, and he cried to her with a gasp of rage and despair,—

"I tell you he is dead!"

She fell face downwards on the ground, and no sound was heard in the dungeon save the sighing of the drop of water which rippled the water in the darkness.

Chapter V

THE MOTHER

I DO not think that there is anything in the world more delightful than the ideas aroused in a mother's heart by the sight of her child's little shoe, especially if it be a best shoe, a Sunday shoe, a christening shoe, a shoe embroidered down to the very sole, a shoe in which the child has never yet taken a step. That shoe is so dainty, so tiny, it is so impossible for it to walk, that it is to the mother as if she saw her child itself. She smiles at it, kisses it, talks to it; she asks it if there can really be so small a foot; and if the child be absent, the pretty shoe is quite enough to bring the sweet and fragile creature before her eyes. She fancies she sees it; she does see it, from head to foot full of life and laughter, with its delicate hands, its round head, its pure lips, its clear eyes, whose very white is blue. If it be winter, it is there; it crawls over the carpet; it laboriously climbs upon a stool, and the mother trembles lest it go too near the fire. If it be summer, it creeps about the courtyard or the garden, pulls up the grass which grows between the paving-stones, gazes innocently and fearlessly at the big dogs and horses, plays with shells and flowers, and makes the gardener scold when he finds sand on his borders and dirt in his paths. All is bright and gay; all is mirth around it like itself, even to the breeze and the sunbeam, which vie with each other in sporting among the light curls of its hair. The shoe shows the mother all this, and makes her heart melt within her like wax before the fire.

But if she has lost her child, these thousand images of bliss, delight, and love which hover around the little shoe become so many horrid visions. The pretty embroidered shoe ceases to be aught but an instrument of torture, forever rending the mother's heart. The same fibre still vibrates,—the deepest and most sensitive fibre; but instead of being caressed by an angel, it is wrenched by a demon.

One morning, as the May sun was rising in a deep-blue sky, such as Garofolo loved to use for the background of his "Descents from the Cross," the recluse of the Tour-Roland heard the noise of wheels, horses' hoofs, and the clink of iron in the Grève. She paid but little heed to it, pulled her hair over her ears to drown it, and again fell to gazing, on her knees, at the inanimate object which she had thus adored for fifteen years. This little shoe, as we have already said, was the entire universe to her. Her every thought was bound up in it, never to be parted until death. The gloomy cavern of the Tour-Roland alone knew how many bitter curses, how many touching lamentations, prayers, and sobs, she had addressed to Heaven on behalf of that dainty pink satin toy. Never was greater despair lavished on a prettier, more graceful object.

On this particular morning it seemed as if her grief burst forth with even greater violence than usual; and those who passed by outside heard her wailing in a loud monotonous tone which pierced their very hearts.

"Oh, my daughter," she moaned, "my daughter! My poor, dear little child, I shall never see you again, then! It is all over! It always seems to me as if it were but yesterday that it happened! My God, my God, it would have been better never to give her to me, if you meant to snatch her from me so soon! Perhaps you did not know that our children are a part of ourselves, and that a mother who loses her child can no longer believe in God! Ah, wretch that I was, to go out that day! Lord! Lord! to take her from me thus, you could never have seen me with her when I warmed her, all rapture, at my fire; when she laughed at my breast; when I helped her little feet to climb up my bosom to my lips! Oh, if you had seen all this, my God, you would have had pity on my joy; you would not have robbed me of the only love left in my heart! Was I, then, so miserable a creature, Lord, that you could not look upon me before you condemned me? Alas! alas! here is the shoe, but where is the foot; where is the rest; where is the child? My daughter, my daughter! what have they done with you? Lord, restore her to me! My knees have been bruised for fifteen years in praying to you, my God! Will that not suffice? Restore her to me for a day, an hour, a single instant,—one instant only, Lord!—and then cast me to the devil for all eternity! Oh, if I did but know where to find the skirts of your garment, I would cling to them with both hands until you gave me back my child! Have you no mercy, when you see her pretty little shoe, Lord? Can you condemn a poor mother to fifteen years of torment? Kind Virgin, gracious Lady of Heaven! they have taken away my child-Jesus; they have stolen her; they devoured her flesh upon the heath, they drank her blood, they gnawed her bones! Gracious Virgin, have pity upon me! My daughter! I must have my daughter! What do I care if she is in paradise? I don't want an angel; I want my child. I am a lioness, roaring for my whelp. Oh, I will writhe upon the ground, I will beat my forehead against the stones, and I will be forever damned, and I will curse you, Lord, if you keep my child from me! You see that my arms are all bitten and torn, Lord! Has the good God no compassion? Oh, give me nothing but salt and black bread, but give me back my daughter, and she will warm me like the sun! Alas! God, my Lord, I am but a vile sinner; but my daughter made me pious. I was full of religion from love of her; and I saw you through her smile as through an opening in the heavens. Oh, if I could only once, once more, just once more, put this shoe on her pretty little rosy foot, I would die, kind Virgin, blessing you! Ah! 'twas fifteen years ago. She would be almost a woman now! Unhappy child! What! then it is indeed true I shall never see her again, not even in heaven, for I shall never go there! Oh, what misery! to think that there is her shoe, and that is all I have left!"

The unhappy woman had flung herself upon the shoe, for so many years her consolation and her despair, and she burst into heartrending sobs as if it were the very day it happened; for to a mother who has lost her child, her loss is ever present. Such grief as that never grows old. The garments of mourning may rust and wear out; the heart remains forever darkened.

At this instant the fresh, gay voices of a band of children were heard outside, passing the cell. Every time that a child met her eye or ear, the poor mother rushed into the blackest corner of her tomb, and seemed trying to bury her head in the stone walls, that she might not hear or see them. But to-day, on the contrary, she sprang up hastily, and listened eagerly. One of the little boys said,—

"They are going to hang a gipsy girl to-day."

With the sudden leap of that spider which we saw rush upon a fly when her web quivered, she ran to her window, which looked, as the reader knows, upon the Grève. A ladder was indeed erected close to the permanent gallows, and the hangman's assistant was arranging the chains rusted by the rain. A number of people stood about watching him.

The laughing group of children had already vanished. The nun looked about for some passer-by, whom she might question. She noticed, close by her cell, a priest, who feigned to be reading the public breviary, but who was far less occupied with the "letters latticed with iron" than with the gibbet, towards which he cast repeated wild and gloomy glances. She recognized him as the archdeacon of Josas, a holy man.

"Father," she asked, "who is to be hanged yonder?"

The priest stared at her, and made no answer; she repeated her question. Then he said,—

"I do not know."

"The children said that it was a gipsy girl," continued the recluse.

"I believe it is," said the priest.

Then Paquette la Chantefleurie burst into a hyena-like laugh.

"Sister," said the archdeacon, "do you hate the gipsies so intensely?"

"Do I hate them!" cried the recluse; "they are witches, child-stealers! They devoured my little girl, my child, my only child! I have no heart now; they ate it!"

She was frightful to look upon. The priest gazed coldly at her.

"There is one whom I hate particularly, and whom I have cursed," she added; "she is young,—about the age that my daughter would have been if her mother had not eaten my girl. Every time that young viper passes my cell, my blood boils!"

"Well, then, sister, rejoice," said the priest, as cold as the statue on a monument; "it is the same girl whose death you are about to witness."

His head fell upon his breast and he moved slowly away.

The recluse wrung her hands with joy.

"I told her she would mount those steps! Thanks, Sir Priest!" she cried.

And she began to stride up and down behind her barred window, with dishevelled hair and flaming eyes, striking her shoulder against the wall as she moved, with the savage air of a caged wolf which has long gone hungry, and knows that feeding-time is at hand.

Chapter VI

Three Men's Hearts, Differently Constituted

Phœbus, however, was not dead. Men of his kind are hard to kill. When Master Philippe Lheulier, advocate extraordinary to the king, said to poor Esmeralda, "He is dying," he was either mistaken or joking. When the archdeacon, in pronouncing her sentence, repeated, "He is dead," the fact was that he knew nothing whatever about it, but that he supposed so, he reckoned upon it, had no doubt of it, sincerely hoped it was so. It would have been too much to expect of him, that he should carry good news of his rival to the woman he loved. Any man would have done the same in his place.

Not that Phœbus's wound was not severe, but it was less so than the archdeacon flattered himself. The surgeon, to whose house the soldiers of the watch had at once carried him, had for a week feared for his life, and even told him so in Latin. However, youth triumphed; and, as frequently happens, prognosis and diagnosis to the contrary, Nature amused herself by saving the patient in spite of the doctor. It was while he still lay upon the surgeon's truckle-bed that he underwent the first examination from Philippe Lheulier and the board of inquiry from the Bishop's Court, which annoyed him exceedingly. Accordingly, one fine morning, feeling better, he left his golden spurs in payment of the doctor, and slipped away. This circumstance, moreover, did not at all disturb the legal proceedings. Justice in those days cared little for precision and accuracy in a criminal suit. Provided the prisoner were hanged, that was all that was necessary. Now, the judges had proof enough against Esmeralda. They believed Phœbus to be dead, and that was the end of the matter.

Phœbus, for his part, had not gone far. He simply rejoined his company, then in garrison at Queue-en-Brie, in the Ile-de-France, a few relays away from Paris.

After all, he had no desire to appear at the trial in person. He had a vague feeling that he should play a ridiculous part in it. In fact, he did not quite know what to think about the matter. Irreligious and superstitious, like most soldiers who are nothing but soldiers, when he questioned himself concerning the affair, he felt somewhat uneasy about the goat, about the strange fashion in which he first met Esmeralda, the no less strange fashion in which she had allowed him to guess her love for him, the fact of her gipsy blood, and lastly the goblin monk. He had a dim idea that there was far more magic than love in the story, that there was probably a witch, perhaps the devil, mixed up in it; it was a very disagreeable farce, or, to use the language of the day, a mystery, in which he played a most awkward part,—that of the butt for cuffs and laughter. He felt quite sheepish about it; he experienced that kind of shame which La Fontaine so admirably defines:—

"Shamefaced as a fox by timid chicken caught."

However, he hoped that the affair would not be noised abroad, and that he being absent, his name would scarcely be mentioned, and in any case would not be known outside the court-room. In this he was not mistaken; for there was no Police Gazette then; and as a week seldom passed but there was some coiner boiled, or witch hanged, or heretic burned, by one of the innumerable justices of Paris, people were so much accustomed to seeing the old feudal Themis at every street corner, with her sleeves tucked up and her arms bare, doing her work at the gibbet, the whipping-post, or the pillory, that they hardly noticed her. The aristocracy of that day scarcely knew the name of the victim who passed them on the street, and at most it was only the mob that regaled itself with this coarse meat. An execution was a common incident in the highways, like a baker's kneading-trough, or the butcher's shambles. The hangman was but a kind of butcher a shade more skilful than the other.

Phœbus accordingly soon set his mind at rest in regard to the enchantress Esmeralda, or Similar, as he called her; to the stab inflicted by the gipsy or the goblin monk (to him it mattered little which); and to the issue of the trial. But no sooner was his heart vacant on that score, than the image of Fleur-de-Lys re-entered it. The heart of Captain Phœbus, like the physics of that time, abhorred a vacuum.

Besides, Queue-en-Brie was a very tedious abode,—a village of farriers, and dairymaids with chapped hands; a long string of huts and hovels bordering the high-road on either side for half a league.

Fleur-de-Lys was his last passion but one,—a pretty girl with a delightful dowry; therefore, one fine morning, completely cured of his wound, and feeling sure that after a lapse of two months the gipsy matter must be past and forgotten, the amorous knight appeared in state at the door of the Gondelaurier house.

He paid no heed to a somewhat numerous crowd which had gathered in the square in front of Notre-Dame; he recollected that it was the month of May; he supposed there was some procession, that it was Pentecost or some other holiday, fastened his horse to the ring at the porch, and went joyously upstairs to see his fair betrothed.

She was alone with her mother.

Fleur-de-Lys ever had upon her mind the scene with the sorceress, her goat, her accursed alphabet, and Phœbus's long absence. Still, when her captain entered, he looked so handsome with his spick-and-span new uniform, his glittering baldric, and his impassioned air, that she blushed for pleasure.

The noble damsel herself was more lovely than ever. Her superb light hair was braided in the most ravishing manner; she was dressed from head to foot in that sky-blue which is so becoming to fair skins,—a piece of coquetry which Colombe had taught her; and her eyes swam in that languor of love which is still more becoming.

Phœbus, who had seen no beauties of any sort since he left the rustic wenches of Queue-en-Brie, was carried away by Fleur-de-Lys, and this lent such cordiality and gallantry to his manner that his peace was soon made. Madame de Gondelaurier herself, still seated maternally in her great arm-chair, had not the courage to scold him. As for the reproaches of Fleur-de-Lys, they died away in tender cooings.

The young girl sat by the window, still working away at her Neptune's cave. The captain leaned against the back of her chair, and she addressed her affectionate complaints to him in an undertone.

"Where have you been for these two months, you naughty fellow?"

"I swear," replied Phœbus, somewhat embarrassed by the question, "that you are handsome enough to disturb the dreams of an archbishop."

She could not help smiling.

"There, there, sir! Leave my beauty out of the question, and answer me. Fine beauty, indeed!"

"Well, dear cousin, I was sent back to garrison."

"And where, pray? And why didn't you come and take leave of me?"

"At Queue-en-Brie."

Phœbus was enchanted that the first question helped him to evade the second.

"But that is close by, sir. Why did you never come to see us?"

Here Phœbus was seriously embarrassed.

"Why — my duties — And then, fair cousin, I have been ill."

"Ill!" she repeated in alarm.

"Yes,—wounded."

"Wounded!"

The poor child was quite overcome.

"Oh, don't be frightened about that!" said Phœbus, indifferently; "it was nothing. A quarrel, a sword-thrust; why should that trouble you?"

"Why should that trouble me?" cried Fleur-de-Lys, raising her lovely eyes bathed in tears. "Oh, you do not really mean what you say! What was this sword-thrust? I insist upon knowing everything."

"Well, then, my dear, I had a row with Mahé Fédy,—you know whom I mean,—the lieutenant from Saint-Germain-en-Laye; and each of us ripped up a few inches of the other's skin. That's all there is about it."

The lying captain was well aware that an affair of honour always exalts a man in a woman's eyes. In fact, Fleur-de-Lys looked him in the face, quivering with terror, delight, and admiration. Still, she was not completely reassured.

"If you are sure that you are quite cured, dear Phœbus!" said she. "I don't know your Mahé Fédy, but he is a bad man. And what did you quarrel about?"

Here Phœbus, whose imagination was only tolerably active, began to wonder how he was to get out of the scrape.

"Oh, I don't know,—a trifle, a horse, a bit of gossip! Fair cousin," cried he, in order to change the conversation, "what can that noise be in the square?" He stepped to the window.

"Heavens! fair cousin, what a crowd there is in the square!"

"I don't know," said Fleur-de-Lys, "but I heard that a witch was to do public penance this morning before the church, and to be hanged afterwards."

The captain felt so sure that Esmeralda's affair was well over, that he took very little interest in Fleur-de-Lys' words. Still he asked her one or two questions.

"What is this witch's name?"

"I do not know," replied she.

"And what do they claim that she has done?"

She again shrugged her white shoulders.

"I don't know."

"Oh, my sweet Saviour!" said the mother, "there are so many sorcerers nowadays that they burn them, I verily believe, without knowing their names. You might as well try to find out the name of every cloud in the sky. After all, we may rest easy. The good God keeps his list." Here the venerable lady rose, and came to the window. "Good Lord!" said she, "you're right, Phœbus. What a rabble! Bless me! if they haven't climbed upon the house-tops! Do you know, Phœbus, it reminds me of my young days. When King Charles VII. entered Paris, there was exactly such a crowd. I've forgotten, now, just what year that was. When I talk to you of such matters, it seems to you like ancient history, doesn't it, while to me it seems quite recent. Oh, that was a much finer-looking crowd than this is! They even hung upon the battlements of the Porte Saint-Antoine. The king had the queen on the crupper behind him, and after their Highnesses came all the ladies riding on the cruppers of all the lords. I remember people laughed well because beside Amanyon de Garlande, who was very short of stature, was my lord Matefelon, a knight of gigantic size, who had killed heaps of Englishmen. It was a splendid sight. A procession of all the gentlemen in France, with their oriflammes blazing in our very eyes. Some bore pennons and some bore banners. How can I tell you who they all were? There was the Lord of Calan, with his pennon; Jean de Châteaumorant with his banner; the Lord of Coucy, with his banner, and a showier one it was, too, than any of the others except that of the Duc de Bourbon. Alas! how sad it is to think that all that has been, and that nothing of it remains!"

The two lovers did not listen to the worthy dowager. Phœbus again leaned on the back of his sweetheart's chair, —a charming position, whence his impudent gaze pierced every opening in Fleur-de-Lys' neckerchief. This neckerchief gaped so opportunely, and permitted him to note so many exquisite things, and to divine so many others, that, dazzled by her skin with its satiny gloss, he said to himself, "How can anybody ever fall in love with any but a fair-skinned woman?"

Both were silent. The young girl occasionally looked up at him with rapture and affection, and their hair mingled in a spring sunbeam.

"Phœbus," suddenly said Fleur-de-Lys in a low voice, "we are to marry in three months; swear to me that you have never loved any other woman but me."

"I swear it, lovely angel!" replied Phœbus, and his passionate gaze combined with the truthful accent of his voice to convince Fleur-de-Lys. Perhaps he even believed it himself at that instant.

Meanwhile the good mother, charmed to see the lovers on such excellent terms, had left the room to attend to some domestic detail. Phœbus perceived this, and solitude so emboldened the adventurous captain that his brain soon filled with very strange ideas. Fleur-de-Lys loved him; he was her betrothed; she was alone with him; his former fancy for her revived, not in all its freshness, but in all its ardour. After all, it is no great crime to eat some of your fruit before it is harvested. I know not whether all these thoughts passed through his mind, but certain it is that Fleur-de-Lys was suddenly frightened by the expression of his eyes. She looked about her, and saw that her mother had gone.

"Heavens!" said she, blushing and confused, "how warm I feel!"

"Indeed, I think," said Phœbus, "that it must be almost noon. The sun is very annoying; I had better close the curtains."

"No, no," cried the poor girl; "on the contrary, I want air."

And like a deer which feels the hot breath of the pack, she rose, ran to the window, opened it, and rushed out upon the balcony.

Phœbus, vexed enough, followed her.

The square before the cathedral of Notre-Dame, upon which, as we know, the balcony looked, at this moment offered a strange and painful spectacle, which quickly changed the nature of the timid Fleur-de-Lys' fright.

A vast throng, which overflowed into all the adjacent streets, completely blocked the square. The little wall, breast-high, which surrounded the central part, known as the Parvis, would not have sufficed to keep it clear if it had not been reinforced by a thick hedge of serjeants of the Onze-Vingts, and hackbuteers, culverin in hand. Thanks to this thicket of pikes and arquebuses, it remained empty. The entrance was guarded by a body of halberdiers bearing the bishop's arms. The wide church-doors were closed, in odd contrast to the countless windows overlooking the square, which, open up to the very gables, revealed thousands of heads heaped one upon the other almost like the piles of cannon-balls in an artillery park.

The surface of this mob was grey, dirty and foul. The spectacle which it was awaiting was evidently one of those which have the privilege of extracting and collecting all that is most unclean in the population. Nothing could be more hideous than the noise which arose from that swarm of soiled caps and filthy headgear. In that crowd there was more laughter than shouting; there were more women than men.

Now and then some sharp, shrill voice pierced the general uproar.

. . . .

"Hollo! Mahiet Baliffre. Will she be hung yonder?"

"Fool! that is where she's to do penance in her shift. The priest will spit a little Latin at her. It's always done here at noon. If you are looking for the gallows, you must go to the Grève."

"I'll go afterwards."

. . . .

"I say, Boucanbry, is it true that she has refused a confessor?"

"So it seems, Bechaigne."

"Look at that, the heathen!"

. . . .

"Sir, it is the custom. The Palace bailiff is bound to deliver over the malefactor, sentence having been pronounced, for execution, if it be one of the laity, to the provost of Paris; if it be a scholar, to the judges of the Bishop's Court."

"I thank you, sir."

. . . .

"Oh, Heavens!" said Fleur-de-Lys, "the poor creature!"

The thought of the unfortunate victim filled with sadness the glance which she cast upon the crowd. The captain, far more absorbed in her than in that collection of rabble, amorously fingered her girdle from behind. She turned with the smiling entreaty,—

"For pity's sake, let me alone, Phœbus! If my mother returned, she would see your hand!"

At this instant the clock of Notre-Dame slowly struck twelve. A murmur of satisfaction burst from the crowd. The last vibration of the twelfth stroke had scarcely died away, when the sea of heads tossed like the waves on a windy day, and a vast shout rose from the street, the windows, and the roofs:—

"There she is!"

Fleur-de-Lys covered her eyes with her hands that she might not see.

"My charmer," said Phœbus, "will you go in?"

"No," replied she; and those eyes which she had closed from fear she opened again from curiosity.

A tumbrel, drawn by a strong Norman cart-horse, and entirely surrounded by cavalry in violet livery with white crosses, had just entered the square from the Rue Saint-Pierre aux Bœufs. The officers of the watch made a passage for it through the people with lusty blows of their whips. Beside the tumbrel rode a number of officers of justice and of police who might be known by their black dress and their awkward seat in the saddle. Master Jacques Charmolue paraded at their head. In the fatal wagon sat a young girl, her arms bound behind her, and no priest at her side. She was in her shift; her long black locks (it was the fashion then not to cut them until the foot of the gibbet was reached) fell upon her breast and over her half-naked shoulders.

Through this floating hair, glossier than the raven's wing, a rough grey cord was twisted and knotted, chafing her delicate skin, and winding about the poor girl's graceful neck like an earthworm around a flower. Beneath this rope glittered a tiny amulet ornamented with green glass beads, which she had doubtless been allowed to keep, because nothing is refused to those about to die. The spectators posted at the windows could see at the bottom of the tumbrel her bare legs, which she tried to hide under her, as if by a last feminine instinct. At her feet was a little goat, also bound. The prisoner held in her teeth her shift, which was not securely fastened.

Even in her misery she seemed to suffer at being thus exposed almost naked to the public gaze. Alas! it is not for such tremors that modesty is made.

"Only see, fair cousin," said Fleur-de-Lys quickly to the captain, "it is that wicked gipsy girl with the goat."

So saying, she turned to Phœbus. His eyes were fixed upon the tumbrel. He was very pale.

"What gipsy girl with the goat?" he stammered.

"Why, Phœbus!" rejoined Fleur-de-Lys; "don't you remember—"

Phœbus interrupted her:—

"I don't know what you mean."

He took a step to re-enter; but Fleur-de-Lys, whose jealousy, already so deeply stirred by this same gipsy, was again revived, cast a suspicious and penetrating look at him. She now vaguely recalled having heard that there was a captain concerned in the trial of this sorceress.

"What ails you?" said she to Phœbus, "one would think that this woman had disturbed you."

Phœbus tried to sneer. "Me! Not the least in the world! Me, indeed!"

"Then, stay," returned she, imperiously; "let us see it out."

The luckless captain was forced to remain. He was somewhat reassured when he found that the prisoner did not raise her eyes from the bottom of her tumbrel. It was but too truly Esmeralda. Upon this last round of the ladder of opprobrium and misfortune she was still beautiful; her large black eyes looked larger ever from the thinness of her cheeks; her livid profile was pure and sublime. She resembled her former self as one of Masaccio's Virgins resembles a Virgin by Raphael,—feebler, thinner, weaker.

Moreover, her whole being was tossed hither and thither, and save for her sense of modesty, she had abandoned everything, so utterly was she crushed by stupor and despair. Her body rebounded with every jolt of the cart, like some shattered, lifeless thing. A tear still lingered in her eye, but it was motionless, and, as it were, frozen.

Meantime the mournful cavalcade had traversed the crowd amid shouts of joy and curious stares. Still, we must confess, as faithful historians, that many, even the hardest hearted, were moved to pity at the sight of so much beauty and so much misery.

The tumbrel had entered the Parvis. Before the central door it stopped. The escort was drawn up in line on either side. The mob was hushed, and amidst this solemn, anxious silence the two leaves of the great door moved, as if spontaneously, upon their creaking hinges. Then the entire length of the deep, dark church was seen, hung with black, faintly lighted by a few glimmering tapers upon the high altar, and opening like the jaws of some cavern in the middle of the square, dazzling with light. At the very end, in the shadows of the chancel, a huge silver cross was dimly visible, standing out in relief against a black cloth which hung from the roof to the floor. The whole nave was empty; but heads of priests were seen moving confusedly among the distant choir-stalls, and, at the moment that the great door was thrown open, a loud, solemn, and monotonous chant proceeded from the church, casting fragments of dismal psalms, like gusts of wind, upon the pristoner's head:—

"*Non timebo millia populi circumdantis me: exsurge, Domine; salvum me fac, Deus!*"

"*Salvum me fac, Deus, quoniam intraverunt aquæ usque ad animam meam.*"

"*Infixus sum in limo profundi; et non est substantia.*"

At the same time another voice, apart from the choir, intoned from the steps of the high altar this mournful offertory:—

"*Qui verbum meum audit, et credit ei qui misit me, habet vitam, æternam et in judicium non venit; sed transit a morte in vitam.*"

This chant, sung afar off by a few old men lost in the darkness, over that beautiful being full of life and youth, caressed by the warm air of spring, bathed in sunshine, was a part of the mass for the dead.

The people listened quietly.

The wretched victim, in her terror, seemed to lose all power of sight and thought in the dark interior of the church. Her pale lips moved as if in prayer, and when the hangman's assistant approached to help her down from the cart, he heard her murmur in an undertone the word "Phœbus."

Her hands were untied, and she alighted, accompanied by her goat, which was also unbound, and which bleated with delight at regaining its freedom; and she was then led barefooted over the hard pavement to the foot of the steps leading to the porch. The cord about her neck trailed behind her, like a serpent pursuing her.

Then the chanting in the church ceased. A great gold cross and a file of tapers began to move in the gloom; the halberds of the beadles in their motley dress clashed against the floor; and a few moments later a long procession of priests in chasubles and deacons in dalmatics marched solemnly towards the prisoner, singing psalms as they came. But her eyes were fixed upon him who walked at their head, immediately after the cross-bearer.

"Oh," she whispered shudderingly, "there he is again! the priest!"

It was indeed the archdeacon. On his left was the assistant precentor, and on his right the precentor himself, armed with the wand of his office. He advanced, with head thrown back, eyes fixed and opened wide, chanting in a loud voice:—

"*De ventre inferi clamavi, et exaudisti vocem meam.*

"*Et projecisti me in profundum in corde maris, et flumen circumdedit me.*"

When he appeared in full daylight under the lofty pointed arch of the portal, wrapped in a vast cope of cloth of silver embroidered with a black cross, he was so pale that more than one of the crowd thought that he must be one of those marble bishops kneeling upon the monuments in the choir, who had risen and come forth to receive on the threshold of the tomb her who was about to die.

She, no less pale and no less rigid, hardly noticed that a heavy lighted taper of yellow wax had been placed in her hand; she did not hear the shrill voice of the clerk reading the fatal lines of the penance; when she was told to answer "Amen," she answered "Amen." Nor was she restored to any slight sense of life and strength until she saw the priest sign to her jailers to retire, and himself advance alone towards her.

Then the blood boiled in her veins, and a lingering spark of indignation was rekindled in that already numb, cold soul.

The archdeacon approached her slowly; even in this extremity she saw him gaze upon her nakedness with eyes glittering with passion, jealousy, and desire. Then he said to her aloud, "Young girl, have you asked God to pardon your faults and failings?"

He bent to her ear and added (the spectators supposed that he was receiving her last confession). "Will you be mine? I can save you even yet!"

She gazed steadily at him: "Begone, demon! or I will denounce you!"

He smiled a horrible smile. "No one will believe you; you would only add a scandal to a crime. Answer quickly! Will you be mine?"

"What have you done with my Phœbus?"

"He is dead!" said the priest.

At this moment the miserable archdeacon raised his head mechanically, and saw at the opposite end of the square, upon the balcony of the Gondelaurier house, the captain standing beside Fleur-de-Lys. He staggered, passed his hand over his eyes, looked again, murmured a curse, and all his features were violently convulsed.

"So be it! die yourself!" he muttered. "No one else shall possess you."

Then, raising his hand above the gipsy girl's head, he exclaimed in funereal tones, *"I nunc, anima anceps, et sit tibi Deus misericors!"*

This was the awful formula with which these sombre ceremonies were wont to close. It was the signal agreed upon between the priest and the executioner.

The people knelt.

"Kyrie, eleison," said the priests beneath the arch of the portal.

"Kyrie, eleison," repeated the multitude with a noise which rose above their heads like the roar of a tempestuous sea.

"Amen," said the archdeacon.

He turned his back upon the prisoner, his head again fell upon his breast, his hands were crossed, he rejoined his train of priests, and a moment later he disappeared, with cross, candles, and copes, beneath the dim arches of the cathedral, and his sonorous voice faded slowly down the choir, chanting these words of despair:—

"Omnes gurgites tui et fluctus tui super me transierunt!"

At the same time the intermittent echo of the iron-bound shaft of the beadles' halberds, dying away by degrees between the columns of the nave, seemed like the hammer of a clock sounding the prisoner's final hour.

Meantime the doors of Notre-Dame remained open, revealing the church, empty, desolate, clad in mourning, silent and unlighted.

The prisoner stood motionless in her place, awaiting her doom. One of the vergers was obliged to warn Master Charmolue, who during this scene had been studying the bas-relief upon the great porch, which represents, according to some, the Sacrifice of Abraham; according to others, the great Alchemical Operation, the sun being typified by the angel, the fire by the fagot, and the operator by Abraham.

He was with some difficulty withdrawn from this contemplation; but at last he turned, and at a sign from him, two men clad in yellow, the executioner's aids, approached the gipsy girl to refasten her hands.

The unhappy creature, as she was about to remount the fatal tumbrel and advance on her last journey, was perhaps seized by some poignant regret for the life she was so soon to lose. She raised her dry and fevered eyes to heaven, to the sun, to the silvery clouds here and there intersected by squares and triangles of azure; then she cast them down around her, upon the ground, the crowd, the houses. All at once, while the men in yellow were binding her elbows, she uttered a terrible shriek,—a shriek of joy. Upon yonder balcony, there, at the corner of the square, she had just seen him, her lover, her lord, Phœbus, the other apparition of her life.

The judge had lied! the priest had lied! It was indeed he, she could not doubt it; he was there, handsome, living, clad in his splendid uniform, the plume upon his head, his sword at his side!

"Phœbus!" she cried; "my Phœbus!" And she strove to stretch out her arms quivering with love and rapture; but they were bound.

Then she saw the captain frown, a lovely young girl who leaned upon him look at him with scornful lip and angry eyes; then Phœbus uttered a few words which did not reach her, and both vanished hastily through the window of the balcony, which was closed behind them.

"Phœbus," she cried in despair, "do you believe this thing?"

A monstrous idea had dawned upon her. She remembered that she had been condemned for the murder of Captain Phœbus de Châteaupers.

She had borne everything until now. But this last blow was too severe. She fell senseless upon the pavement.

"Come," said Charmolue, "lift her into the tumbrel, and let us make an end of it!"

No one had observed, in the gallery of statues of the kings carved just above the pointed arches of the porch, a strange spectator who had until now watched all that happened with such impassivity, with so outstretched a neck, so deformed a visage, that, had it not been for his party-coloured red and violet garb, he might have passed for one of those stone monsters through whose jaws the long cathedral gutters have for six centuries past disgorged themselves. This spectator had lost nothing that had passed since noon before the doors of Notre-Dame. And at the very beginning, unseen by any one, he had firmly attached to one of the small columns of the gallery a strong knotted rope, the end of which trailed upon the ground below. This done, he began to look about him quietly, and to whistle from time to time when a blackbird flew by him.

All at once, just as the hangman's assistants were preparing to execute Charmolue's phlegmatic order, he bestrode the balustrade of the gallery, seized the rope with his feet, knees, and hands; then he slid down the façade as a drop of rain glides down a window-pane, rushed towards the two executioners with the rapidity of a cat falling from a roof, flung them to the ground with his two huge fists, seized the gipsy girl in one hand, as a child might a doll, and with one bound was in the church, holding her above his head, and shouting in a tremendous voice,—

"Sanctuary!"

All this was done with such speed that had it been night, one flash of lightning would have sufficed to see it all.

"Sanctuary! sanctuary!" repeated the mob; and the clapping of ten thousand hands made Quasimodo's single eye flash with pride and pleasure.

This shock restored the prisoner to her senses. She raised her eyelids, looked at Quasimodo, then closed them suddenly, as if alarmed by her saviour.

Charmolue stood stupefied, and the hangman and all the escort did the same. In fact, within the precincts of Notre-Dame the prisoner was secure;

the cathedral was a sure place of refuge; all human justice died upon its threshold.

Quasimodo had paused beneath the great portal, his broad feet seeming as firmly rooted to the pavement of the church as the heavy Roman pillars. His big bushy head was buried between his shoulders like the head of a lion which also has a mane and no neck. He held the young girl, trembling from head to foot, suspended in his horny hands like a white drapery; but he carried her as carefully as if he feared he should break or injure her. He seemed to feel that she was a delicate, exquisite, precious thing, made for other hands than his. At times he looked as if he dared not touch her, even with his breath. Then, all at once, he pressed her close in his arms, upon his angular bosom, as his treasure, his only wealth, as her mother might have done. His gnome-like eye, resting upon her, flooded her with tenderness, grief, and pity, and was suddenly lifted, flashing fire. Then the women laughed and wept, the mob stamped with enthusiasm, for at that instant Quasimodo was truly beautiful. He was beautiful,—he, that orphan, that foundling, that outcast; he felt himself to be august and strong; he confronted that society from which he was banished, and with whose decrees he had so powerfully interfered, that human justice from which he had wrested its prey, all those tigers with empty jaws, those myrmidons, those judges, those executioners, all that royal will which he had crushed, he,— the lowliest of creatures, with the strength of God.

Then, too, how touching was the protection extended by so deformed a creature to one so unfortunate as the girl condemned to die, and saved by Quasimodo! It was the two extreme miseries of Nature and society meeting and mutually aiding each other.

However, after a few moments of triumph, Quasimodo plunged abruptly into the church with his burden. The people, lovers of all prowess, followed him with their eyes, regretting that he had so soon withdrawn from their plaudits. All at once he reappeared at one end of the gallery of the kings of France; he ran along it like a madman, holding his conquest aloft, and shouting, "Sanctuary!" The crowd broke into fresh applause. The gallery traversed, he again rushed into the interior of the church. A moment after, he reappeared upon the upper platform, the gipsy still in his arms, still running frantically, still shouting, "Sanctuary!" and the mob applauded. At last he appeared for the third time upon the summit of the tower of the big bell; from thence he seemed with pride to show the whole city her whom he had saved, and his thundering voice—that voice so rarely heard by any one, and never by himself —repeated thrice, with frenzy that pierced the very clouds: "Sanctuary! Sanctuary! Sanctuary!"

"Noël! Noël!" cried the people in their turn; and that vast shout was heard with amazement by the throng in the Grève on the other bank of the river, and by the recluse, who still waited, her eyes riveted to the gallows.

The Hunchback of Notre-Dame

BOOK IX

ACCUMULATED AFFLICTIONS

CHAPTER I

DELIRIUM

CLAUDE FROLLO was no longer in Notre-Dame when his adopted son so abruptly cut the fatal knot in which the wretched archdeacon had caught the gipsy and was himself caught. Returning to the sacristy, he had snatched off his alb, cope, and stole, flung them all into the hands of the amazed sacristan, fled through the private door of the cloisters, ordered a boatman of the Terrain to set him over to the left bank of the Seine, and plunged in among the hilly streets of the University, not knowing whither he went, meeting at every turn bands of men and women hastening gaily towards the Pont Saint-Michel in the hope that they might yet be in time to see the witch hanged,—pale, haggard, more bewildered, blinder, and fiercer than a night-bird let loose in broad daylight and pursued by a troop of boys. He no longer knew where he was, what he did, whether he was dreaming or awake. He went on, he walked, he ran, taking any street at haphazard, but still urged forward by the Grève, the horrible Grève, which he vaguely felt behind him.

In this way he passed St. Geneviève's Mount, and finally left the town by the Porte Saint-Victor. He continued to flee as long as he could see, on turning, the ring of towers around the University, and the scattered houses of the suburb; but when at last a ridge completely hid that odious Paris, when he could imagine himself a hundred leagues away in the fields, in a desert, he paused, and it seemed as if he breathed again.

Then frightful thoughts crowded upon him. Once more he saw into his soul as clear as day, and he shuddered at the sight. He thought of the unhappy girl who had destroyed him, and whom he had destroyed. He cast a despairing glance at the doubly-crooked path along which Fate had led their destinies, up to the meeting-point where it had pitilessly dashed them against each other. He thought of the folly of eternal vows, of the vanity of chastity, science, religion, virtue, and the uselessness of God. He indulged in evil thoughts to his heart's content, and as he yielded to them he felt himself giving way to Satanic laughter.

And as he thus searched his soul, when he saw how large a space Nature had reserved therein for the passions, he sneered more bitterly still. He stirred up all the hatred and malice from the very depths of his heart; and he recognized, with the cold gaze of a physician studying his patient, that this malice was nothing but love perverted; that love, the source of all virtue in man, turned to horrible things in the heart of a priest, and that a man formed like him, when he became a priest became a demon. Then he laughed fearfully, and all at once he again turned pale, as he considered the most forbidding side of his fatal passion,—of that corrosive, venomous, malignant, implacable love which led but to the gallows for one, to hell for the other: she condemned, he damned.

And then he laughed anew as he reflected that Phœbus was alive; that after all the captain lived, was light-hearted and content, had finer uniforms than ever, a new sweetheart whom he brought to see the old one hanged. His sneers were redoubled when he reflected that, of all the living beings whose death he had desired, the gipsy girl, the only creature whom he did not hate, was the only one who had not escaped him.

Then from the captain his mind wandered to the mob, and he was overcome with jealousy of an unheard-of kind. He thought that the mob, too, the entire mob, had had before their eyes the woman whom he loved, in her shift, almost naked. He writhed as he thought that this woman, whose form, half seen by him alone in darkness would have afforded him supreme delight, had been exposed in broad daylight at high noon to an entire multitude clad as for a night of pleasure. He wept with rage over all those mysteries of love profaned, soiled, exposed, withered forever. He wept with rage, picturing to himself the foul eyes which had revelled in that scanty covering; and that that lovely girl, that virgin lily, that cup of modesty and delight, to which he dared not place his lips without trembling, had been made common property, a vessel from which the vilest rabble of Paris, thieves, beggars, and lackeys, had come to quaff together a shameless, impure, and depraved pleasure.

And when he strove to picture the bliss which he might have found upon earth if she had not been a gipsy and he had not been a priest, if Phœbus had never lived, and if she had loved him; when he imagined the life of peace and love which might have been possible for him also; when he thought that there were even at that very instant here and there on the earth happy couples lost in long talks beneath orange-trees, on the border of streams, beneath a setting sun or a starry heaven; and that, had God so willed, he might have formed with her one of those blest couples, his heart melted within him in tenderness and despair.

Oh, she! it is she! She,—the one idea which returned ever and again, torturing him, turning his brain, gnawing his vitals. He regretted nothing, repented nothing; all that he had done he was ready to do again; he preferred to see her in the hangman's hands rather than in the captain's arms. But he suffered; he suffered so intensely that at times he tore out his hair by handfuls, to see if it had not turned white with anguish.

There was one moment among the rest when it occurred to him that this was possibly the minute when the hideous chain which he had seen that morning was drawing its iron noose closer and ever closer around that slender, graceful neck. This idea made the perspiration start from every pore.

There was another moment when, while laughing devilishly at himself, he pictured at one and the same time Esmeralda as he had first seen her,— alert, heedless, happy, gaily dressed, dancing, winged, and harmonious,—and Esmeralda as he had last seen her, in her shift, with the rope about her neck, slowly approaching with her bare feet the cruel gallows; and this double picture was so vivid that he uttered a terrible cry.

While this whirlwind of despair overwhelmed, crushed, broke, bent, and uprooted everything in his soul, he considered the scene around him. At his feet some hens were pecking and scratching among the bushes, enamelled beetles crawled in the sun; above his head, groups of dappled grey clouds sailed over the blue sky; in the horizon, the spire of the Abbey of Saint-Victor cut the curve of the hill with its slated obelisk; and the miller of the Buttes Copeau whistled as he watched the busy wheels of his mill go round. All this active, industrious, tranquil life, reproduced around him in a thousand forms, hurt him. He again tried to escape.

Thus he ran through the fields until nightfall. This flight from Nature, life, himself, man, God, everything, lasted the entire day. Sometimes he threw himself face downwards upon the earth, and tore up the young corn with his nails: sometimes he paused in some deserted village street; and his thoughts were so unendurable that he seized his head in both hands and tried to snatch it from his shoulders that he might dash it to pieces upon the ground.

Towards sunset he examined himself anew, and found that he was almost mad. The tempest which had been raging within him from the instant that he lost all hope and will to save the gipsy girl had not left a single sane idea, a single sound thought, in his brain. His reason was laid low by it, was almost wholly destroyed by it. His mind retained but two distinct images, —Esmeralda and the scaffold; all else was black. Those two closely connected images presented a frightful group; and the more he fixed upon them such power of attention and intellect as he still retained, the more they seemd to grow, by a fantastic progression,—the one in grace, charm, beauty, light, the other in horror; so that at last Esmeralda appeared to him as a star, the gibbet as an enormous fleshless arm.

It was a remarkable thing that in spite of all this torment he never seriously thought of suicide. The wretch was so constituted. He clung to life. Perhaps he really saw hell lurking in the background.

Meantime, the day continued to decline. That spark of life which still burned within him dreamed dimly of returning home. He fancied himself remote from Paris; but on examination he discovered that he had merely made the circuit of the University. The spire of Saint-Sulpice and the three lofty pinnacles of Saint-Germain des Prés rose above the horizon on his right.

He proceeded in that direction. When he heard the challenge of the abbot's men-at-arms around the battlemented walls of Saint-Germain he turned aside, took a footpath which he saw between the abbey mill and the lazaretto of the suburb, and in a few moments found himself at the edge of the Pré-aux-Clercs. This meadow was famous for the riots going on there continually, day and night; it was the "hydra-headed monster" of the poor monks of Saint-Germain: *"Quod monachis Sancti-Germani pratensis hydra fuit, clericis nova semper dissidiorum capita suscitantibus."* The archdeacon dreaded meeting some one there; he was afraid of any human face; he had shunned the University and the village of Saint-Germain; he was determined not to enter the city streets any earlier than he could help.

He skirted the Pré-aux-Clercs, took the deserted path dividing it from the Dieu-Neuf, and at last reached the bank of the river. There he found a boatman, who for a few farthings rowed him up the Seine as far as the City, where he landed him on that strip of waste land where the reader has already seen Gringoire indulging in a reverie, and which extended beyond the king's gardens, parallel with the island of the Passeur aux Vaches.

The monotonous rocking of the boat and the ripple of the water had somewhat stupefied the unhappy Claude. When the boatman had gone, he stood upon the shore in a dazed condition, staring straight forward, and seeing everything in a sort of luminous mist which seemed to dance before his eyes. The fatigue of great grief often produces this effect upon the brain.

The sun had set behind the tall Tour de Nesle. It was twilight. The sky was silvery, the water in the river was silvery too. Between these two silver whites, the left bank of the Seine, upon which his eyes were riveted, stretched its sombre length, and, tapering in the distance, faded away at last among the hazes of the horizon in the shape of a black spire. It was covered with houses, whose dark outlines only were visible, cast in strong relief against the bright background of cloud and water. Here and there windows began to glow like live embers. The vast black obelisk thus detached between the two white masses of sky and river, the latter very broad just here, produced a strange effect on Don Claude,—such as might be felt by a man lying flat on his back at the foot of the Strasburg cathedral, and gazing up at the huge spire piercing the twilight shadows over his head. Only here, Claude was standing and the obelisk lying low; but as the river, by reflecting the sky, prolonged the abyss beneath, the vast promontory seemed to shoot into space as boldly as any cathedral spire; and the impression produced was the same. The impression was made even stronger and more singular by the fact that it was indeed the Strasburg steeple, but the Strasburg steeple two leagues high,—something unheard-of, gigantic, immeasurable; a structure such as no human eye ever beheld; a Tower of Babel. The chimneys of the houses, the battlements of the wall, the carved gables of the roofs, the spire of the Augustine monastery, the Tour de Nesle, all these projections which marred the outline of the colossal obelisk, added to the illusion by grotesquely counterfeiting to the eye the indentations of some rich and fantastic carving.

Claude, in the state of hallucination in which he then was, believed that he saw—saw with his bodily eyes—the pinnacles of hell; the countless lights scattered from end to end of the awful tower appeared to him like so many doors leading to the vast furnace within; the voices and the sounds which arose from it, like so many shrieks and groans. Then he was terrified; he clapped his hands to his ears that he might not hear them, turned his back that he might not see, and hastened away from the fearful vision.

But the vision was within him.

When he once more entered the city streets, the passing people elbowing each other in the light of the shop windows affected him like the never-ending coming and going of spectres. There were strange noises in his ears; extraordinary images troubled his senses. He saw neither houses, nor pavement, nor chariots, nor men and women, but a chaos of indeterminate objects which melted into one another. At the corner of the Rue de la Barillerie there was a grocer's shop, the sloping roof of which was, according to immemorial custom, hung with tin hoops, from each of which was suspended a circle of wooden candles, which clattered and clashed in the wind like castanets. He fancied he heard the heap of skeletons at Montfaucon knocking their bones against one another in the darkness.

"Oh," he muttered, "the night wind lashes them together, and mingles the sound of their chains with the rattle of their bones! Perhaps she too is there among them!"

Bewildered and distracted, he knew not where he went. After walking a few steps, he found himself upon the Pont Saint-Michel. There was a light at the window of a room on the ground-floor; he went up to it. Through a cracked pane he saw a dirty room, which roused a vague memory in his brain. In this room, dimly lighted by a small lamp, there was a fresh, fair-haired, merry-faced youth, who with loud bursts of laughter kissed a gaudily-dressed girl; and near the lamp sat an old woman spinning and singing in a cracked voice. As the young man occasionally ceased laughing, fragments of the old woman's song reached the priest; it was something unintelligible and frightful:—

"Bark, Grève, growl, Grève!
Spin, spin, my spindle brave,
For the hangman spin a cord,
As he whistles in the prison yard,
Bark, Grève, growl, Grève!

"The lovely hempen cord forevermore!
Sow from Issy e'en to Vanvre's shore
Hemp, and never of corn a grain.
No thief will ever steal for gain
The lovely hempen cord.

"Growl, Grève, bark, Grève!
To see the wanton and the knave
Hanging on the gallows high,
Every window is an eye.
Growl, Grève, bark, Grève!"

Hereupon the young man laughed, and caressed the girl. The old woman was Mother Falourdel; the girl was a woman of the town; the young man was his brother Jehan.

He continued to gaze. As well this sight as another.

He saw Jehan go to a window at the back of the room, open it, cast a glance at the quay, where countless lighted windows gleamed in the distance, and he heard him say, as he closed the window,—

"By my soul! it is night already. The citizens have lighted their candles, and the good God his stars."

Then Jehan went back to the girl and broke a bottle which stood on the table, exclaiming,—

"Empty already, by Jove! and I have no more money! Isabeau, my love, I shall never feel content with Jupiter until he turns your two white breasts into two black bottles, whence I may suck Beaune wine night and day."

This witticism made the girl laugh, and Jehan sallied forth.

Don Claude had barely time to throw himself on the ground, lest he should be encountered, looked in the face, and recognized by his brother. Luckily, the street was dark, and the student was drunk. However, he noticed the archdeacon lying on the pavement in the mire.

"Ho! ho!" said he; "here's a fellow who has led a jolly life to-day."

With his foot he stirred Don Claude, who held his breath.

"Dead drunk," continued Jehan. "Well, he is full,—a regular leech dropped from a cask because he can suck no more. He is bald," he added, stooping; "he is an old man! *Fortunate senex!*"

Then Don Claude heard him move off, saying,—

"All the same, reason is a fine thing, and my brother the archdeacon is very lucky to be both wise and rich."

The archdeacon then rose, and ran at full speed in the direction of Notre-Dame, whose enormous towers rose before him in the darkness above the surrounding houses.

When, quite breathless, he reached the square in front of the cathedral, he shrank back, and dared not raise his eyes to the fatal building.

"Oh," said he in a low tone, "is it indeed true that such a thing can have occurred here to-day,—this very morning?"

Still he ventured to look at the church. The front was dark; the sky behind it glittered with stars. The crescent moon, which had just risen above the horizon, had that instant paused at the summit of the right-hand tower, and seemed to have perched, like a luminous bird, on the edge of the railing, which was cut into black trefoils.

The cloister door was closed, but the archdeacon always carried about him the key to the tower in which was his laboratory. He now used it to let himself into the church.

Inside, all was gloomy and silent as the tomb. By the heavy shadows falling on all sides in broad masses, he knew that the hangings put up for the morning's ceremonies had not yet been removed. The great silver cross gleamed through the darkness, dotted with sparkling points of light, like the milky way of this sepulchral night. The long choir windows showed the tops of their pointed arches above the black drapery, the panes, traversed by a moonbeam, wearing only the doubtful colours of the night,—a sort of violet, white, and blue, in tints which are found nowhere else save on the face of the dead. The archdeacon, seeing these pale points of arches all around the choir, fancied that he beheld the mitres of bishops who had been damned. He shut his eyes, and when he reopened them, he imagined that there was a circle of ashen faces gazing at him.

He fled across the church. Then it seemed to him that the church, too, moved, stirred, breathed, and lived; that each big column became a monstrous leg, which pawed the ground with its broad stone hoof; and that the vast cathedral was only a sort of prodigious elephant, which panted and trampled, with pillars for feet, its two towers for tusks, and the immense black draperies for caparison.

Thus his fever, or mania, had attained such a degree of intensity that the external world had ceased to be to the unfortunate man anything more than a sort of Apocalypse, visible, tangible, terrifying.

For one moment he was comforted. As he entered the aisles, he perceived, behind a group of pillars, a reddish light, towards which he hastened as towards a star. It was the poor lamp which burned day and night above the public breviary of Notre-Dame, under its iron grating. He fell eagerly to reading the sacred book, in the hope of finding some consolation or some encouragement. The volume was open at this passage from Job, over which his fixed eye ran:—

"Then a spirit passed before my face; the hair of my flesh stood up."

On reading this melancholy passage, he felt as a blind man feels who is pricked by the staff which he has picked up. His knees gave way beneath him, and he sank to the ground, thinking of her who had that day perished. Such awful fumes rose up and penetrated his brain that it seemed to him as if his head had become one of the mouths of hell.

He remained some time in this position, incapable of thought, crushed and powerless in the hand of the demon that possessed him. At last, some measure of strength returned to him; it occurred to him to take refuge in the tower with his faithful Quasimodo. He rose, and as he was frightened, he took, to light his steps, the lamp from the breviary. This was a sacrilege, but he had ceased to heed such trifles.

He slowly climbed the tower stairs, full of secret terror, which must have been shared by the few passers-by outside in the square, who saw the mysterious light of his lamp moving at that late hour from loop-hole to loop-hole, to the top of the tower.

All at once he felt a freshness upon his face, and found himself under the door of the uppermost gallery. The air was cold; the sky was overcast with clouds, whose large white masses encroached one upon the other, rounding the sharp corners, and looking like the breaking-up of the ice in a river in winter. The crescent moon, stranded in the midst of the clouds, seemed a celestial ship caught fast among these icebergs of the air.

He cast down his eyes, and looked for a moment between the iron rails of the small columns which connect the two towers, far away, through a mist of fog and smoke, at the silent throng of the roofs of Paris,—steep, numberless, crowded close together, and small as the waves of a calm sea on a summer's night.

The moon shed a faint light, which lent an ashen tint to both heaven and earth.

At this moment the clock raised its shrill, cracked voice; it struck midnight. The priest's thoughts reverted to noonday; it was again twelve o'clock.

"Oh," he whispered, "she must be cold by this time!"

Suddenly a blast of wind extinguished his lamp, and almost at the same instant he saw, at the opposite corner of the tower, a shadow, something white, a figure, a woman. He trembled. By this woman's side was a little goat, which mingled its bleat with the final bleat of the bell.

He had the courage to look at her. It was she.

She was pale; she was sad. Her hair fell loosely over her shoulders, as in the morning, but there was no rope about her neck; her hands were no longer bound. She was free; she was dead.

She was dressed in white, and had a white veil over her head.

She came towards him slowly, looking up to heaven. The supernatural goat followed her. He felt as if turned to stone, and too heavy to escape. At each step that she advanced, he took one backwards, and that was all. In this way he retreated beneath the dark arch of the staircase. He was frozen with fear at the idea that she might perhaps follow him thither; had she done so, he would have died of terror.

She did indeed approach the staircase door, pause there for a few moments, look steadily into the darkness, but without appearing to see the priest, and pass on. She seemed to him taller than in life; he saw the moon through her white robes; he heard her breathe.

When she had passed him, he began to descend the stairs with the same slow motion as the spectre, imagining that he too was a spectre,—haggard, his hair erect, his extinguished lamp still in his hand; and as he went down the spiral stairs, he distinctly heard in his ear a mocking voice, which repeated the words,—

"A spirit passed before my face; the hair of my flesh stood up."

Chapter II

DEFORMED, BLIND, LAME

Every city in the Middle Ages—and up to the time of Louis XII. every city in France—had its places of refuge, its sanctuaries. These places of refuge, amidst the deluge of penal laws and barbarous jurisdictions which flooded the city of Paris, were like so many islands rising above the level of human justice. Every criminal who landed there was saved. In each district there were almost as many places of refuge as gallows. The abuse of a privilege went side by side with the abuse of punishment,—two bad things, each striving to correct the other. Roya palaces, princely mansions, and above all churches, had the right of sanctuary; sometimes an entire town which stood in need of repopulation was given the temporary right. Louis XI. made Paris a sanctuary in 1467.

Having once set foot within the sanctuary, the criminal was sacred; but let him beware how he ventured forth: one step outside his shelter plunged him again in the billows. The wheel, the gibbet, and the strappado kept close guard around the place of refuge, and watched their prey unceasingly, like sharks in a vessel's wake. Thus men have been known to grow grey in a convent, on a palace staircase, in abbey fields, under a church porch; so that the sanctuary became a prison in all save name. It sometimes happened that a solemn decree from Parliament violated the sanctuary, and gave up the criminal to justice; but this occurrence was rare. The Parliaments stood in some awe of the bishops; and when cowl and gown came into collision, the priest usually got the best of it. Sometimes, however, as in the matter of the assassins of Petit-Jean, the Paris hangman, and in that of Emery Rousseau, Jean Valleret's murderer, Justice overrode the Church, and proceeded to carry out her sentences; but, without an order from Parliament, woe to him who violated any sanctuary by armed force! We know what fate befell Robert de Clermont, Marshal of France, and Jean de Châlons, Marshal of Champagne; and yet the case in question was merely that of one Perrin Marc, a money-changer's man, a miserable assassin. But the two marshals broke open the doors of Saint-Méry; therein lay the crime.

Such was the veneration felt for these refuges that, as tradition goes, it occasionally extended even to animals. Aymoin relates that a stag chased by Dagobert, having taken refuge near the tomb of Saint Denis, the pack stopped short, barking loudly.

Churches had usually a cell prepared to receive suppliants. In 1407 Nicolas Flamel had built for them upon the arches of Saint-Jacques de la Boucherie, a chamber which cost him four pounds six pence sixteen Paris farthings.

At Notre-Dame it was a cell built over the aisles under the flying buttresses, on the very spot where the wife of the present keeper of the towers has made a garden, which compares with the hanging gardens of Babylon as a lettuce with a palm-tree, or a porter's wife with Semiramis.

It was here that Quasimodo had deposited Esmeralda after his frantic and triumphal race through the towers and galleries. While that race lasted, the young girl did not recover her senses,—half dozing, half waking, conscious only of being borne upward through the air, whether floating or flying, or lifted above the earth by some unknown power. From time to time she heard the noisy laughter, the harsh voice of Quasimodo in her ear. She half opened her eyes; then beneath her she saw dimly all Paris dotted with countless roofs of slate and tiles, like a red and blue mosaic; above her head the fearful, grinning face of Quasimodo. Her eyelids fell; she thought that all was over, that she had been hanged during her swoon, and that the misshapen spirit which ruled her destiny had again taken possession of her and carried her away. She dared not look at him, but yielded to his sway.

But when the breathless and dishevelled bell-ringer laid her down in the cell of refuge, when she felt his great hands gently untie the rope which bruised her arms, she experienced that sort of shock which wakens with a start the passengers on a ship that runs aground in the middle of a dark night. Her ideas woke too, and returned to her one by one. She saw that she was still in Notre-Dame; she remembered being torn from the hangman's hands; that Phœbus lived, that Phœbus had ceased to love her; and these two ideas, one of which lent such bitterness to the other, presenting themselves simultaneously to the poor victim, she turned to Quasimodo, who stood before her and who terrified her, saying,—

"Why did you save me?"

He looked anxiously at her, as if striving to guess what she said. She repeated her question. He gazed at her with profound sadness, and fled.

She was amazed.

A few moments later he returned, brining a packet which he threw at her feet. It contained clothes left at the door of the church for her by charitable women.

Then she looked down at herself, saw that she was almost naked, and blushed. Life had returned.

Quasimodo appeared to feel something of her shame. He covered his eye with his broad hand, and again departed, but with lingering steps.

She hastily dressed herself. The garments given her consisted of a white gown and veil,—the dress of a novice at the Hôtel-Dieu, the great hospital managed by nuns.

She had scarcely finished when Quasimodo returned. He carried a basket under one arm and a mattress under the other. In the basket were a bottle, a loaf of bread, and a few other provisions. He set the basket down, and said, "Eat!" He spread the mattress on the floor, and said, "Sleep!"

It was his own food, his own bed, which the bell-ringer had brought.

The gipsy lifted her eyes to his face to thank him, but she could not utter a word. The poor devil was hideous indeed. She hung her head with a shudder of fright.

Then he said,—

"I alarm you. I am very ugly, am I not? Do not look at me; only listen to me. During the day, you must stay here; by night, you can walk anywhere about the church; but do not leave the church by day or night. You would be lost. They would kill you, and I should die."

Moved by his words, she raised her head to reply. He had vanished. Alone once more, she pondered the strange words of this almost monstrous being, struck by the sound of his voice, which was so hoarse and yet so gentle.

Then she examined her cell. It was a room of some six feet square, with a little dormer-window and a door opening on the slightly sloping roof of flat stones. Various gutter-spouts in the form of animals seemed bending over her and stretching their necks to look at her through the window. Beyond the roof she saw the tops of a thousand chimneys, from which issued the smoke of all the fires of Paris. A sad spectacle for the poor gipsy girl,—a foundling condemned to death, an unhappy creature, without a country, without a family, without a hearth.

Just as the thought of her forlorn condition struck her more painfully than ever, she felt a hairy, bearded head rub against her hands and knees. She trembled (everything frightened her now) and looked down. It was the poor goat, the nimble Djali, who had escaped with her when Quasimodo scattered Charmolue's men, and who had been lavishing caresses on her feet for nearly an hour without winning a glance. The gipsy girl covered her with kisses.

"Oh, Djali," said she, "how could I forget you! But you never forget me! Oh, you at least are not ungrateful!"

At the same time, as if an invisible hand had lifted the weight which had so long held back her tears, she began to weep; and as her tears flowed, she felt the sharpest and bitterest of her grief going from her with them.

When evening came, she thought the night so beautiful, the moon so soft, that she took a turn in the raised gallery which surrounds the church. She felt somewhat refreshed by it, the earth seemed to her so peaceful, viewed from that height.

Chapter III

DEAF

Next morning she found on waking that she had slept. This strange fact amazed her; it was so long since she had slept! A bright beam from the rising sun came in at her window and shone in her face. With the sun, she saw at the same window an object that alarmed her,—the unhappy face of Quasimodo. Involuntarily she reclosed her eyes, but in vain; she still seemed to see through her rosy lids that one-eyed, gap-toothed, gnome-like face. Then, still keeping her eyes shut, she heard a rough voice say very kindly,—

"Don't be frightened. I am your friend. I came to see if you were asleep. It does you no harm, does it, if I look at you when you are asleep? What does it matter to you if I am here when your eyes are shut? Now I will go. There, I have hidden myself behind the wall. You can open your eyes again."

The tone in which they were uttered was even more plaintive than the words themselves. The gipsy girl, touched by it, opened her eyes. He was no longer at the window. She went to it, and saw the poor hunchback crouched in a corner of the wall, in a painful and submissive posture. She made an effort to overcome the aversion with which he inspired her. "Come here," said she, gently. From the motion of her lips, Quasimodo thought she was ordering him away; he therefore rose and retired, limping slowly, with hanging head, not daring to raise his despairing eye to the young girl's face. "Do come!" she cried. But he still withdrew. Then she ran out of her cell, hurried after him, and took his arm. When he felt her touch, Quasimodo trembled in every limb. He raised his beseeching eye, and finding that she drew him towards her, his whole face beamed with tenderness and delight.

She tried to make him enter her cell; but he persisted in remaining on the threshold. "No, no," said he; "the owl must not enter the lark's nest."

Then she threw herself gracefully upon her bed, with the sleeping goat at her feet. For some moments both were motionless, silently contemplating, he so much grace, she so much ugliness.

Every moment she discovered some additional deformity in Quasimodo. Her gaze roved from his knock knees to his humped back, from his humped back to his single eye. She could not understand why a being so imperfectly planned should continue to exist. But withal there was so much melancholy and so much gentleness about him that she began to be reconciled to it.

He was the first to break the silence: "Did you tell me to come back?"

She nodded her head, as she said, "Yes."

He understood her nod. "Alas!" said he, as if loath to go on, "I am— I am deaf."

"Poor fellow!" cried the gipsy, with a look of kindly pity.

He smiled sadly.

"You think that I only lacked that, don't you? Yes, I am deaf. That's the way I was made. It is horrible, isn't it? And you,—you are so beautiful!"

There was so profound a sense of his misery in the poor wretch's tone, that she had not the strength to say a word. Besides, he would not have heard her. He added:—

"I never realized my ugliness till now. When I compare myself with you, I pity myself indeed, poor unhappy monster that I am! I must seem to you like some awful beast, eh? You,— you are a sunbeam, a drop of dew, a bird's song! As for me, I am something frightful, neither man nor beast,— a nondescript object, more hard, shapeless, and more trodden under foot than a pebble!"

Then he began to laugh, and that laugh was the most heartrending thing on earth. He continued:—

"Yes, I am deaf; but you can speak to me by gestures, by signs. I have a master who talks with me in that way. And then I shall soon know your wishes from the motion of your lips, and your expression."

"Well," she replied, smiling, "tell me why you saved me."

He watched her attentively as she spoke.

"I understand," he answered. "You ask me why I saved you. You have forgotten a villain who tried to carry you off one night,—a villain to whom the very next day you brought succour upon their infamous pillory. A drop of water and a little pity are more than my whole life can ever repay. You have forgotten that villain; but he remembers."

She listened with deep emotion. A tear sparkled in the bell-ringer's eye, but it did not fall. He seemed to make it a point of honour to repress it.

"Listen," he resumed, when he no longer feared lest that tear should flow; "we have very tall towers here; a man who fell from them would be dead long before he touched the pavement; whenever it would please you to have me fall, you need not even say a single word; one glance will be enough."

Then he rose. This peculiar being, unhappy though the gipsy was, yet roused a feeling of compassion in her heart. She signed him to stay.

"No, no," said he. "I must not stay too long. I am not at my ease. It is out of pity that you do not turn away your eyes. I will go where I can see you without your seeing me. That will be better."

He drew from his pocket a small metal whistle.

"There," said he, "when you need me, when you wish me to come to you, when I do not horrify you too much, whistle with this. I hear that sound."

He laid the whistle on the ground, and fled.

Chapter IV

EARTHENWARE AND CRYSTAL

One day followed another. Calm gradually returned to Esmeralda's soul. Excess of grief, like excess of joy, is a violent thing, and of brief duration. The heart of man cannot long remain at any extreme. The gipsy had suffered so much that surprise was the only emotion of which she was now capable. With security, hope had returned. She was far away from society, far from life, but she vaguely felt that it might not perhaps be impossible to return to them. She was like one dead, yet holding in reserve the key to her tomb.

She felt the terrible images which had so long possessed her fading gradually away. All the hideous phantoms, Pierrat Torterue, Jacques Charmolue, had vanished from her mind,—all, even the priest himself.

And then, too, Phœbus lived; she was sure of it; she had seen him. To her, the life of Phœbus was all in all. After the series of fatal shocks which had laid waste her soul, but one thing was left standing, but one sentiment,—her love for the captain. Love is like a tree; it grows spontaneously, strikes its roots deep into our whole being, and often continues to flourish over a heart in ruins.

And the inexplicable part of it is, that the blinder this passion, the more tenacious it is. It is never stronger than when it is utterly unreasonable.

Undoubtedly Esmeralda's thoughts of the captain were tinged with bitterness. Undoubtedly it was frightful that he too should have been deceived, he who should have deemed such a thing impossible,—that he should have believed the stab to come from her, who would have given a thousand lives for him. But, after all, she must not blame him too severely; had she not confessed her crime? Had she not, weak woman that she was, yielded to torture? The fault was wholly hers. She should have let them tear out every nail rather than wrest a single word from her. Well, could she but see Phœbus once more, for one moment only, it would need but a word, a look, to undeceive him, to bring him back. She had no doubts in the matter. She also strove to account to herself for various strange facts,—for the accident of Phœbus's presence on the day of her doing penance, and for the young girl with whom he was. Probably she was his sister. An improbable explanation, but one with which she contented herself, because she must needs believe Phœbus still loved her, and loved her alone. Had he not sworn it to her? What more did she want, simple, credulous girl that she was? And then, in this business, were not appearances much more against her than against him? She therefore waited; she hoped.

Let us add that the church, that vast church which surrounded her on every side, which guarded her, which preserved her, was itself a sovereign anodyne. The solemn lines of its architecture, the religious attitude of every object about the young girl, the calm and pious thoughts which were emitted, as it were, from every pore of its stones, unconsciously acted upon her. Moreover, the building had sounds of such majesty and blessing that they soothed her sick soul. The monotonous chant of the officiating priests, the people's response to them, sometimes inarticulate, sometimes thunderous, the harmonious quiver of the stained-glass windows, the organ loud as the blast of a hundred trumpets, the three belfries, buzzing and humming like hives of great bees,—all this orchestra, with its gigantic gamut perpetually rising and falling, from the crowd to the belfry, lulled her memory, her imagination, her grief. The bells, particularly, soothed her. Those vast machines poured over her broad waves of mighty magnetism.

Thus, each day's rising sun found her more composed, breathing better, less pale. As her inward wounds were healed, her grace and beauty bloomed again, although she was more reserved and quiet. Her former disposition also returned,— something even of her gaiety, her pretty pout, her love for her goat, her passion for singing, and her modesty. She was careful to dress herself every morning in the corner of her cell, lest the inmate of some neighbouring garret should spy her through the window.

When the thoughts of Phœbus gave her time, the gipsy sometimes thought of Quasimodo. He was the only tie, the only bond, the only means of communication left to her with mankind, with the living. Unhappy girl! She was even more completely cut off from the world than Quasimodo. She could not understand the strange friend whom chance had given her. She often reproached herself for not feeling sufficient gratitude to blind her eyes; but, decidedly, she could not accustom herself to the poor ringer. He was too ugly.

She had left the whistle which he gave her on the floor. This did not prevent Quasimodo from appearing now and then during the first few days. She did her best not to turn away with too much aversion when he brought her the basket of food or the jug of water; but he always noticed the slightest movement of the kind, and would then go sadly away.

Once he came up just as she was fondling Djali. He stood for a few moments considering the pretty group of the girl and the goat; at last he said, shaking his heavy, clumsy head,—

"My misfortune is that I am still too much like a human being. I wish I were wholly an animal like that goat."

She looked at him in surprise.

He answered her look:—

"Oh, I very well know why." And he withdrew.

On another occasion he appeared at the door of the cell (which he never entered) as Esmeralda was singing an old Spanish ballad, the words of which she did not understand, but which had lingered in her memory because the gipsies had rocked her to sleep with it when a child. At the sight of his ugly face, coming so suddenly upon her in the midst of her song, the young girl stopped short, with an involuntary gesture of alarm. The wretched ringer fell upon his knees on the door-sill, and clasped his great misshapen hands with a beseeching air. "Oh," said he, sadly, "I pray you, go on, and do not drive me away." She was unwilling to pain him, and, trembling though she was, resumed her song. By degrees, however, her terror subsided, and she gave herself up entirely to the emotions aroused by the slow and plaintive music. He remained on his knees, his hands clasped as if in prayer, attentive, scarcely breathing, his eyes riveted upon the gipsy's sparkling orbs. He seemed to read her song in her eyes.

Another day he came to her with a timid, awkward air. "Listen to me," said he with an effort; "I have something to tell you." She signed to him that she was listening. Then he began to sigh, half opened his lips, seemed just about to speak, looked at her, shook his head, and retired slowly, pressing his hand to his head, leaving the gipsy utterly amazed.

Among the grotesque images carved upon the wall, there was one of which he was particularly fond, and with which he often seemed to exchange fraternal glances. The girl once heard him say to it, "Oh, why am not I of stone, like you!"

Finally, one morning Esmeralda ventured out to the edge of the roof, and looked into the square over the steep top of Saint-Jean le Rond. Quasimodo stood behind her. He stationed himself there to spare the girl as far as possible the annoyance of seeing him. All at once she started; a tear and a flash of joy shone together in her eyes. She knelt on the edge of the roof, and stretched out her arms in anguish towards the square, crying, "Phœbus! Come! Come! One word, only one word, for the love of Heaven! Phœbus! Phœbus!" Her voice, her face, her gesture, her whole person, wore the heartrending expression of a shipwrecked mariner making signals of distress to a ship sailing merrily by in the distance, lit up by a sunbeam on the horizon.

Quasimodo bent over the parapet, and saw that the object of this frenzied entreaty was a young man, a captain, a handsome knight, glittering with arms and ornaments, who pranced and curveted through the square on horseback, waving his plumed helmet to a lovely damsel smiling from her balcony. However, the officer did not hear the unhappy girl's appeal; he was too far away.

But the poor deaf man heard it. A deep sigh heaved his breast; he turned away; his heart swelled with suppressed tears; his clenched fists beat his brow, and when he withdrew them, each of them grasped a handful of red hair.

The gipsy paid no heed to him. He gnashed his teeth, and muttered,—

"Damnation! So that is how one should look! One only needs a handsome outside!"

Meantime, she remained on her knees, crying with great agitation,—

"Oh, now he is dismounting from his horse! He is going into that house! Phœbus! He does not hear! Phœbus! How cruel of that woman to talk to him at the same time that I do! Phœbus! Phœbus!"

The deaf man watched her. He understood her pantomime. The poor bell-ringer's eye filled with tears, but he did not let a single one flow. All at once he plucked her gently by the hem of her sleeve. She turned. He had assumed a tranquil air, and said,—

"Shall I go and fetch him?"

She uttered a cry of joy.

"Oh, go! go! run, quick! that captain! that captain! bring him to me! I will love you!"

She clasped his knees. He could not help shaking his head sadly.

"I will bring him to you," said he in a faint voice. Then he turned his head and hurried quickly down the stairs, choked with sobs.

When he reached the square, he saw nothing but the fine horse tied to the post at the door of the Gondelaurier house; the captain had already entered.

He raised his eyes to the roof of the church. Esmeralda was still in the same place, in the same position. He shook his head sorrowfully, then leaned against one of the posts before the Gondelaurier porch, determined to await the captain's coming.

Within the house, it was one of those gala days which precede a wedding. Quasimodo saw many people go in, and none come out. From time to time he looked up at the roof; the gipsy girl was as motionless as he. A groom came, unfastened the horse, and led him into the stable.

The whole day passed thus,—Quasimodo against the pillar, Esmeralda on the roof, Phœbus, doubtless, at the feet of Fleur-de-Lys.

At last night came,—a moonless night, a dark night. In vain Quasimodo fixed his eyes upon Esmeralda; she soon ceased to be anything more than a white spot in the dusk; then she vanished. Everything faded out; all was dark.

Quasimodo saw the front windows of the Gondelaurier mansion lighted up from top to bottom; he saw the other windows on the square lighted, one by one; he also saw the lights extinguished to the very last, for he remained at his post all the evening. The officer did not come out. When the latest passers had gone home, when all the windows in the other houses were black, Quasimodo was left alone, entirely in the darkness. There were no street lamps in the Parvis then.

But the windows of the Gondelaurier house remained lighted, even after midnight. Quasimodo, motionless and alert, saw countless moving, dancing shadows pass across the many-coloured panes. If he had not been deaf, as the noise of sleeping Paris ceased, he would have heard more and more distinctly, within the house, the sounds of revelry, music and laughter.

About one o'clock in the morning the guests began to go. Quasimodo wrapped in darkness, watched them as they passed beneath the porch brigh with torches. The captain was not among them.

He was filled with sad thoughts; at times he looked up into the air, as if tired of waiting. Great, black, heavy clouds, torn and ragged, hung like masses of crape from the starry arch of night. They seemed like the cobwebs of the vaulted sky.

In one of these upward glances he suddenly saw the long window of the balcony whose stone balustrade was just over his head, mysteriously open. Two persons passed out through the glass door, closing it noiselessly behind them; they were a man and a woman. It was not without some difficulty that Quasimodo succeeded in recognizing in the man the handsome captain; in the woman, the young lady whom he had that morning seen wave a welcome to the officer from that self-same balcony. The square was perfectly dark, and a double crimson curtain, which fell again behind the door as it closed, scarcely permitted a ray of light from the room to reach the balcony.

The young man and the girl, as far as our deaf man could judge without hearing a single one of their words, seemed to give themselves up to a very tender *tête-à-tête*. The young girl had apparently allowed the officer to encircle her waist with his arm, and was making a feeble resistance to a kiss.

Quasimodo looked on from below at this scene, which was all the more attractive because it was not meant to be seen. He beheld that happiness and beauty with bitterness. After all, nature was not mute in the poor devil, and his spinal column, wretchedly crooked as it was, was quite as susceptible of a thrill as that of any other man. He reflected on the miserable part which Providence had assigned him; that woman, love, pleasure, were forever to pass before him, while he could never do more than look on at the happiness of others. But what pained him most in this sight, what added indignation to his annoyance, was the thought of what the gipsy girl must suffer could she see it. True, the night was very dark; Esmeralda, if she had remained at her post (which he did not doubt), was very far away, and it was all he could do himself, to distinguish the lovers on the balcony. This comforted him.

Meantime, their conversation became more and more animated. The young lady seemed to be entreating the officer to ask no more of her. Quasimodo could only make out her fair clasped hands, her smiles blent with tears, her upward glances, and the eyes of the captain eagerly bent upon her.

Luckily,—for the young girl's struggles were growing feebler,—the balcony door was suddenly reopened, and an old lady appeared; the beauty seemed confused; the officer wore a disappointed air, and all three re-entered the house. A moment later a horse was pawing the ground at the door, and the brilliant officer, wrapped in his cloak, passed quickly by Quasimodo.

The ringer let him turn the corner of the street, then ran after him with his monkey-like agility, shouting:

"Hollo there! Captain!"

The captain stopped.

"What can that rascal want?" said he, seeing in the shadow the ungainly figure limping quickly towards him.

Meantime Quasimodo caught up with

him, and boldly seized the horse by the bridle:—

"Follow me, Captain; there is some one here who wishes to speak with you."

"The devil!" muttered Phœbus, "here's an ugly scarecrow whom I think I've seen elsewhere. Hollo, sirrah! will you let my horse's bridle go?"

"Captain," replied the deaf man, "don't you even ask who it is?"

"I tell you to let my horse go!" impatiently replied Phœbus. "What does the fellow mean by hanging to my charger's chamfron thus? Do you take my horse for a gallows?"

Quasimodo, far from loosing his hold on the bridle, was preparing to turn the horse's head in the opposite direction. Unable to understand the captain's resistance, he made haste to say,—

"Come, Captain, it is a woman who awaits you." He added with an effort: "A woman who loves you."

"Arrant knave!" said the captain; "do you think I am obliged to go to all the women who love me, or say they do? And how if by chance she looks like you, you screech-owl? Tell her who sent you that I am about to marry, and that she may go to the devil!"

"Hear me!" cried Quasimodo, supposing that with one word he could conquer his hesitation; "come, my lord! it is the gipsy girl, whom you know!"

These words did indeed make a strong impression upon Phœbus, but not of the nature which the deaf man expected. It will be remembered that our gallant officer retired with Fleur-de-Lys some moments before Quasimodo rescued the prisoner from the hands of Charmolue. Since then, during his visits to the Gondelaurier house he had carefully avoided all mention of the woman, whose memory was painful to him; and, on her side, Fleur-de-Lys had not thought it politic to tell him that the gipsy still lived. Phœbus therefore supposed poor "Similar" to have died some two or three months before. Let us add that for some moments past the captain had been pondering on the exceeding darkness of the night, the supernatural ugliness and sepulchral tones of the strange messenger, the fact that it was long past midnight, that the street was as deserted as on the night when the goblin monk addressed him, and that his horse snorted at the sight of Quasimodo.

"The gipsy girl!" he exclaimed, almost terrified: "pray, do you come from the other world?"

And he placed his hand on the hilt of his dagger.

"Quick! quick!" said the deaf man, striving to urge on the horse; "this way!"

Phœbus dealt him a vigorous kick.

Quasimodo's eyes flashed. He made a movement to attack the captain. Then drawing himself up, he said,—

"Oh, how fortunate it is for you that there is some one who loves you!"

He emphasized the words *some one*, and releasing the horse's bridle, added,—

"Begone!"

Phœbus clapped spurs to his horse, with an oath. Quasimodo saw him plunge down the street and disappear in the darkness.

"Oh," murmured the poor deaf man, "to refuse that!"

He returned to Notre-Dame, lighted his lamp, and climbed the tower. As he had supposed, the gipsy was still in the same place.

As soon as she caught sight of him, she ran to meet him.

"Alone!" she cried mournfully, clasping her lovely hands.

"I could not find him," said Quasimodo, coldly.

"You should have waited all night," she replied indignantly.

He saw her angry gesture, and understood the reproach.

"I will watch better another time," said he, hanging his head.

"Go!" said she.

He left her. She was offended with him. He would rather be maltreated by her than distress her. He kept all the pain for himself.

From that day forth the gipsy saw him no more. He ceased to visit her cell. At most, she sometimes caught a glimpse of the ringer on the top of a tower, gazing sadly at her. But as soon as she saw him, he disappeared.

We must own that she was but little troubled by this wilful absence of the poor hunchback. In her secret heart she thanked him for it. However, Quasimodo did not lie under any delusion on this point.

She no longer saw him, but she felt the presence of a good genius around her. Her provisions were renewed by an invisible hand while she slept. One morning she found a cage of birds on her window-sill. Over her cell there was a piece of carving which alarmed her. She had more than once shown this feeling before Quasimodo. One morning (for all these things occurred at night) she no longer saw it; it was broken off. Any one who had clambered up to it must have risked his life.

Sometimes in the evening she heard a voice, hidden behind the wind-screen of the belfry, sing, as if to lull her to sleep, a weird, sad song, verses without rhyme, such as a deaf person might make:—

> "Heed not the face,
> Maiden, heed the heart.
> The heart of a fine young man is
>   oft deformed.
> There are hearts where Love finds
>   no abiding-place.

> "Maiden, the pine-tree is not fair,
> Not fair as is the poplar-tree
> But its leaves are green in winter
>   bare.

> "Alas! why do I tell you this?
> Beauty alone has right to live;
> Beauty can only beauty love,
> April her back doth turn on
>   January.

> "Beauty is perfect,
> Beauty wins all.
> Beauty alone is lord of all.

> "The raven only flies by day,
> The owl by night alone doth fly,
> The swan by day and night alike
>   may fly."

One morning, on waking, she saw at her window two vases full of flowers. One was a very beautiful and brilliant but cracked crystal vase. It had let the water with which it was filled escape, and the flowers which it held were withered. The other was an earthen jug, coarse and common; but it had retained all its water, and the flowers were fresh and rosy.

I do not know whether it was done purposely, but Esmeralda took the withered nosegay, and wore it all day in her bosom. That day she did not hear the voice from the tower singing. She cared but little. She passed her days in fondling Djali, in watching the door of the Gondelaurier house, in talking to herself about Phœbus, and in scattering crumbs of bread to the swallows.

She had entirely ceased to see or hear Quasimodo; the poor ringer seemed to have vanished from the church. But one night, when she could not sleep, and was thinking of her handsome captain, she heard a sigh close by her cell. Terrified, she rose, and saw by the light of the moon a shapeless mass lying outside across her door. It was Quasimodo sleeping there upon the stones.

Chapter V

THE KEY TO THE PORTE-ROUGE

MEANTIME, public rumour had informed the archdeacon of the miraculous manner in which the gipsy had been saved. When he learned of it, he knew not what he felt. He had accepted the fact of Esmeralda's death. In this way, he made himself perfectly easy; he had sounded the utmost depths of grief. The human heart (Don Claude had mused upon these matters) can hold but a certain quantity of despair. When the sponge is thoroughly soaked, the sea may pass over it without adding another drop to it.

Now, Esmeralda being dead, the sponge was soaked. Everything was over for Don Claude in this world. But to know that she was alive, and Phœbus too, was to endure afresh the torments, shocks, and vicissitudes of life; and Claude was weary of them all.

When he heard this piece of news, he shut himself up in his cloister cell. He did not appear at the chapter meetings or the sacred offices. He barred his door against every one, even the bishop, and remained thus immured for several weeks. He was supposed to be ill, and indeed was so.

What did he do in seclusion? With what thoughts was the unfortunate man battling? Was he waging a final conflict with his terrible passion? Was he plotting a final plan to kill her and destroy himself?

His Jehan, his adored brother, his spoiled child, came once to his door, knocked, swore, entreated, repeated his name half a score of times. Claude would not open.

He passed whole days with his face glued to his window-panes. From this window, in the cloisters as it was, he could see Esmeralda's cell. He often saw herself, with her goat,—sometimes with Quasimodo. He noticed the attentions of the ugly deaf man,—his obedience, his refined and submissive manners to the gipsy. He recalled,—for he had a good memory, and memory is the plague of the jealous,—he recalled the bell-ringer's strange look at the dancer on a certain evening. He asked himself what motive could have led Quasimodo to save her. He witnessed countless little scenes between the girl and the deaf man, when their gestures, seen from a distance and commented on by his passion, struck him as very tender. He distrusted women's whims. Then he vaguely felt awakening within him a jealousy such as he had never imagined possible,—a jealousy which made him blush with rage and shame. "'Twas bad enough when it was the captain; but this fellow!" The idea overwhelmed him.

His nights were frightful. Since he knew the gipsy girl to be alive, the chill fancies of spectres and tombs which had for an entire day beset him, had vanished, and the flesh again rose in revolt against the spirit. He writhed upon his bed at the idea that the dark-skinned damsel was so near a neighbour.

Every night his fevered imagination pictured Esmeralda in all those attitudes which had stirred his blood most quickly. He saw her stretched across the body of the wounded captain, her eyes closed, her beautiful bare throat covered with Phœbus's blood, at that moment of rapture when he himself had pressed upon her pale lips that kiss which had burned the unhappy girl, half dead though she was, like a living coal. He again saw her disrobed by the savage hands of the executioners, exposing and enclosing in the buskin with its iron screws her tiny foot, her plump and shapely leg, and her white and supple knee.

He again saw that ivory knee alone left uncovered by Torterue's horrid machine. Finally, he figured to himself the young girl in her shift, the rope about her neck, her shoulders bare, her feet bare, almost naked, as he saw her on what was to have been her last day on earth. These voluptuous pictures made him clinch his hands, and caused a shudder to run from head to foot.

One night, especially, they so cruelly heated his virgin and priestly blood that he bit his pillow, leaped from his bed, threw a surplice over his shirt, and left his cell, lamp in hand, but half-dressed, wild and haggard, with flaming eyes.

He knew where to find the key to the Porte-Rouge, which led from the cloisters to the church, and he always carried about him, as the reader knows, a key to the tower stairs.

Chapter VI

THE KEY TO THE PORTE-ROUGE (*cont.*)

THAT night Esmeralda fell asleep in her cell, full of peace, hope, and pleasant thoughts. She had been asleep for some time, dreaming, as she always did, of Phœbus, when she fancied she heard a noise. Her sleep was light and restless,—a bird's sleep. A mere trifle roused her. She opened her eyes. The night was very dark. Still, she saw a face peering in at the window; the vision was lighted up by a lamp. When this face saw that Esmeralda was looking at it, it blew out the lamp. Still, the girl had had time to catch a glimpse of it; her eyes closed in terror.

"Oh," said she, in a feeble voice, "the priest!"

All her past misery flashed upon her with lightning speed. She sank back upon her bed, frozen with fear.

A moment after, she felt a touch which made her shudder so that she started up wide awake and furious.

The priest had glided to her side. He clasped her in his arms.

She tried to scream, but could not.

"Begone, monster! Begone, assassin!" she said at last, in a low voice trembling with wrath and horror.

"Mercy! mercy!" murmured the priest, pressing his lips to her shoulders.

She seized his bald head in both hands by the hairs which remained, and strove to prevent his kisses as if they had been bites.

"Mercy!" repeated the unfortunate man. "If you knew what my love for you is! It is fire, molten lead, a thousand knives driven into my heart!"

And he held her arms with superhuman strength. She cried desperately: "Release me, or I shall spit in your face!"

He released her. "Degrade me, strike me, do your worst! do what you will! but have mercy! love me!"

Then she struck him with the impotent fury of a child. She clinched her lovely hands to bruise his face. "Demon, begone!"

"Love me! love me! have pity!" cried the poor priest, clasping her, and returning her blows with caresses.

All at once she felt him stronger than she.

"No more of this!" he exclaimed, gnashing his teeth.

She lay conquered, crushed, and quivering in his arms, at his mercy. She felt a wanton hand wandering over her. She made one last effort, and shrieked: "Help! help! a vampire! a vampire!"

No one came. Djali alone was awakened, and bleated piteously.

"Silence!" said the panting priest.

Suddenly, in her struggle, as she fought upon the floor, the gipsy's hand encountered something cold and metallic. It was Quasimodo's whistle. She seized it with a convulsion of hope, raised it to her lips, and blew with all her remaining strength. The whistle gave forth a sharp, shrill, piercing sound.

"What is that?" said the priest.

Almost as he spoke, he felt himself grasped by a vigorous arm. The cell was dark; he could not distinguish exactly who held him; but he heard teeth chattering with rage, and there was just enough light mingled with the darkness for him to see the broad blade of a cutlass gleam above his head.

He thought he recognized the figure of Quasimodo. He supposed that it could be no other. He remembered having stumbled, as he entered, over a bundle lying across the outside of the door. But as the new-comer did not utter a word, he knew not what to think. He flung himself upon the arm which held the cutlass, crying, "Quasimodo!" He forgot, in this moment of distress, that Quasimodo was deaf.

In the twinkling of an eye the priest was stretched on the floor, and felt a heavy knee pressed against his breast. By the angular imprint of that knee, he knew Quasimodo; but what was he to do? How was he also to be recognized by the hunchback? Night made the deaf man blind.

He was lost. The young girl, pitiless as an enraged tigress, did not interpose to save him. The cutlass came nearer his head; it was a critical moment. All at once his adversary appeared to hesitate.

"No blood upon her!" said he, in a dull voice.

It was indeed the voice of Quasimodo.

Then the priest felt a huge hand drag him from the cell by the heels; he was not to die within those walls. Luckily for him, the moon had risen some moments before.

When they crossed the threshold, its pale rays fell upon the priest. Quasimodo looked him in the face, trembled, relaxed his hold, and shrank back.

The gipsy, who had advanced to the door of her cell, saw with surprise that the actors had suddenly changed parts. It was now the priest who threatened, and Quasimodo who implored.

The priest, who was overwhelming the deaf man with gestures of wrath and reproach, violently signed him to withdraw.

The deaf man bowed his head, then knelt before the gipsy's door. "My lord," said he, in grave, submissive tones, "do what you will afterwards; but kill me first!"

So saying, he offered his cutlass to the priest. The priest, beside himself with rage, rushed upon him. But the young girl was quicker than he. She tore the knife from Quasimodo's hands, and uttered a frenzied laugh.

"Approach now!" she cried.

She held the blade high above her head. The priest stood irresolute. She would certainly have struck.

"You dare not touch me now, coward!" she exclaimed.

Then she added with a pitiless look, and knowing that her words would pierce the priest's heart like a thousand red-hot irons,—

"Ah, I know that Phœbus is not dead!"

The priest threw Quasimodo to the ground with a kick, and rushed down the stairs quivering with rage.

When he had gone, Quasimodo picked up the whistle which had just saved the gipsy.

"It was getting rusty," said he, returning it to her; then he left her alone.

The young girl, overcome by this violent scene, fell exhausted on her bed and burst into a flood of tears. Her horizon was again becoming overcast.

The priest, on his side, groped his way back to his cell.

That was sufficient. Don Claude was jealous of Quasimodo.

He repeated musingly the fatal words: "No one else shall have her!"

BOOK X

THE KING

CHAPTER I

GRINGOIRE HAS SEVERAL CAPITAL IDEAS IN SUCCESSION IN THE RUE DES BERNARDINS

WHEN Pierre Gringoire saw the turn which this whole matter was taking, and that a rope, hanging, and other unpleasant things must certainly be the fate of the chief actors in the play, he no longer cared to meddle with it. The Vagrants, with whom he remained, considering that after all they were the best company to be found in Paris,—the Vagrants still retained their interest in the gipsy. He thought this very natural on the part of people who, like her, had no prospect but Charmolue and Torterue to which to look forward, and who did not, like him, roam through the realms of imagination upon the wings of Pegasus. He learned from their conversation that his bride of the broken jug had taken refuge in Notre-Dame, and he was very glad of it; but he felt no temptation to visit her. He sometimes wondered what had become of the little goat, and that was all. In the daytime he performed feats of juggling for a living, and at night he wrought out an elaborate memorial against the Bishop of Paris; for he remembered being drenched by his mill-wheels, and he bore him a grudge for it. He also busied himself with comments on that fine work by Baudry-le-Rouge, Bishop of Noyon and Tournay, entitled *"De cupa petrarum,"* which had inspired him with an ardent taste for architecture,—a fancy which had replaced in his heart the passion for hermetics, of which indeed it was but a natural corollary, since there is a close connection between hermetics and masonry. Gringoire had turned from the love of an idea to love of the substance.

One day he halted near Saint-Germain-l'Auxerrois, at the corner of a building known as For-l'Evêque, which faces another known as For-le-Roi. This For-l'Evêque contained a charming fourteenth-century chapel, the chancel of which looked towards the street. Gringoire was devoutly studying the outside carvings. He was enjoying one of those moments of selfish, exclusive, supreme pleasure, during which the artist sees nothing in the world but art, and sees the world in art. All at once he felt a hand laid heavily on his shoulder. He turned. It was his former friend, his former master, the archdeacon.

He was astounded. It was a long time since he had seen the archdeacon, and Don Claude was one of those solemn and impassioned men a meeting with whom always upsets the equilibrium of a sceptic philosopher.

The archdeacon was silent for some moments, during which Gringoire had leisure to observe him. He found Don Claude greatly changed,—pale as a winter morning, hollow-eyed, his hair almost white. The priest at last broke the silence, saying in a calm but icy tone,—

"How are you, Master Pierre?"

"As to my health?" answered Gringoire. "Well, well! I may say I am tolerably robust, upon the whole. I take everything in moderation. You know, master, the secret of good health, according to Hippocrates: *'Id est: cibi, potus, somni, venus, omnia moderata sint.'*"

"Then you have nothing to trouble you, Master Pierre?" replied the archdeacon, looking fixedly at Gringoire.

"No, by my faith!"

"And what are you doing now?"

"You see, master, I am examining the cutting of these stones, and the style in which that bas-relief is thrown out."

The priest smiled a bitter smile, which only lifted one corner of his mouth.

"And does that amuse you?"

"It is paradise!" exclaimed Gringoire. And bending over the sculptures with the ravished mien of a demonstrator of living phenomena, he added: "For instance, don't you think that metamorphosis in low-relief is carved with exceeding skill, refinement, and patience? Just look at this little column. Around what capital did you ever see foliage more graceful or more daintily chiselled? Here are three of Jean Maillevin's alto-relievos. They are not the finest works of that great genius. Still, the ingenuousness, the sweetness of the faces, the careless ease of the attitudes and draperies, and that inexplicable charm which is mingled with all their defects, make these tiny figures most delicate and delightful, perhaps almost too much so. Don't you think this is entertaining?"

"Yes, indeed!" said the priest.

"And if you could only see the inside of the chapel!" continued the poet, with his garrulous enthusiasm. "Carvings everywhere, crowded as close as the leaves in the heart of a cabbage! The chancel is fashioned most devoutly, and is so peculiar that I have never seen its like elsewhere."

Don Claude interrupted him,—

"So you are happy?"

Gringoire eagerly replied,—

"Yes, on my honour! At first I loved women, then animals; now I love stones. They are quite as amusing as animals or women, and they are less treacherous."

The priest pressed his hand to his head. It was his habitual gesture.

"Indeed?"

"Stay!" said Gringoire; "you shall see my pleasures!" He took the arm of the unresisting priest, and led him into the staircase turret of For-l'Evêque. "There's a staircase for you! Every time I see it I am happy. It is the simplest and yet the rarest in Paris. Every step is bevelled underneath. Its beauty and simplicity consist in the treads, which, for a foot or more in width, are interlaced, mortised, dovetailed, jointed, linked together, and set into one another in a genuinely solid and goodly way."

"And you desire nothing more?"

"No."

"And you have no regrets?"

"Neither regret nor desire. I have arranged my mode of life."

"What man arranges," said Claude, "circumstances disarrange."

"I am a Pyrrhonian philosopher," replied Gringoire, "and I keep everything equally balanced."

"And how do you earn your living?"

"I still write occasional epics and tragedies; but what brings me in the most, is that trade which you have seen me follow, master,—namely, upholding pyramids of chairs in my teeth."

"That is a sorry trade for a philosopher."

"'Tis keeping up an equilibrium all the same," said Gringoire. "When one has but a single idea he finds it in everything."

"I know that!" responded the archdeacon.

After a pause he added,—

"And yet you are poor enough?"

"Poor! Yes; but not unhappy."

At this instant the sound of horses' hoofs was heard, and our two friends saw a company of archers belonging to the king's ordnance file by at the end of the street, with raised lances, and an officer at their head. The cavalcade was a brilliant one, and clattered noisily over the pavement.

"How you stare at that officer!" said Gringoire to the archdeacon.

"Because I think I have seen him before."

"What is his name?"

"I believe," said Claude, "that his name is Phœbus de Châteaupers."

"Phœbus! a queer name! There is also a Phœbus, Count de Foix. I once knew a girl who never swore save by Phœbus."

"Come with me," said the priest. "I have something to say to you."

Ever since the troops passed by, some agitation was apparent beneath the icy exterior of the archdeacon. He walked on; Gringoire followed, accustomed to obey him, like all who ever approached that man full of such ascendency. They reached the Rue des Bernardins in silence, and found it quite deserted. Here Don Claude paused.

"What have you to tell me, master?" asked Gringoire.

"Don't you think," replied the archdeacon, with a most reflective air, "that the dress of those horsemen whom we just saw is far handsomer than yours and mine?"

Gringoire shook his head.

"I' faith! I like my red and yellow jacket better than those scales of steel and iron. What pleasure can there be in making as much noise when you walk as the Quai de la Ferraille in an earthquake?"

"Then, Gringoire, you never envied those fine fellows in their warlike array?"

"Envied them what, Sir Archdeacon, —their strength, their armour, or their discipline? Philosophy and independence in rags are far preferable. I would rather be the head of a fly than the tail of a lion."

"That's strange," said the priest meditatively. "And yet a handsome uniform is a fine thing."

Gringoire, seeing that he was absorbed in thought, left him in order to admire the porch of a neighbouring house. He came back clapping his hands.

"If you were not so absorbed in the fine uniforms of those soldiers, Sir Archdeacon, I would beg you to take a look at that door. I always said that my lord Aubry's house had the most superb entrance in the world."

"Pierre Gringoire," said the archdeacon, "what have you done with the little gipsy dancer?"

"Esmeralda? What a sudden change of subject!"

"Was she not your wife?"

"Yes, by means of a broken jug. We are married for four years. By the way," added Gringoire, regarding the archdeacon with a half-bantering air, "are you still thinking of her?"

"And you,—do you think of her no longer?"

"Seldom. I have so many other things to occupy me. Heavens! how pretty that little goat of hers was!"

"Did not the girl save your life?"

"She did, indeed, by Jupiter!"

"Well, what has become of her? What have you done with her?"

"I can't say, I fancy that they hanged her."

"You really think so?"

"I'm not sure of it. When I saw that they had taken to hanging people, I withdrew from the game."

"Is that all you know about the matter?"

"Stay. I was told that she had taken refuge in Notre-Dame, and that she was in safety there, and I am delighted to hear it; and I can't find out whether the goat was saved along with her. And that's all I know about it."

"I'll tell you more," cried Don Claude; and his voice, hitherto so low, slow, and almost muffled, became as loud as thunder. "She did indeed take refuge in Notre-Dame. But within three days justice will again overtake her, and she will be hanged upon the Grève. Parliament has issued a decree."

"That's a pity!" said Gringoire.

The priest, in the twinkling of an eye, had recovered his coldness and calm.

"And who the devil," resumed the poet, "has amused himself by soliciting an order of restitution? Why couldn't he have left Parliament in peace? What harm does it do if a poor girl takes shelter under the flying buttresses of Notre-Dame, alongside of the swallows' nests?"

"There are Satans in the world," replied the archdeacon.

"That's a devilish bad job," observed Gringoire.

The archdeacon resumed, after a pause,—

"So she saved your life?"

"From my good friends the Vagrants. A little more, or a little less, and I should have been hanged. They would be very sorry for it now."

"Don't you want to do anything to help her?"

"With all my heart, Don Claude; but what if I should get myself into trouble?"

"What would that matter?"

"What! what would it matter? How kind you are, master! I have two great works but just begun."

The priest struck his forehead. In spite of his feigned calmness, an occasional violent gesture betrayed his inward struggles.

"How is she to be saved?"

Gringoire said: "Master, I might answer, '*Il padelt*,' which is Turkish for, 'God is our hope.' "

"How is she to be saved?" dreamily repeated the archdeacon.

Gringoire in his turn clapped his hand to his head.

"See here, master, I have a lively imagination; I will devise various expedients. Suppose the king were asked to pardon her?"

"Louis XI.,—to pardon!"

"Why not?"

"As well try to rob a tiger of his bone!"

Gringoire set to work to find some fresh solution of the difficulty.

"Well!—stop!—Do you want me to draw up a petition to the midwives declaring the girl to be pregnant?"

This made the priest's hollow eye flash.

"Pregnant, villain! do you know anything about it?"

Gringoire was terrified by his expression. He made haste to say, "Oh, no, not I! our marriage was a true *foris-maritagium*. I was entirely left out. But at any rate, we should gain time."

"Folly! infamy! be silent!"

"You are wrong to be so vexed," grumbled Gringoire. "We should gain time; it would do no one any harm, and the midwives, who are poor women, would earn forty Paris pence."

The priest paid no attention to him.

"And yet she must be got away!" he muttered. "The order will be executed within three days! Besides, even if there were no order, that Quasimodo! Women have very depraved tastes!" He raised his voice: "Master Pierre, I have considered it well; there's but one means of salvation for her."

"What is it? I, for my part, see none."

"Listen, Master Pierre, and remember that you owe your life to her. I will frankly tell you my idea. The church is watched night and day. No one is allowed to come out but those who are seen to go in. Therefore, you can go in. You will come, and I will take you to her. You will change clothes with her. She will put on your doublet; you will put on her gown."

"So far, so good," remarked the philosopher. "What next?"

"What next? She will walk out in your clothes; you will stay behind in hers. Perhaps they may hang you, but she will be saved."

Gringoire scratched his ear, with a very grave look.

"There!" said he; "that's an idea which would never have occurred to me."

At Don Claude's unexpected proposition, the poet's benign and open face had suddenly darkened, like a smiling Italian landscape when some fatal blast sweeps a cloud across the sun.

"Well, Gringoire, what do you say to the plan?"

"I say, master, that they would not hang me *perhaps*, but they would hang me without the slightest doubt."

"That does not concern us!"

"The deuce!" said Gringoire.

"She saved your life. You would only be paying your debt."

"There are plenty of others which I have not paid."

"Master Pierre, it absolutely must be done."

The archdeacon spoke with authority.

"Listen to me, Don Claude," replied the dismayed poet. "You cling to that idea, and you are wrong. I don't see why I should be hanged in another person's stead."

"What makes you so fond of life?"

"Oh, a thousand things!"

"What are they, if you please?"

"What? The air, the sky, morning and evening, moonlight, my good friends the Vagabonds, our larks with the girls, the architectural beauties of Paris to study, three big books to write,—one of which is directed against the bishop and his mills,—and I know not what else. Anaxagoras said that he came into the world to admire the sun; and besides, I have the pleasure of spending all my days, from morning till night, with a man of genius, to wit, myself, and that is a mighty agreeable thing."

"Rattle-pate!" muttered the archdeacon. "Well, speak; who preserved that life of yours which you find so delightful? To whom do you owe it that you still breathe this air, behold that sky, and are still able to amuse your feather-brain with trifles and nonsense? Where would you be now, but for her? Would you have her die, to whom you owe your life,—have her die, that sweet, lovely, adorable creature, necessary to the light of the world, more divine than God himself, while you, half madman and half sage, a mere sketch of something or other, a sort of vegetable growth which fancies that it walks and fancies that it thinks,—you are to go on living with the life of which you have robbed her, as useless as a candle at high noon? Come, have a little pity, Gringoire; be generous in your turn; she set you the example."

The priest was excited. At first Gringoire listened with an air of indecision; then he relented, and ended by pulling a tragic grimace, which made his pallid face look like that of a new-born baby with the colic.

"You are pathetic!" said he, wiping away a tear. "Well, I will consider it. That's an odd idea of yours. After all," he added, after a pause, "who knows? Perhaps they would not hang me. Betrothal is not always marriage. When they find me in her cell, so ridiculously arrayed, in cap and petticoats, perhaps they'll burst out laughing. And then, if they do hang me, why, the rope is like any other death; or, rather, it's not like any other death. It is a death worthy of the wise man who has wavered and swung to and fro all his life,—a death which is neither fish nor flesh, like the spirit of the genuine sceptic; a death fully impressed with Pyrrhonism and uncertainty, a happy medium between heaven and earth, which leaves one in suspense. It is the right death for a philosopher, and perhaps I was predestined to it. It is magnificent to die as one has lived."

The priest interrupted him: "Is it agreed?"

"What is death, after all?" continued Gringoire, with exaltation. "An unpleasant moment, a turnpike gate, the passage from little to nothing. Some one having asked Cercidas, of Magalopolis, if he was willing to die, 'Why not?' he answered: 'for after my death I shall see those great men,—Pythagoras among the philosophers, Hecatæus among the historians, Homer among the poets, Olympus among the musicians.'"

The archdeacon offered him his hand. "It is settled, then? You will come to-morrow."

This gesture brought Gringoire back to reality.

"Oh, no! by my faith!" said he in the tone of a man awakening from sleep. "To be hanged! That is too absurd. I'll not do it."

"Farewell, then!" and the archdeacon added between his teeth, "I shall see you again!"

"I have no desire to see that devil of a man again," thought Gringoire; and he hurried after Don Claude. "Stay, Sir Archdeacon; no malice between old friends! You take an interest in that girl,—in my wife, I should say; it is well. You have planned a stratagem for rescuing her from Notre-Dame; but your scheme is a very disagreeable one for me, Gringoire. Suppose I have another! I warn you that a most brilliant inspiration has just occurred to me. What if I have a suitable plan for getting her out of her evil plight without compromising my own neck in the least of slip-nooses, what would you say? Wouldn't that satisfy you? Is it absolutely necessary that I should be hanged, to suit you?"

The priest impatiently wrenched the buttons from his cassock, saying, "What a flood of words! What is your scheme?"

"Yes," resumed Gringoire, talking to himself, and laying his finger to his nose in token of his absorption, "that's just it! The Vagabonds are brave fellows. The gipsy nation love her! They will rise at a single word! Nothing easier! A sudden attack; amidst the confusion she can readily be carried off. To-morrow night. They will ask nothing better."

"Your plan! speak!" said the priest, shaking him roughly.

Gringoire turned majestically towards him. "Let me alone! Don't you see that I am in the throes of composition?" He reflected for a few moments more, then clasped his hands in delight, exclaiming, "Capital! success is assured!"

"Your plan!" angrily repeated Claude. Gringoire was radiant.

"Come close, and let me whisper it to you. It is really a jolly countermine, and one which will get us all out of difficulty. Zounds! you must confess that I am no fool."

He interrupted himself,—

"Oh, by the way! is the little goat still with the girl?"

"Yes. May the foul fiend fly away with you!"

"They were going to hang her too, were they not?"

"What is that to me?"

"Yes, they would have hanged her. They did hang a sow last month. The hangman likes that; he eats the animal afterwards. Hang my pretty Djali! Poor little lamb!"

"Curses on you!" cried Don Claude. "You are the executioner yourself. What means of saving her have you hit upon, rascal? Must I tear your idea from you with the forceps?"

"Softly, master! It is this."

Gringoire bent to the archdeacon's ear, and whispered to him, casting an anxious glance up and down the street meanwhile, although there was no one in sight. When he ended, Don Claude took his hand and said coldly, "It is well. Until to-morrow, then."

"Until to-morrow," repeated Gringoire. And as the archdeacon departed in one direction, he moved away in the other, muttering. "Here's a pretty business, Master Pierre Gringoire! Never mind! It shall not be said that because a man is little he is afraid of a great enterprise. Biton carried a full-grown bull upon his shoulders; wagtails, blackcaps, and stone-chats cross the sea."

Chapter II

TURN VAGABOND!

THE archdeacon, on returning to the cloisters, found his brother, Jehan du Moulin, awaiting him at the door of his cell. He had whiled away the fatigue of waiting by drawing upon the wall in charcoal his elder brother's profile, enriched with an exaggerated nose.

Don Claude scarcely looked at his brother; he had other cares. That merry roguish face, whose radiance had so often brightened the priest's gloomy countenance, was now incapable of dissipating the clouds which grew daily thicker over that corrupt, mephitic, stagnant soul.

"Brother," timidly said Jehan, "I have come to see you."

The archdeacon did not even deign to look at him.

"Well?"

"Brother," continued the hypocrite, "you are so good to me, and you give me such good advice, that I am always coming back to you."

"Well?"

"Alas! brother, how right you were when you said to me, 'Jehan! Jehan! *cessat doctorum doctrina, discipulorum, disciplina!* Jehan, be prudent; Jehan, be studious; Jehan, do not wander outside the college bounds at night without just cause and leave from your master. Do not quarrel with the Picards (*noli, Joannes, verberare Picardos*). Do not lie and moulder like an illiterate ass (*quasi asinus illiteratus*) amidst the litter of the schools. Jehan, suffer yourself to be punished at the discretion of your master. Jehan, go to chapel every evening, and sing an anthem with a collect and prayer to our Glorious Lady, the Virgin Mary.' Alas! What excellent counsels were these!"

"Well?"

"Brother, you see before you a guilty wretch, a criminal, a miserable sinner, a libertine, a monster! My dear brother, Jehan has trampled your advice beneath his feet. I am fitly punished for it, and the good God is strangely just. So long as I had money I rioted and revelled and led a jolly life. Oh, how charming is the face of Vice, but how ugly and crooked is her back! Now, I have not a single silver coin; I have sold my table-cloth, my shirt, and my towel; no more feasting for me! The wax candle has burned out, and I have nothing left but a wretched tallow dip, which reeks in my nostrils. The girls laugh at me. I drink water. I am tormented by creditors and remorse."

"What else?" said the archdeacon.

"Alas! dearest brother, I would fain lead a better life. I came to you full of contrition. I am penitent. I confess my sins. I beat my breast lustily. You were quite right to wish me to become a licentiate, and submonitor of the Collège of Torchi. I now feel that I have the strongest vocation for that office. But I have no ink, I must buy some; I have no pens, I must buy some; I have no paper, I have no books, I must buy some. I am in great want of a little money for all these things, and I come to you, brother, with a contrite heart."

"Is that all?"

"Yes," said the student. "A little money."

"I have none."

The student then said with a grave and at the same time resolute air, "Very well, brother: I am sorry to be obliged to tell you that very fine offers and propositions have been made me by another party. You will not give me the money? No? In that case, I shall turn Vagabond."

As he uttered this monstrous word, he assumed the expression of an Ajax, expecting to see the thunderbolt descend upon his head.

The archdeacon said coldly,—

"Turn Vagabond!"

Jehan bowed low and hurried down the cloister stairs, whistling as he went.

Just as he passed through the courtyard of the cloisters, under his brother's window, he heard that window open, looked up, and saw the archdeacon's stern face at the aperture.

"Go to the devil!" said Don Claude; "this is the last money which you will ever get from me!"

At the same time he flung at Jehan a purse which raised a large lump on his forehead, and with which he departed, at once angry and pleased, like a dog pelted with marrow-bones.

Chapter III

JOY FOREVER!

THE reader may remember that a part of the Court of Miracles was enclosed by the ancient boundary wall of the city, many of whose towers had at this time begun to fall into ruin. One of these towers had been made into a pleasure-house by the Vagabonds. There was a tavern in the lower portion, and other things above. This tower was the most lively and consequently the most horrible spot in the Vagrant community. It was a sort of monstrous bee-hive, which buzzed and hummed night and day. At night, when all the surplus beggars were asleep, when there was not a window still lighted in any of the dirty houses in the square, when no sound was longer to be heard from any of the innumerable hovels, the abode of swarms of thieves, prostitutes, and stolen children or foundlings, the jolly tower might always be known by the noise which rose from it, by the red light which, beaming alike from chimneys, windows, and cracks in the crumbling walls, escaped, as it were, at every pore.

The cellar, then, was the tavern. It was reached by a low door, and a flight of stairs as steep as a classic Alexandrine verse. Over the door, by way of sign, there was a marvellous daub portraying a number of coins fresh from the mint and fresh-killed chickens, with these punning words above: "The Ringers for the Dead."

One evening, when the curfew-bell was ringing from every belfry in Paris, the serjeants of the watch, had they chanced to enter the much-dreaded Court of Miracles, might have observed that there was even more uproar than usual in the tavern of the Vagabonds; that there was more drinking and more swearing than ordinary. Outside, in the square, numerous groups were chatting together in low tones, as if planning some great enterprise; and here and there some scamp squatted on the ground, sharpening a rusty iron blade upon a paving-stone. Within the tavern itself, however, cards and wine proved so powerful a diversion from the ideas which that evening occupied the minds of the Vagrant community that it would have been hard to guess from the remarks of the drinkers what the scheme on foot really was; they merely seemed somewhat more jovial than usual, and between the legs of every man glistened a weapon,—a pruning-hook, an axe, a big two-edged sword, or the hook of an old hackbut.

The room was circular in shape and very large; but the tables were so closely crowded and the topers so numerous that the entire contents of the tavern—men, women, benches, beer-jugs, drinkers, sleepers, gamblers, able-bodied and crippled—seemed to be heaped together pell-mell, with no more order or harmony than a pile of oyster-shells. A number of tallow dips burned on the tables; but the real luminary of the tavern, which played the same part as the chandelier in an opera-house, was the fire. This cellar was so damp that the fire on the hearth was never suffered to go out, even in midsummer

There was a huge fireplace with carved overhanging mantel, bristling with clumsy iron andirons and kitchen utensils, and one of those tremendous fires of wood and turf mixed, which at night, in village streets, cast such red and spectral images on the opposite walls from the window of a forge. A large dog sat soberly in the ashes, and turned a spit laden with meat before the embers.

In spite of the confusion, after the first glance, three principal groups were readily to be distinguished, pressing about three personages with whom the reader is already acquainted. One of these persons, grotesquely decked with various gaudy Oriental rags, was Mathias Hungadi Spicali, Duke of Egypt and Bohemia. The rascal sat upon a table, with crossed legs and uplifted finger, loudly dispensing his store of black and white magic to the many gaping faces around him. Another mob crowded closely about our old friend, the worthy King of Tunis, or lord of blacklegs, Clopin Trouillefou. Armed to the teeth, he was very seriously, and in low tones, superintending the pillage of an enormous cask full of weapons which stood staved in before him, and from which were disgorged quantities of axes, swords, priming-pans, coats of mail, spear-heads and antique lance-heads, arrows and cross-bow bolts, like so many apples and grapes from a cornucopia. Each took from the heap what he chose,—one a helmet, one a sword-blade, and another a *misericordia*, or cross-handled dagger. The very children armed themselves, and there were even legless cripples, crawling about, barbed and cuirassed, between the legs of the topers, like big beetles.

Lastly a third audience—the noisiest, jolliest, and most numerous of all—thronged the benches and tables, in whose midst held forth and swore a flute-like voice issuing from a heavy suit of armour, complete from helmet to spurs. The individual who had thus imprisoned himself in full panoply was so entirely hidden by his warlike habit that nothing was to be seen of him but an impudent, red, snub nose, a lock of light curly hair, a rosy mouth, and a pair of bold eyes. His belt was stuck full of daggers and knives, a huge sword hung at his side, a rusty cross-bow was on the other thigh, and a vast jug of wine stood before him; not to mention a plump and ragged damsel at his right hand. Every mouth in his vicinity laughed, cursed, and drank.

Add to these twenty secondary groups,—the serving men and maids running about with jugs on their heads; gamblers stooping over their marbles, their hop-scotch, dice, vachette, or exciting game of tringlet; the quarrels in one corner, the kisses in another,—and you will have some idea of the scene over which flickered the glare of a huge roaring fire, which made a myriad monstrous shadows dance upon the walls.

As for the noise, it was like the inside of a big bell ringing a full peal.

The dripping-pan, in which a shower of fat from the spit was crackling, filled up with its constant sputtering the intervals in the endless dialogues going on from one side of the hall to the other.

Amidst this uproar, a philosopher sat at the back of the room on the bench in the chimney-place, musing, with his feet in the ashes and his eyes on the burning brands; it was Pierre Gringoire.

"Come! make haste, arm yourselves! We march in an hour!" said Clopin Trouillefou to his Canters.

A girl hummed,—
  "Good-night, mamma; good-night, my sire;
  Who sits up last, rakes down the fire."

Two card-players disputed together.

"Knave," cried the redder-faced of the two, shaking his fist at the other, "I will mark you with the club; then you can take the place of Pam in the king's own pack of cards."

"*Ouf!*" roared a Norman, readily to be recognized by his nasal twang; "we are crowded together here like so many saints at Caillouville!"

"Boys," said the Duke of Egypt to his followers, speaking in falsetto tones, "the witches of France attend their Sabbath without broomstick, or ointment, or any steed, merely by uttering a few magical words. Italian witches always keep a goat waiting for them at the door. All are obliged to go up the chimney."

The voice of the young scamp armed from head to foot rose above the uproar.

"Noël! Noël!" he shouted. "To-day I wear armour for the first time. A Vagrant! I am a Vagrant, by Christ's wounds! Give me drink! Friends, my name is Jehan Frollo du Moulin, and I am a gentleman born. It is my opinion that if God himself were a dragoon, he would turn plunderer. Brothers, we are about to go on a fine expedition. We are valiant fellows. Assault the church, break open the doors, carry off the lovely damsel in distress, save her from her judges, save her from the priests; dismantle the cloisters, burn the bishop in his palace. We'll do all this in less time than it takes a burgomaster to eat a spoonful of soup. Our cause is just; we will strip Notre-Dame, and that's the end of it. We'll hang Quasimodo. Do you know Quasimodo, ladies? Did you ever see him ring the big bell of a Whit-Sunday until he was out of breath? My word! it's a lovely sight! He looks like a devil astride of a great gaping pair of jaws. Friends, listen to me. I am a Vagrant to my heart's core; I am a Canter in my inmost soul; I was born a Cadger. I have been very rich, and I've devoured my fortune. My mother meant to make a soldier of me; my father, a sub-deacon; my aunt, a member of the Court of Inquiry; my grandmother, prothonotary to the king; my great-aunt, a paymaster in the army; but I,—I turned Vagrant. I told my father that I had made my choice, and he hurled a curse at my head; and my mother,—she, poor old lady, fell to weeping and sputtering, like that log on the fire. A short life and a merry one, say I! I am as good as a whole houseful of lunatics! Landlady, my darling, more wine! I've money enough still to pay for it. No more Surène wine for me; it frets my throat. Zounds! I'd as soon gargle myself with a swarm of bees!"

Meantime, the rabble applauded his words with shouts of laughter; and seeing that the tumult about him increased, the student exclaimed:—

"Oh, what a delightful confusion! *Populi debacchantis populosa debacchatio!*" Then he began to sing, his eyes rolling in feigned ecstasy, in the voice of a canon intoning vespers: "*Quæ cantica; quæ organa! quæ cantilenæ! quæ melodiæ hic sine fine decantantur! Sonant melliflua hymnorum organa, suavissima angelorum melodia cantica canticorum mira—*" He stopped short: "Here, you devil of a tavern-keeper, give me some supper!"

There was a moment of comparative quiet, during which the sharp voice of the Duke of Egypt was heard in its turn, instructing his followers:—

"The weasel is called Aduine, the fox Blue-foot or the Wood-ranger, the wolf Grey-foot, or Gold-foot, the bear Old Man or Grandfather. The cap of a gnome will make its possessor invisible, and enable him to see invisible things. Every toad that is baptized should be clad in black or red velvet, a bell round its neck and another at its feet. The godfather holds it by the head, the godmother by the legs."

The Vagrants continued to arm, whispering together as they did so, at the other end of the tavern.

"Poor Esmeralda!" said a gipsy; "she's our sister. We must rescue her."

"Is she still at Notre-Dame?" asked a Jewish-looking Cadger.

"Yes, in good sooth, she is!"

"Well, then, comrades," cried the Cadger, "on to Notre-Dame! So much the more, that there are two statues in the chapel of Saint Féréol and Saint Ferrution,—one of Saint John the Baptist and the other of Saint Anthony,—of solid gold, the two together weighing seven golden marks and fifteen sterlings, and the silver-gilt pedestals weigh seventeen marks and five ounces. I know all about this; I am a jeweller."

Here Jehan's supper was served. He exclaimed, as he threw himself back upon the bosom of the girl next him:—

"By Saint Voult-de-Lucques, known to the world at large as Saint Goguelu, I am perfectly happy. Before me stands a fool staring at me with as smug a face as any archduke. And at my left elbow sits another, with teeth so long that they hide his chin. And then, too, I'm like Marshal de Gié at the siege of Pontoise,—my right wing rests upon an eminence. Body of Mahomet! comrade, you look very like a dealer in tennis-balls, and yet you dare to take your seat by my side! I am a noble, my friend. Nobility and trade cannot keep company. Get you gone! Hollo there, you fellows! don't fall to fighting. What! Baptiste Croque-Oison, you who have so fine a nose, will you risk it against the heavy fists of yonder lout? Donkey! *non cuiquam datum est habere nasum*. You are indeed divine, Jacqueline Ronge-Oreille! 'Tis a pity you're so bald. Hollo! my name is Jehan Frollo, and my brother is an archdeacon. May the devil take him! Every word I say is true. When I turned vagabond, I cheerfully renounced the half of a house situated in paradise, which my brother promised me (*Dimidiam domum in paradiso*). I quote the Scriptures. I have an estate in fee in the Rue Tire-chappe, and all the women are in love with me as truly as it is true that Saint Aloysius was an excellent goldsmith, and that the five handicrafts of the good city of Paris are those of the tanners, leather-dressers, baldric-makers, purse-makers, and cordwainers, and that Saint Lawrence was broiled over egg-shells. I swear, comrades,—

    'That for a year I'll drink no wine
    If there be any lie in words of mine!'

My charmer, it is moonlight; only look yonder, through that loop-hole; how the wind rumples the clouds,—as I do your tucker! Come, girls! snuff the children and the candles. Christ and Mahomet! what am I eating now, by Jupiter? Ho, there, you fagot! the hairs which are missing on the heads of your women, I find in your omelets. I say, old girl! I like my omelets bald. May the devil put your nose out of joint! A fine hostelry of Beelzebub this, where the wenches comb their heads with forks!"

So saying, he smashed his plate upon the paved floor, and fell to singing at the top of his lungs:—

    "And for this self of mine,
    Now by the Blood Divine!
    No creed I crave,
    No law to save.
    I have no fire,
    I have no hut;
    And I require
    No faith to put
    In monarch high
    Or Deity!"

Meantime, Clopin Trouillefou had finished his distribution of arms. He approached Gringoire, who seemed plunged in deep thought, with his feet upon an andiron.

"Friend Pierre," said the king of blacklegs, "what the deuce are you thinking about?"

Gringoire turned to him with a melancholy smile.

"I love the fire, my dear lord; not for the trivial reason that the fire warms our feet or cooks our soup, but because it throws out sparks. I sometimes spend hours in watching the sparks fly up. I discover a thousand things in these stars that sprinkle the black chimney-back. These stars are worlds as well."

"May I be struck by lightning if I understand you!" said the Vagrant. "Do you know what time it is?"

"I do not," replied Gringoire.

Clopin then went up to the Duke of Egypt:—

"Comrade Mathias, this is not a lucky moment for our scheme. They say that King Louis XI. is in Paris."

"So much the more reason for rescuing our sister from his claws," answered the old gipsy.

"You speak like a man, Mathias," said the King of Tunis. "Moreover, we will act adroitly. We need fear no resistance within the church. The canons are mere hares, and we muster strong. The officers of the Parliament will be nicely taken in to-morrow when they come to seize her! By the Pope's toe! I don't want the pretty maid hanged!"

With these words, Clopin left the tavern.

Meantime, Jehan shouted in hoarse tones,—

"I drink, I eat, I am drunk, I am Jupiter himself! Ha! Pierre l'Assommeur, if you stare at me like that, I'll dust your nose with a fillip or two!"

Gringoire, on his side, roused from his meditations, was contemplating the wild, noisy scene before him, muttering between his teeth: *"Luxuriosa res vinum et tumultuosa ebrietas.* Alas! I have good reasons for not drinking; and how aptly Saint Benedict says: *'Vinum apostatare facit etiam sapientes!'"*

At this instant Clopin returned, and cried in a voice of thunder,—

"Midnight!"

At this word, which had the effect of "Boot and saddle!" upon a regiment at rest, all the Vagrants, men, women, and children, rushed hurriedly from the tavern, with a great clatter of arms and old iron.

The moon was overcast.

The Court of Miracles was quite dark. There was not a light to be seen; and yet it was far from being empty. A crowd of men and women, talking together in low tones, had collected. There was an audible buzz of voices and a glitter of all sorts of weapons in the darkness. Clopin mounted a huge stone.

"To your ranks, Canters!" he cried. "To your ranks, Gipsies! To your ranks, Greeks!"

There was a stir in the gloom. The vast multitude seemed to be forming into line. After a brief pause the King of Tunis again raised his voice:—

"Now, silence as we pass through Paris! *'The chive in the cly'* is the password! The torches will not be lighted until we reach Notre-Dame! Forward, march!"

Ten minutes later the horsemen of the watch fled in terror before a long procession of dark, silent men descending upon the Pont au Change through the crooked streets which traverse the closely built region of the Markets in every direction.

Chapter IV

AN AWKWARD FRIEND

THAT same night Quasimodo did not sleep. He had just made his last round in the church. He did not notice, as he closed the doors, that the archdeacon passed, and seemed somewhat vexed at seeing him so carefully bolt and chain the immense iron bars which made the wide leaves as solid as a wall. Don Claude looked even more preoccupied than usual. Moreover, ever since his nocturnal adventure in the cell he had abused Quasimodo constantly; but though he maltreated him, nay, sometimes even beat him, nothing shook the submission, patience, and humble resignation of the faithful ringer. From the archdeacon he would bear anything and everything, — insults, threats, blows,—without murmuring a reproach, without uttering a complaint. At most he anxiously followed Don Claude with his eye, as he climbed the tower stairs; but the archdeacon had carefully abstained from appearing again in the gipsy's presence.

That night, then, Quasimodo, after giving a glance at his poor forsaken bells,—at Jacqueline, Marie, and Thibauld—had ascended to the roof of the north tower, and there, placing his well-closed dark-lantern upon the leads, gazed out over Paris. The night, as we have already said, was very dark. Paris, which at this time was but scantily lighted, presented to the eye a confused collection of black masses, intersected here and there by the silvery bend of the Seine. Quasimodo saw but a single light, and that in the window of a distant structure, the dim, dark outlines of which were distinctly visible above the roofs, in the direction of Porte Saint-Antoine. There, too, some one was watching.

While his one eye roamed over the expanse of mist and night, the ringer felt within him an inexplicable sense of alarm. For some days he had been upon his guard. He had constantly seen evil-looking men prowling about the church, and never taking their eyes from the young girl's hiding-place. He fancied that there might be some plot brewing against the unfortunate refugee. He imagined that she was a victim to popular hatred like himself, and that something might come of it soon. He therefore stationed himself upon his tower, on the alert, "dreaming in his dreamery," as Rabelais has it, his eye by turns bent upon the cell and upon Paris, keeping faithful watch, like a trusty dog, with a thousand doubts and fears.

All at once, while scrutinizing the great city with the one eye which Nature, by a sort of compensating justice, had made so piercing that it might almost supply the other organs which he lacked, it seemed to him that the outline of the Quai de la Vieille-Pelleterie looked somewhat peculiarly, that there was something moving at that point, that the line of the parapet darkly defined against the white water was not straight and steady like that of the other quays, but that it rippled, as he gazed, like the waves of a river or the heads of a moving multitude.

This struck him as singular. He redoubled his attention. The movement seemed to be towards the City. There was no light to be seen. It continued for some time, upon the quay; then it subsided gradually, as if whatever might be passing had entered the interior of the Island; then it ceased entirely, and the line of the quay became straight and motionless once more.

While Quasimodo was lost in conjectures, it seemed to him as if the movement had reappeared in the Rue du Parvis, which leads into the City directly opposite the front of Notre-Dame. At last, dense as was the darkness, he saw the head of a column emerge from that street, and in an instant fill the square with a crowd in which nothing could be distinguished in the shadows but that it was a crowd.

The spectacle had its terrors. It is probable that this strange procession, which seemed so desirous of stealing along unseen under cover of darkness, was equally careful to observe unbroken silence. And yet some noise appeared inevitable, were it only the tramp of feet. But this sound could not reach our deaf man's ear, and the vast host, so dimly seen, and wholly unheard by him, yet moving and marching onward so near him, produced upon him the effect of an army of ghosts, mute, impalpable, hidden in mists. He seemed to see a fog-bank full of men advancing upon him; to see shadows stirring amid the shades.

Then his fears revived; the idea of an attempt against the gipsy girl again presented itself to his mind. He had a confused sense that a violent scene was at hand. At this critical moment he held counsel with himself with better judgment and more promptness than could have been expected from so ill-organized a brain. Should he awaken the gipsy; help her to escape? Which way? The streets were invested; the church backed up against the river. There was no boat, no outlet! There was but one thing to be done,—to die if need be on the threshold of Notre-Dame; to resist at least until some help should come, if any there were, and not to disturb Esmeralda's sleep. The wretched girl would be wakened soon enough to die. This resolve once taken he began to scan the enemy with greater composure.

The crowd seemed to increase every moment in the square. He presumed that they must be making very little noise, as the windows in the streets and square remained closed. Suddenly a light shone out, and in an instant seven or eight blazing torches rose above the heads of the multitude, shaking out their tufts of flame in the darkness. Quasimodo then plainly saw an eddying, frightful mass of ragged men and women below him in the square, armed with scythes, pikes, bill-hooks, and halberds, whose myriad blades glistened on every hand. Here and there black pitchforks were reared horn-like above those hideous faces. He vaguely recalled this mob, and fancied he recognized the heads of those who had but a few months previous saluted him as Lord of Misrule. A man, grasping a torch in one hand and a whip in the other, climbed upon a post and seemed to be haranguing the crowd. At the same time the strange army went through a number of evolutions, as if taking up their station about the church. Quasimodo picked up his lantern and desscended to the platform between the towers, to get a nearer view and to consider means of defence.

Clopin Trouillefou, having arrived before the great door of Notre-Dame, had indeed drawn up his troops in line of battle. Although he did not expect to meet with any resistance, he desired, like a prudent general, to preserve such order as would enable him, if necessary, to confront a sudden attack from the watch. He had therefore stationed his brigade in such a way that, viewed from above and from a distance, you would have taken them for the Roman triangle of the battle of Ecnoma, the boar's head of Alexander, or the famous wedge of Gustavus Adolphus. The base of this triangle rested upon the farther end of the square, so that it blocked the Rue du Parvis; one side faced the Hôtel-Dieu, the other the Rue Saint-Pierre aux Bœufs. Clopin Trouillefou had placed himself at the head, with the Duke of Egypt, our friend Jehan, and the most daring of the dummy chuckers.

Such an attack as the vagrants were now planning to make upon Notre-Dame was no very uncommon thing in the towns of the Middle Ages. What are now known as police did not then exist. There was no central, controlling power in populous cities, or more particuarly in capitals. The feudal system constructed these large communities after a strange fashion. A city was a collection of a thousand seigniories, or manors, which divided it up into dis-·tricts of all shapes and sizes. Hence arose a thousand contradictory police forces; that is, no police at all. In Paris, for instance, independently of the one hundred and forty-one nobles laying claim to manorial rights, there were twenty-five who also claimed the additional right to administer justice,—from the Bishop of Paris who owned one hundred and five streets, down to the Prior of Notre-Dame des Champs who owned but four. All these feudal justiciaries recognized the supreme power of the king only in name. All had right of way; all were on their own ground. Louis XI., that indefatigable labourer who did such good work in beginning the demolition of the feudal structure, carried on by Richelieu and Louis XIV. to the advantage of royalty, and completed by Mirabeau to the advantage of the people,—Louis XI. had indeed striven to break this network of seigniories which enveloped Paris, by hurling violently athwart it two or three police ordinances. Thus in 1465 the inhabitants were commanded to light their windows with candles at nightfall, and to shut up their dogs, under pain of the halter; during the same year an order was issued that the streets must be closed with iron chains after dark, and citizens were forbidden to wear daggers or any offensive weapons in the street at night. But all these attempts at municipal legislation soon fell into disuse. People let the wind blow out the candles in their windows, and allowed their dogs to roam; the iron chains were only put up in time of siege; the prohibition of daggers led to but little change. The old framework of feudal jurisdiction remained standing,—an immense number of bailiwicks and seigniories, crossing one another throughout the city, crowded, tangled, interlapping, and interwoven; a useless confusion of watches, sub-watches, and counter-watches, in spite of which brigandage, rapine, and sedition were carried on by main force. It was not, therefore, an unheard-of thing, in the midst of such disorder, for a part of the populace to make a bold attack upon a palace, a great mansion, or a house, in the most thickly settled quarters of the town. In the majority of cases the neighbours did not meddle with the matter, unless the pillage extended to their own houses. They turned a deaf ear to the musketry, closed their shutters, barricaded their doors, left the outbreak to be settled with or without the watch, and next day it would be reported: "Last night Etienne Barbette's house was entered." "Marshal Clermont was carried off," etc. Accordingly, not only royal habitations, the Louvre, the Palace, the Bastille, the Tournelles, but the houses of the nobility, the Petit-Bourbon, the Sens mansion, the D'Angoulême mansion, etc., had their battlemented walls and their portcullises. Churches were guarded by their sanctity. Certain of them, however, but not Notre-Dame, were fortified. The abbot of Saint-Germain des Prés was as strongly intrenched as any baron, and more brass was consumed there in bombards than in bells. His fortress was still standing in 1610. Now the church alone exists, and that in ruins.

Let us return to Notre-Dame.

When the first arrangements had been made (and we must say, to the honour of the discipline of the Vagrants, that Clopin's orders were carried out in silence and with admirable precision), the worthy leader of the band mounted the parapet of the Parvis, and raised his hoarse, surly voice, keeping his face turned towards Notre-Dame, and waving his torch, the flame of which, flickering in the wind, and now and again veiled by its own smoke, first revealed and then hid the front of the church, lit up with a reddish glow.

"To you, Louis de Beaumont, Bishop of Paris, Councillor of the Court of Parliament, I, Clopin Trouillefou, king of blacklegs, king of rogues, prince of cant, and bishop of fools, proclaim: Our sister, falsely condemned for magic, has taken refuge in your church. You owe her shelter and safeguard. Now, the Parliamentary Court desire to recover her person, and you have given your consent; so that indeed she would be hanged to-morrow on the Grève were not God and the Vagrants here to aid her. We have therefore come hither to you, O Bishop. If your church be sacred, our sister is likewise sacred; if our sister be not sacred, neither is your church. Wherefore we summon you to deliver over to us the girl if you would save your church, or we will seize upon the girl, and will plunder the church, which will be a righteous deed. In token whereof I here plant my banner; and may God have you in his guard, O Bishop of Paris!"

Unfortunately Quasimodo could not hear these words, uttered as they were with a sort of sombre, savage majesty. A Vagrant handed the banner to Clopin, who planted it solemnly between two flagstones. It was a pitchfork, from whose prongs hung a bleeding mass of carrion.

This done, the King of Tunis turned and glanced at his army,—a fierce host, whose eyes glittered almost as brightly as their pikes. After an instant's pause he cried,—

"Forward, boys! To your work, rebels!"

Thirty stout fellows, with sturdy limbs and crafty faces, stepped from the ranks with hammers, pincers, and crowbars on their shoulders. They advanced towards the main entrance of the church, mounted the steps, and were soon crouching beneath the arch, working away at the door with pincers and levers. A crowd of Vagrants followed them to help or encourage. They thronged the eleven steps leading to the porch.

Still the door refused to yield. "The devil! how tough and obstinate it is!" said one. "It is old, and its joints are stiff," said another. "Courage, comrades!" replied Clopin. "I'll wager my head against an old slipper that you'll have opened the door, captured the girl, and stripped the high-altar before a single sacristan is awake. Stay! I think the lock is giving way."

Clopin was interrupted by a tremendous din behind him. He turned. A huge beam had fallen from the sky; it had crushed a dozen of his Vagrants on the church steps and rebounded to the pavement with the crash of a cannon, breaking the legs of various tatterdemalions here and there in the crowd, which scattered with cries of terror. In the twinkling of an eye the enclosed portion of the square was cleared. The rebels, although protected by the deep arches of the porch, forsook the door, and Clopin himself retired to a respectful distance.

"I had a narrow escape!" cried Jehan. "I felt the wind of it as it passed, by Jove! but Pierre l'Assommeur is knocked down!"

It is impossible to picture the mingled consternation and affright which overcame the bandits with the fall of this beam. They stood for some moments staring into the air, more dismayed by that fragment of wood than by twenty thousand of the king's archers.

"Satan!" growled the Duke of Egypt; "that smells of sorcery!"

"It must be the moon which flung that log at us," said Andry le Rouge.

"Why," replied François Chanteprune, "they say the moon is a friend of the Virgin Mary!"

"By the Pope's head!" exclaimed Clopin; "but you are a parcel of fools!" And yet even he could not explain the fall of the plank.

Meanwhile, nothing was to be seen upon the front of the cathedral, to the top of which the light of the torches did not reach. The heavy plank lay in the middle of the square, and loud were the groans of the wretched men who had received its first shock, and who had been almost cut in two upon the sharp edges of the stone steps.

The King of Tunis, his first dismay over, at last hit upon an explanation which seemed plausible to his companions:—

"Odds bodikins! are the canons defending themselves? Then, sack! sack!"

"Sack!" repeated the rabble, with a frantic cheer. And they discharged a volley of cross-bows and hackbuts at the church.

At this sound the peaceable inhabitants of the houses round about were awakened; several windows were thrown open, and nightcaps and hands holding candles appeared at them.

"Fire at the windows!" roared Clopin. The windows were hastily closed, and the poor citizens, who had barely had time to cast a terrified glance at that scene of glare and tumult, returned to sweat with fear beside their wives, wondering if the witches were holding their revels in the square before Notre-Dame, or if the Burgundians had made another attack, as in '64. Then the husbands thought of robbery, the wives of violence, and all trembled.

"Sack!" repeated the Canters; but they dared not advance. They looked at the church; they looked at the beam. The beam did not bulge, the building retained its calm, deserted look; but something rooted the Vagrants to the spot.

"To work, I say, rebels!" shouted Trouillefou. "Force the door!!"

No one stirred.

"Body o' me!" said Clopin; "here's a pack of fellows who are afraid of a rafter."

"Captain, it's not the rafter that stops us; it's the door, which is entirely covered with iron bars. Our pincers are of no use."

"Well, what would you have to burst it in?" asked Clopin.

"Ah! we need a battering-ram."

The King of Tunis ran bravely up to the much-dreaded beam, and set his foot upon it. "Here you have one," he exclaimed; "the canons themselves have sent it to you." And with a mocking salutation in the direction of the church, he added, "Thanks, gentlemen!"

This piece of bravado proved effective; the charm of the beam was broken. The Vagrants recovered their courage; soon the heavy log, lifted like a feather by two hundred sturdy arms, was furiously hurled against the great door which they had vainly striven to shake. Seen thus, in the dim light cast by the scanty torches of the Vagrants, that long beam borne by that crowd of men, who rapidly dashed it against the church, looked like some monstrous beast with countless legs attacking the stone giantess headforemost.

At the shock of the log, the semi-metallic door rang like a vast drum; it did not yield, but the whole cathedral shook and the deep vaults of the building re-echoed.

At the same moment a shower of large stones began to rain from the top of the façade upon the assailants.

"The devil!" cried Jehan; "are the towers shaking down their balustrades upon our heads?"

But the impulse had been given, the King of Tunis setting the example. The bishop was certainly defending himself; and so they only beat against the door with greater fury, despite the stones which cracked their skulls to right and left.

It is remarkable that these stones all fell singly, but they followed one another in rapid succession. The Canters always felt two at a time,—one at their legs, the other on their heads. Few of them missed their mark, and already a large heap of dead and wounded gasped and bled under the feet of the besiegers, whose ranks, they being now goaded to madness, were constantly renewed. The long beam still battered the door at regular intervals, like the clapper of a bell; the stones still rained down, and the door creaked and groaned.

The reader has doubtless guessed that the unexpected resistance which so enraged the Vagrants came from Quasimodo.

Chance had unluckily served the brave deaf man.

When he descended to the platform between the towers, his head whirled in confusion. For some moments he ran along the gallery, coming and going like a madman, looking down from above at the compact mass of Vagrants ready to rush upon the church, imporing God or the devil to save the gipsy girl. He thought of climbing the south belfry and ringing the alarm; but before he could set the bell in motion, before big Marie's voice could utter a single shriek, the church door might be forced ten times over. This was just the instant when the rebels advanced with their tools. What was to be done?

All at once he remembered that the masons had been at work all day repairing the wall, timbers, and roof of the south tower. This was a ray of light. The wall was of stone, the roof of lead, and the timbers of wood. (The timbers were so huge, and there were so many of them, that they went by the name of "the forest.")

Quasimodo flew to the tower. The lower rooms were indeed full of materials. There were piles of rough stones, sheets of lead in rolls, bundles of laths, heavy beams already shaped by the saw, heaps of plaster and rubbish,—a complete arsenal.

There was no time to be lost. The hammers and levers were at work below. With a strength increased tenfold by his sense of danger, he lifted one of the beams, the heaviest and longest that he could find; he shoved it through a dormer-window, then laying hold of it again outside the tower, he pushed it over the edge of the balustrade surrounding the platform, and launched it into the abyss. The enormous rafter, in its fall of one hundred and sixty feet, scraping the wall, smashing the carvings, turned over and over several times like one of the arms of a windmill moving through space. At last it reached the ground; an awful shriek rose upon the air, and the black beam, rebounding from the pavement, looked like a serpent darting on its prey.

Quasimodo saw the Vagrants scatter, as the log fell, like ashes before the breath of a child. He took advantage of their terror; and while they stared superstitiously at the club dropped from heaven, and put out the eyes of the stone saints over the porch with a volley of arrows and buckshot, Quasimodo silently collected plaster, stones, gravel, even the masons' bags of tools, upon the edge of that balustrade from which the beam had already been launched.

Thus, as soon as they began to batter at the door, the hail of stones began to fall, and it seemed to them as if the church were falling about their heads.

Any one who had seen Quasimodo at that moment would have been frightened. Besides the projectiles which he had piled upon the balustrade, he had collected a heap of stones on the platform itself. As soon as the missiles at the edge of the railing were exhausted, he had recourse to the heap below. He stooped and rose, stooped and rose again, with incredible activity. His great gnome-like head hung over the balustrade, then a huge stone fell, then another, and another. Now and again he followed a particularly fine stone with his eye, and if it did good execution he said, "Hum!"

Meantime the ragamuffins were not discouraged. More than twenty times already the heavy door which they were attacking had trembled beneath the weight of their oaken battering-ram, multiplied by the strength of a hundred men. The panels cracked; the carvings flew in splinters; the hinges, at every blow, shook upon their screw-rings; the boards were reduced to powder, crushed between the iron braces. Luckily for Quasimodo, there was more iron than wood.

Still, he felt that the great door was yielding. Although he could not hear, every stroke of the beam echoed at once through the vaults of the church and through his soul. He saw from above the Vagrants, full of rage and triumph, shaking their fists at the shadowy façade; and he coveted, for himself and for the gipsy girl, the wings of the owls which flew over his head in numbers.

His shower of stones did not suffice to repel the enemy.

At this moment of anguish he observed, a little below the balustrade from which he was crushing the Canters, two long stone gutters, or spouts, which emptied directly over the great door. The inner orifice of these spouts opened upon a level with the platform. An idea flashed into his mind. He ran to the hovel which he occupied as ringer, found a fagot, placed upon this fagot a quantity of bundles of laths and rolls of lead,—ammunition which he had not yet used,—and having carefully laid this pile before the mouth of the two spouts, he set fire to it with his lantern.

During this space of time, the stones having ceased to fall, the Vagrants had also ceased to look up. The bandits, panting like a pack of dogs which have hunted a wild boar to his lair, crowded tumultuously about the door, disfigured by the battering-ram, but still holding firm. They awaited, with a shudder of eagerness, the final blow which should shiver it. Each one strove to be nearest to it, that he might be first, when it opened, to rush into that wealthy cathedral, the vast magazine in which were stored all the riches of three centuries. They reminded each other, with roars of joy and greed, of the beautiful silver crosses, the gorgeous brocade copes, the superb monuments of silver-gilt, the magnificences of the choir, the dazzling holiday displays, the Christmas ceremonies glittering with torches, the Easters brilliant with sunshine,—all the splendid and solemn occasions when shrines, candlesticks, pyxes, tabernacles, and reliquaries embossed the altars with incrusted gold and diamonds. Certainly at this auspicious moment gonnofs and arch-thieves, ruffians and sham Abrams thought far less of freeing the gipsy girl than they did of sacking Notre-Dame. We would even be willing to believe that to a goodly number of them Esmeralda was but a mere pretext,—if thieves require a pretext.

All at once, just as they gathered together about the battering-ram for a final effort, every man holding his breath and straining his muscles so as to lend all his strength to the decisive blow, a howl more frightful even than that which had risen and died away from beneath the rafter, again burst from their midst. Those who did not shriek, those who lived, looked up. Two streams of molten lead fell from the top of the building into the very thickest of the throng. The sea of men had subsided beneath the boiling metal which had made, at the points where it fell, two black and smoking holes in the crowd, as boiling water would in snow. About them writhed the dying, half consumed, and shrieking with agony. Around the two principal jets there were drops of this horrible rain which sprinkled the assailants, and penetrated their skulls like gimlets of flame. A leaden fire riddled the poor wretches as with countless hailstones.

The clamour was heartrending. They fled pell-mell, flinging the beam upon the corpses, the courageous with the timid, and the square was cleared for the second time.

All eyes were turned to the top of the church. What they saw was most strange. Upon the top of the topmost gallery, higher than the central rose-window, a vast flame ascended between the two belfries with whirling sparks,—a vast flame, fierce and strong, fragments of which were ever and anon borne away by the wind with the smoke. Below this flame, below the dark balustrade with its glowing trefoils, two spouts, terminating in gargoyles, vomiting unintermittent sheets of fiery rain, whose silvery streams shone out distinctly against the gloom of the lower part of the cathedral front. As they approached the ground, these jets of liquid lead spread out into sheaves, like water pouring from the countless holes of the rose in a watering-pot. Above the flame, the huge towers, each of which showed two sides, clear and trenchant, one all black, the other all red, seemed even larger than they were, from the immensity of the shadow which they cast, reaching to the very sky. Their innumerable carvings of demons and dragons assumed a mournful aspect. The restless light of the flames made them seem to move. There were serpents, which seemed to be laughing, gargoyles yelping, salamanders blowing the fire, dragons sneezing amid the smoke. And among these monsters, thus wakened from their stony slumbers by the flame, by the noise, there was one that walked about, and moved from time to time across the fiery front of the burning pile like a bat before a candle.

Doubtless this strange beacon would rouse from afar the woodcutter on the hills of Bicêtre, in alarm at seeing the gigantic shadow of the towers of Notre-Dame cast flickering upon his moors.

The silence of terror fell upon the Vagrants, and while it lasted nothing was heard save the cries of consternation uttered by the canons shut up in the cloisters, and more restive than horses in a burning stable, the stealthy sound of windows hastily opened and more hastily closed, the bustle and stir in the Hospital, the wind roaring through the flames, the last gasp of the dying, and the constant pattering of the leaden rain upon the pavement.

Meantime, the leaders of the Vagrants had withdrawn to the porch of the Gondelaurier house, and were holding council. The Duke of Egypt, seated on a post, gazed with religious awe at the magical pile blazing in the air at the height of two hundred feet. Clopin Trouillefou gnawed his brawny fists with rage.

"Impossible to enter!" he muttered between his teeth.

"An old witch of a church!" growled the aged gipsy Mathias Hungadi Spicali.

"By the Pope's whiskers!" added a grey-haired old scamp who had served his time in the army, "here are church-spouts that beat the portcullis of Lectoure at spitting molten lead."

"Do see that demon walking to and fro before the fire!" exclaimed the Duke of Egypt.

"By the Rood!" said Clopin, "it's that damned bell-ringer; it's Quasimodo!"

The gipsy shook his head. "I tell you that it is the spirit Sabnac, the great marquis, the demon of fortifications. He takes the form of an armed soldier, with a lion's head. He turns men to stones, with which he builds towers. He commands fifty legions. It is surely he; I recognize him. Sometimes he is clad in a fine gown of figured gold made in the Turkish fashion."

"Where is Bellevigne de l'Etoile?" asked Clopin.

"He is dead," replied a Vagrant woman.

Andry le Rouge laughed a foolish

laugh. "Notre-Dame makes plenty of work for the hospital," said he.

"Is there no way to force that door?" cried the King of Tunis, stamping his foot.

The Duke of Egypt pointed sadly to the two streams of boiling lead which still streaked the dark façade like two long phosphorescent spindles.

"Churches have been known to defend themselves before," he observed with a sigh. "St. Sophia, at Constantinople, some forty years ago, thrice threw down the crescent of Mahomet merely by shaking her domes, which are her heads. Guillaume de Paris, who built this church, was a magician."

"Must we then go home discomfited like a pack of wretched lackeys?" said Clopin, "and leave our sister here, to be hanged by those cowled wolves to-morrow!"

"And the sacristy, where there are cartloads of gold?" added a Vagabond whose name we regret that we do not know.

"By Mahomet's beard!" cried Trouillefou.

"Let us make one more trial," added the Vagabond.

Mathias Hungadi shook his head.

"We shall not enter by the door. We must find the weak spot in the old witch's armour,—a hole, a back gate, any joint."

"Who'll join us?" said Clopin. "I shall have another try. By the way, where is that little student Jehan, who put on such a coat of mail?"

"He is probably dead," answered some one; "we don't hear his laugh."

The King of Tunis frowned: "So much the worse. There was a stout heart beneath that steel. And Master Pierre Gringoire?"

"Captain Clopin," said Andry le Rouge, "he took to his heels when we had only come as far as the Pont-aux-Changeurs."

Clopin stamped his foot. "By the Mass! he urges us on, and then leaves us in the lurch! A cowardly prater, helmeted with a slipper!"

"Captain Clopin," said Andry le Rouge, who was looking down the Rue du Parvis, "there comes the little student."

"Pluto be praised!" said Clopin. "But what the devil is he lugging after him?"

It was indeed Jehan, running as fast as was possible under the weight of his heavy armour and a long ladder which he dragged sturdily over the pavement, more breathless than an ant harnessed to a blade of grass twenty times its own length.

"Victory! *Te Deum!*" shouted the student. "Here's the ladder belonging to the longshoremen of St. Landry's wharf."

Clopin approached him:—

"Zounds, child! what are you going to do with that ladder?"

"I've got it," replied Jehan, panting and gasping. "I knew where it was,—under the shed at the lieutenant's house. There's a girl there who knows me, who thinks me a perfect Cupid. I took advantage of her folly to get the ladder, and I have the ladder, odds bodikins! The poor girl came down in her shift to let me in."

"Yes," said Clopin; "but what will you do with the ladder now that you have got it?"

Jehan looked at him with a mischievous, cunning air, and cracked his fingers like so many castanets. At that moment he was sublime. He had on his head one of those enormous fifteenth-century helmets, which terrified the foe by their fantastic crests. It bristled with ten iron beaks, so that he might have disputed the tremendous cognomen of δεκέμβολος, with Nestor's Homeric vessel.

"What shall I do with it, august King of Tunis? Do you see that row of statues with their foolish faces yonder, above the three porches?"

"Yes; what then?"

"That is the gallery of the kings of France."

"What is that to me?" said Clopin.

"Wait a bit! At the end of that gallery there is a door which is always on the latch, and with this ladder I will climb to it, and then I am in the church."

"Let me go up first, boy!"

"Not a bit of it, comrade; the ladder is mine. Come, you may be second."

"May Beelzebub strangle you!" said the surly Clopin. "I'll not be second to any man."

"Then, Clopin, seek a ladder for yourself;" and Jehan set out at full speed across the square, dragging his ladder after him, shouting,—

"Help, lads, help!"

In an instant the ladder was lifted, and placed against the railing of the lower gallery, over one of the side doors. The crowd of Vagrants, uttering loud cheers, thronged to the foot of it, eager to ascend; but Jehan maintained his right, and was first to set foot upon the rounds. The journey was long and slow. The gallery of the kings of France is now some sixty feet above the pavement. The eleven steps leading to the door made it still higher at the time of our story. Jehan climbed slowly, hampered by his heavy armour, clinging to the ladder with one hand and his cross-bow with the other. When he reached the middle, he cast a melancholy glance downwards at the poor dead Canters who bestrewed the steps.

"Alas!" said he, "there's a heap of corpses worthy of the fifth book of the Iliad!" Then he resumed his ascent. The Vagrants followed him; there was one upon every round. As this undulating line of cuirassed backs rose through the darkness, it looked like a serpent with scales of steel rearing its length along the church. Jehan, who represented the head, whistled shrilly, thus completing the illusion.

At last the student touched the balcony, and nimbly strode over it, amid the applause of the assembled Vagrants. Thus master of the citadel, he uttered a shout of joy, and all at once paused, petrified. He had seen behind one of the royal statues Quasimodo and his glittering eye lurking in the shadow

Before a second assailant could set foot upon the gallery, the terrible hunchback leaped to the top of the ladder, seized, without a word, the ends of the two uprights in his strong hands, raised them, pushed them from the wall, balancing for a moment, amid screams of agony, the long, pliant ladder loaded with Vagrants from top to bottom, and then suddenly, with superhuman force, hurled the clustering mass of men into the square. There was an instant when the boldest trembled. The ladder plunged backward, for a moment stood erect, and seemed to hesitate, then tottered, then all at once, describing a frightful arc of eighty feet in radius, fell headlong on the pavement with its burden of bandits, more swiftly than a drawbridge when the chains which hold it are broken. There was an awful volley of curses, then all was hushed, and a few mutilated wretches crawled away from under the heap of dead.

A clamour of rage and pain followed the first cries of triumph among the besiegers. Quasimodo looked on unmoved, leaning upon the balustrade. He seemed like some long-haired old king at his window.

Jehan Frollo, for his part, was in a critical situation. He was alone in the gallery with the dreadful ringer, parted from his companions by a perpendicular wall eighty feet high. While Quasimodo juggled with the ladder, the student hurried to the postern, which he supposed would be open. Not at all. The deaf man, on entering the gallery had fastened it behind him. Jehan then hid himself behind a stone king, not daring to breathe, and eyeing the monstrous hunchback with terror, like the man who, making love to the wife of the keeper of a menagerie, went one night to see her by appointment, climbed the wrong wall, and abruptly found himself face to face with a white bear.

For a few moments the deaf man paid no heed to him; but finally he turned his head and started. He had just seen the student.

Jehan prepared for a rude encounter; but the deaf man stood motionless: he had merely turned, and was looking at the youth.

"Ho! ho." said Jehan, "why do you fix that single melancholy eye so steadfastly upon me?"

As he said this, the young scamp slyly adjusted his cross-bow.

"Quasimodo," he cried, "I am going to change your name! Henceforth you shall be called 'the blind!'"

The arrow flew. The winged bolt whizzed through the air, and was driven into the hunchback's left arm. It disturbed Quasimodo no more than a scratch would have done the statue of King Pharamond. He put his hand to the dart, pulled it forth, and quietly broke it across his great knee; then he let the two pieces fall to the ground rather than threw them down. But Jehan had no time to fire a second shot. The arrow broken, Quasimodo drew a long breath, leaped like a grasshopper, and came down upon the student, whose armour was flattened against the wall by the shock.

Then by the dim light of the torches a terrible thing might have been seen. Quasimodo with his left hand grasped both Jehan's arms, the poor fellow making no resistance, so hopeless did he feel that it would be. With his right hand the deaf man removed from him one after the other, in silence and with ominous slowness, all the pieces of his armour,—the sword, the daggers, the helmet, the cuirass, and the brassarts. He looked like a monkey picking a nut as he dropped the student's iron shell, bit by bit, at his feet.

When the youth found himself stripped, disarmed, naked, and helpless in those terrible hands, he did not try to speak to that deaf man, but he laughed impudently in his face, and sang, with the bold unconcern of a lad of sixteen, the song then popular:—

"She's clad in bright array,
The city of Cambray.
Marafin plundered her one day—"

He did not finish. They saw Quasimodo upright on the parapet, holding the boy by the feet with one hand, and swinging him round like a sling over the abyss; then a sound was heard like a box made of bone dashed against a wall, and something fell, but caught a third of the way down upon a projection. It was a dead body which hung there, bent double, the back broken, the skull empty.

A cry of horror rose from the Vagrants.

"Vengeance!" yelled Clopin. "Sack!" replied the multitude. "Assault! assault!"

Then there was an awful howl, intermingled with all languages, all dialects, and all accents. The poor student's death filled the mob with zealous fury. Shame gained the upper hand, and wrath that they had so long been held in check before a church by a hunchback. Rage found ladders, multiplied torches, and in a few moments Quasimodo, in despair, beheld that fearful swarm mounting on all sides to attack Notre-Dame. Those who had no ladders had knotted ropes; those who had no ropes scrambled up by the jutting sculptures. They clung to one another's rags. There was no way to resist this rising tide of awful figures; fury gleamed from their fierce faces; their grimy foreheads streamed with perspiration; their eyes gleamed; all these grimaces, all these deformities beset Quasimodo. It seemed as if some other church had sent its gorgons, its mediæval animals, its dragons, its demons, and its most fantastic carvings, to lay siege to Notre-Dame. A stratum of living monsters seemed to cover the stone monsters of the cathedral front.

Meantime, the square was starred with a thousand torches. The scene of confusion, hitherto lost in darkness, was suddenly ablaze with light. The square shone resplendent, and cast a red glow upon the heavens; the bonfire kindled upon the high platform still burned, and lighted up the city in the distance. The huge silhouette of the two towers, outlined afar upon the housetops of Paris, formed a vast patch of shadow amid the radiance. The city seemed to be aroused. Distant alarm-bells sounded. The Vagrants howled, panted, swore, climbed higher and higher; and Quasimodo, powerless against so many foes, shuddering for the gipsy girl, seeing those furious faces approach nearer and nearer to his gallery, implored Heaven to grant a miracle, and wrung his hands in despair.

Chapter V

THE RETREAT WHERE LOUIS OF FRANCE SAYS HIS PRAYERS

THE reader may remember that a moment before he caught sight of the nocturnal band of Vagrants, Quasimodo, while inspecting Paris from the top of his belfry, saw but one light still burning, and that gleamed from a window in the highest story of a tall dark structure close beside the Porte Saint-Antoine. This building was the Bastille;

that starry light was the candle of Louis XI.

King Louis XI. had actually been in Paris for two days. He was to set out again two days later for his fortress of Montilz-les-Tours. His visits to his good city of Paris were rare and brief; for he never felt that he had enough trap-doors, gibbets, and Scotch archers about him there.

He had that day come to sleep at the Bastille. The great chamber, five fathoms square, which he had at the Louvre, with its huge chimney-piece adorned with twelve great beasts and thirteen great prophets, and his great bed eleven feet by twelve, suited him but ill. He was lost amid all these grandeurs. This good, homely king preferred the Bastille, with a tiny chamber and a simple bed. And then, the Bastille was stronger than the Louvre.

This tiny room, which the king reserved to his own use in the famous state-prison, was spacious enough, after all, and occupied the topmost floor of a turret adjoining the keep. It was a circular chamber, carpeted with mats of lustrous straw, ceiled with beams enriched with *fleurs-de-lis* of gilded metal, with coloured interjoists wainscotted with rich woods studded with rosettes of white metal painted a fine bright green, compounded of orpiment and wood.

There was but one window,—a long arched opening latticed with brass wire and iron bars, and still further darkened by beautiful stained glass emblazoned with the arms of the king and queen, each pane of which was worth twenty-two pence.

There was but one entrance,—a modern door, with surbased arch, hung with tapestry on the inside, and on the outside decorated with a porch of bog-wood, a frail structure of curiously wrought cabinet-work, such as was very common in old houses some hundred and fifty years ago. "Although they are disfiguring and cumbersome," says Sauval, in despair, "still, our old folk will not do away with them, and retain them in spite of everything."

The room contained none of the furniture ordinarily found in such an apartment,—neither b e n c h e s, nor trestles, nor common box stools, nor more elegant stools mounted on posts and counter-posts, at four pence each. There was only one chair,—a folding-chair with arms,—and a very superb one it was: the wood was painted with roses on a red ground, the seat was of scarlet Spanish leather, trimmed with heavy silk fringe and studded with countless golden nails. The solitary chair showed that but one person had a right to be seated in that room. Besides the chair, and very near the window there was a table covered with a cloth embroidered with figures of birds.

Upon this table were a standish spotted with ink, sundry parchments, a few pens, and a chased silver goblet. Farther away stood a stove, and a prayer-desk of crimson velvet embossed with gold. Lastly, at the back of the room there was a simple bed of yellow and carnation-coloured damask, without tinsel or lace,—merely a plain fringe. This bed, famous for having borne the sleep,—or sleeplessness,—of Louis XI., might still be seen two hundred years ago, at the house of a councillor of state, where it was viewed by old Madame Pilou, celebrated in "Cyrus," under the name of "Arricidia" and of "Morality Embodied."

Such was the room known as "the retreat where Louis of France says his prayers."

At the moment when we introduce our reader to it, this retreat was very dark. The curfew had rung an hour before; it was night, and there was but one flickering wax candle placed on the table to light five persons grouped about the room.

The first upon whom the direct rays of the candle fell was a nobleman, magnificently dressed in scarlet breeches and jerkin striped with silver, and a loose coat with padded shoulders, made of cloth of gold brocaded in black. This splendid costume, upon which the light played, seemed to be frosted with flame at every fold. The man who wore it had his armorial bearings embroidered on his breast in gay colours, —a chevron with a deer passant at the base of the shield. The escutcheon was supported by an olive-branch dexter and a buck's horn sinister. This man wore at his belt a rich dagger, the silver-gilt handle of which was wrought in the shape of a crest, and surmounted by a count's coronet. He had an evil expression, a haughty mien, and a proud bearing. At the first glance his face revealed arrogance, at the second craft.

He stood bare-headed, a long scroll in his hand, behind the arm-chair in which sat, his body awkwardly bent, his knees crossed, his elbow on the table, a most ill-attired person. Imagine, indeed, upon the luxurious Spanish leather seat, a pair of knock knees, a couple of slender shanks meagrely arrayed in black woollen knitted stuff, a body wrapped in a fustian coat edged with fur, which had far more skin than hair; finally, to crown the whole, a greasy old hat, of the poorest quality of black cloth, stuck round with a circlet of small leaden images. This, with a dirty skull-cap, which showed scarce a single hair, was all that could be seen of the seated personage. His head was bent so low upon his breast that nothing could be distinguished of his face, which was wholly in shadow, unless it might be the tip of his nose, upon which a ray of light fell, and which was clearly a long one. By the thinness of his wrinkled hand, he was evidently an old man. This was Louis XI.

Some distance behind them, two men clad in Flemish fashion chatted together in low tones. They were not so entirely in the shadow but that any one who had been present at the performance of Gringoire's play could recognize them as two of the chief Flemish envoys, Guillaume Rym, the wise pensionary of Ghent, and Jacques Coppenole, the popular hosier. It will be remembered that these two men were connected with Louis XI.'s secret policy.

Lastly, at the farther end of the room, near the door, stood in the gloom, motionless as a statue, a sturdy man with thickset limbs, in military trappings, his doublet embroidered with armorial bearings, whose square face, with its goggle eyes, immense mouth, and ears hidden under two broad penthouses of straight, lank hair, partook at once of the character of the dog and the tiger.

All were uncovered save the king.

The gentleman nearest to the king was reading a lengthy document, to which his Majesty seemed listening most attentively. The two Flemings whispered together.

"Zounds!" grumbled Coppenole, "I am weary with standing; is there no chair here?"

Rym replied by a shake of the head, accompanied by a prudent smile.

"Zounds!" resumed Coppenole, utterly miserable at being obliged to lower his voice; "I long to sit down on the floor, with my legs crossed, in true hosier style, as I do in my own shop at home."

"Beware how you do so, Master Jacques."

"Bless me! Master Guillaume! must we be on our feet forever here?"

"Or on our knees," said Rym.

At this moment the king spoke. They were silent.

"Fifty pence for the coats of our lackeys, and twelve pounds for the cloaks of the clerks of our crown. That's it! pour out gold by the ton! Are you mad, Olivier?"

So saying, the old man lifted his head. The golden shells of the collar of Saint Michel glistened about his neck. The light of the candle fell full upon his thin, peevish profile. He snatched the paper from his companion's hands.

"You will ruin us!" he cried, running his hollow eye over the scroll. "What is all this? What need have we for so vast an establishment? Two chaplains at ten pounds a month each, and an assistant at one hundred pence! A valet at ninety pounds a year! Four head cooks at six-score pounds a year each; a roaster, a soup-maker, a sauce-maker, an under cook, a keeper of the stores, two stewards' assistants, at ten pounds a month each! Two scullions at eight pounds! A groom and his two helpers at twenty-four pounds a month! A porter, a pastry-cook, a baker, two wagoners, each sixty pounds a year! And the farrier, six-score pounds! And the master of our exchequer chamber, twelve hundred pounds! And the comptroller five hundred! And I know not how many more! 'Tis sheer madness! Our servants' wages plunder France! All the treasures of the Louvre will melt away before such a wasting fire of expense! We will sell our plate! And next year, if God and Our Lady [here he raised his hat] grant us life, we will take our diet-drinks from a pewter pot!"

With these words he cast a glance at the silver goblet which sparkled on the table. He coughed, and continued,—

"Master Olivier, princes who reign over great domains, such as kings and emperors, should never suffer extravagant living in their houses; for thence the fire spreads to the provinces. Therefore, Master Olivier, forget this not. Our expenses increase yearly. The thing displeases us. What, by the Rood! until '79 they never exceeded thirty-six thousand pounds; in '80 they amounted to forty-three thousand six hundred and nineteen pounds,—I have the figures in my head; in '81 they were sixty-six thousand six hundred and eighty pounds; and this year, by my faith! they will come to eighty thousand pounds! Doubled in four years! monstrous!"

He paused for lack of breath; then he went on angrily,—

"I see around me none but people

fattening on my leanness! You suck crowns from me at every pore!"

All were silent. His rage must be allowed free vent. He continued:—

"It is like that petition in Latin from the nobles of France, that we would re-establish what they call the charges on the crown! Charges, indeed! crushing charges! Ah, gentlemen! you say that we are not a king to reign *dapifero nullo, buticulario nullo!* We will show you, by the Rood! whether we be a king or no!"

Here he smiled with a sense of his power; his bad humour moderated, and he turned towards the Flemings:

"Mark you, gossip Guillaume, the head pantler, the chief cellarer, the lord chamberlain, the lord seneschal, are not worth so much as the meanest lackey; remember that, gossip Coppenole. They are good for nothing. As they thus hang uselessly around the king, they remind me of the four Evangelists about the dial of the great clock on the Palace, which Philippe Brille has just done up as good as new. They are gilded over, but they do not mark the hour, and the hands go on as well without them."

For a moment he seemed lost in thought, and added, shaking his aged head:—

"Ho! ho! by Notre-Dame, I am no Philippe Brille, and I will not re-gild my lordly vassals! Go on, Olivier!"

The person thus addressed took the scroll from his royal master's hands, and began to read again in a loud voice:—

"To Adam Tenon, clerk to the keeper of the seals of the provosty of Paris, for the silver, fashioning, and engraving of said seals, which have been new made by reason of the others preceding being old and worn out, and no longer fit for use, twelve Paris pounds.

"To Guillaume Frère, the sum of four pounds four Paris pence for his labour and cost in nourishing and feeding the pigeons in the two dovecots of the Hôtel des Tournelles, for the months of January, February, and March of this present year; for the which he hath expended seven sextaries of barley.

"To a Grey Friar, for confessing a criminal, four Paris pence."

The king listened in silence. From time to time he coughed; then he raised the goblet to his lips, and swallowed a mouthful with a wry face.

"In this year have been made by order of the courts and by sound of trumpet, in the public places of Paris, fifty-six proclamations; the account yet to be made up.

"For quest and search in sundry places, both in Paris and elsewhere, for funds said to be concealed there, but nothing found, forty-five Paris pounds."

"A crown buried to unearth a penny!" said the king.

"For setting six panes of white glass at the Hôtel des Tournelles, in the place where the iron cage is, thirteen pence; for making and delivering, by the king's command, on muster-day, four escutcheons with the arms of our said lord wreathed all around with roses, six pounds; for two new sleeves to the king's old doublet, twenty pence; for a box of grease to grease the king's boots, fifteen farthings; for rebuilding a sty to lodge the king's black swine, thirty Paris pounds; sundry partitions, planks, and gratings made for the safe-keeping of the lions at the Hôtel Saint-Pol, twenty pounds."

"Here be costly beasts," said Louis XI. "Never mind, 't is a luxury which befits a king. There is one big tawny lion that I love for his pretty tricks. Have you seen him, Master Guillaume? Princes must needs keep these rare wild beasts. We kings should have lions for lapdogs, and tigers instead of cats. Grandeur beseems a crown. In the time of Jupiter's pagans, when the people offered an hundred sheep and an hundred oxen to the gods, emperors gave an hundred lions and an hundred eagles. That was fierce and very fine. The kings of France have ever had these roarings round their throne; nevertheless, my subjects must do me the justice to say that I spend far less money in that way than my predecessors, and that I am much more moderate as regards lions, bears, elephants, and leopards. Go on, Master Olivier. We merely wished to say this much to our Flemish friends."

Guillaume Rym bowed low, while Coppenole, with his sullen air, looked like one of those bears to which his Majesty referred.

The king did not notice him. He wet his lips with the liquid in the goblet, and spat the brew out again, saying "Faugh! what a disagreeable diet-drink!" The reader continued:—

"For feeding a rascally tramp, kept under lock and key in the little cell at the shambles for six months, until it should be decided what to do with him, six pounds and four pence."

"What's that?" interrupted the king; "feed what should be hanged! By the Rood! I will not pay one penny for his keep! Olivier, settle the matter with Master d'Estouteville, and this very night make me preparations for this gallant's wedding with the gallows. Go on."

Olivier made a mark with his thumb-nail against the item of the rascally tramp, and resumed:—

"To Henriet Cousin, chief executioner of Paris, the sum of sixty Paris pence, to him adjudged and ordered by the lord provost of Paris, for having bought, by order of the said provost, a broadsword for the execution and decapitation of all persons condemned by the courts for their demerits, and having it furnished with a scabbard and all thereunto appertaining; and likewise for having the old sword sharpened and repaired, it having been broken and notched in doing justice upon my lord Louis of Luxembourg, as herein more fully set down—"

The king interrupted. "Enough; I cheerfully order the sum to be paid. There are expenses which I never regard; I have never regretted such moneys. Continue."

"For repairing a great cage—"

"Ah!" said the king, grasping the arms of his chair with both hands, "I knew that I came here to the Bastille for a purpose. Stay, Master Olivier; I desire to see this cage for myself. You may read the costs while I examine it. Gentlemen of Flanders, come and look at it; it is a curious sight."

Then he rose, leaned upon his reader's arm, signed to the mute who stood at the door to go before him, to the two Flemings to follow him, and left the room.

The royal party was increased at the door of the retreat by men-at-arms weighed down with steel, and slender pages bearing torches. It proceeded for some time through the interior of the gloomy keep, perforated with staircases and corridors in the thickness of the walls. The captain of the Bastille walked at the head of the procession, and ordered the gates to be thrown open before the bent and feeble old king, who coughed as he moved along.

At every wicket gate all heads were forced to stoop, except that of the old man bowed by age. "Hum!" he mumbled, for he had lost all his teeth, "we are all ready for the door of the tomb. A low door needs a stooping passenger."

At last, after passing through a final gate so encumbered with locks that it took a quarter of an hour to open it, they entered a lofty, spacious, vaulted hall, in the middle of which they saw, by the light of the torches, a huge and massive cube of masonry, iron, and wood. The interior was hollow. It was one of those famous cages meant for prisoners of state, which were known by the name of "the king's daughters." In its sides were two or three small windows, so closely grated with heavy iron bars that the glass was entirely hidden. The door was a great flat stone slab, such as are used for tombs,—one of those doors used for entrance only. But here, the dead man was a living being.

The king walked slowly around the little structure, carefully examining it, while Master Olivier, who followed him, read aloud:—

"For repairing a great cage of heavy wooden joists, girders, and timbers, being nine feet long by eight in breadth, and seven feet high between the planks, planed, and clamped with strong iron clamps, which has been placed in a room in one of the towers of the Bastille Saint-Antoine, in which cage is put and kept, by command of our lord the king, a prisoner formerly dwelling in a worn-out and crazy old cage. There were used for the said new cage ninety-six horizontal beams and fifty-two uprights, ten girders eighteen feet long. Nineteen carpenters were employed for twenty days, in the court of the Bastille, to square, cut, and fit all the said wood."

"Quite fine heart of oak," said the king, rapping on the timber with his knuckles.

". . . There were used in this cage," continued the other, "two hundred and twenty large iron clamps, of eight and nine feet, the rest of medium length, with the screws, roller-bolts, and counter-bands requisite for said clamps, all the aforesaid iron weighing three thousand seven hundred and thirty-five pounds; besides eight large iron bolts serving to fasten the said cage, with the nails and clamp-irons, weighing all together two hundred and eighteen pounds; not to mention the iron gratings for the windows of the room wherein the cage was placed, the iron bars on the door, and other items—"

"Here's a mighty deal of iron," said the king, "to restrain the lightness of one mind!"

". . . The whole amounts to three hundred and seventeen pounds five pence and seven farthings."

"By the Rood!" exclaimed the king.

At this oath, which was Louis XI.'s favourite imprecation, some one seemed to waken within the cage: chains rattled loudly against the wood-work, and a faint voice, which appeared to issue from the tomb, cried: "Sire! Sire! Pardon!" But no one could see the person uttering these words.

"Three hundred and seventeen pounds five pence and seven farthings!" repeated Louis XI.

The piteous voice which issued from the cage had chilled the blood of all present, even that of Master Olivier himself. The king alone appeared as if he had not heard it. At his command Master Olivier resumed his reading, and his Majesty calmly continued his inspection of the cage.

"Moreover, there has been paid to a mason who made the holes to receive the window-bars, and the floor of the room in which the cage stands, forasmuch as the floor could not have borne this cage by reason of its weight, twenty-seven pounds and fourteen Paris pence—"

The voice again began its moan:—

"Mercy, Sire! I swear that it was my lord Cardinal of Angers, and not I, who plotted the treason."

"The mason charges well!" said the king. "Go on, Olivier!"

Olivier continued:—

"To a joiner, for window-frames, bedstead, close stool, and other items, twenty pounds two Paris pence—"

The voice continued likewise:—

"Alas! Sire! will you not hear me? I protest that it was not I who wrote that thing to my lord of Guyenne, but his highness Cardinal Balue!"

"The joiner is dear," observed the king. "Is that all?"

"No, Sire. To a glazier, for the window-panes in said chamber, forty-six pence eight Paris farthings."

"Have mercy, Sire! Is it not enough that all my worldly goods were given to my judges, my silver plate to M. de Torcy, my books to Master Pierre Doriolle, my tapestries to the Governor of Roussillon? I am innocent. For fourteen years I have shivered in an iron cage. Have mercy, Sire! You will find your reward in heaven."

"Master Olivier," said the king, "what is the sum total?"

"Three hundred and sixty-seven pounds eight pence three Paris farthings."

"By'r Lady!" cried the king. "What an extravagant cage!"

He snatched the scroll from Master Olivier's hands, and began to reckon up the items himself upon his fingers, looking by turns at the paper and the cage. Meantime, the prisoner's sobs were plainly to be heard. It was a doleful sound in the darkness, and the by-standers paled as they gazed into one another's faces.

"Fourteen years, Sire! full fourteen years! ever since the month of April, 1469. In the name of the Blessed Mother of God, Sire, hear me! You have enjoyed the warmth of the sun all these years. Shall I, poor wretch, never again behold the light of day? Pity me, Sire! Be merciful. Clemency is a goodly and a royal virtue, which turns aside the stream of wrath. Does your Majesty believe that it will greatly content a king in the hour of his death, to reflect that he has never let any offence go unpunished? Moreover, Sire, I never did betray your Majesty; it was my lord of Angers. And I wear about my leg a very heavy chain, and a great ball of iron at the end of it, far heavier than is reasonable. Ah, Sire, have pity upon me!"

"Olivier," said the king, shaking his head, "I observe that these fellows charge me twenty pence the hogshead for plaster, which is worth only twelve. Have this account corrected."

He turned his back on the cage, and prepared to leave the room. The miserable prisoner guessed by the receding torches and noise that the king was departing.

"Sire! Sire!" he cried in tones of despair.

The door closed. He saw nothing more, he heard nothing save the harsh voice of the jailor singing in his ears the song:—

"Master Jean Balue,
Has quite lost view
Of his bishoprics cherished.
My lord of Verdun
Has not a single one;
Every one hath perished."

The king silently reascended to his retreat, and his train followed him, terrified by the prisoner's last groans. All at once his Majesty turned to the governor of the Bastille.

"By the way," said he, "was there not some one in that cage?"

"Zounds, Sire, yes!" replied the governor, lost in amaze at such a question.

"Who, then?"

"The Bishop of Verdun."

The king was better aware of this than any one else; but this was his way.

"Ah!" said he, with an innocent semblance of thinking of it for the first time, "Guillaume de Harancourt, the friend of Cardinal Balue,—a merry devil of a bishop!"

A few moments later the door of the retreat was reopened, then closed again upon the five persons whom we saw there at the beginning of this chapter, and who resumed their places, their low-voiced conversation, and their former attitudes.

During the king's absence a number of despatches had been laid on the table, and he now broke the seals. Then he rapidly read them one after the other, motioned to Master Olivier, who seemed to perform the office of his minister, to take a pen, and without imparting the contents of the despatches to him, began to dictate answers in an undertone, the latter writing them down, kneeling uncomfortably at the table.

Guillaume Rym watched him.

The king spoke so low that the Flemings caught but a few detached and scarcely intelligible fragments, such as:—

". . . keep up fertile places by commerce and sterile ones by manufactures. Show the English lords our four bombards, the London, Brabant, Bourg-en-Bresse, and Saint-Omer. . . Artillery occasions war to be more wisely waged at the present time. . . To Monsieur de Bressuire, our friend. . . . Armies cannot be maintained without tribute," etc.

Once he raised his voice:—

"By the Rood! the King of Sicily seals his letters with yellow wax, like a king of France. We may be wrong to allow him this privilege. My fair cousin of Burgundy gave no armorial bearings upon a field gules. The greatness of a house is ensured by holding its prerogatives intact. Note that, gossip Olivier."

Again:—

"Oho!" said he, "an important message this! What would our brother the emperor have?" And running his eye over the missive, he interrupted his reading with constant exclamations: "Surely the Germans are so great and powerful that 't is scarcely credible. But we are not unmindful of the old proverb: The finest country is Flanders; the fairest duchy, Milan; the most beauteous kingdom, France. Is it not so, Sir Flemings?"

This time Coppenole bowed with Guillaume Rym. The hosier's patriotism was tickled.

The last despatch made Louis XI. frown.

"What's this?" he exclaimed. "Complaints and requisitions against our garrisons in Picardy! Olivier, write with speed to Marshal de Rouault: That discipline is relaxed. That the men-at-arms of the ordnance, the nobles of the ban, the free-archers, and the Swiss guards do infinite injury to the peasants. That the soldiers, not content with the goods which they find in the houses of the tillers of the soil, constrain them, by heavy blows of bludgeons and sticks, to seek throughout the town for wine, fish, spices, and other articles of luxury. That the king is well aware of all this. That we intend to preserve our people from all unseemly acts, larceny, and pillage. That this is our sovereign will by Our Lady! That, moreover, it likes us not that any minstrel, barber, or serving man-at-arms should go arrayed like a prince; in velvet, silken cloth, and rings of gold. That these vanities are hateful in the sight of God. That we content ourselves—we who are a gentleman of high degree—with one cloth doublet at sixteen pence the Paris ell. That soldiers' servants may well come down to that also. We command and order these things. To Monsieur de Rouault, our friend. Good!"

He dictated this letter in a loud voice, in a firm tone, and by fits and starts. Just as he ended it, the door opened and admitted a new personage, who rushed into the room in extreme alarm, shouting,—

"Sire! Sire! the people of Paris have risen in revolt!"

The grave face of Louis XI. was convulsed; but every visible sign of emotion passed away like a flash of lightning. He restrained himself, and said with calm severity,—

"Gossip Jacques, you enter somewhat abruptly!"

"Sire! Sire! there is a revolt!" replied the breathless gossip Jacques.

The king, who had risen, took him roughly by the arm and whispered in his ear in a manner to be heard by him alone, with concentrated rage, and a sidelong glance at the Flemings,—

"Hold your tongue, or speak low!"

The new-comer understood, and began to tell him in a low voice a very incoherent tale, to which the king listened with perfect composure, while Guillaume Rym drew Coppenole's attention to the new-comer's face and dress, his furred hood (*caputia fourrata*), his short epitoge (*epitogia curta*), and his black velvet gown, which bespoke a president of the Court of Accounts.

This person had no sooner given the king a few details, than Louis XI. cried with a burst of laughter,—

"Indeed! Speak up boldly, gossip Coictier! Why do you talk so low? Our Lady knows that we hide nothing from our good Flemish friends."

"But, Sire—"

"Speak up boldly!"

Gossip Coictier was dumb with surprise.

"So," resumed the king,—"speak, sir, —there is a commotion among the common people in our good city of Paris?"

"Yes, Sire."

"And it is directed, you say, against the Bailiff of the Palace of Justice?"

"It looks that way," said the gossip, who still stammered and hesitated, utterly astounded by the sudden and inexplicable change which had been wrought in the king's sentiments.

Louis XI. added: "Where did the watch encounter the mob?"

"Moving from the chief haunt of the beggars and vagrants towards the Pont-aux-Changeurs. I met them myself on my way hither to execute your Majesty's orders. I heard certain of the number shouting, 'Down with the Bailiff of the Palace!'"

"And what is their grievance against the bailiff?"

"Ah!" said gossip Jacques, "that he is their lord."

"Really!"

"Yes, Sire. They are rascals from the Court of Miracles. They have long inveighed against the bailiff, whose vassals they are. They refuse to recognize him either as justiciary or road-surveyor."

"Ay, say you so!" returned the king, with a smile of satisfaction which he vainly strove to disguise.

"In all their petitions to Parliament," added gossip Jacques, "they claim that they have but two masters,—your Majesty and their God, who is, I believe, the devil."

"Hah!" said the king.

He rubbed his hands; he laughed that inward laugh which makes the face radiant; he could not disguise his joy, although he tried at times to compose himself. No one understood his mood, not even Master Olivier. He was silent for a moment, with a pensive but contented air.

"Are they strong in numbers?" he asked suddenly.

"Indeed they are, Sire," replied gossip Jacques.

"How many?"

"At least six thousand."

The king could not help exclaiming, "Good!" He added, "Are they armed?"

"With scythes, pikes, hackbuts, mattocks, and all sorts of dangerous weapons."

The king seemed by no means alarmed at this account. Gossip Jacques felt obliged to add,—

"If your Majesty send not promptly to the bailiff's aid, he is lost."

"We will send," said the king, with an assumed expression of seriousness. "It is well. Certainly we will send. The bailiff is our friend. Six thousand! They are determined knaves. Their boldness is marvellous, and we are greatly wroth at it; but we have few people about us to-night. It will be time enough in the morning."

Gossip Jacques exclaimed, "Straightway, Sire! The bailiff's house may be sacked twenty times over, the seigniory profaned, and the bailiff hanged, ere then. For the love of God, Sire, send before to-morrow morning!"

The king looked him in the face. "I said to-morrow." It was one of those looks which admit of no reply. After a pause, Louis XI. again raised his voice. "Gossip Jacques, you must know— What was—" He corrected himself. "What is the bailiff's feudal jurisdiction?"

"Sire, the Bailiff of the Palace has jurisdiction from the Rue de la Calandre to the Rue de l'Herberie, the Place Saint-Michel, and the places commonly called the Mureaux, situated near the church of Notre-Dame des Champs [here the king lifted the brim of his hat], which residences are thirteen in number; besides the Court of Miracles, the lazaretto known as the Banlieue, and all the highway beginning at this lazar-house and ending at the Porte Saint-Jacques. Of these divers places he is road-surveyor, high, low, and middle justiciary, and lord paramount."

"Hey-day!" said the king, scratching his left ear with his right hand; "that is a goodly slice of my city. And so the bailiff was king of all that?"

This time he did not correct himself. He continued to muse, and as if speaking to himself, said,—

"Have a care, Sir Bailiff! You had a very pretty piece of our Paris in your grasp."

All at once he burst forth. "By the Rood! Who are all these people who claim to be commissioners of highways, justiciaries, lords, and masters in our midst; who have their toll-gate in every bit of field, their gibbet and their hangman at every cross-road among our people, in such fashion that, as the Greek believed in as many gods as there were fountains, and the Persian in as many as he saw stars, the Frenchman now counts as many kings as he sees gallows? By the Lord! this thing is evil, and the confusion likes me not. I would fain know whether it be by the grace of God that there are other inspectors of highways in Paris than the king, other justice than that administered by our Parliament, and other emperor than ourselves in this realm! By the faith of my soul! the day must come when France shall know but one king, one lord, one judge, one headsman, even as there is but one God in paradise!"

He again raised his cap, and went on, still meditating, with the look and tone of a hunter loosing and urging on his pack of dogs: "Good! my people! bravely done! destroy these false lords! do your work. At them, boys! at them! Plunder them, capture them, strip them! Ah, you would fain be kings, gentlemen? On, my people, on!"

Here he stopped abruptly, bit his lip, as if to recall a thought which had half escaped him, bent his piercing eye in turn upon each of the five persons who stood around him, and all at once, seizing his hat in both hands, and staring steadily at it, he thus addressed it: "Oh, I would burn you if you knew my secret thoughts!"

Then again casting about him the

attentive, anxious glance of a fox returning by stealth to his earth, he added,—

"It matters not; we will succour the bailiff. Unfortunately, we have but few troops here to send forth at this moment against so large a populace. We must needs wait until to-morrow. Order shall be restored in the City, and all who are taken shall be strung up on the spot."

"By-the-bye, Sire!" said gossip Coictier, "I forgot it in my first dismay, —the watch has caught two stragglers of the band. If it please your Majesty to see these men, they are here."

"If it please me to see them!" cried the king. "Now, by the Rood! do you forget such things! Run quickly, you, Olivier! go and fetch them."

Master Olivier went out, and returned a moment after with the two prisoners, surrounded by archers of the ordnance. The first had a fat, stupid face, with a drunken and astonished stare. He was dressed in rags, and bent his knee and dragged his foot as he walked. The second was a pale, smiling fellow, whom the reader already knows.

The king studied them for an instant without speaking, then abruptly addressed the first:—

"Your name?"

"Gieffroy Pincebourde."

"Your business?"

"A Vagabond."

"What part did you mean to play in that damnable revolt?"

The Vagabond looked at the king, swinging his arms with a dull look. His was one of those misshapen heads, where the understanding flourishes as ill as the flame beneath an extinguisher.

"I don't know," he said. "The others went, so I went too."

"Did you not intend outrageously to attack and plunder your lord the Bailiff of the Palace?"

"I know that they were going to take something from some one. That's all I know."

A soldier showed the king a pruning-bill, which had been found upon the fellow.

"Do you recognize this weapon?" asked the king.

"Yes, it is my bill; I am a vine-dresser."

"And do you acknowledge this man as your companion?" added Louis XI., pointing to the other prisoner.

"No. I do not know him."

"Enough," said the king. And beckoning to the silent, motionless person at the door, whom we have already pointed out to our readers:—

"Friend Tristan, here is a man for you."

Tristan l'Hermite bowed. He gave an order in a low voice to two archers, who led away the poor Vagrant.

Meantime the king approached the second prisoner, who was in a profuse perspiration. "Your name?"

"Sire, Pierre Gringoire."

"Your trade?"

"A philosopher, Sire!"

"How dared you, varlet, go and beset our friend the Bailiff of the Palace, and what have you to say about this uprising of the people?"

"Sire, I had naught to do with it."

"Come, come, rascal! were you not taken by the watch in this evil company?"

"No, Sire; there is a mistake. It was an accident. I write tragedies. Sire, I entreat your Majesty to hear me. I am a poet. It is the melancholy whim of people of my profession to roam the streets after dark. I passed this way to-night. It was a mere chance. I was wrongfully arrested; I am innocent of this civil storm. Your Majesty sees that the Vagabond did not recognize me. I conjure your Majesty—"

"Silence!" said the king, betwixt two gulps of his diet-drink. "You stun me."

Tristan l'Hermite stepped forward, and pointing at Gringoire, said,—

"Sire, may we hang this one too?"

It was the first time that he had spoken.

"Pooh!" negligently answered the king. "I see no reason to the contrary."

"But I see a great many!" said Gringoire.

Our philosopher was at this moment greener than any olive. He saw by the king's cold and indifferent manner that his only resource was in something very pathetic, and he threw himself at the feet of Louis XI., exclaiming with frantic gestures,—

"Sire, your Majesty will deign to hear me. Sire, let not your thunders fall upon so small a thing as I! The thunderbolts of God never strike a lettuce. Sire, you are an august and very mighty monarch; have pity on a poor honest man, who would find it harder to kindle a revolt than an icicle to emit a spark. Most gracious lord, magnanimity is a virtue meet for kings and royal beasts. Alas! rigour does but anger the minds of men; the fierce blasts of winter could not make the traveller doff his cloak, while the sun shining down, little by little warmed him to such a degree that he stripped to his shirt. Sire, you are the sun. I protest to you, my sovereign lord and master, that I am not of the company of the Vagrants. I am neither disorderly nor a thief. Rebellion and brigandage are not of Apollo's train. I am not one to rush into those clouds which burst in thunders of sedition. I am a faithful vassal of your Majesty. A good subject should feel the same jealousy for the glory of his king that the husband feels for the honour of his wife, the same affection with which the son responds to his father's love; he should burn with zeal for his house; for the increase of his service. Any other passion which possessed him would be mere madness. Such, Sire, are my political maxims. Do not, therefore, judge me to be a rebel and a plunderer, by my ragged dress. If you will but pardon me, Sire, I will wear it threadbare at the knees in praying to God for you night and morning! Alas! I am not exceeding rich, 'tis true. I am indeed rather poor; but not vicious, for all that. It is not my fault. Every one knows that great wealth is not to be derived from literature, and that the most accomplished writers have not always much fire in winter. Pettifoggers get all the grain, and leave nothing but the chaff for the rest of the learned professions. There are forty most excellent proverbs about the tattered cloak of the philosopher. Oh, Sire, clemency is the only light which can illumine the interior of a great soul! Clemency bears the torch for all the other virtues. Without her, they are but blind, and gropers after God. Mercy, which is the same thing as clemency, produces those loving subjects who are the most potent bodyguard of princes. What matters it to you,—to you whose majesty dazzles all who behold it,—if there be one poor man the more upon the earth, a poor innocent philosopher floundering in the darkness of calamity, with an empty stomach and an empty purse? Besides, Sire, I am a scholar. Great kings add a pearl to their crown when they encourage letters. Hercules did not disdain the title of Musagetes. Matthias Corvinus favoured Jean of Monroyal, the ornament of mathematics. Now, it is a poor way of protecting letters, to hang the learned. What a blot upon Alexander's fame if he had hanged Aristotle! The deed would not have been a tiny patch upon the visage of his reputation to enhance its beauty, but a malignant ulcer to disfigure it. Sire, I wrote a most fitting epithalamium for the Lady of Flanders, and my lord the most august Dauphin. That is no fire-brand of rebellion. Your Majesty sees that I am no mere scribbler, that I have studied deeply, and that I have much natural eloquence. Pardon me, Sire. By so doing, you will perform an act of gallantry to Our Lady; and I vow that I am mightily frightened at the very idea of being hanged!"

So saying, the much distressed Gringoire kissed the king's slippers, and Guillaume Rym whispered to Coppenole, "He does well to crawl upon the floor. Kings are like Jupiter of Crete,—they have no ears but in their feet." And, regardless of the Cretan Jove, the hosier responded, with a grave smile, his eye fixed on Gringoire: "Oh, 'tis well done! I fancy I hear Councillor Hugonet begging me for mercy."

When Gringoire paused at last for lack of breath, he raised his head, trembling, to the king, who was scratching with his nail a spot on the knee of his breeches; then his Majesty drank from the goblet of ptisan. He spoke not a word, however, and the silence tortured Gringoire. At last the king looked at him. "What a dreadful bawler!" said he. Then, turning towards Tristan l'Hermite: "Bah! let him go!"

Gringoire fell backwards, overcome with joy.

"Scot-free!" grumbled Tristan. "Don't your Majesty want me to cage him for a while?"

"Friend," rejoined Louis XI., "do you think it is for such birds as these that we have cages made at an expense of three hundred and sixty-seven pounds eight pence three farthings? Let this wanton rascal depart incontinently, and dismiss him with a beating."

"Oh," cried Gringoire, "what a noble king!"

And for fear of a contrary order, he hastened towards the door, which Tristan opened for him with a very bad grace. The soldiers followed, driving him before them with sturdy blows, which Gringoire bore like the true Stoic philosopher that he was.

The king's good humour, since the revolt against the bailiff was announced to him, appeared in everything he did. This unusual clemency was no mean proof of it. Tristan l'Hermite, in his corner, wore the surly look of a dog who has seen a bone, but had none.

The king, meantime, merrily drummed the march of Pont-Audemer with his fingers on the arm of his chair. He was a dissembling prince, but more skilled in hiding his troubles than his joy. These outward manifestations of delight at any good news sometimes went to extraordinary lengths,—as on the death of Charles the Bold, when he vowed a silver balustrade to Saint-Martin of Tours; and on his accession to the throne, when he forgot to order his father's obsequies.

"Ha, Sire!" suddenly exclaimed Jacques Coictier, "what has become of that sharp fit of illness for which your Majesty summoned me?"

"Oh," said the king, "indeed, I suffer greatly, good gossip. I have a ringing in my ears, and cruel pains in my chest."

Coictier took the king's hand, and began to feel his pulse with a knowing air.

"See, Coppenole," said Rym in a low voice; "there he is, between Coictier and Tristan. They make up his entire court,—a doctor for himself, a hangman for the rest of the world!"

As he felt the king's pulse, Coictier assumed a look of more and more alarm. Louis XI. watched him with some anxiety. Coictier's face darkened visibly. The king's feeble health was the worthy man's only source of income, and he made the most of it.

"Oh, oh!" he muttered at last. "This is serious enough."

"Is it not?" said the frightened king.

"*Pulsus creber, anhelans, crepitans, irregularis,*" added the physician.

"By the Rood!"

"This might take a man off in less than three days."

"By'r Lady!" cried the king. "And he remedy, good gossip?"

"I must reflect, Sire."

He examined the king's tongue, shook his head, made a wry face, and in the midst of these affections said suddenly,—

"Zounds, Sire, I must tell you that there is a receivership of regales vacant, and that I have a nephew."

"I give my receivership to your nephew, gossip Jacques," replied the king; "but cool this fire in my breast."

"Since your Majesty is so graciously inclined," rejoined the doctor, "you will not refuse me a little help towards building my house in the Rue Saint-André des Arcs."

"Hey!" said the king.

"I have come to the end of my means," continued the doctor, "and it would really be a pity that my house should have no roof; not for the sake of the house, which is very plain and ordinary, but for the paintings by Jehan Fourbault, which enliven the walls. There is a Diana flying in the air, so excellently done, so delicate, so dainty, so natural in action, the head so nicely coifed and crowned with a crescent, the flesh so white, that she leads into temptation all those who study her too curiously. There is also a Ceres. She, too, is a very lovely divinity. She is seated upon sheaves of grain, and crowned with a gay garland of wheat-ears intertwined with purple goat's-beard and other flowers. Nothing was ever seen more amorous than her eyes, rounder than her legs, nobler than her mien or more graceful than her draperies. She is one of the most innocent and perfect beauties ever produced by mortal brush!"

"Wretch!" groaned Louis XI.; "what are you driving at?"

"I must have a roof over these paintings, Sire; and although it will cost but a trifle, I have no more money."

"How much will your roof cost?"

"Why, a roof of copper, embellished and gilded, two thousand pounds, at the utmost."

"Ah, the assassin!" cried the king; "he never draws me a tooth that is not priceless."

"Am I to have my roof?" said Coictier.

"Yes; and go to the devil! but cure me first."

Jacques Coictier bowed low and said,—

"Sire, a repellant alone can save you. We will apply to your loins the great specific, composed of cerate, Armenian bole, white of egg, vinegar, and oil. You will continue your diet-drink, and we will answer for your Majesty."

A lighted candle attracts more than one moth. Master Olivier, seeing the king so liberally inclined, and thinking the moment opportune, advanced in his turn: "Sire!"

"What is it now?" said Louis XI.

"Sire, your Majesty knows that Master Simon Radin is dead?"

"Well?"

"He was King's Councillor for the Treasury."

"Well?"

"Sire, his post is vacant."

As he said this, the haughty face of Master Olivier lost its arrogant look, and assumed a mean and grovelling expression. This is the only change of which a courtier's features are capable. The king looked him full in the face, and said drily, "I understand."

He added,—

"Master Olivier, Marshal Boucicaut once said, 'There are no good gifts save those from the king, no good fishing save in the sea.' I see that you are quite of ¹ opinion. Now, hear this; we have an excellent memory. In '68, we made you groom of our chamber; in '69, keeper of the castle of the Pont Saint-Cloud, at a salary of one hundred pounds Tours (you wished them to be Paris pounds); in November, '73, by letters given at Gergeole, we appointed you keeper of the woods at Vincennes, in place of Gilbert Acle, esquire; in '75, warden of the forest of Rouvray-lez-Saint-Cloud, in the place of Jacques le Maire; in '78, we graciously settled upon you, by letters-patent sealed with green wax, a rental of ten Paris pounds, for yourself and your wife, to be derived from the Place-aux-Marchands, situated in the Saint-Germain School; in '79, warden of the forest of Senart, in place of that poor Jehan Daiz; then, captain of the Château de Loches; then, governor of Saint-Quentin; then, captain of the Pont de Meulan, of which you style yourself count; of the five pence fine paid by every barber who shall shave a customer upon a holiday, three pence go to you, and we take the remainder. We were pleased to change your name of Le Mauvais, which too strongly resembled your face. In '74, we granted you, to the great displeasure of our nobles, armorial bearings of countless hues, which make your breast shimmer like that of a peacock. By the Rood! are you not sated yet? Is not the draught of fishes fine enough, and miraculous enough; and do you not fear lest another salmon should sin your boat? Pride will be your ruin, my friend. Pride is always hard pressed by ruin and shame. Consider this, and be silent."

These words, uttered in a severe tone, restored its wonted insolence to Master Olivier's face.

"Good!" he muttered almost audibly; "it is plain that the king is ailing to-day; he gives the doctor everything."

Louis XI., far from being irritated by this sally, replied with much gentleness. "Stay; I forgot that I had also made you my ambassador to Mistress Marie at Ghent. Yes, gentlemen," added the king, turning to the Flemings, "this fellow has been an ambassador. There, my gossip," he continued, addressing Master Olivier, "let us not quarrel; we are old friends. It is very late; we have finished our work. Shave me."

Our readers have doubtless ere now recognized in Master Olivier the dread Figaro whom Providence, the greatest of all dramatists, so artistically added to the long and bloody comedy of Louis XI.'s reign. This is not the place for us to attempt any portrait of this strange figure. The royal barber went by three names. At court he was politely termed Olivier le Daim; by the people, Olivier le Diable: his real name was Olivier le Mauvais.

Olivier le Mauvais, then, stood motionless, casting sulky glances at the king, and looking askance at Jacques Coictier.

"Yes, yes; the doctor!" he muttered.

"Well, yes, the doctor!" rejoined Louis XI., with rare good-nature; "the doctor has more influence than you. That is natural enough; he has a hold upon our whole body, while you only take us by the chin. There, my poor barber, cheer up. Why, what would you say, and what would become of your office, if I were such a king as King Chilpêric, whose favourite trick it was to pull his beard through his hand? Come, gossip, look to your work; shave me! Go, fetch the necessary tools."

Olivier, seeing that the king was in a jesting mood, and that it was impossible to put him out of temper, left the room to obey his orders, grumbling as he went.

The king rose, stepped to the window, and suddenly opening it with strange agitation, clapped his hands, exclaiming,—

"Oh, yes, there is a red glow in the sky over the City! The bailiff is burning; it can be nothing else. Ah, my good people! 'tis thus at last you help me to crush their lordships!"

Then turning to the Flemings: "Gentlemen, come and look. Is not that a fire which flares so high?"

The two men of Ghent approached.

"A great fire," said Guillaume Rym.

"Oh," added Coppenole, whose eyes flashed, "that reminds me of the burning of the lord of Hymbercourt's house! There must be a fine riot yonder!"

"Do you think so, Master Coppenole?" And the face of Louis XI. was almost as full of joy as that of the hosier. "'T will be hard to suppress it, eh?"

"By the Mass, Sire! your Majesty will make great gaps in many a company of troops in doing it."

"Oh, I! that's quite another thing," rejoined the king. "If I chose—"

The hosier answered boldly,—

"If this rebellion be what I suppose, you may choose to no purpose, Sire."

"Friend," said Louis XI., "two companies of my ordnance and the discharge of a serpentine would win an easy victory over the groundlings."

The hosier, in spite of the signs made to him by Guillaume Rym, seemed determined to oppose the king.

"Sire, the Swiss were groundlings too. My lord duke of Burgundy was a great gentleman, and he despised that vulgar mob. At the battle of Grandson he cried, 'Gunners, fire upon those low-lived villains!' and he swore by Saint George. But magistrate Scharnachtal fell upon the proud duke with his club and his people, and at the onslaught of the peasants with their bull-hides, the brilliant Burgundian army was broken like a pane of glass by a stone. Many knights were killed that day by base clowns; and my lord of Château-Guyon, the grandest noble in Burgundy, was found dead beside his great grey charger in a small marshy meadow."

"Friend," replied the king, "you talk of battles. This is only a mutiny; and I will quell it with a single frown whenever it pleases me."

The other answered indifferently,—

"That may be, Sire. In that case it will merely be because the people's hour has not yet come."

Guillaume Rym felt obliged to interfere:—

"Master Coppenole, you are speaking to a powerful king."

"I know it," gravely answered the hosier.

"Let him talk, friend Rym," said the king. "I like such frankness. My father, Charles VII., said that Truth was sick. I, for my part, thought she had died, without a confessor. Master Coppenole has undeceived me."

Then, laying his hand familiarly upon Coppenole's shoulder, he added,—

"You were saying, Master Jacques—"

"I was saying, Sire, that perhaps you were right,—that the people's hour had not yet come in this land."

Louis XI. looked searchingly at him:—

"And when will that hour come, sirrah?"

"You will hear it strike."

"By what o'clock, pray?"

Coppenole, with his homely, peaceful face, drew the king to the window.

"Listen, Sire! Here you have a donjon, a bell-tower, cannon, burghers, soldiers. When the bell rings, when the cannon growl, when the donjon falls with a crash, when burghers and soldiers shout and slay one another, then the hour will strike."

The king's face became dark and thoughtful. For an instant he stood silent; then he gently patted the thick donjon wall, as he might have caressed the flank of his favourite horse.

"Oh, no!" he said; "you will not crumble so easily, will you, my good Bastille?"

Then, turning with an abrupt gesture to the daring Fleming,—

"Did you ever see a revolt, Master Jacques?"

"I made one," said the hosier.

"And how," said the king, "do you set to work to make a revolt?"

"Ah!" replied Coppenole, "it is not very difficult. There are a hundred ways of doing it. In the first place, discontent must be rife in the town;

that is not an uncommon occurrence. And then you must consider the character of the inhabitants. The men of Ghent are always ready to rebel; they always love the prince's son, never the prince. Well, I will suppose that one morning somebody comes into my shop and says: Friend Coppenole, this thing or that thing has happened,—the Lady of Flanders is resolved to maintain the Cabinet; the high bailiff has doubled the tax on vegetables or something else; whatever you please. I drop my work on the spot; I leave my shop, and I run out into the street, crying, 'Storm and sack!' There is always some empty hogshead lying about. I mount upon it, and I proclaim aloud, in the first words that come to me, all that distresses me; and when you belong to the people, Sire, there is always something to distress you. Then there is a gathering of the clans; there are shouts; the alarm-bell rings; the people disarm the troops and arm themselves; the marketmen join in; and so it goes on. And it will always be so, so long as there are nobles in the seigniories, burghers in the towns, and peasants in the country."

"And against whom do you rebel in this way?" asked the king. "Against your bailiffs; against your liege-lords?"

"Sometimes; that depends on circumstances. Against the duke, too, at times."

Louis XI. reseated himself, and said with a smile,—

"Ah! here they have got no farther than the bailiffs."

At this instant Olivier le Daim returned. He was followed by two pages carrying various articles of the king's oilet; but what struck Louis XI. was the fact that he was also accompanied by the provost of Paris and the captain of the watch, who seemed dismayed. The spiteful barber also looked dismayed, but was inwardly pleased. He was the first to speak:—

"Sire, I crave your pardon for the disastrous news I bring!"

The king turned so quickly that he tore the matting on the floor with the legs of his chair.

"What do you mean?"

"Sire," replied Olivier le Daim, with the malicious look of a man who rejoices to strike a severe blow, "this rising of the people is not directed against the Bailiff of the Palace."

"And against whom, then?"

"Against you, Sire."

The old king rose to his feet as erect as a young man.

"Explain yourself, Olivier! And look to your head, my friend; for I swear by the cross of Saint-Lô that if you lie to us at this hour, the same sword which cut off the head of my lord Luxembourg is not too dull to chop off yours!"

The oath was a tremendous one; Louis XI. had never but twice in his life sworn by the cross of Saint-Lô.

Olivier opened his lips to answer.

"On your knees!" fiercely interrupted the king. "Tristan, watch this man!"

Olivier knelt, and said coldly,—

"Sire, a witch was condemned to death by your parliamentary court. She took refuge in Notre-Dame. The people desire to take her thence by force. The provost and the captain of the watch, who have just come from the scene of the insurrection, are here to give me the lie if I speak not truly. The people are besieging Notre-Dame."

"Indeed!" said the king in a low voice, pale and trembling with rage. "Notre-Dame! So they lay siege to my good mistress, Our Lady, in her own cathedral! Rise, Olivier; you are right. I give you Simon Radin's office. You are right; it is I whom they attack. The witch is in the safe-keeping of the church; the church is in my safe-keeping; and I was foolish enough to believe that they were assaulting the bailiff. It is myself!"

Then, made young by fury, he began to pace the floor with hasty strides. He laughed no longer; he was terrible to behold; he came and went; the fox was turned to a hyæna. He seemed to have lost all power of speech; his lips moved, and his fleshless hands were clinched. All at once he raised his head, his hollow eye seemed filled with light, and his voice flashed forth like a clarion:—

"Do your work well, Tristan! Do your work well with these scoundrels! Go, Tristan my friend; kill! kill!"

This outburst over, he sat down again, and said with cold and concentrated wrath,—

"Here, Tristan! There are with us in this Bastille Viscount de Gif's fifty lances, making three hundred horse: take them. There is also M. de Châteaupers' company of archers of our ordnance: take them. You are provost-marshal; you have your own men: take them. At the Hôtel Saint-Pol you will find forty archers of the Dauphin's new guard: take them. And with all these soldiers you will hasten to Notre-Dame. Ah, you commoners of Paris, so you would attack the Crown of France, the sanctity of Notre-Dame, and the peace of this republic! Exterminate them, Tristan! exterminate them! and let not one escape but for Montfaucon."

Tristan bowed. "It is well, Sire."

After a pause he added, "And what shall I do with the witch?"

This question gave the king food for thought.

"Ah," said he, "the witch! D'Estouteville, what was the people's pleasure in regard to her?"

"Sire," replied the provost of Paris, "I fancy that as the people desire to wrest her from her shelter in Notre-Dame, it is her lack of punishment that offends them, and they propose to hang her."

The king seemed to muse deeply; then, addressing Tristan l'Hermite: "Very well, good gossip; exterminate the people, and hang the witch!"

"That's it," whispered Rym to Coppenole, "punish the people for their purpose, and then fulfil that purpose."

"It is well, Sire," answered Tristan. "If the witch be still in Notre-Dame, shall we disregard the sanctuary, and take her thence?"

"By the Rood! Sanctuary!" said the king, scratching his ear. "And yet this woman must be hanged."

Here, as if struck by a sudden thought, he fell upon his knees before his chair, doffed his hat, put it on the seat, and gazing devoutly at one of the leaden images with which it was loaded, he exclaimed, with clasped hands: "Oh, Our Lady of Paris, my gracious patroness, pardon me! I will only do it this once. This criminal must be punished. I assure you, Holy Virgin, my good mistress, that she is a witch, and unworthy of your generous protection. You know madame, that many very pious princes have infringed upon the privileges of the Church for the glory of God and the needs of the State. Saint Hugh, Bishop of England, allowed King Edward to capture a magician in his church. Saint Louis of France, my master, for the same purpose violated the church of St. Paul; and Alphonso, son of the King of Jerusalem, the Church of the Holy Sepulchre itself. Forgive me this once, Our Lady of Paris! I will never do so again, and I will give you a fine new silver statue, like the one I gave Our Lady of Ecouys last year. Amen."

He made the sign of the cross, rose, put on his hat, and said to Tristan,—

"Make haste, friend; take Château-pers with you. Ring the alarm! Quell the mob! Hang the witch! That is all. And I expect you to pay the costs of hanging. You will render me an account thereof. Come, Olivier, I shall not go to bed to-night; shave me."

Tristan l'Hermite bowed, and left the room. Then the king dismissed Rym and Coppenole with a gesture, and the words,—

"God help you, my good Flemish friends. Go, take a little rest; the night is passing, and we are nearer morn than evening."

Both retired, and on reaching their apartments under the escort of the captain of the Bastille, Coppenole said to Guillaume Rym,—

"Ahem! I have had enough of this coughing king. I have seen Charles of Burgundy drunk, and he was not so bad as Louis XI. sick."

"Master Jacques," replied Rym, "'tis because the wine of kings is less cruel than their diet-drink."

Chapter VI

"THE CHIVE IN THE CLY"

On leaving the Bastille, Gringoire ran down the Rue Saint-Antoine with the speed of a runaway horse. On reaching the Porte Baudoyer, he walked straight up to the stone cross in the middle of the square, as if he had been able to distinguish in the darkness the figure of a man in a black dress and cowl, who sat upon the steps of the cross.

"Is it you, master?" said Gringoire. The black figure rose.

"'Sdeath! You make my blood boil, Gringoire. The man on the tower of Saint-Gervais has just cried half-past one."

"Oh," rejoined Gringoire, "it is not my fault, but that of the watch and the king. I have had a narrow escape. I always just miss being hanged; it is my fate."

"You just miss everything," said the other; "but make haste. Have you the password?"

"Only fancy, master, that I have seen the king! I have just left him. He wears fustian breeches. It was quite an adventure."

"Oh, you spinner of words! What do I care for your adventure? Have you the watchword of the Vagrants?"

"I have; never fear. It is 'the Chive in the Cly.'"

"Good! Otherwise we could not make our way to the church. The Vagrants block the streets. Luckily, it appears that they met with considerable resistance. We may yet be there in time."

"Yes, master; but how are we to get into Notre-Dame?"

"I have the key to the towers."

"And how shall we get out?"

"There is a small door, behind the cloisters, which opens upon the Terrain, and thence to the water. I have the key, and I moored a boat there this morning."

"I had a pretty escape from being hanged!" repeated Gringoire.

"Come, be quick!" said the other.

Both went hurriedly towards the City.

Chapter VII

CHÂTEAUPERS TO THE RESCUE

The reader may perhaps recall the critical situation in which we left Quasimodo. The brave deaf man, assailed on every hand, had lost, if not all courage, at least all hope of saving not himself (he did not think of himself), but the gipsy. He ran frantically up and down the gallery. Notre-Dame was about to be captured by the Vagrants. Suddenly, the gallop of horses filled the neighbouring streets, and with a long train of torches and a broad column of horsemen riding at full speed with lances lowered, the furious sound burst into the square like a whirlwind:—

"France! France! Hew down the clodpolls! Châteaupers to the rescue! Provosty! provosty!"

The terrified Vagrants wheeled about.

Quasimodo, who heard nothing, saw the naked swords, the torches, the pikeheads, the horsemen, at whose head he recognized Captain Phœbus. He saw the confusion of the Vagrants,—the alarm of some, the consternation of the stoutest-hearted,—and he derived so much strength from this unexpected succour, that he hurled from the church the foremost assailants, who were already bestriding the gallery rails.

The king's troops had actually arrived.

The Vagrants fought bravely; they defended themselves desperately. Taken in flank from the Rue Saint-Pierre aux Bœufs, and in the rear from the Rue du Parvis, driven close against Notre-Dame, which they were still assailing, and which Quasimodo was defending, at once besiegers and besieged, they were in the singular situation in which Count Henri d'Harcourt afterwards found himself at the famous siege of Turin, in 1640,—between Prince Thomas of Savoy, whom he was besieging, and the Marquis de Leganez, who was blockading him. *"Taurinum obsessor idem et obsessus,"* as his epitaph says.

The conflict was frightful. As Père Mathieu puts it, "wolf's flesh needs dog's teeth." The king's cavaliers, among whom Phœbus de Châteaupers comported himself most valiantly, gave no quarter, and the edge of the sword slew those who escaped the thrust of the lance. The Vagrants, ill-armed, foamed and bit. Men, women, and children flung themselves upon the cruppers and breast-pieces of the horses, and clung to them like cats with tooth and nail. Others blinded the archers by blows of their torches; others again struck iron hooks into the riders' necks and pulled them down, cutting into pieces those who fell.

One man had a large shining scythe,

with which he mowed the legs of the horses. It was a frightful sight. He sang a nasal song, and swept his scythe ceaselessly to and fro. At every stroke he cut a broad swath of dismembered limbs. He advanced thus into the thickest of the cavalry, with the calm deliberation, swaying of the head, and regular breathing of a mower cutting down a field of grain. This was Clopin Trouillefou. A shot from an arquebus at last laid him low.

Meantime, windows were again opened. The neighbours, hearing the battle-shouts of the king's men, joined in the skirmish, and from every story bullets rained upon the Vagrants. The square was filled with thick smoke, which the flash of musketry streaked with fire. The front of Notre-Dame was vaguely visible through it, and the decrepit hospital the Hôtel-Dieu, with a few wan patients looking down from the top of its roof dotted with dormer-windows.

At last the Vagrants yielded. Exhaustion, lack of proper arms, the terror caused by the surprise, the musketry from the windows, the brave onslaught of the king's men, all combined to crush them. They broke through the enemy's ranks, and fled in every direction, leaving the square heaped with corpses.

When Quasimodo, who had not stopped fighting for a single instant, saw this rout, he fell upon his knees and raised his hands to heaven; then, mad with joy, he ran, he climbed with the swift motion of a bird to that little cell, all access to which he had so intrepidly defended. He had but one thought now: that was, to kneel before her whom he had saved for the second time.

When he entered the cell he found it empty.

BOOK XI

Marriage

Chapter I

THE LITTLE SHOE

When the Vagrants attacked the church, Esmeralda was asleep.

Soon the ever-increasing noise about the building, and the anxious bleating of her goat, which waked before she did, roused her from her slumbers. She sat up, listened, looked about; then, alarmed by the light and commotion, hurried from her cell to see what it all meant. The aspect of the square, the vision which she beheld, the disorder and confusion of this night attack, the hideous rabble bounding hither and thither like an army of frogs half seen in the darkness, the croaking of the hoarse mob, the few red torches moving and dancing in the darkness like will-o'-the-wisps sporting on the misty surface of a marsh,—the whole scene produced upon her the effect of a weird battle waged by the phantoms of the Witches' Sabbath and the stone monsters of the Church. Imbued from infancy with the superstitious notions of the gipsy tribe, her first thought was that she had surprised the strange beings of the night in their sorceries. Thus she ran back to her cell in affright to hide her head, and implore her pillow to send her some less horrid nightmare.

Little by little, however, the first fumes of fear vanished; from the ever-increasing tumult, and from various other tokens of reality, she felt that she was beset, not by spectres, but by human beings. Then her terror, without being augmented, changed its nature. She reflected upon the possibility of a popular revolt to tear her from her refuge. The idea of again losing life, hope, and Phœbus, whom she still hoped to win in the future, her own absolute defencelessness, all flight cut off, no help at hand, her forlorn condition, her isolation,—these thoughts and countless others overwhelmed her. She fell upon her knees, her face buried in the bedclothes, her hands clasped above her head, full of agony and apprehension, and, gipsy, pagan, and idolater though she was, she began with sobs to entreat mercy of the good Christian God, and to pray to her hostess, Our Lady. For, believe in nothing though one may, there are moments in life when one belongs to the creed of whatever church is nearest.

She lay thus prostrate for a very long time, trembling indeed, far more than she prayed, chilled by the ever-advancing breath of that frantic mob, wholly ignorant of the meaning of their unbridled rage, knowing not what was on foot, what was being done, what object that throng had in view, but foreseeing some terrible issue.

In the midst of her anguish she heard steps close at hand. She turned. Two men, one of whom carried a lantern, entered her cell. She uttered a faint shriek.

"Fear nothing," said a voice which was not unknown to her; "it is I."

"Who are you?" she asked.

"Pierre Gringoire."

That name calmed her fears. She raised her eyes, and saw that it was indeed the poet; but beside him stood a black figure veiled from head to foot, which silenced her.

"Ah!" replied Gringoire in reproachful tones, "Djali knew me before you did!"

The little goat, in fact, did not wait for Gringoire to pronounce his name. He had no sooner entered, than she rubbed herself fondly against his knees, covering the poet with caresses and white hairs,—for she was shedding her coat. Gringoire returned her caresses.

"Who is that with you?" said the gipsy in a low voice.

"Never fear," replied Gringoire; "it's a friend of mine."

Then the philosopher, placing his lantern on the ground, crouched upon the flagstones, and enthusiastically exclaimed, as he clasped Djali in his arms,—

"Oh, 'tis a pretty creature, doubtless more remarkable for her neatness than her size, but ingenious, subtle, and learned as any grammarian of them all! Come, my Djali, let us see if you have forgotten any of your cunning tricks.

Show us how Master Jacques Charmolue does—"

The man in black would not let him finish. He stepped up to him and gave him a rude shove on the shoulder. Gringoire rose.

"True," said he; "I forgot that we are in haste. Still, that's no reason, master mine, for handling people so roughly. My dear child, your life is in danger, and Djali's too. They want to hang you again. We are your friends, and are come hither to save you. Follow us."

"Is it true?" cried she, distractedly.

"Yes, quite true. Come quickly!"

"I will," she stammered. "But why doesn't your friend speak?"

"Ah!" said Gringoire, "that's because his father and mother were queer people, and brought him up to be silent."

She was forced to rest content with this explanation. Gringoire took her by the hand; his companion picked up the lantern and went on before. The girl was dizzy with dread. She let them lead her away. The goat followed them with leaps of delight, so rejoiced to see Gringoire once more that she made him stumble every moment by thrusting her horns between his legs.

"Such is life," said the philosopher at each escape from falling; "it is often our best friends who cause our downfall!"

They rapidly descended the tower stairs, traversed the church, full of solitude and gloom, but echoing with the din without in frightful contrast to the peace within, and came into the cloister courtyard by the Porte-Rouge. The cloister was deserted; the canons had fled to the bishop's palace to pray together; the court was empty, save for a few timid lackeys hiding in dark corners. They made their way towards the door which led from this courtyard to the Terrain. The man in black opened it with a key which he had about him. Our readers know that the Terrain was a strip of ground enclosed with walls on the City side, and belonging to the Chapter of Notre-Dame, which formed the extreme eastern end of the island in the rear of the church. They found this enclosure quite forsaken. Here there was already less noise in the air. The sound of the Vagrant's assault reached them more faintly, less harshly. The fresh wind which followed the course of the stream stirred with a perceptible rustle the leaves of the one tree planted at the tip of the Terrain. However, they were still very close to the danger. The nearest buildings were the Episcopal palace and the church. There was plainly great commotion within the palace. The gloomy mass was furrowed with lights, which flew from one window to another, as when you burn paper a dark structure of ashes remains, upon which bright sparks trace countless grotesque figures. Beside it the huge towers of Notre-Dame, thus viewed from the rear with the long nave upon which they are built, outlined in black against the vast red light which filled the square, looked like two monstrous andirons for a fire of the Cyclops.

In all directions, so much of Paris as could be seen shimmered in blended light and shade. Rembrandt has just such backgrounds in some of his pictures.

The man with the lantern walked straight to the end of the Terrain.

There, on the very edge of the water, were the worm-eaten remains of a picket-fence with laths nailed across, to which a few withered branches of a low vine clung like the fingers of an open hand. Behind, in the shadow of this trellis, a small boat was hidden. The man signed to Gringoire and his companion to enter it. The goat followed them. The man stepped in last; then he cut the hawser, shoved off from the shore with a long boat-hook, and seizing a pair of oars, seated himself in the bow, rowing with all his strength towards the middle of the stream. The Seine runs very swiftly at this point, and he had some difficulty in clearing the end of the island.

Gringoire's first care on entering the boat, was to take the goat upon his knees. He sat down in the stern; and the young girl, whom the stranger inspired with indescribable fears, took her place beside the poet.

When our philosopher felt the boat moving, he clapped his hands, and kissed Djali between her horns.

"Oh," said he, "here we are all four saved!"

He added, with the look of a deep thinker, "One is sometimes indebted to fortune, sometimes to cunning, for the happy issue of a great undertaking."

The boat proceeded slowly towards the right bank. The young girl watched the stranger with secret dread. He had carefully covered the light of his dark-lantern, and was but dimly visible, in the gloom, like a ghost in the bow of the boat. His cowl, still drawn down, formed a sort of mask over his face; and every time that he opened his arms, with their wide hanging black sleeves, in rowing, they looked like the broad wings of a bat. Moreover, he had not yet breathed a word. The only sound in the boat was that of the oars, mingled with the ripple of the water against the side of the boat.

"By my soul!" suddenly exclaimed Gringoire, "we are as gay and lively as so many owls! We're as silent as Pythagoreans or fishes! By the Rood! my friends, I wish one of you would speak to me. The human voice is music to the human ear. I am not the author of that remark, but Didymus of Alexandria is, and famous words they are. Certes, Didymus of Alexandria is no mean philosopher. One word, my pretty child,—say one word to me, I implore. By the way, you used to make a queer, funny little face; do you still make it? Do you know, my darling, that Parliament holds jurisdiction over all sanctuaries, and that you ran great risks in your cell in Notre-Dame? Alas! the little bird trochylus builds its nest in the jaws of the crocodile. Master, there's the moon peeping out again. How I hope they won't see us! We are doing a laudable deed in saving the damsel, and yet we should be hanged in the king's name if we were caught. Alas! human actions may be taken two ways. I am condemned for the same thing for which you are rewarded. Some admire Cæsar and blame Catiline. Isn't that so, master mine? What do you say to that philosophy? For my part, I possess the philosophy of instinct, of Nature (*ut apes geometriam*).— What! nobody answers me! What disagreeable tempers you both have! I must needs talk to myself. That's what we call in tragedy a monologue. By the Rood! —I must tell you that I've just seen King Louis XI., and that I caught that oath from him,—by the Rood, then, they're still keeping up a fine howling in the City! He's a wicked old villain of a king. He's all muffled up in furs. He still owes me the money for my epithalamium, and he came precious near hanging me to-night, which would have bothered me mightily. He is very stingy to men of merit. He really ought to read the four books by Salvien of Cologne, '*Adversus avaritiam*.' In good sooth, he is a very narrow-minded king in his dealings with men of letters, and one who commits most barbarous cruelties. He's a sponge to soak up money squeezed from the people. His economy is like the spleen, which grows fat upon the leanness of all the other members. Thus, complaints of the hardness of the times become murmurs against the sovereign. Under the reign of this mild and pious lord, the gallows crack with their weight of victims, the headsman's blocks grow rotten with blood, the prisons are filled to bursting. This king takes in money with one hand and hangs men with the other. He is pander to my lady Taxes and my lord Gibbet. The great are stripped of their dignities, and the small are ceaselessly loaded with new burdens. 'Tis an extravagant prince. I do not love this monarch. And how say you, my master?"

The man in black suffered the babbling poet to prate his fill. He continued to struggle against the strong and angry current which divides the prow of the City from the stern of the Ile Notre-Dame, which we now know as the Ile Saint-Louis.

"By the way, master," suddenly observed Gringoire, "just as we made our way into the square through the angry Vagabonds, did your reverence note that poor little devil whose brains your deaf friend was about dashing out against the railing of the gallery of kings? I am near-sighted, and did not recognize him. Do you know who it could be?"

The stranger made no answer, but he ceased rowing; his arms fell powerless; his head drooped upon his breast, and Esmeralda heard him heave a convulsive sigh. She shuddered; she had heard similar sighs before.

The boat, left to itself, drifted with the current for some moments. But finally the man in black drew himself up, again seized the oars, and began again to pull against the stream. He rounded the end of the Ile Notre-Dame, and bent his course towards the landing-place of the Hay-market.

"Ah!" said Gringoire, "there's the Barbeau house. There, master, look: that collection of black roofs which form such strange angles; there, beneath that mass of low, stringy, streaked, and dirty clouds, where the moon looks like the yolk of a broken egg. 'Tis a handsome house. It contains a chapel capped by a tiny dome full of daintily wrought decorations. Above it you may see the bell-tower with its delicate tracery. There is also a pleasant garden, consisting of a fish-pond, an aviary, an echo, a mall, a labyrinth, a house for wild beasts, and a quantity of shady alleys most agreeable to Venus. There is also a rascally tree, which goes by the name of the Lovers' Retreat, because it once hid the meetings of a famous French princess and a gallant and witty constable of France. Alas! we poor philosophers are to a constable what a bed of cabbages and radishes is to the gardens of the Louvre. What does it matter, after all? Human life, for the great as well as for us, is made up of mingled good and ill. Grief goes ever hand in hand with gladness, as the spondee with the dactyl. Master, I must tell you the story of this Barbeau house. It ends in tragic fashion. It was in 1319, during the reign of Philip V., the longest of all the French kings. The moral of the story is, that the temptations of the flesh are hurtful and pernicious. Do not look too often at your neighbour's wife, much as your senses may be tickled by her beauty. Fornication is a very libertine thought. Adultery is curiosity about another's pleasure. Hollo! The noise seems to be growing louder over yonder!"

The din around Notre-Dame was indeed increasing rapidly. They paused and listened. They distinctly heard shouts of victory. All at once a hundred torches, which lit up the glittering helmets of men-at-arms, appeared upon all parts of the church,—upon the towers, galleries, and flying buttresses. These torches seemed searching for some one or something; and soon distant cries of, "The gipsy! The witch! Death to the gipsy!" fell plainly on the ears of the fugitives.

The wretched girl hid her face in her hands, and the unknown boatman began to row frantically for the shore. Meantime our philosopher reflected. He hugged the goat in his arms, and edged very gently away from the gipsy, who nestled closer and closer to him, as her only remaining protector.

Gringoire was certainly cruelly perplexed. He considered that the goat too, "according to the existing law," would be hanged if she were recaptured, which would be a great pity,—poor Djali! that it was quite too much of a good thing to have two condemned prisoners clinging to him at once; and, finally, that his companion asked nothing better than to take sole charge of the girl. A violent conflict went on within him, in which, like Jupiter in the Iliad, he alternately weighed the merits of the gipsy and the goat; and he gazed first at the one, then at the other, with tearful eyes, muttering, "After all, I cannot save you both!"

A shock warned them that the boat had reached shore. The ominous uproar still pervaded the City. The stranger rose, approached the gipsy, and tried to take her by the arm to help her to land. She repulsed him, and clung to Gringoire's sleeve, while he, in his turn, absorbed in the goat, almost pushed her from him. Then she sprang from the boat unaided. She was so distressed that she knew not what she was doing, or where she was going. She stood thus stupefied an instant, watching the water as it glided by. When she had somewhat recovered her senses, she was alone upon the wharf with the stranger. It seems that Gringoire had taken advantage of the moment of their landing, and stolen away with the goat into the throng of houses in the Rue Grenier-sur-l'Eau.

The poor gipsy shuddered when she found herself alone with this man. She tried to speak, to cry out, to call Gringoire; her tongue clove to the roof of her mouth, and no sound issued from her lips. All at once she felt the hand of the unknown upon her arm. It was a cold, strong hand. Her teeth chattered, she turned paler than the moonbeams which illumined her face. The man said not a word. He strode rapidly towards the Grève, holding her firmly by the hand. At that moment she vaguely felt that fate is an irresistible power. She had lost all control of her limbs; she suffered him to drag her along, running while he walked. The quay at this point rises abruptly from the river, but it seemed to her is if she were going down hill.

She looked in every direction. Not a single passer. The quay was absolutely deserted. She heard no sound, she perceived no stir save in the tumultuous and blazing City from which she was separated only by an arm of the Seine, and whence her name came to her joined with threats of death. The rest of Paris lay spread around her in great masses of shadow.

Meantime, the stranger drew her on in the same silence and with the same speed. She recognized none of the places through which she passed. As she went by a lighted window she made an effort, suddenly resisted him, and cried, "Help!"

The owner of the house opened the window, appeared in his shirt with his lamp, looked out upon the quay with a drowsy face, pronounced a few words which she did not catch, and closed the shutter. Thus her last glimmer of hope faded.

The man in black did not utter a syllable; he held her fast, and began to increase his speed. She resisted no longer, but followed him helplessly.

From time to time she mustered a little strength, and said in a voice broken by the unevenness of the pavement and the breathless haste with which she was borne along: "Who are you? Who are you?" He made no reply.

In this way they proceeded along the edge of the quay to an open square of considerable size. The moon shone faintly. They were in the Grève. In the middle stood a sort of black cross; it was the gallows. She recognized all this, and knew where she was.

The man stopped, turning to her, and lifted his cowl.

"Oh!" stammered she, frozen with fear; "I was sure that it must be he."

It was the priest. He looked like the ghost of himself. This was due to the moonlight. It seems as if by that light one could see only the spectres of things.

"Listen!" said he; and she trembled at the sound of that fatal voice which she had not heard for so long a time. He went on with the short, quick gasps which betray deep mental emotion: "Listen! We have reached our goal. I must speak with you. This is the Grève. This is a decisive point in our lives. Fate has delivered us over to each other. Your life is in my hands; my soul rests in yours. Beyond this place and this night all is dark. Hear me, then. I am going to tell you— But first, speak not to me of your Phœbus." (As he said this he came and went, like a man who cannot remain quietly in one place, dragging her after him.) "Speak not of him. If you but mention his name, I know not what I shall do, but it will be something terrible."

This said, like a body which has found its centre of gravity, he again stood still, but his words revealed no less emotion. His voice grew lower and lower.

"Do not turn away your head. Listen to me. It is a serious business. In the first place, I will tell you what has happened. It is no laughing matter, I assure you. What was I saying? Remind me! Ah! There is an order from Parliament which returns you to the scaffold. I have rescued you from the hangman's hands; but even now they are in pursuit of you. See!"

He stretched his arm towards the City. The search did, indeed, seem to be continued. The noise drew nearer; the tower of the lieutenant's house, directly facing the Grève, was full of light and bustle, and soldiers were seen running along the opposite quay with torches, shouting: "The gipsy! Where is the gipsy? Death! Death!"

"You see that they are in pursuit of you, and that I do not lie. I love you. Do not open your lips; rather, do not speak to me, if it be to tell me that you hate me. I am resolved never again to hear that. I have saved you.—Let me finish first.—I can save you wholly. Everything is ready. It is for you to choose. I can do as you would have me."

He interrupted himself excitedly: "No, that is not what I meant to say."

Then, running, and making her run after him,—for he did not loose his hold,—he went straight to the gibbet, and pointed to it.

"Choose between us," said he, coldly.

She tore herself from his grasp, and fell at the foot of the gibbet, throwing her arms about that dismal support; then she half turned her lovely head, and looked at the priest over her shoulder. She seemed a Holy Virgin at the foot of the cross. The priest remained motionless, his finger still raised to the gallows, his gesture unchanged as if he were a statue.

At last the gipsy said,—

"It is less horrible to me than you are."

Then he let his arm drop slowly, and gazed at the pavement in deep dejection.

"If these stones could speak," he murmured, "yes, they would say, 'There is a very miserable man.'"

He went on. The girl, kneeling before the gibbet, and veiled by her long hair, let him speak without interruption.

He had now assumed a gentle, plaintive tone, in painful contrast with the proud severity of his features.

"I love you. Oh, it is indeed true! Is there then no visible spark of that fire which burns my soul? Alas! girl, night and day; yes, night and day,—does this deserve no pity? It is a love which consumes me night and day, I tell you; it is torture. Oh, my suffering is too great to be endured, my poor child! It is a thing worthy of compassion, I assure you. You see that I speak gently to you. I would fain have you cease to feel such horror of me. After all, if a man love a woman, it is not his fault! Oh, my God! What! will you never forgive me? Will you always hate me? Is this the end? It is this that makes me wicked, I tell you, and horrible in my own sight! You do not even look at me! You are thinking of other things, perhaps, while I stand and talk to you, and both of us are trembling on the verge of eternity! But do not talk to me of your soldier! What! I might throw myself at your knees; what! I might kiss, not your feet, for that you would not suffer, but the ground beneath your feet; what! I might sob like a child: I might tear from my bosom, not words, but my heart and my very life, to show you how I love you; all would be in vain,— all! And yet your soul is full of gentleness and tenderness; you are radiant with the most beauteous mildness; you are all sweetness, goodness, mercy, and charm. Alas! you are unkind to me alone! Oh, what a freak of fate!"

He buried his face in his hands. The young girl heard his sobs. It was the first time she had seen him weep. Standing thus, shaken by sobs, he appeared more miserable and more suppliant than had he been on his knees. He wept thus for some time.

"Ah, well!" he added, his first tears over, "I can find no words to express my feelings; and yet I pondered well what I should say to you. Now, I tremble and shudder; I give way at the decisive moment; I feel that some superior power surrounds us, and I stammer. Oh, I shall fall to the ground if you do not take pity upon me, upon yourself! Do not condemn us both! If you knew how much I love you; what a heart mine is! Oh, what an abandonment of all virtue! what a desperate desertion of myself! A scholar, I scoff at science; a gentleman, I disgrace my name; a priest, I make my missal a pillow of foul desires, grossly insult my God! All this for your sake, enchantress! to be worthy of your hell! And you reject the damned soul! Oh, let me tell you all! more still, something yet more horrible, oh, far more horrible—"

As he pronounced these last words, his look became quite wild. He was silent an instant, then resumed as if talking to himself, and in a firm voice,—

"Cain, what hast thou done with thy brother?"

There was another pause, and he added,—

"What have I done with him, Lord? I took him in my arms, I brought him up, I fed him, I loved him, I idolized him, and I killed him! Yes, Lord, for they have just now dashed his head, before my very eyes, against the stones of your temple, and it was because of me, because of this woman, because of her—"

His eye was haggard. His voice died away; he still repeated mechanically, over and over, at considerable intervals, like a bell prolonging its last vibration, "Because of her; because of her—"

Here his tongue ceased to articulate any distinct sound, although his lips still moved. All at once he gave way, and sank in a heap, lying motionless upon the ground, his head upon his knees.

A slight movement made by the girl to pull her foot from under him revived him. He slowly drew his hand over his hollow cheeks, and looked in amazement at his fingers, which were wet. "What!" he muttered, "have I wept?"

And turning quickly to the gipsy with indescribable anguish:—

"Alas! and you could coldly see me weep! Child, do you know that those tears are burning lava? Is it then really true,—in the man we hate, nothing moves us? You would see me die, and still laugh! One word,—only one word of pardon! Do not tell me that you love me, only tell me that you will try; that shall suffice, and I will save you. If not,—oh, time passes. I conjure you! by all that you hold sacred, do not wait until I am once more turned to stone, like the gibbet which also claims you! Think, that I hold the destinies of both in my hand; that I am mad,—it is terrible!—that I may let all fall; and that beneath us yawns a bottomless pit, wretched girl, wherein my fall shall follow yours through all eternity! One word of kindness,—but a single word!"

She opened her mouth to answer him. He threw himself upon his knees before her, to receive with adoration the words, perhaps relenting, which were about to fall from her lips. She said to him, "You are an assassin!"

The priest caught her fiercely in his arms, and began to laugh an abominable laugh.

"Well, yes, an assassin!" said he; "and you shall be mine. You will not have me for your slave, you shall have me for your master. You shall be mine! You shall be mine! I have a den whither I will drag you. You must follow me, you must needs follow me, or I will give you up to justice! You must die, my beauty, or be mine,—be the priest's, the apostate's, the assassin's! and that this night; do you hear me? Come! rejoice; come, kiss me, foolish girl! The tomb, or my bed!"

His eyes flashed with rage and desire. His impure lips reddened the neck of the young girl. She struggled in his arms. He covered her with frantic kisses.

"Do not bite me, monster!" she shrieked. "Oh, the hateful, poisonous monk! Let me go! I will tear out your vile grey hair, and throw it by handfuls in your face!"

He flushed, then paled, then released her, and looked at her gloomily. She thought herself victorious, and went on:—

"I tell you that I belong to my Phœbus, that 'tis Phœbus I love, that Phœbus alone is handsome! You, priest, are old! you are ugly! Begone!"

He uttered a violent cry, like the wretch to whom a red-hot iron is applied. "Then die!" he said, gnashing his teeth. She saw his frightful look, and strove to fly. He overtook her, shook her, threw her down, and walked rapidly towards the corner of the Tour-Roland, dragging her after him over the pavement by her fair hands.

Reaching it, he turned to her:—

"For the last time, will you be mine?"

She answered emphatically,—

"No!"

Then he called in a loud voice,—

"Gudule! Gudule! here is the gipsy girl! Avenge yourself!"

The young girl felt herself suddenly seized by the elbow. She looked. A fleshless arm was thrust from a loophole in the wall, and held her with an iron grip.

"Hold her fast!" said the priest; "it's the runaway gipsy. Do not let her go. I will fetch the officers. You shall see her hanged."

A guttural laugh from the other side of the wall replied to these bloody words: "Ha! ha! ha!" The gipsy saw the priest depart in the direction of the Pont Notre-Dame. The tramp of horses was heard coming from that quarter.

The girl recognized the spiteful recluse. Panting with terror, she tried to release herself. She writhed, she twisted herself in agony and despair; but the woman held her with unnatural strength. The thin bony fingers which bruised her flesh fastened about her arm like a vice. That band seemed riveted to her wrist. It was stronger than any chain, stronger than any pillory or iron ring; it was a pair of intelligent and living pincers issuing from a wall.

Exhausted, she sank back, and the fear of death took possession of her. She thought of the beauty of life, of youth, of the sight of the sky, of the various aspects of Nature, of the love of Phœbus, of all that was behind her and of all that was rapidly coming upon her, of the priest who would denounce her, of the hangman who would soon arrive, of the gallows which was already there. Then terror rose to the very roots of her hair, and she heard the melancholy laugh of the recluse, as she whispered in her ear,—

"Ha! ha! ha! You shall be hanged!"

She turned, almost fainting, to the window, and saw the savage face of the nun through the bars.

"What have I done to you?" she asked feebly.

The recluse made no answer; she began to mumble in angry, mocking sing-song, "Gipsy girl! gipsy girl! gipsy girl!"

The luckless Esmeralda veiled her face with her hair, seeing that it was no human being with whom she had to deal.

All at once the recluse exclaimed, as if the gipsy's question had taken all this time to penetrate her troubled brain:—

"What have you done to me, do you say? Ah! What have you done to me, indeed, you gipsy! Well, listen, and I will tell you. I had a child, even I! Do you hear? I had a child,—a child, I say! A pretty little girl! My Agnès," she repeated, her wits wandering for a moment, and kissing something in the gloom. "Well, are you listening, gipsy? They stole my child; they took my child from me; they ate my child! That is what you have done to me."

The young girl answered, as innocently as the lamb in the fable,—

"Alas! I probably was not even born then!"

"Oh, yes!" rejoined the recluse, "you must have been born. You had a hand in it. She would have been about your age! There! For fifteen years I have been in this hole; for fifteen years I have suffered; for fifteen years I have prayed; for fifteen years I have dashed my head against these four walls. I tell you, 'twas the gipsies who stole her from me,—do you hear?—and who gnawed her bones. Have you a heart? Fancy what it is to have a child who plays at your knee; a child who sucks your breast; a child who sleeps in your arms. It is such a helpless, innocent.

thing! Well, that,—that's what they took from me, what they killed for me! The good God knows it well! Now it is my turn; I will slaughter the Egyptians. Oh, how I would bite you, if the bars did not prevent me! My head is too big to pass through them! Poor little thing! they took her while she slept! And if they waked her when they snatched her up, all her shrieks were vain; I was not there! Ah, gipsy mothers, you ate my child! Come, look at yours!"

Then she began to laugh, or gnash her teeth, for the two things were much the same in that frenzied face. Dawn was at hand. An ashen light faintly illumined the scene, and the gallows became more and more distinctly visible in the centre of the square. From the other side, towards the Pont Notre-Dame the poor prisoner imagined she heard the tramp of approaching horsemen.

"Madame," she cried, clasping her hands and falling on her knees, dishevelled, frantic, mad with fright,—"Madame, have pity! they are coming. I never harmed you. Would you see me die so horrible a death before your very eyes? You are merciful, I am sure. It is too awful! Let me save myself! Let me go! Have mercy! I cannot die thus!"

"Give me back my child!" said the recluse.

"Mercy! mercy!"

"Give me back my child!"

"Let me go, in Heaven's name!"

"Give me back my child!"

Upon this, the girl sank down, worn out and exhausted, her eyes already having the glazed look of one dead.

"Alas!" she stammered forth, "you seek your child, and I seek my parents."

"Give me my little Agnès!" continued Gudule. "You know not where she is? Then die! I will tell you all. I was a prostitute; I had a child, they took my child from me. It was the gipsies who did it. You see that you must die. When your gipsy mother comes to claim you, I shall say, 'Mother, look upon that gibbet!—Or else restore my child!' Do you know where she is,—where my little girl is? Stay, I will show you. Here's her shoe,—all that is left me. Do you know where the mate to it is? If you know, tell me, and if it is only at the other end of the world, I will go on my knees to get it."

So saying, with her other hand, stretched through the bars, she showed the gipsy the little embroidered shoe. It was already light enough to distinguish the shape and colours.

"Show me that shoe," said the gipsy shuddering. "My God! my God!"

And at the same time with her free hand she hastily opened the little bag adorned with green glass beads, which she wore about her neck.

"That's it! that's it!" growled Gudule; "search for your devilish spells!"

All at once she stopped short, trembled from head to foot, and cried out in a voice which came from her inmost soul, "My daughter!"

The gipsy had drawn from the bag a tiny shoe, precisely like the other. A strip of parchment was fastened to the little shoe, upon which these verses were written:

"When the mate to this you find,

Her arms to thee shall ope a mother kind."

Quick as a flash of lightning the recluse compared the two shoes, read the inscription on the parchment, and pressed her face, beaming with divine rapture, to the window-bars exclaiming,—

"My daughter! my daughter!"

"Mother!" replied the gipsy.

Here we must forbear to set down more.

The wall and the iron grating parted the two. "Oh, the wall!" cried the recluse. "Oh, to see her and not to kiss her! Your hand! your hand!"

The girl put her arm through the window; the recluse threw herself upon the hand, pressed her lips to it, and stood lost in that kiss, the only sign of life being an occasional sob which heaved her bosom. Yet she wept torrents of tears in silence, in the darkness, like rain falling in the night. The poor mother poured out in floods upon that idolized hand the dark, deep fountain of tears within her heart, into which all her grief had filtered, drop by drop, for fifteen years.

Suddenly she rose, flung her long grey hair back from her face, and without a word began to shake the bars of her cell more fiercely than a lioness. They held firm. Then she brought from one corner a large paving-stone which served her as a pillow, and hurled it against them with such violence that one of them broke, flashing countless sparks. A second blow utterly destroyed the old iron cross which barricaded her window. Then with both hands she pulled out and demolished the rusty fragments. There are moments when a woman's hands seem endowed with supernatural strength.

A passage being cleared,—and it took les than a minute to do the work,—she seized her daughter by the waist and dragged her into the cell. "Come, let me draw you out of the abyss!" she murmured.

When her daughter was in the cell, she placed her gently on the ground, then took her up again, and bearing her in her arms as if she were still her little Agnès, she paced to and fro in the narrow space, frantic, mad with joy, singing, shouting, kissing her daughter, talking to her, bursting into laughter, melting tears, all at once, and with the utmost passion.

"My daughter! my daughter!" she cried. "I've found my daughter! Here she is! The good God has restored her to me. Come, all of you! Is there no one here to see that I've found my daughter? Lord Jesus, how beautiful she is! You made me wait fifteen years, my good God, but it was to make her more beautiful for me! Then the gipsies did not eat her! Who told me so? My little girl! my little girl! kiss me. Those good gipsies! I love gipsies. It is really you. Then that was why my heart leaped within me every time you passed; and I thought it was hate! Forgive me, Agnès, forgive me. You thought me very cruel, didn't you? I love you. Have you still the same little mark on your neck? Let us see. She has it still. Oh, how beautiful you are! It was I who gave you those big eyes, miss. Kiss me. I love you. I care not now if other mothers have children; I can laugh them to scorn. They may come. Here is mine. Here's her neck, her eyes, her hair, her hand. Find me another as lovely! Oh, I tell you she'll have plenty of lovers, this girl of mine! I have wept for fifteen years. All my beauty has left me and gone to her. Kiss me."

She made her a thousand other extravagant speeches, their only merit being in the tone in which they were uttered, disordered the poor girl's dress until she made her blush, smoothed her silken hair with her hand, kissed her foot, her knee, her forehead, her eyes, went into ecstasies over each and all. The young girl made no resistance, but repeated ever and anon, in a low tone and with infinite sweetness, "Mother!"

"Look you, my little one," went on the recluse, interrupting each word with kisses,—"look you; I shall love you dearly. We will go away; we shall be very happy. I have inherited something at Rheims, in our native country. You know, at Rheims? Oh, no! you don't remember; you were too little. If you only knew how pretty you were at four months old! Tiny feet, which people, out of curiosity, came all the way from Epernay, full seven leagues off, to see! We will have a field and a house. I will put you to sleep in my bed. My God! my God! who would ever have believed it? I've found my daughter!"

"Oh, mother!" said the girl, at last recovering sufficient strength to speak in spite of her emotion, "the gipsy woman told me it would be so. There was a kind gipsy woman of our tribe who died last year, and who always took care of me as if she had been my nurse. It was she who hung this bag about my neck. She always said to me, 'Little one, guard this trinket well. It is a precious treasure; it will help you to find your mother. You wear your mother around your neck.' The gipsy foretold it!"

The nun again clasped her daughter in her arms.

"Come; let me kiss you! You said that so prettily. When we are in our own country, we will give these little shoes to the Child Jesus in the church; we surely owe that much to the kind Blessed Virgin. Heavens! what a sweet voice you have! When you spoke to me just now, it was like music. Oh, my Lord God, I have found my child! But is it credible,—all this story? Nothing can kill one, for I have not died of joy."

And then she again began to clap her hands, to laugh, and cry.

"How happy we shall be!"

At this moment the cell rang with the clash of arms and the galloping feet of horses, which seemed to come from the Pont Notre-Dame, and to be advancing nearer and nearer along the quay. The gipsy threw herself into the nun's arms in an agony.

"Save me! save me, mother! I hear them coming!"

The recluse turned pale.

"Heavens! What do you say? I had forgotten; you are pursued! Why, what have you done?"

"I know not," replied the unhappy child; "but I am condemned to die."

"To die!" said Gudule, tottering as if struck by lightning. "To die!" she repeated slowly, gazing steadily into her daughter's face.

"Yes, mother," replied the desperate girl, "they mean to kill me. They are coming now to capture me. That gallows is for me! Save me! save me! They come! Save me!"

The recluse stood for some moments motionless, as if turned to stone; then she shook her head doubtingly, and all at once burst into loud laughter; but her former frightful laugh had returned:—

"Ho! ho! No; it is a dream! Oh, yes; I lost her, I lost her for fifteen years, and then I found her again, and it was but for an instant! And they would take her from me again! Now that she is grown up, that she is so fair, that she talks to me, that she loves me, they would devour her before my eyes,—mine, who am her mother! Oh, no; such things cannot be! The good God would not suffer them."

Here the cavalcade seemed to pause, and a distant voice was heard, saying,—

"This way, Master Tristan; the priest says that we shall find her at the Rat-Hole!" The tramp of horses began again.

The recluse sprang up with a despairing cry.

"Save yourself! save yourself, my child! I remember now! You are right; it is your death! Horror! Malediction! Save yourself!"

She thrust her head from the window, and rapidly withdrew it.

"Stay!" she said in a low, curt, and mournful tone, convulsively clasping the hand of the gipsy, who was more dead than alive. "Stay! do not breathe! There are soldiers everywhere. You cannot go; it is too light."

Her eyes were dry and burning. She stood for a moment speechless; then she strode up and down the cell, pausing at intervals to tear out handfuls of her grey hair. Suddenly she said: "They are coming; I will speak to them. Hide yourself in this corner; they will not see you. I will tell them that you have escaped; that I let you go, by my faith!"

She laid her daughter—for she still held her in her arms—in a corner of the cell which was not visible from without. She made her crouch down, carefully arranged her so that neither hand nor foot protruded beyond the shadow, loosened her black hair, which spread over her white gown to hide it, put before her her jug and pavingstone,—the only articles of furniture which she had,—imagining that they would conceal her; and when this was done, feeling calmer, she knelt and prayed. Day, which was but just breaking, still left many shadows in the Rat-Hole.

At that instant the voice of the priest —that infernal voice—passed very close to the cell, shouting, —

"This way, Captain Phœbus de Châteaupers!"

At that name, at that voice, Esmeralda, huddling in her corner, made a movement.

"Do not stir!" said Gudule.

She had hardly finished speaking when a riotous crowd of men, swords, and horses, halted outside the cell. The mother rose hastily, and placed herself before the window in such a way as to cut off all view of the room. She saw a numerous band of armed men, on foot and on horseback, drawn up in the Grève. The officer in command sprang to the ground and came towards her.

"Old woman," said this man, who had an atrocious face, "we are looking for a witch, that we may hang her. We were told that you had her."

The poor mother assumed the most indifferent air that she could, and answered,—

"I don't know what you mean."

The other replied, "Zounds! Then what was that frightened archdeacon talking about? Where is he?"

"Sir," said a soldier, "he has disappeared."

"Come, now, old hag," resumed the commanding officer, "don't lie! A witch was left in your care. What have you done with her?"

The recluse dared not deny everything, lest she should rouse suspicion, and answered in a surly but seemingly truthful tone,—

"If you mean a tall girl who was thrust into my hands just now, I can only tell you that she bit me, and I let her go. There. Now leave me in peace."

The officer pulled a wry face.

"Don't lie to me, old scarecrow!" he replied. "I am Tristan l'Hermite, and I am the friend of the king. Tristan l'Hermite, do you hear?" he added looking round the Grève, "'Tis a name familiar here."

"You might be Satan l'Hermite," responded Gudule, whose hopes began to rise, "and I could tell you nothing more, and should be no more afraid of you."

"Odds bodikins!" said Tristan, "here's an old gossip for you! Ah, so the witch girl escaped! And which way did she go?"

Gudule answered indifferently,—

"Through the Rue du Mouton, I believe."

Tristan turned his head, and signed to his troop to prepare to resume their march. The recluse breathed more freely.

"Sir," suddenly said an archer, "pray ask this old sorceress how the bars of her window came to be so twisted and broken."

This question revived the miserable mother's anguish. Still, she did not lose all presence of mind.

"They were always so," she stammered.

"Nonsense!" rejoined the archer; "only yesterday they formed a beautiful black cross which inspired pious thoughts in all who looked upon it."

Tristan cast a side-glance at the recluse.

"It seems to me that our friend looks embarrassed."

The unfortunate woman felt that everything depended upon her putting a good face on the matter, and, with death in her soul, she began to laugh. Mothers have such courage.

"Pooh!" said she, "that man is drunk. 'Twas more than a year ago that the tail of a cart full of stones was backed into my window and destroyed the grating. And, what's more, I scolded the carter roundly."

"That's true," said another archer; "I was here at the time."

There are always people everywhere who have seen everything. This unexpected testimony from the archer encouraged the recluse, who during this interrogatory felt as if she were crossing a precipice on the sharp edge of a knife.

But she was condemned to a continual alteration between hope and fear.

"If it was done by a cart," returned the first soldier, "the broken ends of the bars would have been driven inward; but they are bent outward."

"Ho! ho!" said Tristan; "your nose is as sharp as that of any inquisitor at the Châtelet. Answer him, old woman!"

"Good heaven!" she cried, at her wits' end, and in a voice which despite al her efforts was tearful, "I swear, sir, that it was a cart which broke those bars. You heard that man say he saw it; and besides, what has that to do with your gipsy?"

"Hum!" growled Tristan.

"The devil!" added the soldier, flattered by the provost's praises; "the fractures in the iron are quite fresh!"

Tristan shook his head. She turned pale.

"How long ago did you say this affair of the cart occurred?"

"A month,—perhaps a fortnight, sir. I'm sure I don't remember."

"She said it was a year, just now," observed the soldier.

"That looks queer!" said the provost.

"Sir," she cried, still pressing close to the window, and trembling lest their suspicions should lead them to put in their heads and examine the cell,—"sir, I swear it was a cart that broke these bars; I swear it by all the angels in paradise! If it was not a cart, may I be damned forever: and may God renounce me."

"You seem very ready to swear!" said Tristan, with his searching glance.

The poor woman felt her courage sink. She was in a state to commit any folly, and with terror she realized she was saying what she ought not to say.

Here another soldier ran up, shouting,—

"Sir, the old fagot lies. The witch did not escape through the Rue du Mouton. The chain has been stretched across the street all night, and the chain-keeper has seen no one pass."

Tristan, whose face grew more forbidding every instant, addressed the recluse:—

"What have you to say to this?"

She still strove to brave this fresh contradiction.

"I don't know, sir; I may have been mistaken. I dare say, indeed, that she crossed the water."

"That is in the opposite direction," said the provost. "However, it is not very likely that she would wish to return to the City, where she was closely pursued. You lie, old woman!"

"And then," added the first soldier, "there is no boat either on this side of the water or on the other."

"Perhaps she swam across," replied the recluse, disputing the ground inch by inch.

"Can women swim?" said the soldier.

"Odds bodikins! old woman! you lie! you lie!" angrily rejoined Tristan. "I have a great mind to let the witch go, and hang you in her stead. A quarter of an hour of the rack may wring the truth from your lips. Come! follow us!"

She seized eagerly upon his words:—

"As you like, sir. So be it, so be it! The rack. I am willing. Take me. Be quick; be quick. Let us be off at once. Meantime," thought she, "my daughter may escape."

"Zounds!" said the provost; "so greedy for the rack! I don't understand this mad-woman!"

An old grey-headed serjeant of the watch stepped from the ranks, and addressing the provost, said,—

"Mad, indeed, sir! If she let the gipsy go, it was not her fault, for she has no liking for gipsies. For fifteen years I have done duty on the watch, and I have heard her curse the gipsy women nightly with endless execrations. If the girl of whom we are in search is, as I suppose, the little dancer with the goat, she particularly detests her."

Gudule made an effort, and said,—

"Particularly."

The unanimous testimony of the men belonging to the watch confirmed the old serjeant's statement. Tristan l'Hermite, despairing of learning anything from the recluse, turned his back upon her, and with unspeakable anxiety she saw him move slowly towards his horse.

"Come," he muttered, "we must be off. Let us resume our search. I shall not sleep until this gipsy girl be hanged."

Still, he hesitated some time before mounting his horse. Gudule trembled between life and death as she saw him glance about the square with the restless air of a hunting-dog, which scents the lair of the wild beast and refuses to depart. At last he shook his head and leaped into his saddle. Gudule's terribly overladen heart swelled, and she said in a low voice, with a glance at her daughter, at whom she had not dared to look while the soldiers were there, "Saved!"

The poor girl had crouched in her corner all this time, without moving or breathing, staring death in the face. She had lost none of the scene between Gudule and Tristan, and each of her mother's pangs had found an echo in her own soul. She had heard the successive snappings of the thread which held her suspended over the abyss; twenty times she had felt that it must break, and now at last she began to breathe freely, and to hope that her footing was secure. At this instant she heard a voice say to the provost,—

"'Sblood! Mr. Provost, it is no business for a soldier to hang witches. The mob still rages yonder. I must leave you to your own devices. You will not object to my rejoining my company, who are left without a captain."

This voice was that of Phœbus de Châteaupers. She underwent an indescribable revulsion of feeling. So he was there,— her friend, her protector, her stay, her refuge, her Phœbus! She rose, and before her mother could prevent her, flew to the window, crying,—

"Phœbus! help, my Phœbus!"

Phœbus was no longer there. He had just galloped round the corner of the Rue de la Coutellerie. But Tristan was not yet gone.

The recluse flung herself upon her daughter with a roar. She dragged her violently back, digging her nails into her neck. A tigress does not look twice when the safety of her young is in question. But it was too late. Tristan had seen her.

"Ha! ha!" cried he, with a laugh which bared all his teeth, and made his face like the muzzle of a wolf, "two mice in the trap!"

"I thought as much," said the soldier.

Tristan clapped him on the shoulder,—

"You are a famous cat! Come," he added, "where is Henriet Cousin?"

A man who had neither the dress nor the manner of a soldier stepped from the ranks. He wore a motley garb of brown and grey; his hair was smooth and lank, his sleeves were of leather, and in his huge hand was a bundle of rope. This man always accompanied Tristan, who always accompanied Louis XI.

"My friend," said Tristan l'Hermite, "I presume that this is the witch we are seeking. You will hang her for me. Have you your ladder?"

"There is one yonder under the shed of the Pillar House," replied the man. "Are we to do the business on this gallows?" he continued, pointing to the stone gibbet.

"Yes."

"Ho! ho!" rejoined the man, with a coarse laugh even more bestial than that of the provost; "we shan't have far to go."

"Despatch!" said Tristan; "you can laugh afterwards."

Meantime, since Tristan had seen her daughter, and all hope was lost, the recluse had not spoken a word. She had cast the poor gipsy, almost lifeless, into the corner of the cell, and resumed her place at the window, her hands clinging to the sides of the frame like two claws. In this position her eyes wandered boldly over the soldiers, the light of reason having once more faded from them. When Henriet Cousin approached her refuge, she glared so savagely at him that he shrank back.

"Sir," said he, returning to the provost, "which am I to take?"

"The young one."

"So much the better; for the old one seems hard to manage."

"Poor little dancer with the goat!" said the old serjeant of the watch.

Henriet Cousin again advanced to the window. The mother's eye made his own fall. He said somewhat timidly,—

"Madame,—"

She interrupted him in very low but furious tones:

"What do you want?"

"Not you," said he; "it is the other."

'What other?"

"The young one."

She began to wag her head, crying,—

"There's nobody here! there's nobody here! there's nobody here!"

"Yes, there is!" rejoined the hangman, "and you know it well. Let me have the young one. I don't want to harm you."

She said with a strange sneer,—

"Ah! you don't want to harm me!"

"Let me have the other, madame; it is the provost's will."

She repeated with a foolish look,—

"There's nobody here!"

"I tell you there is!" replied the hangman; "we all saw that there were two of you."

"Look then!" said the recluse, with a sneer. "Put your head in at the window."

The hangman scrutinized the mother's nails, and dared not venture.

"Despatch!" cried Tristan, who had ranged his men in a ring around the Rat-Hole, and himself sat on horseback near the gibbet.

Henriet returned to the provost once more, utterly out of countenance. He had laid his rope on the ground, and awkwardly twirled his hat in his hands.

"Sir," he inquired, "how am I to get in?"

"Through the door."

"There is none."

"Through the window."

"It is too small."

"Then make it bigger," angrily exclaimed Tristan. "Have you no pickaxes?"

From the back of her den, the mother, ever on the alert, watched them. She had lost all hope, she knew not what she wished, but they should not have her daughter.

Henriet Cousin went to fetch his box of tools from the shed of the Pillar House. He also brought out the trestles, which he at once set up against the gibbet. Five or six of the provost's men armed themselves with picks and levers, and Tristan moved towards the window with them.

"Old woman," said the provost in a stern voice, "surrender that girl with a good grace."

She looked at him like one who does not understand.

"'Sblood!" added Tristan, "why should you prevent that witch from being hanged, as it pleases the king?"

The wretched woman began to laugh wildly.

"Why? She is my daughter!"

The tone in which she uttered that word made even Henriet Cousin shudder.

"I am sorry," replied the provost, "but it is the king's good pleasure."

She shrieked with redoubled laughter,—

"What is your king to me? I tell you she is my daughter!"

"Make a hole in the wall," said Tristan.

It was only necessary to remove one course of stones under the window, in order to make an opening of sufficient size. When the mother heard the picks and levers undermining her fortress, she uttered an awful scream; then she began to pace her cell with frightful speed,— one of the habits of a wild beast which she had acquired in her cage. She said no more, but her eyes flamed. The soldiers were chilled to the marrow.

All at once she caught up her paving stone, laughed, and hurled it with both hands at the workmen. The stone, ill aimed (for her hands trembled), struck no one and fell at the feet of Tristan's horse. She ground her teeth.

Meantime, although the sun had not yet risen, it was broad daylight; a lovely pink tint illumined the worm-eaten old chimneys of the Pillar House. It was the hour when the windows of the earliest risers in the great city open joyously upon the roofs. Some few country people, some fruiterers going to market on their donkeys, began to pass through the Grève; they paused a moment at sight of this cluster of soldiers huddled in front of the Rat-Hole, looked at them in surprise, then went their way.

The recluse had seated herself beside her daughter, covering her with her body, her eye fixed, listening to the poor girl, who never stirred, but murmured softly the one word, "Phœbus! Phœbus!" As the work of the destroyers progressed, the mother mechanically moved back, pressing the young girl closer and closer against the wall. All at once she saw the stones (for she was on the watch and never took her eyes from them) quiver, and she heard Tristan's voice urging the labourers on. Then she woke from the stupor into which she had sunk, exclaiming,—and, as she spoke, her voice now pierced the ear like a saw, then stammered as if all the curses which she uttered crowded to her lips at once:

"Ho! ho! ho! But this is horrible! You are robbers! Do you really mean to take my daughter from me? I tell you it is my daughter! Oh, cowards! Oh, base hangmen! Vile assassins! Help! help! Fire! Will they thus take my child? Then, what is he whom men call the good God?"

Then turning to Tristan, with foaming mouth, haggard eyes, on all fours like a panther, and bristling with rage:—

"Come and take my daughter! Do you not understand that this woman tells you it is her daughter? Do you know what it is to have a child of your own? Have you no mate, O lynx? Have you never had a cub? And if you have little ones, when they howl does nothing stir within you?"

"Down with the stones," said Tristan; "they are loosened."

The levers lifted the ponderous course of stone. It was, as we have said, the mother's last bulwark.

She threw herself upon it, tried to hold it up. She scratched it with her nails; but the heavy block, set in motion by six men, escaped from her grasp and slid gently to the ground along the iron levers.

The mother, seeing that an entrance was effected, fell across the opening, barricading the breach with her body, wringing her hands, beating her head against the flagstones, and shrieking in a voice hoarse with fatigue and scarcely audible,—

"Help! Fire! Fire!"

"Now, seize the girl," said Tristan, still unmoved.

The mother glared at the soldiers in so terrible a fashion that they would much rather have retreated than advanced.

"Come, come," repeated the provost. "Here, Henriet Cousin!'

No one stirred a step.

The provost swore:—

"By the Cross! my soldiers! Afraid of a woman!"

"Sir," said Henriet, "do you call that a woman?"

"She has a lion's mane!" said another.

"Come!" resumed the provost, "the gap is broad enough. Go in three abreast, as at the breach of Pontoise. Have done with it, by the head of Mahomet! The first who recoils I'll cut in two!"

Thus placed between the provost and the mother, both alike menacing, the soldiers hesitated an instant; then, making their choice, they advanced upon the Rat-Hole.

When the recluse saw this, she rose suddenly to her knees, shook her hair back from her face, then let her thin, bleeding hands fall upon her thighs. Great tears started one by one from her eyes; they trickled down a wrinkle in her cheeks, like a torrent down the bed which it has worn for itself. At the same time she spoke, but in a voice so suppliant, so sweet, so submissive, and so full of pathos, that more than one old fire-eater about Tristan wiped his eyes.

"Gentlemen! soldiers! one word. I must say one thing to you. She is my daughter, you see,—my dear little daughter whom I lost! Listen. It is quite a story. You must know that I was once very friendly with the soldiers. They were always kind to me in the days when little boys threw stones at me because I led a light life. Do you see? You will leave me my child, when you know all! I am a poor woman of the town. The gipsies stole her away from me. I kept her shoe for fifteen years. Stay; here it is. That was the size of her foot. Paquette Chantefleurie, at Rheims,—Rue Folle-Peine! Perhaps you knew her once. That was I. When you were young, you led a merry life; there were fine doings then. You will take pity on me, won't you, gentlemen? The gipsies stole her from me; they kept her hidden from me for fifteen years. I thought she was dead. Only fancy, my kind friends, I thought she was dead. I have spent fifteen years here, in this cave, with never a spark of fire in winter. That was hard to bear, that was. The poor, dear little shoe! I have shed so many tears that the good God heard me. Last night he gave me back my girl. The good God wrought a miracle. She was not dead. You will not take her from me, I am sure. If it were only myself, I would not complain; but for her, a child of sixteen! Let her have time to see the sun! What has she done to you? Nothing at all. No more have I. If you only knew that I have nobody but her, that I am old, that she is a blessing sent down to me by the Holy Virgin! And then, you are all so kind! You did not know that she was my daughter; now you know it. Oh, I love her! Mr. Provost, I would rather have a hole through my heart than a scratch on her finger. You look like a good, kind gentleman! What I tell you, explains the whole thing, doesn't it? Oh, if you ever had a mother, sir! You are the captain; leave me my child! Remember that I pray to you on my knees, as one prays to Jesus Chirst! I ask nothing of any one; I am from Rheims, gentlemen; I have a little field there, left me by my uncle, Mahiet Pradon. I am not a beggar. I want nothing, but I must have my child! Oh, I must keep my child! The good God, who is master of us all, never gave her back to me for nothing! The king! you say the king! It can't give him much pleasure to have my little girl killed! And besides, the king is good! It's my daughter! It's my daughter, my own girl! She is not the king's! she is not yours! I will go away! we will both go away! After all, they will let two women pass,—a mother and her daughter! Let us pass! we are from Rheims! Oh, you are very kind, serjeants! I love you all. You will not take my dear little one from me; it is impossible, isn't it? Utterly impossible! My child, my child!"

We will not try to give any idea of her gestures, of her accent, of the tears which she swallowed as she spoke, of her hands which she clasped and then wrung, of the heartrending smiles, the pathetic glances, the groans, the sighs, the agonizing and piercing cries which she mingled with her wild, incoherent, rambling words. When she ceased, Tristan l'Hermite frowned, but it was to hide a tear that dimmed his tigerish eye. However, he conquered this weakness, and said curtly,—

"It is the king's command."

Then he bent down to Henriet Cousin and said in a low voice,—

"Put an end to this!"

Perhaps the terrible provost himself felt his heart fail him.

The hangman and his men entered the cell. The mother made no resistance. She only dragged herself towards her daughter and threw herself heavily upon her.

The gipsy saw the soldiers coming. The horror of death revived her.

"My mother!" she cried in tones of unspeakable distress; "my mother! They are coming! Defend me!"

"Yes, my love. I will defend you!" replied her mother, in a feeble voice; and clasping her closely in her arms, she covered her with kisses. The two, prostrate on the ground, mother and daughter, were a sight worthy of pity.

Henriet Cousin seized the girl just below her beautiful shoulders. When she felt his hand, she shrieked and fainted. The hangman, whose big tears fell drop by drop upon her, tried to raise her in his arms. He strove to loose her mother's hold, she having, as it were, knotted her hands about her daughter's waist; but she clung so closely to her child that it was impossible to part them. Henriet Cousin therefore dragged the girl from the cell, and her mother after her. The mother's eyes were also closed.

At this moment the sun rose, and there was already a considerable crowd of people in the square, looking on from a little distance to see who was being thus dragged over the pavement to the gallows,—for this was Provost Tristan's way at hangings. He had a mania for hindering the curious from coming too close.

There was no one at the windows. Only, far off, on the top of the Notre-Dame tower overlooking the Grève, two men were to be seen darkly outlined against the clear morning sky, apparently watching the proceedings.

Henriet Cousin paused with his burden at the foot of the fatal ladder, and, scarcely breathing, so strongly was he moved to pity, he passed the rope around the girl's beautiful neck. The unhappy creature felt the horrible contact of the hemp. She raised her eyelids, and saw the fleshless arm of the stone gibbet stretched above her head. Then she shook off her torpor, and cried in a sharp, shrill voice, "No, no, I will not!" Her mother, whose head was buried and lost in her child's garments, did not speak a word; but her entire body was convulsed by a shudder, and she lavished redoubled kisses upon her child. The hangman took advantage of this moment quickly to unclasp her arms from the prisoner. Whether from exhaustion or despair, she submitted. Then he took the girl upon his shoulder, over which the charming creature fell gracefully, bent double over his large head. Then he put his foot upon the ladder to ascend.

At this instant the mother, crouching on the pavement, opened wide her eyes. Without a cry, she sprang up with a terrible look; then, like a wild beast leaping upon its prey, she threw herself upon the hangman's hand, and bit it. It was a flash of lightning. The hangman yelled with pain. They ran to his aid. With some difficulty they withdrew his bleeding hand from between the mother's teeth. She maintained a profound silence. The men pushed her away with some brutality, and observed that her head fell heavily on the pavement. They lifted her up; she fell back again. She was dead.

The hangman, who had not let go his hold of the girl, resumed his ascent of the ladder.

Chapter II

LA CREATURA BELLA BIANCO VESTITA

When Quasimodo saw that the cell was empty, the gipsy gone, that while he was defending her she had been carried off, he tore his hair, and stamped with rage and surprise; then he ran from end to end of the church in search of his sovereign lady, uttering strange howls, as he went, scattering his red hair upon the pavement. It was just at the moment when the royal archers entered Notre-Dame in triumph, also in search of the gipsy. Quasimodo helped them, without suspecting—poor deaf fellow!—their fatal purpose; he supposed that the enemies of the gipsy were the Vagrants. He himself guided Tristan l'Hermite to every possible hiding-place, opened secret doors, false altar-backs, and inner sacristies for him. Had the wretched girl still been there he must have betrayed her.

When the fatigue of unsuccessful search discouraged Tristan, who was not easily discouraged, Quasimodo continued to search alone. Twenty, nay, a hundred times he went the round of the church, from one end to the other, from top to bottom, upstairs, downstairs, running, calling, crying, sniffing, ferreting, rummaging, poking his head into every hole, thrusting a torch into every vault, desperate, mad. No wild beast which had lost its mate could be wilder or more frantic.

Finally when he was sure, very sure, that she was no longer there, that all was over, that she had been stolen from him, he slowly climbed the tower stairs,—those stairs which he had mounted with such eagerness and delight on the day when he saved her. He passed by the same places, with hanging head, voiceless, tearless, almost breathless. The church was again deserted, and had relapsed into its usual silence. The archers had left it to track the witch into the City. Quasimodo, alone in that vast cathedral, so crowded and so noisy but a moment previous, returned to the room where the gipsy had for so many weeks slept under his watchful care.

As he approached it, he fancied that he might perhaps find her there. When, at the turn of the gallery opening upon the roof of the side-aisle, he caught sight of the narrow cell with its tiny door and window nestling under a huge flying buttress, like a bird's nest under a branch, his heart failed him,—poor man!—and he leaned against a pillar lest he should fall. He imagined that she might perhaps have returned; that a good genius had undoubtedly brought her back; that the cell was too quiet, too safe, and too attractive for her not to be there: and he dared not take another step for fear of destroying his illusion. "Yes," he said to himself, "she is asleep, or saying her prayers. I won't disturb her."

At last he summoned up all his courage, advanced on tiptoe, looked, entered. Empty,—the cell was still empty. The unhappy deaf man slowly walked about it, lifted the bed and looked under it, as if she might be hidden between the mattress and the stones; then he shook his head, and stood staring stupidly. All at once he trampled his torch furiously under foot, and without a word, without a sigh, he threw himself headlong against the wall, and fell fainting on the floor.

When he came to his senses, he flung himself upon the bed; he rolled upon it; he kissed frantically the place, still warm, where the young girl had slept; he lay there for some moments as motionless as if about to die; then he rose, streaming with perspiration, panting, insensate, and began to beat his head against the wall with the frightful regularity of the clapper of one of his own bells, and the resolution of a man who is determined to dash out his brains. At last he fell exhausted for the second time; he dragged himself from the cell on his knees, and crouched before the door in an attitude of wonder.

Thus he remained for more than an hour without stirring, his eye fixed upon the empty cell, sadder and more pensive than a mother seated between an empty cradle and a coffin. He did not utter a word; only at long intervals a sob shook his whole body convulsively; but it was a dry, tearless sob, like summer lightning, which is silent.

It seems that it was then that, seeking in his desolate thoughts to learn who could have been the unlooked-for ravisher of the gipsy, his mind reverted to the archdeacon. He remembered that Don Claude alone had a key to the staircase leading to the cell. He recalled his midnight attempts upon the girl,—the first, in which he, Quasimodo, had helped him; the second, which he had foiled. He remembered a thousand details, and soon ceased to doubt that the archdeacon had stolen the gipsy from him. However, such was his respect for the priest, his gratitude, his devotion, his love for the man were so deeply rooted in his heart, that they resisted, even at this moment, the claws of jealousy and despair.

He considered that the archdeacon had done this thing, and the thirst for blood and murder which he would have felt for another were turned in the poor deaf man to added grief where Claude Frollo was concerned.

Just as his thoughts were thus concentrated upon the priest, as dawn whitened the flying buttresses, he saw on the upper story of Notre-Dame, at the angle formed by the outer railing which runs round the chancel, a moving figure. The figure was walking towards him. He recognized it. It was the archdeacon.

Claude advanced with grave, slow pace. He did not look before him as he walked. He was going towards the north tower; but his face was turned aside towards the right bank of the Seine, and he held his head erect, as if trying to see something over the roofs. The owl often carries its head in this crooked position; it flies towards one point, and looks in another. The priest thus passed above Quasimodo without seeing him.

The deaf man, petrified by this sudden apparition, saw him disappear through the door of the staircase in the north tower. The reader knows that this tower is the one from which the Hôtel de Ville is visible. Quasimodo rose, and followed the archdeacon.

Quasimodo climbed the tower stairs, intending to go to the top, to learn why the priest was there; yet the poor ringer knew not what he, Quasimodo, meant to do or say, or what he wished. He was full of fury, and full of fear. The archdeacon and the gipsy struggled for the mastery in his heart.

When he reached the top of the tower, before issuing from the shadow of the stairs and stepping upon the platform, he looked carefully about to see where the priest was. The priest stood with his back to him. There is an open balustrade around the platform of the belfry tower; the priest, whose eyes were riveted upon the city, leaned against that one of the four sides of the railing which overlooks the Pont Notre-Dame.

Quasimodo, stealthily advancing behind him, gazed abroad to see what he was watching so closely.

But the priest's attention was so fully absorbed that he did not hear the deaf man's step at his side.

Paris is a magnificent and charming sight, and especially so was the Paris of that day, viewed from the top of the towers of Notre-Dame in the cool light of a summer dawn. The day might have been one of the early days of July. The sky was perfectly clear. A few tardy stars were fading out at different points, and there was a single very brilliant one in the east, in the brightest part of the sky. The sun was just rising. Paris began to stir. A very white, very pure light threw into strong relief all the outlines which its countless houses present to the east. The monstrous shadows of the steeples spread from roof to roof from one end of the great city to the other. There were already certain quarters filled with chatter and noise,—here the stroke of a bell, there the blow of a hammer, yonder the intricate jingle and clatter of a passing cart. Already smoke rose here and there from the sea of roofs, as from the fissures in a vast volcano. The river, whose waters wash the piers of so many bridges and the shores of so many islands, was rippled with silvery folds. Around the city, outside the ramparts, the view was lost in a wide ring of fleecy vapours, through which the indefinite line of the plains and the graceful swell of the hills were vaguely visible. All sorts of sounds floated confusedly over the half-awakened city. Towards the east, the morning breeze chased across the sky a few white flakes torn from the fleece of mist upon the hills.

In the cathedral square certain good women, milkjug in hand, pointed with amaze to the strange dilapidation of the great door of Notre-Dame, and the two rivulets of lead congealed in the crevices of the sandstone. These were the only remaining signs of the tumult of the night. The bonfire kindled by Quasimodo between the towers had gone out. Tristan had already had the square cleared and the dead bodies thrown into the Seine. Kings like Louis

XI. are careful to wash the pavement quickly after a massacre.

Outside the tower rail, exactly under the point where the priest had paused, there was one of those fancifully carved gutters with which Gothic edifices bristle; and in a chink of this gutter were two pretty gilly-flowers in full bloom, waving and seeming almost alive in the breeze, as they playfully saluted each other. Above the towers, aloft, far away in the depths of the sky, were little twittering birds.

But the priest heard and saw none of these things. He was one of those men for whom there are no day-dreams, or birds, or flowers. In all that immense horizon, which assumed so many and such varied aspects about him, his gaze was centred on a single point.

Quasimodo burned to ask him what he had done with the gipsy; but the archdeacon seemed at this instant to have left the world far behind him. He was evidently passing through one of those critical moments of life when a man would not feel the earth crumble beneath him. His eyes fixed constantly upon a certain spot, he stood motionless and silent; and there was something so fearful about his silence and his motionlessness, that the shy bell-ringer shuddered before it, and dared not disturb him. Only—and this was one way of questioning the archdeacon—he followed the direction of his glance, and in this manner the eye of the unfortunate deaf man fell upon the Grève.

Thus he saw what the priest was watching. The ladder was reared beside the permanent gallows. There were a few people in the square, and a number of soldiers. A man dragged across the pavement a white object to which something black was fastened. This man stopped at the foot of the gallows.

At this point something took place which Quasimodo could not quite make out. Not because his one eye had not retained its great range, but there was a knot of soldiers which hindered him from seeing everything. Besides, at this instant the sun rose, and such a flood of light burst from the horizon that it seemed as if every pinnacle in Paris, spires, chimneys, and gables, were set on fire at once.

Meantime, the man continued to climb the ladder. Then Quasimodo saw him again distinctly. He had a woman across his shoulder,—a young girl dressed in white; this girl had a knotted rope around her neck. Quasimodo recognized her.

It was she!

The man reached the top of the ladder. There he arranged the noose. Here the priest, to see the better, knelt upon the balustrade.

All at once the man pushed the ladder quickly from him with his heel; and Quasimodo, who had scarcely breathed for some moments past, saw the unfortunate girl dangling from the end of the rope, a dozen feet from the ground, the man crouching above her, pressing his feet against her shoulders to weigh her down. The rope revolved rapidly several times, and Quasimodo saw a horrible shudder run through the gipsy's frame. The priest, on his part, with outstretched neck and starting eyes, watched that dreadful group of man and girl,—of the spider and the fly.

At the most awful moment a demoniac laugh—a laugh impossible to a mere man—broke from the livid lips of the priest. Quasimodo did not hear this laughter, but he saw it.

The ringer shrank back a few paces behind the archdeacon, and then, suddenly rushing furiously upon him, with his huge hands he hurled Don Claude into the abyss over which he leaned.

The priest cried, "Damnation!" and fell.

The gutter below arrested his fall. He clung to it with desperate hands, and, as he opened his mouth for a second shriek, he saw, looking over the edge of the balustrade, above his head, the terrible, avenging face of Quasimodo.

Then he was silent.

The abyss was beneath him. A fall of more than two hundred feet,—and the pavement.

In this dreadful situation the archdeacon said not a word, uttered not a groan. He merely writhed about the gutter making incredible efforts to climb up it, but his hands had no grip upon the granite, his feet scratched the blackened wall without finding a foothold. Those who have visited the Towers of Notre-Dame know that the stone projects directly below the balustrade. It was against this swell that the wretched archdeacon exhausted himself in frantic struggles. He was working, not upon a perpendicular wall, but upon a wall which sloped away from beneath him.

Quasimodo had only to stretch forth his hand to save him from the gulf; but he did not even look at him. He looked at the Grève; he looked at the gibbet; he looked at the gipsy girl.

The deaf man leaned his elbows on the railing, in the very place where the archdeacon had been the moment previous, and there, never removing his gaze from the only object which at this instant existed for him, he stood motionless and mute as if struck by lightning, and a river of tears flowed silently from that eye which until then had shed but a single tear.

Meantime, the archdeacon gasped. His bald head streamed with perspiration, his nails bled against the stone, his knees were flayed against the wall.

He heard his cassock, by which he hung to the spout, crack and rip at every jerk he gave it. To complete his misfortunes, this spout terminated in a leaden pipe which was bending beneath the weight of his body. The archdeacon felt this pipe slowly giving way. The miserable creature said to himself that when his cassock was torn through, when the lead bent completely, he must fall; and terror took possession of him. Sometimes he gazed wildly at a sort of narrow platform some ten feet below him, formed by certain carvings which jutted out; and he implored Heaven, from the depths of his distressed soul, to permit him to end his life upon that space two feet square, were it to last a hundred years. Once he looked down into the abyss, into the square; when he raised his head his eyes were shut and his hair was erect.

There was something frightful in the silence of the two men. While the archdeacon, a few feet beneath him, was agonizing in this horrible fashion, Quasimodo wept, and watched the Grève.

The archdeacon, seeing that all his struggles merely weakened the frail support which remained to him, resolved to move no more. He clung there, hugging the gutter, scarcely breathing, never stirring, his only movement being that mechanical heaving of the chest experienced in dreams when we think that we are falling. His eyes were fixed in a wide stare of anguish and amaze. Little by little, however, he lost ground; his fingers slipped from the spout; the feebleness of his arms and the weight of his body increased more and more. The bending lead which supported him, every moment inclined a notch nearer to the abyss.

He saw below him a fearful sight,— the roof of Saint-Jean le Rond as small as a card bent double. He gazed, one after another, at the impassive sculptures on the tower, like him suspended over the precipice, but without terror for themselves or pity for him. All around him was of stone: before his eyes, gaping monsters; below, far down in the square, the pavement; above his head, Quasimodo weeping.

Groups of curious citizens had gathered in the square, calmly trying to guess what manner of madman it might be who amused himself in so strange a manner. The priest heard them say, — for their voices reached him clear and shrill,—"But he will break his neck!"

Quasimodo was weeping.

At last the archdeacon, foaming with rage and fright, knew that all was in vain. However, he summoned up his remaining strength for a final effort. He braced himself against the gutter, set his knees against the wall, hooked his hands into a chink in the stones, and succeeded in climbing up perhaps a foot; but this struggle made the leaden pipe upon which he hung, bend suddenly. With the same effort his cassock tore apart. Then, feeling that everything had failed him, his stiffened and trembling hands alone retaining a hold upon anything, the unfortunate wretch closed his eyes and loosened his grasp of the gutter. He fell.

Quasimodo watched him fall.

A fall from such a height is seldom perpendicular. The archdeacon, launched into space, at first fell head downward, with outstretched arms; then he rolled over and over several times; the wind wafted him to the roof of a house, where the unhappy man broke some of his bones. Still, he was not dead when he landed there. The ringer saw him make another effort to clutch the gable with his nails; but the slope was too steep, and his strength was exhausted. He slid rapidly down the roof, like a loose tile, and rebounded to the pavement. There, he ceased to move.

Quasimodo then raised his eye to the gipsy, whose body he could see, as it swung from the gibbet, quivering beneath its white gown in the last death-throes; then he again lowered it to the archdeacon, stretched at the foot of the tower, without a trace of human shape, and he said, with a sob which heaved his mighty breast, "Oh, all that I ever loved!"

Chapter III

MARRIAGE OF PHŒBUS

Towards evening of the same day, when the bishop's officers came to remove the mangled body of the archdeacon from the pavement, Quasimodo had vanished from Notre-Dame.

Many rumours were rife concerning the accident. No one doubted that the day had come when, according to their compact, Quasimodo—that is to say the devil—was to carry off Claude Frollo, —that is to say the sorcerer. It was supposed that he had destroyed the body in taking the soul, as a monkey cracks the shell to eat the nut.

Accordingly the archdeacon was not buried in consecrated ground.

Louis XI. died the following year, in the month of August, 1483.

As for Pierre Gringoire, he contrived to save the goat, and he achieved some success as a tragic author. It seems that after dipping into astrology, philosophy, architecture, hermetics, and all manner of follies, he returned to writing tragedies, the most foolish of all things. This he called "making a tragic end." In regard to his dramatic triumphs, we read in 1483, in the Accounts of the Ordinary. "To Jehan Marchand and Pierre Gringoire, carpenter and composer, who made and composed the mystery performed at the Châtelet in Paris, on the entry of the legate, ordered the personages, dressed and habited the same as the said mystery required, and likewise made the necessary scaffoldings for the same, one hundred pounds."

Phœbus de Châteaupers also came to a tragic end: he married.

Chapter IV

MARRIAGE OF QUASIMODO

We have already said that Quasimodo disappeared from Notre-Dame on the day of the death of the gipsy and the archdeacon. Indeed, he was never seen again; no one knew what became of him.

During the night following the execution of Esmeralda, the hangman's assistants took down her body from the gibbet, and carried it, as was customary, to the vaults at Montfaucon.

Montfaucon, as Sauval states, was "the most ancient and most superb gibbet in the kingdom." Between the suburbs of the Temple and Saint-Martin, about three hundred and twenty yards from the walls of Paris, a few cross-bow shots from the village of La Courtille, at the top of a gentle, almost imperceptibly sloping hill, yet high enough to be seen for a distance of several leagues, was a building of singular shape, looking much like a Celtic cromlech, and where human sacrifices were also offered up.

Imagine, at the top of a chalk-hill a parallelopipedon of masonry fifteen feet high, thirty broad, and forty long, with a door, an outer railing, and a platform; upon this platform sixteen huge pillars of unhewn stone, thirty feet high, ranged in a colonnade around three of the four sides of the base which supported them, connected at the top by stout beams from which at intervals hung chains; from all these chains swung skeletons; round about it, in the plain, were a stone cross and two gibbets of secondary rank which seemed to spring up like shoots from the central tree; above all this, in the sky, a perpetual flight of ravens: such was Montfaucon.

At the close of the fifteenth century the awful gibbet, which dated from 1328, was already very much decayed; the beams were worm-eaten, the chains rusty, the pillars green with mould; the courses of hewn stone gaped widely at the joints, and grass grew upon the platform where no foot ever trod; the structure cast a horrid shadow against the sky, particularly at night, when the moon shone feebly upon those white skulls, or when the breeze stirred chains and skeletons, and made them rattle in the darkness. The presence of this gibbet was enough to give the entire neighbourhood an evil name.

The stone base of the odious structure was hollow. It had been made into a vast vault, closed by an antique grating of battered iron, into which were cast not only the human remains taken from the chains at Montfaucon, but the bodies of all the unfortunates executed upon the other permanent gallows throughout Paris. In this deep charnelhouse, where so many mortal remains and so many crimes rotted together, many of the great ones of the earth, many innocent beings, have laid their bones, from Enguerrand de Marigni, who was the first victim of Montfaucon, and who was an upright man, down to Admiral de Coligni, who was the last, and who was likewise a good man.

As for the mysterious disappearance of Quasimodo, all that we have been able to discover is this:—

Some two years or eighteen months after the events which close this story, when search was made in the vault at Montfaucon for the body of Olivier le Daim, who had been hanged two days previous, and to whom Charles VIII. had accorded permission to be buried at Saint-Laurent in better company, among all those hideous carcasses two skeletons were found locked in a close embrace. One of the two, which was that of a woman, still had about it some fragments of a gown, of stuff once white, and about its neck was a necklace of grains of adrezarach, with a little silk bag, adorned with green glass beads, which was open and empty. These articles were doubtless of so little value that the hangman had not cared to remove them. The other skeleton, which held this in so close an embrace, was that of a man. It was noticed that his spine was curved, his head close between his shoulder-blades, and one leg shorter than the other. Moreover, his neck was not broken, and it was evident that he had not been hanged. The man to whom these bones belonged must therefore have come hither himself and died here. When an attempt was made to loose him from the skeleton which he clasped, he crumbled into dust.

THE END

Last Days of a Condemned Man

FIRST PAPER

BICETRE PRISON

CONDEMNED to death!

These five weeks have I dwelt with this idea,—always alone with it, always frozen by its presence, always bent under its weight.

Formerly (for it seems to me rather years than weeks since I was free) I was a being like any other; every day, every hour, every minute had its idea. My mind, youthful and rich, was full of fancies, which it developed successively, without order or aim, but weaving inexhaustible arabesques on the poor and coarse web of life. Sometimes it was of youthful beauties, sometimes of unbounded possessions, then of battles gained, next of theatres full of sound and light, and then again the young beauties, and shadowy walks at night beneath spreading chestnut-trees. There was a perpetual revel in my imagination: I might think on what I chose,—I was free.

But now,—I am a Captive! Bodily in irons in a dungeon, and mentally imprisoned in one idea,—one horrible, one hideous, one unconquerable idea! I have only one thought, one conviction, one certitude,—

Condemned to death!

Whatever I do, that frightful thought is always here, like a spectre, beside me, —solitary and jealous, banishing all else, haunting me for ever, and shaking me with its two icy hands whenever I wish to turn my head away or to close my eyes. It glides into all forms in which my mind seeks to shun it; mixes itself, like a horrible chant, with all the words which are addressed to me; presses against me even to the odious gratings of my prison. It haunts me while awake, spies on my convulsive slumbers, and re-appears, a vivid incubus, in my dreams!

I have just started from a troubled sleep in which I was pursued by this thought, and I made an effort to say to myself, "Oh, it was but a dream!"

Well, even before my heavy eyes could read the fatal truth in the dreadful reality which surrounds me,—on the damp and reeking dungeon-walls, in the pale rays of my night-lamp, in the rough material of my prison-garb, on the sombre visage of the sentry, whose cap gleams through the grating of the door,—it seems to me that already a voice has murmured in my ear,—

"*Condemned to death!*"

SECOND PAPER

FIVE weeks have now elapsed since I was tried,—found guilty,—sentenced.

Let me endeavour to recall the circumstances which attended that fatal day.

It was a beautiful morning at the close of August. My trial had already lasted three days; my name and accusation had collected each morning a knot of spectators, who crowded the benches of the Court, as ravens surrounded a corpse. During three days all the assembly of judges, witnesses, lawyers, and officers had passed and repassed as a phantasmagoria before my troubled vision.

The two first nights, through uneasiness and terror, I had been unable to sleep; on the third I had slept, from fatigue and exhaustion. I had left the jury deliberating at midnight, and was taken back to the heap of straw in my prison, where I instantly fell into a profound sleep,—the sleep of forgetfulness. These were the first hours of repose I had obtained after long watchfulness.

I was buried in this oblivion when they sent to have me awakened, and my sound slumber was not broken by the heavy step and iron shoes of the jailor, by the clanking of his keys, or the rusty grating of the lock; to rouse me from my lethargy it required his harsh voice in my ear, his rough hand on my arm.

"Come," shouted he, "rise directly!"

I opened my eyes, and started from my straw bed: it was already daylight.

At this moment, through the high and narrow window of my cell, I saw on the ceiling of the next corridor (the only firmament I was allowed to see) that yellow reflection by which eyes accustomed to the darkness of a prison recognize sunshine. And oh, how I love sunshine!

"It is a fine day!" said I to the jailor.

He remained a moment without answering me, as if uncertain whether it was worth while to expend a word; then, as if with an effort, he coolly murmured, "Very likely."

I remained motionless, my senses half sleeping, with smiling lips, and my eyes fixed on that soft golden reflection which reverberated on the ceiling.

"What a lovely day!" I repeated.

"Yes," answered the jailor; *"they are waiting for you."*

These few words, like a web which stops the flight of an insect, flung me back into the reality of my position. I pictured to myself instantly, as in a flash of lightning, that sombre Court of Justice, the Bench of Judges, in their robes of sanguine hue, the three rows of stupid-looking witnesses, two gendarmes at the extremity of my bench; black robes waving, and the heads of the crowd clustering in the depth of the shadow, while I fancied that I felt upon me the fixed look of the twelve jurymen, who had sat up while I slept.

I rose: my teeth chattered, my hands trembled, my limbs were so weak that at the first step I had nearly fallen; however, I followed the jailor slowly.

Two gendarmes waited for me at the door-way of the cell; they replaced my fetters, to which I yielded mechanically, as in a dream.

We traversed an interior court, and the balmy air of morning reanimated me. I raised my head: the sky was cloudless, and the warm rays of the sun (partially intercepted by the tall chimneys) traced brilliant angles of light on the high and sombre walls of the prison. It was indeed a delicious day.

We ascended a winding staircase; we passed a corridor, then another, then a third, and then a low door was opened. A current of hot air, laden with noise, rushed from it; it was the breath of the crowd in the Court of Justice which I then entered.

On my appearance the hall resounded with the clank of arms and the hum of voices; benches were moved noisily; and while I crossed that long chamber between two masses of people who were walled in by soldiers, I painfully felt myself the centre of attraction to all those fixed and gaping looks.

At this moment I perceived that I was without fetters, but I could not recall where or when they had been removed.

At length I reached my place at the bar, and there was a deep silence. The instant that the tumult ceased in the crowd, it ceased also in my ideas: a sudden clearness of perception came to me, and I at once understood plainly, what until then I could not discover in my confused state of mind, that *the decisive moment was come!* I was brought there to hear my *sentence!*

Explain it who can: from the manner in which this idea came to my mind, it caused me no terror! The windows were open; the air, and the sounds of the City came freely through them; the room was as light as for a wedding; the cheerful rays of the sun traced here and there the luminous forms of the windows, sometimes lengthened on the flooring, sometimes spreading on a table, sometimes broken by the angles of the walls; and from the brilliant square of each window the rays fell through the air in dancing golden beams.

The Judges at the extreme of the hall bore a satisfied appearance, probably from the anticipation of their labours being soon completed. The face of the President, softly lighted by a reflected sunbeam, had a calm and amiable expression; and a young counsel conversed almost gaily with a handsome woman who was placed near him.

The Jury alone looked wan and exhausted, but this was apparently from the fatigue of having sat up all night. Nothing in their countenances indicated men who would pass sentence of death.

Opposite to me a window stood wide open. I heard laughter in the Market for Flowers beneath; and on the sill of the window a graceful plant, illumined by sunshine, played in the breeze.

How could any sinister idea be formed amongst so many soothing sensations? Surrounded by air and sunshine, I could think of nought save freedom. Hope shone within me, as the day shone around me; and I awaited my sentence with confidence, as one daily calculates on liberty and life.

In the meantime my counsel arrived; after taking his place he leaned towards me with a smile.

"I have hopes!" said he.

"Oh, surely!" I replied in the same light tone.

"Yes," returned he; "I know nothing as yet of the verdict, but they have doubtless acquitted you of premeditation, and then it will be only *hard labour for life!*"

"What do you mean, sir?" replied I indignantly; "I would prefer death!"

Then the President, who had only waited for my counsel, desired me to rise. The soldiers carried arms; and, like an electric movement, all the assembly rose at the same instant. The Recorder, placed at a table below the

Tribunal, read the verdict, which the Jury pronounced during my absence.

* * * * * *

A sickly chill passed over my frame; I leaned against the wall to avoid falling.

"Counsel, have you anything to say why this sentence should not be passed?" demanded the President.

I felt that *I* had much to urge, but I had not the power,—my tongue was cleaving to my mouth.

My counsel then rose. His endeavour appeared to be, to mitigate the verdict of the Jury, and to substitute the punishment of hard labour for life,—by naming which he had rendered me so indignant! This indignation must again have been powerful within me to conquer the thousand emotions which distracted my thoughts. I wished to repeat aloud what I had already said to him, but my breath failed, and I could only grasp him by the arm, crying with convulsive strength, "No!"

The Attorney-General replied against my counsel's arguments, and I listened to him with a stupid satisfaction. The Judges then left the Court; soon returned, and the President read my sentence.

"*Condemned to death!*" cried the crowd; and as I was led away the assembly pressed on my steps with avidity, while I walked on, confused, and nearly in unconsciousness. A revolution had taken place within me. Until that sentence of Death I had felt myself breathe, palpitate, exist, like other beings. Now I felt clearly that a barrier existed between me and the world. Nothing appeared to me under the same aspect as hitherto. Those large and luminous windows, that fair sunshine, that pure sky,—all was pale and ghastly, the colour of a winding sheet. Those men, women, and children who pressed on my path seemed to me like phantoms.

At the foot of the stairs a black and dirty prison-cart was waiting; as I entered it, I looked by chance around.

"The Condemned Prisoner!" shouted the people, running towards the cart.

Through the cloud which seemed to me to interpose between me and all things, I distinguished two young girls who gazed at me with eager eyes.

"Well," said the youngest, clapping her hands, "*it will take place in six weeks.*"

THIRD PAPER

CONDEMNED to death!

Well, why not? I remember once reading, "All mankind are condemned to death, with indefinite respites." How then is my position altered?

Since my sentence was pronounced, how many are dead who calculated upon a long life! How many are gone before me, who, young, free, and in good health, had fully intended to be present at my execution! How many, between this and then, perhaps, who now walk and breathe in the fresh air any where they please, will die before me!

And then, what has life for me, that I should regret? In truth, only the dull twilight and black bread of a prison, a portion of meagre soup from the trough of the convicts; to be treated rudely,—*I*, who have been refined by education; to be brutalized by turnkeys without feeling; not to see a human being who thinks me worthy of a word, or whom I could address; incessantly to shudder at what I have done, and what may be done to me,—these are nearly the only advantages of which the executioner can deprive me!

Ah! still it is horrible.

FOURTH PAPER

The black cart brought me here to this hideous Bicêtre Prison.

Seen from afar, the appearance of that edifice is rather majestic. It spreads to the horizon in front of a hill, and at a distance retains something of its ancient splendour,—the look of a Royal Palace. But as you approach it, the Palace changes to a ruin, and the dilapidated gables shock the sight. There is a mixture of poverty and disgrace soiling its royal façades; without glass or shutters to the windows, but massive crossed-bars of iron instead, against which is pressed, here and there, the ghastly face of a felon or a madman.

FIFTH PAPER

When I arrived here the hand of force was laid on me, and numerous precautions were taken: neither knife nor fork was allowed for my repasts; and a strait-waistcoat—a species of sack made of sail-cloth—imprisoned my arms. I had sued to annul my sentence, so the jailors might have for six or seven weeks their responsibility; and it was requisite to keep me safe and healthful for the Guillotine!

For the first few days I was treated with a degree of attention which was horrible to me,—the civilities of a turnkey breathe of a scaffold. Luckily, at the end of some days, habit resumed its influence; they mixed me with the other prisoners in a general brutality, and made no more of those unusual distinctions of politeness which continually kept the executioner in my memory.

This was not the only amelioration. My youth, my docility, the cares of the Chaplain of the prison, and above all some words in Latin which I addressed to the keeper, who did not understand them, procured for me a walk once a week with the other prisoners, and removed the strait-waistcoat with which I was paralyzed. After considerable hesitation they have also given me pens, paper, ink, and a night-lamp. Every Sunday after Mass I am allowed to walk in the Prison-court at the hour of recreation; there I talk with the prisoners, which is inevitable. They make boon companions, these wretches. They tell me their adventures,—enough to horrify one; but I know they are proud of them. They also try to teach me their mystic idioms,—an odious phraseology grafted on the general language, like a hideous excrescence; yet sometimes it has a singular energy, a frightful picturesqueness. To be hung is called "marrying the widow," as though the rope of the gallows were the widow of all who had been executed! At every instant mysterious, fantastic words occur, base and hideous, derived one knows not whence; they resemble crawling reptiles. On hearing this language spoken, the effect is like the shaking of dusty rags before you.

These men at least pity me, and they alone do so. The jailors, the turnkeys, —and I am not angry with them—gossip and laugh, and speak of me in my presence as of a mere animal.

SIXTH PAPER

I SAID to myself, "As I have the means of writing, why should I not do it? But of what shall I write? Placed between four walls of cold and bare stone, without freedom for my steps, without horizon for my eyes, my sole occupation mechanically to watch the progress of that square of light which the grating of my door marks on the sombre wall opposite, and, as I said before, ever alone with one idea,—an idea of crime, punishment, death,—can I have anything to *say,* I who have no more to *do* in this world; and what shall I find in this dry and empty brain which is worthy the trouble of being written?

"Why not? If all around me is monotonous and hueless, is there not within me a tempest, a struggle, a tragedy? This fixed idea which possesses me, does it not take every hour, every instant a new form, becoming more hideous as the time approaches? Why should I not try to describe for myself all the violent and unknown feelings I experience in my outcast situation? Certainly the material is plentiful; and, however shortened my life may be, there will still be sufficient in the anguish, the terrors, the tortures, which will fill it from this hour until my last, to exhaust my pen and ink! Besides, the only means to decrease my suffering in this anguish will be to observe it closely; and to describe it will give me an occupation. And then, what I write may not be without its use. This journal of my sufferings, hour by hour, minute by minute, torment after torment, if I have strength to carry it on to the moment when it will be *physically* impossible for me to continue,—this history necessarily unfinished, yet as complete as possible, of my sensations, may it not give a grand and deep lesson? Will not there be in this process of agonizing thought, in this ever increasing progress of pain, in this intellectual dissection of a condemned man, more than one lesson for those who condemned? Perhaps the perusal may render them less heedless, when throwing a human life into what they call 'the scale of justice.' Perhaps they have never reflected on the slow succession of tortures conveyed in the expeditious formula of a sentence of death. Have they ever paused on the important idea, that in the man whose days they shorten there is an immortal spirit which had calculated on life, a soul which is not prepared for death? No! they see nothing but the execution, and doubtless think that for the condemned there is nothing anterior or subsequent!"

These sheets shall undeceive them. Published, perchance, some day, they will call their attention a few moments to the suffering of the mind; for it is this which they do not consider. They triumph in the power of being able to destroy the body, almost without making it suffer. What an inferior consideration is this! What is mere physical pain compared to that of the mind? A day will come,—and perhaps these memoirs, the last revelations of a solitary wretch, will have contributed—

That is, unless after my death the wind carries away these sheets of paper into the muddy court, or unless they melt with rain when pasted to the broken window of a turnkey.

SEVENTH PAPER

Suppose that what I write might one day be useful to others,—might make the Judge pause in his decision, and might save the wretched (innocent or guilty) from the agony to which I am condemned,—why should *I* do it? What matters it? When my life has been taken, what will it be to me if they take the lives of others? Have I really thought of such folly?—to throw down the scaffold which I had fatally mounted!

* * * * * *

What! sunshine, spring, fields full of flowers and birds, the clouds, trees, nature, liberty, life,—these are to be mine no more!

Ah, it is myself I must try to save! Is it really true that this cannot be, that I must die soon,—to-morrow, to-day perhaps; is it all thus? Oh, heavens! what a dreadful idea,—of destroying myself against the prison wall!

EIGHTH PAPER

Let me consider what time generally elapses between the condemnation and the execution of a prisoner.

Three days of delay, after sentence is pronounced, for the prisoner's final plea to annul it.

The plea forgotten for a week in a Court of Assize, before it is sent to the Minister; a fortnight forgotten at the Minister's, who does not even know that there are such papers, although he is supposed to transmit them, after examination, to the "Cour de Cassation."

Then classification, numbering, registering; the guillotine-list is loaded, and none must go before their turn! A fortnight more waiting; then the Court assembles, rejects twenty pleas together, and sends all back to the Minister, who sends them back to the Attorney-General, who sends them back to the executioner; this would take three more days.

On the morning of the fourth day the Deputies of the Attorney-General and Recorder prepare the order of execution; and the following morning, from day-break, is heard the noise of erecting the scaffold, and in the cross-streets a commotion of hoarse voices.

Altogether *six weeks*. The young girl's calculation was right! I have now been at least five weeks (perhaps six, for I dare not reckon) in this fatal prison; nay, I think I have been even three days more.

NINTH PAPER

I have just made my will; what was the use of this? I have to pay my expenses, and all I possess will scarcely suffice. A forced death is expensive.

I leave a mother, I leave a wife, I leave a child,—a little girl of three years old, gentle, delicate, with large black eyes and chestnut hair. She was two years and one month old when I saw her the last time.

Thus after my death there will be three women without son, without husband, without father,—three orphans in different degrees; three widows by act of law.

I admit that I am justly punished; but these innocent creatures, what have they done? No matter; they will be dishonoured, they will be ruined; and this is justice!

It is not much on account of my poor old mother that I feel thus wretched; she is so advanced in years, she will not survive the blow; or if she still linger a short time, her feelings are so blunted that she will suffer but little.

Nor is it for my wife that I feel the most. She is already in miserable health, and weak in intellect; her reason will give way, in which case her spirit will not suffer while the mind slumbers as in death.

But my daughter, my child, my poor little Mary, who is laughing, playing, singing, at this moment, and who dreams of no evil! Ah, it is the thought of her which unmans me!

TENTH PAPER

HERE is the description of my prison; eight feet square; four walls of granite, with a flagged pavement; on one side a kind of nook by way of alcove, in which is thrown a bundle or straw, where the prisoner is supposed to rest and sleep, dressed, winter, as in summer, in slight linen clothing. Over my head, instead of curtains, a thick canopy of cobwebs, hanging like tattered pennons. For the rest, no windows, not even a ventilator; and only one door, where iron hides the wood. I mistake; towards the top of the door there is a sort of window, or rather an opening of nine inches square, crossed by a grating, and which the turnkey can close at night. Outside, there is a long corridor lighted and aired by means of narrow ventilators high in the wall. It is divided into compartments of masonry, which communicate by a series of doors; each of these compartments serves as an antechamber to a dungeon, like mine. In these dungeons are confined felons condemned by the Governor of the Prison to hard labour. The three first cells are kept for prisoners under sentence of death, as being nearest to the goal, therefore most convenient for the jailor. These dungeons are the only remains of the ancient Bicêtre Castle, such as it was built in the fifteenth centry by the Cardinal of Winchester, he who caused Jeanne of Arc to be burned. I overheard this description from some persons who came to my den yesterday, to gratify their curiosity, and who stared at me from a distance as at a wild beast in a menagerie. The turnkey received five francs for the exhibition.

I have omitted to say that night and day there is a sentry on guard outside the door of my cell; and I never raise my eyes towards the square grating without encountering his eyes, open, and fixed on me.

ELEVENTH PAPER

As there is no appearance of daylight, what is to be done during the night? It occurred to me that I would arise and examine, by my lamp, the walls of my cell. They are covered with writings, with drawings, fantastic figures, and names which mix with and efface each other. It would appear that each prisoner had wished to leave behind him some trace here at least. Pencil, chalk, charcoal,—black, white, grey letters; sometimes deep carvings upon the stone. If my mind were at ease, I could take an interest in this strange book, which is developed page by page, to my eyes, on each stone of this dungeon. I should like to recompose these fragments of thought; to trace a character for each name; to give sense and life to these mutilated inscriptions,—these dismembered phrases.

Above where I sleep there are two flaming hearts, pierced with an arrow; and beneath is written "Amour pour la vie." Poor wretch! it was not a long engagement.

Beyond this, a three-sided cocked hat, with a small figure coarsely done beneath, and the words, "Vive l'Empereur!"

On the opposite wall is the name of "Papavoine." The capital *P* is worked in arabesques and embellished with care.

A verse of a popular drinking-song.

A Cap of Liberty, cut rather deeply into the stone, with the words beneath of "Bories, La République!"

Poor young man! he was one of the four subaltern officers of La Rochelle. How horrible is the idea of their (fancied) political necessity, to give the frightful reality of the guillotine for an opinion, a reverie, an abstraction!—And I! *I* have complained of its severity!—I who have really committed crime—

Ah, what have I seen! I can go no farther in my research! I have just discovered, drawn with chalk in the corner of the wall, that dreadful image, the representation of that scaffold, which even at this moment is perhaps being put up for my execution! The lamp had nearly fallen out of my trembling hands!

TWELFTH PAPER

I RETURNED precipitately to sit on my straw bed; my head sunk on my knees. After a time, my childish fear was dissipated, and a wild curiosity forced me to continue the examination of my walls.

Besides the name of Papavoine, I tore away an enormous cobweb, thick with dust, and filling the angle of the wall. Under this web there were four or five names perfectly legible, among others of which nothing remained but a smear on the wall,—DAUTAN, 1815. POULAIN, 1818. JEAN MARTIN, 1821. CASTAING, 1823.

As I read these names, frightful recollections crowded on me. *Dautan* was the man who cut his brother in quarters, and who went at night to Paris and threw the head into a fountain, and the body into a sewer. *Poulain* assassinated his wife. *Jean Martin* shot his father with a pistol as the old man opened a window. And *Castaing* was the physician who poisoned his friend; and while attending the illness he had caused, instead of antidote, gave him more poison. Then, next to these names, was Papavoine, the horrible madman who stabbed children to death in his phrenzy.

"These," I exclaimed, as a shudder passed over me, "these, then, have been my predecessors in this cell. Here, on the same pavement where I am, they conceived their last thoughts,—these fearful homicides! Within these walls, in this narrow square, their last steps turned and re-turned, like those of a caged wild-beast. They succeeded each other at short intervals; it seems that this dungeon does not remain empty. They have left the place warm,—and it is to me they have left it. In my turn I shall join them in the felons' cemetery of Clamart, where the grass grows so well!"

* * * * *

I am neither visionary nor superstitious, but it is probable these ideas caused in my brain a feverish excitement; for, whilst I thus wandered, all at once these five fatal names appeared as though written in flames on the dark wall; noises, louder and louder, burst on my ears; a dull red light filled my eyes, and it seemed to me that my cell became full of men,—strangers to me. Each bore his severed head in his left hand, and carried it by the mouth, for the hair had been removed; each raised his right hand at me, *except the parricide.*

I shut my eyes in horror, and then I saw all even more distinctly than before!

Dream, vision, or reality, I should have gone mad if a sudden impression had not recalled me in time. I was near fainting, when I felt something cold crawling over my naked foot. It was the bloated spider, whom I had disturbed. This recalled my wandering senses. Those dreadful spectres, then, were only the fumes of an empty and convulsed brain. The sepulchre is a prison from whence none escape. The door of the tomb opens not inwards!

* * * * *

THIRTEENTH PAPER

I HAVE lately witnessed a hideous sight. As soon as it was day, the prison was full of noise, I heard heavy doors open and shut; the grating of locks and bolts; the clanking of bunches of keys; the stairs creaking from top to bottom with quick steps; and voices calling and answering from the opposite extremes of the long corridors. My neighbours in the dungeons, the felons at hard labour, were more gay than usual. All in the prison seemed laughing, singing, running, or dancing; I—alone silent in this uproar, alone motionless in this tumult—listened in astonishment.

A jailor passed; I ventured to call and ask him "if there were a Fête in the Prison."

"A Fête, if you choose to call it so," answered he; "this is the day that they fetter the galley-slaves who are to set off to morrow for Toulon. Would you like to see them? It would amuse you."

For a solitary recluse, indeed, a spectacle of any kind was an event of interest, however odious it might be; and I accepted the "amusement."

The jailor, after taking the usual precautions to secure me, conducted me into a little empty cell, without a vestige of furniture, and only a grated window, —but still a real window, against which one could lean, and through which one could actually perceive the sky! "Here," said he, "you will see and hear all that happens. You will be 'alone in your box,' like the King!"

He then went out, closing on me locks, bolts, and bars.

The window looked into a square and rather wide court, on every side of which was a large six-storied stone edifice. Nothing could seem more wretched, naked, and miserable to the eye than this quadruple façade, pierced by a multitude of grated windows, against which were pressed a crowd of thin and wan faces, placed one above the other, like the stones of a wall; and all, as it were, framed in the intercrossings of iron bars. They were prisoners, spectators of the ceremony, until their turn came to be the actors.

All looked in silence into the still empty court; among these faded and dull countenances there shone, here and there, some eyes which gleamed like sparks of fire.

At twelve o'clock, a large gateway in the court was opened. A cart, escorted by soldiers, rolled heavily into the court, with a rattling of irons. It was the Convict-guard with the chains.

At the same instant, as if this sound awaked all the noise of the prison, the spectators of the windows, who had hitherto been silent and motionless, burst into cries of joy, songs, menaces, and imprecations, mixed with hoarse laughter. It was like witnessing a masque of Demons; each visage bore a grimace, every hand was thrust through the bars, their voices yelled, their eyes flashed, and I was startled to see so many gleams amidst these ashes. Meanwhile the galley-sergeants quietly began their work. One mounted on the cart, and threw to his comrades the fetters, the iron collars, and the linen clothing; while others stretched long chains to the end of the court and the Captain tried each link by striking it on the pavement,—all of which took place under the mocking raillery of the prisoners, and the loud laughter of the convicts for whom they were being prepared.

When all was ready, two or three low doors poured forth into the court a collection of hideous, yelling, ragged men; these were the galley-convicts.

Their entry caused increased pleasure at the windows. Some of them, being 'great names' among their comrades, were saluted with applause and acclamation, which they received with a sort of proud modesty. Several wore a kind of hat of prison straw, plaited by themselves, and formed into some fantastic shape; these men were always the most applauded.

One in particular excited transports of enthusiasm,—a youth of seventeen, with quite a girlish face. In his prison he had made himself a straw dress, which enveloped him from head to foot; and he entered the court, jumping a somerset with the agility of a serpent. He was a mountebank condemned for theft, and there was a furious clapping of hands, and a volley of cheers, for him.

At length the names were called in alphabetical order, and they went to stand two and two, companions by similar initials; so that even if a convict had a friend, most likely their chains would divide them from suffering together.

Whilst they were exchanging their worn-out prison-garments for the thin and coarse clothing of the galleys, the weather, which had been hitherto uncertain, became suddenly cold and cloudy, and a heavy shower chilled their thin forms, and saturated their vesture.

A dull silence succeeded to their noisy bravadoes; they shivered, their teeth chattered, and their limbs shook in the wet clothes.

One convict only, an old man, retained a sort of gaiety. He exclaimed laughing, while wiping away the rain, and shaking his fist at the skies, "This was not in the playbill!"

When they had put on their miserable vestments, they were taken in bands of twenty or thirty to the corner of the court where the long chains were extended. At every interval of two feet in these chains were fastened short transverse chains, and at the extremity of each of the latter was attached a square iron collar, which opened by means of a hinge in the centre and closed by an iron bolt, which is riveted, for the whole journey, on the convict's neck. The convicts were ordered to sit down in the mud on the inundated pavement; the iron collars were fitted on them, and two prison-blacksmiths, with portable anvils, riveted the hard, unheated metal with heavy iron hammers.

This was a frightful operation, and even the most hardy turned pale! Each stroke of the hammer, aimed on the anvil resting on their backs, makes the whole form yield; the failure of its aim, or the least movement of the head, might launch them into eternity.

When this operation was finished, the convicts rose simultaneously. The five gangs joined hands, so as to form an immense circle, and thus ran round and round in the court with a rapidity that the eye could hardly follow. They sung some couplets, in their own idiom, to a melody which was sometimes plaintive, sometimes furious, often interrupted by hoarse cries and broken laughter, like delirious ravings, while the chains, clanking together in cadence, formed an accompaniment to a song more harsh than their own noise. A large trough was now brought in; the guards, striking the convicts to make them discontinue their dance, took them to the trough, in which was swimming I know not what sort of herbs in some smoking and dirty-looking liquid. Having partaken of it, they threw the remainder on the pavement, with their black bread, and began again to dance and sing. This is a liberty which is allowed to them on the day they are fettered and the succeeding night.

I gazed on this strange spectacle with such eager and breathless attention, that I totally forgot my own misery. The deepest pity filled my heart, and their laughter made me weep.

Suddenly, in the midst of a profound reverie into which I had fallen, I observed the yelling circle had stopped, and was silent. Then every eye was turned to the window which I occupied. "The Condemned! the Condemned!" shouted they, pointing their fingers at me; and their bursts of laughter were redoubled.

I was thunderstruck. I know not where they knew me, or how I was recognized.

"Good day! good night!" cried they, with their mocking sneer. One of the youngest, condemned to the Galleys for life, turned his shining, leaden face on me, with a look of envy, saying, "He is lucky! he is to be *clipped!* Good-bye, Comrade!"

I cannot describe what passed within me. I was indeed their "comrade!" The Scaffold is Sister to the Galleys. Nay, I was even lower than they were; the convicts had done me an honour. I shuddered: yes! their "comrade!" I remained at the window, motionless, as if paralyzed; but when I saw the five gangs advance, rushing towards me with phrases of disgusting cordiality; when I heard the horrible din of their chains, their clamours, their steps at the foot of my wall, it seemed to me that this knot of demons were scaling my cell! I uttered a shriek; I threw myself against the door violently, but there was no means of flight. I knocked, I called with mad fury. Then I thought I heard, still nearer, the horrid voices of the convicts. I thought I saw their hideous heads appearing on a level with the window; I uttered another shriek of anguish, and fainted.

* * * * *

FOURTEENTH PAPER

When my consciousness returned it was night; I was lying on a truckle bed; a lamp which swung from the ceiling enabled me to see a line of beds similar to mine, and I therefore judged that I had been taken to the Infirmary. I remained a few moments awake, but without thought or recollection, totally engrossed by the happiness of being again in a bed. Certainly, in former days, this prison-hospital bed would have made me shrink with disgust; but I am no longer the same individual. The sheets were brown, and coarse to the touch, the blanket thin and ragged, and there was but one straw mattress.

No matter! I could stretch my limbs at their ease between these coarse sheets; and under this blanket, thin as it was, I felt the gradual decrease of that horrible chill in the marrow of my bones, to which I had lately been accustomed.—I slept again.

A loud noise awakened me at daylight. The noise came from without; my bed was beside the window, and I sat up to see from what it arose. The window looked into the large Court of the Bicêtre, which was full of people. Two lines of veterans had difficulty in keeping the crowd away from a narrow passage across the Court. Between this double rank of soldiers, five long wagons, loaded with men, were driven slowly jolting at each stone; it was the departure of the convicts.

These wagons were open, and each gang occupied one. The convicts, in consequence of their iron collars being attached to the centre chain, are obliged to sit back to back, their feet hanging over the sides of the wagon; the centre chain stretched the whole length of the cart, and on its unfastened end the Sergeant stood with his loaded musket. There was a continual clanking of the prisoners' chains, and at each plunge of the wagon their heads and pendant limbs were jolted violently. A quick penetrating rain chilled the air, and made their wet slight vesture cling to their shivering forms. Their long beards and short hair streamed with wet; their complexions were saturnine; they were shivering, and grinding their teeth with mingled rage and cold. But they had no power of moving; once riveted to that chain, each becomes a mere fraction of that hideous whole which is called the Gang. Intellect must abdicate,—the fetters condemn it to death; and the mere animal must not even hunger but at certain hours. Thus fixed, the greater part half clad, with bare heads, and no rest for their feet, they begin their journey of twenty-five days; the same sort of wagons, the same portion of dress being used in scorching July as in the cold rains of November. One would almost think that man wishes Heaven to take part in his office of executioner.

Between the crowd and the convicts a horrible dialogue was maintained,—abuse on one side, bravadoes on the other, imprecations from both; but at a sign from the Captain I saw the sticks of the Guard raining indiscriminate blows into the wagon, on heads or shoulders, and all returned to that kind of external calm which is called "order." But their eyes were full of vengeance, and their powerless hands were clenched on their knees.

The five wagons, escorted by mounted gendarmes and guards on foot, passed slowly under the high arched door of the Bicêtre. The crowd followed them: all vanished like a phantasmagoria, and by degrees the sounds diminished of the heavy wheels, clanking fetters, and the yells of the multitude uttering maledictions on the journey of the convicts. And such was their happy beginning!

What a proposition my counsel made! The Galleys! I was right to prefer death; rather the Scaffold than what I had seen!

FIFTEENTH PAPER

UNFORTUNATELY I was not ill; therefore the next day I was obliged to leave the Infirmary to return to my dungeon. Not ill? No truly, I am young, healthful, and strong; the blood flows freely in my veins; my limbs obey my will; I am robust in mind and body, constituted for a long life. Yes, all this is true; and yet, nevertheless, I have an illness, a fatal illness,—an illness given by the hand of man!

Since I came out of the Infirmary a vivid idea has occupied me,—a thought which affects me to madness; namely, that I might have escaped, had they left me there! Those Physicians, those Charity Sisters seemed to take an interest in me. "To die so young! and by such a death!" One would have imagined they pitied me by their pressing round my bed. Bah! it was curiosity! I have no chance now! My plea will be rejected, because all was legal; the witnesses gave correct evidence, the counsel pleaded well, the Judges decided carefully. I do not reckon upon it, unless— No! folly; there is no hope. The plea is a cord which holds you suspended over an abyss, and which you feel giving way at each instant until it breaks. It is as if the axe of the Guillotine took six weeks to fall.

If I could obtain my pardon!—pardon! From whom, for what, and by what means? It is impossible that I should be pardoned. They say *an example is requisite.*

SIXTEENTH PAPER

DURING the few hours I passed at the Infirmary, I seated myself at a window in the sunshine (for the afternoon had become fine), and I enjoyed all the sun which the gratings of the window would allow me.

I sat thus, my heavy and fevered head within my hands, my elbows on my knees, my feet on the bar of the chair; for dejection had made me stoop, and sink within myself, as if I had neither bone nor muscular power.

The stifling air of the prison oppressed me more than ever; I still fancied the noise from the convicts' chains rung in my ears; I was almost overcome. I wished that some guardian spirit would take pity on me, and send even a little bird to sing there, opposite, on the edge of the roof.

I know not if it were a spirit of good or evil which granted my wish; but almost at the moment I uttered it, I heard beneath my window a voice,—not that of a bird, but far better,—the pure, fresh, *velvet* voice of a young girl of fifteen!

I raised my head with a start; I listened with avidity to the song she sung. It was a slow and plaintive air, —a sad yet beautiful melody. As I gathered the sense of the words, I cannot describe my pain and disappointment, while the stanzas of prison-dialect marred the sweet music.

I heard no more. I could listen to no more. The meaning, half-hidden, half-evident, of this horrible lament,—the struggle between the felon and the police; the thief he meets and despatches for his wife; his dreadful explanation to her: "I have sweated an oak" ("I have assassinated a man"); the wife who goes to Versailles with a petition, and the King indignantly exclaiming that he "will make the guilty man dance where there is no floor!"—and all this sung to the sweetest air, and by the sweetest voice that ever soothed human ear! I was shocked, disgusted, overcome. It was a repulsive idea that all these monstrous words proceeded from a fresh rosy mouth: it was like the slime of a snail over a rosebud!

I cannot express what I felt; I was at once pained and gratified. The idiom of crime, a language at once sanguinary and grotesque, united to the voice of a young girl, that graceful transition from the voice of childhood to the voice of woman,—all these deformities of words delightfully sung, cadenced, rounded!

Ah, how infamous is a prison! It contains a venom which assails all within its pestilential reach. Everything withers there, even the song of a girl of fifteen!

If you find a bird within its courts, it has mud on its wing. If you gather a beauteous flower there, it exhales poison!

SEVENTEENTH PAPER

WHILST I was writing, my lamp faded, daylight appeared, and the clock of the chapel struck six.

* * * * *

What can be the meaning of what has since happened? The turnkey on duty came into my cell; he took off his cap, bowed to me, apologized for disturbing me, and making an effort to soften his rough voice, inquired what I wished to have for my breakfast—

A shudder has come over me. *Is it to take place to-day?*

EIGHTEENTH PAPER

I FEEL that it *is* for to-day!
The Governor of the prison himself came to visit me. He asked me how he could serve or accommodate me; he expressed a hope that I had no complaint to make respecting him or his subordinates; and he inquired with interest regarding my health, and how I had

passed the night. On leaving me, he called me "Sir!"

Oh, it surely is for to-day!

NINETEENTH PAPER

The Governor of the prison thinks I have no cause of complaint against him or his jailors. He is right, and it would be wrong of me to complain; they have done their duty, they have kept me safe; and then they have been complaisant at my arrival and departure. Ought I not to be satisfied?

This Governor, with his benign smile, his soft words, his eye which flatters and spies, his coarse heavy hands,—he is the incarnation of a prison!

Ah, hapless creature! what will become of me? What will they do with me?

TWENTIETH PAPER

Lo! I am calm. All is finished—quite finished! I am relieved from the dreadful anxiety into which I was thrown by the Governor's visit; for I confess I still felt hope. Now, thank Heaven! hope is gone.

Let me record what has happened.

At half-past six the door of my cell was opened; an old man with white hair entered, dressed in a brown great-coat.

He unfastened it, and beneath I saw the black cassock and bands of a priest. He was not the usual Chaplain to the prison, and I thought this appeared ominous. He seated himself opposite to me, with a quiet smile; then shook his head, and raised his eyes to heaven. I understood him.

"My son!" said he, "are you prepared?"

I answered, in a low tone, "I am not prepared—but I am ready."

Then my sight became troubled; a chill damp pervaded my frame. I felt the veins on my temples swelling, and a confused murmur in my ears.

Whilst I vacillated on my chair as though asleep, the old man continued speaking,—at least, so it appeared to me, for I think I remember seeing his lips move, and his hand raised.

The door opened again; the noise of the lock roused me from my reverie, and the Priest from his discourse. A person dressed in black entered, accompanied by the Governor of the prison, and bowed profoundly to me; he carried a roll of paper.

"Sir," said he, with a courteous smile, "I have the honour to bring you a message from the Attorney-General."

The first agitation was over; all my presence of mind returned, and I answered in a firm tone, "Read on, Sir."

He then read a long, technically-expressed paper, the purport of which was the rejection of my plea. "The execution will be to-day," added he; "we shall leave this for the Conciergerie Prison at half-past seven. My dear Sir, will you have the extreme goodness to accompany me at that hour?"

For some instants I had no longer listened to him; for while his eyes were fixed on the paper the Governor was occupied talking to the Priest; and I looked at the door which they had left half open! . . . Ah, hapless me! Four sentinels in the corridor. Again I was asked when I would be ready to go.

"When you please," I said; "at your own time."

"I shall have the honour of coming for you, then, in half an hour," said he, bowing; and all the party withdrew.

Oh, for some means of escaping, Good heavens! any means whatever! I *must* make my escape! I must! Immediately! By the doors, by the windows, by the roof! Even though in the struggle I should destroy myself!

Oh, rage! demons! malediction! It would take months to pierce this wall with efficient tools. And I have not one nail, nor one hour!

TWENTY-FIRST PAPER

CONCIERGERIE PRISON.

HERE I am transferred, then. Let me record the details. At half-past seven the messenger again presented himself at the threshold of my dungeon. "Sir," said he, "I wait for you."

Alas! and I saw that four others did the same! I rose, and advanced one step. It appeared to me I could not make a second. My head was so heavy, and my limbs so feeble; but I made an effort to conquer my weakness, and assumed an appearance of firmness.

Prior to leaving the cell, I gave it a final look; I had almost become attached to it. Besides, I left it empty and open, which gives so strange an appearance to a dungeon.

It will not be long untenanted. The turnkeys said they expected some one this evening,—a prisoner who was then being tried at the Court of Assizes.

At the turn of the corridor the Chaplain rejoined us; he had just breakfasted.

At the threshold of the goal, the Governor took me by the hand; he had reinforced my escort by four veterans.

By the door of the Infirmary a dying old man exclaimed, "Good-bye, we shall soon meet again!"

We arrived in the courtyard, where I could breathe again freely, and this refreshed me greatly; but we did not walk long in the open air. The carriage was stationed in the first court. It was the same which had brought me there, —a sort of oblong van, divided into two sections by a transverse grating of close wire. Each section had a door; one in the front, one in the back of the cart; the whole so dirty, so black, so dusty, that the hearse for paupers is a state carriage by comparison! Before I buried myself in this moving tomb, I cast a look round the yard,—one of those despairing looks which seem to ask a miracle. The court was already encumbered with spectators. Like the day when the convicts departed, there was a slight, chilling shower of the season; it is raining still, and doubtless there will be rain all the day,—which will last when I am no more! We entered the van. The messenger and a gendarme, in the front compartment, the Priest, myself, and a gendarme in the other, with four mounted gendarmes around the carriage. As I entered it, an old grey-eyed woman who stood near exclaimed, "I like seeing this, even better than seeing the galley convicts!"

I can conceive this. It is a spectacle more easily taken in at one view. Nothing divides the attention; there is but one man, and on this isolated being there is as much misery heaped as on all the other convicts together. The van passed with a dull noise under the gateway, and the heavy doors of the Bicêtre were closed after us. I felt myself moving, but in stupor, like a man fallen into a lethargy, who can neither move nor cry out, and who fancies he feels that he is being buried alive. I listened vaguely to the peals of bells on the collars of the post-horses which drew the van, the iron wheels grating over various substances in the road, the cracking whips of the postillion, the galloping of the gendarmes round the carriage,— all seemed like a whirlwind which bore me away.

My mind was so stupefied with grief that I only conceived ideas as in a dream. I saw the blue towers of Nôtre-Dame in the distance. "Those who will be on the tower with the flag will see my execution well," said I to myself, smiling stupidly.

I think it was at that moment that the Priest addressed me again; I patiently let him speak. I had already in my ears the noise of the wheels, the galloping horses, and the postillion's whip; therefore it was only one more incomprehensible noise. I listened in silence to that flow of monotonous words, which deadened my thoughts, like the murmur of a brook; and they passed before my torpid mind, always varied yet always the same, like the crooked elms we passed by the roadside. The short and jerking voice of the messenger in the front of the van suddenly aroused me.

"Well, Chaplain," said he, in almost a gay tone, "what news have you to-day?"

The Chaplain, who spoke to me without ceasing, and who was deafened by the carriage, made no answer.

"Well, well! how the van rattles; one can hardly hear oneself. What was I saying to you, Chaplain! Oh, aye!— do you know the great news of Paris to-day?"

I started as if he were speaking to me.

"No," said the priest, who had at last heard him, "I have not had time to read the papers this morning: I shall see them this evening. When I am occupied in this way all day, I order my servant to keep the papers, and I read them on my return."

"Bah!" replied the other, "it is impossible that you have not heard what I mean. The news of Paris—the news of this morning."

It was now my turn to speak; and I said, "I know what you mean."

The Messenger looked at me. "You? really! and pray what is your opinion about it?"

"You are inquisitive," said I.

"How so, sir?" replied he. "Every one should have a political opinion: I esteem you too much to suppose that you are without one. As to myself, I am quite in favour of re-establishing the National Guard. I was a serjeant in my company; and, faith! it was very agreeable to—"

I interrupted him by saying, "I did not think this was the subject in question."

"What did you suppose, then? You professed to know the news."

"I spoke of something else with which Paris is also occupied to-day."

The fool did not understand, and his curiosity was awakened.

"More news! Where the deuce could *you* learn news. What is it, my dear sir? Do you know what it is, Chaplain? Do let me hear all about it, I beg. I like news, you see, to relate to the President; it amuses him."

He looked from one to the other, and obtained no answer.

"Well," said he, "what are you thinking of?"

"I am thinking," said I, "that I shall be past thinking, this evening."

"Oh, that's it," returned he. "Come, come, you are too sad. Mr. Castaing conversed on the day of his execution."

Then, after a pause, he continued: "I accompanied Mr. Papavoine on his last day. He wore his otter-skin cap, and smoked his cigar. As for the young men of La Rochelle, they only spoke among themselves, but still they spoke. As for you, I really think you are too pensive, young man."

"Young man?" I repeated. "I am older than you; every quarter of an hour which passes makes me a year older."

He turned round, looked at me some minutes with stupid astonishment, and then began to titter.

"Come, you are joking; older than I am? why, I might be your grandfather."

"I have no wish to jest," I answered gravely. He opened his snuff-box.

"Here, my good sir, don't be angry. Take a pinch of snuff, and don't bear malice."

"Do not fear," said I; "I shall not have long to bear it against you."

At this moment the snuff-box which he extended to me came against the grating which separated us. A jolt caused it to strike rather violently, and it fell, wide open, under the feet of the gendarme.

"Curse the grating!" said the messenger; then turning to me, he added, "Now, am I not unlucky? I have lost all my snuff!"

"I lose more than you," said I.

As he tried to pick up his snuff, he muttered between his teeth, "More than I! that's very easily said. No more snuff until I reach Paris! It's terrible."

The Chaplain then addressed him with some words of consolation; and I know not if I were pre-occupied, but it seemed to be to be part of the exhortation of which the commencement had been addressed to me.

By degrees conversation increased between the Chaplain and the officer; and I became again lost in thought. The vas was stopped for a minute before the toll-gate, and the inspector examined it. Had it contained a sheep or an ox which was going to be slaughtered, they would have required some money; but a human head pays no duty!

We passed through the gates, and the carriage trotted quickly through those old and crooked streets of the Faubourg St. Marceau and the city, which twist and cross each other like the many paths of an ant-hill. On the pavement of these narrow streets the rolling of the wheels became so noisy and rapid that I could hear no other sound, though I saw that people exclaimed, as the van passed, and bands of children followed its track. I fancied also I occasionally saw in the cross-streets ragged men displaying in their hands a bundle of printed papers, their mouths open as if vociferating something, while the passers stopped to purchase.

Half-past eight struck by the palace clock as we arrived in the court of the Conciergerie Prison. The sight of its wide staircase, its dark chapel, its sombre gates, made me shudder; and when the carriage stopped, I fancied the beatings of my heart stopped also.

But I collected my strength; the door was opened; with the rapidity of lightning I jumped from the moving prison, and passed between two lines of soldiers; already there was a crowd formed on my path.

TWENTY-SECOND PAPER

ALL my resolution abandoned me when I reached the low doors, private stairs, and interior corridors, which are only entered by the condemned. The Officer still accompanied me: the Priest had left me for a couple of hours—perchance to read the papers!

I was then taken to the Governor, into whose charge the Officer gave me. They made an exchange. The Director told him to wait a moment, as he had some "game" for him to take back in the Van to the Bicêtre. No doubt it was the man condemned to-day. He is to sleep to-night on the bundle of straw which I have not had time to wear out.

"Oh, very well," said the Officer to the Governor, "I will wait with pleasure; we can make out the two papers together, and it will be very convenient."

They then placed me in a small room adjoining the Governor's office, and left me, locked in, alone.

I know not of what I was thinking, or how long I had been there, when a sudden and loud burst of laughter in my ear dispersed my reverie.

I raised my eyes with a start. I was no longer alone in the cell; a man was beside me. He was about fifty-five years old, middle-sized, wrinkled, stooping, and bald: with a sinister cast in his grey eyes, and a bitter sneer on his countenance; he was dirty, half clothed, ragged, disgusting.

We looked at each other steadfastly for some moments; he prolonging his bitter laugh, while I felt half astonished, half alarmed.

"Who are you?" said I to him at last.

"That is a funny question," said he. "I am a *friauche*."

"A friauche?" said I; "what does that mean?"

This question redoubled his merriment.

"Why," cried he, in the midst of a shout of laughter, "it means that they will play the same game with my head in six weeks hence, as they will with thine in six hours! Ha! ha! ha! thou seem'st to understand now!"

And truly I was pale, and my hair stood on end. This, then, was the other condemned prisoner, the one just sentenced, whom they expected at the Bicêtre; the heir of my cell.

He continued: "Never mind! Here's *my* history. I am son of a famous thief; it is a pity that they gave him one day a hempen cravat; it was during the 'reign of the Gallows by the grace of Heaven.' At six years of age I had neither father nor mother; in summer I turned somersets in the dust on the high-road, that carriage-travellers might throw me money; in winter I walked with naked feet in the mud, in ragged clothes, and blowing on my purple hands to excite pity. At nine years old I began to use my fingers; at times I emptied a pocket or a reticule; at ten years old I was a pilferer: then I made acquaintances, and at seventeen I became a thief. I broke into a shop, I robbed the till; I was taken and sent to the Galleys. What a hard life that was! Sleeping on bare boards, drinking plain water, eating black bread, dragging a stupid fetter which was of no use; sun-strokes and whip-strokes: and then all the heads are kept shaved, and I had such fine chestnut hair! Never mind! I served my time; fifteen years. That wears one famously!

"I was two-and-thirty years old; one fine morning they gave me a map of the road, a passport, and sixty-six francs, which I had amassed in my fifteen years at the Galleys, working sixteen hours a-day, thirty days a-month, twelve months a-year. Never mind! I wished to be an honest man with my sixty-six francs; and I had finer sentiments under my rags than you might find beneath the cassock of a priest. But deuce take the passport! It was yellow, and they had written upon it 'Freed convict.' I was obliged to show this at every village, and to present it every week to the mayors of the towns through which I was ordered to pass. A fine recommendation! a galley-convict! I frightened all the folk, and little children ran away, and people locked their doors. No one would give me work; I expended the last of my sixty-six francs,—and then— one must live. I showed my arms, fit for labour; the people shut their doors.

I offered my day's work for fifteen sous, for ten sous, for five sous! and no one would have me. What could be done? One day being hungry, I knocked my elbow through a baker's window; I seized on a loaf, and the baker seized on me. I did not eat the loaf, yet I was condemned to the Galleys for life, with three letters branded on my shoulder; I'll show them to you if you like. They call that sort of justice *the relapse*. So here I was, a returned horse. I was brought back to Toulon, —this time among the Green-caps (galley-slaves for life); so now I decided to escape. I had *only* three walls to pierce, two chains to break, and I had one nail! I escaped. They fired the signal gun; for we convicts are, like the Cardinals of Rome, dressed in red, and they fire cannons when we depart! Their powder went to the sparrows! This time, no yellow passport, but then no money either. I met some comrades in the neighbourhood who had also served their time or broken their chains. Their captain proposed to me to join the band. They killed on the highways. I acceded, and I began to kill to live. Sometimes we attacked a Diligence, sometimes it was a post-chaise, sometimes a grazier on horseback. We took the money, we let the horses go, and buried the bodies under a tree, taking care that their feet did not appear; and then we danced on the graves, so that the ground might not seem fresh broken.

I grew old this way, hiding in the bushes, sleeping in the air, hunted from wood to wood, but at least free and my own master. Everything has an end, and this like the rest; the gendarmes one night caught us at our tricks; my comrades escaped; but I, the oldest, remained under the claw of these cats in cocked hats. They brought me here. I had already mounted all the steps of the justice-ladder, except one. Whether I had now taken a handkerchief or a life was all the same for me. There was but one 'relapse' to give me,—the executioner. My business has been short: faith, I began to grow old and good for nothing. My father *married the widow* (was hanged); I am going to retire to the Abbey of Mont-à-Regret (the Guillotine); that's all, comrade!"

I remained stupefied during the recital. He laughed louder than at the beginning, and tried to take my hand. I drew back in horror.

"Friend," cried he, "you don't seem game. Don't be foolish on the scaffold: d' ye see? There is one bad moment to pass on the board, but that's so soon done. I should like to be there to show you the step! Faith, I've a great mind not to plead, if they will finish me with you to-day. The same Priest will serve us both. You see I'm a good fellow, eh? I say, shall we be friends?"

Again he advanced a step nearer to me.

"Sir," I answered, repulsing him, "I decline it."

Fresh bursts of laughter at my answer.

"Ha, ha, ha! Sir, you must be a Marquis."

I interrupted him, "My friend, I require reflection: leave me in peace."

The gravity of my tone rendered him instantly thoughtful. He shook his grey and nearly bald head, while he murmured between his teeth, "I understand now,—the Priest!"

After a few minutes' silence, he said to me, almost timidly,—

"Sir, you are a Marquis; that is all very well; but you have on such a nice great-coat, which will not be of much use to you. The Executioner will take it. Give it to me, and I will sell it for tobacco."

I took off my great-coat, and gave it to him. He began to clap his hands with childish joy; then looking at my shirt-sleeves, and seeing that I shivered, he added, "You are cold, Sir; put on this; it rains, and you will be wet through; besides, you ought to go decently on the wagon!"

While saying this, he took off his coarse, grey woollen jacket, and put my arms into it, which I allowed him to do unconsciously. I then leaned against the wall, and I cannot describe the effect this man had on me. He was examining the coat which I had given him, and uttered each moment an exclamation of delight. "The pockets are quite new! The collar is not in the least worn! It will bring me at least fifteen francs. What luck! I shall have tobacco during all my six weeks."

The door opened again. They were come to conduct me to the room where the condemned finally await their execution; and the guard was also come to take the other prisoner to the Bicêtre. He placed himself, laughingly, amongst them, and said to the gendarmes,—

"I say, don't make a mistake! We have changed skins, the gentleman and I; don't take me in his place. That won't suit me at all, now that I can have tobacco for six weeks!"

TWENTY-THIRD PAPER

THAT old scoundrel! he took my great-coat from me, for I did not give it to him; and then he left me this rag, his odious jacket. For whom shall I be taken?

It was not from indifference, or from charity, that I let him take it. No; but because he was stronger than I! If I had refused, he would have beaten me with those great coarse hands. Charity, indeed! I was full of bad feeling; I should like to have strangled him with my own hands, the old thief! —to have trampled him under my feet.

I feel my heart full of rage and bitterness, and my nature turned to gall: the approach of violent death renders one wicked.

TWENTY-FOURTH PAPER

THEY brought me into an empty cell. I asked for a table, a chair, and writing materials. When all these were brought, I asked for a bed. The turnkey eyed me with astonishment, and seemed mentally to say, "What will be the use of it?" However they made up a chaff bed in the corner. But at the same time a gendarme came to install himself in what was called my chamber. Are they afraid that I would strangle myself with the mattress?

TWENTY-FIFTH PAPER

IT is ten o'clock.

Oh, my poor little girl! In six hours more thy Father will be dead,—something to be dragged about the tables of lecturing rooms; a head to be cast by one party, a trunk to be dissected by another; then all to be thrown together into a bier, and despatched to the felons' burial-ground. This is what they are going to do with thy Father; yet none of them hate me, all pity me, and all could save me! They are going to kill me, Mary, to kill me in cold blood, —a ceremonial for the general good. Poor little girl! thy Father, who loved thee so well, thy Father who kissed thy little white neck, who passed his hands so fondly through the ringlets of thy silken hair, who danced thee on his knee, and every evening joined thy two little hands to pray to God!

Who will do all this for thee in future? Who now will love thee? My darling child, what wilt thou do for my presents, pretty play things, and kisses? Ah, unfortunate Orphan! What wilt thou do for food and raiment?

If the Jury had seen thee, my pretty little Mary, they would have understood it was wrong to kill the Father of a child three years old.

And when she grows up, what will become of her? Her Father will be one of the disgraces of Paris. She will blush for me and at hearing my name; she will be despised, rejected, reviled, on account of him who loved her with all the tenderness of his heart. Oh, my little Mary, whom I so idolized! can it be true that thou wilt encounter shame and horror through me?

Oh! can it be true that I shall die before the close of day? Those distant shouts which I hear, that mass of animated spectators who are already hastening to the Quays, those gendarmes preparing in their barracks,—is it all for me? Yes, I—myself am going to die?—

this actual self which is here, which lives, moves, breathes,—this self which I touch and can feel!

TWENTY-SIXTH PAPER

IF I even knew how *it* is built, and in what way one dies upon it; but it is horrible I do not know this.

The very name of it is frightful, and I cannot understand how I have hitherto been able to write and utter it. The idea I attach to this hateful name is vague, undefined, and therefore more sinister. I construct and demolish in my mind continually its hideous scaffolding.

I dare not ask a question about it; yet it is dreadful not to know what it is, and how to act. I fancy there is a sort of hollow, and that you are laid on your face, and—

Ah, my hair will be white before my head falls!

TWENTY-SEVENTH PAPER

I HAD a glimpse of *it* once. I was passing by the Grève in a carriage, about eleven o'clock, one morning, when a crowd impeded our progress. I looked out of the window; a dense throng of men, women, and children filled the place and the neighbouring streets. Above the crowd I saw a kind of frame of red wood, which three men were building. I turned away my head with disgust. Close to the carriage there was a woman who said to a child, "Now, look! the axe slides badly; they are going to grease the slide with a candle-end."

They are probably doing the same now. Eleven o'clock has just struck. No doubt they are greasing the slide.

Oh, unhappy creature! this time I shall not turn away my head.

TWENTY-EIGHTH PAPER

OH for a pardon! My reprieve! Perhaps I shall be pardoned. The King has no dislike to me. I wish to see my lawyer! He was right, and I should prefer the galleys. Five years of the galleys,—nay, twenty years, or even the galleys for life. Yes, and to be branded with letters! But it would let me have a reprieve of my life! A galley-slave can move, come and go, and see the sunshine.

Oh! I must see my lawyer; he shall discover some new plea to urge in mitigation of my sentence.

How can I thus write when every point of his eloquence has already failed, and been unanswerably refuted!

TWENTY-NINTH PAPER

THE Priest returned. He has white hair, a very gentle look, a good and respectable countenance, and is a charitable man. This morning I saw him empty his purse into the hands of the prisoners. Whence is it then that his voice causes no emotion, and he does not ever seem affected by his own theme? Whence is it that he had as yet said nothing which has won on my intellect or my heart?

This morning I was bewildered; I scarcely heard what he said; his words seemed to me useless, and I remained indifferent; they glided away like those drops of rain off the window-panes of my cell.

Nevertheless, when he came just now to my room, his appearance did me good. Amongst all mankind he is the only one who is still a brother for me, I reflected; and I felt an ardent thirst for good and consoling words.

When he was seated on the chair, and I on the bed, he said to me,—

"My son,—"

This word opened my heart. He continued:

"My son, do you believe in God?"

"Oh, yes, Father!" I answered him.

"Do you believe in the holy Catholic, Apostolic, and Roman Church?"

"Willingly," said I.

"My son," returned he "you have an air of doubt."

Then he began to speak. He spoke a long time; he uttered a quantity of words. Then, when he had finished, he rose, and looked at me for the first time since the beginning of his discourse, and said "Well?"

I protest I had listened to him with avidity at first, then with attention, then with consideration.

I also rose and said, "Sir, leave me for a time, I beg of you."

He asked. "When shall I return?"

"I will let you know, Sir."

Then he withdrew in silence, but shaking his head as though inwardly exclaiming, "An Unbeliever."

No! low as I have fallen, I am *not* an unbeliever. God is my witness that I believe in Him. But how did that old man address me? Nothing to be felt, nothing to affect me, nothing to draw forth tears, nothing which sprung from his heart to enter into mine,— nothing which was addressed from himself to myself.

On the contrary, there was something vague, inaccentuated, applicable to any case and to none in particular: emphatic where it should have been profound, flat where it ought to have been simple; a species of sentimental sermon and theological elegy. Now and then a quotation in Latin; here and there the names of Saint Augustine and Saint Gregory, and others of the Calendar. And throughout he had the air of reciting a lesson which he had already twenty times repeated; seeming to go over a theme almost obliterated in his memory from being so long known; but not one look in his eyes, not one accent in his voice, to indicate that *he* was interested!

And how could it be otherwise? This Priest is the head Chaplain of the Prison; his calling is to console and exhort,—that is, he lives by it. Condemned felons are the spring of his eloquence; he receives their confession, and prays with them, because he keeps his place by it. He had advanced in years in conducting men to death from his youth, he has grown accustomed to that which makes others shudder. The dungeon and scaffold are every-day matters with him.

He receives notice the preceding evening that he will have to attend some one the following day, at a certain hour. He asks, "Is it for the Galleys or an execution?" and he asks no more respecting them, but comes next day as a matter of course.

Oh that they would bring me, instead of this man, some young curate, some aged Priest, taken by chance from the nearest parish! Let them find him at his devotional studies, and without warning, say to him, "There is a man who is going to die, and it is reserved for you to console him. You must be there when they bind his hands; you must take a place in the fatal cart, with your crucifix, and conceal the executioner from him. You must pass with him through that horrible crowd which is thirsting for his execution; you must embrace him at the foot of the scaffold, and you must remain there until his soul has flown!"

When they have said this, let them bring him hither, agitated, palpitating, all shuddering from head to foot. Let me throw myself into his arms; then kneel at his feet, and he will weep, and we will weep together; and he will be eloquent, and I shall be consoled, and my heart will unburthen itself into his heart,—and I shall receive the blessed hope of Redemption, and he will take my Soul!

THIRTIETH PAPER

But that old man, what is he to me? What am I to him? Another individual of an unhappy class, a shadow of which he has seen so many; another unit to add to his list of executions.

I have been wrong, perhaps, not to attend to him more; it is he who is good, while I am the reverse. Alas! it was not my fault. The thought of my violent death has spoiled and hardened all within me.

They have just brought me food, as if I could possibly wish for it! I even tried to eat, but the first mouthful fell untasted from my lips.

THIRTY-FIRST PAPER

Since then a strange circumstance happened. They came to relieve my good old gendarme, with whom, ungrateful egotist that I am, I did not even shake hands. Another took his place; a man with a low forehead, heavy features, and stupid contenance. Beyond this I paid no attention, but seated myself at the table, my forehead resting on my hands, and my mind troubled by thought. A light touch on my shoulder made me look round. It was the new gendarme, with whom I was alone, and who addressed me pretty nearly in these terms:—

"Criminal, have you a kind heart?"

"No!" answered I, impatiently. The abruptness of my answer seemed to disconcert him. Nevertheless, he began again, hesitatingly,—

"People are not wicked for the pleasure of being so?"

"Why not?" answered I. "If you have nothing but that to say to me, leave me in peace. What is your aim?"

"I beg your pardon, Criminal," he returned; "I will only say two words, which are these: If you could cause the happiness of a poor man, and that it cost you nothing, would you not do so?"

I answered gravely, "Surely, you cannot allude to me as having power to confer happiness?"

He lowered his voice and assumed a mysterious air, which ill-suited with his idiotic countenance.

"Yes, Criminal, yes,—happiness! fortune!" whispered he; "all this can come to me through you. Listen here, I am a poor gendarme; the service is heavy, the pay is light; my horse is my own, and ruins me. So I put into the lottery as a counterbalance. Hitherto I have only missed by not having the right numbers. I am always very near them. If I buy seventy-six, number seventy-seven comes up a prize. Have a little patience, if you please; I have almost done. Well, here is a lucky opportunity for me. It appears, Criminal, begging your pardon, that you are to be executed to-day. It is a certain fact that the dead who are destroyed that way see the lottery before it is drawn on earth. Promise that your spirit shall appear to me to-morrow evening, to give me three numbers,—three good ones, eh? What trouble will it be to you? and I am not afraid of ghosts. Be easy on that point. Here's my address: Popincourt Barracks, staircase A, No. 26, at the end of the corridor. You will know me again, won't you? Come even to-night, if it suits you better."

I would have disdained to reply to such an imbecile, if a mad hope had not crossed my mind. In my desperate position there are moments when one fancies that a chain may be broken by a hair.

"Listen," said I to him, acting my part as well as a dying wretch could. "I can indeed render thee richer than the King. I can make thee gain millions, on one condition."

He opened his stupid eyes.

"What, what? I will do anything to please you, Criminal."

"Then instead of three numbers I promise to tell you four. Change coats with me."

"Oh, is that all?" cried he, undoing the first hooks of his uniform cheerfully.

I rose from my chair; I watched all his movements with a beating heart. I already fancied the doors opening before the uniform of a gendarme; and then the prison—the street—the town—left far behind me! But suddenly he turned round with indecision, and asked,—

"I say,—it is not to go out of this?"

I saw that all was lost; nevertheless, I tried one last effort, useless as it was foolish.

"Yes, it is," said I to him; "but as thy fortune will be made—"

He interrupted me.

"Oh, law, no! on account of my numbers! To make them good, you must be dead, you know!"

I sat down again, silent, and more desponding, from all the hope that I had conceived.

THIRTY-SECOND PAPER

I SHUT my eyes, covered them with my hands, and sought to forget the present in the past. In a rapid reverie, the recollections of childhood and youth came back one by one, soft, calm, smiling, like islands of flowers on the black gulf of confused thoughts which whirled through my brain.

I was again a child,—a laughing, healthy schoolboy, playing, running, shouting with my brothers, in the broad green walks of the old garden where my first years were passed.

And then, four years later, behold me there again, still a child, but a passionate dreamer. And there is a young girl in the garden,—a little Spaniard, with large eyes and long hair, her dark polished skin, her rosy lips and cheeks, the Andalusian of fourteen, named *Pepa*. Our mothers had told us to "go and run together;" we had talked instead. Only the year before, we used to play and quarrel and dispute together. I tyrannized over Pepita for the best apple in the orchard; I beat her for a bird's nest. She cried; I scolded her, and we went to complain of each other to our mothers. But now—she was leaning on my arm, and I felt proud and softened. We walked slowly, and we spoke low. I gathered for her some flowers, and our hands trembled on meeting. She spoke to me of the birds, of the sky above us, of the crimson sunset behind the trees; or else of her school-fellows, her gown and ribbons. We talked in innocence, but we both blushed. The child had grown into a young girl. After we had walked for some time, I made her sit down on a bank; she was smiling. I was serious.

"Sit down there," said she, "there is still daylight; let us read something. Have you a book?"

I happened to have a favourite volume with me. I drew near her, and opened it by chance. She leaned her shoulder against mine, and we began to read the same page. Before turning the leaf, she was always obliged to wait for me. My mind was less quick than hers. "Have you finished?" she would ask, when I had only just commenced. Then our heads leaned together, our hair mixed, our breath gradually mingled, and at last our lips met.

When we again thought of continuing our reading it was starlight. I shall remember that evening all my life!

Oh, heaven! All *my* life!

THIRTY-THIRD PAPER

THE clock had just struck some hour, —I do not know which. I do not hear the strokes plainly. I seem to have the peal of an organ in my ears. It is the confusion of my last thoughts. At this final day, when I look back over the events of life, I recall my crime with horror; but I wish to have still longer to repent of it. I felt more remorse after my condemnation; since then it seems as if there were no space but for thoughts of death. But now, oh, how I wish to repent me thoroughly! When I had lingered for a minute on what had passed in my life, and then came back to the thought of its approaching termination, I shuddered as at something new. My happy childhood, my fair youth,—a golden web with its end stained. If any read my history, after so many years of innocence and happiness, they will not believe in this execrable year, which began by a crime, and will close by an execution. It would appear impossible.

And nevertheless, oh, — imperfection of human laws and human nature!— I was not ill-disposed.

THIRTY-FOURTH PAPER

OH! to die in a few hours, and to think that a year ago, on the same day, I was innocent and at liberty, enjoying autumnal walks, wandering beneath the trees! To think that in this same moment there are, in the houses around me, men coming and going, laughing and talking, reading newspapers, thinking of business; shopkeepers selling their wares, young girls preparing their ball-dresses for the evening; mothers playing with their children!

THIRTY-FIFTH PAPER

I REMEMBER once, when a child, going alone to see the belfry of Nôtre-Dame.

I was already giddy from having ascended the dark winding staircase, from having crossed the slight open gallery which unites the two towers, and from having seen Paris beneath my feet; and I entered the cage of stone and woodwork where the great bell is hung. I advanced with trembling steps over the ill-joined planks, examining at a distance that bell, so famous amongst the children and common people in Paris; and it was not without terror that I observed the slated pent-houses, which surrounded the belfry with inclined planes, were just on a level with my feet. Through the openings I saw, in a bird's-eye view, the street beneath, and the passengers diminished to the size of ants.

Suddenly the enormous bell resounded; its deep vibration shook the air, making the heavy tower rock, and the flooring start from the beams. The noise had nearly upset me. I tottered, ready to fall, and seemed on the point of slipping over the pent-houses. In an agony of terror I lay down on the planks, pressing them closely with both my arms,—speechless, breathless, with this formidable sound in my ears, while beneath my eyes was the precipice, a profound abyss, where so many quiet and envied passengers were walking.

Well, it appears to me as if I were again in that belfry; my senses seem again giddy and dazzled; the booming of that bell seems to press on my brain, and around me I no longer see that tranquil and even life which I had quitted (where other men walk still) except from a distance, and beyond a terrible abyss.

THIRTY-SIXTH PAPER

IT is a quarter past one o'clock.

The following are my sensations at present: a violent pain in my head, my frame chilled, my forehead burning. Every time that I rise, or bend forward, it seems to me that there is a fluid floating in my head, which makes my brain beat violently against the bone.

I have convulsive startings, and from time to time my pen falls from my hand as if by a galvanic shock. My eyes ache and burn, and I suffer greatly in all my limbs.

In two hours and three-quarters hence, *all will be cured.*

THIRTY-SEVENTH PAPER

THEY say that it is nothing,—that one does not suffer; that it is an easy death. Ah! then, what do they call this agony of six weeks,—this summing-up in one day? What, then, is the anguish of this irreparable day, which is passing so slowly and yet so fast? What is this ladder of tortures which terminates in the scaffold? Are they not the same convulsions whether life is taken away drop by drop, or intellect extinguished thought by thought?

THIRTY-EIGHTH PAPER

IT is singular that my mind so often reverts to the King. Whatever I do, there is a voice within me which says,—

"There is, in this same town, at this same hour, and not far from hence, in another Palace, a man who also has guards to all his gates; a man alone, like thee, in the crowd,—with this difference, that he is as high as thou art low. His entire life is glory, grandeur, delight. All around him is love, respect, veneration; the loudest voices become low in speaking to him, and the proudest heads are bent. At this moment he is holding a Council of Ministers, where all coincide with his opinions; or else he thinks of the Chase to-morrow, or the Ball for this evening, feeling certain that the Fête will come, and leaving to others the trouble of his pleasures.

"Well, this man is of flesh and blood like thee! And in order that at this instant the scaffold should fall, and thou be restored to life, liberty, fortune, family, it would only be requisite for him to write his name at the foot of a piece of paper; or even that his carriage should meet thy fatal cart! And he is good, too, and perhaps would be glad to do it; and yet it will not be done!"

THIRTY-NINTH PAPER

Well then, let me have courage with death,—let me handle this horrid idea, let me face it boldly. I will ask what it is, know what it demands, turn it in every sense, fathom the enigma, and look before-hand into the tomb.

* * * * *

I have speculated upon Death and Eternity until my mind seems bewildered by its own horrible fantasies. My ideas wander. Oh, for a Priest,—a Priest who could instruct me! I must have a Priest, and a crucifix to embrace. Alas! here is the same Priest again!

FORTIETH PAPER

After a time, I begged of him to let me sleep. I threw myself on the bed. I had a fulness of blood in my head which made me sleep,—my last sleep on earth. I had a horible dream, from which I awoke in terror, shuddering and in agony.

The Chaplain was seated at the foot of my bed, reading prayers.

"Have I slept long?" I inquired of him.

"My son," said he, "you have slept an hour. They have brought your child, who is waiting in the next room; I would not allow them to awaken you."

"Oh," cried I, "my darling child! Let them bring in my idolized child!"

FORTY-FIRST PAPER

My child looked rosy and happy, and her large eyes were bright. Oh, she is so pretty! I drew her towards me; I raised her in my arms, and placing her on my knees, kissed her dear hair. I asked, "Why is her Mother not with her?" And I learnt that she was very ill, and my poor old mother also.

Mary looked at me with astonishment. Caressed, embraced, devoured with kisses, she submitted quietly; but, from time to time, cast an uneasy look towards her Nurse, who was crying in the corner.

At length I was able to speak.

"Mary," I exclaimed. "My own little Mary!" and I pressed her violently gainst my breast, which was heaving with sobs. She uttered a little cry, and then said, "Oh, you hurt me, sir."

"*Sir!*" It is nearly a year since she has seen me, poor child! She has forgotten me, face, words, voice; and then who could know me with this beard, this dress, and this pallor?

What! already effaced from that memory,—the only one where I wished to survive! What! already, no longer a Father, am I condemned to hear no more that word, so soft in the language of children that it cannot remain in the language of men, "Papa?"

And yet to have heard it from that sweet mouth, once more,—only once more,—that is all that I would have asked in payment for the forty years of life they will take from me.

"Listen, Mary," said I to her, joining her two little hands in mine. "Do you not know me?"

She looked at me with her bright beautiful eyes and answered,—

"Oh, no, indeed."

"Look at me well," I repeated. "What! dost thou not know who I am?"

"Yes, sir," she answered. "You are a gentleman."

Alas! while loving one being on earth, loving with all your deep affection, having that being before you, who sees and looks at you, speaks and answers you, and yet knows you not! You wish for consolation but from this one being, who is the only one that does not know that you require it because you are going to die!

"Mary," I continued, "hast thou a papa?"

"Yes, sir," said the child.

"Well, then, dearest, where is he?"

She raised her large eyes in astonishment:—

"Ah, then you don't know, sir? Papa is dead."

Here she began to cry: I nearly let the little angel fall.

"Dead!" I exclaimed: "Mary, knowest thou what it is to be dead?"

"Yes, sir," she answered. "He is in earth and in Heaven;" and she continued of her own accord, "I pray to God for him morning and evening at mamma's knees."

I kissed her on her forehead.

"Mary, say to me thy prayer."

"I could not, sir; a prayer you do not say in the middle of the day. Come to-night to my house, and you shall hear me say it."

This was enough. I interrupted her.

"Darling Mary, it is *I* who am thy papa."

"You!" returned she.

I added, "Wouldst thou like me for thy papa?"

The child turned away. "No, sir; my papa was much prettier."

I covered her with kisses and tears. She tried to escape from my arms, crying,—

"Sir, you hurt me with your beard."

Then I replaced her on my knees, devouring her with my eyes, and continued,—

"Mary, canst thou read?"

"Yes," she answered, "I can read very well. Mamma makes me read my letters."

"Well, then, read a little to me," said I, pointing to a printed paper which she held crumpled in one of her dimpled hands.

She shook her pretty head, saying,—

"Oh, dear me! I can only read fables."

"But try, my darling. Come, open your paper."

She unfolded the paper, and began to spell with her finger, "S E N—sen,—TENCE—tence,—*Sentence.*" I snatched it from her hands. It was my own sentence of death she was reading to me! Her nurse had bought the paper for a penny. To me it had cost more.

No words can convey what I felt; my violence had alarmed the child, who was ready to cry.

Suddenly she said to me,—

"Do give me back my paper; I want to play with it!"

I restored her to her nurse.

"Take her hence!" and I fell back in my chair, gloomy, desolate, in despair! Now they may come: I care for nothing more; the last fibre of my heart is broken.

FORTY-SECOND PAPER

THE Priest is kind; so is the jailor: tears came in their eyes when I sent away my child.

It is done. Now I must fortify myself, and think firmly of the Executioner, the cart, the gendarmes, the crowd in the street and the windows.

I have still an hour to familiarize myself with these ideas. All the people will laugh and clap their hands, and applaud; yet among those men, now free, unknown to jailors, and who run with joy to an execution,—in that throng there is more than one man destined to follow me sooner or later, on the scaffold.

More than one who is here to-day on my account, will come hereafter on his own.

FORTY-THIRD PAPER

MY little Mary. She is gone away to play; she will look at the crowd from the coach window, and already she thinks no more of the "Gentleman." Perhaps I may still have time to write a few pages for her, so that she may read them hereafter, and weep, in fifteen years hence, the sorrows of to-day. Yes, she shall know my history from myself, and why the name I leave her is tarnished.

FORTY-FOURTH PAPER

MY HISTORY

[NOTE. The pages which immediately followed this have not been found. Perhaps, as the next chapter seems to indicate, the Condemned had not time to write his history, as it was so late when he thought of it.]

FORTY-FIFTH PAPER

From a Chamber of the Town Hall.

THE Town Hall. Yes, I am here; the execrable journey is over. The place of execution is before me, and beneath the window, a horrible throng, laughing and yelling, while they await my appearance. My efforts at composure were vain; when above the heads of the crowd I saw the frightful scaffold, my heart failed. I expressed a wish to make my last declaration; so they brought me in here, and have sent for some law-officer to receive it. I am now waiting for him; so there is thus much gained. Here is what occurred, on my removal from the Conciergerie.

At three o'clock they came to tell me it was time. I trembled as if I had thought of any thing else during the last six hours, six weeks, six months. It produced on me the effect of something quite unexpected. They made me cross corridors, and descend stairs, they pushed me through a low door into a sombre room, narrow, arched, and scarcely lighted by a day of rain and fog. A chair was in the centre, on which I seated myself at their desire. Some persons were standing near the door; and beside the Priest and gendarmes, there were three men. The first of these, the tallest and oldest, was stout, with a red countenance. This was HE.

This was the Executioner,—the servant of the Guillotine; the others were his own servants. When I was seated, these walked quietly behind me; then suddenly I felt the cold of steel in my hair, and heard the grating action of scissors. My hair, cut carelessly, fell in heavy locks on my shoulders, and the executioner removed them gently with his coarse hand.

The parties in the room spoke in subdued tones. There was a heavy dull sound from without, which I fancied at first was caused by the river; but a shout of laughter soon proved to me it came from the crowd.

A young man near the window, who was writing with a pencil, in his pocketbook, asked one of the turnkeys, what was the name of the present operation? He was answered "The Toilet of the Condemned." From this I gathered that he was preparing the Report for to-morrow's newspaper. One of the servants then removed my waistcoat, and the other one taking my hands, placed them behind me, and I felt the knots of a cord rolled slowly round my wrists; at the same time the other took off my cravat. My linen,—the only remains of former times,—being of the finest quality, caused him a sort of hesitation for a moment; but at length he began to cut off the collar.

At this dreadful precaution, and the sensation of the steel touching my neck, a tremor passed over me, and a stifled groan escaped; the man's hand trembled.

"Sir," said he, "I beg your pardon; I fear I've hurt you."

The people shouted louder in the street. A tall red-faced man offered a handkerchief, steeped in vinegar, for me to inhale.

"Thank you," said I to him, in the firmest tone I could summon, "it is needless; I am recovered."

Then one man stooped down and fastened a small cord to my ankles, which restricted my steps; and this was again tied to the cord around my wrists; finally, the tall man threw my jacket over my shoullders, and tied the sleeves in front. All was now completed.

Then the Priest drew near with his Crucifix.

"Come, my son," said he.

The man raised me by my arms; and I walked, but my steps were weak and tottering. At this moment the folding doors were thrown open. A furious clamour, a chill breeze, and a strong white light reached me in the shade. From the extreme of the dark chamber I saw through the rain a thousand yelling heads of the expectant mass. On the right of the doorway, a range of mounted gendarmes; in front, a detachment of soldiers; on the left, the back of the cart, with a ladder. A hideous picture, with the appropriate frame of a prison-door.

It was for this dream moment that I had reserved my courage. I advanced a few steps, and appeared on the threshold.

"There he is! there he is!" bellowed the crowd. "He's come out at last!" and the nearest to me clapped their hands. Much as a king might be loved, there could not be more greeting for him.

The tall man first ascended the cart.

"Good morning, *Mr. Sampson!*" cried the children hanging by the lamp-posts. One of his servants next followed. "Bravo, *Tuesday!*" cried out the children, as the two placed themselves on the front seat.

It was now my turn, and I mounted with a firm step.

"He goes well to it!" said a woman beside the gendarmes.

This atrocious commendation gave me courage. The Priest took his seat beside me. They had placed me on the hindmost seat, my back towards the house. I shuddered at that last attention. There is a mixture of humanity in it.

I wished to look around me,—gendarmes before and behind: then crowd! crowd! crowd! A sea of heads in the street. The officer gave the word, and the procession moved on, as if pushed forward by a yell from the populace.

"Hats off! hats off!" cried a thousand voices together, as if for the King. Then I laughed horribly also myself, and said to the Priest, "Their hats—my head."

We passed a street which was full of public-houses, in which the windows were filled with spectators, seeming to enjoy their good places, particularly the women.

There were also people letting out tables, chairs, and carts; and these dealers in human life shouted out, "Who wishes for places?"

A strange rage seized me against these wretches, and I longed to shout out to them, "Do you wish for mine?"

The procession still advanced. At each step the crowd in the rear dispersed; and I saw, with my wandering eyes, that they collected again farther on, to have another view. I know not how it was, that notwithstanding the fog and the small white rain which crossed the air like gossamer, nothing which passed around escaped me; every detail brought its torture; words fail to convey my emotions. My great dread was lest I should faint. Last vanity! Then I endeavoured to confuse myself into being blind and deaf to all, except to the Priest, whose words I scarcely heard amidst the tumult. I took the Crucifix and kissed it.

"Have mercy on me," said I. "O my God!"

And I strove to engross myself with this thought.

But every shake of the cart disturbed me; and then I became excessively chilled, as the rain had penetrated my clothes, and my head was bare.

"Are you trembling with cold, my son?" demanded the Priest.

"Yes," answered I. "Alas! not only from cold."

At the turn to the Bridge, the women expressed pity at my being so young. We approached the fatal Quay. My hearing and sight seemed about to fail me. All those voices, all those heads at the windows, at doors, at shop fronts, on lamp-posts; these thirsting and cruel spectators; this crowd where all knew me, and I knew none; this road paved and welled with human visages,—I was confounded, stupefied, senseless. There is something insupportable in the weight of so many looks being fixed upon one. I could scarcely maintain my place on the seat, and lent no further attention to the Priest. In the tumult which surrounded me, I no longer distinguished exclamations of pity from those of satisfaction, or the sounds of laughter from those of complaint. All formed together a noise in my ears like sounding brass.

My eyes read mechanically the signs over the shops.

Once I felt a painful curiosity to look round on *that* which we were approaching.

It was the last mental bravado, and the body would not aid it; for my neck remained paralyzed, and I could not turn it.

And the cart went on, on. The shops passed away; the signs succeeded each other,—written, painted, gilt; and the populace laughed while they tramped through the mud; and I yielded my mind, as persons do in sleeping. Suddenly this series of shops ended as we turned into the square; the voice of the mob became still more loud, yelling and joyous; the cart stopped suddenly, and I had nearly fallen on my face. The Priest held me up.

"Courage!" murmured he.

They next brought a ladder to the back of my cart. I leaned on the arm of the Priest and descended. I made one step, and turned round to advance another, but I had not the power; beyond the lamp I saw something startling. . . .

Oh, it was THE REALITY!

I stopped as if staggered by a blow.

"I have a last declaration to make," cried I, feebly.

And then they brought me up here. I asked them to let me write my last wishes; and they unbound my hands; but the cord is here, ready to be replaced.

FORTY-SIXTH PAPER

A JUDGE, a Commissioner, a Magistrate,—I know not what was his rank,—has just been here.

I intreated him to procure my pardon; I begged it with clasped hands, and dragging myself on my knees at his feet.

He asked, with a fatal smile, if that were all I had to say to him?

"My pardon, my pardon!" I repeated. "Oh, for mercy's sake, five minutes more! Who knows, my pardon may come. It is so horrible at my age to die in this manner. Reprieves have frequently arrived even at the last moment! And to whom would they show mercy, sir, if not to me?"

That detestable Executioner! He came in to tell the Judge that the execution was ordered for a certain hour, which hour was at hand, and that he was answerable for the event.

"Oh, for mercy's sake! five minutes to wait for my pardon," cried I, "or I will defend myself."

The Judge and the Executioner went out. I am alone,—at least with only two gendarmes present.

That horrible throng, with its hyena cry! Who knows but that I shall escape from it, that I shall be saved? If my pardon,—it is impossible but that they will pardon me! Hark! I hear some one coming upstairs!

FOUR O'CLOCK.

Claude Gueux, King of Thieves

CLAUDE GUEUX was a poor workman, living in Paris about eight years ago, with his mistress and child. Although his education had been neglected, and he could not even read, the man was naturally clever and intelligent, and thought deeply over matters. Winter came with its attendant miseries,—want of work, want of food, want of fuel. The man, the woman, and the child were frozen and famished. The man turned thief. I know not what he stole. What signifies, as the result was the same; to the woman and child it gave three days' bread and warmth; to the man, five years' imprisonment. He was taken to Clairvaux,—the abbey now converted into a prison, its cells into dungeons, and the altar itself into a pillory. This is called progress.

Claude Gueux the honest workman, who turned thief from force of circumstances, had a countenance which impressed you,—a high forehead somewhat lined with care, dark hair already streaked with grey, deep-set eyes beaming with kindness, while the lower part clearly indicated firmness mingled with self-respect. He rarely spoke, yet there was a certain dignity in the man which commanded respect and obedience. A fine character, and we shall see what society made of it.

Over the prison workshop was an inspector, who rarely forgot that he was a jailor also to his subordinates, handing them the tools with one hand, and casting chains upon them with the other. A tyrant, never using even self-reasoning; with ideas against which there was no appeal; hard rather than firm, at times he could even be jocular, doubtless a good father, a good husband, really not vicious, but *bad*. He was one of those men who never can grasp a fresh idea, who apparently fail to be moved by any emotion; yet with hatred and rage in their hearts they look like blocks of wood, heated on the one side but frozen on the other. This man's chief characteristic was obstinacy; and so proud was he of this very stubbornness that he compared himself with Napoleon,—an optical delusion, like taking the mere flicker of a candle for a star. When he had made up his mind to a thing, however absurd, he would carry out that absurd idea. How often it happens, that, when a catastrophe occurs, if we inquire into the cause we find it originated through the obstinacy of one with little ability, but having full faith in his own powers.

Such was the inspector of the prison workshop at Clairvaux,—a man of flint placed by society over others, who hoped to strike sparks out of such material; but a spark from a like source is apt to end in a conflagration.

The inspector soon singled out Claude Gueux, who had been numbered and placed in the workshop, and finding him clever, treated him well. Seeing Claude looking sad (for he was ever thinking of her he termed his wife), and being in a good humour, by way of pastime to console the prisoner he told him the woman had become one of the unfortunate sisterhood, and had been reduced to infamy; of the child nothing was known.

After a time Claude had accustomed himself to prison rule, and by his calmness of manner and a certain amount of resolution clearly marked in his face, he had acquired a great ascendency over his companions, who so much admired him that they asked his advice, and tried in all ways to imitate him. The very expression in his eyes clearly indicated the man's character; besides, is not the eye the window to the soul, and what other result could be anticipated than that the intelligent spirit should lead men with few ideas, who yielded to the attraction as the metal does to the loadstone? In less than three months Claude was the virtual head of the workshop, and at times he almost doubted whether he was king or prisoner, being treated sometimes like a captive pope, surrounded by his cardinals.

Such popularity ever has its attendant hatred; and though beloved by the prisoners, Claude was detested by the jailors. To him two men's rations would have been scarcely sufficient. The inspector laughed at this, as his own appetite was large; but what would be mirth to a duke, to a prisoner would be a great misfortune. When a free man, Claude Gueux could earn his daily four-pound loaf and enjoy it; but as a prisoner he daily worked, and for his labour received one pound and a-half of bread and four ounces of meat; it naturally followed that he was always hungry.

He had just finished his meagre fare, and was about to resume his labours, hoping in work to forget famine, when a weakly-looking young man came towards him, holding a knife and his untasted rations in his hand, but seemingly afraid to address him.

"What do you want?" said Claude, roughly.

"A favour at your hands," timidly replied the young man.

"What is it?" said Claude.

"Help me with my rations; I have more than I can eat."

For a moment Claude was taken aback, but without further ceremony he divided the food in two and at once partook of one half.

"Thank you," said the young man;

"allow me to share my rations with you every day."

"What is your name?" said Claude.

"Albin."

"Why are you here?" added Claude.

"I robbed."

"So did I," said Claude.

The same scene took place daily between this man old before his time (he was only thirty-six) and the boy of twenty, who looked at the most seventeen. The feeling was more like that of father and son than one brother to another; everything created a bond of union between them,—the very toil they endured together, the fact of sleeping in the same quarters and taking exercise in the same court yard. They were happy, for were they not all the world to each other?

The inspector of the workshop was so hated by the prisoners that he often had recourse to Claude Gueux to enforce his authority; and when a tumult was on the point of breaking out, a few words from Claude had more effect than the authority of ten warders. Although the inspector was glad to avail himself of this influence, he was jealous all the same, and hated the superior prisoner with an envious and implacable feeling, —an example of might over right, all the more fearful as it was secretly nourished. But Claude cared so much for Albin that he thought little about the inspector.

One morning as the warders were going their rounds one of them summoned Albin, who was working with Claude, to go before the inspector.

"What are you wanted for?" said Claude.

"I do not know," replied Albin, following the warder.

All day Claude looked in vain for his companion, and at night, finding him still absent, he broke through his ordinary reserve and addressed the turnkey. "Is Albin ill?" said he.

"No," replied the man.

"How is it that he has never put in an appearance today?"

"His quarters have been changed," was the reply.

For a moment Claude trembled, then calmly continued, "Who gave the order?"

"Monsieur D——." This was the inspector's name.

On the following night the inspector, Monsieur D——, went his rounds as usual. Claude, who had perceived him from the distance, rose, and hastened to raise his woollen cap and button his gray woollen vest to the throat, —considered a mark of respect to superiors in prison discipline.

"Sir," said Claude, as the inspector was about to pass him, "has Albin really been quartered elsewhere?"

"Yes," replied the inspector.

"Sir, I cannot live without him. You know the rations are insufficient for me, and Albin divided his portion with me. Could you not manage to let him resume his old place near me?"

"Impossible; the order cannot be revoked."

"By whom was it given?"

"By me."

"Monsieur D——," replied Claude, "on you my life depends."

"I never cancel an order once given."

"Sir, what have I ever done to you?"

"Nothing."

"Why, then," cried Claude, "separate me from Albin?"

"Because I do," replied the inspector, and with that he passed on.

Claude's head sank down, like the poor caged lion deprived of his dog; but the grief, though so deeply felt, in no way changed his appetite,—he was famished. Many offered to share their rations with him, but he steadily refused, and continued his usual routine in silence,—breaking it only to ask the inspector daily, in tones of anguish mingled with rage, something between a prayer and a threat, these two words; "And Albin?"

The inspector simply passed on, shrugging his shoulders; but had he only observed Claude he would have seen the evident change; noticeable to all present, and he would have heard these words, spoken respectfully but firmly:—

"Sir, listen to me; send my companion to me. It would be wise to do so, I can assure you. Remember my words!"

On Sunday he had sat for hours in the courtyard, with his head bowed in his hands, and when a prisoner called Faillette came up laughing, Claude said: "I am judging some one."

On the 25th of October, 1831, as the inspector went his rounds, Claude, to draw his attention, smashed a watch-glass he had found in the passage. This had the desired effect.

"It was I," said Claude. "Sir, restore my comrade to me."

"Impossible," was the answer.

Looking the inspector full in the face, Claude firmly added: "Now, reflect! To-day is the 25th of October; I give you till the 4th of November."

A warder remarked that Claude was threatening Monsieur D——, and ought at once to be locked up.

"No, it is not a case of blackhole," replied the inspector, smiling disdainfully; "we must be considerate with people of this stamp."

The following day Claude was again accosted by one of the prisoners named Pernot, as he was brooding in the courtyard.

"Well, Claude, you are sad indeed; what are you pondering over?"

"I fear some evil threatens that good Monsieur D——," answered Claude.

Claude daily impressed the fact on the inspector how much Albin's absence affected him, but with no result save four-and-twenty hours' solitary confinement. On the 4th of November he looked round his cell for the little that remained to remind him of his former life. A pair of scissors, and an old volume of the "Emile," belonging to the woman he had loved so well, the mother of his child,—how useless to a man who could neither work nor read!

As Claude walked down the old cloisters, so dishonoured by its new inmates and its fresh whitewashed walls, he noticed how earnestly the convict Ferrari was looking at the heavy iron bars that crossed the window, and he said to him: "To-night I will cut through those bars with these scissors," pointing to the pair he still held in his hand.

Ferrari laughed incredulously, and Claude joined in the mirth. During the day he worked with more than ordinary ardour, wishing to finish a straw hat, which he had been paid for in advance by a tradesman at Troyes,—M. Bressier.

Shortly before noon he made some excuse to go down into the carpenters' quarters, a story below his own, at the time the warders were absent. Claude received a hearty welcome, as he was equally popular here as elsewhere.

"Can any one lend me an axe?" he said.

"What for?"

Without exacting any promises of secrecy he at once replied: "To kill the inspector with to-night."

Claude was at once offered several; choosing the smallest, he hid it beneath his waistcoat and left. Now, there were twenty-seven prisoners present, and not one of those men betrayed him; they even refrained from talking upon the subject among themselves, waiting for the terrible even which must follow.

As Claude passed on he saw a young convict of sixteen yawning idly there, and he strongly advised him to learn how to read. Just then Faillette asked what he was hiding.

Claude answered unhesitatingly: "An axe to kill Monsieur D—— to-night; but can you see it?"

"A little," said Faillette.

At seven o'clock the prisoners were locked in their several workshops. It was then the custom for the warders to leave them, until the inspector had been his rounds.

In Claude's workshop a most extraordinary scene took place, the only one of the kind on record. Claude rose and addressed his companions, eighty-four in number, in the following words:—

"You all know Albin and I were like brothers. I liked him at first for sharing his rations with me, afterwards because he cared for me. Now I never have sufficient, though I spend the pittance I earn in bread. It could make no possible difference to the inspector, Monsieur D——, that we should be together; but he chose to separate us simply from a love of tormenting, for he is a bad man. I asked again and again for Albin to be sent back, without success; and when I gave him a stated time, the 4th of November, I was thrust into a dungeon. During that time I became his judge, and sentenced him to death on November the 4th. In two hours he will be here, and I warn you I intend to kill him. But have you anything to say?"

There was a dead silence. Claude then continued telling his comrades, the eighty-one thieves, his ideas on the subject,—that he was reduced to a fearful extremity, and compelled by that very necessity to take the law into his own hands; that he knew full well he could not take the inspector's life without sacrificing his own, but that as the cause was a just one he would bear the consequences, having come to this conclusion after two months' calm reflection; that if they considered resentment alone hurried him on to such a step they were at once to say so, and to state their objections to the sentence being carried out.

One voice alone broke the silence which followed, saying, "Before killing the inspector, Claude ought to give him a chance of relenting."

"That is but just," said Claude, "and he shall have the benefit of the doubt."

Claude then sorted the few things a poor prisoner is allowed, and gave them to the comrades he mostly cared for after Albin, keeping only the pair of scissors. He then embraced them all,—some not being able to withhold their tears at such a moment. Claude continued calmly to converse during this last hour, and even gave way to a trick he had as a boy, of extinguishing the candle with a breath from his nose. Seeing him thus, his companions afterwards owned that they hoped he had abandoned his sinister idea. One young convict looked at him fixedly, trembling for the coming event.

"Take courage, young fellow," said Claude, gently; "it will be but the work of a minute."

The workshop was a long room with a door at both ends, and with windows each side overlooking the benches, thus leaving a pathway up the centre for the inspector to review the work on both sides of him. Claude had now resumed his work,—something like Jacques Clement, who did not fail to repeat his prayers.

As the clock sounded the last quarter to nine, Claude rose and placed himself near the entrance, apparently calm. Amidst the most profound silence the clock struck nine; the door was thrown open, and the inspector came in as usual alone, looking quite jovial and self-satisfied, passing rapidly along, tossing his head at one, grinding words out to another, little heeding the eyes fixed so fiercely upon him. Just then he heard Claude's step, and turning quickly round said,—

"What are you doing here? Why are you not in your place?" just as he would have spoken to a dog.

Claude answered respectfully, "I wish to speak to you, sir."

"On what subject?"

"Albin."

"Again!"

"Always the same," said Claude.

"So then," replied the inspector, walking along, "you have not had enough with twenty-four hours in the blackhole."

Claude, following him closely, replied: "Sir, return my companion to me!"

"Impossible!"

"Sir," continued Claude, in a voice which would have moved Satan, "I implore you to send Albin back to me; you will then see how I will work. You are free, and it would matter but little to you; you do not know the feeling of having only one friend. To me it is everything, encircled by the prison walls. You can come and go at your pleasure; I have but Albin. Pray let him come back to me! You know well he shared his food with me. What can it matter to you that a man named Claude Gueux should be in this hall, having another by his side called Albin? You have but to say 'Yes,' nothing more. Sir, my good sir, I implore you, in the name of Heaven, to grant my prayer!"

Claude, overcome with emotion, waited for the answer.

"Impossible!" replied the inspector, impatiently; "I will not recall my words. Now go, you annoyance!" And with that he hurried on towards the outer door, amidst the breathless silence maintained by the eighty-one thieves.

Claude, following and touching the inspector, gently asked: "Let me at least know why I am condemned to death. Why did you separate us?"

"I have already answered you; because I chose," replied the inspector.

With that he was about to lift the latch, when Claude raised the axe, and without one cry the inspector fell to the ground, with his skull completely cloven from three heavy blows dealt with the rapidity of lightning. A fourth completely disfigured his face, and Claude, in his mad fury, gave another and a useless blow; for the inspector was dead.

Claude, throwing the axe aside, cried out, "Now for the other!"

The other was himself; and taking the scissors, *his wife's*, he plunged them into his breast. But the blade was short, and the chest was deep, and vainly he strove to give the fatal blow. At last, covered with blood he fell fainting across the dead. Which of the two would be considered the victim?

When Claude recovered consciousness he was in bed, surrounded by every care and covered with bandages. Near him were Sisters of Charity, and a recorder ready to take down his deposition, who with much interest inquired how he was. Claude had lost a great deal of blood; but the scissors had done him a bad turn, inflicting wounds not one of which was dangerous; the only mortal blows he had struck were on the body of Monsieur D——. Then the interrogatory commenced.

"Did you kill the inspector of the prison workshop at Clairvaux?"

"Yes," was the reply.
"Why did you do so?"
"Because I did."

Claude's wounds now assumed a more serious aspect, and he was prostrated with a fever which threatened his life. November, December, January, February passed, in nursing and preparations, and Claude in turn was visited by doctor and judge,—the one to restore him to health, the other to glean the evidence needful to send him to the scaffold.

On the 16th of March, 1832, perfectly cured, Claude appeared in court at Troyes, to answer the charge brought against him. His appearance impressed the court favourably; he had been shaved and stood bareheaded, but still clad in prison garb. The court was well guarded by a strong military guard, to keep the witnesses within bounds, as they were all convicts. But an unexpected difficulty occurred; not one of these men would give evidence; neither questions nor threats availed to make them break their silence, until Claude requested them to do so. Then they in turn gave a faithful account of the terrible event; and if one, from forgetfulness or affection for the accused, failed to relate the whole facts, Claude supplied the deficiency. At one time the women's tears fell fast.

The usher now called the convict Albin. He came in trembling with emotion and sobbing painfully, and threw himself into Claude's arms. Turning to the Public Prosecutor, Claude said,—

"Here is a convict who gives his food to the hungry," and stooping, he kissed Albin's hand.

All the witnesses having been examined, the counsel for the prosecution then rose to address the court. "Gentlemen of the jury, society would be utterly put to confusion if a public prosecution did not condemn great culprits like him, who, etc."

After a long address by the prosecution, Claude's counsel rose. Then followed the usual pleading for and against, which ever takes place at the criminal court.

Claude in his turn gave evidence, and every one was astonished at his intelligence; there appeared far more of the orator about this poor workman than the assassin. In a clear and straightforward way he detailed the facts as they were,—standing proudly there, resolved to tell the whole truth. At times the crowd was carried away by his eloquence. This man, who could not read, would grasp the most difficult points of argument, yet treat the judges with all due deference. Once Claude lost his temper, when the counsel for the prosecution stated that he had assassinated the inspector without provocation.

"What!" cried Claude, "I had no provocation? Indeed! A drunkard strikes me,—I kill him; then you would allow there was provocation, and the penalty of death would be changed for that of the galleys. But a man who wounds me in every way during four years, humiliates me for four years, taunts me daily, hourly, for four years, and heaps every insult on my head,— what follows? You consider I have had no provocation! I had a wife for whom I robbed,—he tortured me about her. I had a child for whom I robbed,—he taunted me about this child. I was hungry, a friend shared his bread with me,—he took away my friend. I begged him to return my friend to me,—he cast me into a dungeon. I told him how much I suffered,—he said it wearied him to listen. What then would you have me do? I took his life; and you look upon me as a monster for killing this man, and you decapitate me; then do so."

Provocation such as this the law fails to acknowledge, because the blows have no marks to show.

The judge then summed up the case in a clear and impartial manner,—dwelling on the life Claude had led, living openly with an improper character; then he had robbed, and ended by being a murderer. All this was true. Before the jury retired, the judge asked Claude if he had any questions to ask, or anything to say.

"Very little," said Claude. "I am a murderer, I am a thief; but I ask you, gentlemen of the jury, why did I kill? Why did I steal?"

The jury retired for a quarter of an hour, and according to the judgment of these twelve countrymen—*gentlemen of the jury*, as they are styled—Claude Gueux was condemned to death. At the very outset several of them were much impressed with the name of Gueux (vagabond), and that influenced their decision.

When the verdict was pronounced, Claude simply said: "Very well; but there are two questions these gentlemen have not answered. Why did this man steal? What made him a murderer?"

He made a good supper that night, exclaiming, "Thirty-six years have now passed me." He refused to make any appeal until the last minute, but at the instance of one of the sisters who had nursed him he consented to do so. She in her fulness of heart gave him a five-franc piece.

His fellow-prisoners, as we have already noticed, were devoted to him, and placed all the means at their disposal to help him to escape. They threw into his dungeon, through the air-hole, a nail, some wire, the handle of a pail: any one of these would have been enough for a man like Claude to free himself from his chains. He gave them all up to the warder.

On the 8th of June, 1832, seven months and four days after the murder, the recorder of the court came, and Claude was told that he had but one hour more to live, for his appeal had been rejected.

"Indeed," said Claude, coldly; "I slept well last night, and doubtless I shall pass my next even better."

First came the priest, then the executioner. He was humble to the priest, and listened to him with great attention, regretting much that he had not had the benefit of religious training, at the same time blaming himself for much in the past.

He was courteous in his manner to the executioner; in fact he gave up all, —his soul to the priest, his body to the executioner.

While his hair was being cut, some one mentioned how the cholera was spreading, and Troyes at any moment might become a prey to this fearful scourge. Claude joined in the conversation, saying, with a smile, "There is one thing to be said,—I have no fear of the cholera!" He had broken half of the scissors,—what remained he asked the jailor to give to Albin; the other half lay buried in his chest. He also wished the day's rations to be taken to his friend. The only trifle he retained was the five-franc piece that the sister had given him, which he kept in his right hand after he was bound.

At a quarter to eight, the dismal procession usual in such cases left the prison. Pale, but with a firm tread Claude Gueux slowly mounted the scaffold, keeping his eyes fixed on the crucifix the priest carried,—an emblem of the Saviour's suffering. He wished to embrace the priest and the executioner, thanking the one and pardoning the other; the executioner simply repulsed him. Just before he was bound to the infernal machine, he gave the five-franc piece to the priest, saying, "For the poor."

The hour had scarcely struck its eight chimes, when this man, so noble, so intelligent, received the fatal blow which severed his head from his body.

A market-day had been chosen for the time of execution, as there would be more people about, for there are still in France small towns that glory in having an execution. The guillotine that day remained, inflaming the imagination of the mob to such an extent that one of the tax-gatherers was nearly murdered. Such is the admirable effect of public executions!

We have given the history of Claude Gueux's life, more to solve a difficult problem than for aught else. In his life there are two questions to be considered,—before his fall, and after his fall. What was his training, and what was the penalty? This must interes society generally; for this man was well gifted, his instincts were good. Then what was wanting? On this revolves the grand problem which would place society on a firm basis. *What nature has begun in the individual, let society carry out.* Look at Claude Gueux. An intelligent and most noble-hearted man, placed in the midst of evil surroundings, he turned thief. Society placed him in a prison where the evil was yet greater, and he ended with becoming a murderer. Can we really blame him, or ourselves?—questions which require deep thought, or the result will be that we shall be compelled to shirk this most important subject. The facts are now before us, and if the government gives no thought to the matter, what are the rulers about?

The Deputies are yearly much occupied. It is important to shift sinecures and to unravel the budget; to pass an Act which compels me, disguised as a soldier, to mount guard at the Count de Lobau's, whom I do not know, and to whom I wish to remain a stranger, or to go on parade under the command of my grocer, who has been made an officer. I wish to cast no reflections on the patrol, who keep order and protect our homes, but on the absurdity of making such parade and military hubbub about turning citizens into parodies of soldiers.

Deputies or ministers! it is important that we should sound every subject, even though it end in nothing; that we should question and cross-question what we know but little about. Rulers and legislators! you pass your time in classical comparisons that would make a village schoolmaster smile. You assert that it is the habits of modern civilization that have engendered adultery, incest, parricide, infanticide, and poisoning,—proving that you know little of Jocasta, Phedra, Œdipus, Medea, or Rodoguna, The great orators occupy themselves with lengthy discussions on Corneille and Racine, and get so heated in literary argument as to make the grossest mistakes in the French language. Very important indeed all this is, but we consider there are subjects of far greater consequence. In the midst of such useless arguments, what answer would the Deputies give if one rose and gravely addressed them in the following words:—

"Silence, all those who have been speaking! silence, I say! You consider yourself acquainted with the question? You know nothing about it. The question is this: In the name of justice, scarcely a year ago, a man at Panners was cut to pieces; at Dijon a woman's head was taken off; in Paris, at St. Jacques, executions take place without number. This is the question! Now take your time to consider it, and you who argue over the buttons of the National Guards, whether they should be white or yellow, and if *security* is preferable to *certainty!*

"Gentlemen of the Right, gentlemen of the Left, the great mass of the people suffer! Whether a republic or a monarchy, the fact remains the same,—the people suffer! The people are famished, the people are frozen. Such misery leads them on to crime: the galleys take the sons, houses of ill-fame the daughters. You have too many convicts, too many unfortunates.

"What is the meaning of this social

gangrene? You are near the patient: treat the malady. You are at fault: now study the matter more deeply.

"When you pass laws, what are they but expedients and palliatives? Half your codes result from routine.

"Branding but cauterizes the wound, and it mortifies, and what is the end? You stamp the crime for life on the criminal; you make two friends of them, two companions—inseparables. The convict prison is a blister which spreads far worse matter than ever it extracts; and as for the sentence of death, when carried out it is a barbarous amputation. Therefore, branding, penal servitude, and sentence of death are all of one class; you have done away with the branding, banish the rest. Why keep the chain and the chopper now you have put aside the hot iron? Farinace was atrocious, but he was not ridiculous.

"Take down that worn ladder that leads to crime and to suffering. Revise your laws; revise your codes; rebuild your prisons; replace your judges. Make laws suited to the present time.

"You are bent on economy; do not be so lavish in taking off the heads of so many during the year. Suppress the executioner; you could defray the expenses of six hundred schoolmasters with the wages you give your eighty executioners. Think of the multitude; then there would be schools for the children, workshops for the men.

"Do you know that in France there are fewer people who know how to read than in any other country in Europe? Fancy, Switzerland can read, Belgium can read, Denmark can read, Greece can read, Ireland can read—and France cannot read! It is a crying evil.

"Go into your convict prisons, examine each one of these condemned men, and you will observe by the profile, the shape of the head, how many could find their type in the lower animals. Here are the lynx, the cat, the monkey, the vulture, the hyena. Nature was first to blame, no doubt: but the want of training fostered the evil. Then give the people a fair education, and what there is of good in these ill-conditioned minds, let that be developed. People must be judged by their opportunities. Rome and Greece were educated: then brighten the people's intellect.

"When France can read, then give the people encouragement for higher things. Ignorance is preferable to a little ill-directed knowledge; and remember, there is a book of far greater importance than the 'Compère Mathieu,' more popular than the 'Constitutionnel,' and more worthy of perusal than the charter of 1830,—that is the Bible.

"Whatever you may do for the people, the majority will always remain poor and unhappy. Theirs the work, the heavy burden to carry, to endure: all the miseries for the poor, all the pleasures for the rich.

"As such is life, ought not the State to lean to the weaker and helpless side?

"In the midst of all this wretchedness, if you but throw hope in the balance, let the poor man learn there is a heaven where joy reigns, a paradise that he can share, and you raise him; he feels that he has a part in the rich man's joys. And this was the teaching Jesus gave, and He knew more about it than Voltaire.

"Then give to those people who work, and who suffer here, the hope of a different world to come, and they will go on patiently; for patience follows in the footsteps of hope.

"Then spread the Gospel in all our villages, let every cottage have its Bible; the seed thus sown will soon circulate. Encourage virtue, and from that will spring so much that now lies fallow.

"The man turned assassin under certain circumstances, if differently influenced would have served his country well.

"Then give the people all encouragement; improve the masses, enlighten them, guard their morals, make them useful, and to such heads as those you will not require to use cold steel."

Monster and Infanticide

Guernsey

M. Martin, the queen's provost in Guernsey, came to see me on my arrival. I returned his visit on the 5th of December, 1858. He offered to accompany me to the prison which I was desirous to see.

We had gone by the streets which rise behind the Royal Court. When strolling about Saint Peter's Port, I had already remarked in the town, midway, a high wall, in which was a high gate with a G carved in the granite on the top of it. I said to myself, "That ought to be the prison. So it is."

The jailor received us. He is named Barbet; so the Guernsey malefactors call the prison the Hôtel Barbet. This man had the same frank, firm face, the same pleasant and determined manner which I had already remarked in many other jailors. His wife and daughter were preparing soup in the corner.

Barbet took a heavy key, opened a grated door, and introduced us into a vast empty court, bounded on three sides by the high wall which had already attracted my attention. On the south the court is dominated by a new building of grey granite, the two-storied front of which is composed of two rows of seven arches superposed. Beneath the arches are the windows. Through the glass we perceive the heavy bars, painted white. That is the prison and those are the cells.

"Guernsey is an honest island," said the provost—a distinguished and intelligent man—a Non-comformist, an Independent, as Cromwell and Milton were. And he added, "We have at present only three prisoners, two men and a woman, out of a population of forty thousand."

One of the prisoners entered the court at that moment. He was a young man with a pleasing face, condemned to ten years of Botany Bay for robbery.

He was dressed in cloth trousers, a small blue paletot, and a cap.

The provost, who is also called the sheriff, and who in this capacity is governor of the prison, and accompanies the condemned to the scaffold—a circumstance which makes him averse to capital punishment—explained to me that the young man would not be transported, and that he would be free in a few days from his cellular prison.

The English "cellular prison," imbued and penetrated by the glacial spirit of English Protestantism, proves that severity and cold can be carried to a ferocious pitch. In one of the prisons—Millbank, I think—silence is imposed.

The sheriff told me that when visiting that prison he found in a cell a young man from Guernsey, whom he knew, who had been convicted of theft. When he saw the provost he clasped his hands and cried.

"Ah, monsieur, is my grandmother still alive?"

The provost had scarcely time to reply, when the jailor said to the agonized prisoner, "Hold your tongue!"

The young man died soon after. He passed from the prison to the tomb; from one silence to the other, and scarcely would perceive the change.

Beneath the seven arcades on the ground-floor are the debtors' cells. We entered them. They were unoccupied. A wooden bed, a paillasse, and a rug are all the prison authorities give to a debtor. The last debtor imprisoned was a Guernsey man, whose name has escaped me. He was put there by his wife, who kept him there ten years, gaining her own liberty by his imprisonment. At the end of ten years the husband paid his wife and got out. They lived together again, and the provost says do very well together.

There was no prisoner for debt there at the time; I must repeat this.

This prison is a silent testimony of approval to the Guernsey population. It contains twelve cells: six for debtors, six for ordinary offenders, besides two punishment-cells. There are also for the women two cells only, of which one is a punishment-cell.

One of the seven chambers on the ground-floor is the chapel, a small room without an altar, having a wooden pulpit for the chaplain in the left corner; and in front of the door, back to the window, four or five wooden benches with desks, upon which are scattered a few prayer-books.

On the first floor the criminals are imprisoned. We ascended. The jailor opened a well-lighted cell, furnished only with a wooden bed. At the foot of the bed the coverings were rolled up, and the blankets, like the counterpanes, are of coarse wool, only they seemed to me knitted. The paillasse had been removed, so that one could see the bed-board, on which a number of names and inscriptions had been cut and scratched with knives or nails. These formed a forest of almost obliterated letters. We distinguished among others the following words, which were more legible than the others:—

GUERRE.
HISTOIRE.
CAIN.

Is not all crime included in those words? In a corner of the board there were some rudely-sketched ships in outline.

The cell behind this is a punishment-cell. There is only a plank bed in it, and a small window opening to the north. The last occupant had chalked on the wall a species of labyrinth, which made the jailor very angry. They had soiled the whiteness of his sepulchre for him.

All the cells were whitewashed.

The range of arcades in front of the cells form a sort of gallery, open to the air and southern sun, where the prisoners take exercise in wet weather.

There is in this gallery an old dilapidated bedstead, on which they mount, and can overlook the sea. "That is a great enjoyment for them," said the jailor. I stood upon the bedstead. I could see the island of Sark, and vessels on the horizon. I was desirous of visiting Tapner's cell. The sheriff conducted me thither.

This cell, and the punishment-cell near it, compose the female side.

When one is in the court facing the prison one sees that the first of the seven upper arcades to the left is barred towards the court and walled up towards the gallery. The small space between the railing and the wall was the special paddock of Tapner. There he paced backward and forward all day like a wild beast in a cage, in view of the other prisoners, but separated from them. The window looking into this cage is the window of his cell.

The door is thick, painted black, and bound with iron. Two great bolts above and below and a lock midway.

The jailor opened this door and let us in.

The cell, of the same dimensions as the others, about ten feet square, is clean, white, and well-lighted. The chimney at the bottom of the left angle cantwise, a bucket, a plank fixed to the wall facing the door; on the right of the door under the window is a wooden bedstead, of which one of the four posts is broken. On the bed a paillasse, a rug, and coarse woollen blankets.

This pallet was Tapner's bed. After his death it was given up to the women.

No fire might be lighted in the chimney without the doctor's orders.

At the moment we entered a woman was seated, or rather crouched, upon the bed, with her back to the door. I took my hat off. Mr. Tyrrell, a young English painter, who accompanied me, did the same.

This woman, the only prisoner at the time, was—so the sheriff told me—a thief, and more than that, an Irishwoman, added the jailor. She was a youngish woman, and kept on darning an old stocking, without appearing even to see us.

This woman, in whom the least curiosity was extinct, seemed to personify the sombre indifference of misery.

Tapner suffered in this cold, white, clear cell.

This John Charles Tapner, a kind of gentlemanly employé of the government, not having made use of the advantages of his education, reached the stages of robbery and assassination by drinking and debauchery. He was born of good family and of religious parentage, at Woolwich, in 1823. He died before he was thirty-one, on the 10th of February, 1854.

He lived with two sisters—married

to one, the lover of the other. He had insured his life for the full value of his appointment, £150 sterling, which absorbed all his income, and appeared to announce his intention of living by crime. The assurance was in his wife's name and his own, for the benefit of the survivor.

I asked, "Did the company pay it?"

"Eh? No," replied the sheriff.

"Has it relinquished or given to the poor the annual premiums which it received from Tapner?"

"Oh, no."

Under the virtuous pretext that there had been a crime, the company robbed the widow.

"Tapner appeared indifferent," said the provost, and he therefore concluded the man did not suffer. "That is a mistake," I said. "Do you not believe one is cold under the ice?"

The day before his death his likeness was taken. The apparatus was placed in the cage opening from his cell where there was plenty of sunlight. Tapner could not help laughing as he posed himself. A death's-head might as well have laughed.

"Do not laugh," said the provost to him; "keep serious. They will not recognize your portrait. You cannot laugh today; it is not possible."

It was so possible that he was laughing.

One day the provost lent him a prayer-book. "Read this, Tapner," said he, "if you are guilty." "I am not guilty," replied Tapner. "In any case," replied the provost, "you are a sinner, as we all are. You have not served God. Read this book." Tapner took it, and when the provost entered the cell an hour later he found him, book in hand, bathed in tears.

"His last interview with his wife was most distressing," said the provost. "Nevertheless, the woman was aware of his love-affair with her sister. But who can fathom all the mysteries of pardon?"

The night before my visit to the prison Mr. Pearce, one of the two chaplains who had attended Tapner on the day of his death, came to see me at Hauteville House with the provost. I asked Mr. Pearce, a very venerable and dignified gentleman, "Did Tapner know that I was interested in him?"

"Certainly, sir," replied Mr. Pearce. "He was touched, and very grateful for your intervention, and he particularly wished you to be thanked on his behalf."

I note, as a characteristic detail of the liberty of the English Press, that at the time of Tapner's execution all the journals in the island had more or less demanded it, and were very much shocked by my letter to Lord Palmerston, agreeing in passing over in silence the facts which Mr. Pearce revealed to me.

"There is," said the provost to me, "another thing of which you are ignorant, and which was also passed over in silence. You think you completely failed in your intervention, and, nevertheless, you have gained an enormous victory, of which you have no idea. This island is like all England,—a country of tradition. What has been done yesterday must be done to-day, and done again to-morrow. Now, tradition ordained that the condemned man should go to the gallows with a cord round his neck. Tradition ordained that the gibbet should be erected on the beach, and that the condemned, to reach it, should march through the most public thoroughfares of the town,—there had not been an execution for twenty-five years,—and had been so arranged. So of course Tapner's execution must take place in the same way. After your letter they did not dare to do so. They said, let us hang the man, but in secret. They were ashamed; you did not tie the hands of Death, but you made him blush. They gave up the cord round the neck, the gibbet on the beach, the procession through the streets, and the crowd. They decided that Tapner should be hanged in private in the prison garden. Nevertheless, the law willed that the execution ought to be in public, and the matter was arranged by my signing tickets of admission for two hundred people. Feeling the same distress as they, and more, I agreed to all they decided. I signed the tickets for those who wanted them. Nevertheless, a difficulty presented itself,—the garden adjoining the prison is separated from it by the very wall of the open cell. The door of this garden is in College Street; to reach this door it was necessary for the condemned to leave the prison and walk about one hundred paces in public.

"They did not dare to have this done; so, to avoid it, they made a hole in the wall and let Tapner pass through it. Discretion prevailed."

I do not produce here the exact words of the sheriff, but the sense is the same.

"Well," said I, "conduct me to the garden."

"The breach is closed; the wall is rebuilt; I will take you round by the street."

At the moment of leaving the prison the jailor brought me some of the soup which is supplied to the prisoners, and inviting me to taste it, handed to me a large and very clean tin spoon. I tasted the soup, which is good and wholesome. The bread is excellent. I compared it in my mind to the horrible bread of the French prisons which they showed me at the Conciergerie, which is earthy, damp and viscous and fetid; often full of worms and mouldy.

It was raining; the weather was grey and lowering.

It was not really more than a hundred paces from the prison to the entrance of the garden. We turned to the left, up College Street, along the high black wall. All at once the provost stopped in front of a rather low door. On the panels of the door, which leads to the place where the man lost by drunkenness and ignorance met his death, there are several strips of old bills,—yellow, white, green,—relating to all kinds of things, and on which the rain that effaced them, and the weather that had torn them to pieces, had only left two words distinguishable, — UNIVERSAL EDUCATION — TEMPERANCE.

The provost had a great key in his hand, and unlocked the door, which probably had not been opened since the day of the last execution, and which grated noisily on its hinges. We entered.

The provost shut the door behind us. We found ourselves in a narrow, square space, shut in on three sides by high walls, and opening on the fourth side on a steep staircase, which was dark, though in the open air. Opposite the staircase, the provost pointed out to me the repaired breach in the wall. Through that breach Tapner had passed; the staircase was the first ladder to the gibbet. He had mounted it. We mounted it. I do not know why I counted the steps at that moment; there were fourteen of them. This staircase leads to an oblong and narrow garden, overlooked by another, which forms a terrace. We ascend to this by seven granite steps like the fourteen we have already traversed.

At the top of these seven steps we are in full view of an enclosed open space, a hundred feet square, surrounded by low walls cut by two alleys, which form a cross in the centre. This is what they call the garden. Here Tapner was hanged.

The December sleet continued to fall; a few briers rustled in the wind. There were no flowers nor verdure in the garden, but only one little, thin, stunted fruit-tree at one of the four corners formed by the intersection of the walks. The whole appearance was heartrending. It was one of those sad places which the sun makes melancholy and the rain lugubrious.

There is no house in the garden. It is nobody's garden, except that of the spectre they have left there; it is deserted, abandoned, uncultivated, tragic. Other gardens surround and isolate it. It has no touch with the town, with life, with men—only with the prison. The houses in the low streets which surround it are visible afar off, and seem to have the appearance of looking over the wall into this ill-omened place.

Seeing on one side a sort of little walk, low, narrow, long, and rather deep, on which abutted the first fourteen steps, and on the other this funereal garden, intersected by those two transversal alleys, it was impossible not to think of a ditch near which might be extended the mortuary cloth with the cross.

We have on our right a wall which is as high as the great wall where the gate is, and of which one sees the back from the street. A walk lower than the rest of the garden skirts this wall. A range of thick, rusty tenterhooks, and of long, thin wooden rods, silvered and polished by the frost, were fixed vertically to the wall at intervals of six to eight paces, indicating that formerly there had been an espalier here. It has now disappeared, and nothing of the rods is left, except a sort of skeleton.

A few paces on we reach a flight of three steps, which leads from the garden to the walk. Here we remark more rods on the wall. They reappear again a little farther on, leaving a space of fifteen feet unoccupied.

Here the provost stopped in silence. I saw that the rods were wanting, and I understood. This was where the scaffold had been erected. Looking up, one sees nothing except the broken glass upon the wall, and the round tower of the neighbouring church painted yellow and grey.

The scaffold was raised here. Tapner turned to the left, took the middle walk, and reached by one of the arms of the cross which the walks form the steps of the gibbet placed immediately above the three steps I have mentioned. He mounted on the platform, and thence while he was saying his last prayer, he could see the sea-birds flying in th distance; the pale clouds of February, the ocean, the immensity yonder; and at the same time, by the opening in his mind at that dark hour, he could perceive the mystery, the unknown future, the escarpments of the tomb—God the immensity on high.

The gibbet was composed of two supports and a cross-bar; in the centre of this bar a rope with a knot at the end hung over a closed trap-door. On this trap, the snare of the law, Tapner was placed, and remained standing while the noose was adjusted around his neck. From the street behind the wall, from the College garden at the other side of the street, might have been seen the supports of the gibbet, the cord, the knot, and they could see the back of the condemned man until the trap-door was opened and he fell. Then he disappeared from the view of the spectators outside.

From the interior of the garden, and from the houses of which I have already spoken, they could see the rest.

The punishment was this frightful thing, as I said in my letter to Lord Palmerston. The provost recalled it to my mind, and confirmed all the details. He considered I had rather softened it down than amplified them.

At the moment Tapner fell the cord tightened, and he remained fifteen or twenty seconds motionless, and as if he were dead. The queen's proxy, the chaplain, the magistrates, believing that it was all over, or fancying that it had not commenced, hurried away, and the provost remained alone with the criminal, the executioner, and the curious spectators. I have described the agony of the unhappy wretch, and how the executioner had to drag him down by the feet.

Tapner dead—the law satisfied. It is now the turn of the superstitious; they never failed to come to the rendezvous which the gallows gives them. Epileptics came, and could not be prevented from seizing the convulsive hand of the dead man and passing it frantically over their faces. The dead man was cut down in an hour, and then it was a question who should steal the cord. The assistants threw it down, and each one claimed a piece; but the sheriff took it and threw it in the fire.

When it was burned, the people came and collected the cinders.

The wall against which the gibbet was erected supported a hut which occupied the south-east angle of the garden; thither they carried the corpse. They made ready a table, and a plasterer whom they found there made a cast of the man's face. The visage, violently deformed by strangulation, was recomposed, and had the expression of sleep. The cord removed, calmness returned. It appears as if death, even through punishment, wishes always to be kind, and that its last word should be peace.

I went to this hut; the door was open; it was a miserable cell, scarcely plastered, which served as a garden shed. Some tools were propped against the wall. The chamber was lighted by a window opening into the garden, and by another looking into the street, which had been closed up when Tapner was brought thither, and had not since been reopened. With the exception of the table, which had disappeared, the place was the same as when the corpse had been there. The closed window was then closed; the shutter which had been put up by the hangman remained shut. In front of this window was a piece of furniture, full of little drawers, some of which were missing. On this, beside a broken bottle and some dried flowers, stood one of these drawers full of plaster. It was the same plaster which had been used. I opened at hazard another drawer, and found more plaster, with the imprints of fingers. The floor was littered with yellow herbs and dead leaves. A net was thrown into a corner on a heap of dust. Near the door, in an angle of a wall, was a shovel, the gardener's shovel, probably, or the grave-digger's.

Towards four o'clock in the afternoon, the body being nearly cold, the sheriff put Tapner in the coffin. They did not bury him. They did not go to the expense of a winding-sheet; they simply nailed him down with his clothes on. In Guernsey the clothes of the deceased are his own property; not, as in London, the hangman's perquisite. At nightfall, ten or twelve persons only being present, they carried the coffin to the cemetery, where a grave had been dug in the morning.

"You must see everything," said the provost; so we went out, and I followed him. We plunged into the poor thoroughfares, and arrived in a narrow, steep, angular street lined with hovels, at the corner of which I read Lemarchand Street. The provost left me, went down a dark alley, and came back with the key, which seemed larger than the key of the garden. An instant after we stopped in front of a great black door opening in the centre.

My conductor opened this door, and we found ourselves in a sort of dark and lofty shed.

"Sir," said the provost, "look up; overhead is the gibbet of Beasse."

This Beasse, who was hanged in 1830, was a Frenchman; he had passed as a non-commissioned officer through the Spanish war of 1823 under the Duke of Angoulême; then, enriched by inheritance or otherwise, he retired to Guernsey. There, with his income of fifteen thousand francs, he was a gentleman. He bought a fine house, and became a grandee. In the evening he visited the bailiff, M. Daniel le Brocq.

When one went to see Beasse one found a man working in his garden sometimes. This gardener was the hangman. The hangman of Guernsey was a skilful horticulturist, isolated, and avoided by all. His fellow-creatures having shunned him, he turned to Nature, and was no less skilful in the garden than on the gallows. Beasse, having no prejudices, employed him.

Beasse then was in a good position on account of his money, even in view of the haughty aristocracy of Guernsey, even of the *forty* and the *sixty*.

One day they noticed that his servant was very stout. Then they saw that she was thinner. What had become of the child? The neighbours were aroused; rumours were circulated. The police paid Beasse a visit; two constables came with a doctor. The doctor visited the servant, who was in bed; then the constable said to Beasse, "The woman has been confined. There was a child; we must find it." Beasse, who up to that moment had declared he did not know what they wanted, took a shovel, went into a corner of his garden, and began to dig furiously. One of the constables, thinking that he wished to give a blow with the spade to the object and pass the mark as an accidental wound, took the spade himself and continued to dig more carefully. In a moment or so the child was discovered.

The poor little thing had one larding-pin buried in its throat and another in its anus. Beasse denied that he was the father of the child. He was tried, condemned to be hanged, and it was his friend, the bailiff, Daniel le Brocq, pronounced.

His goods were confiscated.

The provost, after relating this horrible narrative, said: "Beasse was deficient in coolness. By going himself to dig up the ground where the body was, he lost himself. He could easily have saved himself. He had only to say, 'The child is dead. I gave it to a beggar who passed to bury it. I gave him a sovereign. I don't know who he is, and I should not know him again.' No one could have proved the contrary. No one would have known what had become of the child, and they could not have condemned him; Guernsey being still ruled by the Norman custom, which insists on material proof,—*corpus delicti*—before condemnation."

The provost asked me, "Would you have advanced the question of the inviolability of human life for Beasse as you did for Tapner?"

"Unquestionably," I said. "This Tapner and this Beasse are miserable creatures, but the principles never assert their grandeur and beauty so well save when they defend those whom even pity does not defend."

At the time that Beasse was condemned the Revolution of 1830 broke out. He then said to the same M. Martin, now provost, "I would rather remain in France to be shot than in Jersey to be hanged."

Here is a detail. The bailiff was a friend of his, and had to pronounce on him; his gardener was the hangman who executed him. The bailiff did not hesitate. But the gardener was different. Perhaps the gardener had lost touch of hanging. Perhaps his hands, after training roses and lilies, were incapable of making nooses. Perhaps, quite honestly, this legalized slayer was kinder than the law, and was disinclined to stretch the neck of the man with whom he had broken bread. At any rate, the day after the sentence the hangman of Guernsey disappeared. He escaped in some smuggling cutter, and left Saint-Peter's. They sought for him; they searched the island; but he never returned.

It became necessary to advertise.

A man, an Englishman, was in prison for some offence. They offered him pardon if he would become the executioner, and hang Beasse as a commencement. Men call that a pardon. The man accepted. Justice breathed again. She had seen a moment when her death's-head had nothing to devour, not that the upper jaw, the judge, had failed, but because the lower jaw, the hangman, had disappeared.

The day of execution arrived.

They brought Beasse to the gallows, with the cord round his neck, through the streets on to the beach. He was the last who suffered in this way. On the scaffold, at the moment when the white cap was being pulled over his eyes, he turned towards the crowd, and as if he wished to leave one agony behind him, he threw at the spectators this phrase, which might have been spoken by a guilty as well as an innocent man: *"It is only crime that dishonours!"*

The platform was long in falling. They had no trap-door, and had to knock out a whole piece. It was fastened at the extremities to the planks by cords which it was necessary to cut on one side while it remained suspended on the other. The hangman,—the pardoned prisoner,—the same inexperienced wretch, who, twenty-five years later, hanged Tapner,—took an axe and cut the cord; but as he was nervous, he was a long time about it. The crowd murmured, and did not think of saving the culprit, though they nearly stoned the hangman.

I had this scaffold over my head.

I looked up, as the provost requested me to do.

The hut in which we were had a pointed roof, of which the interior framework was naked. Under the beams of this roof, and precisely overhead, were placed two long joists, which had been the support of Beasse's gibbet. At the upper end of those one could see the holes in which the transversal bar had been inserted, to which the cord was fastened. This bar had been taken out, and was lying with the joists. About the centre of these beams were nailed two kinds of wooden cushions, the projecting parts of which had sustained the platform of the gallows. These two beams, supported by the timberwork of the roof, themselves supported a massive, long, narrow plank, from the ends of which ropes hung. This plank was the platform of the gibbet, and those cords were the same which the hangman had been so long cutting. Behind one could perceive a kind of step-ladder, with flat wooden steps, lying near the platform. Beasse had mounted this. All this hideous machine—supports, cross-beams, platform, ladder—were painted iron-grey, and seemed to have been used more than once. The impressions of ropes could be seen on the beams here and there; two or three long ladders of the ordinary form were leaning against the wall.

Near these ladders, in an angle to our right, the provost showed me a species of wooden trellis composed of many panels.

"What is that?" I asked him. "One would say it is a cage. It is, in fact, a cage."

"It is the pillory," he replied. "It is fifteen or twenty years since they used to put that up in the market-place and expose criminals in it. It is now out of date."

Like the gallows of Beasse, this cage was painted a dark grey. Formerly the cage was of iron; then it was made of wood, and painted black to resemble iron; then it was done away with. That is the history of all the old penalty, the future included.

Dust and darkness now cover this apparatus of terror. It might be one of the dark corners of oblivion. Spiders have found this pillory-cage a very good place to spin their webs in and to catch flies.

The platform of the old gibbet having acted badly for Beasse, they built a new one for Tapner. They adopted the English system of the trap, which opens under the patient. "An officer of the garrison invented for the opening of this trap a very ingenious mechanism," said the provost, "and he was executed."

I returned to the scaffold of Beasse. Looking again at one of the ends of the cord, I could see the grooves which the axe in the trembling hands of the hangman had made.

"Now, sir," said the provost, "turn round."

He pointed out in the other compartment of the shed, still up in the roof, a collection of beams having the red colour of the fir-trees. This was like a bundle of planks and beams thrown pell-mell together, among which one could distinguish a long and heavy ladder, with flat steps like the other, and which appeared to me enormous. They were all clean, new, fresh, and forbidding. This was the scaffold of Tapner.

One could see the beams, one might distinguish the cross-beam, one could count the planks of the platform and the steps of the ladder. I was considering from the same point of view the ladder which had borne Beasse and the ladder which Tapner had climbed. My eyes could not detach themselves from those steps, which spectres had ascended, and to which they joined in the distance, in my mind's eye, the sombre steps of the Infinite.

The shed in which we were is composed of two buildings, the geometrical plan of which presents a right angle, forms a T square. The opening of the square is occupied by a little triangular court, which makes one think of the knife of the guillotine. Grass grows between the paving-stones. The rain was falling there; it was formidable.

This funeral shed formerly served as a stable for the country magistrates when they came to sit in the town. One can still see the numbers on the boxes in which they stabled their horses while they were on the bench. I stopped between the two posts marked 3 and 4. An old broken basket was lying on the ground at the bottom of the stall between the two posts; above this stall they had placed the largest beams of the gibbet.

"Why do they keep them there?" I said to the provost. "Why, what you have them do? They would warm a poor family for the whole winter."

Between the figures 3 and 4 one could preceive high up on the roof a startling object—the trap that opened under the feet of Tapner. One could see it underneath,—the massive black bolt, the hinges that turned upon eternity, and the two black joists which united the planks. One also distinguished the ingenious mechanism of which the provost had spoken. It is this too narrow trap which causes the agony. The culprit is caught by the shoulders and suspended. It is scarcely three feet square,—which is not sufficient space, because of the oscillations of the cord. However, the provost explained that Tapner had been badly pinioned, that he had been permitted the movement of his arms; better tied, he would have fallen straight and would not have moved. The guardian of the shed had entered and joined us while the provost was speaking. When he had finished the man added, "Yes, it was the bad pinioning of Tapner that did the mischief, otherwise it would have been magnificent."

Coming out of the shed, the provost begged to take leave of me, and Mr. Tyrrell offered to conduct me to the house of the plasterer who had taken a cast of Tapner. I accepted.

I know still so little of the streets of the town, which seems to be a labyrinth.

We traversed many of the high streets of Saint Peter Port, in which grass grows, and we descended a wide street which plunges into one of the four or five ravines by which the town is intersected. Opposite a house, before which two cypresses, trimmed in the shape of cones, are growing, there is a stonemason's. We entered the yard. At first sight, one is struck by the number of crosses and tomb-stones standing in the passage or against the walls. A workman, the only one in the shed, was fastening together some squares of faience. Mr. Tyrrell spoke to him in English. "Yes, sir," replied the workman, and he went to the planks in tiers at the end of the shed, searched among the plaster and the dust, and brought back in the one hand a mask and in the other a head. These were the mask and the head of Tapner. The mask had been coloured pink—the plaster of the head remained white. The mask had been modelled on the face having still the whiskers and the hair clinging to it; then they had shaved the head and had moulded the skull, the face and the neck naked. Tapner was as celebrated in Guernsey as Lacenaire had been in Paris.

As the provost had said, his face was strangely carved. It recalled to me, in a singular way, the admirable Hungarian violinist Reményi. The physiognomy was youthful and grave, the eyes shut as if in sleep, only a little foam sufficiently thick for the plaster to have taken the impression had remained at the corner of the upper lid, which gives to the face, when regarded for a long while, a sort of ironical sneer. Although the elasticity of the flesh made the neck at the moment of moulding very nearly the natural size, the mark of the cord was plainly visible, and the running knot, distinctly imprinted under the right ear, had left a hideous swelling.

I wanted to carry away this head. They sold it to me for three francs.

It remained to me to make the third pause on this dolorous way, for crime has its own as well as virtue.

"Where is Tapner's grave?" I asked Tyrrell.

He made a gesture and walked on; I followed him.

At Guernsey, as in all English cities, the cemetery is in the town in the midst of the streets. Behind the college, a massive building in English Gothic, which dominates the whole town, there is one of these cemeteries, the largest, perhaps, in Saint Peter Port. A street had been cut through it in the early years of the century, and it is now in two parts. On the western side lie the Guernsey people, on the eastern side the strangers.

We passed up the street through the cemetery, which, planted with trees, has scarcely any houses in it, and above the walls which border it one can see tombstones upright or flat on either side.

Mr. Tyrrell showed me an open door on the right, and said to me, "It is here."

We passed through into the strangers' portion of the cemetery.

We found ourselves in a long parallelogram, enclosed by walls, grass-grown, in which some tombs are scattered. There was no rain, the grass was damp, and the long grey clouds were sweeping slowly along the sky.

As we entered we heard the sound of a pickaxe. The noise ceased, and a living bust seemed to emerge from the ground at the end of the cemetery, and regard us in astonishment.

It was the grave-digger, who was digging a grave, and standing in it waist-deep.

He ceased working when he saw us, not being accustomed to the entrance of living bodies, and not being the landlord except in an hotel of the dead.

We walked towards him over the tombs. He was a young man. There was behind him a stone already mossy, and on which one could read:—

A ANDRÉ JASINSKI,
16th June, 1844.

As we were approaching him he resumed his work. When we reached the edge of the grave he looked up, saw us, and tapped the ground with his spade. The ground sounded hollow. The man said to us, "There is a dead body there which bothers us." Then we understood that he had met with an old grave in the course of digging a new one.

Having said that, without waiting our reply, and as if he were talking less to us than to himself, he bent down and commenced to dig without troubling himself any more about us. One would have said that his eyes were full of the darkness of the grave, and he could see us no longer.

I spoke to him.

"Are you the man," I said, "who buried Tapner?"

He straightened himself, and looked at me like a man who was searching in his memory.

"Tapner?" said he.

"Yes."

"The fellow who was hanged?"

"Yes; did you bury him?"

"No," replied the man. "It was Mr. Morris, the caretaker of the cemetery. I am only a digger myself."

There seems to be a hierarchy among grave-diggers.

I resumed—

"Can you point out the grave to me?"

"Whose grave?"

"Tapner's."

The man replied,—

"Close to the other man who was hanged."

"Show me the place."

He stretched his arm out of the grave, and indicated a spot near the gate by which we had entered,—a grassy corner, about fifteen paces square, where there were no tombs. The tomb-stones which filled the cemetery extended to the borders of this funereal square, and stopped there, as if it were a line it could not pass even in death. The nearest stone backed against the wall of the street bore this epitaph, below which one might read four lines in English, which were hidden by the bushes:—

TO THE MEMORY
OF
AMELIA,
DAUGHTER OF
JOHN AND MARY WINNECOMBE.

I entered into the solitary square which the grave-digger pointed out. I advanced slowly, my gaze bent on the ground. Suddenly I felt under my feet a hillock, which I had not seen because of the height of the grass. This was where they had buried Tapner.

Tapner's grave is very near the entrance to the cemetery, at the foot of a small hut, where the grave-diggers leave their tools. This hut adjoins, gable fashion, to a large building, of which the high door occupies the whole side. The wall which skirts the square in which Tapner is buried is skirted by a penthouse, under which are suspended four or five ladders, fastened with chains and padlocked. At the place where the ladders cease the tombs commence. The benediction and the malediction are side by side in the cemetery, but they do not mingle. Near the shed one distinguishes another eminence, more elongated, and not so prominent as that of Tapner. This is where Beasse is buried.

I spoke to the grave-digger.

"Do you know where the hangman lives who hanged Tapner?"

"The hangman is dead," he replied.

"When did he die?"

"Three months after Tapner."

"Did you bury him?"

"No."

"Is he here?"

"I don't think so."

"Do you know where he is?"

"I do not know."

I snatched a handful of grass from the grave of Tapner, put it in my pocket-book, and came away.

A Woman of the Streets

V. H. WAS elected to the Académie one Tuesday, 1841. Two days afterwards Madame de Girardin, who lived at that time in the Rue Laffitte, invited him to dinner.

At this dinner was Bugeaud, as yet only a general, who had just been appointed governor-general of Algeria, and who was just going out to his post.

Bugeaud was then a man of sixty-five years of age, vigorous, with a very fresh complexion, and pitted with small-pox. He had a certain abruptness of manner which was never rudeness. He was a mixture of rustic and man of the world, old-fashioned and easy mannered, having nothing of the heaviness of the old martinet, witty and gallant.

Madame de Girardin placed the general on her right and V. H. on her left. A conversation sprang up between the poet and the soldier, Madame de Girardin acting as interpreter.

The general was in very bad humour with Algeria. He maintained that this conquest precluded France from speaking firmly to Europe; that nothing was easier to conquer than Algeria, that the forces could easily be blockaded there, that they would be taken like rats, and that they would make but one mouthful; moreover, that it was very difficult to colonize Algeria, and that the soil was unproductive; he had examined the land himself, and he found that there was a distance of a foot and a half between each stalk of wheat.

"So then," said V. H., "that is what has become of what was formerly called the granary of the Romans! But even supposing it were as you say, I think our new conquest is a fortunate and grand affair. It is civilization trampling upon barbarism. It is an enlightened people which goes out to a people in darkness. We are the Greeks of the world; it is for us to illumine the world. Our mission is being accomplished, I only sing Hosanna! You differ from me, it is clear. You speak as a soldier, as a man of action. I speak as a philosopher and a thinker."

V. H. left Madame de Girardin rather early. It was on the 9th of January. It was snowing in large flakes. He had on thin shoes, and when he was in the street he saw that it was impossible to return home on foot. He went along the Rue Taitbout, knowing that there was a cab-rank on the boulevard at the corner of that street. There was no cab there. He waited for one to come.

He was thus waiting, like an orderly on duty, when he saw a young man, well and stylishly dressed, stoop and pick up a great handful of snow, and put it down the back of a woman of the streets who stood at the corner of the boulevard in a low-necked dress. The woman uttered a piercing shriek, fell upon the dandy, and struck him. The young man returned the blow, the woman responded, and the battle went on in a *crescendo,* so vigorously and to such extremities that the police hastened to the spot.

They seized hold of the woman and did not touch the man.

Seeing the police laying hands upon her, the unfortunate woman struggled with them. But when she was securely seized she manifested the deepest grief. While two policemen were pushing her along, each holding one of her arms, she shouted, "I have done no harm, I assure you! It is the gentleman who interfered with me. I am not guilty; I implore you leave me alone! I have done no harm, really, really!"

"Come, move on; you will have six months for this business."

The poor woman at these words, "You will have six months for this business," once more began to defend her conduct, and redoubled her supplications and entreaties. The policemen, not much moved by her tears, dragged her to a police-station in the Rue Chauchat, at the back of the Opéra.

V. H., interested in spite of himself in the unhappy woman, followed them, amid the crowd of people which is never wanting on such an occasion.

Arriving near the station, V. H. conceived the idea of going in and taking up the cause of the woman. But he said to himself that he was well known, that just then the newspapers had been full of his name for two days past, and that to mix himself up in such an affair was to lay himself open to all kinds of disagreeable banter. In short, he did not go in.

The office into which the girl had been taken was on the ground-floor, overlooking the street. He looked through the windows at what was going on. He saw the poor woman lie down upon the floor in despair and tear her hair; he was moved to pity, he began to reflect, and the result of his reflections was that he decided to go in.

When he set foot in the office a man who was seated before a table, lighted by a candle, writing, turned around and said to him in a sharp, peremptory tone of voice, "What do you want, sir?" "Sir, I was a witness of what took place just now; I come to make a deposition as to what I saw, and to speak to you in this woman's favour." At these words the woman looked at V. H. in mute astonishment, and as though dazed. "Your deposition, more or less interested, will be unavailing. This woman has been guilty of an assault in a public thoroughfare. She struck a gentleman. She will get six months' imprisonment for it."

The woman once more began to cry, scream, and roll over and over. Other women, who had come and joined her said to her, "We will come and see you. Never mind. We will bring you some linen things. Take that for the present." And at the same time they gave her money and sweetmeats.

"When you know who I am," said V. H., "you will, perhaps, change your manner and tone, and will listen to me."

"Who are you, then?"

V. H. saw no reason for not giving his name.

He gave his name. The Commissary of Police, for he was a Commissary of Police, was prolific of excuses, and became as polite and deferential as he had before been arrogant; offered him a chair, and begged him to be good enough to be seated.

V. H. told him that he had seen with his own eyes a gentleman pick up a snowball and throw it down the back of the woman; that the latter, who could not even see the gentleman, had uttered a cry indicating sharp pain; that indeed she had attacked the gentleman, but that she was within her right; that apart from the rudeness of the act, the violent and sudden cold occasioned by the snow might, in certain circumstances, do the woman the most serious injury; that so far from taking away from this woman, who had possibly a mother or a child to support, the bread so miserably earned, it should rather be the man guilty of this assault upon her whom he should condemn to pay a fine; in fact, that it was not the woman who should have been arrested, but the man.

During this defence, the woman, more and more surprised, beamed with joy and emotion. "How good the gentleman is!" she said, "how good he is! I never knew so good a gentleman. But then I never saw him. I do not know him at all."

The Commissary of Police said to V. H.: "I believe all that you allege, but the policemen have reported the case, and there is a charge made out. Your deposition will be entered in the charge-sheet, you may be sure. But justice must take its course, and I cannot set the woman at liberty."

"What! After what I have just told you, and what is the truth—truth which you cannot and do not doubt—you are going to detain this woman? Then this justice is a horrible injustice!"

"There is only one condition on which I could end the matter, and that is that you would sign your deposition. Will you do so?"

"If the liberty of this woman depends on my signature, here it is."

And V. H. signed.

The woman continually repeated, "How good the gentleman is! How good he is!"

These unhappy women are astonished and grateful not only when they are treated with sympathy, they are none the less so when they are treated with justice.

Fieschi the Exploder

April 14, 1842.

IN the Boulevard du Temple the house of Fieschi is being pulled down. The rafters of the roof are destitute of tiles. The windows, without glass or frames, lay bare the interior of the rooms. Inside, through the windows at the corner of the yard, can be seen the staircase which Fieschi, Pepin, and Morey went up and down so many times with their hideous project in their hands. The yard is crowded with ladders and carpenter's work, and the ground-floor is surrounded by a timber boarding.

What can be seen of Fieschi's room appears to have been embellished and decorated by the different lodgers who have inhabited it since. The walls and ceilings are covered with a paper sprinkled with a small pattern of greenish hue; and upon the ceiling an ornamental beading, also papered, makes the outline of a Y. This ceiling is, however, already broken in and much cracked by the builder's pickaxe.

Upon the subject of the Fieschi trial I have from the chancellor himself, M. Pasquier, several details which are not known.

As long as Fieschi, after his arrest, thought that his accomplices were in sympathy with him he remained silent. One day he learned through his mistress, Nini Lassave, the one-eyed woman, that Morey said, "What a pity the explosion did not kill him!" From that moment Fieschi was possessed with hatred; he denounced Pepin and Morey, and was as assiduous in ruining them as he had previously been anxious to save them. Morey and Pepin were arrested. Fieschi became the energetic supporter of the prosecution. He entered into the most minute details, revealed everything, threw light on, traced, explained, unveiled, unmasked everything, and failed in nothing, never telling any falsehood, and caring little about putting his head under the knife provided the two other heads fell.

One day he said to M. Pasquier, "Pepin is such a fool that he entered in his account-book the money he gave me for the machine, setting down what it was to be used for. Make a search at the house. Take his account-book for the six first months of 1835. You will find at the head of a page an entry of this kind made with his own hand." His instructions are followed, the search is ordered, the book is found. M. Pasquier examines the book, the procurator-general examines the book; nothing is discovered. This seems strange. For the first time Fieschi was at fault. He is told of it: "Look again." Useless researches, trouble wasted. The commissioners of the court are reinforced by an old examining magistrate whom this affair makes a councillor at the Royal Court in Paris (M. Gaschon, whom the Chancellor Pasquier, in telling me all this, called Gâcon or Cachon). This judge, an expert, takes the book, opens it, and in two minutes finds at the top of a page, as stated, the memorandum which formed the subject of Fieschi's accusation. Pepin had been content to strike it through carelessly, but it remained perfectly legible. The president of the Court of Peers and the procurator-general, from a certain habit readily understood, had not read the passages which were struck through,

and this memorandum had escaped them.

The thing being discovered, Fieschi is brought forward, and Pepin is brought forward, and they are confronted with each other before the book. Consternation of Pepin, joy of Fieschi. Pepin falters, grows confused, weeps, talks of his wife and his three children; Fieschi triumphs. The examination was decisive, and Pepin was lost. The sitting had been long; M. Pasquier dismisses Pepin, takes out his watch, and says to Fieschi, "Five o'clock! Come, that will do for to-day. It is time for you to go to dinner." Fieschi leaped up: "Dinner! O, I have dined to-day. I have cut off Pepin's head!"

Fieschi was correct in the smallest particulars. He said one day that at the moment of his arrest he had a dagger upon him. No mention was to be found of this dagger in any of the depositions. "Fieschi," said M. Pasquier, "what is the use of telling lies? You had no dagger!" "Ah, president," said Fieschi, "when I arrived at the station-house I took advantage of the moment when the policemen had their backs turned to throw the dagger under the camp-bed on which I had to sleep. It must be there still. Have a search made. Those gendarmes are a filthy lot. They do not sweep underneath their beds." A visit was made to the station-house, the camp-bed was removed, and the dagger was found.

I was at the Peers' Court the day before his condemnation. Morey was pale and motionless. Pepin pretended to be reading a newspaper. Fieschi gesticulated while talking loudly and laughing. At one moment he rose and said, "My lords, in a few days my head will be severed from my body; I shall be dead, and I shall rot in the earth. I have committed a crime, and I render a service. As for my crime, I am going to expiate it; as for my service, you will gather the fruits of it. After me no more riots, no more assassinations, no more disturbances. I shall have sought to kill the king; I shall have succeeded in saving him." These words, the gesture, the tone of voice, the hour, the spot, struck me. The man appeared to me courageous and resolute. I said so to M. Pasquier, who answered me: "He did not think he was to die."

He was a bravo, a mercenary, nothing else. He had served in the ranks, and he mixed up his crime with some sort of military ideas. "Your conduct is very dreadful," M. Pasquier said to him; "to blow up perfect strangers, people who have done you no harm whatever,—passers-by." Fieschi coldly replied, "It is what is done by soldiers in an ambush."

Lecomte the Assassin

May 31, 1846.

THE Court of Peers is summoned to try the case of another attempt upon the person of the king.

On the 16th of April last the king went for a drive in the forest of Fontainebleau, in a *char à bancs*. At his side was M. de Montalivet, and behind him were the queen and several of their children. They were returning home towards six o'clock, and were passing by the walls of the Avon enclosure, when two gunshots were fired from the left. No one was hit. Rangers, gendarmes, officers of hussars who escorted the king, all sprang forward. A groom climbed over the wall and seized a man whose face was half masked with a neckerchief. He was an ex-Ranger-general of the forests of the Crown, who had been dismissed from his post eighteen months before for a grave dereliction of duty.

June 1, midday.

The orator's tribune and the president's chair have been removed.

The accused is seated on the spot where the tribune usually stands, and is placed with his back to a green baize curtain, placed there for the trial, between four gendarmes with grenadier's hats, yellow shoulder-straps, and red plumes. In front of him are five barristers, with white bands at their necks and black robes. The one in the centre has the Cross of the Legion of Honour and grey hair. It is Maître Duvergier, the *bâtonnier*. Behind the prisoner red benches, occupied by spectators, cover the semicircle where the chancellor usually presides.

The prisoner is forty-eight years of age; he does not appear to be more than about thirty-six. He has nothing in his appearance which would suggest the deed which he has done. It is one of those calm and almost insignificant countenances, which impress rather favourably than otherwise. General Voirol, who sits beside me, says to me, "He looks a good-natured fellow." However, a dark look gradually overspreads the face, which is somewhat handsome, although of a vulgar type, and he looks like an ill-natured fellow. From the seat which I occupy his hair and moustache appear black. He has a long face with ruddy cheeks. He casts his eyes almost continually downward; when he raises them, every now and then, he looks right up at the ceiling; if he were a fanatic, I should say up to heaven. He has a black cravat, a white shirt, and an old black frockcoat, with a single row of buttons, and wears no ribbon, although belonging to the Legion of Honour.

General Berthuzène leans forward towards me, and tells me that Lecomte yesterday remained quiet all day, but that he became furious when he was refused a new black frock-coat which he had asked for to *appear in before the High Court*. This is a trait of character.

While the names of the Peers were being called over his eyes wandered here and there. To the preliminary questions of the chancellor he replied in a low tone of voice. Some of the Peers called out, "Speak up!" The chancellor told him to look towards the Court.

The witnesses were brought in, among whom were one or two women, very stylishly dressed, and some peasant women. They are on my right, in the lobby on the left of the tribune. M. Decazes walks about among the witnesses. M. de Montalivet, the first witness, is called. He wears a red ribbon, together with two stars, one of a foreign order. He comes in limping, on account of his gout. A footman in a russet livery with a red collar assists him.

I have examined the articles brought forward in support of the indictment, which are in the right-hand passage. The gun is double-barrelled, with twisted barrels, the breech ornamented with arabesques in the style of the Renaissance; it is almost a fancy weapon. The blouse worn by the assassin is blue, tolerably well worn. The neckerchief with which he hid his face is a cotton neckerchief, coffee-coloured, with white stripes. On these articles is hung a small card bearing the signatures of the prosecuting officials and the signature of "Pierre Lecomte."

June 5.

During an interval in the sitting I observed the man from a short distance. He looks his age. He has the tanned skin of a huntsman and the faded skin of a prisoner. When he speaks, when he becomes animated, when he stands upright, his appearance becomes strange. His gesture is abrupt, his attitude fierce. His right eyebrow rises towards the corner of his forehead and gives him an indescribably wild and diabolical appearance. He speaks in a muffled but firm tone.

At one point, explaining his crime, he said,

"I stopped on the 15th of April at the Place du Carrousel. It was raining. I stood under a projecting roof and looked mechanically at some engravings. There was a conversation going on in the shop at the side, where there were three men and a woman. I listened mechanically also. I felt sad. Suddenly I heard the name of the king; they were talking of the king. I looked at these men. I recognized them as servants at the Castle. They said that the king would go the next day to Fontainebleau. At that instant my idea appeared. It appeared to me plainly, dreadfully. It left off raining. I stretched out my hand from beneath the projection of the roof. I found that it no longer rained, and I went away. I returned home to my room, to my little room, bare of furniture and wretched. I remained there alone for three hours. I mused, I pondered, I was very unhappy. My project continually recurred. And then the rain began to come down again. The weather was gloomy; a strong wind was blowing; the sky was nearly black. I felt like a madman. Suddenly I got up. It was settled. I had made up my mind. That is how the idea came into my head."

At another moment, when the chancellor said that the crime was without a motive, he said,—

"How so? I wrote to the king once, twice, three times. The king did not reply. Oh, then—"

He did not finish what he had to say, but his fist clutched the rail fiercely. At this moment he was terrific. He was a veritable wild man. He sits down. He is now composed; calm and fierce.

While the procurator-general spoke, he moved about like a wolf, and appeared furious. When his counsel (Duvergier) spoke, tears came into his eyes. They ran down his cheeks, heavy and perceptible.

June 6.

This is how it takes place. On his name being called in a loud voice by the clerk of the Court, each Peer rises and pronounces sentence also in a loud voice.

The thirty-two Peers who have voted before me have all declared for the parricide's penalty. One or two have mitigated this to capital punishment.

When my turn came, I rose and said,—

"Considering the enormity of the crime and the smallness of the motive, it is impossible for me to believe that the delinquent acted in the full possession of his moral liberty, of his will. I do not think he is a human creature having an exact perception of his ideas and a clear consciousness of his actions. I cannot sentence this man to any other punishment but imprisonment for life."

I said these words in very loud tones. At the first words all the Peers turned round and listened to me in the midst of a silence which seemed to invite me to continue. I stopped short there, however, and sat down again.

The calling of the names continued. The Marquis de Boissy said,—

"We have heard these solemn words. Viscount Victor Hugo has given utterance to an opinion which deeply impresses me, and to which I give my adhesion. I think, with him, that the delinquent is not in full possession of his reason. I declare for imprisonment for life."

The calling of the names continues with the lugubriously monotonous rejoinder: "Capital punishment, parricide's penalty."

Proceeding by seniority, according to the dates at which the members of the House have taken their seats, the list comes down to the names of the oldest Peers. Viscount Dubouchage being called in his turn, said,—

"Being already uneasy in my mind during the trial, owing to the manner of the accused, but fully convinced by the observations of M. Victor Hugo, I declare that, in my opinion, the delinquent is not of sound mind. Viscount Hugo gave the reasons for this opinion in a few words, but in a way which appears to me conclusive. I support him in his vote, and I declare, like himself, for imprisonment for life."

The other Peers, of whom a very small number remained, all voted for the parricide's penalty.

The chancellor, being called on last, rose and said,—

"I declare for the parricide's penalty. Now a second vote will be taken. The first vote is only provisional, the second alone is final. All are, therefore, at liberty to retract or confirm their votes. An opinion worthy of profound consideration in itself, not less worthy of consideration owing to the quarter whence it emanates, has been put forward with authority, although supported by a very small minority, during the progress of the voting. I think it right to declare here that during the continuance of the long inquiry preceding the prosecution, during seven weeks, I saw the accused every day; I examined him, pressed him, questioned him, and, as old Parliamentarians say, 'turned him around' in every direction. Never for a single moment was his calmness of perception obscured. I always found that he reasoned correctly according to the frightful logic of his deed, but without mental derangement, as also without repentance. He is not a madman: he is a man who knows what he wanted to do, and who admits what he has done. Let him suffer the consequences."

The second call has begun. The number of Peers voting for the parricide's penalty has increased. On my name being called I rose. I said,—

"The Court will appreciate the scruples of one in whose conscience such formidable questions are suddenly agitated for the first time. This moment, my lords, is a solemn one for all, for no one more than for myself. For eighteen years past I have had fixed and definite ideas upon the subject of irreparable penalties. Those ideas you are acquainted with. As a mere author I have published them; as a politician, with God's help I will apply them. As a general rule, irreparable penalties are repugnant to me; in no particular instance do I approve of them. I have listened attentively to the observations of the chancellor. They are weighty from so eminent a mind. I am struck by the imposing unanimity of this imposing assembly. But while the opinion of the chancellor and the unanimity of the Court are much, from the point of view of discussion, they are nothing in face of one's conscience. Before the speeches began I read, re-

read, studied all the documents of the trial; during the pleadings I studied the attitude, the looks, the gestures, I scrutinized the soul of the accused. Well, I tell this Court, composed as it is of just men, and I tell the chancellor, whose opinion has so much weight, that I persist in my vote. The accused has led a solitary life. Solitude is good for great, and bad for little minds. Solitude disorders those minds which it does not enlighten. Pierre Lecomte, a solitary man with a small mind, was necessarily destined to become a savage man with a disordered mind. The attempt upon the king, the attempt on a father, at such a time, when he was surrounded by his family; the attempt upon a small crowd of women and children, death dealt out haphazard, twenty possible crimes inextricably added to a crime determined upon,—there is the deed. It is monstrous. Now, let us examine the motive. Here it is: A deduction of twenty francs out of an annual allowance, a resignation accepted, three letters remaining unanswered. How can one fail to be struck by such a reconciliation and such an abyss? I repeat, in conclusion, in the presence of these two extremes, the most monstrous crime, the most insignificant motive, it is evident to me that the thing is absurd, that the mind which has made such a reconciliation and crossed such an abyss is an illogical mind, and that this delinquent, this assassin, this wild and solitary man, this fierce, savage being, is a madman. To a doctor, perhaps, he is not a madman; to a moralist he certainly is. I will add that policy is here in harmony with justice, and that it is always well to deny human reason to a crime which revolts against nature, and shakes society in its foundations. I adhere to my vote."

The Peers listened to me with profound and sympathetic attention. M. de Boissy and M. Dubouchage remained firm, as I did.

There were two hundred and thirty-two voters. This is how the votes were distributed:—

196 for the parricide's penalty;
33 for capital punishment;
3 for imprisonment for life.

The entire House of Peers may be said to have been displeased at the execution of Lecomte. He had been condemned in order that he might be pardoned. It was an opportunity for mercy held out to the king. The king eagerly seized such opportunities, and the House knew this. When it learned that the execution had actually taken place it was surprised, almost hurt.

Immediately after the condemnation, the chancellor and Chief President Franck-Carré, were summoned by the king. M. Franck-Carré was the Peer who had been delegated to draw up the case. They went to the king in the chancellor's carriage. M. Franck-Carré, although he voted for the parricide's penalty, was open in favour of a pardon. The chancellor also leaned in this direction, although he would not declare himself on the subject. On the way he said to President Franck-Carré: "I directed the inquiry, I directed the prosecution, I directed the trial. I had some influence over the vote. I will not give my opinion on the subject of a pardon. I have enough responsibility as it is. They will do what they like."

In the cabinet of the king he respectfully adopted the same tone. He declined to commit himself to a definite opinion on the subject of a pardon. President Franck-Carré was explicit. The king saw what was the real opinion of the chancellor.

Maître Duvergier had conceived an affection for his client, as a barrister always does for the client he has to defend. It is a common result. The public prosecutor ends by hating the accused, and the counsel for the defence by loving him. Lecomte was sentenced on a Friday. On the Saturday M. Duvergier went to see the king. The king received him in a friendly manner, but said, "I will see about it; I will consider it. The matter is a grave one. My danger is the danger of all. My life is of consequence to France, so that I must defend it. However, I will think the matter over. You know that I detest capital punishment. Every time I have to sign the dismissal of an appeal for a pardon I am the first to suffer. All my inclinations, all my instincts, all my convictions are on the other side. However, I am a constitutional king; I have ministers who decide. And then naturally I must think a little of myself too."

M. Duvergier was dreadfully grieved. He saw that the king would not grant a pardon.

The Council of Ministers was unanimously in favour of the execution of the sentence of the Court of Peers.

On the following day, Sunday, M. Duvergier received by express a letter from the Keeper of the Seals, Martin du Nord, announcing to him that "the king thought it right to decide that the law should take its course." He was still under the influence of the first shock of hope definitively shattered when a fresh express arrived. Another letter. The Keeper of the Seals informed the *bâtonnier* that the king, wishing to accord to the condemned man, Pierre Lecomte, a *further* token of his good-will, had decided that the yearly allowance of the said Lecomte should revert to his sister for her lifetime, and that his Majesty had placed an immediate sum of three thousand francs at the disposal of the sister for her assistance. "I thought, M. le Bâtonnier," said the Keeper of the Seals, in conclusion, "that it would be agreeable to you to communicate yourself to the unhappy woman this evidence of the royal favour."

M. Duvergier thought he had made some mistake in reading the first letter. "A *further* token," he said to one of his friends, who was present. "I was mistaken, then. The king grants the pardon." But he re-read the letter, and saw that he had read it only too correctly. A *further token* remained inexplicable to him. He refused to accept the commission which the Keeper of Seals asked him to undertake.

As to the sister of Lecomte, she refused the three thousand francs and the pension; she refused them with something of scorn and also of dignity. "Tell the king," she said, "that I thank him. I should have thanked him better for something else. Tell him that I do not forget my brother so quickly as to take his spoils. This is not the boon that I expected of the king. I want nothing. I am very unhappy and miserable, I am nearly starving of hunger, but it pleases me to die like this, since my brother died like that. He who causes the death of the brother has no right to support the sister."

M. Marilhac plays throughout this affair a lugubriously active part. He was a member of the Commission of the Peers during the preliminaries to the trial. He wanted to omit from the brief for the prosecution the letter of Dr. Gallois, in which he spoke of Lecomte as a madman. It was at one moment proposed to suppress the letter.

Lecomte displayed some courage. At the last moment, however, on the night preceding the execution, he asked, towards two o'clock, to see the procurator-general, M. Hébert; and M. Hébert, on leaving him after an interview of a quarter of an hour, said, "He has completely collapsed; the mind is gone."

June 12.

I dined yesterday at the house of M. Decazes with Lord Palmerston and Lord Lansdowne.

Lord Palmerston is a stout, short, fair man, who is said to be a good talker. His face is full, round, broad, red, merry, and shrewd, slightly vulgar. He wore a red ribbon and a star, which I think is that of the Bath.

The Marquis of Lansdowne affords a striking contrast to Lord Palmerston. He is tall, dark, spare, grave, and courteous, with an air of breeding, a gentleman. He had a star upon his coat, and round his neck a dark-blue ribbon, to which hung a gold-enamelled decoration, round-shaped, and surmounted by the Irish harp.

M. Decazes brought these two gentlemen to meet me. We spoke for some minutes of Ireland, of bread-stuffs, and of the potato disease.

"Ireland's disease is graver still," I said to Lord Palmerston.

"Yes," he replied; "the Irish peasants are very wretched. Now, your country folk are happy. Ah, you are favoured by the skies! What a climate is that of France!"

"Yes, my lord," I rejoined; "but you are favoured by the sea. What a citadel is England!"

Lady Palmerston is graceful and talks well. She must have been charming at one time. She is no longer young. Lord Palmerston married her four years ago, after a mutual passion which had lasted for thirty years. I conclude from this that Lord Palmerston belongs a little to history and a great deal to romance.

At table I was between M. de Mantalivet and Alexandre Dumas. M. de Montalivet wore the cross of the Legion of Honour, and Alexandre Dumas the cross of an order which he told me was that of St. John, and which I believe to be Piedmontese.

I led up in conversation with M. de Montalivet to the event of the 16th of April. He was, it is well known, in the *char à bancs* by the king's side.

"What were you conversing with the king about at the moment of the report?" I said.

"I cannot remember," he replied. "I took the liberty of questioning the king upon this subject. He could not recall it either. The bullet of Lecomte destroyed something in our memory. All I know is that while our conversation was not important, we were very intent upon it. If it had not absorbed our attention we should certainly have perceived Lecomte when he stood up above us to fire; the king, at all events, would have done so, for I myself was turning my back somewhat to speak to the king. All that I remember is that I was gesticulating very much at the moment. When the first shot was fired, some one in the suite cried, 'It is a huntsman unloading his gun.' I said to the king, 'A strange kind of huntsman to fire the remains of his powder at kings.' As I finished speaking the second shot went off. I cried, 'It is an assassin!' 'Oh!' said the king, 'not so fast; do not let us judge too hastily. Wait, we shall see what it means.' You see in that the character of the king, do you not? Calm and serene in the presence of the man who has just fired at him; almost kindly. At this moment the queen touched me gently on the shoulder; I turned round. She showed me, without uttering a word, the wadding of the gun which had fallen upon her lap, and which she had just picked up. There was a certain calmness in this silence which was solemn and touching.

"The queen, when the carriage leans over a little, trembles for fear she will be upset; she makes the sign of the cross when it thunders; she is afraid of a display of fireworks; she alights when a bridge has to be crossed. When the king is fired upon in her presence she is calm."

Henri the Regicide

July 29, midnight, 1846.

Suzanne, the chambermaid, has just returned home.

She has been to the *fête* to see the fireworks. On coming in—she was radiant—she said, "Oh! what a lucky thing, madame! It was my cousin who arrested the man who fired upon the king." "What! Has any one fired at the king?" "Yes, and my cousin arrested the man. What a lucky thing! It was this evening, just now. The king was on the balcony. The man fired two pistol-shots together, and missed the king. Oh, how people applauded! The king was pleased. He pointed out himself where the smoke came from. But my cousin, who is a policeman in plain clothes, was there, close to the man. He only had to turn round. He took the man into custody." "What is his name?" "Joseph Legros." "The assassin?" "No, my cousin. He is a tall fellow. The man is little. I do not know his name. I have forgotten it. He looked sad; he pretended to be crying. When he was taken away he said, 'Oh dear! I must die, then.' He is fifty years old. Some gold was found on him. I should think he will have a bad time of it to-night. My cousin is delighted, and the curé also is delighted." (This is a canon of Nôtre-Dame who resides in the same building as the cousin in the police.) "What luck, eh! Madame, what luck!"

July 30.

There is close to here, in the Rue de Limoges, a house with a carriage-way of solemn and gloomy appearance, some old court-house, with a little square yard. On the left-hand side of the door is a great black board, in the centre of which are the Arms of France. Upon this board is an inscription in wooden letters, formerly gilt, and running thus:—

SOUVENIRS AND USEFUL ARTICLES
for Ladies.
OFFICE REQUISITES
of every kind.
MANUFACTORY OF FANCY ARTICLES
IN EMBOSSED STEEL
AND OTHER GOODS
8 — JOSEPH HENRI — 8

Joseph Henri is the assassin. He has a wife and three children.

On the right-hand side, in the court-yard there is a house-door, above which is seen:—

JOSEPH HENRI
THE WAREHOUSE IS ON THE FIRST FLOOR

The whole house is of a fallen and dismal appearance.

August 1.

The day before yesterday I went to inscribe my name at the palace of the king, who has gone to Eu. This is done upon a kind of register, with a green parchment back like a laundress's book. There are five registers, one for each member of the royal family. Every evening the registers are forwarded to the king, and the queen carefully reads them.

I do not suppose people inscribed their names at the residence of Louis XIV. or of Napoleon.

This reminds me of the first time I dined at the Tuileries. A month afterwards I met M. de Rémusat, who was among the guests, and who says, "Have you paid your visit of digestion?"

Homely manners are charming and graceful, but they go rather too far sometimes. I thoroughly understand royalty living a homely life, but this granted, I prefer the patriarchal style to the home style. Patriarchal life is as simple as homely life, and as majestic as royal life.

M. Lebrun, who came to leave his name at the same time as I did, was telling me that a few years ago the King of the Belgians was at the Tuileries. M. Lebrun goes to see him. He speaks to the hall porter. "Can I see the King of the Belgians, please?" "The King of the Belgians? Oh! yes, Sir, in the second courtyard, through the little door. Go up to the third floor and turn to the left along the corridor. The King of the Belgians is No. 9."

The Prince de Joinville lives in a little attic at the Tuileries. The Duke of Saxe-Coburg is lodged in the Louvre in a corridor. Like the King of the Belgians, he has his card nailed upon the door: "Duke of Saxe-Coburg."

August 25.

The trial of Joseph Henri begins to-day in the Court of Peers.

The prisoner is brought in after the Court is seated by four gendarmes, of whom two hold him by the arms. There were six to Lecomte. Joseph Henri is a little man, who appears over fifty years of age. He is dressed in a black frock-coat; he has a black silk waistcoat and black cravat, whiskers, black hair, a long nose. He wears eye-glasses.

He enters, bows three times to the Court, as an actor bows to the pit, and sits down. During the calling of the names he takes snuff with a profound look of ease.

The chancellor tells him to rise, and asks him his surname and Christian names. He replies in a low tone of voice, in a subdued and timid manner. "Speak louder," said the chancellor. The prisoner repeats his replies loudly and very distinctly. He looks like a worthy citizen who is taking out a passport, and who is being questioned by the government employé. He sits down and whispers a few words to his counsel, M. Baroche, *bâtonnier* of the order of barristers. There are five barristers at the bar. Among the crowd which throngs the semicircle behind the prisoner is a priest. Not far from the priest is a Turk.

The prisoner is so short that when he stands up he does not reach above the heads of the gendarmes seated beside him. From time to time he blows his nose loudly in a white handkerchief with blue squares. He has the appearance of a country registrar. His person altogether suggests something ineffably mild, sad, and subdued. Every now and then, however, he holds his head in his two hands, and a look of despair penetrates through the air of indifference. He is, in fact, despairing and indifferent at one and the same time.

When the procurator-general and the chancellor tell him that he is playing a part, he looks at them without any appearance of resentment, and like a man who does not understand.

He speaks a great deal, rather fast, sometimes in low, at others in very loud, tones. He appears to see things only through a veil, and to hear only through a screen. One would imagine there was a wall, barely transparent, between the real world and himself. He looks fixedly, just as if he is seeking to make out things and distinguish faces from behind a barrier. He utters rambling words in a subdued manner. They have a meaning, however, for a thoughtful person.

He concludes a long explanation thus: "My crime is without a stain. At present my soul is as in a labyrinth."

The procurator-general said to him, "I am not to be imposed on by you. You have an object, and that is to escape the death penalty by appearing to invite it, and in this way to secure some less grave penalty."

"Pooh!" he exclaimed; "how can you say so? Other penalties are a punishment, the penalty of death is annihilation."

He stood musing for a moment, and then added: "For eighteen years my mind has suffered. I do not know what state my mind is in; I cannot say. But you see I am not trying to play the madman."

"You had," the chancellor said, "ferocious ideas."

He replies: "I had no ferocious ideas; I had only ideas" (here he indicates with a gesture an imaginary flight of birds hovering round his head) "which I thought came to me from God."

Then he remains silent for a moment, and continues, almost violently: "I have suffered a great deal,—a great deal" (folding his arms). "And do you think I suffer no longer?"

Objection is made to certain passages of what he has written.

"Just as you please. All that I have written I have written, written, written; but I have not read it."

At another moment he breaks out unexpectedly amid the examination with this: "I have beliefs. My principal belief is that there are rewards and punishments above."

The names of all the regicides, of Fieschi, of Alibaud, of Lecomte, are mentioned to him. His face becomes clouded, and he exclaims, "How is it you speak to me of all those whose names you have just mentioned?"

At this moment Viennet comes up behind me, and says, "He is not a madman, he is a fool."

For myself I should have said the precise contrary.

He is asked, "Why did you write to M. de Lamartine and M. Raspail?"

He replies, "Because I had read some of their writings, and they appeared to me to be philanthropists; and because I thought that philanthropy should not be found only in a pen point."

He frequently concludes his replies with this word, addressed to the Court, and uttered almost in a whisper, *"Appreciate!"*

The procurator-general recapitulates all the charges, and concludes by asking him, "What have you to say in reply?"

"I have no reply to make."

And he places his hand on his forehead as if he had a pain there.

In the midst of a long rambling statement, mingled here and there with flashes of intelligence, and even of thoughtfulness, he stops short to ask for a basin of soup, and gives a number of directions to the attendant who brings it to him. He has a fit of trembling which is plainly perceptible. He drinks a glass of water several times during the examination. He trembles so violently that he cannot carry the glass to his lips without holding it with both hands.

He calls the procurator-general "Monsieur le Procureur." When he speaks of the king he says "his Majesty."

During the very violent speech, for the prosecution, of the procurator-general he makes signs of approval. During the speech for the defence, of his counsel, he makes signs of disagreement. However, he listens to them with profound attention. At one point M. Hébert said, "The prisoner has no political animus. He even protests his respect and admiration for the king." Joseph Henri nods his head twice in token of assent. At another moment the procurator-general says that the prisoner wants to secure a ludicrously inadequate punishment. He says "No," with a shake of his head, and takes snuff.

During the temporary rising of the Court Villemain came to me in the reading-room, and said, "What do you think of all this? It seems to me that no one here is genuine,—neither the prisoner, nor the procurator-general, nor the chancellor. They all look to me as though they are shamming, and as though not one of them says what he thinks. There is something false, equivocal, and confused in this affair."

During the trial Villemain contemplated Joseph Henri with fixed and melancholy interest.

August 27.

The deliberation began at twenty minutes past eight o'clock. The Peers, without swords or hats, sit with closed doors; only the clerks are present. On taking their seats the Peers cried out on all sides, "Open the ventilators; let us have some light; give us some air!"

The heat that was in the hermetically sealed room was over-powering.

Two questions were asked by the chancellor:—

"Is the prisoner Henri guilty of the attempt upon the life of the king? Is he guilty of an attempt upon the person of the king?"

I should not omit to say that during the calling of the names Langrenée said to me, "I shall be the only one of the diplomatic body who will not vote for the sentence of death." I congratulated him, and went and sat down again behind the bench occupied by Bussière.

Another Peer, one of the new ones, whom I did not know, left his seat, came towards me, and seated himself upon the empty chair at the side, saying to me, "You do not know me?" "No." "Well, I nursed you when you were little,—no higher than that, upon my knees. I am a friend of your father's. I am General Rapatel."

I remembered the name, which my father had often mentioned. I shook hands with the general. We conversed affectionately. He spoke to me of my childhood, I spoke to him of his great battles, and both of us became younger again. Then silence took place. The voting had begun.

The voting went on, on the question of an attempt on the life or an attempt on the person, without its being ascertained beforehand whether the difference in the crime involved any difference in the penalty. However, it was soon evident that those Peers who decided that it was an attempt on the person did not desire the death penalty, and the majority of this opinion became larger and larger.

As the second vote was about to be taken, I said: "It results from the deliberation on the whole, and from the earnest views which have been put forward, that, in the opinion of all the judges, the words 'person of the king' have a double sense, and that they signify the physical person and the moral person. These two senses, however, are distinct to the conscience, although they are confounded in the vote. The physical person has not been injured, has not been seriously menaced, as nearly all my noble colleagues are agreed. It is only the moral person who has been not only menaced, but even injured. Having given this explanation, and with this reserve, that it is perfectly understood that it is the moral person only that is injured, I associate myself with the immense majority of my colleagues, who declare the prisoner, Joseph Henri, guilty of an attempt upon the person of the king."

The clerk proclaimed the result:—

One hundred and twenty-two Peers decided for an attempt on the person; thirty-eight for an attempt on the life; four for an act of contempt.

The sitting was suspended for a quarter of an hour. The Peers left the Court, and became scattered in groups in the lobby. I conversed with M. de la Redorte, and I told him that if it came to the point I admitted State policy as well as justice, but on the condition that I should consider State policy as the human voice, and justice as the Divine voice. M. de Mornay came up to me and said that the *Anciens* abandoned the death penalty; that they were sensible of the feeling of the House, and gave way to it; but that, in agreement with the majority, they would vote for penal servitude for life, and I was asked to give my support to this vote. I said that it was impossible for me to do so; that I congratulated our *Anciens* on having abandoned the death penalty, but that I should not vote for penal servitude; that, in my opinion, the punishment exceeded the offence; that, moreover, it was not in harmony with the dignity of the Chamber or its precedents.

The sitting was resumed at half-past four.

When my turn came, I simply said, "Detention for life."

Several Peers gave the same vote. Thirteen in all. Fourteen voted the death penalty; a hundred and thirty-three penal servitude for life.

Several Peers said to me, "You ought to be satisfied; there is no death sentence. The judgment is a good one." I replied, "It might have been better."

The procurator-general and the advocate-general were brought in, in scarlet robes; then the public rushed in noisily. There were a number of men in blouses. Two women who were among the crowd were turned out. The names of the

Peers were called; then the chancellor read the judgment amid profound silence.

P. S.—September 12.

The punishment has not been commuted; the judgment will be carried out.

Joseph Henri, who had been transferred from the Luxembourg and from the Conciergerie to the prison of La Roquette, started the day before yesterday for Toulon in a prison-van with cells, accompanied by eight felons. While the irons were being placed upon him he was weak, and trembled convulsively; he excited the compassion of everybody. He could not believe that he was really a convict. He muttered in an underdone, "Oh dear! if I had but known!"

The Crypt of Pain

I REMEMBER that on Thursday, the 10th of September, 1846, St. Patient's day, I decided to go to the Académie. There was to be a public meeting for the award of the Montyon prize, with a speech by M. Viennet. Arriving at the Institute, I ascended the staircase rather irresolutely. In front of me ran up boldly and cheerfully, with the nimbleness of a schoolboy, a member of the Institute in full dress, with his coat buttoned up, tight-fitting, and nipped in at the waist,—a lean, spare man, with active step and youthful figure. He turned round. It was Horace Vernet. He had an immense moustache, and three crosses of different orders suspended from his neck. In 1846 Horace Vernet was certainly more than sixty years of age.

Arriving at the top of the staircase, he entered. I felt neither so young nor so bold as he, and I did not enter. In the street outside the Institute I met the Marquis of B. "You have just come away from the Académie?" he asked. "No," I replied; "one cannot come away without going in. And you, how is it you are in Paris?" "I have just come from Bourges." The Marquis, a very warm Legitimist, had been to see Don Carlos, son of him who took the title of Charles V. Don Carlos, whom the faithful called Prince of the Asturias, and afterwards King of Spain, and who was known to European diplomacy as the Count de Montemolin, looked with some amount of annoyance upon the marriage of his cousin, Doña Isabella, with the Infante Don Francisco d'Assiz, Duke of Cadiz, which had just been concluded at this very moment He plainly showed the Marquis how surprised he felt, and even let him see a letter addressed by the Infante to him, the Count de Montemolin, in which this phrase occurred, word for word: "I will abandon all thought of my cousin as long as you remain between her and me."

We shook hands, and M. de B. left me.

As I was returning by the Quai des Morfondus, I passed by the lofty old towers of Saint-Louis, and I felt an inclination to visit the prison of the Conciergerie at the Palais de Justice. It is impossible to say how the idea came into my head to go in and see how man had contrived to render hideous in the inside what is so magnificent on the outside. I turned to the right, however, into the little courtyard, and rang at the grating of the doorway. The door was opened; I gave my name. I had with me my peer's medal. A doorkeeper was put at my service to serve as a guide wherever I wished to go.

The first impression which strikes one on entering a prison is a feeling of darkness and oppression, diminished respiration and perception, something ineffably nauseous and insipid intermingled with the funereal and the lugubrious. A prison has its odour as it has its *chiaroscuro*. Its air is not air, its daylight is not daylight. Iron bars have some power, it would seem, over those two free and heavenly things,—air and light.

The first room we came to was no other than the old guard-room of Saint-Louis, an immense hall cut up into a large number of compartments for the requirements of the prison. Everywhere are elliptical-pointed arches and pillars with capitals; the whole scraped, pared, levelled, and marred by the hideous taste of the architects of the Empire and the Restoration. I make this remark once for all, the whole building having been served in the same fashion.

In this warder's room could still be seen on the right-hand side the nook where the pikes were stacked, marked out by a pointed moulding at the angle of the two walls.

The outer office in which I stood was the spot where the *toilet* of condemned criminals took place. The office itself was on the left. There was in this office a very civil old fellow, buried in a heap of cardboard cases, and surrounded by nests of drawers, who rose as I entered, took off his cap, lighted a candle, and said:

"You would like, no doubt, to see Héloïse and Abélard, sir?"

"By all means," I said; "there is nothing I should like better."

The old man took the candle, pushed on one side a green case bearing this inscription, "Discharges for the month," and showed me in a dark corner behind a great nest of drawers a pillar and capital, with a representation of a monk and a nun back to back, the nun holding in her hand an enormous phallus. The whole was painted yellow, and was called Héloïse and Abélard.

My good man continued:—

"Now that you have seen Héloïse and Abélard, you would, no doubt, like to see the condemned cell?"

"Certainly," I said.

"Show the gentleman the way," said the good man to the turnkey.

Then he dived once more into his cases. This peaceful creature keeps the register of the sentences and terms of imprisonment.

I returned to the outer office, where I admired as I passed by a very large and handsome shell-work table in the brightest and prettiest Louis XV. taste, with a marble border, but dirty, unsightly, daubed with colour which had once been white, and relegated to a dark corner. Then I passed through a gloomy room, encumbered with wooden bedsteads, ladders, broken panes of glass, and old window-frames. In this room the turnkey opened a door with a fearful noise of heavy keys and drawn bolts, and said, "That is it, sir."

I went into the condemned cell.

It was rather a large place, with a low, arched ceiling, and paved with the old stone flooring of Saint-Louis,—square blocks of lias-stone alternating with slabs of slate.

Some of the paving-stones were missing here and there. A tolerably large semicircular vent-hole, protected by its iron bars and projecting shaft, cast a pale and wan sort of light inside. No furniture, save an old cast-iron stove of the time of Louis XV., ornamented with panels in relief, which it is impossible to distinguish owing to the rust, and in front of the skylight a large arm-chair in oak, with an opening in the seat. The chair was of the period of Louis XIV., and covered with leather, which was partly torn away so as to expose the horse-hair. The stove was on the right of the door. My guide informed me that when the cell was occupied a folding bedstead was placed in it. A gendarme and a warder, relieved once every three hours, watched the condemned man day and night, standing the whole time, without a chair or bed, so that they might not fall asleep.

We returned to the outer office, which led to two more rooms,—the reception room of the privileged prisoners, who were able to receive their visitors without standing behind a double row of iron bars, and the saloon of the barristers, who are entitled to communicate freely and in private with their clients. This "saloon,"—for so it was described in the inscription placed over the door,—was a long room, lighted by an opening in the wall, and furnished with long wooden benches like the other one. It appears that some young barristers had been guilty of abusing the privilege of a legal *tête-à-tête*. Female thieves and poisoners are occasionally very good-looking. The abuse was discovered, and the "saloon" was provided with a glazed doorway. In this way it was possible to see, although not to hear.

At this juncture the governor of the Conciergerie, whose name was Lebel, came up to us. He was a venerable old man, with some shrewdness in his looks. He wore a long frock-coat, and in his button-hole the ribbon of the Legion of Honour. He begged to be excused for not having ascertained before that I was in the place, and asked me to allow him to accompany me in the tour of inspection which I wished to make.

The outer office led through an iron barrier into a long, wide, and spacious vaulted passage.

"What is that?" I asked M. Lebel.

"That," he said, "was formerly connected with the kitchens of Saint-Louis. It was very useful to us during the riots. I did not know what to do with my prisoners. The Prefect of Police sent and asked me, 'Have you plenty of room just now? How many prisoners can you accommodate?' I replied, 'I can accommodate two hundred.' They sent me three hundred and fifty, and then said to me, 'How many more can you accommodate?' I thought they were joking. However, I made room by utilizing the Women's Infirmary. 'You can,' I said, 'send a hundred prisoners.' They sent me three hundred. This rather annoyed me; but they said, 'How many can you still find room for?' 'You can now send as many as you like.' Sir, they sent me six hundred! I placed them here; they slept upon the ground on trusses of straw. They were very excitable. One of them, Lagrange, the Republican from Lyons, said to me, 'Monsieur Lebel, if you will let me see my sister, I promise you I will make all the men keep quiet.' I allowed him to see his sister; he kept his word, and the place, with all its six hundred devils, became a little heaven. My Lyons men thus continued well behaved and civil until the day when, the House of Peers having begun to move in the matter, they were brought in contact, during the official inquiry, with the Paris rioters, who were of Sainte-Pélagie. The latter said to them, 'You must be mad to remain quiet like that. Why, you should complain, you should shout, you should be furious.' My Lyons men now became furious, thanks to the Parisians. They became perfect Satans! Oh, what trouble I had! They said to me, 'Monsieur Lebel, it is not because of you, but of the Government. We want to show our teeth to the Government.' And Reverchon then undressed himself and stood stark naked."

"He called that showing his teeth, did he?" I asked M. Lebel.

In the meantime the turnkey had opened the great railings at the far end of the corridor, then other railings and heavy doors, and I found myself in the heart of the prison.

I could see through the railed arches the men's exercise-yard. It was a tolerably large, oblong courtyard, above which towered on every side the high walls of Saint-Louis, nowadays plastered and disfigured. A number of men were walking up and down in groups of two or three; others were seated in the corners, upon the stone benches which surround the yard. Nearly all wore the prison dress,—large waistcoats with linen trousers; two or three, however, wore black coats. One of the latter was clean and sedate-looking, and had a certain indescribable air of a town-bred man. It was the wreck of a gentleman.

This yard had nothing repulsive-looking about it. It is true that the sun was shining brightly, and that everything looks smiling in the sun,—even a prison. There were two beds of flowers with trees, which were small, but of a bright green, and between the two beds, in the middle of the yard, an ornamental fountain with a stone basin.

This yard was formerly the cloister of the Palace. The Gothic architect surrounded the four sides with a gallery ornamented with pointed arches. The modern architects have covered these arches with masonry; they have placed steps and partitions in them and made two stories. Each arcade made one cell on the ground-floor and one on the first floor. These cells, clean and fitted with timber floorings, had nothing very repulsive about them. Nine feet long by six feet wide, a door opening on to the corridor, a window overlooking the ground, iron bolts, a large lock, and a railed opening in the door, iron bars to the window, a chain, a bed in the angle on the left of the door, covered with coarse linen and coarse blanketing, but very carefully and neatly made,—that is what these cells were like. It was recreation time. Nearly all the cells were open, the men being in the yard. Two or three, however, remained closed, and some of the prisoners—young workmen, shoemakers and hatters for the most part—were working there, making a great noise with their hammers. They were, I was told, hard-working and well-conducted prisoners, who preferred to do some work rather than go out for exercise.

The quarters of the privileged prisoners were above. The cells were rather larger, and, as a result of the greater liberty enjoyed here at a cost of *sixteen centimes* a day, rather less clean. As a general rule, in a prison, the greater the cleanliness the less liberty there is. These wretched beings are so constituted that their cleanliness is the token of their servitude. They were not alone in their cells; there were, in some cases, two or three together; there was one large room in which there were six. An old man with a kindly and honest-looking face was engaged in reading. He lifted up his eyes from his book when I entered, and looked at me like a country curé reading his breviary and seated upon the grass with the sky above his head. I made inquiries, but I could not discover of what this *good-man* was accused. Upon the whitewashed wall near the door these four lines were written in pencil:—

"Dans la gendarmerie,
Quand un gendarme rit,
Tous les gendarmes rient
Dans la gendarmerie."

Beneath them a parodist had added:—
"Dans la Conciergerie,
Quand un concierge rit,
Tous les concierges rient
Dans la Conciergerie."

M. Lebel called my attention in the yard to the spot where a prisoner had made his escape a few years before. The right angle formed by the two walls of the yard at the northernmost end had sufficed for the accomplishment of the man's purpose. He had planted his back in this angle, and drew himself up solely by the muscular force of his shoulders, elbows, and heels, as far as the roof, where he caught hold of a stove-pipe. Had this stove-pipe given way under his weight he would have been a dead man. On reaching the roof he climbed down again into the outer enclosure and fled. All this in broad daylight. He was captured again in the Palais de Justice. His name was Bottemolle. "Such an escape was deserving of better luck," said M. Lebel. "I was almost sorry to see him brought back."

At the beginning of the men's yard there was, on the left, a little office reserved for the chief warder, with a table placed at a right angle before the window, a leather-covered chair, and all kinds of cardboard cases and papers upon the table. Behind this table and chair was an oblong space of about eight feet by four. It was the site of the cell formerly occupied by Louvel. The wall which divided it from the office had been demolished. At a height of about seven feet the wall ended, and was replaced by an iron grating reaching to the ceiling. The cell was lighted only through this and through the window in the door, the light coming from the corridor of the office and not from the courtyard. Through this grating and through the window of the door Louvel, whose bed was in the corner at the far end, was watched night and day. For all that, moreover, two turnkeys were placed in the cell itself. When the wall was pulled down the architect preserved the door—a low-lying, door, armed with a great square lock and round bolt—and had it built into the outer wall. It was there I saw it.

I remember that in my early youth I saw Louvel cross the Pont-au-Change on the day on which he was taken to the Place de Grève. It was, I think, in the month of June. The sun shone brightly. Louvel was in a cart, with his arms tied behind his back, a blue coat thrown over his shoulders, and a round hat upon his head. He was pale. I saw him in profile. His whole countenance suggested a sort of earnest ferocity and violent determination. There was something harsh and frigid in his appearance.

Before we left the men's quarters M. Lebel said, "Here is a curious spot." And he made me enter a round, vaulted room, rather lofty, about fifteen feet in diameter, without any window or opening in the wall, and lighted only through the doorway. A circular stone bench stretched all round the chamber.

"Do you know where you are now?" asked M. Lebel.

"Yes," I replied.

I recognized the famous chamber of torture. This chamber occupies the ground-floor of the crenellated tower, —the smallest of the three round towers on the quay.

In the centre was an ominous and singular-looking object. It was a sort of long and narrow table of lias-stone, joined with molten lead poured into the crevices, very heavy, and supported on three stone legs. This table was about two and a half feet high, eight feet long, and twenty inches wide. On looking up I saw a great rusty iron hook fastened in the round stone which forms the key-stone of the arch.

This object is the rack. A leather covering used to be put over it, upon which the victim was stretched. Ravaillac remained for six weeks upon this table, with his feet and hands tied, bound at the waist by a strap attached to a long chain hanging from the ceiling. The last ring of this chain was slipped on to the hook which I still saw fixed above my head. Six gentlemen guards and six guards of the provost's department watched him day and night. Damiens was guarded like Ravaillac in this chamber, and tied down upon this table during the whole time occupied by the inquiry and the trial of his case. Desrues, Cartouche, and Voisin were tortured upon it. The Marchioness de Brinvilliers was stretched upon it stark naked, fastened down, and, so to speak, quartered by four chains attached to the four limbs, and there suffered the frightful "extraordinary torture by water," which caused her to ask, "How are you going to continue to put that great barrel of water in this little body?"

A whole dark history is there, having filtered, so to speak, drop by drop, into the pores of these stones, these walls, this vault, this bench, this table, this pavement, this door. There it all is; it has never quitted the place. It has been shut up there, it has been bolted up. Nothing has escaped from it, nothing has evaporated; no one has ever spoken, related, betrayed, revealed anything of it. This crypt, which is like the mouth of a funnel turned upside down, this case made by the hands of man, this stone box, has kept the secret of all the blood it has drunk, of all the shrieks it has stifled. The frightful occurrences which have taken place in this judge's den still palpitate and live, and exhale all sorts of horrible miasms. What a strange abomination is this chamber! What a strange abomination this tower placed in the very middle of the quay, without any moat or wall to separate it from the passer-by! Inside, the saws, the boots, the wooden horses, the wheels, the pincers, the hammers which knock in the wedges, the hissing of flesh touched with the red-hot iron, the spluttering of blood upon the live embers, the cold interrogatories of the magistrates, the despairing shrieks of the tortured man; outside, within four paces, citizens coming and going, women chattering, children playing, tradespeople selling their wares, vehicles rolling along, boats upon the river, the roar of the city, air, sky, sun, liberty!

It is a gloomy reflection that this tower without windows has always seemed silent to the passer-by; it made no more noise then than it does now. What must be the thickness of these walls for the sound of the street not to have reached the tower, and for the sound of the tower not to have reached the street!

I contemplated this table in particular with a curiosity filled with awe. Some of the prisoners had carved their names upon it. Towards the centre eight or ten letters, beginning with an *M*, and forming a word which was illegible, were rather deeply cut. At one end had been written with a punch the name of "Merel." (I quote from memory, and may be mistaken, but I think that is the name.)

The wall was hideous in its nakedness. It seemed as though one felt its fearful and pitiless solidity. The paving was the same kind of paving as in the condemned cell,—that is to say, the old black and white stones of Saint-Louis in alternate squares. A large square brick stove had taken the place of the old heating furnace for the instruments of torture. This chamber is used in winter as a place of warmth for the prisoners.

We then proceeded to the women's building. After being in the prison for an hour, I was already so accustomed to the bolts and bars that I no longer noticed them, any more than the air peculiar to prisons, which suffocated me as I went in. It would be impossible, therefore, for me to say what doors were opened to enable us to walk from the men's to the women's quarters. I do not remember. I only recollect that an old woman, with a nose like a bird of prey, appeared at a railing and opened the gate to us, asking us if we wished to look round the yard. We accepted the offer.

The women's exercise yard was much smaller and much more gloomy than that of the men. There was only one bed of shrubs and flowers, a very narrow one, and I do not think there were any trees. Instead of the ornamental fountain there was a wash-house in the corner. A female prisoner with bare arms was inside washing her clothes. Eight or ten women were seated in the yard in a group, talking, sewing, and working. I raised my hat. They rose and looked at me with curiosity. They were for the most part apparently of the lower middle class, and presented the appearance of small shopkeepers about forty years of age. That appeared to be the average age. There were, however, two or three young girls.

By the side of the yard there was a little chamber into which we entered. There were two young girls there, one seated, the other standing. The one who was seated appeared ill; the other was tending her.

I asked, "What is the matter with that young girl?"

"Oh, it is nothing," said the other, a tall and rather handsome dark girl with blue eyes; "she is subject to it. She is not very well. She was often taken like it at Saint-Lazare. We were there together. I look after her."

"What is she charged with?" I continued.

"She is a servant. She stole six pairs of stockings of her employers."

Just then the invalid turned pale and fainted. She was a poor girl of sixteen or seventeen years of age.

"Give her some air," I said.

The big girl took her in her arms like a child, and carried her into the yard. M. Lebel sent for some ammonia.

"She took six pairs of stockings," he said; "but it is her third offence."

We returned to the yard. The girl lay upon the stones. The women crowded round her, and gave her the ammonia to smell. The old female warder took off her garters, while the big dark girl unlaced her clothing. As she undid her stays she said,—

"This comes over her every time she puts on stays. I will give you stays, you little fool!"

In those words, *little fool*, there was somehow or other a tone which was tender and sympathizing.

We left the place.

One of the peculiarities of the Conciergerie is that all the cells occupied by regicides since 1830 are in the women's quarters.

I entered, first of all, the cell which had been occupied by Lecomte, and which had just been tenanted by Joseph Henri. It was a tolerably large chamber, almost vast, well lighted, and having nothing of the cell about it but the stone floor, the door armed with the biggest lock in the Conciergerie, and the window,—a large railed opening opposite the door. This chamber was furnished as follows: in the corner near the window, a boat-shaped mahogany bedstead, four and a half feet wide, in the most imposing style of the Restoration; on the other side of the window a mahogany writing-table; near the bed a mahogany chest of drawers, with lacquered rings and handles; upon the chest of drawers a looking-glass, and in front of the looking-glass a mahogany clock in the form of a lyre, the face gilded and chased; a square carpet mat at the foot of the bed; four mahogany chairs covered with Utrecht velvet; between the bed and the writing-table a china stove. This furniture, with the exception of the stove, which would shock the taste of common-people, is the very ideal of a rich shopkeeper. Joseph Henri was dazzled by it. I asked what had become of this poor madman. After having been transferred from the Conciergerie to the prison of La Roquette, he had set out that very morning, in the company of eight felons, for the convict prison of Toulon.

The window of this cell looked out on the women's exercise yard. It was ornamented with a rusty old projecting shaft, full of holes. Through these holes could be seen what was going on in the yard,—an amusement for the prisoner not altogether without drawbacks for the women, who thought themselves alone and secluded from observation in the yard.

Near by was the cell formerly occupied by Fieschi and Alibaud. Ouvrard, who was the first to occupy it, had a marble chimney-piece placed in it (Sainte-Anne marble, black with white veins), and a large wooden partition forming a recess and dressing-room. The furniture was of mahogany, and very similar to that of the apartment of Joseph Henri. After Fieschi and Alibaud, this cell had had for its occupants the Abbé de Lamennais and the Marchioness de Larochejacquelein; then Prince Louis Napoleon; and, finally, that "stupid Prince de Berghes," as M. Lebel put it.

Opposite these two cells was the entrance to the Women's Infirmary, a long and broad chamber, too low-lying for its size. There were a score of beds there, with no one in the beds. I expressed surprise at this.

"I hardly ever have any invalids," said M. Lebel. "In the first place, the prisoners only stay here a short time. They come to await their trial, and go away immediately afterwards; if acquitted, at liberty; if convicted, to their destination. As long as they are here, the anticipation of their trial keeps them in a state of excitement which leaves room for nothing else. Yes, they have no time to get ill; they have another sort of feverishness than fever. At the period of the cholera, which was also the great period of riots, I had seven hundred prisoners here. They were everywhere,—in the doorways, in the offices, in the waiting-rooms, in the yards, on the beds, on straw, on the paving-stones. I said, 'Good heavens! It is to be hoped the cholera will not come in addition to all this.' Sir, I did not have a single man invalided."

There is certainly a moral in these facts. They show that strong mental excitement is a preservation against all ailments. In times of pestilence, while sanitary and hygienic measures should not be neglected, the people should be entertained by grand *fêtes*, grand performances, noble impressions. If no one troubled about the epidemic it would disappear.

"When they had, in the cells on the opposite side, a prisoner guilty of an attempt on the person of the king, the Women's Infirmary was converted into a guard-room. Here were installed fifteen or twenty warders, kept secluded from the outer world, like the prisoner himself, seeing no one, not even their wives, and this for the whole time of the preliminaries of the trial, sometimes six weeks, at others two months. That is what is done," added M. Lebel, from whom I had these details, "when I have regicides."

This phrase fell from him in the most natural manner possible; to him it was a sort of habit *to have regicides.*

"You spoke," I said, "in a contemptuous manner of the Prince de Berghes. What do you think of him?"

He wiped his eye-glasses on his sleeve, and replied:

"Oh, as for that, I do not think anything about him; he was a wretched, great simpleton, well-bred, with excellent manners, and a gentle expression, but a fool. When he arrived here I put him at first in this chamber, in this infirmary, which is of a good size, so that he might have space and air. He sent for me. 'Is my case a serious one, sir?' he asked. I stammered a few hesitating words. 'Do you think,' he added, 'that I shall be able to get away this evening?' 'Oh, no,' I said. 'Well, tomorrow, then?' 'Nor to-morrow,' I replied. 'What! do you really think they will keep me here for a week?' 'Perhaps longer.' 'More than a week! More than a week! My case really is a serious one, then? Do you think my case is serious?' He walked about in every direction, continuing to repeat this question, to which I never replied. His family, however, did not abandon him. The duchess his mother, and the princess his wife, came to see him every day. The princess, a very pretty little woman, asked if she might share his prison cell. I gave her to understand that this was impossible. As a matter of fact, what was his offence? Forgery, certainly; but without any motive. It was an act of stupidity, nothing more. The jury found him guilty because he was a prince. If he had been some rich tradesman's son, he would have been acquitted. After he was sentenced to three years' imprisonment, he was left here for some time with me, and then he was transferred to a sanitarium, of which a whole wing was secured for his exclusive use. He has been there nearly a year now, and he will be left there for six months longer; then he will be pardoned. So that his being a prince damaged him at his trial, but it benefits him in his imprisonment."

As we crossed the passage my guide stopped me and called my attention to a low door about four and a half feet in height, armed with an enormous square lock and a great bolt, very similar to the door of Louvel's cell. It was the door of the cell of Marie-Antoinette, —the only thing which had been preserved just as it was, Louis XVIII. having converted her cell into a chapel. It was through this door that the queen went forth to the Revolutionary Court; it was through it also that she went to the scaffold. The door no longer turned on its hinges. Since 1814 it had been fixed in the wall.

I have said that it had been preserved just as it was, but I was mistaken. It was daubed over with a fearful nankeen-coloured picture; but this is of no consequence. What sanguinary souvenir is there which has not been painted either a yellow or a rose-colour?

A moment afterwards I was in the chapel, which had formerly been a cell. If one could have seen there the bare stone floor, the bare walls, the iron bars at the opening, the folding-bedstead of the queen, and the camp-bedstead of the gendarme, together with the historic screen which separated them, it would have created a profound feeling of emotion and an unutterable impression. There were to be seen a little wooden altar, which would have been a disgrace to a village church, a coloured wall (yellow, of course), small stained-glass windows, as in a Turkish *café*, a raised wooden platform, and upon the wall two or three abominable paintings, in which the bad style of the Empire had a tussle with the bad taste of the Restoration. The entrance to the cell had been replaced by an archivault cut in the wall. The vaulted passage by which the queen proceeded to the Court had been walled up. There is a respectful vandalism that is even more revolting than a vindictive vandalism, because of its stupidity.

Nothing was to be seen there of what came under the eye of the queen, unless it was a small portion of the paved flooring, which the boards, fortunately, did not entirely cover. This floor was an old-fashioned, chevroned pavement of bricks, laid on horizontally, with the narrow side uppermost.

A straw chair, placed upon the platform, marked the spot where the bed of the queen had rested.

On coming away from this venerable spot, profaned by a foolish piety, I went into a large apartment at the side, which had been the place of incarceration for the priests during the Terror, and which had been converted into the chapel of the Conciergerie. It was very mean-looking, and very ugly, like the chapel-cell of the queen. The Revolutionary Court held its sittings above this apartment.

While walking about in the depths of the old building, I perceived here and there, through openings in the walls, immense cellars, mysterious and deserted chambers, with portcullises opening on to the river, fearful dungeons, dark passages. In these crypts spiders' webs abounded, as well as mossy stones, sickly gleams of light, vague, and distorted forms. I asked M. Lebel, "What is this place?" He replied, "This is no longer used." What had it been used for?

We had to go back through the men's yard. As we passed through it M. Lebel pointed out to me a staircase near the latrines. It was here that a murderer named Savoye, who had been condemned to the galleys, had hanged himself, not many days previously, to the railings of the baluster. "The jury have made a mistake," said this man; "I ought to have been condemned to death. I will settle the matter." He settled it by hanging himself. He was put under the special supervision of a prisoner who had been raised to the functions of a warder and whom M. Lebel dismissed.

While the governor of the Conciergerie furnished me with these details a decently dressed prisoner came up to us. He seemed to wish to be spoken to. I asked him several questions. He was a young fellow who had been a working embroiderer and lace-maker, afterwards the assistant to the Paris executioner,—what was formerly called the "headsman's valet,"—and finally, he said, a groom in the king's stables.

"Pray, sir, ask the governor not to have me put in the prison-dress, and to leave me my *fainéant*." This word, which has to be pronounced *faignant*, means a cloth coat in the latest slang. He had, in fact, a tolerably good cloth coat. I obtained permission for him to keep it, and I got him into conversation.

He spoke very highly of M. Sanson, the executioner, his former master. M. Sanson lived in the Rue du Marais-du-Temple, in an isolated house, of which the jalousies were always closed. He received many visits. Numbers of English people went to see him. When visitors presented themselves at M. Sanson's they were introduced into an elegant reception-room on the ground-floor, *furnished entirely with mahogany*, in the midst of which there was an excellent piano, always open, and provided with pieces of music. Shortly afterwards M. Sanson arrived, and asked his visitors to be seated. The conversation turned upon one topic and another. Generally the English people asked to see the guillotine. M. Sanson complied with this request, no doubt for some consideration, and conducted the ladies and gentlemen to the adjoining street (the Rue Albouy, I think), to the house of the scaffold-manufacturer. There was a shed at this place, where the guillotine was permanently erected. The strangers grouped themselves around it, and it was made to *work*. Trusses of hay were guillotined.

One day an English family, consisting of the father, the mother, and three pretty daughters, fair and with rosy cheeks, presented themselves at Sanson's residence. It was in order to see the guillotine. Sanson took them to the carpenter's and set the instrument at work. The knife fell and rose again several times at the request of the young ladies. One of them, however,—the youngest,—was not satisfied with this.

She made the executioner explain to her, in the minutest details, what is called the *toilet of the condemned*. Still she was not satisfied. At length she turned hesitatingly towards the executioner.

"Monsieur Sanson," she said.

"Mademoiselle," said the executioner.

"What is done when the man is on the scaffold? How is he tied down?"

The executioner explained the dreadful matter to her, and said, "We call that 'putting him in the oven.'"

"Well, Monsieur Sanson," said the young lady, "I want you to put me in the oven."

The executioner started. He gave an exclamation of surprise. The young lady insisted. "I fancy," she said, "that I should like to be able to say I have been tied down in it."

Sanson spoke to the father and mother They replied, "As she has taken a fancy to have it done, do it."

The executioner had to give in. He made the young Miss sit down, tied her legs with a piece of string, and her arms behind her back with a rope, fastened her to the swinging plank, and strapped her on with the leather strap. Here he wanted to stop. "No, no, that is not yet all," she said. Sanson then swung the plank down, placed the head of the young lady in the dreadful neck-piece, and closed it upon her neck. Then she declared she was satisfied.

When he afterwards told the story, Sanson said, "I quite thought she was going to say at last, 'That is not all; make the knife fall.'"

Nearly all the English visitors ask to see the knife which cut off the head of Louis XVI. This knife was sold for old iron, in the same way as all the other guillotine knives when they are worn out. English people will not believe it and offer to buy it of M. Sanson. If he had cared to trade in them, there would have been as many *knives of Louis XVI.* sold as walking-sticks of Voltaire.

From his anecdotes of Sanson, the fellow who said he had formerly been a groom at the Tuileries, wanted to proceed to anecdotes of the king. He had heard the conferences of the king with the ambassadors, etc. I did not trouble him. I thought of his being a Gascon, and an embroiderer, and his political revelations appeared to be only fancy articles of a superior description.

Up to 1826 the Conciergerie had no other entrance than a grating opening into the courtyard of the Palais de Justice. It was through this that criminals condemned to death came out. In 1826 was made the doorway which is to be seen upon the quay between the two great round towers. These two towers had, upon the ground-floor, like the tower of the torture-chamber, a room without a window. The two grotesque Gothic arches, without any voussoir or equilaterial triangle for a base, which are still admired here to this day, and which are masterpieces of ignorance, were opened in these splendid walls by a sort of stone-mason named Peyre, who held the office of architect to the Palais de Justice, and who mutilated, dishonoured, and disfigured the building as may be seen. These two rooms, thus lighted, make two fine circular apartments. Their walls are ornamented with inlaid Gothic arches of admirable purity, resting upon exquisite brackets. These charming triumphs of architecture and sculpture were never intended to see the light of day, and were made, strange to say, for horror and darkness.

The first of the two rooms—the nearest to the men's yard—had been converted into a dormitory for the warders. There were in it a dozen beds, arranged like the rays of a star, round a stove placed in the centre. Above each bed a plank, fixed in the wall through the delicate mullions of the architecture, held the personal belongings of the warders,— generally represented by a brush, a trunk, and an old pair of boots.

Over one of the beds, however, beside the pair of boots, which was not wanting in any single instance, was a little heap of books. I noticed this; it was explained to me. It was the library of a warder named Peiset, to whom Lacenaire had imparted literary tastes. This man, seeing Lacenaire constantly reading and writing, first admired and then consulted him. He was not without intelligence; Lacenaire advised him to study. Some of the books which were there were those of Lacenaire. Lacenaire gave them to him.

Peiset had bought a few other old books upon the quays; he took the advice of Lacenaire, who said, "Read this," or "Do not read that." By degrees the jailor became a thinker, and it was thus that an intelligence had been awakened and had expanded in this repulsive atmosphere.

The other room could only be entered by a door which bore this inscription: "Entrance reserved for the Governor." M. Lebel opened it for me very politely, and we found ourselves in his sitting-room. This apartment was, in fact, transformed into the governor's sitting-room. It was almost identical with the other, but differently furnished. This sitting-room was made up in extraordinary fashion. The architecture of Saint-Louis, a chandelier which had belonged to Ouvrard, hideous wall-paper in the Gothic arches, a mahogany writing-desk, some articles of furniture with unbleached calico coverings, an old legal portrait without any case or frame and nailed askew upon the wall, some engravings, some heaps of paper, a table loking like a counter; altogether, the room, thus furnished, had the characteristics of a palace, a prison-cell, and a shop-parlour. It was patibulary, magnificent, ugly, ridiculous, sinister, royal, and vulgar.

It was into this apartment that the visitors of the privileged prisoners were shown. At the time of his detention, of which many traces remained at the Conciergerie, M. Ouvrard used to see his friends here. The Prince de Berghes used to see his wife and mother here. "What does it matter to me if they do receive visitors here?" said M. Lebel. "They think themselves in a drawing-room, and they are none the less in a prison." The worthy man looked profoundly convinced that the Duchess and Princess de Berghes must have thought they were in a drawing-room.

It was there also that the chancellor, Duke Pasquier, was in the habit of preparing the preliminaries of the official inquiries confided to him in respect of the prosecutions before the House of Peers.

The governor's room communicated with this apartment. It was very mean and ugly looking. The species of den which served as his bedroom was solely dependent upon the doors for light and air,—that is to say, so far as I could see, for I passed rapidly through. It was clean, although of a rather mouldy-smelling cleanliness, and had all sorts of frames in the corners, and old-fashioned knick-knacks, and all those minutiæ which one sees in the rooms of elderly people. The dining-room was larger, and had windows. Two or three good-looking young ladies were seated there upon straw-bottomed chairs, and were at work under the eye of a lady of about fifty years of age. They rose with a modest and pleasant look as I passed, and their father, M. Lebel, kissed them on the forehead. Nothing stranger could be imagined than this Anglican Presbyterian's home, surrounded by the infamous interior of a prison, and walled round as it were and preserved in all its purity amid every vice, every crime, every disgrace, and every shame.

"But," I said to M. Lebel, "What has become of the hall of the chimney-pieces? Where is it?"

He appeared to turn it over in his mind like a person who fails to understand.

"The hall of the chimney-pieces? Did you say the hall of the chimney-pieces?"

"Yes," I rejoined, "a great hall which was under the *salle des pas perdus*, and there were in the four corners four enormous chimney-pieces, constructed in the thirteenth century. Why, I remember distinctly having come to see it some twenty years ago, in company with Rossini, Meyerbeer, and David d'Angers."

"Ah!" said M. Lebel, "I know what you mean. That is what we call the Kitchens of Saint-Louis."

"Well, the Kitchens of Saint-Louis then, if that is what you call them. But what has become of this hall? Besides the four chimney-pieces, it had some handsome pillars which supported the roof. I have not seen it even now. Has your architect, M. Peyre, hidden it away?"

"Oh, no. Only he has made some alterations in it for us."

These words, quietly uttered, made me shudder. The hall of the chimney-pieces was one of the most remarkable monuments of the Royal and domestic architecture of the Middle Ages. What might not a creature like the architect Peyre have done with it? M. Lebel continued:—

"We scarcely knew where to put our prisoners during the time when they have to undergo their preliminary examination. M. Peyre took the Kitchens of Saint-Louis and made a magnificent *souricière* with three compartments,—one for men, one for women, and one for the juveniles. He contrived this in the best manner possible, and he did not destroy the old hall to any great extent, I assure you."

"Will you take me to it?" I said to M. Lebel.

"By all means."

We passed through long, wide, low, and narrow corridors and passages. Here and there we came across a staircase crowded with gendarmes, and we saw pass, amid a hubbub of policemen and warders, some poor wretch whom the ushers handed to each other, at the same time saying to each other in a loud tone of voice the word *Disponible*.

"What does that word convey?" I said to my guide.

"It means that he has a man whom the examining magistrate has done with, and who is at the disposal of the gendarme."

"To set him at liberty?"

"No, to take him back to prison."

At length the last door opened.

"Here you are," said the governor, "in the room you are looking for."

I look round.

I was in darkness.

I had a wall in front of my eyes.

My eyeballs, however, gradually became accustomed to the darkness, and after a few moments I distinguished on my right, in a recess, a lofty and magnificent chimney-piece in the shape of an inverted funnel, built of stone, and resting, by means of an open buttress of the most exquisite style, against a pillar which stood in face of it.

"Ah," I said, "here is one of the chimney-pieces. But where are the others?"

"This is the only one," replied M. Lebel, "which remains intact. Of the three others, two are completely destroyed, and the third is mutilated; it was necessary for a *souricière*. It is because we had to fill up the intervals between the pillars with stone-work. We had to put up partitions. The architect preserved this chimney-piece as a specimen of the architectural style of the period."

"And," I added, "of the folly of the architects of our time!" Thus there was no hall, but a number of compartments; and out of four chimney-pieces three were destroyed. This was effected under Charles X. This is what the sons of Saint-Louis made of the souvenirs of Saint-Louis.

"It is true," continued M. Lebel, "that this *souricière* might very well have been placed elsewhere. But then, you know, they did not think of that, and they had this hall available. However, they arranged it very well. It is divided by stone walls in longitudinal compartments, lighted each by one of the windows of the old hall. The first is that of the juveniles. Should you like to go in?"

A turnkey opened a heavy door with a peep-hole bored through it, by means of which the interior of the *souricière* could be watched, and we went in.

The juveniles' *souricière* was an oblong room, a parallelogram, provided with two stone benches on the two principal sides. There were three boys there. The eldest was rather a big boy. He appeared to be about seventeen years of age, and was clad in frightful old yellowish clothes.

I spoke to the youngest, who had a rather intelligent, although an enervated and degraded, face.

"What is your age, boy?"
"I am twelve, sir."
"What have you done to be in here?"
"I took some peaches."
"Where?"
"In a garden at Montreuil."
"By yourself?"
"No, with my friend."
"Where is your friend?"

He pointed out the other one, who was clad like himself in the prison material, and was a little bigger than himself, and said, "There he is."

"You got over a wall, then?"
"No, sir. The peaches were on the ground in the road."
"You only stooped down?"
"Yes, sir."
"And picked them up?"

"Yes, sir."

At this point M. Lebel leaned towards me, and said, "He has already been taught his lesson."

It was evident, in fact, that the child was telling a lie. There was neither decision nor candour in his look. He cast his eyes down obliquely as he looked at me, as a sharper examines his victim, and moreover with that delighted expression of a child who makes a man his dupe.

"You are not telling the truth, my lad," I resumed.

"Yes, I am, sir."

This "Yes, I am, sir," was said with that kind of impudence in which one feels that everything is wanting, even assurance. He added boldly, "And for that I have been sentenced to three years' imprisonment. But, *je'n rappelle.*"

"Have not your relatives come to claim you?"

"No, sir."

"And your friend, was he sentenced?"

"No, his relatives claimed him."

"He is a better boy than you, then?"

The boy hung down his head.

M. Lebel said to me, "He has been sentenced to be detained for three years in a House of Correction, to be brought up there,—acquitted, that is to say, for not having acted 'with discretion.' The misfortune and the grief of all the little vagabonds is to be under sixteen years of age. They have a thousand ways of trying to persuade the authorities that they are sixteen years of age, and guilty *with discretion.* In fact, when they are sixteen years and one day old they are punished with a few month's imprisonment for their pranks. If they are a day less than sixteen years old, they have three years' detention at La Roquette."

I gave a small sum of money to these poor little wretches, who perhaps were only wanting in education.

All things considered, society is more guilty towards them than they are guilty towards society. We may ask them, What have you done with our peaches? Very well. But they might reply, what have you done with our intelligence?

"Thank you, sir," said the youngster, putting the money in his pocket.

"I would have given you twice as much," I told him, "if you had not told a lie."

"Sir," said the boy, "I have been sentenced, but *j'en rappelle.*"

"It was bad to take peaches, but it was worse to tell a lie."

The child did not appear to understand.

"Je'n rappelle," he said.

We quitted the cell, and as the door was closed, the boy followed us with a look, while still repeating, "*J'en rappelle.*" The two others did not breathe a word. The jailor bolted the door while muttering, "Keep quiet, my little *rats.*" This word reminded us that we were in a *"souricière."*

The second compartment was set apart for men, and was exactly similar to the first. I did not go in, but contented myself with looking through the peep-hole. It was full of prisoners, among whom the turnkey pointed out to me a youth with a prepossessing countenance, tolerably dressed, and wearing a thoughtful air. This was an individual named Pichery, the ringleader of a gang of thieves who were to be put on their trial in a few days' time.

The third slice cut out of the Kitchens of Saint-Louis was the women's jail. It was thrown open to us. I saw only seven or eight inmates, all more than forty years of age, with the exception of a youngish woman who still retained some remains of good looks. This poor creature hid herself behind the others. I understood this bashfulness, and I neither asked nor permitted any question. All kinds of little articles of women's luggage—baskets, flat baskets, work-bags, pieces of knitting just begun—encumbered the stone benches.

There were also great pieces of brown bread. I took up a piece of this bread. It was of the colour of road scrapings, smelled very nasty, and stuck to the fingers like birdlime.

"What is that?" I said to M. Lebel.

"It is the prison bread."

"Why, it is detestable!"

"Do you think so?"

"Look at it yourself."

"It is a contractor who supplies it."

"And who makes his fortune, does he not?"

"M. Chayet, Secretary at the Prefecture, has to examine the bread; he considers it very good,—so good that he does not have any other on his own table."

"M. Chayet," I said, "is wrong to judge the bread eaten by the prisoners by the bread he receives himself. If the speculator does send him every day a delicacy, that does not prove that he does not send filth to the prisoners."

"You are right; I will speak about it."

I learned afterwards that the quality of the bread had been looked into, and that an improvement had been effected.

On the whole, there was nothing remarkable in this cell, unless it was that the walls were covered all over with inscriptions in black marks. Here are the three which stood out prominently in larger letters than the others: "Corset." "Je suis codanée à six mois pour vacabonage." "Amour pour la vie."

The three doors of the compartments opened on the same passage,—a long dark corridor, at the two extremities of which, like two stone tiaras, were the rounded forms of the two chimney-pieces which had been preserved, and of which, as I had already said, there was only one which was perfect. The second had lost its principal ornament,—its buttress. Of the others all that remained visible was the sites on which they had stood in the corners of the juvenile compartment and the women's compartment.

It was upon the easternmost of these two latter chimney-pieces that the curious figure of the demon Mahidis was carved. The demon Mahidis was a Persian demon which Saint-Louis brought back from the Crusades. It was to be seen upon the chimney-piece with its five heads,—for he had five heads; and each of these five heads had composed one of those songs which are called *ragas* in India, and which are the oldest music known. These ragas are still celebrated and dreaded throughout Hindustan on account of their magic powers. There is no juggler who is bold enough to sing them. One of these ragas sung at nuddar makes the night fall instantly, and to conjure from the ground an immense circle of darkness, which spreads as far as the voice of the singer will carry. Another is called the Ihupuck raga. Whoever sings it perishes by fire. A tradition relates how the Emperor Akbar one day was smitten with a desire to hear this raga sung. He sent for a famous musician named Naïk-Gopaul, and said to him: "Sing me the Ihupuck raga." Thereupon the poor tenor, trembling from head to foot, falls upon the emperor's knees. The emperor had his whim, and was inflexible. The only concession the tenor could obtain was to be allowed to go and see his family for the last time. He sets out, returns to the town in which he lives, makes his will, embraces his old father and mother, says adieu to all that he loves in the world, and returns to the emperor. Six months elapsed. Eastern kings have melancholy and tenacious whims. "Ah, there you are, musician," said Shah Akbar, in a sad but friendly tone. "Welcome! You are going to sing me the Ihupuck raga." Naïk-Gopaul trembles, and implores once more. But the emperor is inexorable. It was winter-time. The Jumna was frozen over; people were skating upon it. Naïk-Gopaul has the ice broken, and gets into the water up to his neck. He begins to sing. At the second verse the water became warm, at the second stanza the ice melted, at the third stanza the river began to boil. Naïk-Gopaul was cooking; he was covered with blisters. Instead of singing, he cried, "Mercy, Sire!"

"Go on," said Akbar, who was no mean lover of music.

The poor wretch went on singing; his face was crimson, his eyes started out of his head, but he continued to sing, the emperor listening meanwhile with ecstasy. At length a few sparks shot out of the hair of the tenor, which stood on end.

"Mercy!" he cried, for the last time. "Sing!" said the emperor.

He began the last stanza amid shrieks. Suddenly the flames burst forth from his mouth, then from his entire body, and the fire consumed him in the midst of the water. That is one of the habitual effects of the music of this demon Mahidis, who was represented upon the demolished chimney-piece. He had a wife named Parbutta, who is the author of what the Hindoos call the *sixth raga*. Thirty raginis, a music of a feminine and inferior character, were dictated by Boimba. It was to these three devils, or gods, that was due the invention of the gamut, composed of twenty-one notes, which forms the basis of the music of India.

As we withdrew three gentlemen in black coats, conducted by a turnkey, passed near us; they were visitors. "Three new members of the Chamber of Deputies," M. Lebel informed me in a whisper. They had whiskers and high cravats, and spoke like Provincial academicians. They were lavish in expressions of admiration; they were in ecstasies, more particularly at the work which had been done in the way of embellishing the prison and making it suitable to the requirements of the police authorities. One of them maintained that Paris was being prodigiously embellished, *thanks to the architects of taste who were modernizing (sic) the ancient buildings;* and he asserted that the Académie Française ought to make these Paris embellishments the subject of a prize competition in poetry. This set me thinking that M. Peyre has done for the Palais de Justice what M. Godde has done for Saint-Germain-des-Prés, and M. Debret for Saint-Denis; and while M. Lebel was giving some instructions to the warders, I wrote with a pencil upon a pillar of the hall of the chimney-pieces these verses, which might be sent in for the competition if ever the Académie should set up the competition desired by these gentlemen, and which, I hope, would secure the prize:—

"Un sizain vaut une longue ode
Pour chanter Debret, Peyre, et Godde;
L'oison gloussant, l'âne qui brait,
Fêtent Godde, Peyre, et Debret;
Et le dindon, digne compère,
Admire Debret, Godde, et Peyre."

As M. Lebel turned round, I finished. He conducted me to the outer door again, and I issued forth. As I went away, some one of a group of men in blouses behind me, who appeared to be waiting on the quay, said, "There is one of them who has been discharged. He is a lucky fellow."

It appears that I looked like a thief. However, I had spent two hours at the Conciergerie, the sitting of the Académie must still be going on, and I reflected, with much inward satisfaction, that if I had gone to it I should not have been "discharged" thus early.

Count Mortier the Madman

November 11, 1846

YESTERDAY Chancellor Pasquier comes to the house of Mme. de Boignes, and finds her in great agitation, holding a letter in her hand. "What is the matter, madame?" "This letter which I have received. Read it." The chancellor took the letter; it was signed "Mortier," and said, in effect, "Madame, when you read this letter my two children and myself will no longer be alive."

It was Count Mortier, a Peer of France, and formerly an ambassador, but where I cannot remember, who wrote. M. Pasquier was much concerned. M. Mortier was known as a confirmed hypochondriac. Four years ago, at Bruges, he ran after his wife with a razor in his hand, with the intention of killing her. A month ago he made a similar attempt, which led to a separation, by the terms of which M. Mortier retained the custody of the children, a little boy of seven years of age and a little girl of five. His hypochondria was caused, it appears, by jealousy, and developed into uncontrollable passion.

The chancellor sends for his carriage, and does not take a chair. "Where does M. Mortier live?" "In the Rue Neuve Saint-Augustin, in the Hôtel Chatham," said Mme. de Boignes.

M. Pasquier arrives at the Hôtel Chatham; he finds the staircase crowded, a commissary of police, a locksmith with his bunch of keys, the door barricaded. The alarm had been given. They were going to break open the door.

"I forbid you," said the chancellor. "You would exasperate him, and if the mischief were not yet done he would do it."

For some time, however, M. Mortier had not answered. There was nothing but a profound silence behind the door, —a terrible silence, for it seemed that if the children were still living they would be crying. "It seemed," said the chancellor, when he told me this to-day, "as if it was the door of a tomb."

The chancellor called out his name: "Count Mortier, it is I, M. Pasquier, the chancellor, your colleague. You know my voice, do you not?"

To this a voice replied, "Yes."

It was the voice of M. Mortier.

The on-lookers breathed again.

"Well," continued M. Pasquier, "you know me; open the door."

"No," replied the same voice. Then it obstinately refused to speak again. All was silent once more.

This happened several times. He replied, the dialogue continued, he refused to open, then he remained silent. Those outside trembled for fear that in these brief intervals of silence he might do the dreadful deed.

In the meantime the prefect of police had arrived.

"It is I, your colleague, Delessert, and your old friend." (They were school-fellows, I think.)

This parleying lasts for more than an hour. At length he consents to open the door provided they give him their word they will not enter. The word is given;

he half opens the door; they go in.

He was in the anteroom, with an open razor in his hand; behind him was the inner door of his rooms, locked and with the key removed. He appeared frenzied.

"If any one approaches me," he said, "there will be an end of him and me. I will remain alone with Delessert and speak to him; I consent to that."

A risky conversation this, with a furious man armed with a razor. M. Delessert, who behaved bravely, asked every one else to withdraw, remained alone with M. Mortier, and after a refusal, which lasted for a space of twenty minutes, persuaded him to put down the razor.

Once disarmed, he was secured.

But were the children dead or living? It was terrible to reflect upon. To all questions on the subject he replied, "It is nothing to do with you."

The inner door is broken open, and what is found at the farther end of the rooms? The two children, crouching under the furniture.

This is what had happened.

In the morning M. Mortier said to his children, "I am very unhappy. You love me, and I love you. I am going to die. Will you die with me?"

The little boy said, resolutely, "No, papa."

As for the little girl, she hesitated. In order to persuade her the father gently passed the back of the razor gently around her neck, and said to her, "There, my dear, it will not hurt you any more than that."

"Well, then, papa," said the child. "I do not mind dying."

The father goes out, probably to fetch a second razor. Directly he goes out, the little boy rushes to the key, lays hold of it, shuts the door, and locks it twice on the inside.

Then he takes his sister to the furthermost end of the rooms and gets under the furniture with her.

The doctors declared that Count Mortier was a melancholy and dangerous madman. He was taken to a mad-house.

He had a mania, in fact, for razors. When he was seized he was searched; besides that which he had in his hand, one was found in each of his pockets.

On the same day the news arrived in Paris that my colleague, Count Bresson, had cut his throat at Naples, where he had recently been appointed Ambassador.

This was a grief to us all, and a great surprise. From a mere worldly point of view, Count Bresson wanted nothing. He was a Peer of France, an ambassador, a Grand Cross of the Legion of Honour. His son had lately been created a Duke in Spain. As an ambassador he had a salary of two hundred thousand francs a year. He was an earnest, kindly, gentle, intelligent, sensible man, very rational in everything, of high stature, with broad shoulders, a good square face, and at fifty-five years of age looked only forty; he had wealth, greatness, dignity, intelligence, health, and was fortunate in private as in public life. He killed himself.

Nourrit also went to Naples and killed himself.

It is the climate? Is it the marvellous sky?

Spleen is engendered just as much under a blue sky as under a gloomy sky, —more so, perhaps.

As the life of even the most prosperous man is always in reality more sad than gay, a gloomy sky is in harmony with ourselves. A brilliant and joyous sky mocks us. Nature in its sad aspects resembles us and consoles us; Nature, when radiant, impassive, serene, magnificent, transplendent, young while we grow old, smiling when we are sighing, superb, inaccessible, eternal, contented, calm in its joyousness, has in it something oppressive.

By dint of contemplating the sky,—ruthless, unrelenting, indifferent, and sublime,—one takes a razor and makes an end of it.

An Over-Night Criminal

THE prison for condemned convicts, built by the side of, and as a comparison to, the prison for youthful offenders, is a living and striking antithesis. It is not only that the beginning and the ending of the evil-doer face each other; there is also the perpetual confronting of the two penal systems,—solitary confinement and imprisonment in common. This is almost enough to decide the question. It is a dark and silent duel between the dungeon and the cell, between the old prison and the new.

On one side were all the condemned, pell-mell,—the child of seventeen with the old man of seventy; the prisoner of thirteen months with the convict for life; the beardless lad who has filched apples and the assassin of the highway, snatched from the Place Saint-Jacques and sent to Toulon in consequence of "extenuating circumstances;" the almost innocent and the quasi-condemned; the blue-eyed and the grey-beard; hideous, pestilential workshops, where they sewed and worked in semi-darkness, amid things dirty and foetid, without air, daylight, speech; without looking at each other; without interest; horrible, mournful spectres, some of whom terrified one by their age, and others by their youth.

On the other side a cloister, a hive, each worker in his cell, each sole in its alveole: an immense edifice of three stories, inhabited by neighbours who never saw each other; a town composed of small hermitages; nothing but children and children who do not know each other, who live years close to each other without ever hearing the echo of each other's foot-falls or the sound of their voices, separated by a wall, by an abyss: work, study, tools, books; eight hours sleep, one hour of repose, one hour of play, in a small walled court; prayers morning and evening: thought ever!

On one side the cesspool, on the other cultivation!

You enter a cell; you find a child standing up before a bench lighted by a dirty window, of which one square pane at the top can be opened. The child is clad in coarse serge; clean, grave, quiet. He ceases working and salutes. You question him; he replies with a serious gaze, and in subdued tones.

Some are making locks, a dozen a day; others are carving furniture, etc., etc. There are as many conditions as stories; as many workshops as corridors. The child can read and write besides. He has in prison a master for his brain as well as for his body.

You must not think that because of its mildness the prison is insufficient punishment. No; it is profoundly sad. All the prisoners have an appearance of punishment which is peculiar.

There are still many more criticisms to be passed; the cell system begins. It has almost all its improvements to come; but, incomplete and imperfect as it is at present, it is admirable when compared with the system of imprisonment in common.

The prisoner—a captive on all sides, and only at all free on the working side —interests himself in what he makes, whatever it may be. Thus, a lad who hated all occupations becomes a most furiously industrious mechanic. When one is in solitary confinement one manages to find light in the darkest dungeon.

The other day I was visiting the convict prison, and I said to the governor, who accompanied me:—

"You have a man condemned to death here now?"

"Yes, sir, a man named Marquis, who tried to murder a girl, Torisse, with intent to rob her."

"I should like to speak to that man," I said.

"Sir," replied the governor, "I am here to take your orders, but I cannot admit you into the condemned cell."

"Why not?"

"Sir, the police regulations do not permit us to introduce everybody into the cells of the condemned."

I replied, "I am not acquainted with the conditions of the police regulations, M. le Directeur de la Prison, but I know what the law permits. The law places the prisons under the authority of the Chambers, and the officials under the *surveillance* of the Peers of France, who can be called upon to judge them. Wherever it is possible that an abuse may exist, the legislature may come in and search for it. Evil may exist in the cell of a man condemned to death. It is therefore my duty to enter, and yours to open it."

The governor made no reply, and led me forward.

We skirted a small courtyard in which were some flowers, and which was surrounded by a gallery. This was the exercise-ground of the condemned prisoners. It was surrounded by four lofty buildings. In the center of one of the sides of the gallery there is a heavy door bound with iron. A wicket opened, and I found myself in a kind of ante-chamber, gloomy, and paved with stone. Before me were three doors,—one directly opposite me, the others on either hand: three heavy doors, pierced with a grating, and cased with iron. These three doors opened into three cells, appropriated to the use of the condemned criminals who awaited their fate after the double appeal to the judge and to the Supreme Courts. This generally means a respite of two months.

"We have never had more than two of these cells occupied at the same time," said the governor.

The door of the centre one was opened. It was that of the condemned cell then occupied.

I entered.

As I crossed the threshold a man rose quickly and stood up.

This man was at the other end of the cell. I saw him at once. A pale gleam of daylight which descended from a wide, deeply-set window above his head lighted it up from the back. His head was bare, his neck was bare; he had shoes on and a strait-waistcoat, and pantaloons of brown woollen stuff. The sleeves of this waistcoat, of thick grey linen, were tied in front. His hand could be distinguished resting on this, and holding a pipe quite full of tobacco. He was on the point of lighting this pipe at the moment the door was opened. This was the condemned man.

Nothing could be seen through the window but a glimpse of the rainy sky.

There was a moment's silence. I was too greatly moved to be able to speak.

He was a young man, evidently not more than twenty-two or twenty-three years old. His chestnut hair, which curled naturally, was cut short; his beard had not been trimmed. He had beautiful large eyes, but his glance was low and villainous, his nose flat, his temples prominent; the bones behind the ears large, which is a bad sign; the forehead low, the mouth coarse, and to the left of the cheek was that peculiar puffing which agony produces. He was pale; his whole face was contracted; nevertheless, at our entry he forced a smile.

He stood upright. His bed was on his left hand,—a kind of truckle-bed, in disorder, on which he had in all probability been extended just previously,—and to his right a small table of wood, coarsely painted a yellow hue, having for a top a plank painted to imitate marble. On this table were glazed earthenware dishes containing cooked vegetables and a little meat, a piece of bread, and a leathern pouch full of tobacco. A straw chair stood beside the table.

This was not the horrible cell of the Conciergerie. It was a good-sized room, fairly light, coloured yellow, furnished with the bed, table, and chair aforesaid, a faïence stove, and a shelf fitted in the angle of the wall opposite the window laden with old clothes and old crockery. In another corner there was a square chair, which replaced the ignoble tub of the old prisons.

Everything was clean, or nearly so, in good order, swept and garnished, and had that indescribable homeliness about it which deprives things of their unpleasantness as well as of their attractiveness. The barred window was open. Two small chains for supporting the sashes hung to two nails above the head of the condemned man. Near the stove two men stood,—a soldier, armed only with his sword, and a warder. Condemned criminals always have this escort of two men, who do not leave them night or day. The attendants are relieved every three hours.

I did not take in all these details at once. The condemned man absorbed all my attention.

M. Paillard de Villeneuve was with me. The governor broke the silence.

"Marquis," he said, pointing to me, "this gentleman is here in your interest."

"Sir," I said, "if you have any complaint to make, I am here to entertain it."

The condemned bowed, and replied with a smile which sat ill upon him, "I have no complaints, sir; I am very well here. These gentlemen [indicating his guardians] are very kind, and would willingly converse with me. The governor comes to see me from time to time."

"How do they feed you?" I asked.

"Very well, sir; I have double rations." Then he added, after a pause, "*We* have a right to double rations; and then I have white bread too."

I glanced at the piece of bread, which was white.

He added, "The prison bread is the only thing to which I have not been able to accustom myself. At Sainte-Pélagie, where I was detained, we formed a society of young men among ourselves, and so as not to mix with the others, to have white bread."

I replied, "Were you better off in Sainte-Pélagie than here."

"I was very well at Sainte-Pélagie, and I am very well here."

I continued, "You said you did not wish to mix with the others. What do you mean by 'the others'?"

"There were a great many common people there," he replied.

The condemned was the son of a porter in the Rue Chabanais.

"Is your bed comfortable?" I asked.

The governor lifted the coverings and said, "Yes, sir; a hair mattress, two mattresses, and two blankets."

"And two bolsters," added Marquis.

"Do you sleep well?" I asked.

He replied without hesitation, "Very well."

There was on the bed an open, torn volume.

"You read?"

"Yes, sir."

I took up the book. It was an "Abridgment of Geography and History," printed in the last century. The first pages and half the binding were wanting. The book was open at a description of the Lake of Constance.

"Sir," said the governor to me, "I lent him that book."

I turned to Marquis.

"Does this book interest you?"

"Yes, sir," he replied. "The governor has also lent me the 'Voyages of La Pérouse' and Captain Cook. I am very fond of the adventures of our great explorers. I have read them already, but I re-read them with pleasure, and I will read them again in one year, or in ten."

He did not say I *could* read them, but I *will* read them. For the rest, the poor young man was a good talker, and was fond of hearing himself speak. "Our great explorers" is textual. He talked like a newspaper. In all the rest of his remarks I remarked this absence of naturalness. Everything disappears in the face of death except affectation. Goodness vanishes, wickedness disappears, the benevolent man becomes bitter, the rude man polite, the affected man remains affected. A strange thing it is that death touches you, but does not give you simplicity.

He was a poor, vain workman; a bit of an artist, too much and too little, who had been destroyed by vanity. He had the idea of coming out and enjoying himself. He had stolen a hundred francs from his father's desk, and next day, after a course of pleasure and dissipation, he had killed a girl in order to rob her. This terrible ladder, which has so many steps that lead from domestic robbery to murder, from the paternal reprimand to the scaffold, criminals like Lacenaire and Poulmann take twenty years to descend; he, this young man, who was a lad but yesterday, had cleared them all in twenty-four hours! He had, as an old convict, a former school-master, said in the courtyard, jumped all the steps.

What an abyss is such a destiny!

He turned over the leaves for a few minutes, and I continued: "Have you never had any means of existence?"

He raised his head, and replied with some pride, "Yes, indeed, sir."

Then he proceeded. I did not interrupt him.

"I was a furniture-designer. I have even studied to be an architect. I am called Marquis. I was a pupil of M. Le Duc."

He referred to M. Viollet Le Duc, the architect of the Louvre. I remarked, in the complacent sequence of the word Marquis, "Le Duc!" However, he had not yet ended.

"I started a 'Journal of Design' for cabinet-makers. I had already made some progress. I wanted to give carpet-manufacturers designs in the Renaissance style, made according to the rules of the trade, which they never had. They are forced to content themselves with engravings of very incorrect styles."

"You had a good idea. Why did you not carry it out?"

"It miscarried, sir."

He spoke the words quickly, and added: "However, I do not mean to say that I wanted money. I had talent, I sold my designs; I would certainly have finished by selling them at my own price."

I could not help saying, "Then why—"

He understood, and answered: "I really cannot say. The idea crossed my mind. I should not be thought capable of that at this fatal day."

At the words "fatal day" he stopped, then continued, with a sort of carelessness:—

"I am sorry I have not some designs here; I would show them to you. I also painted landscapes. M. Le Duc taught me water-colour painting. I succeeded in the Cicéri style. I did things which you would have sworn were Cicéri's. I am very fond of drawing. At Sainte-Pélagie I drew the portraits of many of my companions in crayons only. They would not let me have my box of water-colours."

"Why?" I asked without thinking.

He hesitated. I was sorry I had put the question, for I divined the reason.

"Sir," he said, "it was because they fancied there was poison in the colours. They were wrong. They are water-colours."

"But," remarked the governor, "there is minium in the vermilion?"

"It is possible," he replied. "The fact is, they did not permit it, and I had to content myself with the crayons. The portraits were all good likenesses, too."

"And what do you do here?"

"I occupy myself."

He remained deep in thought after this reply, then he added, "I can draw well. This," indicating the strait-waistcoat, "does not interfere with me. In an extreme case one can draw." He moved his hand beneath his bonds as he spoke. "And then these gentlemen are very kind" (indicating the attendants). They have already offered to let me raise the sleeves. But I do something else,—I read."

"You see the chaplain, of course?"

"Yes, sir; he comes to see me."

Here he turned to the governor, and said, "But I have not yet seen the Abbé Montès."

That name in his mouth had a sinister effect on me. I had seen the Abbé Montès once in my life,—one summer day on the Pont-au-Change, in the cart which was carrying Louvel to the scaffold.

Nevertheless the governor replied, "Ah, dame! He is old; he is nearly eighty-six. The poor man is in attendance when he can."

"Eighty-six!" I exclaimed. "That is what is wanted so long as he has a little strength. At his age one is so near to God that one ought to speak very beautiful words."

"I will see him with pleasure," said Marquis, quickly.

"Sir," said I, "we must have hope."

"Oh!" said he, "do not discourage me. First, I have my petition to the Appeal Court, and then I have my demand *en grâce*. The sentence which has been pronounced may be quashed. I do not say that it is not just, but it is a little severe. They ought to have taken my age into consideration, and given me the benefit of extenuating circumstances. And then I have signed my petition to the king. My father, who comes to see me, bids me be at ease. M. Le Duc himself sent the petition to his Majesty. M. Le Duc knows me well; he knows his pupil Marquis. The king is not in the habit of refusing him anything. It is impossible that they will refuse me a pardon—I do not say a free pardon—but—"

He was silent.

"Yes," I said, "be of good courage; you have here your judges on one side, and your father on the other. But above you have also your father and your judge, who is God, who cannot feel the necessity to condemn you without at the same time experiencing the desire to pardon you. Hope, then."

"Thank you, sir," replied Marquis.

Again silence ensued.

Then I asked, "Do you require anything?"

"I would like to go out and walk in the yard a little oftener. That is all, sir. I only am allowed out for a quarter of an hour a day."

"That is not sufficient." I said to the governor. "Why is it so?"

"Because of our great responsibility," he replied.

"Well!" I exclaimed, "put four guards on duty if two do not suffice, but do not refuse this young man a little air and sunlight. A court in the centre of the prison, stocks and bars everywhere, four lofty walls surrounding it, four guards always there, the strait-waistcoat, sentinels at every wicket, two rounds, and two *enceintes* sixty feet high, what have you to fear? The prisoner ought to be allowed to walk in the courtyard when he asks permission."

The governor bowed, and said, "That is but just, sir. I will carry out your suggestions."

The condemned man thanked me with effusiveness.

"It is time for me to leave you," I said. "Turn to God, and keep up your courage, sir."

"I shall have good courage, sir."

He accompanied me to the door, which was then shut upon him. The governor conducted me into the next cell on the right. It was longer than the other. It contained only a bed and a utensil.

It was in here that Poulmann was confined. In the six weeks which he passed here he wore out three pairs of shoes walking up and down these boards. He never ceased walking, and did fifteen leagues a day in his cell. He was a terrible man.

"You have had Joseph Henri?" I asked.

"Yes, sir; but in the infirmary only. He was ill. He was always writing to the Keeper of the Seals, to the pro- curator-general, to the chancellor, to the Great Refoundary, letters,—letters of four pages, and in small close writing, too. One day I said to him, laughingly, 'It is fortunate that you are not compelled to read what you have written.' No one ever read them, evidently. He was a fool."

As I was leaving the prison the governor indicated to me the two "rounds," or encircling paths: high walls, a scanty herbage, a sentry-box at every thirty paces. He pointed out to me, under the very windows of the condemned cells, a place where two soldiers on duty had shot themselves the year before. They had blown their brains out with their rifles, and we could see the bullet-holes in the sentry-box. The rain had washed away the blood-stains from the wall. One man had killed himself because his officer, seeing him without his rifle, which he had left in the sentry-box, said to him in passing, "fifteen days in the *salle de police.*" We never found out why the other man shot himself.

Praslin, Duchess-Slayer

August 18, 4 P.M., 1846.
I have this instant learned that the Duchess of Praslin was assassinated last night in her own mansion, No. 55 Rue St. Honoré.

August 20.
The Court of Peers is convened for to-morrow, to arraign M. de Praslin.

Saturday, August 21. Written at this sitting.
At seven minutes past two the public sitting opens. The Keeper of the Seals, Hébert, mounts the tribune, and reads the ordinance which constitutes the Court of Peers.

There are women on the benches; a man, stout and bald and white, of ruddy countenance, closely resembling Parmentier, is in the west tribune, and for a moment attracts the attention of the Peers.

The chancellor causes the tribunes to be evacuated; the Procurator-general Delangle is introduced, and the Advocate-general Bresson, in red robes. The chancellor remarks that the tribunes are not all empty, those of the reporters among others; he gets angry, and gives orders to the ushers. The tribunes are cleared with some difficulty.

M. de Praslin was arrested yesterday, and transferred to the prison of the chamber on the chancellor's warrant. He was committed this morning at daybreak. He is in the cell where M. Teste was.

It was M. de Praslin who, on the 17th of July, passed over the pen to sign the warrant for the arrest of MM. Teste and Cubières. A month after, exactly, on the 17th of August, he signed his own warrant with his dagger.

The Duke of Praslin is a man of middle height, and of rather commonplace appearance. He has a very gentle, but a very false, manner. He has a villainous mouth, and a horribly constrained smile. He is a fair, pallid man; pale, washed-out, like an Englishman. He is neither fat nor thin, nor good-looking nor ugly. He has no signs of breeding in his hands, which are fat and thick. He has always the air of being about to say something which he never does say.

I have only spoken to him three or four times in my life. The last time we were ascending the great staircase together. I had informed him that I would interrogate the Minister of War if they did not pardon Dubois de Gennes, whose brother had been the duke's secretary. He said that he would support me.

He had not behaved well towards this Dubois de Gennes. He had put him aside very cavalierly. The duke undertook to present his petitions to the king with his own hands, and he put them in the post!

M. de Praslin did not speak in the Chamber. He voted sternly in the trial. He decided very harshly in the Teste affair.

In 1830 I occasionally met him at the house of the Marquis de Marmier, since duke. He was then only Marquis de Praslin, as his brother was alive. I had noticed the marquise, a good-looking stout woman,—a contrast to the marquis, who was then very thin.

The poor duchess was literally hacked to pieces with the knife, and stunned by the butt of the pistol. Allard, the successor to Vidocq, of the secret police, said, "It was clumsily done; trained assassins would have worked better; a man of the world did that!"

The Comte de Nocé came up to me in the robing-room, and said, "Do you understand? He had made a fire to burn his *robe de chambre.*"

I replied, "He had something to burn! It was not his *robe de chambre,* it was his brain."

A month ago the army received a blow in the case of General Cubières; the magistrature, in President Teste; now the old nobility has had its turn in the Duke of Praslin.

This must be put a stop to.

Sunday, 22.

At the present moment one can perceive, in the window of Mlle. de Luzzy, in Madame Lemaire's house, Rue du Harlay, in the court, the melon, the bouquet, and the basket of fruit which the duke brought from the country the very evening before the murder.

The duke is seriously ill. People say he is poisoned. Just now I heard a flower-girl say, "*Mon Dieu,* if only they do kill him, it will amuse me very much to read all the details in the paper every evening."

In his address to the Court, in secret sitting, the chancellor said the duty which devolved upon the Court, and upon him, was the most painful they had ever been called upon to perform. His voice literally changed while he spoke these words. Before the sitting commenced he came into the reading-room; I bade him good morning, and we shook hands. The old chancellor was overcome.

The chancellor also said, "Rumours of suicide and of escape are in circulation. *Messieurs les Paris* may rest assured. No precaution will be spared to ensure for the culprit, if he be found guilty, the public and legal punishment which he has incurred and deserves, and which he, in that case, cannot by any means escape."

They say that the procurator-general Delangle already repeats to his intimates his little "effective bit"—the description of the room after the crime had been committed there, the sumptuous furniture, the golden fringe, the silken hangings, etc.; there a pool of blood; here the open window, the rising sun, the trees, the garden as far as the eye could reach, the songs of the birds, the sunlight, etc.; then the corpse of the deceased duchess. Contrast! Delangle is astonished at the effect beforehand, and is dazzled by himself.

On the 17th Mlle. de Luzzy had dined at Mme. Lemaire's, at the under-teachers' table. She was pale, and appeared to be suffering. "What is the matter with you?" asked Mlle. Julie Rivière, one of her companions. Mlle. de Luzzy replied that she did not feel very well; that she had fainted that day in the Rue St. Jacques, but the doctor had not thought it necessary to bleed her.

Doctor Louis is the Praslin family practitioner. They called him to see the duke. The prefect of police made the doctor promise that he would only speak to the duke concerning his health. The precaution turned out to be quite needless. The duke would scarcely respond, even by signs, to the doctor's questions. He was in a strange torpor. M. Louis perceived that he had tried to poison himself by swallowing a narcotic.

M. Louis did not think he ought to be moved on the 20th. He thought that if the chancellor had him dragged to Luxembourg, notwithstanding his advice, it was in the hope that the duke would die on the way. I do not think so.

The populace is exasperated against the duke; the family is still more indignant that the populace. If he were to be judged by his family, he would be more severely condemned than by the Court of Peers, and more cruelly tortured than by the people.

August 21.

On Wednesday, when coming from the Académie with Cousin and the Count of Sainte-Aulaire, Cousin said, "You will see Mlle. de Luzzy; she is a rare woman. Her letters are masterpieces of wit and style. Her interrogatory is admirable; still, you will not read it except when translated by Canchy. If you had heard her you would have been astonished. No one has more grace, more tact or intelligence. If she wishes to write some day for us, we will give her, *par Dieu*, the Montyon Prize. For the rest, she is headstrong and impetuous; she is a woman at once wicked and charming."

I said to Cousin, "Ah, so you are in love with her?"

To which he replied, "Hée!"

"What do you think of the affair?" said M. de Sainte-Aulaire, addressing me.

"There must have been some motive. If not, the duke is a madman. The cause is in the duchess or in the mistress; but she is in the swim, otherwise the fact is impossible. There is at the bottom of such a crime as this either a very powerful reason or a great folly."

That was, in effect, my opinion. As for the ferocity of the duke, it is explained by his stupidity; he was a beast —and ferocious.

The populace have already coined the verb *Prasliner*—to *Prasliner* your wife.

The examining Peers visited the Praslin mansion the day before yesterday. The bedroom is still in the state it was left on the morning of the murder. The blood from red has turned to black; that is the only difference. This room gives one the horrors. One can see the terrible struggle and resistance of the duchess as they actually occurred. Everywhere are the prints of bloody hands passing from wall to wall, from one door to another, from one bell-pull to another. The unhappy woman, like a wild animal caught in a snare, must have rushed round and round the room, screaming and seeking an escape from the dagger-blows of the assassin.

From the gate in the Rue de Vaugirard one can see in the prison three windows which have *hottes*. These are the only ones. Three months ago they had neither bars nor *hottes*. The bars were placed for President Teste and the *hottes* for the Duke of Praslin. Doctor Louis told me:

"The day after the murder, at half-past 2 a. m., I was called, and went to M. de Praslin's house. I knew nothing; judge my utter stupefaction. I found the duke in bed; he was already in custody. Eight women, who relieved each other every hour, never took their eyes from him. Four police agents were seated on chairs in a corner. I had noticed his condition, which was terrible. The symptoms declared cholera or poison. People accuse me of not having said at once he is poisoned. That would have denounced him and lost him. Poisoning is a tacit confession of guilt. 'You should have said so,' the chancellor remarked to me. I replied, 'Monsieur le Chancellor, where an opinion implies the condemnation of a person a doctor will not give it.'

"For the rest," continued M. Louis, "the duke was very gentle: he was passionately fond of his children, and passed his life with one of them on his knee, and sometimes one on his back too. The duchess was beautiful and intelligent; she had become an enormous size. The duke suffered terribly, but exhibited the greatest fortitude. Not a word, not a complaint in the midst of the tortures of the arsenic."

It would appear that M. de Praslin was a very well made man.

At the *post-mortem* the doctors were much struck. One of them exclaimed, "What a beautiful corpse!" He was a fine athlete, Doctor Louis told me.

The tomb in which they laid him bears a leaden plate, on which is the number 1054. A number after his death, as convicts have in life, is the only epitaph of the Duke of Choiseul-Praslin.

Mlle. Deluzy—not De Luzzy—is still in the Conciergerie. She walks about every day for two hours in the court-yard. Sometimes she wears a nankeen dress, sometimes a striped silk gown.

She knows that many eyes are fixed on her at the windows. People who watch her say she strikes attitudes. She is a source of amusement for M. Teste, whose window looks in to the court. She was still in confinement on the 31st.

Granier de Cassagnac, who had seen her, has given me a description of her. She has a very low forehead, her nose turns up a great deal, her hair is very light-coloured. Nevertheless, she is pretty. She looks straight at all who pass, seeking observation, and perhaps to fascinate them.

She is one of those women who neglect the heart in order to cultivate the wit. She is capable of follies, not from passion but from egotism.

August 30.

A sitting in which the Court is dissolved. At a quarter past one I enter the Chamber. There are but a few Peers present,—M. Villemain, M. Cousin, M. Thénard; some generals, General Fabvier among them; some former presidents, among them B. Barthe; there is also M. le Comte de Bondy, who bears a singular resemblance to, with better characteristics than, the Duke of Praslin.

I chat with General Fabvier, then for a long time with M. Barthe, of everything, and of those of the Chamber of Peers in particular. It is necessary to take up the subject to make the people sympathetic with it, and to make it sympathetic with the people. We spoke of the suicide of Alfred de Montesquiou.

In the cloak-room it was the general topic, as well as another sad incident: the prince of Eckmühl has been arrested during the night for having stabbed his mistress.

At two o'clock the chancellor rose; he had on his right the Duke Decazes, and on his left the Viscount Pontécoulant. He spoke for twenty minutes. The attorney-general was introduced.

There are about sixty Peers. The Duke of Brancas and the Marquis de Fontis are beside me.

M. Delangle laid down his brief for the prosecution, holding that the Court was dissolved by the death of the duke.

The attorney-general went out. The chancellor said, "Does any one claim the right to speak?"

M. de Boissy rose. He partly approved of what the chancellor had said. The poison had been taken before the Court of Peers had assembled, consequently no responsibility rested on the Court. Public opinion accused the Peers charged with the investigation of having winked at the poisoning.

COUNT LANJUINAIS. An opinion without any foundation.

BOISSY. But universal. [No, no.] I insist that it may be proved that no responsibility for the poisoning rests upon the chancellor, the investigating Peers, nor on the Courts.

THE CHANCELLOR. No one entertains such an opinion; the report of the *post-mortem* quite disposes of the question.

M. Cousin agreed with the chancellor, and, while sharing the anxiety of M. de Boissy, believed that there was no foundation for the rumour.

M. de Boissy persisted. He believed there had been complicity, but he did not accuse any of the officers of the Court.

M. Barthe rose, and gave way to the Duke Decazes, who related the circumstances of his interview with M. de Praslin the Tuesday he died, at 10 a. m.

This is the interview:—

"You suffer a great deal, my dear friend?" M. Decazes had said.

"Yes."

"It is your own fault. Why did you poison yourself?"

Silence.

"You have taken laudanum?"

"No."

"Then you have taken arsenic?"

The sick man looked up and said, "Yes."

"Who procured the arsenic for you?"

"No one."

"What do you mean? Did you buy it yourself at the chemist's?"

"I brought it from Praslin."

Silence. The Duke Decazes continued: "This is the time, for the sake of your family, your memory, your children, to speak. You confess to having taken poison. It is not to be supposed that an innocent person would deprive his nine children of their father when they are already motherless. You are guilty, then?"

Silence.

"At least you regret your crime. I beg of you to say if you deplore it."

The accused raised his eyes and hands to heaven, and said, with an agonized expression, "If I deplore it!"

"Then confess. Do not you wish to see the chancellor?"

The accused made an effort, and said, "I am ready."

"Well, then," said the duke, "I will go and inform him."

"No," replied the sick man, after a pause, "I am too weak to-day. To-morrow. Tell him to come to-morrow."

At half-past four that afternoon he was dead.

This could not be put into the pleadings, as it was a private conversation, which M. Decazes repeated because the Court was, in a sense, informal.

M. Barthe called attention to the fact that the poisoning took place on Wednesday, the 19th, and had not been renewed.

M. de Boissy wished to punish those who watched the duke so carelessly. He poisoned himself on Wednesday, at ten in the evening.

The chancellor said that M. de Boissy was mistaken; it was four in the afternoon. Besides, such things happen frequently in ordinary cases, and in the best guarded prisons.

The decree dissolving the Court was voted unanimously.

The Duke of Massa, after the vote, asked that the words "his wife" should be inserted in the sentence. There was a Dowager Duchess of Praslin. This was allowed.

The procurator-general was recalled, and sentence was read to him. The sitting broke up at five minutes to three.

Many Peers remained to chat in the hall. M. Cousin said to M. de Boissy, "You were right to ask for information. It was excellent."

M. Decazes added to his former statement the following details: When the duke was carried to the Luxembourg he was clad in a dressing-gown and trousers. During the journey he did not vomit; he only complained of a consuming thirst. When he arrived, at five in the afternoon, they undressed him and put him to bed at once. They did not give him back his dress until the next day, when they moved him into an adjacent room to be examined by the chancellor. After the examination they undressed him again, and put him to bed once more. It is therefore impossible that, even if he had some poison in his pockets, he could have taken it. It is true they did not search him; but that would have been futile. They watched his movements closely.

Hubert, The Spy

JERSEY.

YESTERDAY, the 20th of October, 1853, contrary to my custom, I went into the town in the evening. I had written two letters, one to Schœlcher in London, the other to Samuel in Brussels, and I wished to post them myself. I was returning by moonlight, about half-past nine, when, as I was passing the place which we call Tap et Flac, a kind of small square opposite Gosset the grocer's, an affrighted group approached me.

They were four refugees,—Mathé, a representative of the people; Rattier, a lawyer; Hayes, called Sans-Couture, a cobbler; and Henry, called little Father Henry, of whose profession I am ignorant.

"What is the matter with you?" I said, seeing them greatly agitated.

"We are going to execute a man," said Mathé, as he waved a roll of paper which he held in his hand.

Then they rapidly gave me the following details. Having retired since May from the society of refugees, and living in the country, all these facts were new to me.

In the month of April last a political refugee landed in Jersey. The innkeeper Beauvais, who is a generous-hearted fellow, was walking on the quay when the packet came alongside. He saw a man pale, exhausted, and in rags carry a little bundle. "Who are you?" said Beauvais. "A refugee." "What is your name?" "Hubert." "Where are you going?" "I do not know." "You have no inn?" "I have no money." "Come home with me."

Beauvais took Hubert to his house, which is No. 20 Don Street.

Hubert was a man of about fifty, with white hair and black moustache. His face was marked with small-pox. His appearance was robust, his eyes intelligent. He said he had been a schoolmaster and a surveyor. He came from the department of the Eure; he had been exiled on the 2d of December.

He reached Brussels, where he came to see me; driven from Brussels, he went to London, and in London he lived in the last stage of misery. He had lived five months, five winter months, in what they call a *Sociale*, a sort of dilapidated hall, the doors and windows of which permit draughts, and the roof admits the rain. He had slept the two first months side by side with Bourillon, another refugee, on the stone floor in front of the fireplace.

These men lay on the flags without mattress or covering, without even a handful of straw, their wet, ragged clothes on their bodies. There was no fire. It was not till the end of the two months that Louis Blanc and Ledru-Rollin had given them some money to buy coal. When these men had some potatoes they boiled them and dined; when they had none they ate nothing at all.

Hubert, without money or bed, almost without shoes or clothing, lived there, slept on the stone, shivered continually, ate seldom, and never complained. He took his large share of the general suffering stoically, impassible, and in silence. He was a member of the Delegation Society; then he had quitted it, saying, "Félix Pyat is no socialist." Afterwards he joined the Revolutionary Society; but he left it, declaring that Ledru-Rollin was not a Republican.

On the 14th of September, 1852, the Prefect of the Eure wrote to him to agree to send in his submission. Hubert answered the prefect in a letter very outspoken, and full, as regards his "Emperor," of the coarsest terms, such as *clique, canaille, misérable*. He showed this letter, dated the 24th of September, to all the refugees he met, and posted it up in the room where the members of the Revolutionary Society used to meet.

On the 5th of February he saw his name in the "Moniteur" among the pardoned. Hubert was filled with indignation, and instead of returning to France he went to Jersey, declaring that there were better Republicans there than in London. So it came to pass that he disembarked at St. Heliers.

When he reached Beauvais's house, Beauvais showed him a room.

"I told you I had no money," said Hubert. "It is all the same," said Beauvais. "Give me a corner and a truss of straw in the granary." "I will give you my room and my bed in preference," said Beauvais.

At meal-time Hubert did not wish to take his place at table. Many refugees were living in Beauvais's house, where they breakfasted and dined for thirty-five francs a month.

"I have not thirty-five sous," said Hubert. "Give me a morsel at once. I will eat it at a corner of the kitchen-table."

Beauvais was annoyed. "By no means," he said; "you will dine with us, citizen." "And pay you—" "When you can." "Never, perhaps." "Well, then, never."

Beauvais procured for Hubert some pupils in the town, to whom he taught grammar and arithmetic, and with the produce of these lessons he compelled him to buy a coat and some shoes. "I have shoes," said Hubert. "Yes, you have shoes, but they have not any soles."

The refugees were moved at seeing Hubert's condition, and they assigned to him the ordinary assistance allotted to the necessitous who had no wife or child, namely, seven francs a week. With that and his lessons he existed. He had no more. Many people, Gaffney among others, offered him money, but he never would accept it. "No," he would say; "there are people more unfortunate than I."

He made himself very useful in Beauvais's house, occupying the least possible room, rising from the table before dinner was over, drinking no wine or brandy, and refusing to have his glass filled. For the rest, he was an ardent communist, did not recognize any chief, declared the Republic was betrayed by Louis Blanc, Félix Pyat, and Ledru-Rollin; by me, proclaiming at the fall of Napoleon, whom he always called Badinguet, a six months' massacre to finish up with; compelling, by force of suffering and sternness, even from those who avoided him, a kind of respect, having about him some indescribable token of rough honesty. A moderate said of him to an enthusiast, "He is worse than Robespierre." The other replied, "He is better than Marat."

Now the mask was about to fall. The man was a spy.

The fact was discovered in this wise.

Hubert, among the refugees, had an intimate friend named Hayes. One day, in the beginning of September, he took Hayes aside, and said to him, in a low and mysterious tone, "I am going away to-morrow." "You going away?" "Yes." "Where are you going to?" "To France." "What, to France?" "To Paris." "To Paris?" "They expect me there." "What for?" "For a blow." "How will you enter France?" "I have a passport." "From whom?" "From the consul." "In your own name?" "In my own name." "That is very odd." "You forgot that I was pardoned in February." "That's true; and the money?" "I have some." "How much?" "Twenty francs." "Are you going all the way to Paris with twenty francs?" "As soon as I reach Saint-Malo I will go as I can,—on foot, if necessary. If necessary I will not eat anything. I will go straight on by the shortest way."

Instead of taking the shortest, he took the longest way. From Saint-Malo he went to Rennes, from Rennes to Nantes, from Nantes to Angers, from Angers to Paris by the railway. He took six days on the journey. As he proceeded he saw in every town the democratic leaders,—Boué at Saint-Malo, Roche, Dr. Guépin and the Mangins at Nantes; Rioteau at Angers. He announced himself everywhere as being on a mission from the refugees of Jersey, and he easily gained assistance everywhere. He neither hid nor displayed his poverty; people could see it. At Angers he borrowed fifty francs from Rioteau, not having enough to go to Paris.

From Angers he wrote to a woman with whom he had lived in Jersey, one Mélanie Simon, a seamstress, lodging at No. 5 Hill Street, and who had actually lent him thirty-two francs for his journey. He had concealed this money from Hayes. He told this woman that she might write to him to No. 38, Rue de l'Ecole de Médecine; that he did not lodge there, but he had a friend who would forward his letters.

Arrived in Paris he went to see Goudchaux; he found, one knows not how, the dwelling of Boisson, the agent of the Ledru-Rollin faction. The said Boisson lived concealed in Paris. He presented himself to Boisson as an envoy from us, the refugees of Jersey, and entered into all the combinations of the party called the Party of Action.

Towards the end of September he disembarked in Jersey from the steamer "Rose." The day after his arrival he took Hayes aside and declared that a blow was about to be struck, and that if he, Hubert, had arrived some days sooner in Paris, the blow would have been struck then; that his advice, which had almost been accepted, had been to blow up a railway bridge while Badinguet's train was passing; that men and money were both ready, but that the people had no confidence except in the refugees, and that he was going to return to Paris for this purpose. As he had taken part in every blow dealt since 1830, he was not the man to back out of this; but he himself was not sufficient,—he required ten refugees, of good will, to put themselves at the head of the people when the time for action arrived, and he had come to seek them in Jersey. He ended by asking Hayes if he would be one of the ten. *"Parbleu!"* replied Hayes.

Hubert saw the refugees, and made them the same confidences with the same mystery, saying, "I have told no one but you." He enrolled, among others besides Hayes, Jego, who was recovering from typhoid fever, and Gigoux, to whom he declared that his name, Gigoux, would raise the masses.

Those he enlisted thus, with a view of taking them to Paris, said, "But the money?" "Rest easy," replied Hubert, "they have it. They will await you on the landing-stage. Come to Paris, the rest will settle itself. They will undertake to find a place for you."

Besides Hayes, Gigoux, and Jego, he interviewed Jarassé, Famot, Rondeaux, and others.

Since this dissolution of the General Society two societies of refugees were formed in Jersey,—the "Fraternelle" and the "Fraternité."

Hubert belonged to the "Fraternité," of which Gigoux was treasurer. He drew from it, as I have said, seven francs a week. He claimed from Gigoux that he should be paid the fourteen francs for the two weeks he was away, as he had been absent in the service of the Republic.

The day Hubert and those I have mentioned were to leave was fixed for Friday, the 21st of October.

However, a refugee named Rattier, a lawyer of Lorient, being one morning in the shop of Hurel, the tobacconist, saw entering a shop a man to whom he had never spoken, but whom he knew by sight. This man, perceiving him to be a Frenchman, said to him, "Citizen, have you change for a hundred-franc note?" "No," replied Rattier. The man unfolded a yellow paper, which he was holding in his hand, and presented it to the tobacconist, requesting change. The shopkeeper had not sufficient. During the colloquy Rattier recognized the paper as a Bank of France note for one hundred francs. The man went away, and Rattier said to Hurel, "Do you know that man's name?" "Yes," replied Hurel, "he is a French refugee named Hubert."

Almost at the same time Hubert, when paying for his lodging, took from his pocket a handful of shillings and half crowns.

Mélanie Simon claimed the thirty-two francs; he refused to pay her, and at the same time, by a strange sort of contradiction, he permitted her to see a pocketbook full, as Mélanie said afterwards, of yellow and blue papers. "These are bank-notes," said Hubert to her. "I have here three thousand five hundred francs."

Now the contradiction was explained. Hubert, about to return to France, wished to take Mélanie Simon with him; he refused to pay her, in order that she might go with him; and that she might go without anxiety, he showed her that he was rich.

Mélanie Simon did not wish to leave Jersey, and again demanded her thirty-two francs. Disputes arose; Hubert still refused. "Listen to me," said Mélanie;

"if you do not pay me, I have seen your money, I suspect you are a spy, and I will denounce you to the refugees."

Hubert laughed.

"Make them believe that of me," said he. *"Allons donc."*

He hoped to disabuse Mélanie Simon of this idea by putting a good face on the matter.

"My thirty-two francs," said Mélanie.

"Not a sou," replied Hubert.

Mélanie Simon went to find Jarassé, and denounced Hubert.

It seemed at first sight that Hubert was right. Among the refugees the idea was divided.

"Hubert a spy?" they said. "Nonsense!"

Beauvais recalled his sobriety and Gaffney his disinterestedness, Bisson his republicanism, Seigneuret his communism, Bourillon his five months they slept on the stones, Gigoux the assistance they had given him, Roumilhac his stoicism, and all of them his misery.

"I have seen him without shoes," said one.

"And I without a home," said another.

"And I without bread," added a third.

"He was my best friend," remarked Hayes.

Then Rattier related the incident of the one-hundred-franc note; the details of Hubert's journey leaked out by degrees. They asked themselves why this curious journey had been undertaken? They learned that he had passed from place to place with wonderful facility. A resident of Jersey declared that he had seen him walking on the quay of Saint-Malo among the custom-house officers and the gendarmes without their noticing him. Suspicion was awakened: Mélanie Simon proclaimed it on the house-tops; the wine-growing poet, Claude Durand, who was respected by all the proscribed, shook his head when speaking of Hubert.

Mélanie Simon told Jarassé of Hubert's letter, giving his address in Paris at No. 38, Rue de l'Ecole de Médecine, where a friend received his letters. Now, the son of Mathé, the representative, when he went to Paris some months before, had by a curious coincidence lodged in that very same house.

Jarassé having shown to Mathé Hubert's letter to Mélanie, the address and the friend attracted the attention of Mathé's son, who was present, and who declared that it was the house in which he had lodged. Among the lodgers there had been an agent of police named Philippi.

A portentous rumour began to circulate among the refugees.

Hayes and Gigoux, Hubert's friends, whom he had enrolled for Paris, said to him,—

"People are certainly talking." "About what?" said Hubert. "About Mélanie Simon and you." "Well, they say she is my mistress, I suppose." "No, they say that you are a spy." "Well, what of that?" "It will provoke an inquiry," said Hayes. "And a judgment," said Gigoux.

Hubert made no answer. His friends frowned.

Next day they pressed him again. He was silent. They returned to the charge. He almost refused to speak. The more he hesitated, the more they insisted. They finished up by declaring that he must clear the matter up.

Hubert, having no means of avoiding the inquiry, and perceiving that suspicion grew stronger, consented.

The refugees held their club meeting at Beauvais's house, in No. 20, Don Street.

Those idle and those out of work met there in a common room. Hubert posted in this room a declaration addressed to his brothers in exile, in which, in reference to the infamous calumnies spread concerning him, he placed himself at the disposal of all present seeking an inquiry, and demanding that he should be judged by all the refugees.

He wished the inquiry to take place immediately, reminding them that he wished to leave Jersey on Friday, the 21st of October, and concluded by saying, "The justice of the people ought to be prompt."

The last words of this proclamation were, "The Day is approaching. Signed, Hubert."

The society "Fraternité" to which Hubert belonged assembled, called an inquiry, and nominated five of its members to institute this dramatic process of proscription, namely, Mathé, Rattier, Rondeaux, Henry, and Hayes. Mathé, since his son's surprised exclamation, was convinced of the culpability of Hubert.

This commission, a regular judicial one, called witnesses, heard Gigoux and Jego, who had been enrolled by Hubert for Paris, Jarassé, Famot, to whom Hubert had spoken of the six months' massacre to finish up; collected the reports of Rattier and Hayes; called Mélanie Simon, confronted her with Hubert; read in evidence the letter written by Hubert from Angers, which though torn, was pieced together; drew up an official report of everything. When confronted with Hubert, Mélanie Simon confirmed all her statements, and told him plainly that he was a Bonapartist spy.

Suspicions abounded, but the proofs were wanting.

Mathé said to Hubert, "You are going away on Friday?" "Yes." "You have a trunk?" "Yes." "What do you carry in that trunk?" "My old clothes and the copies of the Socialist and Republican publications." "Will you permit your trunk to be searched?" "Yes."

Rondeaux accompanied Hubert to Beauvais's house, where he lodged, and where his trunk was. It was opened. Rondeaux found in it some shirts and handkerchiefs, an old pair of trousers, and an old coat. Nothing more.

The absence of positive proof weakened the suspicions, and the opinion of the refugees went rather in Hubert's favour.

Hayes, Gigoux, and Beauvais defended him warmly.

Rondeaux told what he had found in the trunk.

"And the Socialist publications?" asked Mathé.

"I did not see any of them," replied Rondeaux.

Hubert said nothing.

However, the report of the searching of the trunk got about, and a carpenter of Queen Street said to Jarassé, I think it was. "But have you opened the double bottom?" "What double bottom?" "The double bottom of the trunk." "Do you mean to say that the trunk has a false bottom?" "Certainly."

"How do you know?" "Because I made it."

This was repeated to the commissioners. Mathé said to Hubert, "Your trunk has a false bottom?" "No doubt." "Why this double bottom?" *"Parbleu!* To hide the democratic writings which I carry about." "Why did you not tell Rondeaux of it?" "I did not think about it." "Will you permit us to see it?" "Yes."

Hubert gave his consent in the calmest manner in the world, giving answers in monosyllables and scarcely removing his pipe from his mouth. From his laconic answers his friends argued his innocence.

The commissioners decided that they would all be present at this inspection of the trunk. They set out. It was Thursday,—the day before that fixed by Hubert for his departure. "Where are we going?" asked Hubert.

"To Beauvais's house," said Rondeaux, "since your trunk is there." Hubert replied:—

"We are a numerous body; it will be necessary to break open the false bottom with a hammer; that will cause some commotion at Beauvais's house, where there are always a number of refugees. Let two of you come with me and carry the trunk to the carpenter's house, while the others await us there. As the carpenter made the false bottom, he will be able to remove it better than anybody else. All will then pass in the presence of the commission without scandal."

They consented to this. Hubert, assisted by Hayes and Henry, carried the trunk to the carpenter's shop; the false bottom was opened, a quantity of papers was found; they were Republican writings,—my speeches, the "Bagnes d'Afrique" of Ribeyrolles, the "Couronne Impériale" of Cahaigne.

They found there three or four passports of Hubert's, the last issued in France *on his order*. They found a complete set of documents relative to the interior organization of the revolutionary society organized in London by Ledru-Rollin, all that packed in with a mass of letters and old documents.

Among the latter they found two letters which seemed singular.

The former, dated the 24th of September, was addressed to the Prefect of the Eure, rejecting the amnesty offered with a prodigality of epithets. This was the letter which Hubert had shown to the refugees in London, and fixed up in their meeting-room.

The second letter, dated the 30th, only six days later, was addressed to the same person, and contained, under the guise of asking for money, clear offers of service to the Bonapartist Government.

These two letters contradicted each other; it was evident that only one of them was intended to be sent, and it appeared probable that this was not the former. According to all appearance, the second was the true letter; the first was merely a blind.

They showed them to Hubert, who continued to smoke his pipe calmly.

They put the letters on one side, and continued their examination of the papers.

A letter in Hubert's writing, commencing "My dear mother," fell into the hands of Rattier. He read the opening sentences, but as it seemed a family letter he was about to throw it down, when he perceived that the sheet was double. He opened it almost mechanically, and he felt as if lightning had flashed in his eyes. His gaze fell on the head of the second sheet on these words, in Hubert's handwriting, "To M. de Maupas, Minister of Police. Monsieur le Ministre."

Then followed the letter which they were about to read,—a letter signed "Hubert."

*To M. de Maupas,
Minister of Police at Paris.*

M. LE MINISTRE,—I have received, under date of 14th of September last, with a view of making me return to France, a letter from M. le Préfet de l'Eure.

On the 24th and 30th of the same month I wrote two letters to M. le Préfet, neither of which has been answered.

Since then my name has been figured in the "Moniteur" in the list, according to the decree of the 5th of this month (February), but I was not ready to go at that time, as I wished to finish in London a pamphlet entitled "The Republican Refugees, and the Republic impossible by these same pretended Republicans." This pamphlet, full of truths and facts which no one could deny, will produce, I think, some effect in France, where I wish to have it printed. I had my passport *visé* for France yesterday; nothing of importance will keep me in England except that before leaving, if they will give me what is due to me, what I claim by my letter of the 30th of September.

M. le Préfet de l'Eure who was begged to communicate this letter to the proper person, should have laid it before the Government. I am waiting the solution of the matter, but seeing that so long a time has elapsed and I have received nothing, I have decided to address this letter to you, in the hope of obtaining an immediate settlement.

My address in London, England, is 17 Church Street, Soho Square.

And my name, Hubert Julien Damascène, geometrical surveyor of Henqueville, near Andelys (Eure).

(Signed) HUBERT.
25th of February, 1853.

Rattier raised his eyes and looked at Hubert.

He had dropped his pipe. The perspiration stood on his forehead in great beads.

"You are a spy!" said Rattier.

Hubert, pale as death, fell into a chair without replying.

The members of the commission tied up the papers and went immediately to report the result to the Fraternity Society, which was then assembled.

It was on their way thither that I met them.

When these facts came to light, a sort of electric shock thrilled the refugees in the town. They ran about the streets, they ran against each other; the most excited was the most stupefied. That Hubert, whom they had trusted!

One fact added to the excitement. Thursday is the post-day when the papers from France arrive in Jersey. The news which they brought threw a lurid light upon Hubert. Three hundred arrests had been made in Paris. Hubert had seen Rocher of Nantes at Saint-Malo! Rocher had been arrested. He had seen Guépin and the Mangins at Nantes; the Mangins and Guépin had been arrested. He had seen Rioteau at Angers, and had borrowed money from him; Rioteau was arrested. He had seen Goudchaux and Boisson at Paris; Goudchaux and Boisson were arrested.

Facts and memories came in shoals. Gaffney, one of those who to the last moment had supported Hubert, related that, in 1852, he had forwarded contraband from London to Havre a parcel containing eighty copies of "Napoleon the Little." Hubert and an attorney of Rouen, a refugee named Bachelet, were in his room when he closed the parcel. He had made in their presence a calculation, from which it resulted that the parcel was to be sent to his mother's house to him, Gaffney, on the day when a friend previously notified would come and take it away. Hubert and Bachelet went out. After their departure Gaffney rectified his calculation, and found out that the parcel would arrive at his mother's house at Havre a day too soon. He wrote accordingly to his mother and his friend. The parcel arrived, and was taken away by his friend. On the day following, which had been fixed by Gaffney in the presence of Hubert and Bachelet, the police searched Madame Gaffney's house, with a view of finding the books which they said had been sent to her from London.

About ten o'clock in the evening twelve or fifteen refugees were assembled at Bauvais's house. Pierre Leroux, and a Jersey gentleman, M. Philippe Asplet, a constabulary officer, were seated in a corner. Pierre Leroux conversed with M. Asplet about table-turning.

Suddenly Henry entered and told them about the false bottom in the trunk, the letter to Maupas, the arrests in France; Hayes, Gigoux, and Rondeaux confirmed his statements.

At that moment the door opened and Hubert appeared. He came back to sleep, and as usual took his key from a peg in the common room.

"There he is;" cried Hayes.

They all rushed upon Hubert.

Gigoux struck him, Hayes seized him by the hair, Heurtebise held him by the throat, Beauvais drew his knife, Asplet arrested Beauvais's arm.

Beauvais told me an hour later that, if it had not been for M. Asplet, Hubert would have been a dead man.

M. Asplet, in his official capacity, intervened, and took Hubert from them. Beauvais threw away his knife; they left the spy alone. Two or three went into the corners, dropped their faces into their hands and wept.

Meanwhile I had gone home.

It was close on midnight, as I was going to bed, that I heard a carriage stop at the door. The bell rang, and the moment afterwards Charles came into my room and told me that Beauvais had come.

I went downstairs. All the refugees had united to pronounce sentence on Hubert. They kept him in custody, and they had sent Beauvais to seek for me. I hesitated. To judge this man in this nightly sitting, this *Vehmgericht* of the refugees, all that appeared strange and repugnant to my habits. Beauvais insisted.

"Come," said he to me; "if you do not, I cannot answer for Hubert."

Then he continued, "I cannot answer for myself. If it had not been for Asplet, I should have stabbed him."

I followed Beauvais, taking with me my two sons. As we proceeded we were joined by Cahigne, Ribeyrolles, Frond, Lefèvre the cripple, Cauvat, and many other refugees who lived at Havre-des-pas.

Midnight was striking when we reached our destination.

The room in which they were going to try Hubert is called the Refugee's Club, and is one of those large, square rooms which one finds in almost all English houses. These rooms, not much appreciated by French people, overlook the two façades of the mansion, back and front.

This one, situated on the first floor of Beauvais's house, No. 20, Don Street, has two windows looking into an inner court, and three upon the street opposite the large red front of the building destined for the public halls, which is here called Hôtel de Ville. Some of the inhabitants of the town, aroused by the rumours in circulation, were chattering in low tones beneath the windows. Refugees were arriving from all directions.

When I entered, they had nearly all assembled. They were distributed in the two compartments of the room, and spoke to each other in grave tones.

Hubert had come to see me in Brussels and in Jersey, but I had no recollection of him. When I entered I asked Heurtebise where Hubert was.

"Behind you," said Heurtebise.

I turned round and saw, seated at a table with his back to the wall, near the street, beneath the centre window, a pipe in front of him, his hat on his head, a man about fifty years old, ruddy, marked with smallpox, with very white hair and black moustaches. His eyes were steady and calm. From time to time he raised his hat and wiped his forehead with a large blue handkerchief.

His brown paletot was buttoned to the chin. Now that one knew what he was, one discovered the mien of a serjeant-de-ville.

People passed and repassed before him and round him speaking of him.

"There is the coward," said one.

"Look at the bandit," said another.

He heard these remarks exchanged, and seemed as indifferent to them as if they had been spoken of some one else.

Although the room was crowded by the new arrivals, there was a space left near him. He was alone at the table and on that bench. Four or five refugees stood upright by the window guarding him. One of them was Boni, who teaches us to ride on horseback.

The proscription was nearly complete, although the convocation had been arranged hastily in the middle of the night when the greater number of the refugees were in bed and asleep.

Nevertheless, one remarked some absentees. Pierre Leroux, having assisted at the first collision of Hubert and the refugees, had gone away and had not returned; and of all the numerous family which they call here the Leroux tribe, Charles was the only member present. There was also absent the greater number of those whom we call *les exaltés,* and among them the author of the manifesto entitled "Du Comité Révolutionaire," Seigneuret.

They sent for the commission which had started the proscription. It arrived. Mathé, who had just got out of bed, seemed still half-asleep.

Among the refugees present an old man, grown aged in conspiracy, was conversant with these sorts of summary processes among refugees in the catacombs,—a kind of free-justice meetings, where mystery does not exclude solemnity, and where he more than once had pronounced terrible sentences, which all sanctioned and some carried out. This old man was Cahaigne. Old in face, young in heart, flat nose buried in a grey beard, and white hair, a republican with the face of a Cossack, a democrat with the manners of a gentleman, a poet, a man of the world, a man of action, a fighter at barricades, a veteran in conspiracy. Cahaigne is a personage.

They called on him to preside. For secretaries they gave him Jarassé, who is of the "Fraternité" Society, and Heurtebise, of the "Fraternelle" Society.

These societies do not live fraternally together.

The sitting was open. A deep silence prevailed.

The room at this moment presented a strange aspect. In the two compartments, each lighted, and very feebly, by two gas-jets, were arranged and grouped, seated, standing up, stooping, leaning on their elbows, on benches, chairs, stools, tables, on the window-sills, some with arms folded leaning against the wall, all pale, grave, severe, almost sinister, were the seventy refugees in Jersey. They filled the two compartments of the room, leaving only in the compartment with three windows looking into the street a small space occupied by three tables,—the table by the wall where Hubert sat alone, a table close by, at which were Cahaigne, Jarassé, and Heurtebise, and opposite a very small one, on which Rattier, the reporter, had placed his note-book. Behind this table a bright fire was burning in the grate, and was from time to time attended to by a lad. On the mantelpiece above a pipe-rack, amid a crowd of bills emanating from the refugees, between the announcement of Charles Leroux, recommending his sewing establishment, and the placard of Ribot, inaugurating the hat manufactory of the *Chapeau rouge,* was exhibited, stuck up with some wafers, the placard calling for an inquiry and "prompt justice," signed, Hubert.

Here and there upon the table were glasses of brandy and pots of beer. All round the room hung on hooks were glazed caps, straw and felt hats, and an old draught-board the white squares of which were scarcely whiter than the black ones, was hanging on the wall above Hubert's head.

I was seated with Ribeyrolles and my sons in an angle near the chimney.

Some of the refugees were smoking, —some pipes, others cigars,—so there was little light and much smoke in the room. The upper part of the windows, *en guillotines* English fashion, were open to let out the smoke.

The proceedings commenced by the interrogation of Hubert. At the first words Hubert doffed his cap. Cahaigne questioned him with a somewhat theatrical gravity; but which, whatever the tone, was felt lugubrious and serious.

Hubert gave his two Christian names, Julien Damascène.

Hubert had had time to regain his presence of mind. He answered precisely and without delay. At a certain time, when they were speaking to him concerning his return by the department of the Eure, he rectified some little mistake of Cahaigne's: "Pardon me, Louviers is on the right bank and Andelys on the left." Beyond that he confessed nothing.

The interrogation finished, they passed to the reading of the official report of the commission, the witnesses, and the proofs.

This reading commenced amid profound silence, which was succeeded by a murmur which increased in volume in proportion as the black and odious facts were dragged to light. Stifled murmurs were audible. "Ah, the rascal, the scoundrel, why do not we strangle this blackguard on the spot?"

In the midst of this volley of imprecations the reader was forced to raise his voice. Rattier was reading. Mathé passed him up the sheets of paper. Beauvais was holding a candle to him; the tallow kept dropping on the table.

After the depositions of the witnesses had been read, Rattier announced that he had arrived at a decisive piece of evidence. Silence was renewed,—a feverish, restless silence. Charles whispered to me, "One may learn how to treat a spy."

Rattier read the letter from Hubert to Maupas.

So long as the letter was being read the audience contained itself, hands were clinched, some men bit their handkerchiefs.

When the last word had been read, "The signature?" cried old Fombertaux.

Rattier said, "It is signed, Hubert."

Then the uproar broke out. The silence had only been caused by the expectation mingled with a sort of hesitation to believe such a thing possible. Some had even doubted up till then and said, "It is impossible." When this letter appeared, written by Hubert, dated by Hubert, signed by Hubert, evidently real, indubitable before every one, within every one's reach, the name of Maupas written by Hubert, conviction fell into the middle of the assembly like a thunder-bolt.

Furious faces were turned towards Hubert. Many individuals leaped upon the benches; threatening hands were raised against him. There was a frenzy of rage and grief; a terrible light filled all eyes.

Nothing was heard but cries of "Scoundrel!" "Ah, the miserable Hubert!" "Ah, you brigand of the Rue de Jerusalem!"

Fombertaux, whose son is at Belle Isle, exclaimed, "Those are the scoundrels to whom we give twenty years."

"Yes," added another, "it is, thanks to such creatures as he, that the young are in prison and the old in exile."

A refugee, whose name I forget, a fine, fair-haired young man, leaped upon the table, pointed to Hubert, and cried, "Citizens, death!"

"Death! death!" shouted a chorus of voices. Hubert looked about him with a bewildered air.

The same young man continued:—

"We will keep hold of him, so that he shall not escape us."

One cried, "Throw him into the Seine."

At this there was an explosion of sardonic laughter.

"Do you think you are still on the Pont Neuf?"

Then they continued, "'Throw the spy into the sea, with a stone round his neck.

"Let us send him where all is blue," said Fombertaux.

During the turmoil, Mathé had handed me Hubert's letter, and I was examining it with Ribeyrolles. It was actually written on the second page of a family letter in a rather long, neat, legible hand, with some erasures, but altogether in Hubert's hand. At the bottom of this rough draft, after the manner of an illiterate man, he had signed his name in full.

Cahaigne proclaimed silence, but the tumult was indescribable. Every one spoke at the same time, and it seemed as if a single mind was hurling from sixty mouths the same malediction upon the miserable man.

"Citizens," cried Cahaigne, "you are judges!"

This was sufficient. All was silent, raised hands were lowered, and each man, folding his arms or resting his elbow on his knee, resumed his place with lugubrious dignity.

"Hubert," said Cahaigne, "do you recognize this letter?"

Jarassé presented the letter to Hubert, who replied, "Yes."

Cahaigne continued, "What explanation have you to give?"

Hubert was silent.

"So," pursued Cahaigne, "you confess yourself a spy?"

Hubert raised his head, looked at Cahaigne, struck his fist upon the table, and said, "That—no!"

A murmur pervaded the audience like an angry shiver. The explosion, which had only been suspended, very nearly recommenced, but as they saw that Hubert was about to continue, they kept silence.

Hubert declared, in a thick, broken voice, but which had, nevertheless, a certain firmness and, sad to say, sincerity in it, that he had never done any one any harm; that he was a Republican; that he would die ten thousand deaths before he brought to the ground by his own fault a hair from the head of a Republican. That, if arrests had been made in Paris, he was innocent of them; that they had not paid sufficient attention to the first letter to the Prefect of the Eure. That, as regards the letter to Maupas, it was a draft, a project; that he had written it, but had never sent it. That they would recognize the truth too late, and would regret their action. That, as for the pamphlet, "The Republic impossible because of Republicans," he had written that too, but had not published it.

They all cried out. "Where it is?"

He calmly replied, "I have burned it."

"Is that all you have to say?" inquired Cahaigne.

Hubert shook his head and continued:—

"He owed nothing to Mélanie Simon; those who had seen money in his possession were mistaken. The citizen Rattier was deceived; he (Hubert) had never been in the shop of the tobacconist Hurel. His passports were a very simple matter; being amnestied, he had a right to them. He had paid back the fifty francs to Rioteau of Angers; he was an honest man; he had never had a bank-note. The money he had expended he had received from the woman, about one hundred and sixty francs in all. He had met Citizen Boisson in Paris at a cheap restaurant. It was there he gave his address. If he had intended to bring the refugees to Paris, it was with a view to overturn Badinguet, not to betray his friends. If the gendarmes had allowed him to move freely about in France, it was not his fault. Definitely, there was an understanding among them to get rid of him, and all were victims of it."

He repeated two or three times, without their being able to understand to what this phrase referred, "The carpenter who made the false bottom is here to say so."

"Is that all?" said Cahaigne again.

"Yes," said he.

This word was received with a shudder. They had heard the explanations, but they had explained nothing.

"Take care!" continued Cahaigne. "You yourself have said we can judge you; we do judge you; we can condemn you."

"And execute you," cried a voice.

"Hubert," continued Cahaigne, "you risk all the dangers of punishment. Who knows what will happen to you? Take care! Disarm your judges by candid confession. Our friends are in the hands of Bonaparte, but you are in ours. Tell the facts clearly to us. Aid us to save our friends, or you are lost. Speak."

"It is you," said Hubert, raising his head,—"it is you who lose 'our friends' in Paris by speaking their names as loudly as you do in an assembly" (and he looked around him) "in which there are evidently spies. I have nothing more to say."

Then the uproar was renewed, and with such fury that it was feared some would pass from words to acts.

The cries "to death!" arose anew from a number of angry mouths.

There was in the Assembly a shoemaker of Niort, an old non-commissioned officer of artillery, called Guay, a fanatical Communist, but an excellent and honest workman, nevertheless,—a man with a long black beard, a pale face, rather sunken eyes and slow speech, of grave and resolute demeanour. He rose and said:—

"Citizens, it seems that you wish to condemn Hubert to death. That surprises me. You forgot that we are in a country which has laws that we must not violate, not attempt anything contrary to them. Nevertheless Hubert must be punished, both for the past and for the future, and impress on him an ineffaceable stigma. So, as we must do nothing unlawful, this is what I propose. We will seize Hubert and shave his hair and beard, and as hair will grow again we will cut a small piece out of his right ear. Ears do not grow again."

This proposition, enunciated in the gravest tone and in the most convinced way, was received in that lugubrious assembly with a shout of laughter which continued for some time, and which added another horror to the dread realities of the scene.

Near Guay, at the entrance to the other compartments of the room, beside Dr. Barbier, was seated a refugee named Avias. Avias, a non-commissioned officer in the army of Oudinot, had deserted before Rome, not wishing, as a Republican, to overturn a Republic. He had been caught, tried by court-martial, and condemned to death. He had succeeded in making his escape the day before the execution was to have taken place. He took refuge in Piedmont. On December 2, he crossed the frontier, and joined the Republicans of the Var in arms against the *coup d'état*. In an engagement a bullet broke his ankle. His friends carried him out of action with great difficulty, and his foot was amputated. Expelled from Piedmont he went to England, and thence to Jersey. When he arrived he came to see me. Some friends and myself assisted him, and he had finished by setting up as a dyer and scourer, and so lived.

Avias seemed to have been well acquainted with Hubert. While the extracts were being read he continued to cry, "Ah, *coquin!* ah, j—— f——! Say that he told me Louis Blanc is a traitor! Victor Hugo is a traitor. Ledru-Rollin is a traitor!"

When Guay sat down, Avias rose and stood on his bench, then on the table.

Avias is a man thirty years old, tall, with a wide red face, projecting brows, goggle-eyes, a large mouth, and a Provençal accent. With his furious eyes, his hands discoloured by dye, his foot beating time on the table, nothing more savage than this giant with the harsh voice, and whose head nearly touched the ceiling, can be conceived.

He exclaimed, "Citizens! none of this; let us finish. Let us draw lots who is to give this traitor his *coup-de-grâce*. If no one will, then I will volunteer."

A shout of assent arose: "All! all!"

A small young man with a fair beard, who was seated in front of me said, "I will undertake it. The business of the spy will be settled to-morrow morning."

"Not so," said another, in the opposite corner. "There are four here who will charge themselves with this."

"Yes," added Fombertaux, extending his fist close to Hubert's head. "Justice upon that rascal—death!"

Not a dissenting voice was raised. Hubert, himself terrified, bent his head and seemed to say, "It is just."

I rose.

"Citizens," I said, "in a man whom you have fed, supported, and made friends with, you have found a traitor. In a man you have accepted as a brother you find a spy. This man is still wearing a coat you bought for him, and the shoes with which you provided him. You are shivering with indignation and regret. This indignation I partake, this sorrow I can understand. But take care! What mean these shouts for death? There are two beings in Hubert,—a spy and a man. The spy is infamous, the man is sacred."

Here a voice interrupted me,—the voice of a fine fellow named Cauvet, who is rich and sometimes tipsy, and who abused anything pertaining to Ledru-Rollin, to show himself a fanatic for the guillotine. A deep silence supervened. Cauvet said, in a low voice, "Ah, yes! that's it, always for soft measures."

"Yes," said I, "for moderation. Energy on one side, mildness on the other. Those are the arms which I wish to place in the hands of the Republic."

I resumed:—

"Citizens, do you know what belongs to you in Hubert? The spy, yes! the man, no! The spy is yours; the home of the traitor, the name of the traitor, his moral being, you have the right to do as you please with that; you have the right to crush it, to tear out that, to tread that under foot,—yes, you have the right to tear the name of Hubert to pieces, and to scrape up the hideous fragments in the mud.

"But do you know what you have no right to touch?—not a hair of his head."

I felt the hand of Ribeyrolles pressing mine.

"What MM. Hubert and Maupas have tried to do here is monstrous. To support a spy out of your poor-funds; to keep in the same pocket the police bank-note and the brotherly coins of the refugees; to throw our money in our eyes to blind us; to arrest the men who help us in France by the man we feed in Jersey; to pursue the proscribed in ambush; not to even leave the exile in peace; to attach the thread of an infamous plot to the holiest fibres of our heart; to betray us and rob us at the same time; to pick our pockets and sell us,—that is the snare in which we find the hands of the Imperial police.

"What have we to do? Publish the facts! Take France, Europe, the public conscience, universal probity to witness. Say to the whole world, It is infamous! Sad as the discovery may be, the occasion is fortunate. In this business the moral advantage lies with the proscribed, with the democracy, with the Republic. The situation is excellent. Do not let us spoil it!

"Do you know how we may spoil it? By misconceiving our rights, and behaving like the Venetians of the sixteenth century; instead of like Frenchmen of the nineteenth, in acting like the Council of Ten, in killing a man.

"In principle I am no more anxious about the death of a spy than of a parricide, I assure you. In fact, it is absurd!

"Touch this man, wound him, only beat him, and to-morrow the opinion that is with you will be against you. The English law will arrest you. From judges you will become the accused. M. Hubert gone, M. de Maupas gone, and what remains? You proscribed Frenchmen before a British jury.

"And instead of saying, 'Look at the baseness of that police,' they will say, 'Look at the brutality of those demagogues.'

"Citizens," I added, extending my arms towards Hubert. "I take this man under my protection, not for the man's sake, but for the Republic. I oppose any one who will do him harm now or in the future, here or elsewhere. I sum up your rights in a word: Publish, do not kill! Punishment by publicity, not by violence. A deed in open day, not by night. The skin of Hubert! Great God, what is *it* worth? What can you do with the skin of a spy? I declare no one shall touch Hubert, no one shall ill-treat him. To poniard M. Hubert would be to disgrace the poniard. To whip M. Hubert would only sully the whip."

These words, which I reproduce from memory, were listened to with profound attention and increasing adhesion at each moment. When I reseated myself the question was decided. To tell the truth, I did not think Hubert was in any danger during the sitting; but the morrow might have been fatal.

When I seated myself I distinctly heard a refugee behind me, named Fillion, who had escaped from Africa, say, "That is it. The spy is saved. We should act and not talk. That will teach us to chatter!"

These words were drowned in a general cry of "No violence! Publish the facts, appeal to public opinion, hold the police and Hubert up to execration; that is what we'll do."

Claude, Durand, Bulier, Rattier, Ribeyrolles, Cahaigne congratulated me warmly. Hubert looked at me with a mournful gaze. The sitting had been as it were suspended after my speech. The proscribed of the terrorist school looked at me angrily.

Fillion came up to me and said, "You are right. From the moment they had spoken nothing was more likely. Is it necessary that when you execute a traitor you should proclaim the fact on the house-tops? We are sixty here, fifty-six too many. Four would suffice. In Africa we had a similar case. We discovered that a man named Auguste Thomas was a detective—an old Republican too—and in every plot for the past twenty years. We had proofs of the facts at nine P. M. Next day the man had disappeared, without any one knowing what had become of him. That is the way those things should be managed."

As I was about to reply to Fillion the business was resumed. Cahaigne raised his voice and said, "Seat yourselves, citizens. You have heard Citizen Victor Hugo. What he proposes is moral punishment."

"Yes, yes. Very good," exclaimed a multitude of voices.

Cauvet, the man who had interrupted me, moved upon the table on which he was seated.

"*Parbleu!* that is beautiful, a moral punishment, and you will let him off! To-morrow he will go to France to denounce and sell all our friends. We ought to kill the cur!"

This was one great objection. Hubert at liberty was dangerous.

Beauvais interfered.

"There is no need to kill him, and you need not let him go. I have kept Hubert since April, and lodged him for almost nothing. I was willing to help a refugee, but not to feed a spy. Now M. de Maupas must pay me M. Hubert's expenses,—eighty-three francs. To-morrow morning M. Asplet shall arrest M. Hubert and drop him into prison for debt, at least, unless he produces the bank-notes which M. de Maupas gave him. I shall be glad to see them."

There was laughter at this. Beauvais had in fact settled the question.

"Yes," cried Vincent, "but he will be off to-morrow morning."

"We will guard him," said Boni.

"Search him," cried Fombertaux.

"Yes, yes, search the spy."

A number of men precipitated themselves on Hubert.

"You have neither the right to guard him nor search him. To guard him is to curtail his liberty, to search him is to assault him."

The searching moreover was senseless. It was evident that Hubert, since the investigation, had nothing compromising about him.

Hubert cried, "Let them search me; I consent to it."

This was a little astonishing.

"He consents," they cried. "He consents. Let us search him."

I stopped them, and asked Hubert, "Do you consent?"

"Yes."

"You must give your consent in writing."

"I am quite willing."

Jarassé wrote the consent, and Hubert signed it. Meantime he was being searched, for they had not the patience to wait for the signature.

His pockets were emptied and turned out. Nothing was found except a few coppers, his large handkerchief, and a piece of the "Jersey Chronicle."

"His shoes—search his shoes."

Hubert pulled off his shoes, and put them on the table.

"There was nothing in them," he said, "but the feet of a Republican."

Cahaigne then spoke. He put my proposition, and it was adopted *nem. con.*

While the proposition was being signed, Hubert had put on his shoes and his hat, he had taken up his pipe, and seemed as if he wanted some one to give him a light.

At this moment Cauvet approached him and said, in a low voice, "Would you like a pistol?"

Hubert made no answer.

"Would you like a pistol?" repeated Cauvet.

Hubert kept silence. Cauvet began again: "'I have a pistol at home, a good one. Will you have it?"

Hubert shrugged his shoulders and pushed the table with his elbows.

"Will you?" said Cauvet.

"Leave me alone," said Hubert.

"You don't want my pistol?"

"No."

"Then shake hands."

And Cauvet, quite drunk, held out his hand to Hubert, who did not take it.

Meanwhile I was talking with Cahaigne, who said to me, "You have done well to put them off, but I am afraid that to-morrow their anger will break out again, in two or three like Avias, and that they will kill him in some corner or other."

I had not signed the deposition. All had signed except me.

Heurtebise handed me the pen.

"I will sign it in three days," I said.

"Why?" asked several.

"Because I am afraid of blows. I will sign in three days, when I shall be sure that the threats have not been carried out, and that no ill has come to Hubert."

They shouted on all sides, "Sign, sign; we will not harm him."

"You will guarantee it?"

"We promise you."

I signed.

Half an hour after I reached home; it was six o'clock A.M. The sea-breeze whistled about the Rocher des Proscrits.

The first rays of dawn were lighting up the sky. Some little silver clouds played amid the stars.

At the same hour M. Asplet, directed by Beauvais, arrested Hubert, and put him in prison for debt.

On the morning of October 21, about six o'clock, Sieur Lament, who is French vice-consul here, came to M. Asplet's house. He came, he said, to claim a Frenchman illegally imprisoned.

"For debt," replied M. Asplet. He then produced the order of arrest signed by the deputy, Viscomte M. Horman.

"Will you pay the amount?" said M. Asplet.

The consul bowed and went away.

It seems to be Hubert's destiny to be fed at the refugees' expense. At this moment they are keeping him in his prison at an expense of sixpence a day.

Looking over my papers, I found a letter from Hubert. There is in this letter a sad phrase: "Hunger is a bad counsellor!"

So Hubert has been hungry.

The Ninety-Four Thousand Franc Fraud

July, 1847.

ON the evening of the day when the judicial committee of Peers determined to prosecute M. Teste, Minister of Public Works, chance willed it that the chancellor had to go to Neuilly with the Bureau of the Chamber to present to the king a bill which had been passed.

The chancellor and the Peers of the Bureau (among whom was Count Daru) found the king in a furious state of mind. He had been informed of the prosecution of M. Teste. Immediately he caught sight of them he advanced towards them with rapid strides.

"What! Chancellor," he said, "was not one of my former ministers enough for you? Must you have a second? You have taken Teste now. So that after I have spent seventeen years in

France in setting up authority once more, in one day, in one hour, you have allowed it to be cast down again. You destroy the whole work of my reign. You debase authority, power, the government. And you do that,—you, the chancellor of the House of Peers!" *et cetera.*

The squall was a violent one. The chancellor was very firm. He resolutely refused to give in to the king. He said that, doubtless, policy was to be considered, but that it was necessary also to listen to justice; that the Chamber of Peers also had its independence as a legislative power, and its sovereignty as a judicial power; that this independence and sovereignty must be respected, and if need be, would make themselves respected; that, moreover, in the present state of opinion, it would have been a very serious matter to refuse satisfaction to it; that it would be doing an injury to the country and to the king not to do what this opinion demanded, and what justice required; that there were times when it was more prudent to advance than to retreat; and that finally what had been done was done. "And well done," added Daru. "We shall see," said the king.

And from anger he relapsed into uneasiness.

July 8.

Half-past twelve. The Court enters. A crowd in the galleries. No one in the reserved galleries except Colonel Poizat, governor of the Palace. In the diplomatic galleries two persons only,— Lord Normanby, the English ambassador, and Count de Lœvenhœlm, the Swedish minister.

The accused are brought in. Three tables, with a green baize covering, have been placed facing the Court, to each of these tables there is a chair, and at the back is a bench for the counsel. President Teste sits down at the middle table, General Cubières at the right-hand table, Parmentier at the left-hand table. All three are dressed in black.

Parmentier entered some time after the two Peers. Teste, who is commander of the Legion of Honour, has the rosette of the decoration in his button-hole; Cubières, who is a Grand Officer, the plain ribbon. Before sitting down, the general converses with his counsel, then turns over, with a very busy air, the volume of documents relating to the case. He wears his ordinary look. Teste is pale and calm. He rubs his hands like a man who is pleased. Parmentier is stout, bald, has white hair, a red face, a hooked nose, a mouth like a sabre-cut, thin lips; the appearance of a rascal. He wears a white tie, as does also President Teste. The general wears a black cravat. The three defendants do not look at each other. Parmentier casts his eyes down, and affects to be playing with the gold chain of his watch, which he displays with the ostentation of a country bumpkin against his black waistcoat. A young man with a thin black moustache, who is said to be his son, is seated at his left.

Being questioned as to his position in life, Teste rises and says, "I thought it would not be seemly to bring to this bar the honours which I have had conferred upon me." (Visible impression on the Court.) "I placed them yesterday in the hands of the king." (This makes a manifest favourable impression.)

The indictment is read. It sets forth the following facts:—

Parmentier, Director of the Mines of Gouhenans, alleges that he remitted to General Cubières ninety-four thousand francs for the purpose of obtaining from M. Teste, Minister of Public Works, a grant of a salt-mine. M. Teste emphatically denies having received this sum. Parmentier is quite ready to believe that it was intercepted and that he was thus defrauded of it either by M. Cubières or another shareholder in the mines, M. Pellapra, who, it appears, acted as a go-between from the general to M. Teste. Parmentier is accused of corruption; Cubières and Pellapra of corruption and fraud; Teste of "having received gifts and presents to perform an act of his duty not subject to payment."

Pellapra has fled. Cubières, Teste, and Parmentier appear.

While the indictment is being read Cubières hides his face and forehead in his left hand, and follows the reading of the volume which has been circulated. Teste also follows it, and annotates his copy with a steel pen. He has put on his eye-glasses. From time to time he takes snuff out of a great boxwood snuffbox, and converses with his counsel, M. Paillet. Parmentier appears very attentive.

July 10.

This is what I can make out of it after the two first days.

I have spoken to General Cubières four or five times in my life, and to President Teste once only, and yet, in this affair, I am as much interested in their fate as though they were friends of mine of twenty years' standing. Why? I will say at once. It is because I believe them to be innocent.

I "believe" is not strong; I see them to be innocent. This view may, perhaps, be modified, for this affair changes like the waves, and alters its aspect from one moment to another; but at the present time, after much perplexity, after many transitions, after many painful intervals, in which I have more than once trembled and shuddered in my conscience, I am convinced that General Cubières is innocent of the act of fraud, that President Teste is innocent of the act of corruption.

What is this affair, then? To my mind, it resumes itself in two words,— commission and black-mail; commission deducted by Pellapra, black-mail extorted by Parmentier. A commission, tainted with fraud and swindling, was the cause of the first act alleged in the indictment; black-mail was the cause of the scandal. Hence the whole case.

I have no leaning towards guilt which is not invincibly proved to me. My inclination is to believe in innocence. As long as there remains in the probabilities of a case a possible refuge for the innocence of the accused, all my theories, I will not say incline, but precipitate themselves towards it.

Sunday, July 11.

An adjournment takes place over today. The second and third hearings were devoted to the examination of the accused.

At the opening of Friday's sitting were read communications which had been unexpectedly made by Messrs. Léon de Malleville and Marrast, and which appear to throw a strong light upon this trial. The defendants entered the Court pale and dejected, Parmentier, however, with more assurance than the others. M. Teste listened to the reading of the new documents, while leaning his elbow upon the table and half hiding his face in his hand; General Cubières, with his eyes cast downward; Parmentier with perceptible embarrassment.

The examination began with the general.

M. Cubières has a doll-like face, an undecided look, a hesitating manner of speaking, red cheeks; I believe him to be innocent of fraud; however, I am not deeply impressed with him. During the examination he stood up, and gently beat a tattoo upon the table with the tip of a wooden paper-knife with a look of profound ease. The procurator-general, M. Delangle, a rather commonplace lawyer, treated him once or twice with insolence; Cubières, a Waterloo man, did not venture to say a word in return to make his ears tingle. I felt for him. In the opinion of the Court he is already convicted.

The first part of the examinaton was badly conducted. There was but one expression of opinion at the refreshment-bar. The chancellor is a remarkable veteran,—out of the common,—but then, he is eighty-two years of age; at eighty-two years of age one cannot face either a woman or a crowd.

Parmentier, interrogated by the general, spoke with ease and a sort of vulgar glibness which was sometimes witty, at others shrewd, skilful throughout, never eloquent. He is a man who, to tell the truth, is a scoundrel. He is not aware of it himself. This shameless creature has a twist in his mind, and exposes his nakedness just as Venus would do. A toad who fancies he is beautiful is a repulsive spectacle. He was hissed. At first he either did not hear, or did not understand; however, he ended by understanding; then the perspiration stood in beads upon his face. Every now and then, amid the marks of disgust of the assemblage, he nervously wiped the streaming surface of his bald head, looked about him with a certain air of entreaty and bewilderment, feeling that he was lost, and trying to recover himself. Yet he continues to speak, and to expose his mental defects, while low tones of indignation drowned his utterances, and his anguish increased. At this moment I felt pity for the wretched man.

M. Teste who was examined yesterday, spoke like an innocent man; frequently he was exceedingly eloquent. He was not an advocate; he was a real man, who suffered, who tore out his very vitals and exposed them to view before his judges, saying, "See there!" He profoundly impressed me. While he spoke, a light broke in upon me that this whole affair might be explained by a fraud committed by Pellapra.

Teste is sixty-seven years of age; he has a southern accent, a large and expressive mouth, a tall forehead, giving him a look of intelligence, the eyes deep set and at times sparkling; his whole bodily activity overwhelmed and crushed, but he is energetic withal. He moved about, started, shrugged his shoulders, smiled bitterly, took snuff, turned over his papers, annotated them rapidly, held in check the procurator-general or the chancellor, shielded Cubières, who is his ruin, showed his contempt for Parmentier, who defends him, threw out notes, interruptions, replies, complaints, shouts. He was turbulent, yet ingenuous; overcome with emotion, yet dignified. He was clear, rapid, persuasive, supplicating, menacing, full of anguish without any trepidation, moderate and violent, haughty and tearful. At one point he powerfully affected me. His very soul found expression in the cries which he uttered. I was tempted to rise and say to him, "You have convinced me; I will leave my seat and take up my position on the bench at your side; will you let me be your counsel?" And then I restrained myself, thinking that if his innocence continued to be made manifest to me, I should perhaps be more useful to him as a judge among his judges.

Pellapra is the pivot on which the case turns. Teste appears sincerely grieved at his flight. If Pellapra returns, all will be clear. I ardently hope that Teste is innocent, and that, if innocent, he will be saved.

At the rising of the Court, I followed him with my eyes as he went out. He slowly and sadly crossed the benches of the Peers, looking to right and left upon these chairs, which perhaps he will never occupy again. Two ushers, who guarded him, walked one in front of him, and the other behind him.

July 12.

The aspect of the case has suddenly changed. Some fresh documents are terribly incriminating to Teste. Cubières rises, and confirms the authenticity and importance of these documents. Teste replies haughtily and energetically, but for all that his confidence diminishes. His mouth contracts. I feel uneasy about him. I begin to tremble for fear he has been deceiving us all. Parmentier listens, almost with a smile, and with his arms carelessly folded. Teste sits down again, and takes an immense number of pinches of snuff out of his great boxwood snuffbox, then wipes the perspiration off his forehead with a red silk handkerchief. The Court is profoundly agitated.

"I can imagine what he suffers by what I suffer myself," M. de Pontécoulant said to me. "What torture it is!" said General Neigre. "It is a slow guillotine stroke," said Bertin de Vaux. Apprehension is at its height among the members of the Court and the public. All are anxious not to lose one word. The Peers cry out to those who address them, "Speak up! Speak up! We cannot hear." The chancellor begs the Court to consider his great age.

The heat is insupportable.

The stock-broker Goupil gives his evidence. Teste makes a desperate struggle.

M. Charles Dupin questions the stock-broker. Teste follows him with his eyes, and applauds him with a smile. Anything more doleful than this smile could not be imagined.

On this occasion the private conference was held before the sitting in the old Chamber. The Peers buzzed like a swarm of bees. The chancellor came to the bench on which I was seated, and spoke to me of matters connected with the Académie; then of the trial, of his feeling of fatigue and grief; saying how pleasant was a meeting of the Académie after a sitting of the Court of Peers.

In his evidence M. Legrand, Undersecretary of State for Public Works, described Teste as "a person who is sitting behind me." Teste shrugged his shoulders.

After the serious evidence of the notary Roquebert, the face of Teste assumes an agonized expression.

At the production of the document for the Treasury he turned red, wiped his forehead in anguish, and turned towards his son. They exchanged a few words; then Teste began once more to turn his papers, and the son buried his head in his hands.

In one hour Teste has aged ten years; his head moves, his lower lip twitches. Yesterday he was a lion; to-day he is a booby.

Everything in this affair moves by fits and starts. Yesterday I *saw* that Teste was innocent, to-day I see that he is guilty. Yesterday I admired him, to-day I should be tempted to despise him were he not so miserable. But I no longer feel anything but pity for him.

This trial was one of the most terrible spectacles which I have ever witnessed in my life. It is a moral dismemberment.

That which our forefathers saw eighty years ago in the Place de Grève, on the day of the execution of Damiens, we have seen to-day, on the day of the execution of President Teste in the Court of Peers. We have seen a man tortured with hot irons and dismembered in the spirit. Every hour, every minute, something was torn from him: at twelve o'clock his distinction as a magistrate; at one o'clock his reputation as an upright minister; at two o'clock his conscience as an honest man; half an hour later, the respect of others; a quarter of an hour afterwards, his own self-respect. In the end, he was but a corpse. It lasted for six hours.

For my own part, as I said to the Chief President Legagneur, I doubt whether I should ever have the hardihood, even were Teste convicted and guilty, to add any punishment whatever to this unparalleled chastisement, to this frightful torment.

July 13.

As I entered the cloak-room Viscount Lemercier, who was there, said to me, "Have you heard the news?" "No." "Teste has attempted to commit suicide, and failed."

The fact is as stated. M. Teste, yesterday evening, at nine o'clock, fired two pistol-shots at himself; he fired two shots simultaneously, one with each hand. One he aimed in his mouth, and the cap missed fire; the other at his heart, and the bullet rebounded, the shot being fired from too close a distance.

The chancellor read in the private conference the official documents detailing the occurrence; they were afterwards re-read at the public sitting. The pistols were deposited upon the table of the Court. They were two very little pistols, quite new, with ivory handles.

Teste, not having succeeded in destroying himself, refuses henceforth to appear before the Court. He has written to the chancellor a letter in which he abandons his defence, "the documents produced yesterday leaving no room for contradiction." This is the language of an advocate, not of a man; a man would have said, "I am guilty."

When we entered the Court, M. Dupin the elder, who was seated behind me on the Deputies' bench, said to me, "Guess what book Teste sent for to kill time with?" "I do not know." "'Monte-Cristo!' 'Not the first four volumes,' he said, 'I have read them.' 'Monte-Cristo' was not to be found in the library of the House of Peers. It had to be borrowed from a public reading-room, which only had it in periodical parts. Teste spends his time in reading these parts."

My neighbour, the Duke of Brancas, who is a kind and worthy veteran, says to me, "Do not oppose the condemnation. It is God's justice which will be done."

Yesterday evening, when General Cubières was informed that Teste had fired two pistol-shots at himself, he wept bitterly.

I note that to-day is a fatal day,—the 13th of July. The seat lately occupied by Teste is empty at the sitting. The clerk of the court, La Chauvinière, reads the indictment. M. Cubières listens with an air of profound sadness, then hides his face in his hand. Parmentier holds his head down the whole time. The events of yesterday—the attempted suicide of Teste and his letter to the chancellor—destroy in its very foundations the abominable lines of defence of Parmentier.

At ten minutes past one the Procurator-general Delangle rises to address the Court. He twice repeats, amid the painful impression which prevails, "Messieurs les Pairs"—then stops short, and continues "The trial is ended." The procurator-general spoke only for ten minutes.

It is a curious fact that Teste and Delangle have all their lives been brought into close association, Delangle following Teste, and in the end prosecuting him. Teste was the *bâtonnier* of the bar; Delangle held the office immediately after him. Teste was appointed president of the Court of Cassation; Delangle entered the same court as advocate-general. Teste is accused, Delangle is procurator-general.

I now understand the meaning of the movement of the father and son which I noticed yesterday at the moment of the production of the document from the Treasury; the father said to the son, "Give me the pistols." The son handed them to him, and then sank his head in his hands. It is in this way, I think, the sombre tragedy must have happened.

At the opening of the sitting the chancellor reads a letter, in which Cubières resigns his position as a Peer

The question is put as to whether the accused are guilty.

"Is Cubières guilty of fraud?" Unanimously "No."

Upon the question of corruption:—

"Is Teste guilty?" Unanimously "Yes."

"Is Cubières guilty?" Unanimously, with the exception of three votes, "Yes

"Is Parmentier guilty?" Unanimously "Yes."

Sentences:—

Teste is sentenced to civil degradation unanimously, with the exception of one vote.

Upon the question of the fines, I rose in my turn, and said, "I desire to punish a guilty man; I do not desire to punish a family,—that is to say, innocent persons. The restitution of the money received, to my mind, would be sufficient. No fine. My lords, the example is not in a fine; the example is in the terrible things which you have seen; the example is in the terrible act to which you have just committed yourselves. A fine deteriorates the example. It places a question of money in the place of a question of honour."

Teste was condemned to pay a fine of ninety-four thousand francs.

At half-past six a fresh letter from General Cubières is read, in which he states that he has requested that he may be placed on the retired list. The unhappy man throws something overboard at every moment.

July 15.

At half-past twelve the calling of the names takes place. The Court is profoundly and painfully agitated. The law officials claim the whole law, the whole penalty, against Cubières; the nobles are more humane.

The Court proceeds to pass sentence.

Upon the question whether Teste should be imprisoned, I said, "My lords, the guilty man has already been sufficiently punished. At the present moment he is sixty-seven years of age; in five years he will be seventy-two. I will not add one word. No imprisonment!"

Teste is sentenced to three years' imprisonment.

Respecting Cubières and the penalty of civic degradation, when my turn came, I said, "I feel that the Court is weary, and I am suffering myself from a feeling of agitation which unsettles me; I rise notwithstanding. I have studied, as you have, my lords, with whatever intelligence and power of attention I may have, the whole of the indictment in this deplorable case. I have examined facts. I have contrasted persons. I have endeavoured to penetrate not only into the heart of the case, but into the hearts of these men you are trying at this moment. Well, this is the conclusion I have arrived at: In my opinion, General Cubières was led astray,—led astray by Pellapra, defrauded by Parmentier. Under these circumstances, there has been, I acknowledge, weakness,—a weakness censurable, inexcusable, gravely culpable even, but after all only weakness; and weakness is not baseness, and I do not wish to punish weakness with infamy. I will avow, and the Court will pardon this avowal, that during the many hours that this unfortunate affair has occupied our minds I imagined that you were going to render an altogether different decision in your all-powerful and sovereign justice. I should have wished to leave in his terrible isolation the painful and conspicuous figure of the principal defendant. This man, who, by dint of talent, has contrived—a miracle which, for my part, I should always have thought impossible—to be great in his abasement and touching in his shame; this man I should have liked to punish simply with civic degradation. And I should have wished to add nothing to this fearful penalty; in such a case that which increases diminishes. For the weak and unfortunate General Cubières, I should have wished a sentence of deprivation, for a certain period of time, of the civic and civil rights mentioned in Article 401. And finally, for the men of money, I should have wished money penalties; for the miscreants, humiliating penalties; for Parmentier, fine and imprisonment. For these men of such diversity of guilt I should have wished for a diversity of penalties, which your omnipotence would permit you to decree, and the observance of this proportion between the misdeeds and the punishments appeared to me to be in accordance with conscience, and I will add,—although that concerns me less,—in accordance with public opinion. In your wisdom you have judged otherwise. I bow to it, but I beg of you, nevertheless, to approve my remaining of the same opinion. In an assembly in which there are so many men of importance who have occupied, or who will yet occupy, the highest functions in the State and the government, I appreciate, I honour, I respect that noble feeling of outraged decency which leads you to inflict unusually heavy penalties at this juncture, and to afford not only the most just but also the most cruel satisfaction to public opinion. I, gentlemen, am not a lawyer, I am not a soldier, I am not a public functionary, I am an ordinary tax-payer; I am a member, like any one else, of the great crowd from which emanates that public opinion to which you defer; and it is for this, it is because I am simply this, that I am perhaps qualified to say to you, Enough! Stop! Go as far as the limits of justice; do not overstep them. The example has been set. Do not destroy that isolation of the condemned man Teste, which is the grand aspect, the grand moral lesson of the trial. As long as it was a question only of this unhappy man, I spoke to you merely in the language of pity; I speak to you now in the language of equity, solemn and austere equity. I conjure you, give credit to General Cubières for his sixty years of honourable life, give credit to him for the agony he has suffered for those four years of torture which he endured at the villainous hands of Parmentier, for this public exposure upon that bench during the four days; give credit to him for that unjust accusation of fraud, which was also a torture to him; give credit to him for his generous hesitation to save himself by ruining Teste; give credit to him, finally, for his heroic conduct upon the battle-field of Waterloo, where I regret that he did not remain. I formally propose to sentence M. Cubières to the penalty provided by Article 401, together with Article 42; that is to say, to a suspension of civil and civic rights for ten years. I vote against civic degradation."

At seven o'clock there still remain eighty Peers who have not voted. The chancellor proposes an adjournment until the morrow. Objections are made: An adjournment while the voting is taking place! M. Cauchy reads precedent from the Quénisset trial. Uproar. The adjournment is carried.

July 16.
Continuation of the voting upon the question of the penalty to be inflicted upon General Cubières.

The penalty of civic degradation is carried by 130 votes to 48.

He is condemned besides to a fine of ten thousand francs.

No imprisonment.

It appears that the decision in favour of inflicting the penalty of civic degradation upon General Cubières, which has just been arrived at, has reached the prison. Just now I heard in the street the dreadful cries of Madame de Cubières and Madame de Sampays, her sister, who were with the general at the moment when the news was communicated to him.

July 17.
Sentence upon Parmentier.

Upon the question of civic degradation I said, "I should have wished, as the Court is aware, in order that a great example might be made, that President Teste should have been left in his degrading isolation, alone under the burden of civic degradation." The Court did not agree with me; it thought proper to associate with him General Cubières. I cannot do otherwise than associate with him Parmentier. I vote for civic degradation, while profoundly regretting that I am obliged, after this great social and public penalty has been inflicted upon two ex-Ministers, upon two Peers of France, to whom it is everything, to inflict it upon this wretch to whom it is nothing.

Parmentier is condemned to civic degradation and a fine of ten thousand francs. No imprisonment.

As we were about to leave, and were in the cloak-room, Anatole de Montesquiou, who constantly voted in the most lenient sense, pointed out to me, in the second compartment of the cloakroom near that in which I am putting on my things, an old Peer's robe hanging at the side of the robe of the Minister of Public Instruction. This robe is worn at the elbows, the gilt of the buttons is rubbed off, the embroidery faded; an old ribbon of the Legion of Honour is in the button-hole, more yellow than red, and half untied. Above this coat was written, according to the custom, the name of him to whom it belonged: "M. Teste."

My opinion is that the public will consider the decree of the Court of Peers just in the case of Teste, harsh in that of Cubières, and lenient in that of Parmentier.

At half-past four the doors were thrown open to the public. An immense crowd had been waiting since the morning. In a moment the galleries were noisily filled. It was like a wave. Then profound silence when the calling of the names began. The Peers replied, generally speaking, in a barely audible and weary tone of voice.

Then the chancellor put on his shaped hat of black velvet lined with ermine, and read the decree. The procurator-general was at his post. The chancellor read the decree in a firm tone, very remarkable in an old man of eighty years of age. Whatever may have been said by certain newspapers, he did not shed "silent tears."

The judgment will be read presently by the Chief Clerk of the Court to the condemned men.

It will be just a month ago tomorrow, the 18th, that Teste was arraigned by the judicial committee of the Peers, and that he said to them, "I thank you for placing me in a position which gives me the precious privilege of defending myself."

July 21.

It is a curious fact that M. Teste, who, as Minister of Public Works, had this Luxembourg prison built, is the first minister who has been confined in it. This reminds one of the gibbet of Montfaucon, and of Enguerrand de Marigny.

M. Teste occupies in this prison an apartment separated only by a partition from the apartment of General Cubières. The partition is so thin that, as M. Teste speaks loudly, Mme. de Cubières was obliged on the first day to tap upon the wall to warn M. Teste that she heard all he said. The pistol-shot, too, made General Cubières start as though it had been fired in his own apartment.

The sitting of the 12th had been so decisive that some act of desperation was thought probable. During the very sitting the Duke Decazes had had iron bars put to the windows of the prisoners. They found these bars in the windows on coming back, but did not feel any surprise on seeing them. They also had their razors taken from them, and had to dine without knives.

Policemen were to remain day and night by their side. However, it was thought that M. Teste might be left alone with his son and the counsel who were defending him. He dined with them almost in silence,—a remarkable fact, for he was a great talker. The little he did say was concerning matters foreign to the trial. At nine o'clock the son and the barristers retired. The policeman who was to watch M. Teste received orders to go up directly. It was during the few minutes which elapsed between the departure of his son and the entrance of the policeman that M. Teste made his attempt to commit suicide.

Many persons had doubted whether this attempt was seriously intended. This was the tone of the comments in the Chamber. M. Delessert, the prefect of police, whom I questioned on this subject, told me there could be no doubt about it that M. Teste had tried to kill himself in downright good earnest, but he believes that only one pistol-shot was fired.

After his condemnation, General Cubières received many visits; the sentence of the Court missed its mark by reason of its excessive severity. The general's visitors, in going to his cell, passed before that of Parmentier, which was only closed with a door having, instead of a glass pane, a white curtain, through which he could be seen. All of them in passing by loaded Parmentier with terms of contempt, which obliged the fellow to hide in a corner where he was no longer visible.

During the trial the heat was intense. At every moment the chancellor had to summon back the Peers who went off to the refreshment-bars or the lobbies.

Lord Normanby did not miss a single sitting.

July 22.

The name of Teste has already been removed from his seat in the House of Peers. It is General Achard now who occupies his chair.

Yesterday, Tuesday, the 21st of July, as I was proceeding from the Académie to the House of Peers, towards four o'clock, I met near the exit of the Institute, in the most deserted part of the Rue Mazarin, Parmentier coming out of prison. He was going in the direction of the Quay. His son accompanied him. Parmentier, dressed in black, carried his hat in his hand behind his back; with his other arm he leaned upon his son. The son had a downcast look. Parmentier appeared completely overwhelmed. He had the appearance of exhaustion,—of a man who has just come from a long walk. His bald head seemed to bend beneath his shame. They were walking slowly.

It was stated to-day at the Chamber that Madame de Cubières gave a *soirée* two days after the condemnation. It appears that in reality she simply contented herself with not shutting her door. She has just written to the newspapers a letter, which will not do her husband much good, but in which there is nevertheless one fine passage, as follows: "He has had his peerage, his rank, everything taken from him, even to his dignity as a citizen. He retains his wounds."

The chancellor offered to let M. de Cubières leave the prison by one of the private gates of the chancellor's official residence in the Luxembourg. A hired conveyance would have awaited M. de Cubières, and he would have got in without being seen by any one in the street. M. de Cubières refused. An open carriage, drawn by two horses, came and took up its position at the gate-way of the Rue de Vaugerard, in the midst of the crowd. M. de Cubières got into it, accompanied by his wife and Madame de Sampays, and this is how he came out of prison. Since then he has had, every evening, more than a hundred visitors. There are always some forty carriages at his door.

Ninety-Three

PART I.—AT SEA

BOOK I

THE WOOD OF LA SAUDRAIE

IN the latter part of May, 1793, one of the Paris battalions sent into Brittany by Santerre, searched the much dreaded forest of La Saudraie, in Astillé. There were only about three hundred men in the reconnoitring party, for the battalion had been well-nigh annihilated in the fierce conflicts in which it had engaged.

It was after the battles of Argonne, Jemappes, and Valmy, and of the First Paris Regiment, which consisted originally of six hundred volunteers, only twenty-seven men remained, of the Second Regiment only thirty-three, of the Third only fifty-seven. It was unquestionably a time of epic strife.

Each of the battalions sent from Paris to the Vendée numbered nine hundred and twelve men, and was provided with three field-pieces. The force had been very hastily organized. On the 25th of April,—Gohier being minister of Justice, and Bouchotte minister of war,—the Committee of Public Welfare urged the necessity of immediately dispatching a large body of troops to Vendée. Lubin, a member of the Commune, reported the bill favourably; and on the 1st of May, Santerre had twelve thousand men, thirty cannon, and a corps of gunners ready for the field.

These battalions, though organized so hurriedly, were organized so well that they serve as models even at the present day. Regiments of the Line are yet organized in the same manner; the relative proportion between the number of soldiers and non-commissioned officers has been changed,—that is all.

On the 28th of April, the Commune of Paris gave Santerre's volunteers this order: "No mercy; no quarter." By the end of May, of the twelve thousand men that left Paris, eight thousand were dead.

The troops who were exploring the forest of La Saudraie held themselves on the alert. They advanced slowly and cautiously. Each man cast furtive glances to the right and to the left of him, in front of him and behind him. It was Kléber who said: "A soldier has one eye in his back." They had been marching a long while. What time of day could it be? It was difficult to say, for a dim twilight always pervades these dense forests. It is never really light there.

The forest of La Saudraie was tragic. It was in its copses that, from the month of November, 1792, civil war commenced its crimes. Mousqueton, the ferocious cripple, came out of its fatal shades. The list of murders that had been committed there was enough to make one's hair stand on end. There was no place more to be dreaded. The soldiers moved cautiously forward. The depths were full of flowers; on each side was a trembling wall of branches and dew-wet leaves. Here and there rays of sunlight pierced the green shadows. The gladiola, that flame of the marshes, the meadow narcissus, the little wood daisy, harbinger of spring, and the vernal crocus, embroidered the thick carpet of vegetation, crowded with every form of moss, from that resembling velvet (*chenille*) to that which looks like a star. The soldiers advanced in silence, step by step, pushing the brushwood softly aside. The birds twittered above the bayonets.

In former peaceable times La Saudraie was a favourite place for the *Houicheba*, the hunting of birds by night; now they hunted men there.

The thicket was one of birch-trees, beeches, and oaks; the ground flat; the thick moss and grass deadened the sound of the men's steps; there were no paths, or only blind ones, which quickly disappeared among the holly, wild sloes, ferns, hedges of rest-harrow, and high brambles. It would have been impossible to distinguish a man ten steps off.

Now and then a heron or a moor-hen flew through the branches, indicating the neighbourhood of marshes.

They pushed forward. They went at random, with uneasiness, fearing to find that which they sought.

From time to time they came upon traces of encampments,—burned spots, trampled grass, sticks arranged crosswise, branches stained with blood. Here soup had been made; there, Mass had been said; yonder, they had dressed wounds. But all human beings had disappeared. Where were they? Very far off, perhaps; perhaps quite near, hidden, blunderbuss in hand. The wood seemed deserted. The regiment redoubled its prudence. Solitude — hence distrust. They saw no one; so much more reason for fearing some one. They had to do with a forest with a bad name. An ambush was probable.

Thirty grenadiers, detached as scouts, and commanded by a sergeant, marched at a considerable distance in front of the main body. The vivandière of the battalion accompanied them. The vivandières willingly join the vanguard; they run risks, but they have the chance of seeing whatever happens. Curiosity is one of the forms of feminine bravery.

Suddenly the soldiers of this little advance party started like hunters who have neared the hiding-place of their prey. They had heard something like a breathing from the centre of a thicket, and seemed to perceive a movement among the branches. The soldiers made signals.

In the species of watch and search confided to scouts, the officers have small need to interfere; the right thing seems done by instinct.

In less than a minute the spot where the movement had been noticed was surrounded; a line of pointed muskets encircled it; the obscure centre of the thicket was covered on all sides at the same instant; the soldiers, finger on trigger, eye on the suspected spot, only waited for the sergeant's order. Notwithstanding this, the vivandière ventured to peer through the underbrush, and at the moment when the sergeant was about to cry, "Fire!" this woman cried, "Halt!"

Turning toward the soldiers, she added, "Do not fire, comrades!"

She plunged into the thicket; the men followed.

There was, in truth, some one there.

In the thickest of the brake, on the edge of one of those little round clearings left by the fires of the charcoal-burners, in a sort of recess among the branches, a kind of chamber of foliage, half open like an alcove, a woman was seated on the moss, holding to her breast a nursing babe, while the fair heads of two sleeping children rested on her knees.

This was the ambush.

"What are you doing here, you?" cried the vivandière.

The woman lifted her head.

The vivandière added furiously:—

"Are you mad, that you are there? A little more and you would have been blown to pieces!"

Then she addressed herself to the soldiers,—

"It is a woman."

"Well, that is plain to be seen," said a grenadier.

The vivandière continued,—

"To come into the wood to get yourself massacred! The idea of such stupidity!"

The woman, stunned, petrified with fear, looked about like one in a dream at these guns, these sabres, these bayonets, these savage faces.

The two children awoke, and cried.

"I am hungry," said the first.

"I am afraid," said the other.

The baby was still suckling; the vivandière addressed it.

"You are in the right of it," said she.

The mother was dumb with terror. The sergeant cried out to her:—

"Do not be afraid; we are the battalion of the Bonnet Rouge."

The woman trembled from head to foot. She stared at the sergeant, of whose rough visage there was nothing visible but the moustaches, the brows, and two burning coals for eyes.

"Formerly the battalion of the Red Cross," added the vivandière.

The sergeant continued: "Who are you, madame?"

The woman scanned him, terrified. She was slender, young, pale, and in rags; she wore the large hood and woollen cloak of the Breton peasant, fastened about her neck by a string. She left her bosom exposed with the indifference of an animal. Her feet, shoeless and stockingless, were bleeding.

"It is a beggar," said the sergeant.

The vivandière began anew, in a voice at once soldierly and feminine, but sweet,—

"What is your name?"

The woman stammered so that she was scarcely intelligible.

"Michelle Fléchard."

The vivandière stroked the little head of the sleeping babe with her large hand.

"What is the age of this mite?" demanded she.

The mother did not understand. The vivandière persisted.

"I ask you, how old is it?"

"Ah!" said the mother; "eighteen months."

"It is old," said the vivandière; "it ought not to suckle any longer. You must wean it; we will give it soup."

The mother began to feel a certain confidence. The two children, who had awakened, were rather curious than scared. They admired the plumes of the soldiers.

"Ah," said the mother, "they are very hungry."

Then she added, "I have no more milk."

"We will give them something to eat," cried the sergeant; "and you too. But that's not all. What are your political opinions?"

The woman looked at him, but did not reply.

"Did you hear my question?"

She stammered,—

"I was put into a convent very young —but I am married—I am not a nun. The sisters taught me to speak French. The village was set on fire. We ran away so quickly that I had not time to put on my shoes."

"I ask you, what are your political opinions?"

"I don't know what that means."

The sergeant continued,—

"There are such things as female spies. We shoot spies. Come, speak! You are not a gipsy? Which is your side?"

She still looked at him as if she did not understand.

The sergeant repeated,—

"Which is your side?"

"I do not know," she said.

"How? You do not know your own country."

"Ah, my country! Oh, yes, I know that."

"Well, where is it?"

The woman replied,—

"The farm of Siscoignard, in the parish of Azé."

It was the sergeant's turn to be stupefied. He remained thoughtful for a moment, then resumed: "You say—"

"Siscoignard."

"That is not a country."

"It is my country," said the woman; and added, after an instant's reflection, "I understand, sir. You are from France; I belong to Brittany."

"Well?"

"It is not the same neighbourhood."

"But it is the same country," cried the sergeant.

The woman only repeated,—

"I am from Siscoignard."

"Siscoignard be it," returned the sergeant. "Your family belong there?"

"Yes."

"What is their occupation?"

"They are all dead; I have nobody left."

The sergeant, who thought himself a fine talker, continued his interrogatories:—

"What? the devil! One has relations, or one has had. Who are you? Speak."

The woman listened, astounded by this: *"Or one has had!"* which was more like the growl of an animal than any human sound.

The vivandière felt the necessity of interfering. She began again to caress the babe, and to pat the cheeks of the two other children.

"How do you call the baby?" she asked. "It is a little girl—this one?"

The mother replied, "Georgette."

"And the eldest fellow? For he is a man, the small rascal!"

"René-Jean."
"And the younger? He is a man, too, and chubby-faced into the bargain."
"Gros-Alain," said the mother.
"They are pretty little fellows," said the vivandière; "they already look as if they were somebody."
Still the sergeant persisted. "Now, speak, madame! Have you a house?"
"I had one."
"Where was it?"
"At Azé."
"Why are you not in your house?"
"Because they burned it."
"Who?"
"I do not know—a battle."
"Where did you come from?"
"From there."
"Where are you going?"
"I don't know."
"Get to the facts! Who are you?"
"I don't know."
"You don't know who you are?"
"We are people who are running away."
"What party do you belong to?"
"I don't know."
"Are you Blues? Are you Whites? Who are you with?"
"I am with my children."
There was a pause. The vivandière said,—
"As for me, I have no children; I have not had time."
The sergeant began again:—
"But your parents? See here, madame! give us the facts about your parents. My name is Radoub; I am a sergeant from the street of Cherche Midi; my father and mother belonged there. I can talk about my parents; tell us about yours. Who were they?"

"Their name was Fléchard,—that is all."
"Yes; the Fléchards are the Fléchards, just as the Radoubs are the Radoubs. But people have a calling. What was your parents' calling? What was their business, these Fléchards of yours?"
"They were labourers. My father was sickly, and could not work on account of a beating that the lord—his lord—our lord—had given to him. It was a kindness, for my father had poached a rabbit,—a thing for which one was condemned to death; but the lord showed him mercy, and said, 'You need only give him a hundred blows with a stick;' and my father was left crippled."
"And then?"
"My grandfather was a Huguenot. The curé had him sent to the galleys. I was very little at the time."
"And then?"
"My husband's father smuggled salt. The king had him hung."
"And your husband,—what did he do?"
"Lately, he fought."
"For whom?"
"For the king."
"And afterward?"
"Well, for his lordship."
"And next?"
"Well, then for the curé."
"A thousand names of brutes!" cried a grenadier.
The woman gave a start of terror.
"You see, madame, we are Parisians," said the vivandière, graciously.
The woman clasped her hands, and exclaimed,—
"O my God and blessed Lord!"

"No superstitious ejaculations!" growled the sergeant.

The vivandière seated herself by the woman, and drew the eldest child between her knees. He submitted quietly. Children show confidence as they do distrust, without any apparent reason; some internal monitor warns them.

"My poor, good woman of this neighbourhood," said the vivandière, "your brats are very pretty,—babies are always that. I can guess their ages. The big one is four years old; his brother is three. Upon my word! the little suckling poppet is a greedy one. Oh, the monster! Will you stop eating up your mother? See here, madame, do not be afraid. You ought to join the battalion. Do like me. I call myself Houzarde. It is a nickname; but I like Houzarde better than being called Mamzelle Bicorneau, like my mother. I am the canteen woman; that is the same as saying, 'she who offers drink when they are firing and stabbing.' Our feet are about the same size. I will give you a pair of my shoes. I was in Paris the 10th of August. I gave Westermann drink too. How things went! I saw Louis XVI. guillotined,—Louis Capet, as they call him. It was against his will. Only just listen, now! To think that the 13th of January he roasted chestnuts and laughed with his family. When they forced him down on the see-saw, as they say, he had neither coat nor shoes, nothing but his shirt, a quilted waistcoat, grey cloth breeches, and grey silk stockings. I saw that, I did! The hackney-coach they brought him in was painted green. See here! come with us; the battalion are good fellows. You shall be canteen number two; I will teach you the business. Oh, it is very simple! You have your can and your hand-bell; away you go into the hubbub, with the platoons firing, the cannon thundering,—into the thickest of the row; and you cry, 'Who'll have a drop to drink, my children?' It's no more trouble than that. I give everybody and anybody a sup, yes, indeed,—Whites the same as Blues, though I am a Blue myself, and a good Blue, too; but I serve them all alike. Wounded men are all thirsty. They die without any difference of opinions. Dying fellows ought to shake hands. How silly it is to go fighting! Do you come with us. If I am killed, you will step into my place. You see I am only so-so to look at; but I am a good woman, and a brave chap. Don't you be afraid."

When the vivandière ceased speaking, the woman murmured,—

"Our neighbour was called Marie Jeanne, and our servant was named Marie Claude."

In the mean time the sergeant reprimanded the grenadier:—

"Hold your tongue! You frighten madame. One does not swear before ladies."

"All the same; it is a downright butchery for an honest man to hear about," replied the grenadier; "and to see Chinese Iroquois, that have had their fathers-in-law crippled by a lord, their grandfathers sent to the galleys by the priest, and their fathers hung by the king, and who fight—name of the little Black Man!—and mix themselves up with revolts, and get smashed for his lordship, the priest, and the king!"

"Silence in the ranks!" cried the sergeant.

"A man may hold his tongue, Sergeant," returned the grenadier; "but that doesn't hinder the fact that it's a pity to see a pretty woman like this running the risk of getting her neck broken for the sake of a dirty robber."

"Grenadier," said the sergeant, "we are not in the Pike-club of Paris; no eloquence!"

He turned toward the woman.

"And your husband, madame? What is he at? What has become of him?"

"There hasn't anything become of him, because they killed him."

"Where did that happen?"

"In the hedge."

"When?"

"Three days ago."

"Who did it?"

"I don't know."

"How. You do not know who killed your husband?"

"No."

"Was it a Blue? Was it a White?"

"It was a bullet."

"Three days ago?"

"Yes."

"In what direction?"

"Toward Ernée. My husband fell,— that is all."

"And what have you been doing since your husband was killed?"

"I bear away my children."

"Where are you taking them?"

"Straight ahead."

"Where do you sleep?"

"On the ground."

"What do you eat?"

"Nothing."

The sergeant made that military grimace which makes the moustache touch the nose.

"Nothing?"

"That is to say, sloes and dried berries left from last year, myrtle seeds, and fern shoots."

"Faith! you might as well say 'nothing.'"

The eldest of the children, who seemed to understand, said, "I am hungry."

The sergeant took a bit of regulation bread from his pocket, and handed it to the mother. She broke the bread into two fragments, and gave them to the children, who ate them with avidity.

"She has kept none for herself," grumbled the sergeant.

"Because she is not hungry," said a soldier.

"Because she is a mother," said the sergeant.

The children interrupted the dialogue.

"I want to drink," cried one.

"I want to drink," repeated the other.

"Is there no brook in this devil's wood?" asked the sergeant.

The vivandière took the brass cup which hung at her belt beside her handbell, turned the cock of the can she carried slung over her shoulder, poured a few drops into the cup, and held it to the children's lips in turn.

The first drank and made a grimace. The second drank and spat it out.

"Nevertheless, it is good," said the vivandière.

"Is it some of the old cut-throat?" asked the sergeant.

"Yes, and the best; but these are peasants." And she wiped her cup.

The sergeant resumed:—

"And so, madame, you are trying to escape?"

"There is nothing else left for me to do."

"Across fields—going whichever way chance directs?"

"I run with all my might, then I walk, then I fall."

"Poor villager!" said the vivandière.

"The people fight," stammered the woman. "They are shooting all around me. I do not know what it is they wish. They killed my husband; that is all I understood."

The sergeant grounded the butt of his musket till the earth rang, and cried,—

"What a beast of a war—in the hangman's name!"

The woman continued,—

"Last night we slept in an *émousse*."

"All four?"

"All four."

"Slept?"

"Slept."

"Then," said the sergeant, "you slept standing."

He turned toward the soldiers: "Comrades, what these savages call an *émousse* is an old hollow tree-trunk that a man may fit himself into as if it were a sheath. But what would you? We cannot all be Parisians."

"Slept in a hollow tree?" exclaimed the vivandière. "And with three children!"

"And," added the sergeant, "when the little ones howled, it must have been odd to anybody passing by and seeing nothing whatever, to hear a tree cry, 'Papa! mamma!'"

"Luckily it is summer," sighed the woman.

She looked down upon the ground in silent resignation, her eyes filled with the bewilderment of wretchedness.

The soldiers made a silent circle round this group of misery. A widow, three orphans; flight, abandonment, solitude, war muttering around the horizon; hunger, thirst; no other nourishment than the herbs of the field, no other roof than that of heaven.

The sergeant approached the woman, and fixed his eye on the sucking baby. The little one left the breast, turned its head gently, gazing with its beautiful blue orbs into the formidable hairy face, bristling and wild, which bent toward it, and began to smile.

The sergeant raised himself, and they saw a great tear roll down his cheek and cling like a pearl to the end of his moustache.

He lifted his voice:—

"Comrades, from all this I conclude that the regiment is going to become a father. Is it agreed? We adopt these three children?"

"Hurrah for the Republic!" chorused the grenadiers.

"It is decided!" said the sergeant.

He stretched his two hands above the mother and her babes.

"Behold the children of the battalion of the Bonnet Rouge!"

The vivandière leaped for joy.

"Three heads under one bonnet!" cried she.

Then she burst into sobs, embraced the poor widow wildly, and said to her, "What a rogue the little girl looks already!"

"Vive la République!" repeated the soldiers.

And the sergeant said to the mother:—

"Come, citizeness!"

BOOK II

THE CORVETTE "CLAYMORE."

CHAPTER I

ENGLAND AND FRANCE IN CONCERT

In the spring of 1793, at the moment when France, simultaneously attacked on all its frontiers, suffered the pathetic distraction of the downfall of the Girondists, this was what happened in the Channel Islands.

At Jersey, on the evening of the 1st of June, about an hour before sunset, a corvette set sail from the solitary little Bay of Bonnenuit, in that kind of foggy weather which is favourable to flight because pursuit is rendered dangerous. The vessel was manned by a French crew, though it made part of the English fleet stationed on the lookout at the eastern point of the island. The Prince de la Tour d'Auvergne, who was of the house of Bouillon, commanded the English flotilla; and it was by his orders, and for an urgent and special service, that the corvette had been detached.

This vessel, entered at Trinity House under the name of the "Claymore," had the appearance of a transport or trader, but was in reality a war corvette. She had the heavy, pacific look of a merchantman; but it would not have been safe to trust to that. She had been built for a double purpose,—cunning and strength: to deceive if possible, to fight if necessary. For the service before her this night, the lading of the lower deck had been replaced by thirty carronades of heavy calibre. Either because a storm was feared, or because it was desirable to prevent the vessel having a suspicious appearance, these carronades were housed,—that is to say, securely fastened within by triple chains, and the hatches above shut close. Nothing was to be seen from without. The ports were blinded; the slides closed; it was as if the corvette had put on a mask. Armed corvettes only carry guns on the upper deck; but this one, built for surprise and cunning, had the deck free, and was able, as we have just seen, to carry a battery below. The "Claymore" was after a heavy, squat model, but a good sailer nevertheless,—the hull of the most solid sort used in the English navy,—and in battle was almost as valuable as a frigate, though for mizzen she had only a small mast of brigantine rig. Her rudder, of a peculiar and scientific form, had a curved frame, of unique shape, which cost fifty pounds sterling in the dockyards of Southampton.

The crew, all French, was composed of refugee officers and deserter sailors. They were tried men; not one but was a good sailor, good soldier, and good royalist. They had a threefold fanaticism,—for ship, sword and king.

A half-regiment of marines, that could be disembarked in case of need, was added to the crew.

The corvette "Claymore" had a captain chevalier of Saint Louis, Count du Boisberthelot, one of the best officers of the old Royal Navy; for second, the

Chevalier La Vieuville, who had commanded a company of French guards in which Hoche was sergeant; and for pilot, Philip Gacquoil, the most skilful mariner in Jersey.

It was evident that the vessel had unusual business on hand. Indeed, a man who had just come on board had the air of one entering upon an adventure. He was a tall old man, upright and robust, with a severe countenance, whose age it would have been difficult to guess accurately, for he seemed at once old and young,—one of those men who are full of years and of vigour; who have white hair on their heads and lightning in their glance; forty in point of energy and eighty in power and authority. As he came on deck his sea-cloak blew open, exposing his large loose breeches and top-boots, and a goat-skin vest which had one side tanned and embroidered with silk, while on the other the hair was left rough and bristling,—a complete costume of the Breton peasant. These old-fashioned jackets answered alike for working and holidays: they could be turned to show the hairy or embroidered side, as one pleased,—goat-skin all the week, gala accoutrements on Sunday. As if to increase a resemblance which had been carefully studied, the peasant dress worn by the old man was threadbare at the knees and elbows, and seemed to have been long in use, while his coarse cloak might have belonged to a fisherman. He had on his head the round hat of the period,—high, with a broad rim which, when turned down, gave the wearer a rustic look, but took a military air when fastened up at the side with a loop and a cockade. The old man wore his hat with the brim flattened forward, peasant fashion, without either tassels or cockade.

Lord Balcarras, the governor of the island, and the Prince de la Tour d'Auvergne, had in person conducted and installed him on board. The secret agent of the princes, Gélambre, formerly one of the Count d'Artois's bodyguard, had superintended the arrangement of the cabin; and, although himself a nobleman, pushed courtesy and respect so far as to walk behind the old man, carrying his portmanteau. When they left him to go ashore again, Monsieur de Gélambre saluted the peasant profoundly; Lord Balcarras said to him, "Good luck, General!" and the Prince de la Tour d'Auvergne added, "*Au revoir,* my cousin!"

"The peasant" was the name by which the crew immediately designated their passenger during the short dialogues which seamen hold; but without understanding further about the matter, they comprehended that he was no more a peasant than the corvette was a common sloop.

There was little wind. The "Claymore" left Bonnenuit, and passed in front of Boulay Bay, and was for some time in sight, tacking to windward; then she lessened in the gathering night, and finally disappeared.

An hour after, Gélambre, having returned to his house at Saint Helier, sent by the Southampton express the following lines to the Count d'Artois, at the Duke of York's headquarters,—

MONSEIGNEUR,—The departure has just taken place. Success certain. In eight days the whole coast will be on fire from Granville to Saint Malo.

Four days previous, Prieur, the representative of Marne, on a mission to the army along the coast of Cherbourg, and momentarily residing at Granville, had received by a secret emissary this message, written in the same hand as the dispatch above:—

> CITIZEN REPRESENTATIVE,— On the 1st of June, at the hour when the tide serves, the war corvette "Claymore," with a masked battery, will set sail for the purpose of landing upon the shore of France a man of whom this is a description: tall, old, white hair, peasant's dress, hands of an aristocrat. I will send you more details to-morrow. He will land on the morning of the 2d. Warn the cruisers; capture the corvette; guillotine the man.

CHAPTER II

NIGHT ON THE VESSEL AND WITH THE PASSENGER

THE corvette, instead of going south and making for Saint Catherine's, headed north, then veered to the west, and resolutely entered the arm of the sea between Sark and Jersey, called the Passage de la Deronte. At that time there was no lighthouse upon any point along either coast. The sun had set clear; the night was dark,—darker than summer nights ordinarily are; there was a moon; but vast clouds, rather of the equinox than the solstice, veiled the sky, and according to all appearances the moon would not be visible till she touched the horizon at the moment of setting. A few clouds hung low upon the water and covered it with mist.

All this obscurity was favourable.

The intention of Pilot Gacquoil was to leave Jersey on the left and Guernsey on the right, and to gain, by bold sailing between the Hanois and the Douvree, some bay of the Saint Malo shore,—a route less short than that by the Minquiers, but safer, as the French cruisers had standing orders to keep an especially keen watch between Saint Helier and Granville. If the wind were favourable, and nothing occurred, Gacquoil hoped by setting all sail to touch the French coast at daybreak.

All went well. The corvette had passed Gros-Nez. Toward nine o'clock the weather looked sulky, as sailors say, and there were wind and sea; but the wind was good and the sea strong without being violent. Still, now and then the waves swept the vessel's bows.

The "peasant," whom Lord Balcarras had called "General," and whom the Prince de la Tour d'Auvergne addressed as "My cousin," had a sailor's footing, and paced the deck with tranquil gravity. He did not even seem to notice that the corvette rocked considerably. From time to time he took a cake of chocolate out of his pocket and munched a morsel: his white hair did not prevent his having all his teeth.

He spoke to no one, except now and then a few low quick words to the captain, who listened with deference, and seemed to consider his passenger, rather than himself, the commander.

The "Claymore," ably piloted, skirted unperceived in the fog the long escarpment north of Jersey, hugging the shore on account of the formidable reef,

Pierres de Leeq, which is in the middle of the channel between Jersey and Sark. Gacquoil, standing at the helm, signalled in turn the Grève de Leeq, Gros-Nez, and Plémont, and slipped the corvette along among this chain of reefs, feeling his way to a certain extent, but with certitude, like a man familiar with the course and acquainted with the disposition of the sea. The corvette had no light forward, from a fear of betraying its passage through these guarded waters. The fog was a cause for rejoicing. They reached the Grande Etaque. The mist was so thick that the outlines of the lofty pinnacle could scarcely be made out. Ten o'clock was heard to sound from the belfry of Saint Ouen, a proof that the wind was still abaft. All was yet going well. The sea grew rougher on account of the neighbourhood of La Corbière.

A little after ten. Count de Boisberthelot and the Chevalier La Vieuville reconducted the man in the peasant's garb to his cabin, which was in reality the captain's stateroom. As he went in, he said to them in a low voice:—

"Gentlemen, you understand the importance of secrecy. Silence up to the moment of explosion. You two are the only ones here who know my name."

"We will carry it with us to the tomb," replied Boisberthelot.

"As for me," added the old man, "were I in face of death, I would not tell it."

He entered his cabin.

Chapter III

NOBLE AND PLEBEIAN IN CONCERT

The commander and the second officer returned on deck and walked up and down, side by side, in conversation. They were evidently talking of their passenger, and this was the dialogue which the wind dispersed among the shadows.

Boisberthelot grumbled in a half-voice in the ear of La Vieuville: —

"We shall see if he is really a leader."

La Vieuville replied, "In the mean time he is a prince."

"Almost."

"Nobleman in France, but prince in Brittany."

"Like the La Trémoilles; like the Rohans."

"With whom he is connected."

Boisberthelot resumed:—

"In France, and in the king's carriages, he is marquis, as I am count, and you are chevalier."

"The carriages are far off!" cried La Vieuville. "We have got to the tumbrel."

There was a silence.

Boisberthelot began again:—

"For lack of a French prince, a Breton one is taken."

"For lack of thrushes,—no, for want of an eagle,—a crow is chosen."

"I should prefer a vulture," said Boisberthelot.

And La Vieuville retorted,—

"Yes, indeed! a beak and talons."

"We shall see."

"Yes," resumed La Vieuville, "it is time there was a head. I am of Tinteniac's opinion: '*A true chief, and—*

gunpowder!" See, Commander; I know nearly all the leaders, possible and impossible,—those of yesterday, those of to-day, and those of to-morrow; there is not one with the sort of head-piece we need. In that accursed Vendée it wants a general who is a lawyer at the same time. He must worry the enemy, dispute every mill, thicket, ditch, pebble; quarrel with him; take advantage of everything; see to everything; slaughter plentifully; make examples; be sleepless, pitiless. At this hour there are heroes among that army of peasants, but there are no captains. D'Elbée is *nil;* Lescure is ailing; Bonchampe shows mercy,—he is kind, that means stupid; La Rochejacquelein is a magnificent sub-lieutenant; Silz an officer for open country, unfit for a war of expedients; Cathelineau is a simple carter; Stofflet is a cunning gamekeeper; Bérard is inept; Boulainvilliers is ridiculous; Charette is shocking. And I do not speak of the barber Gaston. For, in the name of Mars! what is the good of opposing the Revolution, and what is the difference between the Republicans and ourselves, if we set hairdressers to command noblemen?"

"You see that beast of a Revolution has infected us also."

"An itch that France has caught."

"An itch of the Third Estate," replied Boisberthelot.

"It is only England that can cure us of it."

"And she will cure us, do not doubt it, Captain."

"In the meanwhile it is ugly."

"Indeed, yes. Clowns everywhere! The monarchy which has for commander-in-chief Stofflet, the gamekeeper of M. de Maulevrier, has nothing to envy in the republic that has for minister, Pache, son of the Duke de Castrie's porter. What men this Vendean war brings out against each other! On one side Santerre the brewer, on the other Gaston the wigmaker!"

"My dear Vieuville, I have a certain respect for Gaston. He did not conduct himself ill in his command of Guemenée. He very neatly shot three hundred Blues, after making them dig their own graves."

"Well and good; but I could have done that as well as he."

"Zounds! no doubt; and I also."

"The great acts of war," resumed La Vieuville, "require to be undertaken by noblemen. They are matters for knights and not hairdressers."

"Still, there are some estimable men among this 'Third Estate,'" returned Boisberthelot. "Take, for example, Joby the clockmaker. He had been a sergeant in a Flanders regiment; he gets himself made a Vendean chief; he commands a coast band; he has a son who is a Republican, and while the father serves among the Whites, the son serves among the Blues. Encounter. Battle. The father takes the son prisoner, and blows out his brains."

"He's a good one," said La Vieuville.

"A royalist Brutus," replied Boisberthelot.

"All that does not hinder the fact that it is insupportable to be commanded by a Coquereau, a Jean-Jean, a Mouline, a Focart, a Bouju, a Chouppes!"

"My dear chevalier, the other side is equally disgusted. We are full of plebeians; they are full of nobles. Do you suppose the *sans-culottes* are content to be commanded by the Count de Canclaux, the Viscount de Miranda, the Viscount de Beauharnais, the Count de Valence, the Marquis de Custine, and the Duke de Biron."

"What a hash!"

"And the Duke de Chartres!"

"Son of Egalité. Ah, then, when will he ever be king?"

"Never."

"He mounts toward the throne. He is aided by his crimes."

"And held back by his vices," said Boisberthelot.

There was silence again; then Boisberthelot continued:

"Still, he tried to bring about a reconciliation. He went to see the king. I was at Versailles when somebody spat on his back."

"From the top of the grand staircase?"

"Yes."

"It was well done."

"We call him Bourbon the Bourbeux."

"He is bald; he has pimples; he is a regicide—poh!"

Then La Vieuville added,—

"I was at Ouessant with him."

"On the 'Saint Esprit'?"

"Yes."

"If he had obeyed the signal that the Admiral d'Orvilliers made him, to keep to the windward, he would have kept the English from passing."

"Certainly."

"Is it true that he was hidden at the bottom of the hold?"

"No; but it must be said all the same."

And La Vieuville burst out laughing.

Boisberthelot observed,—

"There are idiots enough. Hold!

That Boulainvilliers you were speaking of, La Vieuville,—I knew him. I had a chance of studying him. In the beginning, the peasants were armed with pikes: if he did not get it into his head to make pikemen of them! He wanted to teach them the manual of exercise, *de la pique-en biais et de la pique-trainante-le-fer-dévant*. He dreamed of transforming those savages into soldiers of the Line. He proposed to show them how to mass battalions and form hollow squares. He jabbered the old-fashioned military dialect at them; for 'chief of a squad,' he said *un cap d'escade*, which was the appellation of corporals under Louis XIV. He persisted in forming a regiment of those poachers: he had regular companies. The sergeants ranged themselves in a circle every evening to take the countersign from the colonel's sergeant, who whispered it to the sergeant of the lieutenants; he repeated it to his neighbour, and he to the man nearest; and so on, from ear to ear, down to the last. He cashiered an officer because he did not stand bareheaded to receive the watchword from the sergeant's mouth. You can fancy how all succeeded. The booby could not understand that peasants must be led peasant fashion, and that one cannot make drilled soldiers out of woodchoppers. Yes, I knew that Boulainvilliers."

They moved on a few steps, each pursuing his own thoughts.

Then the conversation was renewed.

"By the way, is it true that Dampierre is killed?"

"Yes, Commander."

"Before Condé?"

"At the camp of Pamars, by a gunshot."

Boisberthelot sighed.

"The Count de Dampierre. Yet another of ours who went over to them!"

"A good journey to him," said La Vieuville.

"And the princesses—where are they?"

"At Trieste."

"Still?"

"Still. Ah, this republic!" cried Vieuville. "What havoc from such slight consequences! When one thinks that this revolution was caused by the deficit of a few millions."

"Distrust small outbreaks," said Boisberthelot.

"Everything is going badly," resumed La Vieuville.

"Yes; La Rouarie is dead; Du Dresnay is an idiot. What pitiful leaders all those bishops are,—that Concy, Bishop of Rochelle; that Beaupoil Saint-Aulaire, Bishop of Poitiers; that Mercy, Bishop of Luçon and lover of Madame de l'Eschasserie—"

"Whose name is Servanteau, you know, Commander; L'Eschasserie is the name of an estate."

"And that false Bishop of Agra, who is curé of I know not what."

"Of Dol. He is called Guillot de Folleville. At least he is brave, and he fights."

"Priests when soldiers are needed! Bishops who are not bishops! Generals who are no generals!"

La Vieuville interrupted Boisberthelot.

"Commander, have you the 'Moniteur' in your cabin?"

"Yes."

"What are they playing in Paris just now?"

"'Adèle and Poulin,' and 'The Cavern.'"

"I should like to see that."

"You will be able to. We shall be at Paris in a month."

Boisberthelot reflected a moment, and added,—

"At the latest. Mr. Windham said so to Lord Hood."

"But then, Captain, everything is not going so ill."

"Zounds! everything would go well, on condition that the war in Brittany could be properly conducted."

La Vieuville shook his head.

"Commander," he asked, "do we land the marines?"

"Yes, if the coast is for us, not if it is hostile. Sometimes war must break down doors, sometimes slip in quietly. Civil war ought always to have a false key in its pocket. We shall do all in our power. The most important is the chief."

Then Boisberthelot added thoughtfully:—

"La Vieuville, what do you think of the Chevalier de Dieugie?"

"The younger?"

"Yes."

"For a leader?"

"Yes."

"That he is another officer for open country and pitched battles. Only the peasant understands the thickets."

"Then resign yourself to General Stofflet and to General Cathelineau."

La Vieuville mused a while, and then said, "It needs a prince,—a prince of France, a prince of the blood, a true prince."

"Why? Whoever says prince—"

"Says poltroon. I know it, Captain. But one is needed for the effect on the big stupid eyes of the country lads."

"My dear chevalier, the princes will not come."

"We will get on without them."

Boisberthelot pressed his hand upon his forehead with the mechanical movement of a man endeavouring to bring out some idea. He exclaimed,—

"Well, let us try the general we have here."

"He is a great nobleman."

"Do you believe he will answer?"

"Provided he is strong."

"That is to say, ferocious," said Boisberthelot.

The count and the chevalier looked fixedly at each other.

"Monsieur du Boisberthelot, you have said the word,—ferocious. Yes; that is what we need. This is a war without pity. The hour is to the bloodthirsty. The regicides have cut off Louis XVI.'s head; we will tear off the four limbs of the regicides. Yes, the general necessary is General Inexorable. In Anjou and Upper Poitou the chiefs do the magnanimous; they dabble in generosity: nothing moves on. In the Marais and the country of Retz, the chiefs are ferocious: everything goes forward. It is because Charette is savage that he holds his own against Parrein: it is hyæna against hyæna."

Boisberthelot had no time to reply; La Vieuville's words were suddenly cut short by a desperate cry, and at the same instant they heard a noise as unaccountable as it was awful. The cry and this noise came from the interior of the vessel.

The captain and lieutenant made a rush for the gun-deck, but could not get down. All the gunners were hurrying frantically up.

A frightful thing had just happened.

CHAPTER IV

TORMENTUM BELLI

ONE of the carronades of the battery, a twenty-four pounder, had got loose.

This is perhaps the most formidable of ocean accidents. Nothing more terrible can happen to a vessel in open sea and under full sail.

A gun that breaks its moorings becomes suddenly some indescribable supernatural beast. It is a machine which transforms itself into a monster. This mass turns upon its wheels, has the rapid movements of a billiard-ball; rolls with the rolling, pitches with the pitching; goes, comes, pauses, seems to meditate; resumes its course, rushes along the ship from end to end like an arrow, circles about, springs aside, evades, rears, breaks, kills, exterminates. It is a battering-ram which assaults a wall at its own caprice. Moreover, the battering-ram is metal, the wall wood. It is the entrance of matter into liberty. One might say that this eternal slave avenges itself. It seems as if the power of evil hidden in what we call inanimate objects finds a vent and bursts suddenly out. It has an air of having lost patience, of seeking some fierce, obscure retribution; nothing more inexorable than this rage of the inanimate. The mad mass has the bounds of a panther, the weight of the elephant, the agility of the mouse, the obstinacy of the axe, the unexpectedness of the surge, the rapidity of lightning, the deafness of the tomb. It weighs ten thousand pounds, and it rebounds like a child's ball. Its flight is a wild whirl abruptly cut at right angles. What is to be done? How to end this? A tempest ceases, a cyclone passes, a wind falls, a broken mast is replaced, a leak is stopped, a fire dies out; but how to control this enormous brute of bronze? In what way can one attack it?

You can make a mastiff hear reason, astound a bull, fascinate a boa, frighten a tiger, soften a lion; but there is no resource with that monster,—a cannon let loose. You cannot kill it,—it is dead; at the same time it lives. It lives with a sinister life bestowed on it by Infinity.

The planks beneath it give it play. It is moved by the ship, which is moved by the sea, which is moved by the wind. This destroyer is a plaything. The ship, the waves, the blasts, all aid it; hence its frightful vitality. How to assail this fury of complications? How to fetter this monstrous mechanism for wrecking a ship? How foresee its comings and goings, its returns, its stops, its shocks? Any one of these blows upon the sides may stave out the vessel. How divine its awful gyrations! One has to deal with a projectile which thinks, seems to possess ideas, and which changes its direction at each instant. How stop the course of something which must be avoided? The horrible cannon flings itself about, advances, recoils, strikes to the right, strikes to the left, flees, passes, disconcerts ambushes, breaks down obstacles, crushes men like flies. The great danger of the situation is in the mobility of its base. How combat an inclined plane which has caprices? The ship, so to speak, has lightning imprisoned in its womb which seeks to escape; it is like thunder rolling above an earthquake.

In an instant the whole crew were on foot. The fault was the chief gunner's; he had neglected to fix home the screw-nut of the mooring-chain, and had so badly shackled the four wheels of the carronade that the play given to the sole and frame had separated the platform, and ended by breaking the breeching. The cordage had broken, so that the gun was no longer secure on the carriage. The stationary breeching which prevents recoil was not in use at that period. As a heavy wave struck the port, the carronade, weakly attached, recoiled, burst its chain, and began to rush wildly about. Conceive, in order to have an idea of this strange sliding, a drop of water running down a pane of glass.

At the moment when the lashings gave way the gunners were in the battery, some in groups, others standing alone, occupied with such duties as sailors perform in expectation of the command to clear for action. The carronade, hurled forward by the pitching, dashed into this knot of men, and crushed four at the first blow; then, flung back and shot out anew by the rolling, it cut in two a fifth poor fellow, glanced off to the larboard side, and struck a piece of the battery with such force as to unship it. Then rose the cry of distress which had been heard. The men rushed toward the ladder; the gun-deck emptied in the twinkling of an eye. The enormous cannon was left alone. She was given up to herself. She was her own mistress, and mistress of the vessel. She could do what she willed with both. This whole crew, accustomed to laugh in battle, trembled now. To describe the universal terror would be impossible.

Captain Boisberthelot and Lieutenant Vieuville, although both intrepid men, stopped at the head of the stairs, and remained mute, pale, hesitating, looking down on the deck. Some one pushed them aside with his elbow and descended.

It was their passenger, the peasant,—the man of whom they had been speaking a moment before.

When he reached the foot of the ladder, he stood still.

Chapter V

VIS ET VIR

THE cannon came and went along the deck. One might have fancied it the living chariot of the Apocalypse. The marine-lantern, oscillating from the ceiling, added a dizzying whirl of lights and shadows to this vision. The shape of the cannon was undistinguishable from the rapidity of its course; now it looked black in the light, now it cast weird reflections through the gloom.

It kept on its work of destruction. It had already shattered four other pieces, and dug two crevices in the side, fortunately above the water-line, though they would leak in case a squall should come on. It dashed itself frantically against the frame-work; the solid tie-beams resisted, their curved form giving them great strength, but they creaked ominously under the assaults of this terrible club, which seemed endowed with a sort of appalling ubiquity, striking on every side at once. The strokes of a bullet shaken in a bottle would not be madder or more rapid. The four wheels passed and repassed above the dead men, cut, carved, slashed them, till the five corpses were a score of stumps rolling about the deck; the heads seemed to cry out; streams of blood twisted in and out of the planks with every pitch of the vessel. The ceiling, damaged in several places, began to gape. The whole ship was filled with the awful tumult.

The captain promptly recovered his composure, and at his order the sailors threw down into the deck everything which could deaden and check the mad rush of the gun,—mattresses, hammocks, spare sails, coils of rope, extra equipments, and the bales of false assignats of which the corvette carried a whole cargo; an infamous deception which the English considered a fair trick in war.

But what could these rags avail? No one dared descend to arrange them in any useful fashion, and in a few instants they were mere heaps of lint.

There was just sea enough to render an accident as complete as possible. A tempest would have been desirable,—it might have thrown the gun upside down; and the four wheels once in the air, the monster could have been mastered. But the devastation increased. There were gashes and even fractures in the masts, which, imbedded in the woodwork of the keel, pierce the decks of ships like great round pillars. The mizzen-mast was cracked, and the main-mast itself was injured under the convulsive blows of the gun. The battery was being destroyed. Ten pieces out of the thirty were disabled; the breaches multiplied in the side, and the corvette began to take in water.

The old passenger who had descended to the gun-deck, looked like a form of stone stationed at the foot of the stairs. He stood motionless, gazing sternly about upon the devastation. Indeed, it seemed impossible to take a single step forward.

Each bound of the liberated carronade menaced the destruction of the vessel. A few minutes more and shipwreck would be inevitable.

They must perish or put a summary end to the disaster. A decision must be made—but how?

What a combatant—this cannon!

They must check this mad monster. They must seize this flash of lightning. They must overthrow this thunderbolt.

Boisberthelot said to La Vieuville:—
"Do you believe in God, Chevalier?"
La Vieuville replied,—
"Yes. No. Sometimes."
"In a tempest?"
"Yes; and in moments like this."
"Only God can aid us here," said Boisberthelot.

All were silent: the cannon kept up its horrible fracas.

The waves beat against the ship; their blows from without responded to the strokes of the cannon.

It was like two hammers alternating.

Suddenly, into the midst of this sort of inaccessible circus, where the escaped cannon leaped and bounded, there sprang a man with an iron bar in his hand. It was the author of this catastrophe,—the gunner whose culpable negligence had caused the accident; the captain of the gun. Having been the means of bringing about the misfortune, he desired to repair it. He had caught up a handspike in one fist, a tiller-rope with a slipping-noose in the other, and jumped down into the gun-deck.

Then a strange combat began, a titanic strife,—the struggle of the gun against the gunner; a battle between matter and intelligence; a duel between the inanimate and the human.

The man was posted in an angle, the bar and rope in his two fists; backed against one of the riders, settled firmly on his legs as on two pillars of steel, livid, calm, tragic, rooted as it were in the planks, he waited.

He waited for the cannon to pass near him.

The gunner knew his piece, and it seemed to him that she must recognize her master. He had lived a long while with her. How many times he had thrust his hand between her jaws! It was his tame monster. He began to address it as he might have done his dog.

"Come!" said he. Perhaps he loved it.

He seemed to wish that it would turn toward him.

But to come toward him would be to spring upon him. Then he would be lost. How to avoid its crush? There was the question. All stared in terrified silence.

Not a breast respired freely, except perchance that of the old man who alone stood in the deck with the two combatants, a stern second.

He might himself be crushed by the piece. He did not stir.

Beneath them, the blind sea directed the battle.

At the instant when, accepting this awful hand-to-hand contest, the gunner approached to challenge the cannon, some chance fluctuation of the waves kept it for a moment immovable, as if suddenly stupefied.

"Come on!" the man said to it. It seemed to listen.

Suddenly it darted upon him. The gunner avoided the shock.

The struggle began,—struggle unheard of. The fragile matching itself against the invulnerable. The thing of flesh attacking the brazen brute. On the one side blind force, on the other a soul.

The whole passed in a half-light. It was like the indistinct vision of a miracle.

A soul,—strange thing; but you would have said that the cannon had one also, —a soul filled with rage and hatred. This blindness appeared to have eyes. The monster had the air of watching the man. There was—one might have fancied so at least—cunning in this mass. It also chose its moment. It became some gigantic insect of metal, having, or seeming to have, the will of a demon. Sometimes this colossal grasshopper would strike the low ceiling of the gun-deck, then fall back on its four wheels like a tiger upon its four claws, and dart anew on the man. He, supple, agile, adroit, would glide away like a snake from the reach of these lightning-like movements. He avoided the encounters; but the blows which he escaped fell upon the vessel and continued the havoc.

An end of broken chain remained attached to the carronade. This chain had twisted itself, one could not tell how, about the screw of the breech-button. One extremity of the chain was fastened to the carriage. The other, hanging loose, whirled wildly about the gun and added to the danger of its blows.

The screw held it like a clinched hand, and the chain multiplying the strokes of the battering-ram by its strokes of a thong, made a fearful whirlwind about the cannon,—a whip of iron in a fist of brass. This chain complicated the battle.

Nevertheless, the man fought. Sometimes, even, it was the man who attacked the cannon. He crept along the side, bar and rope in hand, and the cannon had the air of understanding, and fled as if it perceived a snare. The man pursued it, formidable, fearless.

Such a duel could not last long. The gun seemed suddenly to say to itself, "Come, we must make an end!" and it paused. One felt the approach of the crisis. The cannon, as if in suspense, appeared to have, or had,—because it seemed to all a sentient being,—a furious premeditation. It sprang unexpectedly upon the gunner. He jumped aside, let it pass, and cried out with a laugh, "Try again!" The gun, as if in a fury, broke a carronade to larboard; then, seized anew by the invisible sling which held it, was flung to starboard toward the man, who escaped.

Three carronades gave way under the blows of the gun; then, as if blind and no longer conscious of what it was doing, it turned its back on the man, rolled from the stern to the bow, bruising the stem and making a breach in the plankings of the prow. The gunner had taken refuge at the foot of the stairs, a few steps from the old man, who was watching.

The gunner held his handspike in rest. The cannon seemed to perceive him, and, without taking the trouble to turn itself, backed upon him with the quickness of an axe-stroke. The gunner, if driven back against the side was lost. The crew uttered a simultaneous cry.

But the old passenger, until now immovable, made a spring more rapid than all those wild whirls. He seized a bale of the false assignats, and at the risk of being crushed, succeeded in flinging it between the wheels of the carronade. This manœuvre, decisive and dangerous, could not have been executed with more adroitness and precision by a man trained to all the exercises set down in Durosel's "Manual of Sea Gunnery."

The bale had the effect of a plug. A pebble may stop a log, a tree-branch turn an avalanche. The carronade stumbled. The gunner, in his turn, seizing this terrible chance, plunged his iron bar between the spokes of one of the hind wheels. The cannon was stopped.

It staggered. The man, using the bar as a lever, rocked it to and fro. The heavy mass turned over with a clang like a falling bell, and the gunner, dripping with sweat, rushed forward headlong and passed the slipping-noose of the tiller-rope about the bronze neck of the overthrown monster.

It was ended. The man had conquered. The ant had subdued the mastodon; the pigmy had taken the thunderbolt prisoner.

The marines and the sailors clapped their hands.

The whole crew hurried down with cables and chains, and in an instant the cannon was securely lashed.

The gunner saluted the passenger.

"Sir," he said to him, "you have saved my life."

The old man had resumed his impassible attitude, and did not reply.

Chapter VI

THE TWO SCALES OF THE BALANCE

The man had conquered, but one might say that the cannon had conquered also. Immediate shipwreck had been avoided, but the corvette was by no means saved. The dilapidation of the vessel seemed irremediable. The sides had five breaches, one of which, very large, was in the bow. Out of the thirty carronades, twenty lay useless in their frames. The carronade, which had been captured and rechained, was itself disabled; the screw of the breech-button was forced, and the levelling of the piece impossible in consequence. The battery was reduced to nine pieces. The hold had sprung a leak. It was necessary at once to repair the damages and set the pumps to work.

The gun-deck, now that one had time to look about it, offered a terrible spectacle. The interior of a mad elephant's cage could not have been more completely dismantled.

However great the necessity that the corvette should escape observation, a still more imperious necessity presented itself,—immediate safety. It had been necessary to light up the deck by lanterns placed here and there along the sides.

But during the whole time this tragic diversion had lasted, the crew were so absorbed by the one question of life or death that they noticed little what was passing outside the scene of the duel. The fog had thickened; the weather had changed; the wind had driven the vessel at will; it had got out of its route, in plain sight of Jersey and Guernsey, farther to the south than it ought to have gone, and was surrounded by a troubled sea. The great waves kissed the gaping wounds of the corvette,—kisses full of peril. The sea rocked her menacingly. The breeze became a gale. A squall, a tempest perhaps, threatened. It was impossible to see before one four oars' length.

While the crew were repairing summarily and in haste the ravages of the gun-deck, stopping the leaks and putting back into position the guns which had escaped the disaster, the old passenger had gone on deck.

He stood with his back against the main-mast.

He had paid no attention to a proceeding which had taken place on the vessel. The Chevalier La Vieuville had drawn up the marines in line on either side of the main-mast, and at the whistle of the boatswain the sailors busy in the rigging stood upright on the yards.

Count du Boisberthelot advanced toward the passenger.

Behind the captain marched a man, haggard, breathless, his dress in disorder, yet wearing a satisfied look under it all. It was the gunner who had just now so opportunely shown himself a tamer of monsters, and who had got the better of the cannon.

The count made a military salute to the unknown in peasant garb, and said to him:—

"General, here is the man."

The gunner held himself erect, his eyes downcast, standing in a soldierly attitude.

Count du Boisberthelot continued,—

"General, taking into consideration what this man has done, do you not think there is something for his commanders to do?"

"I think there is," said the old man.

"Be good enough to give the orders," returned Boisberthelot.

"It is for you to give them. You are the captain."

"But you are the general," answered Boisberthelot.

The old man looked at the gunner.

"Approach," said he.

The gunner moved forward a step. The old man turned toward Count du Boisberthelot, detached the cross of Saint Louis from the captain's uniform and fastened it on the jacket of the gunner.

"Hurrah!" cried the sailors.

The marines presented arms. The old passenger, pointing with his finger toward the bewildered gunner, added,—

"Now let that man be shot."

Stupor succeeded the applause.

Then, in the midst of a silence like that of the tomb, the old man raised his voice. He said,—

"A negligence has endangered this ship. At this moment she is perhaps lost. To be at sea is to face the enemy. A vessel at open sea is an army which gives battle. The tempest conceals, but does not absent itself. The whole sea is an ambuscade.

"Death is the penalty of any fault committed in the face of the enemy. No fault is reparable. Courage ought to be rewarded and negligence punished."

These words fell one after the other, slowly, solemnly, with a sort of inexorable measure, like the blows of an axe upon an oak.

And the old man, turning to the soldiers, added,—

"Do your duty."

The man upon whose breast shone the cross of Saint Louis bowed his head.

At a sign from Count du Boisberthelot, two sailors descended between decks, then returned, bringing the hammock winding-sheet. The ship's chaplain, who since the time of sailing had been at prayer in the officer's quarters, accompanied the two sailors; a sergeant detached from the line twelve marines, whom he arranged in two ranks, six by six; the gunner, without uttering a word, placed himself between the two files. The chaplain, crucifix in hand, advanced and stood near him.

"March!" said the sergeant.

The platoon moved with slow steps toward the bow. The two sailors who carried the shroud followed.

A gloomy silence fell upon the corvette. A hurricane moaned in the distance.

A few instants later there was a flash; a report followed, echoing among the shadows; then all was silent; then came the thud of a body falling into the sea.

The old passenger still leaned back against the main-mast with folded arms, thinking silently.

Boisberthelot pointed toward him with the forefinger of his left hand, and said in a low voice to La Vieuville:

"The Vendée has found a head!"

Chapter VII

HE WHO SETS SAIL PUTS INTO A LOTTERY

But what was to become of the corvette?

The clouds, which the whole night through had touched the waves, now lowered so thickly that the horizon was no longer visible; the sea seemed to be covered with a pall. Nothing to be seen but fog,—a situation always perilous, even for a vessel in good condition.

Added to the mist came the surging swell.

The time had been used to good purpose: the corvette had been lightened by throwing overboard everything which could be cleared from the havoc made by the carronade,—the dismantled guns, the broken carriages, frames twisted or unnailed, the fragments of splintered wood and iron; the portholes had been opened, and the corpses and parts of bodies, enveloped in tarpaulin, were slid down planks into the waves.

The sea was no longer manageable. Not that the tempest was imminent; it seemed, on the contrary, that the hurricane rustling behind the horizon decreased, and the squall was moving northward; but the waves were very high still, which indicated disturbance in the depths. The corvette could offer slight resistance to shocks in her crippled condition, so that the great waves might prove fatal to her.

Gacquoil stood thoughtfully at the helm.

To face ill-fortune with a bold front is the habit of those accustomed to rule at sea.

La Vieuville, who was the sort of man that becomes gay in the midst of disaster, accosted Gacquoil.

"Well, pilot," said he, "the squall has missed fire. Its attempt at sneezing comes to nothing. We shall get out of it. We shall have wind, and that is all."

Gacquoil replied, seriously, "Where there is wind there are waves."

Neither laughing nor sad, such is the sailor. The response had a disquieting significance. For a leaky ship to encounter a high sea is to fill rapidly. Gacquoil emphasized his prognostic by a frown. Perhaps La Vieuville had spoken almost jovial and gay words a little too soon after the catastrophe of the gun and its gunner. There are things which bring bad luck at sea. The ocean is secretive; one never knows what it means to do; it is necessary to be always on guard against it.

La Vieuville felt the necessity of getting back to gravity.

"Where are we, pilot?" he asked.

The pilot replied,—

"We are in the hands of God."

A pilot is a master; he must always be allowed to do what he will, and often he must be allowed to say what he pleases. Generally this species of man speaks little.

La Vieuville moved away. He had asked a question of the pilot; it was the horizon which replied. The sea suddenly cleared.

The fogs which trailed across the waves were quickly rent; the dark confusion of the billows spread out to the horizon's verge in a shadowy half-light, and this was what became visible:—

The sky seemed covered with a lid of clouds, but they no longer touched the water; in the east appeared a whiteness, which was the dawn; in the west trembled a corresponding pallor, which was the setting moon. These two ghostly presences drew opposite each other narrow bands of pale lights along the horizon, between the sombre sea and the gloomy sky.

Across each of these lines of light were sketched black profiles, upright and immovable.

To the west, against the moonlight sky, stood out sharply three lofty rocks, erect as Celtic cromlechs.

To the east, against the pale horizon of morning, rose eight sail, ranged in order at regular intervals in a formidable array.

The three rocks were a reef; the eight ships, a squadron.

Behind the vessel was the Minquiers, —a rock of an evil renown; before her, the French cruisers. To the west, the abyss; to the east, carnage; she was between a shipwreck and a combat.

For meeting the reef, the corvette had a broken hull, rigging disjointed, masts tottering in their foundations; for facing battle, she had a battery where one-and-twenty cannon out of thirty were dismounted, and whose best gunners were dead.

The dawn was yet faint; there still remained a little night to them. This might even last for some time, since it was principally made by thick, high clouds presenting the solid appearance of a vault.

The wind, which had succeeded in dispersing the lower mists, was forcing the corvette toward the Minquiers.

In her excessive feebleness and dilapidation, she scarcely obeyed the helm; she rolled rather than sailed, and, smitten by the waves, she yielded passively to their impulse.

The Minquiers, a dangerous reef, was still more rugged at that time than it is now. Several towers of this citadel of the abyss have been razed by the incessant chopping of the sea.

The configuration of reefs changes. It is not idly that waves are called the swords of the ocean; each tide is the stroke of a saw. At that period, to strike on the Minquiers was to perish.

As for the cruisers, they were the squadron of Cancale, afterward so celebrated under the command of that Captain Duchesne whom Léquinio called Father Duchesne.

The situation was critical. During the struggle of the unchained carronade, the corvette had, unobserved, got out of her course, and sailed rather toward Granville than Saint Malo. Even if she had been in a condition to have been handled and to carry sail, the Minquiers would have barred her return toward Jersey, and the cruisers would have prevented her reaching France.

For the rest, tempest there was none. But, as the pilot had said, there was a swell. The sea, rolling under a rough wind and above a rocky bottom, was savage.

The sea never says at once what it wishes. The gulf hides everything, even trickery. One might almost say that the sea has a plan. It advances and recoils; it proposes and contradicts itself; it sketches a storm and renounces its design; it promises the abyss, and does not hold to it; it threatens the north, and strikes the south.

All night the corvette "Claymore" had had the fog and the fear of the storm. The sea had belied itself, but in a savage fashion; it had sketched in the tempest, but developed the reef. It was shipwreck just the same, under another form.

So that to destruction upon the rocks was added extermination by combat,— one enemy complementing the other.

La Vieuville cried amid his brave merriment:—

"Shipwreck here—battle there! We have thrown the double fives!"

Chapter VIII

9 = 380

The corvette was little more than a wreck.

In the wan, dim light, midst the blackness of the clouds, in the confused, changing line of the horizon, in the mysterious sullenness of the waves, there was a sepulchral solemnity. Except for the hissing breath of the hostile wind, all was silent. The catastrophe rose with majesty from the gulf. It resembled rather an apparition than an attack. Nothing stirred among the rocks; nothing moved on the vessels. It was an indescribable, colossal silence. Had they to deal with something real? One might have believed it a dream sweeping across the sea; there are legends of such visions. The corvette was in a manner between the demon reef and the phantom fleet.

Count du Boisberthelot gave orders in a half-voice to La Vieuville, who descended to the gun-deck; then the captain seized his telescope and stationed himself at the stern by the side of the pilot.

Gacquoil's whole effort was to keep the corvette to the wind; for if struck on the side by the wind and the sea, she would inevitably capsize.

"Pilot," said the captain, "where are we?"

"Off the Minquiers."

"On which side?"

"The bad one."

"What bottom?"

"Small rocks."

"Can we turn broadside on?"

"We can always die," said the pilot.

The captain levelled his glass toward the west and examined the Minquiers; then he turned to the east and studied the sail in sight.

The pilot continued, as if talking to himself:—

"It is the Minquiers. It is where the laughing sea-mew and the great black-hooded gull rest, when they make for Holland."

In the mean time the captain counted the sail.

There were, indeed, eight vessels, drawn up in line, and lifting their warlike profiles above the water. In the centre was seen the lofty sweep of a three-decker.

The captain questioned the pilot.

"Do you know those ships?"

"Indeed, yes!" replied Gacquoil.

"What are they?"

"It is the squadron."

"Of France?"

"Of the devil."

There was silence. The captain resumed:—

"The whole body of cruisers are there."

"Not all."

In fact, on the 2d of April, Valazé had announced to the Convention that ten frigates and six ships-of-the-line were cruising in the Channel. The recollection of this came into the captain's mind.

"Right," said he; "the squadron consists of sixteen vessels. There are only eight here."

"The rest," said Gacquoil, "are lagging below, the whole length of the coast, and on the look-out."

The captain, still with his glass to his eye, murmured:

"A three-decker, two first-class frigates, and five second-class."

"But I, too," growled Gacquoil, "have marked them out."

"Good vessels," said the captain. "I have done something myself toward commanding them."

"As for me," said Gacquoil, "I have seen them close by. I do not mistake one for the other. I have their description in my head."

The captain handed his telescope to the pilot.

"Pilot, can you make out the three-decker clearly?"

"Yes, Captain; it is the 'Côte d'Or.'"

"Which they have rebaptized," said the captain. "She was formerly the 'Etats de Bourgogne.' A new vessel; a hundred and twenty-eight guns."

He took a pencil and note-book from his pocket, and made the figure 128 on one of the leaves.

He continued,—

"Pilot, what is the first sail to larboard?"

"It is the 'Expérimentée.' The—"

"First-class frigate. Fifty-two guns. She was fitted out at Brest two months since."

The captain marked the figure 52 on his note-book.

"Pilot," he asked, "what is the second sail to larboard?"

"The 'Dryade.'"

"First-class frigate. Forty eighteen-pounders. She has been in India. She has a good naval reputation."

And beneath the 52 he put the figure 40; then lifting his head:—

"Now, to starboard."

"Commander, those are all second-class frigates. There are five of them."

"Which is the first, starting from the three-decker?"

"The 'Résolute.'"

"Thirty-two pieces of eighteen. And the second?"

"The 'Richemont.'"

"Same. The next?"

"The 'Athéiste.'"

"Odd name to take to sea. What next?"

"The 'Calypso.'"

"And then?"

"'La Preneuse.'"

"Five frigates, each of thirty-two guns."

The captain wrote 160 below the first figures.

"Pilot," said he, "you recognize them perfectly."

"And you," replied Gacquoil—"you know them well, Captain. To recognize is something: to know is better."

The captain had his eyes fixed on his note-book, and added between his teeth:—

"One hundred and twenty-eight, fifty-two, forty, a hundred and sixty."

At this moment La Vieuville came on deck again.

"Chevalier," the captain cried out to him, "we are in sight of three hundred and eighty cannon."

"So be it," said La Vieuville.

"You come from the inspection, La Vieuville: how many guns, exactly, have we fit for firing?"

"Nine."

"So be it," said Boisberthelot, in his turn.

He took the telescope from the pilot's hands and studied the horizon.

The eight vessels, silent and black, seemed motionless, but they grew larger.

They were approaching imperceptibly.

La Vieuville made a military salute.

"Commander," said he, "this is my report. I distrusted this corvette 'Claymore.' It is always annoying to embark suddenly on a vessel that does not know you or that does not love you. English ship—traitor to Frenchman. That slut of a carronade proved it. I have made the round. Anchors good. They are not made of half-finished iron, but forged bars soldered under the tilt-hammer. The flukes are solid. Cables excellent, easy to pay out; regulation length, a hundred and twenty fathoms. Munitions in plenty. Six gunners dead. A hundred and seventy-one rounds apiece."

"Because there are but nine pieces left," murmured the captain.

Boisberthelot levelled his telescope with the horizon. The squadron was still slowly approaching.

The carronades possess one advantage,—three men are enough to work them; but they have one inconvenience,—they do not carry so far nor aim so true as guns. It would be necessary to let the squadrons get within range of the carronades.

The captain gave his orders in a low voice. There was silence throughout the vessel. No signal to clear for battle had been given, but it was done. The corvette was as much disabled for combat with men as against the waves. Everything that was possible was done with this ruin of a war-vessel. By the gangway near the tiller-ropes were heaped all the hawsers and spare cables for strengthening the masts in case of need. The cockpit was put in order for the wounded. According to the naval use of that time, the deck was barricaded, which is a guaranty against balls but not against bullets. The ball-gauges were brought, although it was a little late, to verify the calibres; but so many incidents had not been foreseen. Each sailor received a cartridge-box, and stuck into his belt a pair of pistols and a dirk. The hammocks were stowed away, the artillery pointed, the musketry prepared, the axes and grapplings laid out, the cartridge and bullet stores made ready, and the powder-room opened. Every man was at his post. All was done without a word being spoken, like arrangements carried on in the chamber of a dying person. All was haste and gloom.

Then the corvette showed her broadside. She had six anchors, like a frigate. The whole six were cast,—the cockbill anchor forward, the kedger aft, the flood-anchor toward the open, the ebb-anchor on the side to the rocks, the bower-anchor to starboard, and the sheet-anchor to larboard.

The nine carronades still in condition were put into form, the whole nine on one side,—that toward the enemy.

The squadron had on its part not less silently completed its manœuvres. The eight vessels now formed a semicircle, of which the Minquiers made the chord. The "Claymore," enclosed in this semicircle, and into the bargain tied down by her anchors, was backed by the reef,—that is to say, by shipwreck.

It was like a pack of hounds about a wild boar, not yet giving tongue, but showing their teeth.

It seemed as if on the one side and the other they awaited some signal.

The gunners of the "Claymore" stood to their pieces.

Boisberthelot said to La Vieuville:—

"I should like to open fire."

"A coquette's whim," replied La Vieuville.

Chapter IX

SOME ONE ESCAPES

The passenger had not quitted the deck; he watched all the proceedings with the same impassible mien.

Boisberthelot approached.

"Sir," he said to him, "the preparations are complete. We are now lashed fast to our tomb; we shall not let go our hold. We are the prisoners of either the squadron or the reef. To yield to the enemy, or founder among the rocks: we have no other choice. One resource remains to us,—to die. It is better to fight than be wrecked. I would rather be shot than drowned; in the matter of death, I prefer fire to water. But dying is the business of the rest of us; it is not yours. You are the man chosen by the princes; you are appointed to a great mission,—the direction of the war in Vendée. Your loss is perhaps the monarchy lost; therefore you must live. Our honour bids us remain here; yours bids you go. General, you must quit the ship. I am going to give you a man and a boat. To reach the coast by a detour is not impossible. It is not yet day; the waves are high, the sea is dark; you will escape. There are cases when to fly is to conquer."

The old man bowed his stately head in sign of acquiescence.

Count du Boisberthelot raised his voice:—

"Soldiers and sailors!" he cried.

Every movement ceased; from each point of the vessel all faces turned toward the captain.

He continued:—

"This man who is among us represents the king. He has been confided to us; we must save him. He is necessary to the throne of France; in default of a prince he will be—at least this is what we try for—the leader of the Vendée. He is a great general. He was to have landed in France with us; he must land without us. To save the head is to save all."

"Yes! yes! yes!" cried the voices of the whole crew.

The captain continued:—

"He is about to risk, he also, serious danger. It will not be easy to reach the coast. In order to face the angry sea the boat should be large, and should be small in order to escape the cruisers. What must be done is to make land at some safe point, and better toward Fougères than in the direction of Coutances. It needs an athletic sailor, a good oarsman and swimmer, who belongs to this coast, and knows the Channel. There is night enough, so that the boat can leave the corvette without being perceived. And besides, we are going to have smoke, which will serve to hide her. The boat's size will help her through the shallows. Where the panther is snared, the weasel escapes. There is no outlet for us; there is for her. The boat will row rapidly off; the enemy's ships will not see her: and moreover, during that time we are going to amuse them ourselves. Is it decided?"

"Yes! yes! yes!" cried the crew.

"There is not an instant to lose," pursued the captain. "Is there any man willing?"

A sailor stepped out of the ranks in the darkness and said, "I."

Chapter X

DOES HE ESCAPE?

A FEW minutes later, one of those little boats called a "gig," which are especially appropriate to the captain's service, pushed off from the vessel. There were two men in this boat,—the old man in the stern, and the sailor who had volunteered in the bow. The night still lingered. The sailor, in obedience to the captain's orders, rowed vigorously in the direction of the Minquiers. For that matter, no other issue was possible. Some provisions had been put into the boat,—a bag of biscuit, a smoked ox-tongue, and a cask of water.

At the instant the gig was let down, La Vieuville, a scoffer even in the presence of destruction, leaned over the corvette's stern-post, and sneered this farewell to the boat:—

"She is a good one if one want to escape, and excellent if one wish to drown."

"Sir," said the pilot, "let us laugh no longer."

The start was quickly made, and there was soon a considerable distance between the boat and the corvette. The wind and waves were in the oarsman's favour; the little bark fled swiftly, undulating through the twilight, and hidden by the height of the waves.

The sea seemed to wear a look of sombre, indescribable expectation.

Suddenly, amid the vast and tumultuous silence of the ocean, rose a voice, which, increased by the speaking-trumpet as if by the brazen mask of antique tragedy, sounded almost superhuman.

It was the voice of Captain Boisberthelot giving his commands: "Royal marines," cried he, "nail the white flag to the main-mast. We are about to see our last sunrise."

And the corvette fired its first shot.

"Long live the king!" shouted the crew.

Then from the horizon's verge echoed an answering shout, immense, distant, confused, yet distinct nevertheless:—

"Long live the Republic!"

And a din like the peal of three hundred thunderbolts burst over the depths of the sea.

The battle began.

The sea was covered with smoke and fire. Streams of foam, made by the falling bullets, whitened the waves on every side.

The "Claymore" began to spit flame on the eight vessels. At the same time the whole squadron, ranged in a half-moon about the corvette, opened fire from all its batteries. The horizon was in a blaze. A volcano seemed to have burst suddenly out of the sea. The wind twisted to and fro the vast crimson banner of battle, amid which the ships appeared and disappeared like phantoms.

In front the black skeleton of the corvette showed against the red background.

The white banner, with its *fleur-de-lis*, could be seen floating from the main.

The two men seated in the little boat kept silence. The triangular shallows of the Minquiers, a sort of submarine Trinacrium, is larger than the entire island of Jersey. The sea covers it. It has for culminating point a platform which even the highest tides do not reach, from whence six mighty rocks detach themselves toward the northeast, ranged in a straight line, and producing the effect of a great wall, which has crumbled here and there. The strait between the plateau and the six reefs is only practicable to boats drawing very little water. Beyond this strait is the open sea.

The sailor who had undertaken the command of the boat made for this strait. By that means he put the Minquiers between the battle and the little bark. He manœuvred the narrow channel skilfully, avoiding the reefs to larboard and starboard. The rocks now masked the conflict. The lurid light of the horizon, and the awful uproar of the cannonading, began to lessen as the distance increased; but the continuance of the reports proved that the corvette held firm, and meant to exhaust to the very last her one hundred and seventy-one broadsides. Presently the boat reached safe water, beyond the reef, beyond the battle, out of reach of the bullets.

Little by little the face of the sea became less dark; the rays, against which the darkness struggled, widened; the foam burst into jets of light, and the tops of the waves gave back white reflections.

Day appeared.

The boat was out of danger so far as the enemy was concerned, but the most difficult part of the task remained. She was saved from grape-shot, but not from shipwreck. She was a mere egg-shell, in a high sea, without deck, without sail, without mast, without compass, having no resource but her oars, in the presence of the ocean and the hurricane,—an atom at the mercy of giants.

Then, amid this immensity, this solitude, lifting his face, whitened by the morning, the man in the bow of the boat looked fixedly at the one in the stern, and said:

"I am the brother of him you ordered to be shot."

BOOK III

HALMALO

CHAPTER I

SPEECH IS THE "WORD"

THE old man slowly raised his head. He who had spoken was a man of about thirty. His forehead was brown with sea-tan; his eyes were peculiar: they had the keen glance of a sailor in the open pupils of a peasant. He held the oars vigorously in his two hands. His air was mild.

In his belt were a dirk, two pistols, and a rosary.

"Who are you?" asked the old man.
"I have just told you."
"What do you want with me?"

The sailor shipped the oars, folded his arms, and replied,—

"To kill you."
"As you please," said the old man.
The other raised his voice:—
"Get ready!"
"For what?"
"To die."
"Why?" asked the old man.
There was a silence. The sailor seemed for an instant confused by the question. He repeated:—
"I say that I mean to kill you."
"And I ask you, what for?"
The sailor's eyes flashed lightning:—

"Because you killed my brother."

The old man replied with perfect calmness:—

"I began by saving his life."

"That is true. You saved him first, then you killed him."

"It was not I who killed him."

"Who, then?"

"His own fault."

The sailor stared open-mouthed at the old man; then his eyebrows met again in their murderous frown.

"What is your name?" asked the old man.

"Halmalo; but you do not need to know my name in order to be killed by me."

At this moment the sun rose. A ray struck full upon the sailor's face, and vividly lighted up that savage countenance. The old man studied it attentively.

The cannonading, though it still continued, was broken and irregular. A vast cloud of smoke weighed down the horizon. The boat, no longer directed by the oarsman, drifted to leeward.

The sailor seized in his right hand one of the pistols at his belt, and the rosary in his left.

The old man raised himself to his full height.

"You believe in God?" said he.

"Our Father which art in heaven," replied the sailor; and he made the sign of the cross.

"Have you a mother?"

"Yes."

He made a second sign of the cross. Then he resumed:

"It is all said. I give you a minute, my lord." And he cocked the pistol.

"Why do you call me 'my lord'?"

"Because you are a lord. That is plain enough to be seen."

"Have you a lord—you?"

"Yes, and a grand one. Does one live without a lord?"

"Where is he?"

"I don't know. He has left this country. He is called the Marquis de Lantenac, Viscount de Fontenay, Prince in Brittany; he is the lord of the Seven Forests. I never saw him, but that does not prevent his being my master."

"And if you were to see him, would you obey him?"

"Indeed, yes. Why, I should be a heathen if I did not obey him. I owe obedience to God; then to the king, who is like God; and then to the lord, who is like the king. But we have nothing to do with all that. You killed my brother; I must kill you."

The old man replied,—

"Agreed; I killed your brother. I did well."

The sailor clinched the pistol more tightly.

"Come," said he.

"So be it," said the old man. Still perfectly composed, he added, "Where is the priest?"

The sailor stared at him.

"The priest?"

"Yes; the priest. I gave your brother a priest; you owe me one."

"I have none," said the sailor. And he continued, "Are priests to be found out at sea?"

The convulsive thunderings of battle sounded more and more distant.

"Those who are dying yonder have theirs," said the old man.

"That is true," murmured the sailor; "they have the chaplain."

The old man continued: "You will lose me my soul; that is a serious matter."

The sailor bent his head in thought.

"And in losing me my soul," pursued the old man, "you lose your own. Listen. I have pity on you. Do what you choose. As for me, I did my duty a little while ago,—first, in saving your brother's life, and afterward in taking it from him; and I am doing my duty now in trying to save your soul. Reflect. It is your affair. Do you hear the cannon-shots at this instant? There are men perishing yonder, there are desperate creatures dying, there are husbands who will never again see their wives, fathers who will never again see their children, brothers who, like you, will never again see their brothers. And by whose fault? Your brother's—yours! You believe in God, do you not? Well, you know that God suffers in this moment; he suffers in the person of his Most Christian Son the King of France, who is a child as Jesus was, and who is a prisoner in the fortress of the Temple. God suffers in his Church of Brittany; he suffers in his insulted cathedrals, his desecrated Gospels, in his violated houses of prayer, in his murdered priests. What did we intend to do, we, with that vessel which is perishing at this instant? We were going to succour God's children. If your brother had been a good servant, if he had faithfully done his duty like a wise and prudent man, the accident of the carronade would not have occurred, the corvette would not have been disabled, she would not have got out of her course, she would not have fallen in with this fleet of perdition, and at this hour we should be landing in France,—all, like valiant soldiers and seamen as we were, sabre in hand, the white flag unfurled, numerous, glad, joyful; and we should have gone to help the brave Vendean peasants to save France, to save the king; we should have been doing God's work. This was what we meant to do; this was what we should have done. It is what I—the only one who remains—set out to do. But you oppose yourself thereto. In this contest of the impious against the priests, in this strife of the regicides against the king, in this struggle of Satan against God, you are on the devil's side. Your brother was the demon's first auxiliary; you are the second. He commenced; you finish. You are with the regicides against the throne; you are with the impious against the Church. You take away from God his last resource. Because I shall not be there,—I, who represent the king,—the hamlets will continue to burn, families to weep, priests to bleed, Brittany to suffer, the king to remain in prison, and Jesus Christ to be in distress. And who will have caused this? You! Go on; it is your affair. I depended on you to help bring about just the contrary of all this. I deceived myself. Ah, yes! it is true,—you are right: I killed your brother. Your brother was courageous; I recompensed that. He was culpable; I punished that. He had failed in his duty; I did not fail in mine. What I did, I would do again. And I swear by the great Saint Anne of Auray, who sees us, that in a similar case I would shoot my son just as I shot your brother. Now you are master. Yes, I pity you. You have lied to your captain. You, Christian, are without faith; you, Breton, are without honour. I was confided to your loyalty and accepted by your treason; you offer my death to those to whom you had promised my life. Do you know who it is you are destroying here? It is yourself. You take my life from the king, and you give your eternity to the devil. Go on; commit your crime,—it is well. You sell cheaply your share in Paradise. Thanks to you, the devil will conquer; thanks to you, the churches will fall; thanks to you, the heathen will continue to melt the bells and make cannon of them. They will shoot men with that which used to warn souls! At this moment in which I speak to you, perhaps the bell that rang for your baptism is killing your mother. Go on; aid the devil,—do not hesitate. Yes, I condemned your brother; but know this: I am an instrument of God. Ah, you pretend to judge the means God uses! Will you take it on yourself to judge Heaven's thunderbolt? Wretched man, you will be judged by it! Take care what you do. Do you even know whether I am in a state of grace? No. Go on, all the same. Do what you like. You are free to cast me into hell, and to cast yourself there with me. Our two damnations are in your hand. It is you who will be responsible before God. We are alone; face to face in the abyss. Go on—finish—make an end. I am old and you are young; I am without arms and you are armed; kill me!"

While the old man stood erect, uttering these words in a voice louder than the noise of the sea, the undulations of the waves showed him now in the shadow, now in the light. The sailor had grown lividly white; great drops of sweat fell from his forehead; he trembled like a leaf; he kissed his rosary again and again. When the old man finished speaking, he threw down his pistol and fell on his knees.

"Mercy, my lord! Pardon me!" he cried; "you speak like God. I have done wrong. My brother did wrong. I will try to repair his crime. Dispose of me. Command; I will obey."

"I give you pardon," said the old man.

Chapter II

THE PEASANT'S MEMORY IS AS GOOD AS THE CAPTAIN'S SCIENCE

THE provisions which had been put into the boat proved most acceptable. The two fugitives, obliged to make long detours, took thirty-six hours to reach the coast. They passed a night at sea; but the night was fine, though there was too much moon to be favourable to those seeking concealment.

They were obliged first to row away from France, and gain the open sea toward Jersey.

They heard the last broadside of the sinking corvette as one hears the final roar of the lion whom the hunters are killing in the wood. Then a silence fell upon the sea.

The "Claymore" died like the "Avenger," but glory has ignored her. The man who fights against his own country is never a hero.

Halmalo was a marvellous seaman. He performed miracles of dexterity and intelligence; his improvisation of a route amid the reefs, the waves, and the enemy's watch was a masterpiece. The wind had slackened and the sea grown calmer. Halmalo avoided the Caux des Minquiers, coasted the Chaussée-aux-Bœufs, and in order that they might have a few hours' rest, took shelter in the little creek on the north side, practicable at low water; then, rowing southward again, found means to pass between Granville and the Chausey Islands without being discovered by the look-out either of Granville or Chausey.

He entered the bay of Saint-Michel, —a bold undertaking, on account of the neighbourhood of Cancale, an anchorage for the cruising squadron.

About an hour before sunset on the evening of the second day, he left Mont Saint-Michel behind him, and proceeded to land on a beach deserted because the shifting sands made it dangerous.

Fortunately the tide was high.

Halmalo drove the boat as far up as he could, tried the sand, found it firm, ran the bark aground, and sprang on shore. The old man strode over the side after him and examined the horizon.

"Monseigneur," said Halmalo, "we are here at the mouth of the Couesnon. There is Beauvoir to starboard, and Huisnes to larboard. The belfry in front of us is Ardevon."

The old man bent down to the boat and took a biscuit, which he put in his pocket, and said to Halmalo:

"Take the rest."

Halmalo put the remains of the meat and biscuit into the bag and slung it over his shoulder. This done, he said:—

"Monseigneur, must I conduct or follow you?"

"Neither the one nor the other." Halmalo regarded the speaker in stupefied wonder.

The old man continued:—

"Halmalo, we must separate. It will not answer to be two. There must be a thousand or one alone."

He paused, and drew from one of his pockets a green silk bow, rather like a cockade, with a gold *fleur-de-lis* embroidered in the centre. He resumed:—

"Do you know how to read?"

"No."

"That is fortunate. A man who can read is troublesome. Have you a good memory?"

"Yes."

"That will do. Listen, Halmalo. You must take to the right and I to the left. I shall go in the direction of Fougères, you toward Bazouges. Keep your bag; it gives you the look of a peasant. Conceal your weapons. Cut yourself a stick in the thickets. Creep among the fields of rye, which are high. Slide behind the hedges. Climb the fences in order to go across the meadows. Leave passers-by at a distance. Avoid the roads and the bridges. Do not enter Pontorson. Ah! you will have to cross the Couesnon. How will you manage?"

"I shall swim."

"That's right. And there is a ford —do you know where it is?"

"Between Ancey and Vieux-Viel."

"That is right. You do really belong to the country."

"But night is coming on. Where will Monseigneur sleep?"

"I can take care of myself. And you —where will you sleep?"

"There are hollow trees. I was a peasant before I was a sailor."

"Throw away your sailor's hat; it will betray you. You will easily find a woolen cap."

"Oh, a peasant's thatch is to be found anywhere. The first fisherman will sell me his."

"Very good. Now listen. You know the woods?"

"All of them."

"Of the whole district?"

"From Noirmoutier to Laval."

"Do you know their names too?"

"I know the woods; I know their names; I know about everything."

"You will forget nothing?"

"Nothing."

"Good! At present, attention. How many leagues can you make in a day?"

"Ten, fifteen—twenty, if necessary."

"It will be. Do not lose a word of what I am about to say. You will go to the wood of Saint-Aubin."

"Near Lamballe?"

"Yes. On the edge of the ravine between Saint-Reuil and Plédiac there is a large chestnut-tree. You will stop there. You will see no one."

"Which will not hinder somebody's being there. I know."

"You will give the call. Do you know how to give the call?"

Halmalo puffed out his cheeks, turned toward the sea, and there sounded the "to-whit, to-hoo" of an owl.

One would have said it came from the night-locked recesses of a forest. It was sinister and owl-like.

"Good!" said the old man. "You have it."

He held out the bow of green silk to Halmalo.

"This is my badge of command. Take it. It is important that no one should as yet know my name; but this knot will be sufficient. The *fleur-de-lis* was embroidered by Madame Royale in the Temple prison."

Halmalo bent one knee to the ground. He trembled as he took the flower-embroidered knot, and brought it near to his lips, then paused, as if frightened at this kiss.

"Can I?" he demanded.

"Yes, since you kiss the crucifix."

Halmalo kissed the *fleur-de-lis*.

"Rise," said the old man.

Halmalo rose and hid the knot in his breast.

The old man continued,—

"Listen well to this. This is the order: Up! Revolt! No quarter! On the edge of this wood of Saint-Aubin you will give the call. You will repeat it thrice. The third time you will see a man spring out of the ground."

"Out of a hole under the trees. I know."

"This man will be Planchenault, who is also called the King's Heart. You will show him this knot. He will understand. Then, by routes you must find out, you will go to the wood of Astillé; there you will find a cripple, who is surnamed Mousqueton, and who shows pity to none. You will tell him that I love him, and that he is to set the parishes in motion. From there you will go to the wood of Couesbon, which is a league from Ploërmel. You will give the owl-cry; a man will come out of a hole. It will be Thuault, seneschal of Ploërmel, who has belonged to what is called the Constituent Assembly, but on the good side. You will tell him to arm the castle of Couesbon, which belongs to the Marquis de Guer, a refugee. Ravines, little woods, ground uneven,—a good place. Thuault is a clever, straightforward man. Thence you will go to Saint-Guen-les-Toits, and you will talk with Jean Chouan, who is, in my mind, the real chief. From thence you will go to the wood of Ville-Anglose, where you will see Guitter, whom they call Saint Martin; you will bid him have his eye on a certain Courmesnil, who is the son-in-law of old Goupil de Préfeln, and who leads the Jacobinery of Argentan. Recollect all this. I write nothing, because nothing should be written. La Rouarie made out a list; it ruined all. Then you will go to the wood of Rougefeu, where is Miélette, who leaps the ravine on a long pole."

"It is called a leaping-pole."

"Do you know how to use it?"

"Am I not a Breton and a peasant? The *ferte* is our friend. She widens our arms and lengthens our legs."

"That is to say, she makes the enemy smaller and shortens the route. A good machine."

"Once on a time, with my *ferte*, I held my own against three salt-tax men who had sabres."

"When was that?"

"Ten years ago."

"Under the king?"

"Yes, of course."

"Then you fought in the time of the king?"

"Yes, to be sure."

"Against whom?"

"My faith, I do not know! I was a salt-smuggler."

"Very good."

"They called that fighting against the excise officers. Were they the same thing as the king?"

"Yes. No. But it is not necessary that you should understand."

"I beg Monseigneur's pardon for having asked a question of Monseigneur."

"Let us continue. Do you know La Tourgue?"

"Do I know La Tourgue? Why, I belong there."

"How?"

"Certainly, since I come from Parigné."

"In fact, La Tourgue is near Parigné"

"Know La Tourgue! The big round castle that belongs to my lord's family? There is a great iron door which separates the new part from the old that a cannon could not blow open. The famous book about Saint Bartholomew, which people go to look at from curiosity, is in the new building. There are frogs in the grass. When I was little, I used to go and tease them. And the underground passage, I know that; perhaps there is nobody else left who does."

"What underground passage? I do not know what you mean."

"It was made for old times, in the days when La Tourgue was besieged. The people inside could escape by going through the underground passage which leads into the wood."

"There is a subterranean passage of that description in the castle of Jupellière, and the castle of Hunaudaye, and the tower of Champéon; but there is nothing of the sort at La Tourgue."

"Oh, yes, indeed, Monseigneur! I do not know the passages that Monseigneur spoke of; I only know that of La Tourgue, because I belong to the neighbourhood. Into the bargain, there is nobody but myself who does know it. It was not talked about. It was forbidden, because it had been used in the time of Monsieur de Rohan's wars. My father knew the secret, and showed it to me. I know how to get in and out. If I am in the forest, I can go into the tower, and if I am in the tower, I can go into the forest, without anybody's seeing me. When the enemy enters, there is no longer any one there. That is what the passage of La Tourgue is. Oh, I know it!"

The old man remained silent for a moment.

"It is evident that you deceive yourself. If there were such a secret, I should know it."

"Monseigneur, I am certain. There is a stone that turns."

"Ah, good! You peasants believe in stones that turn and stones that sing, and stones that go at night to drink from the neighbouring brook. A pack of nonsense!"

"But since I have made the stone turn—"

"Just as others have heard it sing. Comrade, La Tourgue is a fortress, sure and strong, easy to defend; but anybody who counted on a subterranean passage for getting out of it would be silly indeed."

"But, Monseigneur—"

The old man shrugged his shoulders. "We are losing time; let us talk of what concerns us."

The peremptory tone cut short Halmalo's persistence.

The unknown resumed:—

"To continue. Listen. From Rougefeu you will go to the wood of Montchevrier; Benedicité is there, the chief of the Twelve. There is another good fellow. He says his *Bénédicité* while he has people shot. War and sensibility do not go together. From Montchevrier, you will go—"

He broke off.

"I forgot the money."

He took from his pocket a purse and a pocket-book, and put them in Halmalo's hand.

"There are thirty thousand livres in assignats in the pocket-book (something like three pounds); it is true the assignats are false, but the real ones are just as worthless. In the purse—attention—there are a hundred gold louis. I give you all I have. I have no need of anything here. Besides, it is better that no money should be found on me. I resume. From Montchevrier you will go to Antrain, where you will see Monsieur de Frotté; from Antrain to La Jupellière, where you will see De Rochecotte; from La Jupellière to Noirieux, where you will find the Abbé Baudoin. Can you recollect all this?"

"Like my paternoster."

"You will see Monsieur Dubois-Guy at Saint-Bricen-en-Cogles, Monsieur de Turpin at Morannes, which is a fortified town, and the Prince de Talmont at Château-Gonthier."

"Shall I be spoken to by a prince?"

"Since I speak to you."

Halmalo took off his hat.

"Madame's *fleur-de-lis* will ensure you a good reception everywhere. Do not forget that you are going into the country of mountaineers and rustics. Disguise yourself. It will be easy to do.

These republicans are so stupid that you may pass anywhere with a blue coat, a three-cornered hat, and a tricoloured cockade. There are no longer regiments, there are no longer uniforms; the companies are not numbered; each man puts on any rag he pleases. You will go to Saint-Mhervé; there you will see Gaulier, called Great Peter. You will go to the cantonment of Parné, where the men blacken their faces. They put gravel into their guns, and a double charge of powder, in order to make more noise. It is well done; but tell them, above all, to kill—kill—kill! You will go to the camp of the Vache Noire, which is on a height; to the middle of the wood of La Charnie, then to the camp Avoine, then to the camp Vert, then to the camp of the Fourmis. You will go to the Grand Bordage, which is also called the Haut de Pré, and is inhabited by a widow whose daughter married Treton, nicknamed the Englishman. Grand Bordage is in the parish of Quelaines. You will visit Epineux-le-Chevreuil, Sillé-le-Guillaume, Parannes, and all the men in all of the woods. You will make friends, and you will send them to the borders of the high and the low Maine; you will see Jean Treton in the parish of Vaisges, Sans Regret at Bignon, Chambord at Bonchamps, the brothers Corbin at Maisoncelles, and the Petit-sans-Peur at Saint-John-on-Erve. He is the one who is called Bourdoiseau. All that done, and the watch-word — Revolt! No quarter!—given everywhere, you will join the grand army, the Catholic and royal army, wherever it may be. You will see D'Elbée, De Lescure, De la Rochejacquelein, all the chiefs who may chance to be still living. You will show them my token of command. They all know what it means. You are only a sailor, but Cathelineau is only a carter. This is what you must say to them from me: 'It is time to join the two wars, the great and the little. The great makes the most noise; the little does the most execution. The Vendée is good; *Chouannerie* is worse; and in civil war the worst is the best. The goodness of a war is judged by the amount of bad it does.'"

He paused.

"Halmalo, I say all this to you. You do not understand the words, but you comprehend the things themselves. I gained confidence in you from seeing you manage the boat. You do not understand goemetry, yet you perform sea-manœuvres that are marvellous. He who can manage a boat can pilot an insurrection. From the way in which you have conducted this sea intrigue, I am certain you will fulfil all my commands well. I resume. You will tell the whole to the chiefs, in your own way, of course; but it will be well told. I prefer the war of the forest to the war of the plain; I have no wish to set a hundred thousand peasants in line, and expose them to Carnot's artillery and the grape-shot of the Blues. In less than a month I mean to have five hundred thousand sharpshooters ambushed in the woods. The Republican army is my game. Poaching is our way of waging war. Mine is the strategy of the thickets. Good; there is still another expression you will not catch; no matter, you will seize this: *No quarter, and ambushes everywhere.* I depend more on bush fighting than on regular battles.

You will add that the English are with us. We catch the Republic between two fires. Europe assists us. Let us make an end of the Revolution. Kings will wage a war of kingdoms against it; let us wage a war of parishes. You will say this. Have you understood?"

"Yes. Put all to fire and sword."

"That is it."

"No quarter."

"Not to a soul. That is it."

"I will go everywhere."

"And be careful, for in this country it is easy to become a dead man."

"Death does not concern me. He who takes his first step uses perhaps his last shoes."

"You are a brave fellow."

"And if I am asked Monseigneur's name?"

"It must not be known yet. You will say you do not know it, and that will be the truth."

"Where shall I see Monseigneur again?"

"Where I shall be."

"How shall I know?"

"Because all the world will know. I shall be talked of before eight days go by. I shall make examples; I shall avenge religion and the king, and you will know well that it is I of whom they speak."

"I understand."

"Forget nothing."

"Be tranquil."

"Now go. May God guide you! Go."

"I will do all that you have bidden me. I will go. I will speak. I will obey. I will command."

"Good!"

"And if I succeed?"

"I will make you a knight of Saint Louis."

"Like my brother. And if I fail, you will have me shot?"

"Like your brother."

"Done, monseigneur."

The old man bent his head and seemed to fall into a sombre reverie. When he raised his eyes he was alone. Halmalo was only a black spot disappearing on the horizon.

The sun had just set.

The sea-mews and the hooded gulls flew homeward from the darkening ocean.

That sort of inquietude which precedes the night made itself felt in space. The green frogs croaked; the kingfishers flew whistling out of the pools; the gulls and the rooks kept up their evening tumult; the cry of the shore birds could be heard, but not a human sound. The solitude was complete. Not a sail in the bay, not a peasant in the fields. As far as the eye could reach stretched a deserted plain. The great sand-thistles shivered. The white sky of twilight cast a vast livid pallor over the shore. In the distance, the pools scattered over the plain looked like great sheets of pewter spread flat upon the ground. The wind hurried in from the sea with a moan.

BOOK IV

TELLMARCH

CHAPTER I

THE TOP OF THE DUNE

THE old man waited till Halmalo disappeared, then he drew his fisherman's cloak closely about him and set out on his course. He walked with slow steps, thinking deeply. He took the direction of Huisnes, while Halmalo went toward Beauvoir.

Behind him, an enormous black triangle, with a cathedral for tiara and a fortress for breastplate, with its two great towers to the east, one round, the other square, helping to support the weight of the church and village, rose Mont-Saint-Michel, which is to the ocean what the Pyramid of Cheops is to the desert.

The quicksands of Mont-Saint-Michel Bay insensibly displace their dunes. Between Huisnes and Ardevon there was at that time a very high one, which is now completely effaced. This dune, levelled by an equinoctial storm, had the peculiarity of being very ancient; on its summit stood a commemorative column, erected in the twelfth century, in memory of the council held at Avranches against the assassins of Saint Thomas of Canterbury. From the top of this dune the whole district could be seen, and one could fix the points of the compass.

The old man ascended it.

When he reached the top, he sat down on one of the projections of the stones, with his back against the pillar, and began to study the kind of geographical chart spread beneath his feet. He seemed to be seeking a route in a district which had once been familiar. In the whole of this vast landscape, made indistinct by the twilight, there was nothing clearly defined but the horizon stretching black against the sky.

He could perceive the roofs of eleven towns and villages; could distinguish for several leagues' distance all the bell-towers of the coast, which were built very high, to serve in case of need as landmarks to boats at sea.

At the end of a few minutes the old man appeared to have found what he sought in this dim clearness. His eyes rested on an enclosure of trees, walls, and roofs, partially visible midway between the plain and the wood; it was a farm. He nodded his head in the satisfied way a man does who says to himself, "There it is," and began to trace with his finger a route across the fields and hedges. From time to time he examined a shapeless, indistinct object stirring on the principal roof of the farm, and seemed to ask himself, "What can it be?" It was colourless and confused, owing to the gloom; it floated—therefore it was not a weathercock; and there was no reason why it should be a flag.

He was weary; he remained in his resting-place, and yielded passively to the vague forgetfulness which the first moments of repose bring over a tired man.

There is an hour of the day which may be called noiseless: it is the serene hour of early evening. It was about him now. He enjoyed it; he looked, he listened—to what? The tranquillity. Even savage natures have their moments of melancholy.

Suddenly this tranquillity was not troubled, but accentuated by the voices of persons passing below,—the voices of women and children. It was like a chime of joy-bells unexpectedly ringing amid the shadows. The underbrush hid the group from whence the voices came, but it was moving slowly along the foot of the dune toward the plain and the forest. The clear, fresh tones reached distinctly the pensive old man; they were so near that he could catch every word.

A woman's voice said,—

"We must hurry ourselves, Flécharde. Is this the way?"

"No, yonder."

The dialogue went on between the two voices,—one high-pitched, the other low and timid.

"What is the name of the farm we are stopping at?"

"L'Herbe-en-Pail."

"Will it take us much longer to get there?"

"A good quarter of an hour."

"We must hurry on to get our soup."

"Yes; we are late."

"We shall have to run. But those brats of yours are tired. We are only two women; we can't carry three brats. And you—you are already carrying one, my Flécharde; a regular lump of lead. You have weaned the little gormandizer, but you carry her all the same. A bad habit. Do me the favour to make her walk. Oh, very well—so much the worse! The soup will be cold."

"Oh, what good shoes these are that you gave me! I should think they had been made for me."

"It is better than going barefooted, eh?"

"Hurry up, René-Jean!"

"He is the very one that hindered us. He must needs chatter with all the little peasant girls he met. Oh, he shows the man already!"

"Yes, indeed; why, he is going on five years old."

"I say, René-Jean, what made you talk to that little girl in the village?"

A child's voice, that of a boy, replied,—

"Because she was an acquaintance of mine."

"What, you know her?" asked the woman.

"Yes, ever since this morning; she played some games with me."

"Oh, what a man you are!" cried the woman. "We have only been three days in the neighbourhood; that creature there is no bigger than your fist, and he has found a sweetheart already!"

The voices grew fainter and fainter; then every sound died away.

Chapter II

AURES HABET, ET NON AUDIET

The old man sat motionless. He was not thinking, scarcely dreaming. About him was serenity, rest, safety, solitude. It was still broad daylight on the dune, but almost dark in the plain, and quite night in the forest. The moon was floating up the east; a few stars dotted the pale blue of the zenith. This man, though full of preoccupation and stern cares, lost himself in the ineffable sweetness of the infinite. He felt within him the obscure dawn of hope, if the word hope may be applied to the workings of civil warfare. For the instant it seemed to him that in escaping from that inexorable sea and touching land once more, all danger had vanished. No one knew his name; he was alone, escaped from the enemy, having left no trace behind him, for the sea leaves no track; hidden, ignored; not even suspected. He felt an indescribable calm; a little more and he would have fallen asleep.

What made the strange charm of this tranquil home to that man, a prey within and without to such tumults, was the profound silence alike in earth and sky.

He heard nothing but the wind from the sea; but the wind is a continual bass, which almost ceases to be a noise, so accustomed does the ear become to its tone.

Suddenly he started to his feet.

His attention had been quickly awakened; he looked about the horizon. Then his glance fixed eagerly upon a particular point. What he looked at was the belfry of Cormeray, which rose before him at the extremity of the plain. Something very extraordinary was going on within it.

The belfry was clearly defined against the sky; he could see the tower surmounted by the spire, and between the two the cage for the bell, square, without pent-house, open at the four sides after the fashion of Breton belfries.

Now this cage appeared alternately to open and shut at regular intervals; its lofty opening showed entirely white, then black; the sky could be seen for an instant through it, then it disappeared; a gleam of light would come, then an eclipse, and the opening and shutting succeeded each other from moment to moment with the regularity of a hammer striking its anvil.

This belfry of Cormeray was in front of the old man, about two leagues from the place where he stood. He looked to his right at the belfry of Baguer-Pican, which rose equally straight and distinct against the horizon; its cage was opening and shutting, like that of Cormeray.

He looked to his left, at the belfry of Tanis: the cage of the belfry of Tanis opened and shut, like that of Baguer-Pican.

He examined all the belfries upon the horizon, one after another; to his left those of Courtils, of Précey, of Crollon, and the Croix-Avranchin; to his right the belfries of Raz-sur-Couesnon, of Mordrey, and of the Pas; in front of him, the belfry of Pontorson. The cages of all these belfries were alternately white and black.

What did this mean?

It meant that all the bells were swinging. In order to appear and disappear in this way they must be violently rung.

What was it for? The tocsin, without doubt.

The tocsin was sounding, sounding madly, on every side, from all the belfries, in all the parishes, in all the villages; and yet he could hear nothing.

This was owing to the distance and the wind from the sea, which, sweeping in the opposite direction, carried every sound of the shore out beyond the horizon.

All these mad bells calling on every side, and at the same time this silence; nothing could be more sinister.

The old man looked and listened. He did not hear the tocsin; he saw it. It was a strange sensation, that of seeing the tocsin.

Against whom was this rage of the bells directed?

Against whom did this tocsin sound?

Chapter III

USEFULNESS OF BIG LETTERS

Assuredly some one was snared.

Who?

A shiver ran through this man of steel.

It could not be he? His arrival could not have been discovered. It was impossible that the acting representative should have received information; he had scarcely landed. The corvette had evidently foundered, and not a man had escaped. And even on the corvette, Boisberthelot and La Vieuville alone knew his name.

The belfries kept up their savage sport. He mechanically watched and counted them; and his meditations, pushed from one conjecture to another, had those fluctuations caused by a sudden change from complete security to a terrible consciousness of peril. Still, after all, this tocsin might be accounted for in many ways; and he ended by reassuring himself with the repetition of, "In short, no one knows of my arrival, and no one knows my name."

During the last few seconds there had been a slight noise above and behind him. This noise was like the fluttering of leaves. He paid no attention to it at first, but as the sound continued—one might have said insisted on making itself heard—he turned round at length. It was in fact a leaf, but a leaf of paper. The wind was trying to tear off a large placard pasted on the stone above his head. This placard had been very lately fastened there, for it was still moist, and offered a hold to the wind, which had begun to play with and was detaching it.

The old man had ascended the dune on the opposite side, and had not seen this placard as he came up.

He mounted the coping where he had been seated, and laid his hand on the corner of the paper which the wind moved. The sky was clear, for the June twilights are long; the bottom of the dune was shadowy, but the top in light. A portion of the placard was printed in large letters, and there was still light enough for him to make it out. He read this:—

THE FRENCH REPUBLIC, ONE AND INDIVISIBLE.

We, Prieur, of the Marne, acting representative of the people with the army of the coast of Cherbourg, give notice: The *ci-devant* Marquis de Lantenac, Viscount de Fontenay, so-called Breton prince, secretly landed on the coast of Granville, is declared an outlaw. — A price is set on his head. — Any person bringing him, alive or dead, will receive the sum of sixty thousand livres. — This amount will not be paid in assignats, but in gold. — A battalion of the Cherbourg coast-guards will be immediately dispatched for the apprehension of the so-called Marquis de Lantenac.

The parishes are ordered to lend every assistance.

Given at the Town-Hall of Granville, this 2nd of June, 1793.

(Signed)
PRIEUR, DE LA MARNE.

Under this name was another signature, in much smaller characters, and which the failing light prevented the old man's deciphering.

The old man pulled his hat over his eyes, closed his sea-jacket up to his chin and rapidly descended the dune.

It was unsafe to remain longer on this summit.

He had perhaps already stayed too long; the top of the dune was the point in the landscape which still remained visible.

When he reached the obscurity of the bottom, he slackened his pace.

He took the route which he had traced for himself toward the farm, evidently having reason to believe that he should be safe in that direction.

The plain was deserted. There were no passers-by at that hour.

He stopped behind a thicket of underbrush, undid his cloak, turned his vest the hairy side out, refastened his rag of a mantle about his neck by its cord, and resumed his way.

The moon was shining.

He reached a point where two roads branched off; an old stone cross stood there. Upon the pedestal of the cross he could distinguish a white square, which was most probably a notice like that he had just read. He went toward it.

"Where are you going?" said a voice.

He turned round.

A man was standing in the hedge-row, tall like himself, old like himself, with white hair like his own, and garments even more dilapidated,—almost his double. This man leaned on a long stick.

He repeated,—

"I ask you where you are going."

"In the first place, where am I?" returned he, with an almost haughty composure.

The man replied,—

"You are in the seigneury of Tanis. I am its beggar; you are its lord."

"I?"

"Yes, you, my lord Marquis de Lantenac."

CHAPTER IV

THE CAIMAND

THE Marquis de Lantenac—we shall henceforth call him by his name—answered quietly:—

"So be it. Give me up."

The man continued:—

"We are both at home here: you in the castle, I in the bushes."

"Let us finish. Do your work. Betray me," said the marquis.

The man went on:—

"You were going to the farm of Herbe-en-Pail, were you not?"

"Yes."

"Do not go."

"Why?"

"Because the Blues are there."

"Since how long?"

"These three days."

"Did the people of the farm and the hamlet resist?"

"No; they opened all the doors."

"Ah!" said the marquis.

The man pointed with his finger toward the roof of the farm-house, which could be perceived above the trees at a short distance.

"You can see the roof, Marquis?"

"Yes."

"Do you see what there is above it?"

"Something floating?"

"Yes."

"It is a flag."

"The tricolour," said the man.

This was the object which had attracted the marquis's attention as he stood on the top of the dune.

"Is not the tocsin sounding?" asked the marquis.

"Yes."

"On what account?"

"Evidently on yours."

"But I cannot hear it."

"The wind carries the sound the other way."

The man added,—

"Did you see your placard?"

"Yes."

"They are hunting you;" and casting a glance toward the farm, he added, "There is a demi-battalion there."

"Of republicans?"

"Parisians."

"Very well," said the marquis; "march on."

And he took a step in the direction of the farm.

The man seized his arm.

"Do not go there."

"Where do you wish me to go?"

"Home with me."

The marquis looked steadily at the mendicant.

"Listen, my lord marquis. My house is not fine, but it is safe. A cabin lower than a cave. For flooring a bed of seaweed, for ceiling a roof of branches and grass. Come. At the farm you will be shot; in my house you may go to sleep. You must be tired; and to-morrow morning the Blues will march on, and you can go where you please."

The marquis studied this man.

"Which side are you on?" he asked. "Are you republican? Are you royalist?"

"I am a beggar."

"Neither royalist nor republican?"

"I believe not."

"Are you for or against the king?"

"I have no time for that sort of thing."

"What do you think of what is passing?"

"I have nothing to live on."

"Still you come to my assistance."

"Because I saw you were outlawed. What is the law? So one can be beyond its pale. I do not comprehend. Am I inside the law? Am I outside the law? I don't in the least know. To die of hunger, is that being within the law?"

"How long have you been dying of hunger?"

"All my life."

"And you save me?"

"Yes."

"Why?"

"Because I said to myself. 'There is one poorer than I. I have the right to breathe; he has not.'"

"That is true. And you save me?"

"Of course; we are brothers, monseigneur. I ask for bread; you ask for life. We are a pair of beggars."

"But do you know there is a price set on my head?"

"Yes."

"How did you know?"

"I read the placard."

"You know how to read?"

"Yes; and to write, too. Why should I be a brute?"

"Then, since you can read, and since you have seen the notice, you know that a man would earn sixty thousand livres by giving me up?"

"I know it."

"Not in assignats."

"Yes, I know; in gold."

"Sixty thousand livres! **Do you know** it is a fortune?"

"Yes."

"And that anybody apprehending me would make his fortune?"

"Very well; what next?"

"His fortune!"

"That is exactly what I thought. When I saw you, I said, 'Just to think anybody by giving up that man yonder would gain sixty thousand livres, and make his fortune!' Let us hasten to hide him."

The marquis followed the beggar.

They entered a thicket; the mendicant's den was there. It was a sort of chamber which a great old oak had allowed the man to take possession of within its heart; it was dug down among its roots, and covered by its branches. It was dark, low, hidden, invisible. There was room for two persons.

"I foresaw that I might have a guest," said the mendicant.

This species of underground lodging, less rare in Brittany than people fancy, is called in the peasant dialect a *carnichot*. The name is also applied to hiding-places contrived in thick walls.

It was furnished with a few jugs, a pallet of straw or dried wrack, with a thick covering of kersey; some tallow-dips, a flint and steel, and a bundle of furze twigs for tinder.

They stooped low,—crept rather,— penetrated into the chamber, which the great roots of the tree divided into fantastic compartments, and seated themselves on the heap of dry sea-weed which served as a bed. The space between two of the roots, which made the doorway, allowed a little light to enter. Night had come on; but the eye adapts itself to the darkness, and one always finds at last a little day among the shadows. A reflection from the moon's rays dimly silvered the entrance. In a corner was a jug of water, a loaf of buckwheat bread, and some chestnuts.

"Let us sup," said the beggar.

They divided the chestnuts; the marquis contributed his morsel of biscuit. They bit into the same black loaf, and drank out of the jug, one after the other.

They conversed.

The marquis began to question this man.

"So, no matter whether anything or nothing happens, it is all the same to you?"

"Pretty much. You are the lords, you others. Those are your affairs."

"But after all, present events—"

"Pass away up out of my reach."

The beggar added presently:—

"Then there are things that go on still higher up; the sun that rises, the moon that increases or diminishes; those are the matters I occupy myself about."

He took a sip from the jug, and said,—

"The good fresh water!"

Then he asked,—

"How do you find the water, monseigneur?"

"What is your name?" inquired the marquis.

"My name is Tellmarch. but I am called the Caimand."

"I understand. *Caimand* is a word of the district."

"Which means beggar. I am also nicknamed Le Vieux. I have been called 'the old man' these forty years."

"Forty years! But you were a young man then."

"I never was young. You remain so always, on the contrary, my lord marquis. You have the legs of a boy of twenty; you can climb the great dune. As for me, I begin to find it difficult to walk; at the end of a quarter of a league I am tired. Nevertheless, our age is the same. But the rich, they have an advantage over us,—they eat every day. Eating is a preservative."

After a silence the mendicant resumed:—

"Poverty, riches—that makes a terrible business. That is what brings on the catastrophes,—at least, I have that idea. The poor want to be rich; the rich are not willing to be poor. I think that is about what it is at the bottom. I do not mix myself up with matters. The events are the events. I am neither for the creditor nor for the debtor. I know there is a debt, and that it is being paid. That is all. I would rather they had not killed the king; but it would be difficult for me to say why. After that, somebody will answer, 'But remember how they used to hang poor fellows on trees for nothing at all.' See; just for a miserable gunshot fired at one of the king's roebucks, I myself saw a man hung who had a wife and seven children. There is much to say on both sides."

Again he was silent for a while. Then:—

"I am a little of a bone-setter, a little of a doctor, I know the herbs, I study plants. The peasants see me absent, preoccupied, and that makes me pass for a sorcerer. Because I dream, they think I must be wise."

"You belong to the neighbourhood?" asked the marquis.

"I never was out of it."

"You know me?"

"Of course. The last time I saw you was when you passed through here two years ago. You went from here to England. A little while since I saw a man on the top of the dune,—a very tall man. Tall men are rare; Brittany is a country of small men. I looked close; I had read the notice; I said to myself, 'Ah ha!' And when you came down there was moonlight, and I recognized you."

"And yet I do not know you."

"You have seen me, but you never looked at me."

And Tellmarch the Caimand added,—

"I looked at you, though. The giver and the beggar do not look with the same eyes."

"Had I encountered you formerly?"

"Often; I am your beggar. I was the mendicant at the foot of the road from your castle. You have given me alms. But he who gives does not notice; he who receives examines and observes. When you say mendicant, you say spy. But as for me, though I am often sad, I try not to be a malicious spy. I used to hold out my hand; you only saw the hand, and you threw into it the charity I needed in the morning in order that I might not die in the evening. I have often been twenty-four hours without eating. Sometimes a penny is life. I owe you my life; I pay the debt."

"That is true; you save me."

"Yes, I save you, monseigneur."

And Tellmarch's voice grew solemn as he added,—

"On one condition."

"And that?"

"That you are not come here to do harm."

"I come here to do good," said the marquis.

"Let us sleep," said the beggar.

They lay down side by side on the sea-weed bed. The mendicant fell asleep immediately. The marquis, although very tired, remained thinking deeply for a few moments; he gazed fixedly at the beggar in the shadow, and then lay back. To lie on that bed was to lie on the ground,—which suggested to him to put his ear to the earth and listen. He could hear a strange buzzing underground. We know that sound stretches down into the depths: he could hear the noise of the bells.

The tocsin was still sounding.

The marquis fell asleep.

Chapter V

SIGNED GAUVAIN

It was daylight when he awoke. The mendicant was standing up,—not in the den, for he could not hold himself erect there, but without, on the sill. He was leaning on his stick. The sun shone upon his face.

"Monseigneur," said Tellmarch, "four o'clock has just sounded from the belfry of Tanis. I could count the strokes, therefore the wind has changed: it is the land breeze. I can hear no other sound, so the tocsin has ceased. Everything is tranquil about the farm and hamlet of Herbe-en-Pail. The Blues are asleep or gone. The worst of the danger is over; it will be wise for us to separate. It is my hour for setting out."

He indicated a point in the horizon.

"I am going that way."

He pointed in the opposite direction.

"Go you this way."

The beggar made the marquis a gesture of salute. He pointed to the remains of the supper.

"Take the chestnuts with you, if you are hungry."

A moment after, he disappeared among the trees.

The marquis rose and departed in the direction which Tellmarch had indicated.

It was that charming hour called in the old Norman peasant dialect "the song-sparrow of the day." The finches and the hedge-sparrows flew chirping about. The marquis followed the path by which they had come on the previous night. He passed out of the thicket and found himself at the fork of the road, marked by the stone cross. The placard was still there, looking white, fairly gay, in the rising sun. He remembered that there was something at the bottom of the placard which he had not been able to read the evening before, on account of the twilight and the size of the letters. He went up to the pedestal of the cross. Under the signature "PRIEUR, DE LA MARNE," there were yet two other lines in small characters:—

The identity of the *ci-devant* Marquis de Lantenac established, he will be immediately shot.

(Signed)

GAUVAIN,

Chief of battalion commanding the exploring column.

"Gauvain!" said the marquis. He stood still, thinking deeply, his eyes fixed on the notice.

"Gauvain!" he repeated.

He resumed his march, turned about, looked again at the cross, walked back, and once more read the placard.

Then he went slowly away. Had any person been near, he might have been heard to murmur, in a half-voice, "Gauvain!"

From the sunken paths into which he retreated he could only see the roofs of the farm, which lay to the left. He passed along the side of a steep eminence covered with furze, of the species called long-thorn, in blossom. The summit of this height was one of those points of land named in Brittany a *hure.*

At the foot of the eminence the gaze lost itself among the trees. The foliage seemed bathed in light. All Nature was filled with the deep joy of the morning.

Suddenly this landscape became terrible. It was like the bursting forth of an ambuscade. An appalling, indescribable trumpeting, made by savage cries and gunshots, struck upon these fields and these woods filled with sunlight, and there could be seen rising from the side toward the farm a great smoke, cut by clear flames, as if the hamlet and the farm buildings were consuming like a truss of burning straw. It was sudden and fearful,—the abrupt change from tranquillity to fury; an explosion of hell in the midst of dawn; a horror without transition. There was fighting in the direction of Herbe-en-Pail. The marquis stood still.

There is no man in a similar case who would not feel curiosity stronger than a sense of the peril. One must know what is happening, if one perish in the attempt. He mounted the eminence along the bottom of which passed the sunken path by which he had come. From there he could see, but he could also be seen. He remained on the top for some instants. He looked about.

There was, in truth, a fusillade and a conflagration. He could hear the cries, he could see the flames. The farm appeared the centre of some terrible catastrophe. What could it be? Was the farm of Herbe-en-Pail attacked? But by whom? Was it a battle? Was it not rather a military execution? Very often the Blues punished refractory farms and villages by setting them on fire. They were ordered to do so by a revolutionary decree; they burned, for example, every farm-house and hamlet where the tree-cutting prescribed by law had been neglected, or no roads opened among the thickets for the passage of the republican cavalry. Only very lately, the parish of Bourgon, near Ernée, had been thus destroyed. Was Herbe-en-Pail receiving similar treatment? It was evident that none of the strategic routes called for by the decree had been made among the copses and enclosures. Was this the punishment for such neglect? Had an order been received by the advance-guard occupying the farm? Did not this troop make part of one of those exploring divisions called the "infernal columns"?

A bristling and savage thicket surrounded on all sides the eminence upon which the marquis had posted himself for an outlook. This thicket, which was called the grove of Herbe-en-Pail, but which had the proportions of a wood, stretched to the farm, and concealed, like all Breton copses, a network of ravines, by-paths, and deep cuttings, labyrinths where the republican armies lost themselves.

The execution, if it were an execution, must have been a ferocious one, for it was short. It had been, like all brutal deeds, quickly accomplished. The atrocity of civil wars admits of these savage vagaries. While the marquis, multiplying conjectures, hesitating to descend, hesitating to remain, listened and watched, this crash of extermination ceased, or, more correctly speaking, vanished. The marquis took note of something in the thicket that was like the scattering of a wild and joyous troop. A frightful rushing about made itself heard beneath the trees. From the farm the band had thrown themselves into the wood. Drums beat. No more gunshots were fired. Now it resembled a battue; they seemed to search, follow, track. They were evidently hunting some person. The noise was scattered and deep; it was a confusion of words of wrath and triumph; of indistinct cries and clamour. Suddenly, as an outline becomes visible in a cloud of smoke, something is articulated clearly and distinctly amid this tumult: it was a name,—a name repeated by a thousand voices,—and the marquis plainly heard this cry:—

"Lantenac! Lantenac! The Marquis de Lantenac!"

It was he whom they were looking for.

Chapter VI

THE WHIRLIGIGS OF CIVIL WAR

Suddenly all about him, from all sides at the same time, the copse filled with muskets, bayonets, and sabres, a tricoloured flag rose in the half-light, the cry of "Lantenac!" burst forth in his very ear, and at his feet, behind the brambles and branches, savage faces appeared.

The marquis was alone, standing on a height, visible from every part of the wood. He could scarcely see those who shrieked his name; but he was seen by all. If a thousand muskets were in the wood, there was he like a target. He could distinguish nothing among the brush-wood but burning eyeballs fastened upon him.

He took off his hat, turned back the brim, tore a long, dry thorn from a furze-bush, drew from his pocket a white cockade, fastened the upturned brim and the cockade to the hat with the thorn, and putting back on his head the hat, whose lifted edge showed the white cockade, and left his face in full view, he cried in a loud voice that rang like a trumpet through the forest:—

"I am the man you seek. I am the Marquis de Lantenac, Viscount de Fontenay, Breton prince, lieutenant-general of the armies of the king. Now make an end! Aim! Fire!"

And tearing open with both hands his goat-skin vest, he bared his naked breast.

He looked down, expecting to meet levelled guns, and saw himself surrounded by kneeling men.

Then a great shout arose:—

"Long live Lantenac! Long live Monseigneur! Long live the general!"

At the same time hats were flung into the air, sabres whirled joyously, and through all the thicket could be seen rising sticks on whose points waved caps of brown woollen. He was surrounded by a Vendean band.

This troop had knelt at sight of him.

Old legends tell of strange beings that were found in the ancient Thuringian forests,—a race of giants, more or less than men, who were regarded by the Romans as horrible monsters, by the Germans as divine incarnations, and who, according to the encounter, ran the risk of being exterminated or adored.

The marquis felt something of the sentiment which must have shaken one of those creatures when, expecting to be treated like a monster, he suddenly found himself worshipped as a god.

All those eyes, full of terrible lightnings, were fastened on him with a sort of savage love.

This crowd was armed with muskets, sabres, scythes, poles, sticks; they wore great beavers or brown caps, with white cockades, a profusion of rosaries and amulets, wide breeches open at the knee, jackets of skins, leather gaiters, the calves of their legs bare, their hair long: some with a ferocious look, all with an open one.

A man, young and of noble mien, passed through the kneeling throng, and hurried toward the marquis. Like the peasants, he wore a turned-up beaver and a white cockade, and was wrapped in a fur jacket; but his hands were white and his linen fine, and he wore over his vest a white silk scarf, from which hung a gold-hilted sword.

When he reached the *hure* he threw aside his hat, untied his scarf, bent one knee to the ground, and presented the sword and scarf to the marquis, saying:

"We were indeed seeking you, and we have found you. Accept the sword of command. These men are yours now. I was their leader; I mount in grade, for I become your soldier. Accept our homage, my lord. General, give me your orders."

Then he made a sign, and some men who carried a tricoloured flag moved out of the wood. They marched up to where the marquis stood, and laid the banner at his feet. It was the flag which he had just caught sight of through the trees.

"General," said the young man who had presented to him the sword and scarf, "this is the flag we just took from the Blues, who held the farm of Herbe-en-Pail. Monseigneur, I am named Gavard. I belong to the Marquis de la Rouarie."

"It is well," said the marquis. And, calm and grave, he put on the scarf.

Then he drew his sword, and waving it above his head, he cried,—

"Up! Long live the king!"

All rose. Through the depths of the wood swelled a wild triumphant clamour: "Long live the king! Long live our marquis! Long live Lantenac!"

The marquis turned toward Gavard:—

"How many are you?"

"Seven thousand."

And as they descended the eminence, while the peasants cleared away the furze-bushes to make a path for the Marquis de Lantenac, Gavard continued:—

"Monseigneur, nothing more simple. All can be explained in a word. It only needed a spark. The reward offered by the Republic, in revealing your presence, roused the whole district for the king. Besides that, we had been secretly warned by the mayor of Granville, who is one of our men, the same who saved the Abbé Ollivier. Last night they sounded the tocsin."

"For whom?"

"For you."

"Ah!" said the marquis.

"And here we are," pursued Gavard.

"And you are seven thousand?"

"To-day. We shall be fifteen thousand to-morrow. It is the Breton contingent. When Monsieur Henri de la Rochejacquelein set out to join the Catholic army, the tocsin was sounded, and in one night six parishes,—Isernay, Corqueux, the Echaubroignes, the Aubiers, Saint-Aubin, and Nueil—brought him ten thousand men. They had no munitions; they found in the house of a quarry-master sixty pounds of blasting-powder, and M. de la Rochejacquelein set off with that.

"We were certain you must be in some part of this forest, and we were seeking you."

"And you attacked the Blues at the farm of Herbe-en-Pail?"

"The wind prevented their hearing the tocsin. They suspected nothing; the people of the hamlet, who are a set of clowns, received them well. This morning we surrounded the farm; the Blues were asleep, and we did the thing out of hand. I have a horse. Will you deign to accept it, General?"

"Yes."

A peasant led up a white horse with military caparisons. The marquis mounted without the assistance Gavard offered him.

"Hurrah!" cried the peasants. The cries of the English were greatly in use along the Breton coast, in constant communication as it was with the Channel Islands.

Gavard made a military salute, and asked,—

"Where will you make your headquarters, monseigneur?"

"At first in the Forest of Fougères."

"It is one of your seven forests, my lord marquis."

"We must have a priest."

"We have one."

"Who?"

"The curate of the Chapelle-Erbrée."

"I know him. He has made the voyage to Jersey."

A priest stepped out of the ranks, and said,—

"Three times."

The marquis turned his head.

"Good-morning, Monsieur le Curé. You have work before you."

"So much the better, my lord marquis."

"You will have to hear confessions,— those who wish; nobody will be forced."

"My lord marquis," said the priest, "at Guéménée, Gaston forces the republicans to confess."

"He is a hairdresser," said the marquis; "death ought to be free."

Gavard, who had gone to give some orders, returned.

"General, I wait your commands."

"First, the rendezvous in the Forest of Fougères. Let the men disperse, and make their way there."

"The order is given."

"Did you not tell me that the people of Herbe-en-Pail had received the Blues well?"

"Yes, General."

"You have burned the house?"

"Yes."

"Have you burned the hamlet?"

"No."

"Burn it."

"The Blues tried to defend themselves, but they were a hundred and fifty, and we were seven thousand."

"Who were they?"

"Santerre's men."

"The one who ordered the drums to beat while the king's head was being cut off? Then it is a regiment of Paris?"

"A half-regiment."

"Its name?"

"General, it had on its flag, 'Battalion of the Bonnet Rouge.'"

"Wild beasts."

"What is to be done with the wounded?"

"Put an end to them."

"What shall we do with the prisoners?"

"Shoot them."

"There are about eighty."

"Shoot the whole."

"There are two women."

"Them also."

"There are three children."

"Carry them off. We will see what shall be done with them."

And the marquis rode on.

Chapter VII

"NO MERCY!" (WATCHWORD OF THE COMMUNE). "NO QUARTER!" (WATCHWORD OF THE PRINCES).

WHILE all this was passing near Tanis, the mendicant had gone toward Crollon. He plunged into the ravines, among the vast silent bowers of shade, inattentive to everything and attentive to nothing, as he had himself said; dreamer rather than thinker, for the thoughtful man has an aim, and the dreamer has none; wandering, rambling, pausing, munching here and there a bunch of wild sorrel; drinking at the springs, occasionally raising his head to listen to the distant tumult, again falling back into the bewildering fascination of Nature; warming his rags in the sun; hearing sometimes the noise of men, but listening to the song of the birds.

He was old, and moved slowly. He could not walk far; as he had said to the Marquis de Lantenac, a quarter of a league fatigued him. He made a short circuit to the Croix-Avranchin, and evening had come before he returned.

A little beyond Macey, the path he was following led to a sort of culminating point, bare of trees, from whence one could see very far, taking in the whole stretch of the western horizon to the sea.

A column of smoke attracted his attention.

Nothing calmer than smoke, but nothing more startling. There are peaceful smokes, and there are evil ones. The thickness and colour of a line of smoke marks the whole difference between war and peace, between fraternity and hatred, between hospitality and the tomb, between life and death. A smoke mounting among the trees may be a symbol of all that is most charming in the world,—a heart at home; or a sign of that which is most awful,—a conflagration. The whole happiness of man, or his complete misery, is sometimes expressed in this thin vapour, which the wind scatters at will.

The smoke which Tellmarch saw was disquieting.

It was black, dashed now and then with sudden gleams of red, as if the brasier from which it flowed burned irregularly, and had begun to die out; and it rose above Herbe-en-Pail.

Tellmarch quickened his steps, and walked toward this smoke.

He was very tired, but he must know what this signified.

He reached the summit of a hill, against whose side the hamlet and farm were nestled.

There was no longer either farm or hamlet.

A heap of ruins was burning still; it was Herbe-en-Pail.

There is something which it is more painful to see burn than a palace,—it is a cottage. A cottage on fire is a lamentable sight. It is a devastation swooping down on poverty, the vulture pouncing upon the worms of the ground; there is in it a contradiction which chills the heart.

If we believe the Biblical legend, the sight of a conflagration changed a human being into a statue. For a moment Tellmarch seemed thus transformed. The spectacle before his eyes held him motionless. Destruction was completing its work amid unbroken silence. Not a cry arose; not a human sigh mingled with this smoke. This furnace laboured, and finished devouring the village, without any noise being heard save the creaking of the timbers and the crackling of the thatch. At moments the smoke parted, the fallen roofs revealed the gaping chambers, the brasier showed all its rubies; rags turned to scarlet, and miserable bits of furniture, tinted with purple, gleamed amid these vermilion interiors, and Tellmarch was dizzied by the sinister bedazzlement of disaster.

Some trees of a chestnut grove near the house had taken fire, and were blazing.

He listened, trying to catch a sound of a voice, an appeal, a cry. Nothing stirred except the flames; everything was silent, save the conflagration. Was it that all had fled?

Where was the knot of people who had lived and toiled at Herbe-en-Pail? What had become of this little band? Tellmarch descended the hill.

A funereal enigma rose before him. He approached without haste, with fixed eyes. He advanced toward this ruin with the slowness of a shadow; he felt like a ghost in this tomb.

He reached what had been the door of the farm-house, and looked into the court, which had no longer any walls, and was confounded with the hamlet grouped about it.

What he had before seen was nothing. He had hitherto only caught sight of the terrible; the horrible appeared to him now.

In the middle of the court was a black heap, vaguely outlined on one side by the flames, on the other by the moonlight. This heap was a mass of men; these men were dead.

All about this human mound spread a great pool which smoked a little; the flames were reflected in this pool, but it had no need of fire to redden it, —it was blood.

Tellmarch went closer. He began to examine these prostrate bodies one after another; they were all dead men.

The moon shone; the conflagration also.

These corpses were the bodies of soldiers. All had their feet bare; their shoes had been taken. Their weapons were gone also; they still wore their uniforms, which were blue. Here and there he could distinguish among those heaped-up limbs and heads shot-riddled hats with tri-coloured cockades. They were Republicans. They were those Parisians who on the previous evening had been there, all living, keeping garrison at the farm of Herbe-en-Pail. These men had been executed: this was shown by the symmetrical position of the bodies; they had been struck down in order, and with care. They were all quite dead. Not a single death-gasp sounded from the mass.

Tellmarch passed the corpses in review without omitting one; they were all riddled with balls.

Those who had shot them, in haste probably to get elsewhere, had not taken the time to bury them.

As he was preparing to move away, his eyes fell on a low wall in the court, and he saw four feet protruding from one of its angles.

They had shoes on them; they were smaller than the others. Tellmarch went up to this spot. They were women's feet. Two women were lying side by side behind the wall; they also had been shot.

Tellmarch stooped over them. One of the women wore a sort of uniform; by her side was a canteen, bruised and empty: she had been vivandière. She had four balls in her head. She was dead.

Tellmarch examined the other. This was a peasant. She was livid: her mouth open. Her eyes were closed. There was no wound in her head. Her garments, which long marches, no doubt, had worn to rags, were disarranged by her fall, leaving her bosom half naked. Tellmarch pushed her dress aside, and saw on one shoulder the round wound which a ball makes; the shoulder-blade was broken. He looked at her livid breast.

"Nursing mother," he murmured.

He touched her. She was not cold.

She had no hurts besides the broken shoulder-blade and the wound in the shoulder.

He put his hand on her heart and felt a faint throb. She was not dead.

Tellmarch raised himself and cried out in a terrible voice,—

"Is there no one here?"

"Is it you, Caimand?" a voice replied, so low that it could scarcely be heard.

At the same time a head was thrust out of a hole in the ruin. Then another face appeared at another aperture. They were two peasants, who had hidden themselves,—the only ones who survived.

The well-known voice of the Caimand had reassured them, and brought them out of the holes in which they had taken refuge.

They advanced toward the old man, both still trembling violently.

Tellmarch had been able to cry out, but he could not talk; strong emotions produce such effects.

He pointed out to them with his finger the woman at his feet.

"Is there still life in her?" asked one of the peasants.

Tellmarch gave an affirmative nod of his head.

"Is the other woman living?" demanded the second man.

Tellmarch shook his head.

The peasant who had first shown himself continued:

"All the others are dead, are they not? I saw the whole. I was in my cellar. How one thanks God at such a moment for not having a family! My house burned. Blessed Saviour! They killed everybody. This woman here had three children—all little. The children cried, 'Mother!' The mother cried, 'My children!' Those who massacred everybody are gone. They were satisfied. They carried off the little ones, and shot the mother. I saw it all. But she is not dead,—didn't you say so? She is not dead? Tell us, Caimand, do you think you could save her? Do you want us to help carry her to your *carnichot?*

Tellmarch made a sign, which signified "Yes."

The wood was close to the farm. They quickly made a litter with branches and ferns. They laid the woman, still motionless, upon it, and set out toward the copse, the two peasants carrying the litter, one at the head, the other at the feet, Tellmarch holding the woman's arm, and feeling her pulse.

As they walked, the two peasants talked; and over the body of the bleeding woman, whose white face was lighted up by the moon, they exchanged frightened ejaculations.

"To kill all!"

"To burn everything!"

"Ah, my God! Is that the way things will go now?"

"It was that tall old man who ordered it to be done."

"Yes; it was he who commanded."

"I did not see while the shooting went on. Was he there?"

"No. He had gone. But no matter; it was all done by his orders."

"Then it was he who did the whole."

"He said, 'Kill! burn! no quarter!'"

"He is a marquis."

"Of course, since he is our marquis."

"What do they call him now?"

"He is M. de Lantenac."

Tellmarch raised his eyes to heaven, and murmured:

"If I had known!"

PART II.—IN PARIS

BOOK I

CIMOURDAIN

CHAPTER I

THE STREETS OF PARIS AT THAT TIME

PEOPLE lived in public; they ate at tables spread outside the doors; women seated on the steps of the churches made lint as they sang the "Marseillaise." Park Monceaux and the Luxembourg Gardens were parade-grounds. There were gunsmiths' shops in full work; they manufactured muskets before the eyes of the passers-by, who clapped their hands in applause. The watchword on every lip was, "Patience; we are in revolution." The people smiled heroically. They went to the theatre as they did at Athens during the Peloponnesian war. One saw play-bills such as these pasted at the street corners: "The Siege of Thionville;" "A Mother Saved from the Flames;" "The Club of the Careless;" "The Eldest of the Popes Joan;" "The Philosopher-Soldiers;" "The Art of Village Love-Making."

The Germans were at the gates; a report was current that the King of Prussia had secured boxes at the Opera. Everything was terrible, and no one was frightened. The mysterious law against the suspected, which was the crime of Merlin of Douai, held a vision of the guillotine above every head. A solicitor named Séran, who had been denounced, awaited his arrest in dressing-gown and slippers, playing his flute at his window; Nobody seemed to have leisure; all the world was in a hurry. Every hat bore a cockade. The women said, "We are pretty in red caps." All Paris seemed to be removing. The curiosity-shops were crowded with crowns, mitres, sceptres of gilded wood, and *fleurs-de-lis* torn down from royal dwellings: it was the demolition of monarchy that went on. Copes were to be seen for sale at the old-clothesmen's, and rochets hung on hooks at their doors. At Ramponneau's and the Porcherons, men dressed out in surplices and stoles, and mounted on donkeys caparisoned with chasubles, drank wine at the doors from cathedral ciboria. In the Rue Saint-Jacques, barefooted street-pavers stopped the wheelbarrow of a peddler who had boots for sale, and clubbed together to buy fifteen pairs of shoes, which they sent to the Convention "for our soldiers."

Busts of Franklin, Rousseau, Brutus, and, we must add, of Marat, abounded. Under a bust of Marat in the Rue Cloche-Perce was hung in a black wooden frame, and under glass, an address against Malouet, with testimony in support of the charges, and these marginal lines:

These details were furnished me by the mistress of Silvain Bailly, a good patriotess, who has a liking for me.

(Signed) MARAT

The inscription on the Palais Royal fountain—"*Quantos effundit in usus!*"—was hidden under two great canvases painted in distemper, the one representing Cahier de Gerville denouncing to the National Assembly the rallying cry of the "Chiffonistes" of Arles; the other, Louis XVI. brought back from Varennes in his royal carriage, and under the carriage a plank fastened by cords, on each end of which was seated a grenadier with fixed bayonet.

Very few of the larger shops were open; peripatetic haberdashery and toy shops were dragged about by women, lighted by candles, which dropped their tallow on the merchandise. Open-air shops were kept by ex-nuns, in blond wigs. This mender, darning stockings in a stall, was a countess; that dressmaker, a marchioness. Madame de Boufflers inhabited a garret, from whence she could look out at her own hotel. Hawkers ran about offering the "papers of news." Persons who wore cravats that hid their chins were called "the scrofulous." Street-singers swarmed. The crowd hooted Pitou, the royalist song-writer, and a valiant man into the bargain; he was twenty-two times imprisoned and taken before the revolutionary tribunal for slapping his coat-tails as he pronounced the word *civism*. Seeing that his head was in danger, he exclaimed: "But it is just the opposite of my head that is in fault;"—a witticism which made the judges laugh, and saved his life. This Pitou ridiculed the rage for Greek and Latin names; his favourite song was about a cobbler,

whom he called *Cujus,* and to whom he gave a wife named *Cujusdam.* They danced the Carmagnole in great circles. They no longer said "gentleman and lady," but "citizen and citizeness." They danced in the ruined cloisters, with the church-lamps lighted on the altars, with cross-shaped chandeliers hanging from the vaulted roofs, and tombs beneath their feet. Waistcoats of "tyrant's blue" were worn. There were "liberty-cap" shirt-pins made of white, blue, and red stones. The Rue de Richelieu was called the Street of Law; the Faubourg Saint Antoine was named the Faubourg of Glory; a statue of Nature stood in the Place de la Bastille. People pointed out to one another certain well-known personages,—Chatelet, Didier, Nicholas, and Garnier-Delaunay, who stood guard at the door of Duplay the joiner; Voullant, who never missed a guillotine-day, and followed the carts of the condemned,—he called it going to "the red mass;" Montflabert, revolutionary juryman, and a marquis, who took the name of "Dix Août" [Tenth of August]. People watched the pupils of the Ecole Militaire file past, described by the decrees of the Convention as "aspirants in the school of Mars," and by the crowd as "the pages of Robespierre." They read the proclamations of Fréron denouncing those suspected of the crime of "negotiantism." The dandies collected at the doors of the mayoralties to mock at the civil marriages, thronging about the brides and grooms as they passed, and shouting "Married *municipaliter!*" At the Invalides the statues of the saints and kings were crowned with Phrygian caps. They played cards on the curb-stones at the crossings. The packs of cards were also in the full tide of revolution: the kings were replaced by genii, the queens by the Goddess of Liberty, the knaves by figures representing Equality, and the aces by impersonations of Law. They tilled the public gardens; the plough worked at the Tuileries. With all these excesses was mingled, especially among the conquered parties, an indescribable haughty weariness of life. A man wrote to Fouquier-Tinville, "Have the goodness to free me from existence. This is my address." Champcenetz was arrested for having cried in the midst of the Palais Royal garden: "When are we to have the revolution of Turkey? I want to see the republic *à la Porte.*" Newspapers appeared in legions. The hairdressers' men curled the wigs of women in public, while the master read the "Moniteur" aloud. Others, surrounded by eager groups, commented with violent gestures upon the journal "Listen to Us," of Dubois Crancé, or the "Trumpet" of Father Bellerose. Sometimes the barbers were pork-sellers as well, and hams and chitterlings might be seen hanging side by side with a golden-haired doll. Dealers sold in the open street "wines of the refugees;" one merchant advertised wines of fifty-two sorts. Others displayed harp-shaped clocks and sofas *à la duchesse.* One hairdresser had for sign: "I shave the clergy; I comb the nobility; I arrange the Third Estate."

People went to have their fortunes told by Martin, at No. 173, in the Rue d'Anjou, formerly Rue Dauphine. There was a lack of bread, of coals, of soap. Herds of milch-cows might be seen coming in from the country. At the Vallée, lamb sold for fifteen francs the pound. An order of the Commune assigned a pound of meat per head every ten days. People stood in rank at the doors of the butchers' shops. One of these files has remained famous: it reached from a grocer's shop in the Rue du Petit Carreau to the middle of the Rue Montorgueil. To form a line was called "holding the cord," from a long rope which was held in the hands of those standing in the row. Amid this wretchedness, the women were brave and mild; they passed entire nights awaiting their turn to get into the bakers' shops. The Revolution resorted to expedients which were successful; she alleviated this widespread distress by two perilous means,—the assignat and the maximum. The assignat was the lever, the maximum was the fulcrum. This empiricism saved France. The enemy, whether of Coblentz or London, gambled in assignats. Girls came and went, offering lavender water, garters, false hair, and selling stocks. There were jobbers on the Perron of the Rue Vivienne, with muddy shoes, greasy hair, and fur caps decorated with fox-tails; and there were swells from the Rue Valois, with varnished boots, toothpicks in their mouths, and long-napped hats on their heads, to whom the girls said "thee" and "thou." Later, the people gave chase to them as they did to the thieves, whom the royalists styled "active citizens." For the time, theft was rare. There reigned a terrible destitution and a stoical probity. The barefooted and the starving passed with lowered eyelids before the jewellers' shops of the Palais Egalité. During a domiciliary visit that the Section Antoine made to the house of Beaumarchais, a woman picked a flower in the garden; the crowd boxed her ears. Wood cost four hundred francs in coin per cord; people could be seen in the streets sawing up their bedsteads. In the winter the fountains were frozen; water cost twenty sous: every man made himself a water-carrier. A gold louis was worth three thousand nine hundred and fifty francs. A course in a hackney-coach cost six hundred francs. After a day's use of a carriage, this sort of dialogue might be heard: "Coachman, how much do I owe you?" "Six thousand francs." A green-grocer woman sold twenty thousand francs' worth of vegetables a day. A beggar said, "Help me, in the name of charity! I lack two hundred and thirty francs to finish paying for my shoes." At the ends of the bridges might be seen colossal figures sculptured and painted by David, which Mercier insulted. "Enormous wooden Punches!" said he. The gigantic shapes symbolized Federalism and Coalition overturned.

There was no faltering among this people. There was the sombre joy of having made an end of thrones. Volunteers abounded; each street furnished a battalion. The flags of the districts came and went, every one with its device. On the banner of the Capuchin district could be read, "Nobody can cut our beards." On another, "No other nobility than that of the heart." On all the walls were placards, large and small, white, yellow, green, red, printed and written, on which might be read this motto: "Long live the Republic!" The little children lisped "Ca ira."

These children were in themselves the great future.

Later, to the tragical city succeeded the cynical city. The streets of Paris have offered two revolutionary aspects entirely distinct,—that before and that after the 9th Thermidor. The Paris of Saint-Just gave place to the Paris of Tallien. Such antitheses are perpetual; after Sinai the Courtille appeared.

An attack of public madness made its appearance. It had already been seen eighty years before. The people came out from under Louis XIV. as they did from under Robespierre, with a great need to breathe; hence the regency which opened that century and the directory which closed it,—two saturnalia after two terrorisms. France snatched the wicket-key and got beyond the Puritan cloister just as it did beyond that of monarchy, with the joy of a nation that escapes.

After the 9th Thermidor Paris was gay, but with an insane gaiety. An unhealthy joy overflowed all bounds. To the frenzy for dying succeeded the frenzy for living, and grandeur eclipsed itself. They had a Trimalcion, calling himself Grimod de la Reynière: there was the "Almanac of the Gourmands." People dined in the entresols of the Palais Royal to the din of orchestras of women beating drums and blowing trumpets; the "rigadooner" reigned, bow in hand. People supped Oriental fashion at Méot's surrounded by perfumes. The artist Boze painted his daughters, innocent and charming heads of sixteen, *en guillotinées;* that is to say, with bare necks and red shifts. To the wild dances in the ruined churches succeeded the balls of Ruggieri, of Luquet-Wenzel, Mauduit, and the Montansier; to grave citizenesses making lint succeeded sultanas, savages, nymphs; to the naked feet of the soldiers covered with blood, dust, and mud, succeeded the naked feet of women decorated with diamonds. At the same time, with shamelessness, improbity reappeared; and it had its purveyors in high ranks, and their imitators among the class below. A swarm of sharpers filled Paris, and every man was forced to guard well his *luc*,—that is, his pocketbook. One of the amusements of the day was to go to the Palace of Justice to see the female thieves; it was necessary to tie fast their petticoats. At the doors of the theatres the street boys opened cab doors, saying, "Citizen and citizeness, there is room for two." The "Old Cordelier" and the "Friend of the People" were no longer sold. In their places were cried "Punch's Letter" and the "Rogues' Petition." The Marquis de Sade presided at the Section of the Pikes, Place Vendôme. The reaction was jovial and ferocious. The Dragons of Liberty of '92 were reborn under the name of the Chevaliers of the Dagger. At the same time there appeared in the booths that type, Jocrisse. There were "the Merveilleuses," and in advance of these feminine marvels came "the Incroyables." People swore by strange and affected oaths; they jumped back from Mirabeau to Bobêche. Thus it is that Paris sways back and forth; it is the enormous pendulum of civilization; it touches either pole in turn,—Thermopylæ and Gomorrah. After '93 the Revolution traversed a singular occultation; the century seemed to forget to finish that which it had commenced. A strange orgy interposed itself, took the foreground, swept back to the second place the awful Apocalypse, veiled the immeasurable vision; and laughed aloud after its fright. Tragedy disappeared in parody, and, rising darkly from the bottom of the horizon, a smoke of carnival effaced Medusa.

But in '93, where we are, the streets of Paris still wore the grandiose and savage aspect of the beginning. They had their orators, such as Varlet, who promenaded in a booth on wheels, from the top of which he harangued the passers-by; they had their heroes, of whom one was called the "Captain of the iron-pointed sticks;" their favourites, among whom ranked Guffroy, the author of the pamphlet "Rougiff." Certain of these popularities were mischievous, others had a healthy tone; one among them all was honest and fatal,—it was that of Cimourdain.

Chapter II

CIMOURDAIN

CIMOURDAIN had a conscience pure but sombre. There was something of the absolute within him. He had been a priest, which is a grave matter. A man may, like the sky, possess a serenity which is dark and unfathomable; it only needs that something should have made night within his soul. The priesthood had made night in that of Cimourdain. He who has been a priest remains one.

What makes night within us may leave stars. Cimourdain was full of virtues and verities, but they shone among shadows.

His history is easily written. He had been a village curate, and tutor in a great family; then he inherited a small legacy, and gained his freedom.

He was above all an obstinate man. He made use of meditation as one does of pincers; he did not think it right to quit an idea until he had followed it to the end; he thought stubbornly. He understood all the European languages, and something of others besides. This man studied incessantly, which aided him to bear the burden of celibacy; but nothing can be more dangerous than such a life of repression.

He had from pride, chance, or loftiness of soul been true to his vows, but he had not been able to guard his belief. Science had demolished faith; dogma had fainted within him. Then, as he examined himself, he felt that his soul was mutilated; he could not nullify his priestly oath, but tried to remake himself man, though in an austere fashion. His family had been taken from him; he adopted his country. A wife had been refused him; he espoused humanity. Such vast plenitude has a void at bottom.

His peasant parents, in devoting him to the priesthood, had desired to elevate him above the common people; he voluntarily returned among them.

He went back with a passionate energy. He regarded the suffering with a terrible tenderness. From priest he had become philosopher; and from philosopher, athlete. While Louis XV. still lived, Cimourdain felt himself vaguely Republican. But belonging to what republic? To that of Plato perhaps, and perhaps also to the republic of Draco.

Forbidden to love, he set himself to hate. He hated lies, monarchy, theocracy, his garb of priest; he hated the present, and he called aloud to the future; he had a presentiment of it, he caught glimpses of it in advance; he pictured it awful and magnificent. In his view, to end the lamentable wretchedness of humanity required at once an avenger and a liberator. He worshipped the catastrophe afar off.

In 1789 this catastrophe arrived, and found him ready. Cimourdain flung himself into this vast plan of human regeneration on logical grounds,—that is to say, for a mind of his mould, inexorably; logic knows no softening. He lived among the great revolutionary years, and felt the shock of their mighty breaths,—'89, the fall of the Bastille, the end of the torture of the people; on the 4th of August, '90, the end of feudalism; '91, Varennes, the end of royalty; '92, the birth of the Republic. He saw the Revolution loom into life; he was not a man to be afraid of that giant,—far from it. This sudden growth in everything had revivified him; and though already nearly old,—he was fifty, and a priest ages faster than another man,—he began himself to grow also. From year to year he saw events gain in grandeur, and he increased with them. He had at first feared that the Revolution would prove abortive; he watched it. It had reason and right on its side; he demanded success for it likewise. In proportion to the fear it caused the timid, his confidence strengthened. He desired that his Minerva, crowned with the stars of the future, should be Pallas also, with the Gorgon's head for buckler. He demanded that her divine glance should be able at need to fling back to the demons their infernal glare, and give them terror for terror.

Thus he reached '93.

'93 was the war of Europe against France, and of France against Paris. And what was the Revolution? It was the victory of France over Europe, and of Paris over France. Hence the immensity of that terrible moment, '93,— grander than all the rest of the century. Nothing could be more tragic: Europe attacking France, and France attacking Paris! A drama which reaches the stature of an epic. '93 is a year of intensity. The tempest is there in all its wrath and all its grandeur. Cimourdain felt himself at home. This distracted centre, terrible and splendid, suited the span of his wings. Like the sea-eagle amid the tempest, this man preserved his internal composure and enjoyed the danger. Certain winged natures, savage yet calm, are made to battle the winds,—souls of the tempest: such exist.

He had put pity aside, reserving it only for the wretched. He devoted himself to those sorts of suffering which cause horror. Nothing was repugnant to him. That was his kind of goodness. He was divine in his readiness to succour what was loathsome. He searched for ulcers in order that he might kiss them. Noble actions with a revolting exterior are the most difficult to undertake; he preferred such. One day at the Hôtel Dieu a man was dying, suffocated by a tumour in the throat,—a fetid, frightful abscess,—contagious perhaps,— which must be at once opened. Cimourdain was there; he put his lips to the tumour, sucked it, spitting it out as his mouth was filled, and so emptied the abscess and saved the man. As he still wore his priest's dress at the time, some one said to him, "If you were to do that for the king, you would be made a bishop." "I would not do it for the king," Cimourdain replied. The act and the response rendered him popular in the sombre quarters of Paris.

They gave him so great a popularity that he could do what he liked with those who suffered, wept, and threatened. At the period of the public wrath against monopolists,—a wrath which was prolific in mistakes,—Cimourdain by a word prevented the pillage of a boat loaded with soap at the quay Saint Nicholas, and dispersed the furious bands who were stopping the carriages at the barrier of Saint Lazare.

It was he who, two days after the 10th of August, headed the people to overthrow the statues of the kings. They slaughtered as they fell: in the Place Vendôme, a woman called Reine Violet was crushed by the statue of Louis XIV., about whose neck she had put a cord, which she was pulling. This statue of Louis XIV. had been standing a hundred years. It was erected the 12th of August, 1692; it was overthrown the 12th of August, 1792. In the Place de la Concorde, a certain Guinguerlot was butchered on the pedestal of Louis XV.'s statue for having called the demolishers scoundrels. The statue was broken in pieces. Later, it was melted to coin—into sous. The arm alone escaped,—it was the right arm, which was extended with the gesture of a Roman emperor. At Cimourdain's request the people sent a deputation with this arm to Latude, the man who had been thirty-seven years buried in the Bastille. When Latude was rotting alive, the collar on his neck, the chain about his loins, in the bottom of that prison where he had been cast by the order of that king whose statue overlooked Paris, who could have prophesied to him that this prison would fall, this statue would be destroyed; that he would emerge from the sepulchre and monarchy enter it; that he, the prisoner, would be the master of this hand of bronze which had signed his warrant; and that of this king of Mud there would remain only his brazen arm?

Cimourdain was one of those men who have an interior voice to which they listen. Such men seem absent-minded; no, they are attentive.

Cimourdain was at once learned and ignorant. He understood all science, and was ignorant of everything in regard to life. Hence his severity. He had his eyes bandaged, like the Themis of Homer. He had the blind certainty of the arrow, which, seeing not the goal, yet goes straight to it. In a revolution there is nothing so formidable as a straight line. Cimourdain went straight before him, fatal, unwavering.

He believed that in a social Genesis the farthest point is the solid ground,—an error peculiar to minds which replace reason by logic. He went beyond the Convention; he went beyond the Commune; he belonged to the Evêché.

The society called the Evêché, because its meetings were held in a hall of the former episcopal palace, was rather a complication of men than a union. There, as at the Commune, those silent but significant spectators were present who, as Garat said, "had as many pistols as pockets."

The Evêché was a strange mixture,—a crowd at once cosmopolitan and Parisian. This is no contradiction, for Paris is the spot where beats the heart of the peoples. The great plebeian incandescence was at the Evêché. In comparison to it, the Convention was cold, and the Commune lukewarm. The Evêché was one of those revolutionary formations similar to volcanic ones; it contained everything,—ignorance, stupidity, probity, heroism, choler, spies. Brunswick had agents there. It numbered men worthy of Sparta, and men who deserved the galleys. The greater part were mad and honest. The Gironde had pronounced by the mouth of Isnard, temporary president of the Convention, this monstrous warning:—

"Take care, Parisians! There will not remain one stone upon another of your city, and the day will come when the place where Paris stood shall be searched for."

This speech created the Evêché. Certain men—and we have just said, they were men of all nations—felt the need of gathering themselves close about Paris. Cimourdain joined this club.

The society reacted on the reactionists. It was born out of that public necessity for violence which is the formidable and mysterious side of revolutions. Strong with this strength, the Evêché at once began its work. In the commotions of Paris it was the Commune that fired the cannon; it was the Evêché that sounded the tocsin.

In his implacable ingenuousness, Cimourdain believed that everything in the service of truth is justice, which rendered him fit to dominate the extremists on either side. Scoundrels felt that he was honest, and were satisfied. Crime is flattered by having virtue to preside over it; it is at once troublesome and pleasant. Palloy, the architect who had turned to account the demolition of the Bastille, selling its stones to his own profit, and who, appointed to whitewash the cell of Louis XVI., in his zeal covered the wall with bars, chains, and iron rings; Gonchon, the suspected orator of the Faubourg Saint Antoine, whose quittances were afterward found; Fournier, the American, who on the 17th of July fired at Lafayette a pistol-shot, paid for, it is said, by Lafayette himself; Henriot, who had come out of Bicêtre, and who had been valet, mountebank, robber, and spy before being a general and turning the guns on the Convention; La Reynie, formerly grand-vicar of Chartres, who had replaced his breviary by "The Père Duchesne,"—all these men were held in respect by Cimourdain; and at certain moments, to keep the worst of them from stumbling, it was sufficient to feel his redoubtable and believing candour as a judgment before them. It was thus that Saint-Just terrified Schneider. At the same time the majority of the Evêché, composed principally as it was of poor and violent men who were honest, believed in Cimourdain and followed him. He had for curate or *aide-de-camp*, as you please, that other republican priest, Danjou, whom the people loved on account of his height, and had christened Abbé Six-Foot. Cimourdain could have led where he would that intrepid chief called General La Pique, and that bold Truchon named the Great Nicholas, who had tried to save Madame de Lamballe, and had given her his arm, and made her spring over the corpses,—an attempt which which would have succeeded, had it not been for the ferocious pleasantry of the barber Charlot.

The Commune watched the Convention; the Evêché watched the Commune. Cimourdain, naturally upright and detesting intrigue, had broken more than one mysterious thread in the hand of Pache, whom Beurnonville called "the black man." Cimourdain at the Evêché was on confidential terms with all. He was consulted by Dobsent and Momoro. He spoke Spanish with Gusman, Italian with Pio, English with Arthur, Flemish with Pereyra, German with the Austrian Proly, the bastard of a prince. He created a harmony between these discordances. Hence his position was abscure and strong. Hébert feared him.

In these times and among these tragic groups, Cimourdain possessed the power of the inexorable. He was an impeccable, who believed himself infallible. No person had ever seen him weep. He was Virtue inaccessible and glacial. He was the terrible offspring of Justice.

There is no half-way possible to a priest in a revolution. A priest can only give himself up to this wild and prodigious chance either from the highest or the lowest motive; he must be infamous or he must be sublime. Cimourdain was sublime, but in isolation, in rugged inaccessibility, in inhospitable secretiveness, sublime amid a circle of precipices. Lofty mountains possess this sinister freshness.

Cimourdain had the appearance of an ordinary man, dressed in every-day garments, poor in aspect. When young, he had been tonsured; as an old man he was bald. What little hair he had left was grey. His forehead was broad, and to the acute observer it revealed his character. Cimourdain had an abrupt way of speaking, which was passionate and solemn; his voice was quick, his accent peremptory, his mouth bitter and sad, his eye clear and profound, and over his whole countenance an indescribable indignant expression.

Such was Cimourdain.

No one to-day knows his name. History has many of these great Unknown.

Chapter III

A CORNER NOT DIPPED IN STYX

Was such a man indeed a man? Could the servant of the human race know fondness? Was he not too entirely a soul to possess a heart? This widespread embrace, which included everything and everybody, could it narrow itself down to one. Could Cimourdain love? We answer, Yes.

When young, and tutor in an almost princely family, he had had a pupil whom he loved,—the son and heir of the house. It is so easy to love a child. What can one not pardon a child? One forgives him for being a lord, a prince, a king. The innocence of his age makes one forget the crime of race; the feebleness of the creature causes one to overlook the exaggeration of rank. He is so little that one forgives him for being great. The slave forgives him for being his master. The old negro idolizes the white nursling. Cimourdain had conceived a passion for his pupil. Childhood is so ineffable that one may unite all affections upon it. Cimourdain's whole power of loving prostrated itself, so to speak, before this boy; that sweet, innocent being became a sort of prey for that heart condemned to solitude. He loved with a mingling of all tendernesses,—as father, as brother, as friend, as maker. The child was his son, not of his flesh, but of his mind. He was not the father, and this was not his work; but he was the master, and this his masterpiece. Of this little lord he had made a man,—perhaps a great man; who knows? Such are dreams. Has one need of the permission of a family to create an intelligence, a will, an upright character. He had communicated to the young viscount, his scholar, all the advanced ideas which he held himself; he had inoculated him with the redoubtable virus of his virtue; he had infused into his veins his own convictions, his own conscience and ideal,—into this brain of an aristocrat he had poured the soul of the people.

The spirit suckles; the intelligence is a breast. There is an analogy between the nurse who gives her milk and the preceptor who gives his thought. Sometimes the tutor is more father than is the father, just as often the nurse is more mother than the mother.

This deep spiritual paternity bound Cimourdain to his pupil. The very sight of the child softened him.

Let us add this: to replace the father was easy,—the boy no longer had one. He was an orphan; his father and mother were both dead. To keep watch over him he had only a blind grandmother and an absent great-uncle. The grandmother died; the great-uncle, head of the family, a soldier of high rank, provided with appointments at Court, avoided the old family dungeon, lived at Versailles, went forth with the army, and left the orphan alone in the solitary castle. So the preceptor was master in every sense of the word.

Let us add still further: Cimourdain had seen the child born. The boy, while very little, was seized with a severe illness. In this peril of death, Cimourdain watched day and night. It is the physician who prescribes, it is the nurse who saves; and Cimourdain saved the child. Not only did his pupil owe to him education, instruction, science, but he owed him also convalescence and health; not only did his pupil owe him the development of his mind, he owed him life itself. We worship those who owe us all; Cimourdain adored this child.

The natural separation came about at length. The education completed, Cimourdain was obliged to quit the boy, grown to a young man. With what cold and unconscionable cruelty these separations are insisted upon! How tranquilly families dismiss the preceptor, who leaves his spirit in a child, and the nurse, who leaves her heart's blood!

Cimourdain, paid and put aside, went out of the grand world and returned to the sphere below. The partition between the great and the little closed again. The young lord, an officer of birth, and made captain at the outset, departed for some garrison; the humble tutor (already at the bottom of his heart an unsubmissive priest) hastened to go down again into that obscure ground-floor of the Church occupied by the under clergy, and Cimourdain lost sight of his pupil.

The Revolution came on; the recollection of that being whom he had made a man brooded within him, hidden but not extinguished by the immensity of public affairs.

It is a beautiful thing to model a statue and give it life; to mould an intelligence and instil truth therein is still more beautiful. Cimourdain was the Pygmalion of a soul.

The spirit may own a child.

This pupil, this boy, this orphan, was the sole being on earth whom he loved.

But even in such an affection, would a man like this prove vulnerable?

We shall see.

BOOK II.

The Public House of the Rue Du Paon

Chapter I

MINOS, ÆACUS, AND RHADAMANTHUS

There was a public-house in the Rue du Paon which was called a café. This café had a back room, which is to-day historical. It was there that often, almost secretly, met certain men, so powerful and so constantly watched that they hesitated to speak with one another in public.

It was there that on the 23rd of October, 1792, the Mountain and the Gironde exchanged their famous kiss. It was there that Garat, although he does not admit it in his Memoirs, came for information on that lugubrious night when, after having put Clavière in safety in the Rue de Beaune, he stopped his carriage on the Pont Royal to listen to the tocsin.

On the 28th of June, 1793, three men were seated about a table in this back chamber. Their chairs did not touch; they were placed one on either of the three sides of the table, leaving the fourth vacant. It was about eight o'clock in the evening; it was still light in the street, but dark in the back room, and a lamp, hung from a hook in the ceiling,—a luxury there,—lighted the table.

The first of these three men was pale, young, grave, with thin lips and a cold glance. He had a nervous movement in his cheek, which must have made it difficult for him to smile. He wore his hair powdered. He was gloved; his light-blue coat, well brushed, was without a wrinkle, carefully buttoned. He wore nankeen breeches, white stockings, a high cravat, a plaited shirt-frill, and shoes with silver buckles.

Of the other two men, one was a species of giant, the other a sort of dwarf. The tall one was untidily dressed in a coat of scarlet cloth, his neck bare, his unknotted cravat falling down over his shirt-frill, his vest gaping from lack of buttons. He wore top-boots; his hair stood stiffly up and was disarranged, though it still showed traces of powder; his very peruke was like a mane. His face was marked with small-pox; there was a choleric line between his brows; a wrinkle that signified kindness at the corner of his mouth; his lips were thick, the teeth large; he had the fist of a porter and eyes that blazed. The little one was a yellow man, who looked deformed when seated. He carried his head thrown back; the eyes were injected with blood, there were livid blotches on his face; he had a handkerchief knotted about his greasy straight hair; he had no forehead; the mouth was enormous and horrible. He wore pantaloons instead of knee-breeches, slippers, a waistcoat which seemed originally to have been of white satin, and over this a loose jacket, under whose folds a hard, straight line showed that a poniard was hidden.

The first of these men was named Robespierre; the second, Danton; the third, Marat.

They were alone in the room. Before Danton was set a glass and a dusty wine-bottle, reminding one of Luther's pint of beer; before Marat a cup of coffee; before Robespierre only papers.

Near the papers stood one of those heavy, round-ridged, leaden ink-stands which will be remembered by men who were school-boys at the beginning of this century. A pen was thrown carelessly by the side of the ink-stand. On the papers lay a great brass seal, on which could be read *Palloy fecit*, and which was a perfect miniature model of the Bastille.

A map of France was spread in the middle of the table. Outside the door was stationed Marat's "watch-dog,"—a certain Laurent Basse, porter of No. 18, Rue des Cordeliers, who, some fifteen days after this 28th of June, say the

13th of July, was to deal a blow with a chair on the head of a woman named Charlotte Corday, at this moment vaguely dreaming in Caen. Laurent Basse was the proof-carrier of the "Friend of the People." Brought this evening by his master to the café of the Rue du Paon, he had been ordered to keep the room closed where Marat, Danton, and Robespierre were seated, and to allow no person to enter unless it might be some member of the Committee of Public Safety, the Commune, or the Evêché.

Robespierre did not wish to shut the door against Saint-Just; Danton did not want it closed against Pache; Marat would not shut it against Gusman.

The conference had already lasted a long time. It was in reference to papers spread on the table, which Robespierre had read. The voices began to grow louder. Symptoms of anger arose between these three men. From without, eager words could be caught at moments. At that period the example of the public tribunals seemed to have created the right to listen at doors. It was the time when the copying-clerk of Fabricius Pâris looked through the keyhole at the proceedings of the Committee of Public Safety,—a feat which, be it said by the way, was not without its use; for it was this Pâris who warned Danton on the night before the 31st of March, 1794. Laurent Basse had his ear to the door of the back room where Danton, Marat, and Robespierre were. Laurent Basse served Marat, but he belonged to the Evêché.

Chapter II

MAGNA TESTANTUR VOCE PER UMBRAS

Danton had just risen and pushed his chair hastily back.

"Listen!" he cried. "There is only one thing imminent,—the peril of the Republic. I only know one thing,—to deliver France from the enemy. To accomplish that, all means are fair,—all! all! all! When I have to deal with a combination of dangers, I have recourse to every or any expedient; when I fear all, I have all. My thought is a lioness. No half-measures. No squeamishness in resolution. Nemesis is not a conceited prude. Let us be terrible and useful. Does the elephant stop to look where he sets his foot? We must crush the enemy!"

Robespierre replied mildly,—

"I shall be very glad."

And he added,—

"The question is to know where the enemy is."

"It is outside, and I have chased it there," said Danton.

"It is within, and I watch it," said Robespierre.

"And I will continue to pursue it," resumed Danton.

"One does not drive away an internal enemy."

"What, then, do you do?"

"Exterminate it."

"I agree to that," said Danton in his turn.

Then he continued,—

"I tell you Robespierre, it is without."

"Danton, I tell you it is within."

"Robespierre, it is on the frontier."

"Danton, it is in Vendée."

"Calm yourselves," said a third voice. "It is everywhere, and you are lost."

It was Marat who spoke.

Robespierre looked at him and answered tranquilly: "Truce to generalities. I particularize. Here are facts."

"Pedant!" grumbled Marat.

Robespierre laid his hand on the papers spread before him, and continued,—

"I have just read you the dispatches from Prieur, of the Marne. I have just communicated to you the information given by the Gélambre. Danton, listen! The foreign war is nothing; the civil war is all. The foreign war is a scratch that one gets on the elbow; civil war is the ulcer which eats up the liver. This is the result of what I have been reading: The Vendée, up to this day divided between several chiefs, is concentrating herself. Henceforth she will have one sole captain—"

"A central brigand," murmured Danton.

"Who is," pursued Robespierre, "the man that landed near Pontorson on the 2d of June. You have seen who he was. Remember this landing coincides with the arrest of the acting Representatives, Prieur, of the Côte-d'Or, and Romme, at Bayeux, by the traitorous district of Calvados, the 2d of June,— the same day."

"And their transfer to the castle of Caen," said Danton.

Robespierre resumed,—

"I continue my summing up of the dispatches The war of the Woods is organizing on a vast scale. At the same time, an English invasion is preparing,— Vendeans and English; it is Briton with Breton. The Hurons of Finistère speak the same language as the Topinambes of Cornwall. I have shown you an intercepted letter from Puisaye, in which it is said that 'twenty thousand red-coats distributed among the insurgents will be the means of raising a hundred thousand more.' When the peasant insurrection is prepared, the English descent will be made. Look at the plan; follow it on the map."

Robespierre put his finger on the chart and went on:

"The English have the choice of landing-place from Cancale to Paimbol. Craig would prefer the Bay of Saint-Brieuc; Cornwallis, the Bay of Saint-Cast. That is mere detail.

"The left bank of the Loire is guarded by the rebel Vendean army; and as to the twenty-eight leagues of open country between Ancenis and Pontorson, forty Norman parishes have promised their aid. The descent will be made at three points,—Plérin, Iffiniac, and Pléneuf. From Plérin they can go to Saint-Brieuc, and from Pléneuf to Lamballe. The second day they will reach Dinan, where there are nine hundred English prisoners, and at the same time they will occupy Saint-Jouan and Saint-Méen; they will leave cavalry there. On the third day, two columns will march,— the one from Jouan on Bedée, the other from Dinan on Becheral, which is a natural fortress, and where they will establish two batteries. The fourth day they will reach Rennes. Rennes is the key of Brittany. Whoever has Rennes has the whole. Rennes captured, Châteauneuf and Saint-Malo will fall. There are at Rennes a million of cartridges and fifty artillery field-pieces—"

"Which they will sweep off," murmured Danton.

Robespierre continued,—

"I conclude. From Rennes three columns will fall,—the one on Fougères, the other on Vitré, the third on Redon. As the bridges are cut, the enemy will furnish themselves—you have seen this fact particularly stated—with pontoons and planks, and they will have guides for the points fordable by the cavalry. From Fougères they will radiate to Avranches; from Redon to Ancenis; from Vitré to Laval. Nantes will capitulate. Brest will yield. Redon opens the whole extent of the Vilaine; Fougères gives them the route of Normandy; Vitré opens the route to Paris. In fifteen days they will have an army of brigands numbering three hundred thousand men, and all Brittany will belong to the King of France."

"That is to say, the King of England," said Danton.

"No, to the King of France."

And Robespierre added,—

"The King of France is worse. It needs fifteen days to expel the stranger, and eighteen hundred years to eliminate monarchy."

Danton, who had reseated himself, leaned his elbows on the table, and rested his head in his hands in a thoughtful attitude.

"You see the peril," said Robespierre. "Vitré lays open to the English the road to Paris."

Danton raised his head and struck his two great clinched hands on the map as on an anvil.

"Robespierre, did not Verdun open the route to Paris to the Prussians?"

"Very well!"

"Very well, we will expel the English as we expelled the Prussians." And Danton rose again.

Robespierre laid his cold hand on the feverish fist of the other.

"Danton, Champagne was not for the Prussians, and Brittany is for the English. To retake Verdun was a foreign war; to retake Vitré will be civil war."

And Robespierre murmured in a chill, deep tone,—

"A serious difference."

He added aloud,—

"Sit down again, Danton, and look at the map instead of knocking it with your fist."

But Danton was wholly given up to his own idea.

"That is madness!" cried he,—"to look for the catastrophe in the west when it is in the east. Robespierre, I grant you that England is rising on the ocean; but Spain is rising among the Pyrenees; but Italy is rising among the Alps; but Germany is rising on the Rhine. And the great Russian bear is at the bottom. Robespierre, the danger is a circle, and we are within it. On the exterior, coalition; in the interior, treason. In the south, Servant half opens the door of France to the King of Spain. At the north, Dumouriez passes over to the enemy; for that matter, he always menaced Holland less than Paris. Neerwinden blots out Jemappes and Valmy. The philosopher Rabaut Saint-Etienne, a traitor like the Protestant he is, corresponds with the courtier Montesquiu. The army is destroyed. There is not a battalion that has more than four hundred men remaining; the brave regiment of Deux-Ponts is reduced to a hundred and fifty men; the camp of Pamars has capitulated; there are only five hundred sacks of flour left at Givet; we are falling back on Landau; Wurmser presses Kléber; Mayence succumbs bravely, Condé cowardly. Valenciennes also. But all that does not prevent Chancel, who defends Valenciennes, and old Féraud, who defends Condé, being heroes, as well as Meunier, who defended Mayence. But all the rest are betraying us. Dharville betrays us at Aix-la-Chapelle; Mouton at Brussels; Valence at Bréda; Neuilly at Limbourg; Miranda at Maestricht, Stingel, traitor; Lanou, traitor; Ligonnier, traitor; Menou, traitor; Dillon, traitor,—hideous coin of Dumouriez. We must make examples. Custine's countermarches look suspicious to me. I suspect Custine of preferring the lucrative prize of Frankfort to the useful capture of Coblentz. Frankfort can pay four millions of war tribute; so be it. What would that be in comparison with crushing that nest of refugees? Treason, I say. Meunier died on the 13th of June. Kléber is alone. In the meantime Brunswick strengthens and advances. He plants the German flag on every French place that he takes. The Margrave of Brandenburg is to-day the arbiter of Europe; he pockets our provinces; he will adjudge Belgium to himself,—you will see. One would say that we were working for Berlin. If this continue, and we do not put things in order, the French Revolution will have been for the benefit of Potsdam; it will have accomplished for unique result the aggrandizement of the little State of Frederick II., and we shall have killed the King of France for the King of Prussia's sake."

And Danton burst into a terrible laugh.

Danton's laugh made Marat smile.

"You have each one your hobby," said he. "Danton, yours is Prussia; Robespierre, yours is the Vendée. I am going to state facts in my turn. You do not perceive the real peril; it is this: The cafés and the gaming-houses. The Café Choiseul is Jacobin; the Café Pitou is Royalist; the Café Rendez-Vous attacks the National Guard; the Café of the Porte Saint Martin defends it; the Café Régence is against Brissot; the Café Corazza is for him; the Café Procope swears by Diderot; the Café of the Théâtre Français swears by Voltaire; at the Rotonde they tear up the assignats; the Cafés Saint Marceau are in a fury; the Café Manouri debates the question of flour; at the Café Foy uproars and fisticuffs; at the Perron the hornets of the finance buzz. These are the matters which are serious."

Danton laughed no longer. Marat continued to smile. The smile of a dwarf is worse than the laugh of a giant.

"Do you sneer at yourself, Marat?" growled Danton.

Marat gave that convulsive movement of his lip which was celebrated. His smile died.

"Ah, I recognize you, Citizen Danton! It is indeed you who in full Convention called me, 'the individual Marat.' Listen; I forgive you. We are playing the fool! Ah! *I* mock at myself! See what I have done! I denounced Chazot; I denounced Pétion;

I denounced Kersaint; I denounced Moreton; I denounced Dufriche-Valazé; I denounced Ligonnier; I denounced Menou; I denounced Banneville; I denounced Gensonné; I denounced Biron; I denounced Lidon and Chambon. Was I mistaken? I smell treason in the traitor, and I find it best to denounce the criminal before he can commit his crime. I have the habit of saying in the evening that which you and others say on the following day. I am the man who proposed to the Assembly a perfect plan of criminal legislation. What have I done up to the present? I have asked for the instruction of the sections in order to discipline them for the Revolution; I have broken the seals of thirty-two boxes; I have reclaimed the diamonds deposited in the hands of Roland; I proved that the Brissotins gave to the Committee of the General Safety blank warrants; I noted the omissions in the report of Lindet upon the crimes of Capet; I voted the punishment of the tyrant in twenty-four hours; I defended the battalions of Mauconseil and the Républicain; I prevented the reading of the letter of Narbonne and of Malonet; I made a motion in favour of the wounded soldiers; I caused the suppression of the Commission of Six; I foresaw the treason of Dumouriez in the affair of Mons; I demanded the taking of a hundred thousand relatives of the refugees as hostages for the commissioners delivered to the enemy; I proposed to declare traitor any Representative who should pass the barriers; I unmasked the Roland faction in the troubles at Marseilles; I insisted that a price should be set on the head of Egalité's son; I defended Bouchotte; I called for a nominal appeal in order to chase Isnard from the chair; I caused it to be declared that the Parisians had deserved well of the country. That is why I am called a dancing-puppet by Louvet; that is why Finistère demands my expulsion; why the city of Loudun desires that I should be exiled, the city of Amiens that I should be muzzled; why Coburg wishes me to be arrested, and Lecointe Puiraveau proposes to the Convention to decree me mad. Ah, now, Citizen Danton, why did you ask me to come to your little council if it were not to have my opinion? Did I ask to belong to it? Far from that. I have no taste for dialogues with counter-revolutionists like Robespierre and you. For that matter, I ought to have known that you would not understand me,—you no more than Robespierre; Robespierre no more than you. So there is not a statesman here? You need to be taught to spell at politics; you must have the dot put over the *i* for you. What I said to you meant this: you both deceive yourselves. The danger is not in London as Robespierre believes; nor in Berlin, as Danton believes: it is in Paris. It consists in the absence of unity; in the right of each one to pull on his own side, commencing with you two; in the binding of minds; in the anarchy of wills—"

"Anarchy!" interrupted Danton. "Who causes that, if not you?"

Marat did not pause.

"Robespierre, Danton, the danger is in this heap of cafés, in this mass of gaming-houses, this crowd of clubs,— Clubs of the Blacks, the Federals, the

Women; the Club of the Impartials, which dates from Clermont-Tonnerre, and which was the Monarchical Club of 1790, a social circle conceived by the priest Claude Fauché; Club of the Woollen Caps, founded by the gazetteer Prudhomme, et cætera; without counting your Club of the Jacobins, Robespierre, and your club of the Cordeliers, Danton. The danger lies in the famine which caused the sack-porter Blin to hang up to the lamp of the Hôtel de Ville the baker of the Market Palu, François Denis, and in the justice which hung the sack-porter Blin for having hanged the baker Denis. The danger is in the paper money, which the people depreciate. In the Rue du Temple an assignat of a hundred francs fell to the ground, and a passer-by, a man of the people, said, 'It is not worth the pains of picking it up.' The stock-brokers and the monopolists,—there is the danger. To have nailed the black flag to the Hôtel de Ville,—a fine advance! You arrest Baron Trenck; that is not sufficient. I want this old prison intriguer's neck wrung. You believe that you have got out of the difficulty because the President of the Convention puts a civic crown on the head of Labertèche, who received forty-one sabre cuts at Jemappes, and of whom Chénier makes himself the elephant driver? Comedies and juggling! Ah, you will not look at Paris! You seek the danger at a distance when it is close at hand. What is the use of your police, Robespierre? For you have your spies,—Payan at the Commune, Coffinhal at the Revolutionary Tribunal, David at the Committee of General Security, Couthon at the Committee of Public Safety. You see that I know all about it. Very well, learn this: the danger is over your heads; the danger is under your feet,—conspiracies! conspiracies! conspiracies! The people in the streets read the newspapers to one another and exchange nods; six thousand men, without civic papers, returned emigrants, Muscadins, and Mathevons, are hidden in cellars and garrets and the wooden galleries of the Palais Royal. People stand in a row at the bakers' shops, the women stand in the doorways and clasp their hands, crying, 'When shall we have peace?' You may shut yourselves up as close as you please in the hall of the Executive Council, in order to be alone; every word you speak is known; and as a proof, Robespierre, here are the words you spoke last night to Saint-Just: 'Barbaroux begins to show a fat paunch; it will be a trouble to him in his flight.' Yes; the danger is everywhere, and above all in the centre. In Paris the 'Retrogrades' plot, while patrols go barefooted; the aristocrats arrested on the 9th of March are already set at liberty; the fancy horses which ought to be harnessed to the frontier-cannon spatter mud on us in the streets; a loaf of bread weighing four pounds costs three francs twelve sous; the theatres play indecent pieces; and Robespierre will presently have Danton guillotined."

"Oh, there, there!" said Danton.

Robespierre attentively studied the map.

"What is needed," cried Marat, abruptly, "is a dictator. Robespierre, you know that I want a dictator."

Robespierre raised his head.

"I know, Marat; you or me."

"Me or you," said Marat.

Danton grumbled between his teeth,—

"The dictatorship; only try it!"

Marat caught Danton's frown.

"Hold!" he began again; "one last effort. Let us get some agreement. The situation is worth the trouble. Did we not come to an agreement for the day of the 31st of May? The entire question is a more serious one than that of Girondism, which was a question of detail. There is truth in what you say; but *the* truth, the whole truth, the real truth, is what I say. In the south, Federalism; in the west, Royalism; in Paris, the duel of the Convention and the Commune; on the frontiers, the retreat of Custine and the treason of Dumouriez. What does all this signify? Dismemberment. What is necessary for us? Unity. There is safety; but we must hasten to reach it. Paris must assume the government of the Revolution. If we lose an hour, to-morrow the Vendeans may be at Orleans, and the Prussians in Paris. I grant you this, Danton; I accord you that, Robespierre. So be it. Well, the conclusion is—a dictatorship. Let us seize the dictatorship,—we three who represent the Revolution. We are the three heads of Cerberus. Of these three heads, one talks,—that is you, Robespierre; one roars,—that is you, Danton—"

"The other bites," said Danton; "that is you, Marat."

"All three bite," said Robespierre.

There was a silence. Then the dialogue, full of dark threats, recommenced.

"Listen, Marat; before entering into a marriage, people must know each other. How did you learn what I said yesterday to Saint-Just?"

"That is my affair, Robespierre."

"Marat!"

"It is my duty to enlighten myself, and my business to inform myself."

"Marat!"

"I like to know things."

"Marat!"

"Robespierre, I know what you say to Saint-Just, as I know what Danton says to Lacroix; as I know what passes on the Quay of the Theatins, at the Hôtel Labriffe, the den where the nymphs of the emigration meet; as I know what happens in the house of the Thilles, near Gonesse, which belongs to Valmerange, former administrator of the post where Maury and Cazales went; where, since then, Sieyès and Vergniaud went, and where now some one goes once a week."

In saying "some one," Marat looked significantly at Danton.

Danton cried,—

"If I had two farthings' worth of power, this would be terrible."

Marat continued,—

"I know what I am saying to you, Robespierre, just as I knew what was going on in the Temple tower when they fattened Louis XVI. there, so well that the he-wolf, the she-wolf, and the cubs ate up eighty-six baskets of peaches in the month of September alone. During that time the people were starving. I know that, as I know that Roland was hidden in a lodging looking on a back court, in the Rue de la Harpe; as I know that six hundred of the pikes of July 14th were manufactured by Faure, the Duke of Orleans's locksmith; as I know what they do in the house of the Saint-Hilaire, the mistress of Sillery. On the days when there is to be a ball, it is old Sillery himself who chalks the floor of the yellow saloon of the Rue Neuve des Mathurins; Buzot and Kersaint dined there. Saladin dined there on the 27th, and with whom, Robespierre? With your friend Lasource."

"Mere words!" muttered Robespierre. "Lasource is not my friend."

And he added thoughtfully,—

"In the mean while there are in London eighteen manufactories of false assignats."

Marat went on in a voice still tranquil, though it had a slight tremulousness that was threatening,—

"You are the faction of the All-Importants! Yes; I know everything, in spite of what Saint-Just calls 'the silence of State—'"

Marat emphasized these last words, looked at Robespierre, and continued,—

"I know what is said at your table the days when Lebas invites David to come and eat the dinner cooked by his betrothed, Elizabeth Duplay,—your future sister-in-law, Robespierre. I am the far-seeing eye of the people, and from the bottom of my cave I watch. Yes, I see; yes, I hear; yes, I know! Little things content you. You admire yourselves. Robespierre poses to be contemplated by his Madame de Chalabre, the daughter of that Marquis de Chalabre who played whist with Louis XV. the evening Damiens was executed. Yes, yes; heads are carried high. Saint-Just lives in a cravat. Legendre's dress is scrupulously correct,—new frockcoat and white waistcoat, and a shirt-frill to make people forget his apron. Robespierre imagines that history will be interested to know that he wore an olive-coloured frockcoat *à la Constituante,* and a sky-blue dress coat *à la Convention.* He has his portrait hanging on all the walls of his chamber—"

Robespierre interrupted him in a voice even more composed than Marat's own:—

"And you, Marat, have yours in all the sewers."

They continued this style of conversation, in which the slowness of their voices emphasized the violence of the attacks and retorts, and added a certain irony to menace.

"Robespierre, you have called those who desire the overthrow of thrones 'the Don Quixotes of the human race.'"

"And you, Marat, after the 4th of August, in No. 559 of the 'Friend of the People' (ah, I have remembered the number; it may be useful!), you demanded that the titles of the nobility should be restored to them. You said, 'A duke is always a duke.'"

"Robespierre, in the sitting of December 7th, you defended the woman Roland against Viard."

"Just as my brother defended you, Marat, when you were attacked at the Jacobin Club. What does that prove? Nothing!"

"Robespierre, we know the cabinet of the Tuileries where you said to Garat: 'I am tired of the Revolution!'"

"Marat, it was here, in this publichouse, that, on the 29th of October, you embraced Barbaroux."

"Robespierre, you said to Buzot: 'The Republic! What is that?'"

"Marat, it was also in this public-house that you invited three Marseillais suspects to keep you company."

"Robespierre, you have yourself escorted by a stout fellow from the market, armed with a club."

"And you, Marat, on the eve of the 10th of August you asked Buzot to help you flee to Marseilles disguised as a jockey."

"During the prosecutions of September you hid yourself, Robespierre."

"And you, Marat—you showed yourself."

"Robespierre, you flung the red cap on the ground."

"Yes, when a traitor hoisted it. That which decorates Dumouriez sullies Robespierre."

"Robespierre, you refused to cover Louis XVI.'s head with a veil while soldiers of Chateauvieux were passing."

"I did better than veil his head: I cut it off."

Danton interposed, but it was like oil flung upon flames.

"Robespierre, Marat," said he: "calm yourselves."

Marat did not like being named the second. He turned about.

"With what does Danton meddle?" he asked.

Danton bounded.

"With what do I meddle? With this! That we must not have fratricide; that there must be no strife between two men who serve the people; that it is enough to have a foreign war; that it is enough to have a civil war; that it would be too much to have domestic war; that it is I who have made the Revolution, and I will not permit it to be spoiled. Now you know what it is I meddle with!"

Marat replied, without raising his voice,—

"You had better meddle with getting your accounts ready."

"My accounts!" cried Danton. "Go ask for them in the defiles of Argonne, in Champagne delivered, in Belgium conquered, in the armies where I have already four times offered my breast to the musket-shots. Go demand them at the Place de la Revolution, at the scaffold of January 21st, from the throne flung to the ground, from the guillotine; that widow—"

Marat interrupted him,—

"The guillotine is a virgin Amazon; she does not give birth."

"Are you sure?" retorted Danton. "I tell you I will make her fruitful."

"We shall see," said Marat. He smiled.

Danton saw this smile.

"Marat," cried he, "you are the man that hides; I am the man of the open air and broad day. I hate the life of a reptile. It would not suit me to be a wood-louse. You inhabit a cave; I live in the street. You hold communication with none; whosoever passes may see and speak with me."

"Pretty fellow! Will you mount up to where I live?" snarled Marat.

Then his smile disappeared, and he continued, in a peremptory tone,—

"Danton, give an account of the thirty-three thousand crowns, ready money, that Montmorin paid you in the king's name under pretext of indemnifying you for your post of solicitor at the Châtelet."

"I was of the 14th of July," said Danton, haughtily.

"And the Garde-Meuble, and the crown diamonds?"

"I was of the 6th of October."

"And the thefts of your *alter ego*, Lacroix, in Belgium?"

"I was of the 20th of June."

"And the loans to the Montansier?"

"I urged the people on to the return from Varennes."

"And the opera-house, built with money that you furnished?"

"I armed the sections of Paris."

"And the hundred thousand livres, secret funds of the Ministry of Justice?"

"I caused the 10th of August."

"And the two millions for the Assembly's secret expenses, of which you took the fourth?"

"I stopped the enemy on their march, and I barred the passage to the kings in coalition."

"Prostitute!" said Marat.

Danton was terrible as he rose to his full height.

"Yes!" cried he. "I am a harlot! I sold myself, but I saved the world!"

Robespierre had gone back to biting his nails. As for him, he could neither laugh nor smile. The laugh (the lightning) of Danton, and the smile (the sting) of Marat were both wanting to him.

Danton resumed,—

"I am like the ocean; I have my ebb and flow. At low water my shoals may be seen; at high tide you may see my waves."

"You foam," said Marat.

"My tempest," said Danton.

Marat had risen at the same moment as Danton. He also exploded. The snake became suddenly a dragon.

"Ah!" cried he. "Ah, Robespierre! Ah, Danton! You will not listen to me! Well, you are lost; I tell you so. Your policy ends in an impossibility to go farther; you have no longer an outlet; and you do things which shut every door against you,—except that of the tomb."

"That is our grandeur," said Danton. He shrugged his shoulders.

Marat hurried on:—

"Danton, beware. Vergniaud has also a wide mouth, thick lips, and frowning eyebrows; Vergniaud is pitted, too, like Mirabeau and like thee; that did not prevent the 31st of May. Ah, you shrug your shoulders! Sometimes a shrug of the shoulders makes the head fall. Danton, I tell thee, that big voice, that loose cravat, those top-boots, those little suppers, those great pockets,—all those are things which concern Louisette."

Louisette was Marat's pet name for the guillotine.

He pursued:—

"And as for thee, Robespierre, thou art a Moderate, but that will serve nothing. Go on! powder thyself, dress thy hair, brush thy clothes, play the vulgar coxcomb, have clean linen, keep curled and frizzed and bedizened; none the less thou wilt go to the Place de Grève. Read Brunswick's proclamation. Thou wilt get a treatment no less than that of the regicide Damiens! Fine as thou art, thou wilt be dragged at the tails of four horses."

"Echo of Coblentz!" said Robespierre between his teeth.

"I am the echo of nothing; I am the cry of the whole, Robespierre! Ah, you are young, you! How old art thou, Danton? Four-and-thirty. How many are your years, Robespierre? Thirty-three. Well, I—I have lived always! I am the old human suffering; I am six thousand years old."

"That is true," retorted Danton. "For six thousand years Cain has been preserved in hatred, like the toad in a rock; the rock breaks, Cain springs out among men, and is called Marat."

"Danton!" cried Marat, and a livid glare illuminated his eyes.

"Well, what?" asked Danton.

Thus these three terrible men conversed.

They were conflicting thunderbolts.

Chapter III

A STIRRING OF THE INMOST NERVES

THERE was a pause in the dialogue; these Titans withdrew for a moment each into his own reflections.

Lions dread hydras. Robespierre had grown very pale, and Danton very red. A shiver ran through the frames of both.

The wild-beast glare in Marat's eyes had died out; a calm, cold and imperious, settled again on the face of this man, dreaded by his formidable associates.

Danton felt himself conquered, but he would not yield. He resumed,—

"Marat talks very loud about the dictatorship and unity, but he has only one ability,—that of breaking to pieces."

Robespierre parted his thin lips, and said,—

"As for me, I am of the opinion of Anacharsis Cloots: I say, Neither Roland nor Marat."

"And I," replied Marat, "I say, Neither Danton or Robespierre."

He regarded both fixedly, and added,—

"Let me give you advice, Danton. You are in love, you think of marrying again; do not meddle any more with politics. Be wise."

And moving backward a step toward the door, as if to go out, he made them a menacing salute, and said,—

"Adieu, gentlemen."

Danton and Robespierre shuddered.

At this instant a voice rose from the bottom of the room, saying,—

"You are wrong, Marat."

All three turned about. During Marat's explosion some one had entered unperceived by the door at the end of the room.

"Is it you, Citizen Cimourdain?" asked Marat. "Good-day."

It was indeed Cimourdain.

"I say you are wrong, Marat," he repeated.

Marat turned green, which was his way of growing pale.

"You are useful, but Robespierre and Danton are necessary. Why threaten them? Union, union, citizens! The people expect unity."

This entrance acted like a dash of cold water, and had the effect that the arrival of a stranger does on a family quarrel,—it calmed the surface, if not the depths.

Cimourdain advanced toward the table.

Danton and Robespierre knew him. They had often remarked among the public tribunals of the Convention this obscure but powerful man, whom the people saluted. Nevertheless, Robespierre, always a stickler for forms, asked,—

"Citizen, how did you enter?"

"He belongs to the Evêché," replied Marat, in a voice in which a certain submission was perceptible.

Marat braved the Convention, led the Commune, and feared the Evêché. This is a law.

Mirabeau felt Robespierre stirring at some unknown depth below; Robespierre felt Marat stir; Marat felt Hébert stir; Hébert, Babeuf. As long as the layers underneath are still, the politician can advance; but under the most revolutionary there must be some subsoil, and the boldest stop in dismay when they feel under their feet the earthquake they have created.

To be able to distinguish the movement which covetousness causes from that brought about by principle, to combat the one and second the other, is the genius and the virtue of great revolutionists.

Danton saw that Marat faltered.

"Oh, Citizen Cimourdain is not one too many," said he. And he held out his hand to the new-comer.

Then he said,—

"Zounds! explain the situation to Citizen Cimourdain. He appears just at the right moment. I represent the Mountain; Robespierre represents the Committee of Public Safety; Marat represents the Commune; Cimourdain represents the Evêché. He is come to give the casting vote."

"So be it," said Cimourdain, simply and gravely. "What is the matter in question?"

"The Vendée," replied Robespierre.

"The Vendée!" repeated Cimourdain.

Then he continued: "There is the great danger. If the Revolution perish, she will perish by the Vendée. One Vendée is more formidable than ten Germanys. In order that France may live, it is necessary to kill the Vendée."

These few words won him Robespierre.

Still Robespierre asked this question: "Were you not formerly a priest?"

Cimourdain's priestly air did not escape Robespierre. He recognized in another that which he had within himself.

Cimourdain replied,—

"Yes, citizen."

"What difference does that make?" cried Danton. "When priests are good fellows, they are worth more than others. In revolutionary times the priests melt into citizens, as the bells do into arms and cannon. Danjou is a priest; Daunou is a priest; Thomas Lindet is the Bishop of Evreux. Robespierre, you sit in the Convention side by side with Massieu, Bishop of Beauvais. The Grand Vicar Vaugeois was a member of the Insurrection Committee of August 10th. Chabot is a Capuchin. It was Dom Gerle who devised the tennis-court oath; it was the Abbé Audran who caused the National Assembly to be declared superior to the king; it was the Abbé Goutte who demanded of the Legislature that the dais should be taken away from Louis XVI.'s armchair; it was the Abbé Grégoire who proposed the abolition of royalty."

"Seconded," sneered Marat, "by the actor Collot d'Herbois. Between them they did the work,—the priest overturned the throne; the comedian flung down the king."

"Let us get back to the Vendée," said Robespierre.

"Well, what is it?" demanded Cimourdain. "What is this Vendée doing now?"

Robespierre answered,—

"This: she has found a chief. She becomes terrible.

"Who is this chief, Citizen Robespierre?"

" A *ci-devant* Marquis de Lantenac, who styles himself a Breton prince."

Cimourdain made a movement.

"I know him," said he; "I was chaplain in his house."

He reflected for a moment, then added,—

"He was a man of gallantry before being a soldier."

"Like Biron, who was a Lauzun," said Danton.

And Cimourdain continued, thoughtfully: "Yes, an old man of pleasure. He must be terrible."

"Frightful," said Robespierre. "He burns the villages, kills the wounded, massacres the prisoners, shoots the women."

"The women!"

"Yes. Among others he had the mother of three children shot. Nobody knows what became of the little ones. He is really a captain; he understands war."

"Yes, in truth," replied Cimourdain. "He was in the Hanoverian war, and the soldiers said, 'Richelieu in appearance, Lantenac at the bottom.' Lantenac was the real general. Talk about him to your colleague Dussaulx."

Robespierre remained silent for a moment; then the dialogue began anew between him and Cimourdain.

"Well, Citizen Cimourdain, this man is in Vendée."

"Since when?"

"The last three weeks."

"He must be declared an outlaw."

"That is done."

"A price must be set on his head."

"It is done."

"A large reward must be offered to whoever will take him."

"That is done."

"Not in assignats."

"That is done."

"In gold."

"That is done."

"And he must be guillotined."

"That *will* be done."

"By whom?"

"By you."

"By me?"

"Yes; you will be delegated by the Committee of Public Safety with unlimited powers."

"I accept," said Cimourdain.

Robespierre made his choice of men rapidly,—the quality of a true statesman. He took from the portfolio before him a sheet of white paper, on which could be read this printed heading: "THE FRENCH REPUBLIC ONE AND INDIVISIBLE.—COMMITTEE OF PUBLIC SAFETY."

Cimourdain continued,—

"Yes, I accept. The terrible against the terrible. Lantenac is ferocious; I shall be so too. War to the death against this man. I will deliver the Republic from him, please God."

He checked himself; then resumed,—

"I am a priest; no matter; I believe in God."

"God has gone out of date," said Danton.

"I believe in God," said Cimourdain unmoved.

Robespierre gave a sinister nod of approval.

Cimourdain asked,—

"To whom am I delegated?"

"The commandant of the exploring division sent against Lantenac. Only, —I warn you,—he is a nobleman."

Danton cried out,—

"That is another thing which matters little. A noble! Well, what then! It is with the nobles as with the priests. When one of either class is good, he is excellent. Nobility is a prejudice; but we should not have it in one sense more than the other,—no more against than in favour of it. Robespierre, is not Saint-Just a noble? Florelle de Saint-Just, zounds! Anarchasis Cloots is a baron. Our friend Charles Hesse, who never misses a meeting of the Cordeliers, is a prince, and the brother of the reigning Landgrave of Hesse-Rothenburg. Montaut, the intimate of Marat, is the Marquis de Montaut. There is in the revolutionary tribunal a juror who is a priest,—Vilate; and a juror who is a nobleman—Leroy, Marquis de Montflabert. Both are tried men."

"And you forget," added Robespierre, "the foreman of the revolutionary jury."

"Antonelle?"

"Who is the Marquis Antonelle," said Robespierre.

Danton continued,—

"Dampierre was a nobleman,—the one who lately got himself killed before Condé for the Republic; and Beaurepaire was a noble,—he who blew his brains out rather than open the gates of Verdun to the Prussians."

"All of which," grumbled Marat, "does not alter the fact that on the day Condorcet said, 'the Gracchi were nobles,' Danton cried out, 'All nobles are traitors, beginning with Mirabeau and ending with thee.'"

Cimourdain's grave voice made itself heard—

"Citizen Danton, Citizen Robespierre, you are perhaps right to have confidence, but the people distrusts them; and the people is not wrong in so doing. When a priest is charged with the surveillance of a nobleman, the responsibility is doubled, and it is necessary for the priest to be inflexible."

"True," said Robespierre.

Cimourdain added,—

"And inexorable."

Robespierre replied,—

"It is well said, Citizen Cimourdain. You will have to deal with a young man. You will have the ascendency over him, being double his age. It will be necessary to direct him, but he must be carefully managed. It appears that he possesses military talent; all the reports are unanimous as to that. He belongs to a corps which has been detached from the Army of the Rhine to go into Vendée. He arrives from the frontier, where he was noticeable for intelligence and courage. He leads the exploring column in a superior way.

For fifteen days he has held the old Marquis de Lantenac in check. He restrains and drives him before him. He will end by forcing him into the sea, and tumbling him into it headlong. Lantenac has the cunning of an old general, and the audacity of a youthful captain. This young man has already enemies, and those who are envious of him. The Adjutant-General Léchelle is jealous of him."

"That L'Echelle wants to be commander-in-chief," interrupted Danton. "There is nothing in his favour but a pun: 'It needs a ladder to get on top of a cart.' All the same. Charette beats him."

"And he is not willing," pursued Robespierre, "that anybody besides himself should beat Lantenac. The misfortune of the Vendean war is in such rivalries. Heroes badly commanded,—that is what our soldiers are. A simple captain of hussars, Chérin, enters Saumur with trumpets playing *Ca ira;* he takes Saumur; he could keep on and take Cholet but he has no orders, so he halts. All those commands of the Vendée must be remodelled. The head-quarters are scattered, the forces dispersed. A scattered army is an army paralyzed; it is a rock crumbled into dust. At the camp of Paramé there are only some tents. There are a hundred useless little companies posted between Tréguier and Dinan, of which a division might be formed that could guard the whole cast. Léchelle, supported by Parrein, strips the northern coast under pretext of protecting the southern, and so opens France to the English. A half million peasants in revolt and a descent of England upon France,—that is Lantenac's plan. The young commander of the exploring column presses his sword against Lantenac's loins, keeps it there, and beats him without Léchelle's permission. Now, Léchelle is his general, so Léchelle denounces him. Opinions are divided in regard to this young man. Léchelle wants to have him shot. Prieur, of the Marne, wants to make him adjutant-general."

"This youth appears to me to possess great qualities," said Cimourdain.

"But he has one fault." The interruption came from Marat.

"What is it?" demanded Cimourdain.

"Clemency," said Marat.

Then he added,—

"He is firm in battle, and weak afterward. He shows indulgence; he pardons; he grants mercy; he protects devotees and nuns; he saves the wives and daughters of aristocrats; he releases prisoners; he sets priests free."

"A grave fault," murmured Cimourdain.

"A crime," said Marat.

"Sometimes," said Danton.

"Often," said Robespierre.

"Almost always," chimed in Marat.

"When one has to deal with the enemies of the country—always," said Cimourdain.

Marat turned toward him.

"And what, then, would you do with a republican chief who set a royalist chief at liberty?"

"I should be of Léchelle's opinion; I would have him shot."

"Or guillotined," said Marat.

"He might have his choice," said Cimourdain.

Danton began to laugh.

"I like one as well as the other."

"Thou art sure to have one or the other," growled Marat.

His glance left Danton and settled again on Cimourdain.

"So, Citizen Cimourdain, if a republican leader were to flinch, you would cut off his head?"

"Within twenty-four hours."

"Well," retorted Marat, "I am of Robespierre's opinion; Citizen Cimourdain ought to be sent as delegate of the Committee of Public Safety to the commandant of the exploring division of the coast army. How is it you call this commandant?"

Robespierre answered,—

"He is a *ci-devant* noble."

He began to turn over the papers.

"Get the priest to guard the nobleman," said Danton. "I distrust a priest when he is alone; I distrust a noble when he is alone. When they are together, I do not fear them. One watches the other, and they do well."

The indignant look always on Cimourdain's face grew deeper, but without doubt finding the remark just at bottom, he did not look at Danton, but said in his stern voice:—

"If the republican commander who is confided to me makes one false step the penalty will be death."

Robespierre, with his eyes on the portfolio, said,—

"Here is the name, Citizen Cimourdain The commandant, in regard to whom full powers will be granted you, is a so-called viscount; his name is Gauvain."

Cimourdain turned pale.

"Gauvain!" he cried.

Marat saw his sudden pallor.

"The Viscount Gauvain!" repeated Cimourdain.

"Yes," said Robespierre.

"Well," said Marat, with his eyes fixed on the priest.

There was a brief silence, which Marat broke.

"Citizen Cimourdain, on the conditions named by yourself, do you accept the mission as commissioner delegate near the Commandant Gauvain? Is it decided?"

"It is decided," replied Cimourdain. He grew paler and paler.

Robespierre took the pen which lay near him, wrote in his slow, even hand four lines on the sheet of paper which bore the heading COMMITTEE OF PUBLIC SAFETY, signed them, and passed the sheet and the pen to Danton; Danton signed, and Marat, whose eyes had not left Cimourdain's livid face, signed after Danton.

Robespierre took the paper again, dated it, and gave it to Cimourdain, who read:—

Year II. of the Republic.

Full powers are granted to Citizen Cimourdain, delegated Commissioner of Public Safety to the Citizen Gauvain, commanding the Exploring Division of the Army of the Coasts.

Robespierre. Danton. Marat.

And beneath the signatures:—

June 28, 1793.

The revolutionary calendar, called the Civil Calendar, had no legal existence at this time, and was not adopted by the Convention, on the proposition of Romme, until October 5, 1793.

While Cimourdain read, Marat watched him.

He said in a half-voice, as if talking to himself,—

"It will be necessary to have all this formalized by a decree of the Convention, or a special warrant of the Committee of Public Safety. There remains something yet to be done."

"Citizen Cimourdain, where do you live?" asked Robespierre.

"Court of Commerce."

"So do I, too," said Danton. "You are my neighbour."

Robespierre resumed,—

"There is not a moment to lose. Tomorrow you will receive your commission in form, signed by all the members of the Committee of Public Safety. This is a confirmation of the commission. It will accredit you in a special manner to the acting Representatives, Philippeaux, Prieur of the Marne, Lecointre, Alquier, and the others. We know you. Your powers are unlimited. You can make Gauvain a general or send him to the scaffold. You will receive your commission to-morrow at three o'clock. When shall you set out?"

"At four," said Cimourdain.

And they separated.

As he entered his house, Marat informed Simonne Evrard that he should go to the Convention on the morrow.

BOOK III

The Convention

Chapter I

ONLY ONE

We approach the grand summit. Behold the Convention!

The gaze grows steady in presence of this height.

Never has a more lofty spectacle appeared on the horizon of mankind.

There is one Himalaya, and there is one Convention.

The Convention is perhaps the culminating point of History.

During its lifetime—for it lived— men did not quite understand what it was. It was precisely the grandeur which escaped its contemporaries; they were too much scared to be dazzled. Everything grand possessess a sacred horror. It is easy to admire mediocrities and hills; but whatever is too lofty, whether it be a genius or a mountain,—an assembly as well as a masterpiece,—alarms when seen too near. An immense height appears an exaggeration. It is fatiguing to climb. One loses breath upon acclivities, one slips down declivities; one is hurt by sharp, rugged heights which are in themselves beautiful; torrents in their foaming reveal the precipices; clouds hide the mountain-tops; a sudden ascent terrifies as much as a fall. Hence there is a greater sensation of fright than admiration. What one feels is fantastic enough,—an aversion to the grand. One sees the abyss and loses sight of the sublimity; one sees the monster and does not perceive the marvel. Thus the Convention was at first judged. It was measured by the purblind,—it, which needed to be looked at by eagles.

To-day we see it in perspective, and it throws across the deep and distant heavens, against a background at once serene and tragic, the immense profile of the French Revolution.

Chapter II

THE TRICOLOUR

The 14th of July delivered. The 10th of August blasted. The 21st of September founded.

The 21st of September was the Equinox; was Equilibrium,—*Libra*, the balance. It was, according to the remark of Romme, under this sign of Equality and Justice that the Republic was proclaimed. A constellation heralded it.

The Convention is the first avatar of the peoples. It was by the Convention that the grand new page opened and the future of to-day commenced.

Every idea must have a visible enfolding; a habitation is necessary to any principle; a church is God between four walls; every dogma must have a temple. When the Convention became a fact, the first problem to be solved was how to lodge the Convention.

At first the Riding-school, then the Tuileries, was taken. A platform was raised, scenery arranged,—a great grey painting by David imitating bas-reliefs; benches were placed in order; there was a square tribune, parallel pilasters with plinths like blocks and long rectilinear stems; square enclosures, into which the spectators crowded, and which were called the public tribunes; a Roman velarium, Grecian draperies; and in these right-angles and these straight lines the Convention was installed,—the tempest confined within this geometrical plan. On the tribune the Red Cap was painted in grey. The royalists began by laughing at this grey red cap, this theatrical hall, this monument of pasteboard, this sanctuary of papier-mâché, this Pantheon of mud and spittle. How quickly it would disappear! The columns were made of the staves from hogsheads, the arches were of deal boards, the bas-reliefs of mastic, the entablatures were of pine, the statues of plaster; the marbles were paint, the walls canvas; and of this provisional shelter France has made an eternal dwelling.

When the Convention began to hold its sessions in the Riding-school, the walls were covered with the placards which sprouted over Paris at the period of the return from Varennes.

On one might be read: "The king returns. Any person who cheers him shall be beaten; any person who insults him shall be hanged." On another: "Peace! Hats on! He is about to pass before his judges." On another: "The king has aimed at the nation. He has hung fire; it is now the nation's turn." On another: "The Law! The Law!" It was within those walls that the Convention sat in judgment on Louis XVI.

At the Tuileries, where the Convention began to sit on the 10th of May, 1793, and which was called the Palais-National, the assembly-hall occupied the whole space between the Pavillon de l'Horloge, called the Pavilion of Unity, and the Pavillon Marsan, then named Pavilion of Liberty. The Pavilion of Flora was called Pavillon Egalité. The hall was reached by the grand staircase of Jean Bullant. The whole ground-floor of the palace, beneath the story occupied by the Assembly, was a kind of long guard-room, littered with bundles and camp-beds of the troops of all arms, who kept watch about the Convention. The Assembly had a guard of honour styled "the Grenadiers of the Convention."

A tricoloured ribbon separated the palace where the Assembly sat from the garden in which the people came and went.

Chapter III

ARCHITECTURE

Let us finish the description of that sessions-hall. Everything in regard to this terrible place is interesting.

What first struck the sight of any one entering was a great statue of Liberty, placed between two wide windows. One hundred and forty feet in length, thirty-four feet in width, thirty-seven feet in height,—such were the dimensions of this room, which had been the king's theatre, and which became the theatre of the Revolution. The elegant and magnificent hall built by Vigarani for the courtiers was hidden by the rude timber-work which in '93 supported the weight of the people. This framework, whereon the public tribunes were erected, had (a detail deserving notice) one single post for its only point of support. This post was of one piece, ten metres [32 feet 6 inches] in circumference. Few caryatides have laboured like that beam; it supported for years the rude pressure of the Revolution. It sustained applause, enthusiasm, insolence, noise, tumult, riot,—the immense chaos of opposing rages. It did not give way. After the Convention it witnessed the Council of the Ancients. The 18th Brumaire relieved it.

Percier then replaced the wooden pillar by columns of marble, which did not last so well.

The ideal of architects is sometimes strange. The architect of the Rue de Rivoli had for his ideal the trajectory of a cannon-ball; the architect of Carlsruhe, a fan; a gigantic drawer would seem to have been the model of the architect who built the hall where the Convention began to sit on the 10th of May, 1793; it was long, high, and flat. At one of the sides of the parallelogram was a great semicircle; this amphitheatre contained the seats of the Representatives, but without tables or desks. Garan-Coulon, who wrote a great deal, held his paper on his knee. In front of the seats was the tribune; before the tribune, the bust of Lepelletier Saint-Fargeau; behind was the President's arm-chair.

The head of the bust passed a little beyond the ledge of the tribune, for which reason it was afterward moved away from that position.

The amphitheatre was composed of nineteen semicircular rows of benches, rising one behind the other, the supports of the seats prolonging the amphitheatre into the two corners.

Below, in the horse-shoe at the foot of the tribune, the ushers had their places.

On one side of the tribune a placard nine feet in length was fastened to the wall in a black wooden frame bearing on two leaves, separated by a sort of sceptre, the "Declaration of the Rights of Man;" on the other side was a vacant place, at a later period occupied by a similar frame, containing the Constitution of Year II., with the leaves divided by a sword. Above the tribune, over the head of the orator, from a deep *loge* with double compartments always filled with people, floated three immense tricoloured flags, almost horizontal, resting on an altar upon which could be read the word LAW. Behind this altar there arose, tall as a column, an enormous Roman fasces like the sentinel of free speech. Colossal statues, erect against the wall, faced the Representatives. The President had Lycurgus on his right hand and Solon on his left; Plato towered above the Mountain.

These statues had plain blocks of wood for pedestals, resting on a long cornice which encircled the hall, and separated the people from the Assembly. The spectators could lean their elbows on this cornice.

The black wooden frame of the proclamation of the "Rights of Man" reached to the cornice, and broke the regularity of the entablature,—an infraction of the straight line which caused Chabot to murmur: "It is ugly," he said to Vadier.

On the heads of the statues alternated crowns of oak-leaves and laurel. A green drapery, on which similar crowns were painted in deeper green, fell in heavy folds straight down from the cornice of the circumference, and covered the whole wall of the ground-floor occupied by the Assembly. Above this drapery the wall was white and naked. In it, as if hollowed out by a gigantic axe, without moulding or foliage, were two stories of public tribunes, —the lower ones square, the upper ones round. According to rule, for Vitruvius was not dethroned, the archivolts were superimposed upon the architraves. There were ten tribunes on each side of the hall, and two huge boxes at either end,—in all, twenty-four. There the crowds gathered thickly.

The spectators in the lower tribunes, overflowing their borders, grouped themselves along the reliefs of the cornice. A long iron bar, firmly fixed at a height to lean on, served as a safety rail to the upper tribunes, and guarded the spectators against the pressure of the throngs mounting the stairs. Nevertheless, a man was once thrown headlong into the Assembly; he fell partly upon Massieu, Bishop of Beauvais, and thus was not killed. He said "Hullo! Why, a bishop is really good for something!"

The hall of the Convention could hold two thousand persons comfortably; on the days of insurrection it held three.

The Convention held two sittings, one in the daytime and one in the evening.

The back of the President's chair was curved, and studded with gilt nails. The table was upheld by four winged monsters, with a single foot; one might have thought they had come out of the

Apocalypse to assist at the Revolution. They seemed to have been unharnessed from Ezekiel's chariot to drag the dung-cart of Sanson.

On the President's table was a huge hand-bell almost large enough to have served for a church, a great copper ink-stand, and a parchment folio, which was the book of official reports.

Many times freshly severed heads, borne aloft on the tops of pikes, sprinkled their blood-drops over this table.

The tribune was reached by a staircase of nine steps. These steps were high, steep, and hard to mount. One day Gensonné stumbled as he was going up. "It is a scaffold-ladder," said he. "Serve your apprenticeship," Carrier cried out to him.

In the angles of the hall, where the wall had looked too naked, the architect had put Roman fasces for decorations, with the axe turned to the people.

At the right and left of the tribune were square blocks supporting two candelabra twelve feet in height, having each four pairs of lamps. There was a similar candelabrum in each public box.

On the pedestals were carved circles, which the people called guillotine-collars.

The benches of the Assembly reached almost to the cornice of the tribunes; so that the Representatives and the spectators could talk together.

The outlets from the tribunes led into a labyrinth of sombre corridors, often filled with a savage din.

The Convention overcrowded the palace and flowed into the neighbouring mansions,—the Hôtel de Longueville and the Hôtel de Coigny. It was to the Hôtel de Coigny, if one may believe a letter of Lord Bradford's, that the royal furniture was carried after the 10th of August. It took two months to empty the Tuileries.

The committees were lodged in the neighbourhood of the hall: in the Pavillon Egalité were those of Legislation, Agriculture, and Commerce; in the Pavilion of Liberty were the Marine, the Colonies, Finance, Assignats, and Public Safety; the War Department was at the Pavilion of Unity.

The Committee of General Security communicated directly with that of Public Safety by an obscure passage, lighted day and night with a reflector-lamp, where the spies of all parties came and went. People spoke there in whispers.

The bar of the Convention was several times moved. Generally it was at the right of the President.

At the far ends of the hall the vertical partitions which closed the concentric semicircles of the amphitheatre left between them and the wall a couple of narrow, deep passages, from which opened two dark square doors.

The Representatives entered directly into the hall by a door opening on the Terrace des Feuillants.

This hall, dimly lighted during the day by deep-set windows, took a strange nocturnal aspect when, with the approach of twilight, it was badly illuminated by lamps. Their pale glare intensified the evening shadows, and the lamplight sessions were lugubrious.

It was impossible to see clearly; from the opposite ends of the hall, to the right and to the left, indistinct groups of faces insulted each other. People met without recognizing one another. One day Laignelot, hurrying toward the tribune, hit against some person in the sloping passage between the benches. "Pardon, Robespierre," said he. "For whom do you take me?" replied a hoarse voice. "Pardon, Marat," said Laignelot.

At the bottom, to the right and left of the President, were two reserved tribunes; for, strange to say, the Convention had its privileged spectators. These tribunes were the only ones that had draperies. In the middle of the architrave two gold tassels held up the curtains. The tribunes of the people were bare.

The whole surroundings were peculiar and savage, yet correct. Regularity in barbarism is rather a type of revolution. The hall of the Convention offered the most complete specimen of what artists have since called "architecture Messidor;" it was massive, and yet frail.

The builders of that time mistook symmetry for beauty. The last word of the Renaissance had been uttered under Louis XV., and a reaction followed. The noble was pushed to insipidity, and the pure to absurdity. Prudery may exist in architecture. After the dazzling orgies of form and colour of the eighteenth century, Art took to fasting, and only allowed herself the straight line. This species of progress ends in ugliness, and Art reduced to a skeleton is the phenomenon which results. The fault of this sort of wisdom and abstinence is, that the style is so severe that it becomes meagre.

Outside of all political emotion, there was something in the very architecture of this hall which made one shiver. One recalled confusedly the ancient theatre with its garlanded boxes, its blue and crimson ceiling, its prismed lustres, its girandoles with diamond reflections, its brilliant hangings, its profusion of Cupids and Nymphs on the curtain and draperies, the whole royal and amorous idyll—painted, sculptured, gilded—which had brightened this sombre spot with its smile, where now one saw on every side hard rectilinear angles, cold and sharp as steel; it was something like Boucher guillotined by David.

Chapter IV

GIANTS MEET

But when one saw the Assembly, the hall was forgotten. Whoever looked at the drama no longer remembered the theatre. Nothing more chaotic and more sublime. A crowd of heroes; a mob of cowards. Fallow deer on a mountain; reptiles in a marsh. Therein swarmed, elbowed one another, provoked one another, threatened, struggled, and lived, all those combatants who are phantoms to-day.

A convocation of Titans.

To the right, the Gironde,—a legion of thinkers; to the left, the Mountain, —a group of athletes. On one side Brissot, who had received the keys of the Bastille; Barbaroux, whom the Marseillais obeyed; Kervélégan, who had under his hand the battalion of Brest, garrisoned in the Faubourg

Saint Marceau; Gensonné, who had established the supremacy of the Representatives over the generals; the fatal Guadet, to whom the queen one night, at the Tuileries, showed the sleeping Dauphin; Guadet kissed the forehead of the child, and caused the head of the father to fall. Salles, the crack-brained denouncer of the intimacy between the Mountain and Austria. Sillery, the cripple of the Right, as Couthon was the paralytic of the Left. Lause-Duperret, who, having been called a scoundrel by a journalist, invited him to dinner, saying, "I know that by scoundrel you simply mean a man who does not think like yourself." Rabaut Saint-Etienne, who commenced his almanac for 1790 with this saying: "The Revolution is ended." Quinette, one of those who overthrew Louis XVI.; the Jansenist Camus, who drew up the civil constitution of the clergy; believed in the miracles of the Deacon Paris, and prostrated himself each night before a figure of Christ seven feet high, which was nailed to the wall of his chamber. Fauchet, a priest, who, with Camille Desmoulins, brought about the 14th of July; Isnard, who committed the crime of saying, "Paris will be destroyed," at the same moment when Brunswick was saying, "Paris shall be burned." Jacob Dupont, the first who cried, "I am an Atheist," and to whom Robespierre replied, "Atheism is aristocratic." Lanjuinais, stern, sagacious, and valiant Breton; Ducos, the Euryalus of Boyer-Fonfrède; Rebecqui, the Pylades of Barbaroux (Rebecqui gave in his resignation because Robespierre had not yet been guillotined). Richaud, who combated the permanency of the Sections.

Lasource, who had given utterance to the murderous apothegm, "Woe to grateful nations!" and who was afterwards to contradict himself at the foot of the scaffold by this haughty sarcasm flung at the Mountainists: "We die because the people sleep; you will die because the people awake." Biroteau, who caused the abolition of inviolability to be decreed; who was also, without knowing it, the forger of the axe, and raised the scaffold for himself. Charles Villatte, who sheltered his conscience behind this protest: "I will not vote under the hatchet." Louvet, the author of "Faublas," who was to end as a bookseller in the Palais Royal, with Lodoiska behind the counter. Mercier, author of the "Picture of Paris," who exclaimed, "On the 21st of January, all kings felt for the backs of their necks!" Marec, whose anxiety was "the faction of the ancient limits." The journalist Carra, who said to the headsman at the foot of the scaffold, "It bores me to die. I would have liked to see the continuation." Vigée, who called himself a grenadier in the second battalion of Mayence and Loire, and who, when menaced by the public tribunals, cried, "I demand that at the first murmur of the tribunals we all withdraw and march on Versailles, sabre in hand!" Buzot, reserved for death by famine; Valazé, destined to die by his own dagger; Condorcet, who was to perish at Bourg-la-Reine (become Bourg-Egalité), betrayed by the Horace which he had in his pocket; Pétion, whose destiny was to be adored by the crowd in 1792 and devoured by wolves in 1794; twenty others still,—Pontecoulant, Marboz, Lidon, Saint-Martin, Dussaulx, the translator of Juvenal, who had been in the Hanover campaign; Boileau, Bertrand, Lesterp-Beauvais, Lesage, Gomaire, Gardien, Mainvelle, Duplentier, Lacaze, Antiboul, and at their head a Barnave, who was styled Vergniaud.

On the other side, Antoine Louis Léon Florelle de Saint-Just, pale, with a low forehead, a regular profile, eye mysterious, a profound sadness, aged twenty-three. Merlin of Thionville, whom the Germans called *Feuerteufel,*—"the fire-devil." Merlin of Douai, the culpable author of the "Law of the Suspected." Soubrany, whom the people of Paris at the first Prairial demanded for general. The ancient priest Lebon, holding a sabre in the hand which had sprinkled holy water; Billaud Varennes, who foresaw the magistracy of the future, without judges or arbiters; Fabre d'Eglantine, who fell upon a delightful treasure-trove,—the Republican Calendar,—just as Rouget de Lisle had a single sublime inspiration,—the "Marseillaise;" neither one nor the other ever produced a second. Manuel, the attorney of the Commune, who had said, "A dead king is not a man the less." Goujon, who had entered Tripstadt, Neustadt, and Spires, and had seen the Prussian army flee. Lacroix, a lawyer turned into a general, named Chevalier of Saint Louis, six days before the 10th of August. Fréron Thersites, the son of Fréron Zöilus. Ruth, the inexorable searcher of the iron cupboard, predestined to a great republican suicide,—he was to kill himself the day the Republic died. Fouché, with the soul of a demon and the face of a corpse. Camboulas, the friend of Father Duchesne, who said to Guillotin, "Thou belongest to the Club of the Feuillants, but thy daughter belongs to the Jacobin Club." Jagot, who to such as complained to him of the nudity of the prisoners, replied by this savage saying, "A prison is a dress of stone." Javogues, the terrible desecrator of the tombs of Saint Denis. Osselin, a proscriber, who hid one of the proscribed, Madame Charry, in his house. Bentabolle, who, when he was in the chair, made signs to the tribunes to applaud or hoot. The journalist, Robert, the husband of Mademoiselle Kéralio, who wrote: "Neither Robespierre nor Marat come to my house. Robespierre may come when he wishes—Marat, never." Garan Coulon, who, when Spain interfered in the trial of Louis XVI., haughtily demanded that the Assembly should not deign to read the letter of a king in behalf of a king. Grégoire, a bishop, at first worthy of the Primitive Church, but who afterward, under the Empire, effaced Grégoire the republican beneath the Count Grégoire. Amar, who said: "The whole earth condemns Louis XVI. To whom, then, appeal for judgment? To the planets?" Rouyer, who, on the 21st of January, opposed the firing of the cannon of Pont Neuf, saying, "A king's head ought to make no more noise in falling than the head of another man." Chénier, the brother of André; Vadier, one of those who laid a pistol on the tribunes; Tanis, who said to Momoro,—

"I wish Marat and Robespierre to embrace at my table."

"Where dost thou live?"

"At Charenton."

"Anywhere else would have astonished me," replied Momoro.

Legendre, who was the butcher of the French Revolution, as Pride had been of the English. "Come, that I may knock you down," he cried to Lanjuinais.

"First have it decreed that I am a bullock," replied Lanjuinais.

Collot d'Herbois, that lugubrious comedian who had the face of the antique mask, with two mouths which said yes and no, approving with one while he blamed with the other; branding Carrier at Nantes and defying Châlier at Lyons; sending Robespierre to the scaffold and Marat to the Pantheon. Génissieux, who demanded the penalty of death against whosoever should have upon him a medallion of "Louis XVI. martyred." Léonard Bourdon, the schoolmaster, who had offered his house to the old man of Mont Jura. Topsent, sailor; Goupilleau, lawyer; Laurent Lecointre, merchant; Duhem, physician; Sergent, sculptor; David, painter; Joseph Egalité, prince.

Others still: Lecointe Puiraveau, who asked that a decree should be passed declaring Marat mad. Robert Lindet, the disquieting creator of that devil-fish whose head was the Committee of General Surety, and which covered France with its one-and-twenty thousand arms called revolutionary committees. Lebœuf, upon whom Girez-Dupré, in his "Christmas of False Patriots," had made this epigram,—

"Lebœuf vit Legendre et beugla."

Thomas Paine, the clement American; Anacharsis Cloots, German, baron, millionaire, atheist, Hébertist, candid. The upright Lebas, the friend of the Duplays. Rovère, one of those strange men who are wicked for wickedness' sake,—for the art, from love of the art, exists more frequently than people believe. Charlier, who wished that "you" should be employed in addressing aristocrats. Tallien, elegiac and ferocious, who will bring about the 9th Thermidor from love. Cambacérès, a lawyer, who will be a prince later. Carrier, an attorney, who will become a tiger. Laplanche, who will one day cry, "I demand priority for the alarm-gun." Thuriot, who desired the vote of the revolutionary tribunal to be given aloud. Bourdon of the Oise, who challenged Chambon to a duel, denounced Paine, and was himself denounced by Hébert. Fayau, who proposed the sending of "an army of incendiaries" into the Vendée. Tavaux, who, on the 13th of April, was almost a mediator between the Gironde and the Mountain. Vernier, who proposed that the chiefs of the Gironde and the Mountain should be sent to serve as common soldiers. Rewbell, who shut himself up in Mayence. Bourbotte, who had his horse killed under him at the taking of Saumur. Guimberteau, who directed the army of the Cherbourg coast. Jard Panvilliers, who managed the army of the coasts of Rochelle. Lecarpentier, who led the squadron of Cancale. Roberjot, for whom the ambush of Rastadt was waiting. Prieur, of the Marne, who bore in camp his old rank of major. Levasseur of the Sarthe, who by a word decided Serrent, commandant of the battalion of Saint-Amand, to kill himself. Reverchon, Maure, Bernard de Saintes, Charles Richard, Lequinio, and at the summit of this group a Mirabeau, who was called Danton.

Outside the two camps, and keeping both in awe, rose the man Robespierre.

Chapter V

LOWLANDS

Below crouched Dismay, which may be noble; and Fear, which is base. Beneath passions, beneath heroisms, beneath devotion, beneath rage, was the gloomy cohort of the Anonymous. The shoals of the Assembly were called the Plain. There was everything there which floats; the men who doubt, who hesitate, who recoil, who adjourn, who wait, each one fearing somebody. The Mountain was made up of the Select; the Gironde of the Select; the Plain was a crowd. The Plain was summed up and condensed in Sieyès.

Sieyès, a profound man, who had grown chimerical. He had stopped at the Tiers-Etat, and had not been able to mount up to the people. Certain minds are made to rest half-way. Sieyès called Robespierre a tiger, and was called a mole by Robespierre. This metaphysician had stranded, not on wisdom, but prudence. He was the courtier, not the servitor, of the Revolution. He seized a shovel, and went with the people to work in the Champ de Mars, harnessed to the same cart as Alexandre de Beauharnais. He counselled energy, but never showed it. He said to the Girondists, "Put the cannon on your side." There are thinkers who are wrestlers: those were, like Condorcet, with Vergniaud; or like Camille Desmoulins, with Danton. There are thinkers whose aim is to preserve their lives: such were with Sieyès.

The best working vats have their lees. Underneath the Plain even was the Marsh,—a hideous stagnation which exposed to view the transparencies of egotism. There shivered the fearful in dumb expectation. Nothing could be more abject,—a conglomeration of shames feeling no shame; hidden rage; revolt under servitude. They were afraid in a cynical fashion; they had all the desperation of cowardice; they preferred the Gironde and chose the Mountain; the final catastrophe depended upon them; they poured toward the successful side; they delivered Louis XVI. to Vergniaud, Vergniaud to Danton, Danton to Robespierre, Robespierre to Tallien. They put Marat in the pillory when living, and deified him when dead. They upheld everything up to the day when they overturned everything. They had the instinct to give the decisive push to whatever tottered. In their eyes—since they had undertaken to serve on condition that the basis was solid—to waver was to betray them. They were number; they were force; they were fear. From thence came the audacity of turpitude.

Thence came May 31st, the 11th Terminal, the 9th Thermidor,—tragedies knotted by giants and untied by dwarfs.

Chapter VI

VISIONARIES

Among these men full of passions were mingled men filled with dreams. Utopia was there under all its forms,—

under its warlike form, which admitted the scaffold, and under its innocent form, which would abolish capital punishment; phantom as it faced thrones; angel as it regarded the people. Side by side with the spirits that fought were the spirits that brooded. These had war in their heads, those peace. One brain, Carnot, brought forth fourteen armies; another intellect, Jean Debry, meditated a universal democratic federation.

Amid this furious eloquence, among these shrieking and growling voices, there were fruitful silences. Lakanal remained voiceless, and combined in his thoughts the system of public national education; Lanthenas held his peace, and created the primary schools; Revellière Lépaux kept still, and dreamed of the elevation of Philosophy to the dignity of Religion. Others occupied themselves with questions of detail, smaller and more practical. Guyton Morveaux studied means for rendering the hospitals healthy; Maire, the abolition of existing servitudes; Jean Bon Saint-André, the suppression of imprisonment for debt and constraint of the person; Romme, the proposition of Chappe; Duboë, the putting the archives in order; Coren Fustier, the creation of the Cabinet of Anatomy and the Museum of Natural History; Guyomard, river navigation and the damming of the Scheldt. Art had its monomaniacs. On the 21st of January, while the head of monarchy was falling on the Place de la Revolution, Bézard, the Representative of the Oise, went to see a picture of Rubens, which had been found in a garret in the Rue Saint-Lazare. Artists, orators, prophets, men-giants like Danton, child-men like Cloots, gladiators and philosophers, all had the same goal,—progress. Nothing disconcerted them. The grandeur of the Convention was, the searching how much reality there is in what men call the impossible. At one extreme, Robespierre had his eye fixed on Law; at the other, Condorcet has his fixed on Duty.

Condorcet was a man of reverie and enlightenment. Robespierre was a man of execution; and sometimes, in the final crises of worn-out orders, execution means extermination. Revolutions have two currents,—an ebb and a flow; and on these float all seasons, from that of ice to flowers. Each zone of these currents produces men adapted to its climate, from those who live in the sun to those who dwell among the thunderbolts.

Chapter VII

SENTENCES

PEOPLE showed each other the recess of the left-hand passage where Robespierre had uttered low in the ear of Garat, Clavière's friend, this terrible epigram: "Clavière has conspired wherever he has respired." In this same recess, convenient for words needed to be spoken aside and for half-voiced cholers, Fabre d'Eglantine had quarreled with Romme, and reproached him for having disfigured his calendar by changing "Fervidor" into "Thermidor." So, too, was shown the angle where, elbow to elbow, sat the seven Representatives of the Haute-Garonne, who, first called to pronounce their verdict upon Louis XVI., thus responded, one after the other: Mailhe, "Death;" Delmas, "Death;" Projean, "Death;" Calès, "Death;" Ayral, "Death;" Julien, "Death;" Desaby, "Death,"—eternal reverberation which fills all history, and which, since human justice has existed, has always given an echo of the sepulchre to the wall of the tribunal. People pointed out with their fingers, among that group of stormy faces, all the men from whose mouths had come the uproar of tragic notes,—Paganel, who said: "Death! A king is only made useful by death." Millaud, who said: "To-day, if death did not exist, it would be necessary to invent it." The old Raffon du Trouillet, who said: "Speedy death!" Goupilleau, who cried: "The scaffold at once. Delay aggravates dying." Sieyès, who said, with funeral brevity: "Death!" Thuriot, who had rejected the appeal to the people proposed by Buzot: "What! the primary assemblies! What! Forty-four thousand tribunals! A case without limit. The head of Louis XVI. would have time to whiten before it would fall." Augustin Bon Robespierre, who, after his brother, cried: "I know nothing of the humanity which slaughters the people and pardons despots. Death! To demand a reprieve is to substitute an appeal to tyrants for the appeal to the people." Foussedoire, the substitute of Bernardin de Saint-Pierre, who had said: "I have a horror of human bloodshed, but the blood of a king is not a man's blood. Death!" Jean Bon Saint-André, who said: "No free people without a dead tyrant." Lavicomterie, who proclaimed this formula: "So long as the tyrant breathes, Liberty is suffocated! Death!" Châteauneuf Randon, who had uttered this cry: "Death to the last Louis!" Guyardin, who had said: "Let the Barrière Renversée be executed." (The Barrière Renversée was the Barrière du Trône.) Tellier, who had said: "Let there be forged, to aim against the enemy, a cannon of the calibre of Louis XVI.'s head." And the indulgents,—Gentil, who said: "I vote for confinement. To make a Charles I. is to make a Cromwell." Bancel, who said: "Exile. I want to see the first king of the earth condemned to a trade in order to earn his livelihood." Albouys, who said: "Banishment! Let this living ghost go wander among the thrones." Zangiacomi, who said: "Confinement. Let us keep Capet alive as a scarecrow." Chaillon, who said: "Let him live. I do not wish to make a dead man of whom Rome will make a saint."

While the sentences fell from those severe lips and dispersed themselves one after another into history, women in low-necked dresses and decorated with gems, sat in the tribunes, list in hand, counting the voices and pricking each vote with a pin.

Where tragedy entered, horror and pity remain.

To see the Convention, no matter at what period of its reign, was to see anew the trial of the last Capet. The legend of the 21st of January seemed mingled with all its acts; the formidable Assembly was full of those fatal breaths which blew upon the old torch of monarchy, that had burned for eighteen centuries, and extinguished it. The decisive trials of all kings in that judgment pronounced upon one king was like the point of departure in the great war made against the Past. Whatever might be the sitting of the Convention at which one was present, the shadow of Louis XIV.'s scaffold was seen thrust forward within it. Spectators recounted to one another the resignation of Kersaint, the resignation of Roland Duchâtel, the deputy of the Deux-Sèvres, who, being ill, had himself carried to the Convention on his bed, and dying voted the king's life which caused Marat to laugh; and they sought with their eyes the Representative whom history has forgotten, he who, after that session of thirty-seven hours, fell back on his bench overcome by fatigue and sleep, and when roused by the usher as his turn to vote arrived, half opened his eyes, said "Death," and fell asleep again.

At the moment Louis XIV, was condemned to death, Robespierre had still eighteen months to live; Danton, fifteen months; Vergniaud, nine months; Marat, five months and three weeks; Lepelletier Saint-Fargeau, one day. Quick and terrible blast from human mouths!

Chapter VIII

THE SCENE

The people had a window opening on the Convention,—the public tribunes; and when the window was not sufficient, they opened the door, and the street entered the Assembly. These invasions of the crowd into that senate make one of the most astounding visions of history. Ordinarily these irruptions were amicable. The market-place fraternized with the curule chair; but it was a formidable cordiality,—that of a people who one day took within three hours the cannon of the Invalides and forty thousand muskets besides. At each instant a troop interrupted the deliberations; deputations presented at the bar petitions, homages, offerings. The pike of honour of the Faubourg Saint Antoine entered, borne by women. Certain English offered twenty thousand pairs of shoes for the naked feet of our soldiers. "The citizen Arnoux," announced the "Moniteur," "Curé of Aubignan, Commandant of the Battalion of Drôme, asks to march to the frontiers, and desires that his cure may be preserved for him."

Delegates from the Sections arrived, bringing on hand-barrows, dishes, patens, chalices, monstrances, heaps of gold, silver, and enamel, presented to the country by this multitude in rags, who demanded for recompense the permission to dance the Carmagnole before the Convention. Chenard, Narbonne, and Vallière came to sing couplets in honour of the Mountain. The Section of Mont Blanc brought the bust of Lepelletier, and a woman placed a red cap on the head of the President, who embraced her. The citizenesses of the Section of the Mail "flung flowers" to the legislators. "The pupils of the country" came, headed by music, to thank the Convention for having prepared the prosperity of the century. The women of the Section of the Gardes Françaises offered roses; the women of the Champs Elysées Section gave a crown of oak-leaves; the women of the Section of the Temple came to the bar to swear "only to unite themselves with true Republicans." The Section of Molière presented a medal of Franklin, which was suspended by decree to the crown of the statue of Liberty. The Foundlings, — declared the Children of the Republic —filed through, habited in the national uniform. The young girls of the Section of Ninety-two arrived in long white robes, and the "Moniteur" of the following morning contained this line: "The President received a bouquet from the innocent hands of a young beauty." The orators saluted the crowds, sometimes flattered them: they said to the multitude, "Thou art infallible; thou art irreproachable; thou art sublime." The people have an infantile side: they like those sugar-plums. Sometimes Riot traversed the Assembly: entered furious and withdrew appeased, like the Rhone which traverses Lake Leman, and is mud when it enters and pure and azure when it pours out.

Sometimes the crowd was less pacific, and Henriot was obliged to come with his furnaces for heating shot to the entrance of the Tuileries.

Chapter IX

RESULTS

At the same time that it threw off revolution, this Assembly produced civilization. Furnace, but forge too. In this caldron, where terror bubbled, progress fermented. Out of this chaos of shadow, this tumultuous flight of clouds, spread immense rays of light parallel to the eternal laws,—rays that have remained on the horizon, visible forever in the heaven of the peoples, and which are, one, Justice; another, Tolerance; another, Goodness; another, Right; another, Truth; another, Love.

The Convention promulgated this grand axiom: "The liberty of each citizen ends where the liberty of another citizen commences,"—which comprises in two lines all human social law. It declared indigence sacred; it declared infirmity sacred in the blind and the deaf and dumb, who became wards of the State; maternity sacred in the girl-mother, whom it consoled and lifted up; infancy sacred in the orphan, whom it caused to be adopted by the country; innocence sacred in the accused who was acquitted, whom it indemnified. It branded the slave-trade; it abolished slavery. It proclaimed civic joint responsibility. It decreed gratuitous instruction. It organized national education by the normal school of Paris; central schools in the chief towns; primary schools in the communes. It created the academies of music and the museums. It decreed the unity of the Code, the unity of weights and measures, and the unity of calculation by the decimal system. It established the finances of France, and caused public credit to succeed to the long monarchical bankruptcy. It put the telegraph in operation. To old age it gave endowed almshouses; to sickness, purified hospitals; to instruction, the Polytechnic School; to science, the Bureau of Longitudes; to human intellect, the Institute. At the same time that it was national it was cosmopolitan. Of the eleven thousand two hundred and ten decrees which emanated from the Convention, a third had a political aim; two thirds, a human aim. It declared universal morality the basis of society, and universal conscience the basis of law. And all that servitude abolished, fraternity proclaimed, humanity protected, human conscience rectified, the law of work transformed into right, and from onerous made honourable, — national riches consolidated, childhood instructed and raised up, letters and sciences propagated, light illuminating all heights, aid to all sufferings, promulgation of all principle,—the Convention accomplished, having in its bowels that hydra, the Vendée; and upon its shoulders that heap of tigers, the kings.

Chapter X

GATHERING FOES

Immense place! All types were there, —human, inhuman, superhuman. Epic gathering of antagonisms,—Guillotin avoiding David, Bazire insulting Chabot, Gaudet mocking Saint-Just, Vergniaud disdaining Danton, Louvet attacking Robespierre, Buzot denouncing Egalité, Chambon branding Pache; all execrating Marat. And how many names remain still to be registered!—Armonville, styled Bonnet Rouge, because he always attended the sittings in a Phrygian cap, a friend of Robespierre, and wishing, "after Louis XVI., to guillotine Robespierre in order to restore an equilibrium;" Massieu, colleague and counterpart of that good Lamourette, a bishop fitted to leave his name to a kiss; Lehardy of the Mobihan, stigmatizing the priests of Brittany; Barère, the man of majorities, who presided when Louis XVI. appeared at the bar, and who was to Paméla what Louvet was to Lodoiska; the Oratorian Danou, who said, "Let us gain time;" Dubois Crancé, close to whose ear leaned Marat; the Marquis de Châteauneuf, Laclos, Hérault of Séchelles, who recoiled before Henriot crying, "Gunners, to your pieces;" Julien, who compared the Mountain to Thermopylæ; Gamon, who desired a public tribune reserved solely for women; Laloy, who adjudged the honours of the séance to the Bishop Gobel coming into the Convention to lay down his mitre and put on the red cap; Lecomte, who exclaimed, "So the honours are for whosoever will unfrock himself;" Féraud, whose head Boissy d'Anglas saluted, leaving this question to history "Did Boissy d'Anglas salute the head,—that is to say the victim, —or the pike; that is to say the assassins?" the two brothers Duprat, one a member of the Mountain, the other of the Gironde, who hated each other like the two brothers Chénier.

At this tribune were uttered those mysterious words which sometimes possess unconsciously to those who pronounce them the prophetic accent of revolutions, and in whose wake material facts appear suddenly to assume an inexplicable discontent and passion, as if they had taken umbrage at the things just heard; events seem angered by words; catastrophes follow furious, and as if exasperated by the speech of men. Thus a voice upon a mountain suffices to set the avalanche in motion. A word too much may be followed by a landslip. If no one had spoken, the catastrophe would not have happened. You might say sometimes that events are irascible.

It was thus, by the hazard of an orator's ill-comprehended word, that Madame Elizabeth's head fell.

At the Convention intemperance of language was a right. Threats flew about and crossed one another like sparks in a conflagration.

Pétion: "Robespierre, come to the point."

Robespierre: "The point is yourself, Pétion; I shall come to it, and you will see it."

A voice: "Death to Marat!"

Marat: "The day Marat dies there will be no more Paris, and the day that Paris expires there will be no longer a Republic."

Billaud Varennes rises, and says, "We wish—"

Barère interrupts him: "Thou speakest like a king."

Another day, Philippeaux, "A member has drawn his sword upon me."

Audouin: "President, call the assassin to order."

The President: "Wait."

Panis: "President, I call you to order—I!"

There was rude laughter moreover.

Lecointre: "The Curé of Chant de Bout complains of Fauchet, his bishop, who forbids his marrying."

A voice: "I do not see why Fauchet, who has mistresses, should wish to hinder others from having wives."

A second voice: "Priest, take a wife!"

The galleries joined in the conversation. They said "thee" and "thou" to the members. One day the Representative Ruamps mounted to the tribune. He had one hip very much larger than the other. A spectator, crying out, thus jeered him: "Turn that toward the Right, since thou hast a cheek *à la David*."

Such were the liberties the people took with the Convention. On one occasion, however, during the tumult of the 11th of April, 1793, the President commanded a disorderly person in the tribunes to be arrested.

One day when the session had for witness the old Buonarotti, Robespierre takes the floor and speaks for two hours, staring at Danton, sometimes straight in the face, which was serious; sometimes obliquely, which was worse. He thunders on to the end, however. He closes with an indignant outburst full of menacing words: "The conspirators are known, the corrupters and the corrupted are known; the traitors are known; they are in this assembly. They hear us; we see them, and we do not move our eyes from them. Let them look above their heads, and they will see the sword of the law; let them look into their conscience, and they will see their own infamy. Let them beware!" And when Robespierre has finished, Danton, with his face raised toward the ceiling, his eyes half closed, one arm hanging loosely down, throws himself back in his seat, and is heard to hum,—

"Cadet Roussel fait des discours,
  Qui ne sont pas longs quand ils
    sont courts."

Imprecations followed one another,—conspirator! assassin! scoundrel! factionist! moderate! They denounced one another to the bust of Brutus that stood there, — apostrophes, insults, challenges; furious glances from one side to the other; fists shaken; pistols allowed to be seen; poniards half drawn; terrible blazing forth in the tribune. Certain persons talked as if they were driven back against the guillotine; heads wavered, frightened and awed. Mountainists, Girondists, Feuillantists, Moderates, Terrorists, Jacobins, Cordeliers, eighteen regicide priests,—all these men a mass of vapours driven wildly in every direction.

Chapter XI

DESTINY

SPIRITS which were a prey of the wind. But this was a miracle-working wind. To be a member of the Convention was to be a wave of the ocean. This was true even of the greatest there. The force of impulsion came from on high. There was a Will in the Convention which was that of all, and yet not that of any one person. This Will was an Idea,—an idea indomitable and immeasurable, which swept from the summit of heaven into the darkness below. We call this Revolution. When that Idea passed, it beat down one and raised up another; it scattered this man into foam and dashed that one upon the reefs. This Idea knew whither it was going, and drove the whirlpool before it. To ascribe the Revolution to men is to ascribe the tide to the waves.

The Revolution is a work of the Unknown. Call it good or bad, according as you yearn toward the future or the past, but leave it to the power which caused it. It seems the joint work of grand events and grand individualities mingled, but it is in reality the result of events. Events dispense, men suffer; events dictate, men sigh. The 14th of July is signed Camille Desmoulins; the 10th of August is signed Danton; the 2nd of September is signed Marat; the 21st of September is signed Grégoire; the 21st of January is signed Robespierre; but Desmoulins, Danton, Marat, Grégoire and Robespierre are mere scribes. The great and mysterious writer of these grand pages has a name,—God; and a mask, Destiny. Robespierre believed in God: yea, verily!

The Revolution is a form of the eternal phenomenon which presses upon us from every quarter, and which we call Necessity. Before this mysterious complication of benefits and sufferings arises the Wherefore of history. *Because:* this answer of him who knows nothing is equally the response of him who knows all.

In presence of these climacteric catastrophes which devastate and revivify civilization, one hesitates to judge their details. To blame or praise men on account of the result is almost like praising or blaming ciphers on account of the total. That which ought to happen happens; the blast which ought to blow blows. The Eternal Serenity does not suffer from these north winds. Above revolutions Truth and Justice remain as the starry sky lies above and beyond tempests.

Chapter XII

WIND-SWEPT

SUCH was the unmeasured and immeasurable Convention,—a camp cut off from the human race, attacked by all the powers of darkness at once; the night-fires of the besieged army of Ideas; a vast bivouac of minds upon the edge of a precipice. There is nothing in history comparable to this group, at the same time senate and populace, conclave and street-crossing, Areopagus and public square, tribunal and the accused.

The Convention always bent to the wind; but that wind came from the mouth of the people, and was the breath of God.

And to-day, after eighty-four years have passed away, always when the Convention presents itself before the reflection of any man, whosoever he may be,—historian or philosopher,—that man pauses and meditates. It would be impossible not to remain thoughtfully attentive before this grand procession of shadows.

Chapter XIII

MARAT

MARAT, in accordance with his declaration to Simonne Evrard, went to the Convention the morning after that interview in the Rue du Paon. There was in the Convention a marquis who was a Maratist, Louis de Montaut, the same who afterward presented to the Convention a decimal clock surmounted by the bust of Marat. At the moment Marat entered, Chabot had approached De Montaut. He began:—

"*Ci-devant*—"

Montaut raised his eyes. "Why do you call me *ci-devant?*"

"Because you are so."

"I?"

"For you were a marquis."

"Never."

"Bah!"

"My father was a soldier; my grandfather was a weaver."

"What song is that you are singing, Montaut?"

"I do not call myself Montaut."

"What do you call yourself, then?"

"Maribon."

"In point of fact," said Chabot, "it is all the same to me." And he added between his teeth: "No marquis on any terms."

Marat paused in the corridor to the left and watched Montaut and Chabot. Whenever Marat entered, there was a buzz, but afar from him. About him people kept silence.

Marat paid no attention thereto. He disdained "the croaking of the mud-pool." In the gloomy obscurity of the lower row of seats, Compé of the Oise, Prunelle, Villars, a bishop who was afterward a member of the French Academy, Boutroue, Petit, Plaichard, Bonet, Thibaudeau, and Valdruche pointed him out to one another.

"See Marat!"

"Then he is not ill?"

"Yes, for he is here in a dressing-gown."

"In a dressing-gown!"

"Zounds, yes!"

"He takes liberties enough!"

"He dares to come like that into the Convention!"

"As he came one day crowned with laurels, he may certainly come in a dressing-gown."

"Face of brass and teeth of verdigris."

"His dressing-gown looks new."

"What is it made of?"

"Reps."
"Striped."
"Look at the lapels."
"They are fur."
"Tiger-skin."
"No; ermine."
"Imitation."
"He has stockings on!"
"That is odd."
"And shoes with buckles!"
"Of silver!"
"Camboula's sabots will not pardon that."

People in other seats affected not to see Marat. They talked of indifferent matters. Santhonax accosted Dussaulx.

"Have you heard, Dussaulx?"
"What?"
"The *ci-devant* Count de Brienne?"
"Who was in La Force with the *ci-devant* Duke de Villeroy?"
"Yes."
"I knew them both."
"Well?"
"They were so horribly frightened that they saluted all the red caps of all the turnkeys, and one day they refused to play a game of piquet because somebody offered them cards that had kings and queens among them."
"Well?"
"They were guillotined yesterday."
"The two of them?"
"Both."
"Indeed; how had they behaved in prison?"
"As cowards."
"And how did they show on the scaffold?"
"Intrepid."

Then Dussaulx ejaculated: "It is easier to die than to live!"

Barère was reading a report; it was in regard to the Vendée. Nine hundred men of Morbihan had started with cannon to assist Nantes. Redon was menaced by the peasants. Paimbœuf had been attacked. A fleet was cruising about Maindrin to prevent invasions. From Ingrande, as far as Maure, the entire left bank of the Loire was bristling with royalist batteries. Three thousand peasants were masters of Pornic. They cried, "Long live the English!" A letter from Santerre to the Convention, which Barère was reading, ended with these words:—

"Seven thousand peasants attacked Vannes. We repulsed them, and they have left in our hands four cannon—"

"And how many prisoners?" interrupted a voice.

Barère continued: "Postcript of the letter:—

"We have no prisoners, because we no longer make any."

Marat, standing motionless, did not listen; he appeared absorbed by a stern preoccupation. He held in his hand a paper, which he crumpled between his fingers; had any one unfolded it, he might have read these lines in Momoro's writing,—probably a response to some question he had been asked by Marat:—

"No opposition can be offered to the full powers of delegated commissioners, above all, those of the Committee of Public Safety. Genissieux in vain said, in the sitting of May 6th, 'Each Commissioner is more than a king;' it had no effect. Life and death are in their hands. Massade at Angers; Trullard at Saint-Amand; Nyon with General Marcé; Parrein with the army of Sables; Millier with the army of Niort; they are all-powerful. The Club of the Jacobins has gone so far as to name Parrein brigadier-general. The circumstances excuse everything. A delegate from the Committee of Public Safety holds in check a commander-in-chief."

Marat ceased crumpling the paper, put it in his pocket, and walked slowly toward Montaut and Chabot, who continued to converse, and had not seen him enter.

Chabot was saying: "Maribon, or Montaut, listen to this: I have just come from the Committee of Public Safety."

"And what is being done there?"

"They are setting a priest to watch a noble."

"Ah!"

"A noble like yourself—"

"I am not a noble," interrupted Montaut.

"To be watched by a priest—"

"Like you."

"I am not a priest," said Chabot.

They both begin to laugh.

"Make your story explicit," resumed Montaut.

"Here it is then. A priest named Cimourdain is delegated with full powers to a viscount named Gauvain; this viscount commands the exploring column of the army of the coast. The question will be to keep the nobleman from trickery and the priest from treason."

"It is very simple," replied Montaut. "It is only necessary to bring death into the matter."

"I come for that," said Marat.

They looked up.

"Good morning, Marat," said Chabot. "You rarely attend our meetings."

"My doctor has ordered me baths," answered Marat.

"One should beware of baths," returned Chabot. "Seneca died in one."

Marat smiled.

"Chabot, there is no Nero here."

"Yes, there is you," said a rude voice.

It was Danton who passed and ascended to his seat.

Marat did not turn round. He thrust his head in between Montaut and Chabot.

"Listen; I come about a serious matter. One of us three must propose to-day the draft of a decree to the Convention."

"Not I," said Montaut; "I am never listened to. I am a marquis."

"And I," said Chabot.—"I am not listened to. I am a Capuchin."

"And I," said Marat—"I am not listened to. I am Marat."

There was a silence among them.

It was not safe to interrogate Marat when he appeared preoccupied, still Montaut hazarded a question.

"Marat, what is the decree that you wish passed?"

"A decree to punish with death any military chief who allows a rebel prisoner to escape."

Chabot interrupted,—

"The decree exists; it was passed in April."

"Then it is just the same as if it did not exist," said Marat. "Everywhere, all through Vendée, anybody who chooses helps prisoners to escape, and gives them an asylum with impunity."

"Marat, the fact is, the decree has fallen into disuse."

"Chabot, it must be put into force anew."

"Without doubt."

"And to do that, the Convention must be addressed."

"Marat, the Convention is not necessary; the Committee of Public Safety will suffice."

"The end will be gained," added Montaut, "if the Committee of Public Safety cause the decree to be placarded in all the communes of the Vendée, and make two or three good examples."

"Of men in high position," returned Chabot,—"of generals."

Marat grumbled: "In fact that will answer."

"Marat," resumed Chabot, "go yourself and say that to the Committee of Public Safety."

Marat stared straight into his eyes, which was not pleasant even for Chabot.

"The Committee of Public Safety," said he, "sits in Robespierre's house; I do not go there."

"I will go myself," said Montaut.

"Good!" said Marat.

The next morning an order from the Committee of Public Safety was sent in all directions among the towns and villages of Vendée, enjoining the publication and strict execution of the decree of death against any person conniving at the escape of brigands and captive insurgents. This decree proved only a first step: the Convention was to go further than that. A few months later, the 11th Brumaire, Year II. (November, 1793), when Laval opened its gates to the Vendean fugitives, the Convention decreed that any city giving asylum to the rebels should be demolished and destroyed. On their side, the princes of Europe, in the manifesto of the Duke of Brunswick, conceived by the emigrants and drawn up by the Marquis de Linnon, intendant of the Duke of Orleans, had declared that every Frenchman taken with arms in his hand should be shot, and that, if a hair of the king's head fell, Paris should be razed to the ground.

Cruelty against barbarity.

Ninety-Three

PART III.—LA VENDÉE

BOOK I

La Vendée

Chapter I

THE FORESTS

There were at that time seven ill-famed forests in Brittany. The Vendean war was a revolt of priests. This revolt had the forests as auxiliaries. These spirits of darkness aid one another.

The seven Black Forests of Brittany were the forest of Fougères, which stopped the way between Dol and Avranches; the forest of Princé, which was eight leagues in circumference; the forest of Paimpol, full of ravines and brooks, almost inaccessible on the side toward Baignon, with an easy retreat upon Concornet, which was a royalist town; the forest of Rennes, from whence could be heard the tocsin of the republican parishes, always numerous in the neighbourhood of the cities (it was in this forest that Puysaye lost Focard); the forest of Machecoul, which had Charette for its wild beast; the forest of Garnache, which belonged to the Trémoilles, the Gauvains, and the Rohans; and the forest of Brocéliande, which belonged to the fairies.

One gentleman of Brittany bore the title of Lord of the Seven Forests: this was the Viscount de Fontenay, Breton Prince. For the Breton Prince existed distinct from the French Prince. The Rohans were Breton princes. Garnier de Saintes, in his report to the Convention of the 15th Nivose, Year II., thus distinguishes the Prince de Talmont: "This Capet of the brigands, Sovereign of Maine and of Normandy."

The record of the Breton forests from 1792 to 1800 would form a history of itself, mingling like a legend with the vast undertaking of the Vendée. History has its truth: Legend has hers. Legendary truth is wholly different from historic; legendary truth is invention that has reality for a result. Still history and legend have the same aim,—that of depicting the external type of humanity.

La Vendée can only be completely understood by adding legend to history; the latter is needed to describe its entirety, the former the details. We may say, too, that La Vendée is worth the pains. La Vendée was a prodigy.

This war of the Ignorant, so stupid and so splendid, so abject yet magnificent, was at once the desolation and the pride of France. La Vendée is a wound which is at the same time a glory.

At certain crises human society has its enigmas,—enigmas which resolve themselves into light for sages, but which the ignorant in their darkness translate into violence and barbarism. The philosopher is slow to accuse; he takes into consideration the agitation caused by these problems, which cannot pass without casting about them shadows dark as those of the storm-cloud.

If one wish to comprehend Vendée, one must picture to one's self this antagonism: on one side the French Revolution, on the other the Breton peasant. In face of these unparalleled events— an immense promise of all benefits at once, a fit of rage for civilization, an excess of maddened progress, an improvement that exceeded measure and comprehension—must be placed this grave, strange, savage man, with an eagle glance and flowing hair; living on milk and chestnuts; his ideas bounded by his thatched roof, his hedge, and his ditch, able to distinguish the sound of each village bell in the neighbourhood; using water only to drink; wearing a leather jacket covered with silken arabesques, uncultivated but clad embroidered; tattooing his garments as his ancestors the Celts had tattooed their faces; looking up to a master in his executioner; speaking a dead language, which was like forcing his thoughts to dwell in a tomb; driving his bullocks, sharpening his scythe, winnowing his black grain, kneading his buckwheat biscuit; venerating his plough first, his grandmother next; believing in the Blessed Virgin and the White Lady; devoted to the altar, but also to the lofty mysterious stone standing in the midst of the moor; a labourer in the plain, a fisher on the coast, a poacher in the thicket; loving his kings, his lords, his priests, his very lice; pensive, often immovable for entire hours upon the great deserted sea-shore, a melancholy listener to the sea.

Then ask yourself if it would have been possible for this blind man to welcome that light.

Chapter II

THE PEASANTS

The peasant had two points on which he leaned,—the field which nourished him, the wood which concealed him.

It is difficult to picture to one's self what those Breton forests really were. They were towns. Nothing could be more secret, more silent, and more savage than those inextricable entanglements of thorns and branches; those vast thickets were the home of immobility and silence; no solitude could present an appearance more death-like and sepulchral. Yet if it had been possible to fell those trees at one blow, as by a flash of lightning, a swarm of men would have stood revealed in those shades. There were wells, round and narrow, masked by coverings of stones and branches, the interior at first vertical, then horizontal, spreading out underground like funnels, and ending in dark chambers. Cambyses found such in Egypt, and Westermann found the same in Brittany. There they were found in the desert, here in the forest; the caves of Egypt held dead men, the caves of Brittany were filled with the living. One of the wildest glades of the wood of Misdon, perforated by galleries and cells amid which came and went a mysterious society, was called "the great city." Another glade, not less deserted above ground and not less inhabited beneath, was styled "the place royal."

This subterranean life had existed in Brittany from time immemorial. From the earliest days man had there hidden, flying from man. Hence those hiding-places, like the dens of reptiles, hollowed out below the trees. They dated from the era of the Druids, and certain of those crypts were as ancient as the cromlechs. The larvæ of legend and the monsters of history all passed across that shadowy land,—Toutates, Cæsar, Höel, Neomenes, Geoffrey of England, Alain of the iron glove, Pierre Manclerc; the French house of Blois, the English house of Montfort; kings and dukes, the nine barons of Brittany, the judges of the Great Days, the Counts of Nantes contesting with the Counts of Rennes; highwaymen, banditti, Free Lances; René II., Viscount de Rohan; the governors for the king; "the good Duke of Chaulnes," hanging the peasants under the windows of Madame de Sévigné; in the fifteenth century the butcheries by the nobles, in the sixteenth and seventeenth centuries the wars of religion, in the eighteenth century the thirty thousand dogs trained to hunt men. Beneath these pitiless tramplings the inhabitants made up their minds to disappear. Each in turn—the Troglodytes to escape the Celts, the Celts to escape the Romans, the Bretons to escape the Normans, the Huguenots to escape the Roman Catholics, the smugglers to escape the excise officers—took refuge first in the forest and then underground, the resource of hunted animals. It is this to which tyranny reduces nations. During two thousand years despotism under all its forms—conquest, feudality, fanaticism, taxes—beset this wretched, distracted Brittany: a sort of inexorable battue, which only ceased under one shape to recommence under another. Men hid underground. When the French Republic burst forth, Terror, which is a species of rage, was already latent in human souls, and when the Republic burst forth, the dens were ready in the woods. Brittany revolted, finding itself oppressed by this forced deliverance,— a mistake natural to slaves.

CHAPTER III

CONNIVANCE OF MEN AND FORESTS

THE gloomy Breton forests took up anew their ancient rôle, and were the servants and accomplices of this rebellion, as they had been of all others. The subsoil of every forest was a sort of madrepore, pierced and traversed in all directions by a secret highway of mines, cells, and galleries. Each one of these blind cells could shelter five or six men. There are in existence certain strange lists which enable one to understand the powerful organization of that vast peasant rebellion. In Ille-et-Vilaine, in the forest of Pertre, the refuge of the Prince de Talmont, not a breath was heard, not a human trace to be found, yet there were collected six thousand men under Focard. In the forest of Meulac, in Morbihan, not a soul was to be seen, yet it held eight thousand men. Still, these two forests, Pertre and Meulac, do not count among the great Breton forests. If one trod there, the explosion was terrible. Those hypocritical copses, filled with fighters waiting in a sort of underground labyrinth, were like enormous black sponges whence, under the pressure of the gigantic foot of Revolution, civil war spurted out. Invisible battalions lay there in wait. These untrackable armies wound along beneath the republican troops; burst suddenly forth from the earth and sank into it again; sprang up in numberless force and vanished at will; gifted with a strange ubiquity and power of disappearance, an avalanche at one instant, gone like a cloud of dust the next; colossal, yet able to become pygmies at will; giants in battle, dwarfs in ability to conceal themselves, jaguars with the habits of moles.

There were not only the forests, there were the woods. Just as below cities there are villages, below these forests there were woods and underwoods. The forests were united by the labyrinths (everywhere scattered) of the woods. The ancient castles, which were fortresses; the hamlets, which were camps; the farms, which were enclosures for ambushes and snares, traversed by ditches and palisaded by trees,—were the meshes of the net in which the republican armies were caught.

This whole formed what is called the "Bocage."

There was the wood of Misdon, which had a pond in its centre, and which was held by Jean Chouan. There was the wood of Gennes, which belonged to Taillefer. There was the wood of Huisserie, which belonged to Gouge-le-Bruant; the wood of Charnie, where lurked Courtillé-le-Batard, called Saint-Paul, chief of the camp of the Vache Noire; the wood of Burgault, which was held by that enigmatical Monsieur Jacques, reserved for a mysterious end in the vault of Juvardeil.

There was the wood of Charreau, where Pimousse and Petit-Prince, when attacked by the garrison of Châteauneuf, rushed forward and seized the grenadiers in the republican ranks about the waist and carried them back prisoners; the wood of La Heureuserie, the witness of the rout of the military post of Longue-Faye; the wood of Aulne, whence the route between Rennes and Laval could be overlooked; the wood of La Gravelle, which a prince of La Trémoille had won at a game of bowls; the wood of Lorges, in the Côtes-du-Nord, where Charles de Boishardy reigned after Bernard de Villeneuve; the wood of Bagnard, near Fontenay, where Lescure offered battle to Chalbos, who accepted the challenge, although one against five; the wood of La Durondais, which in old days had been disputed by Alain le Redru and Hérispoux, the son of Charles the Bald; the wood of Croqueloup, upon the edge of that moor where Coquereau sheared the prisoners; the wood of Croix-Bataille, which witnessed the Homeric insults of Jambe d'Argent to Morière and of Morière to Jambe d'Argent; the wood of La Saudraie, which we have seen being searched by a Paris regiment. There were many others besides. In several of these forests and woods there were not only subterranean villages grouped about the burrow of the chief, but also actual hamlets of low huts, hidden under the trees, sometimes so numerous that the forest was filled with them. Frequently they were betrayed by the smoke. Two of these hamlets of the wood of Misdon have remained famous,—Lorrière, near Létang, and the group of cabins called the Rue de Bau, on the side toward Saint-Ouen-les-Toits.

The women lived in the huts, and the men in the cellars. In carrying on the war they utilized the galleries of the fairies and the old Celtic mines. Food was carried to the buried men. Some were forgotten, and died of hunger; but these were awkward fellows, who had not known how to open the mouth of their well. Usually the cover, made of moss and branches, was so artistically fashioned that, although impossible on the outside to distinguish from the surrounding turf, it was very easy to open and close on the inside. These hiding-places were dug with care. The earth taken out of the well was flung into some neighbouring pond. The sides and the bottom were carpeted with ferns and moss. These nooks were called "lodges." The men were as comfortable there as could be expected, considering that they lacked light, fire, bread and air.

It was a difficult matter to unbury themselves and come up among the living without great precaution. They might find themselves between the legs of an army on the march. These were formidable woods, snares with a double trap; the Blues dared not enter, the Whites dared not come out.

Chapter IV

THEIR LIFE UNDERGROUND

The men grew weary of their wild-beast lairs. Sometimes in the night they came forth at any risk, and went to dance upon the neighbouring moor; else they prayed, in order to kill time. "Every day," says Bourdoiseau, "Jean Chouan made us count our rosaries."

It was almost impossible to keep those of the Bas-Maine from going out for the Fête de la Gerbe when the season came. Some of them had ideas peculiar to themselves. "Denys," says Tranche Montagne, "disguised himself as a woman, in order to go to the theatre at Laval, then went back to his hole." Suddenly they would rush forth in search of death, exchanging the dungeon for the sepulchre. Sometimes they raised the cover of their trench, and listened to hear if there were fighting in the distance; they followed the combat with their ears. The firing of the republicans was regular; the firing of the royalists, open and dropping, — this guided them. If the platoon-firing ceased suddenly, it was a sign that the royalists were defeated; if the irregular firing continued, and retreated toward the horizon, it was a sign that they had the advantage. The Whites always pursued; the Blues never, because they had the country against them.

These underground belligerents were kept perfectly informed of what was going on. Nothing could be more rapid, nothing more mysterious, than their means of communication. They had cut all the bridges, broken up all the wagons; yet they found means to tell each other everything, to give each other timely warning. Relays of emissaries were established from forest to forest, from village to village, from farm to farm, from cottage to cottage, from bush to bush. A peasant with a stupid air passed by; he carried dispatches in his hollow stick. An ancient constituent, Boètidoux, furnished them, to pass from one end of Brittany to the other, with republican passports according to the new form, with blanks for the names, of which this traitor had bundles. It was impossible to discover these emissaries. Says Puysaye: "The secrets confided to more than four hundred thousand individuals were religiously guarded."

It appeared that this quadrilateral—closed on the south by the line of the Sables to Thouars, on the east by the line of Thouars to Saumur and the river of Thoué, on the north by the Loire, and on the west by the ocean—possessed everywhere the same nervous activity, and not a single point of this soil could stir without shaking the whole. In the twinkling of an eye Luçon had information in regard to Noirmoutier, and the camp of La Loué knew what the camp of Croix-Morineau was doing. It seemed as if the very birds of the air carried tidings. The 7th Messidor, Year III., Hoche wrote: "One might believe that they have telegraphs." They were in clans, as in Scotland; each parish had its captain. In that war my father fought, and I can speak advisedly thereof.

Chapter V

THEIR LIFE IN WARFARE

Many of them were only armed with pikes. Good fowling-pieces were abundant. No marksmen could be more expert than the poachers of the Bocage and the smugglers of the Loroux. They were strange combatants, terrible and intrepid.

The decree for the levy of three hundred thousand men had been the signal for the tocsin to sound in six hundred villages. The blaze of the conflagration burst forth in all quarters at the same time. Poitou and Anjou exploded on one day. Let us add that a premonitory rumbling had made itself heard on the moor of Kerbader upon the 8th of July, 1792, a month before the 10th of August. Alain Redeler, to-day forgotten, was the precursor of La Rochejacquelein and Jean Chouan. The royalists forced all able-bodied men to march under pain of death. They requisitioned harnesses, carts, and provisions. At once Sapinaud had three thousand soldiers, Cathelineau ten thousand, Stofflet twenty thousand, and Charette was master of Noirmoutier. The Viscount de Scépeaux roused the Haut Anjou; the Chevalier de Dieuzie, the Entre Vilaine et Loire; Tristan l'Hermite, the Bas-Maine; the barber Gaston, the city of Guéménée; and Abbé Bernier all the rest.

It needed but little to rouse all those multitudes. In the altar of a priest who had taken the oath to the republic—a "priest swearer," as the people said—was placed a great black cat, which sprang suddenly out during Mass. "It is the devil!" cried the peasants, and a whole canton rose in revolt. A breath of fire issued from the confessionals. In order to attack the Blues and to leap the ravines, they had their poles fifteen feet in length, called *ferte*, an arm available for combat and for flight. In the thickest of the frays, when the peasants were attacking the republican squares if they chanced to meet upon the battle-field a cross or a chapel, all fell upon their knees and said a prayer under the enemy's fire; the rosary counted, such as were still living sprang up again and rushed upon the foe. Alas! what giants! They loaded their guns as they ran; that was their peculiar talent. They were made to believe whatever their leaders chose. The priests showed them other priests whose necks had been reddened by means of a cord, and said to them, "These are the guillotined who have been brought back to life." They had their spasms of chivalry: they honoured Fesque, a republican standard-bearer, who allowed himself to be sabred without losing hold of his flag. The peasants had a vein of mockery: they called the republican and married priests "Des sans-calottes devenus sans-culottes!" ("The unpetticoated become the unbreeched.")

They began by being afraid of the cannon, then they dashed forward with their sticks and took them. They captured first a fine bronze cannon which they baptized "The Missionary;" then another which dated from the Roman Catholic wars, upon which were engraved the arms of Richelieu and a head of the Virgin; this they named "Marie Jeanne." When they lost Fontenay they lost Marie Jeanne, about which six hundred peasants fell without flinching; then they retook Fontenay in order to recover Marie Jeanne: they brought it back beneath a *fleur-de-lis* embroidered banner, and covered with flowers, and forced the women who passed to kiss it. But two cannon were a small store. Stofflet had taken Marie Jeanne; Catheli-neau, jealous of his success, started out of Pin-en-Mange, assaulted Jallais, and captured a third. Forest attacked Saint-Florent and took a fourth. Two other captains, Chouppes and Saint-Pol, did better; they simulated cannon by the trunks of trees, gunners by mannikins, and with this artillery, about which they laughed heartily, made the Blues retreat to Mareuil. This was their great era. Later, when Chalbos routed La Marsonnière, the peasants left behind them on the dishonoured field of battle thirty-two cannon bearing the arms of England. England at that time paid the French princes, and as Nantiat wrote on the 10th of May, 1794, "sent funds to Monseigneur, because Pitt had been told that it was proper so to do."

Mellinet, in a report of the 31st of March, said, "Long live the English!" is the cry of the rebels. The peasants delayed themselves by pillage. These devotees were robbers. Savages have their vices. It is by these that civilization captures them later. Puysaye says: "I several times preserved the burg of Phélan from pillage." And further on, he recounts how he avoided entering Montfort: "I made a circuit in order to prevent the plundering of the Jacobins' houses."

They robbed Cholet; they sacked Challans. After having failed at Granville, they pillaged Ville-Dieu. They styled the "Jacobin herd" those of the country people who had joined the Blues, and exterminated such with more ferocity than other foes. They loved battle like soldiers, and massacre like brigands. To shoot the "clumsy fellows"—that is, the *bourgeois*—pleased them; they called that "breaking Lent."

At Fontenay, one of their priests, the Curé Barbotin, struck down an old man by a sabre stroke. At Saint-Germain-sur-Ille, one of their captains, a nobleman, shot the solicitor of the commune, and took his watch. At Machecoul, for five weeks they shot republicans at the rate of thirty a day, setting them in a row, which was called "the rosary." Back of the line was a trench, into which some of the victims fell alive; they were buried all the same. We have seen a revival of such actions. Joubert, the President of the district, had his hands sawed off. They put sharp handcuffs, forged expressly, on the Blues whom they made prisoners. They massacred them in the public places, with the hunting cry, "In at the death!"

Charette, who signed "Fraternity, the Chevalier Charette," and who wore for head-covering a handkerchief knotted about his brows after Marat's fashion, burned the city of Pornic, and the inhabitants in their houses. During that time Carrier was horrible. Terror replied to terror. The Breton insurgent had almost the appearance of a Greek rebel, with his short jacket, his gun slung over his shoulder, his leggings, and large breeches similar to the fustanella. The peasant lad resembled the klepht.

Henri de la Rochejacquelein, at the age of one-and-twenty, set out for this war armed with a stick and a pair of pistols. The Vendean army counted a hundred and fifty-four divisions. They undertook regular sieges; they held Bressuire invested for three days. One Good Friday ten thousand peasants cannonaded the town of Sables with red-hot balls. They succeeded in a single day in destroying fourteen republican cantons, from Montigné to Courbeveilles. On the high wall of Thouars this dialogue was heard between La Rochejacquelein and a peasant lad as they stood below:—

"Charles!"
"Here I am."
"Stand so that I can mount on your shoulders."
"Jump up."
"Your gun."
"Take it."

And Rochejacquelein leaped into the town, and the towers which Duguesclin had besieged were taken without the aid of ladders.

They preferred a cartridge to a gold louis. They wept when they lost sight of their village belfry. To run away seemed perfectly natural to them; at such times the leaders would cry: "Throw off your sabots, but keep your guns." When munitions were wanting, they counted their rosaries and rushed forth to seize the powder in the caissons of the republican artillery; later, D'Elbée demanded powder from the English. If they had wounded men among them, at the approach of the enemy they concealed these in the grainfields or among the ferns, and went back in search of them when the fight was ended. They had no uniforms. Their garments were torn to bits. Peasants and nobles wrapped themselves in any rags they could find. Roger Mouliniers wore a turban and a pelisse taken from the wardrobe of the theatre of La Flèche; the Chevalier de Beauvilliers wore a barrister's gown, and set a woman's bonnet on his head over a woolen cap. All wore the white belt and a scarf; different grades were marked by the knots; Stofflet had a red knot; La Rochejacquelein had a black knot; Wimpfen, who was half a Girondist, and who for that matter never left Normandy, wore the leather jacket of the Carabots of Caen. They had women in their ranks,—Madame de Lescure, who became Madame de la Rochejacquelein; Thérèse de Mollien, the mistress of La Rouarie (she who burned the list of the chiefs of the parishes); Madame de la Rochefoucauld (beautiful, young), who, sabre in hand, rallied the peasants at the foot of the great tower of the castle of Puy Rousseau; and that Antoinette Adams, styled the Chevalier Adams, who was so brave that when captured she was shot standing, out of respect for her courage.

This epic period was a cruel one. Men were mad. Madame de Lescure made her horse tread upon the republicans stretched on the ground: *dead*, she averred,—only wounded perhaps. Sometimes the men proved traitors; the women never. Mademoiselle Fleury, of the Théâtre Français, went from La Rouarie to Marat; but it was for love. The captains were often as ignorant as the soldiers. Monsieur de Sapinaud could not spell; he was at fault in regard to the orthography of the commonest word. There was enmity among the leaders; the captains of the Marais cried, "Down with those of the High Country!" Their cavalry was not numerous, and difficult to form. Puysaye writes: "Many a man who would cheerfully give me his two sons grows lukewarm if I ask for one of his horses." Poles, pitchforks, reaping-hooks, guns, old and new, poachers' knives, spits, cudgels bound and studded with iron,— these were their arms; some of them carried slung round them crosses made of dead men's bones. They rushed to an attack with loud cries, springing up suddenly from every quarter, from the woods, the hills, the bushes, the hollows of the roads,—killing, exterminating, destroying; then were gone. When they marched through a republican town they cut down the liberty pole, set it on fire, and danced in circles about it as it burned. All their habits were nocturnal. The Vendean rule was always to appear unexpectedly. They would march fifteen leagues in silence, not as much as stirring a blade of grass as they went. When evening came, after the chiefs had settled what republican posts should be surprised on the morrow, the men loaded their guns, mumbled their prayers, pulled off their sabots, and filed in long columns through the woods, marching barefoot across the heath and moss, without a sound, without a word, without a breath. It was like the march of cats through the darkness.

Chapter VI

THE SPIRIT OF THE PLACE PASSES INTO THE MAN

The Vendée in insurrection did not number less than five hundred thousand, counting men, women, and children. A half-million of combatants is the sum total given by Tuffin de la Rouarie.

The federalists helped them; the Vendée had the Gironde for accomplice. La Lozère sent thirty thousand men into the Bocage. Eight departments coalesced,—five in Brittany, three in Normandy. Evreux, which fraternized with Caen, was represented in the rebellion by Chaumont its mayor, and Gardembas, a man of note. Buzot, Gorsas, and Barbaroux at Caen, Brissot at Moulins, Chassan at Lyons, Rabaut-Saint-Etienne at Nismes, Meillen and Duchâtel in Brittany,—all these mouths blew the furnace.

There were two Vendées,—the great which carried on the war of the forests; and the little, which waged the war of the thickets. It is that shade which separates Charette from Jean Chouan. The little Vendée was honest, the great corrupt; the little was much better. Charette was made a marquis, lieutenant-general of the king's armies, and received the great cross of Saint Louis, Jean Chouan remained Jean Chouan. Charette borders on the bandit; Jean Chouan on the paladin.

As to the magnanimous chiefs Bonchamps, Lescure, La Rochejacquelein,—they deceived themselves. The grand Catholic army was an insane attempt; disaster could not fail to follow it. Let any one imagine a tempest of peasants attacking Paris, a coalition of villages besieging the Pantheon, a troop of herdsmen flinging themselves upon a host governed by the light of intellect. Le Mans and Savenay chastised this madness. It was impossible for the Vendée to cross the Loire; she could do everything except that leap. Civil war does not conquer. To pass the Rhine establishes a Cæsar and strengthens a Napoleon; to cross the Loire killed La Rochejacquelein. The real strength of Vendée was Vendée at home; there she was invulnerable, unconquerable. The Vendean at home was smuggler, labourer, soldier, shepherd, poacher, sharp-shooter, goatherd, bell-ringer, peasant, spy, assassin, sacristan, wild beast of the wood.

La Rochejacquelein is only Achilles; Jean Chouan is Proteus.

The rebellion of the Vendée failed. Other revolts have succeeded,—that of Switzerland, for example. There is this difference between the mountain insurgent like the Swiss and the forest insurgent like the Vendean,—that almost always the one fights for an ideal, the other for a prejudice. The one soars, the other crawls; the one combats for humanity, the other for solitude; the one desires liberty, the other wishes isolation; the one defends the commune, the other the parish,—"Communes! Communes!" cried the heroes of Morat; the one has to deal with precipices, the other with quagmires; the one is the man of torrents and foaming streams, the other of stagnant puddles where pestilence lurks; the one has his head in the blue sky, the other in the thicket; the one is on a summit, the other in a shadow.

The education of heights and shallows is very different. The mountain is a citadel; the forest is an ambuscade: one inspires audacity, the other teaches trickery. Antiquity placed the gods on heights and the satyrs in copses. The satyr is the savage, half man, half brute. Free countries have Apennines, Alps, Pyrenees, and Olympus. Parnassus is a mountain. Mont Blanc is the colossal auxiliary of William Tell. Below and above these immense struggles of souls against the night which fills the poems of India, the Himalayas may be seen. Greece, Spain, Italy, Helvetia have for their likeness the mountain; Cimmeria, Germany, Brittany has the wood. The forest is barbarous.

The configuration of soil decides many of man's actions. The earth is more his accomplice than people believe. In presence of certain savage landscapes one is tempted to exonerate man and criminate creation. One feels a certain hidden provocation on the part of Nature; the desert is sometimes unhealthy for the conscience, especially for the conscience that is little illuminated. Conscience may be a giant,—then she produces a Socrates, a Christ; she may be a dwarf,—then she moulds Atreus and Judas. The narrow conscience becomes quickly reptile in its instincts: forests where twilight reigns; the bushes, the thorns, the marshes beneath the branches,—all have a fatal attraction for her; she undergoes the mysterious infiltration of evil persuasions. Optical illusions, unexplained mirages, the terrors of the hour or the scene, throw man into this sort of fright,—half religious, half bestial, which engenders superstition in ordinary times, and brutality at violent epochs. Hallucinations hold the torch which lights the road to murder. The brigand is dizzied by a vertigo. Nature in her immensity has a double meaning, which dazzles great minds and blinds savage souls. When man is ignorant, when his desert is peopled with visions, the obscurity of solitude adds itself to the obscurity of intelligence; hence come depths in the human soul, black and profound as an abyss. Certain rocks, certain ravines, certain thickets, certain wild openings in the trees through which night looks down, push men on to mad and atrocious actions. One might almost say that there are places which are the home of the spirit of evil. How many tragic sights have been watched by the sombre hill between Baignon and Phélan! Vast horizons lead the soul on to wide, general ideas; circumscribed horizons engender narrow, one-sided conceptions, which condemn great hearts to be little in point of soul. Jean Chouan was an example of this truth. Broad ideas are hated by partial ideas; this is in fact the struggle of progress.

Neighbourhood, country,—these two words sum up the whole of the Vendean war; a quarrel of the local idea against the universal; of the peasant against the patriot.

Chapter VII

LA VENDÉE ENDED BRITTANY

Brittany is an ancient rebel. Each time she revolted during two thousand years she was in the right; but the last time she was wrong. Still, at bottom (against the revolution as against monarchy, against the acting Representatives as against governing dukes and peers, against the rule of assignats as against the sway of excise officers, whosoever might be the men that fought, Nicolas Rapin, François de la Noue, Captain Pluviaut, the Lady of La Garnache or Stofflet, Coquereau, and Lechandelier de Pierreville; under De Rohan against the king, and under La Rochejacquelein for the king) it was always the same war that Brittany waged, —the war of the Local Spirit against the Central. Those ancient provinces were ponds; that stagnant water could not bear to flow; the wind which swept across did not revivify,—it irritated them.

Finistère formed the bounds of France: there the space given to man ended, and the march of generations stopped. "Halt!" the ocean cried to the land, to barbarism and to civilization. Each time that the centre—Paris—gives an impulse, whether that impulse comes from royalty or republicanism, whether it be in the interest of despotism or liberty, it is something new, and Brittany bristles up against it. "Leave us in peace! What is it they want of us?" The Marais seizes the pitchfork, the Bocage its carbine. All our attempts, our initiative movement in legislation and in education, our encyclopedias, our philosophies, our genius, our glories, all fail before the Houroux; the tocsin of Bazouges menaces the French Revolution, the moor of Faou rises in rebellion against the voices of our towns, and the bell of the Haut-des-Prés declares war against the Tower of the Louvre.

Terrible blindness! The Vendean insurrection was the result of a fatal misunderstanding.

A colossal scuffle, a jangling of Titans, an immeasurable rebellion, destined to leave in history only one word,—the Vendée,—word illustrious yet dark; committing suicide for the absent, devoted to egotism, passing its time in making to cowardice the offer of a boundless bravery; without calculation, without strategy, without tactics, without plan, without aim, without chief, without responsibility; showing to what extent Will can be impotent; chivalric and savage; absurdity at its climax, a building up a barrier of black shadows against the light; ignorance making a long resistance at once idiotic and superb against justice, right, reason, and deliverance; the terror of eight years, the rendering desolate fourteen departments, the devastation of fields, the destruction of harvests, the burning of villages, the ruin of cities, the pillage of houses, the massacre of women and children, the torch in the thatch, the sword in the heart, the terror of civilization, the hope of Mr. Pitt,—such was this war, the unreasoning effort of the parricide.

In short, by proving the necessity of perforating in every direction the old Breton shadows, and piercing this thicket with arrows of light from every quarter at once, the Vendée served Progress. The catastrophes had their uses.

BOOK II

THE THREE CHILDREN

CHAPTER I

PLUSQUAM CIVILIA BELLA

THE summer of 1792 had been very rainy; the summer of 1793 was dry and hot. In consequence of the civil war, there were no roads left, so to speak, in Brittany. Still it was possible to get about, thanks to the beauty of the season. Dry fields make an easy route.

At the close of a lovely July day, about an hour before sunset, a man on horseback, who came from the direction of Avranches, drew rein before the little inn called the Croix-Branchard, which stood at the entrance of Pontorson, and which for years past had borne this inscription on its sign: "Good cider on draught." It had been warm all day, but the wind was beginning now to rise.

The traveler was enveloped in an ample cloak which covered the back of his horse. He wore a broad hat with a tri-coloured cockade, which was a sufficiently bold thing to do in this country of hedges and gunshots, where a cockade was a target. The cloak, fastened about his neck, was thrown back to leave his arms free, and beneath glimpses could be had of a tricoloured sash and two pistols thrust in it. A sabre hung down below the cloak.

At the sound of the horse's hoofs the door of the inn opened and the landlord appeared, a lantern in his hand. It was the intermediate hour between day and night: still light along the highway, but dark in the house. The host looked at the cockade.

"Citizen," said he, "do you stop here?"

"No."

"Where are you going, then?"

"To Dol."

"In that case go back to Avranches or remain at Pontorson."

"Why?"

"Because there is fighting at Dol."

"Ah!" said the horseman.

Then he added,—

"Give my horse some oats."

The host brought the trough, emptied a measure of oats into it, and took the bridle off the horse, which began to sniff and eat.

The dialogue continued:—

"Citizen, has that horse been seized?"

"No."

"It belongs to you?"

"Yes. I bought and paid for it."

"Where do you come from?"

"Paris."

"Not direct?"

"No."

"I should think not! The roads are closed, but the post runs still."

"As far as Alençon. I left it there."

"Ah! Very soon there will be no longer any posts in France. There are no more horses. A horse worth three hundred livres costs six hundred, and fodder is beyond all price. I have been postmaster, and now I am keeper of a cookshop. Out of thirteen hundred and thirteen postmasters that there used to be, two hundred have resigned. Citizen, you travelled according to the new tariff?"

"That of the 1st of May—yes."

"Twenty sous a post for a carriage, twelve for a gig, five sous for a van. You bought your horse at Alençon?"

"Yes."

"You have ridden all day?"

"Since dawn."

"And yesterday?"

"And the day before."

"I can see that. You came by Domfront and Mortain."

"And Avranches."

"Take my advice, citizen; rest yourself. You must be tired. Your horse is certainly."

"Horses have a right to be tired; men have not."

The host again fixed his eyes on the traveller, whose face was grave, calm, and severe, and framed by grey hair.

The innkeeper cast a glance along the road, which was deserted as far as the eye could reach, and said,—

"And you travel alone in this fashion?"

"I have an escort."

"Where is it?"

"My sabre and pistols."

The innkeeper brought a bucket of water, and while the horse was drinking, studied the traveller, and said mentally: "All the same, he has the look of a priest."

The horseman resumed: "You say there is fighting at Dol?"

"Yes. That ought to be about beginning."

"Who is fighting?"

"One *ci-devant* against another *ci-devant*."

"You said—"

"I say that an **ex-noble** who is for the Republic is fighting against another ex-noble who is for the king."

"But there is no longer a king."

"There is the little fellow! The odd part of the business is that these two *ci-devants* are relations."

The horseman listened attentively. The innkeeper continued:—

"One is young, the other old. It is the grand-nephew who fights the great-uncle. The uncle is a royalist, the nephew a patriot. The uncle commands the Whites, the nephew commands the Blues. Ah, they will show no quarter, I'll warrant you. It is a war to the death."

"Death?"

"Yes, citizen. Hold! would you like to see the compliments they fling at each other's heads? Here is a notice the old man finds means to placard everywhere, on all the houses and all the trees, and that he has had stuck up on my very door."

The host held up his lantern to a square of paper fastened on a panel of the double door, and as the placard was written in large characters, the traveller could read it as he sat on his horse:—

"The Marquis de Lantenac has the honour of informing his grand-nephew, the Viscount Gauvain, that, if the Marquis has the good fortune to seize his person, he will cause the Viscount to be decently shot."

"Here," added the host, "is the reply."

He went forward, and threw the light of the lantern upon a second placard placed on a level with the first upon the other leaf of the door. The traveller read:—

"Gauvain warns Lantenac that, if he take him, he will have him shot."

"Yesterday," said the host, "the first placard was stuck on my door, and this morning the second. There was no waiting for the answer."

The traveller in a half-voice, and as if speaking to himself, uttered these words, which the innkeeper heard without really comprehending,—

"Yes; this is more than war in the country; it is war in families. It is necessary, and it is well. The grand restoration of the people must be bought at this price."

And the traveller raised his hand to his hat and saluted the second placard, on which his eyes were still fixed.

The host continued:—

"So, citizen, you understand how the matter lies. In the cities and the large towns we are for the Revolution, in the country they are against it; that is to say, in the towns people are Frenchmen, and in the villages they are Bretons. It is a war of the townspeople against the peasants. They call us clowns, we call them boors. The nobles and the priests are with them."

"Not all," interrupted the horseman.

"Certainly not, citizen, since we have here a viscount against a marquis."

Then he added to himself: "And I feel sure I am speaking to a priest."

The horseman continued: "And which of the two has the best of it?"

"The viscount so far. But he has to work hard. The old man is a tough one. They belong to the Gauvain family,— nobles of these parts. It is a family with two branches: there is the great branch, whose chief is called the Marquis de Lantenac! and there is the lesser branch, whose head is called the Viscount Gauvain. To-day the two branches fight each other. One does not see that among trees, but one sees it among men. This Marquis de Lantenac is all-powerful in Brittany; the peasants consider him a prince. The very day he landed, eight thousand men joined him; in a week, three hundred parishes had risen. If he had been able to get foothold on the coast, the English would have landed. Luckily this Gauvain was at hand,—the other's grand-nephew: odd chance! He is the republican commander, and he has checkmated his grand-uncle. And then, as good luck would have it, when this Lantenac arrived, and was massacring a heap of prisoners, he had two women shot, one of whom had three children that had been adopted by a Paris battalion. And that made a terrible battalion; they call themselves the Battalion of the Bonnet Rouge. There are not many of those Parisians left, but they are furious bayonets. They have been incorporated into the division of Commandant Gauvain: nothing can stand against them. They mean to avenge the women and retake the children. Nobody knows what the old man has done with the little ones: that is what enraged the Parisian grenadiers. Suppose those babies had not been mixed up in the matter, the war would not be what it is. The viscount is a good, brave young man; but the old fellow is a terrible marquis. The peasants call it the war of Saint Michael against Beelzebub. You know, perhaps, that Saint Michel is an angel of the district; there is a mountain named after him out in the bay; they say he overcame the demon, and buried him under another mountain near here, which is called Tombelaine."

"Yes," murmured the horseman; "Tumba Beleni, the tomb of Belenus,—Belus, Bel, Belial, Beelzebub."

"I see that you are well informed." And the host again spoke to himself: "He understands Latin! Decidedly he is a priest." Then he resumed: "Well, citizen, for the peasants it is that war beginning over again. For them the royalist general is Saint Michael, and Beelzebub is the republican commander. But if there is a devil, it is certainly Lantenac; and if there is an angel, it is Gauvain. You will take nothing, citizen?"

"I have my gourd and a bit of bread. But you do not tell me what is passing at Dol!"

"This. Gauvain commands the exploring column of the coast. Lantenac's aim was to rouse a general insurrection, and sustain Lower Brittany by the aid of Lower Normandy, open the door to Pitt, and give a shove forward to the Vendean army, with twenty thousand English, and two hundred thousand peasants. Gauvain cut this plan short: he holds the coast, and he drives Lantenac into the interior and the English into the sea. Lantenac was here, and Gauvain has dislodged him; has taken from him the Pont-au-Beau, has driven him out of Avranches, chased him out of Villedieu, and kept him from reaching Granville. He is manœuvring to shut him up again in the forest of Fougères, and to surround him. Yesterday everything was going well; Gauvain was here with his division. All of a sudden, an alarm! the old man, who is skilful, made a point; information comes that he has marched on Dol. If he takes Dol, and establishes a battery on Mount Dol (for he has cannon), then there will be a place on the coast where the English can land, and everything is lost. That is why, as there was not a minute to lose, that Gauvain, who is a man with a head, took counsel with nobody but himself, asked no orders and waited for none, but sounded the signal to saddle, put to his artillery, collected his troop, drew his sabre, and while Lantenac throws himself on Dol, Gauvain throws himself on Lantenac. It is at Dol that these two Breton heads will knock together. There will be a fine shock. They are at it now."

"How long does it take to get to Dol?"

"At least three hours for a troop with cannon; but they are there now."

The traveller listened, and said: "In fact, I think I hear cannon."

The host listened. "Yes, citizen; and the musketry. They have opened the ball. You would do well to pass the night here. There will be nothing good to catch over there."

"I cannot stop. I must keep on my road."

"You are wrong. I do not know your business; but the risk is great, and unless it concern what you hold dearest in the world—"

"In truth, it is that which is concerned," said the cavalier.

"Something like your son—"

"Very nearly that," said the cavalier.

The inkeeper raised his head, and said to himself.

"Still this citizen gives me the impression of being a priest." Then, after a little reflection: "All the same, a priest may have children."

"Put the bridle back on my horse," said the traveller. "How much do I owe you?" He paid the man.

The host set the trough and the bucket back against the wall, and returned toward the horseman. "Since you are determined to go, listen to my advice. It is clear that you are going to Saint Malo. Well, do not pass by Dol. There are two roads,—the road by Dol, and the road along the seashore. There is scarcely any difference in their length. The sea-shore road passes by Saint-Georges-de-Brehaigne, Cherrueix, and Hirèlle-Vivier. You leave Dol to the south and Cancale to the north. Citizen, at the end of the street you will find the branching off of the two routes; that of Dol is on the left, that of Saint-Georges-de-Brehaigne on the right. Listen well to me: if you go by Dol, you will fall into the middle of the massacre. That is why you must not take to the left, but to the right."

"Thanks," said the traveller. He spurred his horse forward. The obscurity was now complete; he hurried on into the night. The innkeeper lost sight of him.

When the traveller reached the end of the street where the two roads branched off, he heard the voice of the innkeeper calling to him from afar,—

"Take the right!"

He took the left.

CHAPTER II

DOL

DOL, a Spanish city of France in Brittany, as the guide-books style it, is not a town; it is a street,—a great old Gothic street, bordered all the way on the right and the left by houses with pillars, placed irregularly, so that they form nooks and elbows in the highway, which is nevertheless very wide. The rest of the town is only a network of lanes, attaching themselves to this great diametrical street, and pouring into it like brooks into a river. The city, without gates or walls, open, overlooked by Mount Dol, could not have sustained a siege; but the street might have sustained one. The promontories of houses, which were still to be seen fifty years back, and the two-pillared galleries which bordered the street, made a battle-ground that was very strong and capable of offering great resistance. Each house was a fortress in fact, and it would be necessary to take them one after another. The old market was very nearly in the middle of the street.

The innkeeper of the Croix-Branchard has spoken truly,—a mad conflict filled Dol at the moment he uttered the words. A nocturnal duel between the Whites, that morning arrived, and the Blues, who had come upon them in the evening, burst suddenly over the town. The forces were unequal: the Whites numbered six thousand; there were only fifteen hundred of the Blues. But there was equality in point of obstinate rage; strange to say, it was the fifteen hundred who had attacked the six thousand.

On one side a mob, on the other a phalanx. On one side six thousand peasants, with blessed medals on their leather vests, white ribbons on their round hats, Christian devices on their braces, chaplets at their belts, carrying more pitchforks than sabres, carbines without bayonets, dragging cannon with ropes; badly equipped, ill disciplined, poorly armed, but frantic. In opposition to them were fifteen hundred soldiers, wearing three-cornered hats, coats with large tails and wide lapels, shoulder-belts crossed, copper-hilted swords, and carrying guns with long bayonets. They were trained, skilled; docile, yet fierce; obeying like men who would know how to command: volunteers also, shoeless and in rags too, but volunteers for their country. On the side of Monarchy, peasants who were paladins; for the Revolution, barefooted heroes, and each troop possessing a soul in its leader: the royalists having an old man, the republicans a young one. On this side, Lantenac; on the other, Gauvain.

The Revolution, side by side with its faces of youthful giants like those of Danton, Saint-Just, and Robespierre, has faces of ideal youth, like those of Hoche and Marceau. Gauvain was one of these.

He was thirty years old; he had a Herculean bust, the solemn eye of a prophet, and the laugh of a child. He did not smoke, he did not drink, he did not swear. He carried a dressing-case through the whole war; he took care of his nails, his teeth, and his hair, which was dark and luxuriant. During halts he himself shook in the wind his military coat, riddled with bullets and white with dust. Though always rushing headlong into an affray, he had never been wounded. His singularly sweet voice had at command the abrupt imperiousness needed by a leader. He set the example of sleeping on the ground, in the wind, the rain, and the snow, rolled in his cloak and with his noble head pillowed on a stone. His was a heroic and innocent soul. The sabre in his hand transfigured him. He had that effeminate air which in battle turns into something formidable. With all that, a thinker and a philosopher, a youthful sage,—Alcibiades in appearance, Socrates in speech.

In that immense improvisation of the French Revolution this young man had become at once a leader. His division, formed by himself, was like a Roman legion, a kind of complete little army. It was composed of infantry and cavalry; it had its scouts, its pioneers, its sappers, pontoniers; and as a Roman legion had its catapults, this one had its cannon. Three pieces, well mounted, rendered the column strong, while leaving it easy to guide.

Lantenac was also a thorough soldier,—a more consummate one. He was at the same time wary and hardy. Old heroes have more cold determination than young ones, because they are far removed from the warmth of life's morning; more audacity, because they are near death. What have they to lose? So very little. Hence the manœuvres of Lantenac were at once rash and skilful. But in the main, and almost always, in this dogged hand-to hand conflict between the old man and the young, Gauvain gained the advantage. It was rather the work of fortune than anything else. All good luck

—even successes which are in themselves terrible—go to youth. Victory is somewhat of a woman.

Lantenac was exasperated against Gauvain,—justly, because Gauvain fought against him; in the second place, because he was of his kindred. What did he mean by turning Jacobin,—this Gauvain, this mischievous dog! his heir (for the marquis had no children), his grand-nephew, almost his grandson! "Ah," said this quasi-grandfather, "if I put my hand on him, I will kill him like a dog!"

For that matter, the Revolution was right to disquiet itself in regard to this Marquis de Lantenac. An earthquake followed his landing. His name spread through the Vendean insurrection like a train of powder, and Lantenac at once became the centre. In a revolt of that nature, where each is jealous of the other, and each has his thicket or ravine, the arrival of a superior rallies the scattered leaders who have been equals among themselves. Nearly all the forest captains had joined Lantenac, and, whether near or far off, they obeyed him. One man alone had departed; it was the first who had joined him,—Gavard. Wherefore? Because he had been a man of trust. Gavard had known all the secrets and adopted all the plans of the ancient system of civil war; Lantenac appeared to replace and supplant him. One does not inherit from a man of trust; the shoe of La Romain did not fit Lantenac. Gavard departed to join Ponchamp.

Lantenac, as a military man, belonged to the school of Frederick II.; he understood combining the great war with the little. He would have neither a "confused mass" (like the great Catholic and Royal army), a crowd destined to be crushed, nor a troop of guerillas scattered among the hedges and copses, —good to harass, impotent to destroy. Guerila warfare finishes nothing, or finishes ill; it begins by attacking a republic and ends by rifling a diligence. Lantenac did not comprehend this Breton war as the other chiefs had done,— neither as La Rochejacquelein, who was all for open country campaigns; nor as Jean Chouan, all for the forest. He would have neither Vendée nor Chouannerie; he wanted real warfare: he would make use of the peasant, but he meant to depend on the soldier. He wanted bands for strategy and regiments for tactics. He found these village armies admirable for attack, for ambush and surprise, quickly gathered, quickly dispersed; but he felt that they lacked solidity,—they were like water in his hand. He wanted to create a solid base in this floating and diffused war; he wanted to join to the savage army of the forests regularly drilled troops that would make a pivot about which he could manœuvre the peasants. It was a profound and terrible conception; if it had succeeded, the Vendée would have been unconquerable.

But would he find regular troops? Where look for soldiers, where seek for regiments, where discover an army ready made? In England. Hence Lantenac's determined idea,—to land the English. Thus the conscience of parties compromises with itself. The white cockade hid the red uniform from Lantenac's sight. He had only one thought,—to get possession of some point on the coast, and deliver it up to Pitt. That was why, seeing Dol defenceless, he flung himself upon it; the taking of the town would give him Mount Dol, and Mount Dol the coast.

The place was well chosen. The cannon of Mount Dol would sweep the Fresnois on one side and Saint-Brelade on the other; would keep the cruisers of Cancale at a distance, and leave the whole beach, from Raz-sur-Couesnon to Saint-Mêloir-des-Oudes, clear for an invasion. For the carrying out of this decisive attempt, Lantenac had brought with him only a little over six thousand men, the flower of the bands which he had at his disposal, and all his artillery, —ten sixteen-pound culverins, a demi-culverin, and a four-pounder. His idea was to establish a strong battery on Mount Dol, upon the principle that a thousand shots fired from ten cannon do more execution than fifteen hundred fired with five. Success appeared certain. They were six thousand men. Toward Avranches, they had only Gauvain and his fifteen hundred men to fear, and Léchelle in the direction of Dinan. It was true that Léchelle had twenty-five thousand men, but he was twenty leagues away. So Lantenac felt confidence! on Léchelle's side he put the great distance against the great numbers; with Gauvain, the size of the force against their propinquity. Let us add that Léchelle was an idiot, who later on allowed his twenty-five thousand men to be exterminated in the *landes* of the Croix-Bataille,—a blunder which he atoned for by suicide.

So Lantenac felt perfect security. His entrance into Dol was sudden and stern. The Marquis de Lantenac had a stern reputation; he was known to be without pity. No resistance was attempted. The terrified inhabitants barricaded themselves in their houses. The six thousand Vendeans installed themselves in the town with rustic confusion; it was almost like a fair-ground, without quartermasters, without allotted camp, bivouacking at hazard, cooking in the open air, scattering themselves among the churches, forsaking their guns for their rosaries. Lantenac went in haste with some artillery officers to reconnoitre Mount Dol, leaving the command to Gouge-le-Bruant, whom he had appointed field-sergeant.

This Gouge-le-Bruant has left a vague trace in history. He had two nicknames, Brise-bleu, on account of his massacre of patriots, and Imânus, because he had in him a something that was indescribably horrible. Imânus, derived from *imanis*, is an old bas-Norman word which expresses superhuman ugliness, something almost divine in its awfulness,—a demon, a satyr, an ogre. An ancient manuscript says, "With my two eyes I saw Imânus." The old people of the Bocage no longer know to-day who Gouge-le-Bruant was, nor what Brise-bleu signifies; but they know, confusedly, Imânus. Imânus is mingled with the local superstitions; they talk of him still at Trémorel and at Plumaugat, two villages where Gouge-le-Bruant has left the trace of his sinister course. In the Vendée the others were savages; Gouge-le-Bruant was the barbarian. He was a species of cacique, tattooed with Christian crosses and *fleur-de-lis;* he had on his face the hideous, almost supernatural glare of a soul which no other human soul resembled. He was infer nally brave in combat; atrocious afterward. His was a heart full of tortuous intricacies, capable of all forms of devotion, inclined to all madnesses. Did he reason? Yes; but as serpents crawl, in a twisted fashion. He started from heroism to reach murder. It was impossible to divine whence his resolves came to him; they were sometimes grand from their very monstrosity. He was capable of every possible unexpected horror; his ferocity was epic. Hence his mysterious nickname, Imânus. The Marquis de Lantenac had confidence in his cruelty. It was true that Imânus excelled in cruelty, but in strategy and in tactics he was less clever, and perhaps the marquis erred in making him his field-sergeant. However that might be, he left Imânus behind him with instructions to replace him and look after everything. Gouge-le-Bruant, a man more of a fighter than a soldier, was fitter to cut the throats of a clan than to guard a town. Still he posted main-guards.

When evening came, as the Marquis de Lantenac was returning toward Dol, after having decided upon the ground for his battery, he suddenly heard the report of cannon. He looked forward. A red smoke was rising from the principal street. There had been surprise, invasion, assault; they were fighting in the town. Although very difficult to astonish, he was stupefied. He had not been prepared for anything of the sort. Who could it be? Evidently it was not Gauvain. No man would attack a force that numbered four to his one. Was it Léchelle? But could he have made such a forced march? Léchelle was improbable; Gauvain impossible.

Lantenac urged on his horse; as he rode forward he encountered the flying inhabitants; he questioned them. They were mad with terror; they cried, "The Blues! the Blues!" When he arrived, the situation was a bad one. This is what had happened.

Chapter III

SMALL ARMIES AND GREAT BATTLES

As we have just seen, the peasants, on arriving at Dol, dispersed themselves through the town, each man following his own fancy, as happens when troops "obey from friendship," a favourite expression with the Vendeans,—a species of obedience which makes heroes, but not troopers. They thrust the artillery out of the way along with the baggage, under the arches of the old market-hall. They were weary; they ate, drank, counted their rosaries, and lay down pell-mell across the principal street, which was encumbered rather than guarded.

As night came on, the greater portion fell asleep, with their heads on their knapsacks, some having their wives beside them, for the peasant women often followed their husbands, and the robust ones acted as spies. It was a mild July evening; the constellation glittered in the deep purple of the sky. The entire bivouac, which resembled rather the halt of a caravan than an army encamped, gave itself up to repose. Suddenly, amid the dull gleams of twilight, such as had not yet closed their eyes saw three pieces of ordnance pointed at the entrance of the street. It was Gauvain's artillery. He had surprised the main-guard. He was in the town, and his column held the top of the street.

A peasant started up, crying, "Who goes there?" and fired his musket; a cannon-shot replied. Then a furious discharge of musketry burst forth. The whole drowsy crowd sprang up with a start. A rude shock,—to fall asleep under the stars and wake under a volley of grape-shot.

The first moments were terrific. There is nothing so tragic as the aimless swarming of a thunderstricken crowd. They flung themselves on their arms; they yelled, they ran; many fell. The assaulted peasants no longer knew what they were about, and blindly shot one another. The townspeople, stunned with fright, rushed in and out of their houses, and wandered frantically amid the hubbub. Families shrieked to one another. A dismal combat ensued, in which women and children were mingled. The balls, as they whistled overhead, streaked the darkness with rays of light. A fusillade poured from every dark corner. There was nothing but smoke and tumult. The entanglement of the baggage-wagons and the cannon-carriages was added to the confusion. The horses became unmanageable; the wounded were trampled under foot. The groans of the poor wretches, helpless on the ground, filled the air. Horror here, stupefaction there. Soldiers and officers sought for one another. In the midst of all this could be seen creatures made indifferent to the awful scene by personal preoccupations. A woman sat nursing her new-born babe, seated on a bit of wall, against which her husband leaned with his leg broken; and he, while his blood was flowing, tranquilly loaded his rifle and fired at random, straight before him into the darkness. Men lying flat on the ground fired across the spokes of the wagon-wheels. At moments there rose a hideous din of clamours, then the great voices of the cannon drowned all. It was awful. It was like a felling of trees; they dropped one upon another. Gauvain poured out a deadly fire from his ambush, and suffered little loss.

Still the peasants, courageous amid their disorder, ended by putting themselves on the defensive; they retreated into the market,—a vast, obscure redoubt, a forest of stone pillars. There they again made a stand; anything which resembled a wood gave them confidence. Imânus supplied the absence of Lantenac as best he could. They had cannon, but to the great astonishment of Gauvain they did not make use of it; that was owing to the fact that the artillery officers had gone with the marquis to reconnoitre Mount Dol, and the peasants did not know how to manage the culverins and demi-culverins. But they riddled with balls the Blues who cannonaded them; they replied to the grape-shot by volleys of musketry. It was now they who were sheltered. They had heaped together the drays, the tumbrels, the casks, all the litter of the old market, and improvised a lofty barricade, with openings through which they could pass their carbines. From these holes their fusillade was murderous. The whole was quickly arranged. In a quarter of an hour the market presented an impregnable front.

This became a serious matter for Gauvain. This market suddenly transformed into a citadel was unexpected

The peasants were inside it, massed and solid. Gauvain's surprise had succeeded, but he ran the risk of defeat. He got down from his saddle. He stood attentively studying the darkness, his arms folded, clutching his sword in one hand, erect, in the glare of a torch which lighted his battery. The gleam, falling on his tall figure, made him visible to the men behind the barricade. He became an aim for them, but he did not notice it. The shower of balls sent out from the barricade fell about him as he stood there, lost in thought. But he could oppose cannon to all these carbines, and cannon always ends by getting the advantage. Victory rests with him who has the artillery. His battery, well manned, insured him the superiority.

Suddenly a lightning-flash burst from the shadowy market; there was a sound like a peal of thunder, and a ball broke through a house above Gauvain's head. The barricade was replying to the cannon with its own voice. What had happened? Something new had occurred. The artillery was no longer confined to one side. A second ball followed the first and buried itself in the wall close to Gauvain. A third knocked his hat off on the ground. These balls were of a heavy calibre. It was a sixteen-pounder that fired.

"They are aiming at you, commandant," cried the artillerymen.

They extinguished the torch. Gauvain, as if in a reverie, picked up his hat. Some one had in fact aimed at Gauvain; it was Lantenac. The marquis had just arrived within the barricade from the opposite side. Imânus had hurried to meet him.

"Monseigneur, we are surprised!"
"By whom?"
"I do not know."
"Is the route to Dinan free?"
"I think so."
"We must begin a retreat."
"It has commenced. A good many have run away."
"We must not run; we must fall back. Why are you not making use of this artillery?"
"The men lost their heads; besides, the officers were not here."
"I am come."
"Monseigneur, I have sent toward Fougères all I could of the baggage, the women, everything useless. What is to be done with the three little prisoners?"
"Ah, those children!"
"Yes."
"They are our hostages. Have them taken to La Tourgue."

This said, the marquis rushed to the barricade. With the arrival of the chief the whole face of affairs changed. The barricade was ill-constructed for artillery; there was only room for two cannon; the marquis put in position a couple of sixteen-pounders, for which loopholes were made. As he leaned over one of the guns, watching the enemy's battery through the opening, he perceived Gauvain.

"It is he!" cried the marquis.

Then he took the swab and rammer himself, loaded the piece, sighted it, and fired. Thrice he aimed at Gauvain and missed. The third time he only succeeded in knocking his hat off.

"Numbskull!" muttered Lantenac; "a little lower, and I should have taken his head." Suddenly the torch went out, and he had only darkness before him.

"So be it!" said he. Then turning toward the peasant gunners, he cried; "Now let them have it!"

Gauvain, on his side, was not less in earnest. The seriousness of the situation increased. A new phase of the combat developed itself. The barricade had begun to use cannon. Who could tell if it were not about to pass from the defensive to the offensive? He had before him, after deducting the killed and fugitives, at least five thousand combatants, and he had left only twelve hundred serviceable men. What would happen to the republicans if the enemy perceived their paucity of numbers? The rôles were reversed. He had been the assailant,—he would become the assailed. If the barricade were to make a sortie, everything might be lost. What was to be done? He could no longer think of attacking the barricade in front; an attempt at main force would be foolhardy: twelve hundred men cannot dislodge five thousand. To rush upon them was impossible; to wait would be fatal. He must make an end. But how?

Gauvain belonged to the neighbourhood; he was acquainted with the town; he knew that the old market-house where the Vendeans were intrenched was backed by a labyrinth of narrow and crooked streets. He turned towards his lieutenant, who was that valiant Captain Guéchamp, afterward famous for clearing out the forest of Concise, where Jean Chouan was born, and for preventing the capture of Bourgneuf by holding the dike of La Chaîne against the rebels.

"Guéchamp," said he, "I leave you in command. Fire as fast as you can. Riddle the barricade with cannon-balls. Keep all those fellows over yonder busy."

"I understand," said Guéchamp.

"Mass the whole column with their guns loaded, and hold them ready to make an onslaught." He added a few words in Guéchamp's ear.

"I hear," said Guéchamp.

Gauvain resumed: "Are all our drummers on foot?"

"Yes."

"We have nine. Keep two and give me seven."

The seven drummers ranged themselves in silence in front of Gauvain. Then he said: "Battalion of the Bonnet Rouge!"

Twelve men, one of whom was a sergeant, stepped out from the main body of the troop.

"I demand the whole battalion," said Gauvain.

"Here it is," replied the sergeant.

"You are twelve!"

"There are twelve of us left."

"It is well," said Gauvain.

This sergeant was the good, rough trooper Radoub, who had adopted, in the name of the battalion, the three children they had encountered in the wood of La Saudraie. It will be remembered that only a demi-battalion had been exterminated at Herbe-en-Pail, and Radoub was fortunate enough not to have been among that number.

There was a forage-wagon standing near; Gauvain pointed toward it with his finger. "Sergeant, order your men to make some straw ropes and twist them about their guns, so that there will be no noise if they knock together."

A minute passed; the order was silently executed in the darkness.

"It is done," said the sergeant.

"Soldiers, take off your shoes," commanded Gauvain.

"We have none," returned the sergeant.

They numbered, counting the drummers, nineteen men; Gauvain made the twentieth. He cried: "Follow me! Single file! The drummers next to me, the battalion behind them. Sergeant, you will command the battalion."

He put himself at the head of the column, and while the firing on both sides continued, these twenty men, gliding along like shadows, plunged into the deserted lanes. The line marched thus for some time, twisting along the fronts of the houses. The whole town seemed dead; the citizens were hidden in their cellars. Every door was barred; every shutter closed; no light to be seen anywhere. Amid this silence the principal street kept up its din; the cannonading continued; the republican battery and the royalist barricade spit forth their volleys with undiminished fury.

After twenty minutes of this tortuous march, Gauvain, who kept his way unerringly through the darkness, reached the end of a lane which led into the broad street, but on the other side of the market-house. The position was turned. In this direction there was no intrenchment, according to the eternal imprudence of barricade builders; the market was open, and the entrance free among the pillars where some baggage-wagons stood ready to depart. Gauvain and his nineteen men had the five thousand Vendeans before them, but their backs instead of their faces.

Gauvain spoke in a low voice to the sergeant; the soldiers untwisted the straw from their guns; the twelve grenadiers posted themselves in line behind the angle of the lane, and the seven drummers waited with their drumsticks lifted. The artillery firing was intermittent. Suddenly, in a pause between the discharges, Gauvain waved his sword, and cried in a voice which rang like a trumpet through the silence: "Two hundred men to the right; two hundred men to the left; all the rest in the centre!"

The twelve muskets fired, and the seven drums beat.

Gauvain uttered the formidable battle-cry of the Blues: "To your bayonets! Down upon them!"

The effect was prodigious. This whole peasant mass felt itself surprised in the rear, and believed that it had a fresh army at its back. At the same instant, on hearing the drums, the column which Guéchamp commanded at the head of the street began to move, sounding the charge in its turn, and flung itself at a run on the barricade. The peasants found themselves between two fires. Panic magnifies: a pistol-shot sounds like the report of a cannon; in moments of terror the imagination heightens every noise; the barking of a dog sounds like the roar of a lion. Add to this the fact that the peasant catches fright as easily as thatch catches fire, and as quickly as a blazing thatch becomes a conflagration, a panic among peasants becomes a rout. An indescribably confused flight ensued.

In a few instants the market-hall was empty; the terrified rustics broke away in all directions; the officers were powerless; Imânus uselessly killed two or three fugitives; nothing was to be heard but the cry, "Save, yourselves!" The army poured through the streets of the town like water through the holes of a sieve, and dispersed into the open country with the rapidity of a cloud carried along by a whirlwind. Some fled toward Châteauneuf, some toward Plerguer, others toward Antrain.

The Marquis de Lantenac watched this stampede. He spiked the guns with his own hands and then retreated,—the last of all, slowly, composedly, saying to himself, "Decidedly, the peasants will not stand. We must have the English."

Chapter IV

"it is the second time"

The victory was complete. Gauvain turned toward the men of the Bonnet Rouge battalion, and said: "You are twelve, but you are equal to a thousand." Praise from a chief was the cross of honour of those times.

Guéchamp, dispatched beyond the town by Gauvain, pursued the fugitives and captured a great number. Torches were lighted and the town was searched. All who could not escape surrendered. They illuminated the principal street with fire-pots. It was strewn with dead and dying. The root of a combat must always be torn out; a few desperate groups here and there still resisted; they were surrounded, and threw down their arms.

Gauvain had remarked, amid the frantic pell-mell of the retreat, an intrepid man, a sort of agile and robust form, who protected the flight of others, but had not himself fled. This peasant had used his gun so energetically—the barrel for firing, the butt-end for knocking down—that he had broken it; now he grasped a pistol in one hand—and a sabre in the other. No one dared approach him. Suddenly Gauvain saw him reel and support himself against a pillar of the broad street. The man had just been wounded; but he still clutched the sabre and pistol in his fists. Gauvain put his sword under his arm and went up to him. "Surrender!" said he.

The man looked steadily at him. The blood ran through his clothing from a wound which he had received, and made a pool at his feet.

"You are my prisoner," added Gauvain. The man remained silent. "What is your name?"

The man answered, "I am called the Shadow-dancer."

"You are a brave man," said Gauvain. And he held out his hand.

The man cried, "Long live the king!" Gathering up all his remaining strength, he raised both arms at once, fired his pistol at Gauvain's heart, and dealt a blow at his head with the sabre.

He did it with the swiftness of a tiger; but some one else had been still more prompt. This was a man on horseback, who had arrived unobserved a few minutes before. This man, seeing the Vendean raise the sabre and pistol, rushed between him and Gauvain. But for this interposition, Gauvain would have been killed.

The horse received the pistol-shot, the man received the sabre-stroke, and both fell. It all happened in the time it would have needed to utter a cry.

The Vendean sank on his side upon the pavement. The sabre had struck the man full in the face; he lay senseless on the stones. The horse was killed.

Gauvain approached. "Who is this man?" said he. He studied him. The blood from the gash inundated the wounded man, and spread a red mask over his face. It was impossible to distinguish his features, but one could see that his hair was grey. "This man has saved my life," continued Gauvain. "Does any one here know him?"

"Commandant," said a soldier, "he came into the town a few minutes ago. I saw him enter; he came by the road from Pontorson."

The chief surgeon hurried up with his instrument-case. The wounded man was still insensible. The surgeon examined him and said: "A simple gash. It is nothing. It can be sewed up. In eight days he will be on his feet again. It was a beautiful sabre-stroke."

The sufferer wore a cloak, a tricoloured sash, pistols, and a sabre. He was laid on a litter. They undressed him. A bucket of fresh water was brought; the surgeon washed the cut: the face began to be visible. Gauvain studied it with profound attention.

"Has he any papers on him?" he asked.

The surgeon felt in the stranger's sidepocket and drew out a pocket-book, which he handed to Gauvain. The wounded man, restored by the cold water, began to come to himself. His eyelids moved slightly.

Gauvain examined the pocket-book; he found in it a sheet of paper, folded four times; he opened this and read:

"Committee of Public Safety.

The Citizen Cimourdain."

He uttered a cry: "Cimourdain!"

The wounded man opened his eyes at this exclamation.

Gauvain was astounded. "Cimourdain! It is you! This is the second time you have saved my life."

Cimourdain looked at him. A gleam of ineffable joy lighted his bleeding face.

Gauvain fell on his knees beside him, crying, "My master!"

"Thy father," said Cimourdain.

Chapter V

THE DROP OF COLD WATER

They had not met for many years, but their hearts had never been parted; they recognized each other as if they had separated the evening before.

An ambulance had been improvised in the town-hall of Dol. Cimourdain was placed on a bed in a little room next the great common chamber of the other wounded. The surgeon sewed up the cut and put an end to the demonstrations between the two men, judging that Cimourdain ought to be left to sleep. Besides, Gauvain was claimed by the thousand occupations which are the duties and cares of victory.

Cimourdain remained alone, but he did not sleep: he was consumed by two fevers,—that of his wound and that of his joy. He did not sleep, and still it did not seem to him that he was awake. Could it be possible that his dream was realized? Cimourdain had long ceased to believe in luck, yet here it was. He had refound Gauvain. He had left him a child, he found him a man; he found him great, formidable, intrepid. He found him triumphant, and triumphing for the people. Gauvain was the real support of the Revolution in Vendée; and it was he, Cimourdain, who had given this tower of strength to the Republic. This victor was his pupil. The light which he saw illuminating this youthful face (reserved perhaps for the Republican Pantheon) was his own thought,—his, Cimourdain's. His disciple—the child of his spirit—was from henceforth a hero, and before long would be a glory. It seemed to Cimourdain that he saw the apotheosis of his own soul. He had just seen how Gauvain made war; he was like Chiron, who had watched Achilles fight. There was a mysterious analogy between the priest and the centaur, for the priest is only half man.

All the chances of this adventure, mingled with the sleeplessness caused by his wound, filled Cimourdain with a sort of mysterious intoxication. He saw a glorious youthful destiny rising; and what added to his profound joy was the possession of full power over this destiny. Another success like that which he had just witnessed, and Cimourdain would only need to speak a single word to induce the Republic to confide an army to Gauvain. Nothing dazzles like the astonishment of complete victory. It was an era when each man had his military dream; each one wanted to make a general. Danton wished to appoint Westermann; Marat wished to appoint Rossignol; Hébert wished to appoint Ronsin; Robespierre wished to put these all aside. Why not Gauvain, asked Cimourdain of himself; and he dreamed. All possibilities were before him: he passed from one hypothesis to another; all obstacles vanished. When a man puts his foot on that ladder, he does not stop, it is an infinite ascent: one starts from earth and one reaches the stars. A great general is only a leader of armies; a great captain is at the same time a leader of ideas. Cimourdain dreamed of Gauvain as a great captain. He seemed to see—for reverie travels swiftly—Gauvain on the ocean, chasing the English; on the Rhine, chastising the Northern kings; on the Pyrenees, repulsing Spain; on the Alps, making a signal to Rome to rouse itself. There were two men in Cimourdain,—one tender, the other stern; both were satisfied, for the inexorable was his ideal; and at the same time that he saw Gauvain noble, he saw him terrible. Cimourdain thought of all that it was necessary to destroy before beginning to build up, and said to himself: "Verily, this is no time for tenderness. Gauvain will be 'up to the mark,'" an expression of the period. Cimourdain pictured Gauvain spurning the shadows with his foot, with a breastplate of light, a meteor-glare on his brow, rising on the grand ideal wings of Justice, Reason, and Progress, but with a sword in his hand: an angel,—a destroyer likewise.

In the height of this reverie, which was almost an ecstasy, he heard through the half-open door a conversation in the great hall of the ambulance which was next his chamber. He recognized Gauvain's voice; through all those years of separation that voice had rung ever in his ear, and the voice of the man had still a tone of the childish voice he had loved. He listened. There was a sound of soldiers' footsteps; one of the men said:—

"Commandant, this is the man who fired at you. While nobody was watching, he dragged himself into a cellar. We found him. Here he is."

Then Cimourdain heard this dialogue between Gauvain and the prisoner:—

"You are wounded?"

"I am well enough to be shot."

"Lay that man on a bed. Dress his wounds; take care of him; cure him."

"I wish to die."

"You must live. You tried to kill me in the king's name; I show you mercy in the name of the Republic."

A shadow passed across Cimourdain's forehead. He was like a man waking up with a start, and he murmured with a sort of sinister dejection: "In truth, he is one of the merciful."

Chapter VI

A HEALED BREAST; A BLEEDING HEART

A cut heals quickly; but there was in a certain place a person more seriously wounded than Cimourdain. It was the woman who had been shot, whom the beggar Tellmarch had picked up out of the great lake of blood at the farm of Herbe-en-Pail.

Michelle Fléchard was even in a more critical situation than Tellmarch had believed. There was a wound in the shoulder-blade corresponding to the wound above the breast; at the same time that the ball broke her collar-bone, another ball traversed her shoulder, but, as the lungs were not touched, she might recover. Tellmarch was a "philosopher,"—a peasant phrase which means a little of a doctor, a little of a surgeon, and a little of a sorcerer. He carried the wounded woman to his forest lair, laid her upon his sea-weed bed, and treated her by the aid of those mysterious things called "simples;" and thanks to him she lived. The collar-bone knitted together, the wounds in the breast and shoulder closed; after a few weeks she was convalescent. One morning she was able to walk out of the carnichot, leaning on Tellmarch, and seat herself beneath the trees in the sunshine. Tellmarch knew little about her; wounds in the breast demand silence, and during the almost death-like agony which had preceded her recovery she had scarcely spoken a word. When she tried to speak, Tellmarch stopped her, but she kept up an obstinate reverie; he could see in her eyes the sombre going and coming of poignant thoughts. But this morning she was quite strong; she could almost walk alone; a cure is a paternity, and Tellmarch watched her with delight. The good old man began to smile. He said to her:—

"We are upon our feet again; we have no more wounds."

"Except in the heart," said she. She added, presently: "Then you have no idea where they are."

"Who are 'they?'" demanded Tellmarch.

"My children."

This "then" expressed a whole world of thoughts; it signified: "Since you do not talk to me, since you have been so many days beside me without opening your mouth, since you stop me each time I attempt to break the silence, since you seem to fear that I shall speak, it is because you have nothing to tell me." Often in her fever, in her wanderings, her delirium, she had called her children, and had seen clearly (for delirium makes its observations) that the old man did not reply to her.

The truth was, Tellmarch did not know what to say to her. It is not easy to tell a mother that her children are lost. And then, what did he know? Nothing. He knew that a mother had been shot; that this mother had been found on the ground by himself; that when he had taken her up she was almost a corpse; that this quasi-corpse had three children; and that Lantenac, after having had the mother shot, carried off the little ones. All his information ended there. What become of the children? Were they even living? He knew, because he had inquired, that there were two boys and a little girl, barely weaned. Nothing more. He asked himself a host of questions concerning this unfortunate group, but could answer none of them. The people of the neighbourhood whom he had interrogated contented themselves with shaking their heads. The Marquis de Lantenac was a man of whom they did not willingly talk. They did not willingly talk *of* De Lantenac, and they did not willingly talk *to* Tellmarch. Peasants have a species of suspicion peculiar to themselves. They did not like Tellmarch. Tellmarch the Caimand was a puzzling man. Why was he always studying the sky? What was he doing and what was he thinking in his long hours of stillness? Yes, indeed, he was odd! In this district in full warfare, in full conflagration, in high tumult; where all men had only one business,—devastation; and one work,—carnage; where whosoever could burned a house, cut the throats of a family, massacred an outpost, sacked a village; where nobody thought of anything but laying ambushes for one another, drawing one another into snares, killing one another,—this solitary, absorbed in Nature, as if submerged in the immense peacefulness of its beauties, gathering herbs and plants, occupied solely with the flowers, the birds, and the stars, was evidently a dangerous man. Plainly he was not in possession of his reason; he did not lie in wait behind thickets; he did not fire a shot at any one. Hence he created a certain dread about him. "That man is mad," said the passers-by.

Tellmarch was more than an isolated man,—he was shunned. People asked him no questions and gave him few answers; so he had not been able to inform himself as he could have wished. The war had drifted elsewhere; the armies had gone to fight farther off; the Marquis de Lantenac had disappeared from the horizon, and in Tellmarch's state of mind for him to be conscious there was a war it was necessary for it to set its foot on him.

After that cry, "My children," Tellmarch ceased to smile, and the woman went back to her thoughts. What was passing in that soul? It was as if she looked out from the depths of a gulf. Suddenly she turned toward Tellmarch, and cried anew, almost with an accent of rage: "My children!"

Tellmarch drooped his head like one guilty. He was thinking of this Marquis de Lantenac, who certainly was not thinking of him, and who probably no longer remembered that he existed. He accounted for this to himself, saying, "A lord, when he is in danger, he knows you; when he is once out of it, he does not know you any longer." And he asked himself: "But why, then, did I save this lord?" And he answered his own question: "Because he was a man." Thereupon he remained thoughtful for some time, then began again mentally: "Am I very sure of that?" He repeated his bitter words: "If I had known!"

This whole adventure overwhelmed him, for in that which he had done he perceived a sort of enigma. He meditated dolorously. A good action might sometimes be evil. He who saves the wolf kills the sheep. He who sets the vulture's wing is responsible for his talons. He felt himself in truth guilty. The unreasoning anger of this mother was just. Still, to have saved her consoled him for having saved the marquis. But the children?

The mother meditated also. The reflections of these two went on side by side; and, perhaps, though without speech, met one another amid the shadows of reverie. The woman's eyes, with a night-like gloom in their depths, fixed themselves anew on Tellmarch. "Nevertheless, that cannot be allowed to pass in this way," said she.

"Hush!" returned Tellmarch, laying his finger on his lips.

She continued: "You did wrong to save me, and I am angry with you for it. I would rather be dead, because I am sure I should see them then. I should know where they are. They would not see me, but I should be near them. The dead,—they ought to have power to protect."

He took her arm and felt her pulse. "Calm yourself; you are bringing back your fever."

She asked him almost harshly, "When can I go away from here?"

"Go away?"

"Yes. Walk."

"Never, if you are not reasonable. To-morrow, if you are wise."

"What do you call being wise?"

"Having confidence in God."

"God! What has he done with my children?" Her mind seemed wandering. Her voice became very sweet. "You understand," she said to him, "I cannot rest like this. You have never had any children, but I have. That makes a difference. One cannot judge of a thing when one does not know what it is. You never had any children, had you?"

"No," replied Tellmarch.

"And I—I had nothing besides them. What am I without my children? I should like to have somebody explain to me why I have not my children. I feel that things happen, but I do not understand. They killed my husband; they shot me: all the same, I do not understand it."

"Come," said Tellmarch, "there is the fever taking you again. Do not talk any more."

She looked at him and relapsed into silence. From this day she spoke no more. Tellmarch was obeyed more absolutely than he liked. She spent long hours of stupefaction, crouched at the foot of an old tree. She dreamed, and held her peace. Silence makes an impenetrable refuge for simple souls that have been down into the innermost depths of suffering. She seemed to relinquish all effort to understand. To a certain extent despair is unintelligible to the despairing.

Tellmarch studied her with sympathetic interest. In presence of this anguish the old man had thoughts such as might have come to a woman. "Oh, yes," he said to himself, "her lips do not speak, but her eyes talk. I know well what is the matter,—what her one idea is. To have been a mother, and to be one no longer! To have been a nurse, and to be so no more! She cannot resign herself. She thinks about the tiniest child of all, that she was nursing not long ago. She thinks of it; thinks, thinks. In truth, it must be sweet to feel a little rosy mouth that draws your very soul out of your body, and who, with the life that is yours, makes a life for itself." He kept silence on his side, comprehending the impotency of speech in face of an absorption like this. The persistence of an all-absorbing idea is terrible. And how to make a mother thus beset hear reason? Maternity is inexplicable; you cannot argue with it. That it is which renders a mother sublime; she becomes unreasoning; the maternal instinct is divinely animal. The mother is no longer a woman, she is a wild creature; her children are her cubs. Hence in the mother there is something at once inferior and superior to argument. A mother has an unerring instinct. The immense mysterious Will of creation is within her and guides her. Hers is a blindness superhumanly enlightened.

Now Tellmarch desired to make this unhappy creature speak; he did not succeed. On one occasion he said to her: "As ill-luck will have it, I am old, and I cannot walk any longer. At the end of a quarter of an hour my strength is exhausted, and I am obliged to rest; if it were not for that I would accompany you. After all, perhaps it is fortunate that I cannot. I should be rather a burden than useful to you. I am tolerated here; but the Blues are suspicious of me, as being a peasant; and the peasants suspect me of being a wizard."

He waited for her to reply. She did not even raise her eyes. A fixed idea ends in madness or heroism. But of what heroism is a poor peasant woman capable? None. She can be a mother, and that is all. Each day she buried herself deeper in her reverie. Tellmarch watched her. He tried to give her occupation; he brought her needles and thread and a thimble; and at length, to the satisfaction of the poor Caimand, she began some sewing. She dreamed, but she worked,—a sign of health; her energy was returning little by little. She mended her linen, her garments, her shoes; but her eyes looked cold and glassy as ever. As she bent over her needle, she sang unearthly melodies in a low voice. She murmured names,— probably the names of children,—but not distinctly enough for Tellmarch to catch them. She would break off abruptly and listen to the birds, as if she thought they might have brought her tidings. She watched the weather. Her lips would move,—she was speaking low to herself. She made a bag and filled it with chestnuts. One morning Tellmarch saw her preparing to set forth, her eyes gazing away into the depths of the forest.

"Where are you going?" he asked.

She replied, "I am going to look for them."

He did not attempt to detain her.

Chapter VII

THE TWO POLES OF THE TRUTH

At the end of a few weeks, which had been filled with the vicissitudes of civil war, the district of Fougères could talk of nothing but the two men who were opposed to each other, and yet were occupied in the same work; that is, fighting side by side the great revolutionary combat.

The savage Vendean duel continued, but the Vendée was losing ground. In Ille-et-Vilaine in particular, thanks to the young commander who had at Dol so opportunely replied to the audacity of six thousand royalists by the audacity of fifteen hundred patriots, the insurrection, if not quelled, was at least greatly weakened and circumscribed. Several lucky hits had followed that one, and out of these successes had grown a new position of affairs. Matters had changed their face, but a singular complication had arisen.

In all this portion of the Vendée the Republic had the upper hand,—that was beyond a doubt. But which republic? In the triumph which was opening out, two forms of republic made themselevs felt,—the republic of terror, and the republic of clemency; the one desirous to conquer by rigour, and the other by mildness. Which would prevail? These two forms—the conciliating and the implacable—were represented by two men, each of whom possessed his special influence and authority: the one a military commander, the other a civil delegate. Which of them would prevail?

One of the two, the delegate, had a formidable basis of support; he had arrived bearing the threatening watchword of the Paris Commune to the battalions of Santerre: "No mercy; no quarter!" He had, in order to put everything under his control, the decree of the Convention, ordaining "death to whomsoever should set at liberty and help a captive rebel chief to escape." He had full powers, emanating from the Committee of Public Safety, and an injunction commanding obedience to him as delegate, signed ROBESPIERRE, DANTON, MARAT. The other, the soldier, had on his side only this strength,—pity. He had only his own arm, which chastised the enemy; and his heart, which pardoned them. A conqueror, he believed that he had the right to spare the conquered.

Hence arose a conflict, hidden but deep, between these two men. The two stood in different atmospheres; both combating the rebellion, and each having his own thunderbolt,—that of the one, victory; that of the other, terror.

Throughout all the Bocage nothing was talked of but them; and what added to the anxiety of those who watched them from every quarter was the fact that these two men so diametrically opposed were at the same time closely united. These two antagonists were friends. Never sympathy loftier and more profound joined two hearts; the stern had saved the life of the clement, and bore on his face the wound received in the effort. These two men were the incarnation,—the one of life, the other of death; the one was the principle of destruction, the other of peace, and they loved each other. Strange problem! Imagine Orestes merciful and Pylades pitiless. Picture Arimanes the brother of Ormus!

Let us add that the one of the pair who was called "the ferocious," was, at the same time, the most brotherly of men. He dressed the wounded, cared for the sick, passed his days and nights in the ambulance and hospitals, was touched by the sight of barefooted children, had nothing for himself, gave all to the poor. He was present at all the battles; he marched at the head of the columns and in the thickest of the fight, armed,—for he had in his belt a sabre and two pistols,—yet disarmed, because no one had ever seen him draw his sabre or touch his pistols. He faced blows, and did not return them. It was said that he had been a priest.

One of these men was Gauvain; the other was Cimourdain. There was friendship between the two men, but hatred between the two principles; this hidden war could not fail to burst forth. One morning the battle began.

Cimourdain said to Gauvain: "What have we accomplished?"

Gauvain replied: "You know as well as I. I have dispersed Lantenac's bands. He has only a few men left. Then he is driven back to the forest of Fougères. In eight days he will be surrounded."

"And in fifteen days?"

"He will be taken."

"You have read my notice?"

"Yes. Well?"

"He will be shot."

"More clemency! He must be guillotined."

"As for me," said Gauvain, "I am for a military death."

"And I," replied Cimourdain, "for a revolutionary death." He looked Gauvain in the face, and added: "Why did you set at liberty those nuns of the convent of Saint-Marc-le-Blanc?"

"I do not make war on women," answered Gauvain.

"Those women hate the people; and where hate is concerned, one woman outweighs ten men. Why did you refuse to send to the revolutionary tribunal all that herd of old fanatical priests who were taken at Louvigné?"

"I do not make war on old men."

"An old priest is worse than a young one. Rebellion is more dangerous preached by white hairs. Men have faith in wrinkles. No false pity, Gauvain! The regicides are liberators. Keep your eye fixed on the tower of the Temple."

"The Temple tower! I would bring the Dauphin out of it. I do not make war on children."

Cimourdain's eyes grew stern. "Gauvain, learn that it is necessary to make war on a woman when she calls herself Marie Antoinette, on an old man when he is named Pius VI. and Pope, and upon a child when he is named Louis Capet."

"My master, I am not a politician."

"Try not to be a dangerous man. Why, at the attack on the post of Cossé, when the rebel Jean Treton, driven back and lost, flung himself alone, sabre in hand, against the whole column, didst thou cry, 'Open the ranks! Let him pass?'"

"Because one does not set fifteen hundred to kill a single man."

"Why, at the Cailleterie d'Astillé, when you saw your soldiers about to kill the Vendean Joseph Bézier, who was wounded and dragging himself along, did you exclaim, 'Go on before! This is my affair!' and then fire your pistol in the air?"

"Because one does not kill a man on the ground."

"And you were wrong. Both are to-day chiefs of bands. Joseph Bézier is Mustache, and Jean Treton is Jambe d'Argent. In saving those two men you gave two enemies to the Republic."

"Certainly I could wish to give her friends, and not enemies."

"Why, after the victory of Landéan, did you not shoot your three hundred peasant prisoners?"

"Because Bonchamp had shown mercy to the republican prisoners, and I wanted it said that the Republic showed mercy to the royalist prisoners."

"But, then, if you take Lantenac you will pardon him?"

"No."

"Why? Since you showed mercy to the three hundred peasants?"

"The peasants are ignorant men; Lantenac knows what he does."

"But Lantenac is your kinsman."

"France is the nearest."

"Lantenac is an old man."

"Lantenac is a stranger. Lantenac has no age. Lantenac summons the English. Lantenac is invasion. Lantenac is the enemy of the country. The duel between him and me can only finish by his death or mine."

"Gauvain, remember this vow."

"It is sworn."

There was silence, and the two looked at each other.

Then Gauvain resumed: "It will be a bloody date, this year '93 in which we live."

"Take care!" cried Cimourdain. "Terrible duties exist. Do not accuse that which is not accusable. Since when is it that the illness is the fault of the physician? Yes, the characteristic of this tremendous year is its pitilessness. Why? Because it is the grand revolutionary year. This year in which we live is the incarnation of the Revolution. The Revolution has an enemy,—the old world,—and it is without pity for it; just as the surgeon has an enemy,—gangrene,—and is without pity for it. The Revolution extirpates royalty in the king, aristocracy in the noble, despotism in the soldier, superstition in the priest, barbarism in the judge; in a word, everything which is tyranny, in all which is the tyrant. The operation is fearful; the Revolution performs it with a sure hand. As to the amount of sound flesh which it sacrifices, demand of Boerhaave what he thinks in regard to that. What tumour does not cause a loss of blood in its cutting away? Does not the extinguishing of a conflagration demand an energy as fierce as that of the fire itself? These formidable necessities are the very condition of success. A surgeon resembles a butcher; a healer may have the appearance of an executioner. The Revolution devotes itself to its fatal work. It mutilates, but it saves. What! you demand pity for the virus? You wish it to be merciful to that which is poisonous? It will not listen. It holds the post,—it will exterminate it. It makes a deep wound in civilization, from whence will spring health to the human race. You suffer?

Without doubt. How long will it last? The time necessary for the operation. After that you will live. The Revolution amputates the world. Hence this hæmorrhage,—'93."

"The surgeon is calm," said Gauvain, "and the men that I see are violent."

"The Revolution," replied Cimourdain, "needs savage workmen to aid it! It pushes aside every hand that trembles. It has only faith in the inexorables. Danton is the terrible, Robespierre is the inflexible; Saint-Just is the immovable, Marat is the implacable. Take care, Gauvain! these names are necessary. They are worth as much as armies to us; they will terrify Europe."

"And perhaps the future also," said Gauvain. He checked himself, and resumed: "For that matter, my master, you err. I accuse no one. According to me, the true point of view of the Revolution is its irresponsibility. Nobody is innocent, nobody is guilty. Louis XVI. is a sheep thrown among lions: he wishes to escape, he tries to flee, he seeks to defend himself; he would bite if he could. But one is not a lion at will; his craze to be one passes for crime. This enraged sheep shows his teeth: 'The traitor!' cry the lions; and they eat him. That done, they fight among themselves."

"The sheep is a brute."

"And the lions, what are they?"

This retort set Cimourdain to thinking. He raised his head, and answered: "These lions are consciences. These lions are ideas. These lions are principles."

"They produce the reign of Terror."

"One day, the Revolution will be the justification of this Terror."

"Beware lest the Terror become the calumny of the Revolution." Gauvain continued: "Liberty, Equality, Fraternity,—these are the dogmas of peace and harmony. Why give them an alarming aspect? What is it we want? To bring the peoples to a universal republic. Well, do not let us make them afraid. What can intimidation serve? The people can no more be attracted by a scarecrow than birds can. One must not do evil to bring about good; one does not overturn the throne in order to leave the gibbet standing. Death to kings, and life to nations! Strike off the crowns; spare the heads! The Revolution is concord, not fright. Clement ideas are ill served by cruel men. Amnesty is to me the most beautiful word in human language. I will only shed blood in risking my own. Besides, I simply know how to fight; I am nothing but a soldier. But if I may not pardon, victory is not worth the trouble it costs. During battle let us be the enemies of our enemies, and after the victory their brothers."

"Take care!" repeated Cimourdain, for the third time. "Gauvain, you are more to me than a son; take care!" Then he added thoughtfully: "In a period like ours, pity may become one of the forms of treason."

Any one listening to the talk of these two men might have fancied he heard a dialogue between the sword and the axe.

Chapter VIII

DOLOROSA

IN the mean while the mother was seeking her little ones. She went straight forward. How did she live? It is impossible to say; she did not know herself. She walked day and night; she begged, she ate herbs, she lay on the ground, she slept in the open air, in the thickets, under the stars, sometimes in the rain and wind. She wandered from village to village, from farm to farm, seeking a clew. She stopped on the thresholds of the peasants' cots. Her dress was in rags. Sometimes she was welcomed, sometimes she was driven away; when she could not get into the houses, she went into the woods. She did not know the district; she was ignorant of everything except Siscoignard and the parish of Azé. She had no route marked out; she retraced her steps, travelled roads already gone over, made useless journeys; sometimes she followed the highway, sometimes a cart-track, as often the paths among the copses. In these aimless wanderings she had worn out her miserable garments; she had shoes at first, then she walked barefoot, then with her feet bleeding. She crossed the track of warfare, among gun-shots, hearing nothing, seeing nothing, avoiding nothing,—seeking her children. Revolt was everywhere; there were no more gendarmes, no more mayors, no authorities of any sort. She had only to deal with chance passers. She spoke to them, she asked,—

"Have you seen three little children anywhere?"

Those she addressed would look at her.

"Two boys and a girl," she would say, Then she would name them: "René-Jean, Gros-Alain, Georgette. You have not seen them?"

She would ramble on thus: "The eldest is four years and a half old; the little girl is twenty months." Then would come the cry: "Do you know where they are? They have been taken from me."

The listeners would stare at her, and that was all.

When she saw that she was not understood, she would say: "It is because they belong to me,—that is why."

The people would pass on their way. Then she would stand still, uttering no further word, but digging at her breast with her nails.

However, one day, a peasant listened to her. The good man set himself to thinking. "Wait, now," said he. "Three children?"

"Yes."

"Two boys—"

"And a girl."

"You are hunting for them?"

"Yes."

"I have heard talk of a lord who had taken three little children, and had them with him."

"Where is this man?" she cried. "Where are they?"

The peasant replied: "Go to La Tourgue."

"Shall I find my children there?"

"It may easily be."

"You say—"

"La Tourgue."

"What is that,—La Tourgue?"

"It is a place."

"Is it a village, a castle, a farm?"

"I never was there."

"Is it far?"

"It is not near."

"In which direction?"

"Toward Fougères."

"Which way must I go?"

"You are at Ventortes," said the peasant; "you must leave Ernée to the left and Coxelles to the right; you will pass by Lorchamps and cross the Leroux." He pointed his finger to the west. "Always straight before you and toward the sunset."

Ere the peasant had dropped his arm, she was hurrying on.

He cried after her: "But take care. They are fighting over there."

She did not answer or turn round; on she went, straight before her.

Chapter IX

A PROVINCIAL BASTILE

1. *La Tourgue.*

Forty years ago, a traveller who entered the forest of Fougères from the side of Laignelet, and left it toward Parigné, was met on the border of this vast old wood by a sinister spectacle. As he came out of the thickets, La Tourgue rose abruptly before him. Not La Tourgue living, but La Tourgue dead,—La Tourgue cracked, battered, seamed, dismantled.

The ruin of an edifice is as much its ghost as a phantom is that of man. No more lugubrious vision could strike the gaze than that of La Tourgue. What the traveller had before his eyes was a lofty round tower, standing alone at the corner of the wood like a malefactor. This tower, rising from a perpendicular rock, was so severe and solid that it looked almost like a bit of Roman architecture, and the frowning mass gave the idea of strength even amid its ruin. It was Roman in a way, since it was Romanic. Begun in the ninth century, it had been finished in the twelfth, after the third Crusade. The peculiar ornaments of the mouldings told its age. On ascending the height, one perceived a breach in the wall; if one ventured to enter, he found himself within the tower,—it was empty. It resembled somewhat the inside of a stone trumpet set upright on the ground, —from top to bottom no partitions, no ceilings, no floors. There were places where arches and chimneys had been torn away; falconet embrasures were seen; at different heights, rows of granite corbels and a few transverse beams marked where the different stories had been; these beams were covered with the ordure of night-birds. The colossal wall was fifteen feet in thickness at the base and twelve at the summit; here and there were chinks and holes which had been doors, through which one caught glimpses of staircases in the shadowy interior of the wall. The passer-by who penetrated there at evening heard the cry of the wood-owl, the goat-suckers, and the bats, and saw beneath his feet brambles, stones, reptiles, and above his head, across a black circle which looked like the mouth of an enormous well, he could perceive the stars.

The neighbourhood kept a tradition that in the upper stories of this tower there were secret doors formed like those in the tombs of the kings of Judah, of great stones turning on pivots, opening by a spring, and forming part of the wall when closed,—an architectural mystery which the Crusaders had brought from the East along with the pointed arch. When these doors were shut, it was impossible to discover them, so accurately were they fitted into the other stones. At this day such doors may still be seen in those mysterious cities of the Anti-Libanus which escaped the burial of the twelve towns in the time of Tiberius.

2. *The Breach.*

THE breach by which one entered the ruin had been the opening of a mine. For a connoisseur, famiilar with Errard, Sardi, and Pagan, this mine had been skilfully planned. The fire-chamber, shaped like a mitre, was proportioned to the strength of the keep it had been intended to disembowel; it must have held at least two hundred-weight of powder. The channel was serpentine, which does better service than a straight one. The crumbling of the mine left naked among the broken stones the saucisse which had the requisite diameter, that of a hen's egg. The explosion had left a deep rent in the wall by which the besiegers could enter.

This tower had evidently sustained at different periods real sieges conducted according to rule. It was scarred with balls, and these balls were not all of the same epoch. Each projectile has its peculiar way of marking a rampart; and those of every sort had left their traces on this keep, from the stone balls of the fourteenth century to the iron ones of the eighteenth. The breach gave admittance into what must have been the ground-floor. In the wall of the tower opposite the breach there opened the gateway of a crypt cut in the rock, and stretching among the foundations of the tower under the whole extent of the ground-floor hall. This crypt, three fourths filled up, was cleared out in 1855 under the direction of ·Monsieur Auguste le Prévost, the antiquary of Bernay.

3. *The Oubliette.*

THIS crypt was the oubliette. Every keep had one. This crypt, like many penal prisons of that era, had two stories. The upper floor, which was entered by the wicket, was a vaulted chamber of considerable size, on a level with the ground-floor hall. On the walls could be seen two parallel and vertical furrows, extending from one side to the other, and passing along the vault of the roof, in which they had left deep ruts like old wheel-tracks. It was what they were in fact; these two furrows had been hollowed by two wheels. Formerly, in feudal days, victims were torn limb from limb in this chamber by a method less noisy than dragging them at the tails of horses. There had been two wheels, so immense that they touched the walls and the arch. To each of these wheels an arm and a leg of the victim were attached; then the wheels were turned in the inverse direction, which crushed the man. It required great force; hence the furrows which the wheels had worn in the wall as they grazed it. A chamber of this kind may still be seen at Vianden.

Below this room there was another. That was the real dungeon. It was not entered by a door; one penetrated into it by a hole. The victim, stripped naked, was let down by means of a rope placed under his armpits into the dungeon, through an opening left in the centre of the flagging of the upper chamber. If he persisted in living, food was flung to him through this aperture. A hole of this sort may yet be seen at Bouillon. The wind swept up through this opening.

The lower room, dug out beneath the ground-floor hall, was a well rather than a chamber. It had water at the bottom, and an icy wind filled it. This wind, which killed the prisoner in the depths, preserved the life of the captive in the room above; it rendered his prison respirable. The captive above, groping about beneath his vault, only got air by this hole. For the rest, whatever entered or fell there could not get out again. It was for the prisoner to be cautious in the darkness. A false step might make the prisoner in the upper room a prisoner in the dungeon below. That was his affair. If he clung to life, this hole was a peril; if he wished to be rid of it, this hole was his resource. The upper floor was the dungeon; the lower, the tomb, a superposition which resembled society at that period. It was what our ancestors called a moat-dungeon. The thing having disappeared, the name has no longer any significance in our ears. Thanks to the Revolution, we hear the words pronounced with indifference.

Outside the tower, above the breach, which forty years since was the only means of ingress, might be seen an opening larger than the other loophole, from which hung an iron grating bent and loosened.

4. *The Bridge-Castle.*

ON the opposite side from the breach a stone bridge was connected with the tower, having three arches still in almost perfect preservation. This bridge had supported a building of which some fragments remained. It had evidently been destroyed by fire; there were left only portions of the framework, between whose blackened ribs the daylight peeped, as it rose beside the tower like a skeleton beside a phantom. This ruin is to-day completely demolished,—not a trace of it is left. It only needs one day and a single peasant to destroy that which it took many centuries and many kings to build.

La Tourgue is a rustic abbreviation for La Tour-Gauvain, just as *La Jupelle* stands for La Jupellière, and *Pinson-le-Tort,* the nickname of a hunchbacked leader, is put for Pinson-le-Tortu. La Tourgue, which forty years since was a ruin, and which is to-day a shadow, was a fortress in 1793. It was the old bastile of the Gauvains; toward the west guarding the entrance to the forest of Fougères,—a forest which is itself now hardly a grove. This citadel had been built on one of the great blocks of slate which abound between Mayenne and Dinan, scattered everywhere among the thickets and heaths, like missiles that had been flung in some conflict between Titans. The tower made up the entire fortress; beneath the tower was the rock, and at the foot of the rock one of those water-courses which the month of January turns into a torrent, and which the month of June dries up.

Thus protected, this fortress was in the Middle Ages almost impregnable.

The bridge alone weakened it. The Gothic Gauvains had built without bridge. They got into it by one of those swinging foot-bridges which a blow of an axe sufficed to break away. As long as the Gauvains remained viscounts they contented themselves with this; but when they became marquises and left the cavern for the court, they flung three arches across the torrent, and made themselves accessible on the side of the plain just as they had made themselves accessible to the king. The marquises of the seventeenth century and the marquises of the eighteenth no longer wished to be impregnable. An imitation of Versailles replaced the traditions of their ancestors.

Facing the tower, on the western side, was a high plateau which ended in two plains; this plateau almost touched the tower, only separated from it by a very deep ravine, through which ran the water-course, which was a tributary of the Couesnon. The bridge which joined the fortress and the plateau was built up high on piers; and on these piers was constructed, as at Chenonceaux, an edifice in the Mansard style, more habitable than the tower. But customs were still very rude; the lords continued to occupy chambers in the keep which were like dungeons. The building on the bridge, which was a sort of small castle, was made into a long corridor, that served as an entrance, and was called the hall of the guards; above this hall of the guards, which was a kind of entresol, a library was built; above the library, a granary. Long windows, with small panes in Bohemian glass; pilasters between the windows; medallions sculptured on the wall; three stories: below, bartizans and muskets; in the middle, books; on high, sacks of oats,—the whole at once somewhat savage and very princely.

The tower rose gloomy and stern at the side. It overlooked this coquettish building with all its lugubrious height. From its platform one could destroy the bridge.

The two edifices—the one rude, the other elegant—clashed rather than contrasted. The two styles had nothing in keeping with each other. Although it should seem that two semicircles ought to be identical, nothing can be less alike than a Romanic arch and the classic archivault. That tower, in keeping with the forests, made a stronger neighbour for that bridge, worthy of Versailles. Imagine Alain Barte-Torte giving his arm to Louis XIV. The juxtaposition was sinister. These two majesties thus mingled made up a whole which had something inexpressibly menacing in it.

From a military point of view, the bridge (we must insist upon this) was a traitor to the tower. It embellished, but disarmed; in gaining ornament, the fortress lost strength. The bridge put it on a level with the plateau. Still impregnable on the side toward the forest, it became vulnerable toward the plain. Formerly it commanded the plateau; now it was commanded thereby. An enemy installed there would speedily become master of the bridge. The library and the granary would be for the assailant and against the citadel. A library and a granary resemble each other in the fact that both books and straw are combustible. For an assailant who serves himself by fire, to burn Homer or to burn a bundle of straw, provided it make a flame, is all the same; the French proved this to the Germans by burning the library at Heidelberg, and the Germans proved it to the French by burning the library of Strasbourg. This bridge, added to the Tourgue, was, therefore, strategically an error; but in the seventeenth century, under Colbert and Louvois, the Gauvain princes no more considered themselves besiegeable than did the princes of Rohan or the princes of La Trémoille. Still, the builders of the bridge had used certain precautions. In the first place they had foreseen the possibility of conflagration: below the three casements that looked down the stream they had fastened transversely to cramp-irons, which could still be seen half a century back, a strong ladder, whose length equalled the height of the two stories of the bridge,—a height which surpassed that of the three ordinary stories. Secondly, they had guarded against assault,—they had cut off the bridge by means of a low, heavy iron door. This door was arched; it was locked by a great key, which was hidden in a place known to the master alone, and, once closed, this door could defy a battering-ram and almost brave a cannon-ball. It was necessary to cross the bridge in order to reach this door, and to pass through the door in order to enter the tower. There was no other entrance.

5. The Iron Door.

The second story of the castle on the bridge was raised by the arches, so that it corresponded with the second story of the tower. It was at this height, for greater security, that the iron door had been placed. The iron door opened toward the library on the bridge side, and toward a grand vaulted hall, with a pillar in the centre, on the side to the tower.

This hall, as has already been said, was the second story of the keep. It was circular, like the tower; a long loop-hole, looking out on the fields, lighted it. The rude wall was naked, and nothing hid the stones, which were however symmetrically laid. This hall was reached by a winding staircase built in the wall,—a very simple thing when walls are fifteen feet in thickness. In the Middle Ages a town had to be taken street by street; a street, house by house; a house, room by room. A fortress was besieged story by story. In this respect La Tourgue was very skilfully disposed, and was very intractable and difficult. A spiral staircase, at first very steep, led from one floor to the other. The doors were askew, and were not of the height of a man. To pass through, it was necessary to bow the head; now, a head bowed was a head cut off, and at each door the besieged awaited the besiegers.

Below the circular hall with the pillar were two similar chambers, which made the first and the ground floor; and above were three. Upon these six chambers, placed one upon another, the tower was closed by a lid of stone, which was the platform, and which could only be reached by a narrow watch-tower. The fifteen feet thickness of wall which it had been necessary to pierce in order to place the iron door, and in the middle of which it was set, embedded it in a long arch; so that the door when closed was, both on the side toward the tower and on that toward the bridge, under a porch six or seven feet deep; when it was open, these two porches joined and made the entrance-arch.

In the thickness of the wall of the porch toward the bridge opened the low gate of Saint Gilles's screw-stairway, which led into the corridor of the first story beneath the library. This offered another difficulty to besiegers. The small castle of the bridge showed, on the side toward the plateau, only a perpendicular wall; and the bridge was cut there. A draw-bridge put the besieged in communication with the plateau; and this draw-bridge (on account of the height of the plateau, never lowered except at an inclined plane) allowed access to the long corridor, called the guard-room. Once masters of this corridor, besiegers, in order to reach the iron door, would have been obliged to carry by main force the winding staircase which led to the second story.

6. *The Library.*

As for the library, it was an oblong room, the width and length of the bridge, with a single door,—the iron one. A false leaf-door hung with green cloth, which it was only necessary to push, masked in the interior the entrance-arch of the tower. The library wall from floor to ceiling was filled with glazed book-cases, in the beautiful style of the seventeenth-century cabinet-work. Six great windows, three on either side, one above each arch, lighted this library. Through these windows the interior could be seen from the height of the plateau. In the spaces between these windows stood six marble busts on pedestals of sculptured oak,—Hermolaüs, of Byzantium; Athenæus, the grammarian of Naucratis; Suidas; Casaubon; Clovis, King of France; and his chancellor, Anachalus, who for that matter was no more chancellor than Clovis was king.

There were books of various sorts in this library. One has remained famous. It was an old quarto with prints, having for title "Saint Bartholomew," in great letters; and for second title, "Gospel according to Saint Bartholomew, preceded by a dissertation by Pantœnus, Christian philosopher, as to whether this gospel ought to be considered apocryphal, and whether Saint Bartholomew was the same as Nathaniel." This book, considered a unique copy, was placed on a reading-desk in the middle of the library. In the last century, people came to see it as a curiosity.

7. *The Granary.*

As for the granary, which took, like the library, the oblong form of the bridge, it was simply the space beneath the woodwork of the roof. It was a great room filled with straw and hay, and lighted by six Mansard windows. There was no ornament except a figure of Saint Bartholomew carved on the door, with this line beneath,—

"Barnabus sanctus falcem jubet
  ire per herbam."

Thus it was a lofty, wide tower of six stories, pierced here and there with loop-holes, having for entrance and egress a single door of iron leading to a bridge-castle closed by a draw-bridge; behind the tower a forest; in front a plateau of heath, higher than the bridge, lower than the tower; beneath the bridge a deep, narrow ravine full of brushwood,—a torrent in winter, a brook in spring-time, a stony moat in summer.

This was the Tower Gauvain, called La Tourgue.

Chapter X

THE HOSTAGES

July passed; August came. A blast, fierce and heroic, swept over France. Two spectres had just passed beyond the horizon,—Marat with a dagger in his heart, Charlotte Corday headless. Affairs everywhere were waxing formidable.

As to the Vendée, beaten in grand strategic schemes, she took refuge in little ones,—more redoubtable, we have already said. This war was now an immense fight, scattered about among the woods. The disasters of the large army, called the Catholic and Royal, had commenced. The army from Mayence had been ordered into the Vendée. Eight thousand Vendeans had fallen at Ancenis; they had been repulsed from Nantes, dislodged from Montaigu, expelled from Thouars, chased from Noirmoutier, flung headlong out of Cholet, Mortagne, and Saumur; they had evacuated Parthenay, abandoned Clisson, fallen back from Châtillon, lost a flag at Saint-Hilaire; they had been beaten at Pornic, at the Sables, at Fontenay, at Doué, at the Château d'Eau, at the Ponts-de-Cé; they were kept in check at Luçon, were retreating from the Chataigneraye, and were routed at the Roche-sur-Yon. But on the one hand they were menacing Rochelle; and on the other an English fleet in the Guernsey waters, commanded by General Craig, and bearing several English regiments and some of the best officers of the French navy, only waited a signal from the Marquis de Lantenac to land. This landing might make the royalist revolt again victorious.

Pitt was in truth a State malefactor. Policy has treasons sure as an assassin's dagger. Pitt stabbed our country and betrayed his own: to dishonour his country was to betray it. Under him and through him England waged a Punic war; she spied, she cheated, she hid. Poacher and forger, she stopped at nothing; she descended to the very minutiæ of hatred. She monopolized tallow, which cost five francs a pound. An Englishman was taken at Lille on whom was found a letter from Prigent, Pitt's agent in Vendée, which contained these lines:—

"I beg you to spare no money. We hope that the assassinations will be committed with prudence; disguised priests and women are the persons most fit for this duty. Send sixty thousand francs to Rouen and fifty thousand to Caen."

This letter was read in the Convention on the first of August by Barère. The cruelties of Parrein, and later the atrocities of Carrier, replied to these perfidies. The republicans of Metz and the republicans of the South were eager to march against the rebels. A decree ordered the formation of eighty companies of pioneers for burning the copses and thickets of the Bocage. It was an unheard-of crisis. The war only ceased on one footing to begin on another. "No mercy! No prisoners!" was the cry of both parties. The history of that time is black with awful shadows.

During this month of August, La Tourgue was besieged. One evening, just as the stars were rising amid the calm twilight of the dog-days, when not a leaf stirred in the forest, not a blade of grass trembled on the plain, across the stillness of the night swept the sound of a horn. This horn was blown from the top of the tower. The peal was answered by the voice of a clarion from below. On the summit of the tower stood an armed man; at the foot, a camp spread out in the shadow.

In the obscurity about the Tower Gauvain could be distinguished a moving mass of black shapes. It was a bivouac. A few fires began to blaze beneath the trees of the forest and among the heaths of the plateau, pricking the darkness here and there with luminous points, as if the earth were studding itself with stars at the same instant as the sky; but they were the sinister stars of war. On the side toward the plateau the bivouac stretched out to the plains, and on the forest side extended into the thicket. La Tourgue was invested.

The outstretch of the besiegers' bivouac indicated a numerous force. The camp tightly clasped the fortress, coming close up to the rock on the side toward the tower, and close to the ravine on the bridge side.

There was a second sound of the horn, followed by another peal from the clarion. This time the horn questioned, and the trumpet replied. It was the demand of the tower to the camp: "Can we speak to you?" The clarion was the answer for the camp; "Yes."

At this period the Vendeans, not being considered belligerents by the Convention, and a decree having forbidden the exchange of flags of truce with "the brigands," the armies supplemented as they could the means of communication which the law of nations authorizes in ordinary war and interdicts in civil strife. Hence on occasion a certain understanding between the peasant's horn and the military trumpet. The first call was only to attract attention; the second put the question, "Will you listen?" If on this second summons the clarion kept silent, it was a refusal; if the clarion replied, it was a consent. It signified, "Truce for a few moments."

The clarion having answered the second appeal, the man on the top of the tower spoke, and these words could be heard:—

"Men, who listen to me, I am Gouge le-Bruant, surnamed Brise-Bleu because I have exterminated many of yours; surnamed also Imânus, because I mean to kill still more than I have already done. My finger was cut off by a blow from a sabre on the barrel of my gun in the attack of Granville; at Laval you guillotined my father, my mother, and my sister Jacqueline, aged eighteen. This is who I am. I speak to you in the name of my lord Marquis Gauvain de Lantenac, Viscount de Fontenay, Breton prince, lord of the Seven Forests,—my master.

"Learn, first, that Monseigneur the Marquis, before shutting himself in this tower where you hold him blockaded, distributed the command among six chiefs, his lieutenants. He gave to Delière the district between the road to Brest and the road to Ernée; to Tréton, the district between Roë and Laval; to

Jacquet, called Taillefer, the border of the Haut-Maine; to Gaulier, named Grand Pierre, Château Gontier; to Lecomte, Craon; to Dubois Guy, Fougères; and to De Rochambeau, all of Mayenne. So the taking of this fortress will not end matters for you; and even if Monseigneur the Marquis should die, the Vendée of God and the king will still live. That which I say—know this—is to warn you. Monseigneur is here by my side; I am the mouth through which his words pass. You who are besieging us, keep silence. This is what it is important for you to hear:—

"Do not forget that the war you are making against us is without justice. We are men inhabiting our own country, and we fight honestly; we are simple and pure,—beneath the will of God, as the grass is beneath the dew. It is the Republic which has attacked us; she comes to trouble us in our fields; she has burned our houses, our harvests, and ruined our farms, while our women and children were forced to wander with naked feet among the woods when the winter robin was still singing. You who are down there and who hear me, you have enclosed us in the forest and surrounded us in this tower; you have killed or dispersed those who joined us; you have cannon; you have added to your troop the garrisons and posts of Mortain, of Barenton, of Teilleul, of Landivy, of Evran, of Tinteniac, and of Vitré—by which means you are four thousand five hundred soldiers who attack us; and we—we are nineteen men who defend ourselves. You have provisions and munitions. You have succeeded in mining and blowing up a corner of our rock and a bit of our wall. That has made a gap at the foot of the tower, and this gap is a breach by which you can enter, although it is not open to the sky; and the tower, still upright and strong, makes an arch above it. Now, you are preparing the assault; and we,—first, Monseigneur the Marquis, who is Prince of Brittany, and secular Prior of the Abbey of Saint Marie de Lantenac, where a daily Mass was established by Queen Jeanne; and, next to him, the other defenders of the tower, who are the Abbé Turmeau, whose military name is Grand Francœur; my comrade Guinoiseau, who is captain of Camp Vert; my comrade Chante-en-Hiver, who is captain of Camp Avoine; my comrade Musette, who is captain of Camp Fourmis; and I, peasant, born in the town of Daon, through which runs the brook Moriandre,—we all, all have one thing to say to you. Men, who are at the bottom of this tower, listen!

"We have on our hands three prisoners, who are three children. These children were adopted by one of your regiments, and they belong to you. We offer to surrender these three children to you, on one condition; it is that we shall depart freely. If you refuse, listen well. You can only attack us in one of two ways,—by the breach, on the side of the forest; or by the bridge, on the side of the plateau. The building on the bridge has three stories; in the lower story, I, Imânus—I who speak to you—have put six hogsheads of tar and a hundred fascines of dried heath; in the top story there is straw; in the middle story there are books and papers. The iron door which communicates between the bridge and the tower is closed and Monseigneur carries the key; I have myself made a hole under the door, and through this hole passes a sulphur slow-match, one end of which is in the tar and the other within reach of my hand, inside the tower. I can fire it when I choose. If you refuse to let us go out, the three children will be placed in the second floor of the bridge, between the story where the sulphur-match touches the tar and the floor where the straw is, and the iron door will be shut on them. If you attack by the bridge, it will be you who set the building on fire; if you attack by the breach it will be we; if you attack by the breach and the bridge at the same time, the fire will be kindled at the same instant by us both, and, in any case, the three children will perish.

"Now, accept or refuse. If you accept, we come out. If you refuse, the children die. I have spoken."

The man speaking from the top of the tower became silent. A voice from below cried: "We refuse!"

This voice was abrupt and severe. Another voice, less harsh, though firm, added: "We give you four-and-twenty hours to surrender at discretion." There was a silence, then the same voice continued: "To-morrow, at this hour, if you have not surrendered, we commence the assault."

And the first voice resumed: "And then no quarter!"

To this savage voice another replied from the top of the tower! Between the two battlements a lofty figure bent forward, and in the starlight the stern face of the Marquis de Lantenac could be distinguished; his sombre glance shot down into the obscurity and seemed to look for some one; and he cried: "Hold, it is thou, priest!"

"Yes, traitor; it is I," replied the stern voice from below.

Chapter XI

TERRIBLE AS THE ANTIQUE

THE implacable voice was, in truth, that of Cimourdain; the younger and less imperative that of Gauvain.

The Marquis de Lantenac did not deceive himself in fancying that he recognized Cimourdain. As we know, a few weeks in this district, made bloody by civil war, had rendered Cimourdain famous; there was no notoriety more darkly sinister than his. People said: Marat at Paris, Châlier at Lyons, Cimourdain in Vendée. They stripped the Abbé Cimourdain of all the respect which he had formerly commanded; that is the consequence of a priest's unfrocking himself. Cimourdain inspired horror. The severe are unfortunate; those who note their acts condemn them, though perhaps, if their consciences could be seen, they would stand absolved. A Lycurgus misunderstood appears a Tiberius. Those two men, the Marquis de Lantenac and the Abbé Cimourdain, were equally poised in the balance of hatred. The maledictions of the royalists against Cimourdain made a counterpoise to the execrations of the republicans against Lantenac. Each of these men was a monster to the opposing camp; so far did this equality go, that while Prieur, of the Marne, was setting a price on the head of Lantenac, Charette at Noirmoutiers set a price on the head of

Cimourdain. Let us add, these two men—the marquis and the priest—were up to a certain point the same man. The bronze mask of civil war has two profiles,—the one turned toward the past, the other set toward the future; but both equally tragic. Lantenac was the first of these profiles, Cimourdain the second; only, the bitter sneer of Lantenac was full of shadow and night, and on the fatal brow of Cimourdain shone a gleam from the morning.

And now the besieged of La Tourgue had a respite. Thanks to the intervention of Gauvain, a sort of truce for twenty-four hours had been agreed upon.

Imânus had, indeed, been well informed. Through the requisitions of Cimourdain, Gauvain had now four thousand five hundred men under his command, part national guards, part troops of the Line; with these he had surrounded Lantenac in La Tourgue, and was able to level twelve cannon at the fortress,—a masked battery of six pieces on the edge of the forest toward the tower, and an open battery of six on the plateau, toward the bridge. He had succeeded in springing the mine and making a breach at the foot of the tower.

This, when the twenty-four hours' truce was ended, the attack would begin under these conditions: On the plateau and in the forest were four thousand five hundred men. In the tower nineteen! History might find the names of those besieged nineteen in the list of outlaws. We shall perhaps encounter them.

As commander of these four thousand five hundred men, which almost made an army, Cimourdain had wished Gauvain to allow himself to be made adjutant-general. Gauvain refused, saying, "When Lantenac is taken, we will see. As yet, I have merited nothing." Those great commands, with low regimental rank, were, for that matter, a custom among the republicans. Bonaparte was, after this, at the same time colonel of artillery and general-in-chief of the army of Italy.

The Tower Gauvain had a strange destiny,—a Gauvain attacked, a Gauvain defended it. From that fact rose a certain reserve in the attack, but not in the defence; for Lantenac was a man who spared nothing. Moreover, he had always lived at Versailles, and had no personal associations with La Tourgue, which he scarcely knew indeed. He had sought refuge there because he had no other asylum,—that was all; he would have demolished it without scruple. Gauvain had more respect for the place.

The weak point of the fortress was the bridge; but in the library, which was on the bridge, were the family archives. If the assault took place on that side, the burning of the bridge would be inevitable. To burn the archives seemed to Gauvain like attacking his forefathers. La Tourgue was the ancestral dwelling of the Gauvains; in this tower centred all their fiefs of Brittany, just as all the fiefs of France centred in the tower of the Louvre. The home associations of Gauvain were there; he had been born within those walls. The tortuous fatalities of life forced him, a man, to attack this venerable pile which had sheltered him when a child. Could he be guilty of the impiety of reducing this dwelling to ashes? Perhaps his very cradle was stored in some corner of the granary above the library. Certain reflections are emotions. Gauvain felt himself moved in the presence of this ancient house of his family. That was why he had spared the bridge. He had confined himself to making any sally or escape impossible by this outlet, and had guarded the bridge by a battery, and chosen the opposite side for the attack. Hence the mining and sapping at the foot of the tower.

Cimourdain had allowed him to take his own way. He reproached himself for it; his stern spirit revolted against all these Gothic relics, and he no more believed in pity for buildings than for men. Sparing a castle was a beginning of clemency. Now, clemency was Gauvain's weak point. Cimourdain, as we have seen, watched him,—drew him back from this, in his eyes, fatal weakness. Still, he himself, though he felt a sort of rage in being forced to admit it to his soul, had not revisited La Tourgue without a secret shock; he felt himself softened at the sight of that study where were still the first books he had made Gauvain read. He had been the priest of the neighbouring village, Parigné; he, Cimourdain, had dwelt in the attic of the bridge-castle; it was in the library that he had held Gauvain between his knees as a child, and taught him to lisp out the alphabet; it was within those four old walls that he had seen grow this well-beloved pupil, the son of his soul, increase physically and strengthen in mind. This library, this small castle, these walls full of his blessings upon the child,—was he about to overturn and burn them? He had shown them mercy,—not without remorse. He had allowed Gauvain to open the siege from the opposite point. La Tourgue had its savage side, the tower, and its civilized side, the library. Cimourdain had allowed Gauvain to batter a breach in the savage side alone.

In truth, attacked by a Gauvain, defended by a Gauvain, this old dwelling returned in the height of the French Revolution to feudal customs. Wars between kinsmen make up the history of the Middle Ages: the Eteocles and Polynices are Gothic as well as Grecian, and Hamlet does at Elsinore what Orestes did in Argos.

Chapter XII

POSSIBLE ESCAPE

The whole night was consumed in preparations on the one side and the other. As soon as the sombre parley which we have just heard had ended, Gauvain's first act was to call his lieutenant.

Guéchamp, of whom it will be necessary to know somewhat, was a man of second-rate, honest, intrepid, mediocre; a better soldier than leader; rigorously intelligent up to the point where it ceases to be a duty to understand; never softened; inaccessible to corruption of any sort,—whether of venality, which corrupts the conscience; or of pity, which corrupts justice. He had on soul and heart those two shades,—discipline and the countersign, as a horse has his blinkers on both eyes; and he walked unflinchingly in the space thus left visible to him. His way was straight, but narrow. A man to be depended on; rigid in command, exact in obedience.

Gauvain spoke rapidly to him. "Guéchamp, a ladder."

"Commandant, we have none."

"One must be had."

"For scaling?"

"No, for escape."

Guéchamp reflected an instant, then answered: "I understand. But for what you want, it must be very high."

"At least three stories."

"Yes, Commandant, that is pretty nearly the height."

"It must even go beyond that, for we must be certain of success."

"Without doubt."

"How does it happen that you have no ladder?"

"Commandant, you did not think best to besiege La Tourgue by the plateau; you contented yourself with blockading it on this side. You wished to attack, not by the bridge, but the tower; so we only busied ourselves with the mine, and the escalade was given up. That is why we have no ladders."

"Have one made immediately."

"A ladder three stories high cannot be improvised."

"Have several short ladders joined together."

"One must have them in order to do that."

"Find them."

"There are none to be found. All through the country the peasants destroy the ladders, just as they break up the carts and cut the bridges."

"It is true; they try to paralyze the Republic."

"They want to manage so that we can neither transport baggage, cross a river, nor escalade a wall."

"Still, I must have a ladder."

"I just remember, Commandant, at Javené, near Fougères, there is a large carpenter's shop. They might have one there."

"There is not a minute to lose."

"When do you want the ladder?"

"To-morrow at this hour, at the latest."

"I will send an express full speed to Javené. He can take a requisition. There is a post of cavalry at Javené which will furnish an escort. The ladder can be here to-morrow before sunset."

"It is well; that will answer," said Gauvain. "Act quickly; go."

Ten minutes after, Guéchamp came back and said to Gauvain: "Commandant, the express has started for Javené."

Gauvain ascended the plateau and remained for a long time with his eyes fixed on the bridge-castle across the ravine. The gable of the building, without other means of access than the low entrance closed by the raising of the draw-bridge, faced the escarpment of the ravine. In order to reach the arches of the bridge from the plateau, it was necessary to descend this escarpment,—a feat possible to accomplish by clinging to the brushwood. But once in the moat, the assailants would be exposed to all the projectiles that might rain from the three stories.

Gauvain finished by convincing himself that at the point which the siege had reached, the veritable attack ought to be by the breach of the tower. He took every measure to render any escape out of the question; he increased the strictness of the investment; drew closer the ranks of his battalions, so that nothing could pass between. Gauvain and

Cimourdain divided the investment of the fortress between them. Gauvain reserved the forest side for himself, and gave Cimourdain the side of the plateau. It was agreed that while Gauvain, seconded by Guéchamp, conducted the assault through the mine, Cimourdain should guard the bridge and ravine, with every match of the open battery lighted.

Chapter XIII

WHAT THE MARQUIS WAS DOING

While without every preparation for the attack was going on, within everything was preparing for resistance.

It is not without a real analogy that a tower is called a "douve;" and sometimes a tower is breached by a mine, as a cask is bored by an auger. The wall opens like a bunghole. This was what had happened at La Tourgue. The great blast of two or three hundredweight of powder had burst the mighty wall through and through. This breach started from the foot of the tower, traversed the wall in its thickest part, and made a sort of shapeless arch in the ground-floor of the fortress. On the outside the besiegers, in order to render this gap practicable for assault, had enlarged and finished it off by cannon-shots.

The ground-floor which this breach penetrated was a great round hall, entirely empty, with a central pillar which supported the keystone of the vaulted roof This chamber, the largest in the whole keep, was not less than forty feet in diameter. Each story of the tower was composed of a similar room, but smaller, with guards to the embrasures of the loop-holes. The ground-floor chamber had neither loop-holes nor air-holes; there was about as much air and light as in a tomb. The door of the dungeon, made more of iron than wood, was in this ground-floor room. Another door opened upon a staircase which led to the upper chambers. All the staircases were contrived in the interior of the wall. It was into this lower room that the besiegers could arrive by the breach they had made, This hall taken, there would still be the tower to take. It had always been impossible to breathe in that hall for any length of time. Nobody ever passed twenty-four hours there without suffocating. Now, thanks to the breach, one could exist there. That was why the besieged had not closed the breach. Besides, of what service would it have been? The cannon would have reopened it. They stuck an iron torch-holder into the wall, and put a torch in it, which lighted the ground-floor.

Now, how to defend themselves? To wall up the hole would be easy, but useless. A retirade would be of more service. A retirade is an intrenchment with a re-entering angle,—a sort of rafted barricade, which admits of converging the fire upon the assailants, and while leaving the breach open exteriorly blocks it on the inside. Materials were not lacking. They constructed a retirade with fissures for the passage of the gun-barrels. The angle was supported by the central pillar; the wings touched the wall on either side.

The marquis directed everything. Inspirer, commander, guide, and master, —a terrible spirit. Lantenac belonged to that race of warriors of the eighteenth century, who at eighty years saved cities. He resembled that Count d'Alberg who, almost a centenarian, drove the King of Poland from Riga. "Courage, friends," said the marquis; "at the commencement of this century, in 1713, at Bender, Charles XII., shut up in a house with three hundred Swedes, held his own against twenty thousand Turks."

They barricaded the two lower floors, fortified the chambers, battlemented the alcoves, supported the doors with joists driven in by blows from a mallet; and thus formed a sort of buttress. It was necessary to leave free the spiral staircase which joined the different floors, for they must be able to get up and down, and to stop it against the besiegers would have been to close it against themselves. The defence of any place has thus always some weak side.

The marquis, indefatigable, robust as a young man, set an example,—lifted beams, carried stones, put his hand to the work, commanded, aided, fraternized, laughed with this ferocious clan, but remained always the noble still,—haughty, familiar, elegant, savage. He permitted no reply to his orders. He said "If the half of you should revolt, I would have them shot by the other half, and defend the place with those that were left." Such things make a leader adored.

Chapter XIV

WHAT IMÂNUS WAS DOING

While the marquis occupied himself with the breach and the tower, Imânus was busy with the bridge. At the beginning of the siege, the escape-ladder which hung transversely below the windows of the second story had been removed by the marquis's orders, and Imânus had put it in the library. (It was, perhaps, the loss of this ladder which Gauvain wished to supply.) The windows of the lower floor, called the guard-room, were defended by a triple bracing of iron bars set in the stone, so that neither ingress nor egress was possible by them. The library windows had no bars, but they were very high.

Imânus took three men with him, who, like himself, possessed capabilities and resolution that would carry them through anything: these men were Hoisnard, called Branche d'Or, and the two brothers Pique-en-Bois. Imânus, carrying a dark lantern, opened the iron door and carefully visited the three stories of the bridge-castle. Branche d'Or was implacable as Imânus, having had a brother killed by the republicans. Imânus examined the upper room filled with hay and straw, and the ground-floor, where he had several fire-pots added to the tuns of tar; he placed the heap of fascines so that they touched the casks, and assured himself of the good condition of the sulphur-match, of which one end was in the bridge and the other in the tower. He spread over the floor, under the tuns and fascines, a pool of tar, in which he dipped the end of the sulphur-match. Then he brought into the library, between the ground-floor where the tar was and the garret filled with straw, the three cribs in which lay René-Jean, Gros-Alain, and Georgette, buried in deep sleep. They carried the cradles very gently in order not to awaken the little ones. They were simple village cribs, a sort of low osier-basket, which stood on the floor so that a child could get out unaided. Near each cradle Imânus placed a porringer of soup, with a wooden spoon. The escape-ladder, unhooked from its cramping-irons, had been set on the floor against the wall; Imânus arranged the three cribs, end to end, in front of the ladder. Then, thinking that a current of air might be useful, he opened wide the six windows of the library; the summer night was warm and starlight. He sent the brothers Pique-en-Bois to open the windows of the upper and lower stories. He had noticed on the eastern façade of the building a great dried old ivy, the colour of tinder, which covered one whole side of the bridge from top to bottom, and framed in the windows of the three stories. He thought this ivy might be left.

Imânus took a last watchful glance at everything; that done, the four men left the châtelet and returned to the tower. Imânus double-locked the heavy iron door, studied attentively the enormous bolts, and nodded his head in a satisfied way at the sulphur-match which passed through the hole he had drilled, and was now the sole communication between the tower and the bridge. This train or wick started from the round chamber, passed beneath the iron door, entered under the arch, twisted like a snake down the spiral stair-case leading to the lower story of the bridge, crept over the floor, and ended in the heap of dried fascines laid on the pool of tar. Imânus had calculated that it would take about a quarter of an hour for this wick, when lighted in the interior of the tower, to set fire to the pool of tar under the library. These arrangements all concluded, and every work carefully inspected, he carried the key of the iron door back to the marquis, who put it in his pocket.

It was important that every movement of the besiegers should be watched. Imânus, with his cowherd's horn in his belt, posted himself as sentinel on the watch-tower of the platform at the top of the tower. While keeping a constant look-out, one eye on the forest and one on the plateau, he worked at making cartridges, having near him, in the embrasure of the watch-tower window, a powder-horn, a canvas-bag full of good-sized balls, and some old newspapers, which he tore up for wadding.

When the sun rose it lighted in the forest eight battalions, with sabres at their sides, knapsacks on their backs, and guns with fixed bayonets, ready for the assault; on the plateau, a battery with caissons, cartridges, and boxes of case-shot; within the fortress, nineteen men loading several guns, muskets, blunderbusses, and pistols,—and three children sleeping in their cradles.

BOOK III

The Massacre of Saint Bartholomew

Chapter I

THE CHILDREN

The children woke. The little girl was the first to open her eyes. The waking of children is like the unclosing of flowers,—a perfume seems to exhale from those fresh young souls.

Georgette, twenty months old, the youngest of the three who was still a nursing baby in the month of May, raised her little head, sat up in her cradle, looked at her feet, and began to chatter. A ray of the morning fell across her crib; it would have been difficult to decide which was the rosiest,—Georgette's foot or Aurora. The other two still slept; the slumber of boys is heavier. Georgette, gay and happy, began to chatter. René-Jean's hair was brown, Gros-Alain's was auburn, Georgette's blond. These tints would change later in life. René-Jean had the look of an infant Hercules; he slept lying on his stomach, with his two fists in his eyes. Gros-Alain had thrust his legs outside his little bed.

All three were in rags. The garments given them by the battalion of the Bonnet Rouge had worn to shreds; they had not even a shirt between them. The two boys were almost naked; Georgette was muffled in a rag which had once been a petticoat, but was now little more than a jacket. Who had taken care of these children? Impossible to say. Not a mother. These savage peasant fighters, who dragged them along from forest to forest, had given them their portion of soup. That was all. The little ones lived as they could. They had everybody for master, and nobody for father. But even about the rags of childhood there hangs a halo. These three tiny creatures were lovely.

Georgette prattled. A bird sings, a child prattles; but it is the same hymn, —hymn indistinct, inarticulate, but full of profound meaning. The child, unlike the bird, has the sombre destiny of humanity before it: this thought saddens any man who listens to the joyous song of a child. The most sublime psalm that can be heard on this earth is the lisping of a human soul from the lips of childhood. This confused murmur of thought which is as yet only instinct, holds a strange unreasoning appeal to eternal justice; perchance it is a protest against life while standing on its threshold,—a protest unconscious, yet heart-rending. This ignorance, smiling at infinity, lays upon all creation the burden of the destiny which shall be offered to this feeble, unarmed creature; if unhappiness comes, it seems like a betrayal of confidence. The babble of an infant is more and less than speech: it is not measured, and yet it is a song; not syllables, and yet a language,—a murmur that began in heaven, and will not finish on earth; it commenced before human birth, and will continue in the sphere beyond! These lispings are the echo of what the child said when he was an angel, and of what he will say when he enters eternity. The cradle has a yesterday, just as the grave has a to-morrow: this morrow and this yesterday join their double mystery in that incomprehensible warbling; and there is no such proof of God, of eternity, and the duality of destiny, as in this awe-inspiring shadow flung across that flower-like soul.

There was nothing saddening in Georgette's prattle; her whole lovely face was a smile. Her mouth smiled, her eyes smiled, the dimples in her cheeks smiled. There was a serene acceptance of the morning in this smile. The soul has faith in the sunlight. The sky was blue, warm, beautiful. This frail creature, who knew nothing, who comprehended nothing, softly cradled in a dream which was not thought, felt herself in safety amidst the loveliness of Nature,—these sturdy trees, this pure verdure, this landscape fair and peaceful, with its noises of birds, brooks, insects, leaves, above which glowed the brightness of the sun.

After Georgette, René-Jean, the eldest, who was past four, awoke. He sat up, jumped in a manly way over the side of his cradle, found out the porringer, considered that quite natural, and so sat down on the floor and began to eat his soup.

Georgette's prattle had not awakened Gros-Alain, but at the sound of the spoon in the porringer he turned over with a start, and opened his eyes. Gros-Alain was the one three years old. He saw his bowl; he had only to stretch out his arm and take it. So, without leaving his bed, he followed René-Jean's example, seized the spoon in his little fists, and began to eat, holding the bowl on his knees.

Georgette did not hear them; the modulations of her voice seemed measured by the cradling of a dream. Her gerat eyes, gazing upward, were divine. No matter how dark the ceiling in the vault above the child's head, heaven is reflected in its eyes.

When René-Jean had finished his portion, he scraped the bottom of the bowl with his spoon, sighed, and said with dignity, "I have eaten my soup."

This roused Georgette from her reverie. "Thoup!" said she. Seeing René-Jean had eaten, and that Gros-Alain was eating, she took the porringer which was placed by her cradle, and began to eat in her turn,—not without carrying the spoon to her ear much oftener than to her mouth. From time to time she renounced civilization, and ate with her fingers.

When Gros-Alain had scraped the bottom of his porringer too, he leaped out of bed and joined his brother.

Chapter II

THE JOURNEY

Suddenly from without, down below, on the side of the forest, came the stern, loud ring of a trumpet. To this clarion-blast a horn from the top of the tower replied. This time it was the clarion which called, and the horn which made answer. The clarion blew a second summons, and the horn again replied. Then from the edge of the forest rose a voice, distant but clear, which cried thus:—

"Brigands, a summons! If at sunset

you have not surrendered at discretion, we commence the attack."

A voice, which sounded like the roar of a wild animal, responded from the summit of the tower: "Attack!"

The voice from below resumed: "A cannon will be fired, as a last warning, half an hour before the assault."

The voice from on high repeated: "Attack!"

These voices did not reach the children, but the trumpet and the horn rose loud and clear. At the first sound of the clarion, Georgette lifted her head, and stopped eating; at the sound of the horn, she dropped her spoon into the porringer; at the second blast of the trumpet, she lifted the little forefinger of her right hand, and, raising and depressing it in turn, marked the cadences of the flourish which prolonged the blast. When the trumpet and the horn ceased, she remained with her finger pensively lifted, and murmured, in a half voice, "Muthic." We suppose that she wished to say, "Music."

The two elders, René-Jean and Gros-Alain, had paid no attention to the trumpet and horn; they were absorbed by something else: a wood-louse was just making a journey across the library floor.

Gros-Alain perceived it, and cried: "There is a little creature!" René-Jean ran up. Gros-Alain continued: "It stings."

"Do not hurt it," said René-Jean.

And both remained watching the traveller.

Georgette proceeded to finish her soup; that done, she looked about for her brothers. René-Jean and Gros-Alain were in the recess of one of the windows, gravely stooping over the wood-louse,—their foreheads touching, their curls mingling. They held their breath in wonder, and examined the insect, which had stopped, and did not attempt to move, though not appreciating the admiration it received.

Georgette seeing that her brothers were watching something, must needs know what it was. It was not an easy matter to reach them; still she undertook the journey. The way was full of difficulties. There were things scattered over the floor. There were footstools overturned, heaps of old papers, packing-cases forced open and empty, trunks, rubbish of all sorts, in and out of which it was necessary to sail,—a whole archipelago of reefs; but Georgette risked it. The first task was to get out of her crib; then she entered the chain of reefs, twisted herself through the straits,—pushed a footstool aside, crept between two coffers, got over a heap of papers, climbing up one side and rolling down the other, regardless of the exposure to her poor little naked legs, and succeeded in reaching what a sailor would have called an open sea,—that is, a sufficiently wide space of the floor which was not littered over, and where there were no more perils; then she bounded forward, traversed this space, which was the whole width of the room, on all fours with the agility of a kitten, and got near to the window. There a fresh and formidable obstacle encountered her: the great ladder lying along the wall reached to this window, the end of it passing a little beyond the corner of the recess; it formed between Georgette and her brothers a sort of cape, which must be crossed. She stopped and meditated; her internal monologue ended, she came to a decision. She resolutely twisted her rosy fingers about one of the rungs, which were vertical, as the ladder lay along its side; she tried to raise herself on her feet, and fell back; she began again, and fell a second time; the third effort was more successful. Then, standing up, she caught hold of the rounds in succession, and walked the length of the ladder. When she reached the extremity there was nothing more to support her; she tottered, but seizing in her two hands the end of one of the great poles, which held the rungs, she rose again, doubled the promontory, looked at René-Jean and Gros-Alain, and began to laugh.

Chapter III

THE GOOD GOD

At that instant, René-Jean, satisfied with the result of his investigations of the wood-louse, raised his head, and announced, "'T is a she-creature."

Georgette's laughter made René-Jean laugh, and René-Jean's laughter made Gros-Alain laugh. Georgette seated herself beside her brothers, the recess forming a sort of little reception chamber; but their guest, the wood-louse, had disappeared. He had taken advantage of Georgette's laughter to hide himself in a crack of the floor.

Other incidents followed the wood-louse's visit. First, a flock of swallows passed. They probably had their nests under the edge of the overhanging roof. They flew close to the window, a little startled by the sight of the children, describing great circles in the air, and uttering their melodious spring song. The sound made the three little ones look up, and the wood-louse was forgotten.

Georgette pointed her finger toward the swallows, and cried, "Chicks!"

René-Jean reprimanded her. "Miss, you must not say 'chicks;' they are birds."

"Birz," repeated Georgette.

And all three sat and watched the swallows.

Then a bee entered. There is nothing so like a soul as a bee. It goes from flower to flower as a soul from star to star, and gathers honey as the soul does light. This visitor made a great noise as it came in; it buzzed at the top of its voice, seeming to say, "I have come! I have first been to see the roses, now I come to see the children. What is going on here?" A bee is a house-wife; its song is a grumble. The children did not take their eyes off the new-comer as long as it stayed with them. The bee explored the library, rummaged in the corners, fluttered about with the air of being at home in a hive, and wandered, winged and melodious, from book-case to book-case, examining the titles of the volumes through the glass doors as if it had an intellect. Its explorations finished, it departed.

"She is going to her own house," said René-Jean.

"It is a beast," said Gros-Alain.

"No," replied René-Jean, "it is a fly."

"A f'y," said Georgette.

Thereupon Gros-Alain, who had just found on the floor a cord with a knot in one end, took the opposite extremity between his thumb and forefinger, and made a sort of windmill of the string, watching its whirls with profound attention.

On her side, Georgette, having turned into a quadruped again, and recommenced her capricious course back and forward across the floor, discovered a venerable tapestry-covered armchair, so eaten by moths that the horse-hair stuck out in several places. She stopped before this seat. She enlarged the holes, and diligently pulled out the long hairs. Suddenly she lifted one finger; that meant, "Listen!"

The two brothers turned their heads. A vague, distant noise surged up from without: it was probably the attacking camp executing some strategic manœuvre in the forest, horses neighed, drums beat, caissons rolled, chains clanked, military calls and responses,— a confusion of savage sounds, whose mingling formed a sort of harmony. The children listened in delight.

"It is the good God who does that," said René-Jean.

Chapter IV

THE GALLOP

The noise ceased. René-Jean remained lost in a dream. How do ideas vanish and reform themselves in the brains of those little ones? What is the mysterious motive of those memories at once so troubled and so brief? There was in that sweet, pensive little soul a mingling of ideas of the good God, of prayer, of joined hands, the light of a tender smile it had formerly known and knew no longer; and René-Jean murmured, half aloud, "Mamma!"

"Mamma!" repeated Gros-Alain.

"Mamma!" cried Georgette.

Then René-Jean began to leap. Seeing this, Gros-Alain leaped too. Gros-Alain repeated every movement and gesture of his brother. Three years copies four years; but twenty months keeps its independence.

Georgette remained seated, uttering a word from time to time. Georgette could not yet manage sentences. She was a thinker; she spoke in apothegms; she was monosyllabic. Still, after a little, example proved infectious and she ended by trying to imitate her brothers; and these three little pairs of naked feet began to dance, to run, to totter amidst the dust of the old polished oak floor, beneath the grave aspects of the marble busts toward which Georgette from time to time cast an unquiet glance, murmuring "Momommes." Probably in Georgette's language this signified something which looked like a man, but yet was not one,—perhaps the first glimmering of an idea in regard to phantoms. Georgette, oscillating rather than walking, followed her brothers, but her favourite mode of locomotion was on all fours.

Suddenly René-Jean, who had gone near a window, lifted his head, then dropped it, and hastened to hide himself in a corner of the wall made by the projecting window recess. He had just caught sight of a man looking at him. It was a soldier, from the encampment of the Blues on the plateau, who profiting by the truce, and perhaps infringing it a little, had ventured to the very edge of the escarpment, whence the interior of the library was visible. Seeing René-Jean hide himself, Gros-Alain hid too; he crouched down beside his brother, and Georgette hurried to hide herself behind them. So they remained, silent, motionless, Georgette pressing her finger against her lips. After a few instants, René-Jean ventured to thrust out his head; the soldier was there still. René-Jean retreated quickly, and the three little ones dared not even breathe. This suspense lasted for some time. Finally the fear began to bore Georgette; she gathered courage to look out. The soldier had disappeared. They began again to run about and play.

Gros-Alain, although the imitator and admirer of René-Jean, had a specialty,— that of discoveries. His brother and sister saw him suddenly galloping wildly about, dragging after him a little cart, which he had unearthed behind some box. This doll's wagon had lain forgotten for years among the dust, living amicably in the neighbourhood of the printed works of genius and the busts of sages. It was, perhaps, one of the toys that Gauvain had played with when a child.

Gros-Alain had made a whip of his string, and cracked it loudly; he was very proud. Such are discoverers. The child discovers a little wagon; the man, an America: the spirit of adventure is the same.

But it was necessary to share the godsend. René-Jean wished to harness himself to the carriage, and Georgette wished to ride in it. She succeeded in seating herself. René-Jean was the horse. Gros-Alain was the coachman. But the coachman did not understand his business; the horse began to teach him. René-Jean shouted, "Say 'Whoa!'"

"Whoa!" repeated Gros-Alain.

The carriage upset. Georgette rolled out. Child-angels can shriek; Georgette did so. She had a vague wish to weep.

"Miss," said René-Jean, "you are too big."

"Me big!" stammered Georgette. And her size consoled her for her fall.

The cornice of entablature outside the windows was very broad; the dust blowing from the plain of heath had collected there; the rains had hardened it into soil, the wind had brought seeds; a blackberry-bush had profited by the shallow bed to grow up there. This bush belonged to the species called fox blackberry. It was August now, and the bush was covered with berries; a branch passed in by the window, and hung down nearly to the floor. Gros-Alain, after having discovered the cord and wagon, discovered this bramble. He went up to it. He gathered a berry and ate.

"I am hungry," said René-Jean.

Georgette arrived, galloping up on her hands and knees. The three between them stripped the branch, and ate all the berries. They stained their faces and hands with the purple juice until the trio of little seraphs was changed into a knot of little fauns, which would have shocked Dante and charmed Virgil. They shrieked with laughter. From time to time the thorns pricked their fingers. There is always a pain attached to every pleasure. Georgette held out her finger to René-Jean, on which showed a tiny drop of blood, and pointing to the bush, said, "P'icks."

Gros-Alain, who had suffered also, looked suspiciously at the branch, and said: "It is a beast."

"No," replied René-Jean; "it is a stick."

"Then a stick is wicked," retorted Gros-Alain.

Again Georgette, though she had a mind to cry, burst out laughing.

Chapter V

THE BOOK

In the mean time René-Jean, perhaps jealous of the discoveries made by his younger brother, had conceived a grand project. For some minutes past, while busy eating the berries and pricking his fingers, his eyes turned frequently toward the chorister's desk mounted on a pivot and isolated like a monument in the centre of the library. On this desk lay the celebrated volume of "Saint Bartholomew." It was in truth a magnificent and priceless folio. It had been published at Cologne by the famous publisher of the edition of the Bible of 1682, Blœuw, or, in Latin, Cœsius. It was printed, not on Dutch paper, but upon that beautiful Arabian paper so much admired by Edrisi, which was made of silk and cotton and never grew yellow; the binding was of gilt leather, and the clasps of silver; the boards were of that parchment which the parchment sellers of Paris took an oath to buy at the Hall Saint Mathurin, "and nowhere else." The volume was full of engravings on wood and copper, with geographical maps of many countries; it had on a fly-leaf a protest of the printers, paper-makers, and publishers against the edict of 1635, which set a tax on "leather, fur, cloven-footed animals, sea-fish, and paper;" and at the back of the frontispiece could be read a dedication to the Gryphes, who were to Lyons what the Elzevirs were to Amsterdam. These combinations resulted in a famous copy almost as rare as the "Apostol" at Moscow.

The book was beautiful; it was for that reason René-Jean looked at it, too long perhaps. The volume chanced to be open at a great print representing Saint Bartholomew carrying his skin over his arm. He could see this print where he stood. When the berries were all eaten, René-Jean watched it with a feverish longing, and Georgette, following the direction of her brother's eyes, perceived the engraving, and said "Pic'-sure."

This exclamation seemed to decide René-Jean. Then, to the utter stupefaction of Gros-Alain, an extraordinary thing happened. A great oaken chair stood in one corner of the library; René-Jean marched toward it, seized and dragged it unaided up to the desk. Then he mounted thereon and laid his two hands on the volume. Arrived at this summit, he felt a necessity for being magnificently generous; he took hold of the upper end of the "pic'sure" and tore it carefully down. The tear went diagonally over the saint, but that was not the fault of René-Jean; it left in the book the left side, one eye, and a bit of the halo of the old apocryphal evangelist. He offered Georgette the other half of the saint and all his skin. Georgette took the saint, and observed, "Momommes."

"And I!" cried Gros-Alain.

The tearing of the first page of a book by children is like the shedding of the first drop of blood by men,—it decides the carnage. René-Jean turned the leaf; next to the saint came Commentator

Pantœnus. René-Jean bestowed Pantœnus upon Gros-Alain. Meanwhile Georgette tore her two large pieces into two little morsels, then the two into four, and continued her work till history might have noted that Saint Bartholomew, after having been flayed in Armenia, was torn limb from limb in Brittany.

CHAPTER VI

EXTERMINATION

THE quartering completed, Georgette held out her hand to René-Jean, and said, "More!" After the saint and the commentator followed portraits of frowning glossarists. The first in the procession was Gavantus: RenéJean tore him out and put Gavantus into Georgette's hand. The whole group of Saint Bartholomew's commentators met the same fate in turn.

There is a sense of superiority in giving. René-Jean kept nothing for himself. Gros-Alain and Georgette were watching him,—he was satisfied with that; the admiration of his public was reward enough. René-Jean, inexhaustible magnanimity, offered Frabricio Pignatelli to Gros-Alain, and Father Stilting to Georgette; he followed these by the bestowal of Alphonse Tostat on Gros-Alain, and Cornelius a Lapide upon Georgette. Then Gros-Alain received Henry Hammond, and Georgette received Father Roberti, together with a view of the city of Douai, where that father was born, in 1619. Gros-Alain received the protest of the stationers, and Georgette obtained the dedication to the Gryphes. Then it was the turn of the maps. René-Jean proceeded to distribute them. He gave Gros-Alain Ethiopia, and Lycaonia fell to Georgette. This done he tumbled the book upon the floor.

This was a terrible moment. With mingled ecstasy and fright Gros-Alain and Georgette saw René-Jean wrinkle his brows, stiffen his legs, clinch his fists, and push the massive folio off the stand. The majestic old tome was fairly a tragic spectacle. Pushed from its resting-place, it hung for an instant on the edge of the desk,—seemed to hesitate, trying to balance itself,—then crashed down, and broken, crumpled, torn, ripped from its bindings, its clasps fractured, flattened itself miserably on the floor. Fortunately it did not fall on the children; they were only bewildered, not crushed. Victories do not always finish so well. Like all glories it made a great noise, and left a cloud of dust.

Having flung the book on the ground, René-Jean descended from the chair. There was a moment of silence and fright; victory has its terrors. The three children seized one another's hands and stood at a distance, looking toward the vast dismantled tome. But after a brief reverie Gros-Alain approached it quickly and gave it a kick. Nothing more was needed. The appetite for destruction grows rapidly. René-Jean kicked it, Georgette dealt it a blow with her little foot which overset her, though she fell in a sitting position, by which she profited to fling herself on Saint Bartholomew. The spell was completely broken. René-Jean pounced upon the saint, Gros-Alain dashed upon him, and joyous, distracted, triumphant, pitiless, tearing the prints, slashing the leaves, pulling out the markers, scratching the binding, ungluing the gilded leather, breaking off the nails from the silver corners, ruining the parchment, making mince-meat of the august text, working with feet, hands, nails, teeth,—rosy, laughing, ferocious, the three angels of prey demolished the defenceless evangelist. They annihilated Armenia, Judea, Benevento, where rest the relics of the saint; Nathaniel, who is perhaps the same as Bartholomew; the Pope Gelasius, who declared the Gospel of Saint Bartholomew (Nathaniel) apocryphal; all the portraits; all the maps; and the inexorable massacre of the old book absorbed them so entirely that a mouse ran past without their perceiving it. It was an extermination. To tear in pieces history, legend, science, miracles, whether true or false, the Latin of the Church, superstitions, fanaticisms, mysteries,—to rend a whole religion from top to bottom would be a work for three giants; but the three children completed it. Hours passed in the labour, but they reached the end; nothing remained of Saint Bartholomew.

When they had finished, when the last page was loosened, the last print lying on the ground, when nothing was left of the book but the edges of the text and pictures in the skeleton of the binding, René-Jean sprang to his feet, looked at the floor covered with scattered leaves, and clapped his hands. Gros-Alain clapped his hands likewise. Georgette took one of the pages in her hand, rose, leaned against the window-sill, which was on a level with her chin, and commenced to tear the great leaf into tiny bits, and scatter them out of the casement. Seeing this, René-Jean and Gros-Alain began the same work. They picked up and tore into small bits, picked up again and tore, and flung the pieces out of the window, as Georgette had done, page by page. Rent by these little desperate fingers, the entire ancient volume almost flew down the wind.

Georgette thoughtfully watched these swarms of little white papers dispersed by the breeze, and said: "Butterf'ies!"

So the massacre ended with these tiny ghosts vanishing in the blue of heaven!

Chapter VII

SLEEP

Thus was Saint Bartholomew for the second time made a martyr,—he who had been for the first time sacrificed in the year of our Lord 49.

Then the evening came on; the heat increased; there was sleep in the air. Georgette's eyes began to close; René-Jean went to his crib, pulled out the straw sack which served instead of a mattress, dragged it to the window, stretched himself thereon, and said, "Let us go to bed." Gros-Alain laid his head against René-Jean, Georgette placed hers on Gros-Alain, and the three malefactors fell asleep.

The warm breeze entered by the open windows, the perfume of wild flowers from the ravines and hills mingled with the breath of evening. Nature was calm and pitiful; everything beamed, was at peace, full of love; the sun gave its caress, which is light, to all creation; everywhere could be heard and felt that harmony which is thrown off from the infinite sweetness of inanimate things. There is a motherhood in the infinite,—

she perfects her grandeur by her goodness; creation is a miracle in full bloom. It seemed as if one could feel some invisible Being take those mysterious precautions which in the formidable conflict of opposing elements of life protect the weak against the strong; at the same time there was beauty everywhere,—the splendour equalled the gentleness. The landscape that seemed asleep had those lovely hazy effects which the changings of light and shadow produce on the fields and rivers; the mists mounted toward the clouds like reveries changing into dreams; the birds circled noisily about La Tourgue; the swallows looked in through the windows, as if they wished to be certain that the children slept well.

They were prettily grouped upon one another, motionless, half-naked, posed like little Cupids; they were adorable and pure; the united ages of the three did not make nine years. They were dreaming dreams of paradise, which were reflected on their lips in vague smiles. Perchance God whispered in their ears. They were of those whom all human languages call the weak and blessed; they were made majestic by innocence. All was silence about them, as if the breath from their tender bosoms was the care of the universe, and listened to by the whole creation; the leaves did not rustle, the grass did not stir. It seemed as if the vast starry world held its breath for fear of disturbing these three humble angelic sleepers, and nothing could have been so sublime as that reverent respect of Nature in presence of this littleness.

The sun was near its setting; it almost touched the horizon. Suddenly, across this profound peace burst a lightning-like glare, which came from the forest; then a savage noise. A cannon had just been fired. The echoes seized upon this thundering, and repeated it with an infernal din; the prolonged growling from hill to hill was terrible. It woke Georgette. She raised her head slightly, lifted her little finger, and said: "Boom!" The noise died away; the silence swept back; Georgette laid her head on Gros-Alain, and fell asleep once more.

BOOK IV

The Mother

Chapter I

DEATH PASSES

When the evening came, the mother whom we saw wandering almost at random had walked the whole day. This was indeed the history of all her days, —to go straight before her without stopping. For her slumbers of exhaustion, given in to in any corner that chanced to be nearest, were no more rest than the morsels she ate here and there (as the birds pick up crumbs) were nourishment. She ate and slept just what was absolutely necessary to keep her from falling down dead. She had passed the previous night in an empty barn; civil wars leave many such. She had found in a bare field four walls, an open door, a little straw beneath the ruins of a roof; and she had slept on the straw under the rafters, feeling the rats slip about beneath, and watching the stars rise through the gaping wreck above. She slept for several hours; then she woke in the middle of the night and set out again in order to get over as much road as possible before the great heat of the day should set in. For any one who travels on foot in the summer, midnight is more fitting than noon.

She had followed to the best of her ability the brief itinerary the peasant of Vautortes had marked out for her; she had gone as straight as possible toward the west. Had there been any one near, he might have heard her ceaselessly murmur, half aloud, "La Tourgue." Except the names of her children, this word was all she knew. As she walked, she dreamed. She thought of the adventures with which she had met; she thought of all she had suffered, all which she had accepted,—of the meetings, the indignities, the terms offered; the bargains proposed and submitted to, —now for a shelter, now for a morsel of bread, sometimes simply to obtain from some one information as to her route. A wretched woman is more unfortunate than a wretched man, for she may be a prey to lust. Frightful wandering march! But nothing mattered to her, provided she could discover her children.

Her first encounter this day had been a village. The dawn was beginning to break; everything was still tinged with the gloom of night. A few doors were already half open in the principal streets, and curious faces looked out of the windows; the inhabitants were agitated like a disturbed bee-hive: this arose from a noise of wheels and chains which had been heard. On the church square a frightened group with their heads raised, watched something descend a high hill along the road toward the village. It was a four-wheeled wagon drawn by five horses, harnessed with chains. On this wagon could be distinguished a heap like a pile of long joists, in the middle of which lay some shapeless object, covered with a large canvas resembling a pall. Ten horsemen rode in front of the wagon, and ten others behind; these men wore three-cornered hats, and above their shoulders rose what seemed to be the points of naked sabres. This whole cortège, advancing slowly, showed black and distinct against the horizon, the wagon looked black, the harness looked black, the horsemen looked black. Behind them gleamed the pallor of the morning. They entered the village and moved toward the square. Daylight had come on while the wagon was going down the hill, and the cortège could be distinctly seen; it was like watching a procession of shadows, for not a man in the party uttered a word. The horsemen were gendarmes; they did in truth carry drawn sabres. The cover was black.

The wretched, wandering mother entered the village from the opposite side, and approached the mob of peasants at the moment the gendarmes and the wagon reached the square. Among the crowd, voices whispered questions and replies:—

"What is it?"
"The guillotine."
"Whence does it come?"
"From Fougères."
"Where is it going?"
"I do not know. They say to a castle in the neighbourhood of Parigné."
"Parigné."
"Let it go where it likes, provided it does not stop here."

This great cart, with its lading hidden by a sort of shroud; this team, these gendarmes, the noise of the chains, the silence of the men, the grey dawn,—all made up a whole that was spectral. The group traversed the square and passed out of the village. The hamlet lay in a hollow between two hills: at the end of a quarter of an hour, the peasants, who had stood still as if petrified, saw the lugubrious procession reappear on the summit of the western hill; the heavy wheels jolted along the ruts, the chains clanked in the morning wind, the sabres shone in the rising sun,—then the road turned off, and the cortège disappeared.

It was at the very moment when Georgette woke in the library by the side of her still sleeping brothers, and wished her rosy feet good-morning.

Chapter II

DEATH SPEAKS

THE mother watched this mysterious procession, but neither comprehended nor sought to understand; her eyes were busy with another vision,—her children, lost amidst the darkness. She went out of the village also, a little after the cortège which had filed past, and followed the same route at some distance behind the second squad of gendarmes. Suddenly the word "guillotine" recurred to her. "Guillotine!" she said to herself. This rude peasant, Michelle Fléchard, did not know what that was, but instinct warned her. She shivered without being able to tell wherefore; it seemed horrible to her to walk behind this thing and she turned to the left, quitted the high-road, and passed into a wood, which was the forest of Fougères. After wandering for some time, she perceived a belfry and some roofs; it was one of the villages scattered along the edge of the forest. She went toward it; she was hungry. It was one of the villages in which the republicans had established military posts. She passed on to the square in front of the mayoralty.

In this village there was also fright and anxiety. A crowd pressed up to the flight of steps. On the top step stood a man escorted by soldiers; he held in his hand a great open placard; at his right was stationed a drummer, at his left a bill-sticker, carrying a paste-pot and brush. Upon the balcony over the door appeared the mayor, wearing a tricoloured scarf over his peasant dress. The man with the placard was a public crier. He wore his shoulder-belt, with a small wallet hanging from it,—a sign that he was going from village to village, and had something to publish throughout the district. At the moment Michelle Fléchard approached, he had unfolded the placard, and was beginning to read. He read in a loud voice:—

"THE FRENCH REPUBLIC ONE AND INDIVISIBLE."

The drum beat. There was a sort of movement among the assembly. A few took off their caps; others pulled their hats closer over their heads. At that time and in that country one could almost recognize the political opinions of a man by his head-gear: hats were royalists; caps republican. The confused murmur of voices ceased; everybody listened; the crier read:—

"In virtue of the orders we have received, and the authority delegated to us by the Committee of Public Safety—"

The drum beat the second time. The crier continued:—

"And in execution of the decree of the National Convention, which puts beyond the law all rebels taken with arms in their hands, and which ordains capital punishment to whomsoever shall give them shelter or help them to escsape—"

A peasant asked, in a low voice of his neighbour: "What is that,—capital punishment?"

His neighbour replied: "I do not know."

The crier fluttered the placard:—

"In accordance with Article 17th of the law of April 30, which gives full power to delegates and sub-delegates against rebels, we declare outlaws—"

He made a pause, and resumed:—

"The individuals known under the names and surnames which follow"—

The whole assemblage listened intently. The crier's voice sounded like thunder. He read:—

"Lantenac, brigand—"

"That is Monseigneur," murmured a peasant. And through the whole crowd went the whisper: "It is Monseigneur." The crier resumed:—

"Lantenac, ci-devant marquis, brigand. Imânus, brigand—"

Two peasants glanced sideways at each other.

"That is Gouge-le-Bruant."

"Yes; it is Brise-Bleu."

The crier continued to read the list:—

"Grand Francœur, brigand—"

The assembly murmured,—

"He is a priest."

"Yes; the Abbé Turmeau."

"Yes; he is a curé somewhere in the neighbourhood of the wood of Chapelle."

"And brigand," said a man in a cap. The crier read:—

"Boisnouveau, brigand. The two brothers, Pique-en-Bois, brigands. Houzard, brigand—"

"That is Monsieur de Quelen," said a peasant.

"Panier, brigand—"

"That is Monsieur Sepher."

"Place Nette, brigand—"

"That is Monsieur Jamois."

The crier continued his reading without noticing these commentaries:—

"Guinoiseau, brigand. Chatenay, styled Robi, brigand—"

A peasant whispered: "Guinoiseau is the same as Le Blond; Chatenay is from Saint Ouen."

"Hoisnard, brigand—" pursued the crier.

Among the crowd could be heard,—

"He is from Ruillé."

"Yes; it is Branche d'Or."

"His brother was killed in the attack on Pontorson."

"Yes; Hoisnard Malonnière."

"A fine young chap of nineteen."

"Attention!" cried the crier. "Listen to the last of the list:—

"Belle Vigue, brigand. La Musette, brigand. Sabretout, brigand. Brin d'Amour—"

A lad nudged the elbow of a young girl. The girl smiled.

The crier continued:—

"Chante-en-Hiver, brigand. Le Chat, brigand—"

A peasant said, "That is Moulard."

"Tabouze, brigand—"

Another peasant said: "That is Gauffre."

"There are two of the Gauffres," added a woman.

"Both good fellows," grumbled a lad.

The crier shook the placard, and the drum beat. The crier resumed his reading:—

"The above-named, in whatsoever place taken, and their identity established, shall be immediately put to death."

There was a movement among the crowd. The crier went on:—

"Any one affording them shelter or aiding their escape, will be brought before a court-martial and put to death. Signed—"

The silence grew profound.

"The Delegate of the Committee of Public Safety,

CIMOURDAIN."

"A priest," said a peasant.

"The former curé of Parigné," said another.

A townsman added, "Turmeau and Cimourdain—A Blue priest and a White."

"Both black," said another townsman.

The mayor, who was on the balcony, lifted his hat, and cried: "Long live the Republic!"

A roll of the drum announced that the crier had not finished.

He was making a sign with his hand. "Attention!" said he. "Listen to the last four lines of the Government proclamation. They are signed by the Chief of the exploring column of the North Coasts, Commandant Gauvain."

"Listen!" exclaimed the voices of the crowd. And the crier read:—

"Under pain of death—"

All were silent.

"It is forbidden, in pursuance of the above order, to give aid or succour to the nineteen rebels above named, at this time shut up and surrounded in La Tourgue."

"What?" cried a voice. It was the voice of a woman; of the mother.

CHAPTER III

MUTTERINGS AMONG THE PEASANTS

MICHELLE FLÉCHARD had mingled with the crowd. She had listened to nothing, but one hears certain things without listening. She caught the words "La Tourgue." She raised her head. "What?" she repeated, "La Tourgue!"

People stared at her. She appeared out of her mind. She was in rags. Voices murmured, "She looks like a brigand." A peasant woman, who carried a basket of buckwheat biscuits, drew near, and said to her in a low voice: "Hold your tongue!"

Michelle Fléchard gazed stupidly at the woman. Again she understood nothing. The name La Tourgue had passed through her mind like a flash of lightning and the darkness closed anew behind it. Had she not a right to ask information? What had she done that they should stare at her in this way?

But the drum had beat for the last time; the bill-sticker posted up the placard; the mayor retired into the house; the crier set out for some other village, and the mob dispersed. A group remained before the placard; Michelle Fléchard joined this knot of people. They were commenting on the names of the men declared outlaws. There were peasants and townsmen among them; that is to say, Whites and Blues.

A peasant said: "After all, they have not caught everybody. Nineteen are only nineteen. They have not got Riou, they have not got Benjamin Moulins, nor Goupil of the parish of Andouillé."

"Nor Lorieul of Monjean," said another.

Others added,—

"Nor Brice Denys."

"Nor François Dudouet."

"Yes, him of Laval."

"Nor Huet of Launey Villiers."

"Nor Grégis."

"Nor Pilon."

"Nor Filleul."

"Nor Ménicent."

"Nor Guéharrée."

"Nor the three brothers Logerais."

"Nor Monsieur Lechandelier de Pierreville."

"Idiots!" said a stern-faced, white-haired old man. "They have all if they have Lantenac."

"They have not got him yet," murmured one of the young men.

The old man added: "Lantenac taken, the soul is taken. Lantenac dead, La Vendée is slain."

"Who, then, is this Lantenac?" asked a townsman.

A townsman replied: "He is a *ci-devant*."

Another added: "He is one of those who shoot women."

Michelle Fléchard heard and said: "It is true."

They turned toward her.

She went on: "For he shot me."

It was a strange speech; it was like hearing a living woman declare herself dead. People began to look at her a little suspiciously. She was indeed a startling object; trembling at everything, scared, quaking, showing a sort of wild-animal trouble, so frightened that she was frightful. There is always something terrible in the feebleness of a despairing woman; she is a creature who has reached the furthest limits of destiny. But peasants have not a habit of noticing details. One of them muttered, "She might easily be a spy."

"Hold your tnogue and get away from here," the good woman who had already spoken to her said in a low tone. Michelle Fléchard replied: "I am doing no harm. I am looking for my children."

The good woman glanced at those who were staring at Michelle, touched her forehead with one finger and winked, saying: "She is a simpleton." Then she took her aside and gave her a biscuit. Michelle Fléchard, without thanking her, began to eat greedily.

"Yes," said the peasants, "she eats like an animal; she is an idiot." So the tail of the mob dwindled away. They all went away, one after another.

When Michelle Fléchard had devoured her biscuit, she said to the peasant woman: "Good! I have eaten. Now where is La Tourgue?"

"It is taking her again!" cried the peasant.

"I must go to La Tourgue! Show me the way to La Tourgue!"

"Never!" exclaimed the peasant. "Do you want to get yourself killed, eh? Besides, I don't know. Oh, see here! You are really crazy! Listen, poor woman, you look tired. Will you come to my house and rest yourself?"

"I never rest," said the mother.

"And her feet are torn to pieces!" murmured the peasant.

Michelle Fléchard resumed: "Don't I tell you that they have stolen my children?—a little girl and two boys. I come from the carnichot in the forest. You can ask Tellmarch the Caimand about me, and the man I met in the field down yonder. It was the Caimand who cured me; it seems I had something broken. All that is what happened to me. Then there is Sergeant Radoub besides,—you can ask him, he will tell thee. Why, he was the one we met in the wood. Three,—I tell you three children! even the oldest one's name,—René-Jean. I can prove all that. The other's name is Gros-Alain, and the little girl's is Georgette. My husband is dead,—they killed him; he was the farmer at Siscoignard. You look like a good woman,—show me the road! I am not crazy; I am a mother! I have lost my children; I am trying to find them,—that is all. I don't know exactly which way I have come. I slept last night in a barn on the straw. La Tourgue, that is where I am going. I am not a thief. You must see that I am telling the truth; you ought to help me find my children. I do not belong to the neighbourhood. I was shot, but I do not know where."

The peasant woman shook her head, and said: "Listen, traveller. In times of revolution you mustn't say things that cannot be understood; you may get yourself taken up in that way."

"But La Tourgue!" cried the mother. "Madame, for the love of the Child Jesus and the Blessed Virgin up in Paradise, I beg you, madame, I entreat you, I conjure you, tell me which way I must go to get to La Tourgue!"

The peasant woman went into a passion. "I do not know! And if I knew I would not tell! It is a bad place. People do not go there."

"But I am going," said the mother. And she set forth again.

The woman watched her depart, muttering, "Still, she must have something to eat." She ran after Michelle Fléchard and put a roll of black bread into her hand: "There is for your supper."

Michelle Fléchard took the buckwheat bread, but did not answer, did not turn her head, but walked on. She went out of the village. As she reached the last houses she met three ragged, barefooted little children. She approached them, and said: "These are two girls and a boy." Noticing that they looked at the bread, she gave it to them. The children took the bread, then grew frightened. She plunged into the forest.

Chapter IV

A MISTAKE

On the same morning, before the dawn appeared, this happened amidst the obscurity of the forest, along the crossroad which goes from Javené to Lécousse.

All the roads of the Breage are between high banks; but of all the routes, that leading from Javené to Parigné by the way of Lécousse is the most deeply embedded. Besides that, it is winding; it is a ravine rather than a road. This road comes from Vitré, and had the honour of jolting Madame de Sévigné's carriage. It is, as it were, walled in to the right and left by hedges. There could be no better place for an ambush.

On this morning, an hour before Michelle Fléchard from another point of the forest reached the first village where she had seen the sepulchral apparition of the wagon escorted by gendarmes, a crowd of men filled the copses where the Javené road crosses the bridge over the Couesnon. The branches hid them. These men were peasants, all wearing jackets of skins, which the kings of Brittany wore in the sixth century and the peasants in the eighteenth. The men were armed,—some with guns, others with axes. Those who carried axes had just prepared in an open space a sort of pyre of dried fagots and billets, which only remained to be set on fire; those who had guns were stationed at the two sides of the road in watchful positions. Anybody who could have looked through the leaves would have seen everywhere fingers on triggers, and guns aimed toward the openings left by the interlacing branches. These men were on the watch. All the guns converged toward the road, which the first gleams of day had begun to whiten. In this twilight low voices held converse:—

"Are you sure of that?"

"Well, they say so."

"*She* is about to pass?"

"They say she is in the neighbourhood."

"She must not go out."

"She must be burned."

"We are three villages who have come out for that."

"Yes; but the escort?"

"The escort will be killed."

"But will she pass by this road?"

"They say so."

"Then she comes from Vitré?"

"Why not?"

"But somebody said she was coming from Fougères."

"Whether she comes from Fougères or Vitré, she comes from the devil."

"Yes."

"And must go back to him."

"Yes."

"So she is going to Parigné?"

"It appears so."

"She will not go."

"No."

"No, no, no!"

"Attention!"

It became prudent now to be silent, for the day was breaking. Suddenly these ambushed men held their breath; they caught a sound of wheels and horses' feet. They peered through the branches, and could perceive indistinctly a long wagon, an escort on horseback, and something on the wagon, coming toward them along the high-banked road.

"There she is," said one who appeared to be the leader.

"Yes," said one of the scouts; "with the escort."

"How many men?"

"Twelve."

"We were told they were twenty."

"Twelve or twenty, *we* must kill the whole."

"Wait until they get within sure aim."

A little later, the wagon and its escort appeared at a turn in the road. "Long live the king!" cried the chief peasant. A hundred guns were fired at the same instant.

When the smoke scattered, the escort was scattered also. Seven horsemen had fallen; five had fled. The peasants rushed up to the wagon.

"Hold!" cried the chief; "it is not the guillotine! It is a ladder."

A long ladder was, in fact, all the wagon carried. The two horses had fallen wounded; the driver had been killed, but not intentionally.

"All the same," said the chief; "a ladder with an escort looks suspicious. It was going toward Parigné. It was for the escalade of La Tourgue, very sure."

"Let us burn the ladder!" cried the peasants.

And they burned the ladder. As for the funereal wagon for which they had been waiting, it was pursuing another road, and was already two leagues off, in the village where Michelle Fléchard saw it pass at sunrise.

Chapter V

VOX IN DESERTO

When Michelle Fléchard left the three children to whom she had given her bread, she took her way at random through the wood. Since nobody would point out the road, she must find it out for herself. Now and then she sat down, then rose, then reseated herself again. She was borne down by that terrible fatigue which first attacks the muscles, then passes into the bones,—weariness like that of a slave. She was a slave in truth,—the slave of her lost children. She must find them; each instant that elapsed might be to their hurt. Whoso has a duty like this woman's has no rights; it is forbidden even to stop to take breath. But she was very tired. In the extreme of exhaustion which she had reached, another step became a question,—can one make it? She had walked all the day, encountering no other village, not even a house. She took first the right path, then a wrong one, ending by losing herself amidst leafy labyrinths, resembling one another precisely. Was she approaching her goal? Was she nearing the term of her Passion? She was in the Via Dolorosa, and felt the overwhelming of the last station. Was she about to fall in the road, and die there? There came a moment when to advance further seemed impossible to her. The sun was declining, the forest growing dark; the paths were hidden beneath the grass, and she was helpless. She had nothing left but God. She began to call; no voice answered.

She looked about; she perceived an opening in the branches; turned in that direction, and found herself suddenly on the edge of the wood. She had before her a valley, narrow as a trench, at the bottom of which a clear streamlet ran along over the stones. She discovered then she was burning with thirst; she went down to the stream, knelt by it, and drank. She took advantage of her kneeling position to say her prayers.

When she rose she tried to decide upon a course. She crossed the brook. Beyond the little valley stretched, as far as the eye could reach, a plateau covered with short underbrush, which, starting from the brook, ascended in an inclined plain, and filled the whole horizon. The forest had been a solitude; this plain was a desert. Behind every bush of the forest she might meet some one; on the plateau, as far as she could see, nothing met her gaze. A few birds, which seemed frightened, were flying away over the heath. Then, in the midst of this awful abandonment, feeling her knees give way under her, and as if gone suddenly mad, the distracted mother flung forth this strange cry into the silence: "Is there any one here?"

She waited for an answer. It came. A low, deep voice burst forth; it proceeded from the verge of the horizon, was borne forward from echo to echo; it was either a peal of thunder or a cannon, and it seemed as if the voice replied to the mother's question, and that it said, "Yes." Then the silence closed in anew.

The mother rose, animated with fresh life. There was some one; it seemed to her as if she had now some person with whom she could speak. She had just drank and prayed; her strength came back; she began to ascend the plateau in the direction whence she had heard that vast and far-off voice. Suddenly she saw a lofty tower start up on the extreme edge of the horizon. It was the only object visible amidst the savage landscape; a ray from the setting sun crimsoned its summit. It was more than a league away. Behind the tower spread a great sweep of scattered verdure lost in the midst: it was the forest of Fougères. This tower appeared to her to be the point whence came the thundering which had sounded like a summons in her ear. Was it that which had given the answer to her cry?

Michelle Fléchard reached the top of the plateau; she had nothing but the plain before her. She walked toward the tower.

Chapter VI

THE SITUATION

The moment had come. The inexorable held the pitiless. Cimourdain had Lantenac in his hand.

The old royalist rebel was taken in his form; it was evident that he could not escape, and Cimourdain meant that the marquis should be beheaded here,— upon his own territory, his own lands,— on this very spot, in sight of his ancestral dwelling-place, that the feudal stronghold might see the head of the feudal lord fall, and the example thus be made memorable. It was with this intention that he had sent to Fougères for the guillotine, which we lately saw upon its road. To kill Lantenac, was to slay the Vendée; to slay the Vendée was to save France. Cimourdain did not hesitate. The conscience of this man was quiet; he was urged to ferocity by a sense of duty.

The marquis appeared lost; as far as that went, Cimourdain was tranquil. But there was a consideration which troubled him. The struggle must inevitably be a terrible one. Gauvain would direct it, and perhaps would wish to take part. This young chief was a soldier at heart; he was just the man to fling himself into the thick of this pugilistic combat. If he should be killed,—Gauvain, his child! the unique affection he possessed on earth! So far fortune had protected the youth; but fortune might grow weary. Cimourdain trembled. His strange destiny had placed him here between these two Gauvains,—for one of whom he wished death, for the other life.

The cannon-shot which had roused Georgette in her cradle and summoned the mother in the depths of her solitude had done more than that. Either by accident, or owing to the intention of the man who fired the piece, the ball, although only meant as a warning, had struck the guard of iron bars which protected the great loop-hole of the first floor of the tower, broken it and half wrenched it away. The besieged had not had time to repair this damage.

The besieged had been boastful, but they had very little ammunition. Their situation, indeed, was much more critical than the besiegers supposed. If they had had powder enough they would have blown up La Tourgue when they and the enemy should be together within it; this had been their dream. But their reserves were exhausted; they had not more than thirty charges left for each man. They had plenty of guns, blunderbusses, and pistols, but few cartridges. They had loaded all the weapons in order to keep up a steady fire; but how long could this steady firing last? They must lavishly exhaust the resources which they required to husband. That was the difficulty. Fortunately (sinister fortune) the struggle would be mostly man to man; sabre and poniard would be more needed than firearms. The conflict would be rather a duel with knives than a battle with guns. This was the hope of the besieged.

The interior of the tower seemed impregnable. In the lower hall, which the mine had breached, the retirade so skilfully constructed guarded the entrance. Behind the retirade was a long table covered with loaded weapons, blunderbusses, carbines, and muskets; sabres, axes, and poniards. Since they had no powder to blow up the tower, the crypt of the oubliettes could not be utilized; therefore the marquis had closed the door of the dungeon. Above the ground-floor hall was the round chamber which could only be reached by the narrow, winding staircase. This chamber (in which there also set a table covered with loaded weapons ready to the hand) was lighted by the great loop-hole, the grating of which had just been broken by the cannon-ball. From this chamber the spiral staircase ascended to the circular room on the second floor, in which was the iron door communicating with the bridge-castle. This chamber was called indifferently the "room with the iron door," or the "mirror-room," from numerous small looking-glasses hung to rusty old nails on the naked stones of the wall,—a fantastic mingling of elegance and savage desolation. Since the apartments on the upper floor could not be successfully defended, this mirror-room became what Manesson Mallet, the law-giver in regard to fortified places, calls "the last post where the besieged can capitulate." The struggle, as we have already said, would be to keep the assailants from reaching this room. This second-floor round chamber was lighted by loop-holes; still, a torch burned there. This torch, in an iron holder like the one in the hall below, had been kindled by Imânus, and the end of the sulphur-match placed near it. Terrible carefulness! At the end of the ground-floor hall was a board placed upon trestles, which held food, like the arrangement in a Homeric cavern; great dishes of rice, furmety of black grain, hashed veal, hotchpotch, biscuits, stewed fruit, and jugs of cider. Whoever wished could eat and drink.

The cannon-shot set them all on the watch. Not more than a half hour of quiet remained to them. From the top of the tower Imânus watched the approach of the besiegers.

Lantenac had ordered his men not to fire as the assailants came forward. He said: "They are four thousand five hundred. To kill outside is useless. When they try to enter, we are as strong as they." Then he laughed, and added: "Equality, Fraternity."

It had been agreed that Imânus should sound a warning on his horn when the enemy began to advance. The little troop, posted behind the retirade or on the stairs, waited with one hand on their muskets, the other on their rosaries.

This was what the situation had resolved itself into: For the assailants a breach to mount, a barricade to force, three rooms (one above the other) to take in succession by main strength, two winding staircases to be carried step by step under a storm of bullets. For the besieged—to die!

Chapter VII

PRELIMINARIES

GAUVAIN on his side arranged the order of attack. He gave his last instructions to Cimourdain, whose part in the action, it will be remembered, was to guard the plateau, and to Guéchamp, who was to wait with the main body of the army in the forest camp. It was understood that neither the masked battery of the wood nor the open battery of the plateau would fire unless there should be a sortie or an attempt at escape on the part of the besieged. Gauvain had reserved for himself the command of the storming column. It was that which troubled Cimourdain.

The sun had just set. A tower in an open country resembles a ship in open sea. It must be attacked in the same manner: it is a boarding rather than an assault. No cannon; nothing useless attempted. What would be the good of cannonading walls fifteen feet thick? A port-hole; men forcing it on the one side, men guarding it on the other; axes, knives, pistols, fists, and teeth,— that is the undertaking.

Gauvain felt that there was no other way of carrying La Tourgue. Nothing can be more murderous than a conflict so close that the combatants look into one another's eyes. He had lived in this tower when a child, and knew its formidable recesses by heart. He meditated profoundly.

A few paces from him his lieutenant, Guéchamp, stood with a spy-glass in his hand, examining the horizon in the direction of Parigné. Suddenly he cried "Ah! at last!"

This exclamation aroused Gauvain from his reverie. "What is it, Guéchamp?"

"Commandant, the ladder is coming."

"The escape-ladder?"

"Yes."

"How? It has not yet got here?"

"No, Commandant. And I was troubled. The express that I sent to Javené came back."

"I know it."

"He told me that he had found at the carpenter's shop in Javené a ladder of the requisite dimensions; he took it, he had it put on a cart; he demanded an escort of twelve horsemen, and he saw them set out from Parigné,—the cart, the escort, and the ladder. Then he rode back full speed, and made his report; and he added that the horses being good and the departure having taken place about two o'clock in the morning the wagon would be here before sunset."

"I know all that. Well?"

"Well, Commandant, the sun has just set, and the wagon which brings the ladder has not yet arrived."

"Is it possible? Still, we must commence the attack. The hour has come. If we were to wait, the besieged would think we hesitated."

"Commandant, the attack can commence."

"But the escape-ladder is necessary."

"Without doubt."

"But we have not got it."

"We have it."

"How?"

"It was that which made me say, 'Ah! at last!' The wagon did not arrive; I took my telescope, and examined the route from Parigné to La Tourgue, and, Commandant, I am satisfied. The wagon and the escort are coming down yonder; they are descending a hill. You can see them."

Gauvain took the glass and looked. "Yes; there it is. There is not light enough to distinguish very clearly. But I can see the escort,—it is certainly that. Only the escort appears to me more numerous than you said, Guéchamp."

"And to me also."

"They are about a quarter of a league off."

"Commandant, the escape-ladder will be here in a quarter of an hour."

"We can attack."

It was indeed a wagon which they saw approaching, but not the one they believed. As Gauvain turned he saw Sergeant Radoub standing behind him, upright, his eyes downcast, in the attitude of military salute.

"What is it, Sergeant Radoub?"

"Citizen commandant, we, the men of the Battalion of the Bonnet Rouge, have a favour to ask of you."

"What?"

"To have us killed."

"Ah!" said Gauvain.

"Will you have that kindness?"

"But—that is according to circumstances," said Gauvain.

"Listen, Commandant. Since the affair of Dol, you are careful of us. We are still twelve."

"Well?"

"That humiliates us."

"You are the reserve."

"We would rather be the advance-guard."

"But I need you to decide success at the close of the engagement. I keep you back for that."

"Too much."

"No. You are in the column. You march."

"In the rear. Paris has a right to march in front."

"I will think of it, Sergeant Radoub."

"Think of it to-day, my commandant. There is an opportunity. There are going to be hard blows to give or to take. It will be lively. La Tourgue will burn the fingers of those that touch her. We demand the favour of being in the party." The sergeant paused, twisted his moustache, and added, in an altered voice: "Besides, look you, my commandant, our little ones are in this tower. Our children are there,—the children of the battalion,—our three children. That abominable beast called Brise-Bleu and Imânus, this Gouge-le-Bruant, this Fouge-le-Truant, this thunder-clap of the devil, threatens our children. Our children,—our pets, Commandant. If all the earthquakes should mix in the business, we cannot have any misfortune happen to them. Do you hear that—authority? We will have none of it. A little while ago I took advantage of the truce, and mounted the plateau, and looked at them through a window; yes, they are certainly there,—you can see them from the edge of the ravine. I did see them, and they were afraid of me, the darlings. Commandant, if a single hair of their little cherub pates should fall, I swear by the thousand names of everything sacred,—I, Sergeant Radoub,—that I will have revenge out of somebody. And that is what all the battalion want: either we want the babies saved, or we want to be all killed. It is our right: yes—all killed. And now, salute and respect."

Gauvain held out his hand to Radoub, and said: "You are brave men. You shall have a place in the attacking column. I will divide you into two parties. I will put six of you in the vanguard to make sure that the troops advance, and six in the rear-guard to make sure that nobody retreats."

"Shall I command the twelve, as usual?"

"Certainly."

"Then, my commandant, thanks. For I am of the vanguard."

Radoub made another military salute, and went back to his company.

Gauvain drew out his watch, spoke a few words in Guéchamp's ear, and the storming column began to form.

Chapter VIII

THE WORD AND THE ROAR

Now, Cimourdain, who had not yet gone to his post on the plateau, approached a trumpeter. "Sound your trumpet!" said he.

The clarion sounded; the horn replied. Again the trumpet and the horn exchanged a blast.

"What does that mean?" Gauvain asked Guéchamp. "What is it Cimourdain wants?"

Cimourdain advanced toward the tower, holding a white handkerchief in his hand. He spoke in a loud voice: "Men who are in the tower, do you know me?"

A voice—the voice of Imânus—replied from the summit: "Yes."

The following dialogue between the two voices reached the ears of those about:—

"I am the Envoy of the Republic."

"You are the late Curé of Parigné."

"I am the delegate of the Committee of Public Safety."

"You are a priest."

"I am the representative of the law."

"You are a renegade."

"I am the commissioner of the Revolution."

"You are an apostate."

"I am Cimourdain."

"You are the demon."

"Do you know me?"

"We hate you."

"Would you be content if you had me in your power?"

"We are here eighteen, who would give our heads to have yours."

"Very well! I come to deliver myself up to you."

From the top of the tower rang a burst of savage laughter, and this cry: "Come!"

The camp waited in the breathless silence of expectancy.

Cimourdain resumed: "On one condition."

"What?"

"Listen."

"Speak."

"You hate me?"

"Yes."

"And I love you. I am your brother."

The voice from the top of the tower replied: "Yes, Cain."

Cimourdain went on in a singular tone, at once loud and sweet: "Insult me; but listen. I come here under a flag of truce. Yes, you are my brothers. You are poor mistaken creatures. I am your friend. I am the light, and I speak to ignorance. Light is always brotherhood. Besides, have we not all the same mother,—our country? Well, listen to me: you will know hereafter, or your children will know, or your children's children will know, that what is done in this moment is brought about by the law above, and that the Revolution is the work of God. While awaiting the time when all consciences, even yours, shall understand this; when all fanaticisms, even yours, shall vanish,—while waiting for this great light to spread, will no one have pity on your darkness? I come to you. I offer you my head. I do more,—I hold out my hand to you. I demand of you the favour to destroy me in order to save yourselves. I have unlimited authority, and that which I say I can do. This is a supreme instant. I make a last effort. Yes, he who speaks to you is a citizen and in this citizen—yes—there is a priest. The citizen defies you, but the priest implores you. Listen to me. Many among you have wives and children. I am defending your children and your wives,—defending them against yourselves. Oh, my brothers,—"

"Go on! Preach!" sneered Imânus.

"My brothers, do not let the terrible horn sound. Throats are to be cut. Many among us who are here before you will not see to-morrow's sun; yes, many of us will perish, and you—you are all going to die. Show mercy to yourselves. Why shed all this blood, when it is useless? Why kill so many men, when it would suffice to kill two?"

"Two?" repeated Imânus.

"Yes. Two."

"Who?"

"Lantenac and myself." Cimourdain spoke more loudly. "Two men are too many. Lantenac for us; I for you. This is what I propose to you, and you will all have your lives safe. Give us Lantenac, and take me. Lantenac will be guillotined, and you shall do what you choose with me."

"Priest," howled Imânus, "if we had thee we would roast thee at a slow fire!"

"I consent," said Cimourdain. He went on: "You, the condemned who are in this tower, you can all in an hour be living and free. I bring you safety. Do you accept?"

Imânus burst forth: "You are not only a villain, you are a madman. Ah, why do you come here to disturb us. Who begged you to come and speak to us? We give up Monseigneur? What is it you want?"

"His head. And I offer—"

"Your skin. Oh, we would flay you like a dog, Curé Cimourdain! Well, no; your skin is not worth his head. Get away with you!"

"The massacre will be horrible. For the last time—reflect."

Night had come on during this strange colloquy, which could be heard without and within the tower. The Marquis de Lantenac kept silence, and allowed events to take their course. Leaders possess such sinister egotism; it is one of the rights of responsibility.

Imânus sent his voice beyond Cimourdain; he shouted: "Men, who attack us, we have submitted our propositions to you: they are settled: we have nothing to change in them. Accept them, else woe to all! Do you consent? We will give you up the three children, and you will allow liberty and life to us all!"

"To all, yes," replied Cimourdain, "except one."

"And that?"

"Lantenac."

"Monseigneur! Give up Monseigneur? Never!"

"We can only treat with you on that condition."

"Then begin."

Silence fell. Imânus descended after having sounded the signal on his horn; the marquis took his sword in his hand; the nineteen besieged grouped themselves in silence behind the retirade of the lower hall and sank upon their knees. They could hear the measured tread of the column as it advanced toward the tower in the gloom. The sound came nearer; suddenly they heard it close to them, at the very mouth of the breach. Then all, kneeling, aimed their guns and blunderbusses across the openings of the barricade, and one of them —Grand Francœur, who was the priest Turmeau—raised himself, with a naked sabre in his right hand and a crucifix in his left, saying, in a solemn voice,—

"In the name of the Father, of the Son, and of the Holy Ghost!"

All fired at the same time, and the battle began.

Chapter IX

TITANS AGAINST GIANTS

The encounter was frightful. This hand-to-hand contest went beyond the power of fancy in its awfulness. To find anything similar, it would be necessary to go back to the great duels of Æschylus or the ancient feudal butcheries; to "those attacks with short-arms" which lasted down to the seventeenth century, when men penetrated into fortified places by concealed breaches, tragic assaults, where, says the old sergeant of the province of Alentejo, "when the mines had done their work, the besiegers advanced bearing planks covered with sheets of tin, and, armed with round shields and furnished with grenades, they forced those who held the intrenchments or retirades to abandon them; and thus become masters, they vigorously drove in the besieged."

The place of attack was terrible; it was what in military language is called "a covered breach,"—that is to say, a crevice traversing the wall through and through, and not an extended fracture open to the sky. The powder had acted like an auger. The effect of the explosion had been so violent that the tower was cracked for more than forty feet above the chamber of the mine. But this was only a crack; the practicable rent which served as a breach, and which gave admittance into the lower hall, resembled a thrust from a lance which pierces, rather than a blow from an axe which gashes. It was a puncture in the flank of the tower; a long cut, something like the mouth of a well; a passage, twisting and mounting like an intestine along the wall fifteen feet in thickness; a misshapen cylinder, encumbered with obstacles, traps, stones broken by the explosion, where any one entering struck his head against the granite rock, his feet against the rubbish, while the darkness blinded him.

The assailants saw before them this black gap, the mouth of a gulf, which had for upper and lower jaws all the stones of the jagged wall: a shark's mouth has not more teeth than had this frightful opening. It was necessary to enter this gap and to get out of it. Within was the wall; without rose the retirade,—without; that is to say, in the hall of the ground-floor.

The encounters of sappers in covered galleries when the countermine succeeds in cutting the mine, the butcheries in the gun-decks of vessels boarded in a naval engagement, alone have this ferocity. To fight in the bottom of a grave,—it is the supreme degree of horror; it is frightful for men to meet in the death-struggle in such narrow bounds. At the instant when the first rush of besiegers entered, the whole retirade blazed with lightnings; it was like a thunder-bolt bursting underground. The thunder of the assailants replied to that of the ambuscade; the detonations answered one another. Gauvain's voice was heard shouting, "Drive them back!" Then Lantenac's cry, "Hold firm against the enemy!" Then Imânus's yell, "Here, you men of the Main!" Then the clash of sabres against sabres, and echo after echo of terrible discharges that killed right and left. The torch fastened against the wall dimly lighted the horrible scene.

It was impossible clearly to distinguish anything; the combatants struggled amidst a lurid night; whoever entered was suddenly struck deaf and blind,—deafened by the noise, blinded by the smoke. The combatants trod upon the corpses; they lacerated the wounds of the injured men lying helpless amidst the rubbish, stamped recklessly upon limbs already broken; the sufferers uttered awful groans; the dying fastened their teeth in the feet of their unconscious tormentors. Then for an instant would come a silence more dreadful than the tumult: the foes collared each other; the hissing sound of their breath could be heard; the gnashing of teeth, death-groans, curses,—then the thunder would recommence. A stream of blood flowed out from the tower through the breach and spread away across the darkness, and formed smoking pools upon the grass. One might have said that the tower had been wounded, and that the giantess was bleeding.

Strange thing! scarcely a sound of the struggle could be heard without. The night was very black, and a sort of funereal calm reigned in plain and forest about the beleaguered fortress. Hell was within, the sepulchre without. This shock of men exterminating one another amidst the darkness, these musket volleys, these clamours, these shouts of rage,—all that din expired beneath that mass of walls and arches; air was lacking, and suffocation added itself to the carnage. Scarcely a sound reached those outside the tower. The little children slept.

The desperate strife grew madder. The retirade held firm. Nothing more difficult than to force a barricade with a re-entering angle. If the besieged had numbers against them, they had at least the position in their favour. The storming-column lost many men. Stretched in a long line outside the tower, it forced its way slowly in through the opening of the breach like a snake twisting itself into its den.

Gauvain, with the natural imprudence of a youthful leader, was in the hall in the thickest of the *mêlée*, with the bullets flying in every direction about his head. Besides the imprudence of his age, he had the assurance of a man who has never been wounded. As he turned about to give an order, the glare of a volley of musketry lighted up a face close beside him. "Cimourdain!" he cried. "What are you doing here?"

It was indeed Cimourdain. He replied: "I have come to be near you."

"But you will be killed!"

"Very well: you—what are you doing, then?"

"I am necessary here; you are not."

"Since you are here, I must be here too."

"No, my master!"

"Yes, my child!"

And Cimourdain remained near Gauvain.

The dead lay in heaps on the pavement of the hall. Although the retirade was not yet carried, numbers would evidently conquer at last. The assailants were sheltered, and the assailed under cover; ten besiegers fell to one among the besieged, but the besiegers were constantly renewed; the assailants increased, and the assailed grew less. The nineteen besieged were all behind the retirade, because the attack was made there. They had dead and wounded among them; not more than fifteen could fight now. One of the most furious, Chante-en-Hiver, had been horribly mutilated. He was a stubby, woolly-haired Breton, little and active; he had an eye shot out, and his jaw broken. He could walk still; he dragged himself up the spiral staircase, and reached the chamber of the first floor, hoping to be able to say a prayer there and die. He backed himself against the wall near the loop-hole in order to breathe a little fresh air.

Beneath, in front of the barricade, the butchery became more and more horrible. In a pause between the answering discharges, Cimourdain raised his voice: "Besieged!" cried he. "Why let any more blood flow? You are beaten. Surrender! Think! we are four thousand five hundred men against nineteen, —that is to say, more than two hundred against one. Surrender!"

"Let us stop these babblings," retorted the Marquis de Lantenac; and twenty balls answered Cimourdain.

The retirade did not reach to the arched roof; this space permitted the besieged to fire upon the barricade, but it also gave the besiegers an opportunity to scale it.

"Assault the retirade!" cried Gauvain. "Is there any man willing to scale the retirade?"

"I!" said Sergeant Radoub.

Chapter X

RADOUB

Then a sort of stupor seized the assailants. Radoub had entered the breach at the head of the column, and of those men of the Parisian battalion of which he made the sixth, four had already fallen. After he had uttered that shout, "I!" he was seen to recoil instead of advance. Stooping, bending forward, almost creeping between the legs of the combatants, he regained the opening of the breach and rushed out. Was it a flight? A man like this to fly! What did it mean?

When he was outside, Radoub, still blinded by the smoke, rubbed his eyes as if to clear them from the horror of the cavernous night he had just left, and studied the wall of the tower by the starlight. He nodded his head, as if to say, "I was not mistaken."

Radoub had noticed that the deep crack made by the explosion of the mine extended above the breach to the loop-hole of the upper story, whose iron grating had been shattered, and by a ball. The net-work of broken bars hung loosely down, so that a man could enter. A man could enter, but could he climb up? By the crevice it might have been possible for a cat to mount. That was what Radoub was. He belonged to the race which Pindar calls "the agile athletes." One may be an old soldier and a young man. Radoub, who had belonged to the French guards, was not yet forty; he was a nimble Hercules.

Radoub threw his musket on the ground, took off his shoulder-belts, laid aside his coat and jacket, guarding his two pistols, which he thrust in his trousers' belt, and his naked sabre, which he held between his teeth; the butt-ends of the pistols protruded above his belt. Thus lightened of everything useless, and followed in the obscurity by the eyes of all such of the attacking column as had not yet entered the breach, he began to climb the stones of the cracked wall as if they had been the steps of a staircase. Having no shoes was an advantage; nothing can cling like a naked foot. He twisted his toes into the holes of the stones; he hoisted himself with his fists, and bore his weight on his knees. The ascent was a hazardous one; it was somewhat like climbing along the teeth of a gigantic saw. "Luckily," thought he, "there is nobody in the chamber of the first story, else I should not be allowed to climb up like this."

Radoub had not more than forty feet left to mount. He was somewhat encumbered by the projecting butt-ends of his pistols; and, as he climbed, the crevice narrowed, rendering the ascent more and more difficult, so that the danger of falling increased as he went on. At last he reached the frame of the loop-hole and pushed aside the twisted and broken grating so that he had space enough to pass through. He raised himself for a last powerful effort, rested his knee on the cornice of the ledge, seized with one hand a bar of the grating at the left, with the other a bar at the right, lifted half his body in front of the embrasure of the loop-hole, and, sabre between his teeth, hung thus suspended by his two fists over the abyss. It only needed one spring more to land him in the chamber of the first floor.

But a face appeared in a loop-hole. Radoub saw a frightful spectacle rise suddenly before him in the gloom,—an eye torn out, a jaw fractured, a bloody mask. This mask, which had only one eye left, was watching him. This mask had two hands; these two hands thrust themselves out of the darkness of this loop-hole and clutched at Radoub; one of them seized the two pistols in his belt, the other snatched the sword from between his teeth. Radoub was disarmed. His knee slipped upon the inclined plane of the cornice; his two fists, cramped about the bars of the grating, barely sufficed to support him, and beneath was a sheer descent of forty feet.

This mask and these hands belonged to Chante-en-Hiver. Suffocated by the smoke which rose from the room below, Chante-en-Hiver had succeeded in entering the embrasure of the loop-hole: the air from without had revived him; the freshness of the night had congealed the blood, and his strength had in a measure come back. Suddenly he perceived the torso of Radoub rise in front of the embrasure. Radoub, having his hands twisted about the bars, had no choice but to let himself fall or allow himself to be disarmed; so Chante-en-Hiver, with a horrible tranquillity, had taken the two pistols out of his belt and the sabre from between his teeth.

Then commenced an unheard-of duel, —a duel between the disarmed and the wounded. Evidently the dying man had the victory in his own hands. A single shot would suffice to hurl Radoub into the yawning gulf beneath his feet. Luckily for Radoub, Chante-en-Hiver held both pistols in the same hand, so that he could not fire either, and was forced to make use of the sabre. He struck Radoub a blow on the shoulder with the point. The sabre-stroke wounded Radoub, but saved his life. The soldier was unarmed, but in full possession of his strength. Regardless of his wound, which indeed was only a flesh-cut, he swung his body vigorously forward, loosed his hold of the bars, and bounded through the loop-hole. There he found himself face to face with Chante-en-Hiver, who had thrown the sabre behind him and was clutching a pistol in either hand. Chante-en-Hiver had Radoub close to the muzzle as he took aim upon his knees, but his enfeebled arm trembled, and he did not fire at once.

Radoub took advantage of this respite to burst out laughing. "I say, ugly face!" cried he, "do you suppose you frighten me with your bloody bullock's jaws? Thunder and Mars, how they have shattered your features!"

Chante-en-Hiver took aim.

Radoub continued: "It is not polite to mention it, but the grape-shot has dotted your mug very neatly. Bellona has disturbed your physiognomy, my lad. Come, come; spit out your little pistol-shot, my good fellow!"

Chante-en-Hiver fired; the ball passed so close to Radoub's head that it carried away part of his ear. His foe raised the second pistol in his other hand.

Radoub did not give him time to take aim. "It is enough to lose one ear!" cried he. "You have wounded me twice. It is my turn now."

He flung himself on Chante-en-Hiver, knocked aside his arm with such force that the pistol went off and the ball whizzed against the ceiling. He seized his enemy's broken jaw in both hands and twisted it about. Chante-en-Hiver uttered a howl of pain and fainted. Radoub stepped across his body and left him lying in the embrasure of the loop-hole.

"Now that I have announced my ultimatum, don't you stir again," said he. "Lie there, you ugly crawling snake! You may fancy that I am not going to amuse myself by massacring you. Crawl about on the ground at your ease,—under foot is the place for you. Die, —you can't get rid of that! In a little while you will learn what nonsense your priest has talked to you. Away with you into the great mystery, peasant!" And he hurried forward into the room. "One cannot see an inch before one's nose," grumbled he.

Chante-en-Hiver began to writhe convulsively upon the floor, and uttered fresh moans of agony.

Radoub turned back. "Hold your tongue! Do me the favour to be silent, citizen, without knowing it. I cannot trouble myself further with you; I should scorn to make an end of you. Just let me have quiet."

Then he thrust his hands into his hair as he stood watching Chante-en-Hiver. "But here, what am I to do now? It is all very fine, but I am disarmed. I had two shots to fire, and you have robbed me of them, animal! and with all that, a smoke that would blind a dog!"

Then his hand touched his wounded ear. "Aïe!" he said.

Then he went on: "You have gained a great deal by confiscating one of my ears! However, I would rather have one less of them than anything else: an ear is only an ornament. You have scratched my shoulder, too; but that is nothing. Expire, villager! I forgive you."

He listened. The din from the lower room was fearful. The combat had grown more furious than ever. "Things are going well down there;" he muttered. "How they howl 'Live the king!' One must admit that they die bravely."

His foot struck against the sabre. He picked it up, and said to Chante-en-Hiver, who no longer stirred, and who might indeed be dead: "See here, man of the woods, I will take my sabre; you have left me that, anyway. But I needed my pistols. The devil fly away with you, savage! Oh, there, what am I to do? I am no good whatever here."

He advanced into the hall trying to guide his steps in the gloom. Suddenly, in the shadow behind the central pillar, he perceived a long table upon which something gleamed faintly. He felt the objects. They were blunderbusses, carbines, pistols, a whole row of firearms laid out in order to his hand; it was the reserve of weapons the besieged had provided in this chamber, which would be their second place of stand, a whole arsenal.

"A sideboard!" cried Radoub; and he clutched them right and left, dizzy with joy. Thus armed, he became formidable.

He could see back of the table the door of the staircase, which communicated with the rooms above and below, standing wide open. Radoub seized two pistols, and fired them at random through the doorway; then he snatched a blunderbuss, and fired that,—then a blunderbuss loaded with buckshot, and discharged it. The blunderbuss, vomiting forth its fifteen balls, sounded like a volley of grape-shot. He got his breath back, and shouted down the staircase, in a voice of thunder,"Long live Paris!" Then seizing a second blunderbuss, still bigger than the first, he aimed it toward the staircase and waited.

The confusion in the lower hall was indescribable. This unexpected attack from behind paralyzed the besieged with astonishment. Two balls from Radoub's triple fire had taken effect: one had killed the elder of the brothers Pique-en-Bois; the other had killed De Quélen, nicknamed Houzard.

"They are on the floor above!" cried the marquis.

At this cry the men abandoned the retirade,—a flock of birds could not have fled more quickly; they plunged madly toward the staircase.

The marquis encouraged the flight. "Quick, quick!" he exclaimed. "There is most courage now in escape. Let us all get up to the second floor. We will begin again there." He left the retirade the last. This brave act saved his life.

Radoub, ambushed at the top of the stairs, watched the retreat, finger on trigger. The first who appeared at the turn of the spiral steps received the discharge of his gun full in their faces, and fell. Had the marquis been among them, he would have been killed. Before Radoub had time to seize another weapon, the others passed him,—the marquis behind all the rest, and moving more slowly.

Believing the first-floor chambers filled with the besiegers, the men did not pause there, but rushed on and gained the room above, which was the hall of the mirrors. There was the iron door; there was the sulphur-match; it was there they must capitulate or die.

Gauvain had been as much astounded as the besieged by the denotations from the staircase, and was unable to understand how aid could have reached him in that quarter; but he took advantage without waiting to comprehend. He leaped over the retirade, followed by his men, and pursued the fugitives up to the first floor. There he found Radoub.

The segreant saluted, and said: "One minute, my commandant. I did that. I remembered Dol; I followed your plan: I took the enemy between two fires."

"A good scholar," answered Gauvain, with a smile.

After one has been a certain length of time in the darkness, the eyes become accustomed to the obscurity like those of a night-bird. Gauvain perceived that Radoub was covered with blood. "But you are wounded, comrade!" he exclaimed.

"Never mind that, my commandant! What difference does it make,—an ear more or less? I got a sabre-thrust, too, but it is nothing. One always cuts one's self a little in breaking a window; it is only losing a little blood."

The besiegers made a halt in the first-floor chamber, which had been conquered by Radoub. A lantern was brought. Cimourdain rejoined Gauvain. They held a council. It was time to reflect, indeed. The besiegers were not in the secrets of their foes; they were unaware of the lack of munitions; they did not know that the defenders of the tower were short of powder, that the second floor must be the last post where a stand could be made; the assailants could not tell but the staircase might be mined. One thing was certain,— the enemy could not escape. Those who had not been killed were as safe as if under lock and key. Lantenac was in the trap.

Certain of this, the besiegers could afford to give themselves time to choose the best means of bringing about the end. Numbers among them had been killed already. The thing now was to spare the men as much as possible in this last assault. The risk of this final attack would be great. The first fire would without doubt be a hot one. The combat was interrupted. The besiegers, masters of the ground and first floors, waited the orders of the commander-in-chief to renew the conflict. Gauvain and Cimourdain were holding counsel.

Radoub assisted in silence at their deliberation. At length he timidly hazarded another military salute. "Commandant!"

"What is it, Radoub?"

"Have I a right to a little recompense?"

"Yes, indeed. Ask what you like."

"I ask permission to mount the first."

It was impossible to refuse him; indeed, he would have done it without permission.

Chapter XI

DESPERATE

While this consultation took place on the first floor, the besieged were barricading the second. Success is a fury; defeat is a madness. The encounter between the foes would be frenzied. To be close on victory intoxicates. The men below were inspired by hope, which would be the most powerful of human incentives if despair did not exist. Despair was above,—a calm, cold, sinister despair.

When the besieged reached the hall of refuge, beyond which they had no resource, no hope, their first care had been to bar the entrance. To lock the door was useless; it was necessary to block the staircase. In a position like theirs, an obstacle across which they could see, and over which they could fight, was worth more than a closed door. The torch which Imânus had planted in the wall near the sulphur-match lighted the room. There was in the chamber one of those great, heavy oak chests which were used to hold clothes and linen before the invention of chests of drawers. They dragged this chest out, and stood it on end in the door-way of the staircase. It fitted solidly and closed the entrance, leaving open at the top a narrow space by which a man could pass; but it was scarcely probable that the assailants would run the risk of being killed one after another by any attempt to pass the barrier in single file.

This obstruction of the entrance afforded the besieged a respite. They numbered their company. Out of the nineteen only seven remained, of whom Imânus made one. With the exception of Imânus and the marquis, they were all wounded. The five wounded men (active still, for in the heat of combat any wound less than mortal leaves a man able to move about) were Chatenay (called Robi), Guinoiseau, Hoisnard (Branche d'Or), Brin d'Amour, and Grand Francœur. All the others were dead. They had no munitions left; the cartridge-boxes were almost empty: they counted the cartridges. How many shots were there left for the seven to fire? Four! They had reached the pass where nothing remained but to fall. They had retreated to the precipice; it yawned black and terrible; they stood upon the very edge. Still, the attack was about to recommence,—slowly, and all the more surely on that account. They could hear the butt-end of the muskets sound along the staircase step by step, as the besiegers advanced. No means of escape. By the library? On the plateau bristled six cannon with every match lighted. By the upper chambers? To what end? They gaze on the platform: the only resource when that was reached would be to fling themselves from the top of the tower.

The seven survivors of this Homeric band found themselves inexorably enclosed and held fast by that thick wall which at once protected and betrayed them. They were not yet taken, but they were already prisoners.

The marquis spoke: "My friends, all is finished." Then after a silence, he added: "Grand Francœur, become again the Abbé Turmeau."

All knelt, rosary in hand. The measured stroke of the muskets sounded nearer. Grand Francœur covered with blood from a wound which had grazed his skull and torn away his leather cap, raised the crucifix in his right hand. The marquis, a sceptic at bottom, bent his knee to the ground.

"Let each one confess his faults aloud," said Grand Francœur. "Monseigneur, speak."

The marquis answered, "I have killed."

"I have killed," said Hoisnard.
"I have killed," said Guinoiseau.
"I have killed," said Brin d'Amour.
"I have killed," said Chatenay.
"I have killed," said Imânus.

And Grand Francœur replied: "In the name of the most Holy Trinity I absolve you. May your souls depart in peace!"

"Amen," replied all the voices.

The marquis raised himself. "Now let us die," he said.

"And kill," added Imânus.

The blows from the butt-end of the besiegers' muskets began to shake the chest which barred the door.

"Think of God," said the priest; "earth no longer exists for you."

"It is true," replied the marquis; "we are in the tomb."

All bowed their heads and smote their breasts. The marquis and the priest were alone standing. The priest prayed, keeping his eyes cast down; the peasants prayed; the marquis reflected. The coffer echoed dismally, as if under the stroke of hammers.

At this instant a rapid, strong voice sounded suddenly behind him, exclaiming: "Did I not tell you so, monseigneur?"

All turned their heads in stupefied wonder. A gap had just opened in the wall. A stone, perfectly fitted into the others, but not cemented, and having a pivot above and a pivot below, had just revolved like a turnstile, leaving the wall open. The stone having revolved on its axis, the opening was double, and offered two means of exit,—one to the right and one to the left; narrow, but leaving space enough to allow a man to pass. Beyond this door, so unexpectedly opened, could be seen the first of a spiral staircase. A face appeared in the opening. The marquis recognized Halmalo.

Chapter XII

DELIVERANCE

"Is it you, Halmalo?"

"It is I, monseigneur. You see there are stones that turn; they really exist; you can get out of here. I am just in time; but come quickly. In ten minutes you will be in the heart of the forest."

"God is great," said the priest.

"Save yourself, monseigneur!" cried the men in concert.

"All of you go first," said marquis.

"You must go first, monseigneur," returned the Abbé Turmeau. "I go the last."

And the marquis added, in a severe tone: "No struggle of generosity; we have no time to be magnanimous. You are wounded; I order you to live and to fly. Quick! Take advantage of this outlet. Thanks, Halmalo."

"Marquis, must we separate?" asked Abbé Turmeau.

"Below, without doubt. We can only escape one by one."

"Does Monseigneur assign us a rendezvous?"

"Yes; a glade in the forest,—La Pierre Gauvain. Do you know the place?"

"We all know it."

"I shall be there to-morrow at noon. Let all those who can walk meet me at that time."

"Every man will be there."

"And we will begin the war anew," said the marquis.

As Halmalo pushed against the turning-stone, he found that it did not stir. The aperture could not be closed again.

"Monseigneur," he said, "we must hasten. The stone will not move. I was able to open the passage, but I cannot shut it."

The stone, in fact, had become deadened, as it were, on its hinges from long disuse. It was impossible to make it revolve back into its place.

"Monseigneur," resumed Halmalo, "I had hoped to close the passage, so that the Blues, when they got in and found no one, would think you must have flown off in the smoke. But the stone will not budge. The enemy will see the outlet open, and can follow. At least, do not let us lose a second. Quick, everybody make for the staircase!"

Imânus laid his hand on Halmalo's shoulder. "Comrade, how much time will it take to get from here to the forest and to safety?"

"Is there any one seriously wounded?" asked Halmalo.

They answered, "Nobody."

"In that case a quarter of an hour will be enough."

"Go," said Imânus; "if the enemy can be kept out of here for a quarter of an hour—"

"They may follow; they cannot overtake us."

"But," said the marquis, "they will be here in five minutes; that old chest cannot hold out against them any longer. A few blows from their muskets will end the business. A quarter of an hour! Who can keep them back for a quarter of an hour?"

"I," said Imânus.

"You, Gouge-le-Bruant?"

"I, monseigneur. Listen. Five out of six of you are wounded. I have not a scratch."

"Nor I," said the marquis.

"You are the chief, monseigneur. I am a soldier. Chief and soldier are two."

"I know we have each a different duty."

"No, monseigneur, we have, you and I, the same duty; it is to save you."

Imânus turned toward his companions. "Comrades, the thing necessary to be done is to hold the enemy in check and retard the pursuit as long as possible. Listen. I am in possession of my full strength; I have not lost a drop of blood; not being wounded, I can hold out longer than any of the others. Fly, all of you! Leave me your weapons; I will make good use of them. I take it on myself to stop the enemy for a good half hour. How many loaded pistols are there?"

"Four."

"Lay them on the floor." His command was obeyed. "It is well. I stay here. They will find somebody to talk with. Now, quick! get away."

Life and death hung in the balance; there was no time for thanks,—scarcely time for those nearest to grasp his hand.

"We shall meet soon," the marquis said to him.

"No, monseigneur; I hope not,—not soon; for I am going to die."

They got through the opening one after another and passed down the stairs, the wounded going first. While the men were escaping, the marquis took a pencil out of a notebook which he carried in his pocket and wrote a few words on the stone, which, remaining motionless, left the passage gaping open.

"Come, monseigneur, they are all gone but you," said Halmalo. And the sailor began to descend the stairs. The marquis followed.

Imânus remained alone.

Chapter XIII

THE EXECUTIONER

The four pistols had been laid on the flags, for the chamber had no flooring. Imânus grasped a pistol in either hand. He moved obliquely toward the entrance to the staircase which the chest obstructed and masked.

The assailants evidently feared some surprise,—one of those final explosions which involve conqueror and conquered in the same catastrophe. This last attack was as slow and prudent as the first had been impetuous. They had not been able to push the chest backward into the chamber,—perhaps would not have done it if they could. They had broken the bottom with blows from their muskets, and pierced the top with bayonet holes; by these holes they were trying to see into the hall before entering. The light from the lanterns with which they had illuminated the staircase shone through these chinks.

Imânus perceived an eye regarding him through one of the holes. He aimed his pistol quickly at the place, and pulled the trigger. To his joy, a horrible cry followed the report. The ball had entered the eye and passed through the brain of the soldier, who fell backward down the stairs.

The assailants had broken two large holes in the cover; Imânus thrust his pistol through one of these and fired at random into the mass of besiegers. The ball must have rebounded, for he heard several cries, as if three or four were killed or wounded; then there was a great tramping and tumult as the men fell back. Imânus threw down the two pistols which he had just fired, and, taking the two which still remained, peered out through the holes in the chest. He was able to see what execution his shots had done.

The assailants had descended the stairs. The twisting of the spiral staircase only allowed him to look down three or four steps; the men he had shot lay writhing there in the death agony. Imânus waited. "It is so much time gained," thought he. Then he saw a man flat on his stomach creeping up the stairs; at the same instant the head of another soldier appeared lower down from behind the pillar about which the spiral wound. Imânus aimed at this head and fired. A cry followed, the soldier fell; and Imânus, while watching, threw away the empty pistol, and changed the loaded one from his left hand to his right. As he did so he felt a horrible pain, and, in his turn, uttered a yell of agony. A sabre had traversed his bowels. A fist (the fist of the man who had crept up the stairs) had just been thrust through the second hole in the bottom of the chest, and this fist had plunged a sabre into Imânus's body. The wound was frightful; the abdomen was pierced through and through.

Imânus did not fall. He set his teeth together and muttered, "Good!" Then he dragged himself, tottering along, and retreated to the iron door, at the side of which the torch was still burning. He laid his pistol on the stones and seized the torch, and while with his left hand he held together the terrible wound through which his intestines protruded, with his right he lowered the torch till it touched the sulphur-match. It caught fire instantaneously; the wick blazed.

Imânus dropped the torch; it lay on the ground still burning. He seized his pistol anew, dropped forward upon the flags, and with what breath he had left blew the wick. The flame ran along it, passed beneath the iron door, and reached the bridge-castle. Then seeing that his execrable exploit had succeeded, —prouder, perhaps, of this crime than of the courage he had before shown,—this man, who had just proved himself a hero, only to sink into an assassin, smiled as he stretched himself out to die, and muttered: "They will remember me. I take vengeance on their little ones for the fate of our little one,— the king shut up in the Temple!"

Chapter XIV

IMÂNUS ALSO ESCAPES

At this moment there was a great noise; the chest was thrown violently back into the hall, and gave passage to a man who rushed forward, sabre in hand, crying,—

"It is I—Radoub! What are you going to do? It bores me to wait. I have risked it. Anyway I have just disembowelled one. Now I attack the whole of you. Whether the rest follow me or don't follow me, here I am. How many are there of you?"

It was indeed Radoub, and he was alone!

After the massacre Imânus had caused upon the stairs, Gauvain, fearing some secret mine, had drawn back his men and consulted with Cimourdain. Radoub, standing sabre in hand upon the threshold, sent his voice anew into the obscurity of the chamber across which the nearly extinguished torch cast a faint gleam, and repeated his question, "I am one. How many are you?"

There was no answer. He stepped forward. One of those sudden jets of light which an expiring fire sometimes sends out, and which seem like its dying throes, burst from the torch and illuminated the entire chamber. Radoub caught sight of himself in one of the mirrors hanging against the wall,—approached it, and examined his bleeding face and wounded ear. "Horrible mutilation!" said he.

Then he turned about, and, to his utter stupefaction, perceived that the hall was empty. "Nobody here!" he exclaimed. "Not a creature!"

Then he saw the revolving stone, and the staircase beyond the opening. "Ah! I understand! The key to the fields. Come up, all of you!" he shouted. "Comrades, come up! They have run away! They have filed off, dissolved, evaporated, cut their lucky! This old jug of a tower has a crack in it. There is the hole they got out by, the beggars! How is anybody to get the better of Pitt and Cobourg while they are able to play such comedies as this? The very devil himself came to their rescue. There is nobody here!"

The report of a pistol cut his words short: a ball grazed his elbow and flattened itself against the wall.

"Aha!" said he. "So there is somebody left. Who was good enough to show me that little politeness?"

"I," answered a voice.

Radoub looked about, and caught sight of Imânus in the gloom. "Ah!" cried he. "I have got one at all events. The others have escaped, but you will not, I promise you."

"Do you believe it?" retorted Imânus.

Radoub made a step forward and paused. "Hey, you, lying on the ground there! Who are you?"

"I am a man who laughs at you who are standing up."

"What is it you are holding in your right hand?"

"A pistol."

"And in your left hand?"

"My entrails."

"You are my prisoner."

"I defy you!"

Imânus bowed his head over the burning wick, spent his last breath in stirring the flame, and expired.

A few seconds after, Gauvain and Cimourdain, followed by the whole troop of soldiers, were in the hall. They all saw the opening. They searched the corners of the room and explored the staircase; it had a passage at the bottom which led to the ravine. The besieged had escaped. They raised Imânus,—he was dead. Gauvain, lantern in hand, examined the stone which had afforded an outlet to the fugitives: he had heard of the turning-stone, but he too had always disbelieved the legend. As he looked he saw some lines written in pencil on the massive block; he held the lantern closer, and read these words:—

"*Au revoir, Viscount.*
"Lantenac."

Guéchamp was standing by his commandant. Pursuit was utterly useless; the fugitives had the whole country to aid them,—thickets, ravines, copses, the inhabitants. Doubtless they were already far away. There would be no possibility of discovering them; they had the entire forest of Fougères, with its countless hiding-places, for a refuge. What was to be done? The whole struggle must begin anew. Gauvain and Guéchamp exchanged conjectures and expressions of disappointment.

Cimourdain listened gravely, but did not utter a word.

"And the ladder, Guéchamp?" said Gauvin.

"Commandant, it has not come."

"But we saw a wagon escorted by gendarmes."

Guéchamp only replied: "It did not bring the ladder."

"What did it bring, then?"

"The guillotine," said Cimourdain.

Chapter XV

NEVER PUT A WATCH AND A KEY IN THE SAME POCKET

The Marquis de Lantenac was not so far away as they believed. But he was none the less in safety, and completely out of their reach. He had followed Halmalo.

The staircase by which they descended in the wake of the other fugitives ended in a narrow vaulted passage close to the ravine and the arches of the bridge. This passage opened upon a deep natural fissure, which led into the ravine on one side and into the forest on the other. The windings of the path were completely hidden among the thickets; it would have been impossible to discover a man concealed there. A fugitive, once arrived at this point, had only to twist away like a snake. The opening from the staircase into the secret passage was so completely obstructed by brambles that the builders of the passage had not thought it necessary to close the way in any other manner.

The marquis had only to go forward now. He was not placed in any difficulty by lack of a disguise. He had not thrown aside his peasant's dress since coming to Brittany, thinking it more in character.

When Halmalo and the marquis passed out of the passage into the cleft, the five other men—Guinoiseau, Hoisnard (Branche d'Or), Brin d'Amour, Chatenay, and the Abbé Turmeau—were no longer there.

"They did not take much time to get away," said Halmalo.

"Follow their example," said the marquis.

"Must I leave, monseigneur?"

"Without doubt. I have already told you so. Each must escape alone to be safe. One man passes where two cannot. We should attract attention if we were together. You would lose my life and I yours."

"Does Monseigneur know the district?"

"Yes."

"Monseigneur still gives the rendezvous for the Pierre Gauvain?"

"Tomorrow,—at noon."

"I shall be there. We shall all be there." Then Halmalo burst out: "Ah, monseigneur! When I think that we were together in the open sea, that we were alone, that I wanted to kill you, that you were my master, that you could have told me so, and that you did not speak! What a man you are!"

The marquis replied: "England! There is no other resource. In fifteen days the English must be in France."

"I have much to tell monseigneur. I obeyed his orders."

"We will talk of all that to-morrow."

"Farewell till to-morrow, monseigneur."

"By-the-way, are you hungry?"

"Perhaps I am, monseigneur. I was in such a hurry to get here that I am not sure whether I have eaten to-day."

The marquis took a cake of chocolate from his pocket, broke it in half, gave one piece to Halmalo, and began to eat the other himself.

"Monseigneur," said Halmalo, "at your right is the ravine; at your left, the forest."

"Very good. Leave me. Go on your way."

Halmalo obeyed. He hurried off through the darkness. For a few instants the marquis could hear the crackling of the underbrush, then all was still. By that time it would have been impossible to track Halmalo. This forest of the Bocage was the fugitive's auxiliary. He did not flee,—he vanished. It was this facility for disappearance which made our armies hesitate before this ever-retreating Vendée, so formidable as it fled.

The marquis remained motionless. He was a man who forced himself to feel nothing; but he could not restrain his emotion on breathing this free air, after having been so long stifled in blood and carnage. To feel himself completely at liberty after having seemed so utterly lost; after having seen the grave so close, to be swept suddenly beyond its reach; to come out of death back into life,—it was a shock even to a man like Lantenac. Familiar as he was with danger, in spite of all the vicissitudes he had passed through he could not at first steady his soul under this. He acknowledged to himself that he was content. But he quickly subdued this emotion, which was more like joy than any feeling he had known for years. He drew out his watch and struck the hour. What time was it?

To his great astonishment, the marquis found that it was only ten o'clock. When one has just passed through some terrible convulsion of existence in which every hope and life itself were at stake, one is always astounded to find that those awful minutes were no longer than ordinary ones. The warning cannon had been fired a little before sunset, and La Tourgue attacked by the storming-party half an hour later, between seven and eight o'clock,—just as night was falling. The colossal combat, begun at eight o'clock, had ended at ten. This whole *épopée* had only taken a hundred and twenty minutes to enact. Sometimes catastrophes sweep on with the rapidity of lightning,—the climax is overwhelming from its suddenness. On reflection, the astonishing thing was that the struggle could have lasted so long. A resistance for two hours of so small a number against so large a force was extraordinary; and certainly it had not been short or quickly finished, this battle of nineteen against four thousand.

But it was time he should be gone. Halmalo must be far away, and the marquis judged that it would not be necessary to wait there longer. He put his watch back into his waistcoat, but not into the same pocket, for he discovered that the key of the iron door given him by Imânus was there, and the crystal might be broken against the key. Then he moved toward the forest in his turn. As he turned to the left, it seemed to him that a faint gleam of light penetrated the darkness where he stood. He walked back, and across the underbrush, clearly outlined against a red background and become visible in their tiniest outlines, he perceived a great glare in the ravine; only a few paces separated him from it. He hurried forward,—then stopped, remembering what folly it was to expose himself in that light. Whatever might have happened, after all it did not concern him. Again he set out in the direction Halmalo had indicated, and walked a little way toward the forest.

Suddenly, deep as he was hidden among the brambles, he heard a terrible cry echo over his head. This cry seemed to proceed from the very edge of the plateau which stretched above the ravine. The marquis raised his eyes and stood still.

BOOK V

In Dæmone Deus

Chapter I

FOUND, BUT LOST

At the moment Michelle Fléchard caught sight of the tower, she was more than a league away. She, who could scarcely take a step, did not hesitate before these miles which must be traversed. The woman was weak, but the mother found strength. She walked on.

The sun set; the twilight came, then the night. Always pressing on, Michelle heard a bell afar off, hidden by the darkness, strike eight o'clock, then nine. The peal probably came from the belfry of Parigné. From time to time she paused to listen to strange sounds like the deadened echo of blows, which might perhaps be the wind in the distance. She walked straight on, breaking the furze and the sharp heath-stems beneath her bleeding feet. She was guided by a faint light which shone from the distant tower, defining its outlines against the night, and giving a mysterious glow to the tower amidst the surrounding gloom. This light became more distinct when the noise sounded louder, then faded suddenly.

The vast plateau across which Michelle Fléchard journeyed was covered with grass and heath; not a house, not a tree appeared. It rose gradually, and, as far as the eye could reach, stretched in a straight hard line against the sombre horizon where a few stars gleamed. She had always the tower before her eyes; the sight kept her strength from failing. She saw the massive pile grow steadily as she walked on.

We have just said the smothered reports and the pale gleams of light starting from the tower were intermittent; they stopped, then began anew, offering an enigma full of agony to the wretched mother. Suddenly they ceased; noise and gleams of light both died. There was a moment of complete silence,—an ominous tranquillity.

It was just at this moment that Michelle Fléchard reached the edge of the plateau. She saw at her feet a ravine, whose bottom was lost in the wan indistinctness of the night; also at a little distance, on the top of the plateau, an entanglement of wheels, metal, and harness, which was a battery; and before her, confusedly lighted by the matches of the cannon, an enormous edifice that seemed built of shadows blacker than the shadows which surrounded it. This mass of buildings was composed of a bridge whose arches were embedded in the ravine, and of a sort of castle which rose upon the bridge; both bridge and castle were supported against a lofty circular shadow,—the tower toward which this mother had journeyed from so far. She could see lights come and go in the loop-holes of the tower, and from the noise which surged up she divined that it was filled with a crowd of men; indeed, now and then their gigantic shadows were flung out on the night. Near the battery was a camp, whose outposts she might have perceived through the gloom and the underbrush, but she had as yet noticed nothing. She went close to the edge of the plateau, so near the bridge that it seemed to her she could almost touch it with her hand. The depth of the ravine alone kept her from reaching it. She could make out in the gloom the three stories of the bridge-castle.

How long she stood there Michelle Fléchard could not have told, for her mind, absorbed in her mute contemplation of this gaping ravine and this shadowy edifice, took no note of time. What was this building? What was going on within? Was it La Tourgue? A strange dizziness seized her; in her confusion she could not tell if this were the goal she had been seeking on the starting-point of a terrible journey. She asked herself why she was there. She looked; she listened.

Suddenly a great blackness shut out every object. A cloud of smoke swept up between Michelle and the pile she was watching; a sharp report forced her to close her eyes. Scarcely had she done so, when a great light reddened the lids. She opened them again. It was no longer the night she had before her; it was the day,—but a fearful day! the day born of fire! She was watching the beginning of a conflagration. From black the smoke had become scarlet, filled with a mighty flame, which appeared and disappeared, writhing and twisting in serpentine coils. The flame burst out like a tongue from something which resembled blazing jaws; it was the embrasure of a window filled with fire. This window, covered by iron bars, already reddening in the heat, was a casement in the lower story of the bridge-castle. Nothing of the edifice was visible except this window. The smoke covered even the plateau, leaving only the mouth of the ravine black against the vermilion flames.

Michelle Fléchard stared in dumb wonder. It was like a dream; she could no longer tell where reality ended, and the confused fancies of her poor troubled brain began. Ought she to fly? Should she remain? There was nothing real enough for any definite decision to steady her mind. A wind swept up and burst aside the curtain of smoke; in the opening the frowning bastile rose suddenly in view,—donjon, bridge, châtelet, —dazzling in the terrible gilding of conflagration which framed it from top to bottom.

The appalling illumination showed Michelle Fléchard every detail of the ancient heap. The lowest story of the castle built on the bridge was burning. Above rose the two other stories, still untouched, but as it were supported on a corbel of flames. From the edge of the plateau where Michelle Fléchard stood, she could catch broken glimpses of the interior between the clouds of smoke and fire. The windows were all open. Through the great casements of the second story she could make out the cupboards stretched along the walls, which looked to her full of books, and by one of the windows could see a little group lying on the floor, in the shadow, indistinct and massed together like birds in a nest, which at times she fancied she saw move. She looked fixedly in this direction. What was that little group lying there in the shadow? Sometimes it flashed across her mind that those were living forms; but she had fever; she had eaten nothing since morning; she had walked without intermission; she was utterly exhausted. She felt herself giving way to a sort of hallucination, which she had still reason enough to struggle against. Still, her eyes fixed themselves ever more steadily upon that one point; she could not look away from that little heap upon the floor,—a mass of inanimate objects, doubtless, that had been left in that room below which the flames roared and billowed.

Suddenly the fire, as if animated by a will and purpose, flung downward a jet of flame toward the great dead ivy which covered the façade whereat Michelle Fléchard was gazing. It seemed as if the fire had just discovered this outwork of dried branches; a spark darted greedily upon it, and a line of flame spread upward from twig to twig with frightful rapidity. In the twinkling of an eye it reached the second story. As they rose, the flames illuminated the chamber of the first floor, and the awful glare threw out in bold relief the three little creatures lying asleep upon the floor. A lovely, statuesque group of legs and arms interlaced, closed eyes, and angelic, smiling faces.

The mother recognized her children! She uttered a terrible cry. That cry of indescribable agony is only given to mothers. No sound is at once so savage and so touching. When a woman utters it, you seem to hear the yell of a sea-wolf; when the sea-wolf cries thus, you seem to hear the voice of a woman. This cry of Michelle Fléchard was a howl. Hecuba howled, says Homer.

It was this cry which reached the Marquis de Lantenac. When he heard it he stood still. The marquis was between the outlet of the passage through which he had been guided by Halmalo and the ravine. Across the brambles which enclosed him he saw the bridge in flames, and La Tourgue red with the reflection. Looking upward through the opening which the branches left above his head, he perceived close to the edge of the plateau on the opposite side of the gulf, in front of the burning castle, in the full light of the conflagration, the haggard, anguish-stricken face of a woman bending over the depth. It was this woman who had uttered that cry.

The face was no longer that of Michelle Fléchard; it was a Gorgon's. She was appalling in her agony; the peasant woman was transformed into one of the Eumenides; this unknown villager, vulgar, ignorant, unreasoning, had risen suddenly to the epic grandeur of despair. Great sufferings swell the soul to gigantic proportions. This was no longer a simple mother,—all maternity's voice cried out through hers: whatever sums up and becomes a type of humanity grows superhuman. There she towered on the edge of that ravine, in front of that conflagration, in presence of that crime, like a power from beyond the grave; she moaned like a wild beast, but her attitude was that of a goddess; the mouth, which uttered imprecations, was set in a flaming mask. Nothing could have been more regal than her eyes shooting lightnings through her tears. Her look blasted the conflagration.

The marquis listened. The mother's voice flung its echoes down upon his head,—inarticulate, heart-rending; sobs rather than words:—

"Ah, my God, my children! Those are my children! Help! Fire! fire! fire! O you brigands! Is there no one here? My children are burning up! Georgette! My babies! Gros-Alain! René-Jean! What does it mean? Who put my children there? They are asleep. Oh, I am mad! It is impossible! Help, help!"

A great bustle of movement was apparent in La Tourgue and upon the plateau. The whole camp rushed out to the fire which had just burst forth. The besiegers, after meeting the grape-shot, had now to deal with the conflagration. Gauvain, Cimourdain, and Guéchamp were giving orders. What was to be done? Only a few buckets of water could be drained from the half-dried brook of the ravine. The consternation increased. The whole edge of the plateau was covered with men whose troubled faces watched the progress of the flames. What they saw was terrible; they gazed, and could do nothing.

The flames had spread along the ivy and reached the topmost story, leaping greedily upon the straw with which it was filled. The entire granary was burning now. The flames wreathed and danced as if in fiendish joy. A cruel breeze fanned the pyre. One could fancy the evil spirit of Imânus urging on the fire, and rejoicing in the destruction which had been his last earthly crime. The library, though between the two burning stories, was not yet on fire; the height of its ceiling and the thickness of the walls retarded the fatal moment; but it was fast approaching. The flames from below licked the stones; the flames from above whirled down to caress them with the awful embrace of death: beneath, a cave of lava; above, an arch of embers. If the floor fell first, the children would be flung into the lava stream; if the ceiling gave way, they would be buried beneath burning coals.

The little ones slept still; across the sheets of flame and smoke which now hid, now exposed the casements, the children were visible in that fiery grotto, within that meteoric glare, peaceful, lovely, motionless, like three confident cherubs slumbering in a hell. A tiger might have wept to see those angels in that furnace, those cradles in that tomb.

And the mother was wringing her hands: "Fire! I say, fire! Are they all deaf, that nobody comes? They are burning my chilldren! Come, come, you men that I see yonder. Oh, the days and days that I have hunted,—and this is where I find them! Fire! Help! Three angels,—to think of three angels burning there! What have they done, the innocents? They shot me; they are burning my little ones! Who is it does such things? Help! save my children! Do you not hear me? A dog,—one would have pity on a dog! My children! my children! They are asleep. O Georgette,—I see her face! René-Jean, Gros-Alain,—those are their names: you may know I am their mother. Oh, it is horrible! I have travelled days and nights! Why, this very morning I talked of them with a woman! Help, help! Where are those monsters? Horror, horror! The eldest not five years old, the youngest not two. I can see their little bare legs. They are asleep, Holy Virgin! Heaven gave them to me, and devils snatch them away. To think how far I have journeyed! My children, that I nourished with my milk! I, who thought myself wretched because I could not find them,—have pity on me! I want my children; I must have my children! And there they are in the fire! See, how my poor feet bleed! Help! It is not possible, if there are men on the earth, that my little ones will be left to die like this. Help! Murder! Oh, such a thing was never seen! O assassins! What is that dreadful house there? They stole my children from me in order to kill them. God of mercy, give me my children! They shall not die; Help! help! help! Oh, I shall curse Heaven itself, if they die like that!"

While the mother's awful supplications rang out, other voices rose upon the plateau and in the ravine.

"A ladder!"

"There is no ladder!"

"Water!"

"There is no water!"

"Up yonder, in the tower, on the second story, there is a door."

"It is iron."

"Break it in!"

"Impossible!"

And the mother, redoubling her agonized appeals: "Fire! Help! Hurry, I say, if you will not kill me! My children, my children! Oh, the horrible fire! Take them out of it, or throw me in!"

In the interval between these clamours the triumphant crackling of the flames could be heard.

The marquis put his hand in his pocket and touched the key of the iron door. Then, stooping again beneath the vault through which he had escaped, he turned back into the passage from whence he had just emerged.

Chapter II

FROM THE DOOR OF STONE TO THE IRON DOOR

A WHOLE army distracted by the impossibility of giving aid; four thousand men unable to succour three children,—such was the situation. Not even a ladder to be had; that sent from Javené had not arrived. The flaming space widened like a crater that opens. To attempt the staying of the fire by means of the half-dried brook would have been mad folly,—like flinging a glass of water on a volcano.

Cimourdain, Guéchamp, and Radoub had descended into the ravine; Gauvain remounted to the room in the second story of the tower, where were the stone that turned, the secret passage, and the iron door leading into the library. It was there that the sulphur-match had been lighted by Imânus; from there the conflagration had started. Gauvain took with him twenty sappers. There was no possible resource except to break open the iron door; its fastenings were terribly secure. They began by blows with axes. The axes broke. A sapper said: "Steel snaps like glass against that iron." The door was made of double sheets of wrought-iron, bolted together; each sheet three fingers in thickness. They took iron bars and tried to shake the door beneath their blows; the bars broke "like matches" said one of the sappers.

Gauvain murmured gloomily: "Nothing but a ball could open that door. If we could only get a cannon up here!"

"But how to do it?" answered the sapper.

There was a moment of consternation. Those powerless arms ceased their efforts. Mute, conquered, dismayed, these men stood staring at the immovable door. A red reflection crept from beneath it; behind, the conflagration was each instant increasing. The frightful corpse of Imânus lay on the floor,—a demoniac victor. Only a few moments more and the whole bridge-castle might fall in. What could be done? There was not a hope left.

Gauvain, with his eyes fixed on the turning-stone and the secret passage, cried furiously: "It was by that the Marquis de Lantenac escaped."

"And returns," said a voice.

The face of a white-haired man appeared in the stone frame of the secret opening. It was the marquis! Many years had passed since Gauvain had seen that face so near. He recoiled. The rest all stood petrified with astonishment.

The marquis held a large key in his hand; he cast a haughty glance upon the sappers standing before him, walked straight to the iron door, bent beneath the arch, and put the key in the lock. The iron creaked, the door opened, revealing a gulf of flame; the marquis entered it. He entered with a firm step, his head erect. The lookers-on followed him with their eyes. The marquis had scarcely moved half a dozen paces down the blazing hall when the floor, undermined by the fire, gave way beneath his feet and opened a precipice between him and the door. He did not even turn his head,—he walked steadily on. He disappeared in the smoke. Nothing more could be seen.

Had the marquis been able to advance further? Had a new gulf of fire opened beneath his feet? Had he only succeeded in destroying himself? They could not tell. They had before them a wall of smoke and flame. The marquis was beyond that, living or dead.

Chapter III

WHERE WE SEE THE CHILDREN WAKE THAT WE SAW GO ASLEEP

The little ones opened their eyes at last. The conflagration had not yet entered the library, but cast a rosy glow across the ceiling. The children had never seen an aurora like that; they watched it. Georgette was in ecstasies.

The conflagration unfurled all its splendours; the black hydra and the scarlet dragon appeared amidst the wreathing smoke in awful darkness and gorgeous vermilion. Long streaks of flame shot far out and illuminated the shadows, like opposing comets pursuing one another. Fire is recklessly prodigal with its treasures; its furnaces are filled with gems which it flings to the winds; it is not for nothing that charcoal is identical with the diamond. Fissures had opened in the wall of the upper story, through which the embers poured like cascades of jewels; the heaps of straw and oats burning in the granary began to stream out of the windows in an avalanche of golden rain, the oats turning to amethyst and the straw to carbuncles.

"Pretty!" said Georgette.

They all three raised themselves.

"Ah!" cried the mother. "They have awakened!"

René-Jean got up, then Gros-Alain, and Georgette followed. René-Jean stretched his arms toward the window and said, "I am warm."

"Me warm," cooed Georgette.

The mother shrieked: "My children! René! Alain! Georgette!"

The little ones looked about. They strove to comprehend. When men are frightened, children are only curious. He who is easily astonished is difficult to alarm; ignorance is intrepidity. Children have so little claim to purgatory that if they saw it they would admire.

The mother repeated: "René! Alain! Georgette!"

René-Jean turned his head; that voice roused him from his reverie. Children have short memories, but their recollections are swift; the whole past is yesterday to them. René-Jean saw his mother; found that perfectly natural; and feeling a vague want of support in the midst of those strange surroundings, he called "Mamma!"

"Mamma!" said Gros-Alain.

"M'ma!" said Georgette. And she held out her little arms.

"My children!" shrieked the mother.

All three went close to the window-ledge; fortunately the fire was not on that side.

"I am too warm," said René-Jean. He added, "It burns." Then his eyes sought the mother. "Come here, mamma!" he cried.

"Tum, m'ma," repeated Georgette.

The mother, with her hair streaming about her face, her garments torn, her feet and hands bleeding, let herself roll from bush to bush down into the ravine. Cimourdain and Guéchamp were there, as powerless as Gauvain was above. The soldiers, desperate at being able to do nothing, swarmed about. The heat was unsupportable, but nobody felt it. They looked at the bridge, the height of the arches, the different stories of the castle,—the inaccessible windows. Help to be of any avail must come at once. Three stories to climb; no way of doing it!

Radoub, wounded, with a sabre-cut on his shoulder and one ear torn off, rushed forward dripping with sweat and blood. He saw Michelle Fléchard. "Hold!" cried he. "The woman that was shot! So you have come to life again?"

"My children!" groaned the mother.

"You are right," answered Radoub, "we have no time to occupy ourselves about ghosts." He attempted to climb the bridge, but in vain; he dug his nails in between the stones and clung there for a few seconds, but the layers were as smoothly joined as if the wall had been new; Radoub fell back.

The conflagration swept on, each instant growing more terrible. They could see the heads of the three children framed in the red light of the window. In his frenzy Radoub shook his clinched hand at the sky, and shouted, "Is there no mercy yonder?"

The mother on her knees, clung to one of the piers, crying, "Mercy, mercy!"

The hollow sound of cracking timbers rose above the roar of the flames. The panes of glass in the book-cases of the library cracked and fell with a crash. It was evident that the timber-work had given way. Human strength could do nothing. Another moment and the whole would fall. The soldiers only waited for the final catastrophe. They could hear the little voices repeat, "Mamma! mamma!" The whole crowd was paralyzed with horror!

Suddenly, at the casement near that where the children stood, a tall form appeared against the crimson background of the flames. Every head was raised, every eye fixed. A man was above there,—a man in the library, in the furnace! The face showed black against the flames, but they could see the white hair; they recognized the Marquis de Lantenac. He disappeared, then appeared again. The indomitable old man stood in the window shoving out an enormous ladder. It was the escape ladder deposited in the library; he had seen it lying upon the floor and dragged it to the window. He held it by one end; with the marvellous agility of an athlete he slipped it out of the casement, and slid it along the wall down into the ravine.

Radoub folded his arms about the ladder as it descended within his reach, crying, "Long live the Republic!"

The marquis shouted, "Long live the King!"

Radoub muttered: "You may cry what you like, and talk nonsense if you please, you are an angel of mercy all the same."

The ladder was settled in place, and communication established between the burning floor and the ground. Twenty men rushed up, Radoub at their head, and in the twinkling of an eye they were hanging to the rungs from the top to the bottom, making a human ladder. He had his face turned toward the conflagration. The little army scattered among the heath and along the sides of the ravine pressed forward, overcome by contending emotions, upon the plateau, into the ravine, out on the platform of the tower.

The marquis disappeared again, then reappeared bearing a child in his arms. There was a tremendous clapping of hands. The marquis had seized the first little one that he found within reach. It was Gros-Alain.

Gros-Alain cried, "I am afraid."

The marquis gave the boy to Radoub; Radoub passed him on to the soldier behind, who passed him to another; and just as Gros-Alain, greatly frightened and sobbing loudly, was given from hand to hand to the bottom of the ladder, the marquis, who had been absent for a moment, returned to the window with René-Jean, who struggled and wept and beat Radoub with his little fists as the marquis passed him on to the sergeant.

The marquis went back into the chamber that was now filled with flames. Georgette was there alone. He went up to her. She smiled. This man of granite felt his eyelids grow moist. He asked, "What is your name?"

"Orgette," said she.

He took her in his arms; she was still smiling, and at the instant he handed her to Radoub, that conscience, so lofty and yet so darkened, was dazzled by the beauty of innocence: the old man kissed the child.

"It is the little girl!" said the soldiers; and Georgette in her turn descended from arm to arm till she reached the ground, amidst cries of exultation. They clapped their hands;

they leaped; the old grenadiers sobbed, and she smiled at them.

The mother stood at the foot of the ladder breathless, mad, intoxicated by this change,—flung, without transition, from hell into paradise. Excess of joy lacerates the heart in its own way. She extended her arms; she received first Gros-Alain, then René-Jean, then Georgette. She covered them with frantic kisses, then burst into a wild laugh and fainted.

A great cry rose: "They are all saved."

All were indeed saved, except the old man. But no one thought of him,—not even he himself, perhaps. He remained for a few instants leaning against the window-ledge lost in a reverie, as if he wished to leave the gulf of flames time to make a decision. Then, without the least haste, slowly indeed and proudly, he stepped over the window-sill, and erect, upright, his shoulders against the rungs, having the conflagration at his back, the depth before him, he began to descend the ladder in silence, with the majesty of a phantom.

The men who were on the ladder sprang off; every witness shuddered. About this man thus descending from that height there was a sacred horror as about a vision; but he plunged calmly into the darkness before him. They recoiled; he drew nearer them. The marble pallor of his face showed no emotion; his haughty eyes were calm and cold. At each step he made out of the darkness, he seemed to tower higher; the ladder shook and echoed under his firm tread: one might have thought him the statue of the "Commendatore" descending anew into his sepulchre.

As the marquis reached the bottom, and his foot left the last rung and planted itself on the ground, a hand seized his shoulder. He turned about.

"I arrest you," said Cimourdain.

"I approve of what you do," said Lantenac.

BOOK VI

After The Victory The Combat Begins

Chapter I

LANTENAC TAKEN

The marquis had indeed descended into the tomb. He was led away.

The crypt dungeon of the ground-floor of La Tourgue was immediately opened under Cimourdain's lynx-eyed superintendence. A lamp was placed within, a jug of water and a loaf of soldier's bread; a bundle of straw was flung on the ground, and in less than a quarter of an hour from the instant when the priest's hand seized Lantenac the door of the dungeon closed upon him. This done, Cimourdain went to find Gauvain; at that instant eleven o'clock sounded from the distant church-clock of Parigné.

Cimourdain said to his former pupil: "I am going to convoke a court-martial;

you will not be there. You are a Gauvain, and Lantenac is a Gauvain. You are too near a kinsman to be his judge; I blame Egalité for having voted upon Capet's sentence. The court-martial will be composed of three judges,—an officer, Captain Guéchamp; a non-commissioned officer, Sergeant Radoub; and myself. I shall preside. Nothing of all this concerns you any longer. We will conform to the decree of the Convention; we will confine ourselves to proving the identity of the *ci-devant* Marquis de Lantenac. To-morrow the court-martial; day after to-morrow the guillotine. The Vendée is dead."

Gauvain did not answer a word, and Cimourdain, preoccupied by the final task which remained for him to fulfil, left the young man alone. Cimourdain had to decide upon the hour, and choose the place. He had—like Lequinio at Granville, like Tallien at Bordeaux, like Châlier at Lyons, like Saint-Just at Strasbourg—the habit of assisting personally at executions; it was considered a good example for the judge to come and see the headsman do his work,—a custom borrowed by the Terror of '93 from the parliaments of France and the Inquisition of Spain.

Gauvain also was preoccupied. A cold wind moaned up from the forest. Gauvain left Guéchamp to give the necessary orders, went to his tent in the meadow which stretched along the edge of the wood at the foot of La Tourgue, took his hooded cloak and enveloped himself therein. This cloak was bordered with the simple galoon which, according to the republican custom (chary of ornament), designated the commander-in-chief. He began to walk about in this bloody field where the attack had begun. He was alone there. The fire still continued, but no one any longer paid attention to it. Radoub was beside the children and their mother, almost as maternal as she. The bridge-castle was nearly consumed; the sappers hastened the destruction. The soldiers were digging trenches in order to bury the dead; the wounded were being cared for; the retirade had been demolished; the chambers and stairs disencumbered of the dead; the soldiers were cleansing the scene of carnage, sweeping away the terrible rubbish of the victory,—with true military rapidity setting everything in order after the battle.

Gauvain saw nothing of all this. So profound was his reverie that he scarcely cast a glance toward the guard about the tower, doubled by the orders of Cimourdain. He could distinguish the breach through the obscurity, perhaps two hundred feet away from the corner of the field where he had taken refuge. He could see the black opening. It was there the attack had begun three hours before; it was by this dark gap that he (Gauvain) had penetrated into the tower; there was the ground-floor where the retirade had stood; it was on that same floor that the door of the marquis's prison opened. The guard at the breach watched this dungeon. While his eyes were absently fixed upon the heath, in his ear rang confusedly, like the echo of a knell, these words: "To-morrow, the court-martial; day after to-morrow, the guillotine."

The conflagration, which had been isolated, and upon which the sappers had thrown all the water that could be procured, did not die away without resistance; it still cast out intermittent flames. At moments the cracking of the ceilings could be heard, and the crash one upon another of the different stories as they fell in a common ruin; then a whirlwind of sparks would fly through the air, as if a gigantic torch had been shaken; a glare like lightning illuminated the farthest verge of the horizon, and the shadow of La Tourgue, growing suddenly colossal, spread out to the edge of the forest.

Gauvain walked slowly to and fro amidst the gloom in front of the breach. At intervals he clasped his two hands at the back of his head, covered with his soldier's hood. He was thinking.

Chapter II

GAUVAIN'S SELF-QUESTIONING

His reverie was fathomless. A seemingly impossible change had taken place. The Marquis de Lantenac had been transfigured.

Gauvain had been a witness of this transfiguration. He would never have believed that such a state of affairs would arrive from any complication of events, whatever they might be. Never would he have imagined, even in a dream, that anything similar would be possible. The unexpected—that inexplicable power which plays with man at will—had seized Gauvain, and held him fast. He had before him the impossible become a reality, visible, palpable, inevitable, inexorable. What did he think of it—he, Gauvain? There was no chance of evasion; the decision must be made. A question was put to him; he could not avoid it. Put by whom? By events. And not alone by events; for when events, which are mutable, address a question to our souls, Justice, which is unchangeable, summons us to reply. Above the cloud which casts its shadow upon us is the star that sends toward us its light. We can no more escape from the light than from the shadow.

Gauvain was undergoing an interrogatory. He had been arraigned before a judge: before a terrible judge,—his conscience. Gauvain felt every power of his soul vacillate. His resolutions the most solid, his promises the most piously uttered, his decisions the most irrevocable, all tottered in this terrible overwhelming of his will. There are moral earthquakes. The more he reflected upon that which he had lately seen, the more confused he became. Gauvain, republican, believed himself, and was, just. A higher justice had revealed itself. Above the justice of revolutions is that of humanity. What had happened could not be eluded; the case was grave; Guavain made part of it; he could not withdraw himself; and although Cimourdain had said, "It concerns you no further," he felt within his soul the pang which a tree may feel when torn upward from its roots.

Every man has a basis; a disturbance of this base causes a profound trouble; it was what Gauvain now felt. He pressed his head between his two hands, searching for the truth. To state clearly a situation like his is not easy; nothing could be more painful. He had before him the formidable ciphers which he must sum up into a total; to judge a human destiny by mathematical rules. His head whirled. He tried; he endeavoured to consider the matter; he forced himself to collect his ideas, to discipline the resistance which he felt within himself, and to recapitulate the facts. He set them all before his mind.

To whom has it not arrived to make such a report, and to interrogate himself in some supreme circumstances upon the route which must be followed,—whether to advance or retreat?

Gauvain had just been witness of a miracle. Before the earthly combat had fairly ended, there came a celestial struggle,—the conflict of good against evil. A heart of adamant had been conquered. Given the man with all that he had of evil within him, violence, error, blindness, unwholesome obstinacy, pride, egotism,—Gauvain had just witnessed a miracle: the victory of humanity over the man. Humanity had conquered the inhuman. And by what means; in what manner? How had it been able to overthrow that colossus of wrath and hatred? What arms had it employed; what implement of war? The cradle!

Gauvain had been dazzled. In the midst of social war, in the very blaze of all hatreds and all vengeances, at the darkest and most furious moment of the tumult, at the hour when crime gave all its blackness,—at that instant of conflict, when every sentiment becomes a projectile; when the *mêlée* is so fierce that one no longer knows what is justice, honesty, or truth,—suddenly the Unknown (mysterious warner of *souls*) sent the grand rays of eternal truth resplendent across human light and darkness. Above that sombre duel between the false and the relatively true, there, in the depths, the face of truth itself abruptly appeared. Suddenly the force of the feeble had interposed. He had seen three poor creatures, almost new born, unreasoning, abandoned, orphans, alone, lisping, smiling; having against them civil war, retaliation, the horrible logic of reprisals, murder, carnage, fratricide, rage, hatred, all the Gorgons,— he had seen them triumph against those powers. He had seen the defeat and extinction of a horrible conflagration that had been charged to commit a crime; he had seen atrocious premeditations disconcerted and brought to naught; he had seen ancient feudal ferocity, inexorable disdain, professed experiences of the necessities of war, reasons of State, all the arrogant resolves of a savage old age, vanish before the clear gaze of those who had not yet lived. And this was natural; for he who has not yet lived has done no evil: he is justice, truth, purity; and the highest angels of heaven hover about those souls of little children.

A useful spectacle, a counsel, a lesson. The maddened, merciless combatants, in face of all the projects, all the outrages of war, fanaticism, assassination, revenge kindling the fagots, death coming torch in hand, had suddenly seen all-powerful Innocence raise itself above this enormous legion of crimes. And Innocence had conquered. One could say: No, civil war does not exist; barbarism does not exist; hatred does not exist; crime does not exist; darkness does not exist. To scatter these spectres it only needed that divine aurora,— innocence. Never in any conflict had Satan and God been more plainly visible.

This conflict had a human conscience for its arena. The conscience of Lantenac. Now the battle began again—more desperate, more decisive still perhaps—in another conscience,—the conscience of Gauvain.

What a battle-ground is the soul of man! We are given up to those gods, those monsters, those giants, — our thoughts. Often these terrible belligerents trample our very souls down in their mad conflict.

Gauvin meditated. The Marquis de Lantenac, surrounded, doomed, condemned, outlawed; shut in like the wild beast in the circus, held like a nail in the pincers, enclosed in his refuge become his prison, bound on every side by a wall of iron and fire,—had succeeded in stealing away. He had performed a miracle in escaping; he had accomplished that masterpiece,—the most difficult of all in such a war,—flight. He had again taken possession of the forest, to intrench himself therein; of the district, to fight there; of the shadow, to disappear within it. He had once more become the formidable, the dangerous wanderer, the captain of the invincibles, the chief of the underground forces, the master of the woods. Gauvain had the victory, but Lantenac had his liberty. Henceforth Lantenac had security before him, limitless freedom, an inexhaustible choice of asylums. He was indiscernible, unapproachable, inaccessible. The lion had been taken in the snare, and had broken through.

Well, he had re-entered it. The Marquis de Lantenac had voluntarily, spontaneously, by his own free act, left the forest, the shadow, security, liberty, to return to that horrible peril: intrepid when Gauvain saw him the first time plunge into the conflagration at the risk of being engulfed therein; intrepid a second time, when he descended that ladder which delivered him to his enemies,—a ladder of escape to others, of perdition to him. And why had he thus acted? To save three children. And now what was it they were about to do to this man? Guillotine him. Had these three children been his own? No. Of his family? No. Of his rank? No. For three little beggars—chance children, foundlings, unknown, ragged, barefooted—this noble, this prince, this old man, free, safe, triumphant (for evasion is a triumph), had risked all, compromised all, lost all; and at the same time he restored the babes, had proudly brought his own head,—and this head, hitherto terrible, but now august, he offered to his foes. And what were they about to do? Accept the sacrifice.

The Marquis de Lantenac had had the choice between the life of others and his own: in this superb option he had chosen death. And it was to be granted him; he was to be killed. What a reward for heroism! Respond to a generous act by a barbarous one! What a degrading of the Revolution, what a belittling of the Republic! As this man of prejudice and servitude, suddenly transformed, returned into the circle of humanity, the men who strove for deliverance and freedom elected to cling to the horrors of civil war, to the routine of blood, to fratricide! The divine law of forgiveness, abnegation, redemption, sacrifice, existed for the combatants of error, and did not exist for the soldiers of truth! What! Not to make a struggle in magnanimity: resign themselves to this defeat? They, the stronger, to show themselves the weaker; they, victorious, to become assassins, and cause it to be said that there were those on the side of monarchy who saved children, and those on the side of the Republic who slew old men?

The world would see this great soldier, this powerful octogenarian, this disarmed warrior,—stolen rather than captured, seized in the performance of a good action; seized by his own permission, with the sweat of a noble devotion still upon his brow,—mount the steps of the scaffold as he would mount to the grandeur of an apotheosis! And they would put beneath the knife that head about which would circle, as suppliants, the souls of the three little angels he had saved! And before this punishment—infamous for the butchers —a smile would be seen on the face of that man, and the blush of shame on the face of the Republic! And this would be accomplished in the presence of Gauvain, the chief. And he who might hinder this would abstain. He would rest content under that haughty absolution, "This concerns thee no longer." And he was not even to say to himself that in such a case abdication of authority was complicity! He was not to perceive that of two men engaged in an action so hideous, he who permits the thing is worse than the man who does the work, because he is the coward!

But this death,—had he, Gauvain, not promised it? Had not he, the merciful, declared that Lantenac should have no mercy; that he would himself deliver Lantenac to Cimourdain? That head,— he owed it. Well, he would pay the debt; so be it. But it was, indeed, the same head.

Hitherto Gauvain had seen in Lantenac only the barbarous warrior, the fanatic of royalty and feudalism, the slaughterer of prisoners, an assassin whom war had let loose, a man of blood. That man he had not feared; he had proscribed that proscriber: the implacable would have found him inexorable. Nothing more simple; the road was marked out and terribly plain to follow; everything foreseen: those who killed must be killed; the path of horror was clear and straight. Unexpectedly that straight line had been broken; a sudden turn in the way revealed a new horizon; a metamorphosis had taken place. An unknown Lantenac entered upon the scene. A hero sprang up from the monster: more than a hero,—a man; more than a soul,—a heart. It was no longer a murderer that Gauvain had before him, but a saviour. Gauvain was flung to the earth by a flood of celestial radiance. Lantenac had struck him with the thunder-bolt of generosity.

And Lantenac transfigured could not transfigure Gauvain! What! Was this stroke of light to produce no counterstroke? Was the man of the Past to push on in front, and the man of the Future to fall back? Was the man of barbarism and superstition suddenly to unfold angel pinions, and soar aloft to watch the man of the ideal crawl beneath him in the mire and the night? Gauvain to lie wallowing in the bloodstained rut of the past, while Lantenac rose to a new existence in the sublime future?

Another thing still. Their family! This blood which he was about to spill,

—for to let it be spilled was to spill it himself,—was not this his blood, his, Gauvain's? His grandfather was dead, but his grand-uncle lived, and this grand-uncle was the Marquis de Lantenac. Would not that ancestor who had gone to the grave rise to prevent his brother from being forced into it? Would he not command his grandson henceforth to respect that crown of white hairs, become pure as his own angelic halo? Did not a spectre loom with indignant eyes between him, Gauvain, and Lantenac? Was, then, the aim of the Revolution to denaturalize man? Had she been born to break the ties of family and to stifle the instincts of humanity? Far from it. It was to affirm these glorious realities, not to deny them, that '89 had risen. To overturn the bastiles was to deliver humanity; to abolish feudality was to found families. The author being the point from whence authority sets out, and authority being included in the author, there can be no other authority than paternity: hence the legitimacy of the queen-bee who creates her people, and who, being mother, is queen; hence the absurdity of the king-man, who not being father, cannot be master. Hence the suppression of the king; hence the Republic that comes from all this! Family, humanity, revolution. Revolution is the accession of the peoples; and, at the bottom, the People is Man. The thing to decide was, whether when Lantenac returned into humanity, Gauvain should return to his family. The thing to decide was, whether the uncle and nephew should meet again in a higher light, or whether the nephew's recoil should reply to the uncle's progress.

The question in this pathetic debate between Gauvain and his conscience had resolved itself into this; and the answer seemed to come of itself,—he must save Lantenac.

Yes; but France? Here the dizzying problem suddenly changed its face. What! France at bay? France betrayed, flung open, dismantled? Having no longer a moat. Germany would cross the Rhine; no longer a wall, Italy would leap the Alps, and Spain the Pyrenees. There would remain to France that great abyss, the ocean. She had for her the gulf; she could back herself against it, and, giantess, supported by the entire sea, could combat the whole earth,—a position, after all, impregnable. Yet no; this position would fail her. The ocean no longer belonged to her. In this ocean was England. True, England was at a loss how to traverse it. Well, a man would fling her a bridge; a man would extend his hand to her; a man would go to Pitt, to Craig, to Cornwallis, to Dundas, to the pirates, and say, "Come!" A man would cry, "England, seize France!" And this man was the Marquis de Lantenac. This man was now held fast. After three months of chase, of pursuit, of frenzy, he had at last been taken. The hand of the Revolution had just closed upon the accursed one; the clinched fist of '93 had seized this royalist murderer by the throat. Through that mysterious premeditation from on high which mixes itself in human affairs, it was in the dungeon belonging to his family that this parricide awaited his punishment. The feudal lord was in the feudal oubliette. The stones of his own castle rose against him and shut him in, and he who had sought to betray his country had been betrayed by his own dwelling. God had visibly arranged all this; the hour had sounded; the Revolution had taken prisoner this public enemy; he could no longer fight, he could no longer struggle, he could no longer harm. In this Vendée, which owned so many arms, his was the sole brains; with his extinction, civil war would be extinct. He was held fast,—tragic and fortunate conclusion! After so many massacres, so much carnage, he was a captive, this man who had slain so pitilessly; and it was his turn to die.

And if some one should be found to save him! Cimourdain, that is to say, '93, held Lantenac, that is to say, Monarchy; and could any one be found to snatch its prey from that hand of bronze? Lantenac, the man in whom concentrated that sheaf of scourges called the Past,—the Marquis de Lantenac,—was in the tomb; the heavy eternal door had closed upon him; would some one come from without to draw back the bolt? This social malefactor was dead, and with him died revolt, fratricidal contest, bestial war; and would any one be found to resuscitate him? Oh, how that death's-head would laugh! That spectre would say, "It is well; I live again,—the idiots!" How he would once more set himself at his hideous work. How joyously and implacably this Lantenac would plunge anew into the gulf of war and hatred, and on the morrow would be seen again houses burning, prisoners massacred, the wounded slain, women shot!

And, after all, did not Gauvain exaggerate this action which had fascinated him? Three children were lost; Lantenac saved them. But who had flung them into that peril? Was it not Lantenac? Who had set those three cradles in the heart of the conflagration? Was it not Imânus? Who was Imânus? The lieutenant of the marquis. The one responsible is the chief. Hence the incendiary and the assassin was Lantenac. What had he done so admirable? He had not persisted,—that was all. After having conceived the crime, he had recoiled before it. He had become horrified at himself. That mother's cry had awakened in him those remains of human mercy which exist in all souls, even the most hardened; at this cry he had returned upon his steps. Out of the night where he had buried himself, he hastened toward the day; after having brought about the crime, he caused its defeat. His whole merit consisted in this,—not to have been a monster to the end.

And in return for so little, to restore him all. To give him freedom, the fields, the plains, air, day; restore to him the forest, which he would employ to shelter his bandits; restore him liberty, which he would use to bring about slavery; restore life, which he would devote to death. As for trying to come to an understanding with him; attempting to treat with that arrogant soul; propose his deliverance under certain conditions; demand if he would consent, were his life spared, henceforth to abstain from all hostilities and all revolt, —what an error such an offer would be! what an advantage it would give him! against what scorn would the proposer wound himself! how he would freeze the questioner by his response, "Keep such shame for yourself: kill me!"

There was, in short, nothing to do with this man but to slay or set him free. He was ever ready to soar or to sacrifice himself; his strange soul held at once the eagle and the abyss. To slay him,—what a pang! To set him free,—what a responsibility! Lantenac saved, all was to begin anew with the Vendée,—like a struggle with a hydra whose heads had not been severed. In the twinkling of an eye, with the rapidity of a meteor, the flame extinguished by this man's disappearance would blaze up again. Lantenac would never stop to rest until he had carried out that execrable plan,—to fling, like the cover of a tomb, Monarchy upon the Republic, and England upon France. To save Lantenac was to sacrifice France. Life to Lantenac was death to a host of innocent beings,—men, women, children, caught anew in that domestic war; it was the landing of the English, the recoil of the Revolution; it was the sacking of the villages, the rending of the people, the mangling of Brittany; it was flinging the prey back into the tiger's claw. And Gauvain, in the midst of uncertain gleams and rays of introverted light, beheld, vaguely sketched across his reverie, this problem rise,—the setting the tiger at liberty.

And then the question reappeared under its first aspect; the stone of Sisyphus, which is nothing other than the combat of man with himself, fell back. Was Lantenac that tiger? Perhaps he had been; but was he still?

Gauvain was dizzy beneath the whirl and conflict in his soul; his thoughts turned and circled upon themselves with serpentine swiftness. After the closest examination, could any one deny Lantenac's devotion; his stoical self-abnegation, his superb disinterestedness? What! to attest his humanity in the presence of the open jaws of civil war! What! in this contest of inferior truths, to bring the highest truth of all! What! to prove that above royalties, above revolutions, above earthly questions, is the grand tenderness of the human soul, —the recognition of the protection due to the feeble from the strong, the safety due to those who are perishing from those who are saved, the paternity due to all little children from all old men! To prove these magnificent truths by the gift of his head! to be a general, and renounce strategy, battle, revenge! What! to be a royalist, and to take a balance and put in one scale the King of France, a monarchy of fifteen centuries, old laws to re-establish, ancient society to restore, and in the other three little unknown peasants, and to find the king, the throne, the sceptre, and fifteen centuries of monarchy too light to weigh against these three innocent creatures! What! was all that nothing? What! could he who had done this remain a tiger! Ought he to be treated like a wild beast? No, no, no! The man who had just illuminated the abyss of civil war by the light of a divine action was not a monster. The sword-bearer was metamorphosed into the angel of day. The infernal Satan had again become the celestial Lucifer. Lantenac had atoned for all his barbarities by one act of sacrifice; in losing himself materially he had saved himself morally; he had become innocent again, he had signed his own pardon. Does not the right of self-forgiveness exist? Henceforth he was venerable.

Lantenac had just shown himself almost superhuman; it was now Gauvain's turn. Gauvain was called upon to answer him. The struggle of good and evil passions made the world a chaos at this epoch: Lantenac, dominating the chaos, had just brought humanity out of it; it now remained for Gauvain to bring forth their family therefrom.

What was he about to do? Was Gauvain about to betray the trust Providence had shown in him? No; and he murmured within himself, "Let us save Lantenac." And a voice answered, "It is well. Go on; aid the English; desert; pass over to the enemy. Save Lantenac and betray France!" And Gauvain shuddered. "Thy solution is no solution, O dreamer!" Gauvain saw the Sphinx smile bitterly in the shadow.

This situation was a sort of formidable meeting-ground where hostile truths confronted one another, and where the three highest ideas of man—humanity, family, country—looked in one another's faces. Each of these voices took up the word in its turn, and each uttered truth. Each in its turn seemed to find the point where wisdom and justice met, and said, "Do this!" Was that the thing he ought to do? Yes: no. Reasoning said one thing, and feeling another: the two counsels were in direct opposition. Reasoning is only reason; feeling is often conscience. The one comes from man himself, the other from a higher source; hence it is that feeling has less clearness and more power. Still, what force stern reason possesses!

Gauvain hesitated. Maddening perplexity! Two abysses opened before him. Should he let the marquis perish? Should he save him? He must plunge into one depth or the other. Toward which of the two gulfs did Duty point?

Chapter III

THE COMMANDANT'S MANTLE

It was, after all, with Duty that these victors had to deal. Duty raised herself,—stern to Cimourdain's eyes; terrible to those of Gauvain. Simple before the one; complex, diverse, tortuous, before the other.

Midnight sounded; then one o'clock. Without being conscious of it, Gauvain had gradually approached the entrance to the breach. The expiring conflagration only flung out intermittent gleams; the plateau on the other side of the tower caught the reflection and became visible for an instant, then disappeared from ivew as the smoke swept over the flames. This glare, reviving in jets and cut by sudden shadows, disproportioned objects, and made the sentinels look like phantoms. Lost in his reverie, Gauvain mechanically watched the strife between the flame and smoke. These appearances and disappearances of the light before his eyes had a strange, subtle analogy with the revealing and concealment of truth in his soul.

Suddenly, between two clouds of smoke, a long streak of flame, shot out from the dying brazier, illuminated vividly the summit of the plateau, and brought out the skeleton of a wagon against the vermilion background. Gauvain stared at this wagon. It was surrounded by horsemen wearing gendarmes' hats; it seemed to him the wagon which he had looked at through Guéchamp's glass several hours before, when the sun was setting and the wagon away off on the verge of the horizon. Some men were mounted on the cart and appeared to be unloading it; that which they took off seem to be heavy, and now and then gave out the sound of clanking iron. It would have been difficult to tell what it was; it looked like beams for a frame-work. Two of the men lifted between them and set upon the ground a box, which, as well as he could judge by the shape, contained a triangular object.

The flame sank; all was again buried in darkness. Gauvain stood with fixed eyes lost in thought upon that which the darkness hid. Lanterns were lighted, men came and went on the plateau; but the forms of those moving about were confused, and, moreover, Gauvain was below and on the other side of the ravine, and therefore could see little of what was passing.

Voices spoke, but he could not catch the words. Now and then came a sound like the shock of timbers striking together. He could hear also a strange metallic creaking, like the sharpening of a scythe.

Two o'clock struck. Slowly, and like one who strove to retreat and yet was forced by some invisible power to advance, Gauvain approached the breach. As he came near, the sentinel recognized in the shadow the cloak and braided hood of the commandant, and presented arms. Gauvain entered the hall of the ground-floor, which had been transformed into a guard-room. A lantern hung from the roof; it cast just light enough so that one could cross the hall without treading upon the soldiers who lay, most of them asleep, upon the straw. There they lay; they had been fighting a few hours before; the grape-shot, partially swept away, scattered its grains of iron and lead over the floor and troubled their repose somewhat, but they were weary, and so slept. This hall had been the battle-ground, the scene of frenzied attack; there men had groaned, howled, ground their teeth, struck out blindly in their death-agony, and expired. Many of these sleepers' companions had fallen dead upon this floor, where they now lay down in their weariness; the straw which served them for a pillow had drunk the blood of their comrades. Now all was ended; the blood had ceased to flow, the sabres were dried; the dead were dead; these sleepers slumbered peacefully. Such is war. And then, perhaps to-morrow, the slumber of all will be the same.

At Gauvain's entrance a few of the men rose,—among others, the officers in command. Gauvain pointed to the door of the dungeon. "Open it," he said to the officer. The bolts were drawn back; the door opened. Gauvain entered the dungeon. The door closed behind him.

BOOK VII

FEUDALITY AND REVOLUTION

Chapter I

THE ANCESTOR

A LAMP was placed on the flags of the crypt at the side of the air-hole in the oubliette. There could also be seen on the stones a jug of water, a loaf of army bread, and a truss of straw. The crypt being cut out in the rock, the prisoner who had conceived the idea of setting fire to the straw would have done it to his own hurt,—no risk of conflagration to the prison, certainty of suffocation to the prisoner.

At the instant the door turned on its hinges the marquis was walking to and fro in his dungeon,—that mechanical pacing natural to wild animals in a cage. At the noise of the opening and shutting of the door he raised his head, and the lamp which set on the floor between Gauvain and the marquis struck full upon the faces of both men. They looked at each other, and something in the glance of either kept the two motionless.

At length the marquis burst out laughing, and exclaimed: "Good-evening, sir. It is a long time since I have had the pleasure of meeting you. You do me the favour of paying me a visit; I thank you. I ask nothing better than to converse a little; I was beginning to bore myself. Your friends lose a great deal of time; proofs of identity, court-martials,—all those ceremonies take a long while; I could go much quicker at need. Here I am in my house; take the trouble to enter. Well, what do you say of all that is happening? Original, is it not? Once on a time there was a king and a queen: the king was the king; the queen was—France. They cut the king's head off, and married the queen to Robespierre; this gentleman and that lady have a daughter named Guillotine, with whom it appears I am to make acquaintance to-morrow morning. I shall be delighted—as I am to see you. Did you come about that? Have you risen in rank? Shall you be the headsman? If it is a simple visit of friendship, I am touched. Perhaps, Viscount, you no longer know what a nobleman is; well, you see one,—it is I. Look at the specimen. It is an odd race; it believes in God, it believes in tradition, it believes in family, it believes in its ancestors, it believes in the example of its father,—in fidelity, loyalty, duty toward its prince, respect to ancient laws, virtue, justice; and it would shoot you with pleasure. Have the goodness to sit down, I pray you,—on the stones, it must be, it is true, for I have no armchair in my salon; but he who lives in the mire can sit on the ground. I do not say that to offend you, for what we call the 'mire' you call the 'nation.' I fancy that you do not insist I shall shout 'Liberty, Equality, Fraternity'? This is an ancient chamber of my house: formerly the lords imprisoned clowns here; now clowns imprison the lords. These stupidities are called a Revolution. It appears that my head is to be cut off in thirty-six hours. I see nothing inconvenient in that; still, if my captors had been polite, they would have sent me my snuff-box: it is up in the chamber of the mirrors, where you used to play when you were a child, where I used to dance you on my knees. Sir, let me tell you one thing: You call yourself Gauvain, and, strange to say, you have noble blood in your veins,—yes, by Heaven! the same that runs in mine; yet the blood that made me a man of honour makes you a rascal. Such are personal idiosyncrasies! You will tell me it is not your fault that you are a rascal; nor is it mine that I am a gentleman. Zounds! one is a malefactor without knowing it: it comes from the air one breathes. In times like these of ours one is not responsible for what one does; the Revolution is guilty for the whole world, and all your great criminals are great innocents. What blockheads! To begin with yourself. Permit me to admire you. Yes, I admire a youth like you, who, a man of quality, well placed in the State, having noble blood to shed in a noble cause, Viscount of this Tower-Gauvain, Prince of Brittany, able to be duke by right, and peer of France by heritage,—which is about all a man of good sense could desire here below,—amuses himself, being what he is, to be what you are; playing his part so well that he produces upon his enemies the effect of a villain, and on his friends of an idiot. By the way, give my compliments to the Abbé Cimourdain."

The marquis spoke perfectly at his ease, quietly, emphasizing nothing, in his polite society voice, his eyes clear and tranquil, his hand in his waistcoat-pocket. He broke off, drew a long breath, and resumed: "I do not conceal from you that I have done what I could to kill you. Such as you see me, I have myself, in person, three times aimed a cannon at you. A discourteous proceeding,—I admit it; but it would be giving rise to a bad example to suppose that in war your enemy tries to make himself agreeable to you. For we are in war, monsieur my nephew; everything is put to fire and sword. Into the bargain, it is true that they have killed the king. A pretty century!"

He checked himself again, and again resumed: "When one thinks that none of these things would have happened if Voltaire had been hanged and Rousseau sent to the galleys! Ah, those men of mind,—what scourges! But there, what is it you reproach that monarchy with? It is true that the Abbé Pucelle was sent to his Abbey of Portigny with as much time as he pleased for the journey; and as for your Monsieur Titon, who had been, begging your pardon, a terrible debauchee, and had gone the rounds of the loose women before hunting after the miracles of the Deacon Paris, he was transferred from the Castle of Vincennes to the Castle of Ham in Picardy, which is, I confess, a sufficiently ugly place. There are wrongs for you! I recollect: I cried out also in my day; I was as stupid as you."

The marquis felt in his pocket as if seeking his snuff-box, then continued: "But not so wicked. We talked just for talk's sake. There was also the mutiny of demands and petitions; and then up came those gentlemen the philosophers, and their writings were burned instead of the authors. The Court cabals mixed themselves in the matter; there were all those stupid fellows. Turgot, Quesnay, Malesherbes, the physiocratists, and so forth,—and the quarrel began. The whole came from the scribblers and the rhymesters. The Encyclopedia; Diderot D'Alembert, —ah, the wicked scoundrels! To think of a well-born man like the King of Prussia joining them! I would have suppressed all those paper-scratchers. Ah, we were justiciaries, our family; you may see there on the wall the marks of the quartering-wheel. We did not jest. No, no; no scribblers! While there are Arouets, there will be Marats; as long as there are fellows who scribble there will be scoundrels who assassinate; as long as there is ink, there will be black stains; as long as men's claws hold a goose's feather, frivolous stupidities will engender atrocious ones. Books cause crimes. The word 'chimera' has two meanings,—it signifies dream, and it signifies monster. How dearly one pays for idle trash! What is that you sing to us about your rights? The rights of man! rights of the people!— is that empty enough, stupid enough, visionary enough, sufficiently void of sense? When I say Havoise, the sister of Conan II., brought the county of Brittany to Hoel Count of Nantes and Cornouailles, who left the throne to Alain Fergant the uncle of Bertha, who espoused Alain-le-noir Lord of Roche-sur-Yon, and bore him Conan the Little, grandfather of Guy, or Gauvain de Thouars, our ancestor,—I state a thing that is clear, and there is a right. But your scoundrels, your rascals, your wretches, what do they call their rights? Deicide and regicide! Is it not hideous? Oh, the clowns! I am sorry for you, sir, but you belong to this proud Brittany blood; you and I had Gauvain de Thouars for our ancestor; we had for another that great Duke of Montbazon who was peer of France and honoured with the Grand Collar of the Orders, who attacked the suburb of Tours, and was wounded at the Battle of Arques, and died Grand Huntsman of France, in his house of Couzières in Touraine, aged eighty-six. I could tell you still further of the Duke de Laudunois, son of the Lady of Garnache; of Claude de Lorraine, Duke of Chevreuse and of Henri de Lenoncourt, and of Françoise de Laval-Boisdauphin,—but to what purpose? Monsieur has the honour of being an idiot, and considers himself the equal of my groom. Learn this: I was an old man while you were still a brat; I remain as much your superior as I was then. As you grew up you found means to belittle yourself. Since we ceased to see each other each has gone his own way: I followed honesty, you went in the opposite direction. Ah, I do not know how all that will finish: those gentlemen, your friends, are full-blown wretches! Verily, it is fine, I grant you, a marvellous step gained in the cause of progress,—to have suppressed in the army the punishment of the pint of water inflicted on the drunken soldier for three consecutive days; to have the Maximum, the Convention, the Bishop Gobel, Monsieur Chaumette, and Monsieur Hébert; to have exterminated the Past in one mass from the Bastille to the peerage! They replace the saints by vegetables! So be it, citizens! you are masters; reign, take your ease, do what you like, stop at nothing! All this does not hinder the fact that religion is religion, that royalty fills fifteen hundred years of our history, and that the old French nobility are loftier than you, even with their heads off. As for your cavilling over the historic rights of royal races, we shrug our shoulders at that. Chilperic, in reality, was only a monk named Daniel; it was Rainfroi who invented Chilperic, in order to annoy Charles Martel; we know those things just as well as you do. The question does not lie there; the question is this: To be a great kingdom, to be the ancient France, to be a country perfectly ordered, wherein were to be considered, first, the sacred person of its monarchs, absolute lords of the State; then the princes; then the officers of the crown for the armies on land and sea, for the artillery, for the direction and superintendence of the finances; after that the officers of justice, great and small, those for the management of taxes and general receipts; and, lastly, the police of the kingdom in its three orders. All this was fine and nobly regulated; you have destroyed it. You have destroyed the provinces, like the lamentably ignorant creatures you are, without even suspecting what the provinces really were. The genius of France held the genius of the entire continent; each province of France represented a virtue of Europe: the frankness of Germany was in Picardy; the generosity of Sweden, in Champagne; the industry of Holland, in Burgundy; the activity of Poland, in Languedoc; the gravity of Spain, in Gascony; the wisdom of Italy, in Provence; the subtlety of Greece, in Normandy; the fidelity of Switzerland, in Dauphiny. You knew nothing of all that; you have broken, shattered, ruined, demolished; you have shown yourselves simply idiotic brutes. Ah, you will no longer have nobles? Well, you *shall* have none! Get your mourning ready; you shall have no more paladins, no more heroes; say good-night to the ancient grandeurs; find me a D'Assas at present! You are all of you afraid for your skins. You will have no more the chivalry of Fontenoy, who saluted before killing one another; you will have no more combatants like those in silk stockings at the siege of Lérida; you will have no more plumes floating past like meteors; you are a people finished, come to an end. You will suffer the outrage of invasion. If Alaric II. could return, he would no longer find himself confronted by Clovis; if Abderaman could come back, he would no longer find himself face to face with Charles Martel; if the Saxons, they would no longer find Pepin before them. You will have no more Agnadel, Rocroy, Lens, Staffarde, Neerwinden, Steinkirke, La Marsaille, Rancoux, Lawfeld, Mahon; you will have no Marignan, with Francis I.; you will have no Bouvines, with Philip Augustus taking prisoner with one hand Renaud Count of Boulogne, and with the other, Ferrand Count of Flanders; you will have Agincourt, but you will have no more the Sieur de Bacqueville, grand bearer of the oriflamme, enveloping himself in his banner to die. Go on, go on; do your work! Be the new men! become dwarfs!"

The marquis was silent for an instant, then began again: "But leave us great. Kill the kings, kill the nobles, kill the priests; tear down, ruin, massacre; trample under foot, crush ancient laws beneath your heels; overthrow the throne; stamp upon the altar of God, dash it in pieces, dance above it! On with you to the end! You are traitors and cowards, incapable of devotion or sacrifice. I have spoken; now have me guillotined, monsieur the viscount. I have the honour to be your very humble servant."

Then he added: "Ah, I do not hesitate to set the truth plainly before you. What difference can it make to me? I am dead."

"You are free," said Gauvain. He unfastened his Commandant's cloak, advanced toward the marquis, threw it about his shoulders, and drew the hood close down over his eyes. The two men were of the same height.

"Well, what are you doing?" the marquis asked.

Gauvain raised his voice, and cried: "Lieutenant, open to me."

The door opened.

Gauvain exclaimed: "Close the door carefully behind me!" And he pushed the stupefied marquis across the threshold.

The hall turned into a guard-room was lighted, it will be remembered, by a horn lantern, whose faint rays only broke the shadows here and there. Such of the soldiers as were not asleep saw dimly a man of lofty stature, wrapped in the mantle and hood of the commander-in-chief, pass through the midst of them and move toward the entrance. They made a military salute, and the man passed on.

The marquis slowly traversed the guard-room, the breach (not without hitting his head more than once), and went out. The sentinel, believing that he saw Gauvain, presented arms. When he was outside, having the grass of the fields under his feet, within two hundred paces of the forest, and before him space, night, liberty, life,—he paused, and stood motionless for an instant like a man who has allowed himself to be pushed on; who has yielded to surprise, and who, having taken advantage of an open door, asks himself if he has done well or ill, hesitates to go farther, and gives audience to a last reflection. After a few seconds' deep reverie he raised his right hand, snapped his thumb and middle finger, and said, "My faith!" And he hurried on.

The door of the dungeon had closed again. Gauvain was within.

Chapter II

THE COURT-MARTIAL

At that period all courts-martial were very nearly discretionary. Dumas had offered in the Assembly a rough plan of military legislation, improved later by Talot in the Council of the Five Hundred; but the definitive code of war-councils was only drawn up under the Empire. Let us add in parenthesis, that from the Empire dates the law imposed on military tribunals to begin receiving the votes by the lowest grade Under the Revolution this law did not exist. In 1793 the president of a military tribunal was almost the tribunal in himself. He chose the members, classed the order of grades, regulated the manner of voting,—was at once master and judge.

Cimourdain had selected for the hall of the court-martial that very room on the ground-floor where the retirade had been erected, and where the guard was now established. He wished to shorten everything,—the road from the prison to the tribunal, and the passage from the tribunal to the scaffold.

In conformity with his orders the court began its sitting at midday, with no other show of state than this: three straw-bottomed chairs, a pine table, two lighted candles, a stool in front of the table. The chairs were for the judges, and the stool for the accused. At either end of the table also stood a stool,—one for the commissioner auditor, who was a quartermaster; the other for the registrar, who was a corporal. On the table were a stick of red sealing-wax, a brass seal of the Republic, two ink-stands, some sheets of white paper, and two printed placards spread open,—the first containing the declaration of outlawry; the second, the decree of the Convention. The tricoloured flag hung on the back of the middle chair: in that period of rude simplicity decorations were quickly arranged, and it needed little time to change a guard-room into a court of justice. The middle chair, intended for the president, stood in face of the prison door. The soldiers made up the audience. Two gendarmes stood on guard by the stool.

Cimourdain was seated in the centre chair, having at his right Captain Guéchamp, first judge; and at his left Sergeant Radoub, second judge. Cimourdain wore a hat with a tricoloured cockade, his sabre at his side, and his two pistols in his belt; his scar, of a vivid red, added to his savage appearance. Radoub's wound had been only partially stanched; he had a handkerchief knotted about his head, upon which a bloodstain slowly widened.

At midday the court had not yet opened its proceedings. A messenger, whose horse could be heard stamping outside, stood near the table of the tribunal. Cimourdain was writing,— writing these lines:—

"CITIZEN MEMBERS OF THE COMMITTEE OF PUBLIC SAFETY,—Lantenac is taken. He will be executed to-morrow."

He dated and signed the dispatch; folded, sealed, and handed it to the messenger, who departed. This done, Cimourdain called in a loud voice: "Open the dungeon!"

The two gendarmes drew back the bolts, opened the door of the dungeon, and entered.

Cimourdain lifted his head, folded his arms, fixed his eyes on the door and cried: "Bring out the prisoner!"

A man appeared between the two gendarmes, standing beneath the arch of the door-way. It was Gauvain.

Cimourdain started. "Gauvain!" he exclaimed. Then he added, "I demanded the prisoner."

"It is I," said Gauvain.

"Thou?"

"I."

"And Lantenac?"

"He is free."

"Free?"

"Yes."

"Escaped?"

"Escaped."

Cimourdain trembled as he stammered: "In truth the castle belongs to him; he knows all its outlets. The dungeon may communicate with some secret opening. I ought to have remembered that he would find means to escape; he would not need any person's aid for that."

"He was aided," said Gauvain.

"To escape?"

"To escape."

"Who aided him?"

"I."

"Thou?"

"I."

"Thou art dreaming!"

"I went into the dungeon; I was alone with the prisoner. I took off my cloak; I put it about his shoulders; I drew the hood down over his face; he went out in my stead, and I remained in his. Here I am!"

"Thou didst not do it!"

"I did it."

"It is impossible!"

"It is true."

"Bring me Lantenac!"

"He is no longer here. The soldiers, seeing the commandant's mantle, took him for me, and allowed him to pass. It was still night."

"Thou art mad!"

"I tell you what was done."

A silence followed. Cimourdain stammered: "Then thou hast merited—"

"Death," said Gauvain.

Cimourdain was pale as a corpse. He sat motionless as a man who had just been struck by lightning. He no longer seemed to breathe. A great drop of sweat stood out on his forehead. He forced his voice into firmness, and said: "Gendarmes, seat the accused."

Gauvain placed himself on the stool.

Cimourdain added: "Gendarmes, draw your sabres." His voice had got back to its ordinary tone. "Accused," said he, "you will stand up." He no longer said "thee" and "thou" to Gauvain.

Chapter III

THE VOTES

Gauvain rose.

"What is your name?" demanded Cimourdain.

The answer came unhesitatingly: "Gauvain."

Cimourdain continued the interrogatory: "Who are you?"

"I am Commander-in-Chief of the Expeditionary Column of the Côtes-du-Nord."

"Are you a relative or a connection of the man who has escaped?"

"I am his grand-nephew."

"You are acquainted with the decree of the Convention?"

"I see the placard lying on your table."

"What have you to say in regard to this decree?"

"That I countersigned it; that I ordered its carrying out; that it was I who had this placard written, at the bottom of which is my name."

"Choose a defender."

"I will defend myself."

"You can speak."

Cimourdain had become again impassible. But his impassibility resembled the sternness of a rock rather than the calmness of a man.

Gauvain remained silent for a moment, as if collecting his thoughts.

Cimourdain spoke again: "What have you to say in your defence?"

Gauvain slowly raised his head, but without fixing his eyes upon either of the judges, and replied: "This: One thing prevented my seeing another; a good action seen too near hid from me a hundred criminal deeds. On one side an old man; on the other, three children,—all these put themselves between me and duty. I forgot the burned villages, the ravaged fields, the butchered prisoners, the slaughtered wounded, the women shot; I forgot France betrayed to England. I set at liberty the murderer of our country; I am guilty. In speaking thus, I seem to speak against myself; it is a mistake,—I speak in my own behalf. When the guilty acknowledges his fault, he saves the only thing worth the trouble of saving,—honour."

"Is that," returned Cimourdain, "all you have to say in your own defence?"

"I add, that being the chief I owed an example; and that you in your turn, being judges, owe one."

"What example do you demand?"

"My death."

"You find that just?"

"And necessary."

"Be seated."

The quartermaster, who was auditor-commissioner, rose and read, first, the decree of outlawry against the *ci-devant* Marquis de Lantenac; secondly, the decree of the Convention ordaining capital punishment against whosoever should aid the escape of a rebel prisoner. He closed with the lines printed at the bottom of the placard, forbidding "to give aid or succour to the below named rebel, under penalty of death;" signed "Commander-in-Chief of the Expeditionary Column,—GAUVAIN." These notices read, the auditor-commissioner sat down again.

Cimourdain folded his arms and said: "Accused, pay attention. Public, listen, look, and be silent. You have before you the law. The votes will now be taken. The sentence will be given according to the majority. Each judge will announce his decision aloud, in presence of the accused, justice having nothing to conceal."

Cimourdain continued: "The first judge will give his vote. Speak, Captain Guéchamp."

Captain Guéchamp seemed to see neither Cimourdain nor Gauvain. His downcast lids concealed his eyes, which remained fixed upon the placard of the decree as if they were staring at a gulf. He said: "The law is immutable. A judge is more and less than a man: he is less than a man because he has no heart; he is more than a man because he holds the sword of justice. In the four hundred and fourteenth year of Rome, Manlius put his son to death for the crime of having conquered without his orders; violated discipline demanded an example. Here it is the law which has been violated, and the law is still higher than discipline. Through an emotion of pity, the country is again endangered. Pity may wear the proportions of a crime. Commandant Gauvain has helped the rebel Lantenac to escape. Gauvain is guilty. I vote—death."

"Write, registrar," said Cimourdain.

The clerk wrote, "Captain Guéchamp: death."

Gauvain's voice rang out, clear and firm. "Guéchamp," said he, "you have voted well, and I thank you."

Cimourdain resumed: "It is the turn of the second judge. Speak, Sergeant Radoub."

Radoub rose, turned toward Gauvain, and made the accused a military salute. Then he exclaimed: "If that is the way it goes, then guillotine me, for I give here, before God, my most sacred word of honour that I would like to have done, first, what the old man did, and, after that, what my commandant did. When I saw that old fellow, eighty years of age, jump into the fire to pull three brats out of it, I said 'Old fellow, you are a brave man!' And when I hear that my commandant has saved that old man from your beast of a guillotine, I say, 'My commandant, you ought to be my general, and you are a true man; and, as for me, thunder! I would give you the Cross of Saint Louis if there were still crosses, or saints, or Louises.' Oh, there! are we going to turn idiots at present? If it was for these things that we gained the Battle of Jemappes, the Battle of Valmy, the Battle of Fleurus, and the Battle of Wattignies, then you had better say so. What! here is Commandant Gauvain, who for these four months past has been driving those asses of royalists to the beat of the drum, and saving the Republic by his sword; who did a thing at Dol which needed a world of brains to do,—and when you have a man like that, you try to get rid of him! Instead of electing him your general, you want to cut off his head! I say it is enough to make a fellow throw himself off the Pont Neuf head foremost! You, yourself, Citizen Gauvain, my commandant, if you were my corporal instead of being my superior, I would tell you that you talked a heap of infernal nonsense just now. The old man did a fine thing in saving children; you did a fine thing in saving the old man; and if we are going to guillotine people for good actions, why, then, get away with you all to the devil, for I don't know any longer what the question is about! There's nothing to hold fast to! It is not true, is it, all this? I pinch myself to see if I am awake! I can't understand. So the old man ought to have let the babies burn alive, and my commandant ought to have let the old man's head be cut off! See here! guillotine me! I would as lief have it done as not. Just suppose: if the children had been killed, the battalion of the Bonnet Rouge would have been dishonoured! Is that what was wished for? Why, then, let us eat one another up and be done! I understand politics as well as any of you: I belonged to the Club of the Section of Pikes. Zounds, we are coming to the end! I sum up the matter according to my way of looking at it. I don't like things to be done which are so puzzling you don't know any longer where you stand. What the devil is it we get ourselves killed for? In order that somebody may kill our chief! None of that, Lisette! I want my chief; I will have my chief; I love him better to-day than I did yesterday. Send him to the guillotine? Why, you make me laugh! Now, we are not going to have anything of that sort. I have listened. People may say what they please. In the first place it is not possible!"

And Radoub sat down again. His wound had reopened. A thin stream of blood exuded from under the kerchief, and ran along his neck from the place where his ear had been.

Cimourdain turned toward the sergeant. "You vote for the acquittal of the accused?"

"I vote," said Radoub, "that he be made general."

"I ask if you vote for his acquittal."

"I vote for his being made head of the Republic."

"Sergeant Radoub, do you vote that Commandant Gauvain be acquitted,— yes or no?"

"I vote that my head be cut off in place of his."

"Acquittal," said Cimourdain. "Write it, registrar."

The clerk wrote, "Sergeant Radoub: acquittal."

Then the clerk said: "One voice for death. One voice for acquittal. A tie."

It was Cimourdain's turn to vote. He rose. He took off his hat and laid it on the table. He was no longer pale or livid. His face was the colour of clay. Had all the spectators been corpses lying there in their winding-sheets, the silence could not have been more profound.

Cimourdain said, in a solemn, slow, firm voice: "Accused, the case has been heard. In the name of the Republic, the court-martial, by a majority of two voices—"

He broke off; there was an instant of terrible suspense. Did he hesitate before pronouncing the sentence of death? Did he hesitate before granting life? Every listener held his breath.

Cimourdain continued: "Condemns you to death."

His face expressed the torture of an awful triumph. Jacob, when he forced the angel, whom he had overthrown in the darkness, to bless him, must have worn that fearful smile. It was only a gleam—it passed; Cimourdain was marble again. He seated himself, put on his hat, and added: "Gauvain, you will be executed to-morrow at sunrise."

Gauvain rose, saluted, and said: "I thank the court."

"Lead away the condemned," said Cimourdain. He made a sign: the door of the dungeon re-opened; Gauvain entered; the door closed. The two gendarmes stood sentinel,—one on either side of the arch, sabre in hand.

Sergeant Radoub fell senseless upon the ground, and was carried away.

Chapter IV

AFTER CIMOURDAIN THE JUDGE COMES CIMOURDAIN THE MASTER

A CAMP is a wasp's nest,—in revolutionary times above all. The civic sting which is in the soldier moves quickly, and does not hesitate to prick the chief after having chased away the enemy.

The valiant troop which had taken La Tourgue was filled with diverse commotions,—at first against Commandant Gauvain when it learned that Lantenac had escaped. As Gauvain issued from the dungeon which had been believed to hold the marquis, the news spread as if by electricity, and in an instant the whole army was informed. A murmur burst forth; it was: "They are trying Gauvain; but it is a sham. Trust *ci-devants* and priests! We have just seen a viscount save a marquis, and now we are going to see a priest absolve a noble!"

When the news of Gauvain's condemnation came, there was a second murmur: "It is horrible! Our chief, our brave chief, our young commander,—a hero! He may be a viscount,—very well; so much the more merit in his being a Republican. What, he, the liberator of Pontorson, of Villedieu, of Pont-au-Beau; the conqueror of Dol and La Tourgue,—he who makes us invincible; he, the sword of the Republic in Vendée; the man who for five months has held the Chouans at bay, and repaired all the blunders of Léchelle and the others!—this Cimourdain to dare to condemn *him* to death! For what? Because he saved an old man who had saved three children! A priest kill a soldier!"

Thus muttered the victorious and discontented camp. A stern rage surrounded Cimourdain. Four thousand men against one,—that should seem a power; it is not. These four thousand men were a crowd; Cimourdain was a will. It was known that Cimourdain's frown came easily, and nothing more was needed to hold the army in respect. In those stern days it was sufficient for a man to have behind him the shadow of the Committee of Public Safety to make that man formidable; to make imprecation die into a whisper, and the whisper into silence.

Before, as after the murmurs, Cimourdain remained the arbiter of Gauvain's fate as he did of the fate of all. They knew there was nothing to ask of him, that he would only obey his conscience,—a superhuman voice audible to his ear alone. Everything depended on him. That which he had done as martial judge, he could undo as civil delegate. He only could show mercy. He possessed unlimited power: by a sign he could set Gauvain at liberty. He was master of life and death; he commanded the guillotine. In this tragic moment he was the man supreme. They could only wait.

Night came.

Chapter V

THE DUNGEON

The hall of justice had become again a guard-room; the guard was doubled as upon the previous evening; two sentinels stood on duty before the closed door of the prison.

Toward midnight, a man who held a lantern in his hand traversed the hall, made himself known to the sentries, and ordered the dungeon open. It was Cimourdain. He entered and the door remained ajar behind him. The dungeon was dark and silent. Cimourdain moved forward a step in the gloom, set the lantern on the ground, and stood still. He could hear amidst the shadows the measured breath of a sleeping man. Cimourdain listened thoughtfully to this peaceful sound.

Gauvain lay on a bundle of straw at the farther end of the dungeon. It was his breathing which caught the newcomer's ear. He was sleeping profoundly.

Cimourdain advanced as noiselessly as possible, moved close, and looked down upon Gauvain. The glance of a mother watching her nursling's slumber could not have been more tender or fuller of love. Even Cimourdain's will could not control that glance. He pressed his clinched hands against his eyes with the gesture one sometimes sees in children, and remained for a moment motionless. Then he knelt, softly raised Gauvain's hand, and pressed it to his lips.

Gauvain stirred. He opened his eyes, full of the wonder of sudden waking. He recognized Cimourdain in the dim light which the lantern cast about the cave. "Ah," said he, "it is you, my master." And he added: "I dreamed that Death was kissing my hand."

Cimourdain started as one does sometimes under the sudden rush of a flood of thoughts. Sometimes the tide is so high and so stormy that it seems as if it would drown the soul. Not an echo from the overcharged depths of Cimourdain's heart found vent in words. He could only say, "Gauvain!"

And the two gazed at each other,— Cimourdain with his eyes full of those flames which burn up tears; Gauvain with his sweetest smile.

Gauvain raised himself on his elbow and said: "That scar I see on your face is the sabre-cut you received for me. Yesterday, too, you were in the thick of that *mêlée*, at my side, and on my account. If Providence had not placed you near my cradle, where should I be today? In utter darkness. If I have any true conception of duty, it is from you that it comes to me. I was born with my hands bound,—prejudices are ligatures: you loosened those bonds; you gave my growth liberty, and of that which was already only a mummy you made anew a child. Into what would have been an abortion you put a conscience. Without you I should have grown up a dwarf. I exist by you. I was only a lord, you made me a citizen; I was only a citizen, you have made me a mind. You have made me, as a man, fit for this earthly life; you have educated my soul for the celestial existence; you have given me human reality, the key of truth, and, to go beyond that, the key of light. O my master! I thank you. It is you who have created me."

Cimourdain seated himself on the straw beside Gauvain, and said: "I have come to sup with thee."

Gauvain broke the black bread and handed it to him. Cimourdain took a morsel; then Gauvain offered the jug of water.

"Drink first," said Cimourdain.

Gauvain drank, and passed the jug to his companion, who drank after him. Gauvain had only swallowed a mouthful. Cimourdain drank great draughts. During this supper, Gauvain ate, and Cimourdain drank,—a sign of the calmness of the one, and of the fever which consumed the other. A serenity so strange that it was terrible reigned in this dungeon. The two men conversed.

Gauvain said: "Grand events are sketching themselves. What the Revolution does at this moment is mysterious. Behind the visible work stands the invisible; one conceals the other. The visible work is savage, the invisible sublime. In this instant I perceive all very clearly. It is strange and beautiful. It has been necessary to make use of the materials of the Past. Hence this marvellous '93. Beneath a scaffolding of barbarism a temple of civilization is building."

"Yes," replied Cimourdain. "From this provisional will rise the definitive. The definitive—that is to say, right and duty—are parallel: taxes proportional and progressive; military service obligatory; a levelling without deviation; and above the whole, making part of all, that straight line, the law,—the Republic of the absolute."

"I prefer," said Gauvain, "the ideal Republic." He paused for an instant, then continued: "O my master! in all which you have just said, where do you place devotion, sacrifice, abnegation, the sweet interlacing of kindnesses, love? To set all in equilibrium, it is well; to put all in harmony, it is better. Above the Balance is the Lyre. Your Republic weighs, measures, regulates man; mine lifts him into the open sky. It is the difference between a theorem and an eagle."

"You lose yourself in clouds."

"And you in calculation."

"Harmony is full of dreams."

"There are such, too, in algebra."

"I would have man made by the rules of Euclid."

"And I," said Gauvain, "would like him better as pictured by Homer."

Cimourdain's severe smile remained fixed upon Gauvain, as if to hold that soul steady: "Poesy! Mistrust poets."

"Yes, I know that saying. Mistrust the zephyrs, mistrust the sunshine, mistrust the sweet odours of spring, mistrust the flowers, mistrust the stars!"

"None of these things can feed man."

"How do you know? Thought is nourishment. To think is to eat."

"No abstractions! The Republic is the law of two and two make four. When I have given to each the share which belongs to him—"

"It still remains to give the share which does not belong to him."

"What do you understand by that?"

"I understand the immense reciprocal concession which each owes to all, and which all owe to each, and which is the whole of social life."

"Beyond the strict law there is nothing."

"There is everything."

"I only see justice."

"And I,—I look higher."

"What can there be above justice?"

"Equity."

At certain instants they paused as if lightning flashes suddenly chilled them.

Cimourdain resumed: "Particularize; I defy you."

"So be it. You wish military service made obligatory. Against whom? Against other men. I,—I would have no military service; I want peace. You wish the wretched succoured; I wish an end put to suffering. You want proportional taxes; I wish no tax whatever. I wish the general expense reduced to its most simple expression, and paid by the social surplus."

"What do you understand by that?"

"This: First, suppose parasitisms,—the parasitisms of the priest, the judge, the soldier. After that, turn your riches to account. You fling manure into the sewer; cast it into the furrow. Three parts of the soil are waste land: clear up France; suppress useless pasture-grounds; divide the communal lands; let each man have a farm and each farm a man. You will increase a hundred-fold the social product. At this moment France only gives her peasants meat four days in the year; well cultivated, she would nourish three hundred millions of men—all Europe. Utilize Nature, that immense auxiliary so disdained; make every wind toil for you, every water-fall, every magnetic effluence. The globe has a subterranean network of veins; there is in this net-work a prodigious circulation of water, oil, fire. Pierce those veins: make this water feed your fountains this oil your lamps, this fire your hearths. Reflect upon the movements of the waves, their flux and reflux, the ebb and flow of the tides. What is the ocean? An enormous power allowed to waste. How stupid is earth not to make use of the sea!"

"There you are in the full tide of dreams."

"That is to say, of full reality"

Gauvain added: "And woman, what will you do with her?"

Cimourdain replied: "Leave her where she is,—the servant of man."

"Yes. On one condition."

"What?"

"That man shall be the servant of woman."

"Can you think of it?" cried Cimourdain. "Man a servant? Never! Man is master. I admit only one royalty,—that of the fireside. Man in his house is king!"

"Yes. On one condition."

"What?"

"That woman shall be queen there."

"That is to say, you wish for man and woman—"

"Equality."

"Equality! Can you dream of it? The two creatures are different."

"I said equality; I did not say identity."

There was another pause, like a sort of truce between two spirits flinging lightnings.

Cimourdain broke the silence: "And the offspring, to whom do you consign them?"

"First to the father who engenders; then to the mother who gives birth; then to the master who rears; then to the city that civilizes; then to the country which is the mother supreme; then to humanity, who is the great ancestor."

"You do not speak of God?"

"Each of those degrees—father, mother, master, city, country, humanity —is one of the rungs in the ladder which leads to God."

Cimourdain was silent.

Gauvain continued: "When one is at the top of the ladder, one has reached God. Heaven opens,—one has only to enter."

Cimourdain made a gesture like a man calling another back: "Gauvain, return to earth. We wish to realize the possible."

"Do not commence by rendering it impossible."

"The possible always realizes itself."

"Not always. If one treats Utopia harshly, one slays it. Nothing is more defenceless than the egg."

"Still, it is necessary to seize Utopia, to put the yoke of the real upon it, to frame it in the actual. The abstract idea must transform itself into the concrete: what it loses in beauty, it will gain in usefulness; it is lessened, but made better. Right must enter into law, and when right makes itself law, it becomes absolute. That is what I call possible."

"The possible is more than that."

"Ah, there you are in dream-land again!"

"The possible is a mysterious bird, always soaring above a man's head."

"It must be caught."

"Living." Gauvain continued: "This is my thought: Constant progression. If God had meant man to retrograde, he would have placed an eye in the back of his head. Let us look always toward the dawn, the blossoming, the birth. That which falls encourages that which mounts; the cracking of the old tree is an appeal to the new. Each century must do its work: to-day civic, to-morrow human; to-day the question of right, to-morrow the question of salary. Salary and right,—the same word at bottom. Man does not live to be paid nothing. In giving life, God contracts a debt. Right is the payment inborn; payment is right acquired."

Gauvain spoke with the earnestness of a prophet. Cimourdain listened. Their *rôles* were changed; now it seemed the pupil who was master.

Cimourdain murmured: "You go rapidly."

"Perhaps because I am a little pressed for time," said Gauvain, smiling. And he added, "O my master! behold the difference between our two Utopias! You wish the garrison obligatory, I the school. You dream of man the soldier; I dream of man the citizen. You want him terrible; I want him a thinker. You found a Republic upon swords; I found—"

He interrupted himself: "I would found a Republic of intellects."

Cimourdain bent his eyes on the pavement of the dungeon, and said: "And while waiting for it, what would you have?"

"That which is."

"Then you absolve the present moment?"

"Yes."

"Wherefore?"

"Because it is a tempest. A tempest knows always what it does. For one oak uprooted, how many forests purified! Civilization had the plague; this great wind cures it. Perhaps it is not so careful as it ought to be; but could it do otherwise than it does? It is charged with a difficult task. Before the horror of miasma, I comprehend the fury of the blast."

Guavain continued: "Moreover, why should I fear the tempest if I had my compass? How can events affect me if I have my conscience?" And he added, in a low, solemn voice: "There is a power that must always be allowed to guide."

"What?" demanded Cimourdain.

Gauvain raised his finger above his head. Cimourdain's eyes followed the direction of that uplifted finger, and it seemed to him that across the dungeon vault he beheld a starlit sky. Both were silent again.

Cimourdain spoke first: "Society is greater than Nature. I tell you, this is no longer a possibility—it is a dream."

"It is the goal. Otherwise of what use is society? Remain in Nature; be savages. Otaheite is a paradise,—only the inhabitants of that paradise do not think. An intelligent hell would be preferable to an imbruted heaven. But, no,—no hell; let us be a human society.

Greater than Nature? Yes. If you add nothing to Nature, why go beyond her? Content yourself with work, like the ant; with honey, like the bee,—remain the working drudge instead of the queen intelligence. If you add to Nature, you necessarily become greater than she: to add is to augment; to augment is to grow. Society is Nature sublimated. I want all that is lacking to bee-hives, all that is lacking to ant-hills,—monuments, arts, poesy, heroes, genius. To bear eternal burdens is not the destiny of man. No, no, no! no more pariahs, no more slaves, no more convicts, no more damned! I desire that each of the attributes of man should be a symbol of civilization and a patron of progress; I would place liberty before the spirit, equality before the heart, fraternity before the soul. No more yokes! Man was made not to drag chains, but to soar on wings. No more of man reptile! I wish the transfiguration of the larva into the winged creature; I wish the worm of the earth to turn into a living flower and fly away. I wish—"

He broke off. His eyes blazed. His lips moved. He ceased to speak.

The door had remained open. Sounds from without penetrated into the dungeon. The distant peal of trumpets could be heard, probably the reveille; then the butt-end of muskets striking the ground as the sentinels were relieved; then, quite near the tower, as well as one could judge, a noise like the moving of planks and beams, followed by muffled, intermittent echoes like the strokes of a hammer.

Cimourdain grew pale as he listened. Gauvain heard nothing. His reverie became more and more profound. He seemed no longer to breathe, so lost was he in the vision that shone upon his soul. Now and then he started slightly. The morning which illuminated his eyes waxed grander.

Some time passed thus. Then Cimourdain asked: "Of what are you thinking?"

"Of the future," replied Gauvain.

He sank back into his meditation. Cimourdain rose from the bed of straw where the two were sitting. Gauvain did not perceive it. Keeping his eyes fixed upon the dreamer, Cimourdain moved slowly backward toward the door and went out. The dungeon closed again.

Chapter VI

WHEN THE SUN ROSE

Day broke along the horizon,—and with the day an object, strange, motionless, mysterious, which the birds of heaven did not recognize, appeared upon the plateau of La Tourgue and towered above the forest of Fougères. It had been placed there in the night; it seemed to have sprung up rather than to have been built. It lifted high against the horizon a profile of straight, hard lines, looking like a Hebrew letter, or one of those Egyptian hieroglyphics which made part of the alphabet of the ancient enigma.

At the first glance the idea which this object roused was its lack of keeping with the surroundings. It stood amidst the blossoming heath. One asked one's self for what purpose it could be useful? Then the beholder felt a chill creep over him as he gazed. It was a sort of trestle, having four posts for feet; at one end of the trestle two tall joists upright and straight, and fastened together at the top by a cross-beam, raised and held suspended some triangular object which showed black against the blue sky of morning. At the other end of the staging was a ladder. Between the joists, and directly beneath the triangle, could be seen a sort of panel composed of two movable sections, which, fitting into each other, left a round hole about the size of a man's neck. The upper section of this panel slid in a groove, so that it could be hoisted or lowered at will; for the time, the two crescents, which formed the circle when closed, were drawn apart. At the foot of the two posts supporting the triangle was a plank turning on hinges, looking like a see-saw. By the side of this plank was a long basket; and between the two beams, in front and at the extremity of the trestle, was a square basket. The monster was painted red. The whole was made of wood except the triangle,—that was iron. One would have known the thing must have been constructed by man, it was so ugly and evil looking; at the same time it was so formidable that it might have been reared there by evil genii. This shapeless thing was the guillotine.

In front of it, a few paces off, another monster rose out of the ravine. La Tourgue,—a monster of stone rising up to hold companionship with the monster of wood. For when man has touched wood or stone they no longer remain inanimate matter; something of man's spirit seems to enter into them. An edifice is a dogma; a machine, an idea. La Tourgue was that terrible offspring of the Past called the Bastille in Paris, the Tower of London in England, the Spielberg in Germany, the Escurial in Spain, the Kremlin in Moscow, the Castle of Saint Angelo in Rome.

In La Tourgue were condensed fifteen hundred years (the Middle Age), vassalage, servitude, feudality; in the guillotine one year,—'93; and these twelve months made a counterpoise to those fifteen centuries. La Tourgue was Monarchy; the guillotine was Revolution,— tragic confrontation! On one side the debtor, on the other the creditor. On one side the inextricable Gothic complication of serf, lord, slave, master, plebeian, nobility, the complex code ramifying into customs, judge and priest in coalition, shackles innumerable, fiscal impositions, excise laws, mortmain, taxes, exemptions, prerogatives, prejudices, fanaticisms, the royal privilege of bankruptcy, the sceptre, the throne, the regal will, the divine right; on the other, this simple thing,—a knife. On one side the noose, on the other, the axe.

La Tourgue had long stood alone in the midst of this wilderness. There she had frowned with her machicolated casements, from whence had streamed boiling oil, blazing pitch, and melted lead; her oubliettes paved with human skeletons, her torture-chamber, — the whole hideous tragedy with which she was filled. Rearing her funereal front above the forest, she had passed fifteen centuries of savage tranquility amidst its shadows; she had been the one power in this land, the one object of respect and fear; she had reigned supreme, she had been the realization of barbarism; and suddenly she saw rise before her and against her, something (more than something) as terrible as herself,—the guillotine.

Inanimate objects sometimes appear endowed with a strange power of sight. A statue notices, a tower watches, the face of an edifice contemplates. La Tourgue seemed to be studying the guillotine. She seemed to question herself concerning it. What was that object? It looked as if it had sprung out of the earth. It was from there, in truth, that it had risen. The sinister tree had germinated in the fatal ground. Out of the soil watered by so much of human sweat, so many tears, so much blood; out of the earth in which had been dug so many trenches, so many graves, so many caverns, so many ambuscades—out of this earth wherein had rolled the countless victims of countless tyrannies—out of this earth spread above so many abysses wherein had been buried so many crimes (terrible germs) had sprung in a destined day this unknown, this avenger, this ferocious sword-bearer, and '93 had said to the Old World, "Behold me!" And the guillotine had the right to say to the donjon tower, "I am thy daughter."

And, at the same time, the tower—for those fatal objects possess a strange vitality—felt herself slain by this newly risen force.

Before this formidable apparition La Tourgue seemed to shudder. One might have said that she was afraid. The monstrous mass of granite was majestic, but infamous; that plank with its black triangle was worse. The all-powerful fallen trembled before the all-powerful risen. Criminal history was studying judicial history. The violence of bygone days was comparing itself with the violence of the present; the ancient fortress, the ancient prison, the ancient seigneury where tortured victims had shrieked out their lives; that construction of war and murder, now useless, defenceless, violated, dismantled, uncrowned, a heap of stones with no more than a heap of ashes, hideous yet magnificent, dying, dizzy with the awful memories of all those by-gone centuries, watched the terrible living Present sweep up. Yesterday trembled before to-day, antique ferocity acknowledged and bowed its head before this fresh horror. The power which was sinking into nothingness opened eyes of fright upon this new-born terror; the phantom stared at the spectre.

Nature is pitiless; she never withdraws her flowers, her music, her fragrance, and her sunlight from before human cruelty or suffering. She overwhelms man by the contrast between divine beauty and social hideousness. She spares him nothing of her loveliness, neither wing of butterfly nor song of bird. In the midst of murder, vengeance, barbarism, he must feel himself watched by holy things; he cannot escape the immense reproach of universal nature and the implacable serenity of the sky. The deformity of human laws is forced to exhibit itself naked amidst the dazzling rays of eternal beauty. Man breaks and destroys; man lays waste; man kills; but the summer remains summer; the lily remains the lily; the star remains the star.

Never had a morning dawned fresher and more glorious than this. A soft breeze stirred the heath, a warm haze rose amidst the branches; the forest of Fougères permeated by the breath of hidden brooks, smoked in the dawn like a vast censer filled with perfumes; the blue of the firmament, the whiteness of the clouds, the transparency of the streams, the verdure, that harmonious gradation of colour from aquamarine to emerald, the groups of friendly trees, the mats of grass, the peaceful fields, all breathed that purity which is Nature's eternal counsel to man. In the midst of all this rose the horrible front of human shamelessness; in the midst of all this appeared the fortress and the scaffold, war and punishment, —the incarnations of the bloody age and the bloody moment; the owl of the night of the Past and the bat of the cloud-darkened dawn of the Future. And blossoming, odour-giving creation, loving and charming, and the grand sky golden with morning spread about La Tourgue and the guillotine, and seemed to say to man, "Behold my work and yours."

Such are the terrible reproaches of the sunlight!

This spectacle had its spectators. The four thousand men of the little expeditionary army were drawn up in battle order upon the plateau. They surrounded the guillotine on three sides in such a manner as to form about it the shape of a letter E; the battery placed in the centre of the largest line made the notch of the E. The red monster was enclosed by these three battle fronts; a sort of wall of soldiers spread out on two sides of the edge of the plateau; the fourth side, left open, was the ravine, which seemed to frown at La Tourgue. These arrangements made a long square, in the centre of which stood the scaffold.

Gradually, as the sun mounted higher, the shadow of the guillotine grew shorter on the turf. The gunners were at their pieces; the matches lighted. A faint blue smoke rose from the ravine, the breath of the expiring conflagration. This cloud encircled without veiling La Tourgue, whose lofty platform overlooked the whole horizon. There was only the width of the ravine between the platform and the guillotine. The one could have parleyed with the other.

The table of the tribunal and the chair shadowed by the tricoloured flags had been set upon the platform. The sun rose higher behind La Tourgue, bringing out the black mass of the fortress clear and defined, and revealing upon its summit the figure of a man in the chair beneath the banners, sitting motionless, his arms crossed upon his breast. It was Cimourdain. He wore, as on the previous day, his civil delegate's dress; on his head was the hat with the tricoloured cockade; his sabre at his side; his pistols in his belt. He sat silent.

The whole crowd was mute. The soldiers stood with downcast eyes, musket in hand,—stood so close that their shoulders touched; but no one spoke. They were meditating confusedly upon this war,—the numberless combats, the hedge-fusillades so bravely confronted; the hosts of peasants driven back by their might; the citadels taken, the battles won, the victories gained; and it seemed to them as if all that glory had turned now to their shame. A sombre expectation contracted every heart. They could see the executioner come and go upon the platform of the guillotine. The increasing splendour of the morning filled the sky with its majesty.

Suddenly the sound of muffled drums broke the stillness. The funeral tones swept nearer. The ranks opened—a cortège entered the square and moved toward the scaffold. First, the drummers with their crape-wreathed drums; then a company of grenadiers with reversed arms; then a platoon of gendarmes with drawn sabres; then the condemned,—Gauvain. He walked forward with a free, firm step. He had no fetters on hands or feet. He was in an undress uniform, and wore his sword. Behind him marched another platoon of gendarmes.

Gauvain's face was still lighted by that pensive joy which had illuminated it at the moment when he said to Cimourdain, "I am thinking of the Future." Nothing could be more touching and sublime than that smile. When he reached the fatal square, his first glance was directed toward the summit of the tower. He disdained the guillotine. He knew that Cimourdain would make it an imperative duty to assist at the execution. His eyes sought the platform; he saw him there.

Cimourdain was ghastly and cold. Those standing near him could not catch even the sound of his breathing. Not a tremor shook his frame when he saw Gauvain.

Gauvain moved toward the scaffold. As he walked on, he looked at Cimourdain, and Cimourdain looked at him. It seemed as if Cimourdain rested his very soul upon that clear glance. Gauvain reached the foot of the scaffold. He ascended it. The officer who commanded the grenadiers followed him. He unfastened his sword, and handed it to the officer; he undid his cravat, and gave it to the executioner. He looked like a vision. Never had he been so handsome.

His brown curls floated on the wind; at the time it was not the custom to cut off the hair of those about to be executed. His white neck reminded one of a woman; his heroic and sovereign glance made one think of an archangel. He stood there on the scaffold lost in thought. That place of punishment was a height too. Gauvain stood upon it, erect, proud, tranquil. The sunlight streamed about him till he seemed to stand in the midst of a halo. But he must be bound. The executioner advanced, cord in hand.

At this moment, when the soldiers saw their young leader so close to the knife, they could restrain themselves no longer, the hearts of those stern warriors gave way. A mighty sound swelled up,—the united sob of a whole army. A clamour rose: "Mercy! mercy!" Some fell upon their knees; others flung away their guns and stretched their arms toward the platform where Cimourdain was seated. One grenadier pointed to the guillotine, and cried, "A substitute! A substitute! Take me!" All repeated frantically, "Mercy! mercy!" Had a troop of lions heard, they must have been softened or terrified, the tears of soldiers are terrible.

The executioner hesitated, no longer knowing what to do.

Then a voice, quick and low, but so stern that it was audible to every ear, spoke from the top of the tower: "Fulfill the law!"

All recognized that inexorable tone. Cimourdain had spoken. The army shuddered.

The executioner hesitated no longer. He approached, holding out the cord.

"Wait!" said Gauvain. He turned toward Cimourdain, made a gesture of farewell with his right hand, which was still free, then allowed himself to be bound.

When he was tied, he said to the executioner: "Pardon. One instant more." And he cried: "Long live the Republic!"

He was laid upon the plank. That noble head was held by the infamous yoke. The executioner gently parted his hair aside, then touched the spring. The triangle began to move,—slowly at first, then rapidly; a terrible blow was heard—

At the same instant another report sounded. A pistol-shot had answered the blow of the axe. Cimourdain had seized one of the pistols from his belt, and as Gauvain's head rolled into the basket, Cimourdain sank back pierced to the heart by a bullet his own hand had fired. A stream of blood burst from his mouth; he fell dead.

And those two souls, united still in that tragic death, soared away together, the shadow of the one mingled with the radiance of the other.

THE END.

Hernani

PERSONAGES OF THE DRAMA

Hernani.
Don Carlos.
Don Ruy Gomez de Silva.
Doña Sol de Silva.
The King of Bohemia.
The Duke of Bavaria.
The Duke of Gotha.
The Baron of Hohenbourg.
The Duke of Lutzelbourg.
Don Sancho.
Don Matias.
Don Ricardo.
Don Garcie Suarez.
Don Francisco.
Don Juan de Haro.
Don Pedro Gusman de Lara.
Don Gil Tellez Giron.
Doña Josefa Duarte.
Jaquez.

A Mountaineer.
A Lady
First Conspirator.
Second Conspirator.
Third Conspirator.

Conspirators of the Holy League, Germans and Spaniards, Mountaineers, Nobles, Soldiers, Pages, Attendants, &c.

SPAIN, A. D. 1519.

ACT FIRST: THE KING

Scene 1.—Saragossa. *A Chamber. Night: a lamp on the table.*

Doña Josefa Duarte, *an old woman dressed in black, with body of her dress worked in jet in the fashion of Isabella the Catholic.* Don Carlos.

Doña Josefa, *alone. She draws the crimson curtains of the window, and puts some armchairs in order. A knock at a little secret door on the right. She listens. A second knock.*

    Doña Josefa. Can it be he already? (*Another knock.*)
T' is, indeed,
At th' hidden stairway. (*A fourth knock.*)
I must open quick.
    (*She opens the concealed door.* Don Carlos *enters, his face muffled in his cloak, and his hat drawn over his brows.*)
Good evening to you, sir!
    (*She ushers him in. He drops his cloak and reveals a rich dress of silk and velvet in the Castilian style of 1519. She looks at him closely, and recoils astonished.*)
What now?—not you,
Signor Hernani! Fire! fire! Help, oh help!
    Don Carlos (*seizing her by the arm*). But two words more, Duenna, and you die!
    (*He looks at her intently. She is frightened into silence.*)

Is this the room of Doña Sol, betrothed
To her old uncle, Duke de Pastrana?
A very worthy lord he is—senile,
White-hair'd and jealous. Tell me, is it true
The beauteous Doña loves a smooth-faced youth,
All whiskerless as yet, and sees him here
Each night, in spite of envious care? Tell me,
Am I informed aright?
(*She is silent. He shakes her by the arm.*)
Will you not speak?

Doña Josefa. You did forbid me, sir, to speak two words.

Don Carlos. One will suffice. I want a yes, or no.
Say, is thy mistress Doña Sol de Silva?

Doña Josefa. Yes, why?

Don Carlos. No matter why. Just at this hour
The venerable lover is away?

Doña Josefa. He is.

Don Carlos. And she expects the young one now?

Doña Josefa. Yes.

Don Carlos. Oh, that I could die!

Doña Josefa. Yes.

Don Carlos. Say, Duenna,
Is this the place where they will surely meet?

Doña Josefa. Yes.

Don Carlos. Hide me somewhere here.

Doña Josefa. You?

Don Carlos. Yes, me.

Doña Josefa. Why?

Don Carlos. No matter why.

Doña Josefa. I hide you here!

Don Carlos. Yes, here.

Doña Josefa. No, never!

Don Carlos (*drawing from his girdle a purse and a dagger*). Madam, condescend to choose
Between a purse and dagger.

Doña Josefa (*taking the purse*). Are you then
The devil?

Don Carlos. Yes, Duenna.

Doña Josefa (*opening a narrow cupboard in the wall*). Go—go in.

Don Carlos (*examining the cupboard*). This box!

Doña Josefa (*shutting up the cupboard*). If you don't like it, go away.

Don Carlos (*re-opening cupboard*). And yet! (*Again examining it.*) Is this the stable where you keep
The broom-stick that you ride on?
(*He crouches down in the cupboard with difficulty.*) Oh! oh! oh!

Doña Josefa (*joining her hands and looking ashamed*). A man here!

Don Carlos (*from the cupboard, still open*). And was it a woman then
Your mistress here expected?

Doña Josefa. Heavens! I hear
The step of Doña Sol! Sir, shut the door!
Quick—quick (*She pushes the cupboard door, which closes.*)

Don Carlos (*from the closed cupboard*). Remember, if you breathe a word
You die!

Doña Josefa (*alone*). Who is this man? If I cry out,
Gracious! there's none to hear. All are asleep
Within the palace walls—Madam and I
Excepted. Pshaw! the other'll come. He wears

A sword: 'tis his affair. And Heav'n keep us
From powers of hell. (*Weighing the purse in her hand.*) At least no thief he is.

Enter DOÑA SOL *in white.* (DOÑA JOSEFA *hides the purse.*)

SCENE 2—DOÑA JOSEFA; DON CARLOS, *hidden;* DOÑA SOL; *afterwards* HERNANI.

DOÑA SOL. Josefa!
DOÑA JOSEFA. Madam?
DOÑA SOL. I some mischief dread,
For 'tis full time Hernani should be here.
(*Noise of steps at the secret door.*)
He's coming up; go—quick! at once, undo
Ere he has time to knock.
(JOSEFA *opens the little door. Enter* HERNANI *in large cloak and large hat; underneath costume of mountaineer of Aragon—grey, with a cuirass of leather; a sword, a dagger, and a horn at his girdle.*)
DOÑA SOL (*going to him*). Hernani! Oh!
HERNANI. Ah, Doña Sol! it is yourself at last
I see—your voice it is I hear. Oh, why
Does cruel fate keep you so far from me?
I have such need of you to help my heart
Forget all else!
DOÑA SOL (*touching his clothes*). Oh! Heav'ns! your cloak is drench'd!
The rain must pour!
HERNANI. I know not.
DOÑA SOL. And the cold—
You must be cold!
HERNANI. I feel it not.
DOÑA SOL. Take off
This cloak then, pray.
HERNANI. Doña, beloved, tell me,
When night brings happy sleep to you, so pure
And innocent—sleep that half opes your mouth,
Closing your eyes with its light finger-touch—
Does not some angel show how dear you are
To an unhappy man, by all the world
Abandoned and repulsed?
DOÑA SOL. Sir, you are late;
But tell me, are you cold?
HERNANI. Not near to you.
Ah! when the raging fire of jealous love
Burns in the veins, and the true heart is riven
By its own tempest, we feel not the clouds
O'erhead, though storm and lightning they fling forth!
DOÑA SOL. Come, give me now the cloak, and your sword too.
HERNANI (*his hand on his sword*). No. 'Tis my other love, faithful and pure.
The old Duke, Doña Sol—your promised spouse,
Your uncle—is he absent now?
DOÑA SOL. Oh, yes;
This hour to us belongs.
HFRNANI. And that is all!
Only this hour! and then comes afterwards!—
What matter! For I must forget or die!
Angel! one hour with thee—with whom I would
Spend life, and afterwards eternity!
DOÑA SOL. Hernani!
HERNANI. It is happiness to know

The Duke is absent. I am like a thief
Who forces doors. I enter—see you
—rob
An old man of an hour of your sweet
voice
And looks. And I am happy, though,
no doubt
He would deny me e'en one hour,
although
He steals my very life.

DOÑA SOL. Be calm. (*Giving the
cloak to the Duenna.*) Josefa!
This wet cloak take and dry it.

(*Exit* JOSEFA.)
(*She seats herself, and makes a sign for*
HERNANI *to draw near.*)
Now come here.

HERNANI (*without appearing to hear
her*). The Duke, then, is not in the
mansion now?

DOÑA SOL. How grand you look!

HERNANI. He is away?

DOÑA SOL. Dear one,
Let us not think about the Duke.

HERNANI. Madam,
But let us think of him, the grave old
man
Who loves—you—who will marry you!
How now?
He took a kiss from you the other day.
Not think of him!

DOÑA SOL. Is't that which grieves
you thus?
A kiss upon my brow—an uncle's kiss—
Almost a father's.

HERNANI. No, not so; it was
A lover's, husband's, jealous kiss. To
him—
To him it is that you will soon belong.
Think'st thou not of it! Oh, the foolish
dotard,
With head drooped down to finish out
his days!
Wanting a wife, he takes a girl; himself
Most like a frozen spectre. Sees he not,
The senseless one! that while with one
hand he
Espouses you, the other mates with
Death!
Yet without shudder comes he 'twixt
our hearts!
Seek out the grave-digger, old man, and
give
Thy measure. Who is it that makes for you
This marriage? You are forced to it,
I hope?

DOÑA SOL. They say the King desires it.

HERNANI. King! this king!
My father on the scaffold died condemned
By his; and, though one may have
aged since then—
For e'en the shadow of that king, his son,
His widow, and for all to him allied,
My hate continues fresh. Him dead,
no more
We count with; but while still a child
I swore
That I'd avenge my father on his son.
I sought him in all places—Charles the
King
Of the Castiles. For hate is rife between
Our families. The fathers wrestled long
And without pity, and without remorse,
For thirty years! Oh, 'tis in vain that
they
Are dead; their hatred lives. For them
no peace
Has come; their sons keep up the duel
still.

HERNANI

Ah! then I find 'tis thou who hast made up
This execrable marriage! Thee I sought—
Thou comest in my way!

DOÑA SOL. You frighten me!

HERNANI. Charged with the mandate of anathema,
I frighten e'en myself; but listen now:
This old, old man, for whom they destine you,
This Ruy de Silva, Duke de Pastrana,
Count and grandee, rich man of Aragon,
In place of youth can give thee, oh! young girl,
Such store of gold and jewels that your brow
Will shine 'mong royalty's own diadems
And for your rank and wealth, and pride and state,
Queens many will perhaps envy you. See, then,
Just what he is. And now consider me.
My poverty is absolute, I say.
Only the forest, where I ran barefoot
In childhood, did I know. Although perchance
I too can claim illustrious blazonry,
That's dimm'd just now by rusting stain of blood.
Perchance I've rights, though they are shrouded still,
And hid 'neath ebon folds of scaffold cloth,
Yet which, if my attempt one day succeeds,
May, with my sword from out their sheath leap forth.
Meanwhile, from jealous Heaven I've received
But air, and light, and water—gifts bestowed
On all. Now, wish you from the Duke, or me,
To be delivered? You must choose 'twixt us,
Whether you marry him, or follow me.

DOÑA SOL. You, I will follow!

HERNANI. 'Mong companions rude,
Men all proscribed, of whom the headsman knows
The names already. Men whom neither steel
Nor touch of pity softens; each one urged
By some blood feud that's personal. Wilt thou
Then come? They'd call thee mistress of my band,
For know you not that I a bandit am?
When I was hunted throughout Spain, alone
In thickest forests, and on mountains steep,
'Mong rocks which but the soaring eagle spied,
Old Catalonia like a mother proved.
Among her hills—free, poor, and stern—I grew;
And now, to-morrow if this horn should sound,
Three thousand men would rally at the call.
You shudder, and should pause to ponder well.
Think what 'twill prove to follow me through woods
And over mountain paths, with comrades like
The fiends that come in dreams! To live in fear,
Suspicious of a sound, of voices, eyes:
To sleep upon the earth, drink at the stream.

And hear at night, while nourishing perchance
Some wakeful babe, the whistling musket balls.
To be a wanderer with me proscribed,
And when my father I shall follow—then,
E'en to the scaffold, you to follow me!

DOÑA SOL. I'll follow you.

HERNANI. The Duke is wealthy, great
And prosperous, without a stain upon
His ancient name. He offers you his hand,
And can give all things—treasures, dignities,
And pleasure——

DOÑA SOL. We'll set out to-morrow. Oh!
Hernani, censure not th' audacity
Of this decision. Are you angel mine
Or demon? Only one thing do I know,
That I'm your slave. Now, listen: wheresoe'er
You go, I go—pause you or move I'm yours.
Why act I thus? Ah! that I cannot tell;
Only I want to see you evermore.
When sound of your receding footstep dies
I feel my heart stops beating; without you
Myself seems absent, but when I detect
Again the step I love, my soul comes back,
I breathe—I live once more.

HERNANI (*embracing her*). Oh! angel mine!

DOÑA SOL. At midnight, then, to-morrow, clap your hands
Three times beneath my window, bringing there
Your escort. Go! I shall be strong and brave.

HERNANI. Now know you who I am?

DOÑA SOL. Only my lord.
Enough—what matters else?—I follow you.

HERNANI. Not so. Since you, a woman weak, decide
To come with me, 'tis right that you should know
What name, what rank, what soul, perchance what fate
There hides beneath the low Hernani here.
Yes, you have willed to link yourself for aye
With brigand—would you still with outlaw mate?

DON CARLOS (*opening the cupboard*). When will you finish all this history?
Think you 'tis pleasant in this cupboard hole?

(HERNANI *recoils, astonished.* DOÑA SOL *screams and takes refuge in* HERNANI'S *arms, looking at* DON CARLOS *with frightened gaze.*)

HERNANI (*his hand on the hilt of his sword*). Who is this man?

DOÑA SOL. Oh, heavens, help!

HERNANI. Be still,
My Doña Sol! you'll wake up dangerous eyes.
Never—whatever be—while I am near,
Seek other help than mine.
(*To* DON CARLOS.) What do you here?

DON CARLOS. I?—Well, I am not riding through the wood,
That you should ask.

HERNANI. He who affronts, then jeers,
May cause his heir to laugh.

DON CARLOS. Each, Sir, in turn.

Let us speak frankly. You the lady love,
And come each night to mirror in her eyes
Your own. I love her too, and want to know
Who 'tis I have so often seen come in
The window way, while I stand at the door.

HERNANI. Upon my word, I'll send you out the way
I enter.

DON CARLOS. As to that we'll see. My love
I offer unto Madam. Shall we then
Agree to share it? In her beauteous soul
I've seen so much of tenderness, and love,
And sentiment, that she, I'm very sure,
Has quite enough for ardent lovers twain.
Therefore to-night, wishing to end suspense
On your account, I forced an entrance, hid,
And—to confess it all—I listened too.
But I heard badly, and was nearly choked;
And then I crumpled my French vest—and so,
By Jove! come out I must!

HERNANI. Likewise my blade
Is not at ease, and hurries to leap out.

DON CARLOS (*bowing*). Sir, as you please.

HERNANI (*drawing his sword*). Defend yourself!

(DON CARLOS *draws his sword.*)

DOÑA SOL. Oh, Heaven!

DON CARLOS. Be calm, Señora.

HERNANI (*to* DON CARLOS). Tell me, Sir, your name.

DON CARLOS. Tell me yours!

HERNANI. It is a fatal secret,
Kept for my breathing in another's ear,
Some day when I am conqueror, with my knee
Upon his breast, and dagger in his heart.

DON CARLOS. Then tell to me this other's name.

HERNANI. To thee
What matters it? On guard! Defend thyself!

(*They cross swords.* DOÑA SOL *falls trembling into a chair. They hear knocks at the door.*)

DOÑA SOL (*rising in alarm*). Oh Heavens! there's some one knocking at the door!

(*The champions pause. Enter* JOSEFA, *at the little door, in a frightened state.*)

HERNANI (*to* JOSEFA). Who knocks in this way?

DOÑA JOSEFA (*to* DOÑA SOL). Madam, a surprise!
An unexpected blow. It is the Duke
Come home.

DOÑA SOL (*clasping her hands*). The Duke! Then every hope is lost!

DOÑA JOSEFA (*looking round*). Gracious! the stranger out! and swords, and fighting!
Here's a fine business!

(*The two combatants sheathe their swords.* DON CARLOS *draws his cloak round him, and pulls his hat down on his forehead. More knocking.*)

HERNANI. What is to be done?

(*More knocking.*)

A VOICE (*without*). Doña Sol, open to me.

(DOÑA JOSEFA *is going to the door, when* HERNANI *stops her.*

HERNANI. Do not open.

DOÑA JOSEFA (*pulling out her ro-*

sary). Holy St. James! now draw us through this broil!

(*More knocking.*)

HERNANI (*pointing to the cupboard*). Let's hide!

DON CARLOS. What! in the cupboard?

HERNANI. Yes, go in; I will take care that it shall hold us both.

DON CARLOS. Thanks. No; it is too good a joke.

HERNANI (*pointing to secret door*). Let's fly
That way.

DON CARLOS. Good night! But as for me I stay
Here.

HERNANI. Fire and fury, Sir, we will be quits
For this. (*To* DOÑA SOL.) What if I firmly barr'd the door?

DON CARLOS (*to* JOSEFA). Open the door.

HERNANI. What is it that he says?

DON CARLOS (*to* JOSEFA, *who hesitates bewildered*). Open the door, I say.

(*More knocking.* JOSEFA *opens the door, trembling.*)

DOÑA SOL. Oh, I shall die!

SCENE 3.—*The same, with* DON RUY GOMEZ DE SILVA, *in black; white hair and beard. Servants with lights.*

DON RUY GOMEZ. My niece with two men at this hour of night!
Come all! The thing is worth exposing here.
(*To* DOÑA SOL.) Now by St. John of Avila, I vow
That we three with you, madam, are by two
Too many. (*To the two young men.*)
My young Sirs, what do you here?
When we'd the Cid and Bernard—giants both
Of Spain and of the world—they travelled through
Castile protecting women, honouring
Old men. For them steel armour had less weight
Than your fine velvets have for you. These men
Respected whitened beards, and when they loved,
Their love was consecrated by the Church.
Never did such men cozen or betray,
For reason that they had to keep unflawed
The honour of their house. Wished they to wed,
They took a stainless wife in open day,
Before the world, with sword, or axe, or lance
In hand. But as for villains such as you,
Who come at eve, peeping behind them oft,
To steal away the honour of men's wives
In absence of their husbands, I declare,
The Cid, our ancestor, had he but known
Such men, he would have plucked away from them
Nobility usurped, have made them kneel,
While he with flat of sword their blazon dashed.
Behold what were the men of former times
Whom I, with anguish, now compare with these
I see to-day! What do you here? Is it
To say, a white-haired man's but fit for youth

To point at when he passes in the street,
And jeer at there? Shall they so laugh at me,
Tried soldier of Zamora? At the least
Not yours will be that laugh.
 HERNANI. But Duke——
 DON RUY GOMEZ. Be still!
What! You have sword and lance, falcons, the chase,
And songs to sing 'neath balconies at night,
Festivals, pleasures, feathers in your hats,
Raiment of silk—balls, youth, and joy of life;
But wearied of them all, at any price
You want a toy, and take an old man for it.
Ah, though you've broke the toy, God wills that it
In bursting should be flung back in your face!
Now follow me!
 HERNANI. Most noble Duke——
 DON RUY GOMEZ. Follow—
Follow me, Sirs. Is this alone a jest?
What! I've a treasure, mine to guard with care,
A young girl's character, a family's fame.
This girl I love—by kinship to me bound,
Pledged soon to change her ring for one from me.
I know her spotless, chaste, and pure.
Yet when
I leave my home one hour, I—Ruy Gomez
De Silva—find a thief who steals from me
My honour, glides unto my house. Back, back,
Make clean your hands, oh base and soulless men,
Whose presence, brushing by, must serve to taint
Our women's fame! But no, 'tis well. Proceed.
Have I not something more?
(*Snatches off his collar.*)
Take, tread it now
Beneath your feet. Degrade my Golden Fleece.
(*Throws off his hat.*)
Pluck at my hair, insult me every way,
And then, to-morrow through the town make boast
That lowest scoundrels in their vilest sport
Have never shamed a nobler brow, nor soiled
More whitened hair.
 DOÑA SOL. My lord——
 DON RUY GOMEZ (*to his servants*).
A rescue! grooms!
Bring me my dagger of Toledo, axe,
And dirk.
(*To the young men.*)
Now follow—follow me—ye two.
 DON CARLOS (*stepping forward a little*). Duke, this is not the pressing thing just now;
First we've to think of Maximilian dead,
The Emperor of Germany.
(*Opens his cloak and shows his face, previously hidden by his hat.*)
 DON RUY GOMEZ. Jest you!
Heavens, the King!
 DOÑA SOL. The King!
 HERNANI. The King of Spain!
 DON CARLOS (*gravely*). Yes, Charles, my noble Duke, are thy wits gone?
The Emperor, my grandsire, is no more.
I knew it not until this eve, and came
At once to tell it you and counsel ask,
Incognito, at night, knowing you well
A loyal subject that I much regard.

The thing is very simple that has caused
This hubbub.

(Don Ruy Gomez *sends away servants by a sign, and approaches* Don Carlos. Doña Sol *looks at* The King *with fear and surprise.* Hernani *from a corner regards him with flashing eyes.*)

Don Ruy Gomez. But oh, why was it the door
Was not more quickly opened?

Don Carlos. Reason good.
Remember all your escort. When it is
A weighty secret of the state I bear
That brings me to your palace, it is not
To tell it to thy servants.

Don Ruy Gomez. Highness, oh!
Forgive me, some appearances——

Don Carlos. Good father,
Thee Governor of the Castle of Figuère
I've made. But whom thy governor shall I make?

Don Ruy Gomez. Oh, pardon——

Don Carlos. 'Tis enough. We'll say no more
Of this. The Emperor is dead.

Don Ruy Gomez. Your Highness's Grandfather dead!

Don Carlos. Ay, Duke, you see me here
In deep affliction.

Don Ruy Gomez. Who'll succeed him?

Don Carlos. A Duke of Saxony is named. The throne
Francis the First of France aspires to mount.

Don Ruy Gomez. Where do the Electors of the Empire meet?

Don Carlos. They say at Aix-la-Chapelle, or at Spire,
Or Frankfort.

Don Ruy Gomez. But our King, whom God preserve!
Has he not thought of Empire?

Don Carlos. Constantly.

Don Ruy Gomez. To you it should revert.

Don Carlos. I know it, Duke.

Don Ruy Gomez. Your father was Archduke of Austria.
I hope 'twill be remembered that you are
Grandson to him, who but just now has changed
The' imperial purple for a winding-sheet.

Don Carlos. I am, besides, a citizen of Ghent.

Don Ruy Gomez. In my own youth your grandfather I saw.
Alas! I am the sole survivor now
Of all that generation past. All dead!
He was an Emperor magnificent
And mighty.

Don Carlos. Rome is for me.

Don Ruy Gomez. Valiant, firm,
And not tyrannical, this head might well
Become th' old German body.

(*He bends over* The King's *hands and kisses them.*)
Yet so young.
I pity you indeed, thus plunged in such
A sorrow.

Don Carlos. Ah! the Pope is anxious now
To get back Sicily—the isle that's mine;
'Tis ruled that Sicily cannot belong
Unto an Emperor; therefore it is
That he desires me Emperor to be made;
And then, to follow that, as docile son
I give up Naples too. Let us but have
The Eagle, and we'll see if I allow
Its wings to be thus clipp'd!

Don Ruy Gomez. What joy 'twould be
For this great veteran of the throne to see
Your brow, so fit, encircled by his crown!
Ah, Highness, we together weep for him,
The Christian Emperor, so good, so great!

Don Carlos. The Holy Father's clever. He will say—
This isle unto my States should come; 'tis but
A tatter'd rag that scarce belongs to Spain.
What will you do with this ill-shapen isle
That's sewn upon the Empire by a thread?
Your Empire is ill-made; but quick, come here,
The scissors bring, and let us cut away!—
Thanks, Holy Father, but if I have luck
I think that many pieces such as this
Upon the Holy Empire will be sewn!
And if some rags from me are ta'en, I mean
With isles and duchies to replace them all.

Don Ruy Gomez. Console yourself, for we shall see again
The dead more holy and more great. There is
An Empire of the Just.

Don Carlos. Francis the First
Is all ambition. The old Emperor dead,
Quick, he'll turn wooing. Has he not fair France
Most Christian? 'Tis a place worth holding fast.
Once to King Louis did my grandsire say—
If I were God, and had two sons, I'd make
The elder God, the second, King of France.
(*To* Don Ruy Gomez.)
Think you that Francis has a chance to win?

Don Ruy Gomez. He is a victor.

Don Carlos. There'd be all to change—
The golden bull doth foreigners exclude.

Don Ruy Gomez. In a like manner, Highness, you would be
Accounted King of Spain.

Don Carlos. But I was born
A citizen of Ghent.

Don Ruy Gomez. His last campaign
Exalted Francis mightily.

Don Carlos. The Eagle
That soon perchance upon my helm will gleam
Knows also how to open out its wings.

Don Ruy Gomez. And knows your Highness Latin?

Don Carlos. Ah, not much.

Don Ruy Gomez. A pity that. The German nobles like
The best those who in Latin speak to them.

Don Carlos. With haughty Spanish they will be content,
For trust King Charles, 'twill be of small account,
When masterful the voice, what tongue it speaks.
To Flanders I must go. Your King, dear Duke,
Must Emperor return. The King of France
Will stir all means. I must be quick to win.
I shall set out at once.

Don Ruy Gomez. Do you then go, Oh Highness, without clearing Aragon Of those fresh bandits who, among the hills,
Their daring insolence show everywhere?

Don Carlos. To the Duke d'Arcos I have orders given
That he should quite exterminate the band.

Don Ruy Gomez. But is the order given to its Chief
To let the thing be done?

Don Carlos. Who is this Chief— His name?

Don Ruy Gomez. I know not. But the people say
That he's an awkward customer.

Don Carlos. Pshaw! I know
That now he somewhere in Galicia hides
With a few soldiers, soon we'll capture him.

Don Ruy Gomez. Then it was false, the rumour which declared
That he was hereabouts?

Don Carlos. Quite false. Thou canst
Accommodate me here to-night.

Don Ruy Gomez (*bowing to the ground*). Thanks! Thanks! Highness! (*He calls his servants.*) You'll do all honour to the King, My guest.

(*The servants re-enter with lights. The Duke arranges them in two rows to the door at the back. Meanwhile Doña Sol approaches Hernani softly. The King observes them.*)

Doña Sol (*to Hernani*). To-morrow, midnight, without fail
Beneath my window clap your hands three times.

Hernani (*softly*). To-morrow night.

Don Carlos (*aside*). To-morrow!

(*Aloud to* Doña Sol, *whom he approaches with politeness.*)
Let me now
Escort you hence, I pray.

(*He leads her to the door. She goes out.*)

Hernani (*his hand in his breast on dagger hilt*). My dagger true!

Don Carlos (*coming back, aside*). Our man here has the look of being trapp'd.

(*He takes* Hernani *aside.*)
I've crossed my sword with yours; that honour, sir,
I've granted you. For many reasons I
Suspect you much, but to betray you now
Would shame the King; go therefore freely. E'en
I deign to aid your flight.

Don Ruy Gomez (*coming back, and pointing to* Hernani). This lord—who's he?

Don Carlos. One of my followers, who'll soon depart.

(*They go out with servants and lights, the* Duke *preceding with waxlight in his hand.*)

Scene 4—Hernani *alone*.

Hernani. One of thy followers! I am, oh King!
Well said. For night and day and step by step
I follow thee, with eye upon thy path
And dagger in my hand. My race in me
Pursues thy race in thee. And now behold
Thou art my rival! For an instant I
'Twixt love and hate was balanced in the scale.
Not large enough my heart for her and thee;

In loving her oblivious I became
Of all my hate of thee. But since 'tis thou
That comes to will I should remember it,
I recollect. My love it is that tilts
Th' uncertain balance, while it falls entire
Upon the side of hate. Thy follower!
'Tis thou hast said it. Never courtier yet
Of thy accursed court, or noble, fain
To kiss thy shadow—not a seneschal
With human heart abjured in serving thee;
No dog within the palace, trained the King
To follow, will thy steps more closely haunt
And certainly than I. What they would have,
These famed grandees, is hollow title, or
Some toy that shines—some golden sheep to hang
About the neck. Not such a fool am I.
What I would have is not some favour vain,
But 'tis thy blood, won by my conquering steel—
Thy soul from out thy body forced—with all
That at the bottom of thy heart was reached
After deep delving. Go—you are in front—
I follow thee. My watchful vengeance walks
With me, and whispers in mine ear. Go where
Thou wilt I'm there to listen and to spy,
And noiselessly my step will press on thine.
No day, shouldst thou but turn thy head, oh King,
But thou wilt find me, motionless and grave,
At festivals; at night, should'st thou look back,
Still wilt thou see my flaming eyes behind.

(*Exit by the little door.*)

SECOND ACT:
THE BANDIT

SARAGOSSA.

SCENE 1.—*A square before the Palace of* SILVA. *On the left the high walls of the Palace, with a window and a balcony. Below the window a little door. To the right, at the back, houses of the street. Night. Here and there are a few windows still lit up, shining in the front of the houses.*

DON CARLOS, DON SANCHO SANCHEZ DE ZUNIGA COMTE DE MONTEREY, DON MATIAS CENTURION MARQUIS D'ALMUNAN, DON RICARDO DE ROXAS LORD OF CASAPALMA.

All four arrive, DON CARLOS *at the head, hats pulled down, and wrapped in long cloaks, which their swords inside raise up.*

DON CARLOS (*looking up at the balcony*). Behold! We're at the balcony—the door.

My heart is bounding.
(*Pointing to the window, which is dark.*)
Ah, no light as yet.
(*He looks at the windows where light shines.*)
Although it shines just where I'd have it not,
While where I wish for light is dark.

DON SANCHO. Your Highness,
Now let us of this traitor speak again.
And you permitted him to go!

DON CARLOS. 'Tis true.

DON MATIAS. And he, perchance, was Major of the band.

DON CARLOS. Were he the Major or the Captain e'en,
No crown'd king ever had a haughtier air.

DON SANCHO. Highness, his name?

DON CARLOS (*his eyes fixed on the window*). Muñoz—Fernan—(*With gesture of a man suddenly recollecting.*)
A name
In i.

DON SANCHO. Perchance Hernani?

DON CARLOS. Yes.

DON SANCHO. 'Twas he.

DON MATIAS. The chief, Hernani!

DON SANCHO. Cannot you recall his speech?

DON CARLOS. Oh, I heard nothing in the vile
And wretched cupboard.

DON SANCHO. Wherefore let him slip
When there you had him?

DON CARLOS (*turning round gravely and looking him in the face*). Count de Monterey,
You question me!
(*The two nobles step back, and are silent.*)
Besides, it was not he
Was in my mind. It was his mistress, not
His head, I wanted. Madly I'm in love
With two dark eyes, the loveliest in the world,
My friends! Two mirrors, and two rays! two flames!
I heard but of their history these words:
"To-morrow come at midnight." 'Twas enough.
The joke is excellent! For while that he,
The bandit lover, by some murd'rous deed
Some grave to dig, is hindered and delayed,
I softly take his dove from out its nest.

DON RICARDO. Highness, 'twould make the thing far more complete
If we, the dove in gaining, killed the kite.

DON CARLOS. Count, 'tis most capital advice. Your hand
Is prompt.

DON RICARDO (*bowing low*). And by what title will it please
The King that I be Count?

DON SANCHO. 'Twas a mistake.

DON RICARDO (*to* DON SANCHO). The King has called me Count.

DON CARLOS. Enough—enough! (*To* DON RICARDO).
I let the title fall; but pick it up.

DON RICARDO (*bowing again*).
Thanks, Highness.

DON SANCHO. A fine Count—Count by mistake!

(THE KING *walks to the back of the stage, watching eagerly the lighted windows. The two lords talk together at the front.*)

DON MATIAS (*to* DON SANCHO). What think you that the King will do, when once

The beauty's taken?

DON SANCHO (*looking sideways at* DON RICARDO). Countess she'll be made;
Lady of honour afterwards, and then,
If there's a son, he will be King.

DON MATIAS. How so?—
My Lord! a bastard! Let him be a Count.
Were one His Highness, would one choose as king
A Countess' son?

DON SANCHO. He'd make her Marchioness
Ere then, dear Marquis.

DON MATIAS. Bastards—they are kept
For conquer'd countries. They for viceroys serve.

(DON CARLOS *comes forward*.)

DON CARLOS (*looking with vexation at the lighted windows*). Might one not say they're jealous eyes that watch? Ah! there are two which darken; we shall do.
Weary the time of expectation seems—
Sirs, who can make it go more quickly?

DON SANCHO. That
Is what we often ask ourselves within
The palace.

DON CARLOS. 'Tis the thing my people say
Again with you. (*The last window light is extinguished.*)
The last light now is gone.
(*Turning towards the balcony of* DOÑA SOL, *still dark.*)
Oh, hateful window! When wilt thou light up?
The night is dark; come, Doña Sol, and shine
Like to a star! (*To* DON RICARDO.)
Is't midnight yet?

DON RICARDO. Almost.

DON CARLOS. Ah! we must finish, for the other one
At any moment may appear.
(*A light appears in* DOÑA SOL'S *chamber. Her shadow is seen through the glass.*)
My friends!
A lamp! and she herself seen through the pane!
Never did daybreak charm me as this sight.
Let's hasten with the signal she expects.
We must clap hands three times. An instant more
And you will see her. But our number, perhaps,
Will frighten her. Go, all three out of sight
Beyond there, watching for the man we want.
'Twixt us, my friends, we'll share the loving pair,
For me the girl—the brigand is for you.

DON RICARDO. Best thanks.

DON CARLOS. If he appear from ambuscade,
Rush quickly, knock him down, and, while the dupe
Recovers from the blow, it is for me
To carry safely off the darling prize.
We'll laugh anon. But kill him not outright,
He's brave, I own;—killing's a grave affair.
(*The lords bow and go.* DON CARLOS *waits till they are quite gone, then claps his hands twice. At the second time the window opens, and* DOÑA SOL *appears on the balcony.*)

SCENE 2.—DON CARLOS. DOÑA SOL.

DOÑA SOL (*from the balcony*). Hernani, is that you?

DON CARLOS (*aside*). The devil! We must
Not parley!
(*He claps his hands again*).

DOÑA SOL. I am coming down.
(*She closes the window and the light disappears. The next minute the little door opens, and she comes out, the lamp in her hand, and a mantle over her shoulders.*)

DOÑA SOL. Hernani!
(DON CARLOS *pulls his hat down on his face, and hurries towards her.*)

DOÑA SOL (*letting her lamp fall*). Heavens! 'Tis not his footstep!
(*She attempts to go back, but* DON CARLOS *runs to her and seizes her by the arm.*)

DON CARLOS. Doña Sol!

DOÑA SOL. 'Tis not his voice! Oh, misery!

DON CARLOS. What voice
Is there that thou could'st hear that would be more
A lover's? It is still a lover here,
And King for one.

DOÑA SOL. The King!

DON CARLOS. Ah, wish, command,
A kingdom waits thy will; for he whom thou
Hast vanquish'd is the King, thy lord—
'tis Charles,
Thy slave!

DOÑA SOL (*trying to escape from him*). To the rescue! Help, Hernani! Help!

DON CARLOS. Thy fear is maidenly, and worthy thee.
'Tis not thy bandit—'tis thy King that holds
Thee now!

DOÑA SOL. Ah, no. The bandit's you. Are you
Not 'shamed? The blush unto my own cheek mounts
For you. Are these the exploits to be noised
Abroad? A woman thus at night to seize!
My bandit's worth a hundred of such kings!
I do declare, if man were born at level
Of his soul, and God made rank proportional
To his heart, he would be king and prince, and you
The robber be!

DON CARLOS (*trying to entice her*). Madam!——

DOÑA SOL. Do you forget
My father was a Count?

DON CARLOS. And you'll make
A Duchess.

DOÑA SOL (*repulsing him*). Cease! All this is shameful;—go!
(*She retreats a few steps.*)
Nothing, Don Carlos, can there 'twixt us be.
My father for you freely shed his blood.
I am of noble birth, and heedful ever
Of my name's purity. I am too high
To be your concubine—too low to be
Your wife.

DON CARLOS. Princess!

DOÑA SOL. Carry to worthless girls,
King Charles, your vile addresses. Or, if me
You treat insultingly, I'll show you well
That I'm a woman, and a noble dame.

DON CARLOS. Well, then but come, and you shall share my throne,

My name—you shall be Queen and
Empress——
　Doña Sol. No. It is a snare. Besides, I frankly speak,
Since, Highness, it concerns you. I avow
I'd rather with my king, Hernani, roam,
An outcast from the world and from the law—
Know thirst and hunger, wandering all the year,
Sharing the hardships of his destiny—
Exile and warfare, mourning hours of terror,
Than be an Empress with an Emperor!
　Don Carlos. Oh, happy man is he!
　Doña Sol. What! poor, proscribed!
　Don Carlos. 'Tis well with him, though poor, proscribed he be,
For he's beloved!—an angel watches him!
I'm desolate. You hate me, then?
　Doña Sol. I love You not.
　Don Carlos (*seizing her violently*).
Well, then, it matters not to me
Whether you love me, or you love me not!
You shall come with me—yes, for that my hand's
The stronger, and I will it! And we'll see
If I for nothing am the King of Spain
And of the Indies!
　Doña Sol (*struggling*). Highness! Pity me!
You're King, you only have to choose among
The Countesses, the Duchesses, the great
Court ladies, all have love prepared to meet
And answer yours; but what has my proscribed

Received from niggard fortune? You possess
Castile and Aragon—Murcia and Léon,
Navarre, and still ten kingdoms more. Flanders,
And India with the mines of gold you own,
An empire without peer, and all so vast
That ne'er the sun sets on it. And when you,
The King, have all, would you take me, poor girl,
From him who has but me alone.
(*She throws herself on her knees. He tries to draw her up.*)
　Don Carlos. Come—come!
I cannot listen. Come with me. I'll give
Of Spain a fourth part unto thee. Say, now.
What wilt thou? Choose.
　Doña Sol (*struggling in his arms*).
For mine own honour's sake
I'll only from your Highness take this dirk.
(*She snatches the poignard from his girdle.*)
Approach me now but by a step!
　Don Carlos. The beauty!
I wonder not she loves a rebel now.
(*He makes a step towards her. She raises the dirk.*)
　Doña Sol. Another step, I kill you—and myself.
(*He retreats again. She turns and cries loudly.*)
Hernani! Oh, Hernani!
　Don Carlos. Peace!
　Doña Sol. One step,
And all is finished.
　Don Carlos. Madam, to extremes

I'm driven. Yonder there I have three men
To force you—followers of mine.
HERNANI (*coming suddenly behind him*). But one
You have forgotten.
(THE KING *turns, and sees* HERNANI *motionless behind him in the shade, his arms crossed under the long cloak which is wrapped round him, and the brim of his hat raised up.* DOÑA SOL *makes an exclamation and runs to him.*)

SCENE 3.—DON CARLOS, DOÑA SOL, HERNANI.

HERNANI (*motionless, his arms still crossed, and his fiery eyes fixed on the* KING). Heaven my witness is,
That far from here it was I wished to seek him.
DOÑA SOL. Hernani! save me from him.
HERNANI. My dear love,
Fear not.
DON CARLOS. Now what could all my friends in town
Be doing, thus to let pass by the chief
Of the Bohemians? Ho! Monterey!
HERNANI. Your friends are in the hands of mine just now,
So call not on their powerless swords; for three
That you might claim, sixty to me would come
Each one worth four of yours. So let us now
Our quarrel terminate. What! you have dared
To lay a hand upon this girl! It was
An act of folly, great Castilian King,
And one of cowardice!
DON CARLOS. Sir Bandit, hold!

There must be no reproach from you to me!
HERNANI. He jeers! Oh, I am not a king; but when
A king insults me, and above all jeers,
My anger swells and surges up, and lifts
Me to his height. Take care! When I'm offended,
Men fear far more the reddening of my brow
Than helm of king. Foolhardy, therefore, you
If still you're lured by hope.
(*Seizes his arm.*)
Know you what hand
Now grasps you? Listen. 'Twas your father who
Was death of mine. I hate you for it. You
My title and my wealth have taken. You
I hate. And the same woman now we love.
I hate—hate—from my soul's depths you I hate.
DON CARLOS. That's well.
HERNANI. And yet this night my hate was lull'd.
Only one thought, one wish, one want I had—
'Twas Doña Sol! And I, absorbed in love,
Came here to find you daring against her
To strive, with infamous design! You —you,
The man forgot—thus in my pathway placed!
I tell you, King, you are demented! Ah!
King Charles, now see you're taken in the snare

Laid by yourself: and neither flight nor help
For thee is possible. I hold thee fast,
Besieged, alone, surrounded by thy foes,
Bloodthirsty ones, what wilt thou do?

Don Carlos (*proudly*). Dare you To question me!

Hernani. Pish! pish! I would not wish
An arm obscure should strike thee. 'Tis not so
My vengeance should have play. 'Tis I alone
Must deal with thee. Therefore defend thyself.
(*He draws his sword.*)

Don Carlos. I am your lord, the King, Strike! but no duel,

Hernani. Highness, thou may'st remember yesterday
Thy sword encountered mine.

Don Carlos. I yesterday
Could do it. I your name knew not, and you
Were ignorant of my rank. Not so to-day.
You know who I am, I who you are now.

Hernani. Perchance.

Don Carlos. No duel. You can murder. Do.

Hernani. Think you that kings to me are sacred? Come,
Defend thyself.

Don Carlos. You will assassinate Me then?

(Hernani *falls back. The* King *looks at him with eagle eyes.*) Ah! bandits, so you dare to think
That your most vile brigades may safely spread
Through towns—ye blood-stained, murderous, miscreant crew—
But that you'll play at magnanimity!
As if we'd deign th' ennobling of your dirks
By touch of our own swords—we victims duped.
No, crime enthralls you! Away! and murder me.

(Hernani, *morose and thoughtful, plays for some instants with the hilt of his sword, then turns sharply towards the* King *and snaps the blade on the pavement.*)

Hernani. Go, then.

(*The* King *half turns towards him and looks at him haughtily.*)
We shall have fitter meetings. Go. Get thee away.

Don Carlos. 'Tis well. I go, Sir, soon
Unto the Ducal Palace. I, your King,
Will then employ the magistrate. Is there
Yet put a price upon your head?

Hernani. Oh, yes.

Don Carlos. My master, from this day I reckon you
A rebel, trait'rous subject; you I warn.
I will pursue you everywhere, and make
You outlaw from my kingdom.

Hernani. That I am Already.

Don Carlos. That is well.

Hernani. But France is near To Spain. There's refuge there.

Don Carlos. But I shall be
The Emperor of Germany, and you
Under the empire's ban shall be.

Hernani. Ah, well!
I still shall have the remnant of the world,

From which to brave you—and with havens safe
O'er which you'll have no power.
DON CARLOS. But when I've gain'd The world?
HERNANI. Then I shall have the grave.
DON CARLOS. Your plots
So insolent I shall know how to thwart.
HERNANI. Vengeance is lame, and comes with lagging steps,
But still it comes.
DON CARLOS (*with a half laugh of disdain*). For touch of lady whom The bandit loves!
HERNANI (*with flashing eyes*). Dost thou remember, King,
I hold thee still? Make me not recollect
Oh, future Roman Cæsar, that despised
I have thee in my all too loyal hand,
And that I only need to close it now
To crush the egg of thy Imperial Eagle!
DON CARLOS. Then do it.
HERNANI. Get away.
(*He takes off his cloak, and throws it on the shoulders of the* KING.)
Go, fly, and take
This cloak to shield thee from some knife I fear
Among our ranks. (*The* KING *wraps himself in the cloak.*)
At present safely go,
My thwarted vengeance for myself I keep.
It makes 'gainst every other hand thy life
Secure.
DON CARLOS. And you who've spoken thus to me
Ask not for mercy on some future day.
(*Exit* DON CARLOS.)

SCENE 4.—HERNANI. DOÑA SOL.

DOÑA SOL (*seizing* HERNANI'S *hand*). Now let us fly—be quick.
HERNANI. It well becomes
You, loved one, in the trial hour to prove
Thus strong, unchangeable, and willing e'en
To th' end and depth of all to cling to me;
A noble wish, worthy a faithful soul!
But Thou, oh God, dost see that to accept
The joy that to my cavern she would bring—
The treasure of a beauty that a king
Now covets—and that Doña Sol to me
Should all belong—that she with me should 'bide,
And all our lives be joined—that this should be
Without regret, remorse—it is too late.
The scaffold is too near.
DOÑA SOL. What is't you say?
HERNANI. This King, whom to his face just now I braved,
Will punish me for having dared to show
Him mercy. He already, perhaps, has reached
His palace, and is calling round him guards
And servants, his great lords, his headsmen—
DOÑA SOL. Heavens!
Hernani! Oh, I shudder. Never mind,
Let us be quick and fly together then.
HERNANI. Together! No; the hour has passed for that.
Alas! When to my eyes thou didst reveal

Thyself, so good and generous, deigning e'en
To love me with a helpful love, I could
But offer you—I, wretched one!—the hills,
The woods, the torrents, bread of the proscribed,
The bed of turf, all that the forest gives;
Thy pity then emboldened me—but now
To ask of thee to share the scaffold! No,
No, Doña Sol. That is for me alone.

DOÑA SOL. And yet you promised even that!

HERNANI (*falling on his knees*). Angel!
At this same moment, when perchance from out
The shadow Death approaches, to wind up
All mournfully a life of mournfulness.
I do declare that here a man proscribed,
Enduring trouble great, profound—and rock'd
In blood-stained cradle—black as is the gloom
Which spreads o'er all my life, I still declare
I am a happy, to-be-envied man,
For you have loved me, and your love have owned!
For you have whispered blessings on my brow
Accursed!

DOÑA SOL (*leaning over his head*). Hernani!

HERNANI. Praiséd be the fate
Sweet and propitious that for me now sets
This flower upon the precipice's brink!
(*Raising himself.*)
'Tis not to you that I am speaking thus;
It is to Heaven that hears, and unto God.

DOÑA SOL. Let me go with you.

HERNANI. Ah, 'twould be a crime
To pluck the flower while falling in the abyss.
Go: I have breathed the perfume—'tis enough.
Remould your life, by me so sadly marred.
This old man wed; 'tis I release you now.
To darkness I return. Be happy thou—
Be happy thou—
Be happy and forget.

DOÑA SOL. No, I will have
My portion of thy shroud. I follow thee.
I hang upon thy steps.

HERNANI (*pressing her in his arms*). Oh, let me go
Alone! Exiled—proscribed—a fearful man
Am I.
(*He quits her with a convulsive movement, and is going.*)

DOÑA SOL (*mournfully, and clasping her hands*). Hernani, do you fly from me!

HERNANI (*returning*). Well, then, no, no. You will it, and I stay.
Behold me! Come into my arms. I'll wait
As long as thou wilt have me. Let us rest,
Forgetting them. (*He seats her on a bench.*)
Be seated on this stone. (*He places himself at her feet.*)
The liquid light of your eyes inundates
Mine own. Sing me some song, such as sometimes
You used at eve to warble, with the tears

In those dark orbs. Let us be happy now,
And drink; the cup is full. This hour is ours,
The rest is only folly. Speak and say,
Enrapture me. Is it not sweet to love,
And know that he who kneels before you loves?
To be but two alone? Is it not sweet
To speak of love in stillness of the night
When nature rests? Oh, let me slumber now,
And on thy bosom dream. Oh, Doña Sol,
My love, my darling! (*Noise of bells in the distance.*)

Doña Sol (*starting up frightened*). Tocsin!—dost thou hear? The tocsin!

Hernani (*still kneeling at her feet*). Eh! No, 'tis our bridal bell They're ringing
(*The noise increases. Confused cries. Lights at all the windows, on the roofs, and in the streets.*)

Doña Sol. Rise—oh, fly—great God! the town Lights up!

Hernani (*half rising*). A torchlight wedding for us 'tis!

Doña Sol. The nuptials these of Death, and of the tombs!
(*Noise of swords and cries.*)

Hernani (*lying down on the stone bench*). Let us sleep again.

A Mountaineer (*rushing in, sword in hand*). The runners, sir.
The alcadés rush out in cavalcades
With mighty force. Be quick—my Captain,—quick.
(Hernani *rises.*)

Doña Sol (*pale*). Ah, thou wert right!

The Mountaineer. Oh, help us!

Hernani (*to* Mountaineer). It is well—
I'm ready. (*Confused cries outside.*) Death to the bandit!

Hernani (*to* Mountaineer). Quick, thy sword—
(*To* Doña Sol.)
Farewell!

Doña Sol. 'Tis I have been thy ruin! Oh, Where can'st thou go? (*Pointing to the little door.*) The door is free. Let us
Escape that way.

Hernani. Heavens! Desert my friends!
What dost thou say?

Doña Sol. These clamours terrify. Remember, if thou diest I must die.

Hernani (*holding her in his arms*). A kiss!

Doña Sol. Hernani! Husband! Master mine!

Hernani (*kissing her forehead*). Alas! it is the first!

Doña Sol. Perchance the last!
(Hernani *exit. She falls on the bench.*)

THIRD ACT:
THE OLD MAN

The Castle of Silva.

In the midst of the Mountains of Aragon.

Scene 1.—*The gallery of family portraits of Silva; a great hall of which these portraits—surrounded with rich frames, and surmounted by ducal coronets and gilt escutcheons—form the decoration. At the back a lofty Gothic door. Between the portraits complete panoplies of armour of different centuries.*

Doña Sol, *pale, and standing near a table.*

Don Ruy Gomez de Silva, *seated in his great carved oak chair.*

Don Ruy Gomez. At last the day has come!—and in an hour
Thou'lt be my Duchess, and embrace me! Not
Thine Uncle then! But hast thou pardoned me?
That I was wrong I own. I raised thy blush,
I made thy cheek turn pale. I was too quick
With my suspicions—should have stayed to hear
Before condemning; but appearances
Should take the blame. Unjust we were. Certes
The two young handsome men were there. But then—
No matter—well I know that I should not
Have credited my eyes. But, my poor child,
What would'st thou with the old?
Doña Sol (*seriously, and without moving*). You ever talk
Of this. Who is there blames you?
Don Ruy Gomez. I myself,
I should have known that such a soul as yours
Never has galants; when 'tis Doña Sol,
And when good Spanish blood is in her veins.
Doña Sol. Truly, my Lord, 'tis good and pure; perchance
'Twill soon be seen.
Don Ruy Gomez (*rising, and going towards her*). Now list. One cannot be
The master of himself, so much in love
As I am with thee. And I am old
And jealous, and am cross—and why? Because
I'm old; because the beauty, grace or youth
Of others frightens, threatens me. Because
While jealous thus of others, of myself
I am ashamed. What mockery! that this love
Which to the heart brings back such joy and warmth,
Should halt, and but rejuvenate the soul,
Forgetful of the body. When I see
A youthful peasant, singing blithe and gay,
In the green meadows, often then I muse—
I, in my dismal paths, and murmur low:
"Oh, I would give my battlemented towers,
And ancient ducal donjon, and my fields
Of corn, and all my forest lands, and flocks

So vast which feed upon my hills, my name
And all my ancient titles—ruins mine,
And ancestors who must expect me soon,
And—all I'd give for his new cot, and brow
Unwrinkled. For his hair is raven black,
And his eyes shine like yours. Beholding him
You might exclaim: A young man this!
And then
Would think of me so old." I know it well.
I am named Silva. Ah, but that is not
Enough; I say it, see it. Now behold
To what excess I love thee. All I'd give
Could I be like thee—young and handsome now!
Vain dream! that I were young again, who must
By long, long years precede thee to the tomb.

DOÑA SOL. Who knows?

DON RUY GOMEZ. And yet, I pray you, me believe,
The frivolous swains have not so much of love
Within their hearts as on their tongues. A girl
May love and trust one; if she dies for him,
He laughs. The strong-winged and gay-painted birds
That warble sweet, and in the thicket trill,
Will change their loves as they their plumage moult.
They are the old, with voice and colour gone,
And beauty fled, who have the resting wings
We love the best. Our steps are slow, And dim
Our eyes. Our brows are furrowed,— but the heart
Is never wrinkled. When an old man loves
He should be spared. The heart is ever young,
And always it can bleed. This love of mine
Is not a plaything made of glass to shake
And break. It is a love severe and sure,
Solid, profound, paternal,—strong as is
The oak which forms my ducal chair. See then
How well I love thee—and in other ways
I love thee—hundred other ways, e'en as
We love the dawn, and flowers, and heaven's blue!
To see thee, mark thy graceful step each day,
Thy forehead pure, thy brightly beaming eye,
I'm joyous—feeling that my soul will have
Perpetual festival!

DOÑA SOL. Alas!

DON RUY GOMEZ. And then,
Know you how much the world admires, applauds,
A woman, angel pure, and like a dove,
When she an old man comforts and consoles
As he is tott'ring to the marble tomb,
Passing away by slow degrees as she
Watches and shelters him, and condescends
To bear with him, the useless one, that seems
But fit to die? It is a sacred work

And worthy of all praise—effort supreme
Of a devoted heart to comfort him
Unto the end, and without loving perhaps,
To act as if she loved. Ah, thou to me
Wilt be this angel with a woman's heart
Who will rejoice the old man's soul again
And share his latter years, and by respect
A daughter be, and by your pity like
A sister prove.

Doña Sol. Far from preceding me,
'Tis likely me you'll follow to the grave.
My lord, because that we are young is not
A reason we should live. Alas! I know
And tell you, often old men tarry long,
And see the young go first, their eyes shut fast
By sudden stroke, as on a sepulchre
That still was open falls the closing stone.

Don Ruy Gomez. Oh cease, my child, such saddening discourse,
Or I shall scold you. Such a day as this
Sacred and joyous is. And, by-the-bye,
Time summons us. Are you not ready yet
For chapel when we're called? Be quick to don
The bridal dress. Each moment do I count.

Doña Sol. There is abundant time.
Don Ruy Gomez. Oh no, there's not.
(*Enter a* Page.)
What want you?

The Page. At the door, my lord, a man—

A pilgrim—beggar—or I know not what,
Is craving here a shelter.

Don Ruy Gomez. Let him in
Whoever he may be. Good enters with
The stranger that we welcome. What's the news
From th' outside world? What of the bandit chief
That filled our forests with his rebel band?

The Page. Hernani, Lion of the mountains, now
Is done for.

Doña Sol (*aside*). God!
Don Ruy Gomez (*to the* Page). How so?

The Page. The troop's destroyed.
The King himself has led the soldiers on.
Hernani's head a thousand crowns is worth
Upon the spot; but now he's dead, they say.

Doña Sol. (*aside*). What! Without me, Hernani!

Don Ruy Gomez. And thank Heaven!
So he is dead, the rebel! Now, dear love,
We can rejoice; go then and deck thyself,
My pride, my darling. Day of double joy.

Doña Sol. Oh, mourning robes!
(*Exit* Doña Sol.)
Don Ruy Gomez (*to the* Page).
The casket quickly send
That I'm to give her. (*He seats himself in his chair.*)
'Tis my longing now
To see her all adorned Madonna like.
With her bright eyes, and aid of my rich gems
She will be beautiful enough to make
A pilgrim kneel before her. As for him

Who asks asylum, bid him enter here.
Excuses from us offer; run, be quick.
  (*The* PAGE *bows and exit.*)
'Tis ill to keep a guest long waiting thus.
  (*The door at the back opens.* HERNANI *appears disguised as a Pilgrim. The* DUKE *rises.*)

SCENE 2.—DON RUY GOMEZ. HERNANI.

(HERNANI *pauses at the threshold of the door.*)
  HERNANI. My lord, peace and all happiness be yours!
  DON RUY GOMEZ (*saluting him with his hand*). To thee be peace and happiness, my guest!
  (HERNANI *enters. The* DUKE *reseats himself.*) Art thou a pilgrim?
  HERNANI (*bowing*). Yes.
  DON RUY GOMEZ. No doubt you come
From Armillas?
  HERNANI. Not so. I hither came
By other road, there was some fighting there.
  DON RUY GOMEZ. Among the troops of bandits, was it not?
  HERNANI. I know not.
  DON RUY GOMEZ. What's become of him—the chief
They call Hernani? Dost thou know?
  HERNANI. My lord,
Who is this man?
  DON RUY GOMEZ. Dost thou not know him then?
For thee so much the worse! Thou wilt not gain
The good round sum. See you a rebel he
That has been long unpunished. To Madrid

Should you be going, perhaps you'll see him hanged.
  HERNANI. I go not there.
  DON RUY GOMEZ. A price is on his head
For any man who takes him.
  HERNANI (*aside*). Let one come!
  DON RUY GOMEZ. Whither, good pilgrim, goest thou?
  HERNANI. My lord,
I'm bound for Saragossa.
  DON RUY GOMEZ. A vow made
In honour of a Saint, or of Our Lady?
  HERNANI. Yes, of Our Lady, Duke.
  DON RUY GOMEZ. Of the Pillar?
  HERNANI. Of the Pillar.
  DON RUY GOMEZ. We must be soulless quite
Not to acquit us of the vows we make
Unto the Saints. But thine accomplished, then
Hast thou not other purposes in view?
Or is to see the Pillar all you wish?
  HERNANI. Yes. I would see the lights and candles burn,
And at the end of the dim corridor
Our Lady in her glowing shrine, with cope
All golden—then would satisfied return.
  DON RUY GOMEZ. Indeed, that's well. Brother, what is thy name?
Mine, Ruy de Silva is.
  HERNANI (*hesitating*). My name——
  DON RUY GOMEZ. You can
Conceal it if you will. None here has right
To know it. Cam'st thou to asylum ask?
  HERNANI. Yes, Duke.
  DON RUY GOMEZ. Remain, and know thou'rt welcome here.

For nothing want; and as for what thou'rt named,
But call thyself my guest. It is enough.
Whoever thou may'st be. Without demur
I'd take in Satan if God sent him me.

(*The folding doors at the back open. Enter* DOÑA SOL *in nuptial attire. Behind her Pages and Lackeys, and two women carrying on a velvet cushion a casket of engraved silver, which they place upon a table, and which contains, bracelets, pearls and diamonds in profusion.* HERNANI, *breathless and scared, looks at* DOÑA SOL *with flaming eyes without listening to the* DUKE.)

SCENE 3.—*The Same:* DOÑA SOL, PAGES, LACKEYS, WOMEN.

DON RUY GOMEZ (*continuing*). Behold my blessed Lady—to have prayed
To her will bring thee happiness.
(*He offers his hand to* DOÑA SOL, *still pale and grave.*)
Come then,
My bride. What! not thy coronet, nor ring!

HERNANI (*in a voice of thunder*). Who wishes now a thousand golden crowns
To win?
(*All turn to him astonished. He tears off his Pilgrim's robe, and crushes it under his feet, revealing himself in the dress of a Mountaineer.*)
I am Hernani.

DOÑA SOL (*joyfully*). Heavens! Oh, He lives!

HERNANI (*to the Lackeys*). See! I'm the man they seek.
(*To the* Duke.)
You wished
To know my name—Diego or Perez?
No, No! I have a grander name—Hernani.
Name of the banished, the proscribed. See you
This head? 'Tis worth enough of gold to pay
For festival.
(*To the Lackeys.*)
I give it to you all.
Take; tie my hands, my feet. But there's no need,
The chain that binds me's one I shall not break.

DOÑA SOL (*aside*). Oh misery!

DON RUY GOMEZ. Folly! This my guest is mad—
A lunatic!

HERNANI. Your guest a bandit is.

DOÑA SOL. Oh, do not heed him.

HERNANI. What I say is truth.

DON RUY GOMEZ. A thousand golden crowns—the sum is large.
And, sir, I will not answer now for all
My people.

HERNANI. And so much the better, should
A willing one be found.
(*To the Lackeys.*)
Now seize, and sell me!

DON RUY GOMEZ (*trying to silence him*). Be quiet, or they'll take you at your word.

HERNANI. Friends, this your opportunity is good.
I tell you, I'm the rebel—the proscribed Hernani!

DON RUY GOMEZ. Silence!

HERNANI. I am he!

DOÑA SOL (*in a low voice to him*). Be still!

HERNANI (*half turning to* DOÑA SOL).

There's marrying here! My spouse awaits me too.
(*To the* DUKE.)
She is less beautiful, my Lord, than yours,
But not less faithful. She is Death.
(*To the Lackeys.*) Not one
Of you has yet come forth!

DOÑA SOL (*in a low voice*). For pity's sake!

HERNANI (*to the Lackeys*). A thousand golden crowns. Hernani here!

DON RUY GOMEZ. This is the demon!

HERNANI (*to a young Lackey*). Come! thou'lt earn this sum,
Then rich, thou wilt from lackey change again
To man. (*To the other Lackeys, who do not stir.*)
And also you—you waver. Ah,
Have I not misery enough?

DON RUY GOMEZ. My friend,
To touch thy life they'd peril each his own.
Wert thou Hernani, or a hundred times
As bad, I must protect my guest,—were e'en
An Empire offered for his life—against
The King himself; for thee I hold from God.
If hair of thine be injured, may I die.
(*To* DOÑA SOL.)
My niece, who in an hour will be my wife,
Go to your room. I am about to arm
The Castle—shut the gates.
(*Exit, followed by servants.*)

HERNANI (*looking with despair at his empty girdle*). Not e'en a knife!

(DOÑA SOL, *after the departure of the* DUKE, *takes a few steps, as if to follow her women, then pauses, and when they are gone, comes back to* HERNANI *with anxiety.*)

SCENE 4.—HERNANI. DOÑA SOL.

HERNANI *looks at the nuptial jewel-case with a cold and apparently indifferent gaze; then he tosses back his head, and his eyes light up.*

HERNANI. Accept my 'gratulations!
Words tell not
How I'm enchanted by these ornaments.
(*He approaches the casket.*)
This ring is in fine taste,—the coronet
I like,—the necklace shows surpassing skill.
The bracelet's rare—but oh, a hundred times
Less so than she, who 'neath a forehead pure
Conceals a faithless heart.
(*Examining the casket again.*)
What for all this
Have you now given? Of your love some share?
But that for nothing goes! Great God! to thus
Deceive, and still to live and have no shame!
(*Looking at the jewels.*)
But after all, perchance, this pearl is false,
And copper stands for gold, and glass and lead
Make out sham diamonds—pretended gems!
Are these false sapphires and false jewels all?
If so, thy heart is like them, Duchess false,
Thyself but only gilded.
(*He returns to the casket.*)
Yet, no, no!

They all are real, beautiful, and good,
He dares not cheat, who stands so
near the tomb.
Nothing is wanting.
(*He takes up one thing after another.*)
Necklaces are here,
And brilliant earrings, and the Duchess'
crown
And golden ring. Oh marvel! Many
thanks
For love so certain, faithful and profound.
The precious box!
  Doña Sol (*She goes to the casket,
feels in it, and draws forth a dagger*).
You have not reached its depths.
This is the dagger which, by kindly aid
Of patron saint, I snatched from Charles
the King
When he made offer to me of a throne,
Which I refused for you, who now insult
me.
  Hernani (*falling at her feet*). Oh,
let me on my knees arrest those tears,
The tears that beautify thy sorrowing
eyes.
Then after thou canst freely take my
life.
  Doña Sol. I pardon you, Hernani.
In my heart
There is but love for you.
  Hernani. And she forgives—
And loves me still! But who can also
teach
Me to forgive myself, that I have used
Such words? Angel, for heaven reserved, say where
You trod, that I may kiss the ground.
  Doña Sol. My love!
  Hernani. Oh, no, I should to thee
be odious.
But listen. Say again—I love thee still!
Say it, and reassure a heart that doubts.
Say it, for often with such little words
A woman's tongue hath cured a world
of woes.
  Doña Sol (*absorbed, and without
hearing him*). To think my love had
such short memory!
That all these so ignoble men could
shrink
A heart, where his name was enthroned,
to love
By them thought worthier.
  Hernani. Alas! I have
Blasphemed! If I were in thy place I
should
Be weary of the furious madman, who
Can only pity after he has struck.
I'd bid him go. Drive me away, I say,
And I will bless thee, for thou hast
been good
And sweet. Too long thou hast myself
endured,
For I am evil; I should blacken still
Thy days with my dark nights. At last
it is
Too much; thy soul is lofty, beautiful,
And pure; if I am evil, is't thy fault?
Marry the old duke then, for he is good
And noble. By the mother's side he has
Olmédo, by his father's Alcala.
With him be rich and happy by one act.
Know you not what this generous hand
of mine
Can offer thee of splendour? Ah, alone
A dowry of misfortune, and the choice
Of blood or tears. Exile, captivity
And death, and terrors that environ me.
These are thy necklaces and jewelled
crown.
Never elated bridegroom to his bride
Offered a casket filled more lavishly,
But 'tis with misery and mournfulness.

Marry the old man—he deserves thee well!
Ah, who could ever think my head proscribed
Fit mate for forehead pure? What looker-on
That saw thee calm and beautiful, me rash
And violent—thee peaceful, like a flower
Growing in shelter, me by tempests dash'd
On rocks unnumber'd—who could dare to say
That the same law should guide our destinies?
No, God, who ruleth all things well, did not
Make thee for me. No right from Heav'n above
Have I to thee; and I'm resigned to fate.
I have thy heart; it is a theft! I now
Unto a worthier yield it. Never yet
Upon our love has Heaven smiled; 'tis false
If I have said thy destiny it was.
To vengeance and to love I bid adieu!
My life is ending; useless I will go,
And take away with me my double dream,
Ashamed I could not punish, nor could charm.
I have been made for hate, who only wished
To love. Forgive and fly from me, these my prayers
Reject them not, since they will be my last.
Thou livest—I am dead. I see not why
Thou should'st immure thee in my tomb.

DOÑA SOL. Ingrate!

HERNANI. Mountains of old Aragon! Galicia!
Estremadura! Unto all who come
Around me I bring misery! Your sons,
The best, without remorse I've ta'en to fight,
And now behold them dead! The bravest brave
Of all Spain's sons lie, soldier-like, upon
The hills, their backs to earth, the living God
Before; and if their eyes could ope they'd look
On heaven's blue. See what I do to all
Who join me! Is it fortune any one
Should covet? Doña Sol, oh! take the Duke,
Take hell, or take the King—all would be well,
All must be better than myself, I say.
No longer have I friend to think of me,
And it is fully time that thy turn comes,
For I must be alone. Fly from me then,
From my contagion. Make not faithful love
A duty of religion! Fly from me,
For pity's sake. Thou think'st me, perhaps, a man
Like others, one with sense, who knows the end
At which he aims, and acts accordingly.
Oh, undeceive thyself. I am a force
That cannot be resisted—agent blind
And deaf of mournful mysteries! A soul
Of misery made of gloom. Where shall I go?
I cannot tell. But I am urged, compelled
By an impetuous breath and wild decree;

I fall, and fall, and cannot stop descent.
If sometimes breathless I dare turn my head,
A voice cries out, "Go on!" and the abyss
Is deep, and to the depths I see it red
With flame or blood! Around my fearful course
All things break up—all die. Woe be to them
Who touch me. Fly, I say! Turn thee away
From my so fatal path. Alas! without
Intending I should do thee ill.

DOÑA SOL. Great God!

HERNANI. My demon is a formidable one.
But there's a thing impossible to it—
My happiness. For thee is happiness.
Therefore go seek another lord for thou
Art not for me. If Heaven, that my fate
Abjures, should smile on me, believe it not:
It would be irony. Marry the Duke!

DOÑA SOL. 'Twas not enough to tear my heart, but you
Must break it now! Ah me! no longer then
You love me!

HERNANI. Oh, my heart—its very life
Thou art! The glowing hearth whence all warmth comes
Art thou! Wilt thou then blame me that I fly
From thee, adored one?

DOÑA SOL. No, I blame thee not,
Only I know that I shall die of it.

HERNANI. Die! And for what? For me? Can it then be
That thou should'st die for cause so small?

DOÑA SOL (*bursting into tears*). Enough.
(*She falls into a chair.*)

HERNANI (*seating himself near her*).
And thou art weeping; and 'tis still my fault!
And who will punish me? for thou I know
Wilt pardon still! Who, who can tell thee half
The anguish that I suffer when a tear
Of thine obscures and drowns those radiant eyes
Whose lustre is my joy. My friends are dead!
Oh, I am crazed—forgive me—I would love
I know not how. Alas! I love with love
Profound. Weep not—the rather let us die!
Oh that I had a world to give to thee!
Oh, wretched, miserable man I am!

DOÑA SOL (*throwing herself on his neck*). You are my lion, generous and superb!
I love you.

HERNANI. Ah, this love would be a good
Supreme, if we could die of too much love!

DOÑA SOL. Thou art my lord! I love thee and belong
To thee!

HERNANI (*letting his head fall on her shoulder*). How sweet would be a poignard stroke
From thee!

DOÑA SOL (*entreatingly*). Fear you not God will punish you
For words like these?

HERNANI (*still leaning on her shoulder*). Well, then, let Him unite us! I have resisted; thou would'st have it thus.

(*While they are in each other's arms, absorbed and gazing with ecstasy at each other, DON RUY GOMEZ enters by the door at the back of the stage. He sees them, and stops on the threshold as if petrified.*)

SCENE 5.—HERNANI. DOÑA SOL. DON RUY GOMEZ.

DON RUY GOMEZ (*motionless on the threshold, with arms crossed*).
And this is the requital that I find
Of hospitality!
DOÑA SOL. Oh Heavens—the Duke!
(*Both turn as if awakening with a start.*)
DON RUY GOMEZ (*still motionless*).
This, then's the recompense from thee, my guest?
Good duke, go see if all thy walls be high,
And if the door is closed, and archer placed
Within his tower, and go the castle round
Thyself for us; seek in thine arsenal
For armour that will fit—at sixty years
Resume thy battle-harness—and then see
The loyalty with which we will repay
Such service! Thou for us do thus, and we
Do this for thee! Oh, blessed saints of Heaven!
Past sixty years I've lived, and met sometimes
Unbridled souls; and oft my dirk have drawn
From out its scabbard, raising on my path
The hangman's game birds: murd'rers I have seen
And coiners, traitorous varlets poisoning
Their masters; and I've seen men die without
A prayer, or sight of crucifix. I've seen
Sforza and Borgia; Luther still I see,
But never have I known perversity
So great that feared not thunder bolt, its host
Betraying! 'Twas not of my age—such foul
Black treason, that at once could petrify
An old man on the threshold of his door,
And make the master, waiting for his grave,
Look like his statue ready for his tomb.
Moors and Castilians! Tell me, who's this man?
(*He raises his eyes and looks round on the portraits on the wall.*)
Oh you, the Silvas who can hear me now,
Forgive if, in your presence by my wrath
Thus stirr'd, I say that hospitality
Was ill advised.
HERNANI (*rising*). Duke——
DON RUY GOMEZ. Silence!
(*He makes three steps into the hall looking at the portraits of the SILVAS.*)
Sacred dead!
My ancestors! Ye men of steel, who know
What springs from heav'n or hell, reveal, I say,
Who is this man? No, not Hernani he,
But Judas is his name—oh, try to speak

And tell me who he is! (*Crossing his arms.*)
In all your days
Saw you aught like him? No.
  HERNANI. My lord——
  DON RUY GOMEZ (*still addressing the portraits*). See you
The shameless miscreant? He would speak to me,
But better far than I you read his soul.
Oh, heed him not! he is a knave—he'd say
That he foresaw that in the tempest wild
Of my great wrath I brooded o'er some deed
Of gory vengeance shameful to my roof.
A sister deed to that they call the feast
Of Seven Heads. He'll tell you he's proscribed,
He'll tell you that of Silva they will talk
E'en as of Lara. Afterwards he'll say
He is my guest and yours. My lords, my sires,
Is the fault mine? Judge you between us now.
  HERNANI. Ruy Gomez de Silva, if ever 'neath
The heavens clear a noble brow was raised,
If ever heart was great and soul was high,
Yours are, my lord; and oh, my noble host,
I, who now speak to you, alone have sinn'd.
Guilty most damnably am I, without
Extenuating word to say. I would
Have carried off thy bride—dishonour'd thee.
'Twas infamous. I live; but now my life

I offer unto thee. Take it. Thy sword
Then wipe, and think no more about the deed.
  DOÑA SOL. My lord, 'twas not his fault—strike only me.
  HERNANI. Be silent, Doña Sol. This hour supreme
Belongs alone to me; nothing I have
But it. Let me explain things to the Duke.
Oh, Duke, believe the last words from my mouth,
I swear that I alone am guilty. But
Be calm and rest assured that she is pure,
That's all. I guilty and she pure. Have faith
In her. A sword or dagger thrust for me.
Then throw my body out of doors, and have
The flooring washed, if you should will it so.
What matter?
  DOÑA SOL. Ah! I only am the cause
Of all; because I love him.
  (DON RUY *turns round trembling at these words, and fixes on* DOÑA SOL *a terrible look. She throws herself at his feet.*)
Pardon! Yes,
My lord, I love him!
  DON RUY GOMEZ. Love him—you love him!
  (*To* HERNANI.)
Tremble! (*Noise of trumpets outside. Enter a* PAGE.)
What is this noise?
  THE PAGE. It is the King,
My lord, in person, with a band complete

Of archers, and his herald, who now sounds.

DOÑA SOL. Oh God! This last fatality—the King!

THE PAGE (*to the* DUKE). He asks the reason why the door is closed,
And order gives to open it.

DON RUY GOMEZ. Admit
The King.

(*The* PAGE *bows and exit.*)

DOÑA SOL. He's lost!

(DON RUY GOMEZ *goes to one of the portraits—that of himself and the last on the left; he presses a spring, and the portrait opens out like a door, and reveals a hiding-place in the wall. He turns to* HERNANI.)

Come hither, sir.

HERNANI. My life
To thee is forfeit; and to yield it up
I'm ready. I thy prisoner am.

(*He enters the recess.* DON RUY *again presses the spring, and the portrait springs back to its place looking as before.*)

DOÑA SOL. My lord,
Have pity on him!

THE PAGE (*entering*). His highness the King!

(DOÑA SOL *hurriedly lowers her veil. The folding-doors open. Enter* DON CARLOS *in military attire, followed by a crowd of gentlemen equally armed with halberds, arquebuses, and crossbows.*)

SCENE 6.—DON RUY GOMEZ, DOÑA SOL *veiled*, DON CARLOS *and Followers.*

DON CARLOS *advances slowly, his left hand on the hilt of his sword, his right hand in his bosom, and looking at the* DUKE *with anger and defiance.*

The DUKE *goes before the* KING *and bows low. Silence. Expectation and terrror on all. At last the* KING, *coming opposite the* DUKE, *throws back his head haughtily.*

DON CARLOS. How comes it then, my cousin, that to-day
Thy door is strongly barr'd? By all the Saints
I thought your dagger had more rusty grown,
And know not why, when I'm your visitor,
It should so haste to brightly shine again
All ready to your hand.

(DON RUY GOMEZ *attempts to speak, but the* KING *continues with an imperious gesture.*)

Late in the day
It is for you to play the young man's part!
Do we come turban'd? Tell me, are we named
Boabdil or Mahomet, and not Charles, That the portcullis 'gainst us you should lower
And raise the drawbridge?

DON RUY GOMEZ (*bowing*). Highness——

DON CARLOS (*to his gentlemen*). Take the keys
And guard the doors.

(*Two officers exeunt. Several others arrange the soldiers in a triple line in the hall from the* KING *to the principal door.* DON CARLOS *turns again to the* DUKE.)

Ah! you would wake to life
Again these crushed rebellions. By my faith,

If you, ye Dukes, assume such airs as these
The King himself will play his kingly part,
Traverse the mountains in a warlike mode,
And in their battlemented nests will slay
The lordlings!

Don Ruy Gomez (*drawing himself up*). Ever have the Silvas been,
Your Highness, loyal.

Don Carlos (*interrupting him*). Without subterfuge
Reply, or to the ground I'll raze thy towers
Eleven! Of extinguished fire remains
One spark—of brigands dead the chief survives,
And who conceals him? It is thou, I say!
Hernani, rebel-ringleader, is here,
And in thy castle thou dost hide him now.

Don Ruy Gomez. Highness, it is quite true.

Don Carlos. Well then, his head
I want—or if not, thine. Dost understand,
My cousin?

Don Ruy Gomez. Well, then, be it so. You shall
Be satisfied.

(Doña Sol *hides her face in her hands and sinks into the arm-chair.*)

Don Carlos (*a little softened*). Ah! you repent. Go seek
Your prisoner.

(*The* Duke *crosses his arms, lowers his head, and remains some moments pondering. The* King *and* Doña Sol, *agitated by contrary emotions, observe him in silence. At last the* Duke *looks up, goes to the* King, *takes his hand, and leads him with slow steps towards the oldest of the portraits, which is where the gallery commences to the right of the spectator.*)

Don Ruy Gomez (*pointing out the old portrait to the* King). This is the eldest one,
The great forefather of the Silva race,
Don Silvius our ancestor, three times
Was he made Roman consul.

(*Passing to the next portrait.*)
This is he
Don Galceran de Silva—other Cid!
They keep his body still at Toro, near
Valladolid; a thousand candles burn
Before his gilded shrine. 'Twas he who freed
Leon from tribute o' the hundred virgins.

(*Passing to another.*)
Don Blas—who, in contrition for the fault
Of having ill-advised the king, exiled
Himself of his own will.

(*To another.*)
This Christoval!
At fight of Escalon, when fled on foot
The King Don Sancho, whose white plume was mark
For general deadly aim, he cried aloud,
Oh, Christoval! And Christoval assumed
The plume, and gave his horse.

(*To another.*)
This is Don Jorge,
Who paid the ransom of Ramire, the King
Of Aragon.

Don Carlos (*crossing his arms and looking at him from head to foot*). By Heavens now, Don Ruy,

I marvel at you! But go on.
  DON RUY GOMEZ. Next comes
Don Ruy Gomez Silva, he was made
Grand Master of St. James, and Calatrava.
His giant armour would not suit our heights.
He took three hundred flags from foes, and won
In thirty battles. For the King Motril
He conquer'd Antequera, Suez,
Nijar; and died in poverty. Highness,
Salute him.
  (*He bows, uncovers, and passes to another portrait. The* KING *listens impatiently, and with increasing anger.*)
Next him is his son, named Gil,
Dear to all noble souls. His promise worth
The oath of royal hands.
  (*To another.*)
Don Gaspard this,
The pride alike of Mendocé and Silva.
Your Highness, every noble family
Has some alliance with the Silva race.
Sandoval has both trembled at, and wed
With us. Manrique is envious of us: Lara
Is jealous. Alencastre hates us. We
All dukes surpass, and mount to Kings.
  DON CARLOS. Tut! tut!
You're jesting.
  DON RUY GOMEZ. Here behold Don Vasquez, called
The Wise. Don Jayme surnamed the
Strong. One day
Alone he stopped Zamet and five score Moors.
I pass them by, and some the greatest.
  (*At an angry gesture of the* KING *he passes by a great number of portraits, and speedily comes to the last three at the left of the audience.*)
This,
My grandfather, who lived to sixty years,
Keeping his promised word even to Jews.
  (*To the last portrait but one.*)
This venerable form my father is,
A sacred head. Great was he, though he comes
The last. The Moors had taken prisoner
His friend Count Alvar Giron. But my sire
Set out to seek him with six hundred men
To war inured. A figure of the Count
Cut out of stone by his decree was made
And dragged along behind the soldiers, he,
By patron saint, declaring that until
The Count of stone itself turned back and fled,
He would not falter; on he went and saved
His friend.
  DON CARLOS. I want my prisoner.
  DON RUY GOMEZ. This was
A Gomez de Silva. Imagine—judge
What in this dwelling one must say who sees
These heroes——
  DON CARLOS. Instantly—my prisoner!
  DON RUY GOMEZ. (*He bows low before the* KING, *takes his hand, and leads him to the last portrait, which serves for the door of* HERNANI'S *hiding-place.* DOÑA SOL *watches him with anxious eyes. Silence and expectation in all.*)
This portrait is my own. Mercy! King Charles!

For you require that those who see it here
Should say, "This last, the worthy son of race
Heroic, was a traitor found, that sold
The life of one he sheltered as a guest!"

(*Joy of* DOÑA SOL. *Movement of bewilderment in the crowd. The* KING *disconcerted moves away in anger, and remains some moments with lips trembling and eyes flashing.*)

DON CARLOS. Your Castle, Duke, annoys me, I shall lay
It low.

DON RUY GOMEZ. Thus, Highness, you'd retaliate,
Is it not so?

DON CARLOS. For such audacity
Your towers I'll level with the ground, and have
Upon the spot the hemp-seed sown.

DON RUY GOMEZ. I'd see
The hemp spring freely up where once my towers
Stood high, rather than stain should eat into
The ancient name of Silva.

(*To the portraits.*)
Is't not true?
I ask it of you all.

DON CARLOS. Now, Duke, this head, 'Tis ours, and thou hast promised it to me.

DON RUY GOMEZ. I promised one or the other.

(*To the portraits.*)
Was't not so?
I ask you all?

(*Pointing to his head.*)
This one I give.

(*To the* KING.)
Take it.

DON CARLOS. Duke, many thanks; but 'twould not do. The head
I want is young; when dead the headsman must
Uplift it by the hair. But as for thine,
In vain he'd seek, for thou hast not enough
For him to clutch.

DON RUY GOMEZ. Highness, insult me not.
My head is noble still, and worth far more
Than any rebel's poll. The head of Silva
You thus despise!

DON CARLOS. Give up Hernani!

DON RUY GOMEZ. I
Have spoken, Highness.

DON CARLOS (*to his followers*).
Search you everywhere
From roof to cellar, that he takes not wing——

DON RUY GOMEZ. My keep is faithful as myself; alone
It shares the secret which we both shall guard
Right well.

DON CARLOS. I am the King!

DON RUY GOMEZ. Out of my house
Demolished stone by stone, they'll only make
My tomb,—and nothing gain.

DON CARLOS. Menace I find
And prayer alike are vain. Deliver up
The bandit, Duke, or head and castle both
Will I beat down.

DON RUY GOMEZ. I've said my word.

DON CARLOS. Well, then,
Instead of one head I'll have two.

(*To the* DUKE D'ALCALA.)
You, Jorge,
Arrest the Duke.

DOÑA SOL (*she plucks off her veil and throws herself between the* KING, *the* DUKE, *and the* GUARDS). King Charles, an evil king
Are you!

DON CARLOS. Good heavens! Is it Doña Sol
I see?

DOÑA SOL. Highness! Thou hast no Spaniard's heart!

DON CARLOS (*confused*). Madam, you are severe upon the King.
(*He approaches her, and speaks low.*)
'Tis you have caused the wrath that's in my heart.
A man approaching you perforce becomes
An angel or a monster. Ah, when we
Are hated, swiftly we malignant grow!
Perchance, if you had willed it so, young girl,
I'd noble been—the lion of Castile;
A tiger I am made by your disdain.
You hear it roaring now. Madam, be still!
(DOÑA SOL *looks at him. He bows.*)
However, I'll obey.
(*Turning to the* DUKE.)
Cousin, may be
Thy scruples are excusable, and I
Esteem thee. To thy guest be faithful still,
And faithless to thy King. I pardon thee.
'Tis better that I only take thy niece
Away as hostage.

DON RUY GOMEZ. Only!

DOÑA SOL. Highness! Me!

DON CARLOS. Yes, you.

DON RUY GOMEZ. Alone! Oh, wondrous clemency!
Oh, generous conqueror, that spares the head
To torture thus the heart! What mercy this!

DON CARLOS. Choose 'twixt the traitor and the Doña Sol;
I must have one of them.

DON RUY GOMEZ. The master you!
(DON CARLOS *appproaches* DOÑA SOL *to lead her away. She flies towards the* DUKE.)

DOÑA SOL. Save me, my lord!
(*She pauses.—Aside.*)
Oh misery! and yet
It must be so. My Uncle's life, or else
The other's!—rather mine!
(*To the* KING.)
I follow you.

DON CARLOS (*aside*). By all the Saints! the thought triumphant is!
Ah, in the end you'll soften, princess mine!
(DOÑA SOL *goes with a grave and steady step to the casket, opens it, and takes from it the dagger, which she hides in her bosom.* DON CARLOS *comes to her and offers his hand.*)

DON CARLOS. What is't you're taking thence?

DOÑA SOL. Oh, nothing!

DON CARLOS. Is't
Some precious jewel?

DOÑA SOL. Yes.

DON CARLOS (*smiling*). Show it to me.

DOÑA SOL. Anon you'll see it.
(*She gives him her hand and prepares to follow him.* DON RUY GOMEZ, *who has remained motionless and absorbed in thought, advances a few steps crying out.*)

Don Ruy Gomez. Heavens, Doña Sol!
Oh, Doña Sol! Since he is merciless,
Help! walls and armour come down on us now!

(*He runs to the* King.)

Leave me my child! I have but her, oh King!

Don Carlos (*dropping* Doña Sol's *hand*). Then yield me up my prisoner.

(*The* Duke *drops his head, and seems the prey of horrible indecision. Then he looks up at the portraits with supplicating hands before them.*)

Oh, now
Have pity on me all of you!

(*He makes a step towards the hiding-place,* Doña Sol *watching him anxiously. He turns again to the portraits.*)

Oh hide
Your faces! They deter me.

(*He advances with trembling steps towards his own portrait, then turns again to the* King.)

Is't your will?

Don Carlos. Yes.

(*The* Duke *raises a trembling hand towards the spring.*)

Doña Sol. Oh God!

Don Ruy Gomez. No!

(*He throws himself on his knees before the* King.)

In pity take my life!

Don Carlos. Thy niece!

Don Ruy Gomez (*rising*). Take her and leave me honour then.

Don Carlos (*seizing the hand of the trembling* Doña Sol). Adieu, Duke.

Don Ruy Gomez. Till we meet again!

(*He watches the* King, *who retires slowly with* Doña Sol. *Afterwards he puts his hand on his dagger.*)

May God
Shield you!

(*He comes back to the front of the stage panting, and stands motionless, with vacant stare, seeming neither to see nor hear anything, his arms crossed on his heaving chest. Meanwhile the* King *goes out with* Doña Sol, *the suite following two by two according to their rank. They speak in a low voice among themselves.*)

Don Ruy Gomez (*aside*). Whilst thou go'st joyous from my house,
Oh King, my ancient loyalty goes forth
From out my bleeding heart.

(*He raises his head, looks all round, and sees that he is alone. Then he takes two swords from a panoply by the wall, measures them, and places them on a table. This done, he goes to the portrait, touches the spring, and the hidden door opens.*)

Scene 7.—Don Ruy Gomez. Hernani.

Don Ruy Gomez. Come out.

(Hernani *appears at the door of the hiding-place.* Don Ruy Gomez *points to the two swords on the table.*)

Now choose.
Choose, for Don Carlos has departed now,
And it remains to give me satisfaction.
Choose, and be quick. What, then! trembles thy hand?

Hernani. A duel! Oh, it cannot be, old man,
'Twixt us.

Don Ruy Gomez. Why not? Is it thou art afraid?
Or that thou art not noble? So or not,

All men who injure me, by hell I count
Noble enough to cross their swords with
mine.
  HERNANI. Old man——
  DON RUY GOMEZ. Come forth, young
man, to slay me, else
To be the slain.
  HERNANI. To die, ah yes! Against
My will thyself hast saved me, and my
life
Is yours. I bid you take it.
  DON RUY GOMEZ. This you wish?
(*To the portraits.*)
You see he wills it. (*To* HERNANI.)
This is well. Thy prayer
Now make.
  HERNANI. It is to thee, my lord, the
last
I make.
  DON RUY GOMEZ. Pray to the other
Lord.
  HERNANI. No, no,
To thee. Strike me, old man—dagger
or sword—
Each one for me is good—but grant
me first
One joy supreme. Duke, let me see her
ere
I die.
  DON RUY GOMEZ. See her!
  HERNANI. Or at least I beg
That you will let me hear her voice
once more—
Only this one last time!
  DON RUY GOMEZ. Hear her!
  HERNANI. Ah well,
My lord, I understand thy jealousy,
But death already seizes on my youth.
Forgive me. Grant me—tell me that
without
Beholding her, if it must be, I yet
May hear her speak, and I will die to-
night.
I'll grateful be to hear her. But in
peace
I'd calmly die, if thou wouldst deign
that ere
My soul is freed, it sees once more the
soul
That shines so clearly in her eyes. To
her
I will not speak. Thou shalt be there
to see,
My father, and canst slay me after-
wards.
  DON RUY GOMEZ (*pointing to the
recess still open*). Oh, Saints of
Heaven! can this recess then be
So deep and strong that he has nothing
heard?
  HERNANI. No, I have nothing heard.
  DON RUY GOMEZ. I was compelled
To yield up Doña Sol or thee.
  HERNANI. To whom?
  DON RUY GOMEZ. The King.
  HERNANI. Madman! He loves her.
  DON RUY GOMEZ. Loves her! He!
  HERNANI. He takes her from us!
He our rival is!
  DON RUY GOMEZ. Curses be on him!
Vassals! all to horse—
To horse! Let us pursue the ravisher!
  HERNANI. Listen! The vengeance
that is sure of foot
Makes on its way less noise than this
would do.
To thee I do belong. Thou hast the
right
To slay me. Wilt thou not employ me
first
As the avenger of thy niece's wrongs?
Let me take part in this thy vengeance
due;

Grant me this boon, and I will kiss thy feet,
If so must be. Let us together speed
The King to follow. I will be thine arm.
I will avenge thee, Duke, and afterwards
The life that's forfeit thou shalt take.

Don Ruy Gomez. And then,
As now, thou'lt ready be to die?

Hernani. Yes, Duke.

Don Ruy Gomez. By what wilt thou swear this?

Hernani. My father's head.

Don Ruy Gomez. Of thine own self wilt thou remember it?

Hernani (*giving him the horn which he takes from his girdle*). Listen! Take you this horn, and whatsoe'er
May happen—what the place, or what the hour—
Whenever to thy mind it seems the time
Has come for me to die, blow on this horn
And take no other care; all will be done.

Don Ruy Gomez (*offering his hand*). Your hand! (*They press hands.*)

(*To the portraits.*)
And all of you are witnesses.

FOURTH ACT

The Tomb. Aix-la-Chapelle.

Scene 1.—*The vaults which enclose the Tomb of Charlemagne at Aix-la-Chapelle. Great arches of Lombard architecture, with semicircular columns, having capitals of birds and flowers. At the right a small bronze door, low and curved. A single lamp suspended from the crown of the vault shows the inscription:* CAROLVS MAGNVS. *It is night. One cannot see to the end of the vaults, the eye loses itself in the intricacy of arches, steps, and columns which mingle in the shade.*

Don Carlos, Don Ricardo de Roxas, Comte de Casapalma, *lanterns in hand, and wearing large cloaks and slouched hats.*

Don Ricardo (*hat in hand*). This is the place.

Don Carlos. Yes, here it is the League
Will meet; they that together in my power
So soon shall be. Oh, it was well, my lord
Of Trèves th' Elector—it was well of you
To lend this place; dark plots should prosper best
In the dank air of catacombs, and good
It is to sharpen daggers upon tombs.
Yet the stake's heavy—heads are on the game,
Ye bold assassins, and the end we'll see.
By heaven, 'twas well a sepulchre to choose
For such a business, since the road will be
Shorter for them to traverse. (*To* Don Ricardo.)
Tell me now
How far the subterranean way extends?

Don Ricardo. To the strong fortress.

Don Carlos. Farther than we need.
Don Ricardo. And on the other side it reaches quite
The Monastery of Altenheim.
Don Carlos. Ah, where
Lothaire was overcome by Rodolf. Once
Again, Count, tell me o'er their names and wrongs.
Don Ricardo. Gotha.
Don Carlos. Ah, very well I know why 'tis
The brave Duke is conspirator: he wills
For Germany, a German Emperor.
Don Ricardo. Hohenbourg.
Don Carlos. Hohenbourg would better like
With Francis hell, than Heaven itself with me.
Don Ricardo. Gil Tellez Giron.
Don Carlos. Castile and our Lady! The scoundrel!—to be traitor to his king!
Don Ricardo. One evening it is said that you were found
With Madame Giron. You had just before
Made him a baron; he revenges now
The honour of his dear companion.
Don Carlos. This, then, the reason he revolts 'gainst Spain?
What name comes next?
Don Ricardo. The Reverend Vasquez,
Avila's Bishop.
Don Carlos. Pray does he resent
Dishonour of his wife!
Don Ricardo. Then there is named
Guzman de Lara, who is discontent,
Claiming the collar of your order.
Don Carlos. Ah!
Guzman de Lara! If he only wants
A collar he shall have one.

Don Ricardo. Next the Duke
Of Lutzelbourg. As for his plans, they say—
Don Carlos. Ah! Lutzelbourg is by the head too tall.
Don Ricardo. Juan de Haro—who Astorga wants.
Don Carlos. These Haros! Always they the headsman's pay
Have doubled.
Don Ricardo. That is all.
Don Carlos. Not by my count. These make but seven.
Don Ricardo. Oh, I did not name
Some bandits, probably engaged by Trèves
Or France.
Don Carlos. Men without prejudice of course,
Whose ready daggers turn to heaviest pay,
As truly as the needle to the pole.
Don Ricardo. However, I observed two sturdy ones
Among them, both new comers—one was young,
The other old.
Don Carlos. Their names?
(Don Ricardo *shrugs his shoulders in sign of ignorance.*)
Their age then say?
Don Ricardo. The younger may be twenty.
Don Carlos. Pity then.
Don Ricardo. The elder must be sixty, quite.
Don Carlos. One seems
Too young—the other, over old; so much
For them the worse 'twill be. I will take care—

Myself will help the headsman, be there need.
My sword is sharpened for a traitor's block,
I'll lend it him if blunt his axe should grow,
And join my own imperial purple on
To piece the scaffold cloth, if it must be
Enlarged that way. But shall I Emperor prove?

Don Ricardo. The College at this hour deliberates.

Don Carlos. Who knows? Francis the First, perchance, they'll name, Or else their Saxon Frederick the Wise. Ah, Luther, thou art right to blame the times
And scorn such makers-up of royalty,
That own no other rights than gilded ones.
A Saxon heretic! Primate of Trèves,
A libertine! Count Palatine, a fool!
As for Bohemia's king, for me he is.
Princes of Hesse, all smaller than their states!
The young are idiots, and the old debauched,
Of crowns a plenty—but for heads we search
In vain! Council of dwarfs ridiculous,
That I in lion's skin could carry off
Like Hercules; and who of violet robes
Bereft, would show but heads more shallow far
Than Triboulet's. See'st thou I want three votes
Or all is lost, Ricardo? Oh! I'd give
Toledo, Ghent, and Salamanca too,
Three towns, my friend, I'd offer to their choice
For their three voices—cities of Castile
And Flanders. Safe I know to take them back
A little later on.

(Don Ricardo *bows low to the* King, *and puts on his hat.*) You cover, Sir!

Don Ricardo. Sire, you have called me thou (*bowing again*).
And thus I'm made
Grandee of Spain.

Don Carlos (*aside*). Ah, how to piteous scorn
You rouse me! Interested brood devour'd
By mean ambition. Thus across my plans
Yours struggle. Base the Court where without shame
The King is plied for honours, and he yields,
Bestowing grandeur on the hungry crew.
(*Musing.*)
God only, and the Emperor are great,
Also the Holy Father! for the rest.
The kings and dukes, of what account are they?

Don Ricardo. I trust that they your Highness will elect.

Don Carlos. Highness—still Highness! Oh, unlucky chance!
If only King I must remain.

Don Ricardo (*aside*). By Jove, Emperor or King, Grandee of Spain I am.

Don Carlos. When they've decided who shall be the one
They choose for Emperor of Germany,
What sign is to announce his name?

Don Ricardo. The guns.
A single firing will proclaim the Duke
Of Saxony is chosen Emperor;
Two if 'tis Francis; for your Highness three.

Don Carlos. And Doña Sol! I'm crossed on every side.
If, Count, by turn of luck, I'm Emperor made,
Go seek her; she by Cæsar might be won.

Don Ricardo (*smiling*). Your Highness pleases.

Don Carlos (*haughtily*). On that subject peace!
I have not yet inquired what's thought of me.
But tell me when will it be truly known
Who is elected?

Don Ricardo. In an hour or so, At latest.

Don Carlos. Ah, three votes; and only three!
But first this trait'rous rabble we must crush,
And then we'll see to whom the Empire falls,
(*He counts on his fingers and stamps his foot.*)
Always by three too few! Ah, they hold power.
Yet did Cornelius know all long ago:
In Heaven's ocean thirteen stars he saw
Coming full sail towards mine, all from the north.
Empire for me—let's on! But it is said,
On other hand, that Jean Trithème Francis
Predicted! Clearer should I see my fate
Had I some armament the prophecy
To help. The Sorcerer's predictions come
Most true when a good army—with its guns
And lances, horse and foot, and martial strains,
Ready to lead the way where Fate alone
Might stumble—plays the midwife's part to bring
Fulfilment of prediction. That's worth more
Than our Cornelius Agrippa or Trithème. He, who by force of arms expounds
His system, and with sharpen'd point of lance
Can edge his words, and uses soldiers' swords
To level rugged fortune—shapes events
At his own will to match the prophecy.
Poor fools! who with proud eyes and haughty mien
Only look straight to Empire, and declare
"It is my right!" They need great guns in files
Whose burning breath melts towns; and soldiers, ships,
And horsemen. These they need their ends to gain
O'er trampled peoples. Pshaw! at the cross roads
Of human life, where one leads to a throne
Another to perdition, they will pause
In indecision,—scarce three steps will take
Uncertain of themselves, and in their doubt
Fly to Necromancer for advice
Which road to take. (*To* Don Ricardo.)
Go now, 'tis near the time
The trait'rous crew will meet. Give me the key.

Don Ricardo (*giving key of tomb*).
Sire, 'twas the guardian of the tomb, the Count
De Limbourg, who to me confided it,

And has done everything to pleasure you.

DON CARLOS. Do all, quite all that I commanded you.

DON RICARDO (*bowing*). Highness, I go at once.

DON CARLOS. The signal then
That I await is cannon firing thrice?

(DON RICARDO *bows and exit*.)

(DON CARLOS *falls into a deep reverie, his arms crossed, his head drooping; afterwards he raises it, and turns to the tomb*.)

SCENE 2.

DON CARLOS (*alone*). Forgive, me, Charlemagne! Oh, this lonely vault
Should echo only unto solemn words.
Thou must be angry at the babble vain
Of our ambition at your monument.
Here Charlemagne rests! How can the sombre tomb
Without a rifting spasm hold such dust!
And art thou truly here, colossal power,
Creator of the world? And canst thou now
Crouch down from all thy majesty and might?
Ah, 'tis a spectacle to stir the soul
What Europe was, and what by thee 'twas made.
Mighty construction with two men supreme
Elected chiefs to whom born kings submit.
States, duchies, kingdoms, marquisates and fiefs—
By right hereditary most are ruled,
But nations find a friend sometimes in Pope
Or Cæsar; and one chance another chance
Corrects; thus even balance is maintained
And order opens out. The cloth-of-gold
Electors, and the scarlet cardinals.
The double, sacred senate, unto which
Earth bends, are but paraded outward show,
God's fiat rules it all. One day HE wills
A thought, a want, should burst upon the world,
Then grow and spread, and mix with every thing,
Possess some man, win hearts, and delve a groove
Though kings may trample on it, and may seek
To gag;—only that they some morn may see
At diet, conclave, this the scorned idea,
That they had spurned, all suddenly expand
And soar above their heads, bearing the globe
In hand, or on the brow tiara. Pope
And Emperor, they on earth are all in all,
A mystery supreme dwells in them both,
And Heaven's might, which they still represent,
Feasts them with kings and nations, holding them
Beneath its thunder-cloud, the while they sit
At table with the world served out for food.
Alone they regulate all things on earth,
Just as the mower manages his field.
All rule and power are theirs. Kings at the door
Inhale the odour of their savoury meats,

Look through the window, watchful on tip-toe,
But weary of the scene. The common world
Below them groups itself on ladder-rungs.
They make and all unmake. One can release,
The other surely strike. The one is Truth,
The other Might. Each to himself is law,
And is, because he is. When—equals they
The one in purple, and the other swathed
In white like winding-sheet—when they come out
From Sanctuary, the dazzled multitude
Look with wild terror on these halves of God,
The Pope and Emperor. Emperor! oh, to be
Thus great! Oh, anguish, not to be this Power
When beats the heart with dauntless courage fill'd!
Oh, happy he who sleeps within this tomb!
How great, and oh! how fitted for his time!
The Pope and Emperor were more than men,
In them two Romes in mystic Hymen joined
Prolific were, giving new form and soul
Unto the human race, refounding realms
And nations, shaping thus a Europe new,
And both remoulding with their hands the bronze
Remaining of the great old Roman world.

What destiny! And yet 'tis here he lies?
Is all so little that we come to this!
What then? To have been Prince and Emperor,
And King—to have been sword, and also law;
Giant, with Germany for pedestal—
For title Cæsar—Charlemagne for name:
A greater to have been than Hannibal
Or Attila—as great as was the world.
Yet all rests here! For Empire strive and strain
And see the dust that makes an Emperor!
Cover the earth with tumult, and with noise
Know you that one day only will remain—
Oh, madd'ning thought—a stone! For sounding name
Triumphant, but some letters 'graved to serve
For little children to learn spelling by.
How high so e'er ambition made thee soar,
Behold the end of all! Oh, Empire, power,
What matters all to me! I near it now
And like it well. Some voice declares to me
Thine—thine—it will be thine. Heavens, were it so!
To mount at once the spiral height supreme
And be alone—the key-stone of the arch,
With states beneath, one o'er the other ranged,
And kings for mats to wipe one's sandall'd feet!
To see 'neath kings the feudal families,
Margraves and Cardinals, and Doges—Dukes,

Then Bishops, Abbés—Chiefs of ancient clans,
Great Barons—then the soldier class and clerks,
And know yet farther off—in the deep shade
At bottom of th' abyss there is Mankind—
That is to say a crowd, a sea of men,
A tumult—cries, with tears, and bitter laugh
Sometimes. The wail wakes up and scares the earth
And reaches us with leaping echoes, and
With trumpet tone. Oh, citizens, oh, men!
The swarm that from the high church towers seems now
To sound the tocsin! (*Musing.*)
Wondrous human base
Of nations, bearing on your shoulders broad
The mighty pyramid that has two poles,
The living waves that ever straining hard
Balance and shake it as they heave and roll,
Make all change place, and on the highest heights
Make stagger thrones, as if they were but stools.
So sure is this, that ceasing vain debates
Kings look to Heaven! Kings look down below,
Look at the people!—Restless ocean, there
Where nothing's cast that does not shake the whole;
The sea that rends a throne, and rocks a tomb—
A glass in which kings rarely look but ill.

Ah, if upon this gloomy sea they gazed
Sometimes, what Empires in its depths they'd find!
Great vessels wrecked that by its ebb and flow
Are stirr'd—that wearied it—known now no more!
To govern this—to mount so high if called,
Yet know myself to be but mortal man!
To see the abyss—if not that moment struck
With dizziness bewildering every sense.
Oh, moving pyramid of states and kings
With apex narrow,—woe to timid step!
What shall restrain me? If I fail when there
Feeling my feet upon the trembling world,
Feeling alive the palpitating earth,
Then when I have between my hands the globe
Have I the strength alone to hold it fast,
To be an Emperor? Oh, God, 'twas hard
And difficult to play the kingly part.
Certes, no man is rarer than the one
Who can enlarge his soul to duly meet
Great Fortune's smiles, and still increasing gifts.
But I! Who is it that shall be my guide,
My counsellor, and make me great?
   (*Falls on his knees before the tomb.*)
'Tis thou,
Oh, Charlemagne! And since 'tis God for whom
All obstacles dissolve, who takes us now
And puts us face to face—from this tomb's depths
Endow me with sublimity and strength.

Let me be great enough to see the truth
On every side. Show me how small the world
I dare not measure—me this Babel show
Where, from the hind to Cæsar mounting up,
Each one, complaisant with himself, regards
The next with scorn that is but half restrained.
Teach me the secret of thy conquests all,
And how to rule. And show me certainly
Whether to punish, or to pardon, be
The worthier thing to do.
Is it not fact
That in his solitary bed sometimes
A mighty shade is wakened from his sleep,
Aroused by noise and turbulence on earth;
That suddenly his tomb expands itself,
And bursts its doors—and in the night flings forth
A flood of light? If this be true indeed,
Say, Emperor! what can after Charlemagne
Another do! Speak, though thy sovereign breath
Should cleave this brazen door. Or rather now
Let me thy sanctuary enter lone!
Let me behold thy veritable face,
And not repulse me with a freezing breath,
Upon thy stony pillow elbows lean,
And let us talk. Yes, with prophetic voice
Tell me of things which make the forehead pale,
And clear eyes mournful. Speak, and do not blind
Thine awe-struck son, for doubtlessly thy tomb
Is full of light. Or if thou wilt not speak,
Let me make study in the solemn peace
Of thee, as of a world, thy measure take,
Oh giant, for there's nothing here below
So great as thy poor ashes. Let them teach,
Failing thy spirit.
(*He puts the key in the lock.*)
Let us enter now.
(*He recoils.*)
Oh, God, if he should really whisper me!
If he be there and walks with noiseless tread,
And I come back with hair in moments bleached!
I'll do it still.
(*Sound of footsteps.*)
Who comes? who dares disturb
Besides myself the dwelling of such dead!
(*The sound comes nearer.*)
My murderers! I forgot! Now enter we.
(*He opens the door of the tomb, which shuts upon him.*)
(*Enter several men walking softly, disguised by large cloaks and hats.*)

SCENE 3.—THE CONSPIRATORS.

(*They take each others' hands, going from one to another and speaking in a low tone.*)

FIRST CONSPIRATOR (*who alone carries a lighted torch*). Ad augusta.

SECOND CONSPIRATOR. Per angusta.

FIRST CONSPIRATOR. The Saints
Shield us.
THIRD CONSPIRATOR. The dead assist
us.
FIRST CONSPIRATOR. Guard us God!
(*Noise in the shade.*)
FIRST CONSPIRATOR. Who's there?
A VOICE. *Ad augusta.*
SECOND CONSPIRATOR. *Per angusta.*
(*Enter fresh* CONSPIRATORS—*noise of footsteps.*)
FIRST CONSPIRATOR *to* THIRD. See! there is some one still to come.
THIRD CONSPIRATOR. Who's there?
(VOICE *in the darkness.*) *Ad augusta.*
THIRD CONSPIRATOR. *Per angusta.*
(*Enter more* CONSPIRATORS, *who exchange signs with their hands with the others.*)
FIRST CONSPIRATOR. 'Tis well. All now are here. Gotha, to you it falls To state the case. Friends, darkness waits for light.
(THE CONSPIRATORS *sit in a half circle on the tombs. The* FIRST CONSPIRATOR *passes before them, and from his torch each one lights a wax taper which he holds in his hand. Then the* FIRST CONSPIRATOR *seats himself in silence on a tomb a little higher than the others in the center of the circle.*)
DUKE OF GOTHA (*rising*). My friends! This Charles of Spain, by mother's side A foreigner, aspires to mount the throne Of Holy Empire.
FIRST CONSPIRATOR. But for him the grave.
DUKE OF GOTHA (*throwing down his light and crushing it with his foot*). Let it be with his head as with this flame.
ALL. So be it.

FIRST CONSPIRATOR. Death unto him.
DUKE OF GOTHA. Let him die.
ALL. Let him be slain.
DON JUAN DE HARO. German his father was.
DUKE DE LUTZELBOURG. His mother Spanish.
DUKE OF GOTHA. Thus you see that he
Is no more one than other. Let him die.
A CONSPIRATOR. Suppose th' Electors at this very hour
Declare him Emperor!
FIRST CONSPIRATOR. Him! oh, never him!
DON GIL TELLEZ GIRON. What signifies? Let us strike off the head, The Crown will fall.
FIRST CONSPIRATOR. But if to him belongs
The Holy Empire, he becomes so great And so august, that only God's own hand
Can reach him.
DUKE OF GOTHA. All the better reason why
He dies before such power august he gains.
FIRST CONSPIRATOR. He shall not be elected.
ALL. Not for him
The Empire.
FIRST CONSPIRATOR. Now, how many hands will't take
To put him in his shroud?
ALL. One is enough.
FIRST CONSPIRATOR. How many strokes to reach his heart?
ALL. But one.
FIRST CONSPIRATOR. Who, then, will strike?
ALL. All! All!

FIRST CONSPIRATOR. The victim is
A traitor proved. They would an Emperor choose,
We've a high-priest to make. Let us draw lots.

(*All the* CONSPIRATORS *write their names on their tablets, tear out the leaf, roll it up, and one after another throw them into the urn on one of the tombs. Afterwards the* FIRST CONSPIRATOR *rises and says,*)

Now let us pray.

(*All kneel, the* FIRST CONSPIRATOR *rises and says,*)

Oh, may the chosen one
Believe in God, and like a Roman strike,
Die as a Hebrew would, and brave alike
The wheel and burning pincers, laugh at rack,
And fire, and wooden horse, and be resigned
To kill and die. He might have all to do.

(*He draws a parchment from the urn.*)

ALL. What name?

FIRST CONSPIRATOR (*in low voice*). Hernani!

HERNANI (*coming out from the crowd of* CONSPIRATORS). I have won, yes won!
I hold thee fast! Thee I've so long pursued
With vengeance.

DON RUY GOMEZ (*piercing through the crowd and taking* HERNANI *aside*). Yield—oh yield this right to me.

HERNANI. Not for my life! Oh, Signor, grudge me not
This stroke of fortune—'tis the first I've known.

DON RUY GOMEZ. You nothing have!
I'll give you houses, lands,
A hundred thousand vassals shall be yours
In my three hundred villages, if you
But yield the right to strike to me.

HERNANI. No—no.

DUKE OF GOTHA. Old man, thy arm would strike less sure a blow.

DON RUY GOMEZ. Back! I have strength of soul, if not of arm.
Judge not the sword by the mere scabbard's rust.

(*To* HERNANI.)

You do belong to me.

HERNANI. My life is yours,
As his belongs to me.

DON RUY GOMEZ (*drawing the horn from his girdle*). I yield her up,
And will return the horn.

HERNANI (*he trembles*). What life! my life
And Doña Sol! No, I my vengeance choose,
I have my father to revenge—yet more,
Perchance I am inspired by God in this.

DON RUY GOMEZ. I yield thee Her—
and give thee back the horn!

HERNANI. No!

DON RUY GOMEZ. Boy, reflect.

HERNANI. Oh, Duke, leave me my prey.

DON RUY GOMEZ. My curses on you for depriving me
Of this my joy.

FIRST CONSPIRATOR (*to* HERNANI).
Oh, brother, ere they can
Elect him—'twould be well this **very** night
To watch for Charles.

HERNANI. Fear nought, I know the way
To kill a man.
FIRST CONSPIRATOR. May every treason fall
On traitor, and may God be with you now.
We Counts and Barons, let us take the oath
That if he fall, yet slay not, we go on
And strike by turn unflinching till Charles dies.
ALL (*drawing their swords*). Let us all swear.
DUKE OF GOTHA (*to* FIRST CONSPIRATOR). My brother, let's decide
On what we swear.
DON RUY GOMEZ (*taking his sword by the point and raising it above his head*).
By this same cross,
ALL (*raising their swords*). And this
That he must quickly die impenitent.
(*They hear a cannon fired afar off. All pause and are silent. The door of the tomb half opens, and* DON CARLOS *appears at the threshold. A second gun is fired, then a third. He opens wide the door and stands erect and motionless without advancing.*)

SCENE 4.—*The* CONSPIRATORS *and* DON CARLOS. *Afterwards* DON RICARDO; SIGNORS, GUARDS, *The* KING OF BOHEMIA, *The* DUKE OF BAVARIA, *afterwards* DOÑA SOL.

DON CARLOS. Fall back, ye gentlemen—the Emperor hears.
(*All the lights are simultaneously extinguished. A profound silence.* DON CARLOS *advances a step in the darkness, so dense, that the silent, motionless* CONSPIRATORS *can scarcely be distinguished.*)
Silence and night! From darkness sprung, the swarm
Into the darkness plunges back again!
Think ye this scene is like a passing dream,
And that I take you now your lights are quenched,
For men's stone figures seated on their tombs?
Just now, my statues, you had voices loud,
Raise, then, your drooping heads for Charles the Fifth
Is here. Strike. Move a pace or two and show
You dare. But no, 'tis not in you to dare.
Your flaming torches, blood-red 'neath these vaults,
My breath extinguished; but now turn your eyes
Irresolute, and see that if I thus
Put out the many, I can light still more.
(*He strikes the iron key on the bronze door of the tomb. At the sound all the depths of the cavern are filled with soldiers bearing torches and halberds. At their head the* DUKE D'ALCALA, *the* MARQUIS D'ALMUÑAN, &c.)
Come on, my falcons! I've the nest—the prey.
(*To* CONSPIRATORS.)
I can make blaze of light, 'tis my turn now,
Behold! (*To the Soldiers.*)
Advance—for flagrant is the crime.
HERNANI (*looking at the Soldiers*).
Ah, well! At first I thought 'twas Charlemagne,

Alone he seemed so great—but after all
'Tis only Charles the Fifth.
 Don Carlos (*to the* Duke d'Alcala).
Come, Constable
Of Spain, (*To* Marquis d'Almuñan.)
And you Castilian Admiral,
Disarm them all.
 (*The* Conspirators *are surrounded
and disarmed.*)
 Don Ricardo (*hurrying in and bowing almost to the ground*). Your Majesty!
 Don Carlos. Alcadé
I make you of the Palace.
 Don Ricardo (*again bowing*). Two Electors,
To represent the Golden Chamber, come
To offer to your Sacred Majesty
Congratulations now.
 Don Carlos. Let them come forth.
 (*Aside to* Don Ricardo.)
The Doña Sol.
 (Ricardo *bows and exit. Enter with flambeaux and flourish of trumpets the* King of Bohemia *and the* Duke of Bavaria, *both wearing cloth of gold, and with crowns on their heads. Numerous followers. German nobles carrying the banner of the Empire, the double-headed Eagle, with the escutcheon of Spain in the middle of it. The* Soldiers *divide, forming lines between which the* Electors *pass to the* Emperor, *to whom they bow low. He returns the salutation by raising his hat.*)
 Duke of Bavaria. Most Sacred Majesty
Charles, of the Romans King, and Emperor,
The Empire of the world is in your hands—
Yours is the throne to which each king aspires!
The Saxon Frederick was elected first,
But he judged you more worthy, and declined.
Now then receive the crown and globe,
oh King—
The Holy Empire doth invest you now,
Arms with the sword, and you indeed are great.
 Don Carlos. The College I will thank on my return.
But go, my brother of Bohemia,
And you, Bavarian cousin.—Thanks; but now
I do dismiss you—I shall go myself.
 King of Bohemia. Oh! Charles, our ancestors were friends. My Sire
Loved yours, and their two fathers were two friends—
So young! exposed to varied fortunes! say,
Oh Charles, may I be ranked a very chief
Among thy brothers? I cannot forget
I knew you as a little child.
 Don Carlos. Ah, well—
King of Bohemia, you presume too much.
 (*He gives him his hand to kiss, also the* Duke of Bavaria, *both bow low.*)
Depart.
 (*Exeunt the two* Electors *with their followers.*)
 The Crowd. Long live the Emperor!
 Don Carlos (*aside*). So 'tis mine,
All things have helped, and I am Emperor—
By the refusal though of Frederick
Surnamed the Wise!

(*Enter* Doña Sol *led by* Don Ricardo.)

Doña Sol. What, Soldiers!—Emperor!
Hernani! Heaven, what an unlooked-for chance!

Hernani. Ah! Doña Sol!

Don Ruy Gomez (*aside to* Hernani). She has not seen me.

(Doña Sol *runs to* Hernani, *who makes her recoil by a look of disdain.*)

Hernani. Madam!

Doña Sol (*drawing the dagger from her bosom*). I still his poignard have!

Hernani (*taking her in his arms*). My dearest one!

Don Carlos. Be silent all.

(*To the* Conspirators.)
Is't you remorseless are?
I need to give the world a lesson now,
The Lara of Castile, and Gotha, you
Of Saxony—all—all—what were your plans
Just now? I bid you speak.

Hernani. Quite simple, Sire,
The thing, and we can briefly tell it you.
We 'graved the sentence on Belshazzar's wall.

(*He takes out a poignard and brandishes it.*)
We render unto Cæsar Cæsar's due.

Don Carlos. Silence!

(*To* Don Ruy Gomez.)
And you! You too are traitor, Silva!

Don Ruy Gomez. Which of us two is traitor, Sire?

Hernani (*turning towards the* Conspirators). Our heads
And Empire—all that he desires he has.

(*To the* Emperor.)
The mantle blue of kings encumbered you;
The purple better suits—it shows not blood.

Don Carlos (*to* Don Ruy Gomez). Cousin of Silva, this is felony,
Attaining your baronial rank. Think well,
Don Ruy—high treason!

Don Ruy Gomez. Kings like Roderick
Count Julians make.

Don Carlos (*to the* Duke d'Alcala). Seize only those who seem
The nobles,—for the rest!——

(Don Ruy Gomez, *the* Duke de Lutzelbourg, *the* Duke of Gotha, Don Juan de Haro, Don Guzman de Lara, Don Tellez Giron, *the* Baron of Hohenbourg *separate themselves from the group of* Conspirators, *among whom is* Hernani. *The* Duke d'Alcala *surrounds them with guards.*)

Doña Sol (*aside*). Ah, he is saved!

Hernani (*coming from among the* Conspirators). I claim to be included!

(*To* Don Carlos.)
Since to this
It comes, the question of the axe—that now
Hernani, humble churl, beneath thy feet
Unpunished goes, because his brow is not
At level with thy sword—because one must
Be great to die, I rise. God, who gives power,
And gives to thee the scepter, made me Duke
Of Segorbe and Cardona, Marquis too
Of Monroy, Albaterra's Count, of Gor
Viscount, and Lord of many places, more
Than I can name. Juan of Aragon

Am I, Grand Master of Avis—the son
In exile born, of murder'd father slain
By king's decree, King Charles, which me proscribed,
Thus death 'twixt us is family affair;
You have the scaffold—we the poignard hold.
Since heaven a Duke has made me, and exile
A mountaineer,—since all in vain I've sharpen'd
Upon the hills my sword, and in the torrents
Have tempered it, (*He puts on his hat.*)
(*To the* CONSPIRATORS.)
Let us be covered now,
Us the Grandees of Spain. (*They cover.*)
(*To* DON CARLOS.)
Our heads, oh! King,
Have right to fall before thee covered thus.
(*To the* PRISONERS.)
Silva, and Haro—Lara—men of rank
And race make room for Juan of Aragon.
Give me my place, ye Dukes and Counts—my place.
(*To the* COURTIERS *and* GUARDS.)
King, headsmen, varlets—Juan of Aragon
Am I. If all your scaffolds are too small
Make new ones. (*He joins the group of* NOBLES.)
DOÑA SOL. Heavens!
DON CARLOS. I had forgotten quite
This history.
HERNANI. But they who bleed remember
Far better. Th' evil that wrong-doer thus

So senselessly forgets, for ever stirs
Within the outraged heart.
DON CARLOS. Therefore, enough
For me to bear this title, that I'm son
Of sires, whose power dealt death to ancestors
Of yours!
DOÑA SOL (*falling on her knees before the* EMPEROR). Oh, pardon—pardon!
Mercy, Sire,
Be pitiful, or strike us both, I pray,
For he my lover is, my promised spouse,
In him it is alone I live—I breathe;
Oh, Sire, in mercy us together slay.
Trembling—oh Majesty!—I trail myself
Before your sacred knees. I love him, Sire,
And he is mine—as Empire is your own.
Have pity! (DON CARLOS *looks at her without moving.*)
Oh what thought absorbs you?
DON CARLOS. Cease.
Rise—Duchess of Segorbé—Marchioness
Of Monroy—Countess Albaterra—and
(*To* HERNANI.)
Thine other names, Don Juan?
HERNANI. Who speaks thus,
The King?
DON CARLOS. No, 'tis the Emperor.
DOÑA SOL. Just Heav'n!
DON CARLOS (*pointing to her*). Duke Juan, take your wife.
HERNANI (*his eyes raised to heaven,* DOÑA SOL *in his arms*). Just God!
DON CARLOS (*to* DON RUY GOMEZ). My cousin,
I know the pride of your nobility,
But Aragon with Silva well may mate.
DON RUY GOMEZ (*bitterly*). 'Tis not a question of nobility.
HERNANI (*looking with love on* DOÑA

Sol *and still holding her in his arms*).
My deadly hate is vanishing away.
(*Throws away his dagger.*)

Don Ruy Gomez (*aside, and looking at them*). Shall I betray myself? Oh, no
—my grief,
My foolish love would make them pity cast
Upon my venerable head. Old man
And Spaniard! Let the hidden fire consume,
And suffer still in secret. Let heart break
But cry not;—they would laugh at thee.

Doña Sol (*still in* Hernani's *arms*). My Duke!

Hernani. Nothing my soul holds now but love!

Doña Sol. Oh, joy!

Don Carlos (*aside, his hand in his bosom*). Stifle thyself, young heart so full of flame,
Let reign again the better thoughts which thou
So long hast troubled. Henceforth let thy loves,
Thy mistresses, alas!—be Germany
And Flanders—Spain (*looking at the banner*).
The Emperor is like
The Eagle his companion, in the place
Of heart, there's but a 'scutcheon.

Hernani. Cæsar you!

Don Carlos. Don Juan, of your ancient name and race
Your soul is worthy (*pointing to* Doña Sol).
Worthy e'en of her.
Kneel, Duke.

(Hernani *kneels.* Don Carlos *unfastens his own Golden Fleece and puts it on* Hernani's *neck.*)
Receive this collar.
(Don Carlos *draws his sword and strikes him three times on the shoulder.*)
Faithful be,
For by St. Stephen now I make thee Knight.
(*He raises and embraces him.*)
Thou hast a collar softer and more choice;
That which is wanting to my rank supreme,—
The arms of loving woman, loved by thee.
Thou wilt be happy—I am Emperor.
(*To* Conspirators.)
Sirs, I forget your names. Anger and hate
I will forget. Go—go—I pardon you.
This is the lesson that the world much needs.

The Conspirators. Glory to Charles!

Don Ruy Gomez (*to* Don Carlos). I only suffer then!

Don Carlos. And I!

Don Ruy Gomez. But I have not like Majesty
Forgiven!

Hernani. Who is't has worked this wondrous change?

All. Nobles, Soldiers, Conspirators.
Honour to Charles the Fifth and Germany!

Don Carlos (*turning to the tomb*). Honour to Charlemagne! Leave us now together.
(*Exeunt all.*)

SCENE 5.—DON CARLOS (alone).

(He bends towards the tomb.)
Art thou content with me, oh, Charlemagne!
Have I the kingship's littleness stripped off?
Become as Emperor another man?
Can I Rome's mitre add unto my helm?
Have I the right the fortunes of the world
To sway? Have I a steady foot that safe
Can tread the path, by Vandal ruins strewed,
Which thou hast beaten by thine armies vast?
Have I my candle lighted at thy flame?
Did I interpret right the voice that spake
Within this tomb? Ah, I was lost—alone
Before an Empire—a wide howling world
That threatened and conspired! There were the Danes
To punish, and the Holy Father's self
To compensate—with Venice—Soliman,
Francis, and Luther—and a thousand dirks
Gleaming already in the shade—snares—rocks;
And countless foes; a score of nations, each
Of which might serve to awe a score of kings.
Things ripe, all pressing to be done at once.
I cried to thee—with what shall I begin?
And thou didst answer—Son, by clemency!

FIFTH ACT

THE NUPTIALS.

SCENE 1.—SARAGOSSA. *A terrace of the palace of Aragon. At the back a flight of steps leading to the garden. At the right and left, doors on to a terrace which shows at the back of the stage a balustrade surmounted by a double row of Moorish arches, above and through which are seen the palace gardens, fountains in the shade, shrubberies and moving lights, and the Gothic and Arabic arches of the palace illuminated. It is night. Trumpets afar off are heard. Masks and Dominoes, either singly or in groups, cross the terrace here and there. At the front of the stage a group of young lords, their masks in their hands, laugh and chat noisily.*

DON SANCHO SANCHEZ DE ZUNIGA, COMTE DE MONTERET, DON MATIAS CENTURION, MARQUIS D'ALMUÑAN, DON RICARDO DE ROXAS, COMTE DE CASAPALMA, DON FRANCISCO DE SOTOMAYOR, COMTE DE VALALCAZAR, DON GARCIE SUAREZ DE CARBAJAL. COMTE DE PENALVER.

DON GARCIE. Now to the bride long life—and joy—I say!

DON MATIAS (*looking to the balcony*). All Saragossa at its windows shows.

Don Garcie. And they do well. A torch-light wedding ne'er
Was seen more gay than this, nor lovelier night,
Nor handsomer married pair.

Don Matias. King Emp'ror!

Don Sancho. When we went with him in the dark that night
Seeking adventure, Marquis, who'd have thought
How it would end?

Don Ricardo (*interrupting*). I, too, was there. (*To the others.*) Now list. Three gallants, one a bandit, his head due
Unto the scaffold; then a Duke, a King,
Adoring the same woman, all laid siege
At the same time. The onset made—who won?
It was the bandit.

Don Francisco. Nothing strange in that,
For love and fortune, in all other lands
As well as Spain, are sport of the cogg'd dice.
It is the rogue who wins.

Don Ricardo. My fortune grew
In seeing the love-making. First a Count
And then Grandee, and next an Alcadé
At court. My time was well spent, though without
One knowing it.

Don Sancho. Your secret, sir, appears
To be the keeping close upon the heels
O' the King.

Don Ricardo. And showing that my conduct's worth
Reward.

Don Garcie. And by chance you profited.

Don Matias. What has become of the old Duke? has he
His coffin ordered?

Don Sancho. Marquis, jest not thus
At him! For he a haughty spirit has;
And this old man loved well the Doña Sol.
His sixty years had turned his hair to grey,
One day has bleached it.

Don Garcie. Not again, they say,
Has he been seen in Saragossa.

Don Sancho. Well?
Wouldst thou that to the bridal he should bring
His coffin?

Don Francisco. What's the Emperor doing now?

Don Sancho. The Emperor is out of sorts just now,
Luther annoys him.

Don Ricardo. Luther!—subject fine
For care and fear! Soon would I finish him
With but four men-at-arms!

Don Matias. And Soliman
Makes him dejected.

Don Garcie. Luther—Soliman
Neptune—the devil—Jupiter! What are
They all to me? The women are most fair,
The masquerade is splendid, and I've said
A hundred foolish things!

Don Sancho. Behold you now
The chief thing.

Don Ricardo. Garcie's not far wrong, I say.
Not the same man am I on festal days.
When I put on the mask in truth I think
Another head it gives me.

Don Sancho (*apart to* Don Matias).
Pity 'tis
That all days are not festivals!
Don Francisco. Are those
Their rooms?
Don Garcie (*with a nod of his head*).
Arrive they will, no doubt, full soon.
Don Francisco. Dost think so?
Don Garcie. Most undoubtedly!
Don Francisco. 'Tis well.
The bride is lovely!
Don Ricardo. What an Emperor!
The rebel chief, Hernani, to be pardoned—
Wearing the Golden Fleece! and married too!
Ah, if the Emperor had been by me
Advised, the gallant should have had a bed
Of stone, the lady one of down.
Don Sancho (*aside to* Don Matias).
How well
I'd like with my good sword this lord to smash,
A lord made up of tinsel coarsely joined;
Pourpoint of Count filled out with bailiff's soul!
Don Ricardo (*drawing near*). What are you saying?
Don Matias (*aside to* Don Sancho).
Count, no quarrel here!
(*To* Don Ricardo.)
He was reciting one of Petrarch's sonnets
Unto his lady love.
Don Garcie. Have you not seen
Among the flowers and women, and dresses gay
Of many hues, a figure spectre-like,
Whose domino all black, upright against
A balustrade, seems like a spot upon
The festival?
Don Ricardo. Yes, by my faith!
Don Garcie. Who is't?
Don Ricardo. By height and mien I judge that it must be——
The admiral—the Don Prancasio.
Don Francisco. Oh, no.
Don Garcie. He has not taken off his mask.
Don Francisco. There is no need;
it is the Duke de Soma,
Who likes to be observed. 'Tis nothing more.
Don Ricardo. No; the Duke spoke to me.
Don Garcie. Who then can be
This Mask? But see—he's here.
(*Enter a* Black Domino, *who slowly crosses the back of the stage. All turn and watch him without his appearing to notice them.*)
Don Sancho. If the dead walk,
That is their step.
Don Garcie (*approaching the* Black Domino). Most noble Mask——
(*The* Black Domino *stops and turns.* Garcie *recoils.*)
I swear,
Good Sirs, that I saw flame shine in his eyes.
Don Sancho. If he's the devil he'll find one he can
Address.
(*He goes to the* Black Domino, *who is still motionless.*)
Ho, Demon! comest thou from hell?
The Mask. I come not thence—'tis thither that I go.
(*He continues his walk and disappears at the balustrade of the staircase. All*

watch him with a look of horrified dismay.)

Don Matias. Sepulchral is his voice, as can be heard.

Don Garcie. Pshaw! What would frighten elsewhere, at a ball
We laugh at.

Don Sancho. Silly jesting 'tis!

Don Garcie. Indeed,
If Lucifer is come to see us dance,
Waiting for lower regions, let us dance!

Don Sancho. Of course it's some buffoonery.

Don Matias. We'll know
To-morrow.

Don Sancho (*to* Don Matias). Look now what becomes of him,
I pray you!

Don Matias (*at the balustrade of the terrace*). Down the steps he's gone. That's all.

Don Sancho. A pleasant jester he! (*Musing.*) 'Tis strange.

Don Garcie (*to a lady passing*). Marquise,
Let us pray dance this time. (*He bows and offers his hand.*)

The Lady. You know, dear sir,
My husband will my dances with you all
Count up.

Don Garcie. All the more reason. Pleased is he
To count, it seems, and it amuses him. He calculates—we dance.

(*The lady gives her hand and they exeunt.*)

Don Sancho (*thoughtfully*). In truth, 'tis strange!

Don Matias. Behold the married pair! Now silence all!

(*Enter* Hernani *and* Doña Sol *hand in hand.* Doña Sol *in magnificent bridal dress.* Hernani *in black velvet and with the Golden Fleece hanging from his neck. Behind them a crowd of Masks and of ladies and gentlemen who form their retinue. Two Halberdiers in rich liveries follow them, and four Pages precede them. Every one makes way for them and bows as they approach. Flourish of trumpets.*)

Scene 2.—*The Same.* Hernani, Doña Sol *and retinue.* Hernani (*saluting*).

Dear friends!

Don Ricardo (*advancing and bowing*). Your Excellency's happiness
Makes ours.

Don Francisco (*looking at* Doña Sol). Now, by St. James, 'tis Venus' self
That he is leading.

Don Matias. Happiness is his!

Don Sancho (*to* Don Matias). 'Tis late now, let us leave.

(*All salute the married pair and retire—some by the door, others by the stairway at the back.*)

Hernani (*escorting them*). Adieu!

Don Sancho (*who has remained to the last, and pressing his hand*).
Be happy!

(*Exit* Don Sancho.)

(Hernani *and* Doña Sol *remain alone. The sound of voices grows fainter and fainter till it ceases altogether. During the early part of the following scene the sound of trumpets grows fainter, and the lights by degrees are extinguished—till night and silence prevail.*)

Scene 3.—Hernani. Doña Sol.

Doña Sol. At last they are all gone.
Hernani (*seeking to draw her to his arms*). Dear love!
Doña Sol (*drawing back a little*). Is't late?—
At least to me it seems so.
Hernani. Angel dear,
Time ever drags till we together are.
Doña Sol. This noise has wearied me. Is it not true,
Dear Lord, that all this mirth but stifling is
To happiness?
Hernani. Thou sayest truly, Love,
For happiness is serious, and asks
For hearts of bronze on which to 'grave itself.
Pleasure alarms it, flinging to it flowers;
Its smile is nearer tears than mirth.
Doña Sol. Thy smile's
Like daylight in thine eyes.
(Hernani *seeks to lead her to the door*.) Oh, presently.
Hernani. I am thy slave; yes, linger if thou wilt,
Whate'er thou dost is well. I'll laugh and sing
If thou desirest that it should be so.
Bid the volcano stifle flame, and 'twill
Close up its gulfs, and on its sides grow flowers,
And grasses green.
Doña Sol. How good you are to me,
My heart's Hernani!
Hernani. Madam, what name's that?
I pray in pity speak it not again!
Thou call'st to mind forgotten things. I know
That he existed formerly in dreams,
Hernani, he whose eyes flashed like a sword,
A man of night and of the hills, a man
Proscribed, on whom was seen writ everywhere
The one word *vengeance*. An unhappy man
That drew down malediction! I know not
The man they called Hernani. As for me,
I love the birds and flowers, and woods
—and song
Of nightingale. I'm Juan of Aragon,
The spouse of Doña Sol—a happy man!
Doña Sol. Happy am I!
Hernani. What does it matter now,
The rags I left behind me at the door!
Behold, I to my palace desolate
Come back. Upon the threshold-sill there waits
For me an Angel; I come in and lift
Upright the broken columns, kindle fire,
And ope again the windows; and the grass
Upon the courtyard I have all pluck'd up;
For me there is but joy, enchantment, love.
Let them give back my towers, and donjon-keep,
My plume, and seat at the Castilian board
Of Council, comes my blushing Doña Sol,
Let them leave us—the rest forgotten is.
Nothing I've seen, nor said, nor have I done.
Anew my life begins, the past effacing.
Wisdom or madness, you I have and love,
And you are all my joy!
Doña Sol. How well upon
The velvet black the golden collar shows!

HERNANI. You saw it on the King ere now on me.

DOÑA SOL. I did not notice. Others, what are they
To me? Besides, the velvet is it, or
The satin? No, my Duke, it is thy neck
Which suits the golden collar. Thou art proud
And noble, my own Lord.
(*He seeks to lead her indoors.*)
Oh, presently,
A moment! See you not, I weep with joy?
Come look upon the lovely night.
(*She goes to the balustrade.*)
My Duke,
Only a moment—but the time to breathe
And gaze. All now is o'er, the torches out,
The music done. Night only is with us.
Felicity most perfect! Think you not
That now while all is still and slumbering,
Nature, half waking, watches us with love?
No cloud is in the sky. All things like us
Are now at rest. Come, breathe with me the air
Perfumed by roses. Look, there is no light,
Nor hear we any noise. Silence prevails.
The moon just now from the horizon rose
E'en while you spoke to me; her trembling light
And thy dear voice together reached my heart.
Joyous and softly calm I felt, oh, thou
My lover! And it seemed that I would then
Most willingly have died.

HERNANI. Ah, who is there
Would not all things forget when listening thus
Unto this voice celestial! Thy speech
But seems a chaunt with nothing human mixed,
And as with one, who gliding down a stream
On summer eve, sees pass before his eyes
A thousand flowery plains, my thoughts are drawn
Into thy reveries!

DOÑA SOL. This silence is
Too deep, and too profound the calm.
Say, now,
Wouldst thou not like to see a star shine forth
From out the depths—or hear a voice of night,
Tender and sweet, raise suddenly in song?

HERNANI (*smiling*). Capricious one!
Just now you fled away
From all the songs and lights.

DOÑA SOL. Ah yes, the ball!
But yet a bird that in the meadow sings,
A nightingale in moss or shadow lost,
Or flute far off. For music sweet can pour
Into the soul a harmony divine,
That like a heavenly choir wakes in the heart
A thousand voices! Charming would it be!
(*They hear the sound of a horn from the shade.*)
My prayer is heard.

HERNANI (*aside trembling*). Oh, miserable man!

DOÑA SOL. An angel read my thought
—'twas thy good angel

Doubtless?

HERNANI (*bitterly*). Yes, my good angel! (*Aside.*)
There, again!

DOÑA SOL (*smiling*). Don Juan, I recognize your horn.

HERNANI. Is't so?

DOÑA SOL. The half this serenade to you belongs?

HERNANI. The half, thou hast declared it.

DOÑA SOL. Ah, the ball
Detestable! Far better do I love
The horn that sounds from out the woods! And since
It is your horn 'tis like your voice to me.

(*The horn sounds again.*)

HERNANI (*aside*). It is the tiger howling for his prey!

DOÑA SOL. Don Juan, this music fills my heart with joy.

HERNANI (*drawing himself up and looking terrible*). Call me Hernani! call me it again!
For with that fatal name I have not done.

DOÑA SOL (*trembling*). What ails you?

HERNANI. The old man!

DOÑA SOL. Oh God, what looks! What is it ails you?

HERNANI. That old man who in
The darkness laughs. Can you not see him there?

DOÑA SOL. Oh, you are wand'ring! Who is this old man?

HERNANI. The old man!

DOÑA SOL. On my knees I do entreat Thee, say what is the secret that afflicts Thee thus?

HERNANI. I swore it!

DOÑA SOL. Swore!

(*She watches his movements with anxiety. He stops suddenly and passes his hand across his brow.*)

HERNANI (*aside*). What have I said? Oh, let me spare her. (*Aloud.*)
I—nought. What was it
I said?

DOÑA SOL. You said——

HERNANI. No, no, I was disturbed——
And somewhat suffering I am. Do not Be frightened.

DOÑA SOL. You need something? Order me,
Thy servant.

(*The horn sounds again.*)

HERNANI (*aside*). Ah, he claims! he claims the pledge!
He has my oath. (*Feeling for his dagger.*)
Not there. It must be done!
Ah!——

DOÑA SOL. Suff'rest thou so much?

HERNANI. 'Tis an old wound
That I thought healed—it has re-opened now. (*Aside.*)
She must be got away. (*Aloud.*)
My best beloved,
Now listen; there's a little box that in Less happy days I carried with me——

DOÑA SOL. Ah,
I know what 'tis you mean. Tell me your wish.

HERNANI. It holds a flask of an elixir which
Will end my sufferings.—Go!

DOÑA SOL. I go, my Lord.

(*Exit by the door to their apartments.*)

SCENE 4.

HERNANI (*alone*). This, then, is how my happiness must end!
Behold the fatal finger that doth shine Upon the wall! My bitter destiny
Still jests at me.
(*He falls into a profound yet convulsive reverie. Afterwards he turns abruptly.*)
Ah, well! I hear no sound.
Am I myself deceiving?——
(*The* MASK *in black domino appears at the balustrade of the steps.* HERNANI *stops petrified.*)

SCENE 5.—HERNANI. THE MASK.

THE MASK. "Whatsoe'er
May happen, what the place, or what the hour,
Whenever to thy mind it seems the time
Has come for me to die—blow on this horn
And take no other care. All will be done."
This compact had the dead for witnesses.
Is it all done?

HERNANI (*in a low voice*). 'Tis he!

THE MASK. Unto thy home
I come, I tell thee that it is the time.
It is my hour. I find thee hesitate.

HERNANI. Well then, thy pleasure say. What wouldst thou
Of me?

THE MASK. I give thee choice 'twixt poison draught
And blade. I bear about me both. We shall
Depart together.

HERNANI. Be it so.

THE MASK. Shall we
First pray?

HERNANI. What matter?

THE MASK. Which of them wilt thou?

HERNANI. The poison.

THE MASK. Then hold out your hand.
(*He gives a vial to* HERNANI, *who pales at receiving it.*)
Now drink,
That I may finish.
(HERNANI *lifts the vial to his lips, but recoils.*)

HERNANI. Oh, for pity's sake
Until to-morrow wait! If thou hast heart
Or soul, if thou art not a spectre just
Escaped from flame, if thou art not a soul
Accursed, for ever lost; if on thy brow
Not yet has God inscribed His "never."
Oh
If thou hast ever known the bliss supreme
Of loving, and at twenty years of age
Of wedding the beloved; if ever thou
Hast clasped the one thou lovedst in thine arms,
Wait till to-morrow. Then thou canst come back!

THE MASK. Childish it is for you to jest this way!
To-morrow! why, the bell this morning toll'd
Thy funeral! And I should die this night,
And who would come and take thee after me!
I will not to the tomb descend alone,
Young man, 'tis thou must go with me!

HERNANI. Well, then,

I say thee nay; and, demon, I from thee
Myself deliver. I will not obey.
  THE MASK. As I expected. Very well. On what
Then didst thou swear? Ah, on a trifling thing,
The mem'ry of thy father's head. With ease
Such oath may be forgotten. Youthful oaths
Are light affairs.
  HERNANI. My father!—father! Oh My senses I shall lose!
  THE MASK. Oh, no—'tis but
A perjury and treason.
  HERNANI. Duke!
  THE MASK. Since now
The heirs of Spanish houses make a jest
Of breaking promises, I'll say Adieu!
  (*He moves as if to leave.*)
  HERNANI. Stay!
  THE MASK. Then——
  HERNANI. Oh cruel man! (*He raises the vial.*)
Thus to return
Upon my path at heaven's door!
  (*Re-enter* DOÑA SOL *without seeing the* MASK, *who is standing erect near the balustrade of the stairway at the back of the stage.*)

SCENE 6.—*The Same.* DOÑA SOL.

  DOÑA SOL. I've failed
To find that little box.
  HERNANI (*aside*). Oh God! 'tis she! At such a moment here!
  DOÑA SOL. What is't, that thus
I frighten him,—e'en at my voice he shakes!
What hold'st thou in thy hand? What fearful thought!
What hold'st thou in thy hand? Reply to me.
  (*The* DOMINO *unmasks, she utters a cry in recognizing* DON RUY.)
'Tis poison!
  HERNANI. Oh, great Heaven!
  DOÑA SOL (*to* HERNANI). What is it
That I have done to thee? What mystery
Of horror? I'm deceived by thee, Don Juan!
  HERNANI. Ah, I had thought to hide it all from thee.
My life I promised to the Duke that time
He saved it. Aragon must pay this debt
To Silva.
  DOÑA SOL. Unto me you do belong, Not him. What signify your other oaths?
  (*To* DON RUY GOMEZ.)
My love it is which gives me strength, and, Duke,
I will defend him against you and all
The world.
  DON RUY GOMEZ (*unmoved*).
Defend him if you can against
An oath that's sworn.
  DOÑA SOL. What oath?
  HERNANI. Yes, I have sworn.
  DOÑA SOL. No, no; naught binds thee; it would be a crime,
A madness, an atrocity—no, no,
It cannot be.
  DON RUY GOMEZ. Come, Duke.
  (HERNANI *makes a gesture to obey.* DOÑA SOL *tries to stop him.*)
  HERNANI. It must be done.
Allow it, Doña Sol. My word was pledged
To the Duke, and to my father now in heaven!

Doña Sol (*to* Don Ruy Gomez).
Better that to a tigress you should go
And snatch away her young, than take from me
Him whom I love. Know you at all what is
This Doña Sol? Long time I pitied you,
And, in compassion for your age, I seemed
The gentle girl, timid and innocent,
But now see eyes made moist by tears of rage.
(*She draws a dagger from her bosom.*)
See you this dagger? Old man imbecile!
Do you not fear the steel when eyes flash threat?
Take care, Don Ruy! I'm of thy family.
Listen, mine Uncle! Had I been your child
It had been ill for you, if you had laid
A hand upon my husband!
(*She throws away the dagger, and falls on her knees before him.*)
At thy feet
I fall! Mercy! Have pity on us both.
Alas! my Lord, I am but woman weak,
My strength dies out within my soul, I fail
So easily; 'tis at your knees I plead,
I supplicate—have mercy on us both!
Don Ruy Gomez. Doña Sol!
Doña Sol. Oh, pardon! With us Spaniards
Grief bursts forth in stormy words, you know it.
Alas! you used not to be harsh! My Uncle,
Have pity, you are killing me indeed
In touching him! Mercy, have pity now,
So well I love him!
Don Ruy Gomez (*gloomily*). You love him too much!
Hernani. Thou weepest!
Doña Sol. No, my love, no, no, it must
Not be. I will not have you die. (*To Don Ruy.*)
To-day
Be merciful, and I will love you well,
You also.
Don Ruy Gomez. After him; the dregs you'd give
The remnants of your love, and friendliness.
Still less and less.—Oh, think you thus to quench
The thirst that now devours me?
(*Pointing to* Hernani.)
He alone
Is everything. For me kind pityings!
With such affection, what, pray, could I do?
Fury! 'tis he would have your heart, your love,
And be enthroned, and grant a look from you
As alms; and if vouchsafed a kindly word
'Tis he would tell you—say so much, it is
Enough,—cursing in heart the greedy one
The beggar, unto whom he's forced to fling
The drops remaining in the emptied glass.
Oh, shame! derision! No, we'll finish. Drink!
Hernani. He has my promise, and it must be kept.
Don Ruy Gomez. Proceed.
(Hernani *raises the vial to his lips,*

Doña Sol *throws herself on his arm.*)
    Doña Sol. Not yet. Deign both of you to hear me.
    Don Ruy Gomez. The grave is open and I cannot wait.
    Doña Sol. A moment only—Duke, and my Don Juan,
Ah! both are cruel! What is it I ask?
An instant! that is all I beg from you.
Let a poor woman speak what's in her heart,
Oh, let me speak——
    Don Ruy Gomez. I cannot wait.
    Doña Sol. My Lord,
You make me tremble! What then have I done?
    Hernani. His crime is rending him.
    Doña Sol (*still holding his arm*). You see full well
I have a thousand things to say.
    Don Ruy Gomez (*to* Hernani). Die—die
You must.
    Doña Sol (*still hanging on his arm*). Don Juan, when all's said indeed
Thou shalt do what thou wilt.
    (*She snatches the vial.*)
I have it now!
    (*She lifts the vial for* Hernani *and the old man to see.*)
    Don Ruy Gomez. Since with two women I have here to deal,
It needs, Don Juan, that I elsewhere go
In search of souls. Grave oaths you took to me,
And by the race from which you sprang.
I go
Unto your father, and to speak among
The dead. Adieu.
    (*He moves as if to depart.* Hernani *holds him back.*)

    Hernani. Stay, Duke. (*To* Doña Sol.) Alas! I do
Implore thee. Would'st thou wish to see in me
A perjured felon only, and e'erwhere
I go "a traitor" written on my brow?
In pity give the poison back to me.
'Tis by our love I ask it, and our souls
Immortal——
    Doña Sol (*sadly*). And thou wilt?
(*She drinks.*)
Now take the rest.
    Don Ruy Gomez (*aside*). 'Twas then for her!
    Doña Sol (*returning the half-emptied vial to* Hernani). I tell thee, take.
    Hernani (*to* Don Ruy). Oh miserable man!
    Doña Sol. Grieve not for me,
I've left thy share.
    Hernani (*taking the vial*). Oh, God!
    Doña Sol. Not thus would'st thou
Have left me mine. But thou! not thine the heart
Of Christian wife! Thou knowest not to love
As Silvas do—but I've drunk first—made sure.
Now drink it, if thou wilt!
    Hernani. What hast thou done, Unhappy one?
    Doña Sol. 'Twas thou who willed it so.
    Hernani. It is a frightful death!
    Doña Sol. No—no—why so?
    Hernani. This philtre leads unto the grave.
    Doña Sol. And ought
We not this night to rest together? Does
It matter in what bed?
    Hernani. My father, thou

Thyself avengest upon me, who did
Forget thee! (*He lifts the vial to his
mouth.*)
    Doña Sol (*throwing herself on him*).
Heavens, what strange agony!
Ah, throw this philtre far from thee!
My reason
Is wand'ring. Stop! Alas! oh, my Don Juan,
This drug is potent, in the heart it wakes
A hydra with a thousand tearing teeth
Devouring it. I knew not that such pangs
Could be! What is the thing? 'tis liquid fire.
Drink not! For much thou'dst suffer!
    Hernani (*to* Don Ruy). Ah, thy soul
Is cruel! Could'st thou not have found for her
Another drug?
    (*He drinks and throws the vial away.*)
    Doña Sol. What dost thou?
    Hernani. What thyself
Hast done.
    Doña Sol. Come to my arms, young lover, now.
    (*They sit down close to each other.*)
Does one not suffer horribly?
    Hernani. No, no.
    Doña Sol. These are our marriage rites! But for a bride
I'm very pale, say am I not?
    Hernani. Ah me!
    Don Ruy Gomez. Fulfilled is now the fatal destiny!
    Hernani. Oh misery and despair to know her pangs!
    Doña Sol. Be calm. I'm better.—
Towards new brighter light
We now together open out our wings.
Let us with even flight set out to reach
A fairer world. Only a kiss—a kiss!
    (*They embrace.*)
    Don Ruy Gomez. Oh, agony supreme!
    Hernani (*in a feeble voice*). Oh bless'd be Heav'n
That will'd for me a life by spectres followed,
And by abysses yawning circled still,
Yet grants, that weary of a road so rough,
I fall asleep my lips upon thy hand.
    Don Ruy Gomez. How happy are they!
    Hernani (*in voice growing weaker and weaker*). Come,—come, Doña Sol,
All's dark. Dost thou not suffer?
    Doña Sol (*in a voice equally faint*). Nothing now.
Oh, nothing.
    Hernani. Seest thou not fires in the gloom?
    Doña Sol. Not yet.
    Hernani (*with a sigh*). Behold——
(*He falls.*)
    Don Ruy Gomez (*raising the head, which falls again*). He's dead!
    Doña Sol (*dishevelled and half raising herself on the seat*). Oh no, we sleep.
He sleeps. It is my spouse that here you see.
We love each other—we are sleeping thus.
It is our bridal. (*In a failing voice.*)
I entreat you not
To wake him, my Lord Duke of Meudocé,
For he is weary. (*She turns round the face of* Hernani.)

Turn to me, my love.
More near—still closer——
(*She falls back.*)

Don Ruy Gomez. Dead! Oh, I am damn'd!
(*He kills himself.*)

Ruy Blas

PERSONAGES OF THE DRAMA

Ruy Blas.
Don Salluste de Bazan.
Don Cæsar de Bazan.
Don Guritan.
The Count de Camporeal.
The Marquis de Santa-Cruz.
The Marquis del Basto.
The Count d'Albe.
The Marquis de Priego.
Don Manuel Arias.
Montazgo.
Don Antonio Ubilla.
Covadenga.
Gudiel.

A Lackey.
An Alcaid.
An Usher.
An Alguazil.
A Page.

Doña Maria de Neubourg, Queen of Spain.
The Duchess d'Albuquerque.
Casilda.
A Duenna.

Ladies, Lords, Privy Councillors, Pages, Duennas, Alguazils, Guards, and Gentlemen Ushers.

Madrid, 169—.

ACT FIRST:

DON SALLUSTE

(*The Hall of Danaé in the King's Palace at Madrid. Magnificent furniture in the half-Flemish Style of Philip IV. At the left, a large window with small squares of glass set in gilt frames. On each side a low door leading to some interior apartments. At the back, a large glass partition with gilt frames opens by a glass door on a long corridor. This corridor, which stretches all along the stage, is concealed by wide curtains that fall from top to bottom of the glass partition. A table with writing materials, and an easy chair.*

Don Salluste *enters by the little door at the left, followed by* Ruy Blas, and by GUDIEL, *who carries a cash-box and other packages as if in preparation for a journey.* DON SALLUSTE *is dressed in black velvet, in the fashion of the Court of Charles II., and wears the Golden Fleece. Over his black dress he has a rich mantle of light velvet embroidered with gold and lined with black satin. A sword with a large hilt. A hat with white feathers.* GUDIEL *is in black and wears a sword.* RUY BLAS *is in livery—leggings and undercoat brown; overcoat turned up with red and gold. Bareheaded and without a sword.*)

SCENE 1.—DON SALLUSTE DE BAZAN, GUDIEL; RUY BLAS *at intervals.*

DON SALLUSTE. That window open,
Ruy Blas—and shut
The door.
  RUY BLAS *obeys, and then, at a sign from* DON SALLUSTE *goes out by the door at the back.* DON SALLUSTE *walks to the window.*
All here still sleep. 'Tis nearly dawn.
(*He turns suddenly towards* GUDIEL.)
It is a thunderbolt! Ah, yes, my reign
Is over, Gudiel! Exiled and disgraced,
All lost in but a day. At present, though,
The thing is secret—speak not of it, pray.
Yes, only for a little love affair,
—At my age senseless folly I admit—
And with a nobody—a serving maid
Seduced—ill luck! because she was about
The Queen, who brought the girl from Neubourg here.
This creature wept, complained of me, and dragg'd

Into the royal chambers her young brat;
Then I was ordered to espouse the girl,
And I refused. They banished me.
Me—me
They exiled! After twenty years of work
So difficult, engaging day and night,
Years of ambition. I, the President,
Abhorr'd by all the Court Alcaids, who named
Me but with dread. Chief of the house Bazan
That is so proud; my credit, power, and all
I did, and had, and dreamed, honours and place
One moment sweeps away, amid the roars
Of laughter of the crowd.
  GUDIEL. None know it yet, My Lord.
  DON SALLUSTE. Ah, but to-morrow!
'Twill be known
To-morrow! We shall then be on our way.
I will not fall. No, no, I'll disappear.
(*He hastens to unbutton his doublet.*)
You always fasten me as if I were
A priest. You strain my doublet; and oh, now
I stifle.
(*He sits down.*)
Ah, with th' air of innocence
I'll dig a deep, dark mine! Chased—chased away!
(*He rises.*)
  GUDIEL. Whence came the blow, my Lord?
  DON SALLUSTE. 'Twas from the Queen.
Oh, Gudiel, I will be revenged. Thou know'st,

Thou understandest me—whom thou hast taught
And aided well for twenty years in things
Long past. Thou know'st where turn my darken'd thoughts,
As a skill'd architect can at a glance
Measure the depth of wells that he has sunk.
I will set out for my Castilian lands,
Estates of Finlas there to brood and plan.
All for a girl! Thou must—for time is short—
Arrange for our departure. First I'd speak
A word at any risk unto the scamp
Thou know'st. It may be that he proves of use.
I know not. But till night I'm master here.
I will have vengeance—how I cannot tell;
But I will make it terrible. Go now,
At once get ready—hasten—silent be!
You shall go with me—hasten.

(GUDIEL *bows and exit.* DON SALLUSTE *calls.*) Ruy Blas!

RUY BLAS (*appearing at the door at the back*). Excellency?

DON SALLUSTE. Within the Palace walls
I sleep no more; thus shutters should be closed,
The keys be left.

RUY BLAS. My Lord, it shall be done.

DON SALLUSTE. Listen, I beg. In two hours will the Queen,
In coming back from mass unto her room
Of state, pass through the corridor; you must
Be there.

RUY BLAS. I will, my Lord.

DON SALLUSTE (*at the window*). See you that man
I' the square—a paper to the guard he shows
And passes? Sign to him without a word
That he may enter by the back stair way.

(RUY BLAS *obeys.* DON SALLUSTE *continues, pointing to the little door on the right.*)
Before you go look in the guard room there—
See if three Alguazils on duty are
As yet awake.

RUY BLAS (*He goes to the door, half opens it and comes back*).
My Lord, they sleep.

DON SALLUSTE. Speak low.
I shall be wanting you, so go not far
Away. Keep watch that we be not disturbed.

(*Enter* DON CÆSAR DE BAZAN. *Hat staved in. A ragged cloak, which conceals all his dress except stockings that hang loose, and shoes that are split open. Sword of a brawler.*
As he enters, he and RUY BLAS *glance at each other from opposite sides with gestures of surprise.*)

DON SALLUSTE (*observing them, aside*). Looks were exchanged! Can they each other know!

(*Exit* RUY BLAS.)

SCENE 2.—DON SALLUSTE—DON CÆSAR.

DON SALLUSTE. So, bandit, you are here!

DON CÆSAR. Yes, cousin, yes. Behold me.

DON SALLUSTE. Great the pleasure 'tis to see

A beggar!

Don Cæsar (*bowing*). I delighted am. . . .

Don Salluste. We know Your doings, sir.

Don Cæsar (*graciously*). Which you approve?

Don Salluste. Oh yes, They're mighty meritorious. Don Charles
De Mira but the other night was robb'd.
They took from him his sword with scabbard chased,
And shoulder belt. As 'twas near Easter Eve,
And he a knight of bless'd St. James, the band
Let him retain his cloak.

Don Cæsar. Just heaven, why?

Don Salluste. Because upon it was embroidered plain
The order. Well, what say you to all this?

Don Cæsar. The devil! I but say we live in times
Most dreadful. Oh, what will become of us
If thieves pay court to good St. James, and count
Him of themselves?

Don Salluste. You were with them.

Don Cæsar. Well, yes;
If I must speak, I was. But your Don Charles
I did not touch. I only gave advice.

Don Salluste. Worse still. Last night, just when the moon had set,
A crowd of low riff-raff,—all sorts of men,
Shoeless and ragged, rushed out from their dens
Pell-mell unto the Mayor Square, and then
Attacked the guard. There you were.

Don Cæsar. Cousin, yes,
'Tis true. But always I disdain to fight
The mere thief-catchers. There I was —that's all;
For during all the row, I walked apart
Beneath th' Arcade, verse making. Ah, they knock'd
Each other about finely.

Don Salluste. That's not all.

Don Cæsar. Well, what is it?

Don Salluste. 'Mong other things, in France
They say that you, with rebels like yourself,
Did force the lock of the strong money box
Of the Excise.

Don Cæsar. Oh, I deny it not,
France is the country of an enemy.

Don Salluste. Again, in Flanders, meeting with Don Paul
Barthélemy, who then had just received
The product of a vineyard he was charged
To carry to Mons' noble Chapter, you
Laid hands upon it, though the gold belonged
E'en to the clergy.

Don Cæsar. In Flanders, was it?
It might be so, for I have travelled much.
And is that all?

Don Salluste. The sweat of shame, Don Cæsar,
To my forehead mounts whene'er I think of you.

Don Cæsar. Well, let it mount.

Don Salluste. Our family ——

Don Cæsar. No, stay;
For only unto you in all Madrid

My real name is known. So do not speak
Of family.

Don Salluste. Only the other day,
A marchioness, when leaving Church, spoke thus:
Who is that brigand there below, who struts
With nose turned up, and eyes upon the watch,
Squaring himself with arms a-kimbo set?
More tatter'd far than Job, and prouder he
Than a Braganza—covering his rags
With arrogance—handling his big sword-hilt
Beneath his sleeve, that's all in slits, the while
The blade about his heels hangs as he steps
With masterful air, his cloak in dented gaps
Resembling saws, his stockings all awry.

Don Cæsar (*glancing at his own attire*).
And then, of course, you promptly answered her,
It is dear Zafari!

Don Salluste. No, Sir, I blush'd.

Don Cæsar. Ah, well, the lady had her laugh. I like
To make a woman laugh.

Don Salluste. Your comrades are Swashbucklers infamous.

Don Cæsar. Mere learners they—Scholars—each one as gentle as a sheep.

Don Salluste. You everywhere are seen with women vile.

Don Cæsar. Oh Love's bright radiance! Oh sweet Isabels!

What fine things now one hears of you!
A shame
It is to treat you thus—beauties with sly
And laughing eyes, to whom I tell at night
The sonnets I have made at morn.

Don Salluste. In short,
The friend you are of Matalobos, that
Galician thief who desolates Madrid,
Defying our police.

Don Cæsar. If you will deign
I beg you let us reason. Without him
Bare-backed I should have been—that would have looked
Unseemly. Seeing me without a coat,
Though it was winter time, he felt for me.—
That amber-perfumed fop, the Count of Albe,
Was robbed but lately of his doublet fine,
His silken one——

Don Salluste. Well?

Don Cæsar. I it is who have it,
Matalobos gave it me.

Don Salluste. The Count's pelisse!
And you are not ashamed?

Don Cæsar. I'm ne'er ashamed
Of wearing a good coat, 'broidered, galloon'd,
That keeps me warm in winter—makes me smart
In summer time. Look, here it is, quite new.
(*He half opens his cloak, and shows a superb doublet of rose-coloured satin embroidered in gold.*)
By scores, love-letters written to the Count
Are cramm'd i' the pockets. Oft, when poor, love-sick,

With nought to eat, a steaming vent hole I
Discover, from the which comes up the smell
Of cooking, cheating then by turns my heart
And stomach, I can sit me down to read
The Count's sweet letters, revelling there alike
I' the scent of feasting, and a dream of love.
    DON SALLUSTE. Don Cæsar——
    DON CÆSAR. Cousin, now a truce, I beg,
Unto reproaches. A grandee I am,
And of your kindred. Cæsar is my name,
The Count Garofa, but upon my birth
'Twas folly crown'd me. Lands and palaces
I had, and well I paid the Célimènes.
Pshaw! Scarcely twenty years I knew before
The whole had vanished, only there remained
Of my good fortune—true or false—a pack
Of creditors to howl about my heels.
Good faith! I took to flight and changed my name.
Now am I but a boon companion found,
Zafari, whom none know by other name
Save you. No money, Master, give you me;
I do without. At night, with head upon
The stones, before the ancient palace walls
Of Tevé, there these nine years past I've stopp'd.
I slumber with the blue sky overhead,
And happy thus. 'Tis a fine fortune, mine!
The world believes me to the Indies gone,
Or to the devil—dead. The fountain near
Supplies my drink, and afterwards I walk
With air of glory. My own palace, whence
My money flew, is tenanted to-day
By the Pope's Nuncio, Espinola. Well,
When I by chance am there, I give advice
Unto the Nuncio's workmen—occupied
In sculpturing a Bacchus o'er the door.—
But will you lend me just ten crowns?
    DON SALLUSTE. Hear me——
    DON CÆSAR (*crossing his arms*).
Now, what is't you would say?
    DON SALLUSTE. I sent for you
That I might serve you. I, childless and rich,
And much the elder, see you, Cæsar, now
With sorrow and regret to ruin dragged,
And fain would save you. Bully that you are,
You are unfortunate. I'll pay your debts,
Restore your palace—place you at the Court,
And make of you again a lady-killer.
Let then Zafari be extinguished now,
And Cæsar newly born. I wish that you
Henceforth should, at your will, my fortune use
Fearless, and taking with both hands, nor care
For future needs. When we have relatives

We must support them, and be pitiful.
(*While* Don Salluste *is speaking*
Don Cæsar's *countenance takes more
and more the expression of astonishment, joyous and hopeful. At last he
bursts out.*)
Don Cæsar. You always had a devil's wit, and what
You've said just now's most eloquently put.
Go on.
Don Salluste. Yes, Cæsar, I will do all this
On one condition. I'll explain it all
A moment hence. First take my purse.
Don Cæsar (*weighing the purse, which is full of gold*). This is
Magnificent!
Don Salluste. And I intend for you
Five hundred ducats.
Don Cæsar (*bewildered*). Marquis!
Don Salluste. From to-day.
Don Cæsar. By Jove, I'm yours to order. Now then tell
Conditions—name them. On a brave man's faith
My sword is at your service to command.
Your slave I am, and, if you wish it so,
I'll cross blades with the Don Spavento, who
A captain is that comes from hell.
Don Salluste. No, not
Your sword can I accept, for reasons good.
Don Cæsar. What then? Right little else have I.
Don Salluste (*drawing nearer and lowering his voice*). You know,
And in this case 'tis lucky, all the rogues
About Madrid.
Don Cæsar. You do me honour.

Don Salluste. You
Can always in your train bring all the pack;
You could raise up a tumult if need be.
I know it. All this may be useful now.
Don Cæsar. Upon my word it seems you would invent
An opera. What part am I to take?
Shall I compose the verse, or symphony?
Command, I for a frolic row am good.
Don Salluste (*gravely*). 'Tis to
Don Cæsar that I speak, and not
Zafari (*lowering his voice more and more*). List! 'Tis for a stern result
I need that some one should in secret work
And aid me with his skill to bring about
A great event. Not mischievous am I,
But times there are when without any shame
One the most delicate turns up his sleeves
And sets to work. Thou shalt be rich, but thou
Must help me silently to spread a net
As in the night bird-catchers do. A web
That's strong, but hid by shining glass, a snare
Such as is set for lark or girl. The plan,
It must be terrible and wonderful.
I think you are not very scrupulous.—
Avenge me.
Don Cæsar. You avenge!
Don Salluste. Yes, me.
Don Cæsar. On whom?
Don Salluste. A woman.
Don Cæsar (*drawing himself up and looking haughtily at* Don Salluste).
Halt! and say no more of this
To me. Now, Cousin, on my soul I'll speak

My mind to you. He who can claim the right
A sword to bear, and yet by stealthy means
Takes vengeance basely—on a woman too,—
Who, born patrician, acts the bailiff's part,
Were he grandee of Old Castile, and did
A hundred clarions follow him, and sound
Their din, were he with orders harness'd, were
He Marquis, Viscount, of the lineal heir
Of blameless, noble sire—for me he'd be
Only a scoundrel of the deepest dye,
Whom for such villainy I'd gladly see
Upon the gallows, hanging by four nails.

Don Salluste. Cæsar!——

Don Cæsar. Add not a word, outrageous 'tis.

(*He throws the purse at the feet of* Don Salluste.)

There—keep your secret and your money too.
Ah, I can comprehend a theft, a stroke
That's murderous, or in darkness of the night
The forcing of prison doors—hatchet in hand
And with a hundred desperate buccaneers,
With howl and thrust, to slaughter jailers there,
Claiming, we bandits, for an eye an eye,
And tooth for tooth—men against men.
That's well.
But stealthily a woman to destroy,
And dig a trap beneath her feet—perchance
Abuse her, for who knows what chance may be?—
To take this poor bird in some hideous snare—
Oh, rather than accomplish such dishonour,
And be at such a price, my noble Lord,
So rich and great—I say before my God,
Who sees my soul, much sooner would I choose—
Than reach such odious infamy—that dogs
Should gnaw my bones beneath the pillory.

Don Salluste. Cousin——

Don Cæsar. Your benefits I shall not need,
So long as I shall find in my free life
Fountains of water—in the fields fresh air,
And in the town a thief who me provides
With winter raiment; in my soul shall be
Forgetfulness of past prosperity,
When, Sir, before your palace's great doors,
At noon I lay me down, my head in shade
And feet in sunshine, without thought for what
May be on waking. So adieu;—'tis God
Can judge between us. Now, Don Salluste, you
I leave with people of the Court, who are
Of your own sort; I with the scamps will stay.

I herd with wolves, but not with serpents.

DON SALLUSTE. Hold
An instant——
DON CÆSAR. Now, my master, cease.
Let us
Cut short this visit; if 'twas meant to trap
And send me off to prison—do it quick.

DON SALLUSTE. I thought you, Cæsar, much more hardened. Ah,
My trial of you has succeeded well.
I now am satisfied. Your hand, I pray.

DON CÆSAR. How—what?

DON SALLUSTE. 'Twas but in jest I spoke to you.
All that I said just now was but a test,
And nothing more.

DON CÆSAR. You've set me dreaming, though,
About a woman, vengeance, and a plot——

DON SALLUSTE. A trap—imagination, that was all.

DON CÆSAR. Ah, well and good!—
But how about my debts?
Is paying them imagination, too?
And the five hundred ducats promised me?

DON SALLUSTE. I'm going now to fetch them.

(*He goes towards the door at the back, and makes a sign to* RUY BLAS *to come in.*)

DON CÆSAR (*aside, at the front, and looking across to* DON SALLUSTE).
Hum! The face
A traitor's is. And when the mouth says yes,
The look implies, perhaps.

DON SALLUSTE (*to* RUY BLAS). Ruy Blas, stay here.

(*To* DON CÆSAR.) I'm coming back.
(*Exit by little door at left. As soon as he is gone,* DON CÆSAR *and* RUY BLAS *approach each other eagerly.*)

SCENE 3.—DON CÆSAR—RUY BLAS.

DON CÆSAR. No, I was not deceived;
Upon my faith, 'tis thou, Ruy Blas!

RUY BLAS. 'Tis thou,
Zafari! But how comest thou within
The palace?

DON CÆSAR. Oh, by chance. But soon I take
Myself away. I am a bird, and like
Free space. But thou? this livery? is it worn
For a disguise?

RUY BLAS (*bitterly*). No, I'm disguised when I
Am otherwise.

DON CÆSAR. What is it that you say?

RUY BLAS. Give me thy hand to press again, as in
The happy time of joy and wretchedness.
When without home I lived, hungry by day
And cold at night, when I at least was free!
Then when thou knew'st me, I was still a man;
Born of the people both of us—alas!
It was life's morn!—So much alike we were
That many thought us brothers, and from dawn
Of day we caroll'd—and at night we slept
Before our God, our Father and our Host,

Beneath starr'd heaven sleeping side by side.
Yes, we shared all things—but at last there came
The day—the mournful hour when we were forced
To go our different ways, but now unchanged,
After four years I find thee still the same;
As joyous as a child, and free as are
The gipsy folk. Always Zafari, rich
Though poor, who never had, and never aught
Desired! But as for me, what change! What can
I say, my brother? Orphan boy, brought up
From charity at College! nursed in pride
And science, it but proved a mournful boon.
Instead of skilful workman I was made
A dreamer. Thou hast known me well. My thoughts
And aspirations lifted I to heav'n
In strophes wild. Against thy railing laugh
I brought a hundred answers. Knowing then
That strange ambition fired my soul, what need
Had I to work? But towards an end unseen
I moved; I thought dreams true and possible,
And hoped all things from fate.—And since I am
Of those who pass long, idle days in thought
Before some palace gorged with wealth —and watch
The Duchesses go in and out—one day,
When torn by hunger in the street, I picked
Up bread where I could find it;—brother, 'twas
By ignominious sluggishness. Oh, when
I was but twenty, full of confidence
In my own powers, I barefoot walked, but lost
In meditations on humanity;
I built up many plans, a mountain made
Of projects. Pitying the ills of Spain
I thought, poor soul, that by the world myself
Was needed. Friend, the issue see—behold,
I am a lackey!

Don Cæsar. Yes, I know full well
That want is a low door, which, when we must
By stern necessity pass through, doth force
The greatest to bend down the most. But fate
Has ever ebb and flow. So hope, I say.

Ruy Blas (*shaking his head*). My master is the Marquis of Finlas.

Don Cæsar. I know him. Is it, then, that you reside
Within this palace?

Ruy Blas. No! until to-day,
Just now, I never have the threshold cross'd.

Don Cæsar. Ah, is it so? Your master from his place,
His duties, must live here himself?

Ruy Blas. Oh yes,
The Court may want him any hour. But he
A little secret dwelling has—where perhaps
In daylight he has never yet been seen.

An unobtrusive house, a hundred steps
Beyond the palace; brother, there I live;
And by the secret door, of which alone
He has the key, sometimes at night he comes
Followed by men whom he lets in. These men
Are masked and speak in whispering tones. They are
Shut in together, and none ever knows
What passes then. Of two black mutes I am
The master and companion. But my name
They know not.

Don Cæsar. Yes, 'tis there that he receives
His spies, as Chief of the Alcaids. 'Tis there
He plans his many snares. Subtle is he,
And holds all in his hand.

Ruy Blas. 'Twas yesterday
He said "you must be at the palace ere
The dawn; and enter by the golden grill."
I came, and then he made me don this suit,
This odious livery which you see me in,
And which to-day I for the first time wear.

Don Cæsar. Still hope!

Ruy Blas. I hope! But you know nothing yet.
To breathe 'neath this degrading garb, to lose
The joy and pride of life—all this is naught.
To be a slave and vile, what matters that!
But listen, brother, well. I do not feel
This servile dress, for at my heart there dwells
A hydra, with the fangs of flame, that binds
Me in its fiery folds. If the outside
Has shocked you—what would be could you but look
Within?

Don Cæsar. What can you mean?

Ruy Blas. Invent—suppose—
Imagine—search your mind for all strange things
Unheard of, mad, and horrible—a fate
Bewildering! Yes, compose a deadly draught,
And dig a pit more black than crime, more dull
Than folly, still my secret thou wilt not
Approach. Thou canst not guess it!
Ah, who could,
Zafari? In the gulf where destiny
Has plunged me—plunge thine eyes! I love the queen!

Don Cæsar. Good heavens!

Ruy Blas. Beneath a splendid canopy,
Adorned at top with the Imperial globe
There is in Aranjuez, or may be
In the Escurial—or sometimes here—
A man that scarce is looked on from below,
Or named, except with dread—before whose eyes
We all of equal meanness seem, as if
That he were God. A man that men gaze on
With trembling, serving him on bended knee.
To in his presence stand with cover'd head
Is token of high honour. If he will'd

Our heads should fall, a sign would be enough.
His every whim is an event. He lives
Alone—superb—encased in majesty,
So bulwark'd and profound, its weight is felt
Through half the world. Well, now thou understand'st
That I the lackey—ah, yes even I
Am jealous of that man—yes, of the king!

Don Cæsar. You jealous of the king!

Ruy Blas. Undoubtedly,
Because I love his wife!

Don Cæsar. Unhappy one!

Ruy Blas. Listen: each day I watch to see her pass,
And like a madman am. And oh, the life
Of this poor thing is one long weariness.
Each night I dream of her. Oh, think what 'tis
For her to live in this dull court of hate,
And base hypocrisies,—married to one
Who in the chase spends all his time!
A king—
A fool—an imbecile! at thirty years
Already old—and less than man—unfit
Alike to live or reign. And of a race
That's dying off. His father could not hold
A parchment, so debilitated he!
What misery for her, so young and fair,
Thus to be wedded to the second Charles!
Unto the sisters of the Rosary
She goes each eve—thou know'st it—traversing
The Ortaleza street,—I cannot tell
How 'twas this madness grew within my heart,
But judge! She loves a little azure flower
Of Germany—I go each day a league
To Caramanchel, where alone I find
It grows. I have sought for it everywhere.
I pluck the finest, and a posy make.
Oh, but I tell you now these foolish things!—
At midnight like a thief I scale the wall
Around the royal park, and place the flowers
Upon her favourite bench. Even last night
I dared to put a letter 'mid the flowers—
Truly a letter! Brother, pity me!
At night to reach this bank I have to mount
The wall where bristle iron spikes. I know
Some time that I shall leave my flesh thereon.
Now will she find my flowers—my letter too?
I know not—but you see how mad I am.

Don Cæsar. It is the devil! Now take care—thy game
Is dang'rous. There's the Count Oñate, he loves
Her also, and keeps guard as Chamberlain
As well as lover. On some night a trooper
Unpitying might despatch you with one blow,
Before your flowers were faded nailing them
Unto your heart. Oh th' idea. I say,

Is quite preposterous—loving thus the queen!
And why? It is a devil's scrape you're in.
RUY BLAS (*with energy*). Do I not know it! I myself! My soul
Is given over, I would sell it might
I thus become like one of those young Lords
That from this window I behold—who are
A live offence, entering with plumèd hats
And haughty brows. Yes, if I could but break
My chain, and could, as they, approach the queen
In garments not degrading. But—oh! rage,
To thus appear to her, and unto them!
To be for her a lackey! pity me,
Oh God!
(*Approaching* DON CÆSAR.)
But I must recollect myself.
Ask'st thou not when and why I loved her thus?
One day—but what's the good of this?
'Tis true
My desperate madness I've made known to thee
And all my thousand tortures made you share,
In showing you my agony—but ask
Not how—or wherefore! only I love her—
Insanely love her, that is all.
DON CÆSAR. There now, Don't fret.
RUY BLAS (*pale and overcome, falling into the arm-chair*). No—no—I suffer—pardon me,
Or rather fly from me, my brother. Go
And leave the wretched madman who but knows

With horror that beneath the lackey's coat
There rage the passions of a king!
DON CÆSAR (*laying his hand on the shoulder of* RUY BLAS). Leave thee!
What, I! who have not suffr'd thus because
I have not loved. Like a poor bell am I
Without a clapper—beggar who e'en begs
For love he knows not where. To whom from time
To time fate throws some paltry coin.
With heart
Extinguished—drawn within itself, as from
The tatter'd play-bill of the yester night.
Seest thou that for this all absorbing love
I envy quite as much as pity thee!
Oh, Ruy Blas!
(*A moment of silence, while with clasped hands they look at each other sorrowfully but with confiding friendship.*
Enter DON SALLUSTE. *He advances softly, looking at* DON CÆSAR *and* RUY BLAS *with profound attention, they not perceiving him. In one hand he holds a hat and a sword, which on entering he places on an arm-chair, and in the other a purse which he lays on the table.*)
DON SALLUSTE (*to* DON CÆSAR). Here is the money.
(*At the voice of* DON SALLUSTE, RUY BLAS, *suddenly aroused, starts up, and with eyes looking down, assumes an attitude of respect.*)
DON CÆSAR (*aside, and looking sideways at* DON SALLUSTE). Ah,

The devil has me! At the door no doubt
The artful one has listened. After all
What matter—Pshaw! (*aloud to* Don Salluste). Don Salluste, thanks.

(*He opens the purse—spreads the money on the table, handling the ducats delightedly. Then he arranges them in two piles on the velvet cover. While he is counting them* Don Salluste *goes to the back, looking behind him to be sure that* Don Cæsar *is not observing him. He opens the little door at the right. At a sign from him three Alguazils, armed with swords and dressed in black, appear.* Don Salluste *points out* Don Cæsar *to them in a mysterious manner.* Ruy Blas *stands upright and motionless as a statue by the table, neither seeing nor hearing anything.*)

Don Salluste (*in a low tone to the Alguazils*). You see
That man who counts the money—follow him
When he goes hence, and seize him silently,
And without violence. And then embark
By shortest way to Denia.
(*He gives them a sealed parchment.*)
Here is writ
The order by my hand. And afterwards,
Without attending to his statements, all
Chimerical, you'll sell him on the sea
To corsairs there will be from Africa,
A thousand piastres for you—but be quick.
(*The three* Alguazils *bow and exeunt.*)

Don Cæsar (*finishing the arrangement of his ducats*).
Surely there's nothing more amusing than
To equally divide the crowns that are One's own.
(*He makes two equal piles, and turns to* Ruy Blas.)
Here, brother, is thy share

Ruy Blas. How—what!

Don Cæsar (*pointing to one of the heaps of gold*). Come—take, be free!

Don Salluste (*aside, looking at them from the back*). The devil!

Ruy Blas (*shaking his head in sign of refusal*). No—the heart
It is that has to be delivered. No,
My lot is here. I must remain.

Don Cæsar. Well—well
Have thine own way. Art thou the crazy one?
And am I wise? God knows.
(*He gathers the money into the bag and puts it in his pocket.*)

Don Salluste (*from the back, watching them*). How near alike
They are in mien and face!

Don Cæsar (*to* Ruy Blas). Adieu!

Ruy Blas. Thy hand!
(*They press hands. Exit* Don Cæsar *without noticing* Don Salluste, *who has kept himself apart.*)

Scene 4.—Ruy Blas. Don Salluste

Don Salluste. Ruy Blas!

Ruy Blas (*turning quickly*). My lord?

Don Salluste. I am not confident
Whether 'twas fully daylight when you came
This morning—tell me.

Ruy Blas. Excellency, no,
Not quite. I gave your pass without a word
To the door-keeper, then came up.

Don Salluste. Wore you
a cloak?
Ruy Blas. I did, my Lord.
Don Salluste. In that case then
None in the Castle yet has seen on you
This livery?
Ruy Blas. Nor person of Madrid.
Don Salluste (*pointing to the door by which* Don Cæsar *had gone out*). That's well. Go, close the door. Take off this coat.
(Ruy Blas *takes off his livery-coat and throws it on a chair.*)
I think your writing's good. Write now for me.
(*He makes a sign to* Ruy Blas *to seat himself at the table where there are writing materials.* Ruy Blas *obeys.*)
My secretary you must be to-day,
And first a love-letter must write; you see
I nothing hide from you—my queen of love
Is Doña Praxedis —witch that's come,
I think, from paradise. There—I'll dictate.
"A danger terrible environs me;
My queen alone can stay the tempest's force
By coming to my house this night. If not,
I'm lost. My life, my heart, my reason now
I lay before the feet I kiss."
(*He laughs, interrupting himself.*)
Danger,
A turn well put to draw her on. I am
Expert. Women like much to save just those
Who fool them most. And now, "Come to the door
That's at the end of the Avenue—at night

You'll not be recognised. And one who is
Devoted will be there to ope the door."
'Tis perfect, on my word.—Sign now.
Ruy Blas. Your name, My Lord?
Don Salluste. Not so—sign Cæsar.
'Tis the name
In such adventures I adopt.
Ruy Blas (*after having obeyed*). Unknown
Will be the writing to the lady?
Don Salluste. Pshaw!
The seal will be enough. Oft thus I write.
I go away at night-fall, Ruy Blas,
And leave you here. I'm planning for you as
A friend sincere. Your state shall change, but then
You must obey me in all things. In you
I've found a servant faithful and discreet.
Ruy Blas (*bowing*). My Lord!
Don Salluste. To better your condition here
I wish.
Ruy Blas (*showing the letter he has just written*). How should the letter be addressed?
Don Salluste. I will attend to that. (*Approaching* Ruy Blas *in a significant manner.*) I wish your good.
(*Silence for a few moments. Then he makes a sign for* Ruy Blas *to seat himself again at the table.*)
Write thus. "I, Ruy Blas, the serving man
Of the most noble Lord the Marquis of Finlas, engage to serve him faithfully
On all occasions as a servant true

In public or in secrecy." (RUY BLAS *obeys*.)
Now sign
Your name. The date. That's well. Give it to me.
(*He folds and puts into his portfolio the letter and the paper which* RUY BLAS *has just written*.)
Just now they brought me in a sword.—
Ah, there
It is upon the chair.
(*He looks towards the arm-chair on which he had placed the sword and hat —goes to it and takes up the sword*.)
The tie's of silk,
Painted and 'broidered in the newest style—
(*He makes* RUY BLAS *admire it*.)
Take it. What say you to this foil, Ruy Blas?
The hilt is workmanship of Gil the famed
Engraver, he who chisels out a box
For sweetmeats in a sword's hilt, to amuse
The pretty girls.
(*He passes the scarf to which the sword is attached over the shoulder of* RUY BLAS.)
Now put it on—I want
To see the effect on you. I do declare
You look a noble every inch. (*Listening*.)
They come—
Ah yes, 't is almost time the queen were here—
The Marquis Basto!—

(*The door at the end of the corridor opens.* DON SALLUSTE *unfastens his cloak and hastily throws it over the shoulders of* RUY BLAS, *just at the moment when the* MARQUIS DEL BASTO *appears; then he goes up to the* MARQUIS, *drawing after him* RUY BLAS *in a stupefied state*.)

SCENE 5.—DON SALLUSTE, RUY BLAS, DON PAMFILO D'AVALOS, MARQUIS DEL BASTO,—*afterwards the* MARQUIS DE SANTA-CRUZ, *then the* COUNT D'ALBE *and all the Court*.

DON SALLUSTE (*to the* MARQUIS DEL BASTO). Let me to your grace
Present my cousin—the Don Cæsar—Count
Of Garofa, near to Velalcazar.
RUY BLAS (*aside*). Oh heav'ns!
DON SALLUSTE (*aside to* RUY BLAS). Silence!
MARQUIS DEL BASTO (*to* RUY BLAS). Sir, I am charm'd——
(*He puts out his hand, which* RUY BLAS *takes in a confused manner*.)
DON SALLUSTE (*in a whisper to* RUY BLAS). Let be—
Salute him.
(RUY BLAS *bows to the* MARQUIS.)
MARQUIS DEL BASTO (*to* RUY BLAS). Ah, I loved your mother much.
(*Aside to* DON SALLUSTE.)
How changed! I scarcely would have known him.
DON SALLUSTE (*speaking lower to the* MARQUIS). Ah!
Ten years away!
MARQUIS DEL BASTO (*in the same manner*). Indeed!
DON SALLUSTE (*slapping* RUY BLAS *on the shoulder*). At last come back!
You recollect the prodigal he was?
And how he squander'd the pistoles? Each night
A dance or fête—a hundred instruments
Of music on Apollo's fish-pond raged.

Concerts and masquerades, and wildest pranks
Dazzled Madrid with sudden scenes. Ruin'd
In just three years! Truly a lion he.—
He came from India in the galleon.

RUY BLAS (*confused*). My Lord——

DON SALLUSTE (*gaily*). Oh, call me cousin—such we are.
We, the Bazans, are an old family,
Our ancestor was Iniguez d'Iviza;
His grandson, Pedro de Bazan, was wed
To Marianne de Gor. Their son was Jean;
Under King Philip he was admiral.
Jean had two sons, who on our ancient tree
Grafted two stocks for blazonry: I am
The Marquis of Finlas, and you the Count
Of Garofa, each equal in degree.
And by the women, Cæsar, 'tis the same.
'Tis Aragon you claim, I Portugal.
Your branch as lofty is as ours. I am
The fruit of one, and of the other you
The offspring are.

RUY BLAS (*aside*). Where is he dragging me?

(*Whilst* DON SALLUSTE *was speaking, the* MARQUIS DE SANTA-CRUZ, DON ALVAR DE BAZAN Y BENAVIDES, *an old man with a white moustache and a thick wig was approaching them.*)

MARQUIS DE SANTA-CRUZ (*to* DON SALLUSTE). You make it clear. If he your cousin is
Mine is he too.

DON SALLUSTE. True, Marquis—for we come
Of the same stock.

(*He presents* RUY BLAS *to the* MARQUIS DE SANTA-CRUZ.) Don Cæsar.

MARQUIS DE SANTA-CRUZ. I opine
It is he whom we thought dead?

DON SALLUSTE. It is.

MARQUIS DE SANTA-CRUZ. He has come back then?

DON SALLUSTE. From the Indies.

MARQUIS DE SANTA-CRUZ (*looking at* RUY BLAS). Ah,
Indeed!

DON SALLUSTE. You then remember him?

MARQUIS DE SANTA-CRUZ. By Heav'ns,
I recollect his birth.

DON SALLUSTE (*aside to* RUY BLAS). Half blind he is—
The good man will not own it. 'Tis to prove
His eyes are good he recognizes you.

MARQUIS DE SANTA-CRUZ (*extending his hand to* RUY BLAS). Your hand, my cousin.

RUY BLAS (*bowing*). My Lord——

MARQUIS DE SANTA-CRUZ (*in a low tone to* DON SALLUSTE, *and pointing to* RUY BLAS). He could not look
Better. (*To* RUY BLAS.) Charmed again to see you.

DON SALLUSTE (*in a low tone and taking the* MARQUIS *aside*). His debts
I mean to pay. I think you can serve him,
In your position, if some place at court
Should vacant be—about the king or queen——

MARQUIS DE SANTA-CRUZ (*in a low tone*). A charming youth he is; I will not fail
To think of it; for he a kinsman is.

DON SALLUSTE. At the Castilian council board I know
You're powerful, I recommend him to you.

(*He quits the* MARQUIS DE SANTA-CRUZ, *and goes to other nobles to whom he presents* RUY BLAS. *Among them is the* COUNT D'ALBE *very superbly dressed,* DON SALLUSTE *introduces* RUY BLAS *to him.*)
My cousin, Cæsar, Count of Garofa, Near to Velalcazar.
(*The nobles gravely exchange bows with* RUY BLAS, *who is abashed.* DON SALLUSTE *to the* COUNT DE RIBAGORZA.)
You missed last night
The Atalanta ballet? Lindamire
Did dance divinely.
(*He goes into ecstasies at the doublet of the* COUNT D'ALBE.)
Count, this is splendid!
COUNT D'ALBE. Ah, I had one was richer—rose-coloured
Satin with golden braid. Matalobos
Stole it.
AN USHER *of the* COURT (*from the back*). The Queen is coming. Gentlemen,
Arrange yourselves.
(*The large curtains at the glazed side of the corridor open. The nobles fall into line near the door. The guards line a passage.* RUY BLAS, *breathless and beside himself, comes to the front as if to take refuge there.* DON SALLUSTE *follows him.*)
DON SALLUSTE (*in a low voice to* RUY BLAS). Are you not 'shamed that with
Expanding fortunes, thus your heart should shrink?
Awake. I quit Madrid. My little house
Near the bridge, where you reside, I leave
For you to use, nothing reserving save
The secret keys. I leave the mutes with you.
Some other orders you will soon receive.
Obey, and I will make your fortune.
Rise,
Fear nothing, for the time is opportune.
The Court's a territory where one moves
With little light. Walk you with bandaged eyes.
I'll see for you, my man!
USHER (*in a loud voice*). The Queen!
RUY BLAS. Queen! oh!
(*The* QUEEN *appears magnificently attired and surrounded by ladies and pages, and under a canopy of scarlet velvet supported by four gentlemen of the chamber bareheaded.* RUY BLAS, *bewildered, gazes as if absorbed by this resplendent vision. All the* Grandees *of* Spain *cover, the* MARQUIS DEL BASTO, *the* COUNT D'ALBE, *the* MARQUIS DE SANTA-CRUZ, DON SALLUSTE. DON SALLUSTE *moves rapidly to the arm-chair, takes from it the hat, which he carries to* RUY BLAS *and puts on his head.*)
DON SALLUSTE. What giddiness has seized you? Cover now,
Cæsar, you are grandee of Spain.
RUY BLAS (*absent, low to* DON SALLUSTE). And next,
My lord, what is 't you order me to do?
DON SALLUSTE (*indicating the* QUEEN, *who is slowly passing along the corridor*). To please that woman, and her lover be.

ACT SECOND:

THE QUEEN OF SPAIN.

A saloon next to the Queen's bedchamber. At the left a little door opening into that room. At the right, in an angle of the wall, another door opening to the external apartments. At the back large open windows. It is the afternoon of a fine day in summer. The face of a saint richly enshrined is against the wall; beneath it is read, "Holy Mary in Slavery." On the opposite side is a Madonna, before which a golden lamp is burning. Near to the Madonna is a full length portrait of Charles the Second.

At the rising of the curtain the QUEEN DOÑA MARIA OF NEUBOURG *is in one corner seated beside one of her ladies, a young and pretty girl. The* QUEEN *is in a white dress of cloth of silver. She is embroidering, but interrupts herself from time to time to chat. In the opposite corner is seated, in a highbacked chair, the* DOÑA JUANA DE LA CUEVA, DUCHESS D'ALBUQUERQUE, *first lady of the Chamber, with tapestry in her hand, an old woman in black. Near to the* DUCHESS *a table where several ladies are engaged in feminine work. At the back stands* DON GURITAN COUNT D'OÑATE, *the Chamberlain, a tall thin man of about fifty-five years of age, with grey moustache, looking the old soldier though dressed with exaggerated elegance, wearing ribbons down to his shoes.*

SCENE 1.—THE QUEEN, THE DUCHESS D'ALBUQUERQUE, DON GURITAN, CASILDA, DUENNAS.

THE QUEEN. He's gone, however!
And I ought to be
At ease. Ah well, I am not, though!
this man,
The Marquis of Finlas, weighs on my soul,
He hates me so.

CASILDA. According to your wish
Is he not exiled?

THE QUEEN. That man hates me.

CASILDA. Oh,
Your majesty——

THE QUEEN. 'Tis true, Casilda.
Strange
This man for me is like an angel bad.
One day—'twas on the morrow he must leave—
He came as usual to kiss hands. The rest,
All the grandees, approach'd the throne in file;
I gave my hand—was sorrowful, and still,
Observing vaguely in the hall's dim light
A battle picture painted on the wall,
When, suddenly, it was, my eyes looked down
Near to the table and perceived this man,
So dreaded, was advancing unto me.
Soon as I saw him nothing more I saw.
Slowly he moved, and fingered all the while
His poignard's sheath, so that at times the blade
I saw. Grave was he, yet he dazzled me

With looks of flame. Sudden he bent, and like
A creeping thing——and then upon my hand
I felt his serpent-mouth!
    CASILDA. He render'd you
His homage;—do not we the same?
    THE QUEEN. His lips
Were not like other lips. 'Twas the last time
I saw him. Often since I've thought of him.
'Tis true that I have other troubles, yet
I tell myself that hell is in that soul.
Only a woman am I to that man.
In dreams of night I meet again this fiend,
And feel his frightful kiss upon my hand;
I see his eyes shine out with hatred's glare;
And as a deadly poison runs from vein
To vein, so e'en within my freezing heart
I feel the shudder of that icy kiss!
What sayest thou to this?
    CASILDA. Madam, they are
But phantoms!
    THE QUEEN. Ah, indeed—sorrows I know
That are more real. (*Aside.*) Oh, but I must hide
That which torments me. (*To* CASILDA.) Those poor mendicants
Who dare not to approach—tell me—
    CASILDA (*going to the window*). Madam,
I know. They still are in the square.
    THE QUEEN. Here then,
Throw them my purse.

(CASILDA *takes the purse and throws it from the window.*)
    CASILDA. Oh, Madam, you who give
Your alms so sweetly,
    (*Pointing to* DON GURITAN *who, standing erect and silent at the back of the stage, looks at the* QUEEN *with an expression of mute adoration.*)
Will you nothing throw
In pity to the Count Oñate—a word,
Only a word. A brave old man is he,
With love beneath his armour, and a heart
More soft than hard the rind!
    THE QUEEN. So tiresome he!
    CASILDA. I know it. Yet I pray you speak to him.
    THE QUEEN (*turning towards* DON GURITAN). Good day unto you, Count.
    (DON GURITAN, *making three bows, approaches the* QUEEN, *sighing, to kiss her hand, which with an indifferent and absent manner she allows him to do. Afterwards he returns to his place beside the chair of the* DUCHESS.)
    DON GURITAN (*in retiring to* CASILDA). How charming is
The Queen to-day!
    CASILDA (*looking at him retreating*).
Oh! the poor heron! near
The stream that tempts, he stays. After a day
Of quiet waiting, he but snatches up
A "good day" or "good night," often a dry
Cold word, and goes away delighted with
This little morsel in his beak.
    THE QUEEN (*with a sorrowful smile*). Be still!
    CASILDA. He only needs for happiness to see

The Queen. To see you means delight for him!
(*Looking with ecstasy at a box on a round table.*)
Oh, what a lovely box!
The Queen. I have the key.
Casilda. This box of calambac is exquisite.
The Queen (*giving her the key*). Now open it and see. I've had it fill'd, My dear, with relics, and 'tis my intent To send it on to Neubourg—well I know My father will be greatly pleased with it.
(*She muses for a moment. Then suddenly forces herself out of the reverie.*)
I will not think! That which is in my mind
I wish to drive from it. (*To* Casilda.) Go to my room
And fetch me thence a book.—— What foolishness!
I don't possess a German book! they all Are Spanish! And the king is at the chase;
Always away. What weariness! Near him,
In six months, I have only pass'd twelve days.
Casilda. Who'd wed a king if she must live this way!
(*The* Queen *again falls into reverie—and again rouses herself by a violent effort.*)
The Queen. I wish to go out now.
(*At these words, pronounced imperiously by the* Queen, *the* Duchess d'Albuquerque, *who till this moment had remained motionless in her chair, lifts up her head, then rising makes a low curtsey to the* Queen.)
Duchess d'Albuquerque (*in a hard, curt manner*). It needs before

The Queen goes out—it is the rule—that all
The doors should opened be by some grandee
Of Spain who has the right to bear the keys;
Now at this hour not one of them remains
Within the palace.
The Queen. Then you shut me up! Duchess, in short, they wish that I should die!
The Duchess (*with another curtsey*). I am duenna of the chamber, so I must fulfil my duty (*reseats herself*).
The Queen (*lifting her hands to her head despairingly, aside*). Well, then, now
To dream again! But no! (*Aloud.*) Ladies, be quick!
A table—let us play at lansquenet!
The Duchess (*to the ladies*). Ladies, stir not (*rising and curtseying to the* Queen). Your
Majesty cannot,
According to the ancient laws, play cards,
Except with kings or with their relatives.
The Queen (*with an air of command*). Well, then, go bring to me these relatives.
Casilda (*looking at the* Duchess). Oh this duenna!
The Duchess (*making the sign of the Cross*). To the King who reigns God has not given, Madam, any kin. The Queen his mother's dead. He's now alone.
The Queen. Let them, then, serve me a collation.
Casilda. Yes,
That were amusing.

THE QUEEN. I invite you now
To it, Casilda.
　　CASILDA (*aside, looking at the*
DUCHESS). Oh, you proper—prim
Old grandmother!
　　THE DUCHESS (*making a reverence*).
When absent is the King,
The Queen eats quite alone (*re-seats
herself*).
　　THE QUEEN (*her patience at an end*).
Oh God! what is 't
That I can do? Not take fresh air,
nor play
A game, nor even eat at mine own will!
Most truly I've been dying all the year
That I've been Queen.
　　CASILDA (*aside, looking at her with
compassion*). Oh the poor woman! thus
To pass her days in weariness in this
Insipid Court! with no distraction, save
To see at border of this sleepy swamp
(*looking at* DON GURITAN)
An old, but love-sick Count, that stands
upon
One leg to dream.
　　THE QUEEN (*to* CASILDA). Think
now of something; say,
What shall we do?
　　CASILDA. Ah, hold! The King away,
'Tis you who rule. Just for amusement's sake
Summon the Ministers.
　　THE QUEEN (*shrugging her shoulders*). A pleasure that!
To see eight gloomy countenances
ranged
For talk with me concerning France,
and its
Declining king, of Rome,—they'd also
tell
About the portrait of the Archduke
which

They bear about at Burgos, 'mid the
show
Of cavalcades, beneath a canopy
Of cloth of gold upheld by four Alcaids!
Oh, think of something else!
　　CASILDA. Well, now, 'twould be
Amusing if some youthful equerry
I made come up.
　　THE QUEEN. Casilda!
　　CASILDA. Oh, I want
So much to look at some young man.
Madam,
This venerable Count is death to me.
I think that through the eyes old age
comes on,
That we, by always looking at the old,
Ourselves age all the sooner.
　　THE QUEEN. Foolishness!
There comes a time the heart asserts
itself.
As it wakes up from sleep, it loses joy.
(*Thoughtfully.*)
My only happiness—ah, that is in
The corner of the park, where I'm
allowed
To go alone.
　　CASILDA. Fine happiness, indeed!
A charming place! where snares are set
behind
The marble forms—and where one
nothing views.
The walls around are higher than the
trees.
　　THE QUEEN. Oh, how I wish I could
go out sometimes!
　　CASILDA (*in a low voice*). Go out?
Well, Madam, listen. Let us, though,
Speak softly. In such a prison's gloomy
shade
Nought is there so worth search and
finding as

One precious sparkling jewel that is called
The key o' the fields. I have it! And whene'er
You wish, in spite of foes, I'll let you out
At night, and through the town we both can go.

THE QUEEN. Heavens! never! Silence!

CASILDA. 'Tis quite easy.

THE QUEEN. Peace!

(*She draws a little away from* CASILDA, *and falls into reverie.*)

Oh would that I, who fear the grandees here,
Were still in my good Germany, beside
My parents, as when with my sister dear
I rambled freely through the fields; and when
We met the peasants trailing their rich sheaves,
We talked to them. 'Twas charming. But alas!
One night a man arrived who said—and he
Was dressed in black, I holding by the hand
My sister, sweet companion—"Madam, you
Are to be Queen of Spain."—My father was
All joyous, but my mother wept. Now they
Both weep.—I mean to send in secret soon
This box unto my father, he'll be pleased.
See you how everything disheartens me.
My birds from Germany all died.

(CASILDA *looks across to the* DUCHESS, *and makes a sign of wringing the birds' necks.*)

And then
They would not let me have the flowers that grew
In mine own country. Never on mine ear
Doth vibrate now a word of love. A Queen
I am to-day. But formerly I knew
What freedom was. Truly thou say'st this park
At eve is dreary—with its walls so high,
One cannot see beyond.—Oh weariness!

(*Singing afar off is heard.*)

What is that sound?

CASILDA. The laundrywomen, they
Are singing, as they pass the heather through.

(*The singers approach. The words are heard. The* QUEEN *listens eagerly.*)

SONG FROM OUTSIDE.

Why should we listen
 To birds that rejoice?
The bird the most tender
 Sings now in thy voice.

Let God show or veil
 The stars in the skies,
The purest of stars
 Shines now in thine eyes.

Let April renew
 All the blossoms around,
The loveliest flower
 In thy heart will be found.

The passionate bird song.
 The day star above,
And the flower of the soul
 But call themselves love!

THE QUEEN (*musing*). Love—love!
Ah, they are happy! And their song,
Their voices, do me harm as well as
good.
THE DUCHESS (*to the ladies*). These
women with their song annoy the Queen.
Drive them away!
THE QUEEN (*eagerly*). How, Madam! scarcely can
I hear them; 'tis my will that they, poor
things,
Should pass in peace.
(*To* CASILDA, *pointing to a casement
at the back.*)
The trees are here less thick,
This window opens to the country;
come
Let us now try to look at them.
(*She goes towards the window with*
CASILDA.)
THE DUCHESS (*rising and curtseying*). Spain's Queen
Must not look out of window.
THE QUEEN (*stopping and retracing
her steps*). Oh, what next!
The lovely sunset filling all the vales,
The golden dust of evening rising o'er
The way, the far-off songs to which all
ears
May listen,—these for me exist no more,
Unto the world I've said adieu. Not
e'en
May I regard the nature made by God!
E'en others' freedom I may not behold!
THE DUCHESS (*making signs to the
assistants to leave*). Go now. To day
is sacred to the Saints,
Th' Apostles.
(CASILDA *goes towards the door. The*
QUEEN *stops her.*)
THE QUEEN. What! You leave me?

CASILDA (*pointing to the* DUCHESS).
Madam, we
Are ordered out.
THE DUCHESS (*curtseying to the
ground*). 'Tis right that we the Queen
To her devotions leave.
(*All go out with profound reverence.*)

SCENE 2.

THE QUEEN (*alone*). To her devotions?
Say rather to her thoughts! How can
I flee
Now from them? All have left me, and
alone
I am, poor soul, without a torch to light
My dusky way! (*Musing.*) That bleeding hand whose print
Was on the wall! Oh God, and could
it be
That he was hurt? If so it was his fault.
Why would he climb the wall so high?
And all
To bring me flowers which they refuse
me here;
For such a little thing to venture thus!
Doubtless his wounds were from the
iron spikes—
A scrap of lace hung there. A drop
of blood
Shed for me claims my tears. (*Losing
herself in reverie.*) Each time I go
Unto to the bench, to seek the flowers,
I say
To God—whose help forsakes me—that
I will
No more return. And yet I still go
back.—
But he! Behold three days have pass'd
and he
Has not been there.—And wounded!—
Oh, young man,

Unknown, whoever thou may'st be, who thus
Dost see me lonely, and afar from them
Who cherish'd me, who without recompense,
Or even hope of aught, comes to me thus
'Mid perils never counted—thou who shed'st
Thy blood, and risk'st thy life to give a flower
Unto the Queen of Spain, whoever thou
May'st be—the friend whose shadow follows me—
Since unto law inflexible my heart
Submits, may'st thou be by thy mother loved,
And bless'd by me!
 (*Energetically, and pressing her hand on her heart.*)
But oh, his letter burns!
 (*Falling again into reverie.*)
And he that other! the implacable
Don Salluste! I by destiny am now
Afflicted and protected too. At once
An angel follows me, and spectre dread.
And without seeing them I feel a stir
Amid the gloom that is perchance about
Moments supreme to bring, in which a man
Who hates me will come near to him who loves.
Shall I by one be from the other saved?
I know not. Oh my fate seems but the sport
Of two opposing winds. To be a Queen
How weak and poor a thing! Ah, I will pray.
 (*She kneels before the Madonna.*)
Oh Blessèd Lady help me! For mine eyes

I dare not raise to look on you! (*She interrupts herself.*) Oh God!
The lace, the letter, and the flowers are fire!
 (*She puts her hand to her bosom and takes out a crumpled letter, some little dried blue flowers, and a morsel of lace stained with blood which she throws on the table; then she again kneels.*)
Oh Virgin, thou the star o' the sea! the hope
Of martyrs! help me now! (*Interrupting herself.*) That letter!
 (*Turns half round to the table.*)
Ah!
'Tis that distracts me. (*She kneels again.*) Not again I'll read
The letter. Queen of sweet compassion! you
Who wert bestowed on all afflicted souls
For sister! Come, I call you!
 (*She rises, advances towards the table, then pauses, but at last grasps the letter as if yielding to an irresistible impulse.*)
Yes, I will
Re-read it one last time, and after that
Destroy it. (*With a sad smile.*) For a month, alas! 'tis this
I've said!
 (*She unfolds the letter resolutely and reads.*)
"Madam, in dull obscurity
Beneath your feet, and hidden in the shade,
A man there is who loves you! he the worm
That suffers, loving thus a star; who would
For you give up his soul, if so must be;

And who lies depths below, while you must shine
On high."
(*She places the letter on the table.*)
When souls are thirsty they must drink,
Though it be poison!
(*She puts the letter and the lace in her bosom.*)
Nought on earth have I.
Ah, but I need some one to love. The King
I would have truly loved, had he so will'd it.
But me he leaves alone, of love bereft.
(*The great folding doors open. An* USHER *of the Chamber in full dress enters.*)
THE USHER (*in a loud voice*). A letter from the King!
THE QUEEN (*as if suddenly awakened, with a joyful cry*). From him! I'm saved!

SCENE 3.—THE QUEEN, THE DUCHESS D'ALBUQUERQUE, CASILDA, DON GURITAN, Ladies in Waiting, Pages, RUY BLAS.

All enter with solemnity, the DUCHESS *at their head, followed by the women.* RUY BLAS *remains at the back of the chamber. He is magnificently dressed. His cloak falls over his left arm and hides it. Two pages, carrying the* KING'S *letter on a cushion of cloth of gold, kneel before the* QUEEN *at a few paces distant.*
RUY BLAS (*at the back—aside*). Where am I now?—How beautiful she is!
Oh, for what purpose am I here?
THE QUEEN (*aside*). 'Tis aid

From heaven! (*Aloud.*) Give it me—be quick!
(*Turning to the portrait of the* KING.)
My thanks,
Your majesty! (*To the* DUCHESS.) Whence comes this letter, say?
THE DUCHESS. From Aranjuez, Madam, where the King
Now hunts.
THE QUEEN. And from my soul I thank him. He
Has understood my need of words of love
From him, in my lone weariness. Come then,
Now give it me.
THE DUCHESS (*curtseying and pointing to the letter*). I must inform you that
The custom is, that whatso'er it be
I first must open it and read.
THE QUEEN. Again!—
Ah well, then read.
(*The* DUCHESS *takes the letter and slowly unfolds it.*)
CASILDA. Let's hear the lines of love.
THE DUCHESS (*reading*). "Madam, the wind is high, and I have killed
Six wolves. Signed, Charles."
THE QUEEN (*aside*). Alas!
DON GURITAN (*to the* DUCHESS). And is that all?
THE DUCHESS. Yes, Count.
CASILDA (*aside*). Six wolves he's killed! How this excites
Th' imagination! Tender is your heart,
Exacting, weary, sick. Six wolves he's killed!
THE DUCHESS (*to the* QUEEN, *presenting the letter to her*). If that your Majesty?——

The Queen (*pushing it away*). Oh no.

Casilda (*to the* Duchess). And this Is really all?

The Duchess. Undoubtedly. What more
Should be? Our king is hunting; on the way
He writes declaring all he's killed, and states
The weather he has had. All this is well. (*Examining the letter again.*)
He writes—ah no, he dictates.

The Queen (*snatching the letter and examining it herself*). Then, in short, 'Tis not his hand, only his signature.
(*She examined it with more attention, and seems struck with stupor. Aside.*) Is it delusion? the hand writing's just
The same as that o' the letter!
(*She indicates with her hand the letter she has just hidden in her bossom.*)
Oh, what's this?
(*To the* Duchess.) Who, then, conveyed the letter?

The Duchess (*pointing to* Ruy Blas). He is there.

The Queen (*half turning towards* Ruy Blas). That young man?

The Duchess. 'Twas he himself who brought it.
He's a new equerry his Majesty
Has given to the Queen. A noble whom,
As from the King, my Lord of Santa Cruz
Has introduced to me.

The Queen. His name?

The Duchess. He is
The noble Cæsar de Bazan—the Count
Of Garofa. If rumour be believed
He is the most accomplish'd gentleman
That can be found.

The Queen. That's well. I'll speak to him.
(*To* Ruy Blas.) Sir——

Ruy Blas (*aside, trembling*). Ah, she sees—she speaks to me. Oh God! I tremble.

The Duchess (*to* Ruy Blas). Count, approach.

Don Guritan (*aside, and looking sideways at* Ruy Blas). I did not dream
Of this,—that young man! he an equerry!
(*Ruy Blas, pale and troubled, slowly advances.*)

The Queen. You come from Aranjuez?

Ruy Blas. Yes, Madam.

The Queen. The king is well?
(*Ruy Blas bows, she points to the royal letter.*) This letter was by him Dictated?

Ruy Blas. He on horseback was when he (*Hesitates a moment.*)
To one of his attendants did the lines Dictate.

The Queen (*aside, looking at* Ruy Blas). His looks so pierce me that I dare
Not ask to whom. (*Aloud.*) 'Tis well, you may depart.
Ah!—
(*Ruy Blas, who had stepped back a few paces, turns again towards the* Queen.) Many nobles were assembled there? (*Aside.*)
Why am I stirr'd on seeing this young man?
(*Ruy Blas bows, and she continues.*)
Who were they?

Ruy Blas. Names I do not know. I was

But there a few short moments, for Madrid
I quitted but three days ago.
  The Queen (*aside*). Three days!
  (*She looks at* Ruy Blas *with a troubled expression.*)
  Ruy Blas (*aside*). Another's wife! Oh frightful jealousy!
Of whom? A gulf has opened in my heart.
  Don Guritan (*approaching* Ruy Blas). You are an equerry unto the Queen.
One word with you. Know you your duty? You
To-night must in the next room stay to be
In readiness to open to the king
Should he arrive.
  Ruy Blas (*trembling, aside*). I open to the king! (*Aloud.*)
But—he is absent now.
  Don Guritan. Yet may he not, Though unexpectedly, return?
  Ruy Blas (*aside*). Ah—how!
  Don Guritan (*aside, observing* Ruy Blas). What ails him?
  The Queen (*who has heard all and is looking at* Ruy Blas). Oh, how pale he grows!
  (Ruy Blas, *tottering, leans his arm on a great chair.*)
  Casilda (*to the* Queen). Madam, This young man's ill!
  Ruy Blas (*supporting himself with difficulty*). I—I—oh, no! But strange
It is, how that—the sun—fresh air—the length
Of road—— (*Aside.*) To open to the King!
  (*He falls fainting on to the arm-chair. His cloak slips aside and shows his left hand to be bound up in blood-stained linen.*)
  Casilda. Great God,
He's wounded, Madam, in the hand!
  The Queen. A wound!
  Casilda. He's losing consciousness! Quick, make him breathe,
Some essence.
  The Queen (*feeling in her ruff*). Here's a flask of mine contains
An extract.
  (*At this moment her glance falls on the ruffle* Ruy Blas *wears on his right arm. ...Aside.*) 'Tis the self same lace!
  (*When she took the flask from her bosom, she in her trouble drew out the morsel of lace which was hidden there.* Ruy Blas, *whose eyes were fixed on her, saw and recognized it.*)
  Ruy Blas (*distracted*). Oh—oh!
  (*The eyes of the* Queen *and* Ruy Blas *meet. Silence.*)
  The Queen (*aside*). 'Tis he!
  Ruy Blas (*aside*). Upon her heart!
  The Queen (*aside*). 'Tis he!
  Ruy Blas (*aside*). Grant God
That now I die!
  (*In the confusion of the women pressing round* Ruy Blas, *no one had remarked what passed between the* Queen *and him.*)
  Casilda (*holding the flask for* Ruy Blas *to inhale from*). How were you injured, say?
Was it just now? Ah no! The wound I see
Must have re-opened on the way. And why,
How happened it, that you were made to bear
The message from the King?
  The Queen. I hope that soon You'll finish questioning.

THE DUCHESS (*to* CASILDA). What's this, my dear,
Unto the Queen?
THE QUEEN. Since it was he who wrote
The letter, it was well he brought it me,
Was it not so?
CASILDA. But he has never said
He wrote it.
THE QUEEN (*aside*). Oh! (*To* CASILDA.) Be still!
CASILDA (*to* RUY BLAS). How is your Grace?
Are you now better?
RUY BLAS. I am restored!
THE QUEEN (*to the Ladies*). 'Tis time
That we retire. To his apartments let
The Count be led. (*To the Pages at the back.*) You know the King will not
Come back to-night. He will remain away
Through all the hunting season.
(*She retires with her attendants to her apartments.*)
CASILDA (*watching her go out*). Ah, the Queen
Has something on her mind.
(*She goes out by the same door as the* QUEEN, *carrying the little casket of relics.*)
RUY BLAS (*remains alone*).
(*He seems as if listening for some time with deep joy to the last words of the* QUEEN, *and lost in reverie. The morsel of lace which the* QUEEN *had let fall in her trouble had remained on the ground. He picks it up, looks at it with emotion, and covers it with kisses. Then he raises his eyes to heaven.*)
Mercy, oh God!
Make me not mad!

(*Looking at the morsel of lace*). 'Twas surely near her heart!
(*He hides it in his bosom.—Enter* DON GURITAN *by the door of the room into which he had followed the* QUEEN. *He walks slowly towards* RUY BLAS. *When close to him, he, without saying a word, half-draws his sword, and compares its appearance with that of* RUY BLAS'. *They are not alike. He puts back his sword into the scabbard.* RUY BLAS *looks at him with surprise.*)

SCENE 4.—RUY BLAS—DON GURITAN.

DON GURITAN (*again pushing back his swords.*) I will bring two that are of equal length.
RUY BLAS. What mean you, Sir——
DON GURITAN (*gravely*). I was most deep in love
In sixteen hundred and fifty. Then I dwelt
In Alicante. There a young man was,
As handsome as the loves; he looked too near
Upon my mistress, passing every day
Beneath her balcony, before the old
Cathedral; he was prouder than a Captain
Of an Admiral's ship; Vasquez his name, and though
Bastard he was ennobled. Him I killed.
(RUY BLAS *tries to interrupt him; but* DON GURITAN *prevents him by a gesture, and continues.*)
And after that—it was towards sixty-six —
Gil, Count of Iscola,—a splendid knight,
Sent to my beauty, named Angelica,
A loving letter which she showed, and a slave
Named Grifel of Viserta. Him I had

Despatched, and slew myself the master.
RUY BLAS. Sir!
DON GURITAN (*continuing*). And later—near the year eighty—I had cause
To think I was deceived by beauty, one
Of easy ways, through Tirso Gamonal,
One of those youths whose haughty faces charm,
And go so well with splendid feathers. 'Twas
The time when mules were shod with purest gold.
I slew Don Tirso Gamonal.
RUY BLAS. But what, Sir, means all this?
DON GURITAN. It means to show you, Count,
That if you draw, there's water in the well,
And that to-morrow morn the sun will rise
At four o'clock; that there's a lonely spot
Behind the chapel, far from any road,
Convenient for men of spirit. You
They call Cæsar, I am named Don Gaspar
Guritan Tassis y Guevarra, Count
Of Oñate.
RUY BLAS (*coldly*). Well, Sir, I will be there.

(*A few moments before,* CASILDA, *out of curiosity, had entered softly by the little door at the back, and had listened to the last words without having been seen by the speakers.*)

CASILDA (*aside*). A duel! I must tell the Queen.

(*She disappears by the little door.*)

DON GURITAN (*still imperturbable*). If, Sir,
It pleases you to study and to know
My tastes, for your instruction I will say
I never much admired a coxcomb, or
A ladies' man with curled moustache, on whom
The women like to look, who sometimes are
All lackadaisical, and sometimes gay.
Who in the house speak with their eyes, and fall
In charming attitudes upon arm-chairs,
Just fainting at some little scratches.
RUY BLAS. But
I do not understand.
DON GURITAN. You understand
Quite well. We both desire the same good things,
And in this palace one of us is one
Too many. You are equerry, in short,
And I the Chamberlain. And so our rights
Are equal. I am ill-provided, though.
Our shares are not the same. I have the right
Of age, and you of youth. This frightens me.
At table where I fast, I see sit down
A hungry youth, with strong terrific teeth
And flaming eyes, and air of conqueror;
This troubles me; for vain contention were
Upon love's territory—that fine field,
Which always trembles with mere trifles,—I
Should make th' assault but badly. I've the gout.
Besides, I am not such an arrant fool
As for the heart of a Penelope
To wrestle with a spark so prompt to faint.
Because you're handsome, tender, winning, 'tis

That I must kill you.

RUY BLAS. Well, then, pray try.

DON GURITAN. Count
Of Garofa, to-morrow morn at hour
Of sunrise, at the place that's named,
without
A servant or a witness, if you please,
We'll slaughter one another gallantly,
With sword and dagger, like true gentlemen
Of houses such as ours.

(*He extends his hand to* RUY BLAS, *who takes it.*)

RUY BLAS. No word of this? (*The* COUNT *makes a sign of assent.*)
Until to-morrow.

(*Exit* RUY BLAS.)

DON GURITAN (*alone*). No—no tremor in
His hand I found. To know he'll surely die,
And be thus calm, proves him to be a brave
Young fellow.

(*Noise of a key in the little door of the* QUEEN'S *room.*)
Some one surely's at that door?

(*The* QUEEN *appears and walks briskly towards* DON GURITAN, *who is surprised and delighted to see her. She holds the little casket in her hands.*)

SCENE 5.—DON GURITAN—THE QUEEN.

THE QUEEN (*smiling*). 'Twas you I sought to find!

DON GURITAN. What brings to me
This honour?

THE QUEEN (*placing the casket on the round table*). Oh, 'tis nothing—or, at least,
A small affair, my Lord (*she laughs*).
Just now 'twas said,
'Mong other things—you know how foolish are
The women—and Casilda said, maintained
That you, for me, aught that I asked would do.

DON GURITAN. And she was right.

THE QUEEN (*laughing*). But I the contrary
Declared.

DON GURITAN. Then, Madam, you were wrong.

THE QUEEN. She said
That you for me would give your soul
—your life——

DON GURITAN. Casilda spoke right well in saying that.

THE QUEEN. But I said No.

DON GURITAN. And I say yes, all things
I for your Majesty would do.

THE QUEEN. All things?

DON GURITAN. Yes, all.

THE QUEEN. Well let us see!—swear now that you
To please me will this instant do the thing
I ask you.

DON GURITAN. By the venerated King
My patron saint, King Gaspar, I do swear!
Command, and I obey or die!

THE QUEEN (*taking up the casket*). Well then,
You will set out and leave Madrid at once,
And carry straight this box of calambac
To Neubourg, to my father th' Elector.
Take it.

DON GURITAN (*aside*). I'm caught, indeed! (*Aloud.*) What! to Neubourg!

The Queen. To Neubourg.
Don Guritan. Ah! six hundred leagues from here!
The Queen. Five hundred 'tis and fifty,—
(*pointing to the silken cover of the box.*)
Pray take care
That on the road the blue fringe does not fade.
Don Guritan. When shall I start?
The Queen. This instant.
Don Guritan. Let it be To-morrow!
The Queen. No, I cannot yield.
Don Guritan (*aside*). Entrapp'd I am. (*Aloud.*) But——
The Queen. Now set off.
Don Guritan. But why is this?——
The Queen. You've promised me.
Don Guritan. Affairs——
The Queen. Impossible.
Don Guritan. The object is so frivolous——
The Queen. Be quick!
Don Guritan. One day alone!
The Queen. No, not a moment.
Don Guritan. For——
The Queen. Now do my bidding.
Don Guritan. I——
The Queen. No.
Don Guritan. But——
The Queen. Set off.
Don Guritan. If—if——
The Queen. Yes, I will kiss you!
(*She puts her arms round his neck and kisses him.*)
Don Guritan (*vexed and yet delighted*). I resist
No more. I will obey you, Madam, (*Aside.*) God
Made Himself man; so be't. As woman 'tis
The devil comes!
The Queen (*pointing to the window*). A carriage there below
Is waiting for you.
Don Guritan. All then is prepared!
(*He writes hurriedly a few words on a piece of paper and rings a little bell. A Page enters.*)
Page, take unto Don Cæsar de Bazan
This letter, and without one moment lost.
(*Aside.*)
This duel must be taken up again
When I return. I shall come back!
(*Aloud.*) I go
At once to satisfy your Majesty.
The Queen. Now I'm contented.
(*He takes the casket, kisses the* Queen's *hand, makes a low bow and exit. The next minute the sound of wheels is heard.*)
The Queen (*falling into a chair*). He shall not be kill'd!

ACT THIRD:

RUY BLAS

The Council Chamber of the King's *palace at Madrid. At the back of a large door above some steps. In the angle to the left an opening closed by tapestry of a raised warp. In the opposite angle a window. To the right a square table with a green velvet cover around which are placed stools for eight or ten persons, corresponding to the number of desks placed on the table. At the side of the table which faces the audience is a large arm-chair, covered with cloth of gold, and surmounted by a canopy of the same material, with the arms of Spain and the royal crown emblazoned. A chair at one side of it. When the curtain rises the Privy Council of the* KING *is about to sit.*

SCENE 1.—DON MANUEL ARIAS, PRESIDENT OF CASTILE; DON PEDRO VELEZ DE GUEVARRA COUNT DE CAMPOREAL, *Knight-Counsellor of the Chief Exchequer.* DON FERNANDO DE CORDOVA Y AGUILAR MARQUIS DE PRIEGO *of the same quality.* ANTONIO UBILLA, *Chief Secretary of the Revenue.* MONTAZGO, *Counsellor of the Black Robe for India.* COVADENGA, *Chief Secretary for the Isles. Many other Counsellors. Those of the Robe in black. The others in Court Dress.* CAMPOREAL *has the Cross of Calatrava on his mantle,* PRIEGO *the Golden Fleece at his neck.* DON MANUEL ARIAS, *President of Castile, and the* COUNT DE CAMPOREAL *chat together in low tones at the front. The others form groups here and there in the Hall.*

DON MANUEL ARIAS. Behind such fortune lurks a mystery.

COUNT DE CAMPOREAL. He has the Golden Fleece. Behold him made Chief secretary—minister—and now Duke d'Olmedo he is!

DON MANUEL ARIAS. All in six months.

COUNT DE CAMPOREAL. In some strange secret way he has been raised.

DON MANUEL ARIAS (*mysteriously*). The Queen!

COUNT DE CAMPOREAL. In fact, the king an invalid,
Insane at heart, lives at his first wife's tomb.
He abdicates the throne, shut up within
Th' Escurial, and leaves the Queen alone
To govern all things.

DON MANUEL ARIAS. Dear Camporeal,
She reigns o'er us—Don Cæsar over her.

COUNT DE CAMPOREAL. His way of life is quite unnatural.
In the first place, he never sees the Queen;
They seem to shun each other. You may doubt
My word, but for six months I've watched them well,
For reasons good, and of it I am sure.
Then, from morose caprice, his dwelling is
A little lodge that's near th' Hôtel Tormez,
With shutters ever closed—where negroes two
Guard well the close-shut doors—Lackeys who could
Tell much, if only that they were not dumb.

DON MANUEL ARIAS. Mutes, then?

COUNT DE CAMPOREAL. Yes, mutes. His other servitors
Remain in those apartments which he has
Within the palace.

DON MANUEL ARIAS. It is strange, indeed.

DON ANTONIO UBILLA (*who joined them a few moments before*).

He comes of an old family,—enough
That is.
 COUNT DE CAMPOREAL. The strange
thing seems that he pretends
To be an honest man.
 (*To* DON MANUEL ARIAS.) Cousin he is
Unto the Marquis Salluste, who last year
Was banished—therefore 'twas that Santa Cruz
Befriended him.—In former years, this man,
Don Cæsar, who to-day our master proves,
Seemed but the greatest fool the moon saw born—
A hare-brained dolt—we know the people well
Who knew him. He for revenue consumed
His fortune—changed his loves, his carriages
Each day. His fancies had ferocious teeth,
That could have eaten in a year Peru.
One day he ran away, 'twas not known where.
 DON MANUEL ARIAS. But time has made of this gay fool a sage
Severe.
 COUNT DE CAMPOREAL. Frail women prudish grow when aged.
 UBILLA. I think the man is honest.
 COUNT DE CAMPOREAL (*laughing*). Simpleton,
Ubilla! to be dazzled thus by such
A probity! (*In a significant tone.*) The household of the Queen,
Civil and ordinary (*looking at some papers*), almost costs
Seven hundred thousand golden ducats now
In yearly charges. Here's assuredly
A shady calm Pactolus, where one might
In safety throw a very certain net;
The water trouble, and the fish is there.
 MARQUIS DE PRIEGO (*coming forward*). Ah, that does not displease you.
But unwise
Are you to speak thus freely. Let me say,
My late grandfather, he who was brought up
With the Count-Duke, did oft advise that we
Should gnaw the king—but kiss the favourite.
Now let us, gentlemen, engage ourselves
With public business.
 (*They sit round the table; some take up pens, others turn over the papers. The remainder are idle. A brief silence.*)
 MONTAZGO (*whispering to* UBILLA). I have asked from you,
Out of the money meant for purchasing
Of relics, just a sum enough to buy
The post of Alcaid that my nephew wants.
 UBILLA (*whispering*). You—you—you said you'd shortly give the place
Of bailiff o' the Ebro to my cousin
Melchior of Elva.
 MONTAZGO (*exclaiming*). Only just now
We dowered your daughter. The festivities
O' the nuptials still proceed.— Without a pause
I am assailed. . . .
 UBILLA (*whispering*). The Alcaid's post is yours.
 MONTAZGO (*whispering*). And yours the bailiff's.
 (*They press hands.*)

COVADENGA (*rising*). Gentlemen, we are
Castilian counsellors, and needful 'tis,
In order that each keeps within his sphere,
To regulate our rights and take our shares.
The revenue of Spain is scatter'd when
A hundred hands control it. We need now
To end this public evil. Some acquire
Too much, the others do not have enough.
The farming of tobacco goes to you,
Ubilla. Indigo and musk belong
To Marquis de Priego. Camporeal
Receives the taxes of eight thousand men,
The import dues, the salt, a thousand sums,
And five per cent. on gold, on jet, and on
The amber.
(*To* MONTAZGO.) You who with a restless eye
Regard me, you have managed for yourself
To have the tax on arsenic, and the rights
Of snow. You have dry docks, and cards, and brass,
The ransoms of the citizens that should
Be punished with the stick—the ocean tithes,
And those on lead and rosewood. Nothing, Sirs,
Have I. Decree me something.

COUNT DE CAMPOREAL (*bursting out laughing*). Oh, the old
Devil! Of all he takes the largest share
Of profits. If the Indies we except,
He has the islands of both seas. What spread
Of wings! He holds Majorca in one claw,
And with the other clutches Teneriffe!

COVADENGA (*growing angry*). I say I've nothing!

MARQUIS DE PRIEGO (*laughing*). He the negroes has.

(*They rise, all speaking at once and quarrelling.*)

MONTAZGO. I should long since have made complaint. I want
The forests.

COVADENGA (*to the* MARQUIS DE PRIEGO). Let me have the arsenic, then
The negroes unto you I will give up.

(*A few moments before* RUY BLAS *had entered by the door at the back, and had witnessed this scene without having been observed by the speakers. He is dressed in black velvet, with a mantle of scarlet velvet; he has a white feather in his hat, and wears the Golden Fleece at his neck. At first he listened to them in silence, but suddenly he advances with soft steps and appears in their midst at the height of the quarrel.*)

SCENE 2.—THE SAME—RUY BLAS

RUY BLAS (*bursting on them*). I wish you joy!

(*All turn round. Silence of surprise and uneasiness.*)

(RUY BLAS *puts on his hat, crosses his arms, and continues looking them full in the face.*)
Oh faithful ministers!
And virtuous counsellors! Behold your mode
Of working, servants you who rob the house!
And without shame the dark hour choose, when Spain

Weeps in her agony!—caring for nought
Except to fill your pockets—afterwards
To flee away! Branded you are before
Your country sinking into ruin. Oh,
Her grave you've dug, and robbed her in it too.
But look—reflect—and have some shame. The worth
Of Spain, her virtue and her greatness pass
Away. Since the Fourth Philip's time we've lost
Not only Portugal and the Brazils
Without a struggle made, but in Alsace
Brisach, Steinfort in Luxembourg, and all
The Comté to its last small town; Rousillon,
Ormuz and Goa, five thousand leagues of coast
And Pernambuc, and the blue mountains' range.
But see—from western shores unto the east
Europe, which hates you, laughs at you as well.
As if your King a phantom only were,
Holland and England share his states, and Rome
Deceives you; half an army is the most
You dare to risk in Piedmont; though supposed
A friendly country, Savoy and its Duke
Abound in subtle dangers. France awaits
The hour propitious to attack and take.
And Austria also watches you. And then
Bavaria's Prince is dying—that you know.
As for your viceroys—your Medina, fool
Of love, fills Naples with such tales as are

A scandal; Milan's sold by Vaudémont,
Legañez loses Flanders. What for this
The remedy? The state is indigent,
The state is drained of troops and money both.
Upon the sea—where God his anger shows—
We have already lost three hundred ships
Without our counting galleys. And you dare!——
Ye Sirs, for twenty years the People—think
Of it—and I have reckoned it is thus—
Have borne the burden under which they bend
For you—your pleasures and your mistresses;—
The wretched people whom you still would grind,
Have sweated for your uses, this I say,
More than four hundred millions of their gold!
And this is not enough for you! and still
My masters!—Ah, I am ashamed! At home
The spoilers, troopers, traverse all the land
And fight, the harvest burning. Carbines too
Are pointed at each thicket, just as 'twere
The war of princes; war is there between
The convents, war between the provinces,
All seeking to devour their neighbours poor,
Eaters o' the famished on a vessel wreck'd!
Within your ruined churches grows the grass,

And they are full of adders. Many great
By ancestry, but workers none. Intrigue
Is all, and nothing springs from loyalty.
A sewer is Spain, to which th' impurity
Of all the nations drains.—In his own pay
Each noble has a hundred cut-throats, who
Do speak a hundred tongues. The Genoese,
Sardinian, Flemish.—Babel's in Madrid.
The magistrates, so stern to poverty,
Are lenient to the rich. When night comes on
There's murder, then each one cries out for help!
But yesterday they robb'd me, yes, myself,
Near the Toledo bridge. One half Madrid
Now robs the other half, judges are bribed,
No soldier gets his pay. Old conquerors
O' the world—the Spaniards that we are—see now
What army have we? It but barely shows
Six thousand men who barefoot go; a host
Made up of beggars, Jews, and mountaineers,
Who, armed with daggers, dress themselves in rags,
And every regiment plies a double trade.
When darkness falls disorder reigns, and then
The doubtful soldier changes to a thief.
The robber Matalobos has more troops
Than any Baron. One of his followers
Made war upon the king of Spain.
Alas!
The country peasantry, unshamed, insult
The carriage of the king. And he, your lord,
Consumed by grief and fear, stays all alone
Within the Escurial, with but the dead
He treads upon, and stoops his anxious brow
From which the empire crumbles fast! Behold,
Alas! all Europe crushing 'neath its heel
This land, once purpled—which is now in rags.
The state is ruined in this shocking age;
And you dispute among yourselves who shall
The fragments take! The Spanish nation, once
So great, lies in the shadow enervate,
And dies while you upon it live—mournful
As a lion that to vermin is a prey!—
Oh, Charles the Fifth, in these dread times of shame
And terror, oh, what dost thou in thy tomb
Most mighty Emperor? Arise,—come, see
The best supplanted by the very worst;
This kingdom, now in agony—that was
Constructed out of Empires—near its fall.
It wants thine arm! Come to the rescue, Charles!
For Spain is dying, blotted out, self slain!
Thy globe, which brightly shone in thy right hand,

A dazzling sun that made the world be-
lieve
That thenceforth at Madrid the day first
dawn'd,
Is now a dead star, that in the gloom
grows less
And less—a moon three quarters gnaw'd
away,
And still decreasing ne'er to rise again
But be effaced by other nations! Oh,
Thy heritage is now put up for sale.
Alas! they make piastres of thy rays,
And soil thy splendours! Giant! can it be
Thou sleepest? By its weight thy scep-
tre now
They sell! A crowd of dwarfs de-
formed cut up
Thy royal robes to make their doub-
lets, while
Th' Imperial Eagle, which beneath thy
rule
Covered the world, and grasped its
thunderbolts
And darted flame, a poor unfeather'd
bird
Is cooking in their stew-pan infamous!

(*The* Counsellors *are silent in their consternation. But the* MARQUIS DE PRIEGO *and the* COUNT DE CAMPOREAL *raise their heads and look angrily at* RUY BLAS. *Then* CAMPOREAL, *after having spoken to* PRIEGO, *goes to the table and writes a few words on a piece of paper which they both sign.*)

COUNT DE CAMPOREAL (*pointing to the* MARQUIS DE PRIEGO *and presenting the paper to* RUY BLAS).
In both our names, your Grace, I tender you
The resignation of our posts.

RUY BLAS (*taking the paper calmly*).
Thanks. You
Will with your family retire,
 (*To* PRIEGO.) You, Sir,
To Andalusia.
 (*To* CAMPOREAL.) You, Count, unto
Castile. To his estates each one. Set out
To-morrow.

(*The two nobles bow and exeunt haughtily wearing their hats.* RUY BLAS, *turning to the other counsellors,*)
Whoso'er declines to go
My road, can follow now those gentle-
men.

(*Silence for awhile.* RUY BLAS *seats himself in a chair with a back, placed by the side of the royal chair, and begins to open letters. While running his eyes over them one after another,* COVADENGA, ARIAS, *and* UBILLA *exchange a few words in low tones.*)

UBILLA (*to* COVADENGA, *indicating* RUY BLAS). A master we have found, my friend. This man
Will rise to greatness.

DON MANUEL ARIAS. Yes, if he has time.

COVADENGA. And if he does not lose himself at view
Of all too near.

UBILLA. He will be Richelieu!

DON MANUEL ARIAS. Unless 'tis Olivarez that he proves!

RUY BLAS (*after having run over in an excited manner a letter he had just opened*). A plot! what's this? Now, Sirs, what did I say?   (*Reading.*)
"Duke d' Olmedo must watch. A snare there is
Preparing to remove a personage,
One of the greatest of Madrid." (*Ex-
amining the letter.*) They say
Not whom. But I will watch.—Anony-
mous
The letter is.

(*Enter a* Court Usher *who approaches* Ruy Blas *with a profound bow.*)
How now—what's this?
  Usher. Unto
Your Excellency, th' Ambassador of France
I now announce.
  Ruy Blas. Ah, Harcourt! at this time
I cannot see him.
  Usher (*bowing*). And the Nuncio Imperial waits in the saloon of honour
To see your Excellency.
  Ruy Blas. Oh, at this hour
It is impossible.
  (*The* Usher *bows and exit. A few moments previously a* Page *dressed in a livery of pinkish-grey and silver, had entered and approached* Ruy Blas.)
  Ruy Blas (*perceiving him*). My Page, to none
Whatever am I visible just now.
  The Page (*in a low voice*). The Count de Guritan, who has return'd
From Neubourg——
  Ruy Blas (*with a gesture of surprise*). Ah!—Page, show to him my house
I' the suburb, saying that to-morrow he
Will find me there—if it should please him. Go.
                (*The* Page *exit.*)
  (*To the* Counsellors.)
We shall have work together soon to do.
In two hours, gentlemen, return.
  (*All exeunt, bowing low to* Ruy Blas.)
  (Ruy Blas *is alone, and walks a few steps, absorbed in deep reverie. Suddenly in the corner of the room the tapestry is raised, and the* Queen *appears. She is dressed in white, with a crown on her head. She seems radiant with joy, and looks at* Ruy Blas *with an expression of respect and admiration. She holds back the tapestry with one arm, behind which is perceptible a dark recess, in which a little door can be distinguished.* Ruy Blas, *in turning round, sees the* Queen, *and remains as if petrified by the apparition.*)

Scene 3.—Ruy Blas—The Queen.

  The Queen. Oh, thanks!
  Ruy Blas. Oh, Heaven!
  The Queen. You have done well to speak them thus.
I can refrain no longer, Duke. I must
Press now that loyal hand so strong and true.
  (*She walks quickly towards him and takes his hand, which she presses before he can prevent her.*)
  Ruy Blas (*aside*). To shun her for six months, and then at once
Thus suddenly behold her!
  (*Aloud.*) Madam, you
Were there——
  The Queen. Yes, Duke, and I heard all you said.
Yes, I was there, and listened with my soul!
  Ruy Blas (*pointing to the hiding-place*).
I never thought——Madam, that hiding-place——
  The Queen. It is unknown to all.
A dark recess
That the Third Philip hollowed in the wall,
By means of which the master heard all things
While, spirit-like, invisible. And oft

From there have I beheld the Second Charles,
Mournful and dull, attend the Councils where
They pillaged him and sacrificed the State.
    Ruy Blas. And what said he?
    The Queen. He nothing said.
    Ruy Blas. Nothing!
What did he, then?
    The Queen. He to the hunting field
Went off. But you! Your threatening words still ring
Upon mine ear. Oh! in what haughty ways
You treated them, and how superbly right
You were! The border of the tapestry
I raised and saw you. Yes, your flashing eyes
With lightning overwhelmed them, and without
Fury. Unto them everything was said.
You seemed to me the only upright one!
But where, then, have you learn'd so many things?
How comes it that you know effects and cause?
That everything you know? Whence cometh it
That your voice speaks as tongues of kings should speak,
Why, then, were you like messenger of God,
So terrible and great?
    Ruy Blas. Because--because
I love you! I whom all these hate. Because
I know full well that what they seek to crush
Must fall on you! Because there's nothing can
Dismay a reverent passion so profound.

Therefore to save you I would save the world!
Unhappy man, who loves you with such love.
Alas! I think of you as think the blind
Of day. Oh, Madam, hear me. I've had dreams
Uncounted. I have loved you from afar,
From the deep depths of shade; I have not dared
To touch your finger-tips. You dazzled me
As sight of angel might. I've suffered much,
Truly I have! Ah, Madam, if you knew!
Six months I hid my love—but now I speak.
I fled—I shunned you, but I tortured was.
I am not thinking of these men at all.
I love you! And, oh God! I dare to speak
The words unto your Majesty. Now say,
What I must do? Should you desire my death,
I'll die. Oh, pardon me—I'm terrified!
    The Queen. Oh, speak! enchant me! Never in my life
Such words I've heard. I listen. 'Tis thy soul
That speaking overwhelms me quite. I need
Thy voice, thine eyes. Oh, if thou knewest! I
It is who suffered! Ah, a hundred times
When in the last six months your eyes shunn'd mine——
But no, I must not say these things so fast——
I'm most unhappy. Silent let me be.
I am afraid!

Ruy Blas (*listening with rapture*).
Oh, Madam, finish. You
With joy fill up my heart.
　The Queen. Well, listen, then.
　(*Raising her eyes to heaven.*)
Yes, I will tell him all. Is it a crime?
So much the worse! But when the heart is torn
One cannot help but show what there was hid.
Thou fled'st the Queen? Ah, well, the Queen sought thee.
Each day she came there to that secret place,
And listened to thee, gathering up thy words.
Silent, in contemplation of thy mind,
Which judged, and resolutely willed.
Thy voice
Enthralled me, and gave interest to all.
To me thou seem'dst the real king, the right
True master. I it was that in six months—
Perchance thou doubtest—made thee mount unto
The summit; where by fate thou should'st have been,
A woman placed thee. All that concerned me
Thou hast considered. First it was a flower,
But now an Empire. Ah, I reverence thee.
At first I thought thee good—but afterwards
I found thee great. My God, 'tis this that wins
A woman! If I now do ill, oh why
Was I incarcerated in this tomb,
As in a cage they put a dove, deprived
Of hope, of love, without one gilded ray?
—Some day, when we have time, I'll tell thee all
That I have suffered, I, ever alone,
As if forgot! humiliated too
Most constantly. Now judge. 'Twas yesterday,——
My chamber I disliked; you know—for you
Know all things—rooms there are where we feel more
Depressed than in some others. Mine I wished
To change. Now see what chains are ours, they would
Not let me. Thus a slave am I. O Duke,
It must have been that heaven sent thee here
To save the tottering state, and from the gulf
To draw the people back—the working ones,
And love me who thus suffer. Ah I tell
Thee all at random, in my simple way.
You must, however, see that I am right
　Ruy Blas (*falling on his knees*).
Madam.——
　The Queen (*gravely*). Don Cæsar—
I to you give up
My soul. The Queen for others, I to you
Am but a woman. By the heart to you
It is that I belong. And I have faith
To know your honour will respect mine own.
Whenever you shall call me I will come.
Ready I am. Sublime thy spirit is,
Oh Cæsar. And be proud, for thou art crown'd
By genius. (*She kisses his forehead.*)
Adieu! (*She raises the tapestry and exit.*)

SCENE 4.—RUY BLAS (*alone*).

(*He is as if absorbed in seraphic contemplation.*)
Before mine eyes
'Tis heaven I see! In all my life, oh God,
This hour stands first. Before me is a world,
A world of light, as if the paradise
We dream about had open'd wide and fill'd
My being with new light and brilliancy!
In me, around me, everywhere is joy,
Intoxication, mystery, and delight,
And pride, and that one thing that on the earth
Approaches most divinity, love—love,
In majesty and power. The Queen loves me!
Oh heavens, it is true—me—me—myself!
Since the Queen loves me I am more than King!
Oh, it is dazzling. Conqueror, happy, loved.
Duke d'Olmedo I am—and at my feet
Is Spain. I have her heart. That angel, whom
Upon my knees I contemplate and name,
Has by a word transfigured me and made
Me more than man. But in my star-lit dream
Do I move waking! Yes, I'm very sure
'Twas she herself who spoke—quite sure 'twas she.
A little diadem of silver lace
She wore; and I observed the while she spoke
—I think I see it still—an eagle 'graved
Upon her golden bracelet. She confides
In me, has told me so.—Poor Angel! Oh,
If it be true that God in granting love
Does by a miracle within us blend
That which can make man great with that which can
His nature soften, I who nothing fear
Since I am loved by her, I, who have power,
Thanks to her choice supreme, I, whose full heart
Might well the envy be of kings, declare—
Before my God who hears me—without fear,
And with loud voice, that Madam you may trust
In me,—unto my arm as Queen, unto
My heart as woman,—for devotion, pure
And loyal dwells i' the depth of my great love.
Ah, fear thou nothing!

(*During this speech a man had entered, by a door at the back, wrapped in a large cloak and with a hat gallooned in silver. He advances slowly towards* RUY BLAS *without being seen, and at the moment when* RUY BLAS, *intoxicated with ecstasy and happiness, raises his eyes to heaven, this man slaps him on the shoulder.* RUY BLAS *turns, startled as if awakening from a dream. The man lets fall his cloak, and* RUY BLAS *recognises* DON SALLUSTE. DON SALLUSTE *is dressed in a pinkish-grey livery, gallooned with silver, like that of the page of* RUY BLAS.)

SCENE 5.—RUY BLAS, DON SALLUSTE.

DON SALLUSTE (*placing his hand on the shoulder of* RUY BLAS). Ah, good day.

RUY BLAS (*aside*). Great God!

I'm lost! It is the Marquis that is here!

Don Salluste. I wager now you did not think of me.

Ruy Blas. Indeed your lordship did surprise me.

(*Aside.*) Oh,
My misery is resumed. When turned towards
An angel, 'twas a demon came!

(*He hurries to the tapestry which conceals the little hiding place, and bolts the door inside. Then he returns trembling to* Don Salluste.)

Don Salluste. Well now,
How are you?

Ruy Blas (*his eyes fixed on* Don Salluste, *who is imperturbable and as if himself incapable of gathering together his ideas*). Why this livery?

Don Salluste (*still smiling*). I desired
To find an entrance to the palace. This
Admits me everywhere. I have assumed
Your livery, and find it suits me well.

(*He puts on his hat.* Ruy Blas *remains bareheaded.*)

Ruy Blas. But I'm alarmed for you.

Don Salluste. Alarmed! What was
That word so ludicrous?

Ruy Blas. Exiled you were!

Don Salluste. You think so? Possibly.

Ruy Blas. If it should be
That in the palace you were recognised
In the broad daylight?

Don Salluste. Nonsense! Happy folks
Who are about the Court, would waste their time,
The time that flies so fast, remembering
A face that's in disgrace. Besides, who looks
Upon a lackey's profile?

(*He seats himself in the arm-chair.* Ruy Blas *remains standing.*)
By the bye,
And if you please, what's this that in Madrid
They say? Is't true, that, burning with a zeal
Extravagant, and only for the sake
Of public funds, you've exiled a grandee,
That dear Priego? You've forgotten quite
That you're relations, for his mother was
A Sandoval—yours also. What the deuce!
A Sandoval doth bear on field of "or"
A bend of "sable." Look to your blazonry,
Don Cæsar, it is very clear. Such things,
My dear, between relations should not be.
The wolves that fight with other wolves, make they
Good leaders? Open wide your eyes for self,
But shut them for the others. For himself
Each one.

Ruy Blas (*recovering himself a little*). However, Sir—permit me, pray.
The Marquis de Priego, of the State
A noble, does great wrong in swelling now
Th' expenses of the kingdom. Soon we shall
Have need to put an army in the field;
We have not money, yet it must be done.
Bavaria's Prince is at the point of death;
And yesterday the Count d'Harcourt, when well

You know, said to me in the Emperor's
His master's name, that if the Archduke should
Assert his claim, war would break out—
  Don Salluste. The air
Seems rather chill—will you be good enough
To close the casement?

(Ruy Blas, *pale with shame and despair, hesitates a moment; then by an effort he goes slowly to the window, and shuts it. He returns to* Don Salluste, *who is still seated in the armchair, watching him in an indifferent manner.*)

Ruy Blas (*continuing his endeavour to convince* Don Salluste). Deign, I beg, to see
How very difficult a war will prove;
What without money can we do? Listen,
My Lord. Spain's safety in her honour lies.
For me—I've to the Emperor said, as if
Our arms were ready, I'd oppose him—
  Don Salluste (*interrupting him, and pointing to his handkerchief, which he had let fall on entering*). Stay,
Pick up my handkerchief.

(Ruy Blas, *as if tortured, again hesitates; then stoops and takes up the handkerchief, giving it to* Don Salluste.)

Don Salluste (*putting the handkerchief in his pocket*). You did observe?——
  Ruy Blas (*with an effort*). Yes,
Spain is at our feet; her safety now
And public interest demand that each
Forgets himself. The nation blesses those
Who would release her. Let us dare be great
And strike and save the people. Let us now
Remove the mask from knaves, and let in light
Upon intrigue.
  Don Salluste (*with indifference*).
First let me say all this
Is wearying,—it of the pedant smacks,
His petty way of making monstrous noise
Concerning everything. What signifies
A wretched million, more or less, devoured,
That all these dismal cries are raised about?
My boy, great Lords are not the pedant class,
Freely they live—I speak without bombast.
The mien of them who would redress abuse
Is pride inflated and with anger red!
Pshaw! now you want to be a famous spark
Adored by traitors and by citizens.
'Tis very droll. Have newer fancies, pray.
The public good! First think now of your own.
Spain's safety is a hollow phrase; the rest
Can shout, my boy, as well as you can do.
And popularity? a rattling noise
Thought glory. Oh, what charming work to prowl
Like barking dog about the taxes! But
I know conditions better. Probity?
And faith? and virtue? faded tinsel, used
Already from the time of Charles the Fifth.

You are no fool. Must you be cured of all
This sentiment? You were a sucking child
When we did gaily and without remorse
By pin-pricks, or a kick, burst all at once
Your fine balloon, and amidst roaring mirth
Let out the wind from all these crotchets.

RUY BLAS. But,
My Lord, however——

DON SALLUSTE (*with icy smile*).
You're astonishing.
Let us be serious now.
(*In an abrupt and imperious manner.*)
To-morrow, all
The morning you will wait at home for me,
Within the house I lent you. What I do
Now nears the end. Only retain the mutes
To wait upon us. In the garden have,
But hidden by the trees, a carriage, well
Appointed, horses, all prepared for use.
I will arrange relays. Do all I wish.
—You will want money, I will send it you.—

RUY BLAS. I will obey you, Sir. I will do all.
But first, oh, swear to me that with this work
The Queen has nought to do.

DON SALLUSTE (*playing with an ivory knife on the table turns half round*).
With what are you
Now meddling?

RUY BLAS (*trembling and looking at him with terror*). Oh, you are a fearful man!
My knees beneath me tremble.——Towards a gulf
Invisible you drag me. Oh, I feel
That in a hand most terrible I am!
You have some monstrous scheme. Something I see
That's horrible.——Have mercy upon me!
Oh, I must tell,—judge alas! yourself
You knew it not. I love that woman!

DON SALLUSTE. Yes.
I knew it.

RUY BLAS. Knew it.

DON SALLUSTE. What, by heaven, can
That signify?

RUY BLAS (*leaning for support against the wall, and as if speaking to himself*). Then for mere sport he has,
The coward! this torture practised upon me!
Ah, this affair will be most horrible!
(*He raises his eyes to heaven.*)
Oh, God, all-powerful! who tries me now,
Spare me, oh God!

DON SALLUSTE. There, that's enough —you dream!
Truly you think in earnest that you are
A personage, but 'tis buffoonery.
I to an end move on which I alone
Should know, an end that happier is for you
Than you can guess. But keep you still. Obey.
I have already said, and I repeat
I wish your good. Proceed, the thing is done.
And after all, what are the woes of love?
We all go through them—troubles of a day.
Know you, an Empire's destiny's concerned?

What's yours beside it? Willingly I'd tell
You all; but have the sense to comprehend.
Your station keep. I'm very good and kind.
A lackey though, of coarse clay or of fine,
Is but an instrument to serve my whims.
With your sort, what one wishes one can do.
Your master did disguise you as his plan
Required, and can unmask you at his will.
I made you a great Lord—fantastic part—
But for the instant—and you have complete
The outfit. But forget not that you are
My servant. You pay court unto the Queen—
An incident—like stepping up behind
My carriage. Therefore reasonable be.
    RUY BLAS (*who has listened distracted, as if he could not believe his ears*). Oh God—oh God! the just! the merciful!
Oh, of what crime is this the punishment?
What have I done? Oh, Thou our Father art,
And would not that a man despair. Behold,
Then, where I am!—And willingly, my Lord,
And without wrong in me—only to see
A victim agonised, in what abyss
You've plunged me! torturing thus a heart replete
With love and faith, to serve alone as means

For vengeance of your own!
    (*As if speaking to himself.*)
For vengeance 'tis!
The thing is certain. I divine too well
It is against the Queen! What can I do?
Go tell her all? Great Heaven! become to her
An object of disgust and horror! Knave
With double face! A Crispin! Scoundrel base
And impudent, such as they bastinade
And drive away! Never!—I grow insane,
My reason totters!
    (*A pause. He ponders.*)
God! behold what things
Are done! To build an engine silently,
To arm it hideously with frightful wheels
Unnumber'd, then to see it work, upon
The stone to throw a livery'd one, a thing,
A serving man, and set in motion all—
And suddenly to watch come out, beneath
The wheels, some muddy blood-stained rags, a head
All broken, and a warm and steaming heart,
And not to shudder then to find, despite
The name they call him, that the livery was
But outward covering of a man.
    (*Turning towards* DON SALLUSTE).
But oh,
There still is time! Truly, my Lord, as yet
Th' horrible wheel is not in motion.
    (*Throws himself at his feet.*)
Oh,
Have pity on me! Mercy! Pity her!
You know that I a faithful servant am,

You often said it. See how I submit!
Oh, grace!

Don Salluste. The man will never understand.
This wearies me!

Ruy Blas (*trailing at his feet*). Oh, mercy!

Don Salluste. Let us now
Have done.
(*He turns towards the window.*)
You badly closed the window there,
I'm sure. A draught comes thence.
(*He goes to the casement and shuts it.*)

Ruy Blas (*rising*). It is too much!
At present I'm Duke d'Olmedo, and still
Th' all-powerful minister! I raise my head
From 'neath the foot which crushes me.

Don Salluste. What's that
You say? Repeat the phrase. Is Ruy Blas
Indeed Duke d'Olmedo? Your eyes are bound.
'Twas only on Bazan that thou wast raised
To be Olmedo.

Ruy Blas. I will order you
To be arrested.

Don Salluste. I'll say who you are.

Ruy Blas (*excitedly*). But——

Don Salluste. You'll accuse me?
I've risked both our heads.
That was foreseen. Too soon do you assume
The air of triumph.

Ruy Blas. I'll deny it all.

Don Salluste. Pshaw! you're a child.

Ruy Blas. You have no proof!

Don Salluste. And you
No memory. I'll do just what I say,
And you had best believe me. But the glove
Are you, I am the hand.
(*Lowering his voice and approaching* Ruy Blas.)
If thou obey'st
Me not, if thou to-morrow do not stay
At home preparing what I wish, if thou
Should'st speak a single word of all which now
Is passing, if by look or gesture thou
Betray—first she, for whom thou fearest, shall,
By this thy folly, in a hundred spots
Be publicly defamed, and ruined quite,
And afterward she shall receive—in this
There's nought obscure—a paper under seal
Which in a place secure I keep; 'twas writ
Thou wilt remember by what hand? and signed
Thou knowest how? These are the words her eyes
Will read: "I, Ruy Blas, the serving-man
Of the most noble Lord the Marquis of
Finlas, engage to serve him faithfully
On all occasions as a servant true
In public or in secrecy."

Ruy Blas (*crushed and in husky voice*). Enough.
I will, my Lord, do what you please.
(*The door at the back opens. One sees the members of the Privy Council re-entering.* Don Salluste *hastens to wrap his cloak round him.*)

Don Salluste (*in a low voice*).
They come.
(*Aloud, and bowing to* Ruy Blas.)
I am your humble servant, my Lord Duke. (*Exit.*)

ACT FOURTH:

DON CÆSAR

A small, gloomy, but sumptuous room. Old-fashioned wainscot and furniture, with old gilding. The walls covered with old hangings of crimson velvet pressed down in places, and at the back of the arm-chairs, and gathered by shining gold galloon into vertical bands. At the back folding doors. At the left angle of the wall, a large corner chimney with sculpture of the time of Philip the Second, and an escutcheon of wrought iron inside. At the opposite angle a little door leading to a dark closet. A single window at the left, placed very high, has bars across it, and an inside splay like the windows of prisons. On the walls are some old portraits smoke-begrimed and half defaced. A chest for clothes and a Venetian looking-glass. Large arm-chairs in the fashion of Philip the Third's time. A highly ornamented cupboard against the wall. A square table with writing materials on it. A little round table with gilt feet in a corner. It is morning.

When the curtain rises RUY BLAS, *dressed in black without his mantle and without the Fleece, is seen walking about the room greatly agitated. At the back stands his* Page *motionless, as if awaiting orders.*

SCENE 1.—RUY BLAS. THE PAGE.

RUY BLAS (*aside, as if speaking to himself*). What is it can be done? She must be saved!
Before all else! Nothing but her to be
Considered! Should my brains from on a wall
Spurt out, or should the gibbet claim, or should
Hell seize me, rescued she must be!
But how?
To give my blood, my heart, my soul, all that
Were nothing—it were easy. But to break
This web! To guess, for guess one must, what schemes
This man constructing has combined!
Sudden
He comes from out the shadow, and therein
Replunges. Lone in darkness what does he?
When I remember that at first to him
For self I pleaded! Oh, 'twas cowardice!
Moreover it was stupid! This is why—
He is a wretch.—The thing has olden date,
No doubt.—How can I think, that when he held
His prey but half devoured, the demon would,
In pity for his lackey, leave the Queen!
Can we subdue wild beasts? Oh misery!
I yet must save her! I, the cause of this!
At any price it must be done. All—all
Is ended. Now behold my fall! From height
So great so low! Have I then dream'd?
—Yet oh!
She must escape! But he! By what door will
He come—and by what trap, oh God, will he,
The traitor black, proceed? As of this house,
So of my life, he is the lord. He can
The gilding all strip off. He has the keys

Of all the locks. Enter and leave he can,
Approaching in the dark to tread upon
My heart as on this floor. Yes, this my dream!
Such fate confuses thought i' the rapid tide
Of things so quickly done. I am distraught.
No one thought have I clear. My mind
—of which
I was so vain—oh God! is now in such
A hurricane of rage and fear 'tis like
A reed storm-twisted!—Oh what can I do?
Let me reflect. At first to hinder her
From stirring from the palace. Yes, 'tis that
Undoubtedly that is the snare. Around
Myself the whirlpool is, and darkness dense.
I feel the mesh but see it not. Oh, how
I suffer!—'Tis decided. To forewarn—
Prevent her going from the palace—this
At once to do. But how? No one I have!

(*He reflects earnestly. Suddenly, as if struck with an idea, and having a ray of hope, he raises his head.*)

Don Guritan! Ah, yes, he loves her well,
And he is loyal!

(*He signs to the Page to approach, then speaks low.*)

Page, this instant go
Unto Don Guritan. Make him from me
Apologies; and beg him then without
Delay to seek the Queen, and pray her in
My name, and in his own, that whatso'er
May happen or be said, on no account
To leave the palace for three days. To stir
Not out. Now run. (*Recalling the Page.*) Ah!

(*He takes a leaf and a pencil from his note case.*)

Let him give these words
Unto the Queen,—and watch!

(*He writes on his knee rapidly.*)

"Believe what says
Don Guritan, as he advises do."

(*He folds the paper and gives it to the* Page.)

As for the duel, tell him I was wrong,
That I am at his feet, that I have now
A trouble, beg of him to pity me,
And take my supplication to the Queen
On th' instant. Tell him that I will to him,
In public, make apologies. And say
There is for her a danger imminent.
She must not venture out for quite three days
Whate'er occurs.—— Exactly do all this;
Go, be discreet, and nothing let appear.

PAGE. I am to you devoted—for you are
A master good.

RUY BLAS. Run fast, my little Page,
Hast thou well understood?

PAGE. Oh yes, my lord.
Be satisfied. (*Exit* Page.)

RUY BLAS (*alone, falling into an armchair*). My thoughts grow calmer now.
Yet I forget, and feel things all confused
As were I mad. Ah yes, the means are sure.
Don Guritan.—— But I myself? Is there
The need to wait Don Salluste here?
Wherefore?
Oh no, I will not wait, and that perchance
Will paralyse him for a day. Within
A church I want to pray. I'll go—I've need

Of help, and God will me inspire!
(*He takes his hat from a side table, and shakes a little bell placed on the table. Two Negroes dressed in pale green velvet brocaded with gold, jackets plaited into great lappets, appear at the door at the back.*)
I leave.
But very soon a man will hither come—
And by an entrance known to him. May be,
When in the house, as if he were indeed
The master, he will act. Let him so do.
And if some others come——
(*After hesitating a moment.*)
My faith, why then
You'll please to let them enter.
(*By a gesture he dismisses the Negroes who bow in token of obedience and exeunt.*)
Now I go!   (*Exit.*)
(*At the moment the door closes on* RUY BLAS *there is heard a great noise in the chimney, from which suddenly falls a man wrapped in a tattered cloak. It is* DON CÆSAR *who throws himself into the room.*)

SCENE 2.—DON CÆSAR.

DON CÆSAR (*scared, out of breath, stupefied, disordered, with an expression of mingled joy and anxiety*). 'Tis I! So much the worse!
(*He rises, rubbing the leg on which he has fallen, and comes into the room hat in hand and bowing low.*)
Your pardon, pray!
But heed me not. I don't attend—go on
With your discourse, continue I entreat,
I enter rather rudely—Sirs, for that
I'm sorry!
(*He stops in the middle of the room, perceiving he is alone.*)
No one here?—When on the roof
Just now I perched, I thought I heard the sound
Of voices.—No one, though!
(*Seats himself in an arm-chair.*)
That's very well.
Let me now gather up my thoughts. And good
Is solitude. Oh, what events!—Marvels
With which I'm charged, just as a wetted dog
Who shakes off water. First those Alguazils
Who seized me in their claws, and that absurd
Embarkment; then the corsairs, and the town
So big where I was beaten sorely. Then
Temptations of that sallow woman; next,
Departure from the prison; travels, too,
And at the last return to Spain. And then—
Oh, what a tale!—The day that I arrived,
Those self-same Alguazils the first I met.
My desperate flight, and their enraged pursuit;
I leaped a wall, and then I saw a house
Half-hidden by the trees; I thither ran;
None saw me, so I nimbly climbed from shed
To roof; at last I introduced myself
Into the bosom of famliy
By coming down a chimney, where I tore
To rags my newest mantle, that now hangs

About my heels. By heav'n, Cousin Salluste,
You are a braggart rogue!

(*Looking at himself in a little Venetian glass placed on the sculptured chest.*)

My doublet here
Has kept to me through these disasters all.
It struggles yet.

(*He takes off his mantle and admires in the glass his rose-coloured doublet, now torn and patched; then he puts his hand sharply to his leg, with a look at the chimney.*)

But in my fall my leg
Has suffer'd horribly!

(*He opens the drawers of the chest. In one of them he finds a mantle of light-green velvet embroidered with gold. The mantle given by* DON SALLUSTE *to* RUY BLAS. *He examines it and compares it with his own.*)

It seems to me
This mantle is more decent than my own.

(*He puts on the green mantle, and leaves his own in the chest, after having carefully folded it up. He adds his hat, which he crushes under the mantle with a blow of his fist. Then he shuts the drawer, and struts about proudly draped in the fine mantle embroidered with gold.*)

'Twill do. Behold me now return'd. All is
Proceeding well. Ah, cousin very dear,
You wished to send me off to Africa,
Where man is mouse unto the tiger! Ah,
I'll be revenged on you most savagely,
My cursed cousin, when I've breakfasted.
In my right name I'll go to you, and drag
With me a troup of rogues, such as can smell
The gibbet a league off—and more, I will
Deliver you alive, thus to appease
The appetites of all my creditors,
These followed by their little ones.

(*He perceives in the corner a pair of splendid boots trimmed with lace. He takes off his shoes in a leisurely manner, and, without scruple, puts on the new boots.*)

But first
Now let me see where all his perfidies
Have led me.

(*After looking all round the room.*)

A mysterious dwelling, fit
For tragedies. Closed doors and shutters barred,
A dungeon quite. Into this charming place
One enters from the top, just as there comes
The wine into the bottles.

(*With a sigh.*)

Ah, good wine
Is very good.

(*He notices the little door at the right, opens it, and hastily enters the closet with which it communicates, and then comes back with a gesture of astonishment.*)

Oh wonders, wonders more!
Where everything is closed, a little room
Without the means of egress!

(*He goes to the door at the back, half-opens it, and looks out; he lets it close and comes to the front.*)

Not a soul!—
Oh, where the deuce am I?—At any rate,

I've managed to escape the Alguazils.
What matters all the rest? Need I be scared
And take a gloomy view, because I ne'er
Before beheld a house like this?
(He seats himself in the arm-chair, and yawns, but soon gets up again.)
Come, though,
I feel the dullness here is horrible!
(Perceiving a little corner cupboard in the wall.)
Let's see, this looks to me a little like
A bookcase.
(He opens it, and finds it to be a well-furnished larder.)
Ah! 'tis just the thing—A pie,
A water-melon, and some wine. A cold
Collation for emergency. By Jove!
I'd prejudices 'gainst this house.
(Examines the flagons one after the other.)
All good.—
Come, now! This place is worthy of great praise.
(He goes to the corner, and brings thence to the front a little round table, on which he places the contents of the larder—bottles, dishes, etc. He adds a glass, plate, fork, etc. Then he takes up one of the bottles.)
Let's read this one the first.
(He fills the glass, and drinks off the wine.)
A work that is
Most admirable. The production fine
Of that so famous poet called the sun!
Xérès-des-Chevaliers can nothing show
More ruby-like.
(He sits, and pours out another glass of wine.)
What book's worth this? Find me
Something that is more spiritual!
(He drinks.)
Ah!
This comforts! Let us eat.
(He cuts the pie.)
I have outstripp'd
Those dogs of Alguazils. They've lost the scent.
(He begins eating.)
The king of pies! and as for him who is
The master here, should he drop in—
(He goes to the sideboard, and brings thence a glass and a plate.)
Why, him
I now invite, if that he does not come
To drive me hence. Let me be very quick.
(He takes large mouthfuls.)
My dinner done, I'll look about the house.
Who can inhabit it? Maybe, he is
A jolly fellow. This place can but hide
Some feminine intrigue. Pshaw! What's the harm
That here I do? What is it, I beseech?
Nought but this worthy's hospitality
After the ancient way,
(He half kneels, surrounding the table with his arms.)
Embracing thus
The altar. *(He drinks.)*
Firstly though, this wine is not
A bad man's wine. And then if any one
Should come, I'd certainly declare myself.
How you would rage, my old accursèd coz!
What, that low fellow, that Bohemian!
That beggarly black sheep Zafari? Yes,
Don Cæsar de Bazan, the cousin he
Of the Don Salluste! What a fine surprise!

And what a hubbub in Madrid! When was't
That he return'd? This morning, or this night?
What tumult everywhere at such a bomb,
The great forgotten name that all at once
Again is heard! Don Cæsar de Bazan!
Yes, if you please, good Sirs. Nobody thought—
Nobody spoke of him,—then he's not dead!
He lives, my dames and gentlemen! The men
Will cry: The deuce! The women they will say,
Indeed! Aye, aye! Soft sound that mingles with
The barking of three hundred creditors
As you go home! Fine part to play! Alas!
I am wanting money for it.
(*A noise is heard at the door.*)
Some one comes!
No doubt t' expel me like a vile buffoon.—
No matter though. Cæsar, do nought by halves!
(*He wraps himself in his cloak up to the eyes. The door at the back opens. A Lackey in livery enters bearing a great courier's bag on his back.*)

Scene 3.—Don Cæsar. A Lackey.

Don Cæsar (*scanning the* Lackey *from head to foot*). Whom seek you here, my friend? (*Aside.*)
I must assume
Great confidence—the peril is extreme.
The Lackey. Don Cæsar de Bazan?
Don Cæsar (*lowering his mantle from his face*). Don Cæsar! That's Myself! (*Aside.*)
Here is the wonderful!
The Lackey. You are, My Lord, Don Cæsar de Bazan?
Don Cæsar. By heav'n
I have the honour so to be. Cæsar, The true and only Cæsar. Count of Gar——
The Lackey (*placing the bag on the arm-chair*). Now deign to see if the amount be right.
Don Cæsar (*dazed—aside*). Some money! Oh, it is too wonderful!
(*Aloud.*)
My man——
The Lackey. You'll condescend to count. It is
The sum that I was told to bring you.
Don Cæsar (*gravely*). Ah! 'Tis well, I understand. (*Aside.*)
The devil now
I wish—— But there we must not disarrange
This admirable story. In the nick
Of time it comes. (*Aloud.*)
Now want you a receipt?
The Lackey. Not so, my Lord.
Don Cæsar (*pointing at the table*). Put there the money bag.
(*The* Lackey *obeys.*)
Whom comes it from?
The Lackey. My Lord knows very well.
Don Cæsar. Undoubtedly, but still——
The Lackey. This money here—
And this is what is needful that I add—
Now comes for purpose that you know, from him
You know.

DON CÆSAR (*satisfied with the explanation*). Ah!
THE LACKEY.   Both of us must careful be—
Hush!
DON CÆSAR.   Hush!—This money comes——The phrase is most
Magnificent! Repeat it once again.
THE LACKEY.   This money——
DON CÆSAR.   All explains itself. It comes
From him I know——
THE LACKEY.   For purpose that you know.
We must——
DON CÆSAR.   The pair of us!
THE LACKEY.   Be guarded now.
DON CÆSAR.   It is quite clear.
THE LACKEY.   I do not understand, I but obey.
DON CÆSAR.   Pshaw—Pshaw!
THE LACKEY.   But you, I know, Do comprehend.
DON CÆSAR.   The deuce!
THE LACKEY.   Sufficient 'tis.
DON CÆSAR.   I take it and I understand, my boy,
Receiving money always easy is.
THE LACKEY.   Hush!
DON CÆSAR.   Hush! Deuce take it—ah, we must not now
Imprudent be!
THE LACKEY.   Count it, my Lord!
DON CÆSAR.   For what, Pray, do you take me?
(*Admiring the rotundity of the bag on the table.*)
Oh! the fine paunch!
THE LACKEY (*insisting*). But——
DON CÆSAR.   I do confide in thee.
THE LACKEY.   The gold is in
Broad quadruples, that weigh their full seven drachms
And six and thirty grains, or good doubloons,
The silver in ،oss-maries.
(DON CÆSAR *opens the great bag and takes from it several small bags of gold and silver, which he opens and empties on to the table admiringly; then he digs his hand into the bags of gold and draws out handfuls, filling his pockets with quadruples and doubloons.*)
DON CÆSAR (*pausing, with majesty. Aside*). Now behold
My fine romance,—the crown of fairy-dreams
Is dying for love of a fat million.
(*He continues filling his pockets.*)
Oh joy! I take in like a galleon!
(*One pocket filled, he passes to another. He seeks everywhere for pockets and seems to have forgotten the Lackey.*)
THE LACKEY (*who looks at him calmly*). And now I wait your orders.
DON CÆSAR (*turning round*). What to do?
THE LACKEY.   To promptly execute without delay
A something which you know, but I do not,
A thing of great importance——
DON CÆSAR (*interrupting him as if understanding*). Public 'tis
And private——
THE LACKEY.   Which this instant should be done.
I say what I was told to say.
DON CÆSAR (*slapping him on the shoulder*). And I
Applaud thee for it—faithful servant thou!

THE LACKEY. That nothing be delayed my master sends
Myself to help you.
DON CÆSAR. Acting in accord,
Let us do what he wishes. (*Aside.*)
Hang me now
If I know what to tell him. (*Aloud.*)
Galleon,
Come here, and first (*He fills the other glass with wine*),
Drink this!
THE LACKEY. Indeed, my Lord——
DON CÆSAR. Drink this.
(*The* Lackey *drinks, and* DON CÆSAR *again fills the glass.*)
'Tis wine of Oropesa!
(*He makes the* Lackey *sit down, and plies him with wine.*)
Now
Let's chat.
(*Aside.*) His eyes already sparkle.
(*Aloud, and stretching himself on his chair.*)
Man
Is nought, dear friend, but black smoke that proceeds
From out the passions' fire. Pshaw! I declare
(*Pours wine for him to drink.*)
'Tis rubbish this I'm telling thee. At first
The smoke, unto blue heav'n recalled, comports
Itself in manner different from when
'Tis in a chimney. It mounts gaily, while
We tumble down.
(*He rubs his leg.*)
Only vile lead is man.
(*He fills the two glasses.*)
Let's drink. All thy doubloons are of less worth
Than is a passing drunkard's song.
(*Approaching nearer to him in a mysterious manner.*)
But see,
Be prudent. The o'erloaded axle breaks;
The wall without foundation suddenly
Gives way.—My mantle's collar please to hook.
THE LACKEY (*haughtily*). My Lord, I'm not a valet.
(*Before* DON CÆSAR *can prevent him, he rings the little bell on the table.*)
DON CÆSAR (*aside—terrified*). Oh, he rings!
The master, perhaps, will come himself. I'm caught!
(*Enter one of the* Negroes. DON CÆSAR, *a prey to the greatest anxiety, turns towards the opposite side, as if not knowing what to do.*)
THE LACKEY (*to the* Negro). Fasten my Lord's clasp.
(*The* Negro *gravely approaches* DON CÆSAR, *who looks at him as if stupefied. Then he fastens the mantle, bows, and goes out, leaving* DON CÆSAR *petrified.*)
DON CÆSAR (*rising from the table—aside*). On my word of honour!
Beelzebub's abode this is!
(*He comes to the front, and strides about.*)
My faith!
Now let things drift, and take what comes. At least,
I'll stir the crowns; a coffer full of them.
The money I have got! What shall I do
With it?
(*Turning towards the* Lackey, *who is still at the table, drinking, and who begins to reel in his chair.*)
Your pardon—stop.
(*Musing—aside.*)

Now, let me see,—
If I should pay my creditors?—for shame!
—At least, to calm their minds that are so prompt
At turning sour,—if I should water them
With something on account? What good is it
To water flowers so villainous? How now
The devil did I think of such a thing?
Nothing there is like money to corrupt
A man, and fill him up unto the throat
With all mean sentiments! E'en if he were
From Hannibal himself descended, him
Who conquered Rome! To see me paying debts
I owe! what would they say? Ah, ah!

THE LACKEY (*emptying his glass*). What now
Do you command of me?

DON CÆSAR. Let be—I am
Reflecting. Drink, while waiting.

(*The* Lackey *begins drinking again.* DON CÆSAR *continues to muse; then suddenly strikes his forehead, as if he had found an idea.*)
Yes!

(*To the* Lackey.)
Get up
Immediately. See now, what must be done.
Thy pockets fill with gold.

(*The* Lackey *rises, stumbling, and fills the pockets of his coat,* DON CÆSAR *helping him as he continues.*)
Go thou unto
The lane which leads from out the Mayor Square,
Enter at Number Nine. A narrow house;
A pleasant dwelling, if it did not hap

The glass panes at the right were paper patched.

THE LACKEY. A one-eyed house?[1]

DON CÆSAR. Oh no, it only squints.[1]
One might be crippled mounting up the stairs,
So take you care.

THE LACKEY. A ladder is't?

DON CÆSAR. Almost,
But steeper. Up above, a beauty dwells,
Easy to know—beneath a threepenny cap
Thickish disordered hair. She's rather short
And red—a charming woman, though. My boy,
You'll be respectful, she my dear love is,
Lucinda fair, with eyes like indigo,
Once she; who danced fandango for the Pope
At eve to see. Count out and give to her
A hundred of the ducats, in my name.
Then, in a hovel near, you'll see a stout
And red-nosed devil, with an old felt hat
Dragged down upon his eyebrows, and a plume,
A feather brush, that tragically hangs
Astonished from it; rapier at his side,
And rags upon his back. Give next, from me,
Unto this creature six piastres.—Then
Go further, thou wilt find a hole, black like
An oven, 'tis a tavern at cross roads;
There smokes and drinks i' the porch, a frequenter,
A gentle-manner'd man who leads a life
That's elegant, a gentleman from whom

---

[1] *Maison borgne* — French slang for a disreputable house; and *louche*, for a suspicious one.—TRANS.

An oath ne'er dropp'd, my heart's friend he; his name
Is Goulatromba. Give him thirty crowns!
And tell him for thanksgiving he alone
Must drink them quick, and he shall have some more.
Give to these rascals in the biggest coins,
And do not wonder at the eyes they'll ope.

THE LACKEY. And afterwards?

DON CÆSAR. Why, keep the rest. And then
At last——

THE LACKEY. What would my Lord?

DON CÆSAR. Then surfeit thou
Thyself, thou scamp. Break many pots, and make
Much noise, and not until to-morrow, in
The night, go home.

THE LACKEY. Enough, my Prince.

(*He moves toward the door in a zig-zag way.*)

DON CÆSAR (*aside—observing his walk*). He is
Abominably drunk!

(*Recalling the other, who turns back.*)
Ah, now—when out
Thou goest, idle folks will follow thee.
Do honour to the drink thou's't had.
Try thou
To bear thyself in noble fashion. If
By chance some crowns from out thy stocking drop,
Then let them fall,—and if assayers, clerks,
Some scholars, or the beggars that one sees
Pass by, should pick them up, let them do so.
Don't be a mortal fierce, that they would dread
T' approach.—And e'en if from thy pocket some
They take—be thou indulgent. They are men
As we And, as you see, it is a law
For us, in this world full of misery,
To give sometimes a little joy to all
Who live.

(*With melancholy.*)
Perchance they will be hang'd some day!
Show, then, the kindness to them which is due!
Go, now.

(*The Lackey goes out. Left alone, DON CÆSAR sits down again, and leans his elbow on the table, appearing to be plunged in deep thought.*)
It is the duty of the sage
And Christian having money that he use
It well. For eight days at the very least
I have enough. These will I live. And should
A little money still remain, I will
Employ it piously. But I must not
Be over confident. Undoubtedly
'Tis all a blunder, and from me it will
Be taken, ah, the thing will all become
Misunderstood. A fine scrape this of mine. . . .

(*The door at the back opens. Enter an old, grey-haired* Duenna *in black dress and mantle, and with a fan.*)

SCENE 4.—DON CÆSAR. A DUENNA.

THE DUENNA (*at the threshold of the door*). Don Cæsar de Bazan?

(DON CÆSAR, *absorbed in his meditations, turns his head suddenly.*)

DON CÆSAR. Now then, what is it?
(*Aside.*)
A woman! Oh!

(*Whilst the* Duenna *makes a low re-*

spectful curtsey at the back he comes to the front wonder-struck.)
The devil or Salluste
Must be mixed up in this! Next I expect
To see my cousin here. Duenna, oh!
(*Aloud.*)
'Tis I, Don Cæsar, tell your business, pray.
(*Aside.*)
Most commonly it is a woman old
That ushers in a young one.
    THE DUENNA (*bowing and making sign of the Cross*). I, my Lord,
Salute you, on this fast day, in the name
Of Him o'er whom there's nothing can prevail.
    DON CÆSAR (*aside*). A galant ending that begins devoutly.
(*Aloud.*)
Amen. Good day.
    THE DUENNA. May God maintain you, e'er
In happiness. (*Mysteriously.*)
Know you of some one who
Has sent me now, with whom you've plann'd to-night
A secret meeting?
    DON CÆSAR. Oh, I'm capable
Of such a thing.
    THE DUENNA (*who takes from her farthingale a folded letter which she shows to him, but without allowing him to take it*). Then you indeed it is,
Galant discreet, who've just addressed to one
Who loves you, for to-night a message, —one
Whom you know well?
    DON CÆSAR. It must be I.
    THE DUENNA. Good—good.
The lady married to some dotard old
Is forced no doubt, to careful be. I was
Desired to hither come. Her I know not,
But you know her—it was her waiting maid
Who told me about things. That was enough,
Without the names.
    DON CÆSAR. Excepting mine.
    THE DUENNA. 'Tis plain,
Th' appointment for the lady has been made
By her soul's friend,—but fearing there may be
Some snare, and knowing too much caution ne'er
Spoiled aught, she sends me here from your own mouth
To have the confirmation——
    DON CÆSAR. Oh the old
And surly thing! What fuss about a sweet
Love letter! Yes, 'tis I myself, I tell You so.
    THE DUENNA (*placing on the table the folded letter, which* DON CÆSAR *looks at with curiosity*).
In that case then, if you it be,
The one word, *Come*, upon the letter you
Will write—but not by your own hand—that so
There may be nothing compromised.
    DON CÆSAR. Indeed!
From mine own hand! (*Aside.*)
A message well conveyed!
(*He puts out his hand to take the letter; but it has been resealed and the* DUENNA *will not let him touch it.*)
    THE DUENNA. You must not open
You will recognize
The fold.

Don Cæsar. By Heaven! (*Aside.*)
I who burn to see!——
But let me play my part!
(*He rings the little bell. One of the Negroes enters.*)
Know'st thou to write?
(*The Negro nods an affirmative sign. Astonishment of* Don Cæsar.) (*Aside.*)
A sign! (*Aloud.*) Art thou then dumb, thou rascal?
(*Again the Negro makes the sign of affirmation. Fresh stupefaction of* Don Cæsar.) (*Aside.*)
Well!
Continue! Mutes appear the latest thing!
(*To the Mute, showing him the letter which the old woman holds down on the table.*)
Write there: Come.
(*The Mute writes.* Don Cæsar *signs to the* Duenna *to take back the letter, and to the Mute to go. Exit the Mute.*)
Ah! he is obedient!
The Duenna (*with an air of mystery again placing the letter in her farthingale, and approaching nearer to* Don Cæsar).
To-night you'll see her. Is she very fair?
Don Cæsar. Oh, charming!
The Duenna. 'Twas the cunning waiting-maid
Who managed it. At sermon-time aside
She took me. Oh, how beautiful was she!
With angel's profile and a demon's eye.
Knowing in love affairs she seemed to be.
Don Cæsar (*aside*). I'd be contented with the maid!
The Duenna. We judge—
For always beauty makes the plain afraid,—
So with Sultana and her slave, and with
The master and his man. Most certainly
Your love is very beautiful.
Don Cæsar. I'm proud,
Indeed, to think so!
The Duenna (*making a curtsey and about to withdraw*). Sir, I kiss your hand.
Don Cæsar (*giving her a handful of doubloons*). I'll grease thy palm. Old woman, stop.
The Duenna (*pocketing them*). Ah, youth
Is gay to-day!
Don Cæsar (*dismissing her*). Now go.
The Duenna (*curtseys*). If you have need——
I'm named Dame Oliva. Saint Isidro, The Convent,——
(*She goes out. Afterwards the door re-opens and her head appears.*)
Always at the right I sit
Of the third pillar entering the church.
(Don Cæsar *turns round with impatience. The door closes; again it half opens and the old woman re-appears.*)
To-night you'll see her! In your prayers, my Lord,
Remember me.
Don Cæsar (*driving her away angrily*). Ah!
(*The* Duenna *disappears and the door closes.*)
Don Cæsar (*alone*). Now I'm resolved, my faith,
At nothing more to be at all surprised.
I'm in the moon. Behold a love affair
Now comes; I am about to satisfy

My heart, after long hunger. (*Musing.*) Oh all this
To me just now seems mighty good. But ah!
Beware the end!
(*The door at the back opens.* Don Guritan *appears with two long naked swords under his arm.*)

Scene 5.—Don Cæsar—Don Guritan.

Don Guritan (*at the back*). Don Cæsar de Bazan?
Don Cæsar (*turning and perceiving* Don Guritan *with the two swords*). And now! Well, well! Events were fine enough,
But better still they are. A dinner good,
Then money; and an assignation—now
A duel! Cæsar in his natural state
Again am I!
(*He greets* Don Guritan *gaily, with demonstrative salutations;* Don Guritan *looks at him impatiently, and advances to the front with a firm step.*)
Here is he, my dear Lord
And will you please to enter—take a chair.
(*He places an arm-chair—*Don Guritan *remains standing.*)
Be seated, pray;—without formality.
As if at home. I'm charm'd to see you, Sir;
There, let us chat a moment. Tell me now
What's doing in Madrid? A charming place!
I nothing know; but I suppose that still
They wonder at the Matalobos, and
The Lindamere! As for myself, I'd fear
The stealer of our hearts as peril more
Than stealer of our money bags. Oh, Sir,
The women! Sex possessed! My brain is crack'd
Where they're concern'd, they so enslave me. Speak,
And tell me what is doing now-a-days;
I am but half alive—an ox—a thing
Absurd—with nought that's human left in him,
A dead man risen, an hidalgo true
Of old Castile. They've robbed me of my plume,
And I my gloves have lost. I come from lands
Most wonderful.
Don Guritan. You come, dear Sir? Ah well,
I've just arrived from farther off than you!
Don Cæsar (*brightening up*). From what distinguished shore?
Don Guritan. Down yonder, in The north.
Don Cæsar. And I from farther in the south.
Don Guritan. I'm furious!
Don Cæsar. Is it so? I am enraged!
Don Guritan. Twelve hundred leagues I've travelled!
Don Cæsar. I have done
Two thousand! Women fair, black, yellow, brown
I've seen. To places bless'd by heaven I've been.
Algiers the happy town, and fair Tunis
Where one may see—such pleasant ways have Turks—
People impaled hooked up above the doors.
Don Guritan. I have been played a trick.
Don Cæsar. And I've been sold.

Don Guritan. Almost exiled I was.
Don Cæsar. I almost hang'd!
Don Guritan. To Neubourg cunningly they sent me off,
To bear these few words written in a box:
"Keep this old fool as long as possible."
Don Cæsar (*bursting out laughing*). And who did this?
Don Guritan. But I will wring the neck
Of Cæsar de Bazan.
Don Cæsar (*gravely*). Ah!
Don Guritan. And to crown
His insolence, he just now sent to me
A lackey to excuse himself, he said,
A serving man, but I refused to see
The varlet, and I made them lock him up.
Now to the master, Cæsar de Bazan,
I come! This most audacious traitor knave!
See now, I'll kill him! Where is he?
Don Cæsar (*still gravely*). I'm he.
Don Guritan. You!—You are joking, Sir?
Don Cæsar. I am Don Cæsar.
Don Guritan. What! This again!
Don Cæsar. Undoubtedly again!
Don Guritan. Leave off this play, you greatly weary me,
E'en if you think that you are droll.
Don Cæsar. And you
Amuse me much. You have to me the air
Of jealousy. Exceedingly, dear Sir,
I pity you. The ills that come to us
From our own vices are more hard to bear
Than those which hap to us from others' sins.
I'd rather be—and so I've often said—
Quite poor than miserly, and be deceived
Rather than jealous. You are both. And now,
Upon my soul, I do to-night expect
Your wife.
Don Guritan. My wife!
Don Cæsar. Oh yes, your wife!
Don Guritan. Come now!
I am not married.
Don Cæsar. Yet you have stirr'd up
This riot! And you're not a married man!
For the last quarter of an hour you have
Assumed the husband's roar, or else the air
Of weeping tiger, so efficiently
That in simplicity I've given you
A heap of precious counsel seeming fit!
But if not married, why, by Hercules,
Have you thus made yourself ridiculous?
Don Guritan. Do you know, Sir, that you exasperate me?
Don Cæsar. Pooh!
Don Guritan. This is too much!
Don Cæsar. Truly?
Don Guritan. Oh, but you
Shall pay for this!
Don Cæsar (*looking in a jeering manner at* Don Guritan's *feet, which are covered by waves of ribbon, according to the new fashion*).
In days gone by it was
That on the head were ribbons worn. I mark
That now—and 'tis an honest mode—they're placed
Upon the boot, and feet are thus adorned.
A charming thing!
Don Guritan. I see that we must fight!
Don Cæsar (*with indifference*). You think so?

DON GURITAN. You're not Cæsar, that concerns
Myself; but I'll commence with you.
DON CÆSAR. Good, good!
Take care with me to finish.
DON GURITAN (*presenting one of the swords to him*). Fop! at once.
DON CÆSAR (*taking the sword*). Immediately. When I've a chance to fight I do not lose it!
DON GURITAN. Where?
DON CÆSAR. Behind the wall. This street's deserted.
DON GURITAN (*trying the point of his sword on the floor*). As for Cæsar, ah! I'll kill him afterwards.
DON CÆSAR. Indeed?
DON GURITAN. Most surely!
DON CÆSAR (*also making his sword bend*). Pshaw! One of us dead, you I then defy
To kill Don Cæsar.
DON GURITAN. Let us out!
(*They go out. The sound of their retreating steps is heard. A little concealed door opens in the right wall and* DON SALLUSTE *enters by it.*)

SCENE 6.

DON SALLUSTE (*dressed in a dark green coat, almost black. He appears anxious and pre-occupied. He looks about, and listens uneasily*). There's nought
Prepared! (*Noticing the table covered with dishes.*)
What means all this?
(*Hearing the noise of* CÆSAR's *and* GURITAN's *steps.*)
What noise is that?
(*He walks about in reverie.*)
This morning Gudiel saw the Page go out
And followed him.—Unto Don Guritan He went.—I see not Ruy Blas. This Page——
Oh Satan! 'Tis some countermine! some word
Of faithful counsel, with the which he charged
Don Guritan for her!—And from the mutes
One can learn nothing! It is that! I had
Not counted on Don Guritan at all.
(*Enter* DON CÆSAR. *In his hand he carries the bare sword, which, on entering, he throws upon an arm-chair.*)

SCENE 7.—DON SALLUSTE—DON CÆSAR.

DON CÆSAR (*from the threshold of the door*). Ah, I was very sure! I see you then,
Old fiend!
DON SALLUSTE (*turning round petrified*). Don Cæsar!
DON CÆSAR (*crossing his arms and bursting out laughing*). You are weaving now
Some frightful scheme! But have I not disturb'd
It all just now, by sprawling heavily Into the midst of it?
DON SALLUSTE (*aside*). Oh, all is lost!
DON CÆSAR (*laughing*). Through all this morning have I come across
Your spider webs. Not one of all your plans
Is now unspoilt. I flung myself on them At hazard; and the whole demolished I. This is delightful!
DON SALLUSTE (*aside*). Demon! What can he
Have done?

Don Cæsar (*laughing louder and louder*). The man you sent with money-bag
For purpose that you know, to whom you know.
(*He laughs.*)
What a good joke!
Don Salluste. What then?
Don Cæsar. I made him drunk.
Don Salluste. About the money that he had?
Don Cæsar. With it
I presents made to divers persons. Well, We all have friends.
Don Salluste. You wrongly me suspect——
Don Cæsar (*rattling the money in his pockets*). I first my pockets filled, you will believe.
(*Laughs again.*)
You understand? the lady!
Don Salluste. Oh!
Don Cæsar (*remarking his anxiety*). You know,—
(Don Salluste *listens with redoubled anxiety.* Don Cæsar *proceeds, laughing.*)
She sent an old duenna—fearful wretch, With sprouting beard and drunkard's ruddy nose——
Don Salluste. What for?
Don Cæsar. To quietly inquire if it Were true—from prudence—that Don Cæsar here
Expected her to-night——
Don Salluste (*aside*). Good Heavens! (*Aloud.*)
And what
Didst thou reply?
Don Cæsar. My master, I said yes! That I awaited her.
Don Salluste (*aside*). It may be all Is not yet lost!

Don Cæsar. And last your swordsman fine,
Your Captain, on the field he gave his name—
'Twas Guritan. (Don Salluste *starts.*)
This morning prudently
He would not see the lackey that was sent
With message from Don Cæsar, and he came
To me demanding satisfaction——
Don Salluste. Well,
And what didst thou?
Don Cæsar. I killed the goose-cap.
Don Salluste. Ah! Indeed?
Don Cæsar. Yea, 'neath the wall he's dying now.
Don Salluste. Art sure he'll die?
Don Cæsar. I fear so.
Don Salluste (*aside*). Oh, again I breathe! By Grace of heaven! nothing he
Has yet disturbed! Quite otherwise. But let me
Be rid of him, this rough assistant, now! The money—as for that, 'tis nought.
(*Aloud.*) Your tale
Is very strange. And have you seen none else?
Don Cæsar. No soul. But soon I shall. I shall go on.
My name will cause sensation through the town.
I'll make a frightful scandal, you may rest
Assured.
Don Salluste (*aside*). The devil!
(*Eagerly, and approaching* Don Cæsar.)
Money you may keep,
But leave this house.
Don Cæsar. Ah, yes, one knows your ways;

You'd have me followed! Then I should return—
Delightful destiny—to contemplate
Thy blue, oh sea Mediterranean!
Not I.
    Don Salluste. Believe me.
    Don Cæsar. No. Besides, within
This palace-prison some one is, I feel,
A prey to your dark treachery. All plots
Of Courts have double ladders. On one side
Arms tied, and gloom, and troubled looks. By one
Ascends the suff'rer, by the other mounts
The executioner.—Now you must be
The headsman——of necessity.
    Don Salluste. Oh! oh!
    Don Cæsar. For me! I pull the ladder, and crack—down
It goes!
    Don Salluste. I swear——
    Don Cæsar. I will to spoil it all
Stay through th' adventure. Oh, I know you sharp
Enough, my subtle cousin, puppets two
Or three to hang up by one cord. Hold, now,
I'm one! and I will here remain!
    Don Salluste. Hark, now——
    Don Cæsar. To rhetoric! Ah, me you sold away
To Afric's pirates! Here you fabricate
Some Cæsar false! And thus you compromise
My name!
    Don Salluste. Mere chance it was.
    Don Cæsar. Mere chance! Excuse
That dish that rogues prepare for fools to gulp;
No chance was it. The worse for you if plans
Break through. But I intend to succour those
Whom you'd destroy. I shall cry out my name
From the house-tops.
    (*He climbs on the window supports and looks out.*) Now wait! Here is good luck!
The Alguazils are 'neath the window now.
    (*He passes his arm through the bars and shakes them, crying out*) Halloa!
    Don Salluste (*aside, and terrified, at the front of the stage*).
All's lost if he be recognized!
    (*The* Alguazils *enter, preceded by an* Alcaid. Don Salluste *appears in great perplexity.* Don Cæsar *goes towards the* Alcaid *with an air of triumph.*)

Scene 8.—The Same, an Alcaid, and the Alguazils.

    Don Cæsar (*to the* Alcaid). You, in your warrant, will take down——
    Don Salluste (*pointing to* Don Cæsar). That this
Man is the famous robber Matalobos!
    Don Cæsar (*amazed*). How!
    Don Salluste (*aside*). All I gain, if I but gain a day.
    (*To the* Alcaid.)
This man in shining daylight dares to come
Into our houses.—Seize the thief.
    (*The* Alguazils *seize* Don Cæsar *by the collar.*)
    Don Cæsar (*furious, to* Don Salluste). Pardon!
You lie outrageously!
    The Alcaid. Who was it, then, That called us?
    Don Salluste. It was I.

Don Cæsar. By heaven, now!
That's bold!
The Alcaid. Be still! I think he's
right.
Don Cæsar. But list,
I am Don Cæsar de Bazan himself!
Don Salluste. Don Cæsar! If you
please, examine now
His mantle—you will find that Salluste's writ
Beneath the collar. 'Tis a mantle which
Just now he stole from me.
(*The* Alguazils *snatch off the mantle, and the* Alcaid *examines it.*)
The Alcaid. Quite right—'tis so.
Don Salluste. The doublet that he wears——
Don Cæsar (*aside*). Accursèd Salluste!
Don Salluste (*continuing*). Belongs
to the Count d'Albe; it was from him
He stole it,
(*showing an escutcheon embroidered on the facing of the left sleeve*)
And whose 'scutcheon you behold!
Don Cæsar (*aside*). Bewitched he must be!
The Alcaid (*examining the blazon*).
Ah, yes—yes; here are
The castles two, in gold——
Don Salluste. Also you'll see
Two cauldrons, Henriquez and Guzman.
(*In struggling,* Don Cæsar *has let fall some doubloons from his pockets.* Don Salluste *points out to the* Alcaid *the manner in which they were filled.*)
There!
Is that the way that money's borne about
By honest men?
The Alcaid (*shaking his head*).
Ahem!

Don Cæsar (*aside*). I'm caught.
The Alcaid. Here are
Some papers.
Don Cæsar (*aside*). Ah, they've
found! Oh, oh, the poor
Love-letters saved through all my scrapes!
The Alcaid (*examining the papers*).
Letters——
What's this?—in different hands are they——
Don Salluste (*making him observe the directions*). But all
Directed to the Count.
The Alcaid. Yes.
Don Cæsar. But——
The Alcaid (*tying his hands*).
Caught now!
What luck!
An Alguazil (*entering to the* Alcaid).
Outside, my Lord, a man has just
Been killed.
The Alcaid. Who is the murderer?
Don Salluste (*pointing to* Don Cæsar). 'Tis he.
Don Cæsar (*aside*). The duel! Oh, that senseless freak!
Don Salluste. Ah, when
He entered, in his hand he had a sword,
And there it is.
The Alcaid (*examining the sword*).
And blood upon it! Ah!
(*To* Don Cæsar.)
There—go with them.
Don Salluste (*to* Don Cæsar, *whom the* Alguazils *are taking away*).
To Matalobos now
Good evening.
Don Cæsar (*making a step towards him and looking at him fixedly*). Earth's
vilest scoundrel you!

ACT FIFTH:

THE TIGER AND THE LION

The same room. It is night. A lamp is on the table. At the rising of the curtain RUY BLAS *is alone. He is dressed in a long black robe, which conceals his other vestments.*

SCENE 1.

RUY BLAS (*alone*). 'Tis ended now.
The dream—the vision—all
Has passed away. All day till eve I've walked
Haphazard through the streets. Just now I've hope.
I'm calm. At night the head is less disturb'd
By noise, and one reflects the better then.
Nought too alarming in these darkened walls
I see; the furniture is 'ranged; the keys
Are in the locks; the mutes sleep overhead;
The house is truly very still. Oh yes,
There is no reason for alarm. All things
Proceed quite well. My page all faithful is.
Don Guritan is sure to stir himself
For her. Oh, God! May I not thank Thee now,
Just God, for suff'ring that advice to reach
Her ears. Thou, gracious God, hast aided me,
'Tis Thou hast helped me to protect and save
This angel, and defeat Don Salluste. Oh
May she have nought to fear, and nought, alas,
To suffer; and may she be ever saved!
And oh, that I may die!
(*He draws from his bosom a little vial which he places on the table.*)
Yes, perish now,
Despised! and sink into the grave!
Yes, die
As one should die, who seeks to expiate
A crime! Die in this dwelling, wretched, vile,
And alone!
(*He throws open the black robe, under which is seen the livery which he wore in the first act.*)
Die with thy livery beneath
Thy winding-sheet! Oh, if the demon comes
To see his victim dead,
(*He pushes a piece of furniture to barricade the secret door.*)
he shall at least
Not enter by this horrid door!
(*He comes back to the table.*)
'Tis sure
The Page has spoken to Don Guritan.
It was not eight o'clock this morn.
(*He gazes on the vial.*)
For me
I have condemned myself, and now prepare
My execution,—on my head I shall
Myself let fall the tomb's so heavy lid.
At least I have the comfort certainly
To know there is no help. My fall must be.
(*Sinking into the arm-chair.*)
And yet she loved me! Oh God, help me now!
I've not the courage!
(*He weeps.*)

Oh! he might in peace
Have left us!
(He hides his face in his hands and sobs.)
Oh, my God!
(Raising his head, as if distraught, and looking at the vial.)
The man who sold
Me this asked me what day o' the month it was.
I could not tell. My head's confused.
Oh, men
Are cruel. You may die, and none will care.
I suffer.—Me she loved!—To know things past
Can never be restored! And to behold
Her nevermore! Her hand that I have press'd!
Her lips that touch'd my brow—Angel adored!
Poor angel! There is need to die, and die
Despairing! Oh, her dress, the folds of which
Each one had grace, her footstep that had power
To stir my soul when it pass'd by, her eyes
That did intoxicate mine own still all
Irresolute, her smile, her voice——and I
Shall see her, hear her never more. Is this
Then possible? Oh, never!
(In anguish he stretches out his hand to the vial; at the moment when he seizes it convulsively the door at the back opens. The QUEEN *appears dressed in white, with a dark mantle, the hood of which having fallen back on her shoulders, shows her pale face. She carries in her hand a dark lantern which she places on the floor and walks rapidly towards* RUY BLAS.)

SCENE 2.—RUY BLAS—THE QUEEN.

THE QUEEN *(entering)*. Don Cæsar!
RUY BLAS *(turning round with a frightened gesture, and closing hurriedly the robe which had hidden his livery)*. Oh God! 'tis she! In a most horrid snare
She's taken. *(Aloud.)* Madam!——
THE QUEEN. Cæsar! What a cry
Of fright——
RUY BLAS. Who was it told you to come here?
THE QUEEN. Thyself.
RUY BLAS. Oh, how?
THE QUEEN. I have received from you——
RUY BLAS *(breathless)*. Speak, quick!
THE QUEEN. A note.
RUY BLAS. From me!
THE QUEEN. By your own hand indited.
RUY BLAS. This is but to dash one's brow
Against the wall! But oh, I have not writ—.
Of that I'm very sure!
THE QUEEN *(drawing from her bosom a letter, which she gives him)*.
Read—read it then.
*(*RUY BLAS *takes the letter eagerly, and bends towards the lamp to read it.)*
RUY BLAS *(reading)*.
"A danger terrible environs me;
My Queen alone can stay the tempest's force——
(He looks at the letter as if in a stupor and unable to read further.)
THE QUEEN *(continuing, and pointing*

with her finger to the lines as she reads).
"By coming to my house this night. If not,
I'm lost."

RUY BLAS (*in a stifled voice*). What treason! Oh, that letter!

THE QUEEN (*continuing to read*). "Come
To the door that's at the end of th' Avenue;
At night you'll not be recognized. And one
Who is devoted will be there to open
The door."

RUY BLAS (*aside*). This note I had forgotten.
(*To the* QUEEN, *in a terrible voice.*)
Go
Away!

THE QUEEN. I'll go, Don Cæsar. You are cruel!
My God! What have I done?

RUY BLAS. Good heavens! What?
You ruin and destroy yourself!

THE QUEEN. But how?

RUY BLAS. Explain I cannot. Fly—fly quick.

THE QUEEN. This morn
I for your safety did precaution take,
And a duenna sent——

RUY BLAS. Oh, God! but now
As from a heart that bleeds, I feel your life
In streams is running out.—Go—go!

THE QUEEN (*as if struck by a sudden idea*). Inspired
I am by that devotion which my love
Suggests. Oh, you approach some dreadful hour,
And would remove me from the danger now!
But I remain!

RUY BLAS. Oh, what sublimity!
What thoughtfulness!—Oh God! to thus remain
At such an hour in such a place!

THE QUEEN. From you
The letter really came. And thus——

RUY BLAS (*raising his arms to heaven in despair*). Oh Power
Divine!

THE QUEEN. You wish me gone.

RUY BLAS (*taking her hands*). Oh, understand!

THE QUEEN. I do. Upon the moment's spur you wrote,
And after——

RUY BLAS. Unto thee I have not writ.
I am a demon. Fly! Ah it is thou,
Poor child, who lead'st thyself into the snare!
Ah, it is true, and hell on every side
Besieges thee! Then nothing can I find
That will persuade thee? Listen—understand;
I love thee well, thou know'st. To save thy mind
From what is imaged, I would pluck my heart
From out my body. Go thou!

THE QUEEN. Don Cæsar——

RUY BLAS. Go—go. But I remember, some one must
Have opened to you?

THE QUEEN. Yes.

RUY BLAS. Oh Satan! Who?

THE QUEEN. One in a mask—and hidden by the wall.

RUY BLAS. What said the man? what was his figure—say?
Oh, was he tall? Who was he? Speak, I wait!

(*A man in black, and masked, appears at the door at the back.*)

THE MASKED MAN. 'Twas I.

(*He takes off his mask. It is* DON SALLUSTE. *The* QUEEN *and* RUY BLAS *recognize him with terror.*)

SCENE 3.—THE SAME, DON SALLUSTE.

RUY BLAS. Great God! Fly, Madam, fly!

DON SALLUSTE. There is
No longer time. Madam de Neubourg now
Has ceased to be the Queen of Spain.

THE QUEEN (*horrified*). Don Salluste!

DON SALLUSTE (*pointing to* RUY BLAS). That man's companion you henceforth must be.

THE QUEEN. Great God! ah yes, it is indeed a snare!
Don Cæsar——

RUY BLAS (*despairingly*). Madam, what alas, is it
You've done?

DON SALLUSTE (*moving slowly towards the* QUEEN). I hold you here.—
But I will speak
Without offence unto your Majesty,
For without wrath am I.—I find you here—
Now listen, do not let us make a stir—
At midnight, in Don Cæsar's room alone.
This fact, if public—for a queen—would be
Enough at Rome the marriage to annul.
And promptly would the Holy Father be
Informed of it.—But by consent the thing
Could be concealed.

(*He draws from his pocket a parchment, which he unrolls and presents to the* QUEEN.)
Sign me this letter then
Unto His Majesty our King. I will
Send it by hand of the grand equerry
To the chief notary, and afterwards—
A carriage, where I've placed a heap of gold

(*Pointing outside.*)
Is there—set out the two of you at once.
I help you. Be not anxious, you can go
Toledo way by Alcantare—so
Reach Portugal. Go where you will—to us
It is the same. We'll shut our eyes.—Obey.
I swear that I alone as yet am 'ware
Of the adventure; but if you refuse,
Madrid to-morrow shall know everything.
Let us be calm. I hold you in my hand.

(*Pointing to the table on which is an ink-stand.*)
Madam, for writing, what you need is there.

THE QUEEN (*overwhelmed, falling into an arm-chair*). I'm in his power.

DON SALLUSTE. From you I only ask
This acquiescence signed, for me to send
To the king.

(*Whispering to* RUY BLAS, *who listens motionless and thunderstruck.*)
Let me alone, it is for thee
I work. (*To the* QUEEN.) Sign now.

THE QUEEN (*aside, trembling*). What can I do?

DON SALLUSTE (*leaning over her, and presenting a pen*). There now!
What is a crown? You happiness will gain,

Though you may lose a throne. My people all
Remain outside. They nothing know of this,
All passes here between us three.
(*Trying to put the pen between the* QUEEN'S *fingers, she neither taking nor rejecting it.*) Well now,
(*The* QUEEN, *distraught and undecided, looks at him with anguish.*)
If you sign not you strike the blow yourself—
The scandal and the cloister!
  THE QUEEN (*overwhelmed*). Oh, my God!
  DON SALLUSTE (*pointing to* RUY BLAS). Don Cæsar loves you. He is worthy you;
Upon my honour he is nobly born;
Almost a prince. Lord of a donjon keep
With walls embattled, holding fee of lands,
He is the Duke d'Olmedo—Count Bazan, Grandee of Spain——
  (*He pushes to the parchment the hand of the* QUEEN, *who, trembling and dismayed, seems ready to sign.*)
  RUY BLAS (*as if suddenly awakening*). My name is Ruy Blas,
And I a lackey am!
  (*Snatching the pen from the hand of the* QUEEN, *and the parchment, which he tears.*)
Madam, sign not!—
At last!—I suffocate!
  THE QUEEN. Oh, what says he? Don Cæsar!
  RUY BLAS (*letting his robe fall, and showing himself in livery without a sword*). Yes, my name is Ruy Blas.
I am the servant of that man! (*Turning to* DON SALLUSTE.)
I say
There's been enough of treason, and that I
Refuse my happiness!—Oh thanks!—
You thought
That you did well to whisper in my ear!
I say that it is time, that I at last
Should waken, though I'm strangled in your web
Of hideous plots—and I no further step
Will go. I say we two together make,
My Lord, a pair that's infamous. I have
The clothing of a lackey—you the soul!
  DON SALLUSTE (*to the* QUEEN *coldly*). This man indeed my servant is.
  (*To* RUY BLAS, *with authority.*)
Not one
Word more.
  THE QUEEN (*letting a cry of despair escape her, and wringing her hands*). Just heav'n!
  DON SALLUSTE (*continuing*). Only he spoke too soon.
  (*He crosses his arms, and holds himself up, speaking with a voice of thunder.*)
Well—yes! now 'tis for me to tell it all.
It matters not, my vengeance in its way
Is all complete.
  (*To the* QUEEN.)
What think you? On my word,
Madrid will laugh! You ruined me! and you
I have dethroned. You banished me, and now
I boast of driving you away. Ha, ha!
You offered me for wife your waiting-maid!

(*Bursting into laughter.*)
My lackey I for lover give to you.
You can espouse him certainly. The King
Sinks fast!—A lover's heart will be your wealth.
(*He laughs.*)
You will have made him Duke, that you might be
His Duchess!
(*Grinding his teeth.*)
Ah, you blighted, ruined me,
And trampled me beneath your feet, and yet—
And yet you slept in peace! Fool that you were!

(*Whilst he has been speaking,* RUY BLAS *has gone to the door at the back and fastened it; then he has approached him by soft steps from behind, without having been perceived. At the moment when* DON SALLUSTE *finishes, fixing his eyes full of hatred and triumph on the annihilated* QUEEN, RUY BLAS *seizes the sword of the* MARQUIS *by the hilt, and draws it out swiftly.*)

RUY BLAS (*with the sword of* DON SALLUSTE *in his hand*). I say you have insulted now your Queen!

(DON SALLUSTE *rushes towards the door.* RUY BLAS *bars the way.*)

—Oh, go not there! 'tis not worth while; long since
I fastened it. Marquis, until to-day,
Satan protected thee; but if he will
From my hands pluck thee, let him show himself.
—'Tis my turn now!—When we a serpent meet,
It must be crush'd. No one can enter here.

No, not thy people, and not hell. Beneath
Mine iron heel I hold thee foaming now!
—This man spoke insolently to you, Madam!
I will explain. He has no human soul.
A monster he. With jibings yesterday
He suffocated me. He crush'd my heart,
For his mere pleasure. Oh, he bade me close
A window, and he martyrized me then!
I prayed—I wept—I cannot tell you all.
(*To the* MARQUIS.)
In these last moments you have counted o'er
Your wrongs. I shall not answer your complaints.
Besides, I comprehend them not. But you,
Oh wretch! you dare your Queen to outrage now
—Woman adorable—whilst I am by!
Hold! for a clever man, in truth you much
Astonish me! And you imagine, too,
That I shall see you do it, and say nought!
But listen,—whatsoe'er his sphere, my Lord,
When a vile, trait'rous, tortuous scoundrel strange
And monstrous acts commits, noble or churl,
All men have right, in coming on his path,
To splutter out his sentence to his face,
And take a sword, a knife, a hatchet——
Oh,
By Heav'n! to be a lackey! When I should
The headsman be!

THE QUEEN. You do not mean to kill
This man?
RUY BLAS. Madam, I am ashamed, indeed,
That I my duty must accomplish here;
But this affair must all be stifled now.
(*He pushes* DON SALLUSTE *towards the closet.*)
'Tis settled. Go you there, my Lord, and pray.
DON SALLUSTE. It is assassination.
RUY BLAS. Think you so?
DON SALLUSTE (*unarmed, and looking around him with rage*).
Nothing upon these walls! No arms!
(*To* RUY BLAS.)
A sword,
At least!
RUY BLAS. Marquis, you jest! What! Master! is 't
That I'm a gentleman? a duel! fie!
One of thy servants am I, in galloon
And red, a knave to be chastised and whipp'd,
And one who kills! Yes, I shall kill you, Sir——
Believe you it?—as villain infamous!
As craven! as a dog!
THE QUEEN. Have mercy on him!
RUY BLAS (*to the* QUEEN, *and seizing the* MARQUIS). Madam, each one takes vengeance for himself.
The demon cannot any longer be
Saved by an Angel!
THE QUEEN (*kneeling*). Mercy!
DON SALLUSTE (*calling for help*). Murder! help!
RUY BLAS (*raising the sword*). How soon will you have done?

DON SALLUSTE (*throwing himself on* RUY BLAS). Demon! I die
By murder!
RUY BLAS (*pushing him into the closet*). No, in rightful punishment!
(*They disappear in the cabinet, the door of which closes on them.*)
THE QUEEN (*alone, and falling half dead into the arm-chair*). Oh heavens!
(*A moment of silence.* RUY BLAS *re-enters, pale, and without the sword.*)

SCENE 4.—THE QUEEN—RUY BLAS.

RUY BLAS *totters a few steps towards the* QUEEN, *who remains motionless and as if frozen. Then he falls on both knees, his eyes fixed on the ground, as if he dared not raise them to her.*

RUY BLAS (*in a grave low voice*).
Now, Madam, must I speak to you.
But I will not come near. I frankly speak.
I'm not as guilty as you think I am.
I know my treason, as to you it seems,
Must horrible appear. Oh, to explain
It is not easy. Yet not base my soul,—
At heart I'm honest. 'Tis this love which has
Destroyed me. Not that I defend myself,
For well I know I should have found some means
T' escape. The sin is consummated now!
But all the same, I've loved you truly well.
THE QUEEN. Sir——
RUY BLAS (*still on his knees*). Fear not. I will not approach. Yet would I to your Majesty from step to step

The whole declare. Believe I am not vile!
To-day—all day I paced about the town
Like one possessed. Often the people looked
At me. And near the 'spital that by you
Was founded, vaguely did I feel, athwart
My brain delirious, that silently
A woman of the crowd did wipe away
The sweat from off my brow. Have mercy, God!
My heart is broken!

THE QUEEN. What is't that you wish?

RUY BLAS (*joining his hands*). That, Madam, you would pardon me!

THE QUEEN. Never.

RUY BLAS. Never!
(*He rises, and walks slowly towards the table.*)
Very sure?

THE QUEEN. No, never—never!

RUY BLAS (*he takes the vial that was placed on the table, carries it to his lips, and empties it at one draught*). Sad flame, extinguished be!

THE QUEEN (*rising and rushing to him*). What have you done?

RUY BLAS (*showing the vial*). Nothing. My woes are ended. Nothing. You Curse me—and I bless you. There—that is all.

THE QUEEN (*overcome*). Don Cæsar!

RUY BLAS. When I think, poor angel, that
You loved me!

THE QUEEN. Oh, what was that philtre strange?
What have you done? Speak—answer—tell to me.
I do forgive and love thee, Cæsar. I Believe in thee.

RUY BLAS. My name is Ruy Blas.

THE QUEEN (*throwing her arms around him*). I do forgive thee, Ruy Blas. But speak,
Say what it is you've done? 'Tis my command!
That frightful draught—it was not poison? Say?

RUY BLAS. Yes; it was poison. But my heart is glad.
(*Holding the* QUEEN *in his arms and raising his eyes to heaven.*)
Permit, oh God,—the Sovereign Justice Thou—
That the poor lackey pours out blessings on
This Queen, who did console his tortured heart
By—in his life—her love, and pity gives
In death.

THE QUEEN. Poison! Oh God! 'tis I Have killed thee! Ah, I love thee! If I had
But pardoned!

RUY BLAS (*sinking*). I had done the same.
(*His voice fails. The* QUEEN *supports him.*)
I could
No longer live! Adieu! (*Pointing to the door.*)
Fly hence, and all
Will secret be. I die. (*He falls.*)

THE QUEEN (*throwing herself on his body*). RUY BLAS!

RUY BLAS (*at the point of death, rousing himself at his name pronounced by the* QUEEN). I thank thee!

Capital Punishment

I avow openly, that "The Last Days of a Condemned" is only a pleading, direct or indirect, for *the abolition of punishment by death*. My design herein (and what I would wish posterity to see in my work, if its attention should ever be given to so slight a production) is, not to make out the special defence of any particular criminal, such defence being transitory as it is easy. I would plead generally and permanently for *all* accused persons, present and future; it is the great point of Human Right stated and pleaded before society at large,—that highest judicial court; it is the sombre and fatal question which breathes obscurely in the depths of each capital offence, under the triple envelopes of pathos in which legal eloquence wraps them; it is the question of life and death, I say, laid bare, denuded of the sonorous twistings of the bar, revealed in daylight, and placed where it should be seen, in its true and hideous position,—not in the law courts, but on the scaffold,—not among the judges, but with the Executioner!

This is what I have desired to effect. If futurity should award me the glory of having succeeded,—which I dare not hope,—I desire no other crown.

I proclaim and repeat it, then, in the name of all accused persons, innocent or guilty, before all courts, juries, or judges. And in order that my pleadings should be as universal as my cause, I have been careful, while writing "The Last Days of a Condemned," to omit any thing of a special, individual, contingent, relative, or modifiable nature, as also any episode, anecdote, known event, or real name,—keeping to the limit (if "limit" it may be termed!) of pleading the cause of *any* condemned prisoner whatever, executed at any time, for any offence; happy if, with no other aid than my thoughts, I have mined sufficiently into my subject to make a heart bleed, under the *æs triplex* of a magistrate! happy if I could render merciful those who consider themselves just! happy if I penetrate sufficiently deep within the Judge to reach the man.

When this book first appeared, some people thought it was worth while to dispute the authorship. Some asserted that it was taken from an English work, and others that it was borrowed from an American author. What a singular mania there is for seeking the origin of matters at a great distance,—trying to trace from the source of the Nile the streamlet which flows through our village! In this work there is no English, American, or Chinese assistance. I formed the idea of "The Last Days of a Condemned" where you all might form it,—where perhaps you may all have formed it (for who is there that has not reflected and had reveries of "the last day of a condemned"?—there, on the public walk, the place of execution!

It was there, while passing casually during an execution, that this forcible idea occurred to me; and, since then, after those funeral Thursdays of the Court of Cassation, which send forth through Paris the intelligence of an approaching execution, the hoarse voices of the assembling spectators, as they hurried past my windows, filled my mind with the prolonged misery of the person about to suffer, which I pictured to myself, from hour to hour, according to what I conceived was its actual progress. It was a torture which commenced from daybreak, and lasted, like that of the miserable being who was tortured at the same moment, until *four o'clock*. Then only, whence once the *ponens caput expiravit* was announced by the heavy toll of the clock, I breathed again freely, and regained comparative peace of mind.

One day at length—I think it was after the execution of Ulbach—I commenced writing this work; and since then I have felt relieved. When one of those public crimes called *legal executions* is committed, my conscience now acquits me of participation therein. This, however, is not sufficient; it is well to be freed from self-accusation, but it would be still better to endeavour to save human life. I do not know any aim more elevated, more holy, than that of seeking the abolition of capital punishment; with sincere devotion I join the wishes and efforts of those philanthropic men of all nations who have laboured, of late years, to throw down the patibulary tree,—the only tree which revolution fails to uproot! It is with pleasure that I take my turn to give my feeble stroke, after the all-powerful blow which, seventy years ago, Beccaria gave to the ancient gibbet, which had been standing during so many centuries of Christianity.

I have just said that the scaffold is the only edifice which revolutions do not demolish. It is rare indeed that revolutions are temperate in spilling blood; and although they are sent to prune, to lop, to reform society, the punishment of death is a branch which they have never removed! I own, however, if any revolution ever appeared to me capable and worthy of abolishing capital punishment, it was the Revolution of July, 1830. It seemed, indeed, as if it belonged to the merciful popular rising of modern times to erase the barbarous enactments of Louis the Eleventh, of Richelieu, and of Robespierre, and to inscribe at the head of the code, "the inviolability of human life!" 1830 was worthy of breaking the axe of 1793.

At one time we really hoped for it. In August, 1830, there seemed so much generosity afloat, such a spirit of gentleness and civilization in the multitude, that we almost fancied the punishment of death was abolished, by a tacit and unanimous consent, with the rest of the evils which had oppressed us. For some weeks confiding and credulous, we had faith in the inviolability of life, for the future, as in the inviolability of liberty.

In effect, two months had scarcely passed, when an attempt was made to resolve into a legal reality the sublime Utopia of Cæsar Bonesana. Unfortunately, this attempt was awkward, imperfect, almost hypocritical, and made in a different spirit from the general interest.

It was in the month of October, 1830, as may be remembered, that the question of capital punishment was brought before the Chamber of Deputies, and discussed with much talent, energy, and apparent feeling. During two days there was a continued succession of impressive eloquence on this momentous subject; and what was the subject?—to abolish the punishment of death? Yes and No! Here is the truth.

Four "gentlemen,"—four persons well known in society,—had attempted in the higher range of politics one of those daring strokes which Bacon calls *crimes,* and which Machiavel calls *enterprises.* Well! crime or enterprise,—the law, brutal for all, would punish it by death; and the four unfortunates were prisoners, legal captives guarded by three hundred tricoloured cockades at Vincennes. What was now to be done? You understand the impossibility of sending to the place of execution, in a common cart, ignobly bound with coarse ropes, seated back to back with that functionary who must not be named,— four men of our own rank,—four "gentlemen!"

If there were even a mahogany Guillotine!

Well, to settle the matter, they need only *abolish the punishment of death;* and thereupon the Chamber set to work!

Only yesterday they had treated this abolition as Utopian,—as a theory, a dream, poetic folly. This was not the first time that an endeavour had been made to draw their attention to the cart, the coarse ropes, and the fatal machine. How strange it is that these hideous details acquired such sudden force in their minds!

Alas! it was not on account of the general good that they sought to abolish capital punishment, but for their own sakes,—as Deputies, who might become Ministers. And thus an alloy of egotism alters and destroys the fairest social combinations. It is the dark vein of statuary marble, which, crossing everywhere, comes forth at each moment unexpectedly under the chisel!

It is surely unnecessary for me to declare that I was not among those who desired the death of the Ministers. When once they were imprisoned, the indignant anger I had felt at their attempt changed with me, as with every one else, into profound pity. I reflected on the prejudices of education of some among them; on the ill-developed head of their chief (fanatic and obstinate relapse of the conspiracies of 1804), whitened before its time, in the damp cells of state prisons; on the fatal necessity of their common position; on the impossibility of their placing a drag on that rapid slope down which monarchy rushed blindly on the 8th of August, 1829; on the influence of personal intercourse with Royalty over them, which I had hitherto under-rated; and finally I reflected, above all, on the dignity which one among them spread, like a purple mantle, over their misfortunes! I was among those who sincerely wished their lives saved, and would have readily lent my aid to that effect.

If a scaffold had been raised for them in Paris, I feel quite certain (and if it be an illusion, I would preserve it) that there would have been an insurrection to pull it down; and I should have been one of the rioters.

Here I must add that, in each social crisis, of all scaffolds, the political one is the most abominable, the most fatal, the most mischievous, the most necessary to extirpate.

In revolutionary times, beware of the first execution. It excites the sanguinary passions of the mob.

I therefore agreed thoroughly with those who wished to spare the four Ministers, both as a matter of feeling and of political reasoning. But I should have liked better that the Chamber had chosen another occasion for proposing the abolition of capital punishment. If they had suggested this desirable change not with reference to those four Ministers, fallen from a Palace to a Prison, but in the instance of the first highwayman,—in the case of one of those wretches to whom you neither give word nor look, and from whom you shrink as they pass; miserable beings, who, during their ragged infancy, ran barefoot in the mud of the crossings; shivering in winter near the quays, or seeking to warm themselves outside the ventilator from the kitchens of the hotels where you dine; scratching out, here and there, a crust of bread from the heaps of filth, and wiping it before eating; scraping in the gutter all day, with a rusty nail, in the hopes of finding a farthing; having no other amusement than the gratuitous sight of the King's fête, and the public executions,—that other gratuitous sight,—poor devils! whom hunger forces on theft, and theft to all the rest; children disinherited by their stepmother, the world; who are adopted by the House of Correction in their twelfth year,—by the Galleys at eighteen,—and by the Guillotine at forty! unfortunate beings whom, by means of a school and a workshop, you might have rendered good, moral, useful; and with whom you now know not what to do,—flinging them away like a useless burthen, sometimes into the red ant-heaps of Toulon, sometimes into the silent cemetery of Clamart; cutting off life after taking away liberty.

If it had been in the instance of one of these outcasts that you had proposed to abolish the punishment of death, oh, then your councils would have indeed been noble, great, holy, majestic! It has ever belonged to those who are truly great and truly powerful, to protect the lowly and weak. How grand would be a Council of Bramins advocating the cause of the Paria! And with us the cause of the Paria is the cause of the people. In abolishing the penalty of death for sake of the people, and without waiting until you were personally interested in the question, you would have done more than a political work, —you would have conferred a social benefit.

Instead of this, you have not yet even completed a political act, while seeking to abolish it not for the abolition's sake, but to save four unfortunate Ministers detected in political delinquency. What has happened? As you were not sincere, the people were distrustful; when they suspected the cause of your change, they became angry at the question altogether, and, strange to say, they declared in favour of that condign punishment, the weight of which presses entirely on themselves.

Immediately after the famous discussion in the Chamber, orders were given to respite, indefinitely, all executions. This was apparently a great step gained; the opponents of punishment by death were rendered happy; but the illusion was of short duration. The lives of the Ministers were spared, and the fortress of Ham was selected as a medium, between death and liberty. These different arrangements once completed, all fear was banished from the minds of the ruling statesmen; and along with fear humanity was also banished. There was no farther question of abolishing capital punishment; and, when they no longer wished to prove to the contrary, Utopia became again Utopia!

There were yet in the prisons some unfortunate condemned wretches, who, having been allowed during five or six months to walk about the prison-yards and breathe the fresh air, felt tranquil for the future, sure of life, mistaking their reprieve for pardon.

There had indeed been a reprieve for six months for these hapless captives, whose sufferings were thus gratuitously aggravated, by making them cling again to life: then, without reason, without necessity, without well knowing why, the respites were all revoked, and all these human beings were launched into eternity.

Let me add, that never were executions accompanied by more atrocious circumstances than since that revocation of the reprieve of July. Never have the "anecdotes" been more revolting, or more effectual to prove the execration of capital punishment. I will cite here two or there examples of the horrors which have attended recent executions. I must shock the nerves of the wives of king's counsel. *A wife is sometimes a conscience!*

In the South, towards the close of last September, the following circumstances occurred: I think it was at Pamiers. The officers went to a man in prison, whom they found quietly playing at cards, and gave him notice that he was to die in two hours. The wretched creature was horror-struck; for during the six months he had been forgotten, he had no longer thought of death; he was confessed, bound, his hair cut off, he was placed in the fatal cart, and taken to the place of execution. The Executioner took him from the Priest; laid him down and bound him on the Guillotine, and then let loose the axe. The heavy triangle of iron slowly detached itself, falling by jerks down the slides, until, horrible to relate, it wounded the man, without killing him! The poor creature uttered a frightful cry. The disconcerted Executioner hauled up the axe, and let it slide down again. A second time, the neck of the malefactor was wounded, without being severed. Again he shrieked, the crowd joining him. The Executioner raised the axe a third time, but no better effect attended the third stroke. Let me abridge these fearful details. Five times the axe was raised and let fall, and after the fifth stroke, the condemned was still shrieking for mercy. The indignant populace commenced throwing missiles at the Executioner, who hid himself beneath the Guillotine, and crept away behind the gendarmes' horses: but I have not yet finished. The hapless culprit, seeing he was left alone on the scaffold, raised himself on the plank, and there standing, frightful, streaming with blood, he demanded with feeble cries that some one would unbind him! The populace, full of pity, were on the point of forcing the gendarmes to help the hapless wretch, who had five times undergone his sentence. At this moment the servant of the Executioner, a youth under twenty, mounted on the scaffold, told the sufferer to turn round, that he might unbind him: then taking advantage of the posture of the dying man, who had yielded himself without any mistrust, sprang on him, and slowly cut through the neck with a knife! All this happened; all this was seen.

According to law, a judge was obliged to be present at this execution; by a sign he could have stopped all. Why was he leaning back in his carriage then, this man, while they massacred another man? What was he doing, this punisher of assassins, while they thus assassinated, in open day, his fellow-creature? And the Judge was not tried for this; nor the Executioner was not tried for it; and no tribunal inquired into this monstrous violation of all law on one of God's creatures.

In the seventeenth century, that epoch of barbarity in the criminal code, under Richelieu, under Chistophe Fouquet, Monsieur de Chalais was put to death at Nantes by an awkward soldier, who, instead of a sword-stroke, gave him thirty-four strokes of a cooper's adze. But at last it was considered execrable by the parliament of Paris, there was an inquest and a trial; and, although Richelieu and Fouquet did not suffer, the soldier was punished,—an injustice doubtless, but in which there was some show of justice.

In the modern instance, nothing was done. The fact took place after July, in times of civilization and march of intellect, a year after the celebrated lamentation of the Chamber on the penalty of death. The circumstance attracted no attention; the Paris papers published it as an anecdote, and no one cared about it. It was only known that the Guillotine had been put out of order by a dismissed servant of the Executioner, who, to revenge himself, had taken this method of action.

Another instance. At Dijon, only three months ago, they brought to the scaffold a woman (a woman!). This time again the axe of the Guillotine failed of its effect, and the head was not quite detached. Then the Executioner's servants pulled the feet of the woman; and, amidst the yells of the populace, thus finished the law!

At Paris, we have come back to the time of secret executions; since July they no longer dare to decapitate in the town, for they are afraid. Here is what they do. They took lately from the Bicêtre prison a man, under sentence of death, named Desandrieux, I think; they put him into a sort of panier on two wheels, closed on every side, bolted and padlocked; then with a gendarme in front, and another at the back, without noise or crowd, they proceeded to the deserted barrier of St. James. It was eight in the morning when they arrived, with but little light. There was a newly erected Guillotine, and for spectators, some dozens of little boys, grouped on the heaps of stones around the unexpected machine. Quickly they withdrew the man from the basket; and without giving him time to breathe, they furtively, secretly, shamefully deprived him of life! And that is called a public and solemn act of high justice! Infamous derision! How then do the lawgivers understand the word civilization? To what point have we attained? Justice reduced to stratagems and frauds! The law reduced to expedient! Monstrous! A man condemned to death, it would seem, was greatly to be feared, since they put an end to him in this traitorous fashion!

Let us be just, however; the execution was not quite secret. In the morning people hawked and sold, as usual, the sentence of death through the streets. It appears there are people who live by such sales. The crime of a hapless fellow-creature, its punishment, his torture, his agony, forms their stock in trade—a paper that they sell for a penny. Can one conceive anything more hideous than this coin, *verdisgrised* in blood?

Here are enough facts; here are too many. Is not all this horrible? What can be alleged in favour of punishment by death?

I put this question seriously. I ask it that it may be answered; I ask it of Legislators, and not of literary gossips. I know there are people who take "the excellence of punishment by death" for a text of paradoxes, like any other theme; there are others who only advocate capital punishment because they hate so-and-so who attack it. It is for them almost a literary question, a question of persons, and proper names; these are the envious, who do not find more fault with good lawyers than with good artists. The Joseph Grippas are no more wanting to the Filangieri than the Torregiani to the Michael Angelos, and the Scuderies to the Corneilles.

It is not to these that I address myself, but to men of law, properly so called,—to logicians, to reasoners; to those who love the penalty of death for its beauty, its goodness, its grace!

Let them give their reasons.

Those who judge and condemn say that "punishment by death is necessary, —first, because it is requisite to remove from the social community a member which has already injured it, and might injure it again."

If this be all, perpetual imprisonment would suffice. What is the use of inflicting death? You argue that a prisoner may escape from jail,—keep watch more strictly! If you do not believe in the solidity of iron bars, how do you venture to have menageries? Let there be no executioner where the jailer can be sufficient.

They continue, "But society must avenge itself, society must punish."

Neither one nor the other; *vengeance* is an individual act, and *punishment* belongs to God. Society is between the two; punishment is above its power, retaliation beneath it. Society should not punish, to avenge itself; it should correct, to ameliorate others!

Their third and last reason remains, the theory of example. "We must make examples. By the sight of the fate inflicted on criminals, we must shock those who might otherwise be tempted to imitate them!"

Well, in the first place, I deny the power of the example. I deny that the sight of executions produces the desired effect. Far from edifying the common people, it demoralizes and ruins their feeling, injuring every virtue; proofs of this abound and would encumber my argument if I chose to cite them. I will allude to only one fact, amongst a thousand, because it is of recent occurrence. It happened only ten days back from the present moment when I am writing; namely, on the 5th of March, the last day of the Carnival. At St. Pol, immediately after the execution of an incendiary named Louis Camus, *a group of Masqueraders came and danced round the still reeking scaffold!*

Make, then, your fine examples! Shrove Tuesday will turn them into jest.

If, notwithstanding all experience, you still hold to the theory of example, then give us back the Sixteenth Century; be in reality formidable. Restore to us a variety of suffering; restore us Farinacci; restore us the sworn torturer; restore us the gibbet, the wheel, the block, the rack, the thumb-screw, the live-burial vault, the burning cauldron; restore us in the streets of Paris, as the most open shop among the rest, the hideous stall of the Executioner, constantly full of human flesh; give us back Montfaucon, its cave of bones, its beams, its crooks, its chains, its rows of skeletons; give us back, in its permanence and power, that gigantic outhouse of the Paris Executioner! This indeed would be wholesale example; this would be a system of execution in some proportion,—which, while it is horrible, is also terrible!

But do you seriously suppose you are making an example, when you take the life of a poor wretch, in the most deserted part of the exterior Boulevards, at eight o'clock in the morning?

Do not you see then, that your public executions are done in private? That fear is with the execution, and not among the multitude? One is sometimes tempted to believe, that the advocates for capital punishment have not thoroughly considered in what it consists. But place in the scales, against any crime whatever, this exorbitant right, which society arrogates to itself, of taking away that which it did not bestow: that most irreparable of evils!

The alternatives are these: First, the man you destroy is without family, relations, or friends, in the world. In this case, he has received neither education nor instruction; no care has been bestowed either on his mind or heart; then, by what right would you kill this miserable orphan? You punish him because his infancy trailed on the ground, without stem, or support; you make him pay the penalty of the isolated position in which you left him! you make a crime of his misfortune! No one taught him to know what he was doing; this man lived in ignorance: the fault was in his destiny, not himself. You destroy one who is innocent.

Or, Secondly,—the man has a family; and then do you think the fatal stroke wounds him alone?—that his father, his mother, or his children will not suffer by it? In killing him, you vitally injure all his family: and thus again you punish the innocent.

Blind and ill-directed penalty; which, on whatever side it turns, strikes the innocent!

Imprison for life this culprit who has a family: in his cell he can still work for those who belong to him. But how can he help them from the depth of the tomb? And can you reflect without shuddering, on what will become of those young children, from whom you take away their father, their support? Do you not feel that they must fall into a career of vice?

In the Colonies, when a slave is condemned to public execution, there are a thousand francs of indemnity paid to the proprietor of the man! What, you compensate a master, and you do not indemnify a family! In this country, do you not take the man from those who possess him? Is he not, by a much more sacred tie than master and slave, the property of his father, the wealth of his wife, the fortune of his children?

I have already proved your law guilty of assassination; I have now convicted it of robbery!

And then another consideration. Do you consider the soul of this man? Do you know in what state it is, that you dismiss it so hastily?

This may be called "sentimental reasoning," by some disdainful logicians, who draw their arguments only from their minds. I often prefer the reasonings of the heart; and certainly the two should always go together. Reason is on our side, feeling is on our side, and experience is on our side. In those States where punishment by death is abolished, the mass of capital crime has yearly a progressive decrease. Let this fact have its weight.

I do not advocate, however, a sudden and complete abolition of the penalty of death, such as was so heedlessly attempted in the Chamber of Deputies. On the contrary, I desire every precaution, every experiment, every suggestion of prudence: besides, in addition to this gradual change, I would have the whole penal code examined, and reformed; and time is a great ingredient requisite to make such a work complete. But independently of a partial abolition of death in cases of forgery, incendiarism, minor thefts, et cætera, I would wish that, from the present time, in all the greater offences, the Judge should be obliged to propose the following question to the Jury: "Has the accused acted from Passion, or Interest?" And in case the Jury decide "the accused acted from Passion," then there should be no sentence of death.

Let not the opposite party deceive themselves; this question of the penalty of death gains ground every day. Before long, the world will unanimously solve it on the side of mercy. During the past century, punishments have become gradually milder: the rack has disappeared, the wheel has disappeared; and now the Guillotine is shaken. This mistaken punishment will leave France; and may it go to some barbarous people,—not to Turkey, which is becoming civilized, not to the savages, for they will not have it; but let it descend some steps of the ladder of civilization, and take refuge in Spain, or Russia!

In the early ages, the social edifice rested on three columns, Superstition, Tyranny, Cruelty. A long time ago a voice exclaimed, "Superstition has departed!" Lately another voice has cried, "Tyranny has departed!" It is now full time that a third voice shall be raised to say, "The Executioner has departed!"

Thus the barbarous usages of the olden times fall one by one; thus Providence completes modern regeneration.

To those who regret Superstition, we say, "GOD remains for us!" To those who regret Tyranny, we say, "OUR COUNTRY remains!" But to those who could regret the Executioner we can say nothing.

Let it not be supposed that social order will depart with the scaffold; the social building will not fall from wanting this hideous keystone. Civilization is nothing but a series of transformations. For what then do I ask your aid? The civilization of penal laws.

The gentle laws of CHRIST will penetrate at last into the Code, and shine through its enactments. We shall look on crime as a disease, and its physicians shall displace the judges, its hospitals displace the Galleys. Liberty and health shall be alike. We shall pour balm and oil where we formerly applied iron and fire; evil will be treated in charity, instead of in anger. This change will be simple and sublime.

THE CROSS SHALL DISPLACE THE GIBBET.

The Minds and the Masses

THE PEOPLE

FOR the last eighty years memorable things have been done. A wonderful heap of demolished materials covers the pavement.

What is done is but little by the side of what remains to be done.

To destroy is the task: to build is the work. Progress demolishes with the left hand; it is with the right hand that it builds.

The left hand of Progress is called Force; the right hand is called Mind.

There is at this hour a great deal of useful destruction accomplished; all the old cumbersome civilization is, thanks to our fathers, cleared away. It is well, it is finished, it is thrown down, it is on the ground. Now, up with you all, intellects! to work, to labour, to fatigue, to duty; it is necessary to construct.

Here three questions: To construct what? To construct where? To construct how?

We reply: To construct the people. To construct the people according to the laws of progress. To construct the people according to the laws of light.

SOCIALISM

To work for the people,—that is the great and urgent necessity.

The human mind—an important thing to say at this minute—has a greater need of the ideal even than of the real.

It is by the real that we exist; it is by the ideal that we live. Now, do you wish to realize the difference? Animals exist, man lives.

To live, is to understand. To live, is to smile at the present, to look toward posterity over the wall. To live, is to have in one's self a balance, and to weigh in it the good and the evil. To live, is to have justice, truth, reason, devotion, probity, sincerity, common-sense, right, and duty nailed to the heart. To live, is to know what one is worth, what one can do and should do. Life is conscience. Cato would not rise before Ptolemy. Cato lived.

Literature is the secretion of civilization, poetry of the ideal. That is why literature is one of the wants of societies. That is why poetry is a hunger of the soul. That is why poets are the first instructors of the people. That is why Shakespeare must be translated in France. That is why Molière must be translated in England. That is why comments must be made on them. That is why there must be a vast public literary domain. That is why all poets, all philosophers, all thinkers, all the producers of the greatness of the mind must be translated, commented on, published, printed, reprinted, stereotyped, distributed, explained, recited, spread abroad, given to all, given cheaply, given at cost price, given for nothing.

Poetry evolves heroism. M. Royer-Collard, that original and ironical friend of routine, was, taken all in all, a wise and noble spirit. Some one we know heard him say one day, "Spartacus is a poet."

That wonderful and consoling Ezekiel —the tragic revealer of progress—has all kinds of singular passages full of a profound meaning: "The voice said to me: Fill the palm of thy hand with red-hot coals, and spread them on the city." And elsewhere: "The spirit having gone into them, everywhere the spirit went, they went." And again:

"A hand was stretched towards me. It held a roll which was a book. The voice said to me: Eat this roll. I opened the lips and I ate the book. And it was sweet in my mouth as honey." To eat the book is a strange and striking image,—the whole formula of perfectibility, which above is knowledge, and below, teaching.

We have just said, "Literature is the secretion of civilization." Do you doubt it? Open the first statistics you come across.

Here is one which we find under our hand: Bagne de Toulon, 1862. Three thousand and ten prisoners. Of these three thousand and ten convicts, forty know a little more than to read and write, two hundred and eighty-seven know how to read and write, nine hundred and four read badly and write badly, seventeen hundred and seventy-nine know neither how to read nor write. In this wretched crowd all the merely mechanical trades are represented by numbers decreasing according as they rise toward the enlightened pursuits, and you arrive at this final result: goldsmiths and jewellers, four; ecclesiastics, three; lawyers, two; comedians, one; artist musicians, one; men of letters, not one.

The transformation of the crowd into the people,—profound labour! It is to this labour that the men called socialists have devoted themselves during the last forty years. The author of this book, however insignificant he may be, is one of the oldest in this labour; "Le Dernier Jour d'un Condamné" dates from 1828, and "Claude Gueux" from 1834. He claims his place among these philosophers because it is a place of persecution. A certain hatred of socialism, very blind, but very general, has been at work for fifteen or sixteen years, and is still at work most bitterly among the influential classes. (Classes, then, are still in existence?) Let it not be forgotten, socialism, true socialism, has for its end the elevation of the masses to the civic dignity, and therefore its principal care is for moral and intellectual cultivation. The first hunger is ignorance; socialism wishes then, above all, to instruct. That does not hinder socialism from being calumniated, and socialists from being denounced. To most of the infuriated, trembling cowards who have their say at the present moment, these reformers are public enemies. They are guilty of everything that has gone wrong. "O Romans!" said Tertullian, "we are just, kind, thinking, lettered, honest men. We meet to pray, and we love you because you are our brethren. We are gentle and peaceable like little children, and we wish for concord among men. Nevertheless, O Romans! if the Tiber overflows, or if the Nile does not, you cry, 'to the lions with the Christians!'"

LIBERTY

The democratic idea, the new bridge of civilization, undergoes at this moment the formidable trial of overweight. Every other idea would certainly give way under the load that it is made to bear. Democracy proves its solidity by the absurdities that are heaped on, without shaking it. It must resist everything that people choose to place on it. At this moment they try to make it carry despotism.

The people have no need of liberty,—such was the pass-word of a certain innocent and duped school, the head of which has been dead some years. That poor honest dreamer believed in good faith that men can keep progress with them when they turn out liberty. We have heard him put forth, probably without meaning it, this aphorism: Liberty is good for the rich. These kinds of maxims have the disadvantage of not being prejudicial to the establishment of empires.

No, no, no! Nothing out of liberty.

Servitude is the blind soul. Can you figure to yourself a man blind voluntarily? This terrible thing exists. There are willing slaves. A smile in irons! Can anything be more hideous? He who is not free is not a man; he who is not free has no sight, no knowledge, no discernment, no growth, no comprehension, no will, no faith, no love; he has no wife, he has no children: he has a female and young ones; he lives not,—*ab luce principium*. Liberty is the apple of the eye. Liberty is the visual organ of progress.

Because liberty has inconveniences, and even perils, to wish to create civilization without it is just the same as to try cultivation without the sun; the sun is also a censurable heavenly body. One day, in the too beautiful summer of 1829, a critic, now forgotten,—and wrongly, for he was not without some talent,—M. P., suffering from the heat, sharpened his pen, saying, "I am going to excoriate the sun."

Certain social theories, very distinct from socialism such as we understand and want it, have gone astray. Let us discard all that resembles the convent, the barrack, the cell and the straight-line system. Paraguay, minus the

Jesuits, is Paraguay just the same. To give a new fashion to evil is not a useful task. To recommence the old slavery is idiotic. Let the nations of Europe beware of a despotism made anew from materials they have to some extent themselves supplied. Such a thing, cemented with a special philosophy, might well last. We have just mentioned the theorists, some of whom otherwise right and sincere, who, by dint of fearing the dispersion of activities and energies, and of what they call "anarchy," have arrived at an almost Chinese acceptation of absolute social concentration. They turn their resignation into a doctrine. Provided man eats and drinks, all is right. The happiness of the beast is the solution. But this is a happiness which some other men would call by a different name.

We dream for nations something else besides a felicity solely made up of obedience. The bastinado procures that sort of felicity for the Turkish fellah, the knout for the Russian serf, and the cat-o'-nine-tails for the English soldier. These socialists by the side of socialism come from Joseph de Maistre, and from Ancillon, without suspecting it perhaps; for the ingenuousness of these theorists rallied to the *fait accompli* has —or fancies it has—democratic intentions, and speaks energetically of the "principles of '89." Let these involuntary philosophers of a possible despotism think a moment. To teach the masses a doctrine against liberty; to cram intellects with appetites and fatalism, a certain situation being given; to saturate it with materialism; and to run the risk of the construction which might proceed from it,—that would be to understand progress in the fashion of the worthy man who applauded a new gibbet, and who exclaimed, "This is all right! We have had till now but the old wooden gallows. To-day the age advances; and here we are with a good stone gibbet, which will do for our children and grandchildren!"

LIGHT

To enjoy a full stomach, a satisfied intestine, a satiated belly, is doubtless something, for it is the enjoyment of the brute. However, one may place one's ambition higher.

Certainly, a good salary is a fine thing To tread on this firm ground, high wages, is pleasant. The wise man likes to want nothing. To insure his own position is the characteristic of an intelligent man. An official chair, with ten thousand sesterces a year, is a graceful and convenient seat. Great emoluments give a fresh complexion and good health.. One lives to an old age in pleasant, well-paid sinecures. The high financial world, rich in plentiful profits, is a place agreeable to live in. To be well at Court settles a family well and brings a fortune. As for myself, I prefer to all these solid comforts the old leaky vessel in which Bishop Quodvultdeus embarks with a smile.

There is something beyond gorging one's self. The goal of man is not the goal of the animal.

A moral enhancement is necessary. The life of nations, like the life of individuals, has its minutes of depression; these minutes pass, certainly, but no trace of them ought to remain. Man, at this hour, tends to fall into the stomach. Man must be replaced in the heart; man must be replaced in the brain. The brain,—behold the sovereign that must be restored! The social question requires to-day, more than ever, to be examined on the side of human dignity.

To show man the human end, to ameliorate intelligence first, the animal afterward, to disdain the flesh as long as the thought is despised, and to give the example on their own flesh,—such is the actual, immediate urgent duty of writers.

It is what men of genius have done at all times.

You ask in what poets can be useful? In imbuing civilization with light,—only that.

LITERATURE

Up to this day there has been a literature of *literati*. In France, particularly, as we have said, literature had a disposition to form a caste. To be a poet was something like being a mandarin. Words did not all belong by right to the language. The dictionary granted or did not grant the registration. The dictionary had a will of its own. Imagine the botanist declaring to a vegetable that it does not exist, and Nature timidly offering an insect to entomology, which refuses it as incorrect. Imagine astronomy cavilling at the stars. We recollect having heard an Academician, now dead, say in full academy that French had been spoken in France only in the seventeenth century, and then for only twelve years,—we do not remember which twelve. Let us give up, for it is time, this order of ideas; democracy requires it. The actual enlarging of thoughts needs something else. Let us leave the college, the conclave, the cell, the weak taste, weak art, the small chapel. Poetry is not a coterie. There is at this hour an effort made to galvanize dead things. Let us strive against this tendency. Let us insist on the truths which are urgent. The *chefs-d'œuvre* recommended by the manual of bachelorship, compliments in verse and in prose, tragedies soaring over the head of some king, inspiration in full official dress, the brilliant nonentities fixing laws on poetry, the *Arts poétiques* which forget La Fontaine, and for which Molière is doubtful, the Planats castrating the Corneilles, prudish tongues, the thoughts enclosed between four walls, and limited by Quintilian, Longinus, Boileau, and La Harpe,—all that, although official and public teaching is filled and saturated with it, all that belongs to the past. Some particular epoch, which is called the grand century, and for a certainty the fine century, is nothing else in reality but a literary monologue. Is it possible to realize such a strange thing,—a literature which is an aside? It seems as if one read on the frontal of art "No admittance." As for ourselves, we understand poetry only with the door wide open. The hour has struck for hoisting the "All for All." What is needed by civilization, henceforth a grown-up woman, is a popular literature.

1830 has opened a debate, literary on the surface, at the bottom social and human. The moment is come to close the debate. We close it by asking a literature having in view this purpose: "The People."

The author of these pages wrote, thirty-one years ago, in the preface to "Lucrèce Borgia," a few words often repeated since: "Le poëte a charge d'âmes." He would add here, if it were worth saying, that, allowing for possible error, the words, uttered by his conscience, have been his rule throughout life.

MACCHIAVELLI

MACCHIAVELLI had a strange idea of the people. To heap the measure, to overflow the cup, to exaggerate horror in the case of the prince, to increase the crushing in order to stir up the oppressed to revolt, to cause idolatry to change into a curse, to push the masses to extremities,—such seems to be his policy. His "yes" signifies "no." He loads the despot with despotism in order to make him burst. The tyrant becomes in his hands a hideous projectile, which will break to pieces. Macchiavelli conspires. For whom? Against whom? Guess. His apotheosis of kings is just the thing to make regicides. On the head of his prince he places a diadem of crimes, a tiara of vices, a halo of baseness; and he invites you to adore his monster, with the air of a man expecting an avenger. He glorifies evil with a squint toward the darkness,— the darkness wherein is Harmodius. Macchiavelli, the getter-up of princely outrages, the valet of the Medici and of the Borgias, had in his youth been put to the rack for having admired Brutus and Cassius. He had perhaps plotted with the Soderini the deliverance of Florence. Does he recollect it? Does he continue? His advice is followed, like the lightning, by a low rumbling in the cloud,—alarming reverberation. What did he mean to say? On whom has he a design? Is the advice for or against him to whom he gives it? One day, at Florence, in the garden of Cosmo Ruccelaï, there being present the Duke of Mantua and John de Medici, who afterward commanded the Black Bands of Tuscany, Varchi, the enemy of Macchiavelli, heard him say to the two princes: "Let the people read no book,—not even mine." It is curious to compare with this remark the advice given by Voltaire to the Duke de Choiseul,—at the same time advice to the minister, and insinuation for the king: "Let the boobies read our nonsense. There is no danger in reading, my lord. What can a great king like the King of France fear? The people are but rabble, and the books are but trash." Let them read nothing, let them read everything: these two pieces of contrary advice coincide more than one would think. Voltaire, with hidden claws, is purring at the feet of the king, Voltaire and Macchiavelli are two formidable indirect revolutionists, dissimilar in everything, and yet identical in reality by their profound hatred, disguised in flattery, of the master. The one is malignant, the other is sinister. The princes of the sixteenth century had as theorist on their infamies, and as enigmatical courtier, Macchiavelli, an enthusiast dark at heart. The flattery of a sphinx,—terrible thing! Better yet be flattered, like Louis XV., by a cat.

Conclusion: Make the people read

Macchiavelli, and make them read Voltaire.

Macchiavelli will inspire them with horror of, and Voltaire with contempt for, crowned guilt.

But the hearts should turn, above all, toward the grand pure poets, whether they be sweet like Virgil or bitter like Juvenal.

PROGRESS

THE progress of man by the education of minds,—there is no safety but in that. Teach! learn! All the revolutions of the future are enclosed and imbedded in this phrase: Gratuitous and obligatory instruction.

It is by the unfolding of works of the highest order that this vast intellectual teaching should be crowned. At the top the men of genius.

Wherever there is a gathering of men, there ought to be in a special place, a public expositor of the great thinkers.

By a great thinker we mean a beneficent thinker.

The perpetual presence of the beautiful in their works maintains poets at the summit of teaching.

No one can foresee the quantity of light which will be brought forth by letting the people be in communication with men of genius. This combination of the hearts of the people with the heart of the poet will be the Voltaic pile of civilization.

Will the people understand this magnificent teaching? Certainly. We know of nothing too lofty for the people. The people are a great soul. Have you ever gone on a fête-day to a theatre open gratuitously to all? What do you think of that auditory? Do you know of any other more spontaneous and intelligent? Do you know, even in the forest, of a vibration more profound? The court of Versailles admires like a well-drilled regiment; the people throw themselves passionately into the beautiful. They pack together, crowd, amalgamate, combine, and knead themselves in the theatre,—a living paste that the poet is about to mould. The powerful thumb of Molière will presently make its mark on it; the nail of Corneille will scratch this ill-shaped heap. Whence does that heap come? Whence does it proceed? From the Courtille, from the Porcherons, from the Cunette; it is shoeless, it is bare-armed, it is ragged. Silence! This is the human block.

The house is crowded, the vast multitude looks, listens, loves; all consciences, deeply moved, throw off their inner fire; all eyes glisten; the huge beast with a thousand heads is there,—the Mob of Burke, the *Plebs* of Titus Livius, the *Fex urbis* of Cicero. It caresses the beautiful; smiling at it with the grace of a woman. It is literary in the most refined sense of the word; nothing equals the delicacy of this monster. The tumultous crowd trembles, blushes, palpitates. Its modesty is surprising; the crowd is a virgin. No prudery however; this brute is not brutal. Not a sympathy escapes it; it has in itself the whole keyboard, from passion to irony, from sarcasm to sobbing. Its compassion is more than compassion; it is real mercy. God is felt in it. All at once the sublime passes, and the sombre electricity of the abyss heaves up suddenly all this pile of hearts and entrails;

enthusiasm effects a transfiguration. And now, is the enemy at the gates, is the country in danger? Appeal to that populace, and it would enact the sublime drama of Thermopylæ. Who has called forth such a metamorphosis? Poetry.

The multitude (and in this lies their grandeur) are profoundly open to the ideal. When they come in contact with lofty art they are pleased, they shudder. Not a detail escapes them. The crowd is one liquid and living expanse capable of vibration. A mass is a sensitive-plant. Contact with the beautiful agitates ecstatically the surface of multitudes,—sure sign that the depth is sounded. A rustling of leaves, a mysterious breath, passes, the crowd trembles under the sacred insufflation of the abyss.

And even where the man of the people is not in a crowd, he is yet a good hearer of great things. His ingenuousness is honest, his curiosity healthy. Ignorance is a longing. His near connection with Nature renders him subject to the holy emotion of the true. He has, toward poetry, secret natural desires which he does not suspect himself. All the teachings are due to the people. The more divine the light, the more it is made for this simple soul. We would have in the villages a pulpit from which Homer should be explained to the peasants.

THE IDEAL

Too much matter is the evil of our day. Hence a certain dulness.

It is necessary to restore some ideal in the human mind. Whence shall you take your ideal? Where is it? The poets, the philosophers, the thinkers are the urns. The ideal is in Æschylus, in Isaiah, in Juvenal, in Alighieri, in Shakespeare. Throw Æschylus, throw Isaiah, throw Juvenal, throw Dante, throw Shakespeare into the deep soul of the human race.

Pour Job, Solomon, Pindar, Ezekiel, Sophocles, Euripides, Herodotus, Theocritus, Plautus, Lucretius, Virgil, Terence, Horace, Catullus, Tacitus, Saint Paul, Saint Augustine, Tertullian, Petrarch, Pascal, Milton, Descartes, Corneille, La Fontaine, Montesquieu, Diderot, Rousseau, Beaumarchais, Sedaine, André Chénier, Kant, Byron, Schiller,— pour all these souls into man. And with them pour all the wits from Æsop up to Molière, all the intellects from Plato up to Newton, all the encyclopædists from Aristotle up to Voltaire.

By that means, while curing the illness for the moment, you will establish forever the health of the human mind.

You will cure the middle class and found the people.

As we have said just now, after the destruction which has delivered the world, you will construct the edifice which shall make it prosper.

What an aim,—to make the people! Principles combined with science; every possible quantity of the absolute introduced by degrees into the fact; Utopia treated successively by every mode of realization,—by political economy, by philosophy, by physics, by chemistry, by dynamics, by logic, by art; union replacing little by little antagonism, and unity replacing union; for religion God, for priest the father, for prayer virtue, for field the whole earth, for language the verb, for law the right, for motive-power duty, for hygiene labour, for economy universal peace, for canvas the very life, for the goal progress, for authority liberty, for people the man,—such is the simplification.

And at the summit the ideal.

The ideal!—inflexible type of perpetual progress.

To whom belong men of genius if not to thee, people? They do belong to thee; they are thy sons and thy fathers. Thou givest birth to them, and they teach thee. They open in thy chaos vistas of light. Children, they have drunk thy sap. They have leaped in the universal matrix, humanity. Each of thy phases, people, is an avatar. The deep essence of life, it is in thee that it must be looked for. Thou art the great bosom. Geniuses are begotten from thee, mysterious crowd.

Let them therefore return to thee.

People, the author, God, dedicates them to thee.

FRATERNIZATION

The nineteenth century springs from itself only; it does not receive its impulse from any ancestor; it is the offspring of an idea. Doubtless, Isaiah, Homer, Aristotle, Dante, Shakespeare, have been or could be great starting-points for important philosophical or poetical formations; but the nineteenth century has an august mother,—the French Revolution. It has that powerful blood in its veins. It honours men of genius. When denied it salutes them, when ignored it proclaims them, when persecuted it avenges them, when insulted it crowns them, when dethroned it replaces them upon their pedestal; it venerates them, but it does not proceed from them. The nineteenth century has for family itself, and itself alone. It is the characteristic of its revolutionary nature to dispense with ancestors.

Itself a genius, it fraternizes with men of genius. As for its source, it is where theirs is,—beyond man. The mysterious gestations of progress succeed each other according to a providential law. The nineteenth century is born of civilization. It has a continent to bring into the world. France has borne this century; and this century bears Europe.

The Greek stock bore civilization, narrow and circumscribed at first by the mulberry leaf, confined to the Morea; then civilization, gaining step by step, grew broader, and formed the Roman stock. It is to-day the French stock,—that is to say, all Europe,—with young shoots in America, Africa, and Asia.

The greatest of these young shoots is a democracy,—the United States, the sprouting of which was aided by France in the last century. France, sublime essayist in progress, has founded a republic in America before making one in Europe. *Et vidit quod esset bonum.* After having lent to Washington an auxiliary, Lafayette, France, returning home, gave to Voltaire, dismayed within his tomb, that formidable successor, Danton. In presence of the monstrous past, hurling every thunder, exhaling every miasma, breathing every darkness, protruding every talon, horrible and terrible, progress, constrained to use the same weapons, has had suddenly a hundred arms, a hundred heads, a hundred tongues of fire, a hundred roarings. The good has transformed itself into a hydra. It is this that is termed the Revolution.

Nothing can be more august.

The Revolution ended one century and began another.

An intellectual awakening prepares the way for an overthrow of facts,—and this is the eighteenth century. After which the political revolution, once accomplished, seeks expression, and the literary and social revolution completes it: this is the nineteenth century. With ill-will, but not unjustly, has it been said that romanticism and socialism are identical: hatred, in its desire to injure, very often establishes, and, so far as is in its power, consolidates.

A parenthesis. This word, *romanticism*, has, like all war-cries, the advantage of readily summing up a group of ideas. It is brief,—which pleases in the contest; but it has, to our idea, through its militant signification, the objection of appearing to limit the movement that it represents to a warlike action. Now, this movement is a matter of intellect, a matter of civilization, a matter of soul; and this is why the writer of these lines has never used the words *romanticism* or *romantic*. They will not be found in any of the pages of criticism that he has had occasion to write. If to-day he derogates from his usual prudence in polemics, it is for the sake of greater rapidity and with all reservation. The same observation may be made on the subject of the word *socialism*, which admits of so many different interpretations.

The triple movement—literary, philosophical, and social—of the nineteenth century, which is one single movement, is nothing but the current of the revolution in ideas. This current, after having swept away facts, is perpetuated in minds with all its immensity.

This term, *"literary '93,"* so often quoted in 1830 against contemporaneous literature, was not so much an insult as it was intended to be. It was certainly as unjust to employ it as characterizing the whole literary movement as it is iniquitous to employ it to describe all the political revolutions; there is in these two phenomena something besides '93. But this term, *"literary '93,"* was relatively exact, insomuch as it indicated, confusedly but truthfully, the origin of the literary movement which belongs to our epoch, while endeavouring to dishonour that movement. Here again the clairvoyance of hatred was blind. Its daubings of mud upon the face of truth are gilding, light, and glory.

The Revolution, turning climacteric of humanity, is made up of several years. Each of these years expresses a period, represents an aspect, or realizes a phase of the phenomenon. Tragic '93 is one of those colossal years. Good news must sometimes have a mouth of bronze. Such a mouth is '93.

Listen to the immense proclamation proceeding from it. Give attention, remain speechless, and be impressed. God himself said the first time *Fiat lux,* the second time he has caused it to be said.

By whom?

By '93.

Therefore, we men of the nineteenth century hold in honour that reproach, "You are '93."

But do not stop there. We are '89 as well as '93. The Revolution, the whole Revolution,—such is the source of the literature of the nineteenth century.

On these grounds put it on its trial, this literature, or seek its triumph; hate it or love it. According to the amount of the future that you have in you, outrage it or salute it; little do animosities and fury affect it. It is the logical deduction from the great chaotic and genesiacal fact that our fathers have witnessed, and which has given a new starting-point to the world. He who is against the fact is against that literature; he who is for that fact is on its side. What the fact is worth the literature is worth. The reactionary writers are not mistaken; whenever there is revolution, patent or latent, the Catholic and royalist scent is unfailing. Those men of letters of the past award to contemporaneous literature an honourable amount of diatribe; their aversion is convulsive. One of their journalists, who is, I believe a bishop, pronounces this word *poet* with the same accent as the word *Septembrist;* another, less of a bishop, but quite as angry, writes, "I feel in all this literature Marat and Robespierre." This last writer is rather mistaken; there is in "this literature" Danton rather than Marat.

But the fact is true: democracy is in this literature.

The Revolution has forged the clarion; the nineteenth century sounds it.

Ah, this affirmation suits us, and, in truth, we do not recoil before it; we avow our glory,—we are revolutionists. The thinkers of the present time,—poets, writers, historians, orators, philosophers, —all are derived from the French Revolution. They come from it, and it alone. It was '89 that demolished the Bastille; it was '93 that took the crown from the Louvre. From '89 sprung Deliverance, and from '93 Victory. From '89 and '93 the men of the nineteenth century proceed: these are their father and their mother. Do not seek for them another affiliation, another inspiration, another insufflation, another origin. They are the democrats of the idea, successors to the democrats of action. They are the emancipators. Liberty bent over their cradles,—they all have sucked her vast breast; they all have her milk in their entrails, her marrow in their bones, her sap in their will, her spirit of revolt in their reason, her flame in their intellect.

Even those among them (there are some) who were born aristocrats, who came to the world banished in some degree among families of the past, who have fatally received one of those primary educations whose stupid effort is to contradict progress, and who have commenced the words that they had to say to our century with an indescribable royalist stuttering,—these, from that period, from their infancy (they will not contradict me), felt the sublime monster within them. They had the inner ebullition of the immense fact. They had in the depth of their conscience a whispering of mysterious ideas; the inward shock of false certainties troubled their mind; they felt their sombre surface of monarchism, catholicism, and aristocracy tremble, shudder, and by degrees split up. One day, suddenly and powerfully, the swelling of truth within them prevailed, the hatching was completed, the eruption took place; the light flamed in them, causing them to burst open,—not falling on them, but (more beautiful mystery!) gushing out of these amazed men, enlightening them, while it burned within them. They were craters unknown to themselves.

This phenomenon has been interpreted to their reproach as a treason. They passed over, in fact, from right divine to human right. They turned their back on false history, on false tradition, on false dogmas, on false philosophy, on false daylight, on false truth. The free spirit which soars up,—bird called by Aurora,—offends intellects saturated with ignorance and the fœtus preserved in spirits of wine. He who sees offends the blind; he who hears makes the deaf indignant; he who walks offers an abominable insult to cripples. In the eyes of dwarfs, abortions, Aztecs, myrmidons, and pygmies, forever subject to rickets, growth is apostasy.

The writers and poets of the nineteenth century have the admirable good fortune of proceeding from a genesis, of arriving after an end of the world, of accompanying a reappearance of light, of being the organs of a new beginning. This imposes on them duties unknown to their predecessors—the duties of intentional reformers and direct civilizers. They continue nothing; they remake everything. For new times, new duties. The function of thinkers in our days is complex; to think is no longer sufficient,—they must love; to think and love is no longer sufficient,—they must act; to think, to love, and to act, no longer suffices,—they must suffer. Lay down the pen, and go where you hear the grapeshot. Here is a barricade; be one on it. Here is exile; accept it. Here is the scaffold; be it so. Let John Brown be in Montesquieu, if needful. The Lucretius required by this century in labour should contain Cato. Æschylus, who wrote the "Orestias," had for a brother Cynegyrus, who fastened with his teeth on the ships of the enemies: that was sufficient for Greece at the time of Salamis, but it no longer suffices for France after the Revolution. That Æschylus and Cynegyrus are brothers is not enough; they must be the same man. Such are the actual requirements of progress. Those who devote themselves to great and pressing things can never be too great. To set ideas in motion, to heap up evidence, to pile up principles, that is the redoubtable movement. To heap Pelion on Ossa is the labour of infants beside that work of giants, the placing of right upon truth. To scale that afterward, and to dethrone usurpations in the midst of thunders,—such is the work.

The future presses. To-morrow cannot wait. Humanity has not a minute to lose. Quick! quick! let us hasten; the wretched ones have their feet on red-hot iron. They hunger, they thirst, they suffer. Ah, terrible emaciation of the poor human body! Parasitism laughs, the ivy grows green and thrives, the mistletoe is flourishing, the tapeworm is happy. What a frightful object the prosperity of the tapeworm! To destroy that which devours,—in that is safety. Your life has within itself death, which is in good health. There is too much misery, too much desolation, too much immodesty, too much nakedness, too many brothels, too many prisons, too many rags, too many crimes, too much weakness, too much darkness, not enough schools, too many little innocents growing up for evil! The trucklebeds of poor girls are suddenly covered with silk and lace,—and in that is worse misery; by the side of misfortune there is vice, the one urging the other. Such a society requires prompt succour. Let us seek for the best. Go all of you in this search. Where are the promised lands? Civilization would go forward; let us try theories, systems, ameliorations, inventions, progress, until the shoe for that foot shall be found. The attempt costs nothing, or costs but little,—to attempt is not to adopt,—but before all, above all, let us be lavish of light. All sanitary purification begins in opening windows wide. Let us open wide all intellects. Let us supply souls with air.

Quick, quick, O thinkers! Let the human race breathe; give hope, give the ideal, do good. Let one step succeed another, horizon expand into horizon, conquest follow conquest. Because you have given what you promised do not think you have performed all that is required of you. To possess is to promise; the dawn of to-day imposes on the sun obligations for to-morrow.

Let nothing be lost. Let not one strength be isolated. Every one to work! there is vast urgency for it. No more idle art. Poetry the worker of civilization, what more admirable? The dreamer should be a pioneer; the strophe should mean something. The beautiful should be at the service of honesty. I am the valet of my conscience; it rings for me: I come. "Go!" I go. What do you require of me, O truth, sole majesty of this world? Let each one feel in haste to do well. A book is sometimes a source of hoped-for succour. An idea is a balm, a word may be a dressing for wounds; poetry is a physician. Let no one tarry. Suffering is losing its strength while you are idling. Let men leave this dreamy laziness. Leave the kief to the Turks. Let men labour for the safety of all, and let them rush into it and be out of breath.

Do not be sparing of your strides. Nothing useless; no inertia. What do you call dread nature? Everything lives. The duty of all is to live; to walk, to run, to fly, to soar, is the universal law. What do you wait for? Who stops you? Ah, there are times one might wish to hear the stones murmur at the slowness of man!

Sometimes one goes into the woods. To whom does it not happen at times to be overwhelmed?—one sees so many sad things. The stage is a long one to go over, the consequences are long in coming, a generation is behindhand, the work of the age languishes. What! so many sufferings yet? One might think he has gone backward. There is everywhere increase of superstition, of cowardice, of deafness, of blindness, of imbecility. Penal laws weigh upon brutishness. This wretched problem has been set,—to augment comfort by putting off right; to sacrifice the superior side of man to the inferior side; to yield up principle to appetite. Cæsar takes charge for the belly, I make over to him the brains,—it is the old sale of a birth-right for the dish of porridge. A little more, and this fatal anomaly would cause a wrong road to be taken toward civilization. The fattening pig would no longer be the king, but the people. Alas! this ugly expedient does not even succeed. No diminution whatever of the malady. In the last ten years—for the last twenty years—the low water-mark of prostitution, of mendicity, of crime, has been stationary, below which evil has not fallen one degree. Of true education, of gratuitous education, there is none. The infant nevertheless requires to know that he is man, and the father that he is citizen. Where are the promises? Where is the hope? Oh, poor wretched humanity! one is tempted to shout for help in the forest; one is tempted to claim support, assistance, and a strong arm from that grand mournful Nature. Can this mysterious *ensemble* of forces be indifferent to progress? We supplicate, appeal, raise our hands toward the shadow. We listen, wondering if the rustlings will become voices. The duty of the springs and streams should be to babble forth the word "Forward!" One could wish to hear nightingales sing new Marseillaises.

Notwithstanding all this, these times of halting are nothing beyond what is normal. Discouragement would be puerile. There are halts, repose, breathing spaces in the march of peoples, as there are winters in the progress of the seasons. The gigantic step, '89, is all the same a fact. To despair would be absurd, but to stimulate is necessary.

To stimulate, to press, to chide, to awaken, to suggest, to inspire,—it is this function, fulfilled everywhere by writers, which impresses on the literature of this century so high a character of power and originality. To remain faithful to all the laws of art, while combining them with the law of progress,—such is the problem, victoriously solved by so many noble and proud minds.

Thence this word *deliverance,* which appears above everything in the light, as if it were written on the very forehead of the ideal.

The Revolution is France sublimed. There was a day when France was in the furnace,—the furnace causes wings to grow on certain warlike martyrs,—and from amid the flames this giant came forth archangel. At this day by all the world, France is called Revolution; and henceforth this word *revolution* will be the name of civilization, until it can be replaced by the word *harmony.* I repeat it: do not seek elsewhere the starting-point and the birth-place of the literature of the nineteenth century. Yes, as many as there be of us, great and small, powerful and unknown, illustrious and obscure, in all our works good or bad, whatever they may be,—poems, dramas, romances, history, philosophy,—at the tribune of assemblies as before the crowds of the theatre, as in the meditation of solitudes; yes, everywhere; yes, always; yes, to combat violence and imposture; yes, to rehabilitate those who are stoned and run down; yes, to sum up logically and to march straight onward; yes, to console, to succour, to relieve, to encourage, to teach; yes, to dress wounds in hope of curing them; yes, to transform charity into fraternity, alms into assistance, sluggishness into work, idleness into utility, centralization into a family, iniquity into justice, the *bourgeois* into the citizen, the populace into the people, the rabble into the nation, nations into humanity, war into love, prejudice into free examination, frontiers into solderings, limits into openings, ruts into rails, vestry-rooms into temples, the instinct of evil into the desire of good, life into right, kings into men; yes, to deprive religions of hell and societies of the galley; yes, to be brothers to the wretched, the serf, the fellah, the *prolétaire,* the disinherited, the banished, the betrayed, the conquered, the sold, the enchained, the sacrificed, the prostitute, the convict, the ignorant, the savage, the slave, the negro, the condemned, and the damned, —yes, we are thy sons, Revolution!

Yes, men of genius; yes, poets, philosophers, historians; yes, giants of that great art of previous ages which is all the light of the past,—O men eternal, the minds of this day salute you, but do not follow you; in respect to you they hold to this law,—to admire everything, to imitate nothing. Their function is no longer yours. They have business with the virility of the human race. The hour which makes mankind of age has struck. We assist, under the full light of the ideal, at that majestic junction of the beautiful with the useful. No actual or possible genius can surpass you, ye men of genius of old; to equal you is all the ambition allowed: but, to equal you, one must conform to the necessities of our time, as you supplied the necessities of yours. Writers who are sons of the Revolution have a holy task.

O Homer, their epic poem must weep; O Herodotus, their history must protest; O Juvenal, their satire must dethrone; O Shakespeare, their "thou shalt be king," must be said to the people; O Æschylus, their Prometheus must strike Jupiter with thunderbolts; O Job, their dunghill must be fruitful; O Dante, their hell must be extinguished; O Isaiah, thy Babylon crumbles, theirs must blaze forth with light! They do what you have done; they contemplate creation directly, they observe humanity directly; they do not accept as a guiding light any refracted ray,— not even yours. Like you, they have for their sole starting-point, outside them, universal being: in them, their soul. They have for the source of their work the one source whence flows Nature and whence flows art, the infinite. As the writer of these lines said forty years ago: "The poets and the writers of the nineteenth century have neither masters nor models." No; in all that vast and sublime art of all peoples, in all those grand creations of all epochs, —no, not even thee, Æschylus, not even thee, Dante, not even thee, Shakespeare, —no, they have neither models nor masters. And why have they neither masters nor models? It is because they have one model, Man, and because they have one master, God.

The Face of Cain

THE ADVENT

Here is the advent of the new constellation.

It is certain that at the present hour that which has been till now the light of the human race grows pale, and that the old flame is about to disappear from the world.

The men of brutal force have, since human tradition existed, shone alone in the empyrean of history; theirs was the only supremacy. Under the various names of kings, emperors, captains, chiefs, princes,—summed up in the word heroes,—this group of an apocalypse was resplendent. They were all dripping with victories. Terror transformed itself into acclamation to salute them. They dragged after them an indescribable tumultuous flame. They appeared to man in a disorder of horrible light. They did not light up the heavens,—they set them on fire. They looked as if they meant to take possession of the Infinite. Rumbling crashes were heard in their glory. A red glare mingled with it. Was it purple? Was it blood? Was it shame? Their light made one think of the face of Cain. They hated one another. Flashing shocks passed from one to the other; at times these enormous planets came into collision, striking out lightnings. Their look was furious. Their radiance stretched out into swords. All that hung terrible above us.

That tragic glare fills the past. To-day it is in full process of waning.

There is decline in war, decline in despotism, decline in theocracy, decline in slavery, decline in the scaffold. The blade becomes shorter, the tiara is fading away, the crown is simplified; war is raging, the plume bends lower, usurpation is circumscribed, the chain is lightened, the rack is out of countenance. The antique violence of the few against all, called right divine, is coming to an end. Legitimacy, the grace of God, the monarchy of Pharamond, nations branded on the shoulder with the *fleur-de-lis*, the possession of peoples by the right of birth, the long series of ancestors giving right over the living,—these things are yet striving in some places; at Naples, in Prussia, etc.; but they are struggling rather than striving, —it is death that strains for life. A stammering which to-morrow will be utterance, and the day after to-morrow a full declaration, proceeds from the bruised lips of the serf, of the vassal, of the *prolétaire,* of the pariah. The gag breaks up between the teeth of the human race. The human race has had enough of the sorrowful path, and the patient refuses to go farther.

From this very time certain forms of despotism are no longer possible. The Pharaoh is a mummy, the sultan a phantom, the Cæsar a counterfeit. This stylite of the Trajan columns is anchylosed on its pedestal; it has on its head the excrement of free eagles; it is nihility rather than glory; the bands of the sepulchre fasten this crown of laurels.

The period of the men of brutal force is gone. They have been glorious, certainly, but with a glory that melts away. That species of great men is soluble in progress. Civilization rapidly oxidizes these bronzes. At the point of maturity to which the French Revolution has already brought the universal conscience, the hero is no longer a hero without a good reason; the captain is discussed, the conqueror is inadmissible. In our days Louis XIV. invading the Palatinate would look like a robber. From the last century these realities began to dawn. Frederick II., in the presence of Voltaire, felt and owned himself somewhat of a brigand. To be a great man of matter, to be pompously violent, to govern by the sword-knot and the cockade, to forge right upon force, to hammer out justice and truth by blows of accomplished facts, to make brutalities of genius,—is to be grand, if you like; but it is a coarse manner of being grand, —glories announced with drums which are met with a shrug of the shoulders. Sonorous heroes have deafened human reason until to-day; that pompous noise begins now to weary it. It shuts its eyes and ears before those authorized slaughters that they call battles. The sublime murderers of men have had their time; it is in a certain relative forgetfulness that henceforth they will be illustrious and august; humanity, become greater, requires to dispense with them. The food for guns thinks; it reflects, and is actually losing its admiration for being shot down by a cannon-ball.

A few figures by the way may not be useless.

All tragedy is part of our subject. The tragedy of poets is not the only one; there is the tragedy of politicians and statesmen. Would you like to know how much that tragedy costs?

Heroes have an enemy; that enemy is called finance. For a long time the amount of money paid for that kind of glory was ignored. In order to disguise the total, there were convenient little fireplaces like that in which Louis XIV. burned the accounts of Versailles. That day the smoke of one thousand millions of francs passed out the chimney of the royal stove.

The nation did not even take notice. At the present day nations have one great virtue,—they are miserly. They know that prodigality is the mother of abasement. They reckon up; they learn bookkeeping by double entry. Warlike glory henceforth has its debit and credit account: that renders it impossible.

The greatest warrior of modern times is not Napoleon, it is Pitt. Napoleon carried on warfare; Pitt created it. It is Pitt who willed all the wars of the Revolution and of the empire; they proceeded from him. Take away Pitt and put Fox in his place, there would then be no reason for that exorbitant battle of twenty-three years, there would be no longer any coalition. Pitt was the soul of the coalition, and he dead, his soul remained amidst the universal war. What Pitt cost England and the world, here it is. We add this bas-relief to his pedestal.

In the first place, the expenditure in men. From 1791 to 1814 France alone, striving against Europe, coalesced by England,—France constrained and compelled, expended in butcheries for military glory (and also, let us add, for the defence of territory) five millions of men; that is to say, six hundred men per day. Europe, including the total of France, has expended sixteen millions, six hundred thousand men; that is to say, two thousand deaths per day during twenty-three years.

Secondly, the expenditure of money. We have, unfortunately, no authentic total, save the total of England. From 1791 to 1814 England, in order to make France succumb to Europe, became indebted to the extent of eighty-one millions, two hundred and sixty-five thousand, eight hundred and forty-two pounds sterling. Divide this total by the total of men killed, at the rate of two thousand per day for twenty-three years, and you arrive at this result,—that each corpse stretched on the field of battle has cost England alone fifty pounds sterling.

Add the total of Europe,—total unknown, but enormous.

With these seventeen millions of dead men, they might have peopled Australia with Europeans. With the eighty millions expended by England in cannon-shots, they might have changed the face of the earth, begun the work of civilization everywhere, and suppressed throughout the entire world ignorance and misery.

England pays eighty millions for the two statues of Pitt and Wellington.

It is a fine thing to have heroes, but it is an expensive luxury. Poets cost less.

SPLENDOUR IN THE DISTANCE

The discharge of the warrior is signed: it is splendour in the distance. The great Nimrod, the great Cyrus, the great Sennacherib, the great Sesostris, the great Alexander, the great Pyrrhus, the great Hannibal, the great Cæsar, the great Timour, the great Louis, the great Frederic, and more great ones,—all are going away.

It would be a mistake to think that we reject these men purely and simply. In our eyes five or six of those that we have named are legitimately illustrious; they have even mingled something good in their ravages; their definitive total embarrasses the absolute equity of the thinker, and they weigh nearly even weights in the balance of the injurious and the useful.

Others have been only injurious. They are numerous, innumerable even; for the masters of the world are a crowd.

The thinker is the weigher. Clemency suits him. Let us therefore say, Those others who have done only evil have one attenuating circumstance,—imbecility.

They have another excuse yet,—the mental condition of the human race itself at the moment they appeared; the medium surrounding facts, modifiable, but encumbering.

It is not men that are tyrants, but things. The real tyrants are called frontier, track, routine; blindness under the form of fanaticism, deafness and dumbness under the form of diversity of languages; quarrel under the form of diversity of weights, measures, and moneys; hatred resulting from quarrel, war resulting from hatred. All these tyrants may be called by one name,—separation. Division, whence proceeds irresponsible government,—this is despotism in the abstract.

Even the tyrants of flesh are mere things. Caligula is much more a fact than a man; he is a result more than an existence. The Roman proscriber, dictator, or Cæsar, refuses the vanquished fire and water,—that is to say, puts his life out. One day of Gela represents twenty thousand proscribed, one day of Tiberius thirty thousand, one day of Sylla seventy thousand. One evening Vitellius, being ill, sees a house lighted up, where people were rejoicing. "Do they think me dead?" says Vitellius. It is Junius Blesus who sups with Tuscus Cæcina, the emperor sends to these drinkers a cup of poison, that they may realize by this sinister end of too joyous a night that Vitellius is living. (Reddendam pro intempestiva licentia mœstam et funebrem noctem qua sentiat vivere Vitellium et imperare.) Otho and this same Vitellius forward assassins to each other. Under the Cæsars, it is a marvel to die in one's bed; Pison, to whom this happened, is noted for that strange incident. The garden of Valerius Asiaticus pleases the emperor; the face of Statilius displeases the empress,—state crimes: Valerius is strangled because he has a garden, and Statilius because he has a face. Basil II., Emperor of the East, makes fifteen thousand Bulgarians prisoners; they are divided into bands of a hundred, and their eyes are put out, with the exception of one, who is charged to conduct his ninety-nine blind comrades. He afterward sends into Bulgaria the whole of this army without eyes. History thus describes Basil II.: "He was too fond of glory." Paul of Russia gave out this axiom: "There is no man powerful save him to whom the emperor speaks; and his power endures as long as the word that he hears." Philip V. of Spain, so ferociously calm at the *auto-da-fés*, is frightened at the idea of changing his shirt, and remains six months in bed without washing and without trimming his nails, for fear of being poisoned, by means of scissors, or by the water in the basin, or by his shirt, or by his shoes. Ivan, grandfather of Paul, had a woman put to the torture before making her lie in his bed; had a newly married bride hanged, and placed the husband as sentinel by her side, to prevent the rope from being cut; had a father killed by his son; invented the process of sawing men in two with a cord; burns Bariatinski himself by slow fire, and while the patient howls, brings the embers together with the end of his stick. Peter, in point of excellence, aspires to that of the executioner; he exercises himself in cutting off heads. At first he cuts off but five per day,—little enough; but, with application, he succeeds in cutting off twenty-five. It is a talent for a czar to tear away a woman's breast with one blow of the knout.

What are all those monsters? Symptoms,—running sores, pus which oozes from a sickly body. They are scarcely more responsible than the sum of a column is responsible for the figures in that column. Basil, Ivan, Philip, Paul, etc., are the products of vast surrounding stupidity. The clergy of the Greek Church, for example, having this maxim, "Who can make us judges of those who are our masters?" what more natural than that a czar,—Ivan himself,—should cause an archbishop to be sewn in a bear's skin and devoured by dogs? The czar is amused,—it is quite right. Under Nero, the man whose brother was killed goes to the temple to return thanks to the gods; under Ivan, a Boyard empaled employs his agony, which lasts for twenty-four hours, in repeating, "O God! protect the czar." The Princess Sanguzko is in tears; she presents, upon her knees, a supplication to Nicholas: she implores grace for her husband, conjuring the master to spare Sanguzko (a Pole guilty of loving Poland) the frightful journey to Siberia. Nicholas listens in silence, takes the supplication, and writes beneath it, "On foot." Then Nicholas goes into the streets, and the crowd throw themselves on his boot to kiss it. What have you to say? Nicholas is a madman, the crowd is a brute. From "khan" comes "knez;" from "knez" comes "tzar;" from "tzar" the "czar,"—a series of phenomena rather than an affiliation of men. That after this Ivan you should have this Peter, after this Peter this Nicholas, after this Nicholas this Alexander, what more logical? You all rather contribute to this result. The tortured accept the torture. "The czar, half putrid, half frozen," as Madame de Staël says,—you made him yourselves. To be a people, to be a force, and to look upon these things, is to find them good. To be present, is to give one's consent. He who assists at the crime, assists the crime. Unresisting presence is an encouraging submission.

Let us add that a preliminary corruption began the complicity even before the crime was committed. A certain putrid fermentation of pre-existing baseness engenders the oppressor.

The wolf is the fact of the forest; it is the savage fruit of solitude without defence. Combine and group together silence, obscurity, easy victory, monstrous infatuation, prey offered from all parts, murder in security, the connivance of those who are around, weakness, want of weapons, abandonment, isolation,—from the point of intersection of these things breaks forth the ferocious beast. A dark forest, whence cries cannot be heard, produces the tiger. A tiger is a blindness hungered and armed. Is it a being? Scarcely. The claw of the animal knows no more than does the thorn of a plant. The fatal fact engenders the unconscious organism. In so far as personality is concerned, and apart from killing for a living, the tiger does not exist. Mouravieff is mistaken if he thinks that he is a being.

Wicked men spring from bad things. Therefore let us correct the things.

And here we return to our starting-point: An attenuating circumstance for despotism is—idiocy. That attenuating circumstance we have just pleaded.

Idiotic despots, a multitude, are the mob of the purple; but above them, beyond them, by the immeasurable distance which separates that which radiates from that which stagnates,—there are the despots of genius; there are the captains, the conquerors, the mighty men of war, the civilizers of force, the ploughmen of the sword.

These we have just named. The truly great among them are called Cyrus, Sesostris, Alexander, Hannibal, Cæsar, Charlemagne, Napoleon; and, with the qualifications we have laid down, we admire them.

But we admire them on the condition of their disappearance. Make room for better ones! Make room for greater ones!

Those greater, those better ones, are they new? No. Their series is as ancient as the other; more ancient, perhaps, for the idea has preceded the act, and the thinker is anterior to the warrior. But their place was taken, taken violently. This usurpation is about to cease; their hour comes at last; their predominance gleams forth. Civilization, returned to the true light, recognizes them as its only founders; their series becomes clothed in light, and eclipses the rest; like the past, the future belongs to them; and henceforth it is they whom God will perpetuate.

HISTORY

THAT history has to be re-made is evident. Up to the present time, it has been nearly always written from the miserable point of view of accomplished fact; it is time to write it from the point of view of principle,—and that, under penalty of nullity.

Royal gestures, warlike uproars, princely coronations; marriages, baptisms, and funerals, executions and fêtes; the finery of one crushing all; the triumph of being born king, the prowess of sword and axe; great empires, heavy taxes; the tricks played by chance upon chance; the universe having for a law the adventures of any being, provided he be crowned; the destiny of a century changed by a blow from the lance of a fool through the skull of an imbecile; the majestic *fistula in ano* of Louis XIV.; the grave words of the dying Emperor Mathias to his doctor, trying for the last time to feel his pulse beneath his coverlet and making a mistake,—"Erras, amice hoc est membrum nostrum imperiale sacrocæsareum;" the dance, with castanets of Cardinal Richelieu, disguised as a shepherd before the Queen of France, in the private villa of the Rue de Gaillon; Hildebrand completed by Cisneros; the little dogs of Henri III.; the various Potemkins of Catherine II.,—Orloff here, Godoy there, etc.; a great tragedy with a petty intrigue,—such was history up to our days, alternating between the throne and the altar, lending one ear to Dangeau and another to Dom Calmet, sanctimonious and not stern, not comprehending the true transitions from one age to the other, incapable of distinguishing the climacteric crises of civilization, making the human race mount upward by ladders of silly dates, well versed in puerilities while ignorant of right, of justice, and of truth, and modelled far more upon Le Ragois than upon Tacitus.

So true is this, that in our days Tacitus has been the object of strong attack.

Tacitus on the other hand,—we do not weary of insisting upon it,—is, like Juvenal, like Suetonius and Lampridius, the object of a special and merited hatred. The day when in the colleges professors of rhetoric shall put Juvenal above Virgil, and Tacitus above Bossuet, will be the eve of the day in which the human race shall have been delivered; when all forms of oppression shall have disappeared,—from the slave-owner up to the pharisee, from the cottage where the slave weeps to the chapel where the eunuch sings. Cardinal Duperron, who received for Henri IV. blows from the Pope's stick, had the goodness to say, "I despise Tacitus."

Up to the epoch in which we live, history has been a courtier. The double identification of the king with the nation and of the king with God, is the work of courtier history. The grace of God begets the right divine. Louis XIV. says, "I am the State!" Madame du Barry, plagiarist of Louis XIV., calls Louis XV. "France;" and the pompously haughty saying of the great Asiatic king of Versailles ends with "France, your coffin taints the camp!"

Bossuet writes without hesitation, though palliating facts here and there, the frightful legend of those old thrones of antiquity covered with crimes, and, applying to the surface of things his vague theocratic declamation, satisfies himself by this formula: "God holds in his hand the hearts of kings." That is not the case, for two reasons,—God has no hand, and kings have no heart.

We are only speaking, of course, of the kings of Assyria.

History, that old history of which we have spoken, is a kind of person for princes. It shuts its eyes when a highness says, "History, do not look this way." It has, imperturbably, with the face of a harlot, denied the horrible skull-breaking casque with an inner spike, destined by the Archduke of Austria for the Swiss magistrate Gundoldingen. At the present time this machine is hung on a nail in the Hôtel de Ville of Lucerne; anybody can go and see it: yet history repeats its denial. Moréri calls St. Bartholomew's day " a disturbance." Chaudon, another biographer, thus characterizes the author of the saying to Louis XV., cited above: "A lady of the court, Madame du Barry." History accepts for an attack of apoplexy the mattress under which John II. of England stifled the Duke of Gloucester at Calais. Why is the head of the Infant Don Carlos separated from the trunk in his bier at the Escurial? Philip II., the father, answers: "It is because the Infant having died a natural death, the coffin prepared for him was not found long enough, and they were obliged to cut off the head." History blindly believes in the coffin being too short. What! the father to have his son beheaded! Oh, fie! Only demagogues would say such things.

The ingenuousness with which history glorifies the fact, whatever it may be, and however impious it may be, shines nowhere better than in Cantemir and Karamsin,—the one a Turkish historian, the other a Russian historian. The Ottoman fact and the Muscovite fact evidence, when confronted and compared with each other, the Tartar identity. Moscow is not less sinisterly Asiatic than Stamboul. Ivan is in the one as Mustapha is in the other. The gradation is imperceptible between that Christianity and that Mahometanism. The Pope is brother of the Ulema, the Boyard of the Pacha, the knout of the bowstring, and the moujik of the mute. There is to men passing through the streets little difference between Selim who pierces them with arrows, and Basil who lets bears loose on them. Cantemir, a man of the South, an ancient Moldavian hospodar, long a Turkish subject, feels, although he has passed over to the Russians, that he does not displease the Czar Peter by deifying despotism, and he prostrates his metaphors before the sultans: this crouching upon the belly is Oriental, and somewhat Western also. The sultans are divine; their scimitar is sacred, their dagger is sublime, their exterminations are magnanimous, their parricides are good. They call themselves merciful, as the furies are called Eumenides. The blood that they spill smokes in Cantemir with an odour of incense, and the vast slaughtering which is their reign blooms into glory. They massacre the people in the public interest. When some padischah (I know not which)—Tiger IV. of Tiger VI.—causes to be strangled one after the other his nineteen little brothers running frightened round the chamber, the Turkish native historian declares that "it was executing wisely the law of the empire." The Russian historian, Karamsin, is not less tender to the Tzar than was Cantemir to the Sultan; nevertheless, let us say it, in comparison with Cantemir's the fervency of Karamsin is lukewarmness. Thus Peter, killing his son Alexis, is glorified by Karamsin, but in the same tone in which we excuse a fault. It is not the acceptation pure and simple of Cantemir, who is more upon his knees. The Russian historian only admires, while the Turkish historian adores. No fire in Karamsin, no nerve,—a dull enthusiasm, greyish apotheoses, good-will stuck into an icicle, caresses benumbed with cold. It is poor flattery. Evidently the climate has something to do with it. Karamsin is a chilled Cantemir.

Thus is the greater part of history made up to the present day; it goes from Bossuet to Karamsin, passing by the Abbé Pluche. That history has for its principle obedience. To what is obedience due? To success. Heroes are well treated, but kings are preferred. To reign is to succeed every morning. A king has to-morrow: he is solvent. A hero may be unsuccessful,—such things happen,—in which case he is but a usurper. Before this history, genius itself, even should it be the highest expression of force served by intelligence, is compelled to continual success. If it fails, ridicule; if it falls, insult. After Marengo, you are Europe's hero, the man of Providence, anointed by the Lord; after Austerlitz, Napoleon the Great; after Waterloo, the ogre from Corsica. The Pope anointed an ogre.

Nevertheless, impartial Loriquet, in consideration of services rendered, makes you a marquis. The man of our day who has best executed that surprising gamut from Hero of Europe to Ogre of Corsica, is Fontanes, chosen during so many years, to cultivate, develop, and direct the moral sense of youth.

Legitimacy, right divine, negation of universal suffrage, the throne a fief, the nation an entailed estate, all proceed from that history. The executioner is also part of it; Joseph de Maistre adds him, divinely, to the king. In England such history is called "loyal" history. The English aristocracy, to whom similar excellent ideas sometimes occur, have imagined a method of giving to a political opinion the name of virtue,—*Instrumentum regni*. In England, to be a royalist, is to be loyal. A democrat is disloyal; he is a variety of the dishonest man. This man believes in the people,—shame! He would have universal suffrage,—he is a chartist! are you sure of his probity? Here is a republican passing,—take care of your pockets! That is clever. All the world is more witty than Voltaire: the English aristocracy has more wit than Macchiavelli.

The king pays, the people do not pay,—this is about all the secret of that kind of history. It has also its own tariff of indulgences. Honour and profit are divided,—honour to the master, profit to the historian. Procopius is perfect, and, what is more, Illustrious by special decree (which does not prevent him from being a traitor); Bossuet is bishop, Fleury is prelate prior of Argenteuil, Karamsin is senator, Cantemir is prince. But the finest thing is to be paid successively by For and by Against, and, like Fontanes, to be made senator through idolatry of, and peer of France through spitting upon, the same idol.

What is going on at the Louvre? What is going on at the Vatican, in the Seraglio, Buen Retiro, at Windsor, at Schoenbrünn, at Potsdam, at the Kremlin, at Oranienbaum? Further questions are needless; for there is nothing interesting for the human race beyond those ten or twelve houses, of which history is the door-keeper.

Nothing can be insignificant that relates to war, the warrior, the prince, the throne, the court. He who is not endowed with grave puerility cannot be an historian. A question of etiquette, a hunt, a gala, a grand levee, a procession, the triumph of Maximilian, the number of carriages the ladies have followed the king to the camp before Mons, the necessity of having vices congenial with the faults of his majesty, the clocks of Charles V., the locks of Louis XVI.; how the broth refused by Louis XV. at his coronation, showed him to be a good king; how the Prince of Wales sits in the Chamber of the House of Lords, not in the capacity of Prince of Wales, but as Duke of Cornwall; how the drunken Augustus has appointed Prince Lubormirsky, who is starost of Kasimirow, under-cupbearer to the crown; how Charles of Spain gave the command of the army to Pimentel because the Pimentels have the title of Benavente since 1308; how Frederic of Brandenburg granted a fief of forty thousand crowns to a huntsman who enabled him to kill a fine stag; how Louis Antoine, grand-master of the Teutonic Order and Prince Palatine, died at Liége from displeasure at not being able to make the inhabitants choose him bishop; how the Princess Borghèse, dowager of Mirandole and of the Papal House, married the Prince of Cellamare, son of the Duke of Giovenazzo; how my Lord Seaton, who is a Montgomery, followed James II. into France; how the Emperor ordered the Duke of Mantua, who is vassal of the empire, to drive from his court the Marquis Amorati; how there are always two Cardinal Barberins living, and so on,—all that is the important business. A turned-up nose becomes an historical fact. Two small fields contiguous to the old Mark and to the duchy of Zell, having almost embroiled England and Prussia, are memorable. In fact, the cleverness of the governing and the apathy of the governed have arranged and mixed things in such a manner that all those forms of princely nothingness have their place in human destiny; and peace and war, the movement of armies and fleets, the recoil of the progress of civilization, depend on the cup of tea of Queen Anne or the fly-flap of the Dey of Algiers.

History walks behind those fooleries, registering them.

Knowing so many things, it is quite natural that it should be ignorant of others. If you are so curious as to ask the name of the English merchant who in 1612 first entered China by the north; of the worker in glass who in 1663 first established in France a manufactory of crystal; of the citizen who carried out in the States General at Tours, under Charles VIII.: the sound principle of elective magistracy (a principle which has since been adroitly obliterated); of the pilot who in 1405 discovered the Canary Islands; of the Byzantine lutemaker who in the eighth century invented the organ and gave to music its grandest voice; of the Campanian mason who invented the clock by establishing at Rome on the temple of Quirinus the first sundial; of the Roman lighterman who invented the paving of towns by the construction of the Appian Way in the year 312 B. C.; of the Egyptian carpenter who devised the dove-tail, one of the keys of architecture, which may be found under the obelisk of Loxor; of the Chaldean keeper of flocks who founded astronomy by his observation of the signs of the zodiac, the starting-point taken by Anaximenes; of the Corinthian calker who, nine years before the first Olympiad, calculated the power of the triple lever, devised the trireme, and created a tow-boat anterior by two thousand six hundred years to the steamboat; of the Macedonian ploughman who discovered the first gold mine in Mount Pangæus,—history does not know what to say to you: those fellows are unknown to history. Who is that,—a ploughman, a calker, a shepherd, a carpenter, a lighterman, a mason, a lutemaker, a sailor and a merchant? History does not lower itself to such rabble.

There is at Nüremberg, near the Egydienplatz, in a chamber on the second floor of a house which faces the church of St. Giles, on an iron tripod, a little ball of wood twenty inches in diameter, covered with darkish vellum, marked with lines which were once red, yellow, and green. It is a globe on which is sketched out an outline of the divisions of the earth in the fifteenth century. On this globe is vaguely indicated, in the twenty-fourth degree of latitude, under the sign of the Crab, a kind of island named Antilia, which one day attracted the attention of two men. The one who had constructed the globe and drawn Antilia showed this island to the other, placed his finger upon it, and said, "It is there." The man who looked on was Christopher Columbus; the man who said, "It is there," was called Martin Behaim. Antilia is America. History speaks of Fernando Cortez, who ravaged America, but not of Martin Behaim, who divined it.

Let a man have "cut to pieces" other men; let him have "put them to the sword;" let him have made them "bite the dust,"—horrible expressions, which have become hideously familiar,—and if you search history for the name of that man, whoever he may be, you will find it. But search for the name of the man who invented the compass, and you will not find it.

In 1747, in the eighteenth century, under the gaze even of philosophers, the battles of Raucoux and Lawfield, the siege of Sas-de-Gand and the taking of Bergop-Zoom, eclipse and efface that sublime discovery which to-day is in course of modifying the world,—electricity. Voltaire himself, about that year, celebrated passionately some exploit of Trajan.

A certain public stupidity is the result of that history which is superimposed upon education almost everywhere. If you doubt it, see, among others, the publications of Périsse Brothers, intended by the editors, says a parenthesis, for primary schools.

A prince who gives himself an animal's name makes us laugh. We rail at the Emperor of China, who makes people call him "His Majesty the Dragon," and we placidly say "Monseigneur le Dauphin."

History is the record of domesticity. The historian is no more than the master of ceremonies of centuries. In the model court of Louis the Great there are four historians, as there are four chamber violinists. Lulli leads the one, Boileau the others.

In this old method of history,—the only authorized method up to 1789, and classic in every acceptation of the word, —the best narrators, even the honest ones (there are few of them), even those who think themselves free, place themselves mechanically in drill, stitch tradition to tradition, submit to accepted custom, receive the pass-word from the ante-chamber, accept, pell-mell with the crowd, the stupid divinity of coarse personages in the foreground,—kings, "potentates," "pontiffs," soldiers,—and, all the time thinking themselves historians, end by donning the livery of historiographers, and are lackeys without knowing it.

This kind of history is taught, is compulsory, is commended and recommended; all young intellects are more or less saturated with it, its mark remains upon them, their thought suffers through it and releases itself only with difficulty, —we make schoolboys learn it by heart, and I who speak, when a child, was its victim.

In such history there is everything except history. Shows of princes, of "monarchs," and of captains, indeed; but of the people, of laws, of manners, very little; and of letters, of arts, of sciences, of philosophy, of the universal movement of thought,—in one word, of man,—nothing. Civilization dates by dynasties and not by progress; some king or other is one of the stages along the historical road; the true stages, the stages of great men, are nowhere indicated. It explains how Francis II. succeeds to Henri II., Charles IX. to Francis II., and Henri III. to Charles IX.; but it does not tell us how Watt succeeds to Papin, and Fulton to Watt; behind the heavy scenery of the hereditary rights of kings a glimpse of the mysterious sovereignty of men of genius is scarcely obtained. The lamp which smokes on the opaque façades of royal accessions hides the starry light which the creators of civilization throw over the ages. Not one of this series of historians points out the divine relation of human affairs,—the applied logic of Providence; not one makes us see how progress engenders progress. That Philip IV. comes after Philip III., and Charles II. after Philip IV., it would indeed be shameful not to know; but that Descartes continues Bacon, and that Kant continues Descartes; that Las Casas continues Columbus, that Washington continues Las Casas, and that John Brown continues and rectifies Washington; that John Huss continues Pelagius, that Luther continues John Huss, and that Voltaire continues Luther,—it is almost a scandal to be aware of this!

CHANGE

It is time that all this should be altered. It is time that the men of action should take their place behind, and the men of ideas come to the front. The summit is the head. Where thought is there is power. It is time that men of genius should precede heroes. It is time to render to Cæsar what is Cæsar's, and to the book what is the book's: such or such a poem, such a drama, such a novel, does more work than all the Courts of Europe together. It is time that history should proportion itself to the reality, that it should allow to each influence its true measure, and that it should cease to place the masks of kings on epochs made in the image of poets and philosophers. To whom belongs the eighteenth century,—to Louis XV. or to Voltaire? Confront Versailles with Ferney, and see from which of these two points civilization flows.

A century is a formula; an epoch is a thought expressed,—after which, civilization passes to another. Civilization has phrases: these phrases are the centuries. It does not repeat here, what it says there; but its mysterious phrases are bound together by a chain,—logic (*logos*) is within,—and their series constitutes progress. All these phrases, expressive of a single idea,—the divine idea,—write slowly the word Fraternity.

All light is at some point condensed into flame; in the same way every epoch is condensed into a man. The man having expired, the epoch is closed,— God turns the page. Dante dead, is the full-stop put at the end of the thirteenth century: John Huss can come. Shakespeare dead, is the full-stop put at the end of the sixteenth century; after this poet, who contains and sums up every philosophy, the philosophers Pascal, Descartes, Molière, Le Sage, Montesquieu, Rousseau, Diderot, Beaumarchais can come. Voltaire dead, is the full-stop put at the end of the eighteenth century: the French Revolution, liquidation of the first social form of Christianity, can come.

These different periods, which we name epochs, have all their dominant points. What is that dominant point? Is it a head that wears a crown, or is it a head that bears a thought? Is it an aristocracy, or is it an idea? Answer yourself. Do you see where the power is? Weigh Francis I. in the scales with Gargantua: put all chivalry in the scale against "Don Quixote."

Therefore, every one to his right place. Right about face! and let us now regard the centuries in their true light. In the first rank, minds; in the second, in the third, in the twentieth, soldiers and princes. To the warrior the darkness, to the thinker the pedestal. Take away Alexander, and put in his place Aristotle. Strange thing, that up to this day humanity should have read the Iliad in such a manner as to annihilate Homer under Achilles!

I repeat it, it is time that all this should be changed. Moreover, the first impulse is given. Already, noble minds are at work; future history begins to appear. some specimens of the new and magnificent though partial treatments of the subject being already in existence; a general recasting is imminent,—*ad usum populi*. Compulsory education demands true history; and true history will be given: it is begun.

Effigies must be stamped afresh. That which was the reverse will become the face, and that which was the face will become the reverse. Urban VIII. will be the reverse of Galileo.

The true profile of the human race will re-appear on the different proofs of civilization that the successive ages will offer.

The historical effigy will no longer be the man-king; it will be the man-people.

Doubtless,—and we shall not be reproached for not insisting on it,—real and veracious history, in indicating the sources of civilization wherever they may be, will not lose sight of the appreciable utility of the sceptre-bearers and sword-bearers at given periods and in special states of humanity. Certain wrestling matches necessitate some resemblance between the two combatants; barbarity must sometimes be pitted against savageness. There are cases of progress by violence. Cæsar is good in Cimmeria, and Alexander in Asia; but for Alexander and Cæsar the second rank suffices.

Veracious history, real history, definitive history henceforth charged with the education of the royal infant,—namely, the people,—will reject all fiction, will fail in complaisance, will logically classify phenomena, will unravel profound causes, will study philosophically and scientifically the successive commotions of humanity, and will take less account of the great strokes of the sword than of the grand strokes of the idea. The deeds of light will pass first; Pythagoras will be a much greater event than Sesostris. We have just said it,—heroes, men of the twilight, are relatively luminous in the darkness; but what is a conqueror beside a sage? What is the invasion of kingdoms compared with the opening up of intellects? The winners of minds efface the gainers of provinces. He through whom we think, he is the true conqueror. In future history, the slave Æsop and the slave Plautus will have precedence over kings; and there are vagabonds who will weigh more than certain victors, and comedians who will weigh more than certain emperors.

Without doubt, to illustrate what we are saying by means of facts, it is useful that a powerful man should have marked the halting-place between the ruin of the Latin world and the growth of the Gothic world; it is also useful that another powerful man, coming after the first, like cunning on the footsteps of daring, should have sketched out under the form of a catholic monarchy the future universal group of nations, and the beneficial encroachments of Europe upon Africa, Asia, and America. But it is more useful yet to have written the "Divina Commedia" and "Hamlet." No bad action is mixed up with these great works; nor is here to be charged to the account of the civilizer a debt of nations ruined. The improvement of the human mind being given as the result to be obtained, Dante is of greater importance than Charlemagne, and Shakespeare of greater importance than Charles the Fifth.

In history, as it will be written on the pattern of absolute truth, that intelligence of no account, that unconscious and trivial being,—the *Non pluribus impar*, the Sultan-sun of Marly,—will appear as nothing more than the almost mechanical preparer of the shelter needed by the thinker disguised as a buffoon, and of the environment of ideas and men required for the philosophy of Alceste. Thus Louis XIV. makes Molière's bed.

These exchanges of parts will put people in their true light; the historical optic, renewed, will re-adjust the *ensemble* of civilization, at present a chaos; for perspective, that justice of geometry, will size the past,—making such a plan to advance, placing another in the background. Every one will assume his real stature; the head-dresses of tiaras and of crowns will only make dwarfs more ridiculous; stupid genuflexions will vanish. From these alterations will proceed right.

That great judge We ourselves,—We all,—having henceforth for measure the clear idea of what is absolute and what is relative, deductions and restitutions will of themselves take place. The innate moral sense within man will know its power; it will no longer be obliged to ask itself questions like this,—Why, at the same minute, do people revere in Louis XV. and all the rest of royalty the act for which they burn Deschauffours on the Place de Grève? The quality of kingship will no longer be a false moral weight. Facts fairly placed will place conscience fairly. A good light will come, sweet to the human race, serene, equitable, with no interposition of clouds henceforth between truth and the brain of man, but a definitive ascent of the good, the just, and the beautiful toward the zenith of civilization.

Nothing can escape the law which simplifies. By the mere force of things, the material side of facts and of men disintegrates and disappears. There is no shadowy solidity; whatever may be the mass, whatever may be the block, every combination of ashes (and matter is nothing else) returns to ashes. The idea of the atom of dust is in the word "granite,"—inevitable pulverizations. All those granites of oligarchy, aristocracy, and theocracy, are doomed to be scattered to the four winds. The idea alone is indestructible. Nothing lasts save the mind.

In this indefinite increase of light which is called civilization, the processes of reduction and levelling are accomplished. The imperious morning light penetrates everywhere,—enters as master, and makes itself obeyed. The light is at work; under the great eye of posterity, before the blaze of the nineteenth century, simplifications take place, excrescences fall away, glories drop like leaves, reputations are riven to pieces. Do you wish for an example,—take Moses. There is in Moses three glories, —the captain, the legislator, the poet.

Of these three men contained in Moses, where is the captain to-day? In the shadow, with brigands and murderers. Where is the legislator? Amidst the waste of dead religions. Where is the poet? By the side of Æschylus.

Daylight has an irresistible corroding power on the things of night. Hence appears a new historic sky above our heads, a new philosophy of causes and results, a new aspect of facts.

Certain minds, however, whose honest and stern anxiety please us, object: "You have said that men of genius form a dynasty; now, we will not have that dynasty any more than another." This is to misapprehend, and to fear the word where the thing is reassuring. The same law which wills that the human race should have no owners, wills that it should have guides. To be enlightened is quite different from being enslaved. Kings possess; men of genius conduct,—there is the difference. Between "I am a Man" and "I am the State" there is all the distance from fraternity to tyranny. The forward-march must have a guide-post. To revolt against the pilot can scarcely improve the ship's course; we do not see what would have been gained by throwing Christopher Columbus into the sea. The direction "this way" has never humiliated the man who seeks the road. I accept in the night the guiding authority of torches. Moreover, a dynasty of little encumbrance is that of men of genius, having for a kingdom the exile of Dante, for a palace the dungeon of Cervantes, for a civil list the wallet of Isaiah, for a throne the dunghill of Job, and for a sceptre the staff of Homer.

Let us resume.

GUIDANCE

Humanity, no longer owned but guided,—such is the new aspect of facts.

This new aspect of facts history henceforth is compelled to reproduce. To change the past, that is strange; yet it is what history is about to do. By falsehood? No, by speaking the truth. History has been a picture; she is about to become a mirror. This new reflection of the past will modify the future.

The former king of Westphalia, who was a witty man, was looking one day at an inkstand on the table of some one we know. The writer, with whom Jerome Bonaparte was at that moment, had brought home from an excursion among the Alps, made some years before in company with Charles Nodier, a piece of steatitic serpentine carved and hollowed in the form of an inkstand, and purchased of the chamois-hunters of the Mer de Glace. It was this that Jerome Bonaparte was looking at. "What it this?" he asked. "It is my inkstand," said the writer; and he added, "it is steatite. Admire how Nature with a little dirt and oxide has made this charming green stone." Jerome Bonaparte replied, "I admire much more the men who out of this stone made an inkstand."

That was not badly said for a brother of Napoleon, and due credit should be given for it; for the inkstand is to destroy the sword. The decrease of warriors,—men of brutal force and of prey; the undefined and superb growth of men of thought and peace; the re-appearance on the scene of the true colossals,—in this is one of the greatest facts of our great epoch. There is no spectacle more pathetic and sublime,—humanity delivered from on high, the powerful ones put to flight by the thinkers, the prophet overwhelming the hero, force routed by ideas, the sky cleaned, a majestic expulsion.

Look! raise your eyes! the supreme epic is accomplished. The legions of light drive backward the hordes of flame.

The masters are departing; the liberators are arriving! Those who hunt down nations, who drag armies behind them,—Nimrod, Sennacherib, Cyrus, Rameses, Xerxes, Cambyses, Attila, Genghis Khan, Tamerlane, Alexander, Cæsar, Bonaparte,—all these immense wild men are disappearing. They die away slowly,—behold them touch the horizon; they are mysteriously attracted by the darkness; they claim kindred with the shade,—thence their fatal descent. Their resemblance to other phenomena of the night restores them to that terrible unity of blind immensity, a submersion of all light; forgetfulness, shadow of the shadow, awaits them.

But though they are thrown down, they remain formidable. Let us not insult what has been great. Hooting would be unbecoming before the burying of heroes; the thinker should remain grave in presence of this donning of shrouds. The old glory abdicates, the strong lie down: mercy for those vanquished conquerors! peace to those warlike spirits now extinguished! The darkness of the grave interposes between their glare and ourselves. It is not without a kind of religious terror that one sees planets become spectres.

While in the engulfing process the flaming pleiad of the men of brutal force descends deeper and deeper into the abyss with the sinister pallor of approaching disappearance, at the other extremity of space, where the last cloud is about to fade away, in the deep heaven of the future, henceforth to be azure, rises in radiancy the sacred group of true stars,—Orpheus, Hermes, Job, Homer, Æschylus, Isaiah, Ezekiel, Hippocrates, Phidias, Socrates, Sophocles, Plato, Aristotle, Archimedes, Euclid, Pythagoras, Lucretius, Plautus, Juvenal, Tacitus, Saint Paul, John of Patmos, Tertullian, Pelagius, Dante, Gutenberg, Joan of Arc, Christopher Columbus, Luther, Michael Angelo, Corpernicus, Galileo, Rabelais, Calderon, Cervantes, Shakespeare, Rembrandt, Kepler, Milton, Molière, Newton, Descartes, Kant, Piranesi, Beccaria, Diderot, Voltaire, Beethoven, Fulton, Montgolfier, Washington. And this marvellous constellation, at each instant more luminous, dazzling as a glory of celestial diamonds, shines in the clear horizon, and ascending mingles with the vast dawn of Jesus Christ.

The Souls

PRODUCTION

The production of souls is the secret of the unfathomable depth. The innate, what a shadow! What is that concentration of the unknown which takes place in the darkness, and whence abruptly bursts forth that light, a genius? What is the law of these events, O Love? The human heart does its work on earth, and that moves the great deep. What is that incomprehensible meeting of material sublimation and moral sublimation in the atom, indivisible if looked at from life, incorruptible if looked at from death? The atom, what a marvel! No dimension, no extent, nor height, nor width, nor thickness, independent of every possible measure, and yet, everything in this nothing! For algebra, the geometrical point. For philosophy, a soul. As a geometrical point, the basis of science; as a soul, the basis of faith. Such is the atom. Two urns, the sexes, imbibe life from the infinite; and the spilling of one into the other produces the being. This is the normal condition of all, animal as well as man. But the man more than man, whence comes he?

The Supreme Intelligence, which here below is the great man, what is the power which invokes it, incorporates it, and reduces it to a human state? What part do the flesh and the blood take in this prodigy? Why do certain terrestrial sparks seek certain celestial molecules? Where do they plunge, those sparks? Where do they go? How do they manage? What is this gift of man to set fire to the unknown? This mine, the infinite, this extraction, a genius, what more wonderful! Whence does that spring up? Why, at a given moment, this one and not that one? Here, as everywhere, the incalculable law of affinities appears and escapes. One gets a glimpse, but sees not. O forger of the unfathomable, where art thou?

Qualities the most diverse, the most complex, the most opposed in appearance, enter into the composition of souls. The contraries do not exclude each other,—far from that; they complete each other. More than one prophet contains a scholiast; more than one magian is a philologist. Inspiration knows its own trade. Every poet is a critic: witness that excellent piece of criticism on the theatre that Shakespeare puts in the mouth of Hamlet. A visionary mind may be at the same time precise,—like Dante, who writes a book on rhetoric, and a grammer. A precise mind may be at the same time visionary,—like Newton, who comments on the Apocalypse; like Leibnitz, who demonstrates, *nova inventa logica,* the Holy Trinity. Dante knows the distinction between the three sorts of words, *parola piana, parola sdrucciola, parola tronca;* he knows that the *piana* gives a trochee, the *sdrucciola* a dactyl and the *tronca* an iambus. Newton is perfectly sure that the Pope is the Antichrist. Dante combines and calculates; Newton dreams.

No law is to be grasped in that obscurity. No system is possible. The currents of adhesions and of cohesions cross each other pell-mell. At times one imagines that he detects the phenomenon of the transmission of the idea, and fancies that he distinctly sees a hand taking the light from him who is departing, to give it to him who arrives. 1642, for example, is a strange year. Galileo dies, Newton is born, in that year. Good. It is a thread; try and tie it, it breaks at once. Here is a disappearance: on the 23rd of April, 1616, on the same day, almost at the same minute, Shakespeare and Cervantes die. Why are these two flames extinguished at the same moment? No apparent logic. A whirlwind in the night.

Enigmas constantly. Why does Commodus proceed from Marcus Aurelius?

These problems beset in the desert Jerome, that man of the caves, that Isaiah of the New Testament. He interrupted his deep thoughts on eternity, and his attention to the trumpet of the archangel, in order to meditate on the soul of some Pagan in whom he felt interested. He calculated the age of Persius, connecting that research with some obscure chance of possible salvation for the poet, dear to the cenobite on account of his strictness; and nothing is so surprising as to see this wild thinker, half naked on his straw, like Job, dispute on this question, so frivolous in appearance, of the birth of a man, with Rufinus and Theophilus of Alexandria,—Rufinus observing to him that he is mistaken in his calculations, and that Persius having been born in December under the consulship of Fabius Persicus and Vitellius, and having died in November, under the consulship of Publius Marius and Asinius Gallus, these periods do not correspond rigorously with the year II. of the two hundred and third Olympiad, and the year II. of the two hundred and tenth, the dates fixed by Jerome. The mystery thus attracts deep thinkers.

These calculations, almost wild, of Jerome, or other similar ones, are made by more than one dreamer. Never to find a stop, to pass from one spiral to another like Archimedes, and from one zone to another like Alighieri, to fall, while fluttering about in the circular well, is the eternal lot of the dreamer. He strikes against the hard wall on which the pale ray glides. Sometimes certainty comes to him as an obstacle, and sometimes clearness as a fear. He keeps on his way. He is the bird under the vault. It is terrible. No matter, the dreamer goes on.

To dream is to think here and there, —*passim*. What means the birth of Euripides during that battle of Salamis where Sophocles, a youth, prays, and where Æschylus, in his manhood fights? What means the birth of Alexander in the night which saw the burning of the temple of Ephesus? What tie between that temple and that man? Is it the conquering and radiant spirit of Europe which, destroyed under the form of the *chef-d'œuvre*, revives under the form of the hero? For do not forget that Ctesiphon is the Greek architect of the temple of Ephesus. We have mentioned just now the simultaneous disappearance of Shakespeare and Cervantes. Here is another case not less surprising. The day when Diogenes died at Corinth, Alexander died at Babylon. These two cynics, the one of the tub, the other of the sword, depart together; and

Diogenes, longing to enjoy the immense unknown radiance, will again say to Alexander: "Stand out of my sunlight!"

What is the meaning of certain harmonies in the myths represented by divine men? What is this analogy between Hercules and Jesus which struck the Fathers of the Church, which made Sorel indignant, but edified Duperron, and which makes Alcides a kind of material mirror of Christ? Is there not a community of souls, and, unknown to them, a communication between the Greek legislator and the Hebrew legislator, creating at the same moment, without knowing each other, and without their suspecting the existence of each other, the first the Areopagus, the second the Sanhedrim? Strange resemblance between the jubilee of Moses and the jubilee of Lycurgus! What are these double paternities,—paternity of the body, paternity of the soul, like that of David for Solomon? Giddy heights, steeps, precipices.

He who looks too long into this sacred horror feels immensity racking his brain. What does the sounding-line give you when thrown into that mystery? What do you see? Conjectures quiver, doctrines shake, hypotheses float; all the human philosophy vacillates before the mournful blast rising from that chasm.

The expanse of the possible is, so to speak under your eyes. The dream that you have in yourself, you discover it beyond yourself. All is indistinct. Confused white shadows are moving. Are they souls? One catches, in the depths below, a glimpe of vague archangels passing along; will they be men at some future day? Holding your head between your hands, you strive to see and to know. You are at the window looking into the unknown. On all sides the deep layers of effects and causes, heaped one behind the other, wrap you with mist. The man who meditates not lives in blindness; the man who meditates lives in darkness. The choice between darkness and darkness, that is all we have. In that darkness, which is up to the present time nearly all our science, experience gropes, observation lies in wait, supposition moves about. If you gaze at it very often, you become *vates*. Vast religious meditation takes possession of you.

Every man has in him his Patmos. He is free to go or not to go on that frightful promontory of thought from which darkness is seen. If he goes not, he remains in the common life, with the common conscience, with the common virtue, with the common faith, or with the common doubt; and it is well. For the inward peace it is evidently the best. If he ascends to that peak, he is caught. The profound waves of the marvellous have appeared to him. No one sees with impunity that ocean. Henceforth he will be the thinker enlarged, magnified, but floating,—that is to say, the dreamer. He will partake of the poet and of the prophet. A certain quantity of him now belongs to darkness. The boundless enters into his life, into his conscience, into his virtue, into his philosophy. He becomes extraordinary in the eyes of other men, for his measure is different from theirs. He has duties which they have not. He lives in a sort of vague prayer, attaching himself, strangely enough, to an indefinite certainty which he calls God. He distinguishes in that twilight enough of the anterior life and enough of the ulterior life to seize these two ends of the dark thread, and with them to tie up his soul again. Who has drunk will drink; who has dreamed will dream. He will not give up that alluring abyss, that sounding of the fathomless, that indifference for the world and for life, that entrance into the forbidden, that effort to handle the impalpable and to see the invisible; he returns to them, he leans and bends over them; he takes one step forward, and two,—and thus it is that one penetrates into the impenetrable; and thus it is that one plunges into the boundless chasms of infinite meditation.

He who walks down them is a Kant; he who falls down them is a Swedenborg.

To keep one's own free will in that dilatation, is to be great. But, however great one may be, the problems cannot be solved. One may ply the fathomless with questions. Nothing more. As for the answers, they are there, but mingled with shadows. The huge lineaments of truth seem at times to appear for one moment, then go back, and are lost in the absolute. Of all those questions, that among them all which besets the intellect, that among them all which rends the heart, is the question of the soul.

Does the soul exist? Question the first. The persistency of the self is the thirst of man. Without the persistent self, all creation is for him but an immense *cui bono?* Listen to the astounding affirmation which bursts forth from all consciences. The whole sum of God that there is on the earth, within all men, condemns itself in a single cry,— to affirm the soul. And then, question the second: Are there great souls?

It seems impossible to doubt it. Why not great minds in humanity as well as great trees in the forest, as well as great peaks in the horizon? The great souls are seen as well as the great mountains. Then, they exist. But here the interrogation presses further; interrogation is anxiety: Whence come they? What are they? Who are they? Are these atoms more divine than others? This atom, for instance, which shall be endowed with irradiation here below, this one which shall be Thales, this one Æschylus, this one Plato, this one Ezekiel, this one Macchabœus, this one Apollonius of Tyana, this one Tertullian, this one Epictetus, this one Marcus Aurelius, this one Nestorius, this one Pelagius, this one Gama, this one Copernicus, this one John Huss, this one Descartes, this one Vincent de Paul, this one Piranesi, this one Washington, this one Beethoven, this one Garibaldi, this one John Brown,—all these atoms, souls having a sublime function among men, have they seen other worlds, and do they bring on earth the essence of those worlds? The master souls, the leading intellects, who sends them? Who determines their appearance? Who is judge of the actual want of humanity? Who chooses the souls? Who musters the atoms? Who ordains the departures? Who premeditates the arrivals? Does the atom conjunction, the atom universal, the atom binder of worlds, exist? Is not that the great soul?

To complete one universe by the other; to pour upon the too little of the one the too much of the other; to increase here liberty, there science, there the ideal; to communicate to the inferiors patterns of superior beauty; to exchange the effluvia; to bring the central fire to the planet; to harmonize the various worlds of the same system; to urge forward those which are behind; to mix the creations,—does not that mysterious function exist?

Is it not fulfilled, unknown to them, by certain elects, who momentarily and during their earthly transit, partly ignore themselves? Is not the function of such or such atom, divine motive power called soul, to give movement to a solar man among earthly men? Since the floral atom exists, why should not the stellar atom exist? That solar man will be, in turn, the savant, the seer, the calculator, the thaumaturge, the navigator, the architect, the magian, the legislator, the philosopher, the prophet, the hero, the poet. The life of humanity will move onward through them. The volutation of civilization will be their task; that team of minds will drag the huge chariot. One being unyoked, the others will start again. Each completion of a century will be one stage on the journey. Never any solution of continuity. That which one mind will begin, another mind will finish, soldering phenomenon to phenomenon, sometimes without suspecting that welding process. To each revolution in the fact will correspond an adequate revolution in the ideas, and reciprocally. The horizon will not be allowed to extend to the right without stretching as much to the left. Men the most diverse, the most opposite, sometimes will adhere by unexpected parts; and in these adherences will burst forth the imperious logic of progress. Orpheus, Buddha, Confucius, Zoroaster, Pythagoras, Moses, Manou, Mahomet, with many more, will be the links of the same chain. A Gutenberg discovering the method for the sowing of civilization and the means for the ubiquity of thought, will be followed by a Christopher Columbus discovering a new field. A Christopher Columbus discovering a world will be followed by a Luther discovering a liberty. After Luther, innovator in the dogma, will come Shakespeare, innovator in art. One genius completes the other.

But not in the same region. The astronomer follows the philosopher; the legislator is the executor of the poet's wishes; the fighting liberator lends his assistance to the thinking liberator; the poet corroborates the statesman. Newton is the appendix to Bacon; Danton originates from Diderot; Milton confirms Cromwell; Byron supports Botzaris; Æschylus, before him, has assisted Miltiades. The work is mysterious even for the very men who perform it. Some are conscious of it, others not. At great distances, at intervals of centuries, the correlations manifest themselves, wonderful. The modification in human manners, begun by the religious revealer, will be completed by the philosophical reasoner, so that Voltaire follows up Jesus. Their work agrees and coincides. If this concordance rested with them, both would resist, perhaps,—the one, the divine man, indignant in his martyrdom, the other, the human man, humiliated in his irony; but that is so. Some one who is very high orders it in that way.

Yes, let us meditate on these vast obscurities. The characteristic of revery is to gaze at darkness so intently that it brings light out of it.

Humanity developing itself from the interior to the exterior is, properly speaking, civilization. Human intelligence becomes radiance, and step by step, wins, conquers and humanizes matter. Sublime domestication! This labour has phases; and each of these phases, marking an age in progress, is opened or closed by one of those beings called geniuses. These missionary spirits, these legates of God, do they not carry in them a sort of partial solution of this question, so abstruse, of free will? The apostolate, being an act of will, is related on one side to liberty, and on the other, being a mission, is related by predestination to fatality. The voluntary necessary. Such is the Messiah; such is Genius.

Now let us return—for all questions which append to mystery form the circle, and one cannot get out of it,—let us return to our starting-point, and to our first question: What is a genius? Is it not perchance a cosmic soul, a soul imbued with a ray from the unknown? In what depths are such souls prepared? How long do they wait? What medium do they traverse? What is the germination which precedes the hatching? What is the mystery of the ante-birth? Where was this atom? It seems as if it was the point of intersection of all the forces. How come all the powers to converge and tie themselves into an indivisible unity in this sovereign intelligence? Who has bred this eagle? The incubation of the fathomless on genius, what an enigma! These lofty souls, momentarily belonging to earth, have they not seen something else? Is it for that reason that they arrive here with so many intuitions? Some of them seem full of the dream of a previous world. Is it thence that comes to them the sacred wildness that they sometimes have? Is it that which inspires them with wonderful words? Is it that which gives them strange agitations? Is it thence that they derive the hallucination which makes them, so to speak, see and touch imaginary things and beings? Moses had his fiery thicket; Socrates his familiar demon; Mahomet his dove; Luther his goblin playing with his pen, and to whom he would say, "Be still, there!" Pascal his gaping chasm that he hid with a screen.

Many of those majestic souls are evidently conscious of a mission. They act at times as if they knew. They seem to have a confused certainty. They have it. They have it for the mysterious *ensemble*. They have it also for the detail. John Huss dying predicts Luther. He exclaims, "You burn the goose [Huss], but the swan will come." Who sends these souls? Who creates them? What is the law of their formation anterior and superior to life? Who provides them with force, patience, fecundation, will, passion? From what urn of goodness have they drawn sternness? In what region of the lightnings have they culled love? Each of these great newly arrived souls renews philosophy of art or science or poetry, remakes these worlds after its own image. They are as though impregnated with creation. At times a truth emanates from these souls which lights up the questions on which it falls. Some of these souls are like a star from which light would drip. From what wonderful source, then, do they proceed, that they are all different? Not one originates from the other, and yet they have this in common that they all bring the infinite. Incommensurable and insoluble questions. That does not stop the good pedants and the clever men from bridling up, and saying, while pointing with the finger at the sidereal group of geniuses on the heights of civilization: "You will have no more men such as those. They cannot be matched. There are no more of them. We declare to you that the earth has exhausted its contingent of master spirits. Now for decadence and general closing. We must make up our minds to it. We shall have no more men of genius."— Ah, you have seen the bottom of the unfathomable, you!

BOUNDLESSNESS

No, Thou art not worn out. Thou hast not before thee the bourn, the limit, the term, the frontier. Thou hast nothing to bound thee, as winter bounds summer, as lassitude the birds, as the precipice the torrent, as the cliff the ocean, as the tomb man. Thou art boundless. The "Thou shalt not go farther," is spoken *by* thee, and it is not said *of* thee. No, thou windest not a skein which diminishes, and the thread of which breaks; no, thou stoppest not short; no, thy quantity decreaseth not; no, thy thickness becometh not thinner; no, thy faculty miscarrieth not; no, it is not true that they begin to perceive in thy all-powerfulness that transparence which announces the end, and to get a glimpse behind thee of another thing besides thee. Another thing! And what then? The obstacle. The obstacle to whom? The obstacle to creation, the obstacle to the everlasting, the obstacle to the necessary! What a dream!

When thou hearest men say, "This is as far as God advances,—do not ask more of him; he starts from here, and stops there. In Homer, in Aristotle, in Newton he has given you all that he had; leave him at rest now,—he is empty. God does not begin again; he could do that once, he cannot do it twice; he has spent himself altogether in this man,—enough of God does not remain to make a similar man;" when thou hearest them say such things, if thou wast a man like them, thou wouldst smile in thy terrible depth; but thou art not in a terrible depth, and being goodness, thou hast no smile. The smile is but a passing wrinkle, unknown to the absolute.

Thou struck by a powerful chill; thou to leave off; thou to break down; thou to say "Halt!" Never. Thou shouldst be compelled to take breath after having created a man! No; whoever that man may be, thou art God. If this weak swarm of living beings, in presence of the unknown, must feel wonder and fear at something, it is not at the possibility of seeing the germ-seed dry up and the power of procreation become sterile; it is, O God, at the eternal unleashing of miracles. The hurricane of miracles blows perpetually. Day and night the phenomena surge around us on all sides, and, not less marvellous, without disturbing the majestic tranquillity of the Being. This tumult is harmony.

The huge concentric waves of universal life are boundless. The starry sky that we study is but a partial apparition. We steal from the network of the Being but some links. The complication of the phenomenon, of which a glimpse can be caught, beyond our senses, only by contemplation and ecstasy, makes the mind giddy. The thinker who reaches so far, is, for other men, only a visionary. The necessary entanglement of the perceptible and of the imperceptible strikes the philosopher with stupor. This plenitude is required by thy all-powerfulness, which does not admit any blanks. The permeation of universes into universes makes part of thy infinitude. Here we extend the word universe to an order of facts that no astronomer can reach. In the Cosmos that the vision spies, and which escapes our organs of flesh, the spheres enter into the spheres without deforming each other, the density of creations being different; so that, according to every appearance, with our world is amalgamated, in some inexplicable way, another world invisible to us, as we are invisible to it.

And thou, centre and place of all things, as though thou, the Being, couldst be exhausted! that the absolute serenities could, at certain moments, fear the want of means on the part of the Infinite! that there would come an hour when thou couldst no longer supply humanity with the lights which it requires! that mechanically unwearied, thou couldst be worn out in the intellectual and moral order! that it would be proper to say, "God is extinguished on this side!" No! no! no! O Father!

Phidias created does not stop you from making Michael Angelo. Michael Angelo completed, there still remains to thee the material for Rembrandt. A Dante does not tire thee. Thou art no more exhausted by a Homer than by a star. The auroras by the side of auroras, the indefinite renewing of meteors, the worlds above the worlds, the wonderful passage of these incandescent stars called comets, the geniuses and again the geniuses, Orpheus, then Moses, then Isaiah, then Æschylus, then Lucretius, then Tacitus, then Juvenal, then Cervantes and Rabelais, then Shakespeare, then Molière, then Voltaire, those who have been and those who will be,—that does not weary thee. Swarm of constellations! there is room in thy immensity.

Mirabeau

I

In 1781, there was a serious debate in the bosom of a family in France between a father and an uncle. The subject in dispute was a good-for-nothing whom this family did not know what to do with. He had already passed the first hot stage of youth and yet was still wholly plunged in all the frantic excesses of that passionate time. Overwhelmed by debts, ruined by follies, and separated from his wife, he had carried off the wife of another, had been condemned to death for the act, had been decapitated in effigy, had fled from France and now was back again having, according to his own account, seen the error of his ways; and purged of his contumacy, he was now asking to be restored to his family and to regain possession of his wife. The father desired such an arrangement, for he wanted to have grandchildren to perpetuate his name; and he hoped besides, to be more lucky as a grandfather than he had been as a father.

But the prodigal son was thirty-three years old, and he had to be made over again from top to bottom. A difficult task that! After he took his place again in society, to whose hands should he be confided? Who would undertake to straighten the backbone of such a character? Hence the controversy between his two relatives. The father wished to give him to the uncle, the uncle wished to leave him to the father.

"Take him," said the father.

"I won't have him," said the uncle.

"Now, in the first place," returned the father, "lay this to heart. This man is nothing,—nothing at all. He is a mixture of good taste and charlatanism, has the air of knowing everything, has action, turbulence, daring, is the life and soul of a company, and has some dignity too. In authority he is neither harsh nor hateful. Well, with all this he takes no note of the day or the morrow, the impulse of the moment is his guide; a parrot sort of fellow he, an abortive man, taking thought neither of the possible nor of the impossible, careless of comfort or discomfort, of pleasure or pain, of action or repose, and giving up at once as soon as things become too tough for him. Yet I think he might be made an excellent tool of, if one laid hold of him by the sleeve of his vanity. You would not let him slip. I do not spare him my ratiocinations in the morning. He grasps my well-founded code of ethics and my perennially enduring lessons, because they revolve on an ever-real pivot; namely, that our nature can rarely be changed, but that reason serves to protect the weak side, and by knowing the weak side we prevent people from running foul thereon."

"Oh, there you are again," replied the uncle, "with your posteromania, hard at work tutoring a game-cock of thirty-three! A nice task it is to undertake the rounding of a character that is only a hedgehog, all points and all too little body!"

The father insisted: "Have pity on your nephew Whirlwind (l'Ouragan). He confesses all his follies,—indeed, he is the greatest hand at confessing in the universe; but no one could have more wit and aptitude. He is a very thunderbolt of labour and activity. At bottom, he is no more thirty-three than I am sixty-six; and it is not stranger to see a man of my years able, though grown grey from mishaps, to weary the legs and the minds of the young folk by hunting and studying eight hours a day, than to see a great bloated barrel, pitted with small-pox, and looking like an old man, call me "papa" and not know how to conduct himself. He has an immense need of being governed. He feels it very well. Oh, you must take charge of him. He knows you have always been my pilot and compass, and you must be the same to him. He is vain of nothing so much as of his uncle. I give him to you as a rare fellow to be trained for the future. You have all the saturnine qualities to balance his mercurial ones. But when you hold him, don't let him slip. Though he did miracles, hold him still and pluck him by the sleeve; the poor devil has need of it. If you be a father to him, you will be well pleased with him; if only an uncle, he is lost. Love this young man."

"No," said the uncle. "I know that fellows of a certain stamp can be all smirks and smiles betimes; and he himself when he lived near me was as timid as a daughter-in-law if I only wrinkled my forehead. But I won't have him. I'm not young enough to collar the impossible, and it is not my taste, either."

"O brother!" replied the suppliant old man, "If this hackled creature is ever to be patched up again, you alone are the one to do it. Since he has to be set to rights, I could not think of giving him a better master than you. Take him, be kind and firm, and you'll be his saviour; he will be the best piece of work you ever turned out. Let him know that in that long body of yours and under your cold, stiff demeanour dwells the best man that ever was,—a man formed of the odds and ends left after the angels were made! Sound his heart, raise his head. *Tu es omnis spes et fortuna nostri nominis!*"

"No," returned the uncle, "nor is it because he has committed so great a crime under the circumstances. Quite too much has been made of that business. A young and pretty woman gets in the way of a young man of twenty-six. Where is the young man who would not pick up a thing like that if he found it in his path? But he is a turbulent spirit, a haughty, pretentious, insubordinate fellow, a malicious and vicious character! He does his very best to please you. It is right. I know he is seductive and that he is the rising sun. All the more reason for me not to expose myself to be his dupe. Youth always gets the upper hand when it is dealing with the old."

"You did not always think so," sadly answered the father; "there was a time when you wrote to me; 'As for me, this child unlocks my heart.'"

"Yes," said the uncle, and your answer was: 'Be cautious, be on your guard against the gilding of his beak.'"

"What would you have me do, then?" cried the father, driven to his last stand. "You are too equitable not to feel that one does not cut off a son as one would an arm. If that was possible I would have been one-armed long ago. After all, many a race has sprung from a fellow ten thousand times weaker and madder than he. Now, brother, as far as we are concerned, he is as he is. I leave myself out of the question. If I had not you, I would be but a poor broken-down old man. And as long as we are with him still, we must help him."

But the uncle, that peremptory man, cut short all prayers at last by these plain words:—

"I won't have him! It is madness to want to have anything to do with that man. Send him, as his good wife says, to the insurgents, and let him get his head broken. Your posteromaniac fury has possession of you now; but just think how lucky Cyrus and Marcus Aurelius would have been if neither of them had a Cambyses or a Commodus!"

Does it not seem to you, while reading this, as if you were present at one of the fine scenes of high domestic comedy in which the gravity of Molière almost reaches the grandeur of Corneille? Is there anything in Molière more striking for beauty and distinction of style, more profoundly human and true than these two imposing old men whom the seventeenth century seems to have left behind it in the eighteenth as two exemplars of the grand manner? Do you not see them meet, full of important business, stiff and rigid in their demeanour, resting on their long canes, recalling by their costume Louis the XIV. more than Louis XV., and Louis XIII. more than Louis XIV.?

Is not the language they speak the very language of Molière and Saint-Simon? That father and that uncle are the two eternal types of comedy; they are the two austere mouths by which she scolds, instructs, and moralizes, amid so many other mouths which only make us laugh; it is the Marquis and the Commander, Géronte and Ariste, wisdom and goodness, the admirable duo to which Molière always returns.

THE UNCLE.

Where would you run?

THE FATHER.

Alas! what do I know?

THE UNCLE.

Methinks 't were well that we advise each other
As to what should be done in this event.

The scene is complete; it lacks nothing, not even the *rascal of a nephew*.

But the most striking circumstance of all in the present case is that the scene we have just described is a real thing, that this dialogue of the father and the uncle took place, as we have recorded it, by letters,—letters which the public may read at this very hour; that, all unknown to these two old men, the subject of their grave discussion was one of the greatest men of our history; that the *marquis* and the *commander* are here a real marquis and a real commander. The one was named Victor de Riquetti, Marquis de Mirabeau; the other, Jean Antoine de Mirabeau, Bailli of the Order of Malta; the *rascal of a nephew* was Honoré Gabriel de Riquetti whom his family in 1781 called Whirlwind, and whom the world to-day calls Mirabeau.

So, what Mirabeau was for his family in 1781 was an *abortive man*, a *hackled creature*, a fellow *with whom nothing could be done*, a head good *to get broken* by the insurgents, and a scourge besides.

Ten years after, on the 1st of April, 1791, an immense crowd thronged the approaches of a house in the Chaussée d'Antin. This crowd was gloomy, silent, panic-stricken, and profoundly sad. In that house a man was in his last agony.

All this crowd inundated the street, the court, the staircase, and the antechamber. Several had remained there for three days. Men spoke low, they seemed afraid to breathe, they questioned anxiously those who came and went. The feeling of this crowd for this man was that of a mother for her child. The doctors no longer hoped. From time to time bulletins, wrested from their bearers by a thousand hands, were scattered among the multitude, and the sobs of women were heard. A young man, raging with grief, offered in a loud voice to open an artery so that his rich and pure blood might be infused into the veins of the dying. All, even the least intelligent, seemed weighted to the earth under the thought that it was not merely a man, it was a people, that was about to die.

The citizens addressed but one question to each other. This man expired.

Some minutes after the physician who stood at the head of his bed had said, "He is dead!" the president of the National Assembly rose in his seat and said, "He is dead!" such the fatal cry that in a few moments filled all Paris. One of the principal orators of the Assembly, M. Barrère de Vienzac, rose weeping, and said in a voice broken by sobs: "I ask that the Assembly record on the minutes of this calamitous day the testimony of the sorrow it feels at the loss of this great man, and that there be given, in the name of the country, an invitation to all the members of the Assembly to be present at his funeral."

A priest, a member of the Right, cried, "Yesterday, in the midst of his sufferings, he caused the Bishop of Autun to be summoned to his presence, and handing him a work he had just finished on inheritances, asked him as a last mark of friendship to read it to the Assembly. It is a sacred duty. The Bishop of Autun must exercise here the functions of testamentary executor of the great man we all lament."

Trouchet, the president, proposed that a deputation attend the funeral. The Assembly replied, "We shall all go!"

The Sections of Paris demanded that he should be entombed "in the Plain of the Federation, under the Altar of the County."

The Directory of the Department proposed to give him for his tomb the "new church of Saint Genevieve," and to decree that "this edifice be henceforward destined to receive the ashes of great men."

On this subject, M. Pastoret, the procurator-general syndic of the commune, said, "The tears that the loss of a great man cause us to shed ought not to be barren tears. Several ancient peoples provided separate monuments for their priests and heroes. The species of adoration they rendered to piety and courage, let us to-day render to the love of the happiness and the liberty of men. Let the temple of liberty become the temple of the country! Let the tomb of a great man become the altar of liberty!"

The Assembly applauded.

Barnave exclaimed, "He has, indeed, merited the honours which ought to be decreed by the nation to the great men who have served her well."

Robespierre, that is to say, Envy, rose also, and said, "It is not at the moment when we hear from all parts the regrets excited by the loss of this illustrious man, who in the most critical times displayed so much courage against despotism, that we could oppose the marks of honour which ought to be decreed him. I support the proposal with all my energies, or rather with all my sensibilities."

On that day there was neither Left nor Right in the Natinoal Assembly. All with one voice passed the following decree:—

"The new edifice of Saint Genevieve shall be destined to receive the ashes of great men. There shall be engraved above its front these words,—

TO GREAT MEN

THE COUNTRY GRATEFUL

"The Legislative Body alone shall decide to what men this honour shall be decreed.

"Honoré Riquetti Mirabeau is judged worthy of receiving this honour."

The man who had just died was Honoré de Mirabeau. The *great man* of 1791 was the *abortive man* of 1781.

On the next day the procession of the people at his funeral extended for more than a league. His father was not there; he had died, as was proper in the case of an old gentleman of his kind, on the 13th of July, 1789, the eve of the fall of the Bastille.

It is not without an object that we have brought together these two dates, 1781 and 1791, their memories and their history,—Mirabeau before and Mirabeau after, Mirabeau judged by his family and Mirabeau judged by the people. There is an inexhaustible source of meditation in this contrast. How was it that in ten years the demon of a family became the god of a nation? A profound question this.

II

WE must not believe, however, that at the moment this man issued from the family to make his appearance before the people, he was immediately and by acclamation hailed as a *god*. Things of themselves never march in this fashion. Where genius rises, Envy rears her head. On the contrary, until the very hour of his death, never was man so constantly and so thoroughly gainsaid in every sense as Mirabeau.

When he arrived at the States General as Deputy of Aix, he excited the jealousy of nobody. Obscure and disreputable, he was little sought after by those of good report; ugly and awkward, he inspired the graceful and well-proportioned lords with pity. His nobility vanished under the black habit, his physiognomy under the small-pox. Who, then, could dream of being jealous of this species of adventurer, this released convict, deformed in body and feature, ruined besides, whom the rabble of Aix had sent as deputy to the States General in a moment of frenzy, thoughtlessly, no doubt, and without knowing why? This man, in truth, did not count. Beside him the most commonplace person was handsome, rich, and worthy of consideration. He did not offend any vanity, he did not elbow any pretention. He was a mere cipher which the ambitious, however jealous of one another they might be, scarcely reckoned in their calculations. Little by little, however, as the twilight of all ancient things was approaching, a sufficient shadow was created around the monarchy for the sombre splendour, peculiar to the great men or revolutions, to become visible to the eye. Mirabeau was beginning to radiate.

Then Envy came to this radiance as every bird of night does to the light. To date from that moment, Envy seized on Mirabeau and never let go her hold. And above all, a thing happened which seems strange and yet is not strange. What she refused to his last breath, what she denied him incessantly to his face, was precisely that which crowns him in the eye of posterity,—his oratorical genius. This is the method that Envy always pursues besides; it is at the finest front of a building that she hurls her stones. And, then, it must be admitted that Envy had an inexhaustible supply of good reasons for her work. *Probitas*, the orator should be a man without reproach,—M. de Mirabeau deserves reproach in every direction; *præstantia*, the orator ought to be handsome,—M. de Mirabeau is ugly; *vox amœna*, the orator should have a pleasing organ,—M. de Mirabeau's voice is harsh, dry, shrill, thundering always and never speaking; *subrisus audientium*, the orator ought to be welcome to his hearers,—M. de Mirabeau is hated by the Assembly, etc.; and a crowd of people very well content with themselves, came to this conclusion: *M. de Mirabeau is not an orator.*

Now, far from proving this, all these reasonings prove only one thing; that is, that the Mirabeaus are not foreseen by the Ciceros.

Certainly, he was not an orator after the fashion understood by those people; he was an orator according to his own nature, his organization, his soul, his life. He was an orator because he was hated, just as Cicero was an orator because he was loved. He was an orator because he was ugly, just as Hortensius was an orator because he was well-favoured. He was an orator because he had suffered, because he had failed, because he had been while still young and at that period of life when the heart expands to every influence, repulsed, mocked, humiliated, despised, defamed, banished, robbed, exiled, imprisoned, and condemned; because, like the people of 1789 whose perfect symbol he was, he had been kept in leading-strings long after the age of reason; because a father's hand had been as heavy for him as royalty had been for the people, because, like the people, he had been badly reared; because, like the people, a bad education caused a vice to grow on the root of every virtue. He was an orator, because the wide issues opened by 1789 enabled him at last to pour out into society all the ebullitions that had been so long repressed in his family; because from the very fact that he was abrupt, unequal, violent, vicious, cynical, sublime, diffuse, incoherent, full of instincts still more than of thoughts, with his feet soiled and his head radiant, he was in everything like the ardent years in which he shone, and in which every day passed away, marked on the brow with one of his words. In fine, to those fatuous men who understood their time so poorly as to ask him, at the same time raising a thousand objections often ingenious enough, if he seriously believed he was an orator, he might have simply answered "Inquire of the monarchy that is ending, inquire of the revolution that is beginning!"

It is hard to believe to-day that it is a certain fact many people of 1790, and among those people a number of fair-spoken friends, advised Mirabeau, "to abandon the tribune in his own interest; he would never be entirely successful in it," or at least, "to appear there less often." We have the words under our eyes. It is hard to believe that, during those memorable sessions, when he stirred the Assembly like water in a vase, when the resounding ideas of the moment were dashed together under the impulse of his mighty hand, when he beat out and amalgamated with his powerful eloquence his own personal passion and the passion of all, after he had spoken and while he was speaking and before he spoke, the applause was always mingled with hooting, laughter, and hisses. Miserable petty details which his glory has discounted to-day! The journals and pamphlets of the time are but insults, outrages, and indignities directed against the genius of this man. He is reproached with every offence at every turn. But the reproach that is never for a moment silent, that appears to spring from some kind of mania is "his rough and harsh voice" and the "thundering tones in which he always speaks." What answer can be given to this? His voice is rough, because apparently the time for smooth voices has passed. His tones are thundering, because great issues are thundering beside him, and it is the property of great men to rise to the height of great events.

And then, and this too is a policy that has always been used against men of genius; he was attacked not only by supporters of the monarchy, but by those of his own party—for one is nowhere better hated than in his own party —who were ever agreed, by a sort of tacit convention, on opposing him incessantly and on giving the preference to some other orator, adroitly selected by envy among those who held the same opinions as Mirabeau and Barnave. And it will be always so. It often happens that, in a given period, the same idea is represented in different degrees at the same time by a man of genius and a man of talent. This position offers a happy chance to the man of talent. He is sure of present and undisputed success; this success, it is true, proves nothing and quickly fades. Jealousy and hate at once cross the path of the strongest. Mediocrity would be very much troubled by the presence of the man of talent, if the man of genius were not there; but the man of genius is there, and so she supports the man of talent, and makes use of him against the master of both. She deludes herself with the chimerical hope of overthrowing the one, and in that case (which, however, cannot be realized) she reckons on making a good bargain with the second. Meanwhile she supports the latter, and elevates him as high as she can. Mediocrity is in favour of him who annoys her the least and resembles her the most. In this circumstance, all that is hostile to the man of genius is friendly to the man of talent. The comparison which should crush the latter exalts him. Out of all the stones that pickaxe and spade and calumny and diatribe and insult can tear away from the base of the great man, a pedestal is erected for the second-rate man. What is made to fall from the one serves for the construction of the other. It was in that way that, towards 1790, Barnave was built up with the materials taken from as much of the ruin of Mirabeau as was available.

Rivarol said, "M. Mirabeau is more of a writer, M. Barnave is more of an orator."—Pelletier said, "Barnave yes, Mirabeau no."—"The memorable session of the 13th," wrote Chamfort, "has proved more than ever the pre-eminence, already demonstrated long before, of Barnave to Mirabeau as an orator."—"Mirabeau is dead," murmured M. Target, grasping the hand of Barnave; "his discourse on the formula of promulgation has killed him."—"Barnave, you have buried Mirabeau," added Duport, supported by the smile of Lameth, who was to Duport as Duport was to Barnave,—a diminutive.—"M. Barnave gives pleasure," said M. Goupil, "and M. Mirabeau gives pain."—"The Count de Mirabeau has flashes," said M. Camus, "but he will never make a discourse; he will never even know what a discourse is. Talk to me of Barnave!" —"It is useless for M. de Mirabeau to sweat and weary himself," cackled Robespierre, "he will never reach Barnave, who does not seem to have so much pretension, but is far superior." Such poor little samples of injustice stung Mirabeau and caused him suffering in the midst of his power and his triumphs. Pin-pricks of the kind do make a giant wince.

And if hatred, when it determined to get some one to oppose him, no matter whom, had not found a man of talent suitable for the purpose, she would have taken a man of mediocrity. The equality of the stuff out of which she makes her flag never embarrasses her. Mairet has been preferred to Corneille, Pradon to Racine, and not a hundred years ago Voltaire exclaimed:—

"And dare they then
Prefer the barbarous Crebillon to me!"

In 1808, Geoffroy, the best known critic in Europe, placed "M. Lafon very much about M. Talma." Marvellous instinct of cliques! In 1798, Moreau was thought superior to Bonaparte; in 1815, Wellington ranked higher than Napoleon.

We repeat, because in our opinion the thing is singular, that Mirabeau stooped to be irritated by these petty miseries. The parallel with Barnave offended him. If he could have looked into the future he would have smiled; but it is the special defect of political orators, who are above all men of the present, to keep their eyes too much fixed on contemporaries and not enough on posterity. These two men, Barnave and Mirabeau, presented besides a perfect contrast. When either rose in the Assembly, Barnave was always received with a smile, and Mirabeau with a storm. Barnave possessed as his property the ovation of the moment, the triumph of the quarter of an hour, the glory of the report in the "Gazette," the applause of all, even of the Right. To Mirabeau were allotted the struggle and the turmoil. Barnave was a rather handsome young man, and a very fine speaker. Mirabeau, as Rivarol ingeniously observed, was a *monstrous babbler*. Barnave was one of those men who take each morning the measure of their hearers; who handle the pulse of their audience; who never venture outside the possibility of being applauded; who always humbly kiss the feet of success; who ascend the tribune, sometimes with the idea of to-day, oftenest with that of yesterday, never—from dread of the risk,—with that of to-morrow; who have an even, smooth, easy fluency of speech on which they jog along, making little noise, and pass round with their other baggage, the commonplace ideas of their times; who, fearing that their thoughts might not be sufficiently impregnated with the atmosphere of everybody, unceasingly adjust and arrange their opinions in front of the street as they would a thermometer at the window. Mirabeau, on the contrary, was the man of the new idea, of the sudden illumination, of the risky proposition; fiery, hare-brained, imprudent, always saying something unexpected everywhere, jostling, wounding, overturning, obeying only himself, seeking success undoubtedly, but after many other things, and preferring the applause of the passions of his heart to that of the people in the tribune; noisy, agitated, rapid, profound, seldom transparent, never fordable, and rolling along confusedly in his foamy current all the ideas of his era,—ideas that often suffered a rude shock when coming into collision with his own.

The fame of Mirabeau is to-day so great and so universally recognized, that there is considerable difficulty in forming an idea of the fashion in which he was treated by his colleagues and contemporaries. We have M. de Guillermy exclaiming during one of the great tribune's harangues: "M. Mirabeau is a scoundrel, an assassin!" MM. d'Ambly and de Lautrec vociferating, "This Mirabeau is a great scoundrel!" And then M. de Foucault shook his fist at him, and M. de Virien said, "Monsieur Mirabeau, you insult me!" When hatred did not speak, contempt did. "This shabby Mirabeau!" said M. de Castellanet of the Right. "That extravagant fellow!" said M. Lapoule of the Left. And when he had spoken, Robespierre mumbled between his teeth: "His words have no value."

Sometimes his eloquence showed traces of the effect exercised on him by the hostility of so large a part of his audience, and—in the midst of his magnificent discourse on the Regency, for example—his scornful lips gave vent to such words as these, words at once simple and resigned, melancholy and proud, which every man placed in similar circumstances would do well to meditate on:—

"While I was giving my ideas on the Regency, I have heard some of my hearers say, with the charming sense of incapability of error to which I have been long accustomed: 'That is absurd! that is extravagant! that is unworthy of being brought before us!' But a little serious reflection would not be out of place either."

He spoke these words on the 25th of March, 1791, seven days before his death.

Outside the Assembly, the press tore him to pieces with a strange fury. A hailstorm of pamphlets beat on this man. The extreme parties put him on the same pillory. His name was pronounced in the same tone in the barrack of the Royal Guards and in the club of the Cordeliers. M. de Champcenetz said, "That man has the small-pox in his soul." M. de Lambesc proposed to have him seized and *taken to the galleys* by twenty horsemen. Marat shouted, "Citizens, raise eight hundred gibbets, hang all these traitors on them, and at their head the infamous Riquetti the elder!" And Mirabeau refused to consent to his prosecution by the National Assembly. He contented himself with saying, "It seems a great deal of extravagant nonsense is published. The man who wrote that must have been drunk."

Thus, up to April the 1st, 1791, Mirabeau is a scoundred, an extravagant fellow, a rascal, an assassin, a madman, an orator of the second rank, a mediocre man, a man dead, a man buried, a monstrous babbler, hooted, hissed, scouted more than applauded; Larmbesc would send him to the galleys, Marat to the gibbet. On the 2nd of April he dies. On the 3d the Pantheon was invented for his behoof.

III

THE people, however, which has a peculiar sense and a visual ray always singularly straight, which is not hateful because it is strong, which is not envious because it is great, the people, which knows men, although itself a child,—the people was for Mirabeau. There are no finer spectacles for the thinker than those close embraces of genius and the multitude.

The influence of Mirabeau was gainsaid, and it was immense. It was always he, after all, that had the upperhand; but he won his victories over the Assembly only through the people, and he governed the curule chairs through the tribunes. The precise words which Mirabeau uttered were re-uttered by the crowd accompanied by applause; and under the dictation of this applause the Legislature, often against its will, wrote. Libels, pamphlets, calumnies, insults, interruptions, menaces, hoots, roars of laughter, hisses, were all but pebbles flung into the current of his words, which at times served to make him foam. That was all.

When this sovereign orator, smitten by some sudden thought, mounted the tribune; when this man found himself face to face with his people; when he was standing there and walking on the envious Assembly, as the Man-God on the waters, without sinking; when his sardonic and luminous glance, reaching from the elevation of his tribune the men and ideas of his time, seemed to measure the littleness of the men on the scale of the greatness of the ideas, then was he no longer calumniated, nor hooted, nor insulted. All their deeds, all their words, all the slanders heaped up against him, were vain; the first breath from his mouth as he opened it to speak, scattered them to the winds. On the tribune he was transfigured, and detraction vanished in his presence.

Mirabeau, in 1789, was, then, loved and hated at the same time,—as a genius, hated by the wits; as a man, beloved by the people. His was an illustrious and desirable existence, for he swayed at will all hearts then opening to the future, converted by magic words and by some mysterious kind of alchemy the vague instincts of the multitude into thoughts and systems, into well-planned methods and rational schemes of amelioration and reform, fed the spirit of his time with all the ideas which his great intelligence crumbled into fragments and flung among the crowd, beat and threshed on the table of the tribune, like the wheat on the threshing-floor, the men and things of his century, without rest, and with all his might and main, separating the straw the Republic was to consume from the wheat the Revolution was to fructify, causing sleepless nights to Louis XVI. and to Robespierre at the same time,—to Louis XVI., whose throne he destroyed; to Robespierre, whose guillotine he would have attacked, saying every morning as he awoke, "What ruin shall my words bring about to-day?" a pope in this sense, that he guided souls; a god in this sense, that he guided events.

He died in time. His was a sovereign and sublime head, '91 crowned it. '93 would have cut it off.

IV

As we follow Mirabeau step by step, from the humble baptismal font of Bignon to the Pantheon, we see that like all men of his stamp and stature he was predestined.

Such a child could not fail to be a great man.

At the moment when he came into the world, the enormous size of his head placed the life of his mother in peril. When the old French monarchy, his other mother, brought forth his fame, she too nearly died of it.

At the age of five, Poisson, his tutor, told him to write on whatever came into his head. The "little one," as we are told by his father, wrote literally as follows:—

"Monsieur *Me*, I beg that you will pay attention to your writing and not make blots on your copy. Pay attention to what you are doing; obey your father, your tutor, and your mother; never contradict; no double-dealing on the point of honour above all. Attack no one, except you are attacked yourself. *Defend your country.* Do not be unkind to the servants. Do not be familiar with them. Hide the faults of your neighbour, because you may want them to do the same for you."

When he was eleven, the Duke de Nivernois wrote of him to the Bailli de Mirabeau, in a letter dater from St. Maur, on the 11th of September, 1760:—

"The other day he won a prize at a running-match. It was a hat. He turned round to a youth who had a cap, and giving him his own, which was a very good one, said: 'Here, I haven't two heads!' This stripling appeared to me then worthy to be the emperor of the world. There was something or other godlike about him. I mused on it, I wept, and the lesson did me good."

At twelve, his father said of him: "There is a noble heart under the jacket of that bantling. He has a strange instinct of pride, but of a generous character. This little bit of a man is a bully in a flurry, and would swallow the whole world before he is twelve years old."

At fifteen, he had an air of such daring and haughtiness that the Prince de Conti asked: "What would you do if I slapped your face?" He answered. "That question might have been embarrassing before the invention of pistols for two."

At twenty-one (1770), he began writing a history of Corsica, when some one else was being born there. Singular instinct of great men!

At the same time his father, who held a very tight rein over him, uttered this strange prognostic: "He is a bottle that has been corked and corded for twenty-one years. If he is ever uncorked suddenly, and without great care, there will be a fine evaporation."

At twenty-two, he was presented at court. Madame Elizabeth, then a child of six, asked him *if he had been inoculated*. And all the court laughed. No, he had not been inoculated. He bore within him the germ of a contagion that later on was to spread through a whole people.

He presented himself at court with extreme assurance, with a head as high as the king's, a strange object to all, a hateful one to many. "He is as insinuating as I was shy," said the father, who had never desired to "dance attendance on Versailles," not he; "he was a wild bird that nested between four turrets."—"He turns the great round. and round as if they were a bundle of fagots. He has 'that terrible gift of familiarity' as Gregory the Great used to say." And then the proud old gentleman adds, "Well, as the Mirabeaus, who have never been built like other people, have been endured for the last five hundred years, I suppose they will be endured still."

At twenty-four, the father, as a philosophic agriculturist, wishes to take his son away with him, "and make him rural." He cannot succeed in this. "It is a very hard thing to handle the mouth of that fiery animal!" exclaims the old man.

The uncle, the Bailli, coolly examines the young man, and says, "If he is not worse than Nero, he will be better than Marcus Aurelius."

"After all, we must let this green fruit ripen," replies the marquis.

The father and the uncle corresponded with each other constantly on the future of the young man who had already advanced so far on the road of a bad life. "Your nephew Whirlwind," said the father. "Your son, Monsieur le Comte de la Bourrasque," (squall) replied the uncle.

The Bailli, an old sailor, adds, "The thirty-two winds of the compass are in his head."

At thirty, *the fruit was ripe*. Already strange things are glistening in the deep eyes of Mirabeau. It is seen that he is full of thoughts. "That brain is an overloaded furnace," says the prudent Bailli. At another time, the Bailli, in his alarm, makes this observation: "When anything passes into his head, he pushes it forward, and looks nowhere."

The father, on his side, is astonished at "his tearing of ideas piecemeal and only seeing by flashes." He exclaims, "Rummage in his head, and you find a library all topsy-turvy, a talent for dazzling by superficialities; he has swallowed all formulas and can't substantiate!" He adds, no longer comprehending this creature of his own making: "In childhood he was nothing but a monster of the male species, morally and physically." To-day, he is a man "all reflex and reverberation," a madman "drawn on the right by his heart and on the left by his head, which is always four yards away from him." And then the old man adds, with a melancholy and resigned smile: "I am trying to empty out into this man my brains, my soul, and my heart." At last, like the uncle, he has also his presentiments, his terrors, his anxieties, and his doubts. The father feels all that is stirring in the head of the son, "as the root feels the quivering of the leaves."

Such was Mirabeau at thirty. He was the son of a father who has thus described himself: "And I too, madame, stiff and dull-witted as you see me now, preached when I was three years old; at six, I was a prodigy; at twelve, an object of hope; at twenty, a fire-brand; at thirty, a theoretical statesman; at forty, I am merely a good-natured old fellow."

At forty, Mirabeau is a great man.

At forty, he is the man of the Revolution.

At forty, there breaks out around him in France one of those formidable anarchies of ideas in which societies that have had their day are melted down. Mirabeau was its master.

It was he who, silent till then, cried out to M. de Brézé, on the 23d of June, 1789: "Go tell YOUR MASTER . . . " *Your master!* It was to declare the King of France a foreigner. A whole frontier was traced between the throne and the people. It was the Revolution giving utterance to its cry. Nobody before Mirabeau would have dared this. Only great men pronounce the decisive words of the epochs.

Later on, Louis XVI. shall be insulted more gravely in appearance, shall be beaten to the earth, mocked in his chains, hooted on the scaffold. The Republic, with arms akimbo, will coif herself in her red bonnet, and speak coarse words to him, and call him Louis Capet; but nothing can ever be spoken to Louis XVI. so terrible and effective as that fatal sentence of Mirabeau. Louis Capet!—it is royalty smote on the face; *your master!*—it is royalty stricken to the heart.

And so, to date from these words, Mirabeau is the man of the country, the man of the great social convulsion, the man the end of that century had need of. To be popular and yet not plebeian is a rare thing in such times. His private life is then absorbed in his public life. Honoré de Riquetti, that abandoned man, is henceforth illustrious, worthy of attention and worthy of consideration. The love of the people is his armour against the sarcasms of his enemies. His person is the cynosure of every eye. The passers-by stop as he crosses the street; and, for two years that are left him, the little children of the people write his name unrebuked on all the corners of the walls of Paris, —that name which Saint-Simon eighty years before wrote Mirebaut, with the scorn natural to a peer and duke, and without suspecting that Mirebaut would become Mirabeau.

There are very striking parallels in the lives of certain men. Cromwell while still obscure, despairing of his future in England, wishes to embark for Jamaica; the orders of Charles I. prevent him. The father of Mirabeau, not seeing any possible existence for his son in France, wishes to send the young man to the Dutch Colonies. An order from the king forbids it. Now, take away Cromwell from the English Revolution, take away Mirabeau from the French Revolution, and you perhaps take away from the two revolutions two scaffolds. Who knows if Jamaica would not have saved Charles I., and Batavia Louis XVI.?

But no, the King of England will keep Cromwell; the King of France will keep Mirabeau. When a king is condemned to death, Providence bandages his eyes.

Strange that what is greatest in the history of a society should depend on what is least in the life of a man!

The first part of the life of Mirabeau is filled up with Sophie, the second with the Revolution.

A domestic storm, then a political storm, such was the destiny of Mirabeau. When we give a closer examination of this destiny, we gain an idea of whatever was fatal and necessary in it. The deviations of his heart are explained by the shock of his life.

For just consider the matter. Never have causes been more closely joined to effects than here. Chance gave him a father who taught him to despise his mother; a mother who taught him to hate his father; a tutor, Poisson, who did not like children, and who used him harshly because he was small and ugly; a valet, Grévin, who was the base spy of his enemies; a colonel, the Marquis de Lambert, who was as pitiless for the youth as Poisson had been for the child; a step-mother (not married though), Madame de Pailly, who hated him because he was not her own; a wife, Mademoiselle de Marignane, who repulsed him; a caste, the *noblesse*, which repudiated him; judges, the parliament of Besançon, who condemned him to death; a king, Louis XV., who bastilled him.

Thus, father, mother, wife, his tutor, his colonel, the magistracy, the *noblesse*, the king, that is to say, all that surrounds and skirts the existence of a man in the legitimate and natural order, was for him a cross, an obstacle, a stumbling-block, an occasion of wounds and bruises, a stone hard to his naked feet, a thicket of thorns tearing him on his way. Family and society were both his step-mothers. He met in life only two things that treated him well and loved him, two irregular things in revolt against order,—a mistress and a revolution.

Do not be astonished then, if for the mistress he broke all domestic ties, if for the revolution he broke all social bonds.

Do not be astonished to solve the question in the terms we have laid down at the beginning, if this demon of a family becomes the idol of a mistress in rebellion against her husband, and the god of a nation divorced from its king.

V

THE grief caused by the death of Mirabeau was a grief general, universal, and national. It was felt that something of the public thought had vanished with that soul. But a striking fact, and one necessary to speak of, because it would be artless to attribute it to the hasty and unreflecting admiration of his contemporaries, is that the court wore mourning for him as well as the people.

An insurmountable feeling of shame hinders us from sounding here certain mysteries, certain shameful qualities of the great man, which besides, in our opinion are lost in the colossal proportions of the *ensemble;* but it appears proved that in the latter part of his days the court had, as it affirmed, something to hope from him. It is patent that at this period he fired up angrily more than once at the excess of revolutionary enthusiasm; that he manifested at times the desire to cry halt and bring back somewhat of the past; that he who had such powerful lungs did not follow without breathlessness the march of new ideas becoming ever more and more accelerated, and that on some occasions he essayed to spoke the wheels of the Revolution, though he himself had forged them.

Fatal wheels, which crush so many venerable things on their passage!

There are still to-day many persons who think that if Mirabeau had lived longer he would have finally subdued the movement he had unchained. In their sense, the French Revolution might have been arrested by a single man; and that man was Mirabeau. According to this opinion, founded on some words of Mirabeau on his death-bed, which he surely never uttered, the death of Mirabeau was the ruin of the monarchy; if Mirabeau had lived, Louis XVI. would not have died; and the 2d of April, 1791, has brought to life the 21st of January, 1793.

According to us, those who believed so at the time, Mirabeau himself among the number, were mistaken, and so are those who believe so to-day. A pure optical illusion in Mirabeau as in others, proving that a great man has not always a plain idea of the kind of power that is in him.

The French Revolution was not a simple fact. There was more in it than Mirabeau.

The going out from it of Mirabeau would not suffice to empty it.

There was in the French Revolution something of the past and something of the future. Mirabeau was but the present.

To indicate here only two culminating points the French Revolution was complicated with Richelieu in the past and with Bonaparte in the future.

There is this peculiarity about revolutions, that they cannot be killed when they are still pregnant.

Moreover, even supposing the question more trivial than it really is, it is to be observed that, in political matters especially, what a man has done can rarely be undone except by another man.

The Mirabeau of '91 was impotent against the Mirabeau of '89. His work was stronger than he.

And then, men like Mirabeau are not the lock with which the gates of revolutions can be closed. They are but the hinge on which it turns, to close, it is true, as well as to open. To shut that fatal door, on whose panels are ever beating all the restless ideas, all the restless interests, and all the restless passions of society, a sword in guise of a bolt must be thrust into the iron-work.

VI

WE have attempted to characterize what Mirabeau was in the family and what he has been in the nation. It now remains for us to examine what he will be among posterity.

Notwithstanding certain reproaches of which he has deservingly been made the target, we believe that Mirabeau will continue great.

In presence of posterity every man and everything is absolved by greatness.

To-day, when almost all the things he has sown have given us their fruits which we have tasted, the greater part good and healthful, some bitter; to-day, when the successes and failures of his life have nothing incongruous in our eyes, so much do the years that pass place men in their true perspective; to-day, when there is for his genius neither adoration nor execration, and this man, so furiously tossed about from post to pillar while he lived, has taken the calm and serene attitude that death gives to great historic figures; to-day, when his memory, so long dragged in the mud and kissed on the altar, has been withdrawn from the Pantheon of Voltaire and the sewer of Marat, we may coldly say, "Mirabeau is great." The odour of the Pantheon and not the odour of the sewer clings to him. Impartial history in wiping his locks, sullied in the gutter, has not taken from him his aureole. The mud has been washed from that visage, and it still continues to shine.

After rendering an account of the immense political consequences produced by the sum total of his faculties, we may consider Mirabeau under a twofold aspect, as a writer and as an orator. Here we take the liberty of differing with Rivarol,—we believe Mirabeau was greater as an orator than as a writer.

The Marquis de Mirabeau, his father, had two kinds of style,—two pens, as it were, in his inkstand. When he wrote a book, a good book for the public, for effect, for the court, for the Bastille, for the grand staircase of the Palace of Justice, the worthy patrician draped himself, stiffened his limbs, swelled out his proportions, veiled his thoughts, already obscure enough of themselves, with all the pomps of expression; and it is impossible to fancy under what a style, at once flat and bombastic, heavy and languid, with interminable phrases dragging at its tail, loaded with neologies to such an extent as to banish all cohesion from the tissue,—under what a style, we repeat, altogether colourless and incorrect, the natural and indisputable originality of this strange writer is travestied; writer, half gentleman and half philosopher, preferring Quesnay to Socrates and Lefranc de Pompignan to Pindar; disdaining Montesquieu as behind the times, and submitting to be scolded by his curé; an amphibious dweller among the reveries of the eighteenth century and the prejudices of the sixteenth. But when this man, this same man, wished to write a letter, when he forgot the public and addressed himself only to *the long, stiff, and rigid demeanour* of his venerable brother, the Bailli, or his daughter, *little Saillanette,* "the most emollient woman that ever was," or to the pretty, smiling face of Madame de Rochefort, then that spirit, inflated with pretension, relaxed; no more effort, no more fatigue, no more apopletic distention in the expression; his thoughts, as they are scattered over the family letter become vivid, original, highly coloured, curious, amusing, profound, gracious,—in fine, natural; the echo of that grand aristocratic style of the time of Louis XIV., which Saint-Simon spoke with all the qualities of the man and Madame de Sévigné with all the qualities of the woman. An idea may be formed of it from the fragments we have quoted. After a book of the Marquis de Mirabeau, a letter of his is a revelation. We can hardly believe our eyes. Bouffon would not comprehend such contrasts in the same writer. You have two styles and only one man.

In this respect the son bore some likeness to the father. It might be said, though with certain limitations and modifications, that there is the same difference between his written style and his spoken style. Let us only remark this, that the father was at his ease in a letter, the son in a discourse. To be himself, to be natural, to be in his proper environment, the one needed a family, the other a nation.

The Mirabeau that writes is something less than Mirabeau. Whether he demonstrates to the young American Republic the folly of its "Order of Cincinnatus," and the inconsistency of an order of chivalry among ploughmen; or with his "Sur la liberté de l'Escaut" plagues Joseph II., the philosophic emperor, the Titus of Voltaire, the bust of a Roman Cæsar after the Pompadour style; or rummages in both bottoms of the cabinet at Berlin and draws therefrom that *Histoire secrète* which the court of France ordered to be judicially consigned to the flames on the steps of the Palace of Justice (a noteworthy blunder; for from those books burned by the hand of the executioner there always escaped some little flakes and sparks, which scattered at the will of the wind and alighted on the worm-eaten roof of the great European society, on the carpentry of monarchies, on all minds full of inflammable ideas, on all heads made of tow at that period); or casually inveighs against that cart-load of charlatans which made so much noise on the pavement of the eighteenth century,—Necker, Beaumarchais, Lavater, Calonne, and Cagliostro; in fine, whatever be the book he writes, his thought is always adequate to the subject, but his style is not always adequate to the thought. His ideas are ever grand and lofty; but to get out of his brain they have to stoop and shrink as if under a door too low. Except in his eloquent letters to Madame de Monnier, in which he is his real self, speaking rather than writing, and which are harangues of love quite as much as his discourse to the Constituant are harangues of revolution,—except these, we repeat, the style he discovers in his inkstand is in general commonplace in form, badly connected, pithless, nerveless at the end of his phrases, dry besides, coloured in dull fashion by means of trite epithets, poor in images, or offering here and there only ecccentric mosaics of incoherent metaphors. We feel while reading that the ideas of this man are not, like those of the great prose-writers to the manner born, made up of that peculiar substance which, soft and subtle, lends itself to all the chisellings of expression which finds its way boiling and liquid into all the nooks of the mould into which the writer pours it, and then hardens; lava first, granite after. We feel while reading that many things have remained in his head which it were as well had not stayed there, that this genius has not been so fashioned as to express itself completely in a book, and that a pen is not the best possible conductor for all the fluids compressed in that brain filled with thunders.

The Mirabeau who speaks is the real Mirabeau. The Mirabeau who speaks is the water running, the wave foaming, the fire sparkling, the bird in its flight, something that makes its own peculiar noise, a nature fulfilling its own law. A spectacle of eternal sublimity and harmony!

On the tribune all his contemporaries are unanimous on this point, Mirabeau was something magnificent. There he was himself, wholly himself, a self all-powerful. There, no more table, no more paper, no more inkstand bristling with pens, no more solitary cabinet, no more silence and meditation; but a marble which can be smote, a ladder which can be mounted, a tribune that is a species of cage for this wild beast, on which he can come and go, walk, stop, breathe, gasp, cross his arms, clinch his fists, paint his words by a gesture, and illumine his idea by a glance; a heap of men he can gaze on eye to eye; a great tumult,—magnificent accompaniment for a great voice; a crowd that hates the orator (the Assembly) enveloped in a crowd that loves him (the people); around him all these intelligencies, all these passions, all these mediocrites, all these ambitions, all these diverse natures which he knows, and from which he can draw whatever sound he wills as from an immense harpsichord; above him the vault of the hall of the Constituent Assembly, towards which his eyes are often raised as if to seek there his thoughts, for monarchies are overthrown by the ideas that fall from such a vault on such a head.

Oh, how much that man is at ease there, on his own ground! How sure and firm his footing! How great is that genius in a discourse which becomes so small in books! How happily the tribune has changed the conditions of exterior production for that thought! After Mirabeau the writer, Mirabeau the orator,—what a transfiguration!

In him everything was potent. His abrupt and sudden gestures were full of empire. In the tribune he had a colossal movement of the shoulders, like the elephant that carries an armed tower in battle. He too was carrying his thought. His voice, even at the time he but thundered a word from his bench, had a formidable and revolutionary tone which was recognized in the Assembly as like the roar of the lion in the menagerie. His locks, when he shook his head, were not unlike a mane. The movement of his eyebrows agitated all around him, like that of Jupiter, *cuncta superalio moventis*. His hands sometimes seemed to knead the marble of the tribune. His whole countenance, his whole attitude, his whole person, was swollen with a plethoric arrogance that had its grandeur. His head had a grandiose and thunderous ugliness whose effect was at moments electric and terrible. In the early stages, when nothing was visibly decided for or against royalty; when the contest seemed still nearly equal between the monarchy, still strong, and the theories, which were still weak; when none of the ideas which were, later on, to hold the future had yet arrived at their perfect growth; when the Revolution, badly guarded and badly armed, could apparently be easily taken by assault, it sometimes happened that the Right, believing it had thrown down some wall of the fortress, rushed on in *en masse* with cries of victory; then the monstrous head of Mirabeau appeared at the breach and petrified the assailants. The genius of the Revolution had forged an ægis with all the amalgamated doctrines of Voltaire, Helvetius, Diderot, Bayle, Montesquieu, Hobbes, Locke, and Rousseau, and had fixed the head of Mirabeau in the middle.

He was not only great on the tribune, he was great in his seat; in him the interrupter was equal to the orator. He often put as much in a word as in a discourse. "Lafayette has an army," he said to M. de Suleau, "but I have my head." He interrupted Robespierre with this profound remark: "That man will go far, he believes every word he says."

He dealt thus with the court when an occasion arose: "The court is starving the people. Treason! The people will sell it to the Constitution for bread!" All the instinct of the great revolutionist is in that word.

"The Abbé Sieyès!" he said, "a metaphysician travelling on a map." A keen thrust at the man of theory ever ready to bestride seas and mountains.

His simplicity at times was admirable. One day, or rather one evening, in his discourse of the 3d of May, at the moment when he was struggling, like an athlete with a cestus on each hand, with his left arm aimed at the Abbé Maury and his right at Robespierre, M. de Cazalès, with all the assurance of mediocrity, interrupted him in this fashion: "You are a babbler, and that is all." Mirabeau turned towards the Abbé Gontes, who was in the chair: "Monsieur le President," he said with childlike grandeur, "please stop M. de Cazalès, who is calling me a babbler."

The National Assembly wanted to begin an address to the king with these words: "The Assembly brings to the feet of your Majesty an offering," etc. "Majesty has no feet," said Mirabeau coldly.

A little farther on the Assembly wished to say that "it is intoxicated with the glory of its king." "Really?" objected Mirabeau; "people who make laws and who are intoxicated!"

Sometimes with a phrase that might have been translated from Tacitus, he characterized the history and nature of an entire sovereign house. He cried out to the ministers, for example: "Speak not to me of your Duke of Savoy, a bad neighbour to all liberty!"

Sometimes he laughed,—a formidable thing the laugh of Mirabeau.

He ridiculed the Bastille. "There have been," he said, "fifty-four *lettres de cachets* in my family, and I have had seventeen for my share. So you see I was treated as an elder brother of Normandy." He ridiculed himself. He was accused by M. de Valfond of having gone through the ranks of the Regiment of Flanders on the 6th of October, with a naked sabre in his hand, and of speaking to the soldiers. Some one proved that the matter concerned M. de Gamaches, and not Mirabeau; and Mirabeau added, "So everything having been weighed, everything having been examined, the deposition of M. de Valfond contains nothing very unpleasant for any one except M. de Gamaches, who finds himself legally and vehemently suspected of being very ugly, since he resembles me."

Sometimes he smiled. When the question of the Regency was on debate before the Assembly, the Left thought of the Duke of Orleans, and the Right of the Prince of Condé, then an *émigré* in Germany. Mirabeau moved that no prince can be regent, except he took the oath to the Constitution. M. de Montlosier objected that a prince might have reasons for not having taken the oath; for instance, he might have made a journey beyond the sea. Mirabeau answered, "The discourse of the last speaker will be printed. I demand leave to correct an error in it. For 'beyond the sea,' read, 'beyond the Rhine.'" And this pleasantry decided the question. Thus did the great orator sometimes play with what he killed. To believe the naturalist, there is something of the cat in the lion.

On another occasion, when the *procureurs* of the Assembly had muddled a text of law with their bad editing, Mirabeau rose: "I ask leave to make a few timid reflections on the propriety of the National Assembly speaking French, and even writing in French the laws it proposes."

At moments, in the midst of his most violent popular harangues, he suddenly recalled who he was, and there would be some flashes of the patrician from him. It was at that time an oratorical custom to interject into every discourse some imprecation or other on the massacres of Saint Bartholomew. Mirabeau uttered his imprecation like everybody else; but he said, in passing: "The Admiral de Coligny, who, by way of parenthesis, was my cousin." The parenthesis was worthy of the man whose father wrote: "There has been only one misalliance in my family, the Medicis."—"My cousin, the Admiral de Coligny," would have been pointless at the court of Louis XIV.; it was sublime at the court of the people of 1791. At another time he spoke of his "worthy cousin the Keeper of the Seals," but it was in a different tone.

On the 22d September, 1789, the king made an offer of his gold and silver plate for the needs of the State. The Right fell into ecstasies of admiration and wept. "As for myself," cried Mirabeau, "I do not easily become tearful over the faïence of the great."

His disdain was fine, his laugh was fine, but his anger was sublime.

When an effort to irritate him succeeded, when one of those keen blades that make the orator and the bull bound from the earth, was plunged into his side, if this, for example, occurred in the middle of a discourse, he at once abandoned everything, left his ideas still incomplete, troubled himself little that the edifice of reasoning he had been building up crumbled behind him for want of the final crowning stone; he gave up the question on the spot, and rushed with lowered head on the incident. Then, woe to the interrupter! woe to the toreador who has flung the banderilla! Mirabeau was on him at once, seized him by the waist, raised him in the air, and trampled him under his feet. He drew back from him, returned, bruised and mangled him. He took hold of the entire man in the words he uttered, whoever he was, great or small, wicked or worthless, mud or dust, and caught him up with his life, his character, his ambition, his vices, his follies; he omitted nothing, he spared nothing, he missed nothing; he knocked him against the four corners of the tribune in his desperation; he made his hearers tremble, he made them laugh. Every word told, every phrase was an arrow; he had fury in his heart; he was terrible and superb. His was the anger of the lion. A great and potent orator, but never so fine as then! Then was the time to see in what fashion he chased away all clouds from the discussion! Then was the time to see how his stormy breath made every head in the assembly bristle with terror! Strange fact! he never reasoned better than when he was in a rage. The most violent irritation, far from disuniting the chain of his eloquence in the shocks which it caused him, set free a sort of superior logic within his mind, and he found arguments in fury as others do metaphors. Whether the sharp-pointed teeth of his sarcasm left their mark on the pale forehead of Robespierre, who, two years later, was to treat heads as Phocion treated discourses; or whether he chewed in his rage the wearisome dilemmas of the Abbé Maury and spat them back at the Right, twisted, torn, dislocated, half devoured, and all covered with the foam of his wrath; or plunged the claws of his syllogism into the soft and flabby phrase of the advocate Target, he was great and magnificent, and had a sort of formidable majesty that the most frantic bounds never disordered. Our fathers have told us that they who had not seen Mirabeau in anger had not seen Mirabeau. In anger his genius was at its best and displayed all its splendours. Anger suited this man, as the tempest does the ocean. And, without intending, in what we have just written for the purpose of shadowing forth the supernatural eloquence of Mirabeau, we have painted him by a confusion of images even. Mireabeau was, in fact, not merely the bull, or the lion, or the tiger, or the athlete, or the archer, or the eagle, or the peacock, or the tempest, or the ocean; he was, by an indefinite series of surprising metamorphoses, all this at once; he was Proteus.

For whoever has seen or heard him, his discourses are to-day a dead letter. The colour, the breath, the life, the soul, the flash, the relief, have all disappeared. Everything in these fine harangues lies to-day flat on the earth. Where is the inspiration that whirled all these ideas around like leaves in a hurricane? The word is there, but where is the gesture? The cry is there, but where is the accent? The language is there, but where is the look? The discourse is there, but where is the drama of that discourse? For it is necessary to say that in every orator there are two things,—the actor and the man.

Talma is entirely dead. Mirabeau is half dead.

In the Constituent Assembly there was one thing that frightened those who regarded it attentively,—it was the Convention. To all who have studied this epoch, it was evident that from 1789 the Convention was in the Constituent Assembly. It was there in the state of germ, in the state of fœtus, in the state of outline. To the multitude it was still something indistinct; for him who could see, it was already something terrible. A nothing doubtless; a shade blacker than the general colour; a note sometimes thundering in the orchestra; a surly refrain in a chorus of hopes and illusions; a detail in which there was a certain want of concord with the *ensemble;* a sombre group in an obscure corner; some mouths giving a certain accent to certain words; thirty voices (only thirty voices), which later were to branch out, according to an appealing law of multiplication, into Girondins, the Plain and the Mountains,—'93 in a word; the dark spot in the azure sky of '89. Everything was already in this dark spot: the 21st of January, the 31st of May, the 9th Thermidor,—a bloody trilogy; Buzot, who was to devour Louis XVI., Robespierre, who was to devour Buzot, Vadier, who was to devour Robespierre,—a sinister trinity. Among these men the most vulgar and the most ignorant, Hébrard and Putraink, for example, smiled strangely during the discussions, and seemed to have some thought on the future which they did not tell. In our opinion, the historian ought to have microscopes for the purpose of examining the formation of one assembly in the womb of another. It is a species of gestation which is often reproduced in history, and which, as far as we can see, has not been sufficiently observed. In the present case this mysterious excrescence on the surface of the legislative body was no insignificant detail, containing as it did the scaffold already prepared for the King of France; a vulture's egg born by an eagle. From that time several sound minds in the Constituent Assembly were frightened at the presence of these few impenetrable men who seemed to be holding themselves in reserve for another epoch. They felt that there were many whirlwinds in these breasts from which scarcely a breeze escaped. They asked themselves whether or not these tempests would be let loose some day, and what then should become of all the things essential to civilization which '89 had not uprooted. Rabaut Saint-Etienne, who believed the Revolution terminated, and said so quite aloud, gave anxious attention to Robespierre, who did not believe it begun, and said so quite low. The present demolishers of the monarchy trembled before the future demolishers of society. The latter, like all men who hold the future and who know it, were supercilious, morose, arrogant, and the lowest among them disdainfully elbowed the leaders of the Assembly. The most worthless and the most obscure hurled insolent interruptions at the most thoughtful orators, as their humour and fancy led them; and as every one knew that there were events ready at hand for these men to deal with in the near future, none dare reply to them. It was in such moments, when the Assembly that one day was to be, terrified the Assembly that was,—it was then that the exceptional power of Mirabeau shone in all its splendour. With the feeling of his omnipotence, and with no suspicion that he was doing a great thing, he cried to the sinister group, which was preventing a speaker from being heard: "Silence among the thirty voices!" and the Convention held its peace.

That cave of Æolus remained still and was curbed as long as Mirabeau held his foot on the cover.

When Mirabeau was dead, all the ulterior anarchic projects broke loose.

As we said before, we believe Mirabeau died seasonably. After unchaining many tempests in the State, it is evident that for a time he crushed under his weight all the divergent forces for which the completion of the ruin he had begun was reserved. But the very pressure on them condensed them, and sooner or later the revolutionary explosion must, in our opinion, have found an issue, and would have hurled Mirabeau far in the distance, giant though he was.

Let us conclude.

If we had to sum up Mirabeau in one word, we would say: Mirabeau is not a man, is not a people, but an event, —an event which speaks.

An immense event,—the fall of the monarchical government in France!

With Mirabeau, neither the monarchy nor the republic were possible. The monarchy excluded him by its hierarchy, the republic by its level. Mirabeau is a man that passes through an epoch in a state of preparation. In order that the wings of Mirabeau should unfold at their ease, it was necessary for the social atmosphere to be in that condition in which there is nothing fixed, nothing rooted in the soil which can resist, in which every obstacle to the free course of theories is easily stemmed, in which the principles that are one day to make the solid basis of future society are yet in suspension, without too much form of consistency, waiting, in their intermediate state, where they float confusedly in eddies, till the moment comes for falling and crystallizing. Every institution firmly established has corners against which the genius of Mirabeau would have broken its wings. Mirabeau had a profound sense of things; he also had a profound understanding of men. After his arrival at the States General, he studied with close attention and silence the various groups, so picturesque at the time of the different parties, outside the Assembly as well as within. He detected the incapacity of Mounier, Malouet, and De Rabaut Saint-Etienne, who all were pondering a settlement on English constitutional lines. He estimated with calmness the passion of Chapelier, the succinctness of Pétion, the literary magniloquence of Volney, the Abbé Maury, who sought a place; D'Eprémenil and Adrian Duport, parliamentarians in ill-humour and not tribunes; Roland, that zero, whose wife was the numeral; Gregoire, who was in a condition of political somnambulism. He looked into the depths of the soul of Sieyès, hard though it was to fathom. He intoxicated Camille Desmoulins with his ideas, whose head was not strong enough to bear them. He fascinated Danton, who resembled him in being less great and more ugly. He did not attempt to win the Guillermys, the Lautrecs, or the Cazalès, for these characters irresolvable in revolutions. He felt that everything was going on so fast that there was no time to lose. Besides being full of courage and never afraid of the man of the day, which is rare, nor of the man of the morrow, which is rarer still, he was during all his life bold with those who were powerful; he attacked in succession and during their periods of authority, Maupeon and Terray, Calonne and Necker. He approached the Duke of Orleans, touched him, and left him at once. He looked Robespierre in the face and askance at Marat.

He had been locked up successively in the Ile de Rhé, in the Castle of If, in the fort of Joux, and the keep of Vincennes. He had revenge for all in the taking of the Bastille.

In his captivities he read Tacitus; he devoured him; he lived on him; and when he ascended the tribune in 1789, he had his mouth still full of this marrow of lions. The first words he uttered showed it.

He had no understanding of the aims of Robespierre and Marat. He looked on the one as a lawyer without cases, and on the other as a doctor without patients, and he supposed their disappointments had driven them insane,—an opinion which had its true side also. He turned his back completely on the things that were advancing with such rapid strides behind him. Like all great radical regenerators, his eyes were much more firmly fixed on social questions than on political questions. His work was not the Republic, it was the Revolution.

That he was the truly great, the essential man of those times, is proved by the fact that he has remained greater to-day than any of the men who became great after him in the same order of ideas.

His father, who no more understood him, although he had begotten him, than the Constituant understood the Convention, said of him: "That man is neither the end nor the beginning of a man." He was right. "That man" was the end of one society and the beginning of another.

Mirabeau was not of less importance to the general work of the eighteenth century than Voltaire had been. These two men had like missions,— to destroy what was old and to prepare what was new. The labours of the one were continued, and occupied him during his whole life, and that before the eyes of Europe. The other appeared upon the scene but a few instants. To do their common work, Voltaire was granted years and Mirabeau days; yet Mirabeau has not done less than Voltaire. Each attacked the life of the social body after his fashion. Voltaire decomposed; Mirabeau crushed. The method of Voltaire is in some sort chemical, that of Mirabeau is entirely physical. After Voltaire, a society is in a state of dissolution; after Mirabeau, it is dust. Voltaire is an acid, Mirabeau a club.

VII

IF now, in order to complete the sketch we have endeavoured to give of Mirabeau and his epoch, we give a glance to our situation, it is easy to see, on viewing the point the social movement begun in '89 has reached to-day, that we shall no longer have men like Mirabeau; nor can any one tell us what proportions the great statesmen reserved for us by the future, may take.

The Mirabeaus are no longer necessary; besides, they are no longer possible.

Providence does not create such men when they are useless. It does not fling such seed to the wind.

And in fact, what service could a Mirabeau render now? A Mirabeau is a thunderbolt; what is there to strike with the thunder? Where are there objects in the political regions so highly placed that they attract the thunder? We are no longer in 1789, when inequalities in the social order were so enormous.

To-day the soil is pretty nearly level; everything is smooth, open and even. A tempest like Mirabeau passing over us would not find a single summit on which to lay hold.

But we must not say that, because we shall no longer need a Mirabeau, therefore, we no longer need great men. Quite the reverse. There is surely much work to be done yet. Everything has been unmade, nothing has been made anew.

In times like those in which we live, the party of the future is divided into two classes,—the men of revolution and the men of progress. It is the men of revolution who tear up the old political ground, dig the furrow and scatter the seed; but their day is short. To the men of progress belong the slow and laborious culture of principles, the study of the seasons favourable to the grafting of such and such an idea, the watering of the young plant, the manuring of the soil, the harvest for all. They are bent and patient, under sun or rain, in the public field, removing the stones from that land covered with ruins, grubbing up the stumps of the past, which still keep their hold here and there, uprooting the dead stocks of the old *régimes*, hoeing out abuses, those weeds that grow so quick in all the swamps of the law. To do this they require a good eye, a good foot, and a good hand. Worthy and conscious toilers, often very badly paid!

Now, in our opinion, the men of the revolution have accomplished their task at this very time. They have recently had their Three Days of July. Let them, then, permit the men of progress to accomplish theirs. After the furrow, the ear of corn.

Mirabeau was the great man of revolution. We want now the great man of progress.

We will have him. France has too important an initiative in the civilization of the globe, to ever experience the need of special men for her special work. France is the majestic mother of all the ideas that are to-day doing their mission among all the nations. We may say that France, for two centuries, has been feeding the nations with the milk of her breasts. The blood of the great nation is generous and rich and her womb fruitful; her supply of genius is inexhaustible; she draws out of her bosom all the great intellects she needs; she has always men who rise to the height of her issues; and when the occasion calls, she lacks neither Mirabeaus to begin her revolutions nor Bonapartes to end them.

Providence is sure not to refuse the great social man she feels the want of; the political man she requires no longer.

While hoping for his advent, we must admit that the men who are making history to-day, are, with very few exceptions, small; undoubtedly the great bodies of the State lack general ideas and broad sympathies, and it is sad that they should do so; undoubtedly it is melancholy to see the time that should be employed in rearing structures employed in mere plastering; undoubtedly it is strange men should forget that the true sovereignty is that of the intellect, that, above all, the masses should be enlightened, and that when the people shall be intelligent, then only shall it be sovereign; undoubtedly it is shameful that the magnificent premises of '89 should have brought in their train certain corollaries, just as the head of the mermaid brings in its train the tail of the fish, and that bricklayers should have laid so many laws of plaster over walls of granite; undoubtedly it is deplorable that the French Revolution should have so many unskilful accoucheurs; undoubtedly all this is to be lamented.

But nothing has yet been done that cannot be repaired. No essential principle has been stifled in the revolutionary childbirth; no abortion has taken place; all the ideas important to future civilization have been born with a capacity for living, and are each endowed with strength, beauty, and health. Assuredly, when 1814 arrived, all these ideas, the daughters of the Revolution, were still very young and very small, and, indeed, quite in the cradle; and the restoration was, we must admit, but a lean and sorry nurse for them. But we must admit also that she killed none of them. The group of principles is complete.

All criticism is possible at the present hour; still, the wise man ought to view his whole epoch with a benevolent eye. He ought to hope, to trust, to wait. He ought to have consideration for the men of theory, on account of the slowness with which they urge their ideas; for the men of practice, on account of their narrow and useful love of the things that are, without which successive experiments would disorganize society; for the passions, with their fruitful and generous digressions; for self-interest, because its calculations, in the absence of creeds, bind the classes together; for governments, on account of their tentative gropings in the dark towards the general good; for the opposing parties, because the goad they have ever in their hands forces the oxen to trace the furrow; for the moderate parties, because of the mildness they bring to transitions; for the extreme parties, because of the activity they give to the circulation of ideas, which are the life-blood of civilization; for the friends of the past, because of the care they take of such roots as still live; for the zealots of the future, because of their love of those fine flowers which will one day be fine fruits; for middle-aged men, because of their moderation; for young men, because of their patience; for some, on account of what they are doing; for others, on account of what they wish to do; for all, on account of the difficulty of everything.

Nor shall we deny either all that is stormy and troubled in the age in which we live. Most of the men who are doing something in the State do not know what they are doing. They are working in the night, and do not see. To-morrow, when it is day, they will be, perhaps, surprised at their work. Charmed or frightened, who knows? There is no longer anything settled in political science. All compasses are lost; society is dragging its anchors; during the last twenty years that great mast which is called *dynasty*, and which is always the first stricken by the lightning, has been changed three times.

The final law of anything is not yet revealed. The government, such as it is, is not the affirmation of anything; the press, otherwise so great and useful, is only the perpetual negation of everything. No clear formula of civilization and progress has so far been drawn up.

The French Revolution opened for all social theories an immense book, a sort of grand testament. There Mirabeau wrote his word, Robespierre his, Napoleon his. Louis XVIII. made an erasure, Charles IX. tore out a page. The Chamber of the 2d of August pasted it in again, almost; but this is all. The book is there, the pen is there. Who will dare write?

The men of the present seem of little account, no doubt; yet every one who thinks ought to fix on the present effervescence an attentive look.

Certainly, our confidence is firm and our hope assured.

Who among us does not feel, amid the tumult and the tempest, amid the conflicts of all the systems and all the ambitions that raise so much smoke and dust, that under yonder veil still hiding from our eyes the social and providential statue hardly yet hewn, behind that cloud of theories, passions, and chimeras, crossing, jostling, and devouring one another in the fog lit up only by their flashes, beyond that sound of the human word which speaks all tongues at the same time through all mouths, under that violent whirlwind of things, men, and ideas called the nineteenth century, who does not feel that something great is being accomplished?

God remains calm and does his work

Voltaire

FRANÇOIS MARIE AROUET, so celebrated under the name of Voltaire, was born at Chatenay on the 20th of February, 1694. His family belonged to the magistracy. He was educated by the Jesuits at the college of Louis le Grand, and one of his teachers, Father Lejay, we are told, predicted that he would be the corypheus of deism in France.

Hardly had Arouet left college, where his faculties had sprung to life with all the strength and ingenuousness of youth, when he encountered an inflexible father on the one hand, and a suave corrupter on the other. The latter was his godfather, the Abbé de Châteauneuf. The father condemned all literary studies without knowing why, and consequently with insurmountable obstinacy. The godfather, on the contrary, encouraged the essays of Arouet, and showed a great liking for verses, especially such as breathed a decided savour of licentiousness or impiety. The one would imprison the poet in a lawyer's office; the other led, or rather misled, the young man into all the salons. M. Arouet forbade all reading to his son. Ninon de Lenclos bequeathed a library to the pupil of her friend Châteauneuf. Thus at its birth the genius of Voltaire was unfortunately subjected to two opposite and equally fatal forces, one tending to stifle that sacred fire which cannot be extinguished; the other feeding it thoughtlessly at the expense of all that is noble and worthy in the intellectual order as well as in the social order. These are the two contrary impulses, stamped at the same time on the first flight of this powerful imagination, which vitiated its direction forever. At least we may attribute to them the first aberrations of the talent of Voltaire, vexed in this fashion at once by the bridle and the spur.

We need not be astonished then, if at the very beginning of his career, certain verses, poor and pointless enough, were attributed to him and lodged him in the Bastille,—a somewhat rigorous punishment for bad rhymes. It was during this enforced leisure that Voltaire, at the age of twenty-two, sketched the outline of his tiresome poem the "Ligue," afterwards the "Henriade," and finished his noteworthy drama "Oedipe." After some months in the Bastille, he was freed and pensioned at the same time by the Regent Orleans, whom he thanked for taking care of his board,

but begged that he might be allowed henceforth to take care of his lodging himself.

"Oedipe" was played with success in 1718. Lamotte, the oracle of the period, deigned to consecrate the triumph by a few sacramental words, and the fame of Voltaire began its course. Today, Lamotte is immortal only perhaps because he is named in the writings of Voltaire.

The tragedy of "Artémise" succeeded the "Oedipe." It fell flat. Voltaire went on a trip to Brussels to see J. B. Rousseau, to whom, oddly enough, the epithet great has been attached. The two poets were full of respect for each other before meeting. They separated enemies. It has been said that they were mutually jealous, which could hardly be a sign of superiority in either.

"Artémise," recast and played in 1724 under the name of "Marianne," had considerable success, though its new form was by no means an improvement on the old. France had not so far had an epic poem; but the "Ligue" or the "Henriade" appeared at this time. Voltaire substituted Mornay for Sully in his work, because he had grounds of complaint against the descendant of the great minister. The vengeance seems hardly worthy of a philosopher; there is, however, some excuse for Voltaire, who had been insulted in a cowardly fashion in front of the Hôtel de Sully by a certain Chevalier de Rohan, and finding no redress in the law, he adopted the only retaliation in his power.

Justly indignant at the refusal of the courts to deal with his contemptible antagonist, Voltaire, who was now a celebrity, withdrew into England where he devoted himself to the study of some of the sophists of that nation. Still all his leisure was not wasted; he composed two new tragedies, "Brutus" and "César," many scenes of which Corneille might have acknowledged.

After returning to France, he gave in succession the "Eryphile," which was a failure, and "Zaïre," a masterpiece planned and finished in eighteen days. It is defective only in local colouring and from the absence of a certain severity of style. The success of "Zaïre," was prodigious, and it was well deserved. The tragedy of "Adélaïde du Guesclin" (afterwards the "Duc de Foix") succeeded "Zaïre," but was far from attaining the same success. Some publications of a less important character, the "Temple du Goût," "Lettres sur les anglais," etc., troubled the life of Voltaire for several years.

However, his name was already spreading over Europe. Retiring to Cirey, where he lived in the household of the Marquise du Châtelet, a lady, in the words of Voltaire, fit for all sciences except the science of life, he tried to dull his fine imagination by studying algebra and geometry, wrote "Alzire," "Mahomet," the sprightly "Histoire de Charles XII.," collected materials for the "Siècle de Louis XIV," prepared the "Essai sur les mœurs des nations," and sent madrigals to Frederick, Crown Prince of Prussia. "Mérope," also composed at Cirey, set the seal on the dramatic reputation of Voltaire. He thought he might now present himself for admission to the French Academy and fill the chair of Cardinal de Fleury. He was not received. So far he had nothing but genius to back him. But some time after, he set himself the task of flattering Madame de Pompadour, and this with such obstinate and complacent servility that he obtained, at the same time, the academic chair, the post of gentleman of the bedchamber, and the office of historiographer of France. His favour was not of long duration. Voltaire found a refuge now at Lunéville with Stanislas, the good King of Poland and Duke of Lorraine; now with Madame du Maine, at Sceaux, where he wrote the "Sémiramis, Oreste," and "Rome Sauvée;" and again at Berlin with Frederick, become King of Prussia. He passed several years in the last retreat with the title of chamberlain, the Prussian cross of merit and a pension. He was admitted to the royal suppers along with Maupertuis, D'Argens, and Lamettrie, atheist of the king,—of that king, who, like Voltaire himself, lived without court, without council, and without worship. It was not the sublime friendship of Aristotle and Alexander, of Terence and Scipio. A few years of friction sufficed to wear out all that the soul of the despot philosopher and the soul of the sophist poet had in common. Voltaire wished to escape from Berlin. Frederick hunted him.

Dismissed by Prussia, rejected by France, Voltaire spent two years in Germany, where, to oblige the Duchess of Saxe-Gotha, he compiled and published the "Annales de l'Empire;" then he planted himself at the gates of Geneva with his niece, Madame Denis.

The "Orphelin de la Chine," a tragedy in which nearly every characteristic of his talent is conspicuous, was the first fruit of this retreat, in which he would have lived in peace, if greedy booksellers had not published his odious "Pucelle." It was also at this period and in his different residences of Les Délices, Tournay, and Ferney, that he wrote the poem on the "Earthquake of Lisbon," the tragedy of "Tancrède," some tales, and a number of his minor productions. It was then he defended, with a generosity in which there was too great an admixture of ostentation, Calas, Sirven, La Barre, Montballi, and Lalli, those lamentable victims of judicial mistakes. It was then he quarrelled with Jean Jacques, gained the friendship of Catherine of Russia, for whom he wrote the history of her ancestor Peter the Great, and became reconciled to Frederick. It is from the same time that his co-operation in the "Encyclopédie" dates,—a work in which men who tried to show their strength have only shown their weakness, a monstrous monument of which the "Montieur" of our Revolution is the frightful sequel.

When borne down by the weight of years, Voltaire wished to see Paris once more. He returned to that Babylon which was in sympathy with his genius. Hailed by universal acclamations the unhappy old man was enabled to see before his death how much his work had advanced, was enabled to be delighted or terrified by his glory. His vital power no longer sufficed to support the emotions of the journey, and Paris witnessed his death on the 30th of May, 1778. The freethinkers claimed that he carried with him his infidelity to the tomb. We shall not follow him there.

We have related the private life of Voltaire: we must now try to paint his public and private existence.

To name Voltaire is to characterize the whole eighteenth century; it is to fix at one stroke the historical and literary physiognomy of this epoch, which was, after all, only a period of transition, for society as well as for poetry. The eighteenth century will always appear in history as a century stifled between the age that precedes and the age that follows it. Voltaire is its principal and in some sort its typical representative, and, however prodigious the man may be, his proportions seem paltry enough between the great image of Louis XIV. and the gigantic figure of Napoleon.

There are two beings in Voltaire. His life had two influences. His writings had two results. It is on this twofold action, controlling literature on the one side, manifested in events on the other, we wish to dwell for a moment. We shall study separately each of these two influences of the genius of Voltaire. We must not forget, however, that their double power was intimately co-ordinated, and that the effects of this power, rather intermingled than interlinked, have always had something simultaneous and common. If, in this note, we examine them separately, it is solely because it would be beyond our strength to embrace at a single glance a unity that eludes our grasp. In this we imitate the artifice of those oriental artists, who, finding that they are incapable of representing an entire face, succeed in giving a tolerable idea of the human countenance by painting two profiles and enclosing them in a frame.

In literature Voltaire has left one of those monuments whose appearance is astonishing from its size rather than imposing from its grandeur. There is nothing august in the edifice he has constructed. It is not the palace of kings, nor is it the shelter of the poor. It is a bazaar, vast and elegant, irregular and convenient; making a display of countless wealth amid surrounding filth; supplying all interests, all vanities, and all passions with what exactly suits them; dazzling and fetid; an exchange of prostitutions and pleasures; peopled by vagabonds, merchants, and idlers, but seldom the resort of the priest or of the needy. Here, you see brilliant galleries thronged incessantly by astonished crowds; there, secret caverns which no one cares to boast of having entered. Under these sumptuous arcades you will find a thousand masterpieces of taste and art, everything resplendent with gold and diamonds; but do not look for the statue of bronze with its antique and severe lines. You will find ornaments for your salons and boudoirs; do not look for such decorations as beseem the sanctuary. And woe to the weakling whose soul is his entire fortune, if he expose it to the seductions of this magnificent den,—this monstrous temple in which there are testimonies for all that which is not truth, adoration for all that which is not God!

Certainly though we may wish to speak of a monument of this kind with admiration, we cannot be required to speak of it with respect.

We would pity a city in which the bazaar was crowded, and the church deserted; we would pity a literature that abandoned Corneille and Bossuet to run in the traces of Voltaire.

Far from us the thought, nevertheless, of denying the genius of this extraordinary man. It is because of our conviction that this genius was perhaps one of the finest ever bestowed on a writer that we deplore with the greater bitterness its frivolous and destructive employment. We regret, for his own sake as for the sake of literature, that he turned against Heaven the intellectual power he had received from Heaven. We bewail the glorious genius that did not comprehend its sublime mission. We sorrow over the ingrate who has profaned the chastity of his Muse and the sanctity of his country, over the deserter who did not remember that the tripod of the poet has its place close by the altar. And, it is a profound and inevitable truth, his very crime contained its chastisement. His glory is much less great than it might have been, because he aimed at every species of glory, even at that of Erostates. He has cleared all fields, he cannot be said to have cultivated any. And because he had the guilty ambition of sowing in them nutritive germs and venomous germs with equal impartiality, to his eternal shame, it is the poisons that have borne most fruit. The "Henriade," as a literary composition, is very inferior to the "Pucelle,"—which does not at all mean that this vicious work is among the best, even of its shameful class. His satires, sometimes branded with an infernal impress, are very much superior to his most innocent comedies. His lighter verses, often instinct with shameless cynicism, are preferred to his lyric poems, in which religious and weighty verses are occasionally found. His tales, in fine, so cheerless in their incredulity and scepticism, are far above his histories, where the same defect is felt a little less perceptibly, but where the perpetual absence of dignity is out of harmony with the very nature of this class of literature. As to his tragedies, in which he really shows himself a great poet, often finding the true touches of character and words fresh from the heart, it cannot be denied that, in spite of some admirable scenes, he is still very far from Racine, and still farther from Corneille. And our opinion on this point will be the less suspected, as a deep study of the dramatic work of Voltaire has convinced us of his signal superiority on the theatre. We are inclined to believe that if Voltaire, instead of scattering the colossal forces of his thought over twenty different points, had combined them in one single direction, tragedy, he might have surpassed Racine and, perhaps, equalled Corneille. But he expended his genius in witty sallies. He was, therefore, marvellously sprightly and sparkling, and the seal of his genius is impressed rather on the vast entirety of his works than on any one of them in particular. Ever absorbed by his age, he was too neglectful of posterity, that austere image which should tower above all the meditations of the poet. Engaged in a capricious and frivolous struggle with his capricious and frivolous contemporaries, he wished at once to please and flout them. His Muse, who would have been so beautiful if she had been content to rely on her beauty, often borrowed her charms from the colours of the paint-box and the grimaces of coquetry, and we are constantly tempted to address her in these words of the jealous lover:—

"Why give yourself such trouble? Art for you was not invented, you require it not."

Voltaire appeared to ignore the fact that there is much grace in strength, and that whatever is sublimest in the works of the human intellect is also, perhaps, that which is most simple. Imagination can reveal its heavenly origin without having recourse to foreign artifices. She has but to walk to show that she is a goddess. *Et vera incessu patuit dea.*

If it were possible to summarize the manifold idea which the literary existence of Voltaire presents, we could only class it among those prodigies which the Latins call *monstra*. Voltaire, in truth, is a phenomenon,—a phenomenon perhaps unique which could only arise in France and in the eighteenth century. There is this difference between his literature and that of the great century preceding him, that Corneille, Molière, and Pascal belonged more to society, Voltaire to civilization. We feel, when reading him, that he is the writer of an enervated and feeble age. He has a certain pleasantness but no grace, a certain brilliancy but no real charm, a certain lustre but no majesty. He can flatter but he cannot console. He fascinates but does not persuade. Except in tragedy, which was his native element, he lacks tenderness and sincerity. We feel that everything is the result of an organization, and not the effect of an inspiration; and, though it is an atheist physician who tells you that all Voltaire was in his sinews and in his nerves, you acknowledge with a shudder that he is right. Moreover, like another ambitious personage of later days, who aspired to political supremacy, it is in vain that Voltaire has aimed at literary supremacy. Absolute monarchy is not suitable to man. If Voltaire had understood what is true greatness, he would have placed his glory in unity rather than in universality. Strength is not revealed by a perpetual changing of place, by indefinite metamorphoses, but rather by a majestic immobility. Force is Jupiter not Proteus.

Here begins the second part of our task: it will be shorter, because, thanks to the French Revolution, the political results of Voltaire's philosophy are unfortunately frightfully notorious. It would, however, be supremely unjust to attribute that fatal revolution to the writings of the "patriarch of Ferney" alone. We must above all see in it the effect of a social decomposition commenced long before. Voltaire and the age in which he lived may reciprocally accuse and excuse each other. Too strong to obey his time, Voltaire was also too weak to control it. From this equality of influence there resulted a perpetual reaction between himself and his century, a mutual exchange of impieties and follies, a continual flux and reflux of innovations, which in their oscillations always carried away some old pillar of the social edifice. Let us only consider the political features of the eighteenth century, the scandals of the Regency, the turpitudes of Louis XV.; violence in the ministry, violence in the parliaments, force nowhere; moral corruption descending by degrees from the head to the heart, from the great to the people; the prelates of the court and the abbés of the boudoir; the ancient monarchy, the ancient society staggering on their common foundation, and no longer opposing to the attacks of the innovators anything except the magic of that glorious name Bourbon; let us fancy Voltaire flung into this society in dissolution like a serpent into a swamp, and we shall no longer be astonished at seeing the contagious action of his thought hasten the end of that political order which Montaigne and Rabelais in vain assailed in its youth and vigour. It was not he who rendered the disease mortal, but it was he who developed its germ, and increased the malignity of the outburst. All the venom of Voltaire was needed in order to set this dung-heap in effervescence; and, therefore, a great many of the monstrous occurrences of the Revolution may be justly attributed to this unhappy man. As to the Revolution itself, it was natural that it should be unprecedented. Providence wished to place it between the most formidable of the sophists and the most formidable of the despots. At its dawn, Voltaire appeared in a funereal saturnalia; at its decline, Bonaparte arose amid a massacre.

Sir Walter Scott

SURELY there is something strange and marvellous in the talent of this man, who disposes of his reader as the wind disposes of a leaf; who leads him at his will into all places and into all times; unveils for him with ease the most secret recesses of the heart, as well as the most mysterious phenomena of nature, as well as the obscurest pages of history; whose imagination caresses and dominates all other imaginations, clothes with the same astonishing truth the beggar with his rags and the king with his robes, assumes all manners, adopts all garbs, speaks all languages; leaves to the physiognomy of the ages all that is immutable and eternal in their lineaments, traced there by the wisdom of God, and all that is variable and fleeting, planted there by the follies of men; does not force, like certain ignorant romances, the personages of the past to colour themselves with our brushes and smear themselves with our varnish; but compels, by his magic power, the contemporary reader to imbue himself, at least for some hours, with the spirit of the old times, to-day so much scorned, like a wise and adroit adviser inviting ungrateful children to return to their father. The skilful magician desires above all, however, to be correct. He does not refuse his pen to any truth, not even to that which springs from the portraiture of error,—that daughter of men who might be believed immortal if her changing and capricious humour left us at all in doubt as to her claims to eternity. Few historians are as faithful as this romancer. We feel that he wishes his portraits to be pictures and his pictures portraits. He paints for us our forefathers with all their passions, their vices, and their crimes, but in such sort that the instability of superstition and the impiety of fanaticism but serve to show forth more vividly the perpetuity of religion and the sanctity of beliefs. We delight in finding again our ancestors with their prejudice, often so noble and salutary, as well as with their splendid plumes and stout breastplates.

Walter Scott has been able to draw from the springs of nature and truth an unknown species. It is new to us, because he makes himself as ancient as he wills. He unites to the minute exactness of the chronicles the majestic grandeur of history and the all-compelling interest of romance. His potent and curious genius divines the past; his true pencil traces a faithful portrait after a confused shadow, and forces us to recognize even what we have not seen; his flexible and solid mind takes the peculiar impress of every age and of every country, like soft wax, and preserves this impress for posterity like imperishable bronze.

Few writers have so well fulfilled as Walter Scott the duties of the romancer in relation to his art and to his age; for it would be an almost culpable error in the man of letters to believe himself above the general interest and above national needs, to exempt his mind from all action over the minds of his contemporaries, and to isolate his life from the great life of the social body. What voice is likely to rise in the tempest if not that of the lyre which can calm it? And who will brave the hatreds of anarchism and the disdain of despotism, if not he to whom ancient wisdom assigned the task of reconciling nations and kings, and to whom modern wisdom has given that of dividing them?

It is not, then, to mawkish gallantries, to paltry intrigues, or coarse adventures that Walter Scott devotes his talent. Warned by the instinct of his glory, he has felt that something else was needed by a generation that has just written with its blood and with its tears the most extraordinary page of all human histories. The times which immediately preceded and immediately followed our convulsive Revolution were such periods of weakness as persons in a fever experience before and after their paroxysms. Then books the most stupidly atrocious, the most vapidly impious, the most monstrously obscene, were greedily devoured by a diseased society, whose depraved tastes and blunted faculties rejected all palatable and healthy nourishment. It is this which explains those scandalous triumphs awarded at the time by the plebeians of the drawing-room and the patricians of the coffee-house to certain insipid or obscene writers whom we disdain to name, who are to-day reduced to the necessity of begging the applause of lackeys and the smiles of prostitutes. Now, popularity is no longer distributed by the populace; it springs from the only source that can impress on it a character of immortality as well as of universality,—from the suffrage of that minority of discriminating minds, of exalted souls and sober heads, that represent morally all civilized peoples. It is this which Scott has obtained, borrowing as he does from the annals of nations compositions made for all nations, and from the records of ages works written for all ages. No romancer ever hid so much teaching under so much witchery, so much truth under so much fiction. There is a visible alliance between the form he has made his own and all the literary forms of the past and of the future, and the epic romances of Scott may be considered as a transition from the literature of the present to the grand romances, the grand epics in verse or in prose which our poetic era promises and will give us.

What should be the intention of the romancer? It should be to express through the medium of an interesting fable a useful truth. And when once this fundamental idea is chosen, this explanatory action is invented, should not the author seek for its development a method of execution which gives to his romance the semblance of life, which gives to the imitation the likeness of its model? And is not life a singular drama in which the good and the bad, the beautiful and the ugly, the high and the low are intermingled,—a law whose power only expires beyond creation? Should, then, the writer limit himself, like some Flemish painters, to the composition of pictures altogether dark, or like the Chinese, to that of pictures entirely luminous, since Nature everywhere shows the struggle between light and darkness? Now romancers, before Walter Scott, adopted two distinctly antagonistic methods of composition; both vicious precisely because they are antagonistic. The one class gave to their work the form of a narrative arbitrarily divided into chapters, without very well knowing why, or for the purpose of relaxing the tension of the reader, as the title *descanso* (rest), placed at the head of his chapters by an old Spanish author, innocently confesses. The others unfold their fable in a series of letters, supposed to be written by the different actors in the romance. In the narrative, the characters disappear, the author is ever in front; in the letters, the author passes out of sight so that the characters alone may come into view. The narrative romancer cannot give place to natural dialogue, to real action; he must substitute for these a certain monotonous movement of style, which is as it were a mould in which the most diverse events take the same form, and under which the most elevated creations, the most profound inventions, are lost, just as the inequalities of a field are levelled under the roller. In the romance by letters, the same monotony springs from another cause. The several characters arrive each in their turn with their several epistles after the manner of those strolling actors, who, as they can only appear after one another, appear in succession with a big placard above their heads which informs the public of their various rôles. Again, the romance by letters may be compared to those laborious conversations of deaf-mutes who write in turn what they have to say to each other, so that to express their anger or their joy they must have constantly a pen in the hand and a note-book in the pocket. Now I ask, where is the appropriateness of a tender reproach which you must carry to the post-office? And is not the stormy explosion of passion a little hampered between the obligatory preamble and the polite formula which are the vanguard and the rearguard of every letter written by the well-born? Do you believe that the procession of the compliments and the baggage of the civilities accelerate the progress of the interest and hasten on the march of the action? Ought we not, then, to suppose some radical and insurmountable defect in a kind of composition which has sometimes succeeded in chilling even the eloquence of Rousseau?

Now let us assume that for the narrative romance, in which everything would seem to be thought of except the interest, in which the absurd custom is adopted of ushering in every chapter by a summary, often very detailed,— the story of a story as it were; let us assume that for the epistolary romance, whose very form forbids all vehemence and all rapidity, some creative mind should substitute the dramatic romance, in which the dramatic action is unfolded in true and varied tableaux, just as the events of real life are unfolded; which should know of no other vision than that of the different scenes to be developed; which, in fine, would be a long drama, where descriptions take the place of decorations and costumes, where the characters are delineated by themselves, and represent, by their various and multiplied movements, all the forms of the individual idea of the work. You will find in this new species the advantages of the two old species united without their drawbacks. Having at your disposal the picturesque and, in some sort, magical activities of the drama, you can leave behind the scene those thousand tedious and transitory details which the mere narrator, obliged to follow his actors step by step, as if they were children in leading strings, must expound at length, if he does not wish to be obscure; and you can turn to account those intense and sudden strokes more fruitful for meditation than entire pages flashing from the movements of a scene, but excluded by the rapidity of a tale.

After the picturesque but prosaic romance of Walter Scott, another kind of romance will have still to be created, in our opinion of a finer and more finished kind. It will be the romance which is at once dramatic and epic, picturesque but poetic, real but ideal, true but grand, Walter Scott and Homer in combination.

Like every creator, Walter Scott has up to the present hour been assailed by infuriate critics. He who drains a swamp must resign himself to the croaking of the frogs around him.

For our part, we fulfil a conscientious duty in placing Sir Walter Scott very high among romancers, and "Quentin Durward" in particular, very high among romances. It would be hard to find a book better interwoven, and one in which the moral effect is better linked with the dramatic effect.

The author has wished, in our view, to demonstrate how much more certain loyalty, though found among the obscure, the young and the poor, is likely to obtain its purpose than perfidy, though aided by all the resources of power, riches, and experience. The first of these rôles is embodied by a young Scotchman, Quentin Durward, an orphan, wrecked on all kinds of shoals, exposed to the best laid snares, without other compass to guide him than the love of one whom to love is madness; but it often happens that when love resembles insanity it is really a virtue. The second is intrusted to Louis XI., a king more adroit than the most adroit courtiers, an old fox armed with the lion's claws, powerful and crafty, served in the shadow as well as in the light, covered by his guards as by a buckler, and accompanied by his executioners as by a sword. These two personages, so different in all respects, act and react on each other so as to express the fundamental idea with singularly striking truth. It is by his faithful obedience to the King that the loyal Quentin serves without knowing it, his own interests, while the projects of Louis XI., of which Quentin was to be at once the instrument and the victim, all turn out to the confusion of the cunning old man and the advantage of his simple-minded agent.

A superficial examination would at first sight lead to the belief that the primary intention of the poet is shown in the historic contrast, painted with such talent, of the King of France, Louis of Valois, with Charles the Bold, Duke of Burgundy. This fine episode is perhaps after all a defect in the composition of the work, as it rivals in interest the subject of the romance. But this fault, if it be a fault, in no way diminishes the imposing and comical aspects of the situation in which these two princes are set in opposition; the one, a subtle and ambitious despot, despising the other, a harsh and warlike tyrant, who would scorn him if he dared. They both hate each other. But Louis braves the hatred of Charles, because it is rude and savage; Charles dreads the hatred of Louis, because it is caressing. The Duke of Burgundy, in the midst of his camp and his states, is disturbed by the presence of the King of France, who is defenceless, as the bloodhound is in the neighbourhood of the cat.

The cruelty of the duke springs from his passions, that of the king from his character. The Burgundian is loyal, because he is violent; he never dreams of hiding his bad deeds; he feels no remorse; for he has forgotten his crimes as speedily as his angers. Louis is superstitious, perhaps because he is a hypocrite; mere religion does not suffice the man who is tormented by his conscience and who will not repent; but it is vain for him to believe in useless expiations; the memory of the evil he has done ever lives within him close to the thought of the evil he is about to do, because we always remember what we have long meditated on, and crime, when it has been a desire and a hope, becomes also a memory. The two princes are very devout; but Charles swears by his sword before swearing by God, and Louis tries to gain the good-will of the saints by gifts of money or offices at court,—mingles diplomacy with his prayers, and intrigues even with Heaven. In case of war, Louis is measuring its danger, while Charles is already resting after victory. The policy of the one is in the might of his arm, but the eye of the other reaches farther than the arm of the duke. In fine, Walter Scott proves, by engaging the two rivals in action, that prudence is stronger than daring, and that he who appears to dread nothing is really afraid of him who seems to fear everything.

With what art the illustrious writer paints for us the King of France when, by a refinement of trickery, he presents himself to his fair cousin of Burgundy, and asks his hospitality at the very moment the haughty vassal was about to make war on him! And what can be more dramatic than the news of a revolt fomented in the states of the duke by the agents of the king falling like a thunderbolt between the two rulers at the very moment when the same table united them! Thus fraud is foiled by fraud, and the prudent Louis is delivered into the hands of an enemy justly irritated. History tells us something about this; but at this point I prefer to believe in romance rather than in history, because I count moral truth more desirable than historic truth. A still more remarkable scene perhaps is that where the two princes, whom the safest counsel has failed to bring together, are reconciled by an act of cruelty imagined by the one and executed by the other. For the first time they burst into a laugh of mutual cordiality and enjoyment. And this laugh, excited by the torture of a poor wretch, effaces for a moment their discord. This terrible idea makes the reader thrill with admiration.

We have heard the picture of the debauch criticized as hideous and revolting. It is in our opinion one of the finest chapters of the book. As Walter Scott had undertaken the task of painting that famous cut-throat, surnamed the Boar of Ardennes, his description would have been a failure if it did not excite horror. We must always enter frankly into a dramatic idea, and in everything search out the end to be attained. In this, emotion and interest have their source. It belongs only to timid spirits to capitulate with a strong conception and recoil before the path they themselves have traced.

We shall justify on the same principle two other passages which do not seem to us less worthy of meditation and praise. The first is the execution of Hayraddin,—a singular personage whom the author might perhaps have made more of. The second is the chapter in which Louis XI., arrested by the Duke of Burgundy, arranges with Tristan l'Hermite in his prison the punishment of the astrologer who has deceived him. It is a singularly fine idea to show us this cruel king finding his dungeon even wide enough for his vengeance, seeking for agents to deal justice on those who were lately his servants, and testing all the authority left him by an execution.

We might multiply these observations and try to show in what direction the new drama of Sir Walter Scott seems to us defective, particularly in the denouncement; but the romancer could doubtless supply much better reasons for his justification than we could for attacking him, and against such a formidable champion our weak arms would scarcely be at an advantage. We shall confine ourselves to saying that the witticism put in the mouth of the Duke of Burgundy's fool on the arrival of King Louis XI. at Peronne, really belongs to the fool of Francis I., who uttered it at the time of the passage of Charles V. through France in 1535. As the immortality of this poor Triboulet depends entirely on this quip, it is but fair to let him have it. We think also that the ingenious expedient imagined by Galeotti for the escape of Louis XI. had been tried a thousand years before by the philosopher who wished to put Dionysius of Syracuse to death. We do not attach to these remarks more importance than they deserve; a romancer is not a chronicler. We are astonished only that the king should, in the council of Burgundy, address certain knights of the Holy Ghost, as this Order was not founded for a century later, by Henri III. We believe that even the Order of Saint Michael, with which the noble author decorates the brave Lord Crawford, was not instituted by Louis XI. until after his captivity. Sir Walter Scott must permit us these little chronological quibbles. By winning a slight triumph of a somewhat pedantic kind over so illustrious an *antiquary,* we are not able to refrain from feeling some of that harmless delight which transported his Quentin Durward, when he unhorsed the Duke of Orleans and held Dunois in check, and we are tempted to ask his pardon for our victory in the words of Charles V. to the Pope: *Sanctissime Pater, indulge victori.*